D0099739

THE CHRONICLE OF THE MOVIES

A YEAR-BY-YEAR HISTORY FROM *THE JAZZ SINGER* TO TODAY

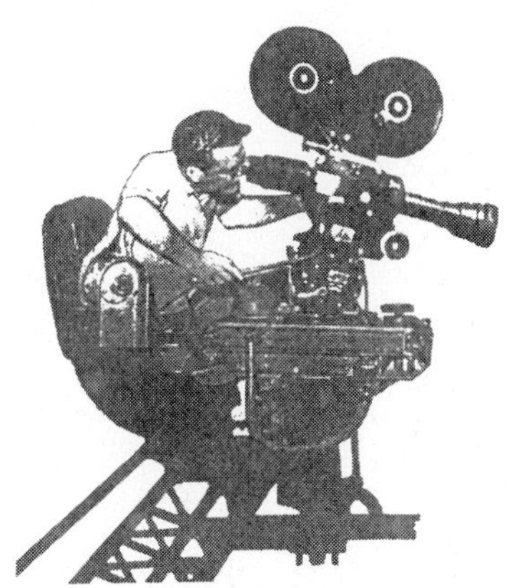

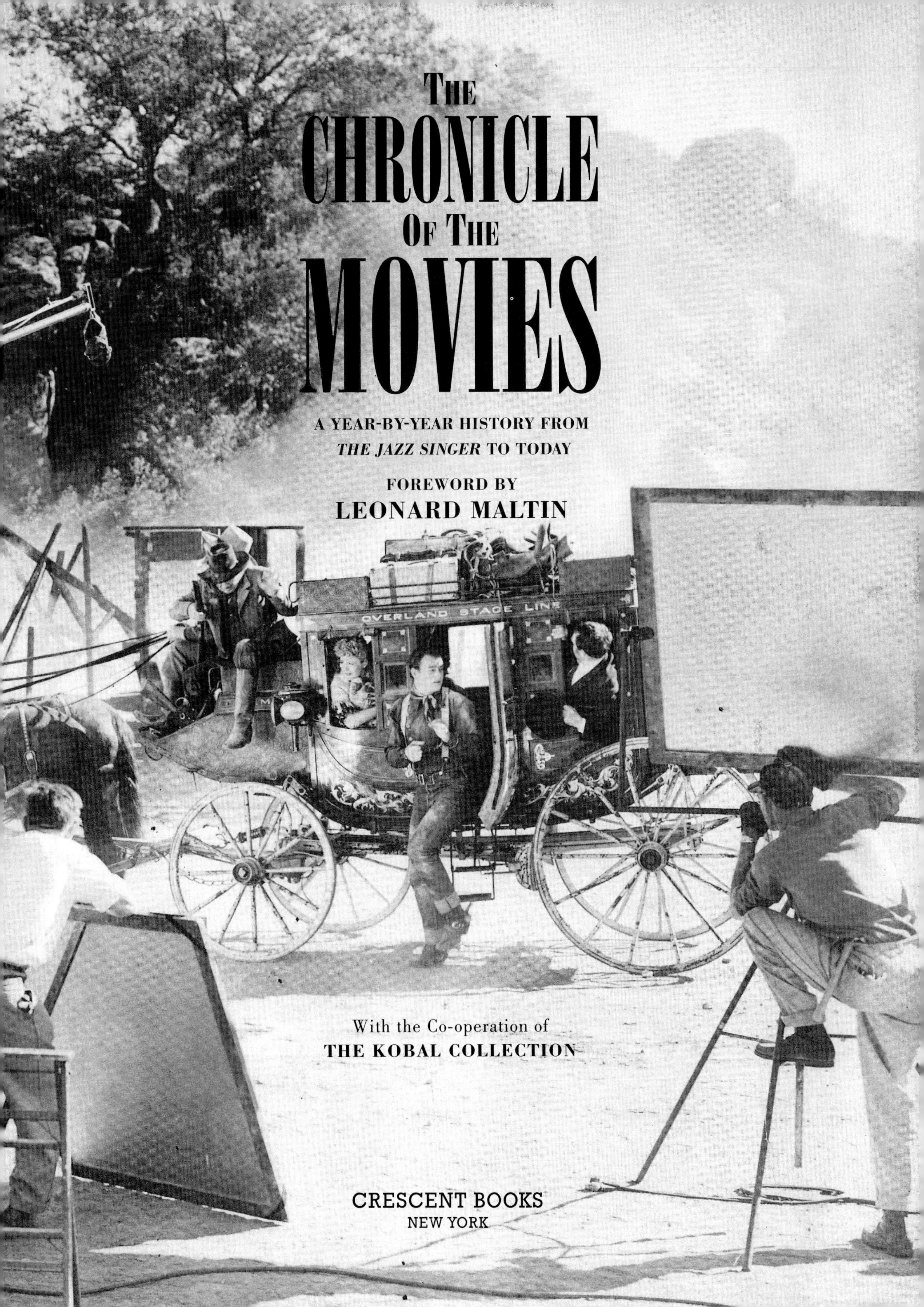

THE CHRONICLE OF THE MOVIES

A YEAR-BY-YEAR HISTORY FROM *THE JAZZ SINGER* TO TODAY

FOREWORD BY

LEONARD MALTIN

With the Co-operation of
THE KOBAL COLLECTION

CRESCENT BOOKS
NEW YORK

Consultant Editor

Derek Elley

Contributors

David Shipman Robin Cross Tony Sloman Adrian Turner
Neil Sinyard Alan Stanbrook

Editor

Julian Brown

Art Editor

Leigh Jones

Designer

Christopher Matthews

Picture Researcher

Jenny Faithfull

Production Controller

Garry Lewis

This 1991 edition published by Crescent Books,
distributed by Outlet Book Company, Inc.,
a Random House Company, 225 Park Avenue South,
New York, New York 10003.

First edition published by
The Hamlyn Publishing Group
part of Reed International Books Limited,
Michelin House, 81 Fulham Road, London SW3 6RB

ISBN 0-517-05689-5

8 7 6 5 4 3 2 1

Produced by Mandarin Offset
Printed and bound in Hong Kong

CONTENTS

Foreword by Leonard Maltin 7

1929 8-15

Talkies, Talkies, Talkies 9

1930s 16-83

Broadway Babies 29
Lounge Lizards and Dizzy Dames 42
Swash & Buckle 56
Public Enemies 70

1940s 84-151

Bette & Co. 90
Oh! What A Lovely War 111
The Big Kiss-Off 124
A Whiff of Wolfbane 138

1950s 152-221

I Got Rhythm 159
Rockin 'n' Rollin' 173
The New Breed 186
Watch The Skies! 200
Ridin' The Range 214

1960s 222-291

Epic Hollywood 229
High, Wide & Handsome 242
Angry Young Brits 251
Play It Again, Man 270
Mogul Power 284

1970s 292-361

High Anxiety 299
Fatal Attractions 313
Something To Shout About 327
Brat Power 340
Uncle Oscar 355

1980s 362-431

The Force Was With Them 374
Anything You Can Do 383
Gore Blimey 396
Beyond the Megasphere 410
The Young Ones 424

1990s 432-439

Index 440

Photographic Acknowledgments 448

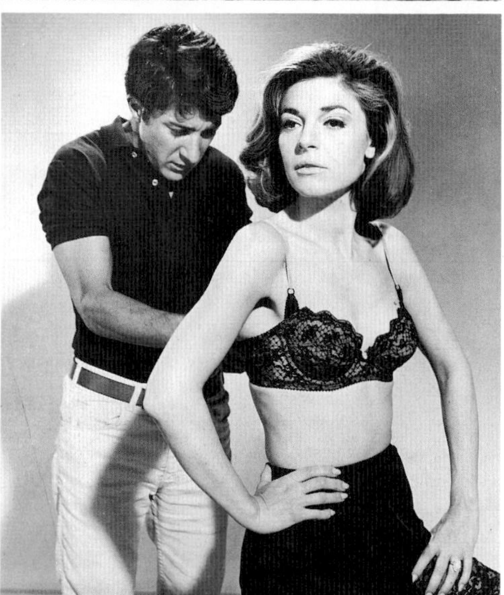
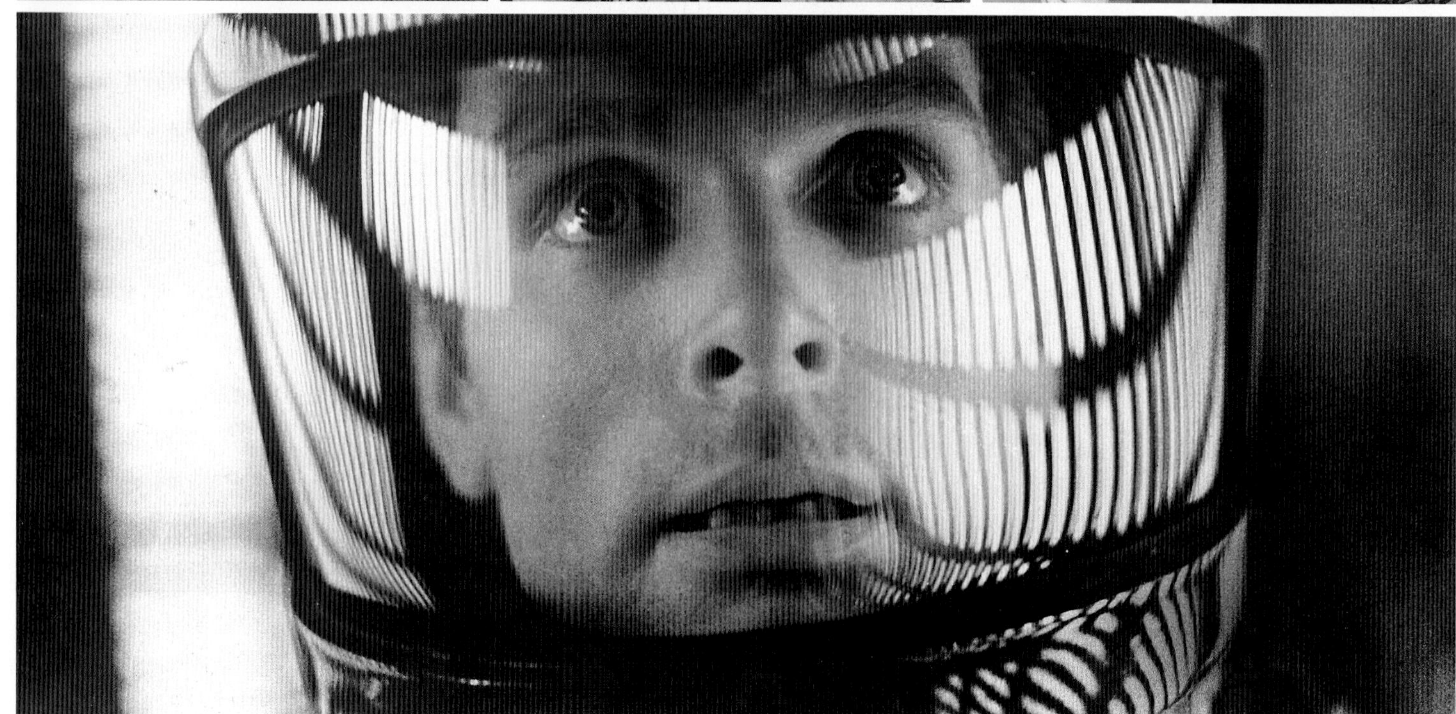

FOREWORD

First, a warning: if you love movies, and you have other plans for this evening (or afternoon, or morning) *don't open this book!* Unless you possess incredible will-power, you will become hooked, as I did, and find yourself unable to break away.

It's not just that the authors have compiled an interesting volume of news, notes, observations, and gossip; they have. But they have done so in a most unusual manner: a month-by-month, year-by-year chronicle, written and reported in the present tense.

With this format we get to experience, vicariously, the way people must have felt at the time of the first talkies, the opening of Radio City Music Hall, and the hearings of the House UnAmerican Activities Committee. We learn the way moviegoers (and movie critics) greeted the initial appearances of many great stars – and various turning points in their careers, as well, from Garbo's talkie debut to John Wayne's acceptance as an actor of standing.

And we can see, with hindsight, the outcome of news that was reported without the benefit of crystal balls: from the first citations by the fledgling Academy of Motion Picture Arts and Sciences (which originally didn't even plan to give out awards!) in 1929 to the 1965 announcement that Stanley Kubrick is to make an outer-space saga called *Journey Beyond the Stars* (which the president of M-G-M hastens to add is nothing like Buck Rogers) set in the year 2001.

Diving into this whirlpool of facts and fanciful trivia is indeed a heady experience, but as much fun as it is to learn about the early days, and compare notes on favourite films, one of the book's real draws for me is allowing the reader to engage in a bit of time-travel.

James Stewart once spoke about the impact of movies in terms of giving people "pieces of time," and that's what struck me most as I read through the section on the late 1950s and early 1960s, the period when I began going to the movies on a regular basis. Movies were already a big part of my life, and the memories are burnished in my head, so that I can remember not just the films I saw but where I saw them: for *West Side Story,* it was the extreme right-hand side of the balcony at the now-departed Rivoli Theater on Broadway in New York City; for *How the West Was Won,* it was smack-dab in the middle of my neighbourhood cinema, the Teaneck Theater on Cedar Lane in Teaneck, New Jersey (the Teaneck, a modest theater, wasn't equipped to show the film in Cinerama, the way it had been filmed, with three separate cameras side by side, so I saw the "standard" release version, with wavy lines joining each third of the picture together).

I remember how Peter O'Toole became an overnight household name when *Lawrence of Arabia* came along, and how Dustin Hoffman was hailed as Hollywood's unlikeliest new leading man after the sensation of *The Graduate.* It's fun to isolate and recall those moments.

And, of course, it's great fun to learn things I didn't know about movies of both the recent and distant past (I remembered that Montgomery Clift was originally set to star in *Sunset Blvd.,* but I didn't know the role was also offered to Gene Kelly. There are scores of other examples).

Chronicle of the Movies can be used as a reference book, to be sure, but I don't think that will be its fate. I suspect that, laid out on a coffee table, it will be browsed by every visitor who comes upon it; it will spark an avalanche of memories and fuel untold conversations.

And it will stop a lot of conversations dead in their tracks, as people get lost in its pages, the way I did. What a wonderful way to relive a lifetime of moviegoing.

Leonard Maltin

Top: *Indians sweep out of the mountains to ambush a wagon train in* How the West Was Won.
Centre, left to right: *Gloria Swanson and William Holden in* Sunset Blvd.*; Russ Tamblyn (centre) with the Jets in* West Side Story*; Dustin Hoffman and Anne Bancroft get acquainted in* The Graduate.
Bottom: *Keir Dullea in* 2001: A Space Odyssey.

Janet Gaynor and Charles Farrell in Seventh Heaven *(1927).*

John Barrymore in the experimental sound movie Don Juan *(1926).*

Victor McLaglen and Edmund Lowe in What Price Glory? (1926).

Talkies, Talkies, Talkies!

Experiments with sound are almost as old as movies themselves but they didn't look like getting anywhere till Warner Bros. took the gamble with *Don Juan*. This 1926 super-spectacle, starring John Barrymore as the great lover, was the first movie issued with a soundtrack.

Warners and Western Electric had formed Vitaphone, which recorded a score played by the New York Philharmonic, accompanied by sound effects. The system was sound-on-disc, which meant synchronization. The film was premiered on 6 August at the Warners' Theatre in New York, supported by some musical short subjects, also synchronized. *Don Juan* was warmly received, but the company wound up in the red because cinema-owners did not want the expense of converting to sound.

Only one other movie mogul was interested at that time – William Fox of Fox Pictures (later 20th Century-Fox), who was experimenting with a sound-on-film system later called Movietone. This was added to *What Price Glory?* (1926) and *Seventh Heaven* (1927), both war stories.

Cinemas that had wired for sound to book these could now also book Movietone or Vitaphone shorts – and they found large, appreciative audiences. Warners decided to add six songs to *The Jazz Singer*, based on a sentimental Broadway play about a Jewish boy who prefers show business to becoming a cantor. The title role went to Al Jolson but the first voice actually heard in a feature was that of Bobbie Gordon, playing Jolson as a child. This film also premiered at the Warner in New York, and the auspicious date 6 October 1927.

The film raked in the sensational sum of $3.5 million and the following year the public flocked to another Jolson vehicle, *The Singing Fool* (1928). The studio had been experimenting with dialogue, for one reel and sometimes two, but it was still too clumsily recorded or spoken to be effective. *The Singing Fool* had dialogue and songs – including the phenomenally popular "Sonny Boy". As those cinemas playing it held it over for week after week, rival houses were forced to convert to sound. And so were the studios.

But recording techniques were still primitive and the camera had to be placed in a sound-proof box. Many of the silent-movie stars spoke in accents unsuitable for talkies – so back to Europe went stars like Emil Jannings and Pola Negri and into retirement went the Bronx-twanged Talmadge sisters, Constance and Norma.

Dashing silent hero John Gilbert was laughed off the screen when he opened his mouth; others, like Ramon Novarro and Charles Farrell, also had voices pitched so high that their days were numbered. The body count was so alarming that moviegoers sighed with relief when favourites like Greta Garbo and Ronald Colman proved to have ideal voices for the new medium.

"King Mike" ruled. For a while Hollywood issued films in two versions – with sound and with intertitles – but the silent movie was dead as 1929 dawned. The panic was on: the public would have nothing but talkies. By the time of its death, the silent screen had found a visual language and vocabulary that were accomplished, beautiful and rich. But all that went unmourned, even as audiences began to tire of the incessant talk, talk, talk which had replaced it. But there was no going back: sound was here to stay.

Theatre hoarding for the first talkie The Jazz Singer (1927).

Main picture: Al Jolson in The Singing Fool (1928), an early talkie musical.

JANUARY
FEBRUARY
1929
MARCH
APRIL

THE ACADEMY PRESENTS . . .

Just over two years after it was formed, the International Academy of Motion Picture Arts & Sciences has announced its first awards. Top prize has gone to Fox studio, for *Sunrise* (1927). King Vidor had originally been told that his movie, *The Crowd* (1928), had scooped the award for "Artistic Quality of Production," but even M-G-M's head, Louis B. Mayer, objected to that on the grounds it was about ordinary people and pessimistic.

It was Mayer who originally came up with the idea of the academy – an association of the elite which would mediate in all labour disputes. On 11 January 1927, the Academy was formally announced. It was to be divided into five branches – actors, writers, producers, directors and technicians. But nothing was said about prizes.

That was president Douglas Fairbanks' idea. A system was devised by which each academy member could cast one nominating vote within his own branch. And then the fun began: what were to be the categories; who would or would not be eligible; and, indeed, what form the trophy was to take.

The awards will be handed out by Douglas Fairbanks at a banquet in the Hollywood Roosevelt Hotel on 19 May.

Noah (played by Paul McAllister) and family lift their arms in prayer in a scene from Michael Curtiz's epic story of the great flood, Noah's Ark.

THE ROAR OF THE WATER

Wunderkind Darryl F. Zanuck provided the story for the latest spectacle from Warners, which brought us the first-ever talking picture, and it's called *Noah's Ark*. Looking back at some of the cinema's milestones like D. W. Griffith's *Intolerance* and Cecil B. DeMille's *The Ten Commandments*, it tells both ancient and modern stories, finding parallels between them – today's tale taking place just a few years ago, with some recruits in Europe fighting the Hun.

The first third of the 135 minutes is silent, with music accompaniment; and rest of it is "all-talkie" and you won't believe how loud the waters roar as they swell and bring whole buildings down. Directed by Hungarian-born Michael Curtiz, it boasts Dolores Costello, Noah Beery and a cast of thousands – some of whom were drowned when one of the giant temples crashed under the impact of the flood.

THE SOUND OF FRYING!

Warner Baxter and Edmund Lowe in the first "outdoor talkie" In Old Arizona.

There's a close-up of ham and eggs, sizzling away in the pan, and the sound is so realistic you can almost eat them. It's a moment delighting all audiences as they watch the first "outdoor all-talkie", *In Old Arizona*, out now from Fox Pictures. It started shooting with Raoul Walsh both directing and playing the lead, but an accident during filming meant the loss of one eye, so Irving Cummings took over the direction and he was replaced in the star-role by Warner Baxter, one of a dozen actors who tested for it. His success in the role looks set to have him berthed at Fox under a long-term contract.

Baxter plays the Cisco Kid, a laughing bandit, and he's in love with a dusky-skinned maiden, Tonia Maria (Dorothy Burgess) – till he overhears her planning to betray him for $5,000 to the sergeant, top-billed Edmund Lowe.

CAPRA ON POVERTY ROW

When Columbia was started by the Cohn brothers in 1922, four major studios were already happily in existence – Fox, Universal, Paramount and First National. Warners and United Artists later joined them as purveyors of first-class entertainment. Exhibitors at first played Columbia's product on the lower half of double bills.

All that has changed thanks to a bright young 31-year-old of Sicilian origin, Frank Capra, who came into prominence at the Mack Sennett studio as gag-man for comic Harry Langdon. After he was sacked by Langdon, Capra eventually ended up at Columbia, for whom he directed a quickie, *That Certain Thing* (1928). Five films later, Columbia invested $150,000 in Capra's *Submarine* (1928) – only the second of the studio's movies to be given a New York premiere. This season sees Capra's first all-talkie – *The Donovan Affair*, based on Owen Davis's popular stage whodunnit. The Cohns are now looking at the sums earned by Capra's films and wondering whether they shouldn't be making more "A" pictures.

BRITAIN LOVES BROADWAY TOO

After triumphing in New York, the "All-Singing! All-Dancing! All-Talking" thrill, *The Broadway Melody*, has broken records across the Atlantic at M-G-M's London flagship, the Empire, Leicester Square, playing for an unprecedented nine weeks to over 500,000 people. Its success has convinced even die-hard exhibitors that they will have to wire for sound.

It's a story of backstage strife and heartache, with a vaudeville sister-act (Anita Page, Bessie Love) aiming for Broadway, where they meet up again with Eddie (Charles King), who shows off his gold tie-pin, his platinum watch-chain and his garters with gold attachments. Harry Beaumont directed, on a 28-day shoot and at a cost of $379,000 – and the film is expected to take six times that in the USA alone.

THE WORLD'S SWEETHEART

We fell in love with her as "The Girl with the Curls" 27 years ago. Toronto-born Mary Pickford came to the fore in the two-reelers of D. W. Griffith and then a star at Famous Players, which later became Paramount. In 1916 she was guaranteed earnings of over $1 million during a two-year period. Only Chaplin earned as much and drew as many people into theatres.

But whenever she played an adult, audiences fell away. In 1919 she formed United Artists to produce her own pictures, in partnership with Douglas Fairbanks, Chaplin and Griffith. "The inmates have taken over the asylum" said one Hollywood wag. The first film Pickford produced was *Pollyanna* (1920), followed by such high spots as *Little Lord Fauntleroy* (1921), in which she played both the little lord and his mother, *Little Annie Rooney* (1925) and *Sparrows* (1926). But enough was enough, and in 1927 she played a store-clerk in love with the boss's son: *My Best Girl*, certainly her most winning performance. Encouraged by the response, 36-year-old Pickford now plays another adult role in her first talkie, *Coquette*, which was a big success on stage for Helen Hayes.

THE MAN WHO NEVER SMILES

Charlie Chaplin has said that he will never ever make a talkie, and Harold Lloyd is still struggling over *Welcome Danger*, which will reportedly use sound in a novel way, to create menace. Meanwhile, Buster Keaton can be seen in *Spite Marriage*, a hilarious tale of a pants-presser who hero-worships a star – only to find himself married to her because she wants to teach her true love a lesson.

Keaton apparently wanted to make this a talkie, but M-G-M refused; other rumours emanating from the studio insist that he no longer has artistic control over his own films – and that he had to fight to keep this film's funniest sequence, in which he tries to put his tipsy bride to bed.

Kansas-born Keaton, 33, has been popular since he first appeared as "Fatty" Arbuckle's side-kick. Given two-reelers of his own and then features like *Sherlock, Jr.* (1924), *The Navigator* (1925) and *The General* (1927),

"The Great Stone Face" has long been recognized as one of the three great clowns of the silent era. In the eyes of many, the ex-vaudevillian is the only one who may be a genius.

MAY
JUNE

JULY
AUGUST

CHORUS GIRLS AND GANGSTERS

Each season the big studios compete to see who can produce the biggest all-talkie. This time it's the turn of Universal, hoping to match the huge revenues still pouring into Metro's coffers for *The Broadway Melody*. Universal's bet is on the more simply titled *Broadway*, based on the smash that lit up the Great White Way itself back in 1927. The studio paid $225,000 for the rights to the play by George Abbott and Philip Dunning, and then poured another tidy sum into the production.

Noted art director Charles D. Hall was commissioned to design a vast nightclub set, and direction was entrusted to Paul Fejos, riding high after his small-scale prestige success, *Lonesome*. Hal Mohr's camera roams around the set, finding as many bootleggers as chorus girls, both factions fighting it out with, in the foreground, a hoofer (Glenn Tryon) trying to make it to the big time with a girl (Merna Kennedy, from Chaplin's *The Circus*).

You note the similarity to the M-G-M film? Universal is advertising this as "The First Million Dollar Talkie" – but there may be moviegoers who don't want to see the same thing twice.

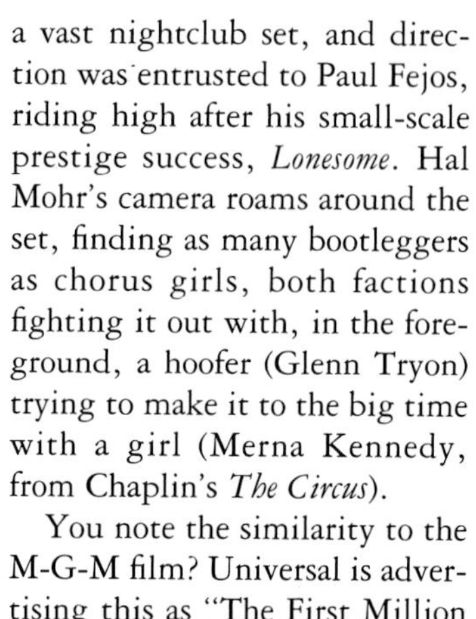

Merna Kennedy and Glenn Tryon in the Paradise Nightclub for a routine in Universal's Broadway.

BRITAIN'S FIRST TALKIE

It took British studios a while to realize that talkies were here to stay. Once they did, there was nothing for it but to ship the casts and crews to where the equipment was – the USA! So Victor Saville re-directed the last three reels of *Jenny* for BIP, and Herbert Wilcox made all of *Black Waters* across the Atlantic. But all this didn't bother Alfred Hitchcock, the rotund young 29-year-old considered the country's leading director since *The Lodger* in 1927.

"Hitch" was filming the thriller *Blackmail* quite happily till he realized that the BIP studio at Elstree was being wired for sound. So he scrapped some of the silent footage. But there was a problem with Czech actress Anny Ondra: her accent was inpenetrable and none of the silent footage could be used if she was replaced – so Joan Barry spoke her dialogue in a microphone off-camera.

What Hitch proves is how imaginatively sound can be used in the hands of the right people: as when the heroine hears nothing but the word "knife" as neighbours gossip about the murder, or when the blackmailer whistles "The Best Things in Life Are Free" as we watch a close-up of money being handed over.

THE GREAT JOLIE

Al Jolson is said to be getting $2.5 million a film. This seems only fair for the man who ushered in the talkies, babbling between songs in *The Jazz Singer* (1927), and who had theatre turnstiles clicking again with *The Singing Fool* (1928).

The Russian-born, 43-year-old star of vaudeville and Broadway is now kept busy by movies. But his new one, *Say It with Songs*, is little more than a reprise of *The Singing Fool*.

THE "IT" GIRL

Britain's not-staid *Picturegoer* magazine has been telling its readers that it was dreading hearing Clara Bow speak, but she has made an effortless transition to sound in *The Wild Party*.

The film itself is little more than a piece of fluff, permitting the 24-year-old star to strut her stuff, smoking after lights out and wandering around in her step-ins. She lets everyone believe that she's man-crazy, whereas the only man she's crazy about is the new professor of anthropology – played by Fredric March, a newcomer from Broadway.

The Brooklyn beauty retains her position as the screen's premier flapper. Love her or leave her, she's Paramount's biggest star, and has been since novelist Elinor Glyn called her "The 'It' Girl" in 1927.

A scene from King Vidor's all-black musical Hallelujah! *in which cotton pickers sing a Negro spiritual as they work.*

AN ALL-BLACK MUSICAL

Lavish, starry M-G-M has gone to the other extreme. Why? Because last year director King Vidor had the critics raving with his tale of an ordinary fella who wants to escape from *The Crowd*, and finds that the powers-that-be don't smile on him.

The "ordinary" folk in *Hallelujah!* are black – cotton-pickers whose lives revolve around revivalist meetings and jazz (and Irving Berlin has composed two new songs for them to sing).

The critics have raved again but in many big cities it has attracted so few spectators that it has been withdrawn after three days. No one, however, can doubt the sincerity of the director, who wanted to show a side of American life hitherto ignored by the movies.

THE LAST SILENT PICTURE

Paramount executives are wondering what to do with *The Four Feathers*, which was started so long ago that the talkie revolution overtook it. This one couldn't be reshot, given the expensive location filming in Africa. (It took almost a year to get a few shots of monkeys and a herd of hippo plunging into a river.)

In charge of the project were Merian C. Cooper and Ernest B. Schoedsack, still big with the studio after their success with *Chang* (1927), a tale of marauding elephants. Paramount added Lothar Mendes to take care of the acting side. *Feathers* is A. E. W. Mason's yarn about the British officer who, accused of cowardice, goes off to the Sudan to redeem his honour. He rescues two colleagues (William Powell, Clive Brook) – and returns home to glory and reconciliation with his fiancee (Fay Wray).

COLMAN SPEAKS

It could be argued that Ronald Colman was the screen's most dashing hero – handsome, courtly, debonair, the very model of an English gentleman. But would talkies be his downfall, as with so many other stars of the silents?

Producer Sam Goldwyn said he had no worries. He chose for Colman's talkie debut not the role of suave lover but of gentleman-adventurer *Bulldog Drummond*, based on Sapper's novel (the first of a series) about an ex-army officer whose exploits keep getting him into big heaps of trouble. The film, directed by F. Richard Jones, is only passable mayhem, and the sound recording is far from the best. But the film is one of the hits of the season, because Colman's voice is exactly what we might have imagined – low, beautifully modulated, a blend of the best American and English.

ACADEMY AWARDS

PRESENTED ON 19 MAY 1929

Best Picture
Broadway Melody

Best Director
Frank Lloyd
The Divine Lady

Best Actor
Warner Baxter
In Old Arizona

Best Actress
Mary Pickford
Coquette

A SWEET SINGING STAR

Old moviegoers will remember her as Harold Lloyd's leading lady – and they, too, will recall Bebe Daniels when she vamped for Cecil B. DeMille. She was Valentino's leading lady in *Monsieur Beaucaire* (1924). More recently she starred delightfully in a series of comedies for Paramount – *Miss Bluebeard* (1925), *Stranded in Paris* (1926), *She's a Sheik* (1928) and *Feel My Pulse* (1928).

Then suddeny Paramount lost interest. After months of inactivity, without even a test for the talkies, the Dallas-born star, 28, bought up her contract.

But RKO supremo William Le Baron had heard her sing at a party and thought she might be ideal for the lead in *Rio Rita*, a restaging of the Ziegfeld musical. The Texas Rangers western has the biggest budget yet by this fledgling studio; it's partly filmed in Technicolor; and Bebe has some fine songs to sing. A Paramount executive said "You never told me you could sing", to which she replied "You never asked me."

A MUSICAL MAESTRO

Ernst Lubitsch, whose comedies have been delighting us since he arrived from Germany in 1923, has used the arrival of sound to prove he's equally a master of the musical sort. Unlike most directors Lubitsch moves his camera – and his people.

And what pretty people they are! Jeanette MacDonald, fresh from the musical stage, plays a Ruritanian queen who makes Paramount's new French heart-throb Maurice Chevalier into her Prince Consort, pampered because he pleases her, as she eventually admits, not "from morning to night" but "from night to morning". Like most of Lubitsch's silents, *The Love Parade* is about the battle of the sexes – and sex is what they are fighting over, slyly, nimbly and wittily.

A LOST QUEEN

Impressed by Erich von Stroheim's ability to turn Mae Murray into an actress in *The Merry Widow*, Gloria Swanson thought he might bring out new riches in her own ability. So began the saga of *Queen Kelly*. She was encouraged by her financier (and, some say, lover) Joseph P. Kennedy, who agreed on a budget of $800,000. That was for a 40-week shooting schedule to make a 30-reel film, hardly economic for exhibitors.

Filming began in autumn 1928, and stopped that winter with only 10 reels completed. The world wanted talkies and, while Swanson hesitated about adding some sound sequences, Kennedy began to get cold feet.

Von Stroheim's story was about an innocent Catholic schoolgirl, Kitty Kelly (Swanson), who enchants a lecherous prince when she loses her bloomers. He intends to seduce her – without the knowledge of his fiancee, the Queen, who is as debauched and depraved as he is. She horse-whips Kitty, who attempts suicide and then goes to Dar-es-Salaam, taking over the hotel her aunt had been running. In the original script that was a brothel, before Hollywood's appointed censor Will Hays stepped in. But whenever Swanson wasn't looking von Stroheim was filming dance-hall girls taking their clients upstairs. Kennedy, a Catholic, hesitated to get into a hassle with Hays, and the film was never restarted.

Swanson brought in another director to shoot a new ending, but von Stroheim insists his contract forbids this version to be shown in the United States. Word is out that it has just been seen in Europe and South Africa – without exciting the least interest.

Below: *Richard Arlin and Gary Cooper in Victor Fleming's* The Virginian. *Cooper plays a ranch foreman who sees his best friend hanged for rustling, and defeats the local bad man.*

A NATURAL IN THE SADDLE

We've seen Gary Cooper several times in Western duds, but in the talkie *The Virginian* he's an even more natural cowboy, for he speaks in a slow, laconic but deliberate drawl. "You long-legged son-of-a –" says Walter Huston. "If you wanna call me that, smile", says Cooper. It's the most memorable line of dialogue the talkies have given us.

This is the third movie version of Owen Wister's classic novel of the old West. Huston is the villainous chief of the rustlers, and Cooper is foreman to Judge Henry, whose cattle is being rustled. Victor Fleming directed for Paramount, which has another success on its hands.

"THE MAN YOU LOVE TO HATE"

On view this season is a familiar figure, elegant in military-style clothes, peering haughtily through a monocle: none other than Erich von Stroheim.

Doubts have been cast as to whether he is the Austrian aristocrat he claims to be – but that is what he played, after a varied career in Hollywood as horse master, extra and actor. Length, cost and sexual excess marked Stroheim's work through a series of films which left Hollywood gasping and critics cheering: *Merry-Go-Round* (1922), *Greed* (1923), *The Merry Widow*, (1925) and *The Wedding March* (1928). He regarded accusations of extravagance as of no consequence in view of his own towering talent: but these, along with his autocratic manner, eventually caused his downfall as a director.

He's now with us in the title role of *The Great Gabbo*, a melodrama about a ventriloquist and his dummy directed by James Cruze, who in 1923 gave us one of the greatest of Westerns, *The Covered Wagon*. Will Hollywood ever permit Stroheim to direct again? *The Great Gabbo* is a bargain-basement job, and that's all that may be available in future to the director once known as "The Man You Love to Hate".

Erich von Stroheim and puppet in The Great Gabbo.

Charles Farrell plays a wealthy socialite and Janet Gaynor the slum girl made good in the delightful musical Sunny Side Up.

GOSSIP COLUMN

■ **Audiences are chortling over John Gilbert's first talkie, *His Glorious Night*. It certainly wasn't for him!**

STAR QUOTES

Mary Pickford

"I have no qualms about admitting that Katharine was one of my worst performances. Instead of being a forceful tiger-cat, I was a spitting little kitten."

YOU CAN'T KEEP A GOOD SONG DOWN

Sunny Side Up is the second movie of the year – after *The Broadway Melody* – to give errand-boys two huge hits to whistle – the title song and "If I Had a Talking Picture of You". They're by the Broadway team of Brown, De Sylva and Henderson, who gave Jolson his great movie hit, "Sonny Boy", and they are already helping this film to be the year's biggest hit after *The Broadway Melody* and more comic adventures for the Victor McLaglen-Edmund Lowe team, *The Cockeyed World*.

Of course, the public has already shown much partiality to the romantic team of Janet Gaynor and Charles Farrell, from *Seventh Heaven* (1927) onwards. So no matter that this is Musical Comedy Plot Number One, with Janet as a poor girl from Yorkville and Charlie as a Long Island heir who eventually make it to the altar, after the usual objections of his ritzy family. The songs enchant, and one of them, "Turn on the Heat", has the most elaborate production number since talkies came in.

DOUG AND MARY – TOGETHER AT LAST

When Douglas Fairbanks wed Mary Pickford in 1924 it was a mating made in heaven. Their first marriages were dismissed as mistakes we all make, and as a couple they entered into the stratosphere of fame and fortune. They were mobbed in every city they visited, from London to Moscow. At home they held court at their mansion, "Pickfair".

Their fans implored them to star in a film together but this was unlikely to happen as long as Pickford continued to play juveniles. It became possible only after *My Best Girl* (1927) and this year's *Coquette* showed the public would accept her in adult roles.

Fairbanks turned to Shakespeare for the right vehicle, but only one play ruled itself in – *The Taming of the Shrew*. Fairbanks would be ideal as Petruchio, and Pickford would be okay as the uppity lady he tames. She accepted the part against her better judgement, and the critics confirmed it wasn't right for her (though a few of them admired the sets). Huge crowds turned up to see Doug and Mary during the first week but the film has since been withdrawn. It may be remembered for the credit, "Additional dialogue by Sam Taylor".

A NEW SCREEN SENSATION

It was soon clear that actor Emil Jannings had no future in talkies. But when he went home to make the first German sound film, for UFA, he took with him Paramount director Josef von Sternberg. His old studio agreed to distribute the English version in the States (the two versions were shot on alternate days). Now it's here – *The Blue Angel*.

Jannings chose the 1905 novel by Heinrich Mann against the wishes of UFA owner Alfred Hugenberg, but he was awed by his talents and by world-famous producer Erich Pommer, he of *The Cabinet of Dr Caligari* (1919), *The Last Laugh* (1924) and *Variete* (1925). It was decided to ignore the latter part of the book, with its various socialist overtones, and concentrate on the early downfall of Professor Unrath (played by Jannings).

This happens when he visits a nightclub, "The Blue Angel", to discover why his pupils are so crazy about its cabaret singer, Lola-Lola (played by new sensation Marlene Dietrich). One look at her garters and he's enslaved, too; they eventually marry, but one humiliation follows another till he becomes a candidate for a straitjacket.

This is America's first view of La Dietrich, a nightclub singer who has recently been promoted to leading roles in local movies. Tough and slightly plump, she lets us know that sex is her business and she likes it: as she sings "Falling in Love Again" audiences, too, are at her feet. When Jannings realised Sternberg was turning the movie into a Dietrich vehicle, it was open war on the set. But she's had the last laugh: she is going to make a film for Paramount.

Emil Jannings plays an old professor infatuated with Marlene Dietrich, a nightclub singer, in The Blue Angel.

GARBO TALKS!

M-G-M has great problems with Swedish-born actress Greta Garbo speaking English.

In selecting *Anna Christie* as her first talkie, Metro is congratulating itself on giving her a different sort of role – a bad lot who finds redemption in a pure love. She actually plays a hooker but the Hays Office overlooked the fact as the original play was by Eugene O'Neill.

Garbo doesn't speak for the first 30 minutes. When she does, she says "Gimme a visky with chincher aile on the side – and don't be stingy." Everyone's breathing a sigh of relief: her voice is low but absolutely right for her image.

Garbo is said not to like either the film or her performance. She prefers the German version made simultaneously. We don't know how much that cost, but the budget on the English one was $376,000.

THE FIRST GENTLEMAN OF THE SCREEN

George Arliss, born in London in 1868, has worked in the United States since 1901 and won Broadway stardom in 1908. He first appeared in the play *Disraeli* in 1911, and he appeared in a film version 10 years later; indeed, he made six pictures around this time, with only moderate success. *Disraeli* was one of the plethora of photographed plays which limped out of Hollywood last year as a result of the coming of sound; and on 30 April the Academy of Motion Pictures honoured Arliss with a statuette for Best Actor.

The film itself is a harmless thing. Academy members seem to have been dazzled by Arliss's classical background and Warners' soubriquet "The First Gentleman of the Screen", for he's monotonous and hammy at the same time. This season Warners has released *The Green Goddess*, in which he is an evil Eastern potentate. It is difficult to know which is the more ludicrous, the film or his performance.

RHAPSODY IN GREEN

The Technicolored *King of Jazz* was no doubt devised in imitation of the other all-star talkie revues, but since Universal has few stars of its own it's made a virtue out of that fact.

The movie is a tribute to the USA's most famous bandleader, Paul Whiteman. Universal players like Laura La Plante, Slim Summerville and Glenn Tryon appear in sketches, while John Boles returns to sing "It Happened in Monterey" and the stirring "Song of the Dawn". This last was to have been sung by one of Paul Whiteman's Rhythm Boys, Bing Crosby, but he was in jail (for being drunk) when shooting was scheduled, so you can only see him as part of the famous close-harmony trio.

Most people will want to see *King of Jazz* to hear Whiteman's celebrated rendition of "Rhapsody in Blue" – for which Universal paid the composer, George Gershwin, an amazing $50,000. There's one glaring anomaly: because the Technicolor palette does not extend to blue, the decor for the "Rhapsody" sequence is green. Broadway's John Murray Anderson was brought to the West Coast to devise and direct.

King of Jazz is a stylish musical revue devised by John Murray Anderson as a tribute to the bandleader Paul Whiteman.

THE "NEW" WOMAN

Ursula Parrot's novel *Ex-Wife* is so notorious that the Hays Office refused to allow M-G-M to use the title. But Wonder Boy producer Irving Thalberg thought it would provide a vehicle for his wife, Norma Shearer, who likes to alternate her goody-goody roles with those in which she is a sophisticated woman of the world.

So in *The Divorcee* she goes to the ultimate, taking a lover (Robert Montgomery) from her country-club set after discovering that her husband (Chester Morris) has been unfaithful. She soon finds that what was sauce for the goose is not for the gander. So will they be reunited? What can be said is that the elegant Shearer represents the "new" woman in this post-flapper era. It can also be reported that the film cost $341,000.

PARAMOUNT'S PLAYBOY OF PARIS

From the moment Maurice Chevalier sang – in his first American film, *Innocents of Paris* (1929) – "Every leetle breeze seems to whisper Louise" he captivated women everywhere.

Born in Paris in 1888 into a poor family, he began to entertain in cafes during his teens. He became a headliner in the Paris music halls, made occasional film appearances, and was delighted when M-G-M tested him. They said no, but let him keep the test; he showed it to Paramount – and now M-G-M is kicking itself.

He's in two movies this season. In *Paramount on Parade* his three sequences were directed by Ernst Lubitsch: two songs and a sketch with Evelyn Brent which includes a mutual striptease. The other is *The Big Pond*, in which Claudette Colbert is his leading lady. She plays a wealthy manufacturer's daughter who has him cross the Atlantic to get a job in her father's factory.

Maurice Chevalier in *The Big Pond*.

FAREWELL TO LOUISE

Lovely Louise Brooks was about to achieve top stardom at Paramount when she took off for Europe to make two films for esteemed German director G.W. Pabst. No studio likes its top stars to work in European studios, but Pabst had assured Paramount that these were outstanding roles. With the studios in turmoil over the arrival of sound and the closure of markets where English is not spoken, Paramount thought it not a bad idea to have Brooks as a star attraction in Germany.

Reports coming out of Germany indicate that Pabst has transformed Louise. In *Pandora's Box* (1929) and *Diary of a Lost Girl* (1929) she has been described as "incandescent", "radiant" and "unique"; she is regarded as a terrific actress and a great beauty.

When she took herself back to Europe for *Prix de Beaute* in France she and Paramount called it quits. Columbia offered her a contract worth $500 a week, not bad for a star thought washed-up in Hollywood, but when she refused to test for a Buck Jones Western, Columbia lost interest too.

BIRTHS, DEATHS AND MARRIAGES

BIRTHS

Rod Taylor
11 Jan, Sydney, Australia

Gene Hackman
30 Jan, San Bernardino, California

Robert Wagner
10 Feb, Detroit

John Frankenheimer
19 Feb, Malba, New York

Joanne Woodward
27 Feb, Thomasville, GA

Silvana Mangano
23 Apr, Rome

Cloris Leachman
30 Apr, Des Moines, IA

DEATHS

Kenneth Hawks
2 Jan, Santa Monica
Plane crash

Mabel Norman
23 Feb, Los Angeles
Tuberculosis

MARRIAGES

Loretta Young
26 Jan, *to* Grant Withers

A GREAT WAR MOVIE

As usual Universal needs a hit. The studio paid a packet for the rights to Erich Maria Remarque's bestseller *All Quiet on the Western Front*. It then poured in a further $1 million so director Lewis Milestone could bring authentic German tanks from Europe. Universal cast the little-known Lew Ayres as the protagonist, and that fine character actor Louis Wolheim as the experienced veteran who takes him under his wing. ZaSu Pitts was cast as Ayres's mother for the silent version. Beryl Mercer took the role for the talkie.

It's bold to tell of the War from the Huns' point of view. The film is long, too, at 140 minutes, but it has been praised as no other war film since *The Big Parade* (1925) and *What Price Glory?* (1926). As *The New York Times* put it, "It is a notable achievement, sincere and earnest, with glimpses that are vivid and graphic . . . It is a vocalised screen offering that is pulsating and harrowing."

THE SCREEN'S IMPISH REDHEAD

We know she's redheaded, because Paramount have promised that we'll see it as they photograph her in Technicolor in *Follow Thru*. We know that she is impish, both in comedy and emotional drama, because she's been a stylish, vivacious, friendly constant in our lives since she joined Paramount in 1928.

We also know she has a reputation for temperament. Born in 1904, diminutive Nancy Carroll was a chorus girl before arriving in Hollywood a year before her bow for Paramount, after making her movie debut for Fox in *Ladies Must Dress* (1927). She showed her mettle last year in movies like *The Shopworn Angel* and *The Dance of Life*. At the moment she's riding high with her performance as a gold digger in *Devil's Holiday* and previews are so promising on the cheeky comedy *Laughter* that she is firmly entrenched at Paramount.

Spectacular flying sequence from Hell's Angels, *a drama about two Americans becoming fliers in the First World War.*

AND THE WAR IN THE AIR

Few films have been more eagerly awaited than *Hell's Angels*, which went into production as long ago as the summer of 1927, just after the success of *Wings*. Its long and troubled history has included several changes of writer and director. The latter include Marshall Neilan, who quit because he couldn't take the constant interference of producer Howard Hughes, who is now the credited director.

There were further complications when it was decided to reshoot the dialogue sequences with sound. Sweden's Greta Nissen was replaced by sexy newcomer Jean Harlow, who has an incongruous nasal twang. The two buddies who josh each other and scrap over her and then go off to fight the Boche are played by Ben Lyon and James Hall.

The aerial photography is often amazing. Early reports indicate a big success for United Artists, which is releasing it. The money in it is mostly Hughes' – to the tune of $3.2 million.

STAR QUOTES

Herman J. Mankiewicz
Screenwriter

"If people don't sit at Chaplin's feet, he goes out and stands where they're sitting."

Chester Morris and Wallace Beery are convicts who attempt a break-out in M-G-M's The Big House.

CHANEY DIES

"Don't step on it" someone once said of a spider, "it may be Lon Chaney". We think the Master of Make-Up might like that as his epitaph. He died in Los Angeles on 25 August, not long after the release of the remake of *The Unholy Three*, his only talkie.

"The Man of a Thousand Faces" was born in 1883 in Colorado Springs, the son of deaf-mute parents. He went on the stage at the age of 16, mainly touring in tank-towns and without much success, and took himself to Hollywood in 1913 hoping to get work as a bit-player. He soon made his movie debut, in the two-reeler *Poor Jake's Demise*, and worked his way up through serials and features, usually as a villain.

He heard Paramount was looking for a contortionist to play a bogus cripple, and it was *The Miracle Man* (1919) which made him a star. Goldwyn made him a ruthless, legless king of the underworld in *The Penalty* (1920) and he was a memorable, pathetic Quasimodo for Universal in *The Hunchback of Notre Dame* (1923). That studio didn't think to put him under long-term contract, and had to pay M-G-M a great deal to borrow him later for *The Phantom of the Opera* (1925).

Chaney became one of Metro's leading stars. He went to extraordinary lengths to perfect his "disguises", and it is believed that the nature of his work in this respect caused the bronchial tumour of which he died – not long after signing a new M-G-M contract.

INSIDE THE SLAMMER

Neither of Metro's supremos, Mayer and Thalberg, like "rough" drama, but Lon Chaney's popularity was such that they had to find vehicles for him. When Chaney died as *The Big House* was about to go into production, they had to replace him with Wallace Beery, a tough guy whose career had been floundering since he left Paramount over a year ago. As spectators line up to see this movie, M-G-M is soon going to cover the $414,000 budget – they are also signing Wally to a long-term contract.

He plays a murderer, sharing his cell with a counterfeiter, Chester Morris, and a newcomer, Robert Montgomery, a guy from a good family jailed for drunken driving. The plot tells, with no holds barred, how Montgomery gets to be a hardened old lag like them. Morris is also a revelation, making up for some weak work on recent outings.

STARRY NIGHTS

Last year M-G-M decided to reassert its superiority over Warners with a "new" form of entertainment, *The Hollywood Revue of 1929*, a showcase for their players with Technicolor sequences. Comperes are Conrad Nagel and Jack Benny; among the stars singing, dancing and clowning are Marion Davies, Buster Keaton, Marie Dressler, Joan Crawford and Laurel & Hardy, while Norma Shearer and John Gilbert do the balcony scene from *Romeo and Juliet* – first seriously, then as comedy.

While the film was in production, Fox hastily assembled *Fox Movietone Follies* and rushed it out before the M-G-M film. Warners followed suit a few months later with *The Show of Shows*, which had Frank Fay in several songs and sketches, and stars like Richard Barthelmess, Douglas Fairbanks Jr, Beatrice Lillie, Loretta Young, Myrna Loy and Rin-Tin-Tin popping up. Not to be outdone, Fox came up earlier this year with *Happy Days*, which featured contractees like Gaynor and Farrell and McLaglen and Lowe, plus some stars from Broadway and vaudeville.

Paramount tried a little harder than its rivals with *Paramount on Parade*, coming up with a starry line-up including Chevalier, Gary Cooper, Clive Brook, Ruth Chatterton and Clara Bow.

Business was only so-so, but Fox has persisted and brought out *Fox Movietone Follies of 1930*. Its box-office performance has been so poor, however, that RKO has cancelled plans for a *Radio Revue of 1930*.

DICK OF THE DAWN PATROL

Another silent favourite who looks set for a long career in talkies is Richard Barthelmess. He's now one of the top stars at Warners.

He was born in New York City in 1895, and used to haunt theatres while still in school. His mother was drama coach to the great Nazimova. That was why he appeared with her in 1916 in *War Brides*; and he's hardly stopped filming since.

The Dawn Patrol is another milestone in his career. It's the third outstanding war movie of the year (less moving than *All Quiet*, more serious than *Hell's Angels*), and tells of the bravery and growing cynicism of the men of the Royal Flying Corps.

BIRTHS, DEATHS AND MARRIAGES

BIRTHS

Clint Eastwood
31 May, San Francisco

Claude Chabrol
24 June, Paris, France

Sean Connery
25 Aug, Edinburgh

Ben Gazzara
28 Aug, New York

DEATHS

Arthur Conan Doyle
7 Jul, London

Rudolph Schildkraut
15 Jul, Hollywood
Heart attack

Lon Chaney
25 Aug, Hollywood
Cancer

SEPTEMBER
OCTOBER

NOVEMBER
DECEMBER

THE BIG SCREEN

Both Fox and M-G-M wanted to be the first to present a film in 70mm. Fox calls its process "Fox Grandeur"; Metro's is "Realife". Their two films have reached cinemas at the same time – but not many of them.

Both have chosen Westerns. *The Big Trail* crew faced and eventually overcame almost every obstacle known to location-shooting except a plague of locusts. Fox's movie was also filmed in a German version.

But M-G-M wins hands down. *Billy the Kid* has a better director (King Vidor), a stronger hero in Johnny Mack Brown, and a really hissable villain in Wallace Beery. And much more suspense. For the record, *The Big Trail* is directed by Raoul Walsh, and Tyrone Power is the villain. Its fine young hero is a newcomer, John Wayne, but Fox does not seem interested in picking up his option.

Unfortunately theatres which have just wired for sound are not prepared to go to the further expense of adapting their projection booths to show wide screen. Neither Fox nor M-G-M has converted more than a handful of their own theatres. So don't lay odds on anything changing when United Artists release *their* widescreen movie in the New Year, *The Bat Whispers*.

Harold Lloyd in Feet First

CLIMBING HIGH

High and Dizzy (1920) was the title of one of Harold Lloyd's early shorts, and that's how he's liked best. Of all his wonderful comedies the best remembered is *Safety Last* (1923), in which he was the "human fly" who climbed the skyscraper. Now he's high up on the roof again in *Feet First*.

Lloyd was born, as the movies were, in 1893 (in Burchard, Nebraska). Arriving in Hollywood in 1912, he started as an extra, and a while later he became friendly with another such, Hal Roach. When Roach inherited $3,000 he started his own company, inviting Lloyd to join him – with Lloyd playing a character called Willie Work. Later that year, 1914, they dropped Willie, and Lloyd became Lonesome Luke, with about 40 shorts a year until he evolved his well-known character.

But it was not until he started making features in 1921 that Lloyd began to come into his own. He's very hard-working, and the elaborate final sequences of his films are all carefully worked out. Anyone who has seen *Grandma's Boy* (1922), *Girl Shy* (1924), *The Freshman* (1925) and *The Kid Brother* (1927) will know that he never repeats himself.

His first talkie, *Welcome Danger* (1929), was a comparative failure. He's now threatened to quit if he can no longer attract audiences.

GOING NOWHERE

Warners is banging the big drum about *Outward Bound*, which starts with a lengthy prologue about the many people who have become interested in "life, death and the hereafter" since Sutton Vane's play was first produced in London in 1923. It's about a motley group of passengers on an outgoing liner, each of whom begins to realize that he or she is dead; the pilot (Dudley Digges), who is due to come aboard is to decide their ultimate destination – or whether to send anyone back to the land of the living. The star is Leslie Howard; the "half-ways" are nicely played by Douglas Fairbanks, Jr and Helen Chandler. But what does it all mean – and does it matter? There is little here to justify the hyperbole of the brothers Warner.

ACADEMY AWARDS

PRESENTED ON 5 NOVEMBER 1930

Best Picture
All Quiet on the Western Front

Best Director
Lewis Milestone
All Quiet on the Western Front

Best Actor
George Arliss
Disraeli

Best Actress
Norma Shearer
The Divorcee

BOX OFFICE

US

1 Whoopee
2 Min and Bill
3 Common Clay

OTHER TOP BOX OFFICE FILMS

All Quiet on the Western Front
Anna Christie
The Big House
The Divorcee
Sunny Side Up
Hell's Angels
Trader Horn

Marie Dressler and Wallace Beery are a riot in the M-G-M comedy Min and Bill.

COPING WITH THE DEPRESSION

What M-G-M had in mind with *Min and Bill* is anyone's guess, but as it lasts only just over an hour it was clearly going to be consigned to the lower half of double-bills (it wasn't cheap, though, with a budget of $327,000). It was also destined to keep in work the most unexpected of this year's new stars. Marie Dressler and Wallace Beery were both making movies almost 20 years ago, and a while back both looked washed up. They're a riot here.

Spectators are rolling up in droves: they've turned their backs on tales of the idle rich to watch people much like themselves coping with problems like their own. Min runs a waterfront tavern and barbershop somewhere near 'Frisco. All Bill wants to do is laze or booze it up, which leads to at least one epic battle in which the best he can do is to fail to get killed.

BIRTHS, DEATHS AND MARRIAGES

BIRTHS

Richard Harris
1 Oct, Limerick

Jean-Luc Godard
3 Dec, Paris

Maximilian Schell
8 Dec, Vienna

DEATHS

Milton Sills
15 Sep, Santa Monica, California
Heart attack

MARRIAGES

Bing Crosby
29 Sep, *to* Dixie Lee

BANJO EYES

Eddie Cantor, seen now in *Whoopee*, has been a star on Broadway since 1916 – often for Flo Ziegfeld, considered Manhattan's leading impresario. He was born in New York in 1893 and was orphaned young; he left school to become an office boy and began performing at amateur nights, taking a chance to turn professional in 1912.

He made his first movie in 1926, when Paramount decided to film one of his Ziegfeld hits, *Kid Boots*, but neither that nor the follow-up, *Special Delivery* (1927), did more than middling business. Cantor showed what he had for talkies when he did his "Jewish tailor" sketch as one of the guest stars in *Glorifying the American Girl* (1929), so now Sam Goldwyn is trying again.

Goldwyn has done little more than reproduce the stage show. There is Technicolor and there are lots of girls, in the midst of whom Cantor sings, dances and rolls his eyes as usual. Goldwyn has an option on his services. The betting is that he'll take it up.

GOODBYE NORMA

Norma Talmadge is the latest to announce she is quitting pictures because she doesn't like the way her voice records. Perhaps she should have retired before inflicting *Du Barry, Woman of Passion* on audiences. It's not that her voice is bad, or her Brooklyn accent too strong for an 18th-century French courtesan. It's just dull.

She and her sister Constance have had a long innings. They were both in films by 1914, and by 1916, before Norma was 20, she had her husband Joseph M. Schenck to guide her career. He kept her a star for 15 years, even though they separated in 1926, perhaps because he was too busy running United Artists.

GOSSIP COLUMN

- **Silent films are as dead a a dodo. As the year finishes 13,128 theatres are wired for sound.**
- **Paramount and Sergei Eisenstein have called it quits. The great Russian director was getting $2,000 a week; but after six months with no concensus on story or script the agreement has been cancelled.**

STAR QUOTES

Maurice Chevalier

"I think women like me because I make them smile, but they do not say 'Oh, that Chevalier!'"

THE WAY TO THE TOP

Warners' *Little Caesar* doesn't have "class" written all over it like *Outward Bound*. But in this hard-hitting and fast-moving version of the mobster novel by W.R. Burnett everything is real. Many of its incidents are taken from yesterday's papers.

Judging by his brilliant performance as the egotistic racketeer, Edward G. Robinson, who has been around movies a time or two before, is here to stay. The strong cast supporting him includes Douglas Fairbanks Jr, Glenda Farrell and William Collier Jr.

Edward G. Robinson, a racketeer, threatens William Collier Jr. in Little Caesar.

JANUARY
FEBRUARY

MARCH
APRIL

TWO EPICS

The year has kicked off with two spectacles – one, of course, from M-G-M, but the other from new challenger RKO. It's the biggest movie in that young studio's existence.

M-G-M's *Trader Horn* has been directed by W.S. Van Dyke – they've been looking for something special for him to do ever since he came back from the South Pacific with *White Shadows of the South Seas* (1928). They sent him to Africa for this one, but as costs mounted the company ordered the crew to return, and a new screenplay was constructed around the footage they had, with more being shot on the studio lot and in Mexico. The eventual cost was $1,322,000 – but they'll get it back, for this is an exciting tale of a man (Harry Carey) who goes searching for a white girl (Edwina Booth) brought up by cannibals. It's based on an autobiographical book by Trader Horn.

RKO's *Cimarron* is based on Edna Ferber's sprawling novel of pioneer days – the springing up of new townships, the land rush, all beautifully managed by director Wesley Ruggles. The budget ended up at $1,433,000 – but they'll get that back, too. At the centre of the action is a newspaper proprietor/editor, Richard Dix. His lovelorn wife is played by Irene Dunne, a newcomer who is plainly in Hollywood to stay.

RKO's Trader Horn *is the story of a Harry Carey (centre) searching for a white girl (Edwina Booth) who has been brought up by cannibals.*

BIRTHS, DEATHS AND MARRIAGES

BIRTHS

Robert Duvall
5 Jan, San Diego, California

James Earl Jones
17 Jan, Arkabutla, Mississipi

James Dean
8 Feb, Marion, Indiana

Claire Bloom
15 Feb, London

Leonard Nimoy
26 Mar, Boston

DEATHS

Anna Pavlova
1 Jan, The Hague
Pleurisy

Will Evans
11 Apr, London

MARRIAGES

Kay Francis
17 Jan, *to* Kenneth McKenna

Melvyn Douglas
5 Apr, *to* Helen Gahagan

DIETRICH VS. GARBO!

M-G-M never expected anyone to topple the great Garbo. It hasn't happened yet, but she is being given a run for her money. The film that's throwing the punches is *Morocco*, in which the slimmed-down, Hollywood-style Marlene Dietrich (from the little-seen but much talked-about *The Blue Angel*) emotes as she dallies with young legionnaire Gary Cooper. She plays a cabaret singer who gives a little after-hours solace to customers. "Every time a man has helped me there has been a price. What's yours?" she asks Adolphe Menjou, who rewards her with expensive trinkets.

She's said to be the creation of her director, Josef von Sternberg. If she improves as much again in her next picture, M-G-M may be putting in a bid for the Austrian Svengali's services.

YESTERDAY'S STAR

Easy-going Richard Dix made the transition to talkies all right, but when he asked for a raise to play the lead in *The Virginian* Paramount said "No deal".

Born in 1894 in St. Paul, Minnesota, Dix intended to be a doctor, but the acting bug got him. Dix became Paramount's leading male star, equally adept in comedy and drama, in such films as *The Ten Commandments* (1923), and *The Vanishing American* (1925). In the latter he played a red Indian, as he did again in *Redskin* (1929).

It was just after that that Dix and Paramount quarrelled. RKO's William Le Baron signed him. His third film for the studio is *Cimarron*, and such is the film's success that Dix will never regret parting from Paramount.

ALL THE NEWS FIT TO PRINT

You couldn't count the number of journalists hired for the movies since talkies arrived, with a brief to provide zingy dialogue. Prominent among them are Ben Hecht and Charles MacArthur, whose play *The Front Page* is the most famous and successful written on that subject – journalism. Howard Hughes's company produced and the direction is in the capable hands of Lewis Milestone, who worked speedily – as did United Artists, who put the film into release only three weeks after completion.

The plot concerns a mild murderer (George E. Stone) and a reporter (Pat O'Brien) covering his execution, not willingly, but because he is being alternately bullied and chivvied by his ruthless editor (Adolph Menjou). Most of the action takes place in the press room of the prison, with the other reporters dashing in and out as they file their stories.

THE GREAT PROFILE

Preview audiences have been talking enthusiastically about John Barrymore's performance in *Svengali*. It's about time, since the great actor hasn't exactly been a success in movies.

He was born into a theatrical family in Philadelphia in 1882, and after a spell in journalism he followed his elder sister Ethel on to the stage in 1903. He was considered one of Broadway's leading light comedians when Famous Players signed him for his first movie, *An American Citizen* (1913). But his film career did not get off the ground until his much-admired *Dr Jekyll and Mr Hyde* (1920). About this time he also consolidated his stage reputation, playing Hamlet and Richard III.

Warners signed him to play the title-role in *Beau Brummell* (1924) but the company found that he couldn't draw the great unwashed. The fans preferred Ronald Colman! Warners decided to give him another chance.

STAR QUOTES

Carl Laemmle
on Bette Davis

"She has as much sex-appeal as Slim Summerville."

JANET AND CHARLIE TOGETHER AGAIN

The team of petite Janet Gaynor and huge-framed Charles Farrell in *Seventh Heaven* (1927) was a heaven-sent gift to Fox's accountants. He's big and protective, she's defenceless and waiflike, though with an odd habit of letting us see her bloomers. Maybe someone high up in the studio also likes seeing them. When Janet quarrelled over her scripts it seemed to spell the end to "America's Favourite Lovebirds", but they are reunited in Raoul Walsh's *The Man Who Came Back*, which Fox are giving the trumpet treatment.

TWO GANGSTERS

This season's gangsters are played by two dynamic newcomers from Broadway: on my right, James Cagney in Warners' *The Public Enemy*, and on my left, Spencer Tracy in Fox's *Quick Millions*. Both play kids from the back streets who make it to the Derby-hat stakes via bootlegging.

Warners' film has the more acrid tone, gritty and unrelenting, with fine support from Joan Blondell, Jean Harlow and Mae Clarke, who gets a grapefruit in the kisser. The more genial Fox movie generates a similar power by insisting that corruption is widespread throughout society.

Spencer Tracy and Sally Eilers in Fox's *Quick Millions*.

MAY
JUNE

JULY
AUGUST

THE SCREEN'S HOTTEST NEW STAR

His first three films were all reviewed by *Photoplay* in March – *The Painted Desert*, *The Easiest Way* and *Dance, Fools, Dance* – and he wasn't even mentioned. But now Clark Gable's name is on the lips of every moviegoer in the United States. M-G-M, which has him on a $350 weekly, two-year contract, foolishly loaned him to Warners for two more support-jobs, a gangster in *The Finger Points* and the cruel chauffeur who is his mistress's lover in *Night Nurse*. The fan mail poured in; and after he slapped Norma Shearer around in *A Free Soul* M-G-M's post room was snowed under.

Now Ohio-born Gable, 30, is to star opposite the studio's other two great ladies – with Joan Crawford in *Possessed* and, before that, with no less than Garbo in *Susan Lenox: Her Fall and Rise.* This last role was earmarked for John Gilbert, who's very different from the uncouth, ungentlemanly, slug-it-to-them Gable. With James Cagney, he marks a new breed of star.

Norma Shearer and newcomer Clark Gable in a clinch from A Free Soul.

If Gilbert's career doesn't get going again, Gable could be the new male star M-G-M badly needs. The studio is said to regard him as only a passing attraction, but one important executive hasn't been too keen on Gilbert since he negotiated a huge rise after threatening to go to Fox. With Clark Gable on show as the tough-guy gambler in *Sporting Blood*, the smart money's on him.

THE END OF THE STRUGGLE

D.W. Griffith has been a hallowed name since he was turning out a two-reeler a week for Biograph. He made the whole industry sit up with his spectacular Civil War tale, *The Birth of a Nation* (1915) – though it upset many with its denigrating portrait of coloured folk. He answered critics with the lavish, four-part *Intolerance* (1916), which the critics liked and the public didn't. When praise was lacking, Griffith provided it himself, brazenly taking ads in the trade press claiming to have invented every innovation in the new medium. An industry in a hurry neither cared nor contradicted, and when he hit form with some melodramas – *Broken Blossoms* (1919), *Way Down East* (1920) and *Orphans of the Storm* (1921) – he was taken at his own word.

Those who praised him did him an injustice, as he couldn't rid himself of his taste for barnstorming blood-and-thunder even as the industry told him he was old-fashioned. He had a failure too many, and he lost his independence to Joseph M. Schenck, who chose his material, stars and writers. Griffith's movies improved and his first talkie, last year's *Abraham Lincoln* with Walter Huston in the title role, was at least respectable.

Before making the last film under his contract to Schenck, he found he had made some lucky investments; there was one film he was burning to do, and so with a bank loan and some money from United Artists he made *The Struggle*, a tract on the Evils Wrought by the Demon Drink. Advance reports say it makes his earlier *A Drunkard's Reformation* (1909) look sophisticated. United Artists doesn't want to release it, but Griffith is insisting they do. It could be the 56-year-old Kentuckian's last stand.

THE LOST GENERATION

It may have passed you by, but *The Last Flight* is one of the most exciting movies of the year. It didn't raise a lot of steam, yet it has exactly the same plot as Ernest Hemingway's novel *The Sun Also Rises*, a bestseller a couple of years back. Since the eminent author hasn't sued for plagiarism, the participants in both must be the same.

It's about a group of American flyers who stop off in Paris after the war to try and drink themselves into oblivion. They're "spent bullets". But where Hemingway was earnest, this film is resolutely casual. William Dieterle (just arrived after a distinguished career in Germany) directs from a novel by John Monk Saunders (he of last summer's *The Dawn Patrol*).

The dour personality of the group's leader fits Richard Barthelmess like a glove; the others are David Manners, John Mack Brown, Elliott Nugent and Walter Byron. Their mascot – the girl who takes to them like a puppy – is the brittle and delightful Helen Chandler, trading flippancy for flippancy. "I'll take vanilla" is her response to most questions. We'll take more from Saunders and Dieterle.

BIRTHS, DEATHS AND MARRIAGES

BIRTHS

Carroll Baker
28 May, Johnstown, Pennsylvania

Leslie Caron
1 Jul, Paris

MARRIAGES

Clark Gable
19 Jun, *to* Ria Langham

William Powell
26 Jun, *to* **Carole Lombard**

Ralph Bellamy
6 Jul, *to* Catherine Willard

Dramatic sequence from The Last Flight, *with Richard Barthelmess (right).*

Josef von Sternberg on the set of An American Tragedy, *about a man who murders his pregnant fiancee when he has the chance to marry a rich girl.*

THE "VON"

The credit on the titles of *An American Tragedy*, now doing the rounds, isn't really a "von". He was born in Vienna (in 1894) to a bourgeois family, but when a producer suggested adding the "von" as marquee bait the autocratic Josef Sternberg was not about to disagree. He came to the United States at the age of seven and entered films as a dogsbody with the World Film Company in New Jersey.

His first movie proper was *The Salvation Hunters* (1925), made on location for $5,000 from its star, George K. Arthur, who wanted to get a footing in America. M-G-M was impressed and signed Sternberg, but he left after two movies were taken out of his hands and reshot by others. Chaplin invited him to direct *A Woman of the Sea*, designed to show what his former co-star, Edna Purviance, could do as an actress. It didn't, because Chaplin suppressed it (some say from professional jealousy).

Paramount signed up Sternberg and, after directing some scenes for others uncredited, he was given *Underworld* (1927). Since then he's done *The Last Command*, *The Docks of New York* (both 1928), *Thunderbolt* (1929) and three with German sizzler Marlene Dietrich. The latest was *Dishonored* earlier this year.

Now comes *An American Tragedy*, based on the novel by Theodore Dreiser, which was originally on Paramount's schedule for Soviet wonder Sergei Eisenstein. The story of a poor boy (Phillips Holmes) who jilts his pregnant girlfriend (Sylvia Sidney) when he's taken up by a rich girl (Frances Dee), it's sombre but absorbing entertainment. The scenes on the lake when he plans to drown Sylvia are stunningly shot – and may be copied if the film is ever remade.

BAD GIRL, GOOD PICTURE

On Broadway last year *Bad Girl* starred Paramount's Sylvia Sidney, and the studio must be kicking itself for not picking up the screen rights. This Fox production, directed by Frank Borzage, has been picking up merry notices and business to match. The *New York Times* thought it superior to Borzage's Oscar-winning *Seventh Heaven* (1927). "Tender and appealing" it called it. "Blessed with truth and simplicity, and yet there is the necessary suspense in all its episodes."

The title gives no indication that the film is actually the story of a marriage, from the couple's first meeting to their first baby. But it does refer to the suspicions of the girl's brother when she stays out till four with her boyfriend. She's actually a good girl.

Hollywood can certainly turn out fine movies about people who live in tenements when it wants to. Edwin Burke wrote the screenplay and the original novel was by Vina Delmar. In his first film James Dunn is terrific – not film-starry, but with a gosh-oh-darn ordinariness. As the girl Sally Eilers is sweet, if not his match as an actress. As her friend, Minna Gombell seizes every chance for a laugh, and there are many.

GOSSIP COLUMN

- **Constance Bennett's salary for *Bought* is said to be the largest in pictures – $30,000 a week in what would normally be her vacation. Don't tell Connie, but Will Rogers gets $35,000 a week at Fox.**
- **Alma Rubens has died of pneumonia. The beautiful 33-year-old star of silents, and ex-wife of Ricardo Cortez, was earlier arrested for possession of narcotics. Her doctor said she'd been an addict for years.**

A POOR LITTLE DEVIL?

That's what Norma Shearer's grandmother calls her in *A Free Soul*, but the title says it better. She's the daughter of a drunken lawyer (Lionel Barrymore) and she has a stuffy fiance (Leslie Howard). Then she meets Ace (Clark Gable). "You're a new kind of man in a new kind of world," she tells him with stars in her eyes. Dad offers to give up liquor if she'll give up Ace. Huh! But when Ace asks her to marry him her answer is a provocative "Why?" – for, as he reminds her, her clothes are hanging in his closet. "You're swine walking with swine," she reminds him, but he's not fazed: "You're talking to the man you love."

Gable, fourth on the cast-list, acts as if he had top-billing: he's not only Norma's big thrill, but every woman's in the audience as well. The original novel was by Adela Rogers St. John, who clearly knows a bit about "the new woman", and the film was directed by Clarence Brown on a budget of $529,000.

STAR QUOTES

Joan Crawford
on Norma Shearer

"How can I compete with her, when she sleeps with the boss?"

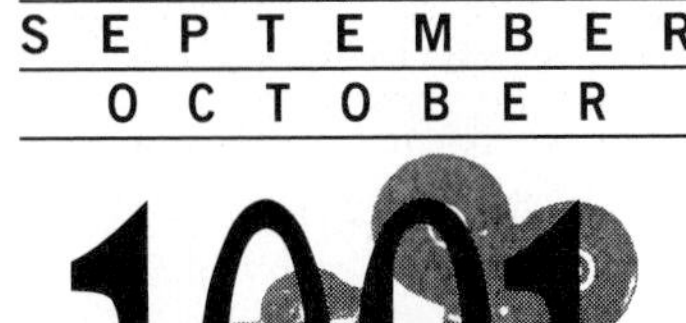

SEPTEMBER OCTOBER

NOVEMBER DECEMBER

BOX OFFICE

US

1 Cimarron
2 Palmy Days

OTHER TOP BOX OFFICE FILMS

The Champ
City Lights
Daddy Long Legs
Frankenstein
Little Caesar
Public Enemy
Skippy
The Smiling Lieutenant

BIRTHS, DEATHS AND MARRIAGES

BIRTHS

Anne Bancroft
17 Sep, New York

Anthony Newley
24 Sep, London

Angie Dickinson
30 Sep, Kulm, North Dakota

Lee Grant
31 Oct, New York

Mike Nichols
6 Nov, Berlin

DEATHS

Arthur Schitzler
21 Oct, Vienna

Lya de Puti
27 Nov, New York
Pneumonia

Tyrone Power Sr.
31 Dec, Hollywood
Heart attack

MARRIAGES

Lew Ayres
15 Sep, *to* Lola Lane

Gloria Swanson
9 Nov, *to* Michael Farmer

Constance Bennett
22Nov, *to* Marquis de la Coudraye

Henry Fonda
25 Dec, *to* **Margaret Sullavan**

THE REPORTER AND THE DEBUTANTE

There have been several comedies about the Press this year, but none funnier than the latest from Columbia's white-haired boy, Frank Capra. *Platinum Blonde* has debutante Jean Harlow meeting reporter Robert Williams and falling head over heels for him. He has been drawn to pretty colleague Loretta Young, but he's flattered by Harlow's attentions. Only trouble is, her ritzy set doesn't mix with his dice-rolling crowd. There is also the matter of his garters: he doesn't wear any. But neither does Einstein, he says. She keeps harping on it and eventually presents him with a pair, initialled.

As he walks away into the sunset with Young at the end, he hands them to a bum. "Hey, what about the socks?" yells the bum.

Harlow is hardly a convincing socialite, but Williams is a delight. This movie dotes on its journalists – it's not interested in stuffed shirts.

Wallace Beery, Jackie Cooper and Roscoe Ates in The Champ.

A FOUR-HANDKERCHIEF JOB

All the world loves a good cry, and that's what you'll get from *The Champ*, a well-crafted movie from M-G-M's King Vidor, costing $356,000. The material could have made something more than a tear jerker, but then it might not have been the crowd-pleaser it is. Europe will get the original unhappy ending, with the Champ dying, rather than the one studio boss Irving Thalberg ordered for Americans.

Wallace Beery has the title role, an old mugg hoping for a comeback. His joy is his kid, Jackie Cooper – till wealthy Irene Rich hoves into view. She was married to Beery in his championship days and wants the child back. A battle ensues.

You could argue that poverty doesn't make people lovable, open-hearted and understanding. But no one's arguing about the teaming of Cooper and Beery.

SELZNICK ARRIVES AT RKO

In its short but troubled history RKO has had only two real hits, *Rio Rita* (1929) and *Cimarron* (1931). It's all a long way from the high hopes expressed when the company was set up in 1928.

Prime mover was businessman Joseph P. Kennedy, who had bought minor studio FBO in 1926. Two years later RCA invested in FBO because its rival, Western Electric, was affiliated to the other studios in supplying sound equipment. RCA decided to build up FBO by acquiring vaudeville circuit Radio-Keith-Orpheum. Its theatres could display the product of the new corporation, owned by RCA and said to be worth $300 million.

The studio made profits from its movies in 1930 and 1931, but was buying up theatres in a big way. When the Depression began to bite this summer it was losing hundreds of thousands of dollars weekly.

In January it had assimilated Pathe Exchange, adding popular players like Ann Harding and Constance Bennett to its own stable of stars like Joel McCrea, Irene Dunne, Evelyn Brent, Mary Astor and Richard Dix. It also bagged Dolores del Rio.

Now comes David O. Selznick, son of the producer Lewis J. Selznick, who was going great guns over at Paramount. He plans to upgrade the studio's product and, if his work at Paramount is anything to go by, RKO's troubles will be over.

ACADEMY AWARDS

PRESENTED ON 10 NOVEMBER 1931

Best Picture
Cimarron

Best Director
Norman Taurog
Skippy

Best Actor
Lionel Barrymore
A Free Soul

Best Actress
Marie Dressler
Min and Bill

Edward G. Robinson, as a ruthless and sensation-seeking newspaper editor, and Boris Karloff in Five Star Final.

THE MAD MONSTER

When Bela Lugosi starred on Broadway in *Dracula*, audiences shivered. They screamed when he toured in it; and when Universal filmed it earlier this year moviegoers ran all the way home, keeping clear of dark places. Tod Browning directed this tale of a Transylvanian count who is also a vampire, but Universal has given its follow-up to James Whale.

It is called *Frankenstein*, from an 1818 novel by Mary Shelley, and doesn't star Lugosi (the Hungarian refused because he has plans of his own to do a *Quasimodo*). The monster is played by British-born Boris Karloff, now coming into his own after being around since 1919. His make-up job is one of the most stunning ever seen on the screen – a creature manufactured by Frankenstein (Colin Clive), in thrall to the theories of a mad doctor.

LITTLE CAESAR HIMSELF

Born in 1893 in Bucharest, Romania, Edward G. Robinson moved to America at the age of nine. He planned to become a rabbi or a lawyer, but instead turned to acting, changing his name from Emanuel Goldenberg. From 1915 he carved out a fair position in the New York theatre. After a supporting role as an elderly revolutionary in *The Bright Shawl* (1923), a Richard Barthelmess vehicle, he made no other movies till 1929, when Paramount put him into a creaky old melodrama called *The Hole in the Wall*.

Five movies followed, including two in which he played a gangster, but it was not until his memorable performance in *Little Caesar* that he became a real star. It was great to see him share the screen with Jimmy Cagney in this summer's *Smart Money*. Shame is, they're both too big at Warners to be teamed again.

In real life Robinson is the opposite of the hard-driving types he's so far played on screen. Off the lot the ruthless editor of *Five Star Final* and the small-time chiseller of *Smart Money* likes to relax with painting and literature.

THE PROBLEMS OF GLORIA

Fine artist though she is, Gloria Swanson is in danger of turning into yesterday's potatoes. Born in 1897, in Chicago, she got into movies as an extra while on a visit to Essanay Studio. She was married to Wallace Beery (for about a month) and appeared as the innocent in Keystone shorts. It was Cecil B. DeMille who made her name in *Don't Change Your Husband* (1919) and other sophisticated maritil comedies, and she went on to be Paramount's chief female star in the next decade, extravagantly gowned, feted everywhere – the first Hollywood star to marry into European aristocracy.

Swanson's attire sometimes got in the way of her acting, but she was wonderful playing shopgirls in *Manhandled* (1924) and *Stage Struck* (1925) – and her *Sadie Thompson* (1928) was a fine piece of acting. However, those amorous entanglements among the Long Island set in *Indiscreet* earlier this year had audiences yawning. Now comes *Tonight or Never*, with Swanson as a temperamental diva who is told to find herself a lover or she will never achieve greatness. Really!

THE LUNTS BRING GLORY TO THE SCREEN

Or so M-G-M says. Irving Thalberg has finally wooed the famous husband-and-wife team of Alfred Lunt and Lynn Fontanne away from Broadway into a version of Ferenc Molnar's *The Guardsman*, the second play in which they appeared together.

It's a bubble of froth about an acting couple: the jealous husband disguises himself as an amorous Russian guardsman in order to test his wife's fidelity. But the public is refusing to go, so the movie is unlikely to get back its $322,000 budget. Everyone is keeping mum about a second film due under the agreement.

They used a fair amount of gauze over the lens for Fontanne, but you can still see she's not in the same class as Garbo, Chatterton or Shearer. Lunt, however, is a fine light comedian. More of *him*, please.

Featuring Tyrone Power and Alice Faye, Alexander's Ragtime Band *(1938) was a cavalcade of Irving Berlin songs.*

MacDonald and Chevalier in The Love Parade *(1929).*

The triumphant finale from 42nd Street *(1933).*

Ruby Keeler is the pivot in this scene from Gold Diggers of 1933.

Bevy of bathing beauties from Footlight Parade *(1933).*

BROADWAY BABIES

It wasn't enough to talk: they had to sing too. As Hollywood scoured Broadway and vaudeville for artists who could sing and dance, the studios were giving lessons in both to those stars who had weathered the talkie revolution. Everybody sang: Joan Crawford, Gloria Swanson, Ramon Novarro, even sturdy heroes Richard Dix and Richard Barthelmess, the dainty Janet Gaynor and the daintier Nancy Carroll.

"All-Talking! All-Singing! All-Dancing!" went the boast, and for a while audiences revelled in musicals. Even Douglas Fairbanks made one, *Reaching for the Moon* (1931), but he didn't sing (an unbilled Bing Crosby did). Each studio turned out a movie review in which all their stars strutted their stuff.

Of the new intake only Broadway's Eddie Cantor and France's Maurice Chevalier really took. Chevalier made the more memorable movies, partnered by Jeanette MacDonald – like *The Love Parade* (1929), *One Hour with You* and *Love Me Tonight* (both 1932). Broadway favourites like Marilyn Miller and Sophie Tucker returned to the stage, while Al Jolson quickly wore out his welcome in some lachrymose tales. From radio in 1932 came Bing Crosby, who was to settle down to a comfortable two-decade reign as Paramount's musical king.

After Warners had almost killed off the screen musical with their two-tone Technicolor operettas, the studio then revitalized them with a smashing trio in 1933, *42nd Street, Gold Diggers of 1933* and *Footlight Parade*. Each featured go-get-'em showgirls, lascivious Broadway "angels", hard-driving dance directors and the cooing, singing love team of Dick Powell and Ruby Keeler. Each contained elaborate numbers by Busby Berkeley, with large choruses of lacquered blondes in geometric patterns. His masterpiece was the foot-tapping "Lullaby of Broadway" finale of *Gold Diggers of 1935*.

Meanwhile, M-G-M followed suit with the gutsy *Dancing Lady*, with Joan Crawford as an ambitious showgirl and Clark Gable as her producer. She even got to dance with Fred Astaire, signed from Broadway by an unenthusiastic RKO, which had loaned him out because it didn't know what to do with him.

The studio teamed him with former Broadway chorine Ginger Rogers, who had been going nowhere fast in movies, for a novelty number in *Flying Down to Rio* (1933). The public liked it, and the couple were reteamed for Cole Porter's *The Gay Divorcee* (1934). Irving Berlin wrote the songs for the two films which would send them into box-office orbit, *Top Hat* (1935) and *Follow the Fleet* (1936), while Jerome Kern composed those for *Swing Time* (1936), which marked their peak as a team.

MacDonald teamed with Chevalier for the last time in the entrancing *The Merry Widow* (1934) and then with the wooden Nelson Eddy in another old show from Broadway, *Naughty Marietta* (1935). They became the second popular musical team of the period for M-G-M. 20th Century-Fox had under contract Alice Faye, who rose to prominence in films like *On the Avenue* (1937) and *Alexander's Ragtime Band* (1938), both with scores by Irving Berlin. The Studio's child star, Shirley Temple, she was probably the biggest box-office attraction of the decade. Her reign ended as two other youngsters of real talent emerged. Deanna Durbin's straightforward playing and clear soprano voice were a boon to Universal from her feature debut in *Three Smart Girls* (1937); Judy Garland took longer to mature. But in 1939 the world lost its heart to her as she chanted "Over the Rainbow" in *The Wizard of Oz*, – a curtain raiser to the Hollywood musical's greatest two decades.

Main picture: Top Hat *(1935), the archetypal Fred Astaire and Ginger Rogers film.*

JANUARY
FEBRUARY

1932

MARCH
APRIL

THE SAGA OF SHANGHAI LILY

Marlene Dietrich, Clive Brook and Anna May Wong in Shanghai Express.

"It took more than one man to change my name to Shanghai Lily," says Marlene Dietrich to old flame Clive Brook before the *Shanghai Express* begins to get up steam. The passenger list is pretty steamy, too. As one of them says: "I suppose every train has its cargo of sin, but this train has more than its share. . . ." They include favourites like Warner Oland as a revolutionary leader, Gustaf Von Seyffertitz as an opium dealer, Anna May Wong as a slyboots and Eugene Pallette as an irascible businessman. At the centre is La Dietrich, fascinating from the first moment we see her, coolly advancing along the platform amidst the crowds.

"Why, she's wrecked a dozen men," exclaims one character. The director – of course – is Josef von Sternberg.

THE MAN OF THE TREES

You can't blame M-G-M for wanting to capitalize on the success of last year's *Trader Horn* – or wanting to re-use the studio jungle when location-shooting went horribly wrong. The surprise is that under the same director, W.S. Van Dyke, the studio has come up with such a winner.

Tarzan the Ape Man is the latest attempt to film Edgar Rice Burroughs' creation, the superhuman brought up by the simians. He's played by former Olympic swimming champ Johnny Weissmuller, who wins no medals as an actor but looks handsome and athletic on screen. The girl he kidnaps and who falls in love with him is Irish colleen Maureen O'Sullivan. Their scenes together have a charge which will leave most viewers weak.

Johnny Weissmuller in his first starring role as Tarzan the Ape Man.

BIRTHS, DEATHS AND MARRIAGES

BIRTHS

Richard Lester
19 Jan, Philadelphia

Piper Laurie
22 Jan, Detroit

Elizabeth Taylor
27 Feb, London

Debbie Reynolds
1 Apr, El Paso, Texas

Anthony Perkins
4 Apr, New York

John Gavin
8 Apr, Los Angeles

Omar Sharif
10 Apr, Alexandria, Egypt

Elaine May
21 Apr, Philadelphia

DEATHS

Edgar Wallace
10 Feb, Hollywood
Heart ailment

Norman McKinnel
29 Mar, London
Heart disease

MARRIAGES

Joan Bennett
12 Mar, *to* Gene Markey

Ann Dvorak
17 Mar, *to* Leslie Fenton

GOSSIP COLUMN

■ Two of the stars of *Grand Hotel* are not on speaking terms – after one of the male stars told one of the two female stars to go home and learn to act. Only one guess allowed.

■ The citizens of Hollywood and Beverly Hills are getting the heebie jeebies about the banks closing. Wallace Beery was one of the worst hit, losing over $100,000.

FIVE STARS! COUNT 'EM

Whether or not Garbo still wants to be alone, she's no longer lonely on her pedestal. In *Grand Hotel* she's billed above the title with John Barrymore, Joan Crawford, Wallace Beery and Lionel Barrymore. The movie is already one of the year's biggest topics of conversation.

The one-star-one-film concept was always a bit daft. And with the emergence of screen teams like Colman-Danky, Gaynor-Farrell and Garbo-Gilbert they found some strange ways to get round it.

M-G-M boss Irving Thalberg was typically bold in casting the movie. Vicki Baum's book (and the play based on it) is a cross-section affair, and once the studio's writers got to work on it they found they had five parts of equal importance. There's the disillusioned ballerina (Garbo), the playboy thief (John Barrymore) who pretends he loves her, the stenographer (Crawford), the tycoon (Beery) who employs her with an eye to more than shorthand, and the accountant (Lionel Barrymore) who checks in for one last spree. Stand by for more all-star movies.

Maurice Chevalier and Jeanette MacDonald in One Hour With You.

AN HOUR (OR SO)

Maurice (Chevalier) and Jeanette (MacDonald) are back together in the witty sex-romp *One Hour With You*, as a married couple. When he sings the title-song to her, we know how they would like to spend that hour. But he can't resist being tempted by a vamp (Genevieve Tobin) on the verge of a divorce, and she is prey to that lady's husband (Charlie Ruggles) – though for the moment he's happy with the maidservant.

In other words, a typical confection from director Ernst Lubitsch – a chocolate-box of delights, written by his usual collaborator, Samson Raphaelson. The credits say Lubitsch was "assisted by George Cukor". Cukor is claiming (rather quietly) that he directed it, under Lubitsch's supervision.

A REAL PRO

Everyone is talking about Barbara Stanwyck. She's no great beauty but she has an understated intensity which should guarantee her a long, long career. She just gets on with the job. She's a real pro.

Born in Brooklyn in 1907, she went to work in a department store at 13, taking dancing lessons at night; at 15 she was a chorus girl in speakeasies. In 1928 she married vaudeville star Frank Fay and when he went into films he tried to get her a contract. But without success: she made two movies in New York, *Broadway Nights* (1927) and *The Locked Door* (1930), her talkie debut.

Then Fay persuaded Frank Capra into casting her in *Ladies of Leisure* (1930), as the chief party girl – the sort who checks a guy's wallet before agreeing to go to his apartment to pose for him. Both Columbia and Warners (Capra's studio) gave her contracts.

Now she's back in her third Capra outing, *Forbidden*, a more conventional but lovingly made tale of a spinster librarian who falls for an older married man (Adolphe Menjou) and rejects her young suitor (Ralph Bellamy). True to form, she's a real pro.

HARDLY DAUNTING

Ann Harding's new movie is called *Prestige* – and she's covered in it. Pathe and now RKO insist she is a "great lady"; but here she's not daunting at all – just warm, beautiful and with a fetching way of playing drama as if it were comedy.

She was born in 1902 at Fort Sam Houston, Texas. While working for Paramount as a script reader, she was persuaded by her colleagues to join the Provincetown Players for fun. By 1927 she was starring on Broadway in *The Trial of Mary Dugan* and when her husband, Harry Bannister, was offered movie work she went with him to the West Coast – to a flock of offers. She chose to do *Paris Bound* (1929) at Pathe, with Fredric March, and then accepted a long-term offer from the studio.

Prestige is one of those overheated triangles that RKO likes so much: she goes out East to visit her drunken husband, only to find that his caddish C.O. (Adolphe Menjou) is making eyes at her. Her next leading man, in *Westward Passage*, will be young British import, Laurence Olivier.

THE RETURN OF POLA

Pola Negri's Hollywood career was kaput before the talkies. She got out with dignity, saying she was never coming back. But after making one movie and walking out of another in France, she's back all right. RKO decided that Pola could be their own continental temptress.

Paramount overdid the publicity when she first arrived in Hollywood back in 1923. The femme fatale image began to seem foolish; and her much-publicised passion for Valentino (after his death) didn't help. Negri's two good films, *Hotel Imperial* and *Barbed Wire* (both 1927), came too late.

It looks as though her latest, *A Woman Commands*, will end up in the red in the ledger books. She has a pretty song and solid support from Basil Rathbone and Roland Young, but the story isn't appealing to American audiences.

MAY JUNE 1932 JULY AUGUST

A DISTINGUISHED ACTOR

Walter Huston recently wrote in *Film Weekly*: "Whenever people saw my name outside the cinema, they knew what to expect: Huston, the hard and heartless man of iron."

Born in Toronto in 1884, Huston first appeared on the New York stage in 1905. He and his then-wife did a song-and-dance act in vaudeville till 1924, when he began to act regularly on Broadway. Paramount brought him into films in 1929, in *Gentlemen of the Press*, and although Hollywood has been reluctant to let him go he has had to scout around for good parts. They have included his kindly prison governor in *The Criminal Code* (1931), the father of a family trapped by gangsters in *The Star Witness* (1931) and his crusty old seadog in *A House Divided* (1932).

Earlier this year he signed with M-G-M, who promise better roles – which he has had in *The Beast of the City*, as an over-zealous top cop, and *The Wet Parade*, as a drunken hotel proprietor.

THE SHAME OF A NATION

A hornet's nest has been stirred up by *Scarface*. Like last year's *Little Caesar*, it's based on the life of Al Capone, but is officially from a novel by Armitage Trail. W.R. Burnett, the author of the book on which *Little Casear* was based, was one of the writers on the movie, which also borrows from *The Public Enemy* (1931). All that has gone unnoticed. The fuss is because many of the incidents in *Scarface* are recognisably from real life, such as the St Valentine's Day Massacre.

Producer Howard Hughes had already had many battles with the Hays Office, which refused to let the gangster chief (Paul Muni) be mown down at the end, insisting that he be publicly hanged. After press criticism, Hughes withdrew the film to add a preface featuring the Police Commissioner of New York pleading for greater arms controls. Also inserted was a scene in which the Chief of Detectives complains to a newspaper editor that the press glamorises gangsters; the editor replies that the public has a right to know the truth. Hughes even added a subtitle to the film – *The Shame of A Nation*. But all this is making little difference to the box-office, which varies from town to town. Some exhibitors still refuse to show the picture, which is a pity. It's a pacy item, directed by Howard Hawks, and with a memorable role by young George Raft as Muni's coin-flipping henchman.

STAR QUOTES

James Cagney
on being refused a raise by Warners

"I guess movies and I are washed up for good."

A particularly menacing Boris Karloff in The Old Dark House, *a horror comedy about a traveller taking refuge in the house of a family of eccentrics.*

KARLOFF IN DEMAND

Only a few years ago he was just another supporting actor on the books of Central Casting, but with his sonorous, deep voice, Boris Karloff has appeared in no fewer than 12 films last year. When *Frankenstein* made him a star Universal gave him a contract, and since this year began he's been seen in six more including *The Cohens and Kellys in Hollywood*, in which he had a guest spot as himself. That's fame!

His busy schedule will see him in three more horror movies over the next months: first as a deadly deaf-mute servant in *The Old Dark House*, and then as the famous yellow peril in M-G-M's *The Mask of Fu Manchu*; then back at Universal as *The Mummy*, returning to life after 3,700 years in an Egyptian tomb.

But first comes *The Most Dangerous Game* from RKO. In this a mad Baron Zaroff (Leslie Banks) sets his hounds out to hunt in the jungle – human prey, kidnapped by him!

"FREAKS" FREAKS OUT

M-G-M doesn't like being second to anyone, so when Universal grasped the horror crown with *Dracula* and *Frankenstein* Irving Thalberg sent for the studio's own specialist, Tod Browning, and told him to go even further.

Even Thalberg was astonished when he saw the result, which is about the passions of the physically deprived among circus folk – the armless, the legless, pinheads, the bearded lady. He ordered the film to be called *Freaks* so that audiences would know what they were in for; he ordered it to be cut to just over an hour as anything more would have been too gruelling, and he ordered a preface to say that it was offered "with humility" to those who have suffered.

Gossip columnist Louella Parsons is still appalled but as her boss William R. Hearst is a buddy of Mayer she has been guarded in what she's said. "For sheer sensationalism *Freaks* tops any picture yet made," she wrote. M-G-M has had the gall to use this in its ads. But it hasn't prevented many states and the U.K. from banning the film.

WEEP ON

John Boles and Irene Dunne in Back Street.

There are two weepies around at the moment which are just about perfect.

Universal's *Back Street*, based on a novel by Fannie Hurst and directed by John M. Stahl, tells of a high-toned small town girl (Irene Dunne) who, after being seduced by a visiting "drummer" (John Boles), goes to the Big City to be with him. She loves him desperately; he returns her love – but not enough to divorce his wife, which might wreck his career. For the next 30 years she is content to live in a back street and have an hour with him on his way home from work.

Warners' *One Way Passage*, directed by Tay Garnett, concerns another impossible love – between a man (William Powell) returning to America to fry in the electric chair, and a woman (Kay Francis) with an incurable disease. This one has a demotic humour to counterbalance the romance, and a supporting cast that includes such old reliables as Frank McHugh, Warren Hymer and the invaluable Aline MacMahon, known to her friends as "Barrelhouse Betty" but here posing as a countess.

Shopgirl and the boss in Red-Headed Woman, *with Jean Harlow and Chester Morris.*

"WHY DON'T YOU CALL IT BY ITS REAL NAME?"

In *Red-Headed Woman* Jean Harlow is so single-minded in pursuit of Chester Morris that he finally asks her what she wants. When she replies, he is astonished: "Love? Why don't you call it by its real name?"

In a season which has seen several female stars playing hookers, Harlow is something else. The others have gone on the streets to pay the bills, but you can be pretty sure that if Jean did the same thing she would be paying the men for the privilege. Morris is her boss, and married, but that doesn't stop her; after she has managed to disgrace him before his wife and married him, she is looking for other people to seduce.

Katharine Brush's novel was so notorious that only a shameless M-G-M would have bought the rights. Harlow got the role by default after Norma Shearer and Joan Crawford, known for playing "independent", turned down the project as too scandalous. Jack Conway directs for humour, and they're trying to sell it as a comedy. We hear the British censor has turned it down flat, and if the Empire follows suit this won't look so funny in the M-G-M ledgers.

BIRTHS, DEATHS AND MARRIAGES

BIRTHS

Peter O'Toole
2 Aug, Ireland

DEATHS

Louis Mercanton
2 May, Paris
Heart disease

Florenz Ziegfeld
26 Jul, Los Angeles
Pneumonia

MARRIAGES

Jean Harlow
Jul, *to* Paul Bern

John Gilbert
Aug, *to* Virginia Bruce

George Brent
13 Aug, *to* Ruth Chatterton

Bette Davis
18 Aug, *to* Harmon Nelson

GOSSIP COLUMN

- **The *Motion Picture Herald* has named the stars who'll bring 'em in regardless of the picture. The women, from the top: Marie Dressler, Janet Gaynor, Joan Crawford, Greta Garbo, Norma Shearer, Sally Eilers, Constance Bennett, Marlene Dietrich. The men: Wallace Beery, Will Rogers, Clark Gable, Chevalier, Buck Jones, John Barrymore, Johny Weissmuller and Ramon Novarro.**
- **Ann Harding's career could be heading for the rocks. Not only has she ignored studio politics but she's also demanding a hand in story and direction. That can't be done – as Gloria Swanson proved.**

SEPTEMBER
OCTOBER

NOVEMBER
DECEMBER

PARAMOUNT'S BIG SEASON

Paramount's had it all its way this season. It's brought Broadway's fabled George M.Cohan bang to the screen, in *The Phantom President*, for the first time since 1918; it's made stars of Mae West and Bing Crosby, in *Night After Night* and *The Big Broadcast*; and it's presented the novel all-star five-story feature, *If I Had a Million*. Director Ernst Lubitsch has furthered his reputation with what may be his most delightful film, *Trouble in Paradise*, while *Blonde Venus* has carried the Sternberg-Dietrich team into even sleazier, more exotic waters.

But the most significant event for the studio was the return of Cecil B. DeMille after an unhappy spell at M-G-M. He's rebounded with a tale of pagan Rome, *The Sign of the Cross*, in which Nero (Charles Laughton) fiddles and Poppaea (Claudette Colbert) bathes in asses' milk.

Paramount's biggest achievement, under Frank Borzage's direction, is a near-perfect love story, *A Farewell to Arms*, based on the novel by Ernest Hemingway. Gary Cooper is the American fighting with the Italian army, and Helen Hayes is the nurse who tends him when he is wounded. Neither has done better work since coming to Hollywood.

Kay Francis and Herbert Marshall in Ernst Lubitsch's Trouble in Paradise.

ACADEMY AWARDS

PRESENTED ON 18 NOVEMBER 1932

Best Picture
Grand Hotel

Best Director
Frank Borzage
Bad Girl

Best Actor
Wallace Beery
The Champ
Fredric March
Dr. Jekyll and Mr. Hyde

Best Actress
Helen Hayes
The Sin of Madelon Claudet

THE ACADEMY'S BEST ACTORS

The Oscars are now four years old and no one is under-estimating their importance. That's why they keep changing the rules. Last year there were five nominees in most categories, including Best Picture, Best Actor and Best Actress. This year no fewer than eight films were listed on the ballot papers, but only six thespians, three of each sex.

That should have made it easier, but in fact two of the actors tied – Wallace Beery in *The Champ* and Fredric March in *Dr Jekyll and Mr Hyde* (the one who missed out was Alfred Lunt in *The Guardsman*). Beery did his lovable old codger act so well that it's no surprise Academy members voted for him. But March was exceptional as both Jekyll and Hyde, under master director Rouben Mamoulian. The film has been so praised that it's overlooked that it was aimed at the same public as *Frankenstein*. At the awards ceremony March quipped that this statuette should have gone to his make-up man.

GOSSIP COLUMN

■ **M-G-M executive Paul Bern, husband of Jean Harlow, shot himself at his Beverly Hills home on 4 September, after only two months of marriage. His naked body was found doused in perfume; Harlow herself was away for the night. He left a suicide note with a vague apology.**

MARSHALL AIRS

What is it about Herbert Marshall that makes all Hollywood's big female stars want him as their leading man? Do they sense smouldering fires beneath his urbane, airy manner? Norma Shearer said, after seeing him in a film with Claudette Colbert, that she had "never seen a lady so thoroughly and convincingly loved. He is both manly and wistful."

He was born in London in 1890, and he took up acting in 1911 after working for a theatre impresario as an accountant. Wounded in the war (he has a wooden leg) he became a West End star, often playing opposite his wife, Edna Best. They prefer Britain, but the movie opportunities are better in Hollywood, and his film career proper began opposite Jeanne Eagels in *The Letter* (1929).

Last year he made movies on both sides of the Atlantic. Paramount hurried him into *Blonde Venus*, as Marlene Dietrich's husband, and then upped him to star status in Ernst Lubitsch's glittering *Trouble in Paradise*, as a confidence trickster teamed with Miriam Hopkins in an attempt to trick wealthy Kay Francis out of her fortune.

BIRTHS, DEATHS AND MARRIAGES

BIRTHS

Roy Scheider
10 Nov, Orange County, New Jersey

Robert Vaughn
22 Nov, New York

Ellen Burstyn
7 Dec, Detroit

DEATHS

Paul Bern
4 Sep, Hollywood
Suicide

Belle Bennett
4 Nov, Hollywood

MARRIAGES

Ray Milland
30 Sep, *to* Malvina Muriel Webber

Vivien Leigh
20 Dec, *to* Leigh Holman

BOX OFFICE

US

1 The Kid from Spain
2 Grand Hotel
3 Emma

OTHER TOP BOX OFFICE FILMS

Dr. Jekyll and Mr. Hyde
If I Had a Million
The Man Who Played God
One Hour With You
Shanghai Express
Shopworn
Tarzan The Ape Man

A CHILLING SOCIAL DOCUMENT

I Am a Fugitive from a Chain Gang may be one of the greatest films ever to come out of Hollywood. It's the tale of a recruit (Paul Muni) who fought for the United States in France. He's placed on the scrapheap when he gets back and finally gets 10 years on the chain gang after a petty crime. Muni escapes the chain gang, makes his way to the head of Chicago society, only to find that he must still expiate his crime.

This grim, persuasive document has been movingly and excitingly filmed by director Mervyn LeRoy from Robert E. Burns's novel. Muni proves outstanding, with excellent support from Glenda Farrell and Helen Vinson. And the outcry has been so large that Congress is re-examining the penal laws on chain gangs.

Paul Muni in a powerful role in I Am a Fugitive from a Chain Gang.

A BAD YEAR FOR THE STUDIOS

It's been a year when the Depression really bit into Hollywood. Paramount posted record losses of $20 million and is now in receivership. Fox did only marginally better, with a loss of $17 million. And despite its mass lay-off last year, Warners saw $14 million of red ink on its books. RKO, despite many changes, lost over $10 million.

But there were smiles of relief elsewhere: Columbia out-goings are small, and the same can be said of Universal, whose *Frankenstein* continued to be profitable in release. So, confounding the pundits, did *City Lights*, the silent which Chaplin made against the wishes of his United Artists partners. It brought in $5 million from world sales.

But the only people really laughing have been at M-G-M, which racked up a profit of $8 million – despite the fact it tends to spend a third more on its productions than its rivals.

WHAT M-G-M'S TWO HE-MEN HAVE BEEN UP TO

It's stretching the term a bit because the public's not wild about John Gilbert any more. He may not have been wild himself about being in *Downstairs*, in which he's the new chauffeur, working his way through the female staff of an Austrian schloss, before turning his attention to its mistress. But it's a good if amoral movie from director Monta Bell.

Red Dust, once intended for Gilbert, went to a real he-man – Clark Gable. His co-star is Jean Harlow and they make a tremendous team as they sass each other, though he thinks he prefers snooty, married Mary Astor. They're all on a rubber plantation in Malaya where the plumbing is primitive (see Harlow take a shower) but the spirits are high. Victor Fleming directed this highly entertaining movie for $408,000.

STAN AND OLLIE

Laurel & Hardy have been everyone's favourites since Hal Roach first teamed then in *Putting Pants on Philip* (1927). In November their *The Music Box* won Best Comedy short at the Oscars, a few weeks after their second feature-length film, *Pack Up Your Troubles*, proved there's more in life to them than short pants, they still make about 10 two-reelers a year.

The rotund, indignant Oliver Hardy was born in Atlanta in 1893, and he went from running a cinema to appearing in them – on screen, usually as a villain. The slender, befuddled Stan Laurel was born in Lancashire in 1890 into a theatrical family, and followed the family trdition into vaudeville. While touring in the United States in 1918 he was offered a short, *Nuts in May*, and he stayed in Hollywood, at this point a better-known name than Hardy.

They were both working on the Roach lot when he made them part of his "Comedy All-Stars" team. Their first short was in no way a *teaming*. But Laurel sensed the contrast worked, adding the sense of conspiracy and complicity between their scraps and arguments.

Stan Laurel and Oliver Hardy, a very successful comedy duo!

A MODERN MAIDEN

Joan Crawford's very happy this season: she's now on screen playing Sadie Thompson in United Artists' *Rain*. When she was loaned out at the beginning of her career she was furious, she said, because big stars weren't loaned. But *Rain* is different: Sadie is a challenge for any actress, and she's directed by Lewis Milestone, no less.

She was born in Texas in 1906. Determined to make it in the movies, she became a professional dancer after winning a Charleston contest, and was a New York showgirl when "discovered" by an M-G-M executive. She played a showgirl in her first film, *Pretty Ladies* (1925) and for a while was just pretty decor for the studio's leading men.

But certain that she was worth something better, she begged for a part in *Our Dancing Daughters* (1928), flapper drama. A follow-up, *Our Modern Maidens* (1929), was her last silent. She soon tired of playing flappers, and last year *Possessed* consolidated her position as queen of drama. With her ambition and cold will, she's not likely to leave the top of the heap for a long while yet.

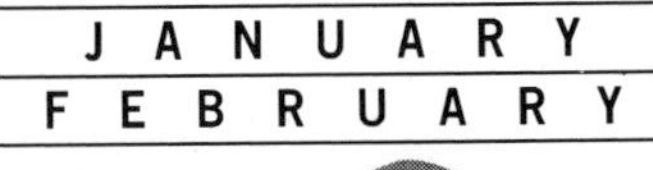

JANUARY FEBRUARY

MARCH APRIL

WARNERS' BEAUTIFUL WORKHORSE

Loretta Young is a paradox. She's meltingly beautiful and dresses as a movie star should – glamorous from head to toe. But Warners see her as just another working girl – the sort who is easily seduced or who takes up with gangsters. She's quite handy with a gun herself and has played a murderess several times.

There's no place for M-G-M type luxury at Warners. This season she's been seen as a shopgirl in *Employees Entrance*, married to nice Wallace Ford but getting drunk with her boss, Warren William, and going to bed with him. But we've also seen her (on loan to Fox) as the innocent girl from an orphanage who shelters with zoo-keeper Gene Raymond in *Zoo in Budapest*. After they separated, her husband, Grant Withers, called her "the steel butterfly."

She was born in Salt Lake City in 1912, but when her parents separated her mother moved to Los Angeles. Her movie debut was in 1926; two years later she was selected from 50 applicants for the role of the high-wire performer loved by Lon Chaney in *Laugh, Clown, Laugh*. Warners signed her and groomed her for star roles, often opposite Douglas Fairbanks Jr. With six movies in 1930 and 1932 and nine in 1931, Young has complained of being overworked. Joan Blondell should be told.

KONG ARRIVES

Willis O'Brien, who masterminded the model monsters in *The Lost World* (1925), was taken on by RKO to make something called *Creation*, but the money ran out by the time David Selznick arrived at the studio as head of production. He showed the assembled material to Merian C. Cooper and Ernest B. Schoedsack, responsible for *Grass* (1925) and *Chang* (1927), and that was how *King Kong* was born.

But it was no nine-month pregnancy. The combination of models, process work, glass shots and normal photography took 55 weeks in all. Selznick assigned the movie a buget of $670,000, large by RKO standards, certain that the studio had a surefire winner. Since opening simultaneously at New York's two biggest cinemas, Radio City Music Hall and the Roxy, on 2 March, it's shattered all world records in its first four days by taking almost $90,000.

Kong, the giant gorilla, doesn't appear for a while, as a New York movie crew somewhere "west of Sumatra" learn of a huge beast feared by natives. The crew's leading lady (Fay Wray) is captured by Kong, and the excitement doesn't let up till Kong is beseiged on the top of the Empire State Building.

BIRTHS, DEATHS AND MARRIAGES

BIRTHS

John Boorman
18 Jan, London

Kim Novak
13 Feb, Chicago

Michael Caine
14 Mar, London

Jean-Paul Belmondo
9 Apr, Neuilly-sur-Seine, France

DEATHS

Jack Pickford
3 Jan, Paris
Multiple neuritis

Lewis J. Selznick
25 Jan, Hollywood
Heart attack

MARRIAGES

Buster Keaton
Jan, *to* Mae Scribbens

Larry "Buster" Crabbe
13 Apr, *to* Adah Virginia Held

Walter Huston, Franchot Tone and Karen Morley in Gabriel over the White House, *the story of a crook who becomes president and mysteriously reforms.*

A TALE FOR THE TIMES

After overseeing *The Bitter Tea of General Yen* at Columbia, Walter Wanger moved to M-G-M, for whom his production of *Gabriel over the White House* is even more controversial. It has upset boss Louis B. Mayer, as it implicitly criticizes Republican president Herbert Hoover whom he supported. But now Hoover's just been succeeded by Democrat Franklin D. Roosevelt, and he's said to love the picture.

The whimsical plot is about a corrupt, cynical president (Walter Huston) who, when killed in an accident, is replaced by a lookalike who pursues opposite policies. He rids America of the Depression and ensures world peace for the immediate future.

A new ending was shot to please Mayer, in which the replacement dies and the old, corrupt policies are resumed. That is the version being shown in the United States. The rest of the world will see the original ending, which shows that any changes in the White House are due either to divine intervention or temporary aberration.

The Bitter Tea of General Yen.

NEVER THE TWAIN SHALL MEET?

Frank Capra continues to surprise, and each time he does so Hollywood grows up a little. The last time we saw an upright American girl fall in love with a Chinaman – way back in *Broken Bloosoms* (1919) – it ended in tragedy. Capra's *The Bitter Tea of General Yen* takes a similar but much more complex look at the same situation.

Barbara Stanwyck plays a girl of Puritan stock who comes to China to marry a missionary. The wicked General Yen (silent star Nils Asther) is fascinated by her and manages to make her his prisoner, initially on the grounds that she must be protected from the riots in Shanghai. In showing the girl and the General – a pathetic beast, in traditional fashion – thinking about the other's proximity, Capra maintains an extraorinary sexual tension; he even manages to suggest that the mutual attraction the couple experience is more important to both of them than either making war or preaching the word of God.

RADIO CITY OPENS

The era of super-cinemas has surely reached its apogee with the opening of Radio City Music Hall. It was intended as an opera house, but the Metropolitan was not interested. When John D. Rockefeller planned the commercial centre to be named after him he envisaged two auditoriums, with the smaller one showing films with live shows. In the event, the smaller of the two, with 3,509 seats, was named the RKO Roxy; the larger, with 5,945, became "Radio City Music Hall", a new home for vaudeville.

It opened on 27 December last year with an all-star bill which ran into the early hours; manager Samuel L. "Roxy" Rothafel landed up in hospital from exhaustion, and a quick decision was made to turn the 5,945-seater Music Hall over to movies. In fact, the plan was so quickly changed that they didn't wait till an RKO film was ready: when it re-opened on 11 January it was with Columbia's *The Bitter Tea of General Yen*.

CONTRASTING PICTURES FROM FOX

Fox has kicked off the year with two beautiful, heartwarming pictures which could not be less alike.

Cavalcade is based on the panoramic play by Noel Coward which has been enthralling London audiences for the past year or so. Fox filmed it in the theatre to reproduce it as accurately as possible – one British family (and their servants) from the Boer War to the sinking of the *Titanic* to the Great War to the jazz age to the present. Frank Lloyd directs and Clive Brook and Diana Wynyard head a fine cast of mainly British players.

In contrast, *State Fair* features the studio's biggest stars, Janet Gaynor and, as her father, Will Rogers. Completing the family are Norman Foster and, as mother, Louise Dresser. Lew Ayres and Sally Eilers play the city types who tempt the youngsters when the family visits the Fair – and that just about sums up the unambitious plot. Henry King directs, and, as ever when handling Americana, he's on top form.

GOSSIP COLUMN

- **Joan Crawford and young Douglas Fairbanks, Jr, long believed to be Hollywood's ideal marrieds, are calling it quits. It's said that Doug's illustrious family never cared for Joan. But it's she who's giving him the heave-ho.**
- **Mary Pickford is packing it in. Following the box-office failure of *Secrets*, America's Sweetheart says she's retiring from movies.**

James Cagney enjoys the attentions of Ruth Donnelly and Mary Brian in Hard To Handle.

HARD TO HANDLE

The title of James Cagney's new film, *Hard to Handle*, could well refer to his battles with Warners for more money (though he's a much bigger draw than either Kay Francis or Douglas Fairbanks Jr, his salary was less than half of what they were being paid). It can't be said to apply to this sparkling, racy piece about an enterprising guy always one step ahead of Depression blues.

Cagney, born in 1899 in New York City, began in show business as a female impersonator. He became an actor after a spell as a chorus boy, and his success in *Penny Arcade* brought him an offer to appear in the film version, *Sinner's Holiday* (1930). After three other credits, he was cast in a supporting role in *The Public Enemy* (1931), but was upped to the lead after three days shooting. That proved him to be a gigantic star, and this soft-spoken, pugnacious actor now has the pick of roles at Warners.

MAY JUNE 1933 JULY AUGUST

BIRTHS, DEATHS AND MARRIAGES

BIRTHS

Roman Polanski
18 Aug, Paris

Debra Paget
19 Aug, Denver

DEATHS

Ernest Torrence
15 May.

Roscoe "Fatty" Arbuckle
29 Jun, New York
Heart attack

MARRIAGES

Constance Cummings
3 Jul, *to* Benn V. Levy

Fred Astaire
12 Jul, *to* Phyllis Baker Potter

THE CHIC OF CONNIE

An alluring Constance Bennett as a hooker with a scheme in Bed of Roses.

Constance Bennett is the personification of Hollywood chic – elegant, sophisticated and soignee. In 1931 American exhibitors voted her second only to Garbo, and in 1932 British cinemagoers voted her second to Norma Shearer. Her salary demands have reflected all this.

She was born in New York City in 1905, the daughter of famed actor Richard Bennett (her sister Joan is also a Hollywood star), who got her small roles in two 1922 movies. Her film career proper began in 1924 when Sam Goldwyn cast for one of the leads in *Cytherea*, and she became an in-demand leading lady, already glamorous, over the next two years. M-G-M signed her, but she eloped with a millionaire and gave up filming.

When she returned in 1929 it was to Pathe, who seemed to cast her either as a kept woman or one bent on sinning. *Lady With a Past* (1932) says it all.

She's currently opposite Joel McCrea, for the nth time, in *Bed of Roses* in which he is an honest Mississippi seaman and she a hooker with a scheme – to get a rich man drunk and accuse him in the morning of such crimes that he will marry her. The oldest profession looks new in Connie's hands.

SEXUAL CLIMBING

Anything goes these days, but Barbara Stanwyck's antics in *Baby Face* are still raising some eyebrows. When the film begins she's a waitress and part-time hooker in a factory-workers' speakeasy. But there are better ways than that of beating the Depression, so she goes to work in the stock-room of a city trust corporation: how she progresses from there to the penthouse suite is the subject of the film. Alfred E. Green directs the Warners movie, with George Brent and, in a brief role, John Wayne, who hasn't made much impression since starring in *The Big Trail* back in 1930.

Wallace Beery and Jean Harlow are guests at a society dinner in Dinner at Eight.

MARIE, WALLY AND OTHERS

Marie Dressler and Wallace Beery have another slug-it-out fest in *Tugboat Annie*, directed by Mervyn LeRoy. They operate a tugboat and, apart form preparing for the visit of their naval officer son (Robert Young) and his fiancee (Maureen O'Sullivan), Dressler spends most of the time trying to find the bottles Beery has hidden. Unlike in *Min and Bill* (1930), the pair try to upstage each other this time.

They have no scenes together in another M-G-M "special", *Dinner at Eight*, but with an all-name cast there's an awful lot of upstaging going on here, too. Joint winners are Dressler, as a down-on-her-luck actress hoping for a loan, and Jean Harlow as the sluttish wife of a tycoon (Beery) who is having an affair with her doctor (Edmund Lowe).

The film in fact concludes at eight, but up till then we've witnessed the plans of the hostess (Billie Burke), the business troubles of her husband (Lionel Barrymore) and the illicit passion of their daughter (Madge Evans) for a failed matinee idol (John Barrymore). George Cukor directs, from the long-running play by George S. Kaufman and Edna Ferber.

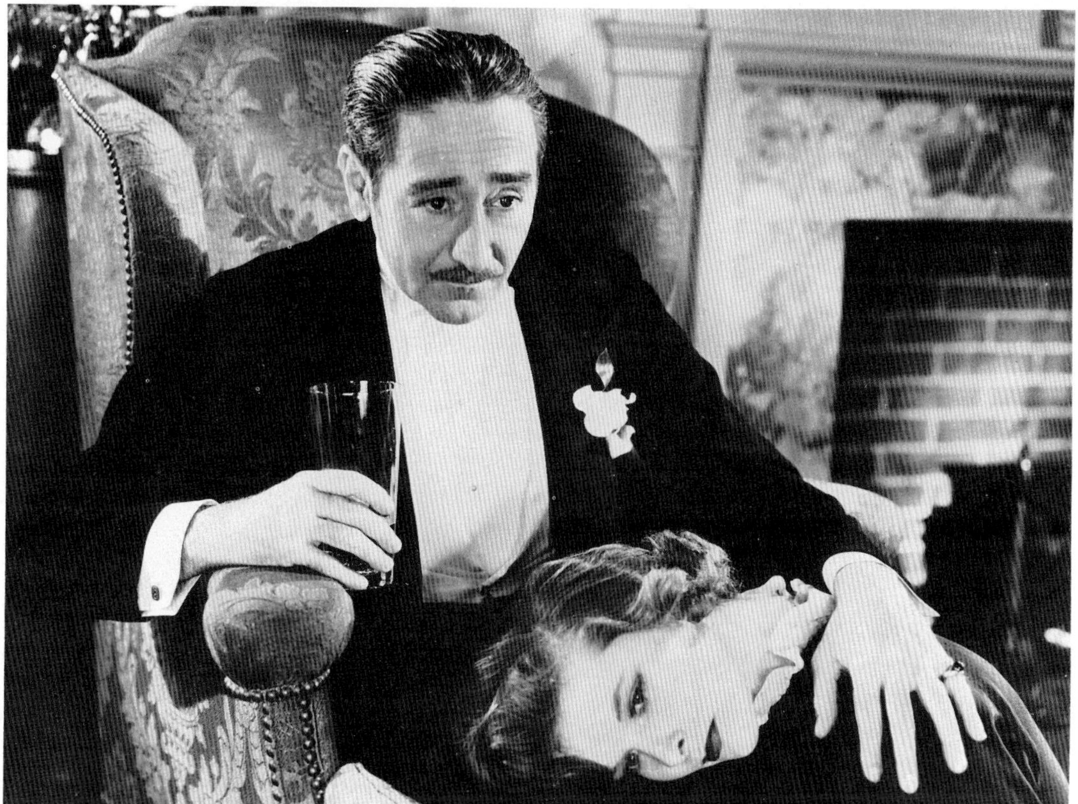

Adolphe Menjou and Katharine Hepburn in Morning Glory, *the story of a young Broadway hopeful who makes it to the top.*

OH, RARE KATE!

With only three films to her name Katharine Hepburn is already at the forefront of Hollywood actresses. She's being praised for her individuality, her drive, her directness.

She was born in 1909 in Connecticut, and studied at prestigious Bryn Mawr, where she got the acting bug. Her professional career started in 1928 and suffered several reversals before she became the rage of Broadway in 1932 in *The Warrior Husband*. She said that if she went to Hollywood she'd go on her own terms – in other words, if she wasn't an instant success she wouldn't hang around to be humiliated. What attracted her to RKO and *A Bill of Divorcement* (1932) was the chance of playing daughter to John Barrymore and fearing (in the plot) that she is as mad as he. Under George Cukor's direction she made a stunning bow.

Next she was a determined British aviatrix in *Christopher Strong* earlier this year; but it is the current *Morning Glory* which has sealed her success, as the ardent young Broadway hopeful who makes it to the top. Her qualities would make her a wonderful Jo in *Little Women*, which is precisely her next role.

WHO'S AFRAID OF THE BIG BAD WOLF?

Mickey Mouse isn't the only animal in Walt Disney's menagerie; he was joined in 1929, a year after his own debut, by some more – and other animated objects – in the "Silly Symphonies". Last year the ever-courageous Walt turned the Symphonies over to the new three-strip Technicolor process, with *Flowers and Trees*.

Now all of the United States is going wild about *The Three Little Pigs*, which was popped into the Radio City Music Hall bill on 25 May. It returned for two more weeks, and as release has widened out, there isn't a cinema which hasn't had *Three Little Pigs* doesn't want it.

It's a simple tale: three little pigs build their houses of a) straw b) twigs and c) bricks. The Big Bad Wolf happens along and huffs and puffs till he blows the first two down. The little piggies take refuge in their wiser brother's brick-built house and the Wolf can't blow that down.

THE END OF FATTY

Remember Roscoe "Fatty" Arbuckle? He was the round, lune-faced clown who appeared in shorts and features for Paramount in the late teens and early 1920s. Now he's dead, of a heart attack, on 29 June.

One day in September 1921 Arbuckle went to a party in a San Francisco hotel: it seems to have been fairly wild and one of the girls, actress Virginia Rappe, was rushed to hospital. Someone came up with the idea that Arbuckle had injured her – and the press deemed him guilty.

Friends and collegues believed in his innocence, as did the other guests at the party, except for the dead girl's best friend. After three trials for manslaughter, Arbuckle was acquitted but exhibitors and the public boycotted his films. Led by his friend Buster Keaton, industry bigwigs funded a company so he could make a comeback when the fuss died down. But he was a broken man.

In 1932 Warners signed him to make 12 two-reelers, but in the middle of his contract the fat man has died. He was only 36.

HOLLYWOOD ALCHEMY

Every so often an alchemist turns up in Hollywood. The current one is an Englishman called James Whale, fresh from his success with *The Old Dark House*. He had no difficulty with its English setting, and even though his Vienna in *The Kiss before the Mirror* is never-never land, it's enchanting nonetheless.

It's the Vienna not of sugary romance but of luxury, wealth and infidelity, as Paul Lukas shoots the man (Walter Pidgeon) he has seen kissing his wife (Gloria Stuart) before a mirror. Frank Morgan also finds himself kissing his wife (Nancy Carroll) before a mirror, and wonders whether, because she is so much younger, she has a lover. She has; and Morgan tells Lukas that he will lie to get him acquitted.

The combination of dreamlike story and racy dialogue has made this one of the most successful films of the season. It's from a story of Laszlo Fodor, who no doubt liked the comment in *Motion Picture Magazine* that "this delicately woven drama seems more like a foreign-made picture than a product of Hollywood."

GOSSIP COLUMN

- **Stripper Sally Rand, who started a riot at the World's Fair in Chicago, has been signed to a $2,500-a-week contract by Paramount. She wants to play the sort of roles they give to Helen Hayes, she says.**
- **Nancy Carroll's been dropped by Paramount. Falling box-office and Nancy's temperament are to blame – she was once one of the studio's top draws. Columbia or Universal may take her on (she's recently been loaned out to both), but first she's off to do a play in New York.**

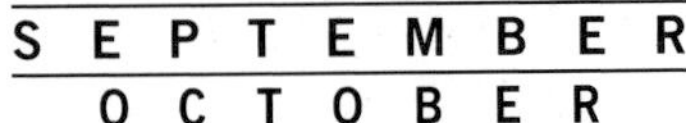

SEPTEMBER
OCTOBER

NOVEMBER
DECEMBER

COME UP AND SEE HER SOMETIME

"Come up and see me" said Mae West, and so many did that Paramount was saved from bankruptcy. After the sensation she created in a supporting role in last year's *Night After Night*, Paramount was prepared to give the Broadway star what she asked for – a leading role and artistic control. But she still couldn't persuade the Hays Office to let her keep the original title of her notorious play, *Diamond Lil*, so it became *She Done Him Wrong* when it opened earlier this year.

In the opening sequence she is seen in a carriage and as she descends a passer-by says to her, "You're a fine woman, Lady Lil", a sentiment she agrees with. "The finest woman who ever worked the streets," she says.

Her leading man in that was Cary Grant, and now they're re-teamed in *I'm No Angel*. She's a lion-tamer, but for the rest it's mostly about male bees buzzing round her honeypot. Mae, who has a quip for every occasion, sings the title song and obviously means it.

For the record, she was born in 1893 in Brooklyn and was a professional child actor; she first caused a furore on Broadway with the play *Sex* in 1926, and she's now doing the same on the country's screens.

Mae West as a lady saloon keeper in She Done Him Wrong.

HENRY VIII RULES AGAIN

When the British picture *The Private Life of Henry VIII* premiered at New York's Radio City Music Hall, Americans finally got to see what the fuss was all about – a lighthearted look at the amours of a king.

Producer-director Alexander Korda had failed in his native Hungary, Germany, the United States, France and finally Britain. Paris was dissatisfied with its British operation and put him in charge – to his delight, because he is an anglophile and because he feels he could make *British* pictures. After five failures Paramount was ready to pull the plug, but Korda was Hungarian enough to think he could proceed by getting bigger. So he formed London Film Productions, whose first offering was to star Charles Laughton, a British character actor enjoying great success in the U.S.

For a historical picture, the budget of *Henry VIII* is small, but Korda's extravagances have sent it soaring. Paramount, which owned Laughton's contract, refused to offer money to complete the picture; but United Artists stepped in, and liked the result so much they're signing an agreement with London Films.

No British picture has been so widely seen in the United States as this one. But it's Laughton who makes it a triumph – as the wily, capricious and crusty old buffer.

BIRTHS, DEATHS AND MARRIAGES

BIRTHS

Daniel Massey
10 Oct, London

DEATHS

Sime Silverman
22 Sep, Los Angeles

Renee Adoree
5 Oct, Hollywood
Respiratory ailment

Texas Guinan
5 Nov, Vancouver
Colitis

MARRIAGES

Joel McCrea
20 Oct, *to* Frances Day

Lupe Velez
28 Oct, *to* Johnny Weissmuller

Bruce Cabot
31 Oct, *to* Adrienne Ames

Gary Cooper
24 May, *to* Veronica Balfe

SOMETHING TO DANCE ABOUT

Warners almost killed off the musical with their operettas. But the studio brought it stunningly back to form earlier this year with *42nd Street*, as "gaudy, sporty, bawdy, naughty" as the thoroughfare it celebrates. It was followed by *Gold Diggers of 1933* and now *Footlight Parade*. All three feature singing lovebirds Dick Powell and Ruby Keeler, rotund Guy Kibbee, songs by Harry Warren and Al Dubin, and staging and choreography Busby Berkeley.

They're also all about putting on a show when times are hard – lecherous Broadway angels, hard-tapping, gold-digging chorus girls, gigolos and fancy women, and a driving, directing producer.

The first was directed by Lloyd Bacon, with a cast including Bebe Daniels, Warner Baxter, Ginger Rogers, Ned Sparks and Una Merkel. In charge of the second was Mervyn LeRoy, with Warren William, Aline MacMahon, Joan Blondell, Sparks and Rogers. The third, directed by Bacon again, has Ruth Donnelly, Claire Dodd, Frank McHugh, Blondell – and, as the brains of it all, James Cagney. For a change he gets to sing and dance rather than pack a pistol.

THREE DIVERSE METRO LADIES

John Gilbert and Greta Garbo in Queen Christina.

They're as different as chalk from cheese, but they must all be rejoicing. Jean Harlow, Joan Crawford and Greta Garbo have each made their best film yet.

Harlow's vehicle is *Bombshell*, in which she plays a put-upon movie star who yearns for domesticity but isn't allowed to have it – by either her hangers-on or the studio. Victor Fleming directs this brilliant satire on Hollywood, partly written by Jules Furthman, with a cast headed by Lee Tracy, Pat O'Brien, Franchot Tone, Una Merkel and Frank Morgan.

Crawford also has a fine cast in *Dancing Lady* – Tone (again), Robert Benchley and, in speciality acts as themselves, screen newcomers Fred Astaire and Nelson Eddy. Crawford is reunited with Clark Gable as the fast-talking, fast-moving producer. It's a copy of Warners' musicals, but none the worse for that.

But topping them all is the great Greta, in a role worthy of her – *Queen Christina*, the Swedish monarch who abdicated out of love for a Spanish ambassador (John Gilbert). It's regal filmmaking by director Rouben Mamoulian, and audiences won't forget the way he has her look in the final sequence.

THE MAD MARXES

You never know where you are with the Marx Brothers or what they are going to do next. But you know you will be laughing.

They were all born in New York City – Chico in 1891, Harpo in 1893, Groucho in 1895 and Zeppo, the straight man, in 1901. Their stage-crazy mother trained them, and by 1912 they were a vaudeville act. Their first Broadway success was a book show, *I'll Say She Is* in 1924, and the following two became their first two talkies, *The Cocoanuts* (1929) and *Animal Crackers* (1930). The first was little more than a film of the stage show, but they began to develop as movie performers in the second, the one in which Groucho was a fake big-game hunter.

In *Monkey Business* (1931) they stowed away on a liner, and in *Horse Feathers* (1932) Groucho was dean of a college. The majestic Margaret Dumont wasn't in those two for Groucho to insult, but she's back in *Duck Soup*, being told that he's fighting for her honour, "which is something you never did." As usual he's a coward and a braggart – but also the President of Freedonia, Rufus T. Firefly. His incompetence gets the country involved in war, aided and abetted by the dumb, inconsequential Harpo and his ally Chico. *Duck Soup* was directed by a master of the genre, Leo McCarey.

GOSSIP COLUMN

■ Popular fast-talking star Lee Tracy has been dropped by M-G-M from *Viva Villa*, allegedly for urinating from the balcony of his hotel while on location in Mexico. Lee is said to have over-indulged in the grape, and Louis B. Mayer is furious – especially as the incident attracted the attention of the local police.

BOX OFFICE

US

1. Cavalcade
2. Roman Scandals
3. 42nd Street
4. I'm No Angel
5. Little Women
6. She Done Him Wrong
7. State Fair
8. Footlight Parade
9. Gold Diggers of 1933
10. State Fair

A NEW STUDIO

At last Hollywood has a new studio. One reason that United Artists invested in London Films was that it was starved of quality product. Joseph M.Schenck was looking for more, and he found a putative provider in Darryl F. Zanuck, the dynamic and imaginative Warners production chief who was unhappy with studio policy (especially over pay cuts).

Zanuck was invited to form 20th Century with Schenck as partner, a company turning out formula films, but of a high polish and with star names. They knew who was discontented elsewhere and planned to sign them up for two films while they got going, with an option for more. But, most importantly, they would have the cooperation of M-G-M, since Schenck's brother Nicholas was the president of its parent company, Loews.

That's why there are two Metro stars – Wallace Beery and Jackie Cooper – in 20th's first release, *The Bowery*. Others will be Ronald Colman, Loretta Young, Ann Harding, Constance Bennett, George Arliss and Fredric March.

HEROES FOR SALE

Earlier in the year Warners offered *Heroes for Sale*, which had enough resemblances to *I Am a Fugitive from a Chain Gang* (1932) to suggest the studio wanted to repeat its success. But, as directed by William A. Wellman and played by Richard Barthelmess, it was an even grimmer affair, liked by neither press nor public. This is surprising, given the conviction and passion with which it was made – qualities Wellman has repeated now in *Wild Boys of the Road*, a tale of the youngsters who ride the freights, looking for work because they know their parents can't feed them.

Both films prove there are people in Hollywood who care about the jobless and homeless. But you'd never think it looking at *Hallelujah, I'm a Bum*, which in rhyming couplets and song (by Richard Rodgers and Lorenz Hart) examines the hoboesville which has sprung up in Central Park. Al Jolson stars, with Harry Langdon and Frank Morgan, under the direction of Lewis Milestone.

Another title, *Man's Castle*, takes a romantic view of the Depression, but under director Frank Borzage it's a very touching one. The setting is a shanty in old shanty town, which is where Spencer Tracy brings Loretta Young after saving her from the cold river. Their jolly, and equally jobless, friends include Walter Connolly and Marjorie Rambeau.

Spencer Tracy and Loretta Young.

LOUNGE LIZARDS AND DIZZY DAMES

Hollywood's most enduring achievement of the 1930s was the "screwball comedy" but it evolved by chance. Its roots lie partly in the early comedies of W. C. Fields and the Marx Brothers, and partly in two slam-bang comedies featuring middle-aged "uglies" Marie Dressler and Wallace Beery, whose antics made audiences forget their Depression blues.

Then in 1934 two unheralded comedies cleaned up at the box office – the snazzy *The Thin Man*, with William Powell and Myrna Loy as a take-it-or-leave-it detective couple, and *It Happened One Night*, in which hard-luck reporter Clark Gable accompanies scatty, spoiled heiress Claudette Colbert on a cross-country bus trip.

The director of the latter, Frank Capra, had already made *Platinum Blonde* (1931), in which debutante Jean Harlow pursues reporter Robert Williams because she is nuts about him. Harlow's personality made her single-minded, but she was nothing if not illogical, and in *Bombshell* (1935) she got in many a scrape as a Hollywood star unconcerned with those about her.

These strong but sexy heroines were quite different from either the vamps or the dim-witted heroines of the 1920s. They were joined in 1934 by Carole Lombard, also playing a wilful, petulant movie star, in *Twentieth Century*, usually regarded as the first true screwball comedy.

Crazy families were a staple of these films, and none was crazier than that in *My Man Godfrey* (1936), in which Lombard plays a spoiled daughter who invites bum William Powell to work for the family. In *Mr Deeds Goes to Town* (1936) it is new millionaire Gary Cooper who wants to help the have-nots for idealistic reasons; and in Jean Arthur, as the conniving reporter out to "get" Mr Deeds, Capra had another of the brilliant comediennes of the period.

Arthur also appeared in *Easy Living* (1937), as a stenographer involved with a wealthy family after a fur coat has fallen on her while she is riding on an open-air Fifth Avenue bus. The film was scripted by Preston Sturges, who took his comic vision unharmed into the 1940s with the last great flowerings of screwball comedy, *The Lady Eve* (1941) and *The Palm Beach Story* (1942), both of which he also directed.

The director of *Easy Living*, Mitchell Leisen, also made the equally superb *Midnight* (1939), in which penniless showgirl Colbert pretends to be the mistress of rich Frenchman John Barrymore to make wife Mary Astor give up her current protegee. Other films that fit the bill include: *True Confession* (1937), with Lombard as a wife who confesses to a murder in order to promote lawyer husband Fred MacMurray; *Nothing Sacred* (1937), with Lombard as a hick stranded and exploited in New York; *Topper* (1937), with Cary Grant and Constance Bennett as ghosts; and *Merrily We Live* (1938), with Billie Burke as a feckless lady who employs bum Brian Aherne, as a butler.

Add to those *Bringing Up Baby* (1938), with Katharine Hepburn as an heiress involving professor Grant with her pet leopard; *A Slight Case of Murder* (1938), with Edward G. Robinson as a reformed gangster trying to hide the bodies in the cellar; *It's a Wonderful World* (1939), with Colbert and James Stewart also caught up in a murder-hunt; and last but not least, *His Girl Friday* (1940), with Grant as an unscrupulous editor who inveigles ex-wife Rosalind Russell into covering a murder trial. Brief though its life was, the screwball comedy left a legacy of players and performances whose like were never to be seen again.

Gary Cooper in Mr Deeds Goes To Town *(1936).*

Carole Lombard, Fredric March and Walter Connolly in Nothing Sacred *(1937).*

Cary Grant (left) and Rosalind Russell in the fast-paced His Girl Friday *(1940).*

Lombard and Powell, My Man Godfrey.

Grant and Hepburn Bringing Up Baby.

McCrea and Colbert in Palm Beach Story.

Gable and Colbert It Happened One Night.

JANUARY
FEBRUARY

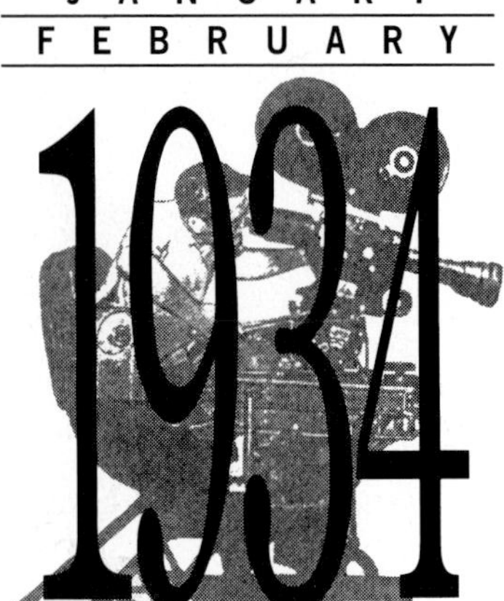

MARCH
APRIL

NORMA, THE BOSS' WIFE

Joan Crawford's envy of Norma Shearer has sparked much gossip, especially her comment, "How can I compete? She sleeps with the boss." Being the wife of M-G-M honcho Irving Thalberg (since 1927) certainly hasn't hurt Shearer, but Crawford should have a look at the popularity polls, in which her rival's rating can't really be blamed on better star vehicles.

Shearer was born in Montreal in 1900 and brought to New York, after her father's busines failed, by a mother anxious to get her into films. Only modelling work was to be found for a while, but that led to movie offers, including *The Stealers* (1920), which attracted Thalberg's attention. He was unable to find her until 1923, when he cast her in *Pleasure Mad*. Dissension between them over her roles resulted in many loan-outs but, as with all good movie plots, their quarrels turned to romance.

Norma Shearer in Riptide.

She's on screens now as audiences most admire her – as a smart, sophisticated woman of the world, in *Riptide*. She marries into the British aristocracy on a whim but loves her husband (Herbert Marshall) dearly; only when he suspects her of infidelity with an old flame (Robert Montgomery) does she make it real, even though her heart is breaking underneath. The plot is hardly original but Shearer's professionalism and her understanding of the medium are, as always, exemplary.

ACADEMY AWARDS

PRESENTED ON 16 MARCH 1934

Best Picture
Cavalcade

Best Director
Frank Lloyd
Cavalcade

Best Actor
Charles Laughton
The Private Life of Henry VIII

Best Actress
Katharine Hepburn
Morning Glory

GRAND NIGHTCLUB

Wonder Bar is that *Grand Hotel* formula again, as taken from a Broadway play, and it comes to the screen with more gloss and glamour than expected from Warners. Set in a nightclub, the bar of the title, it's basically a melodrama, but everyone has a wisecrack for every occasion. The club's owner-emcee is Al Jolson and its stars are a dance-duo, Dolores Del Rio and Ricardo Cortez. Bandleader Dick Powell is in love with Dolores; she is madly in love with Ricardo, who plans to go missing with a necklace owned by his mistress, Kay Francis. Robert Barratt is a suicidal gambler, while Ruth Donnelly, Guy Kibbee and Hugh Herbert are customers. Lloyd Bacon directed this entertaining tale.

PARAMOUNT'S "GRAND HOTEL"

Paramount's hotel is not grand, actually, but a tavern in the wilds of Nevada – and half the fun is in getting there. Mary Boland and Charlie Ruggles decide to go on a cross-country trip, and she advertises for a couple to share expenses – George Burns and Gracie Allen, complete with Great Dane. Boland and Ruggles, ditherers themselves, are bewildered and then exasperated by Allen, who has never been daffier. The all-star cast is completed by W.C. Fields as "Honest" John and Alison Skipworth as the hotel manageress – and you don't need to be told that these two are up to no good: so they're not really *Six of a Kind*, since the other four are as harmless as they are feckless. Leo McCarey, who learnt his trade with Mack Sennett, has directed the funniest film that he – or Paramount – has yet made.

For those who cannot get enough of the Great Man, Fields is also on view this season in *You're Telling Me*. He plays a man universally despised – especially by his wife – until he returns with a princess from an out-of-town visit. He's also an inventor, and is especially proud of his keyhole-finder for drunken home-comers. Erle C. Kenton directed.

W.C. Fields in Paramount's comedy Six of a Kind.

THE LOVEBIRDS SEPARATE

It's taken longer than the pundits predicted, but Janet Gaynor and Charlie Farrell have finally gone their separate ways.

First revealed as a magical team by *Seventh Heaven* (1927), the couple made it together in talkies, but after a while Farrell's high-pitched voice, coupled with his bounciness, made an unelevating combination. Fox experimented by casting them opposite other contract players, but while Gaynor's public stayed faithful, no matter who her leading man, Farrell's began to fall away. Fox probably prolonged his career by casting them together in four out of the five films Gaynor made in the 1931-2 season. Until now they have not been reunited since she signed her new contract in 1932 – and the forthcoming *Change of Heart* is not so much a Gaynor-Farrell vehicle as a romantic roundabout whose other riders include James Dunn and Ginger Rogers. It's their 12th film together – and probably the last. The word is that Fox will not be renewing Farrell's contract when it expires.

TWO BIOGRAPHICAL FILMS

Movie biographies are usually either travesties or hagiographies, so all praise to M-G-M for treating Pancho Villa with the ambiguity this controversial figure deserves: the Mexican bandit who joined the rebel forces, was humiliated when they came to power, but who survived to become president himself. Wallace Beery plays him in *Viva Villa!*, which was directed by Jack Conway.

The House of Rothschild, directed by Alfred Werker, moves more quickly, as it has to, to cover most of the 19th century in 88 minutes. It also flatters audiences by disclosing the methods by which the great banking family came to prominence. George Arliss plays *two* of them, in the same unvaried manner which has marked all his historical portrayals. Loretta Young and Robert Young provide the romantic interest.

Florence and George Arliss, Loretta Young, Robert Young and C. Aubrey Smith in The House of Rothschild.

THE ELEGANT MISS FRANCIS

Mandalay is hardly a great movie – in fact, it's the same old oriental eyewash audiences have been swallowing for years. But it has one breath-catching moment, when Kay Francis appears at the top of a flight of stairs in silver lame and a white feather boa.

Francis was born in Oklahoma City in 1905 to a mother who was a vaudeville star; theatrical contacts brought her the job of understudying Katharine Cornell in *The Green Hat*. She was appearing with Walter Huston in a play, when he recommended her for an important role in *Gentlemen of the Press* (1929). Paramount liked her work in that enough to offer her a contract and, by the time Warners filched her, she was one of the studio's biggest stars.

Like Norma Shearer, she's not a great actress, but she is determined to be thought so. Like Shearer, she is always on the list of best-dressed stars. And like Shearer again, she's not easy to photograph.

BIRTHS, DEATHS AND MARRIAGES

BIRTHS

George Segal
13 Feb, New York

Alan Bates
17 Feb, Allestree, Derbyshire

Alan Arkin
26 Mar, New York

Shirley Jones
31 Mar, Smithton, Pensylvannia

Diane Cilento
2 Apr, Queensland, Australia

Shirley MacLaine
24 Apr, Richmond, Virginia

DEATHS

Lilyan Tashman
21 Mar, New York
Cancer

Gerald du Maurier
11 Apr, London
Complications following surgery

MARRIAGES

Charles Boyer
Feb, *to* Pat Patterson

Cary Grant
9 Feb, *to* Virginia Cherill

JEAN vs BETTE

"All the world turns to adoration of a new Warner Bros star," say the ads for *As the Earth Turns*. "It takes high talent to take a place in the selected ranks of 'The Star Company'" – and there, in the ads, are pictures of Kay Francis, William Powell, Edward G. Robinson, James Cagney, Ruby Keeler, Paul Muni, Richard Barthelmess, Ruth Chatterton and Leslie Howard. The new star is Jean Muir: she's quite capable and pleasant, but not made of the stuff of stardom.

It's surprising the powers-that-be at Warners place her above Joan Blondell, and astonishing they prefer her to a little lady who has been doing sterling work for them ever since Universal dropped her two years ago. She's called Bette Davis and Warners didn't think RKO was serious when it asked to borrow her for one of the most coveted roles of the year, the vicious cockney waitress in *Of Human Bondage*, opposite Leslie Howard. Davis fought like a tigress for the loan-out and reports from the set indicate that she'll be the biggest star in it.

GOSSIP COLUMN

■ **Lilian Harvey, English-born star of German movie musicals, has fallen out with Broadway's George White during filming of *George White's Scandals*. Fox has replaced her with Alice Faye. The word is that, after the weedy box-office for Lilian's first two American films – *My Weakness* and *I Am Suzanne* – the studio isn't losing any sleep over her departure.**

MAY
JUNE

JULY
AUGUST

THE PUBLIC HAS ITS SAY

William Powell and Myrna Loy in The Thin Man.

Earlier this year a little item appeared from Columbia called *It Happened One Night* which no one gave much thought to. This was despite the fact that the director was Frank Capra and the stars, Claudette Colbert and Clark Gable, were in roles turned down by some of Tinseltown's biggest names. Colbert played an heiress who runs away to elope, and Gable was the reporter who chases her across the country for a story. Audiences took the picture to their hearts, and it returned time and time again to the same theatres, attracting growing business all the while.

Now the same thing is happening to *The Thin Man*, based on Dashiell Hammett's thriller and directed by W.S. Van Dyke for M-G-M. Its prime attraction is seen as the reunion (after the recent *Manhattan Melodrama*) of William Powell and Myrna Loy as the sleuthing couple Nick and Nora Charles, urbane, hard-drinking and engagingly cynical. Movie fans everywhere are demanding to see this couple together again. Loy, until recently a sloe-eyed vamp, is now a major star. So, too, is Powell after an equally unrewarding past as a meanie in silents: fortunately for Metro, Warners recently dropped him, so he now goes to pride of place on their contract list.

THE SINGING SWEETHEARTS

That dandy duo, Dick Powell and Ruby Keeler, can be seen again this season amid some more Busby Berkeley routines in *Dames*, the latest musical extravaganza from Warners. And very pretty they are, too.

Keeler was born in Nova Scotia in 1909, and moved with her family to New York when she was three. Only 10 years later she began her career as a dancer, staying in the chorus for some years till given a speaking part. In 1928 she met and married Al Jolson, who wanted her to be a star alongside himself at Warners. But only after he'd left the studio did it give her a contract. She made her movie debut in *42nd Street* (1933) with Powell, and *Dames* is their fourth consecutive movie together. She's winsome and cute, but when she and Powell endlessly duet on "I Only Have Eyes for You" it's just as well to remember what a good dancer she is.

Powell, who can warble with the best of them, was born in 1904 in Arkansas, and sang in the local church choir. In his teens he joined a band and a while later was spotted by a talent scout for Warners, then looking for someone to play the title-role in *The Crooner*. That went to David Manners, but Powell was offered a similar, if smaller, role in *Blessed Event* (1932). *Dames* is the 10th film in which we have been able to enjoy his eager, puppy-like personality.

PUT THE BLAME ON MAE

It was in 1922 that the industry, shaken by some serious scandals – notably the "Fatty" Arbuckle affair and the death from drugs of popular Wallace Reid – appointed Will H. Hays, former Postmaster General under President Harding, to head a newly-formed organization, the Motion Picture Producers & Distributors of America Inc. It became known as the Hays Office, whose job was to defend the industry from attack and demands for censorship.

With the coming of talkies Hays drew up a Production Code in 1930; but fearful of losing audiences as the Depression worsened, the studios did nothing to implement it. Since then movies have become ever more frank, with Mae West's innuendos causing preachers to denounce her from the pulpit.

On 1 July Hays announced the code must be strictly adhered to, so "no picture shall be produced which will lower the standards of those who see it. Hence the sympathy of the audience should never be thrown to the side of crime, wrongdoing, evil or sin." In other words, movies could be a lot less fun.

THE DEATH OF MARIE DRESSLER

Hollywood is mourning the death of Marie Dressler who died in Santa Barbara on 28 July, aged 65. After several years as a has-been, she'd found a new career in talkies as a character actress. Only that? Last year both the *Motion Picture Herald* and *The Hollywood Reporter* named this unlikely star the biggest draw in pictures, even though insiders already knew she was suffering from the cancer that killed her.

Born in Ontario in 1869, she worked in both vaudeville and theatre, making her screen debut with Charlie Chaplin in *Tillie's Punctured Romance* (1914) as Tillie, the lovable battle-axe which she had often played on stage. Though that movie is still being played (due to Chaplin's popularity), other cinema ventures brought little success, and her contribution in founding the actors' union Equity caused theatre managers to neglect her comic gifts. By 1926 she was on the breadline, and according to one report was contemplating suicide when director Allan Dwan, meeting her by chance, offered a role in *The Joy Girl* (1927). The scenarist Frances Marion, remembering past kindnesses, constructed a couple of vehicles for her at M-G-M, but neither that studio nor any other was interested in keeping her till she had successfully tested for a role in *Anna Christie*.

The public liked her as this low-life drunk, and they adored her in tandem either with Polly Moran or Wallace Beery. The world mourns the passing of a grand comedienne.

BIRTHS, DEATHS AND MARRIAGES

BIRTHS

Alan Bennett
9 May, Leeds

DEATHS

Lew Cody
31 May, Beverly Hills
Heart attack

Marie Dressler
28 Jul, Santa Barbara, California
Cancer

DEPRESSION BLUES

Universal has shown no great interest in the Depression, and *Little Man, What Now?* takes place in Germany. It does suggest that ordinary people are coping, hoping that good things are just around the corner, but what attracted the studio is the fact that Hans Fallada's novel provides the basis of a strong vehicle for their new star, Margaret Sullavan. Douglass Montgomery plays her husband, Catherine Doucet is her mother who shelters them when he is jobless, and Alan Hale is the lodger, helping to run the house as a brothel. Directed by Frank Borzage.

Two more great directors have also been looking at the Depression this season: King Vidor, in his independently produced *Our Daily Bread*, about deprived farm-workers starting a collective, and Germany's G.W. Pabst, in *A Modern Hero*, which optimistically finds Richard Barthelmess rising to the top in these troubled times.

FUN ON THE RAILS

Twentieth Century, based on a Broadway play, takes its name from the high-speed luxury train which plies between New York and Chicago. On board for this trip are such merry pranksters as Walter Connolly, Roscoe Karns and, as a religious maniac, Etienne Girardot. Travelling up front, however, are John Barrymore, as a theatre bigwig, and Carole Lombard, as the girl he made a star. She, ungratefully, went off to Hollywood and now, to save his bacon, he wants her back. She has no intention of coming back, so they fight and toss tantrums throughout the journey – most amusingly, as directed by Howard Hawks.

Lombard, hitherto just another Hollywood also-ran, emerges as a major comic talent – the best he has ever worked with, according to Barrymore.

Opera singer Grace Moore and Tulio Carminati in One Night of Love.

A DIVA IN MOVIES

Grace Moore, the prima diva of the Metropolitan Opera, has desperately wanted to be a movie star – all the more so after failing at M-G-M with a couple in 1930, *A Lady's Morals* and *New Moon*. Thinking (rightly) that she is one of the few opera singers slim enough to be in movies, she was delighted when M-G-M approached her to appear in their new version of *The Merry Widow*, but that idea went out of the window when neither she nor Maurice Chevalier would accept second billing. She was consoled when Columbia offered her the film *One Night of Love*, about a girl determined to become an opera star, which has become one of the hits of the summer.

Born in Tennessee in 1903, she showed a remarkable voice early on. She first appeared in New York in revues and made her Metropolitan debut in 1928. Now it looks as if she's in movies to stay, with the critics raving and the public turning up in droves.

Twentieth Century *with Carole Lombard and John Barrymore.*

GOSSIP COLUMN

- **After failing on Broadway in *The Lake*, Katharine Hepburn is back in Hollywood preparing to play Joan of Arc. After the flop of *Spitfire*, it had better be good!**
- **Sales of undershirts are plummeting all over the country since Clark Gable shunned one in *It Happened One Night*.**

STAR QUOTES

Adolphe Menjou
on Shirley Temple

"She knows all the tricks. She's Ethel Barrymore at six."

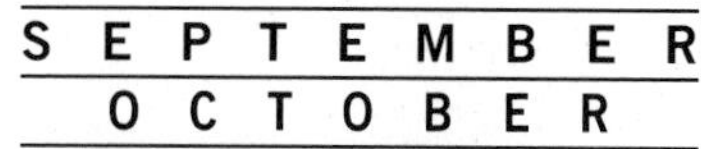

SEPTEMBER
OCTOBER

NOVEMBER
DECEMBER

THE GREAT MAN HIMSELF

General store owner, W.C. Fields, transports family to new life in It's a Gift.

ENGLISH FIELDS

The British took her to their hearts some time ago, before radio and then talkies made her phenomenally popular. Now her reputation is reaching the other side of the pond as well. She's Lancashire lass Gracie Fields.

She was born in 1898 and began singing in a local cinema; she joined a troupe of kiddie entertainers, later touring the music halls as a solo act. After touring in the revue *Mr Tower of London*, she and the show came to London in 1922, and the capital was at her feet. Her great virtues are her sheer joy at entertaining, her manifest love of her audience, her ability to switch from comic to serious songs and a complete absence of pretension.

In her fifth film, *Sing As We Go*, she plays a factory girl on vacation at the seaside resort of Blackpool. Although specially written for her by novelist J.B. Priestley, it is strictly a non-export item. But the British have already adopted the title song as their anthem against the Depression.

STAR QUOTES

George Bernard Shaw

"Cedric Hardwicke is my fifth favourite actor, the first four being the Marx Brothers."

It's a Gift is the fifth film with W.C. Fields that Paramount has released this year. It's also his best movie yet, a compendium of Fieldsian situations in which everything conspires to make his life a misery – nagging wives, rude neighbours, troublesome children and inefficient assistants at the pharmacy where he works. He faces up to them all with resignation but also cowardice, deceit and cunning, admitting defeat only at the hands of his wife (Kathleen Howard). And then he finds solace in a swig from his flask.

The great man was born in Philadelphia in 1879; he ran away from home as a child and slept rough, till he took up juggling, which got him into vaudeville. By the time he was 20 he was getting top billing, and in 1915 he made a short, *Pool Sharks*, based on his current "act." He was comic relief in his first feature *Janice Meredith* (1924) and was signed by Paramount not long afterwards. His comic vehicles for the studio had limited success, so they were not displeased when they could not agree on terms to renew his contract.

As Fields in real life is not unlike the on-screen Fields Paramount took him back reluctantly when it was clear he was a success in talkies.

BOX OFFICE

US

TOP BOX OFFICE FILMS

The Barretts of Wimpole Street
Chained
It Happened One Night
Judge Priest
One Night of Love
Queen Christina
Riptide
Sons of the Desert
Wonderbar
The Thin Man

A VERY SEXY WIDOW

Erich von Stroheim's silent version of *The Merry Widow* (1925) contained a number of sexual irregularities which would never get past the Hays Office in its present mood. Ernst Lubitsch's new version wouldn't bring a blush to the cheek of your maiden aunt, but such is his celebrated "touch" that it's the most sensual movie in an age.

Prince Danilo (Maurice Chevalier) and the widow (Jeanette Macdonald) are already attracted when he is asked to woo her by the King (Frank Morgan) because she is very wealthy and the state coffers are empty. From that outline Lubitsch has fashioned a picture which is dreamy, romantic, amusing and utterly enchanting.

Franz Lehar's songs are wonderfully staged and sung; the brilliant cast also includes Una Merkel as the Queen and Edward Everett Horton as the ambassador; and Chevalier's charm is such that you could carve it with an ice-cream scoop. The only trouble is that with a budget of over $1.6 million, M-G-M will be looking anxiously at the box-office figures; it has to do exceptionally well to get that back.

BIRTHS, DEATHS AND MARRIAGES

BIRTHS

George Chakiris
16 Sep, Norwood, Ohio

Sophia Loren
20 Sep, Rome

Brigitte Bardot
28 Sep, Paris

Sylvia Sims
3 Dec, London

DEATHS

Arthur Wing Pinero
23 Nov, London
Complications following surgery

Lowell Sherman
28 Dec, Hollywood
Pneumonia

MARRIAGES

Orson Welles
Nov, *to* Virginia Nicholson

Lew Ayres
14 Nov, *to* **Ginger Rogers**

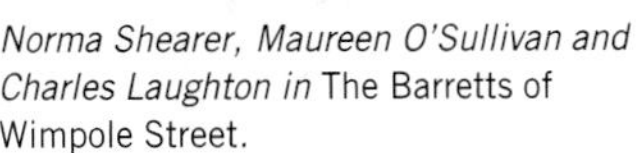

Norma Shearer, Maureen O'Sullivan and Charles Laughton in The Barretts of Wimpole Street.

A HEROINE AND TWO HUSSIES

The vogue for biographical movies continues, with M-G-M offering a typically classy version of the long-running Broadway play, *The Barretts of Wimpole Street*. Norma Shearer is Elizabeth Barrett, whose mysterious illness is cured when she receives visits from a fellow poet, Robert Browning (Fredric March), and Charles Laughton is the cruel father from whom the growing romance must be hidden.

The critics have raved over that; but they are unimpressed by *The Scarlet Empress* and *Cleopatra* from Paramount. They're both characteristic of their directors, Josef von Sternberg and Cecil B. DeMille, especially in their lavish decor and free use of anachronisms. Someone called Manuel Komroff is credited with the dialogue of the Sternberg and you can't imagine why anyone would want their name on the other one. Both concern lady monarchs renowned for their amorous encounters, and particularly unforgettable is the scene in the Sternberg when Marlene Dietrich, as Catherine the Great, picks up a hussar in the garden. In the DeMille the equally exotic Claudette Colbert plays the Queen of the Nile.

GARBO AGAIN

Crafty Greta Garbo is the only one of M-G-M's major stars not under long-term contract; she renegotiates a film or two at a time. When the studio balked at her playing Queen Christina she simply took off for Sweden till it capitulated: part of the bargain was that she should then do a subject of its choosing. That's why this season we're seeing her in *The Painted Veil*. It's her old familiar role of the unfaithful wife who repents, but taken from a novel by W. Somerset Maugham, it's a little more complex and adult than some past excursions into this territory.

Most notably the credits are imposed over her surname, to indicate the exceptional place she holds in the movie hierarchy.

In Imitation of Life *Claudette Colbert becomes rich through the pancake recipe of her black servant (Louise Beavers).*

ADVANCING SLOWLY

The public approves of the slushy portmaneau novels of Fannie Hurst – and so does Hollywood. This is good, as she likes to reflect real-life problems. Two years ago RKO presented the story of a Jewish doctor who leaves the ghetto in *Symphony of Six Million*, and now in *Imitation of Life* Universal offers a tale about a business partnership between two women, one white and one black. True, the black woman (Louise Beavers) is first maid to the other (Claudette Colbert), and when they go into business marketing pancakes you will recognize "Aunt Jemima." The real problems arise when their daughters reach adulthood, and they're handled in mature fashion by director John M. Stahl.

GOSSIP COLUMN

- **Cameraman Hal Rosson is already Harlow's ex; but they're not yet divorced. Her new beau is Clark Gable; but he's still married. But so was he (and she too) while he was making love to Joan Crawford. Joan isn't too sorry to see Clark go; she's now showing an interest in Franchot Tone.**
- **Screenwriter John Monk Saunders socked Herbert Marshall at the party Ernst Lubitsch threw for Max Reinhardt, but nobody's telling why.**
- **Hollywood stars are being wooed to Britain, where producers are tempting them by offering a share in the profits.**
- **Gloria Swanson has divorced her fourth husband, Michael Farmer. Her current escort is Herbert Marshall; but no one expects wedding bells to ring.**
- **They fought on the set of *The Good Fairy*. No one knew anything about a romance till William Wyler and Margaret Sullavan turned up married.**

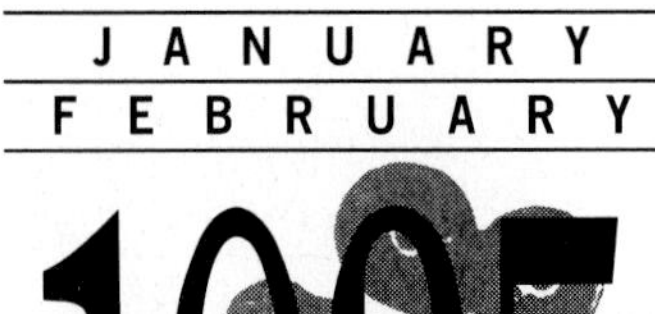

JANUARY
FEBRUARY

MARCH
APRIL

THE MOUSE IN COLOUR

Walt Disney, so often an innovator, has been so encouraged by the success of the *Silly Symphonies* series in Technicolor that he has now decided to make all his animated cartoons in that process. So Mickey Mouse becomes the first Hollywood celebrity to appear in Technicolor.

The film is called *The Band Concert*, and it features Mickey in a resplendent scarlet uniform, conducting the overture to *William Tell*. Donald Duck, so often a thorn in Mickey's flesh, is the flute-player who would rather be performing "Turkey in the Straw." Donald, not by nature a docile creature, is amusing and, of all the animals in the Walt Disney menagerie, seems the most likely to rival the Mouse in popularity if given a starring vehicle of his own.

ACADEMY AWARDS

PRESENTED ON 27 FEBRUARY 1935

Best Picture
It Happened One Night

Best Director
Frank Capra
It Happened One Night

Best Actor
Clark Gable
It Happened One Night

Best Actress
Claudette Colbert
It Happened One Night

KING OF THE BOX-OFFICE

It's one of the curiosities of the career of Clark Gable that his contract does not guarantee him top-billing. He popped into the top 10 box-office draws in his second year in films (1932), moved from seventh place in 1933 to second place last year – in the *Motion Picture Herald* – after Will Rogers (though *The Hollywood Reporter* afterwards reversed these positions).

Yet once again he takes second billing to his leading lady – and Constance Bennett isn't even an M-G-M star. She's passing through. The movie is *After Office Hours*, a pretty slight affair, a comedy to cash in on his success in *It Happened One Night.*

Gable was born in Ohio in 1901; he followed his father into the Oklahoma oil fields, but ran away when he was old enough to join a travelling theatre troupe. Stranded, at one point he became a lumberjack, but later he joined another troupe and married its leader, Josephine Dillon, 14 years his senior. She took him to Hollywood, where he got work as an extra, but they separated in 1930 so that he could marry another much older woman, Rita Langham. And that was the year Hollywood noticed Clark Gable, when he starred in the West Coast stage production of *The Last Mile*.

His new film is proof enough of why women fall all over him. It's a piece of fluff involving an editor (him), a socialite (Bennett) and a scandal, but his masculine sex-appeal has never been more striking.

Fredric March and Charles Laughton star in Darryl F. Zanuck's production of Victor Hugo's Les Miserables.

EVERYBODY'S HAPPY

Hollywood has now had a bash at Victor Hugo's novel *Les Miserables*, the source of at least seven movies to date. Last year's version from France had superlative performances by Harry Baur as Valjean, the wrongly convicted prisoner struggling for rehabilitation, and Charles Vanel as Javert, his nemesis. Fredric March and Charles Laughton – respectively in these roles in 20th Century's new version – are not their equals, but they are still magnificent. And they are splendidly supported, under Richard Boleslawki's direction, by Cedric Hardwicke, Jessie Ralph, Florence Eldridge and others.

It's easy to see why this old tale has so often attracted moviemakers, since it's full of action and emotion, in this case moved along at a fast clip. Moviegoers are likely to be anything but miserable.

STAR QUOTES

Lillian Gish

"Douglas wanted to live in the world, Mary liked to stay at home."

"THE DANCING DIVINITY"

No one ever thought that Britain would challenge Hollywood's domination of the world's cinemas, but it has recently made surprising inroads into the American market. In the light of Korda's success his chief limey rival, Michael Balcon, persuaded his bosses to open a distribution office in the United States, and Gaumont-British, as it is called, is clearly not ashamed of its origin. It is named for Balcon's production company, scoring a notable achievement in getting *Evergreen* into New York's showplace, Radio City Music Hall.

Its charms are very British, despite a couple of songs by Rodgers and Hart and another, "When You've Got a Little Springtime in Your Heart" also by an American. But its chief virtue is the handling of these numbers by its star, Jessie Matthews, who dances as prettily as she sings. Gaumont-British are advertising her as "The Dancing Divinity", and the American public – at least in the big cities – seems to have taken her to its heart. She's now reported to be Hollywood-bound, to partner none other than Fred Astaire.

BIRTHS, DEATHS AND MARRIAGES

BIRTHS

Dean Stockwell
5 Mar, Hollywood

Richard Chamberlain
31 Mar, Los Angeles

Dudley Moore
19 Apr, London

Charles Grodin
21 Apr, Pittsburgh, Pennsylvania

MARRIAGES

Zachary Scott
21 Feb, *to* Elaine Anderson

W. C. Fields and Freddie Bartholomew in M-G-M's adaptation of Charles Dickens's David Copperfield.

ASSORTED ECCENTRICS

It would be hard to imagine a better film made of a novel by Dickens than M-G-M's *David Copperfield*. The sprawling story has been greatly compressed, but as produced by David O. Selznick and directed by George Cukor the original spirit is all there. Some have questioned the playing of David himself – Freddie Bartholomew as a boy and Frank Lawton as a man – but the rest of the cast is wonderful, as they help or hinder David in his path from orphaned childhood through marriage to success as a novelist: Elizabeth Allen (Mrs Copperfield), Jessie Ralph (Peggotty), Basil Rathbone and Violet Kemple Cooper (the monstrous Murdstones), Edna May Oliver (Aunt Betsy), Lennox Pawle (Mr. Dick), Roland Young (Uriah Heep), Maureen O'Sullivan (Dora), Madge Evans and Lewis Stone (the Wickfords) and last but not least W.C. Fields and Jean Cadell (the Micawbers).

Charles Laughton, who was originally contracted to play Mr. Micawber, told M-G-M after three days shooting that Fields was the only person who could do it. Laughton himself promptly moved over to Paramount for another plum role – in *Ruggles of Red Gap*, as the British manservant transported to the Old West by a vulgar American couple, splendidly played by Charlie Ruggles and Mary Boland. Here are some great character players giving moviegoers a grand time; they also include Roland Young again, and ZaSu Pitts as the shy spinster to whom Ruggles the butler takes a fancy.

GOSSIP COLUMN

- **The Pickford-Fairbanks divorce is finally certain. Rumours of separation have been denied for years, but on 10 January Mary went to court.**
- **Hollywood is in uproar over the Academy Award nominations. John Barrymore is furious at not being up for *Twentieth Century*, and everyone else is astounded that Bette Davis' work in *Of Human Bondage* has been overlooked.**

Tribute to the British in Lives of a Bengal Lancer, with Gary Cooper, Richard Cromwell and Franchot Tone.

WHERE THE SUN NEVER SETS

The sun never sets on the British Empire – and Hollywood likes it that way. This season the movie capital has paid two tributes to the British rule in India; of the two, *Lives of a Bengal Lancer*, directed by Henry Hathaway, is by far the more exciting and satisfying. This is a stirring tale of battles fought against local maharajahs on the North-West Frontier by the likes of conscientious Gary Cooper, easy-going Franchot Tone and new recruit Richard Cromwell.

Clive of India may seem equally ambitious, for Ronald Colman (without his famous moustache) doesn't come cheap. But 20th Century doesn't seem to have spent much imagination on this picture: it's a perfunctory run-through of some events in the life of the famed Empire-builder. Loretta Young plays his wife under Richard Boleslawski's direction. C. Aubrey Smith is in both movies – Hollywood cannot make its Empire-loving films without him.

AN ENGLISHMAN AT HOME

Hollywood seems to like Leslie Howard a good deal more than he likes it. He has said that it's a place which pays ridiculous sums for a job which is hardly acting at all . . . and between films he always returns to England.

He was born in London in 1893 – but to a Hungarian couple who had lately arrived there. Suffering from shell-shock during the First World War, he was encouraged to take up acting as therapy. He made his film debut in a minor role in 1917, establishing himself as a stage actor five years later. Curiously, he spent most of the 1920s starring in New York, and was one of the Broadway actors brought into films when talkies arrived. His easy, gentlemanly manner and quiet speaking voice made him an instant success. He has been able to sign deals with several studios, but with so much choice (which few stars have) in what he does and doesn't do, he makes far fewer films than the movie moguls would like.

His participation was one reason that Paramount and then Columbia were willing to produce *Service for Ladies* (1932) and *The Lady Is Willing* (1934) in England, but both had too many of the faults of other British films to succeed in America. But now Howard, like many others, has been impressed by the movies coming from Alexander Korda's London Films: he has signed to do at least one for them, and audiences can currently see him in *The Scarlet Pimpernel*, in which he does a grand job as the foppish Sir Percy whipping away French aristos from the clutches of rabble who have sentenced them to the guillotine.

ANYONE FOR COLOUR?

Of all the attempts to manufacture a colour process in the silent era the most successful was that of Technicolor, but it was not without its hazards. Its palette was limited, while the process of sticking together two negatives was complex – and liable to cause fires in the projector.

Under the aegis of president Herbert Kalmus, Technicolor perfected its "safe" three-strip colour system in 1932, but Walt Disney was the only industry figure with any real enthusiasm for it, so Kalmus granted him exclusive rights. But Kalmus also put some finance into a new production company, Pioneer Pictures, formed to exploit the Technicolor process.

On Pioneer's board are two East Coast millionaires from the Whitney family and Merian C. Cooper. Cooper's involvement with RKO is the reason why that company is distributing Pioneer's first feature, *Becky Sharp*, based on Thackeray's novel *Vanity Fair*, with Miriam Hopkins in the title role.

It's directed by Rouben Mamoulian, who took over, throwing out much of the shot footage, when Lowell Sherman died. The film imaginatively uses the new system, beginning with credits in greys and whites, bursting into colour when a girl pokes her head through grey curtains. As a whole it proves that colour can be as much of a boon to movies as was the arrival of sound, but its reception by both the public and the industry seems to suggest that Technicolor may still have a bumpy ride ahead. It should be ideal for musicals and costume dramas – even though this particular costume drama is not drawing the crowds.

ARCTIC ADVENTURES

RKO, looking for something to top *King Kong*, has turned to Rider Haggard's novel, *She*. But fearing the author had been to Africa once too often, producer Merian C. Cooper has transferred the action to the Arctic, which allows for an avalanche or so.

Randolph Scott hears from his dying grandfather of an ancestor who went exploring and never returned: following his trail he and his companions arrive in the kingdom of Kor, ruled over by Hash-A-Mo-Tep, or "She Who Must be Obeyed" – played by Helen Gahagan (who in private life is Mrs. Melvyn Douglas). She is 500 years old, having stepped into the sacred flame to secure immortality – and she sees in Scott a reincarnation of her former lover, his ancestor, whom she has lovingly preserved.

And so on. It's all great fun but there's no disguising the fact that there are some mediocre special effects and some dreadful dialogue.

STAR QUOTES

Herman J. Mankiewicz
on Louis B. Mayer

"He has the memory of an elephant and the hide of an elephant. The only difference is that elephants are vegetarians and Mayer's diet is his fellow men."

STEPS ACROSS THE POND

Robert Donat and Madeleine Carroll in the thriller The 39 Steps, *adapted from John Buchan's novel.*

The British continue to make inroads in the American market and the latest film from across the Atlantic expected to delight audiences (when it opens in September) is a thriller, *The 39 Steps*. Based on the novel by John Buchan, it features Robert Donat as a Secret Service agent who flees London for Scotland when he finds a corpse on his bed. His attempts to find the real murderer are helped and hindered by a beautiful blonde (Madeleine Carroll).

Both players have already demonstrated their appeal to American audiences, but the real "find" is said to be the director, Alfred Hitchcock, whose 1934 movie, *The Man Who Knew Too Much*, wowed American critics when it opened in March. "Hitch," as the British call him, has a quirky sense of humour, and a sure ability to build suspense. It's a sure bet that Hollywood has already put him on its acquisitions list.

BIRTHS, DEATHS AND MARRIAGES

BIRTHS

Gene Wilder
11 Jun, Milwaukee, Wisconsin

Donald Sutherland
17 Jul, New Brunswick, Canada

DEATHS

George Grossmith
6 Jun, London

Will Rogers
15 Aug, Point Barrow, Alaska
Plane crash

MARRIAGES

Dorothy Lamour
10 May, *to* Herbie Kaye

Errol Flynn
19 Jun, *to* Lili Damita

AN AMERICAN FOLK HERO DEPARTS

Will Rogers, like the late Marie Dressler, was an unlikely star, but like her he seemed to provide an answer to the Depression blues. This ex-cowpuncher had long been popular in vaudeville and journalism, dispensing his home-spun philosophy when he became a star for Ziegfeld on Broadway and for Goldwyn in films. But the intertitles needed to be long to convey his cracker-barrel wit, and he didn't catch on with the public at large.

He was another of the stage performers re-examined when talkies came in, and he was an immediate hit for Fox in *They Had to See Paris*. In 1932 he was the ninth-ranking star at the box-office and in 1933 his salary, at $15,000 a week, exceeded Garbo's. Apart from *State Fair* (1933), perhaps his best two pictures were for director John Ford, *Doctor Bull* (1933) and *Judge Priest* (1934). A third film for Ford, *Steamboat 'round the Bend*, will be released posthumously this autumn – Rogers died in an aviation accident with air pioneer Wiley Post, in Alaska, on 15 August. He was 53, but to judge from the box-office response to his last few films, he had several more years of popularity ahead.

Rogers was no freak success: he was a grand actor who could bring warmth, subtlety and wit to characters only too clearly based on what he himself was supposed to be like – which was reason he always improvised after reading the script, for he had to find his own truth.

THE GREAT GARBO

She has transfixed audiences since her first Hollywood film; and many think no other actress can hold a candle to her. She is Greta Garbo, born in Stockholm in 1903. Her father died when she was 13 and she went to work making lather in a barber-shop. While working for the city's largest department store she was chosen to make a publicity film, an experience which caused her to enroll in dramatic school. There she was discovered by director Mauritz Stiller, who made her a star in *The Atonement of Gosta Berling* (1924). When M-G-M signed him, it took Greta Garbo merely as part of the package: but he was soon dropped – and she was to become the studio's greatest glory.

Now they have cast her as Tolstoy's heroine *Anna Karenina*, the lady who fell in love with a handsome officer (Fredric March), abandoning her unfeeling husband (Basil Rathbone) but also her beloved child (Freddie Bartholomew). Under the direction of Clarence Brown she gives her most complete performance yet, though without extinguishing memories of *Love*, the modern-dress version she did in 1927 with John Gilbert.

GOSSIP COLUMN

■ Sam Goldwyn has given up on Anna Sten. His "Million-Dollar Discovery" is said to have cost him much more than that after all the stops and starts on her three movies. Anna may have dazzled in her Russian and German movies; for Goldwyn she only fizzled.

■ See Jean Harlow and William Powell in *Reckless*, based on the true case of a Broadway star thought to have killed her husband. Joan Crawford got the heave-ho.

Cecil B. DeMille, master of the screen epic, and some of his camera equipment.

DOING WHAT HE DOES BEST

That master of screen spectacle, Cecil B. DeMille, has out his most ambitious film yet, *The Crusades* (even if that plural is not strictly accurate).

Born in Massachusetts in 1881, DeMille was originally an actor overshadowed by the fame of his dramatist brother William DeMille; but when the company which became Paramount was formed he directed one of its first successes, *The Squaw Man* (1914) - and his name was made. That was a western made on location, and he did a number of others, always with a strong moral tone; he also had hits with a tale of high society, *The Cheat* (1915), and with the story of Joan of Arc, *Joan the Woman* (1917). A series of sophisticated marital comedies began with *Don't Change Your Husband* (1918) and it included, somewhat surprisingly, a version of *The Admirable Crichton* called *Male and Female*. DeMille included a sequence set in ancient Babylon, and several of his subsequent epics have managed to contrast past and present.

The Ten Commandments (1923) consisted of two stories, ancient and modern – the modern one illustrating what happens to those who disobey the word of God. It was one of the studios greatest successes; but his films were often dangerously expensive, so no tears were shed when he went independent in 1925. But the only film of this period which was successful was *The King of Kings*.

Three films for M-G-M were disastrous, but he returned to the top at his old studio with *The Sign of the Cross*. A modern morality, *This Day and Age* (1933) and an adventure tale, *Four Frightened People* (1934), also failed, but *Cleopatra* and now *The Crusades* show DeMille doing what he does best – spectacle. If only he paid as much attention to the dialogue as he does to the decor.

A VOYAGE NOT WITHOUT INCIDENT

"It is not sufficiently adroit in its handling to make its coarseness and brutality even slightly palatable" says *Photoplay* of the film *China Seas*. Surely not. Blessed with witty dialogue by Jules Furthman and James Kevin McGuinness and jaunty, fast-paced direction by Tay Garnett, this is as fine an adventure movie as we've had in ages.

A ship sails from Hong Kong to Singapore, captained by Clark Gable, who thinks he loves a hoity-toity English widow (Rosalind Russell) when he is really drawn to an old flame, China Doll (Jean Harlow). She's in cahoots with an adventurer (Wallace Beery) who is scheming to promote a mutiny in order to steal the gold aboard. Hattie McDaniel, Lewis Stone, Akim Tamiroff, Ed Brophy and Robert Benchley are among the other entertaining passengers.

SEPTEMBER
OCTOBER

NOVEMBER
DECEMBER

CLEVER CLAUDETTE

Clever Claudette Colbert runs her career with great acumen. She likes money, and when Frank Capra couldn't interest any other big star in *It Happened One Night* (1934) he offered it to her as a vacation job, at much more than her usual fee. Its success and her Oscar caused Colbert to have her contract with Paramount revised, enabling her to accept outside offers.

She was born in Paris in 1905, but brought up chiefly in New York, to which the family moved when she was six. She became a stenographer, but a chance meeting with a Broadway dramatist brought an acting offer. She was a name in New York when she made her first film, *For the Love of Mike* (1927) – curiously, directed by Capra – but its failure brought no further offers. She was another of the stars brought into movies with the coming of sound, and was one of a handful who, for a while, were acting on the Broadway boards at night and Paramount's Astoria Studios by day.

She is equally at home in comedy and drama, and this year we have seen her in both, directed by Gregory La Cava. *Private Worlds*, set in a home for the mentally handicapped, is one of the best serious films of the year, with Colbert on top form as a work-obsessed doctor. In *She Married Her Boss* she is delightful. The plot tells you the title; Melvyn Douglas, himself no slouch at light comedy, is the husband who still treats Colbert like a secretary.

BIRTHS, DEATHS AND MARRIAGES

BIRTHS

Julie Andrews
1 Oct, Walton-on-Thames, Surrey

Michael Winner
30 Oct, London

Alain Delon
8 Nov, Sceaux, France

Woody Allen
1 Dec, New York

Lee Remick
14 Dec, Boston

Russ Tamblyn
30 Dec, Los Angeles

DEATHS

Thelma Todd
15 Dec, Hollywood
Suicide

MARRIAGES

Jean Harlow
Sep, *to* Hal Rossen

Sylvia Sidney
1 Oct, *to* Bennett Cerf

Joan Crawford
11 Oct, *to* **Franchot Tone**

June Havoc
Winter, *to* Donald S. Gibbs

Claudette Colbert
24 Dec, *to* Joel Pressman

BOX OFFICE

US

TOP BOX OFFICE FILMS

Anna Karenina
China Seas
David Copperfield
The Crusades
In Old Kentucky
Les Miserables
The Littlest Rebel
The Lives of a Bengal Lancer
A Night at the Opera
Top Hat

A scene from Warners' screen version of William Shakespeare's classic, A Midsummer Night's Dream.

WARNERS BLOWS ITS TRUMPET

Warners was never a studio to hide its light under a bushel and there can be few literate people who have not heard that they have come up with an epoch-making movie: "Three hours of Entertainment that was Three Centuries in the Making!"

'Tis a question of the Bard of Avon and his *A Midsummer Night's Dream*, directed jointly by William Dieterle and the famed German theatrical producer, Max Reinhardt, whose production of the play at the Hollywood Bowl caused a sensation a while back. But it is hard to imagine why, if it was anything like this film. Dripping with prancing fairies, it gives a new meaning to the word "kitsch". The text has been mangled to allow for loads of Mendelssohn's music – which is probably for the better, as this cast wouldn't be capable of handling it. But there's some fun from the rustics, played by enterprising types like James Cagney, Joe E. Brown and Hugh Herbert. Young Mickey Rooney, now making a name for himself, is an acceptable Puck.

SELZNICK GOES INDEPENDENT

David O. Selznick, the son of former producer Lewis J. Selznick, has been the white-haired boy of Hollywood ever since he rejuvenated Paramount with the coming of the talkies. Officially executive assistant to B.P. Schulberg, he was initiating many more successful pictures than Schulberg himself. When he left in 1931 he said he was going independent, but RKO needed a new head of production. He was filched from that studio by his father-in-law, Louis B. Mayer, for M-G-M, in case Irving Thalberg leaves or reduces activity.

But Selznick's irritation at being answerable to Mayer, despite several massive hits, has been industry gossip for a while; and United Artists, after losing Zanuck, approached him with a view to releasing any independent productions he cared to make. In October the producer announced the formation of Selznick International Productions – with private financing from several sources, including Mr and Mrs Thalberg and the Whitney brothers, whose involvement with both the new company and Pioneer is one reason why most Selznick pictures will be in Technicolor. But Technicolor is expensive to use and the new company wants a quick return on its first product, so *Little Lord Fauntleroy*, a remake of Mary Pickford's old vehicle will, after all, be made in monochrome. It still cost a mighty $500,000, high by industry standards, but that may well be proof of Selznick's promise to deliver only quality movies. As he said himself, "The day of mass production has ended."

A Night at the Opera.

MIGHTY M-G-M

When it comes to the biggest and best, M-G-M really does deserve the praise its publicists lavish upon it. This season it has come up with two films every moviegoer wants to see.

First, there's *Mutiny on the Bounty*, a rip-roaring tale of life on the Ocean wave, as First Mate Clark Gable and Captain Charles Laughton clash on their voyage back from the South Seas: a minor page in British naval history, perhaps, but a major event on celluloid, as directed by Frank Lloyd and done with all of Metro's know-how.

Then there is the second of the studio's excursions into the world of Charles Dickens this year, *A Tale of Two Cities*, with Ronald Colman (moustacheless) doing a far, far better thing than he has ever done before. He plays the dissolute Sydney Carton, British victim of the French Revolution – often thrillingly recreated by director Jack Conway. A prime cast also includes Edna May Oliver, Basil Rathbone and Elizabeth Allen.

Finally the mad Marxes have arrived at Metro to create further havoc in *A Night at the Opera*. Actually, that's the climax: much of it takes place on an ocean crossing. We wonder why the boat didn't sink – with all those folks shaking with laughter. Sam Wood directed.

HEPBURN'S REVELS

Katharine Hepburn's reign at the RKO studio has not always been of positive benefit, but this summer she decided to film Booth Tarkington's novel *Alice Adams* and chose George Stevens to direct it. His previous most notable work had been a Wheeler & Woolsey comedy. Between them Hepburn and Stevens brought poignancy to this tale of a stuck-up small town girl who falls in love with a wealthy young man (Fred MacMurray) – though the scene where he comes to a disastrous dinner is played, rightly, for nonstop laughter.

Just previewed is another pet project of Hepburn, *Sylvia Scarlett*, in which she disguises herself as a boy, attracting the amorous attention of a con-man (Cary Grant) and an artist (Brian Aherne). The preview went so badly that Hepburn and director George Cukor told head of RKO production Pandro S. Berman that they would do another film at once for no salary. He told them he didn't want either of them to work for him again. His loss, we fear.

Katharine Hepburn and Fred MacMurray in Alice Adams.

ZANUCK'S IN CHARGE

Where, one wondered, would United Artists be without its films from Darryl F. Zanuck's 20th Century Pictures? Also wondering was Joseph Schenck, who sat on the board of both companies. The films were delivered on schedule and of high quality, so when the UA board refused to offer 20th Century a stock interest in gratitude, he resigned from UA. A solution was already at hand, for Zanuck had been approached by Sidney Kent, the head of Fox.

William Fox, founder of one of the oldest surviving movie companies, had been forced out in 1930, and since then Kent had not always seen eye to eye with Winfield R. Sheehan, the head of production. The merger of Fox and 20th Century announced on 29 May, is an attractive one for both parties, since it means no duplication of facilities. And they all announce that Darryl Zanuck is in charge.

M-G-M'S NEW HEART-THROB

M-G-M has a new star, but it's no thanks to themselves. Listen to this: Robert Taylor, born in Nebraska in 1911, was studying at dramatic school in Los Angeles when signed by M-G-M after he had been noticed by a talent scout. They loaned him to Fox for a Will Rogers vehicle, *Handy Andy*, and to Universal for *There's Always Tomorrow* (both 1934). After one picture the same year on his home lot, *A Wicked Woman*, he was put into the first of the studio's new crime shorts with the series title *Crime Does Not Pay*. His work in that encouraged the studio to put him in some B-pictures, which led to his first leading-role in a major picture, this season's *Broadway Melody of 1936*.

But it's a role any competent juvenile could have played, and it was another loan-out to Universal which has made him the new idol of every female filmgoer in the land – as the playboy who accidentally blinds Irene Dunne in *Magnificent Obsession*, and who atones by becoming a famous surgeon who will one day operate on her eyes. It has to be said that he is good, but then this actress does have a habit of bringing her leading men up to her level.

GOSSIP COLUMN

■ Thelma Todd, the "Ice-Cream Blonde", was found dead in her Santa Monica garage a week before Christmas, slumped over the wheel of her car with its ignition on. She was 31. "Either she went to sleep with the motor running or was overcome before she could help herself," said the coroner. He obviously hadn't heard that former director Roland West, her partner in a restaurant, had locked her out of their home because of her nocturnal habits.

Swash & Buckle

The very first feature films, made in Italy in 1912, were epics of Roman times in which strong men were pitted against strong men. When the American cinema made longer pictures, they looked to stage properties for respectability – and came up with *The Prisoner of Zenda* (1913), which included a spectacular sword fight. Looking to the stage for actors, movies found Douglas Fairbanks, who became the screen's first real swashbuckler.

The enormous success of *The Mark of Zorro* (1920) led to *The Three Musketeers* (1921), *Robin Hood* (1922), *The Thief of Bagdad* (1924), *Don Q, Son of Zorro* (1925), *The Black Pirate* (1926) and *The Gaucho* (1927). Fairbanks produced the films himself, with lavish sets and casts of thousands. But some of his famous stunts, like sliding from the topmast through the sails in *The Black Pirate*, were faked, while – in the best-kept secret in Hollywood – he used a double.

After playing a grey-haired d'Artagnan in *The Iron Mask* (1929), Fairbanks hung up his sword. John Barrymore, John Gilbert and Ramon Novarro had followed him into the duelling field, the last in yet another *The Prisoner of Zenda* (1922) and in *Scaramouche* (1923). After the coming of talkies, Hollywood could only "see" one American actor in tights – Fredric March; but he took sword in hand only for *The Affairs of Cellini* (1934) and *The Buccaneer* (1938).

An unknown English actor, Robert Donat, was brought over for *The Count of Monte Cristo* (1934). American audiences fell madly in love with him, but because Donat refused to leave Britain again Warners cast an Australian-born Irishman who had played a couple of small parts (including a corpse) as *Captain Blood* (1935). So Errol Flynn became the famous pirate of the Seven Seas, with Olivia de Havilland, also a newcomer, as the haughty milady he tames.

They were teamed again in *The Charge of the Light Brigade* (1936) and, magically, in the Technicolor success *The Adventures of Robin Hood* (1938). In *The Sea Hawk* (1940) Flynn's climactic duel with Henry Daniell ranked with the magnificent one against Basil Rathbone in *Robin Hood*. During his first flush of success Flynn had a rival at M-G-M, Robert Taylor, and another at 20th Century-Fox, Tyrone Power. But only Power challenged Flynn in buckling a swash – in a fine remake of *The Mark of Zorro* (1940) and in the rousing pirate tale *The Black Swan* (1942).

As wartime escapism Jon Hall duelled for Universal in some action pictures with an oriental flavour, *Arabian Nights* (1941) and *Ali Baba and the 40 Thieves* (1944). Postwar audiences frowned on the genre, till M-G-M, looking for something to repeat the success of their 1931 jungle epic *Trader Horn*, decided to remake *King Solomon's Mines* (1950). Having signed the British actor Stewart Granger for the lead, M-G-M followed with new versions of *Scaramouche* (1952) and *The Prisoner of Zenda* (1952).

At this time Burt Lancaster was showing himself no slouch with a sword in *The Flame and the Arrow* (1950) and, more memorably, *The Crimson Pirate* (1952). Even Gene Kelly had had a go in the musical *The Pirate* (1948). But with these movies the swashbuckler died – not completely, but there were no more masterpieces.

The new *Robin Hood: Prince of Thieves*, with Kevin Costner, is the latest attempt, but the cost of remaking a *Sea Hawk*, with its teaming hordes, is now virtually prohibitive. Yet, if the swashbuckler finally died with the 1952 *Scaramouche*, it did so on a high note: the climactic duel inside a theatre is not only the longest on film (seven minutes) but perhaps the most exciting.

Douglas Fairbanks as The Thief of Bagdad *(1924).*

Errol Flynn being pursued by the Sheriff (Basil Rathbone) and his men in The Adventures of Robin Hood *(1938).*

Errol Flynn in The Sea Hawk (1940).

Stewart Granger in Scaramouche (1952).

Fredric March as The Buccaneer (1938).

Walter Matthau and crew in Roman Polanski's Pirates (1986).

Douglas Fairbanks in The Mark of Zorro (1920).

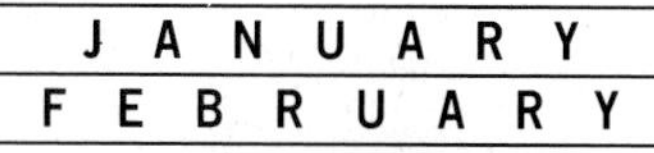

JANUARY
FEBRUARY

MARCH
APRIL

GILBERT DEAD

John Gilbert, dashing star of a string of silents, has died at his Hollywood home on 9 January, of a heart attack. He was 38. His name was from another era – an era of movies like *The Merry Widow* and *The Big Parade* (both 1925), *La Boheme* (1926) and *Flesh and the Devil* (1927). He's best remembered, however, as the most prominent victim of the talkies, after audiences laughed at his high-pitched voice.

The rumour was that Gilbert had offended his boss at M-G-M, Louis B. Mayer, who had ordered the sound engineers to record his voice badly. Certainly Mayer resented the huge fee paid to Gilbert (negotiated before the arrival of talkies) as his box-office tumbled. It was a tragic mess: to prove that he was a talkie *actor*, one of range, Gilbert accepted "tough" roles he hadn't played before – a drunkard in *West of Broadway* (1931), a lecher in *Downstairs* (1932), a braggart in *Fast Workers* (1933). He left the studio, returned at a much reduced fee when Garbo wanted him in *Queen Christina* – and then, after a while, he placed an announcement in the trade press to the effect that M-G-M would neither offer him work nor release him from contract.

But the studio obliged, and Gilbert turned up at Columbia in *The Captain Hates the Sea* (1934), fourth-billed as a drunken writer. This wasn't hard for him to play – days were lost during shooting because Gilbert was on benders. His off-screen companion, Marlene Dietrich, was trying to arrange a comeback when he died.

BIRTHS, DEATHS AND MARRIAGES

BIRTHS

Alan Alda
28 Jan, New York

Burt Reynolds
11 Feb, Waycross, Georgia

Jim Brown
17 Feb, St. Simon's Island, Georgia

Ursula Andress
19 Mar, Berne, Switzerland

Jill Ireland
24 Apr, London

DEATHS

John Gilbert
9 Jan, Hollywood
Heart attack

Marilyn Miller
7 Apr, Hollywood
Toxic poisoning

MARRIAGES

Frances Farmer
8 Feb, *to* **Leif Erikson**

Douglas Fairbanks Sr.
7 Mar, *to* Sylvia Ashley

HOODS ON THE RUN

Who ever expected to see a gangster movie set in the Arizona desert? But that is the venue for Warners' *The Petrified Forest*, based on the play by Robert E. Sherwood and directed by reliable Archie Mayo. The action in fact takes place in and around a lonely gas station, whose proprietor (Porter Hall) has a dreamy daughter (Bette Davis) who has just found a soul-mate in a passing stranger (Leslie Howard).

Into this milieu bursts a gang of ruthless hoods on the run, led by a dour Humphrey Bogart. Warners wanted this role for Edward G. Robinson, but Howard insisted on Bogart, who had played the role with him on Broadway. Bogart, who was not a great success as a contract player at Fox, looks as if he's back in movies to stay.

ACADEMY AWARDS

PRESENTED ON 5 MARCH 1936

Best Picture
Mutiny on the Bounty

Best Director
John Ford
The Informer

Best Actor
Victor McLaglen
The Informer

Best Actress
Bette Davis
Dangerous

A STUNNING OPENING

At the beginning of *Desire* Marlene Dietrich walks into a Paris jewellery store to look at an expensive bauble for which she has no intention of paying. She walks out with it, quite calmly, but soon hops it to the Spanish border – where customs officers are waiting. She gets it past them by slipping it into the pocket of a stranger, but the problem is: how to get it back?

Since the stranger is played by Gary Cooper it's a cinch that sooner or later they will fall into each other's arms. But getting the necklace back proves a more difficult task.

GOSSIP COLUMN

■ **Douglas Fairbanks has married Lady Sylvia Ashley and set her up in his Santa Monica beach home. Seems Lady Ashley – as Doug introduces her – would like to become Hollywood's leading hostess – as Mary once was.**

Marlene Dietrich falls into Gary Cooper's arms in Desire.

BAXTER REVIVED

Worthy, ageing Warner Baxter has never been among the more charismatic of stars, but this season he's in two terrific movies and one fairly good one.

Born in 1891 in Ohio, he was working with success in various stock companies when he decided to try his luck in movies. He made his film debut in *All Woman* (1918), starring Mae Marsh, and went on to be steadily employed, most notably in the title role of *The Great Gatsby* (1926), based on Scott Fitzgerald's bestseller. But stardom eluded him till he played the lead in *In Old Arizona* in 1929.

He is a sturdy, reliable fellow, probably appealing to the more mature spectators, who have kept him near the top of the heap the past six years for Fox.

Warner Baxter takes charge as a producer of a Broadway show in King of Burlesque.

First up this year, in January, was *King of Burlesque*, in a tailor-made role, that of a Broadway producer who goes Fifth Avenue while all the time his heart is with show business and Alice Faye. Second, in February, was John Ford's noble and exciting *The Prisoner of Shark Island*, in which he played the surgeon convicted of setting the leg of John Wilkes Booth after the accident he sustained when fleeing the theatre in which he had killed Abraham Lincoln. A second tale of injustice followed in March, when Baxter was on loan to M-G-M. In *Robin Hood of Eldorado*, under the direction of William A. Wellman, he took the role of Joaquin Murietta, one of the Mexicans who were dispossessed after the Americans annexed California. Baxter can be proud of these two movies.

THE LAST SILENT PICTURE

Charlie Chaplin was among the most vociferous of those who said that talkies were just a flash-in-the pan. Even the great Chaplin can be wrong – but when he released *City Lights* in 1931, long after silents were supposed to be dead and buried, he had a great success on his hands.

He's now done it again, refusing to let "The Little Fellow" speak, though he does have a song in gibberish. *Modern Times* may be silent, but it is often very funny, as the Tramp becomes involved with factory politics and assembly lines. Ignore the glutinous score, composed by Chaplin himself, and the fact that much has been borrowed from the 1931 French comedy, *A Nous la Liberte*. That's easy with Paulette Goddard on hand as the waif befriended by the Tramp. In private life Chaplin's companion, she is probably the most bewitching of all his leading ladies.

CAPRA SCORES AGAIN

Consider the plot of *Mr. Deeds Goes to Town*. Mr Deeds (Gary Cooper) is a hick who arrives in New York to collect a large inheritance. Ridiculed as "The Cinderella Man" by the press and taken for a ride in particular by one cynical reporter (Jean Arthur), he confounds everyone by wanting to give the money away when he discovers her duplicity.

As the film has it, he is "pixilated," a new word for the language. The film may or may not be a new step towards director Frank Capra's belief that movies can have a social conscience (in considering the needy in this post-Depression era); but, as written by his usual writer, Robert Riskin, it is very, very funny. Cooper and Arthur are at their formidable best, and supported by stalwarts like Ruth Donnelly, Raymond Walburn and Walter Catlett.

Margaret Sullavan and Henry Fonda.

FOND OF FONDA

Young Henry Fonda – he of the soft voice and smile, all integrity – looks like a valuable addition to Hollywood's roster of stars. Born in Nebraska in 1905, he had valuable experience in stock before becoming a Broadway name – notably in *The Farmer Takes a Wife*. When Fox decided to film it they discovered that neither Gary Cooper nor Joel McCrea was available – so they negotiated for Fonda's services with William Wanger, who had already placed him under contract. Wanger has him back for two movies this season, both released by Paramount: *The Trail of the Lonesome Pine*, the first outdoor Technicolor movie, in which he plays a backwoods type vying with city slicker Fred MacMurray for Sylvia Sidney; and *The Moon's Our Home*, where he's a shy best-seller writer who tangles with a movie star, Margaret Sullavan. They marry, but are unhappy till the final reel. All very piquant: the two were married in real life before they hit the big time.

MAY

JUNE

JULY

AUGUST

THE SCREEN'S GREAT DANCE TEAM

The names of Fred Astaire and Ginger Rogers are now inseparable. They were fourth and fifth-billed – almost an afterthought – in RKO's big 1933 musical, *Flying Down to Rio*, with only one number, "The Carioca". The studio liked them together and cast Ginger, against Fred's wishes (he thought her miscast as an English divorcee) in a film of one of his stage hits, Cole Porter's *The Gay Divorcee* (1934). They teamed up again the following year in *Roberta* and *Top Hat*. In the former they took second billing to Irene Dunne. But in *Top Hat*, wonderfully scored by Irving Berlin, only the names of Astaire and Rogers appeared above the title.

Astaire, born in 1899 in Nebraska, was a dancer from childhood, partnered by his sister Adele. By 1918 they were Broadway stars, with shows written especially for them and equally successful in London. After Adele married into the British aristocracy Fred turned to movies. and RKO signed him with little enthusiasm, loaning him first to M-G-M for a guest spot in *Dancing Lady* (1933).

Rogers, born in 1911 in Missouri, had a stage mother determined to see her make it in show business; so she pushed her into vaudeville after the girl won a Charleston contest. She was a showgirl and then an ingenue on Broadway, with a Paramount contract which began with *Young Man of Manhattan* (1930). Sixteen films later, she still hadn't made it, despite several leading roles. A return trip to RKO – for *Professional Sweetheart* (1933) – resulted in an RKO contract and the eventual teaming with Astaire.

Earlier this year the plotting of *Follow the Fleet* was an improvement on their earlier marital misunderstandings. Now the songs by Jerome Kern (who also scored *Roberta*) for *Swing Time* are so rich and abundant that the movie looks like the peak of their work together.

Astaire is said to fight RKO over every new teaming, but it's the studio's only surefire seal of success. And Ma Rogers is said to fight everyone so her talented daughter won't be overlooked.

MY LADY LOMBARD

With *My Man Godfrey* Carole Lombard takes her place as the most beautiful and the most accomplished comedienne in Hollywood.

Born in 1908 in Indiana, she moved to Los Angeles and was seen playing in a neighbour's yard by director Allan Dwan, who cast her as Monte Blue's daughter in *A Perfect Crime* (1921). There were further offers – and contracts with Fox and Mack Sennett; and another in the talkie period with Paramount, which cast her in star roles without regarding her as anything special. She was loosening up, growing more beautiful, dressing more elegantly – and getting a reputation as a Good Joe on and around the set.

Throwing tantrums in the screwball *Twentieth Century* (1934) made the big difference, and she had another good role last year in *Hands across the Table* with Fred MacMurray. *My Man Godfrey* is as funny as both put together, as Lombard takes a Depression-hit bum to a ritzy scavenger hunt and finds that he's staying on as the butler. Her scattiness takes on divine dimensions and she's beautifully partnered by William Powell, her real-life partner (for a brief spell) at the beginning of the decade.

M-G-M BIGUNS

M-G-M has a knack of coming up with the big ones – and since Florenz Ziegfeld was Broadway's most flamboyant showman, the studio has called its tribute to him *The Great Ziegfeld*. It's certainly spectacular – especially when the giant wedding-cake of a set turns to "A Pretty Girl Is Like a Melody." William Powell is Flo, with Luise Rainer as his first wife and Myrna Loy as his second (Billie Burke, Flo's real second wife, was to have played herself when this project was on the drawing-board at Universal). Fanny Brice does play herself, while others play such Ziegfeld luminaries as Eddie Cantor and Will Rogers.

More spellbinding is the other Metro biggie of the season, *San Francisco* – or at least the second half, which features the great 1906 earthquake. The first chunk is some nonsense about a nightclub king (Clark Gable), his singer (Jeanette MacDonald), and his boyhood chum, a priest (Spencer Tracy). But the climax is spectacular.

Spencer Tracy and Clark Gable walk through a makeshift camp after the 1906 earthquake that was the story for San Francisco.

Fredric March and Olivia de Havilland in the costume drama Anthony Adverse.

SPECTACLE FROM WARNERS

A lot of people preferred Warners movies in their wham, bam, slam days – fast-moving, realistic comedies and dramas about journalists, mobsters and showgirls. But the studio which brought *A Midsummer Night's Dream* to American screens is not neglecting the more romantic past. It has been putting in bids for the big bestsellers – and at present they don't come any bigger, or at last longer, than Hervey Allen's *Anthony Adverse*.

Compressing it all into one movie must have been daunting enough, but it's a rousing adventure covering much of France and Italy, with a side-trip to Africa, at the end of the 18th century. Fredric March is the hero with the odds so much stacked against him – many of them placed there by scheming Claude Rains and Gale Sondergaard. Olivia de Havilland is the girl he loves.

BRING ON THE "B"S

After experimenting for more than a decade with live shows and shorts of all sorts, cinemas now seem to be giving audiences what they want: one "big" film, one "little" film, and assorted central matter.

The last will always include newsreels and the trailers to whet spectators' appetites. And it may also include a comic or animated short, a travelogue, a documentary like the new *March of Time* series, or true-life stories like *Crime Does Not Pay* or *Great Moments from History*. Moviegoers' attention span may run to a couple of these, but they appear not to like a surfeit.

So all the studios are now producing "B" pictures to support the main feature. It makes economic sense when so many properties are swallowed in Hollywood's maw. And they can provide a splendid training ground for new talent, both in front of and behind the cameras.

THAT BARD AGAIN

Norma Shearer wanted to play Juliet, and when you're Mrs Irving Thalberg you usually get your way at M-G-M. But the studio took no chances. George Cukor, considered Hollywood's leading literary director after *Little Women* (1933) and *David Copperfield* (1935), was brought in to direct, and famed British stage designer Oliver Messel was sent for to give the piece a distinctive look, no expense spared ($2,066,000 in fact). When Fredric March refused Romeo, M-G-M went after Leslie Howard, scheduled to play Hamlet in New York later this year; and Howard wasn't interested until he discovered that Warners wouldn't loan him – and then he insisted on playing the part!

So how is this *Romeo and Juliet*? Over-age – with John Barrymore as Mercutio and Basil Rathbone as Tybalt. Of the major players, only Edna May Oliver as the Nurse is a delight.

A SINGULAR ACHIEVEMENT

No one is more prone to sound off about his own achivements than Sam Goldwyn, but his record on the whole is not too hot. *Arrowsmith* (1931) was good, as directed by John Ford and written by Sidney Howard from the novel by Sinclair Lewis. Howard recommended another of Lewis' novels to Goldwyn, *Dodsworth*, which could have been bought for $20,000. When Goldwyn refused, Howard and Lewis turned it into a play – which Goldwyn bought for $160,000. "I bought a successful play," he said. "Before it was just a novel."

Repeating his success on Broadway is Walter Huston, as the middle-aged factory proprietor who takes his wife (Ruth Chatterton) to Europe, where she succumbs to a set of phony values – while he still cleaves to the standards of the Middle West. Both players are fine, as is Mary Astor as the kindly woman who befriends Sam Dodsworth as his marriage breaks up.

The key to the success of *Dodsworth* may be the pacy but thoughtful direction of William Wyler. A former director of routine westerns, Wyler did excellent work at Universal before being signed by Goldwyn. His work on this and *These Three* suggests that William Wyler is a valuable acquisition.

BIRTHS, DEATHS AND MARRIAGES

BIRTHS

Glenda Jackson
9 May, Birkenhead

Albert Finney
9 May, Salford

Dennis Hopper
17 May, Dodge City, Kansas

Joan Collins
23 May, London

Louis Gosset Jr.
27 May, Brooklyn, New York

Keir Dullea
30 May, Cleveland, Ohio

Bruce Dern
4 Jun, Chicago

Kris Kristofferson
22 Jun, Brownsville, Texas

DEATHS

Thomas Meighan
8 Jul, New York

MARRIAGES

Ann Sheridan
26 Aug, *to* Edward Norris

GOSSIP COLUMN

■ **At its sales convention Warners has announced a series of pictures starring James Cagney, despite the courts backing him (because of a technicality) when he walked out of his contract. He wanted more money, and fewer and better movies. Neither side is giving in and no major studio will employ Cagney (it might encourage their own players to rebel).**

Walter Huston as the middle-aged factory proprietor Dodsworth.

SEPTEMBER
OCTOBER

NOVEMBER
DECEMBER

THE SCREEN'S PERFECT COUPLE

When you see William Powell and Myrna Loy together, you know no couple will ever better their brand of verbal cut-and-thrust. He's urbane and cynical, she's brittle and unfazed. They reached some sort of apotheosis as the husband-and-wife detective team of *The Thin Man* (1934), and now they are reunited for a sequel, *Another Thin Man*.

Both were in films long before enjoying today's success. Powell, born in 1892 in Pittsburgh, was on Broadway in 1912, making his screen debut a decade later as the villain in *Sherlock Holmes* (1922). He remained nasty throughout the decade, usually in supporting roles, but his comic finesse and excellent speaking voice made him a star in talkies, often as a detective or a suave man-about-town.

Loy, born in a Montana village in 1905, learned dancing as a girl – which she taught after the family moved to Los Angeles; she was noticed by a photographer while in the chorus at Grauman's Chinese Theatre; she made her film debut in a bit part in 1925, and with his help was signed to a contract at Warners.

For the next five years she played shady ladies and vamps, usually of an Oriental persuasion. Although her voice proved ideal for talkies, Warners dropped her in 1931, by which time she had proved herself a reliable leading woman, particularly good in sophisticated roles. M-G-M signed her the following year and began grooming her for stardom – which she attained emphatically with *The Thin Man*.

She and Powell have been teamed several times since – most delightfully this season in *Libeled Lady*, in which she has the title-role. Spencer Tracy is the journalist who cannot marry Jean Harlow while he has a $5 million libel suit hanging over him, so he brings in Powell, an old colleague, to compromise Loy.

ANOTHER SLICE OF HISTORY

It's now the turn of 20th Century-Fox to see what they can make of Britain's historical past, and they've done a fine job in *Lloyds of London*, which takes the famous insurance company through 50 years of its early history from 1770. The characters include Benjamin Franklin, Dr Johnson, Lord Nelson and the Prince Regent. Under the confident direction of Henry King it is packed with exciting incident; and at the heart is the romance of Tyrone Power and Madeleine Carroll, both beautiful creatures, who get quite a bit of Hollywood passion going.

BIRTHS, DEATHS AND MARRIAGES

BIRTHS

Jim Henson
24 Sep, Greenville, Massachusetts

Frederic Forrest
23 Dec, Waxahachie, Texas

Mary Tyler Moore
29 Dec, Brooklyn, New York

DEATHS

Irving Thalberg
14 Sep, Hollywood
Pneumonia

MARRIAGES

Henry Fonda
17 Sept, *to* Frances Seymour Brokaw

Signe Hasso
12 Oct, *to* Harry Hasso

John Barrymore
8 Nov, *to* Elaine Barrie

Brian Donlevy
22 Dec, *to* Margorie Lane

Errol Flynn in Charge of the Light Brigade.

A FAMOUS BLUNDER

If you've ever wondered what it was like to be at Balaclava when the Light Brigade made its famous, doomed charge, go and see Warners' new picture. It is excitingly brought to life – at the end of a story of the British Imperial Army.

In fact, *The Charge of the Light Brigade* is somewhat misnamed. What precedes the re-enactment of that famous blunder is a splendid Victorian adventure in the manner of G.A. Henty. It takes in quite a bit of history, but suffice to say that the setting is that old favourite, the North West frontier, where the fierce Afghan tribesmen are looking to Russia to help them in their attacks on British rule. That's only one reason why the 27th Lancers winds up in the Crimea – when Tennyson's ringing phrases retain their power.

Errol Flynn is much in prominence, unaccountably rejected by Olivia de Havilland for his brother, Patric Knowles; others include David Niven, C. Aubrey Smith, Donald Crisp and J. Carroll Naish. Director Michael Curtiz has done a cracking job – though one of the credits suggests that the Charge itself is the work of B. Reeves Eason, responsible for the chariot race in *Ben-Hur* (1925).

KORDA'S PROGRESS

Alexander Korda continues to run London Films on the lines of a Hollywood company. With great fanfare in May he opened his massive new studio complex at Denham, north of London. Among the stars coming to work for him are Marlene Dietrich, Miriam Hopkins and Edmund Lowe. Charles Laughton has just returned in *Rembrandt*, which at least is a prestige success.

But United Artists is complaining that of the 10 films delivered since *The Private Life of Henry VIII* (1933) only one has been a success – Rene Clair's *The Ghost Goes West*, earlier this year. Some of the other pictures have failed horribly, including *The Private Life of Don Juan* (1934), the last picture to date of Douglas Fairbanks, and this year's much-touted futuristic tale written by H.G. Wells, *Things To Come*. Korda in turn is complaining that UA has not handled his films well in America. But the quarrel is likely to be patched up: – Korda is more important than other British suppliers, whom UA claims are not making pictures of high enough quality to attract American audiences. Meanwhile, Gaumont-British continues to make small inroads into the American market.

THE ARTY CROWD

John Ford has been directing movies since 1918 and many remember his silent westerns with affection. He has branched out into other fields in recent years, turning out such interesting movies as *Pilgrimage* (1933) and *The Lost Patrol* (1934). The industry didn't care for *The Informer* (1935), though it wowed the East Coast critics. As a result, RKO, which produced, allowed Ford carte blanche to make two of this year's horrors, *Mary of Scotland* and *The Plough and the Stars*. The first is a dull, pretentious and anachronistic account of Mary Queen of Scots, played laughably by Katharine Hepburn; the second, a return to the Dublin of *The Informer*, is a tedious and perfunctory account of Sean O'Casey's play.

The Informer is not a bad movie, but it's a bad influence: witness *Winterset*, directed by Alfred Santell and based on the prize-winning play by Maxwell Anderson that was loosely inspired by the Sacco and Vanzetti case; as a film it was all fog, arty shadows, an atmosphere of doom, and the downtrodden masses. The critics have raved, but both films are lifeless copies of the sort of movies coming out of Germany in the silent era. When Hollywood gets arty and "European," why do the critics always start to cheer?

IRENE LETS HER HAIR DOWN

The always ladylike Irene Dunne became a star in a series of weepies and marital dramas which she made palatable by never seeming to take them too seriously. Once a star of musical comedy, she's recently begun to sing on screen as well – notably in renditions of Jerome Kern songs in last year's *Sweet Adeline* and *Roberta* and this summer's *Show Boat*. She appeared in the last during her stage days.

She was born in Kentucky in 1904, and studied music in Chicago. She first starred on Broadway in 1923 and made her first movie in 1930 – *Leatherneck-ing*, for RKO. In recent years, much in demand, she has moved from studio to studio, presumably with control over her material, but the publicity line on *Theodora Goes Wild* is that she made it against her will, since she has never seen herself as a comedienne.

She couldn't have been more wrong. As a prissy small town girl who writes a sizzling best-seller and then is humanized by the designer (Melvyn Douglas) of the book's jacket, she is a mistress of her (new) craft – especially when she lets her hair down to meet him on his own terms. Stand by for many more comedies in Irene's future.

Gary Cooper and Jean Arthur in Cecil B. DeMille's big budget western The Plainsman.

THE RETURN OF THE WESTERN

You can spend any Saturday matinee watching Poverty Row westerns with cowboys and Indians chasing each other around trees. The memorable westerns of the silent era were about the pioneers pushing west or making the frontier safe – and Cecil B. DeMille has returned to that tradition with *The Plainsman*, the first big-budget western from a major studio since *Cimarron* (1931).

Some of the names are famous – Wild Bill Hickock (Gary Cooper), Calamity Jane (Jean Arthur), Buffalo Bill Cody (James Ellison) and General George Custer (John Miljan). Surrounding these are Indians and even more treacherous traders. The film has been described by British critic Graham Greene as "perhaps the finest western in the history of films." He seems surprised to find something so good coming from DeMille. So may you.

BOX OFFICE

UK

1 Mr. Deeds Goes to Town
2 Mutiny on the Bounty
3 The Ghost Goes West

OTHER TOP BOX OFFICE FILMS

Anna Karenina
Broadway Melody of 1936
First a Girl
The Littlest Rebel
Rose Marie
Secret Agent
A Tale of Two Cities

BOX OFFICE

US

1 San Francisco
2 Modern Times
3 Strike Me Pink
4 The Trail of the Lonesome Pine
5 Dodsworth
6 A Midsummer Night's Dream

OTHER TOP BOX OFFICE FILMS

Mr. Deeds Goes to Town
Rose Marie
Swing Time
A Tale of Two Cities

JANUARY FEBRUARY 1937 MARCH APRIL

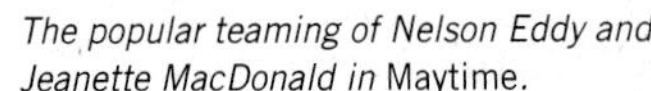

The popular teaming of Nelson Eddy and Jeanette MacDonald in Maytime.

M-G-M'S SINGING SWEETHEARTS

As with Astaire and Rogers, the teaming of popular Jeanette MacDonald and Nelson Eddy came about by chance. MacDonald was cast in *Naughty Marietta* (1935) but, with no obvious leading man, M-G-M cast Nelson Eddy who had languished since being signed two years earlier. His reception told the studio it had a new star and he was put into two more versions of old operettas, *Rose Marie* (1936) and now *Maytime*. In both his original co-star was Grace Moore; but thanks to a conflict of schedules, MacDonald replaced her.

She was born in Philadelphia in 1901, and was a Broadway soprano when Paramount signed her in 1929. She teamed felicitously with Maurice Chevalier in several pictures, but was then dropped and was about to make a film in England when M-G-M came calling. The plan was to make *I Married an Angel*, with Rodgers and Hart songs, but that was cancelled because the script was disliked by the Hays Office. She made *The Cat and the Fiddle* instead, and Metro put her under long-term contract.

Eddy was born in Providence, Rhode Island, in 1901, and after a spell as a journalist won a competition to sing with the Philadelphia Civic Opera. He was quite well known when M-G-M signed him.

Their latest, *Maytime*, is a florid tearjerker in which two student lovers are swept apart by her jealous impresario (John Barrymore). The public is lapping it up so much that M-G-M has now forgotten Moore and is planning more vehicles for the singing sweethearts.

But none of them may be as good as *Rose Marie*, in which Jeannete MacDonald showed her old Paramount style as a temperamental prima donna. In *Maytime* she already seems to be taking the saccharine stuff as seriously as stolid Eddy.

BIRTHS, DEATHS AND MARRIAGES

BIRTHS

Troy Donahue
21 Jan, New Jersey

Vanessa Redgrave
30 Jan, London

Suzanne Pleshette
31 Jan, New York

Tom Courtenay
25 Feb, Hull

Jack Nicholson
22 Apr, Neptune, New Jersey

Sandy Dennis
27 Apr, Hastings, Nebraska

DEATHS

Richard Boleslawski
17 Jan, Hollywood
Heart attack

Marie Prevost
23 Jan, Hollywood
Alcoholism

Guy Standing
24 Feb, Hollywood
Heart attack

MARRIAGES

Ann Harding
17 Jan, *to* Werner Janssen

TECHNICOLOR COMES TO BRITAIN

As Britain prepares for the Coronation of King George VI and Queen Elizabeth after the shock of the Abdication, another milestone has been passed. The British have got their first Technicolor picture, *Wings of the Morning*.

The movie is only partly British, in fact, as it's one of the films produced by New World for international release by 20th Century-Fox. The stars are Henry Fonda, who crossed the Atlantic for the job, and France's Annabella, pausing en route as she goes in the opposite direction, to Hollywood. The complicated and forgettable story has Annabella as a Spanish gypsy and also as her granddaughter, who poses as a boy on arriving in Ireland. If you're in Ireland, you have to have Count John McCormack, and when he sings "Killarney" the Technicolor camera leaves him to roam around the lake of that name. "Wings of the Morning"? That's the name of a horse.

FOX'S NEW SINGING STAR

Since Alice Faye arrived at 20th Century-Fox she's shown a way with a torch song that rivals Broadway's Helen Morgan. But all Fox could see in her – as an actress – was another cutie in the Jean Harlow manner. Until now, that is.

She was born in New York's Hell's Kitchen in 1915 and began her career as a chorus girl. Rudy Vallee gave her a weekly song on his radio show and she accompanied him to Hollywood when he was signed by Fox to co-star with Lilian Harvey in *George White's Scandals* (1934). Instead of singing one song, as intended, she was upped to leading lady when Harvey and George White quarrelled.

Harvey – the British-born singer who had become a star in German movie musicals – departed whence she came, and Faye became Fox's new musical star. When mogul Darryl F. Zanuck took over the studio last year he decreed an end to her plucked eyebrows and platinum blonde hair. Much softened, she had a new kind of appeal last year in *Sing, Baby, Sing* and in a Shirley Temple vehicle, *Stowaway*.

Still billed below the title, she steals *On the Avenue* from its official stars, Dick Powell and Madeleine Carroll, as she sings such Irving Berlin ditties as "This Year's Kisses" and "You're Laughing at Me". She's not a great actress but she's pretty and has the sort of gentle personality which can also burn up the screen. She won't be billed under the title again.

Alice Faye in On the Avenue.

Greta Garbo with Robert Taylor in George Cukor's Camille.

MORE METRO GREATS

You have to hand it to M-G-M, which has come up with three more great movies this season. Pride of place at any time would go to *Camille*, directed by George Cukor from the play by Alexander Dumas, *The Lady of the Camelias*. The star is Greta Garbo, at her most luminous in what may be her greatest triumph. As the boy for whom she deserts her wealthy lover, Robert Taylor is boyish; as the lover, Henry Daniell is superb. It is as well to draw a veil over some others in the cast, but they cannot break the spell of the Garbo magic.

A less expected success is *The Good Earth*, considering the few things there are in common between M-G-M and a Chinese peasant family. But the film encompasses the sweep of Pearl S. Buck's book with ease and without affectation, as directed by Sidney Franklin. Paul Muni and Luise Rainer are strong in the leads, and are well supported by a cast which gives a reasonable impression of being Chinese.

A SAGA OF LIFE IN HOLLYWOOD

In 1932 *What Price Hollywood?* presented a picture of the movie capital that was not all glitter and tinsel. Its producer, David O. Selznick, uses elements of the plot in *A Star Is Born*. And why not? Industry insiders recognize in both films characters and incidents from real life.

A young Hollywood hopeful (Janet Gaynor) arrives in town hoping for a career in pictures: she meets a star (Fredric March) whose own career has begun a gentle decline. It accelerates, worsened by his addiction to the bottle, as her fame begins to build. She continues to love him but there are too many people in the old town glad to see him finished.

It's strong stuff, despite the unusual use of colour for such a subject. And it's eloquently directed by William A. Wellman.

DEANNA SAVES UNIVERSAL

A 15-year-old girl has done the trick and looks like putting Universal back into the black after a bad run. She's Canadian-born Deanna Durbin, a last-minute addition to *Three Smart Girls*, a comedy about a divorcing couple reunited by their children. Her role was built up during shooting, and audiences are now endorsing the enthusiasm of Universal executives (which is more than M-G-M's – the studio dropped her last year after putting her in a short with young Judy Garland). But the movie's benefits to the studio coffers are being severely tested by a musical that was one of Universal's head of production Charles Rogers' pet projects, *Top of the Town*. Everyone's calling that "Flop of the Town".

ACADEMY AWARDS

PRESENTED ON 4 MARCH 1937

Best Picture
The Great Ziegfeld

Best Director
Frank Capra
Mr. Deeds Goes to Town

Best Actor
Paul Muni
The Story of Louis Pasteur

Best Actress
Luise Rainer
The Great Ziegfeld

Best Sup Actor
Walter Brennan
Come and Get It

Best Sup Actress
Gale Sondergaard
Anthony Adverse

Janet Gaynor in A Star Is Born.

FIGHT AGAINST FATE

The great German director Fritz Lang has not had a great deal of success since he arrived in the United States in 1935. *Fury*, a scorching account of mob rule with Spencer Tracy, was praised by the press last year; but the reception didn't impress the right-wing M-G-M boss Louis B. Mayer, who did not feel inclined to extend Lang's contract.

Now independent producer Walter Wanger (releasing through UA) has given Lang the chance to make a second film. *You Only Live Once* is another striking but unflattering picture of American life. Henry Fonda is an ex-convict determined to go straight but finding his past just won't go away; Sylvia Sidney is his wife. Critics are called the movie the most honest portrait of America in this post-Depression era, but Lang himself sees its subject running through all his pictures – "this fight against destiny, against fate."

GOSSIP COLUMN

■ Don't mess with Bette. After walking out on her Warners contract and journeying to Britain – where two film projects and an injunction awaited her – Bette Davis is back with her studio. Although it won its case, Warners has handsomely paid her court costs and promised her better pictures. It seems to have kept its word so far.

PRESENTING MR MUNI

He's no longer Paul Muni in Warners adverts, but *Mr* Paul Muni. The studio has no doubt it has the greatest actor in Hollywood under contract.

He was born in Lemberg, then part of the Austrian Empire, in 1895 into a family of strolling players, who "strolled" all the way to the United States. He joined the Yiddish Theater when just out of his teens and it was not till 1926 that he first acted in English. Fox signed him when talkies came in, but after two films, *The Valiant* and *Seven Faces* (both 1929), he returned to Broadway, where his performance in *Counseller-at-Law* brought him the lead in *Scarface* (1932).

While making *I Am a Fugitive from a Chain Gang* (1932) for Warners the studio offered him a contract. It had the unique clause that if he turned down three of its projects it was bound to do the fourth – of his choosing. That's how *The Story of Louis Pasteur* (1936) came about – and Warners loathed it, till it read the notices. Muni won an Oscar and as a follow-up there's now *The Life of Emile Zola*, which has been even more extravagantly praised. Muni's magisterial presence, his attention to detail and his liking for elaborate make-up – remember his Chinese peasant in *The Good Earth* earlier this year? – all make for "great" acting of a sort. But some still prefer the cheery, extrovert and unpretentious star of programmers like *Hi, Nellie!* (1934) and *Dr. Socrates* (1935).

THE DELECTABLE MISS ARTHUR

Like those outstanding light comediennes Myrna Loy and Carole Lombard, Jean Arthur has sort of crept up on audiences. She was born in New York City in 1905, the daughter of a photographer, for whom she modelled as a youngster. One of these pictures was seen by a Fox talent scout, and with a contract in her pocket she made her screen debut in *Cameo Kirby* (1923). Her career as an ingenue in silents was checkered, and talkies revealed her as still rather awkward. In 1931 she took herself east to work on the stage.

The Jean Arthur who returned was not exactly a transformation, but after four more movies she landed a Columbia contract. Her comic skills were first apparent in John Ford's *The Whole Town's Talking* (1935) and they were finely honed by the time she did *Mr. Deeds Goes to Town* (1936). Earlier this year they were on display again in the comedy-drama, *History Is Made at Night* and now she can be seen in the wonderful *Easy Living* from Paramount.

Budding newcomer Judy Garland and Buddy Ebsen in M-G-M's third in the "Broadway" series Broadway Melody of 1938.

ANOTHER BROADWAY MELODY

Broadway Melody of 1938, M-G-M's third of the series, has the same stars as the last one – Robert Taylor and Eleanor Powell – and the same sort of plot about Broadway hopefuls. It has some other pleasing performers in George Murphy, Sophie Tucker, Robert Benchley and Buddy Ebsen. It also has Judy Garland - and thereby hangs a tale.

Judy, just 15 and a former vaudeville youngster, was signed by M-G-M two years ago, but she didn't fit into the Shirley Temple category of child stars. So the studio allowed her to languish after putting her into one short with Deanna Durbin, *Every Sunday* (1936). It loaned her to 20th Century-Fox for a small role in a college musical, *Pigskin Parade* (1936), but that was all. Music arranger Roger Edens, impressed by her natural talent, wrote a special version of "You Made Me Love You" for her to sing to Clark Gable at his birthday luncheon at the studio. At last M-G-M realised she was something special, and rushed her into this movie to sing it all over again to a picture of Mr. G. It's the highlight of the piece and a guarantee she won't be neglected again.

BIRTHS, DEATHS AND MARRIAGES

BIRTHS

Dustin Hoffman
8 Aug, Los Angeles

Robert Redford
18 Aug, Santa Monica, California

DEATHS

Jean Harlow
7 Jun, Hollywood
Uremic poisoning

Colin Clive
26 Jun, New York
Intestinal ailments

George Gershwin
11 Jul, Hollywood
Brain tumour

MARRIAGES

Jeanette MacDonald
16 Jun, *to* Gene Raymond

Mary Pickford
26 Jun, *to* Buddy Rogers

Ingrid Bergman
Jul, *to* Petter Lindstrom

Barbara Stanwyck, as an uncouth woman who loses both husband and daughter, in Stella Dallas.

A MODERN STELLA

No one who saw Belle Bennett in the 1925 *Stella Dallas* is ever likely to forget her, but that grand actress Barbara Stanwyck is her equal in the remake, directed by King Vidor. Sam Goldwyn's writers have done their best to iron out those aspects of the plot which were old-fashioned then, so Stella can face the day as a lady of 1937. The plot? A toff (John Boles), hiding out in the middle-West, marries Stella, his landlord's daughter. But she is not refined – and so in sad middle-age she loses her daughter (Anne Shirley) as surely as she lost her husband.

M-G-M IN BLIGHTY

The seriousness with which Hollywood regards British talent has been given ample proof by M-G-M's decision to start production at Alexander Korda's Denham studio. To head the operation they have appointed Michael Balcon, who has long guided Gaumont-British and Gainsborough Pictures.

Balcon, who produced his first film in 1923, *Woman to Woman*, introduced or developed talents like Alfred Hitchcock, Jessie Matthews and Will Hay. He has recently presided over the British work of imports like George Arliss and Conrad Veidt. His insistence on quality and the ability to make movies of world class are among the reasons M-G-M hired him. Robert Taylor has arrived to make *A Yank at Oxford*, the first M-G-M film under Balcon's aegis, and brought with him Maureen O'Sullivan and Lionel Barrymore. Joining them as Oxford's chief flirt is a 23-year-old British star, Vivien Leigh.

FAREWELL TO THE PLATINUM BLONDE

Platinum blonde Jean Harlow died in Hollywood of uremic poisoning on 7 June, aged 26. She had been in poor health for about a year, and was taken ill while making *Saratoga* opposite Clark Gable. After some indecision M-G-M is completing the film with a stand-in.

A Kansas City girl, she had a brief marriage in her teens before arriving in Hollywood in 1928, when she found work as an extra. As a decorative blonde she decorated some Laurel & Hardy shorts, but then Howard Hughes signed her for *Hell's Angels* (1930). Hughes had no further plans to make movies, but loaned her out – till her agent objected. He wanted her at M-G-M, and M-G-M wanted her. It had Norma Shearer and Joan Crawford, but no obvious glamour girl. Harlow was obvious, all right, but the studio knew how to use her rather cheap, vampish quality – and it knew how to change her when her frank approach to sex was outlawed by the Hays Code. The new Harlow as still a fine comedienne but it's doubtful whether she would have made it as a serious actress – though Myrna Loy has said she was more intelligent than she was ever allowed to appear.

WE, THE PEOPLE

This season the movies have left the ballrooms, dressing-rooms and newsrooms they love so much to make three fine films about the way most of us live. Best of the bunch is Leo McCarey's sympathetic *Make Way for Tomorrow*, from Paramount, which concerns an ageing couple (Beulah Bondi, Victor Moore) who, finding themselves penniless, have to be billetted separately on their children and their spouses, none of whom really wants them.

Dead End, from producer Sam Goldwyn and director William Wyler, looks at New York's slums, as originally envisaged in Sidney Kingsley's Broadway play. There is a gangster (Humphrey Bogart) raised in these parts, his care-worn mother (Marjorie Main) and his girlfriend (Claire Trevor), plus those who aspire to higher things, like Joel McCrea and Sylvia Sidney.

The most potentially explosive of the three is *They Won't Forget*, directed by Mervyn LeRoy for Warners. It's based on the Leo Frank case of 1913 but set in the contemporary South. A corrupt District Attorney (Claude Rains) uses a murder trial to advance his political ambitions, and in so doing shows the bigotry down in those parts – against blacks and Northerners alike. It's the weakest film of the three, with gaping holes in the plot and much overacting.

The "dead end kids" in Dead End.

SEPTEMBER
OCTOBER

NOVEMBER
DECEMBER

DISNEY'S TRIUMPH

"Disney's folly" the sceptics originally called it. Five years after its inception, and four-and-a-half since drawing began, *Snow White and the Seven Dwarfs* is here.

Under survising director David Hand, Grimm's fairy story has been brought enchantingly Technicolored to life. The film went over budget by $250,000 to finish at just under $1.7 million. The Disney studio is now poised to start on more full-length cartoons. But none could surpass the excitement created by *Snow White*. It's the movie event not just of the year but also of the decade – unless David O. Selznick ever manages to get started on *Gone with the Wind*.

BIRTHS, DEATHS AND MARRIAGES

BIRTHS

Virna Lisi
8 Nov, Ancona, Italy

Jane Fonda
21 Dec, New York

Anthony Hopkins
31 Dec, Port Talbot, Wales

DEATHS

Ruth Roland
22 Sep, Los Angeles
Cancer

MARRIAGES

Alice Faye
3 Sep, *to* Tony Martin

Miriam Hopkins
4 Sep, *to* Anatole Litvak

Cornel Wilde
21 Sep, *to* Patricia Knight

SHIRLEYMANIA

The success of litle Shirley Temple has been phenomenal. She's in *Who's Who*, she's imitated by millions of youngsters, she's visited by every VIP who goes to Hollywood, her every move is headline news. And there are Shirley Temple dolls and books in every toy store.

She was born in 1928 in Santa Monica, near enough to Hollywood for her movie-minded mother, who began hawking her services before she was barely out of diapers. By the age of four she was appearing in the "Baby Burlesks" shorts made by Educational and getting small parts in movies. When a tot was required to sing at the end of the anti-Depression musical at Fox, *Stand Up and Cheer* (1934), she got the job – and a contract. She was already set for the title role in Paramount's *Little Miss Marker* (1934) and by the time it came out Shirleymania had begun. At the end of the year she was the eighth box-office star – and this year she's numero uno.

For those who can stand her, the current *Heidi* is an excellent movie. Most of her vehicles have been mush, but this tells the old story of the Swiss orphan girl with verve – and with two splendid villainesses in Mary Nash and Mady Christians.

Shirley Temple as Heidi.

BOX OFFICE

UK

1 Lost Horizon

OTHER TOP BOX OFFICE FILMS
Camille
The Great Ziegfeld
Libelled Lady
My Man Godfrey
San Francisco
Shall We Dance
Three Smart Girls
Victoria the Great
Wings of the Morning

BOX OFFICE

US

TOP BOX OFFICE FILMS
Dead End
The Good Earth
Hurricane
The Life of Emile Zola
Lost Horizon
Maytime
Saratoga
Stella Dallas
Wells Fargo
Wee Willie Winkie

Jack Smart and Deanna Durbin in One Hundred Men and a Girl.

THE DELIGHTFUL DEANNA

Deanna Durbin is Hollywood's most talented find in a long while. She acts naturally and directly as a child star closer to a brat; but after disposing those who get in her way she sings like an angel.

She was born in Winnipeg, Canada, in 1921 to British parents and came to Los Angeles when her father was advised by the medics to seek a warmer climate. With her remarkable singing voice it was only a matter of time before a studio scout heard her; and she was signed by M-G-M and became a famous singing on The Eddie Cantor Radio Hour. Universal signed her to star in *Three Smart Girls*, but before it started M-G-M borrowed her back for a short with Judy Garland, *Every Sunday*.

The public is lining up to see her in *One Hundred Men and a Girl*. In this she bulldozes the great conductor Leopold Stokowski into giving work to some out-of-work musicians.

STAR QUOTES

Gary Cooper

"I hate glamorous people. They annoy me."

HIGH SUMMER FOR SCREWBALL COMEDY

Some call it screwball comedy – the stuff that Hollywood is making today. And this season there's been no less than five crackerjacks.

Top of the tree is *The Awful Truth*, directed for Columbia by Leo McCarey, in which Irene Dunne and Cary Grant split up, but continue to meet because he has visiting rights to their dog. The really want each other back, so she pretends to be his vulgar sister, to "warn off" his snobbish prospective in-laws.

Second best is *Stand-In*, a sharp satire on Hollywood directed by Tay Garnett for Walter Wanger and United Artists, with Leslie Howard as an accountant appointed to bail out an ailing studio, and learning the ropes from a snappy stand-in (Joan Blondell) and a cynical, drunken director (Humphrey Bogart).

Next comes *True Confession*, directed by Wesley Ruggles for Paramount. Here Carole Lombard confesses to a murder she didn't commit in order to get a job for her unsuccessful lawyer husband (Fred MacMurray).

Then there's the Technicolored *Nothing Sacred*, made by William A. Wellman for Selznick and UA. It has Lombard again, deliriously funny as a small town girl exploited by the New York press (notably Fredric March and Walter Connolly) because it thinks she has an incurable disease. But she knows she hasn't.

Finally, *Topper*, directed by Norman Z. McLeod for Hal Roach and M-G-M, based on a spicy novel by Thorne Smith. This one is about two playful, facetious ghosts (Cary Grant and Constance Bennett) who haunt a respectable banker (Roland Young). His wife can't see them, and since she's played by Billie Burke she's *very* flustered.

Irene Dunne and Cary Grant in the screwball comedy The Awful Truth.

Five comedies? Maybe that ought to be six. *Stage Door*, directed by Gregory La Cava for RKO, from the play by Edna Ferber and George S. Kaufman has some bitchy dialogue in the theatrical boarding-house that makes it the funniest of the lot. As delivered by Katharine Hepburn, Ginger Rogers, Eve Arden, Lucille Ball and other experts, it's wonderful stuff.

Four westerners are taken to a hidden valley in Lost Horizon.

ADVENTURER AND LOVER

It's been a vintage season for Ronald Colman, Hollywood's favourite Englishman.

The most discussed is Frank Capra's *Lost Horizon*, partly because at $2 million it's by far Columbia's most costly film, and partly because of the concept of Shangri-La, from the novel by James Hilton – a hidden paradise on earth, where pain, illness and tyranny are unknown. Colman is the British diplomat who guides some passengers after an air-crash – which may have been deliberately contrived, as he's been chosen to be the next ruler of Shangri-La.

Colman also stars in another romantic fantasy, *The Prisoner of Zenda* in which, as a Britisher on vacation in Ruritania and a dead ringer for the dissolute king, he's persuaded to take his place during the kingdom's darkest days. John Cromwell directs for Selznick and United Artists, from the novel by Anthony Hope. Raymond Massey and Douglas Fairbanks, Jr are splendid villains, David Niven and C. Aubrey Smith are Colman's comrades-in-arms and Madeleine Carroll and Mary Astor are the lovelies involved. This is proving the more popular of the two films, but both stories have been skilfully translated into movies.

Jon Hall and Dorothy Lamour in The Hurricane.

GONE WITH THE STORM

Sam Goldwyn has a big one out now, *The Hurricane*, directed by John Ford from the novel by Nordhoff and Hall, of *Mutiny on the Bounty* fame. Dorothy Lamour, borrowed from Paramount, dons a sarong for the first time since her debut to play the bride of Jon Hall, both of them natives of the South Seas. He's imprisoned for hitting a white man who mocked his skin, and there's much ado about that and his escape – enough to maintain interest till the tremendous climax, created by James Basevi at a cost of $400,000. A fine cast is at risk when this hurricane strikes, including Raymond Massey as the martinet governor, Mary Astor as his wife, Thomas Mitchell and C. Aubrey Smith.

PUBLIC ENEMIES

"Torn From Today's Headlines" said their trailers, and so they were. The gang wars of the 1920s and early 1930s were so full of intrigue, drama and violence that scriptwriters did not have to invent anything. *The Musketeers of Pig Alley* (1912) has been called the first gangster film, but it is really the story of two lovers caught in the crossfire between cops and robbers. The gangster film as we know it begins with *Underworld* (1927), a tale of some drifters in Chicago written by former journalist Ben Hecht.

There were no follow-ups till 1930 when M-G-M presented *The Big House*, a study of gangsters behind bars. The studio attempted no follow-up because its executives disliked action movies; but that year Warners production chief Darryl F. Zanuck commissioned two movies to depict the sort of events picturegoers were reading about in their papers: *Doorway to Hell* (1930) and *Little Caesar* (1930). The second, loosely based on Al Capone, overshadowed the earlier one and gave Edward G. Robinson the famous last line, "Mother of God, is this the end of little Rico?"

The other great Warners gangster melodrama at this time was *The Public Enemy* (1931), in which young actor James Cagney was promoted to the lead after three days" shooting. The pushy personalities of Robinson and Cagney made them ideal to play gang bosses, but most of the melodramas they made thereafter had only an element of crime in them. For although this was the great age of gangster movies, because they reflected what was happening on the streets, there were only two other full-scale films of that type, Fox's *Quick Millions* (1931) with Spencer Tracy and United Artist's *Scarface* (1932) with Paul Muni.

The government complained to Hollywood, and Robinson and Cagney were shifted to the other side of the law – or, if villainous, in some more petty capacity now that the big-time gangsters were being put away. So we find Robinson, in *Bullets or Ballots* (1936), playing an undercover cop investigating the "numbers" racket. One of those running it is Humphrey Bogart, who had made his first impact as a gangster in *The Petrified Forest* (1936), otherwise a romantic tale. Like his two great contemporaries at Warners, he was so perfectly cast as the ruthless gunman. The last flowering of the gangster film at that studio found him partnered with, or pitted against, Cagney, in *Angels with Dirty Faces* (1938) and *The Roaring Twenties* (1939).

Cagney returned to the studio for one strange and powerful last gasp for the gangster movie, *White Heat* (1949). The last few villains Bogart played were simple psychopaths.

In this period there were two notable films about heists, John Huston's *The Asphalt Jungle* (1950) and Stanley Kubrick's *The Killing* (1956). Both involved assorted underworld toughs but were hardly gangster movies as such. There were many other good films featuring the underbelly of American society, but only Fritz Lang's *The Big Heat* (1953) featured villains engaged in organised crime.

The genre was revived by *Bonnie and Clyde* (1967), based on two young punk killers who robbed banks in the mid-West in the 1930s. It led to a score of imitations – and a revival of the genre with *The Godfather* (1972). The gangster films that followed, including two sequels (1974, 1990) were ever-bloodier and seemingly more realistic, with Brian De Palma's operatic *The Untouchables* (1987), set in Prohibition-era Chicago, capping the lot. But with various Dirty Harrys (with or without badges) cleaning up the streets of modern-day America, the traditional Hollywood gangster movie seemed old hat.

James Cagney as a mother-fixated hoodlum in the powerful White Heat *(1949).*

Bette Davis, Leslie Howard and Humphrey Bogart in The Petrified Forest *(1936).*

Kevin Costner as Elliot Ness in The Untouchables *(1987).*

Faye Dunaway and Warren Beatty in Bonnie and Clyde *(1967).*

Sterling Hayden in John Huston's The Asphalt Jungle *(1950).*

agney and Jean Harlow *in* The Public Enemy *(1931).*

Paul Muni in the title role of Scarface *(1932).*

JANUARY
FEBRUARY

MARCH
APRIL

CLAWS AT THE READY

Many await Louella Parsons' syndicated column in the Hearst newspapers – movie fans, for the latest Hollywood gossip, and movie stars, to see whom she has got it in for this time. She's been a columnist with Hearst since the 1922 weekend house party on his yacht which ended in the mysterious death of director Thomas Ince. She is not known to have been on the yacht, but what happened that weekend has been said by her enemies to have led to her present power. She has always been a great admirer of Marion Davies, whose films Hearst has backed; and since M-G-M refused to give *The Barretts of Wimpole Street* (1934) to Davies she has hardly had a good word to say about Norma Shearer or any other Metro player.

Among Parsons' radio rivals has been Hedda Hopper, who has a habit of correcting Parsons' "factual" information. For a couple of years ex-actress Hopper has been casting around for a newspaper column of her own – and now she's got one, on the *Los Angeles Times*, starting on 14 February. Almost certainly she will soon find herself in other newspapers, since one of those promoting her is Louis B. Mayer, who is hoping to break Louella's power.

BATTLING BETTE

While Bette Davis fought Warners for better roles, the studio's plum female roles went to Kay Francis. But stealthily Davis proved her worth and is now regarded as not only the company's leading female star but also a great actress in her own right. Take a look at *Jezebel* for confirmation of that.

Born in Massachusetts in 1908, Davis acted in stock after leaving dramatic school. She made her film debut for Universal in *Bad Sister* (1931), but the studio dropped her a year later. Warners signed her to star opposite George Arliss in *The Man Who Played God* (1932) and found her a useful contract actress, able to play at will an heiress, a vamp, or an ordinary working girl. Her chance came when she played the vicious waitress in *Of Human Bondage* (1934), after fighting the studio to do it on loan-out. She consolidated her position as the two-timing wife in *Bordertown* and as the alcoholic actress in *Dangerous*, for which she won an Oscar.

In her celebrated battle in the British courts in 1936 for better roles, she lost technically; but she emerged the victor as Warners granted her request. She still wants to play Scarlett O'Hara, but is now on view as another spoilt Southern belle in *Jezebel*. It's her best film to date. Warners borrowed William Wyler to direct, with the result that Davis will now be given the challenging roles she longs to play.

Edward G. Robinson as a beer baron who wants to legitimize his business in A Slight Case of Murder.

A zany family hires a butler who is actually a famous writer posing as a tramp in Merrily We Live.

SCREWBALL STILL TOPS

Try this one for size. A reformed gangster (Edward G. Robinson) wants to impress his neighbours but finds that his new house has five corpses stashed away which have to be disposed of pronto. That's Warners' *A Slight Case of Murder*, from a play by Damon Runyon and Howard Lindsay. It's achingly funny as played by Robinson, the divine Ruth Donnelly as his wife, and Ed Brophy and Allen Jenkins – the sort of cohorts no ex-gangster should have.

If that isn't enough, there's also M-G-M's *Merrily We Live*, which borrows beautifully from *My Man Godfrey* (1936) in having another crazy family "adopt" a bum as a butler. He is played by Brian Aherne and the cast includes such other excellent farceurs as Constance Bennett and Billie Burke.

And Katharine Hepburn, whose comedy expertise in last year's *Stage Door* surprised everyone, is as mad as a hatter in *Bringing Up Baby*. She's an heiress who involves Cary Grant, as a paleontologist, in the pursuit of her pet leopard. Howard Hawks directs for RKO Pictures at a fast and hilarious pace.

THE LUBITSCH TOUCH

There's no mistaking the "Lubitsch touch" – subtle and witty images to make an often saucy point.

Ernst Lubitsch was born in Berlin in 1892, and before he was 20 was playing bit roles with the Max Reinhardt company. Within two years he was directing himself – as a comic actor – in shorts. Progressing to features, he became known abroad with some not too serious films about Madam Dubarry (*Passion*, 1919) and Ann Boleyn (*Deception*, 1920). While Hollywood sought to sign him he lingered in his own country, most notably to make *Die Bergkatze* (1921) in which the "touch" can be seen in its first fine flowering.

Mary Pickford brought him to Hollywood for *Rosita* (1923), a historical film which failed to impress anyone; but he stayed on to make a series of scintillating comedies on marital life. His only serious sound film has been *The Man I Killed* (1932), about war-guilt, which was a gallant failure. But his comedies have continued to delight both audiences and Paramount's accountants. The latest, *Bluebeard's Eighth Wife*, has Gary Cooper pursuing Claudette Colbert over much of the French Riviera - or is it the other way round?

The movie concludes his Paramount contract, and it's said that he will move to any studio which does not require him to mine the same saucy situations.

Ernst Lubitsch (centre) directs David Niven and Claudette Colbert on the set of Bluebeard's Eighth Wife.

DAREDEVILS OF THE AIR

Test Pilot isn't quite up to some other recent M-G-M epics, but it will do to be going on with. Or more so, perhaps, to fans of its three stars – the "King" Clark Gable, Myrna Loy and Spencer Tracy, the last fast becoming the best actor in movies. Gable, at his best, has the title role; Loy is the farmer's daughter whom he woos and marries; and Tracy is his mechanic. Moviegoers can't get enough of these daredevils of the air, and with Victor Fleming at the joystick they know they'll see them at their most adventurous.

LINCOLN GREEN

In a blaze of glorious Technicolor the legendary hero of Olde Englande leaps on the screen in *The Adventures of Robin Hood*. It's a movie for all ages and all seasons. Warners planned it for James Cagney and retailored it for Errol Flynn as he became a big star. But with a budget of $2 million Jack Warner still wanted to fire Flynn for constantly forgetting his lines – and for his over-ardent wooing scenes with Olivia de Havilland, which had to be re-shot. He is merely perfect; but she, as Maid Marion, is a story-book heroine come to life.

Eugene Pallette is Friar Tuck and Alan Hale Little John (as he was to Fairbanks Sr's Robin in 1922). And the film has two outstanding villains, Basil Rathbone as Sir Guy of Gisbourne and Claude Rains as Prince John. The director credit is shared by William Keighley, whose lackadaisical work didn't please the studio, and Michael Curtiz, who replaced him.

STAR QUOTES

Cary Grant

"I don't care how ugly they make me in pictures if they just let me play a part with character and substance."

Clark Gable, Myrna Loy and Spencer Tracy in Test Pilot.

ACADEMY AWARDS

PRESENTED ON 10 MARCH 1938

Best Picture
The Life of Emile Zola

Best Director
Leo McCarey
The Awful Truth

Best Actor
Spencer Tracy
Captains Courageous

Best Actress
Luise Rainer
The Good Earth

Best Sup Actor
Joseph Schildkraut
The Life of Emile Zola

Best Sup Actress
Alice Brady
In Old Chicago

BIRTHS, DEATHS AND MARRIAGES

BIRTHS

Margaret O'Brien
15 Jan, Los Angeles

Oliver Reed
13 Feb, London

Warren Beatty
30 Mar, Richmond, Virginia

Ali McGraw
1 Apr, New York

FRESH FIELDS

Darryl F. Zanuck has astonished the movie world by signing Britain's Gracie Fields to a multi-million-dollar contract – "the highest salary ever paid to a human being" as 20th Century-Fox's publicists are calling it.

In 1936 and 1937 Fields was Britain's No. 1 box-office star among home-grown performers, and she was No. 3 on the lists which included Hollywood names. Parliament has been known to adjourn when she is on the radio.

M-G-M's British head, Sam Eckman, compared her with Will Rogers a while back and found them "two of the greatest comedians of their time, but their humour is strictly national."

In trying to make Fields an international name (only one of her previous films has been shown in the USA), Zanuck has been giving her the glamour treatment in Hollywood. Tinseltown's elite turned out to meet her, but she didn't like the place and asked for her first Fox film to be made in Britain. So her leading men, Brian Donlevy and Victor McLaglen, crossed the pond and the three have just completed *We're Going to Be Rich.*

MAY
JUNE

1938

JULY
AUGUST

SHEARER'S FOR THE CHOP!

Tyrone Power and Norma Shearer in Marie Antoinette.

Now that M-G-M has finally released *Marie Antoinette*, Norma Shearer is back on screens for the first time since *Romeo and Juliet* (1936). She's not the foolish queen of history but a spirited and beautiful woman who just happened to be in the wrong place at the wrong time.

M-G-M had no qualms about duplicating the splendours of 18th-century Versailles: the costumes are probably more sumptuous than those worn at the Bourbon court. And the film gives an eloquent account of the series of events which led to Marie Antoinette ending up on the guillotine.

Britain's Robert Morley plays husband Louis XVI, as a booby, so it's no surprise she takes Tyrone Power as her lover. The fine cast also includes Gladys George and Joseph Schildkraut, while W.S. Van Dyke – "One Shot Woody" – took over direction from Sidney Franklin who was said to be working too slowly. The final cost was $2.8 million, which seems to be recoverable. It's the only film of the year so far to be roadshown – exhibitors are nervous of this "hard-ticket" gimmick after the mixed returns of the past year.

BOX-OFFICE POISON

A bombshell's been thrown into the Hollywood arena since *Time* magazine publicized an article in the little-read *Independent Film Journal*. In May it published the names of some stars it considered "box-office poison" and it's causing furrowed brows because the author is Harry Brandt, a New York exhibitor who is also spokesman for the Independent Theater Owners of America. He writes: "Among those players whose dramatic ability is unquestioned, but whose box-office draw is nil, can be numbered Mae West, Edward Arnold, Greta Garbo, Joan Crawford, Katharine Hepburn and many, many others." Those others include Marlene Dietrich and Fred Astaire.

Katharine Hepburn in Bringing Up Baby.

ALEXANDER'S NO DISASTER

Earlier this year 20th Century-Fox came up with *In Old Chicago* which was their equivalent of M-G-M's *San Francisco* (1936) or Goldwyn's *The Hurricane* (1937). In this case there was a strong story, capped off with a spectacular climax of the Chicago fire. Its stars were the three biggest on the Fox lot, Tyrone Power, Alice Faye and Don Ameche; director was Henry King, who's done some fine work and is particularly admired by Darryl F. Zanuck, who produced.

Now these five talented people have come up with another extravaganza, and it's a good deal more original. The musical *Alexander's Ragtime Band* takes the three stars, as friends and lovers, from honky-tonk days to the present. Their triumphs and troubles are interspersed with no less than 26 songs by Irving Berlin, many of them given the big treatment by Ethel Merman and Faye. The film cost $2 million but, with 192,520 customers in its first week at New York's Roxy, Fox's shareholders will be looking for handsome dividends.

MAGGIE THE ENCHANTRESS

In the old days Margaret Sullavan might have been burnt as a witch – she's more enchanting than 10 other actresses put together.

She was born in 1911 in Virginia and studied acting at university; after some experience in stock she found herself on Broadway in *Dinner at Eight*, in which she was seen by director John M. Stahl. He invited her to make a picture turned down by Irene Dunne and Claudette Colbert, *Only Yesterday* (1933). Universal, which produced, offered a long-time contract.

She married the powerful agent Leland Hayward who got her a new contract with M-G-M, and two new films. *The Shopworn Angel* is a remake of an old Nancy Carroll-Gary Cooper vehicle, with Jimmy Stewart filling Coop's old shoes. He plays an army recruit who falls for a kept woman, never guessing that she's less than 100 percent pure.

Three Comrades is. It's the story of friendship between Robert Taylor, Robert Young and Franchot Tone and the girl they all love, set against the terrible events in Germany from the end of the war to the present, from the novel by Erich Maria Remarque.

GOSSIP COLUMN

- **Humphrey Bogart and Mary Phillips have called it quits. No. 3 wife for grizzled Bogart will be Mayo Methot, featured player on the Warners lot.**

Margaret Sullavan in Three Comrades.

THOSE CRAZY VANDERHOFS

Jean Arthur (centre) is the daughter of an eccentric New York family in You Can't Take It with You.

Hollywood's crazy families have been running amok for a while, but Broadway dramatists George S. Kaufman and Moss Hart reclaimed them for the stage with their 1936 play *You Can't Take It with You*. Though a pretty insubstantial affair, it won a Pulitzer Prize – and that's justified not by the play but by this film version.

In deciding to film it, Frank Capra saw an opportunity for several of his favourite themes. But these seem sententious in the mouth of Lionel Barrymore's Grandpa Vanderhof. And the introduction of new themes (an armaments factory, land developers) merely adds weight to the scenario without improving it. Barrymore aside, the Vanderhofs and their boarders are delightfully played by Jean Arthur, Spring Byington, Ann Miller and others. James Stewart is the daughter's wealthy beau and Edward Arnold his pompous father.

THE HARDY HARDYS

In March last year M-G-M released *A Family Affair*, based on an unsuccessful Broadway play about a Judge Hardy and his family, typical small-town Americans. The film was liked enough for the studio to plan a "B" series about the family. But Lewis Stone replaced Lionel Barrymore as the judge, because Barrymore did not fancy seeing the series stolen from him by Mickey Rooney, as his son Andy.

You're Only Young Once and *Judge Hardy's Children* followed earlier this year. The films are supposed to embody true American values, now that Europe is re-arming and we have to consider what role the country will play. But do people really prefer honour to money, and would trouble-prone Andy fall so quickly back in line?

But the latest, *Love Finds Andy Hardy*, does justify the popularity of the series, if only thanks to the presence of little Judy Garland. Despite her wistful songs of love, Andy prefers Polly – cute newcomer Lana Turner, 16. Judy won't be in the next one, *Out West with the Hardys*. She could be missed.

BIRTHS, DEATHS AND MARRIAGES

BIRTHS

Bill Cosby
12 Jul, Philadelphia

DEATHS

Pearl White
4 Aug, Paris
Liver ailment

Warner Oland
6 Aug, Stockholm
Pneumonia

MARRIAGES

Sylvia Sidney
3 Aug, *to* Luther Adler

CASBAH CHARLES

Charles Boyer in a scene from Algiers.

Impersonators are already imitating the way Charles Boyer says "Come wiz me to the Casbah" in *Algiers*, perhaps because up to now even he's never had such a full-blown romantic role.

Hollywood's favourite foreign lover was born in south-west France in 1899 and trained at the Conservatoire; he was still there when engaged for his first film, *L'homme du large* (1920). His first "American" role was as Jean Harlow's chauffeur-lover in *Red Headed Woman* (1932) and his Hollywood career began two years later with a Fox contract and *Caravan*. His romantic allure was at its most pronounced with Dietrich in *The Garden of Allah* (1936) and Jean Arthur in *History Is Made at Night* (1937). Late last year *Tovarich*, with Claudette Colbert, showed him adept at comedy, and his Napoleon in *Conquest* this year is one of Garbo's few partners of equal stature.

Now, in *Algiers* he's a wanted man, tempted to leave the safety of the Casbah for society beauty Hedy Lamarr. He's a more soulful and appealing figure than Jean Gabin, who played the role in last year's original French version, *Pepe Le Moko*.

SEPTEMBER
OCTOBER

NOVEMBER
DECEMBER

FLYNN BRANCHES OUT

It's been Errol Flynn's year, what with *The Adventures of Robin Hood* and now three more films on release. The handsome star was born in 1909 in Tasmania, the son of a professor. He did a variety of odd-jobs before playing Fletcher Christian in a local semi-documentary, *In the Wake of the Bounty* (1933). Its producer advised him to go into rep in England if he wanted to act. One production transferred to London's West End and he was offered the lead in a "quota quickie", *Murder at Monte Carlo* (1935). Warners produced, and when filming finished transferred him to their Hollywood base – and cast him as a corpse with one flashback scene in the Perry Mason murder mystery *The Case of the Curious Bride*. His wife, French-born Lili Damita who he married in 1935, was then a bigger star and campaigned for him to get the title role in *Captain Blood* when Warners had difficulty in casting it. When the movie opened that Christmas, stardom was assured.

He's no great actor, nor even a versatile one. But he was genial in this summer's comedy, *Four's a Crowd* with Olivia de Havilland, Rosalind Russell and Patric Knowles. In *The Sisters* he's the blithe, uncaring newspaper man who marries and then deserts Bette Davis – the sort of role he can play effortlessly. But he is very fine in the very different *The Dawn Patrol*, as a doomed flyer, courageous but insubordinate.

REFORM SCHOOL

In *The Young in Heart* a family of confidence tricksters (Roland Young, Billie Burke, Janet Gaynor and Douglas Fairbanks, Jr) brings help to an old lady (Minnie Dupree), in the assumption her wealth will be rightfully theirs when she leaves this life. But there are problems when the men have to find work and love enters the picture in the persons of Richard Carlson and Paulette Goddard. Could reform be in the air? This sentimental comedy from David O. Selznick may well be a testament to the producer's quest for perfection. It's a gem of a movie.

BIRTHS, DEATHS AND MARRIAGES

BIRTHS

Stella Stevens
1 Oct, Yazoo City, Massachusetts

Christopher Lloyd
22 Oct, Stamford, Connecticut

Jon Voight
29 Dec, Yonkers, New York

DEATHS

Conway Tearle
1 Oct, Los Angeles
Heart attack

F. E. Spencer
11 Nov, Hollywood
Road accident

Florence Lawrence
27 Dec, Beverly Hills, California
Suicide

MARRIAGES

Ronald Colman
30 Sep, *to* Benita Hume

Ida Lupino
17 Nov, *to* Louis Hayward

A SCARLETT AT LAST!

It's official: the search for Scarlett O'Hara is over. The role has gone to little-known British actress Vivien Leigh, who was a college vamp earlier this year in *A Yank at Oxford*, with Robert Taylor.

When David O. Selznick bought the novel *Gone with the Wind* in 1936, his first choices for Scarlett and Rhett were Tallulah Bankhead and Ronald Colman.

Vivien Leigh in A Yank at Oxford.

He next thought of Gary Cooper, and there was a brief plan to borrow Bette Davis and Errol Flynn from Warners as a package. But the public made it clear that there was only one possible Rhett: Clark Gable. There were several possibilities for Melanie and Ashley, but Olivia de Havilland and Leslie Howard are popular choices.

Although the Selznick publicity machine made much of the search for Scarlett, the task was difficult. At one point the role belonged to Norma Shearer, who asked the readers of *Photoplay*: "Will I be hated by my fans if I put all the shallowness of Scarlett into the role?" Katharine Hepburn wanted the part and hoped to get it via her friendship with George Cukor, who is to direct; but Selznick is reputed to have said that he just couldn't imagine Rhett Butler chasing her for several reels.

In the end the choice narrowed down to Paulette Goddard, Jean Arthur and Joan Bennett – till Leigh flew over from London to visit her friend Laurence Olivier, who's making *Wuthering Heights*. Filming had already begun without a Scarlett, and the cameras were turning on the burning of Atlanta, when Olivier and Leigh visited the set with Myron Selznick, Olivier's agent and David's brother. David took one look at her, had her tested – and . . .

THE BRITISH RIDE HIGH

Two wholly British films have been attracting attention in America. Leslie Howard stars in Bernard Shaw's *Pygmalion*, and the man who charmed him into it is Hungarian-born producer Gabriel Pascal. Both Howard and Anthony Asquith are credited with direction and Eliza, the flower-girl whom professor Howard turns into a lady, is played by Wendy Hiller.

The only talent well-known to Americans in *The Lady Vanishes* is director Alfred Hitchcock, who's crafted another cunning thriller. This time it is set on a train travelling across a Europe threatened by war; the young leads are Michael Redgrave and Margaret Lockwood.

Charles Laughton's British films are also being shown in America, and RKO put some money into *Sixty Glorious Years* after the success last year of *Victoria the Great*. The sequel is virtually a remake, sometimes with different incidents, of the life of the Queen-Empress. Producer-director Herbert Wilcox seems to think that the addition of Technicolor will make nobody notice. He and his star, Anna Neagle, are now under contract to RKO and will soon be filming in Hollywood.

THE DOCTOR'S DILEMMA

Ralph Richardson and Robert Donat in The Citadel.

Earlier this year M-G-M's first British production, *A Yank at Oxford*, got a warm welcome on both sides of the Atlantic – but that's nothing compared with the raves for its second one, *The Citadel*. A.J. Cronin's best-seller has been intelligently compressed; Robert Donat is first-rate as the Welsh miners' doctor who loses his sense of values after rising to be one of Harley Street's top medics. M-G-M sent over director King Vidor, and Rosalind Russell to play Donat's wife; among the locals are Ralph Richardson, Rex Harrison, Emlyn Williams and Felix Aylmer.

BOX OFFICE

UK

1 Snow White and the Seven Dwarfs
2 A Yank at Oxford
3 Captains Courageous

OTHER TOP BOX OFFICE FILMS

Firefly
The Good Earth
Oh, Mr. Porter!
One Hundred Men and A Girl
The Prisoner of Zenda
Sixty Glorious Years
A Star Is Born

BOX OFFICE

US

TOP BOX OFFICE FILMS

The Adventures of Robin Hood
Alexander's Ragtime Band
Boys Town
Goldwyn's Follies
Happy Landing
In Old Chicago
Kentucky
Out West with the Hardys
Test Pilot
You Can't Take It with You

STAR ON SKATES

Sonja Henie is a determined lady. A film star was what she decided to be and a film star is what she is. That's not bad for someone whose acting is best overlooked till she puts on her ice-skates.

She was born in 1913 in Oslo and studied dancing and skating. At the Olympic Games of 1928, 1932 and 1936 she broke records and won gold medals; she also underwent extensive beauty treatment in an attempt to interest Hollywood – which said no to her asking price, $75,000 a film. So she hired an ice-rink in Los Angeles, and when she played to sold-out houses Darryl F. Zanuck signed her. With *One in a Million* (1936) the public endorsed his decision, and when *Thin Ice* (1937) and *Happy Landing* (1938) both proved popular Henie renegotiated her contract. Her business sense is as renowned as her tantrums, but while she keeps pulling in the crowds Zanuck will put up with them.

Spencer Tracy and Mickey Rooney in Boys Town.

BOYS WILL BE BOYS

But they often end up as delinquents. Still, "No boy is bad, if given the chance" says Spencer Tracy in M-G-M's *Boys Town*. He plays real-life Father Flanagan, a Nebraskan priest who founded a home to prevent abandoned children from drifting into crime. Cocky Mickey Rooney is his chief problem, but he too reforms in the end.

Over at Warners the boys, played by the Dead End Kids, are already delinquents – or, as the studio has it, *Angels with Dirty Faces*. This is the old one about boyhood friends who grow up to be different – Pat O'Brien becomes a priest and James Cagney a hoodlum, so hero-worshipped by the boys that O'Brien persuades him to scream with cowardice as he's escorted to the electric chair. Michael Curtiz directs, and it is by far the better of the two films – if only because Ann Sheridan and Humphrey Bogart are also around.

Humphrey Bogart and James Cagney in Angels with Dirty Faces.

JANUARY
FEBRUARY

MARCH
APRIL

CLARK AND CAROLE MARRY

After a long and colourful courtship, Clark Gable and Carole Lombard came under heavy pressure from M-G-M boss Louis B. Mayer to "regularize" their relationship. Gable's divorce from his second wife Ria Langham (from whom he had been separated since 1935) was finally granted at a hearing on 8 March.

On the same day Lombard told columnist Louella Parsons that she and Gable would be married soon. But, in characteristically salty fashion, she was determined that the nuptials would not be turned into a "****ing circus". Publicist Otto Winkler chose the First Methodist-Episcopal Church in Kingman, Arizona (pop. 2,000), 300 miles southeast of Los Angeles. Gable, on a two-day furlough from *Gone with the Wind*, had to hide in the rumble seat of Winkler's blue De Soto coupe when they stopped for gas; Lombard, in pigtails, jeans and no make-up passed for an ordinary traveller.

Carole Lombard.

Laurence Olivier and Merle Oberon in the screen version of Emily Bronte's Wuthering Heights.

WITHERING HEIGHTS!

True to form, Sam Goldwyn led everyone a dance on his latest production, the screen version of Emily Bronte's *Wuthering Heights*.

Not satisfied with the Ben Hecht-Charles MacArthur script, he hired John Huston to make the characters of Cathy and Heathcliff more "likable". He suggested a string of new titles, including *Bring Me the World* and *The Wild Heart*, while stubbornly referring to the original as *Withering Heights*.

Encouraged by director William Wyler, he went off on a wild goose chase for the actor to play Heathcliff, fixing for a while on Robert Newton before choosing Laurence Olivier, who until now has never hit it off in Hollywood. Merle Oberon is Cathy.

Goldwyn ordered the Yorkshire moors to be recreated in California and, at huge expense, 14,000 tumbleweeds were anchored to a 540-acre tract in the Canejo hills and then sprayed with purple sawdust to resemble heather. For more intimate scenes, 1,000 real heather plants were bought from nurseries.

Filming was punctuated by frequent rows between William Wyler and Olivier, who initially refused to modify his theatrical approach for the cameras. Relations between Olivier and Oberon are said to have been equally strained.

The movie came in 13 days over schedule and $100,000 over budget. After a sneak preview Goldwyn added a "happy ending" in which the ghostly figures of Cathy and Heathcliff (actually Olivier and Oberon's doubles) "cloud walk" hand in hand from the moors to heaven. Wyler hated it, and the movie has got off to a slow start.

CUKOR GOES WITH THE WIND

Principal shooting on *Gone with the Wind* began at the end of January, but has quickly run into trouble. George Cukor, a "woman's director", was enchanted with Vivien Leigh. But co-star Clark Gable was less than enchanted with Cukor. On his insistence Cukor has been removed and replaced by Gable's friend Victor Fleming, a more "masculine" director.

GOSSIP COLUMN

■ **Fastidious architect-turned-director Mitchell Leisen was appalled by the behaviour of alcoholic John Barrymore on the set of *Midnight*. "The Great Profile" had no qualms about noisily relieving himself behind the bushes of the picture's terrace set, and insisted on reading his lines from monster idiot boards – a measure that required wholesale rebuilding of the sets.**

ACADEMY AWARDS

PRESENTED ON 3 MARCH 1939

Best Picture
You Can't Take It with You

Best Director
Frank Capra
You Can't Take It with You

Best Actor
Spencer Tracy
Boys Town

Best Actress
Bette Davis
Jezebel

Best Sup Actor
Walter Brennan
Kentucky

Best Sup Actress
Fay Bainter
Jezebel

THOSE NASTY THUGS

"Kill, kill, kill for the love of Kali!" chant the blood-crazed Thugs of India's Northwest Frontier. But it's easier said than done when they find themselves up against Cary Grant, Victor McLaglen and Douglas Fairbanks, Jr in RKO's *Gunga Din*.

Inspired by one of Rudyard Kipling's *Barrack Room Ballads*, it's a spectacular celebration of the heyday of the British Empire.

Director George Stevens handles the stirring action sequences and comic relief with equal flair.

RKO's publicity claims *Gunga Din* is "too big for words". So is the budget – at $1.9 million it's the most expensive movie the studio has made.

STAR QUOTES

Carole Lombard

"Clark's a wonder. I'm really nuts about him. I'm nuts about him. *Not just nuts about his* nuts."

Above: Indians menace the carriage in John Ford's western *Stagecoach*. Inset: John Wayne, Ford's hero.

BLAZING A NEW TRAIL

The fortunes of the "A" western, in the doldrums since the mid-1930s, are given a shot in the arm by John Ford's *Stagecoach*, produced for United Artists by Walter Wanger.

Based on a novel by Ernest Haycox, it stars former "B" movie cowpoke John Wayne as the outlawed Ringo Kid who joins a mixed bunch of passengers for an eventful trip west.

The movie's dramatic exteriors, shot in Utah's Monument Valley, bring a new scenic grandeur to the western, particularly in the highlight as the stagecoach careers across salt flats pursued by Indians. With brilliant stunt work by Yakima Canutt, the chase climaxes with the U.S. Cavalry riding to the rescue, banners flying, bugles and swords outstretched for the charge. (Veteran cowboy star William S. Hart has sourly commented that the Indians would have shot the stagecoach's horses first and ended the chase before it had begun.)

Sharing acting honours with Wayne are Claire Trevor as the whore with the heart of gold; Thomas Mitchell as the whisky-sodden Doc Boone; John Carradine as a sardonic, doomed gambler; and Andy Devine as the fat, cheerfully cowardly stage driver Buck.

FROM "SINGIN' SANDY" TO STAR

Stagecoach is the making of husky John Wayne, 31, a former UCLA gridiron star who broke into the movies when Tom Mix found him a job in Fox's property department.

Iowa-born Wayne made his screen debut in John Ford's *Mother Machree* (1928) but muffed his first big chance for stardom in Raoul Walsh's ambitious western *The Big Trail* (1930). By 1932 he was consigned to the treadmill of Mascot serials and low-budget horse sagas, including a stint as a (dubbed) range warbler "Singin' Sandy" in Monogram's *Riders of Destiny* (1933) and a spell as one of Republic's *Three Mesquiteers* (1937). Now he's hit the jackpot in the role of the Ringo Kid that Gary Cooper turned down.

REWRITING HISTORY

20th Century-Fox has scored two firsts with *Jesse James*, starring Tyrone Power as the legendary outlaw and Henry Fonda as his brother Frank. It's the first film about the James gang to attempt historical authenticity, with location shooting around Pineville, Missouri – the heart of James country – and Jesse's grand-daughter is credited as a consultant. Directed by Henry King, it's also the first western to be filmed in Technicolor.

On location, ace stuntman Cliff Lyons was paid a small fortune to take two horses over a 75ft drop into a lake. This killed both animals and resulted in a court case against the studio by the Missouri Humane Association. But it doesn't seem to have harmed the box-office success of *Jesse James*. The western is back with a vengeance.

BIRTHS, DEATHS AND MARRIAGES

BIRTHS

Samantha Eggar
5 Mar, London

Chuck Norris
10 Mar, Ryan, Oklahoma

Francis Ford Coppola
7 Apr, Detroit, Michigan

Claudia Cardinale
15 Apr, Italy

MARRIAGES

Jennifer Jones
2 Jan, *to* **Robert Walker**

Clark Gable
29 Mar, *to* **Carole Lombard**

Tyrone Power
1 Apr, *to* Annabella

Douglas Fairbanks Jr.
22 Apr, *to* Mary Lee Epling Hartford

PARIS, HOLLYWOOD-STYLE

In Paramount's sophisticated *Midnight* Claudette Colbert is a penniless American gold-digger masquerading as a Hungarian countess. It's a delicate web of deception and marital intrigue set in a fanciful Hollywood version of Paris, expertly directed by Mitchell Leisen.

Don Ameche co-stars as a taxi-driving Hungarian aristocrat; Mary Astor plays a snooty bitch to the manner born; and a quizzical John Barrymore is one of Colbert's partners-in-crime on the marriage merry-go-round.

Colbert, as ever, ensures the camera catches only the famous left profile; Barrymore pretends to be sober, watched over by real-life wife Elaine Barrie, who has a small part in the picture; and Mary Astor, cunningly costumed, pretends she isn't pregnant. It's a sparkling concoction – chic, cynical and bracing as an early-morning glass of champagne.

Don Ameche, Claudette Colbert and John Barrymore in *Midnight*.

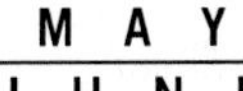

MAY
JUNE

JULY
AUGUST

WE'RE OFF TO SEE THE WIZARD!

Ray Bolger as the Scarecrow tries to save Judy Garland from the apple tree in The Wizard of Oz.

Judy Garland takes a Kansas "twister" to stardom in M-G-M's *The Wizard of Oz*, a $3 million Technicolor fairy tale from the much-loved book by L. Frank Baum. But she wasn't always the first choice.

The studio had bought the rights for $5,000 from Sam Goldwyn, who had been considering *Oz* as a vehicle for Eddie Cantor. Louis B. Mayer first toyed with casting 20th Century-Fox's Shirley Temple as Dorothy, the little girl magically transported from the Middle West to Munchkinland. But there's not a juvenile in Hollywood who can match Garland's appeal and uncanny sense of timing.

Perhaps she's a little old for the part: to play a 10-year-old she had to wear a special corset and yards of tape to flatten her budding bosom. But at barely five feet in her socks, 17-year-old Garland cuts a remarkable figure – an adolescent with an adult's voice playing the part of a child.

She was not the only one to suffer physical discomfort during the filming. M-G-M contract player Buddy Ebsen was the original choice to play the Tin Woodman but was confined to an iron lung after being sprayed with aluminium dust. He was replaced by Jack Haley and his make-up changed.

Joining Haley are the great vaudeville star Bert Lahr as the Cowardly Lion, Ray Bolger as the Scarecrow in search of a brain, Margaret Hamilton as the Wicked Witch of the West, and delightful Billie Burke as the Good Fairy Glinda. And then there are the Munchkins – 350 midgets recruited by the studio, whose bawdy behaviour on and off the set terrorized and charmed the cast and crew.

The rich sepia opening and closing scenes were shot last. Director Victor Fleming had left the picture by then to work on David O. Selznick's *Gone with the Wind*. Some scenes, including Garland's magical singing of "Over the Rainbow", were handled by King Vidor.

"Over the Rainbow" nearly failed to get into the movie: M-G-M's front office thought it made the film too long. Fortunately, producer Mervyn LeRoy, associate producer Arthur Freed and songwriters Harold Arlen and E.Y. "Yip" Harburg persuaded Mayer to keep it. But the studio still isn't sure whether the public will take to the daring extravaganza: there's been heavy pre-release promotion and a record number of 550 prints have been made for nationwide saturation.

ELEMENTARY, MY DEAR WATSON

The greatest detective of them all, Sherlock Holmes, returns to the screen in Fox's lavish *The Hound of the Baskervilles*. Director Sidney Lanfield, more noted for light comedy than period thrillers, has said that "Sherlock Holmes has to be made a more up-to-date character" and that he's tried to "pep up the story".

Holmes buffs were alarmed by Lanfield's threat to "modernize" Arthur Conan Doyle's master sleuth. But the result is a handsome production in which the fog-machine works overtime to disguise the fact that much of the outdoor action takes place on the same master set.

Top-billing goes to Richard Greene as Sir Henry Baskerville, but the picture is dominated by aquiline Basil Rathbone, playing Holmes as if to the manner born. Nigel Bruce is the bluff Dr Watson and Lionel Atwill, bearded and bespectacled, is outstanding.

Holmes fans are delighted that despite the Production Code the great detective still asks Watson to bring him the needle at the successful conclusion of the case.

STAR QUOTES

Hedy Lamarr

"Any girl can look glamorous. All she has to do is stand around and look stupid."

BIRTHS, DEATHS AND MARRIAGES

BIRTHS

James Fox
19 May, London

Terence Stamp
23 Jul, London

Peter Bogdanovich
30 Jul, Kingston, New York

George Hamilton
12 Aug, Memphis, Tennessee

DEATHS

Owen Moore
9 Jun, Beverly Hills, California

MARRIAGES

Barbara Stanwyck
13 May, *to* **Robert Taylor**

Merle Oberon
3 Jun, *to* **Alexander Korda**

Maureen O'Hara
12 Jun, *to* George Brown

Joan Fontaine
Aug, *to* **Brian Aherne**

Cyd Charisse
12 Aug, *to* Nico Charisse

Janet Gaynor
14 Aug, *to* Gilbert Adrian

The Battle of Omdurman as filmed for Zoltan Korda's The Four Feathers.

KORDA'S CONQUESTS

Director Zoltan Korda, younger brother of British film magnate Alexander Korda, has produced an epic picture worthy of Cecil B. DeMille. *The Four Feathers* was two years in the making, was shot on location in the Sudan, and climaxes with a magnificently staged re-enactment of the 1898 Battle of Omdurman with a cast of thousands.

John Clements stars as disgraced army officer Harry Faversham, who as a mark of his cowardice receives the four feathers of the title. He redeems himself, disguised as a native, in Kitchener's reconquest of the Sudan and defeat of the fanatical rebel leader, the Khalifa.

For the climactic battle sequence Korda used 4,000 Arabs and tribesmen. The latter were descendants of the warriors who threw themselves with shields and spears against the British Gatling guns.

NEIGHBOURHOOD FARE

Series movies are one of the bread-and-butter mainstays of the business, providing a steady stream of work for the studios' "B" units and a testing ground for young directors and actors. M-G-M, for example, has been putting a long line of starlets through their paces in its *Andy Hardy* and *Dr. Kildare* series since they began last year. Series also absorb overheads by offering regular work to studios' contract players and enabling expensive standing sets to be re-used.

Handy sources for a series producer are popular fiction (Tarzan, Charlie Chan, Bulldog Drummond, The Saint, The Lone Wolf, Mr. Moto) and comic strips (Blondie, Joe Palooka and, in serial form, Flash Gordon). Some series are spun off from "A" feature hits, notably the Dead End Kids, who first appeared in the 1937 *Dead End*.

Detectives and cowboys (singing and gunslinging) make up the bulk of series heroes. King of the cowboys is prolific William Boyd's Hopalong Cassidy, silver-haired owner of the Bar-20 ranch and star of dozens of brisk hour-long horse operas. Galloping hard behind are the Three Mesquiteers, the Rough Riders, and a posse of sagebrush stars including Charles Starrett, Johnny Mack Brown and Dick Foran.

HELLO AND GOODBYE

"Ageing 60 years over lunch was a bit trying at first, but I finally became used to it." So quips British star Robert Donat of his role in M-G-M's British-shot *Goodbye, Mr. Chips*, in which he ages from 25 to 85.

Adapted from James Hilton's story and directed by Sam Wood, the movie follows the marathon career of a modest public-school pedagogue, Mr. Chipping, at ivy-covered Brookfield College. There's his early days as a teacher in the 1870s; a middle-aged courtship of and marriage to charming Greer Garson; his retirement and return to duty in the First World War; and finally his snowy-haired dotage and death.

It's a great role for handsome, Manchester-born Donat, 34, who's been building quite a reputation in films like *The 39 Steps* (1935), *Knight without Armour* (1937) and *The Citadel* (1938) while steadfastly ignoring the repeated calls of Hollywood. His current contract with M-G-M stipulates he can stay in Britain. Paul Muni – no stranger to layers of make-up himself – has hailed him as "the greatest actor we have today".

Chips is 25-year-old, Irish-born Garson's screen debut. Spotted on the London stage by Louis B. Mayer last year, she had signed with M-G-M but spent several months kicking her heels in Hollywood before returning to England at Sam Wood's insistence to co-star with Donat.

Greer Garson and Robert Donat in Goodbye, Mr. Chips.

NASTY NAZIS

As war clouds gather in Europe, the Hollywood majors are flinching from producing anything with an anti-Nazi message, fearing political and economic reprisals. But there's one exception. Warners hates the Nazis more than it cares for German grosses, not least because the studio's Berlin representative, Joe Kauffman, was beaten up and killed by Nazi thugs. Warners closed their Berlin office.

Apparently backed by J. Edgar Hoover, the studio has come up with the anti-Nazi *Confessions of a Nazi Spy*. Edward G. Robinson stars as real-life agent Leon Turrou who infiltrated a German network in the States.

GOSSIP COLUMN

■ **Edward G. Robinson threw a remarkable sixth birthday party for his son Manny. Manny's mad about jails – he's seen so many on the Warners lot – so dad ordered a child's version of Alcatraz, complete with locks and bars, and sent out invitations on State of California subpoena forms.**

SEPTEMBER
OCTOBER

NOVEMBER
DECEMBER

Left: Hattie McDaniel, as Mammy, and Clark Gable, as Rhett Butler, in Gone with the Wind.

Right: Vivien Leigh plays the heroine Scarlett O'Hara in Gone with the Wind.

DANCING TO SELZNICK'S TUNE

Gone with the Wind is about to take America by storm. Many hands have been involved in the $3.8 million production, including four directors (George Cukor, Sam Wood, William Cameron Menzies and Victor Fleming) and 15 screenwriters (among them F. Scott Fitzgerald and Ben Hecht, who was paid $15,000 for a week's work). But the mighty enterprise has been dominated throughout by producer David O.Selznick, who wrote much of the script himself and even shot some of its scenes.

A final battle was over Clark Gable's concluding line as he takes his leave of Scarlett: "Frankly, my dear, I don't give a damn". Censor Joseph Breen vetoed it but Selznick appealed to Will Hays, head of the Hays Office, who let it through. But Selznick was fined $5,000 for being in technical violation with the word "damn."

Gone with the Wind was premiered on 15 December in Atlanta, Georgia, whose population of 300,000 swelled to 1.5 million as huge crowds lined the streets to see the stars parade in 50 flower-bedecked cars.

Similar scenes were repeated in Manhattan when the movie opened in New York. And on 27 December, in the most spectacular premier ever seen in Hollywood, *Gone with the Wind* finally hit the West Coast. It rings down the curtain on one of the greatest years in the history of Tinseltown – and a decade that's seen silents give way to sound, the ravages of the Depression, and the consolidation of glorious Technicolor.

LEIGH'S LABOURS

From the moment principal shooting began on *Gone with the Wind* in January, Vivien Leigh was under mounting pressure.

Some Southern women threatened to boycott the movie if she didn't measure up to their expectations of how fiery Southern belle Scarlett O'Hara should be portrayed. Initially her relations with Clark Gable were wary, and she had a major row with producer David O. Selznick when, after two weeks of shooting, he fired director George Cukor. But, unknown to Selznick (or to each other), Leigh and Olivia de Havilland (cast as Melanie) continued to take secret night-time coaching from Cukor.

It's all a change of pace for the 26-year-old British actress, who was born in Darjeeling, India. After small roles in English movies in the mid-1930s, she gradually made a name for herself as a stage player in productions like *Richard II, Hamlet, A Midsummer Night's Dream* and the title role in *Serena Blandish*. She's been married since 1931 to Herbert Leigh Holman, by whom she has a daughter and whose middle name she took to replace her own Hartley. But given her friendship with Olivier, divorce seems on the cards.

GARBO LAUGHS!

M-G-M cast around for a film to restore Greta Garbo's fortunes after she was named by U.S. exhibitors in May last year as one of the "box-office poison" stars.

The studio's answer was to switch her into a romantic comedy which guys her own image. In *Ninotchka*, directed by Ernst Lubitsch, she's a humourless Soviet emissary, all hunched shoulders and dowdy clothes, despatched to Paris to obtain currency for the purchase of tractors. In Paris she meets the Grand Duchess Swana (Ina Claire) and her playboy friend Leon (Melvyn Douglas). Under the influence of champagne, glum Garbo is unfrozen by debonair Douglas and – wait for it – laughs. In fact, she's laughed on screen many times before; but this time it's for real. Audiences (and M-G-M's accountants) are doing the same.

The publicity for Ninotchka *centred on the fact that "Garbo laughs!"*

GOSSIP COLUMN

■ **Vivien Leigh's tears and tantrums during the filming of *Gone with the Wind* were not helped by the stream of minor indignities at producer David O. Selznick's hands. Wads of cotton wool were inserted into her corsage to "improve" her bosom. But at least there was one happy moment for the bristly Briton. When Selznick finally gave her permission to meet lover Laurence Olivier in Kansas City, she told him afterwards: "Oh, David, I'm so grateful. Larry met me in the hotel lobby and we went upstairs and we ****ed and ****ed and ****ed the whole weekend."**

CAPRA PREACHES A SERMON

James Stewart and Jean Arthur in Mr. Smith Goes to Washington.

Frank Capra has ruffled a few feathers on Capitol Hill with *Mr. Smith Goes to Washington*, a political parable adapted from *The Man from Montana* by Lewis R. Foster.

James Stewart is Jefferson Smith, a gangling Boy Scout leader and embodiment of shy, soft-spoken provincial virtue, who is cynically installed as a junior senator by a gang of venal politicians who have a crooked land deal going. When their innocent stooge smells the stench of corruption, they attempt to break him. But, with the support of his spunky secretary Jean Arthur, Stewart saves himself, and shames his chief persecutor Claude Rains into a public confession of guilt.

Politicians have protested that Capra's portrait of the Senate as place where "you have to check your ideals outside the door" is not helpful when the rest of the world is looking to the U.S. for a lead over the crisis in Europe.

DOUG DEAD

While the city of Atlanta whips itself up into a frenzy over the premiere of *Gone with the Wind*, mourners are gathering for the funeral of Douglas Fairbanks, Sr.

"Doug", athletic star of the silent screen, died in bed early on the morning of 12 December, aged 55, following a heart attack the day before. His last words were "never felt better." But the star of 1920s swashbucklers and co-founder of United Artists had not been his old self for several years. His marriage to Mary Pickford ended in 1935, but the golden years with "America's sweetheart" haunted him for the rest of his life. A subsequent marriage (his third) was no substitute for the adulation of the 1920s, when his appearance with Pickford would stop the traffic in any city in the world – and brought 300,000 Muscovites out to see them at a time when their films were officially banned in Soviet Russia. The distraction he sought in ferocious physical exercise damaged his circulation, a process hastened by bouts of heavy drinking.

BIRTHS, DEATHS AND MARRIAGES

BIRTHS

Lily Tomlin
1 Sep, Detroit

William Devane
5 Sep, New York

John Cleese
27 Oct, Weston-Super-Mare

Jane Alexander
28 Oct, Boston

Brenda Vaccaro
18 Nov, Brooklyn, New York

Liv Ullmann
16 Dec, Japan

DEATHS

Pauline Frederick
19 Sep, Beverly Hills, California
Asthma

Alice Brady
28 Oct, New York
Cancer

Douglas Fairbanks Sr.
12 Dec, Santa Monica, California
Heart attack

BOX OFFICE

UK

1 The Citadel
2 The Lion Has Wings

OTHER TOP BOX OFFICE FILMS

The Adventures of Robin Hood
Boys Town
The Dawn Patrol
The Four Feathers
Goodbye, Mr. Chips
Gunga Din
The Lady Vanishes
Pygmalion

BOX OFFICE

US

TOP BOX OFFICE FILMS

Babes in Arms
Drums Along the Mohawk
Goodbye, Mr. Chips
The Hunchback of Notre Dame
Jesse James
Mr. Smith Goes to Washington
The Old Maid
The Rains Came
Stagecoach
Three Smart Girls Grow Up

STEWART AND DIETRICH GO WEST

Max Brand's 1930 novel *Destry Rides Again* was originally adapted for the screen by Universal in 1932 as a vehicle for Tom Mix. Now the studio has reworked the story to provide James Stewart and Marlene Dietrich with their first major western roles.

The movie gently mocks the conventions of the western and exploits the stars' contrasting styles. She plays sultry Frenchy, principal attraction at Bottleneck's Last Chance saloon, belting out "See What the Boys in the Back Room Will Have" and scrapping with Una Merkel over Mischa Auer's trousers. He – the son of a famous fighting sheriff – is the unlikeliest of lawmen, preferring anecdotes to gunplay, who's brought in to deal with crooked saloon owner Brian Donlevy. The result has certainly given Dietrich's sagging career a shot in the arm.

ANOTHER NORDIC BEAUTY

The latest in the long line of foreign imports to arrive in Hollywood is 24-year-old Swedish star Ingrid Bergman. She was spotted by David O. Selznick's story buyer Katharine Brown in a Swedish film, *Intermezzo* (1936), in which she was a pianist falling for her child pupil's father, a violin virtuoso. It was her sixth movie.

Ingrid Bergman.

Brown persuaded Selznick to remake it in Hollywood, with Bergman reprising her role, this time opposite Leslie Howard. She arrived in California in the spring, and gave Selznick an option on one further film if her first was a success. Selznick was charmed by the young Stockholmer's healthy, outdoor beauty – a marked contrast to the sophisticated charms of other European stars like Hedy Lamarr. (He even chastised Vivien Leigh for wearing too much lipstick.) And, so that American audiences won't think the movie is an opera, Selznick has added the tag *A Love Story* beneath the title.

JANUARY
FEBRUARY
1940
MARCH
APRIL

HOLLYWOOD HOOPLA

Since the late 1930s it's been fashionable to hold the premieres of major films in locations associated with the theme of the picture. For *Young Tom Edison*, starring Mickey Rooney as the great inventor, M-G-M pulled out all the stops. Rooney and Spencer Tracy, currently filming the sequel, *Edison the Man*, were the guests of Henry Ford in Michigan, where they were photographed intently studying items of "Edisonia" in Greenfield Village. Port Huron, where the movie is to be premiered, threw a civic banquet for Rooney and studio boss Louis B. Mayer. Ford dusted off an old wood-burning locomotive and sent it chugging along the route it took when the youthful Edison peddled candy to the passengers, with Rooney re-enacting the scene. The train pulled in two hours late after a 75-mile run on which it was held up by huge crowds at every whistle stop.

On the day of the premiere Ford, his son Edsel, Mayer and Rooney took an unlikely photo-call riding a bicycle made for four. Rooney was slated to take a bow at each of the three theatres sharing the premiere, but when he arrived at the last one, the Desmond, the crowd was two blocks solid and the pint-sized star was forced to slip in through a side door. Unfortunately the movie also seems to have slipped through a hole in the box-office: it's Rooney's first flop as a star.

"THE PEOPLE THAT LIVE"

Director John Ford and screenwriter Nunnally Johnson have combined to produce a superb adaptation of John Steinbeck's Zola-esque novel *The Grapes of Wrath* for 20th Century-Fox.

At the centre of the film is the Joad family, share-croppers driven from the Oklahoma dustbowl to seek work in California, where they find not the promised land of milk and honey, but the dirt, despair and corruption of the transit camps for migrant labour. As Tom Joad, Henry Fonda gives a superb performance, unshaven and hollow-cheeked and moving with a touchingly angular solemnity.

Also memorable is Jane Darwell as the defiant Ma Joad, symbolically burning her belongings before leaving her lifelong home and proclaiming the indestructibility of "the people that live." It's a powerful document of American social history to set alongside another impressive Steinbeck adaptation, United Artists' *Of Mice and Men*, directed by Lewis Milestone, in which Lon Chaney, Jr is a revelation as the hulking half-witted Lennie, fleeting across an American Gothic landscape with fellow escaped convict Burgess Meredith.

Burgess Meredith and Betty Field in the United Artists adaptation of John Steinbeck's novel Of Mice and Men.

Joan Fontaine and Laurence Olivier in Alfred Hitchcock's Rebecca.

HITCH'S HOLLYWOOD FIRST

Alfred Hitchcock makes his U.S. debut this spring with *Rebecca*, a David O. Selznick production adapted from Daphne du Maurier's Gothic romance. Selznick insisted that the movie should stick closely to the novel, following his experiences on *Gone with the Wind*. After a protracted search for the right actress to play du Maurier's mousy heroine, Hitch chose Joan Fontaine, his own original choice but much against Selznick's wishes. Thus the crafty British director ensured that Fontaine came to the part full of the self-doubt that afflicts her character.

Fontaine co-stars with Laurence Olivier, perfectly cast as her husband, the brooding Max de Winter. He's master of Manderley, the house presided over by Judith Anderson's sinister housekeeper Mrs Danvers and drenched in the poisonous memory of Max's first wife, Rebecca. Outstanding in a strong supporting cast is George Sanders, as the suave Savile Row-suited blackmailer Jack Favell, his insinuating drawl lingering in Manderley's panelled rooms long after he has left them.

BIRTHS, DEATHS AND MARRIAGES

BIRTHS

John Hurt
22 Jan, Shirebrook, Derbyshire

Peter Fonda
23 Feb, New York

Rita Tushingham
14 Mar, Liverpool

James Caan
26 Mar, Bronx, New York

Julie Christie
14 Apr, Assam, India

Al Pacino
25 Apr, New York

MARRIAGES

Celeste Holm
Jan, *to* Francis Davies

William Powell
5 Jan, *to* Diana Lewis

Joan Bennett
12 Jan, *to* **Walter Wanger**

Ronald Reagan
26 Jan, *to* **Jane Wyman**

Lana Turner
13 Feb, *to* **Artie Shaw**

GOSSIP COLUMN

■ Suave William Powell has eloped with young actress Diana Lewis after a 21-day whirlwind romance. It's rumoured that, in the week before, Bill proposed to three different women, and it was the *last* one who said yes.

GONE WITH THE OSCARS

The 1940 Academy Awards ceremony, held on 29 February at the Cocoanut Grove of Hollywood's Ambassador Hotel, was, in the words of Bob Hope, "a benefit night for David Selznick."

Gone with the Wind scooped nine Oscars, including Best Picture, Best Director (Victor Fleming), Best Actress (Vivien Leigh) and Best Supporting Actress (Hattie McDaniel, who played Mammy). McDaniels' award was especially well received, but special permission had to be given for the marvellous black actress to sit at Selznick's table.

At 1.15 a.m. Vivien Leigh stepped up to receive the Oscar which seemed destined to be hers since shooting began on 26 January last year. However, Clark Gable was pipped at the post for Best Actor by Robert Donat, in *Goodbye, Mr. Chips*. Gable is said to be furious, convinced that his strained relations with Selznick cost him the Oscar after the best work of his career.

ACADEMY AWARDS

PRESENTED ON 29 FEBRUARY 1940

Best Picture
Gone with the Wind

Best Director
Victor Fleming
Gone with the Wind

Best Actor
Robert Donat
Goodbye, Mr. Chips

Best Actress
Vivien Leigh
Gone with the Wind

Best Sup Actor
Thomas Mitchell
Stagecoach

Best Sup Actress
Hattie McDaniel
Gone with the Wind

SEX-SWITCH SCREWBALL

Rosalind Russell spars with Cary Grant in His Girl Friday.

Howard Hawks hits the heights of screwball comedy with Columbia's *His Girl Friday*. Set in the wild and woolly world of tabloid journalism, it's brilliantly adapted by Charles Lederer from the stage hit *The Front Page*, first filmed in 1931.

Hawks makes one major change, switching the sex of star reporter Hildy Johnson from male to female – reportedly after a read-through of the play with friends in which his girlfriend took on the role of Hildy to make up the numbers. So Hildy is now stylish sob-sister Rosalind Russell, sparring with her news editor and ex-husband Cary Grant, an inspired manipulator who will stop at nothing to keep her on his paper and sabotage her engagement to stolid insurance man Ralph Bellamy.

This is cold-eyed comedy at its more dazzling, conducted at top speed and supported by a cracking cast of character actors.

BOB AND BING HIT THE ROAD

Paramount has hit the jackpot, teaming Bob Hope and Bing Crosby with Dorothy Lamour in *Road to Singapore*, a property originally slated for George Burns and Fred MacMurray.

It's the flimsiest of plots. Brawling buddies Bing and Bob forswear women and take off for the Far East, where they fetch up on the island of Kaigoon, a small piece of Hollywood Polynesia anchored off the coast of Java.

In no time at all they acquire a new friend and housekeeper, exotic dancer Dorothy Lamour, who has wisely decided to ring down the curtain on her act with Anthony Quinn, whose speciality is flicking cigarettes from her mouth with a bullwhip. Murmurs Bing: "I think he wants her to give up smoking."

This is a movie of the frothiest kind, but audiences response means a sequel is likely.

Bob Hope and Bing Crosby in Road to Singapore.

W.C. Fields and Mae West in My Little Chickadee.

SHOOT-OUT IN GREASEWOOD CITY

In Universal's *My Little Chickadee* comedy heavyweights Mae West and W.C. Fields are teamed as a pair of competing con-artists in a spoof Wild West reminiscent of the studio's *Destry Rides Again*.

Not least of the problems facing the film's director, Keystone Kops veteran Edward F. Cline, was that of marrying the two stars' diametrically opposed styles. Fields has always treated scripts as a barely necessary evil, to be sidestepped with a series of hair-trigger ad-libs. West, whose drawling innuendo has been watered down by the Hays Office in recent years, positions her polished *bon mots* with all the precision of a watchmaker.

Relations between the two stars on set were said to be brittle at best. West's considered comment on the proceedings? "There's no one quite like Bill. And it would be snide of me to add, 'Thank God.' A great performer. My only doubts about him come in bottles."

MAY
JUNE

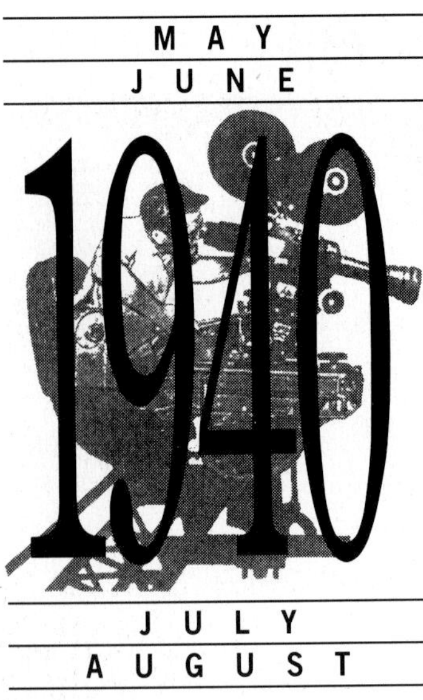

JULY
AUGUST

THE PROFILE SAGS

Few stars have fallen from as great a height as John Barrymore. In 1925 he was at his peak: a triumphant Hamlet on the London stage and, at 43, a romantic screen swashbuckler to rival Fairbanks. Ten years later Barrymore was in the grip of alcoholism, the celebrated matinee idol looks which earned him the nickname "The Great Profile" growing blurred almost beyond recognition.

By the end of the 1930s he was relegated to supporting roles and leads in "B" movies. He survived by parodying his own image as a drunken lecher. With his fourth wife Elaine Barrie he toured America in a grisly play, *My Dear Children*, and audiences flocked to see the star fluff his lines and fall over the furniture.

Now 20th Century-Fox has turned this into a picture whose very title, *The Great Profile*, mocks Barrymore's decline. But Barrymore seems to revel in the joke of playing a has-been old Shakespearian ham.

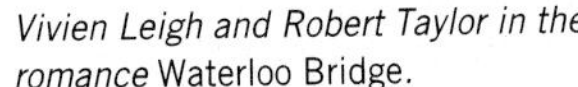
Vivien Leigh and Robert Taylor in the romance Waterloo Bridge.

DOOMED ROMANCE

With husband-to-be Laurence Olivier busy in Hollywood, Vivien Leigh remained in Tinseltown, co-starring with Robert Taylor in M-G-M's *Waterloo Bridge*. Now out, it's her first picture since *Gone with the Wind* (1939). The last time the pair worked together – in England on *A Yank at Oxford* (1938) – Leigh was well down the cast-list; now she gets top billing over Taylor.

Based on Robert E. Sherwood's glum tale of a Canadian soldier who falls in love with a prostitute in London in the First World War, *Waterloo Bridge* has been filmed before, in 1931 with Mae Clarke.

This time around M-G-M has applied a lick of gloss to the story, casting Taylor as an aristocratic British officer and Leigh as the ballet dancer who loves him and is then convinced she's lost him, killed in France.

BIRTHS, DEATHS AND MARRIAGES

BIRTHS

Michael Sarrazin
22 May, Quebec

Jill St. John
19 Aug, Los Angeles

DEATHS

Ben Turpin
1 Jul, Santa Monica, California
Heart disease

MARRIAGES

Buster Keaton
May, *to* Eleanor Norris

Loretta Young
31 Jul, *to* Thomas Lewis

Laurence Olivier
31 Aug, *to* **Vivien Leigh**

STAR QUOTES

Joan Crawford

"Sex is part of what keeps me young."

GOSSIP COLUMN

■ **Celebrated Viennese skin specialist Dr Laszlo has revealed one of Greta Garbo's beauty secrets. He taught her how to mix a raw egg with either hamburger or milk and apply it to her face. The doc swears the treatment gives Greta's skin that special glow.**

TECHNICOLOR RULES

Colour is slowly but surely taking hold of Hollywood. The three-strip system is dominated by Technicolor, used by most of the major studios and displayed in movies like M-G-M's *Gone with the Wind* and *The Wizard of Oz* last year.

Two-strip systems – Cinecolor, Magnacolor, Trucolor – are also in widespread use, although their quality is not so warm and they are largely confined to "B"pictures and subjects like westerns. But only some 18 pictures are planned to be made in Technicolor this year – not exactly galloping progress since the 1935 release of *Becky Sharp*, the first feature made in the perfected three-strip system. But all that could change if Eastman Kodak finally succeeds in developing a system which combines all three colours on one strip of film. Insiders say we can expect a major announcement as soon as next year.

SHORT BUT SWEET

20th Century-Fox is set to end its highly profitable association with Shirley Temple, for five years the studio's box-office mainstay.

All child stars have to grow up and Shirley is now 11 (the studio claims she is 10). This is positively geriatric by the ruthless standards of the business. Her salary of $300,000 a film is no longer matched by her waning box-office appeal, and relations between the studio and her formidable mother Gertrude have reached breaking-point.

However, on the credit side there is the $20 million which Shirley has earned for the studio and the $3 million she has pocketed herself (not counting the trust fund the studio set up for her). Only Mary Pickford, in a considerably longer career, has outgrossed the talented tot from Santa Monica.

LIZARDS AND LOINCLOTHS

A row has brewed up over Hal Roach's *One Million B.C.*, an everyday story of prehistoric folk, with pretty Carole Landis and muscular Victor Mature as star-crossed lovers when dinosaurs ruled the Earth.

The movie's most spectacular special effects – live lizards standing in for dinosaurs and back-projected behind the scantily-clad stars – have incurred the wrath of none less than the American Society for the Prevention of Cruelty to Animals.

Keystone Kops veteran Roach was inspired to make the film by D.W. Griffith's silent one-reeler *Man's Genesis* (1912). He hired Griffith, now 64, disillusioned and unemployed, as a consultant on the movie. Word has it that the veteran director may even have directed some sequences himself.

Victor Mature and Carol Landis battle a "prehistoric" creature in One Million B.C.

Jackie Cooper and Henry Fonda in The Return of Frank James.

Preston Sturges (right) on the set of The Great McGinty *with Brian Donlevy.*

BADMAN'S TERRITORY

Heavyweight German director Fritz Lang makes his western (and colour) debut with 20th Century-Fox's *The Return of Frank James*, the sequel to the studio's immensely successful *Jesse James* (1939).

This time Henry Fonda takes centre stage, repeating his portrayal of Frank James, now hell-bent on avenging the death of his brother. Lang has an intellectual turn of mind to match his monocle, and claims the western "is not only the history of this country, it's what the saga of the Nibelungen is for Europeans".

So it's not surprising that he emphasizes the mythical elements of Frank James' life rather than the historical facts. This is the opposite of the approach by Henry King in *Jesse James*, when a great fuss was made over the movie's factual authenticity.

Also making her debut, as a young reporter, is lynx-eyed Gene Tierney, 20, daughter of a New York socialite family who flirted with Universal, Warners and Columbia before taking up a long-term offer from Fox.

SCRIPT FOR SALE

Freewheeling screenwriter Preston Sturges, 41, one of the most urbane practitioners of his craft in Hollywood, offered Paramount one of his screenplays for $10 if he could direct it himself. Since the Chicago playwright moved to Hollywood in 1930 he has penned a succession of frothy comedies and dramas.

Provisionally titled *The Vagrant*, it told the story of a bum who is manipulated into a state governorship by a crooked political machine.

The studio grudgingly agreed, offering a modest budget of $325,000 and a second-rank star, Brian Donlevy, whose stolid approach to acting amused sophisticated Sturges. Donlevy starts his working day by inserting his false teeth, then squeezing into a girdle, climbing into platform shoes and a jacket with padded shoulders and finally donning a toupee.

But he's perfect as the amiable rough diamond at the centre of Sturges' first directorial outing. It's called *The Great McGinty*, and it's out on screens now.

BREAKING THE SOUND BARRIER

It was Walt Disney's career plans for his biggest star, Mickey Mouse, that led him to the innovative feature-length cartoon *Fantasia*. In 1938 Disney decided to star Mickey in a cartoon version of the old fairy tale *The Sorcerer's Apprentice*, around which French composer Paul Dukas had composed a concert piece. Mickey was to be the hapless apprentice whose misuse of his master's powers creates havoc.

Planned as a two-reeler, the project changed radically after Disney had a chance meeting with Leopold Stokowski, celebrated conductor of the Philadelphia Symphony. When Disney told him of his plans, Stokowski volunteered to conduct the Dukas score.

Like Topsy, the project grew and grew. Stokowski suggested other works which could be suitable and *The Sorcerer's Apprentice* became just one segment in an ambitious project to visualize classics like Stravinsky's *The Rite of Spring* and Beethoven's *Pastoral Symphony*.

Disney encouraged his sound department to develop a system to give the soundtrack concert-hall quality. The result is Fantasound, which records music with a number of microphones and reproduces it on an equal number of loudspeakers to create a stereophonic effect. The music bill alone for *Fantasia* was over $400,000 and the total tab was almost $2.3 million. At New York's Broadway Theater, where the picture is showing with an interval, engineers spent six weeks installing the special RCA sound equipment.

FOX'S BRAZILIAN BOMBSHELL

With much of the European market cut off by the war, the Hollywood majors have decided to woo Latin American audiences with a celluloid avalanche of escapist fare set "south of the border".

Nominal stars of 20th Century-Fox's Technicolored musical-cum-travelogue *Down Argentine Way* are Don Ameche and Betty Grable, who stepped in after Alice Faye had appendicitis. But upstaging everyone is flamboyant Carmen Miranda, 26, the Portuguese-born Brazilian chanteuse who's been wowing New York audiences at the Waldorf-Astoria. Her scenes were shot in New York between shows.

Eyes popping over a mile-wide grin, she sashays through "South American Way" on three-inch platform heels and with several pounds of fruit on her head. No wonder that, as soon as studio heads saw the rushes, they signed the "Brazilian Bombshell" to a long-term contract.

MADE (MOSTLY) IN ENGLAND

In 1937, while Walt Disney was working on his first feature-length cartoon, *Snow White and the Seven Dwarfs*, colourful British-based Hungarian film magnate Alexander Korda announced: "I will do with living players what Disney has done with drawings."

The result is *The Thief of Bagdad*, a freewheeling remake of the 1924 Douglas Fairbanks silent classic. It's Korda's attempt to challenge Hollywood from his Denham studios, near London.

Enchanting young Indian star Sabu is the thief of the title, battling the memorably evil Conrad Veidt, who's scheming to usurp the kingdom of desert prince John Justin. From the opening moment when a massive galley, with crimson sails and a huge glaring eye on its prow, carves its way majestically through blue-green seas, *The Thief of Bagdad* is a treat for the ear and the eye.

It's the first time special effects have been tried on a major scale in Technicolor. Rex Ingram is a playfully malevolent genie the size of an office block; an eight-armed robot assassin slices up doddering sultan Miles Malleson; and there are mechanical toys, giant spiders, flying horses and, of course, a flying carpet.

Several directors have been involved, but the dominant mood is set by Britain's Michael Powell. German director Ludwig Berger began the movie and it was finished in Hollywood by Tim Whelan when Korda shifted production across the Atlantic at the approach of war in Europe.

BOX OFFICE

UK

1 Rebecca
2 Foreign Correspondent
3 Ninotchka

OTHER TOP BOX OFFICE FILMS

Babes in Arms
Convoy
Contraband
Let George Do It!
Pinnochio
Waterloo Bridge
The Women

BOX OFFICE

US

TOP BOX OFFICE FILMS

Arizona
The Fighting 69th
Kitty Foyle
Northwest Mounted Police
North West Passage
Rebecca
The Road to Singapore
Santa Fe Trail
Strange Cargo
Strike Up the Band

Sabu, as the boy theif who helps a deposed king thwart an evil usurper, is in danger in The Theif of Bagdad.

MIX'S LAST ROUND-UP

On 12 October the silent screen's most colourful cowboy star, Tom Mix, bit the dust when his custom-built roadster overturned on a desert road 18 miles south of Florence, Arizona, killing him instantly. He was 69.

Rumours have been circulating recently that Mix was planning a Hollywood comeback. At the height of his popularity in 1925 he was earning $20,000 a week, and his total showbiz earnings are said to have been at least $4 million. A huge neon sign winking his famous initials guided visitors to the mile-long drive to his palatial home. But the coming of sound killed his movie career and he signed off with a rock-bottom Mascot serial *The Miracle Rider* (1935).

Mix made some 400 movies in a career stretching over 24 years, and even wrote for the showbiz paper *Variety* as a roving correspondent. Before entering films he'd worked as a Texas Ranger and soldier of fortune. Recently he had had his own touring Wild West show.

Gary Cooper and Doris Davenport in The Westerner.

CHAPLIN BLASTS FASCISM

Prompted by Alexander Korda's observation on the physical similarity between Charlie Chaplin's Tramp and Adolf Hitler, Chaplin has produced his first all-talking picture, *The Great Dictator*. It's a powerful broadside against Europe's fascists and all their works, and is already proving a hit with moviegoers and critics.

Back on screens for the first time since *Modern Times* (1936), Chaplin is both Adenoid Hynkel, the ranting, vainglorious dictator of Tomania, and his double, a downtrodden Jewish barber. Inevitably, their identities become confused and it is the barber rather than Hynkel who delivers the film's long concluding speech to the world, pleading for an end to tyranny.

Much of Chaplin's anti-Nazi message is muffled by the movie's sentimentality and the music-hall clowning of the supporting players, notably Jack Oakie as the Mussolini-like Benzino Napaloni, dictator of Bacteria. The most striking sequences are those of inspired pantomime: a scene in the Jewish barber's shop in which Chaplin shaves a customer to the strains of Brahms; and a sinister little ballet in which the capering Hynkel toys with a balloon globe of the world, an image both delicate and macabre.

Charles Chaplin in his satire on Hitler The Great Dictator.

WEST OF THE PECOS

William Wyler began directing in the late 1920s with a string of action-packed, two-reel horse operas. But since then he's become better known for dramas like *Dodsworth* (1936), with Walter Huston, *Jezebel* (1938), and last year's *Wuthering Heights*. Now he's back in the great outdoors with *The Westerner*, a lushly photographed story of conflict between cattlemen and farmers.

Gary Cooper is the drifter who falls into the hands of Walter Brennan's self-appointed, despotic Judge Roy Bean. He's based on the real life justice of the peace who exercised his own bizarre form of law and order "west of the Pecos".

Luckily for Cooper, Bean has a weakness for legendary actress Lillie Langtry (Lilian Bond), and Cooper bargains for his life by pretending to be the owner of a lock of Lillie's hair. Bean's fetish establishes an alliance between the two but also proves his own undoing.

Producer Sam Goldwyn poured some extra dollars into this one to give it a better look than most outdoor epics. And his campaign with distributor United Artists to nab newspaper space around the country looks like paying off. The word is that Brennan could be in the awards line-up next year.

BIRTHS, DEATHS AND MARRIAGES

BIRTHS

Pauline Collins
3 Sep, Devon

Raquel Welch
5 Sep, Chicago

Brian De Palma
11 Sep, Newark, New Jersey

David Carradine
8 Oct, Hollywood

Elke Sommer
5 Nov, Germany

Sam Waterston
15 Nov, Cambridge, Massachusetts

Richard Pryor
1 Dec, Illinois

DEATHS

Marguerite Clark
25 Sep, New York
Cerebral hemorrhage

Tom Mix
12 Oct, Arizona
Road accident

MARRIAGES

David Niven
21 Sep, *to* Primula Rollo

Veronica Lake
Nov, *to* John Detlie

Lucille Ball
11 Nov, *to* Desi Arnaz

Bette Davis
31 Dec, *to* Arthur Farnsworth

STAR QUOTES

Judy Garland

"Busby Berkeley made me feel as if he had a big black bullwhip and he was lashing me with it."

Bette & Co.

The early 1940s were the heyday of "women's pictures", lavish productions built around one of the big female stars – notably Bette Davis, Joan Crawford, Barbara Stanwyck, Greer Garson, Ann Sheridan, Gene Tierney, Ida Lupino – and aimed at the massive audience of women separated from their husbands by the war.

Saddled with plots of the purest melodrama, and frequently set against backgrounds of impossible wealth and elegance, "women's pictures" were the quintessence of escapism and wish-fulfilment whose audiences could identify with a scarred Joan Crawford suffering mightily in *A Woman's Face* (1941); Greer Garson "doing her bit" in *Mrs Miniver* (1942), in a Beverly Hills version of the English Home Counties; and Bette Davis, transformed from dowdy spinster by Paul Henreid in *Now, Voyager* (1942).

In the 1930s the fashioning of a full-scale drama around a leading lady had largely been restricted to M-G-M's careful packaging of Greta Garbo. Later in the decade Davis and Crawford began to receive similar treatment, and it was the success of Davis' Oscar-winning performance in *Jezebel* (1938) which convinced the studios of the rich potential of similar vehicles.

Davis opened the decade, quite literally, with a bang, emptying her revolver into her hapless lover at the beginning of *The Letter* (1940); returned to steamy goings-on in Southern mansions as the ferocious Regina Giddens – passionate, thwarted and tyrannical – in *The Little Foxes* (1941); and sailed imperiously through the grand soap of *Mr Skeffington* (1944), discovering the meaning of marriage after she has lost her looks and he has lost his sight.

While Davis paraded her credentials as an actress, Joan Crawford played the part of movie star right down to her lacquered fingernails. The very words might have been invented for her as she progressed from 1920s Jazz Baby to the Shopgirl's Dream of the Depression Years to the Bitch Goddess of the 1940s.

Unlike Stanwyck, the light touch was foreign to her. She was at her best in trash, soaking up the cliches like blotting paper. Crawford's inspired humourlessness immunized her against absurdities of dialogue which verged on the surreal. In *A Woman's Face* (1941) we find her at the piano, closely observed by her evil Svengali, Conrad Veidt. He asks, "Do you like music? Symphonies, concertos?" Joan is equal to the challenge, replying, "Some symphonies, most concertos."

In 1943 Crawford left M-G-M for Warners and came back with a bang in *Mildred Pierce* (1945). In *Humoresque* (1946) she bears down on working-class violin virtuoso John Garfield, barking, "Bad manners, Mr Boray, the infallible sign of talent." In *Possessed* (1947) she succumbs to schizophrenia. In *Flamingo Road* (1949) she strides through Joan Crawford Plot No.1: determined girl from the wrong side of the tracks claws her way to the top and sacrifices love and happiness to stay there. By the end of the decade the appeal of these pulsating soap operas was on the wane, undermined by postwar affluence and the popularity of neo-realist crime films.

By now, Greer Garson's career at M-G-M had all but petered out. Ida Lupino had left Warners, as had Davis, who had bowed out with a clinker, *Beyond The Forest* (1949). A year later she was to confound the cynics who had written her off with a performance of pop-eyed opulence in *All About Eve* (1950). Ever the consummate professionals, Stanwyck and Crawford soldiered on into wintry middle age, now hunted by increasingly younger leading men, magnificent relics of a studio system on the brink of collapse.

Greer Garson, Teresa Wright, Walter Pidgeon and Richard Ney inspect their bomb-damaged home in Mrs Miniver.

Joan Crawford in Possessed *(1947), with Van Heflin in the background.*

Bette Davis, Anne Baxter and George Sanders in All About Eve *(1950).*

Now, Voyager *(1942) with Bette Davis and Paul Henreid.*

Bette Davis in the Somerset Maugham drama The Letter *(1940).*

Melvyn Douglas studies Joan Crawford in A Woman's Face *(1941).*

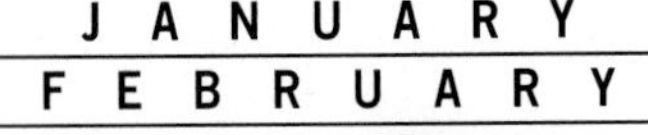

JANUARY
FEBRUARY

MARCH
APRIL

THE HEARST IS YET TO COME

Like a large stone lobbed into placid waters, *Citizen Kane* is stirring ripples far and wide. Tyro director Orson Welles arrived in Hollywood back in 1939, trailing clouds of glory from his triumphs on stage and radio. Amid much ballyhoo the 25-year-old boy wonder was signed by RKO, which gave him virtually complete artistic freedom and $100,000 for one film a year, the budget of which was not to exceed $500,000.

After a couple of false starts, Welles decided to play the lead in an original story suggested by screenwriter Herman J. Mankiewicz. It's a thinly disguised portrait of the life of newspaper baron William Randolph Hearst. Despite the risks, RKO president George J. Schaefer backed Welles, who assembled a cast drawn largely from his own Mercury Theater.

Hearst's gossip columnist Louella Parsons saw a pre-release print and told her boss the movie was nothing more than an unflattering version of his liaison with Marion Davis. Hearst newspapers have refused to carry advertising for RKO, which is teetering on the edge of bankruptcy, and many circuits have refused to book the film. It will finally be released in May, and public response could be lukewarm. But many citics have filed rave reviews, placing Welles in the vanguard of a new group of writer-directors emerging in Hollywood, including Preston Sturges, John Huston and Billy Wilder.

Director and star Orson Welles, with co-star Joseph Cotton, as Hearst-like newspaper tycoon Citizen Kane.

HAYWORTH HITS PAYDIRT

Cast in the title role of Warners' *The Strawberry Blonde*, Rita Hayworth has scored a big hit as the glamorous gold-digger playing fast and loose with infatuated dentist James Cagney in *One Sunday Afternoon*.

Hayworth, on loan from Columbia, was a last-minute replacement for Warners' "Oomph Girl" Ann Sheridan. Born in New York in 1918, the daughter of a Latin American dancer, Hayworth took the traditional studio route to stardom, working her way through a long string of "B" – movies, then strong support parts in *Only Angels Have Wings* (1939) and *Susan and God* (1940) to leads opposite Brian Aherne in *The Lady in Question* and Douglas Fairbanks, Jr in *Angels over Broadway* (both 1940).

Now she's on her way. Warners held on to her to add spice to *Affectionately Yours*, a comedy with Merle Oberon and Dennis Morgan. That one will be in the neighbourhood theatres this summer.

Bud Abbott and Lou Costello, a very popular comedy pairing, clown in an army kitchen in Buck Privates.

BIG BUCKS FOR BUCK PRIVATES

Following their successful debut in *One Night in the Tropics* last year, cross-talk comedy duo Bud Abbott and Lou Costello have been given star billing in Universal's *Buck Privates*, a $90,000 programmer which has yielded a $10 million dividend. Weasel-faced Bud and chubby Lou are in third place in the U.S. popularity ratings, after Mickey Rooney and Clark Gable.

The duo are street-corner necktie salesmen who take cover from the cops in a movie theatre only to find – too late – that it's now an army induction centre. Enlistment and much madcap nonsense follow in this fast-paced comedy capably hustled along by director Arthur Lubin.

Nat Pendleton plays the grizzled sergeant driven to distraction by unsoldierly Lou's original approach to rifle drill. The inevitable love interest is provided by recruits Lee Bowman and Alan Curtis tangling over the favours of sparky Jane Frazee, one of the queens of the "B" musical.

CHURCHILL'S FAVOURITE FILM

The easiest way that Hollywood can tackle the war in Europe without offending the strong element of isolationist opinion in the United States is to make films about the British, for whom sympathy is running high.

United Artist's *That Hamilton Woman!* (in the UK as *Lady Hamilton*), produced and directed in Hollywood by Alexander Korda, stars glamorous husband-and-wife team Laurence Olivier and Vivien Leigh, who finally tied the knot last year. He's Admiral Lord Nelson and she's his mistress, flamboyant Lady Hamilton. Their romance, set against the background of the Napoleonic Wars, is cut short by Nelson's death at the Battle of Trafalgar in 1805, in which the French and Spanish fleets were decisively defeated. The movie draws a clear parallel between Britain's triumph over Napoleon and its current struggle against a new European dictator.

One of the film's biggest fans is British Prime Minister Winston Churchill. He took time off from conducting the war to bombard Korda with helpful messages. And he's since gone on record that it's his favourite film.

Gangster Humphrey Bogart with his moll Ida Lupino in *High Sierra.*

BREAKTHROUGH FOR BOGART

Edward G. Robinson, George Raft and Paul Muni all turned down the role of Roy "Mad Dog" Earle (a member of the Dillinger gang) in Warner's *High Sierra.* The beneficiary was Humphrey Bogart, who establishes himself as a front-rank star as an aging hoodlum on the run in the Sierra Madre mountains and wearily resigned to his fate. Raoul Walsh directs.

Ida Lupino gets top billing as the mobster's moll, but it's Bogart who's stealing the notices. Torn between loyalty to his old boss – who engineers his escape from prison for one last job - and the desire to start afresh with a young crippled woman (Joan Leslie) for whom he has fallen, Bogart's "Mad Dog" Earle is neither hero nor villain but a doomed man condemned to die by the weight of his past.

A taut script by John Huston and W.R. Burnett (who wrote *Little Caesar*), plus strong support from Arthur Kennedy, Henry Hull and Cornel Wilde, make this one of the most powerful dramas of the year.

BATTLE DAMAGE

While the war rages in Europe, it's having a serious effect on Hollywood's overseas revenues.

In Belgium and Holland about 1,400 theatres closed following Hitler's victory – which means millions of dollars lost in revenue. When this is added to the losses already sustained from the closed markets in Poland, Norway, Denmark, Italy, Spain and the Balkans, the gloomy conclusion is that Hollywood will lose about a quarter of its annual revenue.

GOSSIP COLUMN

■ **Sparky Carole Lombard, starring in Alfred Hitchcock's comedy *Mr. and Mrs. Smith*, is the queen of Hollywood pranksters. Not long ago Hitch made the infamous remark that "all actors are cattle." So when the portly director turned up on the set for the first day of filming, he found three cows in a corral, each tagged with the name of a star.**

BIRTHS, DEATHS AND MARRIAGES

BIRTHS

Susannah York
9 Jan, London

Faye Dunaway
14 Jan, Bascom, Florida

David Puttnam
25 Feb, London

Bernardo Bertolucci
16 Mar, Parma, Italy

Ryan O'Neal
20 Apr, Los Angeles

Ann-Margret
28 Apr, Valsjobyn, Sweden

MARRIAGES

Glenda Farrell
19 Jan, *to* Henry Ross

James Mason
Feb, *to* Pamela Ostrer

Constance Bennett
Apr, *to* **Gilbert Roland**

ACADEMY AWARDS

PRESENTED ON 21 FEBRUARY 1941

Best Picture
Rebecca

Best Director
John Ford
The Grapes of Wrath

Best Actor
James Stewart
The Philadelphia Story

Best Actress
Ginger Rogers
Kitty Foyle

Best Sup Actor
Walter Brennan
The Westerner

Best Sup Actress
Jane Darwell
The Grapes of Wrath

Below: Henry Fonda and Barbara Stanwyck in The Lady Eve.

STANWYCK THE MAGNIFICENT

Having found his feet in last year's *The Great McGinty* and *Christmas in July*, writer-director Preston Sturges delivers an immaculate comedy of manners with Barbara Stanwyck and Henry Fonda.

Stanwyck is *The Lady Eve* – ruthless cardsharp Jean Harrington who preys on the smart set with her father "Handsome Harry" Harrington (Charles Coburn). The Adam in her sights is Fonda's sappy amateur naturalist and brewery heir Charlie Pike ("Pike's Pale, the Ale that Won for Yale").

Stanwyck is superb as con-woman Jean, sophisticated, hard as diamonds and quite capable of posing convincingly as a titled Englishwoman when the need arises. Sturges makes every shot count, filling the background with a host of memorable character players, among whom is pop-eyed Eric Blore. He's outstanding as a fellow-fraudster posing as "Sir Alfred McGlennon Keith", salivating at the rich pickings to be had on the Connecticut bridge belt – "simply oozing with millionaires." *The Lady Eve* simply oozes with class.

MAY
JUNE

JULY
AUGUST

MR NATURAL

On set he seems all fingers and thumbs and awkward silences; but on the screen he's Mr. Natural. Gary Cooper is top of the Hollywood tree.

Born of British parents in Montana in 1901, he was educated in Britain. On his return to Montana he studied agriculture and worked as a ranch hand before moving to Los Angeles, where he put his equestrian skills to good use as an extra in dozens of westerns. Paramount steadily built him up into one of their biggest stars: three years after working as an extra in a Florence Vidor vehicle, *The Enchanted Hill* (1925), he was her co-star in *Doomsday* (1928).

His first all-talking picture was *The Virginian* (1929), back in the saddle in the title role. But he exchanged buckskins for lounge suits opposite Carole Lombard in *I Take This Woman* (1931).

By the mid-1930s he was one of Hollywood's top earners. Simultaneously he struck a rich vein which began with the imperial fairy tale *The Lives of a Bengal Lancer* (1935). Frank Capra's *Mr. Deeds Goes to Town* (1936) confirmed his position as major star, an American Everyman and the personification of shy simplicity and honour. A string of hits followed, including *The Plainsman* (1937), *Beau Geste* (1939), *The Westerner* (1940), tangling once again with Walter Brennan, and this year's *Meet John Doe*, playing another one of Capra's political innocents. He'll next be seen in *Ball of Fire* a comedy version of *Snow White*, with Barbara Stanwyck.

GOSSIP COLUMN

■ **Labour troubles are continuing to disrupt film production in Hollywood. There has been so much violence on the picket lines that the new President of the Screen Actors Guild, Ronald Reagan, has taken to wearing a .32 Smith & Wesson in a shoulder holster.**

YORK ON SCREEN

For years Hollywood has wanted to film the story of *Sergeant York*, about the pacifist farm boy from Tennessee who became the most decorated American soldier of the First World War. In the Argonne in October 1918 he single-handedly killed 25 and captured 132 of the enemy.

York's stubborn resistance was finally broken down by producer Jesse L. Lasky, who agreed to the soldier supervising every stage of the picture. York also wanted Gary Cooper in the title role.

Cooper was loaned to Warners by M-G-M boss Sam Goldwyn in exchange for Bette Davis. The screenplay, written by Abem Finkel, Howard Chandler, Howard Koch and John Huston, is fairly faithful to the facts and provides plenty of patriotic uplift at a time when many Americans are still divided over entering the war. Direction, in the capable hands of Howard Hawks, is briskly efficient, but a syrupy ending undercuts the excellent biopic.

BIRTHS, DEATHS AND MARRIAGES

BIRTHS

Stephen Frears
20 Jun, Leicester

David Warner
29 Jul, Manchester

MARRIAGES

Gene Tierney
1 Jun, *to* Oleg Cassini

Tallulah Bankhead
Jun, *to* John Emery

William Holden
12 Jul, *to* Brenda Marshall

Gary Cooper and George Tobias in Sergeant York, *the story of a war hero.*

SOUND-STAGE SLUGFEST

On many a set a boxing referee might be more useful than a director. It was certainly a case of "seconds out" during the filming of *Manpower*, a retread of *Tiger Shark* (1932), in which high-voltage linemen Edward G. Robinson and George Raft fight over the favours of night-club "hostess" Marlene Dietrich.

The scrapping was carried over into a feud between the two stars, both of whom reportedly have the hots for Dietrich. But neither fit the bill of lanky all-American types like John Wayne. The needle between Raft and Robinson was increased by the latter's advice to the former on the best way to deliver his lines and handle business. The tension finally exploded into a punch-up on the set, graphically caught by a *Life* photographer.

Edward G. Robinson and George Raft as power linemen in Manpower.

SWORD AND CAPE

20th Century-Fox seems to have a penchant for starring handsome Tyrone Power in lavish remakes of silent classics. In last year's *The Mark of Zorro*, a spectacular re-run of the 1920 Douglas Fairbanks, Sr. hit, Power's rapier wiped the sneer off Basil Rathbone's face in a masterpiece of screen swordplay.

Now the Cincinnati-born 27-year-old – Fox's answer to Warners' resident swashbuckler Errol Flynn – steps into the shoes of Rudolph Valentino in *Blood and Sand*. The adaptation of Vicente Blasco Ibanez' bullfighting saga was a runaway success for the Great Lover in 1922.

Zorro director Rouben Mamoulian is again at the helm, drenching the screen in lush Technicolor as Power plays the gifted but naive matador led astray by public adulation and exotic dancer Rita Hayworth. But true love Linda Darnell stands by him to the end.

Rita Hayworth, Tyrone Power and Anthony Quinn in Blood and Sand.

Spencer Tracy in a powerful role as both Dr. Jekyll and Mr. Hyde.

STAND UP, SIGMUND FREUD

In its handsome remake of *Dr. Jekyll and Mr. Hyde*, M-G-M eschews the elaborate transformation scenes which distinguished Paramount's 1932 version with Fredric March. Instead, Spencer Tracy's misguided scientist changes into his bestial *alter ego* in a surrealist montage created by Peter Ballbusch.

Ingrid Bergman – now firmly established in Hollywood – is superb as the barmaid who becomes the object of Hyde's desires. A wooden Lana Turner plays Jekyll's well-bred fiancee. Originally the studio cast the two actresses the other way round, but Bergman argued for a switch on the grounds that playing against type would make the movie more interesting.

Equally interesting is the Freudian montage in which Tracy is a charioteer enthusiastically lashing his "horses", Bergman and Turner, with an outsize whip. The Hays Office, normally alert to naughtiness on screen, seems to have left Siggy F off its reading list.

BETTE'S BITCH ON WHEELS

RKO has launched an association with Sam Goldwyn with the distribution of *The Little Foxes*. It's adapted from Lillian Hellman's Broadway play that starred Tallulah Bankhead.

Set among a genteelly decaying Southern family, the movie features the monstrous Regina Giddens, a passionate, thwarted woman who will let nothing stand in the way of her greed.

When Goldwyn first announced he wanted the rights to the play – *The Three Little Foxes*, as he insisted on calling it – he was told by script editor Edward Knopf that it was "a very caustic play." Snapped Goldwyn: "I don't give a damn how much it costs – buy it."

He also wanted Bette Davis to step into Bankhead's shoes as Regina. Davis had long opposed being loaned out by Warners but Goldwyn got her services by trading Gary Cooper for *Sergeant York*.

Making her screen debut in the role of Alexandra, Regina's teenage daughter, is 23-year-old Teresa Wright, who was snapped up by Goldwyn after he saw her on stage in New York. His fatherly concern for her was revealed on set when, in an attempt to relax her, he cried from behind the camera: "Teresa, just let your breasts flow in the breeze."

Many of the cast are from the original Broadway company. Regina's wheelchair-bound husband is played by Herbert Marshall, who played Davis' husband in *The Letter* last year.

Davis and director William Wyler rowed over her interpretation of Regina – Wyler felt it owed too much to Bankhead's original – but the result is one of Davis' most powerful bitches on wheels.

Bette Davis as a passionate and bitter southern woman in The Little Foxes.

SEPTEMBER
OCTOBER

NOVEMBER
DECEMBER

THE STUFF THAT DREAMS ARE MADE OF

Two debutants are striking gold for Warners with *The Maltese Falcon*, an atmospheric detective thriller from the story by Dashiell Hammett. It's been filmed twice already – first in 1931 with Ricardo Cortez and Bebe Daniels and then in 1936, retitled *Satan Met a Lady*, with Bette Davis and Warren William.

Making his debut behind the camera is actor Walter Huston's 35-year-old son John who has led a colourful life as a boxer, actor, artist, officer in the Mexican cavalry, tramp and screenwriter. Making his screen debut is 61-year-old Sydney Greenstreet, a 300lb English import who has had a long association with the Lunts at the Theatre Guild.

Villainous Greenstreet was so nervous before his first scene that he asked co-star Mary Astor to hold his hand and tell him that "I won't make an ass of meself".

Huston's father Walter appears in a walk-on and Elisha Cook Jr is Greenstreet's vicious gun-toting servant, perpetually surprised by Humphrey Bogart's private eye Sam Spade and finally tossed to the wolves when the going gets tough in the scramble for the bird of the title.

Warners gave *The Maltese Falcon* a "gangster flick" budget of $300,000 and a brisk six-week shooting schedule. Associate producer Henry Blanke told Huston to "make every shot count". He's done that.

Lon Chaney Jr. as The Wolf Man, *which established a new Universal monster, being attacked by Claude Rains.*

BOX OFFICE

UK

1 49th Parallel
2 The Great Dictator
3 Pimpernel Smith
4 All This, and Heaven Too
5 Lady Hamilton (*U.S. title*: That Hamilton Woman)
6 South American George

OTHER TOP BOX OFFICE FILMS

Down Argentine Way
Fantasia
Love on the Dole
Major Barbara

BOX OFFICE

US

1 Gone With the Wind
2 Sergeant York
3 The Great Dictator
4 How Green Was My Valley
5 The Philadelphia Story

OTHER TOP BOX OFFICE FILMS

A Yank in the RAF
Abbott and Costello in the Navy
Hellzapoppin'
The Little Foxes
The Road to Zanzibar

A HAIRY HORROR STALKS THE MOORS

Lon Chaney Jr has emerged as a horror star in his own right in Universal's *The Wolf Man*, co-starring Claude Rains and Evelyn Ankers. In the process he's dropped the "Jr".

It took six hours for Jack Pierce to transform Chaney into the hirsute Wolf Man, pasting him over with yak-hair and stranded kelp before fitting him with a T-shaped nose-piece of rubber and fangs over his teeth.

GOSSIP COLUMN

■ This year two thirds of all U.S. families earned between $1,000 and $3,000. Film stars earn a little more, as Inland Revenue Service statistics show. Claudette Colbert has to rub along on $390,000, James Cagney $367,500, Clark Gable $357,500, Gary Cooper $287,671 and Joan Crawford $266,538. M-G-M boss Louis B. Mayer outstrips them all on $704,452.

KEEPING A WELCOME IN THE CALIFORNIA HILLSIDES

Walter Pidgeon, Donald Crisp and Anna Lee in How Green Was My Valley.

20th Century-Fox and director John Ford built a Welsh mining village in the hills north of Los Angeles and peopled it with several hundred actors and extras, including all the Welsh singers they could find on the West Coast.

The object of the exercise was the movie of Richard Llewellyn's best-selling novel *How Green Was My Valley*. Set in Wales at the turn of the century, it tells the tale of the Morgan family, headed by stern Donald Crisp and gentle Sarah Allgood, whose five oldest sons are coalminers. Youngest son Huw, charmingly played by child actor Roddy McDowall, narrates the story in flashback.

Slightly less than truthful is Ford's rhapsodic tribute to a community which was steeped in squalor and exploitation before the advent of unionization. But protests from Welsh critics have been drowned by the sound of ticket-buyers pouring in to see the picture.

DAY OF INFAMY

Before the Japanese bombed Pearl Harbor on 7 December, the U.S. Congress still had a small but influential group of isolationists dedicated to keeping the country out of the war.

In October they introduced Senate Resolution 152 which proposed a committee to investigate "any propaganda disseminated by motion pictures to influence public sentiment in the direction of participation of America in the European war".

They hadn't liked anti-Nazi movies like *Confessions of a Nazi Spy* (1939), *Escape*, *The Mortal Storm* (both 1940) and even *Sergeant York* (1941). Now, however, all doubts about Uncle Sam's entry have gone. And Hollywood has "joined up" in a blaze of patriotic fervour (and commercial calculation).

Paramount has changed the title of *Midnight Angel* to *Pacific Blackout* (it's still a lousy film). David O. Selznick has copyrighted the title *V for Victory*. But the prize for fastest off the blocks goes to M-G-M's B-movie, *A Yank on the Burma Road*, the first picture to incorporate Pearl Harbor into its storyline.

GARBO SWIMS . . . AND SINKS

Having got her to laugh in *Ninotchka* (1939), M-G-M tells us that in *Two-Faced Woman* "Garbo Rhumbas, Garbo Skiis, Garbo Swims, Garbo originates the New Short Bob" and, to cap it all, "Garbo is Twins!"

All this for a so-so comedy, directed by George Cukor, in which Garbo plays a woman who marries New York tycoon Melvyn Douglas and then turns vamp to outwit his old flame Constance Bennett by seducing him afresh in the guise of her soignee twin sister.

The movie had the Catholic Church's League of Decency frothing at the mouth over the mildly risque storyline. M-G-M had to spend $15,000 on a new scene showing Douglas is aware of the deception.

The final blow was delivered by Adrian, M-G-M's costume guru whose creations have played a major part in the Garbo myth. He's left the studio to set up as a freelance couturier. As Garbo says in the movie: "In this harsh world there is no new place for me anymore."

Ronald Reagan and Anne Sheridan in King's Row.

RONNIE'S BUSY YEAR

It's been a busy year for Ronald Reagan, the breezy 30-year-old Warners contract player who makes up with application what he clearly lacks in talent.

On 4 January his wife Jane Wyman gave birth to their first child, a daughter. Three months later his alcoholic father died. His filming schedule has included programmers like *Nine Lives Are Not Enough* (as a newspaperman) and the ludicrous *International Squadron* (as a Yank stunt pilot with the RAF). Latest is the big-budget *Kings Row*, from Henry Bellamann's 1940 best-seller about the rotten underbelly of small-town America. Warners previewed the picture soon after the Japanese bombing of Pearl Harbor; but it's now decided to hold back general release until next spring.

BIRTHS, DEATHS AND MARRIAGES

BIRTHS

David Hemmings
19 Nov, Guildford, Surrey

Beau Bridges
19 Dec, Hollywood

Sarah Miles
31 Dec, Ingatestone, Essex

MARRIAGES

Alice Faye
22 Sep, *to* Phil Harris

Gene Kelly
22 Sep, *to* Betty Blair

Gale Storm
5 Oct, *to* Lee Bonnell

Rosalind Russell
25 Oct, *to* Frederick Brisson

Maureen O'Hara
24 Dec, *to* Will Price

JANUARY
FEBRUARY

MARCH
APRIL

LAUGHING AT THE NAZIS

Critical controversy has been stirred up by director Ernst Lubitsch's *To Be or Not to Be*, starring Jack Benny and Carole Lombard as husband-and-wife Shakespearian actors Joseph and Maria Tura, who use their wits and stage skills to outmanoeuvre the Gestapo in occupied Poland.

Some critics accuse the biting comedy of tastlessness. Says *Life*: "In years to come the fact that Hollywood could convert part of the world crisis into such a cops and robbers charade will certainly be regarded as a remarkable phenomenon."

Sig Ruman, Hollywood's favourite Nazi buffoon, plays the consummately incompetent Gestapo chief "Concentration Camp" Ehrhardt – "I do the concentrating, they do the camping." When Benny, in disguise, asks him what he thinks of Joseph Tura, Ruman replies, "Ah, yes, I saw him once before the war. Believe me, what he did to Shakespeare we are now doing to Poland."

Tragically, the film's release has been overshadowed by the death of Carole Lombard, killed in a plane crash on 16 January in the mountains west of Las Vegas while on a war bonds tour. The small-town girl from Indiana was 34, and at the peak of her career. Her husband, Clark Gable, is devastated and Hollywood has lost an irreplaceable talent that began as a Mack Sennett bathing beauty in the late 1920s. Formerly married to William Powell, she'll be remembered for a string of screwball comedies, the best of which were *Twentieth Century* (1934), *My Man Godfrey* (1936) and *Nothing Sacred* (1937). The acid-tongued party-thrower, who preferred mixing with studio grips and extras to Tinseltown's high-flyers, will be sadly missed.

ACADEMY AWARDS

PRESENTED ON 26 FEBRUARY 1942

Best Picture
How Green Was My Valley

Best Director
John Ford
How Green Was My Valley

Best Actor
Gary Cooper
Sergeant York

Best Actress
Joan Fontaine
Suspicion

Best Sup Actor
Donald Crisp
How Green Was My Valley

Best Sup Actress
Mary Astor
The Great Lie

WHAT KATIE DID NEXT

To follow up her success in *The Philadelphia Story*, Katharine Hepburn bought a script by Ring Lardner Jr and Michael Kanin (brother of Garson), then cannily sold it to M-G-M for $100,000. The condition was she got the leading man of her choice, Spencer Tracy, and the director she wanted, George Stevens.

Woman of the Year is the story of an unlikely romance between Tess Harding, a hyperkinetic political columnist, and Sam Craig, a tough sportswriter on the same paper. They fall in love, marry, then fall out. Sam decides to leave on the night Tess wins the award of Woman of the Year. The movie ends on a note of poignant optimism as Tess tries to win Sam back with a catastrophically inept display of her skills in the kitchen.

Tracy and Hepburn struck up an immediate rapport during filming. When introduced to each other, she observed, "I'm afraid I'm rather tall for you, Mr Tracy." To which he replied, "Don't worry, I'll soon cut you down to size."

Tracy's hard-drinking sportswriter and Hepburn's brisk political pundit reflect the two stars' off-screen personalities. The sparks they struck on set have fanned the flames of romance, although Tracy is a married man with two children.

Katharine Hepburn and Spencer Tracy in Woman of the Year.

UNMAGNIFICENT ORSON

Word is that RKO is in a tizzy over young genius-in-a-hurry Orson Welles' new movie, *The Magnificent Ambersons*, a family saga starring Joseph Cotten and Dolores Costello. To get the studio to back his version of the 1918 Booth Tarkington novel, he let RKO have greater control over script and casting, plus the right to final cut. That's proving a real boomerang.

The tyro director of last year's *Citizen Kane* finished shooting *Ambersons* in late January, but then had to go off to Brazil for a project requested by the US State Department. RKO editor Robert Wise assembled a 131-minute version of the movie (keeping in touch with Welles through cables), and this was previewed in Pomona on 17 March.

Now the studio is panicking over the poor reaction – and exercising its right to final cut. Inside reports say that 50 minutes could be hacked out, and some extra scenes put in behind Welles' back. Expect this one to go out as a support, sometime in June. Is this the end of young Orson?

Alan Ladd as a young and ruthless professional killer who becomes involved with a fifth columnist plot in This Gun for Hire.

A LADD NO LONGER

Since the late 1930s a cool, unsmiling young actor, Alan Ladd, has been slowly climbing the movie ladder, pushed upward by his agent and soon-to-be wife, former actress Sue Carol. Born in Arkansas in 1913, he moved to California at the age of eight. His entry into the business was as a grip at Warners.

A long line of B-movies was followed by a small part at the end of Orson Welles' *Citizen Kane* (1941), when as one of the bunch of reporters packing up, pipe in mouth, hands in pockets, he intones from the shadows the words, "Or Rosebud."

Ladd had his first success in RKO's *Joan of Paris* (1942), a Resistance drama starring Michele Morgan and Paul Henreid in which he played an airman shot down over occupied Europe.

Now Paramount has him opposite Veronica Lake as the enigmatic hired killer Raven in *This Gun for Hire*, from a Graham Greene novel. Although Ladd and Lake did not get on with each other off the set, on camera they melt into a perfect miniature embrace – he's only 5ft 6in and she's three inches shorter. As the cat-loving gunman Ladd carries himself with the ferocity of a cold angel. He's perfectly complemented by Lake's sultry style, all little-girl-lost voice and "peek-a-boo" curtain of blonde hair tumbling over one eye.

The movie's sensational success has already prompted Paramount to rush the pair into a new thriller, *The Glass Key*. Ladd looks like he's a lad no longer.

RED TAPE IN THE SUNSET

Now that Uncle Sam has entered the conflict, wartime regulations have hit Hollywood. Within 48 hours of the attack on Pearl Harbor last December, Army officials moved into all the studios, commandeering the firearms used in production and handing them over to civil defence units.

The studios have been put on a daylight shift of 8am to 5pm to enable employees to beat the blackout on the way home. Night filming is temporarily halted. A Japanese invasion of California is seen by many as imminent, and the government has agreed a detailed set of guidelines on the stance Hollywood should adopt on certain subjects. These include the depiction of the enemy and their leaders, the task of boosting morale on the home front, and the need to increase wartime industrial output.

COOK COUNTY LAW

Ginger Rogers enjoys herself hugely in 20th Century-Fox's *Roxie Hart*, directed by William Wellman, as the brassy showgirl of the title confessing to murder as a publicity stunt.

A fast-moving spoof of the Roaring Twenties, based on the 1927 silent *Chicago*, the movie gives Rogers the chance to strut her comedy stuff, shimmy through the Black Bottom and bounce salty one-liners off dapper Adolphe Menjou, who plays the silver-tongued shyster lawyer hired to defend her.

Menjou prefers his clients guilty, but he takes one look at Ginger's gorgeous gams – "her best defence" – and decides to make an exception for "the prettiest woman ever tried for murder in Cook County."

BIRTHS, DEATHS AND MARRIAGES

BIRTHS

Michael York
27 Mar, Fulmer, Buckinghamshire

Sandra Dee
23 Apr, Batonne, New Jersey

Barbra Streisand
24 Apr, New York

DEATHS

Carole Lombard
16 Jan, Nevada
Aircrash

MARRIAGES

George Brent
5 Jan, *to* **Ann Sheridan**

Mickey Rooney
10 Jan, *to* **Ava Gardner**

Betty Field
12 Jan, *to* Elmer Rice

Cecil B DeMille's Reap the Wild Wind, starring Ray Milland, Paulette Goddard and John Wayne.

SQUID AHOY!

Cecil B DeMille celebrates 30 years in the business with Paramount's *Reap the Wild Wind*, a high, wide and handsome slice of costume hokum set off 19th-century Florida, whose waters seethe with assorted pirates, wreckers and attendant salvage boats.

John Wayne is the salty salvage man tangling with Ray Milland over Southern belle Paulette Goddard and getting entangled in the tentacles of a giant squid guarding a wreck in the murky depths of the studio tank.

Big John doesn't need a diving suit to cuddle up to Paulette, with whom he became very friendly during filming. Ray Milland, on the other hand, ran into a problem. For authenticity he submitted himself to the electric rollers of a studio hairdresser, after which his hair began to fall out in handfuls. It looks like another job for Hollywood's master "rugmakers."

THE KING JOINS UP

Seven months after Carole Lombard's tragic death in January, Clark Gable is still desolated. Having finished *Somewhere I'll Find You* with Lana Turner, the King of Hollywood has become a private in the U.S. Army. He's already on a basic training course in Florida, accompanied by his close friend, studio cameraman Andrew J. McIntyre, who has also enlisted.

Republic's top star, Gene Autry, has also traded in his cowboy duds for the uniform of the Army Air Service. The studio's production programme now has a gaping hole – the singing cowpoke was slated for eight westerns in a row.

GOODNIGHT, SWEET PRINCE

During the last three years of his life, John "The Great Profile" Barrymore, kept himself afloat on a sea of booze by parodying his own drunken decline. He died poverty-stricken on 29 May, aged 60, of complications arising from a chronic liver and kidney ailment. His funeral at Calvary Cemetery was attended by a celebrity crowd, including his old drinking and shooting companion Clark Gable, who made his first public appearance since the death in January of his wife Carole Lombard.

Barrymore's last film was a wretched RKO programmer, *Playmates* (1941), in which he gave band leader Kay Kyser a crash course in Shakespeare. When the time came to film a scene in which he recited Hamlet's famous soliloquy, the theatre's once-great Prince of Denmark could not remember the lines. Turning from the camera he mumbled, "It's been a long time."

MRS. MINIVER DOES HER BIT

M-G-M has channelled the upsurge of American support for the embattled British into *Mrs. Miniver*. Directed by William Wyler, it opens at Radio City Music Hall, NY, on 4 June.

Mrs. Miniver, set in a fantasy England, is full of village flower shows, comic servants and crusty aristocrats with hearts of gold. Greer Garson's Mrs. M. reads *Alice in Wonderland* to the children in the air-raid shelter and pluckily rounds up a downed German airman (Helmut Dantine) who has parachuted into her garden. Walter Pidgeon's tweedily phlegmatic Mr. M. sucks his pipe pensively and sails his little boat across the Channel to pluck Tommies from the Dunkirk beaches.

The role of Mrs. Miniver was originally offered to Norma Shearer, who turned it down as she did not want to play a mother. Garson was less choosy, and during production, which coincided with America's entry into the war, she fell in love with her screen son, Richard Ney. At the studio's insistence the marriage – her second – is to be delayed until the film has done the rounds.

GOSSIP COLUMN

■ When John Barrymore died, his old drinking buddy Errol Flynn went out to drown his sorrows. Returning home considerably the worse for wear, he found Barrymore sitting in his favourite chair, glass fully charged. On closer inspection, the thunderstruck Flynn discovered his old buddy had not risen from the grave. His corpse had been spirited away from a Sunset Boulevard mortuary by roistering director Raoul Walsh.

■ Marlene Dietrich, owner of the loveliest pair of gams in Hollywood, has insured them for £1 million with Lloyd's of London.

James Cagney doing his bit for patriotism in Yankee Doodle Dandy.

BORN ON THE 4TH OF JULY

Smarting from accusations that he has Communist leanings, James Cagney has seized the chance to demonstrate his patriotism by starring in Warners' biopic of the All-American Broadway showman and superpatriot George M. Cohan. His song "Yankee Doodle Dandy" proclaimed that he had been "born on the 4th of July" – well, on the 3rd actually, but who's counting?

Yankee Doodle Dandy is also the title of the movie, dominated by Cagney's performance as the swaggering, strutting lord of the dance. Walter Huston and Rosemary De Camp play Cohan's parents and Cagney's own sister Jeanne makes one of her rare screen appearances as his sister Josie. Joan Leslie is the romantic interest.

FACING UP TO DEFEAT

Although the United States has been at war for nearly nine months, Paramount's *Wake Island* is Hollywood's first serious attempt to dramatize seriously the deeds of American troops at a time when the victorious Japanese were cutting a swathe through vast tracts of the Pacific.

Directed by John Farrow, it's a heavily fictional account of the last-ditch defence by the U.S. Marine Corps of the tiny Pacific island of Wake, which fell to the Japanese after heavy fighting on 23 December 1941.

California's Salton Sea stands in for the Pacific, and a sturdy cast, including Brian Donlevy, Robert Preston, Macdonald Carey and William Bendix, issue the rallying cry for Americans determined to "remember Pearl Harbor".

BIRTHS, DEATHS AND MARRIAGES

BIRTHS

Stacy Keach
2 Jun, Savannah, Georgia

Genevieve Bujold
1 Jul, Montreal

Richard Roundtree
9 Jul, New Rochelle, New York

Harrison Ford
13 Jul, Chicago

DEATHS

John Barrymore
29 May, Hollywood
Liver and kidney failure

James Cruze
4 Aug, Hollywood
Heart ailment

MARRIAGES

Laraine Day
16 May, *to* James Ray Hendricks

Marilyn Monroe
19 Jun, *to* Jim Dougherty

Cary Grant
26 Jun, *to* Barbara Hutton

Lana Turner
17 Jul, *to* Stephen Crane

Ruth Hussey
2 Aug, *to* C. Robert Longenecker

Fay Wray
23 Aug, *to* Robert Riskin

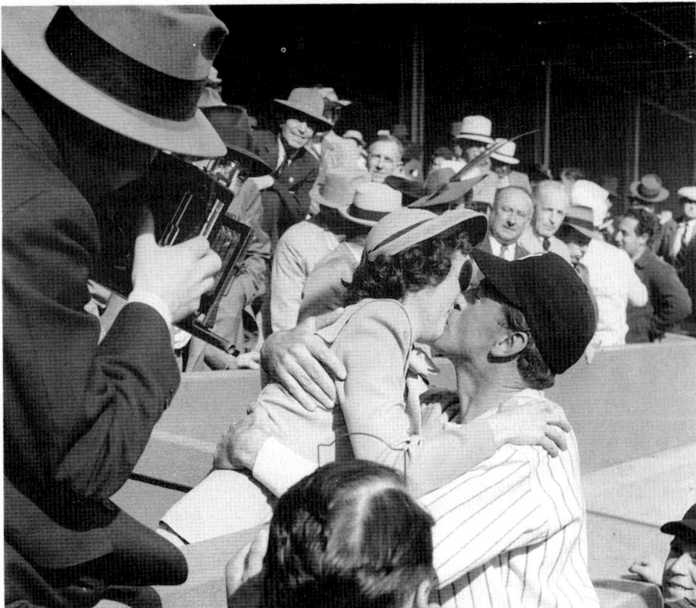

Gary Cooper as baseball hero Lou Gehrig in Pride of the Yankees.

HOME RUN FOR "COOP"

Gary Cooper scores an emotional triumph in *Pride of the Yankees*, a Sam Goldwyn production in which he plays Lou Gehrig, the legendary New York Yankees first baseman who played 2,130 consecutive games for the Yankees before being felled by a fatal neurological disease. It forced him to quit the game on 4 July 1939 at Yankee Stadium in front of 62,000 grief-stricken fans. He died on 2 June 1941, only 37 years old.

Cooper, perfectly cast as the quietly spoken, self-effacing Gehrig, who is taught how to throw left-handed by Lefty O'Dowd and is joined on screen by baseball immortal Babe Ruth. Teresa Wright provides sterling support as Gehrig's wife Truly.

On 19 August all gala floodlit premieres were banned for the duration of the war. But the night before Hollywood went dim, *Pride of the Yankees* had the honour of closing the floodlit series – which had begun in 1923 with James Cruze's *The Covered Wagon*. Proceeds went to the Naval Aid Auxiliary. Among the stars attending were Ava Gardner, Mickey Rooney, Victor Mature (in his coastguard uniform), Lieutenant Ronald Reagan and Jane Wyman, Hedy Lamarr, Jean-Pierre Aumont, Bobe Hope, Ginger Rogers, Jack Benny and Charles Boyer.

A PLACE IN THE COUNTRY

Bing Crosby and Fred Astaire in the very successful Holiday Inn.

Paramount have paired Bing Crosby and Fred Astaire for the first time in *Holiday Inn*, from an idea by Irving Berlin.

The duo play song-and-dance men who split up when Bing decides to establish a country inn that's open only on public holidays. Each of the eight holidays in the movie's easy-going format is provided with an apppropriate song, but the stand-out number is Crosby's rendition of Berlin's "White Christmas", delivered in his deceptively casual style.

Holiday Inn has filmgoers queuing round the block and – an unusual commercial accolade – has had a chain of motels named after it.

CAD FOR HIRE

"I'm beastly but I'm never coarse. I'm a high-class sort of cad." Thus George Sanders about the silky villains he so often plays, men whose patrician hauteur is a guarantee of their evil intentions.

Born of a British father and Russian mother in St. Petersburg in 1906, Sanders led a chequered early life, selling tobacco in Argentina, then drifting into radio drama before being brought to Hollywood by 20th Century-Fox to play the Lord Everett Stacy in *Lloyds of London* (1936).

In the past two years he's appeared in over 20 movies, stealing scenes in the good ones and surviving the stinkers.

Recently, suave sleuths have been his stock-in-trade. At RKO he played the Saint in four films, beginning with *The Saint Strikes Back* (1939). Then he slipped on the role of Michael Arlen's debonair gentleman detective, the Falcon, like an expensive leather glove. After three entries in the series Sanders became bored with the role, so the studio has him bumped off in the autumn release *The Falcon's Brother* (1942), enabling his real-life brother Tom Conway, an actor only marginally less svelte, to take over the part in this popular B-series.

SEPTEMBER OCTOBER 1942 NOVEMBER DECEMBER

"EVERYBODY GOES TO RICK'S"

Claude Rains and Humphrey Bogart help Paul Henreid and Ingrid Bergman escape the clutches of the Nazis in Warner's Casablanca.

Toying with the problem of casting an espionage melodrama based on an unproduced play, "Everybody Goes to Rick's", Warners considered Dennis Morgan and Ann Sheridan. Before the cameras rolled a number of other players floated in and out of the frame, among them Ronald Reagan, George Raft and Hedy Lamarr. But it's Humphrey Bogart who presides over Rick's Cafe Americain, to which Ingrid Bergman beats a fateful path.

In *Casablanca*, Bogart plays disillusioned gun-runner Rick Blaine, a bruised idealist turned cynical nightclub owner, still haunted by a bitter-sweet Paris romance with Ingrid Bergman. Now the wife of a Resistance hero (Paul Henreid), she walks into Rick's nightspot and persuades reluctant pianist Dooley Wilson to play "As Time Goes By", a request calculated to disturb even Bogart's hardboiled equanimity. Her next request is for two exit visas.

Swirling around the star-crossed lovers are enough subplots and salty supporting players to sustain half a dozen movies: Peter Lorre as the cringing, fidgety black marketeer Ugarte; Sydney Greenstreet, as the acceptable face of corruption; Claude Rains as the dapper, amiably immoral Vichy chief of police, forever confiding "I'm only a poor corrupt official"; and Conrad Veidt's thin-lipped Nazi emissary Major Strasser.

The film is released to coincide with the big Allied conference at Casablanca in mid-January.

THE STORY OF A SHIP

In Britain the war has breathed new life into a film industry which was in deep crisis only two years ago. Output is down, as a number of studios have been turned over to war use, but quality is up.

Proof of a regenerated industry is provided by Noel Coward's *In Which We Serve*. In a display of versatility rivalling that of Orson Welles in *Citizen Kane*, Coward wrote and produced the picture, took the starring role and collaborated on direction with former editor David Lean.

Using flashback, *In Which We Serve* tells of a warship, HMS *Torrin*, from her commissioning, through action in the North Sea, to her sinking during the evacuation of Crete. Coward plays the ship's commander, Captain Kinross, whose character is closely modelled on that of his friend Louis Mountbatten, whose destroyer, HMS *Kelly*, was sunk off Crete in 1941.

Noel Coward in In Which We Serve.

BIRTHS, DEATHS AND MARRIAGES

BIRTHS

Britt Ekland
29 Sep, Stockholm

Bob Hoskins
26 Oct, Bury St. Edmunds, Suffolk

Stephanie Powers
2 Nov, Hollywood

Martin Scorsese
17 Nov, New York

DEATHS

May Robson
20 Oct, Beverly Hills, California

George M. Cohan
5 Nov, New York
Intestinal ailments

Buck Jones
30 Nov, Boston, Massachusetts
Fire accident

MARRIAGES

Gregory Peck
Oct, *to* Greta Konen

THE HOLLYWOOD CANTEEN

Following the huge success of New York's Stage Door Canteen, the Hollywood Canteen has been set up in Los Angeles. Principal founder-members are Bette Davis and John Garfield, who raised the initial capital from the sale of $25 tickets for a premiere and a party.

The building is equipped and decorated by volunteers from all the guilds and unions in Hollywood. It opened on 3 October with the public paying $100 a head to watch the first troops crossing the threshold.

The aim of the Canteen is to give GIs a chance to meet the stars. They can eat from a menu prepared by the famous chef Milani and served by Hedy Lamarr, listen to a song from Bing Crosby and take a twirl round the floor with Rita Hayworth.

BOX OFFICE

UK

1 Mrs. Miniver
2 The First of the Few
3 How Green Was My Valley
4 Reap the Wild Wind
5 Holiday Inn
6 Captains of the Clouds
7 Sergeant York

OTHER TOP BOX OFFICE FILMS

Bambi
The Fleet's In
One of Our Aircraft is Missing

BOX OFFICE

US

1 Mrs. Miniver
2 My Gal Sal
3 To the Shores of Tripoli

OTHER TOP BOX OFFICE FILMS

Babes on Broadway
Captains of the Clouds
The Fleet's In
King's Row
My Favorite Blonde
Woman of the Year
Yankee Doodle Dandy

MEMORY LANE

Greer Garson flashes a handsome pair of legs as the music-hall star who marries amnesiac ex-serviceman Ronald Colman twice in M-G-M's *Random Harvest*, adapted from James Hilton's novel and directed by Mervyn LeRoy.

A "woman's picture" set in a Hollywood England festooned with cherry blossom, *Random Harvest*'s romantic absurdities are smoothed away by Colman's tact, timing and incomparable restraint. M-G-M originally slated Spencer Tracy for the role, but Colman seizes the chance to re-establish himself as a front-rank romantic star after a string of indifferent films.

NICE WORK, IF YOU CAN GET IT

RKO looks like cleaning up with one of the biggest "sleepers" in the studio's history, *Hitler's Children*. It's based on the book *Education for Death* by Gregor Ziemer and directed by Edward Dmytryk, one of the most hard-working hands in RKO's B-hive.

A lurid account of the indoctrination of German youth with Nazi ideology, the movie stars Bonita Granville as a young woman deemed unfit to bear illegitimate children for the glory of the Fuhrer and marked down for sterilization. Tim Holt is cast as her boyfriend, a Nazi Youth leader who comes to see the error of his ways, at the cost of his own life.

The movie's setting has enabled RKO to drive a coach and horses through the rules of the censorship office. The publicity department's masterstroke is an advertising still featuring an anguished Bonita in a state of undress about to be publicly flogged by a bunch of sneering Nazis for refusing to submit to their bestial demands.

INTO THE SUNSET

The career of colourful cowboy star Charles "Buck" Jones has ended in Boston. On 28 November he died, with over 400 others, in a blaze at the Cocoanut Grove nightclub, where a testimonial dinner was being held in his honour. He was 53.

Indiana-born Jones, whose adventurous pre-Hollywood career included stints as a cowboy with the 101 Wild West Show, a cavalry sergeant in the Philippines, aviation mechanic, sheepherder and horse-breaker for the French government in the First World War, had thrown himself into the war bonds drive.

His career had gradually wound down since its heyday in the 1920s. In 1940 he joined "Poverty Row" studio Monogram to co-star in their low-budget *Rough Riders* series.

Ronald Colman and Greer Garson in the romantic feature Random Harvest.

M-G-M FINDS A NEW STAR

Gene Kelly makes his screen debut at the advanced age of 30 in M-G-M's *For Me and My Gal*.

Kelly is cast here in a role similar to that of heel-hero Pal Joey. He plays egotistical dancer Harry Palmer, who teams up with George Murphy and Judy Garland (who gets top billing) but finds the First World War getting in the way of his ambition to play the Palace Theater, New York.

Although directed by Busby Berkeley, the film's musical numbers are staged by Bobby Connolly. Outstanding among them are Kelly and Garland singing "Oh, You Beautiful Doll" and Garland singing "After You've Gone", "When Johnny Comes Marching Home".

OF CIGARETTES AND PSYCHIATRISTS

Bette Davis's mailbag is bulging after her latest performance in Warners' *Now, Voyager* as Charlotte Vale, the dowdy, neurotic, mother-dominated spinster who is transformed by silky psychiatrist Claude Rains and suave man of the world Paul Henreid into a chic socialite and understanding Other Woman. And a generation of youthful males are aping Henreid's prelude to seduction – lighting two cigarettes in his mouth with a single match before passing one to Davis.

Now, Voyager is wish-fulfilment in overdrive. As Bette tells the unhappily married Henreid as the film ends, "Let's not ask for the moon when we have the stars."

FRANCES FREAKS OUT

The troubled life of turbulent Paramount star Frances Farmer, one of the studio's hottest properties in the late 1930s, has been steadily falling apart since her conviction on a drunk-driving charge in October last year.

At the time of her arrest her mental balance was already unhinged by a combination of amphetamines (to control her weight) and alcohol (to steady her nerves). Soon after her conviction she dislocated a studio hairdresser's jaw, and later got separated from her sweater during a night club thrash and raced topless down Sunset Strip.

On 13 January she was pulled from her bed in the Knickerbocker Hotel, charged with breaking her parole terms. All hell broke loose from the moment when, at the LA police headquarters, she gave her occupation as "cocksucker".

Kicking and screaming, she was dragged from court, placed in a straitjacket and certified as "mentally incompetent".

OUTLAW OUTLAWED

There's a storm of controversy around the RKO Western *The Outlaw*, the pet project of millionaire-aviator, movie dilettante and odd-ball Howard Hughes.

Producer-director Hughes has built the project around his 22-year-old protegee, busty former chiropodist's assistant Jane Russell. Early in the nine months of filming in 1941 (at the start of which Hughes fired director Howard Hawks), Hughes decided "we're not getting enough production from Jane's breasts." Whereupon, the designer of monster aircraft like the "Spruce Goose" repaired to the drawing board to engineer a brassiere enhancing Russell's formidable cleavage.

For two years Hughes has fought a bitter battle with Joseph Breen's Production Code Administration for a code seal.

In February he got a token San Francisco showing but the hullabaloo over Russell's high-voltage sex scenes with newcomer Jack Buetel has ruled out any general release. At one point she clambers into bed with him "to keep him warm."

Meanwhile, the wild and woolly Western, with Buetel as Billy the Kid and Walter Huston as "Doc" Holliday, has gone back on the shelf.

Jane Russell in the controversial The Outlaw, *the pet project of millionaire Howard Hughes.*

BIRTHS, DEATHS AND MARRIAGES

BIRTHS

Gayle Hunnicut
6 Feb, Fort Worth, Texas

Christopher Walken
21 Mar, Astoria, New York

DEATHS

Conrad Veidt
3 Apr, Hollywood
Heart attack

MARRIAGES

Ginger Rogers
6 Jan, *to* Jack Briggs

Rex Harrison
25 Jan, *to* **Lilli Palmer**

Dorothy Lamour
7 Apr, *to* William Ross Howard

Jane Russell
24 Apr, *to* Bob Waterfield

Peter Finch
24 Apr, *to* Tamara Tchinarowa

CONRAD VEIDT DIES

Conrad Veidt, everyone's favourite German villain, died of a heart attack while playing golf in Hollywood on 3 April. He was 50, and had just completed M-G-M's *Above Suspicion*, with Joan Crawford and Basil Rathbone.

Born in Berlin of Jewish parents, the great silent star of *The Cabinet of Dr Caligari* (1924) and *The Student of Prague* (1926) arrived in Hollywood in 1927, but the coming of sound and his thick German accent cut short his first stint in Tinseltown. He returned to Germany where he quickly became *persona non grata* with the Nazis. He went to England to work for Gaumont British, but a visit to Germany in 1934 nearly ended in internment, and he was saved only by the swift intervention of the British studio.

He was well cast by Michael Powell as a sympathetic German agent in *The Spy in Black* (1939) before travelling to Hollywood to complete *The Thief of Bagdad* (1940), in which he was superb as the Grand Vizier. Joan Crawford's sinister mentor in *A Woman's Face* (1941), he will always be remembered as Major Strasser, thwarted at the last by Humphrey Bogart and Claude Rains in *Casablanca* (1942).

Kent Smith and Ruth Warwick in Forever and a Day.

THERE'LL ALWAYS BE AN ENGLAND

A once-in-lifetime cast is in RKO's *Forever and a Day*, an all-star charity film whose proceeds are going to the British War Relief fund.

The idea was dreamed up back in 1940 by Cedric Hardwicke. The British actors agreed to give their services free and RKO provided studio and distribution facilities.

Filming began in 1941 and was completed only because of the determination of Hardwicke and directors Frank Lloyd and Herbert Wilcox. Featuring 78 name actors and directed by seven leading stars, it's the story of a London house and its occupants from 1804 to the present. C. Aubrey Smith is the fire-breathing admiral who builds the house, Charles Laughton plays a comic butler, Hardwicke and Buster Keaton are a couple of slapstick plumbers, and Gladys Cooper and Roland Young play the parents of a fighter ace killed in the First World War.

Those seven directors? They're Rene Clair, Edmund Goulding, Hardwicke himself, Frank Lloyd, Victor Saville, Robert Stevenson and Herbert Wilcox.

IN LIKE FLYNN

Swashbuckling Errol Flynn has been charged with statutory rape. But there's a suspicion the whole affair is part of a shakedown of the studios by a number of highly placed bent cops.

The "victims" are two teenagers, Betty Hansen and Peggy Satterlee. Hansen claims Flynn had his way at a "swim-and-sex" party. Satterlee says she spliced the mainbrace with the handsome Tasmanian on his yacht *Sirocco*.

The all-woman jury has been locked up all night debating their verdict. Says Peggy Satterlee: "Here I am, two days less than 17 years old and I feel like a broken old woman." No one expects a verdict of guilty, and the hilarious court-room revelations haven't dented Flynn's popularity in the least.

ACADEMY AWARDS

PRESENTED ON 4 MARCH 1943

Best Picture
Mrs. Miniver

Best Director
William Wyler
Mrs. Miniver

Best Actor
James Cagney
Yankee Doodle Dandy

Best Actress
Greer Garson
Mrs. Miniver

Best Sup Actor
Van Heflin
Johnny Eager

Best Sup Actress
Teresa Wright
Mrs. Miniver

Eddie Anderson, Rex Anderson, Lena Horne, Kenneth Spencer in Cabin in the Sky.

DAZZLING DEBUT

After a two-year apprenticeship at M-G-M, former designer and stage director Vincente Minnelli has his first feature assignment with *Cabin in the Sky*, an all-black musical adapted from a 1940 Broadway show.

Given a handsome sepiatone surface, it's a fantasy about the agents of Heaven and Hell struggling for possession of the soul of happy-go-lucky gambler "Little Joe" (Eddie "Rochester" Anderson) who has been felled in a barroom brawl. He's all too easily tempted by the pleasures of the flesh, here embodied by the delicious Lena Horne, with whom he duets delightfully in "Life's Full of Consequences".

The remarkable Ethel Waters repeats her Broadway role as "Little Joe's" wife, and the cast also includes Louis Armstrong and Duke Ellington and his Orchestra.

Like Warners' all-black *Green Pastures* (1936), *Cabin in the Sky* is attracting criticism for its portrayal of blacks as folksy stereotypes, but it's lively entertainment all the same.

THE MERRY WIDOW MURDERER

Alfred Hitchcock's latest skilfully marries a sardonic celebration of small-town America with the elements of a psychological thriller.

In *Shadow of a Doubt*, Hitch's trick is to show the effect of the arrival from New York of raffish Uncle Charlie (Joseph Cotten) on a surburban Californian family. It is only his niece (Teresa Wright) who senses she's given over her bedroom to a murderer – the "Merry Widow" murderer to be precise.

Joseph Cotten is impressive as the psychopathic uncle, but the film is stolen by Hume Cronyn as a noisy connoisseur of crime fiction, eagerly barking up the wrong tree as a real murderer strolls through the sunlit streets of his home town.

GOSSIP COLUMN

■ **The fur flew on the set of Paramount's *So Proudly We Hail*, a tribute to the front-line nurses at Corregidor (the island fortress in the Philippines), starring Claudette Colbert, Veronica Lake and Paulette Goddard. When an interviewer asked Goddard which of her co-stars she preferred, she replied: "Veronica, I think. After all, we're closer in age."**

MAY
JUNE

JULY
AUGUST

SELLING STALIN IN THE STATES

Seeking to drum up popular support for America's Soviet allies, the Office of War Information approached Warners – who had made the ground-breaking anti-Nazi film *Confessions of a Nazi Spy* (1939) – to produce *Mission to Moscow*, adapted from a laudatory book about the Russian people written by the former U.S. ambassador to the Soviet Union Joseph E. Davies.

Conscious of the fuss over *Confessions of a Nazi Spy*, Warners dragged its feet but eventually agreed. It cast Walter Huston as Joseph E. Davies and concocted a semi-fictitious script by Howard Koch which made free with the facts of interwar history. In the finished result, now on release, Moscow show trials of the 1930s, staged in a palace of Babylonian proportions, are glossed over in a mildly critical manner, although by now Davies, who introduces the film, and many others are aware of their true enormity. Similarly, the Nazi-Soviet pact of 1939 is explained in terms of the hostility displayed towards the Soviet Union by France and Britain, whose leader Winston Churchill turns up in a flabby burlesque by Dudley Field Malone.

However, Michael Curtiz's bravura direction, which combines documentary footage with dazzling set-pieces, driven along by Max Steiner's stirring score, wins the day. In the spirit of wartime solidarity, suspicions about the movie's political stance have been swept under the carpet.

LOST LEADER

Mystery surrounds the death of suave British actor Leslie Howard. On 1 June, flying back from Lisbon, his aircraft was shot down by German fighters. Winston Churchill was at a conference in Algiers at the time and there is speculation that Howard's plane may have been a decoy, suspected by the Luftwaffe of carrying the British Prime Minister.

After *Intermezzo* (1939), Howard had returned to England to become one of Britain's busiest producer-directors.

He directed himself in *Pimpernel Smith* (1941), playing a whimsical, scholarly secret agent; and in Michael Powell's *49th Parallel* he was an effete anthropologist, finally rounding on his Nazi captors. He directed and starred in *The First of the Few* (1942), as R.J. Mitchell, the man who designed the Spitfire, and this year helmed two warm tributes to women at war, *The Lamp Still Burns* (nurses) and *The Gentle Sex* (the women of the Auxiliary Territorial service).

LYNCHING PEOPLE IS WRONG

20th Century-Fox's attempt to provide the public with a "thoughtful" Western in the mould of Greek tragedy looks like it has flopped with moviegoers.

The Ox-Bow Incident is about three drifters (Dana Andrews, Anthony Quinn and Francis Ford) who, without any evidence against them, are summarily tried for cattle rustling and then lynched. To ram home the movie's anti-mob law message, Henry Fonda provides the voice of conscience at the end, shaming the lynch party with a letter written by one of the men they have just hanged.

The movie is hampered by a speechifying script (from Walter van Tilburg Clark's 1940 novel) and a low budget which forced director William Wellman to shoot the whole thing in the studio. The lynch mob have all the best lines, notably Frank Conroy as a bogus Southern colonel with a shameful secret and Jane Darwell as a blood-curdling virago. The studio's front office virtually disowned the film until it started to get favourable notices and awards. But the public's staying away in droves.

Dana Andrews, Anthony Quinn and Francis Ford in The Ox-Bow Incident.

Peter Van Eyck, Anne Baxter and Erich von Stroheim in *Five Graves to Cairo*.

GOSSIP COLUMN

■ **During the filming of M-G-M's *A Guy Named Joe*, Van Johnson suffered a badly fractured skull in a motorcycle accident. Louis B. Mayer considered replacing him, but co-star Spencer Tracy persuaded Mayer to suspend the picture until Johnson recovered. He returned with a metal plate in his head and a lump on his forehead which was concealed with clever camerawork.**

SONS OF THE DESERT

In the silent days Erich von Stroheim was "The Man You Love to Hate", sneering away as a bullet-headed Prussian beast, glinting monocle screwed permanently in place.

Now, in Billy Wilder's *Five Graves to Cairo*, he's cast as "The Man You Can't Help but Admire" – the dashing Desert Fox, General Erwin Rommel, the Allies' most chivalrous Nazi opponent.

There's more intrigue than tank action in the movie, which is basically a witty reworking of *Hotel Imperial* (1939) by Wilder and co-screenwriter Charles Brackett, with Akim Tamiroff's Afrika Korps-occupied desert hostelry providing the listening post in which British agent Franchot Tone uncovers the secrets which secure victory for Montgomery at El Alamein.

In a well-crafted slice of hokum, the only regret is that one of the graves of the title, courtesy of a German firing squad, is filled by charming Anne Baxter.

BIRTHS, DEATHS AND MARRIAGES

BIRTHS

Malcolm McDowell
13 Jun, Leeds

Robert De Niro
17 Aug, New York

Tuesday Weld
27 Aug, New York

DEATHS

Leslie Howard
1 Jun, near Lisbon
Plane shot down

MARRIAGES

Richard Conte
21 May, *to* Ruth Strohm

Charlie Chaplin
16 Jun, *to* Oona O'Neill

Betty Grable
11 Jul, *to* Harry James

SLAVERY IN PARADISE

Feisty stars like Bette Davis and James Cagney have famously kicked against the studio pricks, but most go along with the system. Better to be a slave in mink than Mamie Glutz from Nowheresville. But not Olivia de Havilland, who has joined battle with Warners over her contract.

She signed a standard seven-year contract with the studio in 1935. After finishing *Princess O'Rourke* this year she considered the contract at an end. But the studio begged to differ, claiming an extra six months because of disciplinary suspensions.

It's long been a weapon in any studio's armoury (other weapons include loan-outs, demoted billing, one-sided options and B-movie work). De Havilland's victory would be good news for actors. In future, seven years will be the limit for any film contract and, furthermore, this will be inclusive of any suspensions.

THE PUBLICITY MILL GRINDS EXCEEDINGLY SMALL

Claudia is typical of David O. Selznick's post-*Gone with the Wind* wheeling and dealing. It's based on a Broadway comedy hit about a "child-bride", packaged and sold by Selznick to 20th Century-Fox.

To whip up the kind of press interest which accompanied his "search for Scarlett", Selznick announced he had no intention of using the star of the Broadway show, Dorothy McGuire, and fed stories to the press that several big names, including Margaret Sullavan, were being tested for the part of the eponymous heroine. Sullavan's flat shoes and cardigan style might have been the original for Claudia, but Selznick was merely bluffing. McGuire duly made her film debut, co-starring with Robert Young. He skilfully handles the role of the older husband charmed by Claudia's waif-like innocence – slightly risque subject matter whose pitfalls veteran director Edmund Goulding has negotiated with consummate skill.

GREER GARSON DISCOVERS RADIUM

Since the mid-1930s Hollywood has told many a tale of scientific endeavour: Paul Muni battled TB in *The Story of Louis Pasteur* (1936); Don Ameche invented the telephone in *The Story of Alexander Graham Bell* (1939); Spencer Tracy invented just about everything in *Edison the Man* (1940), and Edward G. Robinson found a cure for syphilis in *Dr Ehrlich's Magic Bullet* (1940).

Now stately Greer Garson, currently M-G-M's biggest star, can be seen as *Madame Curie*, her hands unstained by chemicals as she discovers radium.

The part of Marie Curie had originally been slated for Greta Garbo rather than Garson. She shares the limelight with dependable Walter Pidgeon, transformed by a beard from Mr Miniver to Monsieur Curie. They make a handsome couple, although a little underpowered when compared with screen partnerships like Ladd-Lake or Tracy-Hepburn.

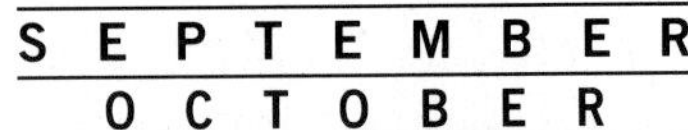

SEPTEMBER OCTOBER 1943 NOVEMBER DECEMBER

BIRTHS, DEATHS AND MARRIAGES

BIRTHS

Catherine Deneuve
22 Oct, Paris

Sam Shepard
5 Nov, Fort Sheridan, IL

Lauren Hutton
17 Nov, Charleston, South Carolina

Ben Kingsley
31 Dec, Yorkshire

DEATHS

Charles Ray
23 Nov, Hollywood
Heart attack

MARRIAGES

Yul Brynner
6 Sep, *to* Virginia Gilmore

Orson Welles
7 Sep, *to* Rita Hayworth

Kirk Douglas
2 Nov, *to* Diana Dill

Lynn Bari
28 Nov, *to* Sid Luft

STAR QUOTES

Ray Milland

"Hedda Hopper was venomous, vicious, a pathological liar, and quite stupid."

GOSSIP COLUMN

■ Veronica Lake's tumbling waterfall of blonde hair is no more. She has shorn her shoulder-length page-boy at the request of the War Department because female munitions workers with copycat hairstyles are getting them caught in the machinery.

BETTE AND MIRIAM SLUG IT OUT

Battle royal was joined on the set of Warners' *Old Acquaintance* when feuding co-stars Bette Davis and Miriam Hopkins snarled their way through the shooting schedule.

Studios have often invented imaginary feuds between stars in the 1920s Paramount pitted but this time the hate was for real.

Old Acquaintance is based on John Van Druten's play about two women, friends from childhood, who become bitter literary enemies before making it up and drinking a toast to beckoning middle age. The original director, Edmund Goulding, suffered a heart attack brought on by endless hour-long telephone harangues from the tantrum-prone Hopkins. Although she was being paid far more than Davis, she resented her rival's status as queen of the Warner lot.

Vincent Sherman took over as director, and the tone was set on the first day of filming when Hopkins turned up on set wearing a copy of Davis' costume in *Jezebel*.

Cigarette smoke blown casually into Davis' eyes and a tendency to rearrange flowers, rewind clocks and plump cushions every time Davis began an important speech were just two of the weapons in Hopkins armoury. The film is a hit with the public. But for both stars *Old Acquaintance* is likely to be quickly forgot and never brought to mind.

Jennifer Jones in The Song of Bernadette.

I GOTTA GROTTO

Jennifer Jones, the young Oklahoma-born actress 'discovered' by David O. Selznick in 1940 and held back from Hollywood 'until exactly the right role comes along', has been launched in 20th Century-Fox's *The Song of Bernadette*. She's the sickly French peasant girl whose vision of the Virgin Mary in a grotto by a rubbish dump turns Lourdes into the pilgrimage centre of France.

Fox claims the hugely expensive production is "a motion picture no human words can describe." But a few choice ones could be found for Bernadette's vision of the Virgin, played by an uncredited Linda Darnell and lit up like a Rockefeller Center Christmas Tree.

Jones, 23, is being pushed hard as an exciting "newcomer". Selznick must have conveniently forgotten her 1939 foray in Hollywood which landed her roles in the Republic B-Western *New Frontier*, starring John Wayne, and the same studio's serial *Dick Tracy's G-Men*.

BOX OFFICE

UK

1 Random Harvest
2 In Which We Serve
3 Casablanca
4 The Life and Death of Colonel Blimp
5 Hello, Frisco, Hello
6 The Black Swan
7 The Man in Grey

OTHER TOP BOX OFFICE FILMS

The Adventures of Tartu
Coney Island
The Gentle Sex

BOX OFFICE

US

1 This Is the Navy
2 For Whom the Bell Tolls
3 Random Harvest
4 Stagedoor Canteen
5 Hitler's Children

OTHER BOX OFFICE SUCCESSES

Casablanca
The Commandos Strike at Dawn
Hello, Frisco, Hello
Now, Voyager
Star Spangled Rhythm

Spencer Tracy and Barry Nelson as ghosts watch over Van Johnson, Irene Dunne and Ward Bond in *A Guy Named Joe*.

DEATH, WHERE IS THY STING?

It takes more than a willing suspension of disbelief to accept Spencer Tracy as a ghost in M-G-M's *A Guy Named Joe*.

Down-to-earth Tracy is a fighter pilot killed in a flying accident who is sent back to Earth by God – or M-G-M's equivalent, Lionel Barrymore – to guide young airman Van Johnson through the pitfalls of service life and into the arms of his old flame, intrepid ferry pilot Irene Dunne.

During filming relations between Tracy and Dunne were somewhat less than ethereal. The sweet nothings he whispers in her ear were more of the raunchy kind. Grumpy, hard-drinking Tracy is strongly attracted to *noli me tangere* types like Dunne, so when the script called for canoodling Tracy gave her a graphic description of what he really wanted to do with her. Starchy Dunne was so upset that studio boss Louis B. Mayer had to read the riot act to his straight-talking star.

FAIR SHARES

Art imitates life in RKO's *Tender Comrade*, a three-handkerchief weepie about "war wives" starring Ginger Rogers. She's now a war wife herself, having met and married Marine Jack Briggs while she was on tour entertaining the troops.

Ginger plays a "chin-up" war widow and aircraft assembly-line worker who pools her pay cheque to live communally with other war wives for the duration. They spend the day at the Douglas plant and their nights mooning over photographs of their absent husbands and absorbing endless sermons on freedom and the glories of the American way of life and the iniquities of violating the rationing regulations.

This sugary slice of uplift, written by Dalton Trumbo and director Edward Dmytryk, is already attracting whispers in some quarters that it is insidious Communist propaganda, not least because of the line uttered by Ginger, "Share and share alike – that's democracy". But the public doesn't seem to care: on the circuits *Tender Comrade* has netted a tidy profit of $850,000. That's showbusiness.

STAR QUOTES

Joan Crawford

"I think what the public wants on the screen is more of those old-fashioned caresses that established love scenes as something real and vital."

MORE STARS THAN THERE ARE IN THE HEAVENS

M-G-M has hit paydirt with *Thousands Cheer*, a star-spangled morale-booster strung around the paper-thin story of trapeze artist-turned GI Gene Kelly romancing colonel's daughter Kathryn Grayson.

The all-stops-out finale is hosted by Mickey Rooney, who repeats his sidesplitting impressions of Clark Gable and Lionel Barrymore (first seen in the 1939 *Babes in Arms*) and then introduces a roster of the studio's brightest talents, including Red Skelton, Margaret O'Brien, Lena Horne, Eleanor Powell and Judy Garland, who is accompanied by classical pianist Jose Iturbi on "The Joint is Really Jumping in Carnegie Hall".

Kelly has only one chance to dance, waltzing with a mop while confined to barracks for insubordination. By the final reel the Army has made a man of the rebellious Kelly, convincing him that "I want to be the most important man in the world – a private in the United States Army". After that it just remains for Grayson and a massed choir to sing "Make Way for a Day Called Tomorrow", surrounded by the billowing flags of the Allies.

Robert Ryan and Ginger Rogers in RKO's weepie *Tender Comrade*.

Gary Cooper as Sergeant York *(1941).*

Kenneth More as the beachmaster on Sword Beach in The Longest Day *(1962).*

Peter Sellers as a mad German-American scientist in Dr Strangelove *(1964).*

Alec Guinness in the Academy Award-winning The Bridge on the River Kwai *(1952).*

James Mason as Africa Korps commander Rommel in The Desert Fox *(1951).*

John Wayne and Robert Montgomery discuss plans in They Were Expendable *(1945).*

The French advance in this scene from Stanley Kubrick's Paths of Glory *(1957) which graphically depicted the horrors of battle in the First World War.*

Oh! What A Lovely War

When war broke out in Europe in 1939 the Hollywood studios were gripped by a moral paralysis, reluctant to court box-office disaster by offending the strong isolationist sentiment prevalent in America by overt attacks on Nazi Germany. But in 1941, with its lucrative European markets cut off, Hollywood embarked on a string of films which celebrated America's military preparedness (*I Wanted Wings, Dive Bomber*), paid tribute to the British (*A Yank in the RAF*), criticized isolationism (*Sergeant York*) and made a start on the service comedy (*Buck Privates, Caught in the Draft*).

After the Japanese attack on Pearl Harbor on 7 December 1941, Hollywood threw itself into the war effort, discovering with relief that patriotism could be immensely profitable. Unlike some industries, it required a minimum of conversion, effortlessly adapting all the stock genres to accommodate popular war themes.

In 1943 the number of films dealing either directly or indirectly with the war reached a peak. There was a greater honesty about the reality of battle in movies like *Guadalcanal Diary, Bataan* and *The Immortal Sergeant*, while the moral complexities of war were tackled in *The Moon Is Down* and *This Land Is Mine*. There was life on the home front in *Swing Shift Maisie* (war workers), *Tender Comrade* (war widows) and *The More the Merrier* (Washington's acute housing shortage). In *The Miracle of Morgan's Creek* (1944), Preston Sturges mercilessly caricatured the upheavals that war brought to small-town America. The surge of support for America's Russian allies was reflected in films like *The North Star* (1943), *Mission to Moscow* (1943) and *Days of Glory* (1944). By 1944, the number of war films made in Hollywood was falling. The outcome of the war was no longer in doubt and the majors were transferring their big budgets to more popular escapist entertainment.

Soon the United States was readjusting to the Cold War, which became hot in Korea in 1950 and stimulated a new burst of films either looking back to the Second World War – *Flying Leathernecks* (1951), *The Desert Fox* (1951), *Stalag 17* (1952) – or covering Korea with varying degrees of flag-waving fervour – *Korea Patrol* (1950), *Fixed Bayonets* (1951), *The Steel Helmet* (1951), *The Bridges at Toko-Ri* (1954). These films usually summoned up uncomplicated images of heroism, strongly influenced by Allan Dwans' *Sands of Iwo Jima* (1949), but a growing number of films began to deal with the casualties of war and the ambiguous price of both victory and defeat: *The Men* (1950), *The Caine Mutiny* (1954), *Attack!* (1955), *Paths of Glory* (1957) and *The Bridge on the River Kwai* (1957).

Towards the end of the decade the changing politics of international alliances altered the way movies told the story of the Second World War. Now there was room for 'good Germans' as well as Nazis (a point originally acknowledged in the 1944 *The Seventh Cross*) and these archetypes can be found in most of the war films of the 1960s. These movies fell into three distinct strands: ponderous spectaculars like *The Longest Day* (1962); 'anti-war' tracts like *Castle Keep* (1969); and violent hymns to the power of group solidarity in films like *The Dirty Dozen* (1967).

These boys' war games were played out under the shadow of the H-bomb. And the nightmare logic of mutually assured destruction was earnestly unfolded in *Fail-Safe* (1964) and gleefully exploded in *Dr Strangelove or: How I Learned to Stop Worrying and Love the Bomb* (1964). When Strangelove was released the United States was gearing itself up for a new war, this time in Vietnam.

JANUARY
FEBRUARY

MARCH
APRIL

HOLLYWOOD JOINS UP

M-G-M has been fighting a long behind-the-scenes battle to keep one of their biggest assets, Mickey Rooney, out of the services. But he has to report for enlistment in May.

One of the first stars to join up was James Stewart, as a private in the United States Army Air Force (USAAF) in March 1941, long before Pearl Harbor. He is now in Europe with 445th Bomb Group, Eighth Air Force, piloting B-24 Liberator bombers against targets in Germany.

Another star to fly combat missions over Europe is Captain Clark Gable, who doubled as an air gunner and cameraman while filming footage for the gunnery training programme. The story goes that Hermann Goring, commander of the Luftwaffe, offered $5,000 to the fighter pilot who shot Gable down. Popular action star Wayne Morris is another aviator, serving with distinction in the Naval air arm in the Pacific.

Robert Taylor, a qualified civilian pilot, is assigned to the Navy's Aviation Volunteer Division, making training films. Lieutenant-Commander Robert Montgomery, a pre-war reservist, has seen action aboard a PT-boat in the Pacific and on a destroyer during the D-Day landings.

Tyrone Power joined the Marine Corps after completing *Crash Dive* (1943), and Henry Fonda is serving in the Navy. Director John Ford is head of the Field Photographic Branch of the Office of Strategic Services (OSS) with the rank of lieutenant-commander. Director Woody Van Dyke, another pre-war reservist, served overseas as commander of 22nd Battalion, U.S. Marine Corps, with many Hollywood personnel in its ranks. But Van Dyke, nicknamed "The Steam Engine in Breeches", drove himself too hard, had a heart attack and was forced to resign his commission. 20th Century-Fox production chief Darryl F. Zanuck is a lieutenant in charge of a documentary unit. Along with many other well-known Hollywood names who are serving as non-combatants, entertaining the troops or selling war bonds, and the many thousands of Hollywood personnel in the armed services, they're all doing their bit to win the war.

BIRTHS, DEATHS AND MARRIAGES

BIRTHS

George Lucas
1 Jan, Modesta, Calif

Rutger Hauer
23 Jan, Breukelen, Netherlands

Stockard Channing
13 Feb, New York

Alan Parker
14 Feb, London

Roger Daltry
1 Mar, London

Diana Ross
26 Mar, Detroit

Jill Clayburgh
30 Apr, New York

MARRIAGES

Charlton Heston
17 Mar, *to* Lydia Marie Clarke

ACADEMY AWARDS

PRESENTED ON 2 MARCH 1944

Best Picture
Casablanca

Best Director
Michael Curtiz
Casablanca

Best Actor
Paul Lukas
Watch on the Rhine

Best Actress
Jennifer Jones
The Song of Bernadette

Best Sup Actor
Charles Coburn
The More the Merrier

Best Sup Actress
Katina Paxinou
For Whom the Bell Tolls

Bing Crosby as an amiable young Catholic priest in Going My Way.

HOLLYWOOD GETS RELIGION

Hard on the heels of *The Song of Bernadette* has come a spate of films striking a religious note.

In Paramount's *Going My Way*, directed by Leo McCarey, Bing Crosby stars as the amiable young Catholic priest Father Chuck O'Malley who is despatched to bail out bankrupt St Dominic's Church, which is run on distinctly old-fashioned lines by Barry Fitzgerald's crusty, aging Father Fitzgibbon.

As Bing is the perfect embodiment of all-singing, all-dancing Christianity, it takes him only a little over two hours to haul St Dominic's out of debt, charm the local teenage toughs into forming a choir, persuade diva Rise Stevens to sing one of his songs at the Met, save Jean Heather from the streets by marrying her off to James Brown, teach Barry Fitzgerald how to play golf and then reunite him with his incredibly ancient Irish mother. All this without breaking sweat. *Going My Way* looks well placed to garner a rich haul of Oscars.

George Sanders, with police help, corners Laird Cregar in The Lodger.

LONDON BY NIGHT

A dead prostitute's hand trails in a water-filled gutter. Fog-shrouded streets echo to the clatter of mounted police and are fitfully penetrated by flashing torches. Jack the Ripper is going about his grim work in old London Town.

This time he's played by the menacingly bulky Laird Cregar in 20th Century-Fox's *The Lodger*, directed by German-born John Brahm, who arrived in Hollywood in 1937. In Cregar's hands the Ripper is a fat, moist-eyed, Bible-quoting doctor with a pathological hatred of women who goes down to the Thames at night to bathe his blood-soaked hands.

Brahm's direction and Lucien Ballard's photography suggest rather than reveal the horrors the Ripper commits. And the soundtrack is filled with Cregar's heavy panting and his victims' last desperate cries.

MURDER PACT

Director Billy Wilder knew he had a good film on his hands – an adaptation of hardboiled writer James M. Cain's *Double Indemnity* – when it was turned down by George Raft, one of the worst judges of a script in Hollywood.

Instead, Wilder secured easy-going Fred MacMurray, exactly the kind of actor he wanted to play the idly philandering insurance salesman drawn by surburban Medusa Barbara Stanwyck into a plot to dispose of her husband in a "perfect murder" and then collect on his life policy.

Stanwyck, too, was reluctant to play an "out-and-out cold-blooded killer" kitted out with a blonde wig because Wilder wanted to make her look "as sleazy as possible". Paramount boss Buddy De Sylva took one look at Barbara and blurted: "We've hired Stanwyck and we get George Washington."

But there's no one more professional than Stanwyck, and she gives a superb performance as the icy murderess. Wilder's direction and screenplay (written over a stormy six months with a grouchy Raymond Chandler) brilliantly builds up the tension as the murderers' nemesis – insurance investigator Edward G. Robinson – closes in on them.

SINGING FOR UNCLE SAM

Sam Goldwyn's newest screen star is 30-year-old Danny Kaye, a graduate of the "Bortsch Belt" and Broadway, whose hyper-energetic style and machine-gun delivery of "patter songs" is on show in *Up in Arms*.

Kaye plays a hypochondriac lift operator drafted into the army and despatched to the Pacific with hilarious results. The outstanding musical number is a frantic burlesque of the movies set in the lobby of Radio City Music Hall, "Manic Depressive Pictures Presents". Kaye also sings a jive duet with Dinah Shore and completes the film off by rounding up job-lots of Japanese in a Mack-Sennett-inspired finale. Adding lashings of leggy charm are the Goldwyn Girls. When one recruit spies them romping on the deck of his troopship, he claims, "We didn't have anything like that in World War I". To which his buddy replies, "We don't have anything like that in this war either!"

GOSSIP COLUMN

■ Movie stars' mothers are a potent factor in Hollywood and Sarah Southern, mother of child star Elizabeth Taylor, is no exception. She's always there behind the camera (and the director), communicating with her small daughter by means of a complicated set of hand signals.

THE FORCES' FAVOURITE

She's the leggy blonde in the war's most popular pin-up, poured into a creamy white bathing costume and looking coyly back over her shoulder from the inside of a million servicemen's lockers. She's the girl with the "million-dollar legs" insured by Lloyd's of London. She's Betty Grable, 28, the butter blonde from St Louis, who was rescued from the "B" movie treadmill by 20th Century-Fox, wrapped in a Technicolor package and mailed to the troops at the front.

She admits she can act "just enough to get by", and predictably she's the cheerful centrepiece of *Pin Up Girl*, as a Washington stenographer who pretends to be a Broadway star. The critics have given the movie the thumbs down but at present Grable has other things on her mind. By the time she filmed the picture's military-parade finale, she was seven months pregnant (she is married to bandleader Harry James).

MUG SHOTS

"This mug of mine is as plain as a barn door. Why should poor people want to pay 35 cents to look at it?" asks Spencer Tracy. He's an unlikely star but one of the biggest. After his success in *The Seventh Cross*, M-G-M has dubbed him "the perfect actor".

Born in Milwaukee in 1900, he nursed ambitions to become a priest but, after service in the navy in the First World War and spells at the Northwestern Military Academy and Ripon College, he enrolled at New York's Academy of Dramatic Art.

He was already 30 when he went to Hollywood, encouraged by director John Ford, who cast him in a prison drama, *Up the River* (1930), alongside another newcomer, Humphrey Bogart. Says Ford: "Spence was as natural as if he didn't know a camera was there, or as if there had *always* been a camera when he had acted before."

In four restless years with Fox, he rapidly gained a reputation for irascibility and heavy drinking. His best work was done on loan-out – like Warners' *20,000 Years in Sing Sing* (1932) and Columbia's *A Man's Castle* (1933). Then he moved to M-G-M.

At first the studio was as flummoxed as Fox about what to do with such a difficult talent. The breakthrough came as the innocent man facing a lynching in Fritz Lang's *Fury* (1936) – a rugged, decent American brought up in the school of hard knocks, who has kept his pride and emotions in check.

Tracy soon shot to the top. At M-G-M he chose his roles carefully and paced his appearances, winning consecutive Oscars for *Captains Courageous* (1937) and *Boys Town* (1938). He made his first appearance in the Box Office Top Ten in 1940, fast outstripping Gable, with whom he sparred energetically in *Boom Town* that year. Two years later, in the comedy *Woman of the Year*, he was teamed for the first time with Katharine Hepburn, a remarkable partnership that's very different from her earlier duos with suave Cary Grant.

Spencer Tracy as a "good German" fleeing a Nazi camp in The Seventh Cross.

GOOD AND BAD GERMANS

Hollywood has not been very subtle so far in its depiction of the enemy. The Japanese are usually shown as sadistic, grinning monkeys, and Germans bullet-headed and brainless or thin-lipped and sadistic.

The balance is partially redressed in M-G-M's *The Seventh Cross*, with Spencer Tracy as a fugitive from a Nazi concentration camp. It dares to suggest there are "good Germans" as well as bad and firmly addresses the treatment of the Jews, a subject which was handled like a hot potato in the early 1940s. Tracy gives a gritty performance, a haunted figure moving through a world which looks much more German than the standard Hollywood Ruritanian landscape.

STARS IN BATTLEDRESS

The troops in the front line don't have to depend on the silver screen for distraction. They can expect a personal appearance by one of their favourite stars under the auspices of the United States Entertainments Organization (USO).

On 21 June Marlene Dietrich perched on a table at USO Camp Show headquarters in New York and told the press of her five-week tour entertaining troops in North Africa and Italy. Hers was the first show to play on the Anzio beachhead, and among many highlights she singled out the moment in Italy when she told GIs that the D-Day landings had begun: "I was getting ready for a show when an officer told me that the Normandy coast had been invaded. I was still in my travelling uniform, but I dashed out on the stage and made the announcement. There was a vast audience out in the open. It was their first news of the invasion. . . . They went wild – but not over me!"

Other tireless entertainers have included Al Jolson, who was among the first to answer USO's call; Joe E. Brown, who's travelled thousands of miles through the jungles of the Pacific theatre to provide shows for audiences in their thousands and sometimes just an isolated platoon; and Bing Crosby and Bob Hope.

BIRTHS, DEATHS AND MARRIAGES

BIRTHS

Geraldine Chaplin
3 Jul, Santa Monica, California

Peter Weir
21 Aug, Sydney, Australia

DEATHS

Mildred Harris
20 Jul, Los Angeles
Pneumonia following surgery

MARRIAGES

Craig Stevens
8 Jun, *to* Alexis Smith

Susan Hayward
23 Jul, *to* Jess Barker

Claudette Colbert, Jennifer Jones and Shirley Temple on the US "home front" in Since You Went Away.

FORTRESS AMERICA

David O. Selznick is never a man to employ understatement when full-blown hyperbole will do. So the publicity slogan for *Since You Went Away* claims that these are "The Four Most Important Words Since *Gone with the Wind*". Selznick's greatest triumph looks like becoming an albatross around his neck.

In *Since You Went Away*, he turns to "the story of that unconquerable fortress – the American Home Front, 1943". Written by Selznick himself and directed with smooth skill by John Cromwell, the movie is a masterpiece of lush sentimentality, starring Claudette Colbert as a fashion plate Mrs. Average America steering her family (Jennifer Jones and a Shirley Temple moving into anonymous adolescence) through the heartaches of war while Mr. Average America is away at the front. This is the war in glowing soft focus; but like its "English" counterpart *Mrs. Miniver* (1942), *Since You Went Away* looks set to be a huge hit.

WILSON OR BUST

20th Century-Fox's production chief Darryl F. Zanuck overreached himself in pouring over $5 million into a "thinking man's blockbuster". *Wilson* is a long, laboured biopic of Woodrow Wilson, the president who reluctantly took the United States into the First World War and then helped set up the League of Nations.

And there it seems to have stayed for *Wilson*. So confident of its success is Zanuck that he vowed that if it flopped he would never make another film without Betty Grable. But it has – to the tune of $2 million.

MAKING A SPLASH

Adolf Hitler robbed swimming star Esther Williams of what might have been a triumphant progress through the 1940 Olympics. But M-G-M stepped into the breach, signing the shapely 18-year-old Angelino five years ago, when she was appearing in Billy Rose's San Francisco Aquacade.

Like starlets Lana Turner, Judy Garland and Katharine Grayson, she was eased gently into the limelight via the Andy Hardy series – in her case, *Andy Hardy's Double Life* (1942). Following a small part in *A Guy Named Joe* (1943), M-G-M has launched her in her first starring vehicle, *Bathing Beauty*. Originally planned as a medium-budget vehicle for comedian Red Skelton, it was revamped to showcase Williams in glowing Technicolor.

STAR QUOTES

Betty Grable

"I've got two reasons for success, and I'm standing on both of them."

A HANDSOME NEWCOMER

Hollywood's love affair with the Soviet Union has continued in RKO's *Days of Glory*, the first film of 28-year-old stage actor Gregory Peck. He plays a Russian partisan leader in love with ballerina Tamara Toumanova, wife of the movie's writer-producer Casey Robinson. Heading a cast of unknowns, Peck and Toumanova make a handsome couple, enthusiastically lobbing grenades at German tanks.

The picture has flopped at the box office but the young Californian's sincere, chiselled good looks have been attracting the interest of the major studios. They're eager to plug the gaps created by established stars serving with the forces. 20th Century-Fox has snapped up Peck at $750 a week and cast him as the high-minded missionary-priest hero of *The Keys of the Kingdom*. Adapted from the novel by A.J. Cronin, the movie should be out by Christmas.

Tamara Toumanova and Gregory Peck as Russian partisans in Days of Glory.

Lauren Bacall and Humphrey Bogart in Howard Hawk's To Have and to Have Not.

THE LOOK OF LOVE

During pre-production of Warners' version of Ernest Hemingway's *To Have and Have Not*, Nelson Rockefeller's American Affairs Committee insisted the studio changed the story from Chinese immigrants being smuggled into the United States from Cuba to Free French resistance fighters being smuggled into Vichy-controlled Martinique.

Having sorted out the propaganda angles, producer-director Howard Hawks turned his attention to finding a co-star for Humphrey Bogart, who's cynical gun-runner Harry Morgan, first cousin to Rick Blaine in *Casablanca* (1942).

Hawks didn't have to go far. Last autumn his wife spotted 18-year-old model Betty Perske on the cover of *Harper's Bazaar* and within a month she was signed to a seven-year contract.

Now re-named Lauren Bacall, she makes a sensational debut as the independent drifter Slim (named after Mrs. Hawks), languidly propositioning Bogie for a match and teaching him how to whistle - "You just put your lips together and blow." Her cool, husky sexiness – dubbed "The Look" by Warners – is the mirror image of Bogart's sardonic masculinity.

When their on-screen affair turned into off-screen love, Hawks and screenwriter Jules Furthman rewrote whole sequences to give a relaxed, intimate banter to the actors' crackling rapport.

BAD BRUNETTE

Since her change from blonde to brunette in *Trade Winds* (1938) Joan Bennett has developed into a purveyor of sultry sexuality which makes some of her love goddess rivals look distinctly anaemic.

In RKO's *The Woman in the Window*, it's her portrait in a gallery window which draws ineffectual family man Edward G. Robinson into a deadly foursome with Bennett, the body of her keeper (accidentally killed by Robinson) and slyly villainous Dan Duryea. Director Fritz Lang is less concerned with the improbable plot than with the sight of Robinson disintegrating like a battered old Teddy Bear in Bennett's hands.

Joan Bennett and Edward G. Robinson in The Woman in the Window.

BIRTHS, DEATHS AND MARRIAGES

BIRTHS

Jacqueline Bisset
13 Sep, Weybridge, Surrey

Michael Douglas
25 Sep, New Brunswick, New Jersey

Chevy Chase
8 Oct, New York

Tom Conti
22 Oct, Glasgow

Danny DeVito
17 Nov, Asbury Park, New Jersey

DEATHS

Laird Cregar
14 Dec, Beverly Hills
Heart attack

Lupe Velez
14 Dec, Beverly Hills
Suicide

Harry Langdon
22 Dec, Los Angeles
Stroke

MARRIAGES

Mickey Rooney
30 Sep, *to* Betty Jane Rase

Ricardo Montalban
26 Oct, *to* Georgiana Foster

Paulette Goddard
30 Oct, *to* **Burgess Meredith**

Veronica Lake
16 Dec, *to* Andre de Toth

ADIOS, LUPE; SO LONG, HARRY

Fiery Lupe Velez, temperamental star of RKO's *Mexican Spitfire* series, whose marriage to Johnny Weissmuller in the 1930s was one long public brawl, died of an overdose of sleeping tablets at her Beverly Hills home on 14 December. She was 36.

The series sputtered to a close last year with *Mexican Spitfire's Blessed Event*. Abandoned by lover Harald Ramond, pregnant, and saddled with huge debts, the Catholic star who first raised eyebrows with her wild mountain girl in Douglas Fairbanks' *The Gaucho* (1927) decided to end it all, swallowing an entire bottle of Seconal.

Fewer column inches have been devoted to silent comedy star Harry Langdon, who died on 22 December, aged 60. From the late 1920s, the whey-faced star who had briefly rivalled Chaplin and Keaton in films like *Tramp, Tramp, Tramp* and *The Strong Man* (both 1926) had slid into bankruptcy and ever-deeper obscurity. His last film role was a bit part in a Republic "B", *Swingin' on a Rainbow*.

Laurence Olivier as King Harry in his own production of William Shakespeare's Henry V.

CRY GOD FOR LARRY

Laurence Olivier fought his own war with the making of *Henry V*, winning a cinematic victory which confirms the renaissance of British cinema during these war years.

When William Wyler and Carol Reed turned down the project, Olivier took the helm himself. The result is a stirring screen version of Shakespeare, boldly combining stylized and naturalistic sequences in one of the first British films in Technicolor.

Henry V reaches a thrilling climax with the ten-minute Battle of Agincourt sequence, which took six weeks to film in County Wicklow, Ireland. This was a gruelling assignment for Olivier, who did all his own stunt work and was often quite literally in the firing line: "At one point I was walking around with a crutch under my right arm, my left in a sling and a plaster bandage right round my face." The last was the result of narrowly avoiding a toppling Technicolor camera, at the time the only one in Britain.

The movie cost £475,000, a record for a British film, and was completed only with the help of film magnate J. Arthur Rank, who baled out the original production company, Filippo Del Giudice's Two Cities. It opened to unanimous critical praise in London in November, at the height of Hitler's V-2 rocket campaign against the city.

BOX OFFICE

UK

1 For Whom the Bell Tolls
2 This Happy Breed
3 The Song of Bernadette
4 Going My Way
5 This Is the Army
6 Jane Eyre
7 The Story of Dr. Wassell
8 Cover Girl
9 The White Cliffs of Dover
10 Sweet Rosie O'Grady

BOX OFFICE

US

1 Going My Way
2 The Song of Bernadette
3 Thirty Seconds over Tokyo
4 Hollywood Canteen

OTHER BOX OFFICE SUCCESSES

Cover Girl
A Guy Named Joe
Lady in the Dark
Madame Curie
The Miracle of Morgan's Creek
Thousands Cheer

M-G-M MAGIC

The M-G-M musical machine has created pure magic with Vincente Minnelli's *Meet Me in St.Louis*, the talented director's first assignment in Technicolor.

Based on Sally Benson's *New Yorker* reminiscences of turn-of-the-century St. Louis, the movie follows the life of the Smith family through the four seasons of 1903 as the city prepares to host the World's Fair and father threatens to shatter their provincial happiness by taking a job in New York.

But beneath the movie's loving recreation of a fondly remembered recent past there is a hard edge. Margaret O'Brien, playing the youngest child, Tootie, dances an enchanting front-parlour cakewalk but also finds herself shuddering with fear at the end of a Halloween prank. She is comforted by her big sister - Judy Garland, who's captivating as Esther Smith, mooning over callow Tom Drake in "The Boy Next Door" and stopping the show with "The Trolley Song".

Judy Garland in Vincente Minnelli's Meet Me in St. Louis.

Gene Tierney as Laura.

EVERY PICTURE TELLS A STORY

In *The Woman in the Window* Edward G. Robinson was bewitched by a painting of Joan Bennett. In 20th Century-Fox's *Laura*, directed by Otto Preminger, a portrait of Gene Tierney casts an equally powerful spell over detective Dana Andrews.

The lovely 24-year-old Fox star, with the heart-shaped face and hooded eyes, was born to a wealthy insurance broker in a select part of Brooklyn. She's steadily climbed the ladder since her debut in *The Return of Frank James* (1940).

In *Laura* she's the mysterious career girl whose life-size portrait gazes ominously down on Dana Andrews, who is investigating her murder. Then, halfway through the picture, she suddenly walks through the door.

GOSSIP COLUMN

■ It's been a vintage year for fist-fights between members of the movie colony. One of the best was beween Errol Flynn and John Huston, who slugged it out for nearly an hour in David O. Selznick's garden after disagreeing about war service. Flynn broke Huston's, but the feisty director, who boxed professionally in his youth, broke two of Flynn's ribs.

AN ENGLISH ROSE

Making her mark in M-G-M's *National Velvet* is 12-year-old Elizabeth Taylor, a beguiling juvenile with a pale face, big eyes and a soft voice.

Born in London in 1932, she was evacuated to California at the beginning of the war with her parents, art dealer Francis Taylor and actress Sara Southern. According to columnist Hedda Hopper, a family friend who held a big block of shares at Universal got Elizabeth a small part in a "B" picture, *There's One Born Every Minute* (1942). She then became an M-G-M baby, attending the Little Red House School with Mickey Rooney and Judy Garland, looking cute in *Lassie Come Home* (1943) and last year playing a girl dying of pneumonia in *Jane Eyre* and a pert country lass with a crush on Roddy McDowall in *The White Cliffs of Dover*.

National Velvet is from Edith Bagnold's novel about a girl, Velvet Brown, who is determined to own and train horses. Elizabeth got the part only after a crash weight- and height-gaining course, during which she shot up 3 inches in three months.

ACADEMY AWARDS

PRESENTED ON 15 MARCH 1945

Best Picture
Going My Way

Best Director
Leo McCarey
Going My Way

Best Actor
Bing Crosby
Going My Way

Best Actress
Ingrid Bergman
Gaslight

Best Sup Actor
Barry Fitzgerald
Going My Way

Best Sup Actress
Ethel Barrymore
None But the Lonely Heart

BIRTHS, DEATHS AND MARRIAGES

BIRTHS

Tom Selleck
29 Jan, Detroit

Mia Farrow
9 Feb, Los Angeles

DEATHS

Mark Sandrich
5 Mar, Hollywood
Heart attack

MARRIAGES

Esther Williams
29 Jan, *to* Benjamin Gage

Gloria Swanson
29 Jan, *to* William N. Davey

Mario Lanza
13 Apr, *to* Betty Hicks

Dick Powell as Raymond Chandler's hard-boiled private eye Philip Marlowe in Murder, My Sweet.

WARBLER TURNS GUMSHOE

Hoofer Dick Powell, previously best known for his musical partnership at Warners with Ruby Keeler, exchanges evening dress for a trenchcoat and a dramatic change of image. He's Raymond Chandler's world-weary shamus Philip Marlowe in RKO's *Murder, My Sweet*, directed by Edward Dmytryk and adapted from Chandler's 1940 mystery *Farewell, My Lovely*.

In the past, screen gumshoes have tended to be suave dilletantes – Philo Vance, The Saint and The Falcon – who in the smooth person of George Sanders negotiated a modified version of *Farewell, My Lovely* called *The Falcon Takes Over* (1942). But Powell is the genuine article, hardboiled and wisecracking, walking down LA's meaner streets for "$25 a day and expenses".

Powell's Marlowe has to contend with a deck stacked with Hollywood low-life: drink-sodden Esther Howard, double-crossing vamp Claire Trevor, Mike Mazurki as giant Moose Malloy, and Otto Kruger as a high-class blackmailer.

THE KING'S COMEBACK

"Gable's Back, and Garson's Got Him!" shriek the posters for *Adventure*, the King of Hollywood's comeback movie. It's prompted one unkind pressman to quip: "And they deserve each other."

But Gable's long-awaited return to the screen after leaving the air force in 1944 is a damp squib. Some of the old magic seems to have flaked off, and he is not well served by a dim romance – a property which, incredibly, had originally been acquired for Freddie Bartholomew – in which prim librarian Greer Garson turns hard-boiled sailor Gable into a family man. The sickly ending, complete with babe-in-arms, was added on the insistence of M-G-M boss Louis B. Mayer.

Shortly after the preview, Gable told the press: "It's lousy. I could tell because I had to work so hard. A picture that is going to turn out well is easy to do. It just seems to flow along by itself." The King has immediately entered a second, self-imposed exile from filmmaking.

Dorothy McGuire and Peggy Ann Garner in A Tree Grows in Brooklyn.

A NEW TALENT EMERGES

A new talent has come to the fore in Hollywood: Elia Kazan, a Turkish immigrant of Armenian descent and graduate of New York's Group Theater. Though he's only in his mid-30s, Kazan already has such a formidable reputation that 20th Century-Fox has offered him a contract which stipulates only occasional films.

The first is *A Tree Grows in Brooklyn*, adapted from Betty Smith's novel of life in a working-class district of Brooklyn at the turn of the century. Although some studio gloss still clings to the production, Kazan avoids sentimentality and gets excellent performances from all the principals. James Dunn, who has long chafed at his "B" movie status, is moving as the family's feckless, alcoholic father; his death is made all the more heart-wrenching by the restraint of young Peggy Ann Garner as his daughter, of whom Kazan says, "She's not pretty at all, or cute or picturesque – only true."

Dorothy McGuire struggles a little as the family's Irish Catholic mother, but there's strong support from Joan Blondell, Lloyd Nolan and James Gleason.

A SONG TO FORGET?

Columbia has pulled out all the stops on *A Song to Remember*, ostensibly a biopic of Frederic Chopin, with muscular Cornel Wilde as the tubercular Pole. Glacial Merle Oberon is his girlfriend George Sand, who puffs a cigar under a top hat and tells him, "You could make miracles of music in Majorca."

Miracles of over-acting are provided by Paul Muni as Chopin's professor, buried beneath a small forest of whiskers and unwisely attempting an impression of S.Z. "Cuddles" Sakall.

Sidney Buchman's script and Charles Vidor's unrestrained direction shoot the movie into the stratosphere of absurdity, with the music of the real Chopin confined to short bursts and dubbed by keyboard wizard Jose Iturbi. To judge by audience response so far, a lot of moviegoers seem to think this is "class".

Merle Oberon and Cornel Wilde in A Song to Remember.

"KING OF THE COWBOYS"

Admiring his slim outline, a Beverly Hills hostess once observed that Roy Rogers has "the purtiest backside in Hollywood". The boyish 32-year-old singing cowboy looks as if he has been poured into his skintight pants, and rides the range in shirts embroidered with roses. But he's the epitome of clean-cut wholesomeness, right down to his hand-tooled boots.

Rogers made his screen debut in 1935 as a member of the Sons of the Pioneers singing group in *The Old Homestead*. His first film as Roy Rogers, *Under Western Stars*, followed three years later.

Until 1942 Republic's No. 1 western star was poker-faced Gene Autry, but his years of military service have enabled Rogers to slip into the top spot. He's now firmly established as "The King of the Cowboys".

Roy's regular partners include his wonder horse Trigger and faithful dog Bullet.

STAR QUOTES

Errol Flynn

"I can't understand why a quiet, reserved fellow like me should be involved in the news so much."

GOSSIP COLUMN

■ **While filming *The Spanish Main*, Maureen O'Hara revealed her secret for foiling the censors. After submitting herself to a cleavage check before filming a scene, she would pull down her waistband and then take a deep breath until her breasts almost jumped out of her peasant blouse.**

Errol Flynn leads a troop of American parachutists against the Japanese in Objective Burma.

A GRAVE MISTAKE

Warners' *Objective Burma* directed by Raoul Walsh and starring Errol Flynn, has landed the dashing star in hot water.

Flynn plays the leader of a band of 50 US paratroopers trapped behind Japanese lines in the Burmese jungle. A stab at gritty realism? In fact, much of the movie was made on a Santa Anita ranch.

It's also enraging British cinemagoers, who complain the picture gives the impression that the war in Burma – where there are very few American personnel – is being won singlehandedly by Flynn. London's *Daily Mirror* newspaper has published a cartoon showing Flynn in battledress seated in a director's chair while a ghostly British soldier whispers over his shoulder: "Excuse me, Mr. Flynn, you're sitting on some graves."

The star can't understand what all the fuss is about – it's only a movie. Says Flynn: "Why blame the actor? He doesn't produce the picture or write the screenplay."

THE BOTTOM OF THE BOTTLE

Ray Milland plays acoholic writer Don Birnam in The Lost Weekend.

For years Ray Milland was the suavely smiling escort to a succession of Paramount leading ladies – nonchalant, immaculately tailored, never less than the model squire, but unlikely to set the screen alight.

Along the way there have been hints of a wider range – his amused performance opposite Ginger Rogers in Billy Wilder's first film, *The Major and the Minor* (1942); and in Fritz Lang's *The Ministry of Fear* (1944), as a man freed from an insane asylum and plunged into wartime intrigue.

Impressed by his first collaboration, Wilder chose him to play the alcoholic writer Don Birnam in *The Lost Weekend*, from Charles Jackson's novel.

Milland gives a memorably bleak performance, revealing all the flaws in his deceptive attractiveness: cadging drinks off long-suffering barman Howard Da Silva; trudging through dusty, drab New York streets, trying to hock his typewriter; resorting to ever more frantic ploys to hide his liquor from fiancee Jane Wyman; and menaced by bats while in the hallucinatory grip of DTs.

BIRTHS, DEATHS AND MARRIAGES

BIRTHS

Steve Martin
1 Aug, Waco, Texas

Nigel Terry
Aug, Bristol

DEATHS

Alla Nazimova
12 Jul, Los Angeles
Coronary thrombosis

MARRIAGES

Humphrey Bogart
21 May, *to* **Lauren Bacall**

Judy Garland
15 Jun, *to* **Vincente Minnelli**

Dick Powell
19 Aug, *to* **June Allyson**

Gloria Grahame
29 Aug, *to* Stanley Clements

TRIBUTE TO GERSHWIN

Music speaks louder than words in Warners' *Rhapsody in Blue*, a largely fictional biopic of George Gershwin, played by vaudeville entertainer Robert Alda in his screen debut.

Crammed with every showbiz cliche in the book, and then some more (right down to the one about it being lonely at the top), the movie is salvaged by the maestro's music.

Ferde Grofe, who worked with Gershwin, arranged "Rhapsody in Blue", which is performed by Paul Whiteman as it was first heard by audiences in Universal's early Technicolor production *King of Jazz* (1930). Al Jolson appears as himself to be thanked for singing "Swanee", and the original Bess (Anne Brown) sings "Summertime", although this was not one of her songs in the musical. Oscar Levant, pianist, hypochondriac, self-declared genius and close associate of Gershwin, provides some mordant comic relief.

V FOR VICTORY

The distant honking of auto horns in Los Angeles on 15 August was the first sign that the war against Japan was over.

But war subjects still play an important part in Hollywood movie-making. Quick to cash in on the Hiroshima bombing is RKO which simply added a couple of scenes after the completion of principal photography on *The First Yank into Tokyo* and claimed the honour of releasing the first movie to incorporate the A-bomb into its storyline. It's a typically ramshackle B-movie, with low-budget stalwart Tom Neal as an American agent who undergoes plastic surgery before being smuggled into Japan to rescue a captured weapons expert. Only in the rough and tumble world of the B-units can such deft last-minute surgery be contemplated.

KELLY AND JERRY

In M-G-M's *Anchors Aweigh* rising stars Gene Kelly and Frank Sinatra are teamed as a couple of navy buddies who spend an energetic shore leave in Hollywood helping would-be singer Kathryn Grayson to stardom.

It's a perfect pairing – the former brash and bouncy, the latter projecting a scrawny soulfulness which has won him millions of bobby-soxer fans across America. Sinatra is now making the transition from crooner to fully fledged movie star which began in RKO's *Higher and Higher* (1943); Kelly is changing from hoofer to dancer, a process accelerated by his success in Columbia's *Cover Girl* (1944), in which he danced magically with his own mirror image.

For *Anchors Aweigh*, Kelly devised his own routines. The most technically demanding combines live action and cartoon as he teaches a recalcitrant mouse – "Jerry" from Tom and Jerry – how to dance "The Worry Song". No worries for M-G-M, who look set to clean up with this lively piece of wartime escapism.

THE MEN OF COMPANY C

General Dwight D. Eisenhower has hailed United Artists' *The Story of GI Joe* as "the greatest war picture I've seen". Based on the exploits of the distinguished war correspondent Ernie Pyle, played in the film by Burgess Meredith, it shows the war from the point of view of the foot soldier – the men of Company C – slogging through North Africa and then up the road to Rome.

At the end of the film there is a desperate assault on a German-held monastery. As the survivors from Company C slump exhausted by the road they have cleared to Rome, the body of their captain (Robert Mitchum) is brought down from the hilltop by mule to be buried in a field of neat white crosses.

Pyle died shortly after the release of the movie but it remains a testimony to his own first-hand view of a war in which "the GI lives so miserably and dies so miserably".

Journalists discuss war strategy over a game of cards in The Story of GI Joe.

HEALING THE SCARS OF WAR

From the attack on Pearl Harbor to V-J Day this August, Warners has been *the* war propaganda studio. Its output topped its rivals' in quantity and quality. In 1943 alone Warners' war-related pictures included *Air Force*, *Mission to Moscow*, *Action in the North Atlantic*, *Watch on the Rhine*, *This Is the Army* and *Destination Tokyo*.

Now Warners has tackled the pertinent theme of post-war readjustment in *Pride of the Marines*, based on the true story of Al Schmid and starring John Garfield as a young Marine blinded at Guadalcanal and now facing a harrowing new battle back in the United States. This is a brave film, but the studio is hedging its bets with posters showing Garfield and co-stars Eleanor Parker and Dane Clark grinning broadly and walking arm-in-arm in best musical comedy fashion. It's the kind of publicity guaranteed to undercut *Pride of the Marine*'s semi-documentary shot at social comment.

Anthony Caruso, Dane Clark and John Garfield face the enemy in Pride of the Marines.

SEPTEMBER
OCTOBER

1945

NOVEMBER
DECEMBER

HITCHCOCK MEETS DALI

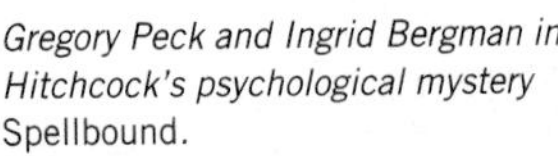
Gregory Peck and Ingrid Bergman in Hitchcock's psychological mystery Spellbound.

FREED HAS A FLOP

M-G-M producer Arthur Freed, one of the most influential figures in the development of the film musical, has had his first flop with *Yolanda and the Thief*, directed by Vincente Minnelli.

Over $1.5 million has gone straight down the plughole in Freed's ambitious attempt to push back the boundaries of the musical. Fred Astaire – recently signed by M-G-M – stars in the whimsical fairy tale of a conman romancing gullible heiress Lucille Bremer. But moviegoers are refusing to be conned.

Astaire is beginning to show his age. And although the sets are a dream, the project has turned into a nightmare for the studio and star.

Fred Astaire and Lucille Bremer.

Sam Goldwyn once said: "Anyone who sees a psychiatrist needs his head examined." But psychoanalysis is all the rage in Hollywood. Last year it even formed the basis of a musical, *Lady in the Dark*, with Ginger Rogers as a chic career woman who undergoes analysis to sort out her tangled love life, her dreams transformed into the movie's big set-pieces. Now here comes producer David Selznick's couch movie *Spellbound*, directed by Alfred Hitchcock.

Gregory Peck plays the new head of a psychiatric hospital who is suspected of being an imposter and possibly a murderer. He is also tortured by a strange recurrent nightmare involving the colour white and parallel lines. His trauma is exposed and innocence established by Ingrid Bergman, severely spectacled and with her hair scraped back for the role of a fellow shrink.

Hitchcock brought in Spanish surrealist painter Salvador Dali to design the dream sequence which helps Bergman unravel the mystery. Cut from its planned length of 20 minutes, it still provides audiences with a succession of haunting images. Hitchcock added his own Freudian flourishes, not least when Bergman and Peck first kiss, which is followed by a shot of doors opening one after the other. There's also a striking use of colour for a single scene in which the murderer shoots himself.

The combination of Bergman and Peck, the latter on the threshold of major stardom, is making *Spellbound* a huge success. According to Selznick, "We could not keep the audience quiet from the moment Peck's name came on the screen until we had shushed the audience three or four times."

BOX OFFICE

UK

1. The Seventh Veil
2. They Were Sisters
3. I Live in Grosvenor Square
4. Perfect Strangers
5. Madonna of the Seven Moons
6. Waterloo Road
7. The Way to the Stars
8. I'll Be Your Sweetheart
9. Dead of Night
10. Waltz Time

BOX OFFICE

US

1. Leave Her to Heaven
2. Meet Me in St. Louis
3. Weekend at the Waldorf
4. Anchors Aweigh
5. The Road to Utopia
6. Thrill of a Romance
7. The Valley of Decision
8. The Dolly Sisters
9. State Fair

OTHER BOX OFFICE SUCCESS

Wonder Man

LOVE IN THE SUBURBS

Love in the suburbs has been an endlessly attractive theme for novelists, playwrights and film-makers. But seldom has it been approached with the sincerity of David Lean and Noel Coward's *Brief Encounter*.

Expanded from a one-act play written by Coward, the movie is the story of Laura Jessop (Celia Johnson), a provincial housewife who comes into the town of Milford once a week to change her library books and go to a cinema matinee. Trevor Howard is Alec Harvey, a doctor who comes every week on the same day to local hospital. He catches the 5.40 down, she catches the 5.43 up. A speck of grit in Laura's eye is the small incident which leads to the blossoming of a doomed love affair amid the Virol advertisements and steamy fug of the station buffet.

Some critics have been comparing *Brief Encounter* with French cinema. But it's utterly English in its portrayal of a discreetly tentative affair stifled by middle-class conventions.

BIRTHS, DEATHS AND MARRIAGES

BIRTHS

Henry Winkler
30 Oct, New York

Roland Joffe
Nov, London

Goldie Hawn
21 Nov, Washington, DC

Bette Midler
1 Dec, Honolulu

DEATHS

Robert Benchley
21 Nov, New York
Cerebral hemorrhage

MARRIAGES

Betty Hutton
2 Sep, *to* Ted Briskin

Shirley Temple
19 Sep, *to* John Agar

Angela Lansbury
27 Sep, *to* Richard Cromwell

Ava Gardner
17 Oct, *to* Artie Shaw

Deborah Kerr
27 Nov, *to* Anthony Bartley

Bette Davis
29 Nov, *to* William Grant

Eddie Albert
5 Dec, *to* Margo

Jeanne Crain
31 Dec, *to* Paul Brinkman

Celia Johnson and Trevor Howard, waiting for a train, are interrupted by garrulous Beverly Gregg in Brief Encounter.

CRAWFORD CONFOUNDS THE CRITICS

Joan Crawford left M-G-M in 1943, written off as "box-office poison". She told studio boss Louis B. Mayer that she "felt like I was yesterday's newspapers because I'd been at Metro so long. I needed a new start somewhere else."

Released from the last 16 months of her contract – M-G-M was not sorry to see her go – Crawford moved over to the Warners lot and bided her time. Apart from a brief appearance in *Hollywood Canteen* last year, she's stayed off the screen until now, making a comeback with *Mildred Pierce*. Crawford, naturally, plays Mildred – a relentless business-woman who suffers at the hands of rat-like lover Zachary Scott and daughter Ann Blyth.

GOSSIP COLUMN

■ Joan Crawford would drive a saint to homicidal thoughts with her behaviour on set. But it never takes much to excite peppery Hungarian director Michael Curtiz. While directing *Mildred Pierce* he grew so fed up with La Crawford's tantrums that he tore the shoulder pads off her dress.

LABOUR DISPUTES ROCK HOLLYWOOD

Renewed fears of Communist infiltration of Hollywood have been stirred up by a series of labour disputes at the major studios. The most serious originated in a quarrel over membership between two large union groupings, the left-wing-led, 10,000-strong Conference of Studio Unions (CSU) and the 16,000-strong International Alliance of Theatrical and Stage Employees (IATSE), which in the 1930s had been run by the Mafia.

Other unions were divided over which of the two rivals to support when the CSU began picketing the studios in March. In October this culminated in several days of rioting outside Warners' Burbank lot, with vicious skirmishing between pickets, police and IATSE members. Burbank police beat back the pickets and sprayed them with fire hoses while Jack Warner and his executives watched the battle from the studio roof.

At the end of October the National Labour Board found in favour of the CSU, but its leader Herbert Sorrell may have won a pyrrhic victory. The studios have suffered but the workers have lost a lot more – an estimated $15 million in wages. Now California's anti-left forces, relatively dormant throughout the war, are once again massing for a counter-attack.

UNSUNG HEROES

"In a war anything can be expendable – money or gasoline or equipment or, most usually, men." These words by a young naval lieutenant formed the basis of William L. White's best-selling novel of the early days of the war in the Pacific, *They Were Expendable*. It's now director John Ford's first film since leaving the U.S. Navy and his first for M-G-M since *Flesh* (1932). John Wayne stars. The "expendable" units are the PT-boat flotillas which in the opening weeks of the Pacific war were the only surface vessels available to fight a delaying action against the Japanese. Robert Montgomery, also returning from distinguished naval service, co-stars in a role closely modelled on Lieutenant John Buckley, who pioneered the use of the PT-boat in combat, and the spare screenplay is by Frank "Spig" Wead, a navy aviation hero of the interwar years who turned screenwriter after being crippled.

THE BIG KISS-OFF

Night in the city. The camera tracks down mean streets to rest on the neon light of a sleazy bar winking fitfully on a sidewalk slick with sin and sudden rain. A double-dealing *femme fatale*, emerges from the shadows gun in hand to give another sucker the big kiss-off. It's the territory of the *film noir* (literally "black film"), a term originally given by French critics to the anguished mood and sombre tone of a cycle of Hollywood movies which reached a climax in the late 1940s and early 1950s but which continues to influence filmmakers in the 1990s.

Harbingers of the full-blown *film noir* appeared at the beginning of the 1940s when Hollywood's discovery of psychoanalysis enabled writers and directors to give characters more shaded, complex motivations in landmark B-thrillers like *Stranger on the Third Floor* (1940) and *Among the Living* (1941) and bigger-budget productions like *I Wake Up Screaming* (1941), in which an infatuated psychopathic cop (sinister Laird Cregar) stalks Betty Grable.

More prosaic influences were also at work. Wartime restrictions on building materials led to the multiple use of cheaply constructed sets which were ideally shot in a low-key light. *When Strangers Marry* (1944), *He Walked by Night* (1948), *Gun Crazy* (1949) and *D.O.A.* (1949) – were B-movies conjured up on a shoestring and a prayer.

In *film noir* women spell trouble. The more glamorous the dame, the more certain that she is mad, bad (sometimes both) and dangerous to know: Mary Astor, wide-eyed and venomous in *The Maltese Falcon* (1941); Barbara Stanwyck's bangled Medusa in *Double Indemnity* (1944), ensnaring the lazily philandering Fred MacMurray in a murder plot; ruthless seductress Joan Bennett picking Edward G. Robinson apart in *The Woman in the Window* (1944).

The conventions and imagery of the *film noir* effortlessly crossed boundaries: into the western with *Pursued* (1947) and *Blood on the Moon* (1948), both infused with Robert Mitchum's brooding presence; into costume melodrama with *The Lodger* (1944) and *Hangover Square* (1945); even into the "women's picture", whose traditional ingredients were cunningly collided with the *film noir* by Michael Curtiz in *Mildred Pierce* (1945).

The *noir* cycle ran on strongly into the 1950s with films such as *In a Lonely Place* (1950), *Angel Face* (1953), *Pickup on South Street* (1953), *The Big Heat* (1954), and *Kiss Me Deadly* (1955). But by the time director Fritz Lang rounded off his Hollywood career with *While the City Sleeps* and *Beyond a Reasonable Doubt* (both 1956), the *noir* film was disappearing into the shadows whence it came.

Elements of the *noir* film can nevertheless be seen in many subsequent films: Orson Welles' *Touch of Evil* (1958), Don Siegel's *Baby Face Nelson* (1957), Peter Yates' *Bullitt* (1968), John Boorman's *Point Blank* (1967), Roman Polanski's *Chinatown* (1974) and Arthur Penn's *Night Moves* (1975). Dick Richards' *Farewell My Lovely* (1975) was an affectionate evocation of the 1940s in which Robert Mitchum finally got to play Marlowe 25 years too late.

In the 1980s writers and directors paid elaborate homage to *film noir*. *Body Heat* (1981) fanned the glowing embers of *Double Indemnity*, while in *Black Widow* (1987) Theresa Russell played a *femme fatale* every bit as deadly as Stanwyck. *Against All Odds* (1984) was a loose remake of *Out of the Past*. *Blood Simple* (1984) was a gory amorality tale in the best tradition of "poverty row"; and *Kill-off* (1990) from a 1957 Jim Thompson novel, caught the authentically rank flavour of doomed obsession and wasted lives.

Main picture: William Hurt and Kathleen Turner sizzle in Body Heat *(1981).*

Fred MacMurray and Barbara Stanwyck in Double Indemnity *(1944).*

Jack Nicholson as J.J. Gittes in Roman Polanski's Chinatown *(1974).*

Charlton Heston and Orson Welles in the sleazy Touch of Evil *(1958).*

Bogart, Peter Lorre, Mary Astor, Sydney Greenstreet in The Maltese Falcon *(1941).*

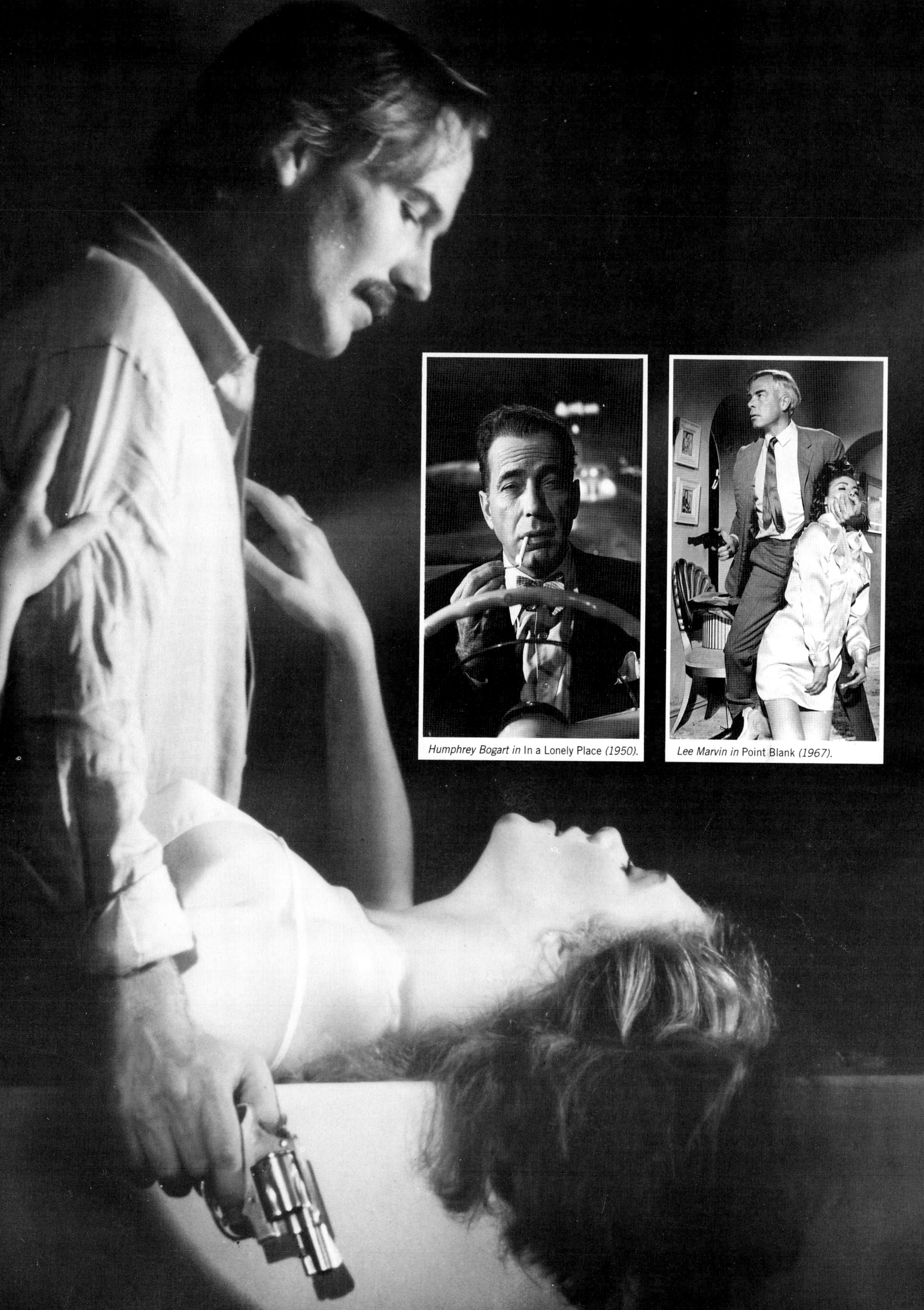

Humphrey Bogart in In a Lonely Place *(1950).*

Lee Marvin in Point Blank *(1967).*

John Garfield, Lana Turner, Cecil Kellaway in The Postman Always Rings Twice.

MURDER PACT

In M-G-M's *The Postman Always Rings Twice* Lana Turner has murder on her mind. Clad in burning white, she lets her lipstick roll slowly across the floor of a greasy diner to rest at the feet of doomed drifter John Garfield.

Twenty-five-year-old Turner couldn't be more voluptuous. No matter that she can't act – evidence of which has abounded in pictures like the all-star *Ziegfeld Girl* (1941) and *Somewhere I'll Find You* (1942), where she played a war correspondent. She simply radiates sexuality.

And like the broad she's playing in *Postman*, she's said to be man-hungry after divorcing second husband, Columbia contract actor Stephen Crane, in 1944. Who better for the role of the poisonous floozie plotting to kill her middle-aged husband? And who better to help her carry it out than handsome Garfield?

GOSSIP COLUMN

■ **Director Tay Garnett, who gave up drinking three years ago, went on a binge while making *The Postman Always Rings Twice* when location shooting was held up by bad weather. As the fog banks rolled in, Tay rolled off the wagon. Says the picture's star Lana Turner: "Nobody could control him. He was a roaring, mean, furniture-smashing drunk."**

HOLD THAT SWEATER

Legend has it that, as a sexy 16-year-old, Lana Turner was spotted sitting on a stool at Schwab's drugstore by Billy Wilkerson, publisher of *The Hollywood Reporter*. She signed with the Zeppo Marx agency and was first seen in a small part in Warners' *They Won't Forget* (1937). Director Mervyn LeRoy signed her to a personal contract and took her with him to M-G-M.

The studio was looking for a new Harlow, but Turner's slow-burning carnality was light years from Harlow's explosive style. She idled through a number of minor films and married band leader Artie Shaw after co-starring with him in *Dancing Co-Ed* (1939). The partnership lasted only a matter of months.

When M-G-M began to push her as "The Sweater Girl", she began to seep into the public consciousness. But was there an actress of similar prominence to match the garment in question? The western *Honky Tonk* (1941) and war drama *Somewhere I'll Find You* (1942), both with Clark Gable, showed she was no Harlow. So M-G-M tried to revamp her as the successor to Joan Crawford, who had packed her bags and moved to Warners.

Turner's stormy private life has kept her in the headlines as much as her movies. And in *The Postman Always Rings Twice* image and actress have finally come together. Throughout the length and breadth of redneck America small-town waitresses are drinking in the movie and yearning to be just like peroxided Lana.

Lana Turner.

DIMPLE-CHIN'S DEBUT

Producer Hal Wallis' discovery Kirk Douglas makes his movie debut in Paramount's *The Strange Love of Martha Ivers*, directed by Lewis Milestone.

The son of Russian immigrants, Douglas, 29, gained some stage experience before and after his war service in the navy and was brought to Wallis' attention by Lauren Bacall.

Signed at $500 a week, he's cast in *Martha Ivers* as Barbara Stanwyck's weak, alcoholic husband. The movie's a wild and woolly melodrama in which Stanwyck plays a rich bitch with a homicidal past fast catching up with her. She takes a fatal shine to childhood sweetheart Van Heflin – a big mistake as Heflin is enamoured of nice, non-murdering Lizabeth Scott, who has just finished a five-year stretch in the slammer.

There was almost a major hitch in Douglas' debut. After seeing the first rushes, Paramount's front office was horrified by the huge dimple in his chin. At first executives tried to fill it with putty, but this proved as hopeless as M-G-M's efforts to pin back Clark Gable's ears. Protested Douglas: "What is this crap? For God sakes, I'm not a good-looking guy." The small crater in Kirk's chin looks like becoming something of a movie landmark.

Kirk Douglas.

DUMB SHOW

Robert Siodmak, master of the moody melodrama, has fashioned a gothic chiller with RKO's *The Spiral Staircase*. It's a property packaged for the studio by David O. Selznick.

Dorothy McGuire is the deaf-and-dumb damsel in distress, the companion-servant of bedridden Ethel Barrymore in the Old Dark House of Ethel Lina White's turn-of-the-century tale. She's all set to become the latest victim of a maniac whose obsession with perfect beauty leads him into the killing of disfigured women.

McGuire suspects that one of Barrymore's two weakling sons is the murderer but she locks up the wrong one (Gordon Oliver) leaving the maniac (suave George Brent) at large. Will she negotiate the spiral staircase between safety and danger? Will she recover her voice in time to summon help? The tension is wound up to screaming pitch in this small masterpiece of terror.

Dorothy McGuire and George Brent in The Spiral Staircase.

ACADEMY AWARDS

PRESENTED ON 7 MARCH 1946

Best Picture
The Lost Weekend

Best Director
Billy Wilder
The Lost Weekend

Best Actor
Ray Milland
The Lost Weekend

Best Actress
Joan Crawford
Mildred Pierce

Best Sup Actor
James Dunn
A Tree Grows in Brooklyn

Best Sup Actress
Anne Revere
National Velvet

BIRTHS, DEATHS AND MARRIAGES

BIRTHS

Diane Keaton
5 Jan, Santa Ana, California

David Lynch
20 Jan, Missoula, Missouri

Charlotte Rampling
5 Feb, London

Gregory Hines
14 Feb, New York

Liza Minnelli
12 Mar, Los Angeles

Timothy Dalton
21 Mar, Colwyn Bay, Wales

Hayley Mills
18 Apr, London

DEATHS

George Arliss
5 Feb, London
Bronchial ailment

Mae Busch
19 Apr, Woodland Hills, California

Lionel Atwill
22 Apr, Pacific Palisades, California
Pneumonia

MARRIAGES

John Wayne
Jan, *to* Esperanza Baur

Rita Hayworth as a casino-owner's wife meets old flame Glenn Ford in the sensuous Gilda.

PUT THE BLAME ON RITA

Posters for Columbia's *Gilda* proclaim "There Never Was a Woman Like Gilda!", prompting a British critic to observe "Blimey! There Never Was!"

As incarnated by Rita Hayworth, Gilda Mundsen represents the height of Hollywood eroticism. Sheathed in black, lustrous hair tumbling over one eye, and with glistening lips slightly parted, she taunts Glenn Ford to "Put the Blame on Mame" in husband George Macready's Buenos Aires casino.

Hayworth is no actress – and no singer, either (her singing voice is actually that of Anita Ellis). But she sails through "Put the Blame on Mame". Says director Charles Vidor: "She sauntered on to the stage holding her head high, in that magnificent way she does, stepping along like a sleek young tiger cub, and the whistles that sounded would have shamed a canary's convention. She enjoyed every second of it. Then she did that elaborate, difficult number in two takes."

THE "MAD DOCTOR" DIES

British-born character actor Lionel Atwill, a key figure in Universal's horror revival of the 1940s, died of pneumonia at his Pacific Palisades home on 22 April aged 61. One of the screen's most accomplished "mad doctors", he never rescued his career from the bizarre scandal which engulfed him in 1941.

During a sensational rape trial two women – a Cuban dress designer and a 16-year-old unmarried mother – recounted tales of an orgy they had attended at Atwill's home the previous December. After watching pornographic movies the guests were invited to strip and repeat the screen action on a tiger-skin rug while Viennese waltzes tinkled away on the piano. Atwill eventually pleaded guilty, and later to perjury.

The studios turned their back on him but Universal kept him working in their "B" factory. It was a sad end for the man who had conquered Broadway after arriving in the U.S. in 1915 and had later co-starred with Marlene Dietrich in *The Devil Is a Woman* (1935). As he told a reporter shortly before his death: "But for the courage and magnanimity of one particular studio, I guess I should have been a dead egg by now."

MAY
JUNE

JULY
AUGUST

DON'T ASK THE WRITERS!

Humphrey Bogart takes on the role of Marlowe in The Big Sleep, *another adaptation of a Chandler novel.*

Even screenwriters William Faulkner, Leigh Brackett and Jules Furthman couldn't make head or tail of the plot of Warners' *The Big Sleep*. It's another convoluted case for Raymond Chandler's cynical shamus, Philip Marlowe.

Chandler, who's under contract to Paramount, wasn't able to help. He agreed the book had more loose ends flapping around than a circus tent in a storm. But he liked the idea of Humphrey Bogart as Marlowe. As he told a friend: "Bogart can be tough without a gun."

And play merry hell with the women, too. There's insolent divorcee Lauren Bacall; her thumb-sucking, nymphomaniac sister Martha Vickers; and bookstore assistant Dorothy Malone, who lets down her hair, takes off her glasses and shuts up shop to entertain Bogart one thundery Los Angeles afternoon.

Director Howard Hawks has distilled the brilliant if tangled screenplay into pure essence of Chandler. It's a world in which the fleshpots of the rich and the sleazy streets of the underworld are equally dangerous. Says Hawks: "It's the first time I've made a picture and just decided that I wasn't going to explain things. I was just going to try and made good scenes."

In the scene at the end Bogart and Bacall find themselves together. "What's wrong with you?" he asks. "Nothing you can't fix," she replies. That's appropriate, as Bogie and Betty are now man and wife.

Lauren Bacall.

SLIM & STEVE

The dynamic screen chemistry between Humphrey Bogart and Lauren Bacall in *To Have and Have Not* (1944) sparked an off-screen romance that had all of Tinseltown talking. The cool innuendos they traded in the Warners movie clearly reflected their true feelings for each other.

But Bogart's affair with the former *Harper's Bazaar* cover-girl and minor stage player initially caused anguish, as he was unable to make a clean break with his third wife, tempestuous Mayo Methot. The liaison between the two attracted so much attention that at one point director Howard Hawks tried to pair Bacall off with Clark Gable.

Eventually Bogart obtained the divorce and "Slim" and "Steve" – they coyly adopted the names of the characters they played in *To Have and Have Not* – were married in May last year. She was 20 and he was 45.

As a couple their publicity value has been colossal. But critics seem reluctant to warm to Bacall, even though the static between her and Bogart crackles again in *The Big Sleep*. Bacall's sultry teasing has summoned up a small army of imitators, most notably Lizabeth Scott.

BIRTHS, DEATHS AND MARRIAGES

BIRTHS

Bruce Robinson
2 May, London

Candice Bergen
9 May, Beverly Hills

Cher
20 May, El Centro, California

Sylvester Stallone
6 Jul, New York

Lesley Ann Warren
16 Aug, New York

DEATHS

William S. Hart
23 Jun, Los Angeles
Stroke

Florence Turner
28 Aug, Woodland Hills, California

MARRIAGES

Louise Allbritton
11 May, *to* Charles Cummings Collingwood

Merle Oberon
26 Jun, *to* Lucien Ballard

Anne Baxter
7 Jul, *to* **John Hodiak**

Olivia de Havilland
26 Aug, *to* Marcus A. Goodrich

FAREWELL, BILL

First it was Tom Mix, now it's William S. Hart. Six years after the silent sagebrush star bit the dust, his biggest rival has also gone to the great corral in the sky. Hart died on 23 June in a Los Angeles hospital after a long illness. His age is reckoned to have been somewhere between 75 and 83.

At his peak Hart was paid $1,000 a day, and he also made some 27 pictures as an independent producer for Famous Players-Lasky, earning a sum thought to be over $4 million. He began his career on the New York stage in early 1880 and went on to play in anything from Shakespeare to a two-year run as Messala in *Ben-Hur* (in 1899).

He entered films in 1914 and became inseparably linked with his famous pinto pony, Paint. His stern-faced western hero became an idol for millions of kids worldwide.

CARTOON MAGIC

Lonely little boy Bobby Driscoll, moping around the old southern plantation, finds happiness at the feet of James Baskett's Uncle Remus, tailspinner extraordinary, in Disney's *Song of the South*, due out later this year.

This framework is providing Disney's animators with the chance to parade their technical mastery in three sequences featuring Brer Rabbit, Brer Fox and Brer Bear, based on the 19th-century stories of Joel Chandler Harris. Live action is being combined skilfully with cartoon at the Disney factory, and the picture's songs will include the catchy "Zip-adee-do-da". Stand by for a tuneful Yuletide.

Cary Grant auditions Jane Wyman while Mary Martin looks on in the biopic of Cole Porter, Night and Day.

ANYTHING GOES

Last year Warners splashed out on *Rhapsody in Blue*, a highly inventive biopic of George Gershwin. Now Cole Porter gets the same fanciful biographical treatment in *Night and Day*, directed by Michael Curtiz.

Warners script department has mixed a colourful cocktail about the life of the sensitive tunesmith. Cary Grant is cast as an improbably red-blooded version of the high-society wit and bon viveur. And the screenplay reduces Porter's musical genius to bathos, particularly in the moment at the piano when he cries "Wait a minute, I think I've got it" as the muse descends for the title song. But urbane Porter is delighted. "It must be good - none of it's true," he quips.

ACROBAT TO ACTOR

In a small darkened room a boxer-turned small-town-garage-attendant waits for the two hoods who will kill him. He's rugged New Yorker Burt Lancaster, 32, a former circus acrobat and war veteran of the Special Services now under contract to producer Hal Wallis, who has an independent outfit at Paramount.

Wallis lent Lancaster to Universal for his debut as the grimly resigned victim in *The Killers*. It's adapted from an Ernest Hemingway story and directed by Robert Siodmak, currently enjoying a purple patch.

The reasons for Lancaster's fate are explained in flashback as insurance investigator Edmond O'Brien unearths his involvement with a gang of very ugly thieves and a very beautiful woman. She's Ava Gardner at her most alluring and treacherous.

Lancaster's acting range is somewhere between morose and more morose. But he strikes enough sparks off Gardner to mark him as a talent worth watching.

Burt Lancaster as Swede, a gangster waiting to be hit, with Ava Gardner in The Killers.

SEPTEMBER OCTOBER

NOVEMBER DECEMBER

BIRTHS, DEATHS AND MARRIAGES

BIRTHS

Nicholas Clay
18 Sep, London

Susan Sarandon
1 Oct, New York

Charles Dance
10 Oct, Worcestershire

Sally Field
6 Nov, Pasadena, California

DEATHS

W. C. Fields
25 Dec, Los Angeles
Cerebral haemorrhage

MARRIAGES

Janet Leigh
5 Oct, *to* Stanley Reames

Robert Hutton
20 Oct, *to* Cleatus Caldwell Murray

PROBLEMS OF PEACE

Fredric March as a returned soldier in The Best Years of Our Lives.

The year's main theme has been postwar readjustment. And the year's best picture is Sam Goldwyn's *The Best Years of Our Lives*. It's directed by William Wyler, who saw combat himself as a lieutenant-colonel while directing a 40-minute documentary about an Eighth Air Force B-17, *Memphis Belle* (1944).

The Best Years of Our Lives condenses the experiences of millions of U.S. servicemen who've returned to a world which has moved on since they went to war. In the Middle West town of Boone City three veterans try to pick up the threads of their former lives: bank clerk Fredric March, former soda-jerk Dana Andrews, and maimed sailor Harold Russell.

March finds he's grown away from wife Myrna Loy and is a stranger to daughter Teresa Wright. Andrews, reduced from officer to soda-jerk, is disillusioned with the wife (Virginia Mayo) he knew for only 20 days. And Russell, giving a poignant performance (the actor lost both his arms in the war), rejects his fiancée Cathy O'Donnell because he fears her pity. The movie is striking a chord with audiences across America and looks set to reap a rich harvest of Oscars next year.

CHRISTMAS CRACKERS

Hard on the heels of *The Best Years of Our Lives* comes Frank Capra's *It's a Wonderful Life*. The famed writer-director took the title from a poem on a Christmas card – which gives an idea of the saccharine quality of his reassuring fable about the "basic decency" of Americans.

Angel (2nd Class) Henry Travers persuades suicidal bank manager James Stewart not to kill himself by showing him a vision of his home town as it might have been if he had never been born – a sly pastiche of all those urban thrillers, with a peaceful community transformed into a blaring hell-hole of clip-joints and dingy bars.

Stewart, in his first picture after distinguished service in the air force, dispenses bags of gangling charm, and there is a remarkably candid performance from Gloria Grahame as a good-time girl gone to the bad. But Capra's sunny view of small-town America seems out of step with moviegoers' demands for more realism. They're staying away in droves. After all the advance ballyhoo, Liberty Films' first production looks like ringing few bells on its way down.

FIELDS DEAD

In 1941 W.C. Fields bade farewell to Tinseltown in his last great comedy, Universal's *Never Give a Sucker an Even Break*, diving from an aeroplane to catch a bottle of booze. Now the "world's greatest living comic" has bade farewell to life itself. Fields died on Christmas Day in a sanatorium at Pasadena, California, aged 67.

His constant companion, Carlotta Monti, was at his bedside. Shortly before his death Fields was visited by actor Thomas Mitchell, who was surprised to find him propped up in bed reading the Bible. When he asked Fields what he was doing, he received the rasping reply: "Looking for loopholes."

UNDER-POWERED COMEBACK

Originally slated as a vehicle for Gregory Peck, 20th Century-Fox's *The Razor's Edge* is Tyrone Power's comeback after his wartime service in the navy.

Adapted from Somerset Maugham's novel, it casts Power as a young(ish) man returning from the First World War and searching for "the Meaning of Life". He drifts disconsolately between spoiled society girl Gene Tierney and alcoholic Anne Baxter, but the film's ending is leaving no one the wiser. Maybe the space devoted to the movie's making in *Life* magazine – for which Fox paid handsomely in advertising – explains its success with the public.

Gene Tierney and Tyrone Power in The Razor's Edge.

Larry Parks doing "Mammy" as Jolson in The Jolson Story.

JOLIE-POLY

Columbia has hit the jackpot with *The Jolson Story*, a tribute to the self-styled "world's greatest entertainer". Eye-rolling Jolie introduced sound to the movies in Warners' *The Jazz Singer* (1927), telling audiences "You ain't heard nothing yet."

Jolson nearly torpedoed the new project at the outset by insisting on playing himself. But he was eventually confined to dubbing Columbia contract player Larry Parks, who impersonates the great man in his first major screen role.

The Jolson Story plays fast and loose with certain facts of Jolson's life. His splicing to Ruby Keeler, which ended in a messy divorce in 1940, is transformed into a marriage to "Julie Benson" (Evelyn Keyes) because Keeler refused to allow her name to be used. Keyes resembles her not one bit.

But Larry Parks makes a creditable stab at conveying the legendary Jolson magic, even if his performance stops well short of the original – the vaudeville equivalent (at its height) of a Blitzkrieg.

BOX OFFICE

UK

1 The Wicked Lady
2 The Bells of St. Mary's
3 Piccadilly Incident

OTHER TOP BOX OFFICE FILMS

Anchors Aweigh
Brief Encounter
Caesar and Cleopatra
Gilda
Mildred Pierce
Spellbound
Wonder Man

BOX OFFICE

US

1 The Bells of St. Mary's
2 Leave Her to Heaven
3 Blue Skies
4 Road to Utopia
5 Spellbound
6 The Green Years
7 Adventure
8 Easy to Wed
9 Notorious
10 Two Years Before the Mast

MYTHS OF THE WEST

Seven years after *Stagecoach*, director John Ford returns to the western with 20th Century-Fox's *My Darling Clementine*. It's about legendary lawman Wyatt Earp (Henry Fonda) and "Doc" Holliday (Victor Mature) and their shoot-out with the Clanton gang at the O.K. Corral.

Ford claims he knew the real Earp, who died in 1929 when Ford was already an experienced director of silent westerns at Universal and Fox. The crusty director is adamant he shot the shootout "just the way Earp said it happened". So why is Old Man Clanton (Walter Brennan) killed at the O.K. Corral when he died several months earlier?

Fonda's lanky dignity contrasts sharply with Mature's irascible, tubercular "Doc" Holliday, lurking behind a huge bloodstained handkerchief. Moviegoers are surprised by Big Vic's, erudition when he completes Hamlet's soliloquy after drunken travelling player Alan Mowbray forgets his lines.

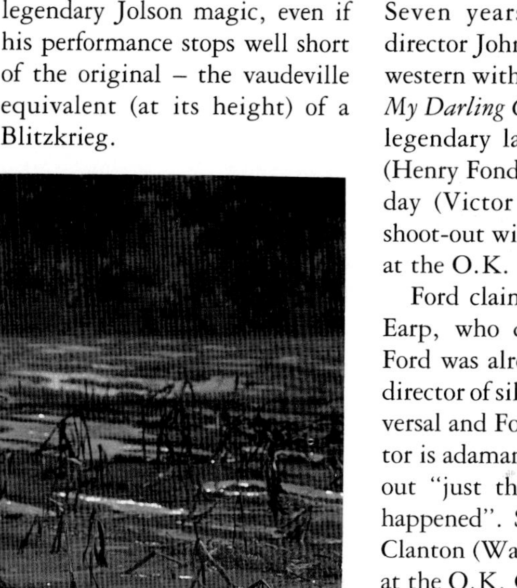

Gregory Peck, Claude Jarman Jr. and Jane Wyman in The Yearling.

SECOND TIME LUCKY, MA

It's second time around for M-G-M with *The Yearling*, from Marjorie Kinnan Rawlings' novel about a family living on the edge of poverty in the Florida Everglades.

The studio first tried to film the book back in 1941 with Spencer Tracy and Anne Revere as Ma and Pa, but the project was abandoned. Five years on the roles have been taken by Gregory Peck and Jane Wyman. Both stars seem ill-at-ease with their corn-pone accents; but more convincing is tow-headed newcomer Claude Jarman, Jr as their adolescent son. He dotes over a fawn and takes over running the farm when Pa gets sick from a snakebite.

Peck and Wyman found the fawn even more trying than their country accents. Minded to skitter gaily off at crucial moments, the little critter stretched one key scene out to 72 takes over two days. But now the film is in the can, director Clarence Brown is providing audiences with a Technicolor treat, the beautiful swampland location bathed in a loving glow.

Director John Ford.

JANUARY
FEBRUARY

1947

MARCH
APRIL

LUST IN THE DUST

After *Gone with the Wind* David O. Selznick seemed to lose interest in production. He functioned largely through loaning out stars he created – like Ingrid Bergman, Gregory Peck, Joan Fontaine, Joseph Cotten – by selling packages like Alfred Hitchcock's *Notorious* (1946) and by taking a 2 per cent interest in United Artists.

But a lingering desire to top his 1939 triumph has now resulted in a $6 million western, *Duel in the Sun*. Conceived on an operatic scale, *Duel in the Sun* is a kind of Texan *Twilight of the Gods*, with Selznick protegee Jennifer Jones as Pearl Chavez, a tempestuous half-breed Scarlett O'Hara, and Gregory Peck as the satanic Lewt McCanles. Selznick reckons he's "the biggest son of a bitch that's ever been seen on a motion picture screen".

Shot in searing Technicolor, *Duel in the Sun* reaches a high-octane climax on Squaw's Head bluff. Lewt and Pearl consummate their love-hate relationship after a fatal gun battle, crawling towards each other across the sun-blasted stones.

Driven to distraction by Selznick's meddling, King Vidor walked off the film two days before the scheduled end of shooting. Final credit for the film is hard to assign as two other directors, Otto Brower and William Dieterle have also handled parts of the picture.

Critics have already dubbed Selznick's folly *Lust in the Dust*. But as with Howard Hughes' *The Outlaw* (1943), the hullabaloo has helped to fan public interest, and the picture's proving a big hit.

Jennifer Jones and Gregory Peck in Duel in the Sun.

SUSAN GETS SOZZLED

Pugnacity is the key to Susan Hayward's character, both on screen and off. The five-foot-three Brooklyn dynamo has always been in there pitching since she screen-tested for Scarlett O'Hara back in 1938.

After her debut, aged 20, in the Ronald Reagan "B" movie *Girls on Probation* (1938), she alternated between spunky heroines in actioners and tart little bitches in melodramas. She first showed her gritty streak in RKO's *Deadline at Dawn* (1946), clearing sailor Bill Williams of a murder charge, and has recently signed a seven-year contract with independent producer Walter Wanger.

The first major challenge for Wanger's new leading lady is *Smash-Up, The Story of a Woman*. It's a female version of *The Lost Weekend* (1945), based on a *New Yorker* study of alcoholism by Frank Cavett and Dorothy Parker.

Hayward is Angie Evans, a torch singer who gives up husband Lee Bowman for the booze and wrecks her family. Characteristically, she undertook gruelling research for the part, attending meetings of Alcoholics Anonymous, touring dozens of bars, and even going on a binge herself. Says Hayward: "It's a hard world, and a saloon is the best place to watch people trying to forget. This movie deals with a serious social problem. I've seen it happen to my own friends."

Susan Hayward in Smash-Up, The Story of a Woman.

ACADEMY AWARDS

PRESENTED ON 13 MARCH 1947

Best Picture
The Best Years of Our Lives

Best Director
William Wyler
The Best Years of Our Lives

Best Actor
Fredric March
The Best Years of Our Lives

Best Actress
Olivia de Havilland
To Each His Own

Best Sup Actor
Harold Russell
The Best Years of Our Lives

Best Sup Actress
Anne Baxter
The Razor's Edge

TROUBLE WITH JUDY

M-G-M's boss Louis B. Mayer has never flinched from driving young Judy Garland to the limit and beyond. But now a terrible price is being paid.

Plagued by weight problems since her teens, Garland has been existing on a diet of chicken soup and Dexedrine during her gruelling schedule of filming, recording and radio work, and personal appearances. Soon after her marriage to bandleader David Rose in 1941, her mother and Mayer forced her to have an abortion. It was a child she desperately wanted. The marriage broke up and ended in divorce in 1945. Now she's said to be shuttling between the studio and her shrink.

CONTRASTING COMEBACKS

Two giants of silent cinema have tried to hit the comeback trail. Harold Lloyd, who retired from acting after *Professor Beware* (1938), makes an ill-advised attempt to revive his brand of "thrill comedy" in RKO's *The Sin of Harold Diddlebock*, and Charles Chaplin directs himself in *Monsieur Verdoux*, his first since *The Great Dictator* (1940).

In *Verdoux*, Chaplin is transformed from the Tramp into a dapper, Latinate little murderer in the tradition of mass-killer Henri Landru, fastidiously disposing of a string of wealthy women to support his crippled wife (a typically Chaplinesque sentimental touch). It's exacting work, particularly if the intended victim is murder-proof, like lusty Martha Raye.

Nor can Harold Lloyd rekindle past glories. The movie is directed by a flagging Preston Sturges, whose powers of comic invention are fast waning after his triumphs of the early 1940s. And the opening sequence, from one of Lloyd's greatest triumphs, *The Freshman* (1925), shows that over 20 years on he's too old to play the charming, bespectacled young go-getter of his heyday. He's just a middle-aged man in a silly suit with a lion on a lead.

GOSSIP COLUMN

■ **Joan Crawford still knows how to throw a party in the style of Tinseltown's heyday. To honour Noel Coward, she hired the whole of the Papillon Restaurant, turned into a miniature version of Versailles by Joan's chum, silent-star-turned-interior-decorator Bill Haines. All Hollywood was there with the exception of Joan's latest ex-husband, Philip Terry**

Arthur Kennedy and Karl Malden in Boomerang.

TRUE TO LIFE

March of Time producer Louis de Rochemont and director Elia Kazan are ruffling a few consciences with 20th Century-Fox's *Boomerang*. It's based on the real-life unsolved murder of a Connecticut priest.

In the screen version an innocent drifter (Arthur Kennedy) is accused of the crime, but is saved from the chair by dogged district attorney Dana Andrews who, as he assembles the case for the prosecution, becomes increasingly stricken by doubts. Piece by piece he proves Kennedy's innocence, at the cost of his own political ambitions. It's a powerful story with a strong, unstarry cast. And Andrews, Kennedy, Karl Malden and Lee J. Cobb give gritty performances.

BIRTHS, DEATHS AND MARRIAGES

BIRTHS

David Bowie
8 Jan, London

Farrah Fawcett
2 Feb, Corpus Christi, Texas

Marisa Berenson
15 Feb, New York

Billy Crystal
14 Mar, Los Angeles

Glenn Close
19 Mar, Greenwich, Connecticut

Peter Riegert
11 Apr, New York

James Woods
18 Apr, Vernal, Utah

DEATHS

Grace Moore
26 Jan, Copenhagen
Air crash

MARRIAGES

Laraine Day
21 Jan, *to* Leo Durocher

Van Johnson
25 Jan, *to* Eve Abbott Wynn

Bonita Granville
5 Feb, *to* John Devereaux Wrather Jr.

June Haver
9 Mar, *to* Jimmy Zito

Carmen Miranda
17 Mar, *to* David Sebastian

Sterling Hayden
25 Apr, *to* Betty De Noon

Left: Martha Raye and Charlie Chaplin in Monsieur Verdoux.

Below: Humphrey Bogart and Lizabeth Scott in Dead Reckoning.

DEAD RIGHT

Lizabeth Scott – she of the husky voice and hunched shoulders – is the deadly dame with whom Humphrey Bogart tangles in Columbia's *Dead Reckoning* as he unravels the murder of a wartime buddy. It's an independent production by Bogart's own company, Santana, handled by Columbia as a snub to Warners.

But sultry Scott was not wildly impressed with Bogie's approach to his work. Says the blonde thespian: "He set the pace. He would arrive on the set totally unprepared at nine. He would then proceed to learn his lines before his martini and lunch. Then he would work till five and leave, the scene completed or not. These were his rules and, although I was equally the star of the picture, I abided by them, as did the crew, director John Cromwell and the studio." Miaow.

MAY
JUNE

JULY
AUGUST

BRAVE NEW WORLD

Since the end of the war, the British film industry has been in optimistic mood. The overall quality of its movies is improving and several of the best have enjoyed critical and commercial success in the United States.

A new wave of British stars has emerged, including Deborah Kerr, John Mills, Stewart Granger, James Mason and Margaret Lockwood. Both Lockwood and Mason scored a big Stateside hit in *The Wicked Lady* (1945), a rip-roaring costume movie in which they made a handsome pair of highwaymen (Lockwood's plunging cleavage had to be adjusted for American consumption). Mason and Kerr are now set for Hollywood careers.

Laurence Olivier's *Henry V* (1944) scooped a special Oscar and ran 11 months at the City Center Theater, New York – a record for a British film.

The box-office success in America of Anthony Asquith's *The Way to the Stars* (1945), Compton Bennett's enjoyably trashy melodrama *The Seventh Veil* (1945) and David Lean's masterly *Great Expectations* (1946) has convinced British mogul J. Arthur Rank that he can take on the U.S. majors in their own market.

ENTER THE GIGGLER

Making one of the most sensational debuts of the year in 20th Century-Fox's *Kiss of Death* is Richard Widmark, a 32-year-old former drama teacher and stage and radio actor.

Cast as giggling hoodlum Tommy Udo in Henry Hathaway's urban thriller, Widmark quickly establishes his psychopathic credentials. He tips crippled Mildred Dunnock down a flight of stairs and terrorizes small-time stoolie Victor Mature.

The chilling sadism, the fearful laugh, the skin stretched tight across the skull – Widmark is the most frightening thing on the screen. Now Fox has the problem of how to soften his gleefully malicious screen presence.

John Payne and Edmund Gwenn in the charming comedy about Santa Claus, *Miracle on 34th Street*.

THREE CHEERS FOR SANTA

There's always been something grating about the "lovable" qualities of tubby English character actor Edmund Gwenn, 72, who settled permanently in America in 1940.

He has carved a cosy niche for himself in avuncular roles. So it's not surprising to find him as the genial but mysterious old cove Kris Kringle in 20th Century-Fox's *Miracle on 34th Street*.

Hired by harassed advertising executive Maureen O'Hara as Macy's Yuletide Santa Claus, he alarms the store's management with his frank criticism of their goods. The saintly old codger soon finds himself in court. But is he a candidate for Bellevue or may he just possibly be the real Santa Claus?

Making her debut in *Miracle on 34th Street* as a satisfied mother is Broadway actress Thelma Ritter, 41, a friend of director George Seaton. It's a late start in the movies for the worn-looking, wisecracking character actress, but it looks as if she will become a fixture.

BIRTHS, DEATHS AND MARRIAGES

BIRTHS

Anthony Higgins
9 May, Northampton

Sondra Locke
28 May, Shelbyville, Tennessee

Jonathan Pryce
1 Jun, North Wales

Candy Clark
20 Jun, Oklahoma

Arnold Schwarzenegger
30 Jul, Graz, Austria

MARRIAGES

Virginia Mayo
5 Jul, *to* Michael O'Shea

LOST IN A DREAM

Danny Kaye is all the rage these days. *Wonder Man* (1945) and *The Kid from Brooklyn* (1946) were big hits, and in both his leading lady was Virginia Mayo, who was a chorus girl in Kaye's first film, *Up in Arms* (1944).

Mayo joins Kaye again for *The Secret Life of Walter Mitty*, a tuppence-coloured version of James Thurber's story about a compulsive daydreamer. The movie gives him the chance to slip into all manner of mock heroic disguises, including fearless cowboy, Mississippi gambler and devil-may-care R.A.F. fighter ace. Say goodbye to Thurber's gentle fantasy and hello to a new sub-plot that suggests Mitty's own life is anything but dull. So why the daydreaming, Danny?

Danny Kaye in The Secret Life of Walter Mitty.

Robert Ryan and Robert Young in the tense thriller Crossfire.

UN-AMERICAN ACTIVITIES

RKO is having a big critical and commercial impact with a murder mystery-cum-morality tale, *Crossfire*, adapted from Richard Brooks' novel *The Brick Foxhole*.

The novel focused on a psychopathic soldier whose violent hatred of homosexuals drove him to murder. But for the movie producer Adrian Scott, director Edward Dmytryk and screenwriter John Paxton have substituted a Jewish war hero (Sam Levene) as the victim. He's beaten up and killed by rabid Jew-hater Robert Ryan, an American G.I. on bar-crawling leave in Washington.

The why of the crime is the main business of the movie. This enables police captain Robert Young to diagnose the fear that leads to hatred and then violence – and to label it "un-American".

Ryan is outstanding as the resentful bully, fear flickering in his eyes as the net closes in. Robert Mitchum gives a sympathetic performance as Young's G.I. confederate. And pouting Gloria Grahame, borrowed from M-G-M, is a sultry, spoiled cutie with a pathologically lying boyfriend (Paul Kelly) perpetually in tow.

John Garfield and Lilli Palmer in Body and Soul.

THE IGNOBLE ART

"Fight for something, not for money" pleads Jewish mother Anne Revere to her prizefighter son John Garfield in M-G-M's *Body and Soul*, directed by Robert Rossen and written by Abraham Polonsky.

But money talks louder than Momma. As Garfield slugs his way to the top, he is corrupted by success, throws over nice artist-girlfriend Lilli Palmer and takes up with leggy showgirl Hazel Brooks. Soon he's nothing but a "no-goodnik", owned "body and soul" by the Mob, which controls the fight game.

But when he is asked to throw the big fight, his conscience stirs. In Europe Jews are being sent to the gas chambers while at home all the Jews in his neighbourhood are betting their life savings on him. And so comes the crucial last round of a savage bout, brilliantly photographed on roller skates by cameraman James Wong Howe. Tough stuff (with a soft centre) from writer Polonsky and director Rossen.

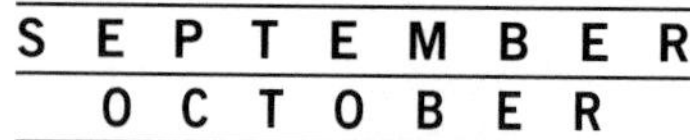

NOVEMBER
DECEMBER

DARK DAYS IN TINSELTOWN

Hollywood's wartime celebrations of the Soviet way of life have become deeply embarrassing to studio bosses. The sweat stands out on Jack Warner's brow every time he thinks of *Mission to Moscow* (1943). Red-baiting politics are spreading through Hollywood, encouraged by a series of bitter labour disputes at the major studios.

Now the House Un-American Activities Committee (HUAC), formed in 1938, has moved in on Hollywood, convinced that the labour unrest is Communist-inspired. Prominent among HUAC's supporters in the press is columnist Hedda Hopper, recently elected vice-president of the Motion Picture Alliance for the Preservation of American Ideals. Its leading lights are director Leo McCarey and actors Ward Bond, John Wayne, Robert Taylor and Hollywood's self-appointed "expert" on Communism, Adolphe Menjou.

Chaired by J. Parnell Thomas, HUAC opened its hearings with the testimony of 23 "friendly" witnesses. Gary Cooper confessed he didn't know much about Communism: "But from what I hear of it, I don't like it, because it isn't on the level."

Next came the turn of the "unfriendly" witnesses – of whom 10 declined to testify before the committee and were held in contempt. The "Hollywood Ten" are writers John Howard Lawson, Lester Cole, Alvah Bessie, Albert Maltz, Samuel Ornitz, Herbert J. Biberman, Dalton Trumbo, Ring Lardner, Jr, director Edward Dmytryk and producer Adrian Scott.

There was a brief flurry of support for the Ten from some of Tinseltown's big names, including Humphrey Bogart, Lauren Bacall and Danny Kaye. But they were quickly warned off.

In November, at a meeting in New York, the Association of Motion Picture Producers pledged that the industry would not "knowingly employ a Communist or a member of any party or group which advocates the overthrow of the Government of the United States by force or by any illegal or unconstitutional method." Writers, directors and actors who are suspected of the slightest trace of left-wing sympathies are being placed on an unofficial "blacklist".

YOUNG MR PECK

Few actors have been blessed with such unnervingly good looks as Gregory Peck. A monument to well-bred decency and grave sincerity, Peck camouflages his sex appeal with lanky, boyish reserve.

Born in California in 1916, he began acting while studying at Berkeley, worked as a barker at the 1939 New York World's Fair and then signed a two-year contract with the Neighbourhood Playhouse, supplementing his income with work as a mail-order-catalogue model.

After his Broadway debut in 1941, in Emlyn Williams' *The Morning Star*, Peck was tested and turned down by David O. Selznick, who wrote: "I am so sorry to say that I don't see what we can do with Gregory Peck. We would have great difficulty in either using him or getting other studios to use him. He photographs like Abe Lincoln, but if he has great personality, I don't think it comes through."

Pronounced medically unfit for war service, Peck finally made it to the screen in RKO's *Days of Glory* (1944), a small-scale follow-up to Paramount's *For Whom the Bell Tolls* (1943), with Peck in the Gary Cooper role of partisan/guerrilla fighter. In his next film, *Keys of the Kingdom* (1944), he was more impressive as an ageing priest recalling his youthful good deeds.

Peck shot to the top when many of Hollywood's leading men were away in the services, and he was in the lucky position of being able to choose his own roles. Under the guidance of agent Leland Hayward he's cannily declined to tie himself down to a single studio or sign a long-term contract.

OH, GOY!

"Oh God, I've got it. It's the only way. It's the only way. I'll *be* Jewish." Thus crusading Gentile journalist Gregory Peck declares his intention of exposing American anti-Semitism in 20th Century-Fox's *Gentleman's Agreement*.

Gregory Peck as a crusading journalist in Gentleman's Agreement.

Directed by Elia Kazan and based on Laura Z. Hobson's best-selling book, the movie charts the effects of Peck's six-month incognito investigation on himself, his family and his friends.

It's just the sort of "fearless" but commercial expose beloved of Darryl F. Zanuck, whose fingerprints are all over the production. As writer Ring Lardner, Jr quipped after seeing a preview: "The movie's moral is that you should never be mean to a Jew, because he might turn out to be a Gentile."

GOSSIP COLUMN

■ It's official: M-G-M boss Louis B. Mayer has a new mate. Mayer's marriage to Margaret Shenburg had collapsed in the early 1940s. By then Maggie was spending increasingly lengthy spells in mental homes, afflicted with "involutional melancholia." The couple separated in 1944 and, after a number of false starts, Mayer settled on the matronly form of former Warners hoofer Lorena Danker. The happy couple were spliced in Yuma, Arizona, this December.

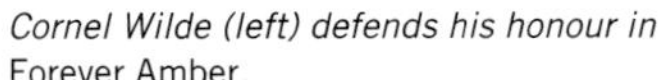

Cornel Wilde (left) defends his honour in Forever Amber.

OH, LINDA!

The American Legion of Decency is working itself up into a lather of moral outrage at the prospect of 20th Century-Fox's version of Kathleen Winsor's bodice-ripper *Forever Amber*.

This is the least of the studio's worries. After spending $2 million, Fox dumped the original director John Stahl and leading lady Peggy Cummins, a disastrous choice for the bounteous 17th-century courtesan of the title. Darryl F. Zanuck replaced them with Otto Preminger and Linda Darnell.

A further $2 million dollars later Preminger is said to have turned in a gaudy, broken-backed epic, with even Darnell singularly lacklustre. Insiders say the only player to survive intact is George Sanders as a languid Charles II, gazing sceptically at the foothills of Darnell's Technicolored cleavage.

BOX OFFICE

UK

1 The Courtneys of Curzon St.
2 The Jolson Story
3 Great Expectations

OTHER TOP BOX OFFICE FILMS

Blue Skies
Duel in the Sun
Frieda
Holiday Camp
Jassy
A Matter of Life and Death
Odd Man Out

BOX OFFICE

US

1 The Best Years of Our Lives
2 Duel in the Sun
3 The Jolson Story
4 Forever Amber
5 Unconquered
6 Life with Father
7 Welcome Stranger
8 The Egg and I
9 The Yearling
10 Green Dolphin Street
The Razor's Edge

BOGART IN BANDAGES

Humphrey Bogart is now Hollywood's highest paid star, at an annual salary of $467,361. So Warners hardly get their money's worth in *Dark Passage*, written and directed by Delmer Daves – Bogart's face is off the screen for the opening 40 minutes.

That's because the first third of the picture is shot entirely from his point of view. This isn't new. Robert Montgomery managed the same stunt for the entire length of last year's *The Lady in the Lake*.

In *Dark Passage* Bogart is a man falsely convicted of murder who breaks out of San Quentin, undergoes a grisly plastic surgery operation and emerges looking like – well, Humphrey Bogart. Fortunately Lauren Bacall is on hand as a teasingly ambiguous guardian angel. But before they can melt into each other's arms, Bogart has to unmask the real murderer.

Humphrey Bogart and Lauren Bacall in Dark Passage.

BIRTHS, DEATHS AND MARRIAGES

BIRTHS

Kevin Kline
24 Oct, St. Louis

Richard Dreyfuss
29 Oct, Brooklyn, New York

Mandy Patinkin
20 Nov, Chicago

Ben Cross
16 Dec, London

Steven Spielberg
18 Dec, Cincinnati

Ted Danson
29 Dec, Flagstaff, Arizona

DEATHS

Harry Carey
21 Sep, Brentwood, California
Heart attack

Olive Borden
1 Oct, Los Angeles
Stomach ailment

Ernst Lubitsch
30 Nov, Los Angeles
Heart attack

MARRIAGES

Gower Champion
5 Oct, *to* **Marge Bell**

Louis B. Mayer
Dec, *to* Lorena Danker

George Brent
17 Dec, *to* Janet Michael

LUBITSCH DIES

Ernst Lubitsch, Berlin-born director of some of the most sophisticated movies of the 1920s and 1930s, died at his Bel Air home on 30 November, aged 55. Creator of the so-called "Lubitsch touch", he was one of the few directors whose name on theatre marquees was a box-office pull.

In 1943 he signed a lucrative producer-director's contract with 20th Century-Fox, but his work was limited by failing health. Towards the end of 1944 he suffered a heart attack in the middle of filming *A Royal Scandal*, a costume comedy starring Tallulah Bankhead as Catherine the Great. The movie was completed by Otto Preminger.

He recovered sufficiently to direct *Cluny Brown* (1946), a charming comedy with Charles Boyer and Jennifer Jones. But a final heart attack claimed him during filming a fantasy starring Betty Grable and Douglas Fairbanks, Jr. Preminger again is to finish the picture.

A Whiff of Wolfbane

Old monsters never die – they just lie unloved and abandoned, disassembled, frozen in glaciers or staked through the heart, awaiting the electric kiss of a new Dr Frankenstein, a young virgin's blood or a full moon and a whiff of wolfbane in the air.

By the late 1930s the momentum had gone from the horror cycle initiated by the huge success of *Dracula* and *Frankenstein* (both 1931). Universal reissued these classics in 1938 and the box-office returns prompted them to re-invest in horror in the following year with the Expressionist *Son of Frankenstein* (1939).

Next to be brought out of retirement was the Invisible Man, in *The Invisible Man Returns* (1940). Scenting box-office blood, Universal delivered *The Wolf Man* (1941), an everyday tale of werewolves, starring Lon Chaney Jr, the son of the Man of a Thousand Faces, as luckless Larry Talbot, a hulking sprig of the British aristocracy who sprouts surplus hair and fangs. Universal pressed their new horror star into the roles made famous in the 1930s by Boris Karloff and Bela Lugosi: as a robotic monster in *The Ghost of Frankenstein* (1942); as the Mummy in *The Mummy's Tomb* (1942); and as a well-fed, sleek Count Dracula in *Son of Dracula* (1943). Chaney tried hard but his limited range prevented him from investing his monsters with the pathos and deliberation of Karloff or the exotic menace of Lugosi in his prime.

Big budgets were the exception rather than the rule in horror films of the 1940s. Universal turned *The Phantom of the Opera* (1943) into an ersatz musical with an uneasy performance from Claude Rains as the hideously scarred Phantom. M-G-M's plush production values overwhelmed *Dr Jekyll and Mr Hyde* (1941), with Spencer Tracy metamorphosing from the good man of science into his demonic alter ego amid a welter of Freudian imagery. Equally handsome and slow-moving was the same studio's *The Picture of Dorian Gray* (1945), which introduced the icily handsome Hurd Hatfield as the joyless, decadent swell who lets the portrait in the attic do the ageing for him.

It was left to a small low-budget unit headed by producer Val Lewton at RKO to produce the finest horror films of this or any other decade. The first was *Cat People* (1942), starring Simone Simon, which suffused the screen with dark feline images. Others were such minor masterpieces as *I Walked With a Zombie* (1943), described as "Jane Eyre in the West Indies", *The Seventh Victim* (1943), *Isle of the Dead* (1945) and *Curse of the Cat People* (1944).

In the 1950s the horror film was supplanted by the science fiction features which fed off the queasy uncertainties of the Cold War. It was left to a British Studio, Hammer, to regenerate the Gothic horror movie with *The Curse of Frankenstein* (1957), starring Peter Cushing as a Byronically feverish Dr F and Christopher Lee as his monstrous creation.

The horror film flourished in the following decade, nourished by the work of Roger Corman and the enormous box-office success of Roman Polanski's *Rosemary's Baby* (1968), the forerunner of a string of big-budget "religious-horror" films of the 1970s initiated by *The Exorcist* (1973).

The 1980s were dominated by two hugely popular "teen-jeopardy" horror series which prompted a myriad of imitators. The first flowed from *Halloween* (1978) and the second was based on *A Nightmare on Elm Street* (1984), which introduced a new horror superstar to swell the ranks of the "undead", the taloned trespasser in teenage dreams, Freddy Kreuger.

Main picture: Robert Englund as Freddy from the Nightmare on Elm Street *series.*

Mia Farrow in Roman Polanski's chiller Rosemary's Baby *(1968).*

Bela Lugosi in Dracula *(1931), a film which started a horror trend.*

Ellen Burstyn battles the demon inside Linda Blair in The Exorcist *(1973).*

Boris Karloff in another ground-breaking horror flick Frankenstein *(1931).*

Spencer Tracy as Dr Jekyll and Mr Hyde *(1943).*

A victim in John Carpenter's seminal horror film Halloween *(1978).*

Tim Holt, Humphrey Bogart and Walter Huston in The Treasure of the Sierra Madre.

*B*IRTHS, DEATHS AND MARRIAGES

BIRTHS

John Carpenter
16 Jan, Carthage, New York

Bernadette Peters
28 Feb, New York

Dianne Wiest
28 Mar, Kansas City, Missouri

MARRIAGES

David Niven
14 Jan, *to* Hjordis Tersmeden

Googie Withers
24 Jan, *to* John McCallum

Anne Shirley
9 Feb, *to* **Adrian Scott**

Lana Turner
26 Apr, *to* Henry J. Topping

*A*CADEMY AWARDS

PRESENTED ON 20 MARCH 1948

Best Picture
Gentleman's Agreement

Best Director
Elia Kazan
Gentleman's Agreement

Best Actor
Ronald Colman
A Double Life

Best Actress
Loretta Young
The Farmer's Daughter

Best Sup Actor
Edmund Gwenn
Miracle on 34th Street

Best Sup Actress
Celeste Holm
Gentleman's Agreement

FOOL'S GOLD

Written and directed by John Huston, from a novel by the mysterious writer B. Traven, Warners' *The Treasure of the Sierra Madre* is a powerful parable about the corrosive effects of greed.

An ill-assorted trio of prospectors – grizzled old-timer Walter Huston (father of John), youthfully optimistic Tim Holt and morose drifter Humphrey Bogart – strike it rich, but not lucky, in the Mexican mountains.

The picture was shot on location in Mexico at a cost of $3 million, and the going was often rugged. When director Huston offered to double the fee for extras prepared to fall off their horses, he was told by the local agent: "For 50 pesos, senor, you can shoot them in the arms and legs. But, mind you, no killing."

During filming Bogart suffered from a vitamin deficiency which caused his hair to fall out in handfuls; he had to wear three wigs of varying lengths. Jack Warner is said to have hated the film and tried to insist that Bogart survive at the end. Huston blithely ignored his demand.

BELVEDERE'S PROGRESS

Balancing the would-be "realism" of pictures like *The Naked City* are successful "family" movies like 20th Century-Fox's *Sitting Pretty*. Here Clifton Webb is let loose as self-declared genius Lynn Belvedere, who decides to add baby-sitting to the list of his accomplishments.

He takes a job with suburban couple Robert Young and Maureen O'Hara, whose three brats are all but unmanageable. Belvedere – actually a writer researching a book on suburbia – soon has the moppets eating out of his hand.

The success of the picture is a further boost for the waspish Webb, 54, who made a late entry into movies four years ago with *Laura* after being spotted by director Otto Preminger in a stage performance of Noel Coward's *Blithe Spirit*. Prior to that he'd had a long career on the boards, starting as a seven-year-old singer and dancer in New York and progressing to Broadway and nightclub work. It looks like the elegant star, who's already famed for his devotion to his mother, will be delighting moviegoers for some time to come.

Clifton Webb as the baby-sitting genius in Sitting Pretty.

TALES OF THE CAVALRY

Henry Fonda and John Wayne in John Ford's epic western Fort Apache.

Once again John Ford magically manipulates myth and truth in RKO's *Fort Apache*, in which the U.S. cavalry is pitted against Cochise's Apache braves. Henry Fonda is an arrogant lieutenant-colonel despatched from the East to take command of a remote Arizona outpost. A martinet and Indian-hater, he ignores the advice of frontier veteran John Wayne and launches a death-or-glory attack on the Apache.

Fort Apache paints a vivid picture of service life in the 1870s. But it's marred by Ford's indulgence of the clowning of two favourite members of his "stock company" – Victor McLaglen and Ward Bond – and the introduction of a romance between John Agar and Shirley Temple.

McLaglen co-starred in skirts with Temple in Ford's *Wee Willie Winkie* (1937), in which he played a bekilted NCO on India's Northwest Frontier. But now Temple is a grown-up 19 – and married to Agar both in the movie and in real-life.

ORSON'S REVENGE

Orson Welles and Rita Hayworth in a dramatic scene from The Lady from Shanghai.

Director Orson Welles gives his estranged wife Rita Hayworth ("she bores me") the big kiss-off in Columbia's *The Lady from Shanghai*. He's cast her as a venomous manipulator of men and himself as the chief victim. To add insult to injury, he's cropped her locks, dyed them blonde, denied her any close-ups, and made sure she's bumped off in the final reel.

The filming of the tangled melodrama – made by Welles to pay off a debt to studio boss Harry Cohn – took a farcical turn on location in Acapulco. Welles rewrote the script every day, quarrelled with the cast and then went AWOL to watch bullfighting in Mexico City.

With costs spiralling, the undeveloped film was shipped to California, where editor Viola Lawrence hacked it into some shape. That was almost a year ago. Now Welles' marriage to Hayworth is terminally over – and so, maybe, is the wunderkind's Hollywood career.

HUGHES SWALLOWS RKO

RKO recorded a loss of $2 million at the end of last year, largely thanks to two box-office flops – John Ford's allegorical *The Fugitive* and a hugely expensive adaptation of Eugene O'Neill's *Mourning Becomes Electra*.

The studio has also been demoralized by the HUAC hearings which have ensnared two of its top talents, director Edward Dmytryk and producer Adrian Scott. No help, too, have been the looming threat of the divorce of the studios from their theatre circuits, and the "freezing" of Hollywood's overseas revenue by a number of countries, notably the U.K.

So RKO chairman Floyd Odlum decided to sell the studio in a move described as "the biggest motion picture transaction since 20th Century took over Fox". Multi-millionaire Howard Hughes has bought just under one million RKO shares for $8.8 million. But production has virtually ground to a halt while Hughes gathers the reins of power.

THE STREETS OF NEW YORK

The never-ending war against crime takes a documentary-tinged turn in Universal's *The Naked City*. It's produced by former newsman Mark Hellinger and directed with gusto by Jules Dassin.

Hellinger himself introduces the movie, which was filmed entirely on location in and around Manhattan. The story follows a Homicide Squad manhunt led by Barry Fitzgerald as leprechaun-like Lieutenant Muldoon.

Barry Fitzgerald (centre) in the documentary-style The Naked City.

The Naked City owes something to old-style racket-busting journalism, something to the so-called "neo-realist" films coming out of Italy, and something to semi-documentary predecessors Stateside: remember 20th Century-Fox's Nazi spy thriller *The House on 92nd St.* (1945) or last year's pacy gangland "B" movie *T-Men*? Looks like we could be in for a string of imitators.

MAY
JUNE

JULY
AUGUST

DEATH OF A GIANT

Since his brief involvement with Hal Roach's *One Million B.C.* (1940) David Wark Griffith remained an observer of the American film industry which he had dominated in its formative years. Now the man who invented the fadeout is himself only a memory. On 23 July, at Hollywood's Knickerbocker Hotel, he was seized by an agonizing pain and collapsed in the lobby. He was pronounced dead of a cerebral haemorrhage at Hollywood's Temple Hospital at 8.24 the following morning. He was 73.

Only a handful of people paid their respects at the funeral parlour where Griffith lay in state, the most famous being Cecil B. DeMille. The funeral service was held on 27 July at Hollywood's Masonic Temple. Among the mourners were Lionel Barrymore, Mack Sennett, Richard Barthelmess, Erich von Stroheim and Raoul Walsh. Sam Goldwyn and Louis B. Mayer were honorary pallbearers.

In his eulogy, Donald Crisp told the mourners: "It was the tragedy of his later years that this active, brilliant mind was given no chance to participate in the advancement of the industry. Difficult as it might have been for him to have played a subordinate role, I do not believe that the fault was entirely his own. I cannot help feeling that there should always have been a place for him in motion pictures."

LANDIS DEAD

Hollywood has claimed another casualty. Carole Landis, whose career never really took off after *One Million B.C.* (1940), was found dead of an overdose of sleeping pills at her Pacific Palisades home on 5 July. A note to her mother concluded: "Goodbye, my angel. Pray for me." She was 29. Her body was discovered by her friend, Rex Harrison.

The only other film in which she caused a stir was *Four Jills in a Jeep* (1944), based on a USO tour she made with Martha Raye, Mitzi Mayfair and Kay Francis. Sadly this morale-booster, in which the girls played themselves, was given the thumbs down by the troops. When it was shown in Iceland, G.I.s staged a mass walk-out.

BIRTHS, DEATHS AND MARRIAGES

DEATHS

Dame May Whitty
29 May, Beverly Hills, California

Carole Landis
5 Jul, Los Angeles
Overdose of sleeping pills

King Baggot
11 Jul, Los Angeles
Stroke

David W. Griffith
23 Jul, Hollywood
Cerebral haemorrhage

MARRIAGES

Gloria Grahame
2 Jun, *to* **Nicholas Ray**

Lucille Bremer
Jul, *to* Abalardo Rodriguez

Ida Lupino
5 Aug, *to* Collier H. Young

Red River, the story of the opening of the Chisholm Trail, stars Montgomery Clift, John Ireland and John Wayne.

MUTINY ON THE RANGE

A western reworking of *Mutiny on the Bounty*, Howard Hawks' *Red River* stars John Wayne as a ruthlessly inflexible cattle baron who clashes with his adopted son on a huge trail drive to Abilene.

Wayne's young adversary is played by handsome newcomer Montgomery Clift, seen earlier this year in the postwar Berlin drama *The Search*. Another interesting new face is John Ireland, first seen in the 1945 war film, *A Walk in the Sun*. Cast as young gunslinger Cherry Valance, Ireland became very friendly during shooting with leading lady Joanne Dru, much to the annoyance of director Hawks, who had marked her out for his own personal branding.

Hawks took his revenge by leaving large amounts of Ireland's footage on the cutting-room floor. Thus he disappears for long stretches of the film and, when he reappears at the end, it is only to be casually gunned down by Wayne. But Hawks' revenge was short-lived: Dru and Ireland married soon after *Red River* was completed.

STAR QUOTES

Robert Mitchum

"I always made the same film. They just kept moving new leading ladies in front of me."

'I've been smoking marijuana since I was a kid.'

IF YOU HAVE TEARS . . .

Since winning the Best Actress Oscar for her performance in Alfred Hitchcock's *Suspicion* (1941), Joan Fontaine has settled for a string of conventional, lady-like roles.

The younger sister of Olivia de Havilland was born in Tokyo in 1917 but was raised in California (the Fontaine is from her mother's second husband). After steadily working in "B" pictures from the mid-1930s, and trying unsuccessfuly for Scarlett O'Hara in *Gone with the Wind* (1939), she hit the big time in Hitchcock's *Rebecca* (1940), a role originally intended for her sister. Now, in *Letter from an Unknown Woman*, director Max Ophuls touches on that same chord of romantic vulnerability that Hitchcock located.

German emigre Ophuls has waited seven years for this opportunity since arriving in Hollywood in 1941.

The letter of the title is written on her deathbed by Fontaine to the famous pianist who has loved and left her and whose child she has borne. It's a story as old as love itself, but secondary to Ophuls' poignant evocation of the bitter-sweet beauty of a lost Imperial Vienna. But the movie has been rejected by audiences thirsting for the "realism" of films like *The Naked City*.

MITCHUM GRASSED

RKO, already reeling from the power-play mounted by Howard Hughes, suffered a further blow on 31 August when rising star Robert Mitchum was charged with possession of marijuana after a raid on the home of starlet Lila Leeds. Ironically, Mitchum had an appointment the next day to address a National Youth Week gathering at Los Angeles' City Hall.

Since his start in the movies as a heavy in Hopalong Cassidy westerns, Mitchum has cultivated a "go to hell" attitude towards the studio and its publicity department. Will he beat the rap – or watch his burgeoning career fall apart at the seams?

Robert Mitchum.

GOSSIP COLUMN

■ **Deanna Durbin, one of Universal's biggest money-earners of the late 1930s and early 1940s, is to retire. Everyone's idea of the perfect teenager, she was at her peak in 1939 when, amid much ballyhoo, she received her first screen kiss, from Robert Stack, in *First Love*. But her popularity fell in mid-decade as her weight soared. Says a weary Deanna: "I'm tired of being the highest paid star with the poorest material."**

Gene Tierney and Dana Andrews in Iron Curtain, *about a Russian who reveals a spy network to the Americans.*

NEW WARS TO FIGHT

Three years after the defeat of the Axis, the Soviet Union has replaced Germany as the main international villain. The Cold War has begun – and with it a cycle of anti-Soviet melodramas.

First off the blocks is 20th Century-Fox's *The Iron Curtain*, directed by William Wellman and allegedly based on the story of Igor Gouzenki, a cypher clerk in the Soviet Embassy in Ottawa who defected to the West. Dana Andrews plays the defector and Gene Tierney his wife – the unlikeliest Russians since the Barrymores were let loose in *Rasputin and the Empress* in 1932.

Humphrey Bogart is a war veteran who fights local gangsters in Key Largo, *which also stars Lauren Bacall.*

CAESAR'S PALACE

Little Caesar has made a comeback as squat, snarling Edward G. Robinson's mobster Johnny Rocco in Warners' *Key Largo*, written and directed by John Huston.

Updated from a Maxwell Anderson play set in the aftermath of the Civil War, *Key Largo* stars Humphrey Bogart as a disillusioned Second World War veteran who finds himself on the wrong end of cigar-chomping Robinson's gun. The mobster and his degenerate gang take over a resort hotel and terrorize its owner (Lionel Barrymore) and occupants.

Lauren Bacall slinks sexily around, trying to play a nice home-town girl. But the acting honours go to Claire Trevor as Johnny Rocco's drink-sodden moll, croaking her way through "Moanin' Low" for a shot of whisky.

SEPTEMBER
OCTOBER

NOVEMBER
DECEMBER

CRISIS AT METRO

In 1944 Mickey Rooney, one of M-G-M's most valuable assets, went to war. When he returned, the world had changed. Audiences stayed away from the homely *Love Laughs at Andy Hardy* (1946) and now *Words and Music*, a sanitized biopic of confirmed bachelor composer Lorenz Hart, is Rooney's last for the studio. He's no longer box-office.

Nor is M-G-M. Although this year's gross of $185 million is a new record for the studio, profits have slumped to little over $5 million, the worst since the Great Depression of 1932/3. The studio is actually running at an operating loss of $6.5 million. Louis B. Mayer is still the highest paid man in the United States at $733,024, but he's losing his grip on the reins of power.

M-G-M is also buckling under government pressure on all the majors to separate their exhibition and production/distribution sides. The studio empires are now threatened with being broken up to conform with anti-trust legislation.

During the summer M-G-M president Nicholas Schenck wooed writer and producer Dore Schary back to his old studio from RKO, where he was in charge of production. The once-mighty M-G-M lion is looking a little mangy as the studio approaches its 25th anniversary.

BIRTHS, DEATHS AND MARRIAGES

BIRTHS

Judy Geeson
10 Sep, Arundel, Sussex

Jeremy Irons
19 Sep, Isle of Wight

Gerard Depardieu
27 Dec, Chateauroux, France

DEATHS

Elissa Landi
22 Oct, Hollywood
Cancer

Edgar Kennedy
9 Nov, Hollywood
Cancer

C. Aubrey Smith
20 Dec, Beverly Hills, Calif
Pneumonia

MARRIAGES

Anne Shirley
19 Oct, *to* **Charles Lederer**

Susanna Foster
23 Oct, *to* Wilbur Evans

BOX OFFICE

UK

1 The Best Years of Our Lives
2 Spring in Park Lane
3 My Brother Jonathan
4 Road to Rio
5 Oliver Twist
6 The Red Shoes

OTHER TOP BOX OFFICE FILMS

The Fallen Idol
Forever Amber
It Always Rains on Sunday
The Winslow Boy

BOX OFFICE

US

1 Road to Rio
2 Easter Parade
3 Red River
4 The Three Musketeers
5 Johnny Belinda
6 Cass Timberlane
7 The Emperor Waltz
8 Gentleman's Agreement
9 A Date with Judy
10 Captain from Castile
Homecoming

TRIUMPH AND TRAGEDY

Agnes Moorhead (left), Lew Ayres and Charles Bickford in Johnny Belinda.

Jane Wyman, previously an anodyne actress, is scoring a huge personal success as the deaf-mute rape victim in Warners' *Johnny Belinda*, directed by Jean Negulesco.

Wyman studied for the role at a school for the deaf and dumb, and put plastic plugs in her ears on the set. But her efforts to be true to the part have been fought against a background of personal unhappiness. Earlier in the year she lost a prematurely born baby. And her eight-year marriage to Ronald Reagan seems to have broken down irretrievably. She's now seeing Lew Ayres, her co-star in *Johnny Belinda*. Sighs Reagan: "If this comes to divorce, I think I'll name *Johnny Belinda* co-respondent."

ENGLISH DREAMER

Since 1939 *Red Shoes* director Michael Powell, 43, and screenwriting partner Emeric Pressburger, 46, have been one of the most quirky, talented teams in British cinema.

Powell gained his first film experience as a young man in the 1920s, working as an assistant at the Nice studios of Hollywood exile Rex Ingram. He joined forces with emigre Hungarian Pressburger for *The Spy in Black* (1939).

Working as "The Archers", Powell and Pressburger quickly became leading filmmakers in wartime Britain, although their richly textured pictures swam against the documentary tide which influenced many feature films of the time. Critics found their cinematic tricks and romantic visual imagery faintly "vulgar". They even managed to arouse political opposition. Churchill tried (unsuccessfully) to ban *The Life and Death of Colonel Blimp* (1943), because he felt its warm portrayal of the club-land boor (created by cartoonist David Low and brilliantly played by Roger Livesey) would be bad for morale.

After the war Powell continued to go his own way, progressing steadily towards a movie in which the talents of musicians, painters, designers and dancers could be fused. The process was seen vividly at work in last year's *Black Narcissus*, an extraordinary fable about the sexual fantasies of nuns in a Himalayan convent whose feverish climax was choreographed to a remarkable score by Brian Easdale.

Bob Hope and Jane Russell in the comedy-western The Paleface.

BITE THE BULLET, BOB

Bob Hope takes time off from partnering Bing Crosby in the *Road* films (the latest of which was last year's *Road to Rio*) to star in one of his best solo vehicles of recent years.

Paramount's *The Paleface*, directed by comedy specialist Norman Z. McLeod, despatches him way out West as Painless Potter, a cowardly toothpuller who tangles with the big guns of Calamity Jane Russell.

Curvaceous Russell is now maturing into an amiable comedienne. She's not simply the top-heavy siren paraded in *The Outlaw* (1943). She's now a big, luscious broad relishing all the nonsense going on around her.

Kirk Douglas and Ann Sothern, one of the ladies in A Letter to Three Wives.

TAKE A LETTER, DEAR

Tart and talkative are the words best applied to writer-producer Joseph L. Mankiewicz's scintillating comedy for 20th Century-Fox, *A Letter to Three Wives*.

The letter in question is delivered to three suburban housewives as they prepare to take a boat trip up the Hudson. Read to us by an un-credited Celeste Holm, the letter informs them that the writer, a bitchy gossip called Addie, will by the end of the day leave with one of their husbands. In flashback each of the women – Jeanne Crain, Ann Sothern and Linda Darnell – reflects on her marriage.

Smart dialogue and snappy playing mark Mankiewicz as one of the freshest new directing talents in Hollywood.

GREENBACKS AND RED SHOES

Robert Helpmann and Moira Shearer in Red Shoes.

Controversial British director Michael Powell, a fervent admirer of Walt Disney, has created his own *Fantasia* with *The Red Shoes*. It ran £200,000 over budget but could become a big dollar-earner for Britih film magnate J. Arthur Rank.

The shoes of the title are those of Hans Christian Andersen's fairy tale, the diabolic ballet shoes which dance their wearer to death. The doomed ballerina is ravishing redhead Moira Shearer, making her screen debut as the protegee of Diaghilev-like impresario, Anton Walbrook.

Shearer is the sole interpreter of the *Red Shoes* ballet, penned by Brian Easdale and choreographed by Leonid Massine, who appears in the film. Drenched with succulent colours and emotions which move in time with the soundtrack, *The Red Shoes* is Powell's attempt at totally integrated cinema.

A CLOUD ON THE HORIZON

As the decade draws to a close, Hollywood's horizons are shrinking and its future is shrouded in uncertainty. Audiences are falling, costs are spiralling and a new competitor has appeared on the horizon – television.

Cinema is still the biggest medium of mass entertainment, but the little box is beginning to catch up. The 10 local TV stations which were closed in 1942 reopened two years ago. They were regarded with contempt by the film industry – the quality of the programmes was execrable – but now the sale of TV sets has quadrupled to 1 million while the average weekly cinema audience has plummeted from 90 million to 66 million. It's only a matter of time before movies and television will be locked in battle for the same audience.

JANUARY
FEBRUARY

1949

MARCH
APRIL

HOME RUN FOR KELLY & CO

Frank Sinatra and Gene Kelly do a "shuffle off to Buffalo" routine for Take Me Out to the Ball Game.

Busby Berkeley shows that he's lost none of his old choreographic flair in M-G-M's Technicolor treat *Take Me Out to the Ball Game*. On-set rumour, though, says much of the film was actually directed by dance directors Gene Kelly and Stanley Donen, who also came up with the original screen story because Kelly was horrified at M-G-M's next proposed project co-starring his *Anchors Aweigh* shipmate Frank Sinatra. "It was the sort of thing they dreamed up 10 years ago for Mickey Rooney and Judy Garland," says Kelly, "and in self-defence I decided I'd write something more suitable myself. The fact that Stanley and I blissfully refused to realize that few people outside America knew or cared about what a ball game was is irrelevant." Despite that, *Ball Game* fairly bubbles along, with highlights including Sinatra being pursued in song by zesty Betty Garrett, and there's a great duet called "Yes, Indeedy!" from Kelly and Sinatra, who are also joined in trio by moonfaced Jules Munshin. Esther Williams swims along to the title number, but generally stays out of the water in this one.

As a reward, producer Arthur Freed has given the long-optioned *On the Town* to Kelly and Donen to direct. Let's see if they can lick that stage show's awkward, stylized book into cinematic shape.

JOHN DEREK – JUVENILE DELINQUENT

Knock on Any Door (1949), the searing study of incipient juvenile delinquency, has made a new bobby-sox idol of John Derek.

Derek's clean-cut good looks have been seen in movies for some time. Born in 1926, he's the son of writer-director Lawson Harris and actress Dolores Johnson; David O. Selznick put him under contract prior to the Second World War, changing his name from Derek Harris. Selznick gave him bit parts in *Since You Went Away* (1944) and *I'll Be Seeing You* (1945), but you'd have had to peer hard at the screen to spot him. Derek also features prominently in the long-gestating *All the King's Men* (1949), the Huey Long story directed by Robert Rossen. Derek plays Tom Stark, adopted son of Willie Stark (the character based on Long), played by Broderick Crawford.

Derek says his principal hobby is still photography, with a strong bias towards taking photographs of beautiful women.

ACADEMY AWARDS

PRESENTED ON 24 MARCH 1949

Best Picture
Hamlet

Best Director
John Huston
The Treasure of the Sierra Madre

Best Actor
Laurence Olivier
Hamlet

Best Actress
Jane Wyman
Johnny Belinda

Best Sup Actor
Walter Huston
The Treasure of the Sierra Madre

Best Sup Actress
Claire Trevor
Key Largo

DIRECTOR OF "GONE WITH THE WIND" DIES

Victor Fleming, the former chauffeur who rose in Hollywood to become the only credited director on *Gone with the Wind* (1939), passed away at the age of 64, on 6 January. It's rumoured that the pressures of filming *Joan of Arc* (1948) contributed to his demise: the 92-day shoot was complicated by the fact that Fleming had fallen in love with his star, Ingrid Bergman. A stack of discovered love letters from the director to the actress reveals that the affair was as mutual as it was intense.

Fleming will be remembered for two movies – *Gone with the Wind* and *The Wizard of Oz* (both 1939). On both he was the replacement director, for George Cukor on *GWTW* and Richard Thorpe on *Wizard*, and on both he revealed a superb sense of cinema, fine craftsmanship and an understanding of the needs of actors. His considerable achievements were often credited to the film's producers, David O. Selznick and Mervin LeRoy.

Among Fleming's other notable films were a remarkable series of movies starring Spencer Tracy, including *Captains Courageous* (1937), for which Tracy won an Oscar, *Dr. Jekyll and Mr. Hyde* (1941), where Fleming first met Ingrid Bergman, *Tortilla Flat* (1942) and *A Guy Named Joe* (1943). Fleming also had a special rapport with Clark Gable, and it was Gable who got him on to *GWTW*, fearing that Cukor was throwing the balance away from Rhett Butler.

Kirk Douglas, with trainer Paul Stewart, is an ambitious prizefighter in Champion.

KIRK TAKES IT ON THE CHIN

"Champion", Ring Lardner's short story about corruption in the fight-promotion racket, has become the fine picture *Champion*, from new producer Stanley Kramer and young director Mark Robson, who used to work for Val Lewton's "B" unit over at RKO. As Midge Kelly, Kirk Douglas achieves fully-fledged stardom as his unpleasant screen character sells out his loyal manager, abandons his devoted wife, and punches out his invalid brother on his way to the middleweight title. Arthur Kennedy, currently playing Biff on Broadway in *Death of a Salesman*, scores heavily as the brother, and Marilyn Maxwell, Ruth Roman and Lola Albright make up an attractive distaff side in a downbeat story. The screenplay is by Carl Foreman, whose socially aware tale clearly indicates he has much to say about man being the product of his environment, and what he must do to overcome it. Dimitri Tiomkin's score tiresomely rams home the message.

Olivia de Havilland experiences the horrors of a mental institution in The Snake Pit.

OLIVIA GOES BANANAS

Olivia de Havilland's performance as Virginia Cunningham in *The Snake Pit* has got to be the most discussed of the season, if not the decade. Mary Jane Ward's noted novel was autobiographical, and in the movie de Havilland plays a woman who becomes insane and is institutionalized for treatment. *The Snake Pit*'s depiction of the mental home is truly harrowing. Although Mark Stevens as a sympathetic hubby and Leo Genn as caring Dr. Kik are on hand, it's the performances of patients Betsy Blair, Isabel Jewell, Beulah Bondi, and especially Jan Clayton (from Broadway's *Carousel*) that stun with their power. Anatole Litvak's movie is a high watermark in Hollywood's new policy of making adult-themed movies for adults.

FRED AND GINGER ARE BACK

Fred Astaire and Ginger Rogers are dancing cheek-to-cheek again, this time in M-G-M's *The Barkleys of Broadway*, their first movie in Technicolor. After their "official" last film together, RKO's *The Story of Vernon and Irene Castle* (1939), Astaire left RKO to freelance. He'd co-starred with Rogers in nine movies, and felt it was enough.

After the tremendous success of last year's *Easter Parade* (1948), producer Arthur Freed wanted to co-star Fred again with Judy Garland, and on 1 May 1948, rehearsals started on *Barkleys*. But Garland was unwell, and after three weeks of rehearsals withdrew from the picture.

But what a joyous return it has been. Will Fred and Ginger dance together again? Who can say?

M-G-M'S NEW IRVING THALBERG?

"The guts, gags, and glory of a lot of wonderful guys!" yells the advertising for *Battleground* (1949), and the public have duly responded, making this sombre and realistic story of the 101st Airborne Division's part in the bloody Battle of the Bulge one of M-G-M's surprise hits of the year, with a domestic gross of over $5 million.

For producer Dore Schary, it's a massive vindication of his faith in the project. At RKO, where Schary had been studio head since 1947, after the sudden death of Charles Koerner, the studio changed from a purveyor of mostly B action movies to a socially aware film-making factory, and produced such memorable movies as *Crossfire* (1947), *I Remember Mama* (1948) and *Sister Kenny* (1946).

But after RKO was sold in 1947, new owner Howard Hughes swiftly upset Schary by cancelling *Battleground*. Schary resigned.

He then got a call from Louis B. Mayer, offering him the immediate job of vice-president in charge of production, effectively Mayer's own job. Schary asked for $6,000 a week and complete autonomy. In June 1948, Schary arrived at Metro with the script of *Battleground*, which he had purchased from RKO.

Under William Wellman's taut direction, *Battleground* has emerged as one of the year's top hits. With a cast including Van Johnson, John Hodiak, George Murphy and Ricardo Montalban, Schary had star-power he could never hope to raise at RKO. Let's see where the wunderkind goes from here.

BIRTHS, DEATHS AND MARRIAGES

BIRTHS

Nigel Havers
6 Jan, London

John Belushi
24 Jan, Chicago

Jessica Lange
20 Apr, Cloquet, Minnesota

Meryl Streep
22 Apr, Bernardsville, New Jersey

DEATHS

Wallace Beery
15 Apr, Hollywood
Heart ailment

Victor Fleming
6 Jan, Hollywood

MARRIAGES

Tyrone Power
24 Jan, *to* Linda Christian

Richard Burton
5 Feb, *to* Sybil Williams

GOSSIP COLUMN

- **Robert Mitchum, sentenced to 60 days in prison, plus two years probation, on a charge of "conspiracy to possess marijuana" on the night of 31 August, 1948, has served his spell – and emerged a folk hero. Lawyer Jerry Giesler said it was a set up: Mitchum was invited to a party, handed a reefer, and then arrested. Also the place was bugged.**
- **Judy Garland repeatedly failed to show up on the set of *Annie Get Your Gun*. So on 10 May, M-G-M suspended her services. A few days later she was taken to the Brigham Hospital, Boston, for a complete rest. And a massive detox.**

WAYNE QUITS THE CAVALRY

John Wayne salutes the flag before going on a dangerous mission in She Wore a Yellow Ribbon.

Director John Ford's *She Wore a Yellow Ribbon* is a stirring account of the last days as a serving US Cavalry Officer of Captain Nathan Brittles, played with mature understanding by John Wayne, following up his marvellous character role in last year's *Red River*. Wayne makes of Brittles a moving, wise old buzzard, and Ford leavens the tension by including a dash of Irish humour involving Victor McLaglen, and a charming romance between Joanne Dru and a couple of beaus, John Agar (Mr. Shirley Temple) and Harry Carey Jr.

The outdoor use of Technicolor by cameraman Winton Hoch certainly deserves its prized Academy Award: the compositions and hues are breathtaking. It's difficult to imagine the well-established team of star Wayne and director Ford ever topping this one. That title? It's a riding-out song of the US 7th Cavalry, and was suggested to Ford by Annapolis graduate Laurence Stallings, better known for writing probably the First World War's greatest play, *What Price Glory?*. He reckoned the movie's original title, *War Party*, was not romantic enough.

Wayne says of Ford: "Jack never respected me as an actor until I made *Red River*." But with this latest performance, and his Oscar-nominated starring role in *Sands of Iwo Jima* (1949), Wayne is odds-on favourite to top the *Motion Picture Herald* poll of most popular stars next year.

MAN OF CONVICTIONS

Producer Stanley Kramer has always believed movies should do more than simply entertain. With *Champion* and *Home of the Brave*, both directed by Mark Robson, he's proved his point with a vengeance. In *Champion* the fight-promotion business is revealed as a gangster-dominated racket, and in *Home of the Brave* the U.S. Army is depicted as a hotbed of racism and bigotry. Kramer next plans a study of paraplegics and a couple of Broadway adaptations, *Death of a Salesman* and *Cyrano de Bergerac*, the latter with Orson Welles. He has set up a company called Screen Plays to make "message" pictures.

Kramer was born in New York in 1913 and has worked in cinema since the mid-1930s, as researcher, writer, and occasional film editor. He worked his way up to associate producer on *So Ends Our Night* (1941) and *The Moon and Sixpence* (1942), both courageous challenges to mainstream movie-making. After Second World War service with the Army Signal Corps, he produced the charming period comedy *So This Is New York* (1948), with a team including director Richard Fleischer and screenwriter Carl Foreman, adapted like *Champion* from a Ring Lardner original.

BIRTHS, DEATHS AND MARRIAGES

BIRTHS

Keith Carradine
8 Aug, San Mateo, Calif

Shelley Long
23 Aug, Ft. Wayne, IN

John Savage
25 Aug, Long Island, New York

Richard Gere
29 Aug, Philadelphia

MARRIAGES

Rita Hayworth
27 May, *to* Aly Khan

Mickey Rooney
3 Jun, *to* Martha Vickers

Jennifer Jones
13 Jul, *to* David O. Selznick

James Stewart
9 Aug, *to* Gloria Hatrick McLean

STUDIOS SPLIT FROM THEATRES

Back in May 1948 the Supreme Court decided that Hollywood was a monopolistic conspiracy, and ordered the studios to divest themselves of their exhibition interests.

But instead of breaking up the monopolies immediately, the Supreme Court threw the case back to the district court of New York. There was considerable pressure to render the decision nullified, but in October the Justice Department formally announced that the five major studios must give up their interests in over 1,400 movie theatres, and notice was served on Paramount, Loew's (M-G-M), RKO, Warners and Fox.

In November of last year, a so-called "consent decree" was approved by the Justice Department, the Supreme Court, and the remaining studios, and now we are finally seeing the result of a "trust-bust" started as long ago as 16 January 1933, when the tiny Victoria Amusement Company of London, New Jersey, filed against trade restraint in the area. Surely the Sherman Anti-Trust Act of 1890 was never meant to smash the movie business?

AGAIN, AND AGAIN, AND . . .

Larry Parks does a remarkable impersonation in Jolson Sings Again.

Jolson Sings Again literally begins where *The Jolson Story* (1946) left off, so it's entirely possible to run the two films consecutively as a complete saga. Once again, Larry Parks gives an uncanny performance as the ego-ridden Al Jolson, miming to new recordings by Jolson of the latter's greatest hits. Indeed, it's getting hard not to think of Parks whenever Jolson is recalled. In this sequel, Parks, as Jolson, actually meets Parks as Parks, about to play Jolson in *The Jolson Story*! Barbara Hale portrays the nurse who became Jolie's latest wife, and once again, as in the earlier movie, previous wives, various relatives, awkward business associates, and other inconvenient characters are all eliminated or telescoped beyond recognition. But it's the music that matters, and *Jolson Sings Again* is proving to be just as big a screen hit as *The Jolson Story*, suggesting that audiences can never have too much of a Technicolored good thing.

BACK ON TOP OF THE WORLD

James Cagney returns to the gangster movie, which he made his own in *The Public Enemy* (1931) – only this time there's a difference. In *White Heat* his character, Cody Jarrett, has a severe case of mother fixation, and not even blonde Virginia Mayo as Cody's wife can get closer to him than old Mrs. Jarrett, portrayed by Margaret Wycherly. The Feds, led by informer Edmond O'Brien, infiltrate Cody's gang, and he eventually goes to jail after confessing to a minor indiscretion. But he breaks out and is finally cornered by the cops in a chemical plant, where, trapped and alone, he's blown to smithereens. Director Raoul Walsh keeps this steamy melodrama at boiling point, and Cagney's last shriek of "Made it, Ma, Top of the World!" looks like going down in the annals as one of the movies' famous last lines.

COMIC CUTS

Arriving this summer is the sparkling debut of nightclub and radio comedians Dean Martin and Jerry Lewis. They have been an astounding success since their first pairing in Atlantic City in 1946, and Paramount have rushed them into the Marie Wilson vehicle *My Friend Irma* (1949) with a tentative plan to follow with *My Friend Irma Goes West*. Martin and Lewis are more than a match for blonde Marie, and virtually take over the movie when they're on the screen.

Martin is the tall, darkly handsome one who croons, and Lewis is the zany, shrill-voiced loon who disrupts things. The next step has to be starring them, *a la* Bing and Bob, in a series in their own right.

Over at Universal, where veterans Marjorie Main and Percy Kilbride have already established a new-found success as Ma and Pa Kettle – from the comedy hit *The Egg and I* (1947) – a talking mule named Francis seems set for a long run. In his first outing *Francis*, the critter is voiced by character actor Chill Wills, and makes Donald O'Connor's life a misery in the U.S. Army. *Francis* is the creation of director Arthur Lubin, who also has plans, he says, if television proves successful, for a TV series based around a talking horse.

MR. VERSATILITY

In only his fourth movie, Britain's Alec Guinness has proven that he's a character actor worthy of inheriting the mantle of Emil Jannings or Charles Laughton. In the black comedy *Kind Hearts and Coronets* Guinness plays no fewer than eight parts, all members of the D'Ascoyne family, including suffragette Lady Agatha D'Ascoyne.

Although Guinness had appeared in *Evensong* (1934), it was director David Lean who launched him on his screen career, casting him as Herbert Pocket in *Great Expectations* (1946), a role he had already played in his own 1939 stage adaptation of Dickens' novel. Guinness next turned up, virtually unrecognizable, as Fagin in Lean's *Oliver Twist* (1948). His vivid caricature was considered so anti-Semitic that release of the film in America was swiftly curtailed.

Guinness started as an advertising copywriter and studied acting at the Fay Compton Studio of Dramatic Art. Actor John Gielgud hired him to join his company in 1935 and in 1936 he joined London's Old Vic, starring in a distinguished modern-dress *Hamlet*. He joined the Royal Navy in 1941, but was allowed to play in *Flare Path* on Broadway for propaganda purposes. Fox offered him a screen test in 1942 but he admirably refused.

A quiet, learned man, he affects not to court publicity. But come Oscar time, watch out for Alec Guinness, Britain's Mr. Versatility.

Alec Guiness as General D'Ascoyne.

SEPTEMBER
OCTOBER

NOVEMBER
DECEMBER

VIC HAS A HAIRCUT

With the box-office smash *Samson and Delilah* Cecil B. DeMille has done it again, and there could be no better casting than Victor Mature as the biblical beefcake.

He was born the son of a Swiss scissors-grinder, in Louisville, Kentucky, in 1915. He arrived in Hollywood broke, and worked for a while at the Pasadena Playhouse, where he was spotted by a talent scout, and made his movie debut in *The Housekeeper's Daughter* (1939), a Hal Roach comedy starring Joan Bennett. He was well-liked, and played starry roles in films as diverse as *One Million B.C.* (1940), as a caveman, and musicals like *No, No, Nanette* (also 1940) and *My Gal Sal* (1942) where he met and wooed Rita Hayworth.

After the war, Mature played a consumptive Doc Holliday for director John Ford in *My Darling Clementine* (1946) and revealed new depths. But he was more often cast for his looks. Samson will be a hard part to follow.

WONDERFUL TOWN!

Frank Sinatra, Gene Kelly and Jules Munshin On the Town.

M-G-M's Christmas present is the most exciting, and revolutionary, screen musical to emerge from the Culver City studios in years. In *On the Town* tyro directors Gene Kelly and Stanley Donen have actually taken their Technicolor cameras off the sound stage and on to the streets of New York for this tale of three sailors on a 24-hour spree. The opening is total joy as Kelly, Frank Sinatra and Jules Munshin (O'Brien, Ryan and Goldberg from *Take Me Out to the Ball Game* earlier this year) airily declare "New York, New York, It's a Wonderful Town" – the music's by Leonard Bernstein.

It's amazing that all the New York exteriors were shot in only three days (two others were lost because of bad weather). Says Kelly: "I desperately wanted one extra day in New York to wrap up shooting. But our cameraman on location was very much an old studio man who didn't realise what I was after, and told Louis B. Mayer we were getting nothing we couldn't have got on the backlot, so we came home as arranged."

Betty Garrett, Ann Miller and Vera-Ellen all have wonderful moments as the sailors' girl friends, but the triumph really belongs to producer Arthur Freed, for having the guts to give Kelly and Donen their directing break. Surely nothing can hold back this talented duo now.

LAUGHTER IN AUSTERITY

Four years after the war ended for Britain, a film company seems to have touched a nerve with its people. Ealing Studios, situated west of London, was set up in 1902, but the films produced by pioneers Will Barker and Basil Dean – comedies with either Gracie Fields or George Formby – didn't export too well.

Then Michael Balcon, who had produced for M-G-M in Britain, joined Ealing in 1938 as an independent producer. Over the next ten years he built a strong team of collaborators, encouraged to contribute to each other's projects. The laughter in the studio canteen was said to be contagious, and this year it's erupted on the screen.

Passport to Pimlico is a gem about an ancient document that reveals London's Pimlico district still belongs to the Duke of Burgundy. The local inhabitants declare themselves Burgundians, no longer subject to British post-war austerity rulings.

Compton MacKenzie's novel *Whisky Galore!* has an equally simple plot: a cargo of Scotch whisky goes aground on a wartime Hebridean island and the English soldiery attempts to stop the wily Scots from seizing the alcoholic haul.

But with *Kind Hearts and Coronets* Balcon's Ealing have a minor masterpiece. A witty, literate black comedy about a young man trying to knock off the 10 people who stand in his way to a title, the movie may turn out to be too dark for most people's taste. But for three such gems from one small studio in a year, we must be grateful to the foresight and experience of the Birmingham-born Michael Balcon.

GET THE REDS!

Now that union boss Roy Brewer has organized the Motion Picture Industry Council to deal with the "Communist problem", the first results of the anti-Red drive are starting to reach the screens. Hot on the heels of last year's Republic melodrama *The Red Menance* come two movies from the majors, tradeshown on successive days in New York City.

On 14 September industry veterans had first sight of M-G-M's *The Red Danube*, an all-star drama set in the Vienna of 1945, where unwilling Soviet repatriates are shipped off to Russia. George Sidney directs a sterling cast headlined by Walter Pidgeon, Ethel Barrymore, Peter Lawford and Angela Lansbury, but there's too much dialogue and not enough action.

The following day *I Married a Communist* (1949) was unveiled. Howard Hughes was anxious to produce it to show that his new baby, RKO, was no longer prone to such "liberal" product as *Crossfire* (1947). Hughes worked his way through several directors before ending up with the reliable Robert Stevenson, who has produced an exciting thriller featuring Robert Ryan battling a communist labour boss. There's talk of changing the title to *The Woman on Pier 13* for the overseas market.

Roy Brewer should be pleased. "Communists", he once told the press, "want to use the movies to soften the minds of the world".

Montgomery Clift and Olivia de Havilland in The Heiress.

SPINSTER SNARES SUITOR

There's no stopping the transformed Olivia de Havilland these days. Under William Wyler's skilled direction she's just a shade too pretty for vengeful spinster Catherine Sloper in this immaculate screen version of Henry James' novel *Washington Square*. As *The Heiress* of the title, de Havilland more than holds her own with Ralph Richardson as her father and newcomer Montgomery Clift as her predatory suitor. Clift seems rather anachronistic in looks and behaviour for the 19th-century setting, but there's no denying the power of his personality.

OSCARS FOR OLIVIA

With *The Snake Pit* and *The Heiress* hotly following her work in *The Dark Mirror* (1946) and her Oscar-winning performance in *To Each His Own* (1946), Olivia de Havilland has laid to rest her reputation as Errol Flynn's pretty little leading lady.

Like baby sister Joan Fontaine, she was born in Tokyo of British parents. In 1921, at the age of five, she moved to California and eventually appeared in local talent shows. Spotted by a scout as Puck in *A Midsummer Night's Dream*, she was recommended to Max Reinhardt, who cast her as Hermia in his marvellous 1935 film version, which led to a Warners contract. She went on to co-star with Flynn in eight romantic epics, most notably as a Technicolored Maid Marian to his Robin Hood, but more affectingly as the widow of Flynn's General Custer.

But it was *Gone with the Wind* (1939) that turned her career around. De Havilland made of the goody-goody Melanie Wilkes a warm and moving screen character, and she began her fight for better parts. After moving to Paramount, she began to play heavier roles.

Her Oscars for *To Each His Own* and *The Heiress* richly justify her confidence in her ability. Right now, however, she's temporarily deserted the silver screen to play both Juliet and Candida on Broadway. Let's hope she isn't away for long.

BOX OFFICE

UK

1. The Third Man
2. Johnny Belinda
3. The Secret Life of Walter Mitty
4. The Paleface
5. Scott of the Antarctic
6. The Blue Lagoon
7. Maytime in Mayfair
8. Easter Parade
9. Red River
10. You Can't Sleep Here (*U.S. title*: I Was an American War Bride)

BOX OFFICE

US

1. Jolson Sings Again
2. Pinky
3. I Was A Male War Bride
4. The Snake Pit
5. Joan of Arc
6. The Stratton Story
7. Mr. Belvedere Goes to College
8. Little Women
9. Words and Music
10. Neptune's Daughter

BIRTHS, DEATHS AND MARRIAGES

BIRTHS

Twiggy
19 Sep, London

Sigourney Weaver
8 Oct, New York

Jeff Bridges
4 Dec, Los Angeles

Sissy Spacek
25 Dec, Quitman, Texas

DEATHS

Frank Morgan
18 Sep, Hollywood

Richard Dix
20 Sep, Hollywood
Heart attack

Sam Wood
22 Sep, Hollywood
Heart attack

Bill Robinson
25 Nov, New York
Heart ailment

Maria Ouspenskaya
3 Dec, Hollywood
Fire accident

MARRIAGES

Clark Gable
20 Dec, *to* Sylvia Ashley

Cary Grant
25 Dec, *to* Betsy Drake

TRACY AND HEPBURN COURT LAUGHS

Spencer Tracy and Katharine Hepburn excel in their sixth movie together, as married (to each other) lawyers in husband and wife Garson Kanin and Ruth Gordon's *Adam's Rib* from M-G-M. He's prosecuting a man-shooting dumb-belle, and she's on the defence, believing a woman has the right to take potshots at an errant hubby. The casting, under director George Cukor, is superb throughout, and especially notable is newcomer Judy Holliday who, in one marvellous long take in jail when visited by lawyer Hepburn, suggests she's destined for a great screen career as a comedienne.

Billy Wilder on Hollywood: Sunset Blvd, *starring William Holden and silent cinema star Gloria Swanson.*

SOME CAN OF BEANS

Director Billy Wilder's much-discussed *Sunset Blvd.* has finally opened to critical acclaim. For a long while Wilder, exercising his right under a new Paramount contract, showed the script to no one and referred to it as *A Can of Beans*. But on 12 April, in Tinseltown itself, the Gothic Hollywood saga was finally unveiled. It's more a can of worms than a can of beans.

Montgomery Clift was cast as the young writer, Joe Gillis, but pulled out two weeks before the start of shooting. "I don't think I could be convincing making love to a woman twice my age," he told Wilder via his agent. That's odd, since he had been involved in real life with torch-singer Libby Holman. Wilder then tried for Fred MacMurray, who turned him down, and Gene Kelly, who was busy. William Holden was the last-minute choice, and he's perfect in the world-weary part.

Gloria Swanson was fourth choice for the role of faded star Norma Desmond ("I am big. It's the pictures that got small"). She was suggested by director George Cukor after Wilder had propositioned May West, Mary Pickford and Pola Negri.

The mordant movie begins with the body of the writer floating in the movie star's pool and, astoundingly, the corpse relates the story – how he was hired to "ghost" a script to restore her to former glory.

Guest stars Erich von Stroheim, Buster Keaton, Anna Q. Nilsson, H.B. Warner and Cecil B. DeMille all add to the sense of Hollywood-on-Hollywood.

STAR QUOTES

Louis B. Mayer
to Billy Wilder on seeing *Sunset Blvd.*

"You should be tarred and feathered and run out of Hollywood."

A LONG STORY

After nearly a year in the cutting rooms, director Robert Rossen's *All the King's Men* has finally arrived on the screen. It's a thinly-disguised biopic of Louisiana's infamous political demagogue Huey Long, from Robert Penn Warren's Pulitzer Prize-winning novel. The book's main character was fictional journalist Jack Burden, but in the movie the focus of attention is Long himself, fictionalized as Willie Stark.

Columbia boss Harry Cohn was unhappy with the original result, an overheated, overlength movie that was hard to cut down. Cohn sent for editor-turned-director Robert Parrish who, working closely with Rossen, ruthlessly cut the movie to 109 minutes, necessitating many dialogue changes. Cohn is said to be so pleased with Parrish's work that he's offered him a series of films to direct.

As Willie Stark, Broderick Crawford gives a chillingly believable study of a country lawyer who becomes a power-crazed despot.

John Ireland is also effective as Burden, and Joanne Dru (Mrs. Ireland) plays Burden's girl friend, who falls under the dangerous spell of Stark. Mercedes McCambridge is Stark's cynical and disillusioned mistress, Sadie Burke.

VIENNESE FANCY

The film that everyone is talking about this season is a British movie that picked up the 1949 Grand Prix at Cannes for the best film in competition, Carol Reed's *The Third Man*.

Based on a marvellous screenplay by Graham Greene, the Alexander Korda-David O. Selznick production went into wide release only this January in the United States, despite the fact that it opened at London's Plaza late last August. It's about an evil black-marketeer in post-war Vienna who specialises in diluted penicillin and is thought to be dead when his one-time friend, pulp writer Holly Martins (Joseph Cotten), comes looking for him. Orson Welles plays marketeer Harry Lime and, though he's only on screen for some 20 minutes, he dominates the movie. He, not Greene, wrote Lime's main speech given in a ferris wheel high above the city.

Orson Welles as Harry Lime in Carol Reed's romantic thriller The Third Man.

Director Reed attributes the movie's success to the fact that it's one of the few British productions made on location. Even the haunting zither theme was chosen (by editor Oswald Hafenrichter) from a pile of music that Reed brought back from Vienna's Cafe Mozart. Trevor Howard plays British military policeman Major Calloway, all moustache and beret, and the lovely Alida Valli is the mysterious Anna, who once loved Harry Lime.

So why has *The Third Man* taken so long to play a wide U.S. release? Well, David Selznick wanted to tinker with it a bit. The 104 minute movie has become 93 minutes in its North American version, and the opening narration is now spoken by Joseph Cotten rather than Reed.

Alastair Sim and Michael Wilding in Hitchcock's creaky backstage thriller Stage Fright.

MICHAEL WILDING

Britain's most popular male star, Michael Wilding, is currently romancing Jane Wyman on screen in Alfred Hitchcock's new thriller *Stage Fright*. But off-screen he's said to be huddling with the movie's *femme fatale*, Marlene Dietrich. They often double date with Stewart Granger and his lovely lady Jean Simmons on the yacht that Wilding owns with best pal Granger. Wilding's marriage to pretty Kay Young is said to be on the rocks.

In the meantime, he's turned producer with a film version of the West End play *Into the Blue*, directed by Herbert Wilcox. The subject matter is the amorous adventures of a young man on a yacht, with Wilding himself in the lead. . . . Co-star, however, is glamorous French import Odile Versois.

It's all a long way from the Essex seaside town where he was born in 1912. The son of an actress and an army officer, Wilding started as a commercial artist, specializing in portraits. But he soon discovered that being a film extra was more fun than being stuck in an art department. "You get a guinea a day," he said, "and the best crumpet in the world."

After a series of small roles, he hit lucky when producer Herbert Wilcox took a chance and co-starred him with Anna Neagle in the romantic froth *Piccadilly Incident* (1946). After that, Wilcox paired them again, and again, in hit after hit – *The Courtneys of Curzon Street* (1947), *Spring in Park Lane* (1948) and *Maytime in Mayfair* (1949). Filmgoers loved his good looks, suave delivery and breezy confidence.

Next up is a co-starring role opposite Greer Garson in a remake of *The Last of Mrs Cheyney*, this time in a Western setting. It's the start of Wilding's seven-year M-G-M contract – not bad going for a boy from Westcliff-on-Sea.

FROM LACHLAN MCLACHLAN TO ALFRED HITCHCOCK

It's shaping up to be quite a year for ABPC's new heart-throb Richard Todd, as he follows last year's Oscar-nominated part in *The Hasty Heart* with the principal suspect role in the new Alfred Hitchcock thriller, *Stage Fright*. Next he's off to Hollywood, working with the veteran director King Vidor.

Todd was born in Dublin in 1919, the son of an Irish rugby player. At 17 he gained entrance to the famed Italia Conti stage school, and made his movie debut in an athletics meeting with Robert Taylor in *A Yank at Oxford* (1938). After war service – he was the first man of the 6th Airborne Division to parachute out over Normandy on D-Day – he played the young thug in Cavalcanti's *For Them That Trespass* (1949) and was then cast by American director Vincent Sherman opposite Ronald Reagan and Patricia Neal in *The Hasty Heart*, as the stubborn Scot Lachlan McLachlan. After being placed under ABPC contract he was loaned out for *Interrupted Journey* (1949), opposite beautiful Valerie Hobson, and the fan mail started pouring in.

Todd sends *Picturegoer* magazine a regular "Hollywood Diary" and he's about to sign a multi-picture deal with Walt Disney. It's a sparkling year for the actor who was so sickly as a child that he couldn't move from an invalid bed.

TI AMO

On 9 February Ingrid Bergman was finally granted a Mexican divorce from devoted husband Petter Lindstrom. But it was a little too late: on 2 February she had given birth to a bouncing baby boy by Italian art-film director Roberto Rossellini, the man to whom she'd once written: "If you need a Swedish actress who in Italian knows only 'ti amo' (I love you), I am ready to come and make a film with you."

The outrage in her adoptive America has been deafening. On 14 March, in the U.S. Senate, Colorado's Edwin C. Johnson denounced her as "one of the most powerful women on earth today – I regret to say, a powerful influence for evil." And all because she once learned two words of Italian to say to Charles Boyer in *Arch of Triumph* (1948).

BIRTHS, DEATHS AND MARRIAGES

BIRTHS

Cybill Shepherd
18 Feb, Memphis, Tennessee

Julie Walters
22 Feb, Birmingham

Neil Jordan
25 Feb, Sligo, Ireland

Brad Dourif
18 Mar, Huntington, West Virginia

William Hurt
20 Mar, Washington, DC

DEATHS

Monty Banks
7 Jan, Arona, Italy
Heart attack

John M. Stahl
12 Jan, Hollywood

Alan Hale
22 Jan, Hollywood
Heart attack

Marguerite de la Motte
11 Mar, San Francisco
Complications after surgery

Walter Huston
7 Apr, Beverly Hills, California
Heart attack

MARRIAGES

Sidney Poitier
26 Apr, *to* Juanita Hardy

Joan Caulfield
29 Apr, *to* Frank Ross

ACADEMY AWARDS

PRESENTED ON 23 MARCH 1950

Best Picture
All the King's Men

Best Director
Joseph L. Mankiewicz
A Letter to Three Wives

Best Actor
Broderick Crawford
All the King's Men

Best Actress
Olivia de Havilland
The Heiress

Best Sup Actor
Dean Jagger
Twelve O'Clock High

Best Sup Actress
Mercedes McCambridge
All the King's Men

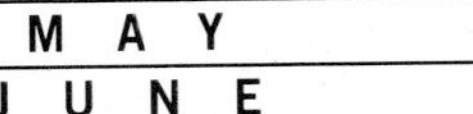

J U L Y
A U G U S T

NO BREED APART

The current trend for "problem" pictures dealing with black-white racial antagonism – *Pinky* (1949), *No Way Out* (1950), *Home of the Brave* (1949) – has had a sobering effect on the Western. Earlier this year, in M-G-M's offbeat *Devil's Doorway*, Robert Taylor was cast as an Indian who served in the Civil War, returning to find that injustice had been done to his people.

Now, in 20th Century-Fox's *Broken Arrow* James Stewart, tired of whites and Indians constantly killing each other, seeks out Apache leader Cochise to attempt a mutual peace. In so doing, he falls in love with an Indian maiden. Once again, the Indians are played by white actors, but Debra Paget (wearing brown contact lenses) as the girl, and Jeff Chandler (borrowed from Universal) as Cochise, play with great dignity in an intelligent script (by Michael Blankfort, recently accused of being a Communist sympathizer by the House UnAmerican Activities Committee). M-G-M is currently shooting Edna Ferber's *Show Boat*.

STAR QUOTES

Elizabeth Taylor

6 May 1950, on the occasion of her first marriage to Nicky Hilton

"I just love everything about getting married."

HOT JEWELS

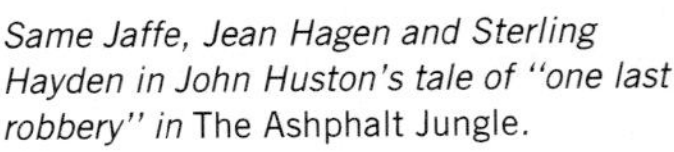

Same Jaffe, Jean Hagen and Sterling Hayden in John Huston's tale of "one last robbery" in The Ashphalt Jungle.

The film version of W.R. Burnett's thriller *The Asphalt Jungle* is a tough caper movie, especially surprising since it emanates from that slickest of studios, M-G-M. Director John Huston tells the story of a jewellery heist that goes wrong, as $500,000 worth of gems stolen from Belletier's find their way into the hands of a disreputable "fence" (Louis Calhern).

As the gunman on the caper, Huston bravely cast Sterling Hayden who was recently dropped by Paramount – allegedly over declining box office appeal but really because of his left-wing sympathies. Metro wanted a bigger box-office draw, but Huston was adamant and told Hayden: "The next time somebody says you can't act, tell them to call Huston".

As Calhern's "niece" Huston cast a girl he met at one of producer Sam Spiegel's card-party nights, a girl who wasn't there as a player that evening. Her name is Marilyn Monroe, and she's a protege of agent Johnny Hyde: she's been in a few movies, but this time she registers with a real impact.

The Asphalt Jungle is a tough movie, and indicative of a new regime at M-G-M. Says studio boss Louis B. Mayer: "That *Asphalt Pavement* thing is full of nasty, ugly people doing nasty, ugly things. I wouldn't walk across the road to see a thing like that." But production head Dore Schary and the public think otherwise.

BIRTHS, DEATHS AND MARRIAGES

BIRTHS

Tom Berenger
31 May, Chicago

Nancy Allen
24 Jun, New York

Susan George
26 Jul, Surrey

DEATHS

Rex Ingram
22 Jul, Hollywood
Cerebral haemorrhage

MARRIAGES

Elizabeth Taylor
6 May, *to* Nicky Hilton

Ingrid Bergman
25 May, *to* Roberto Rossellini

Bette Davis
28 Jul, *to* Gary Merrill

Errol Flynn
Aug, *to* Patrice Wymore

BETTY GETS HER GUN

Betty Hutton's appearance on the cover of *Time* magazine this spring is a sure sign the world has taken her portrayal of Annie Oakley to heart. "Frankly, I know a lot of people don't want me to play this," said Paramount's top blonde. But she wasn't M-G-M's first choice for the film version of Irving Berlin's 1946 Broadway hit *Annie Get Your Gun*. Judy Garland had recorded the score and shot some scenes, but proved unstable, and Republic's Judy Canova, Warners' Doris Day, and M-G-M's own Betty Garrett were all considered as likely contenders. Then producer Arthur Freed hijacked Hutton from Paramount to co-star with handsome Howard Keel, "Curly" from the London production of *Oklahoma!*

And what a choice it was! Hutton is tomboyish and tender by turns, her raucous voice absolutely apt for "You Can't Get a Man with a Gun" and "Doin' What Comes Naturally," and surprisingly tender in her duets with baritone Keel. George Sidney's direction is polished, and the Technicolor is a real joy. M-G-M should be proud of *Annie*. Its success has prompted the studio to mount a roster of new musicals with a promise to deliver a regular supply to exhibitors.

Marlon Brando, a paraplegic war veteran, is helped by Teresa Wright in The Men.

BOB, LAD

The most impersonated performance of the year has got to be Robert Newton's eye-rolling, vowel-stretching Long John Silver in Walt Disney's *Treasure Island*. It's a barnstorming role guaranteed to put the Shaftesbury-born English actor in the world market. Newton revels in the role, as he brings to life every schoolchild's image of Robert Louis Stevenson's immortal villain. Young Bobby Driscoll plays "Jim, lad," and he and Newton create a pairing that couldn't be bettered. And if "Long John Silver" reminds adult audiences of Shakespeare's "Pistol" and Charles Dickens' "Bill Sikes" perhaps that's because those literary characters were also played by Newton, in *Henry V* (1944) and *Oliver Twist* (1948).

Allegedly an actor with a liking for alcohol, Newton, 44, has often been hard to cast, but in *This Happy Breed* (1944) and *Odd Man Out* (1947) he showed a subtle and sensitive talent. It would be a shame if Stevenson's peg-legged pirate type-cast Robert Newton, Britain's wild man of the movies.

MEN UN-MANNED

Producer Stanley Kramer has done it again. For his third hit in a row Kramer and writer Carl Foreman (the team of last year's *Champion*) have chosen the most unlikely of subjects, and, aided by director Fred Zinnemann, have fashioned a touching drama.

The title of *The Men* is laden with irony. These are "men" who have lost their manhood: paraplegics, paralysed from the waist down. In the opening scene Lieutenant Ken Wilozek (Marlon Brando) is hit by a gunshot, and the film follows him as he realizes that not only will he never walk again, but that he'll never be able to father a child, unable to control his bladder or bowels, unable to make love to his fiancee, Ellen (Teresa Wright).

Broadway's Marlon Brando makes an impressive screen debut. Critics have been mixed but his understated, naturalistic performance seems absolutely right. Alongside seasoned veterans like Wright and Everett Sloane, Brando proves that if he can find the right parts for his nervous, edgy talent, he's got a brilliant future in movies.

Judy Holliday, Broderick Crawford and William Holden in Born Yesterday.

TRUMBO AND LAWSON JAILED

On 8 June John Howard Lawson and Dalton Trumbo, two of Hollywood's most talented scriptwriters, were handcuffed together and driven to the District of Columbia jail in Washington by United States marshals. Although a thousand demonstrators gathered in New York to protest, the sentence of $1,000 as a fine and one year in jail was firmly upheld by the Supreme Court. Of the court's sentence said Trumbo: "I am angry and resentful at having to go to jail. But I don't see how we can do otherwise in all conscience."

The charge was Contempt of Congress, indicted by a senatorial majority on 5 December 1948. It's taken two years of fighting to get "The Unfriendly Ten's" appeals heard in the Supreme Court, and eventually those appeals were thrown out.

So the sentences begin. Are Trumbo and Lawson in jail for contempt, or for being Communist Party members? One thing's for sure, it's going to be a long, long time before either writes professionally again.

WALT'S CRITTERS

Walt Disney has hit on the perfect solution to support his new feature product. Along with *Cinderella* and *Treasure Island* are showing the first two of what Disney terms "True-Life Adventures." Lasting a little over half-an-hour, they consist of wonderful natural footage.

Seal Island was the first, and *Beaver Valley* has swiftly followed. The format is virtually identical: local animal life is identified and a Winston Hibler narration comments on the action, often imbuing the critters with human characteristics. The results are delightful. Composer Paul Smith's "Frog Symphony" from *Beaver Valley* is very cleverly integrated, as it accompanies a twilight serenade of nocturnal bullfrogs. At 30 minutes or so, these shorts are great fun, but Disney also plans some True-Life features. Won't that be stretching the material?

SEPTEMBER OCTOBER

NOVEMBER DECEMBER

ALL ABOUT BETTE

Tallulah Bankhead won't be pleased when she sees Bette Davis in *All About Eve*, a jaundiced look at Broadway folk. If Davis isn't exactly playing Bankhead, she's pretty damn close in this cleverly constructed fable of Broadway folk. Davis got the part when both Rosalind Russell and Claudette Colbert were unavailable, and she seizes the role with relish: her Margo Channing is a wickedly bitchy portrayal that'll be slogging it out with Gloria Swanson among the Academy voters.

Anne Baxter is Eve, a ruthless, star-struck youngster who'll stop at nothing to achieve success. Other great characters in Joseph L. Mankiewicz's literate movie include George Sanders as world-weary theatre critic Addison de Witt ("Television? It's nothing but auditions"), Celeste Holm and Gary Merrill (soon to become Mr Bette Davis) as Broadway sophisticates. There's also that fabulous blonde Marilyn Monroe as a Miss Casswell, described by Addison de Witt as "a graduate of the Copacabana School of Dramatic Art."

All About Eve is yet another superb example of the Darryl F. Zanuck production regime at 20th Century-Fox. As long as the spectacular *David and Bathsheba* continues to make money for the studio, there's plenty of room to plough back the profits into movies like this.

A NEW HERO

Deborah Kerr and Stewart Granger as Rider Haggard's Allan Quartermain in the African adventure King Solomon's Mines.

M-G-M's *King Solomon's Mines* allows no doubt that the new decade had ushered in its first major star. Stewart Granger is exactly what audiences need: a 6ft 2in, sun-bronzed hero to combat the angst-ridden movie leads filling our black-and-white screens.

Granger is made for Technicolor, his whitened sideburns setting female hearts a-flutter, his heroic manner an example to schoolboys the world over as he incarnates Rider Haggard's Allan Quartermain. His contract specifies he remakes the silent Ramon Navarro swashbuckler *Scaramouche* (1923), but *King Solomon's Mines* is proving so successful that M-G-M is grooming him as the successor to Clark Gable himself, with remakes of *The Prisoner of Zenda*, *Quo Vadis*, and *Ben-Hur* for the handsome Brit.

The co-director of *Mines*, Compton Bennett, has complained that Granger was "monstrously difficult to work with." And those who have worked with "Jimmy" – his real name (no joke) is James Stewart – testify to his Taurean blend of arrogance and stubbornness.

But as long as 37-year-old Granger can deliver the goods the public will flock to his movies. He may not be the world's finest actor, but there's no question he's a real movie star.

THAT DARN RABBIT

In 1947 James Stewart made a welcome return to Broadway in a play by Mary Chase entitled *Harvey*, taking over from vaudevillian Frank Fay, who had created the role of Elwood P. Dowd, a likable, befuddled gent whose best friend is a large, invisible white rabbit, "Harvey".

Stewart's stage appearance was a dry run for the movie, and this year he's starred in the film of the same name. There was great speculation whether or not Harvey would actually appear on screen: but no, only Elwood P. Dowd saw Harvey, even though the lovable rabbit (or his agent) managed to secure a solo screen credit at the film's end.

NO DUMB BLONDE

It's easy to confuse the real Judy Holliday with her role of Billie Dawn in *Born Yesterday*. But she's far from the dumb blonde she plays so superbly.

As the world mimics her "Do me a favour will ya, Harry? – Drop Dead" line, the actress with an I.Q. of 172 prefers to socialize with New York buddies Leonard Bernstein, Betty Comden and Adolph Green.

Holliday made her film debut in *Greenwich Village* (1944), but most of her part ended up on the cutting-room floor. It wasn't until *Adam's Rib* (1949) that she made a real impact with movie audiences, and she nearly didn't appear in the Broadway version of *Born Yesterday*. In the play's tryout, star Jean Arthur was having trouble with the role, wanting to play it too intelligent at first, and the producers sent for Holliday, whom they had seen play a similar role on stage in *Kiss Them For Me* opposite Richard Widmark. Holliday went on in Boston with minimal rehearsal – and became inseparable from Billie Dawn, playing her from 1946 until 1950, and now on screen.

GOSSIP COLUMN

- **The privately-printed "Red Channels" unofficial Hollywood blacklist is said to name 151 names, including stars like Gene Kelly, Humphrey Bogart, Lauren Bacall, and Danny Kaye.**
- **Rita Hayworth is in dispute with Uncle Sam. The income tax people say she owes about $250,000 in back taxes from when she was married to Orson Welles. She backed his stage show *Around the World*. Now she's Princess Aly Khan, perhaps he can help her out?**

BIRTHS, DEATHS AND MARRIAGES

BIRTHS

Howard Rollins
17 Oct, Baltimore, Maryland

John Candy
31 Oct, Toronto

Don Johnson
15 Dec, Flat Creek, Missouri

DEATHS

Sara Allgood
13 Sep, Hollywood

Al Jolson
23 Oct, San Francisco
Heart attack

Maurice Costello
28 Oct, Hollywood

MARRIAGES

Robert Montgomery
9 Dec, *to* Elizabeth Harkness

Shirley Temple
16 Dec, *to* Charles Black

Stewart Granger
20 Dec, *to* **Jean Simmons**

JOLIE DEAD

The great Al Jolson has died, of a heart attack, on 23 October in a San Francisco hotel room. He was 64. Jolson is best remembered for speaking the first dialogue ever heard on the screen in *The Jazz Singer* (1927). He came to movies trailing a reputation as "The World's Greatest Entertainer", the man who stopped shows on Broadway, who threw away the book, turned up the house lights, and proceeded to sing requests into the wee small hours.

Jolson had several careers: as a Broadway star, as a movie great and, most recently, as the first man to entertain the troops when the Second World War broke out. His trips abroad brought him new audiences, and paved the way for the double-decker saga of his life.

SCHNOZ APPEAL

Jose Ferrer's bravado theatrical performance as the swashbuckler with the big conk has been brought to the screen with remarkable fidelity in *Cyrano de Bergerac*. Carl Foreman's screenplay, using the Brian Hooker translation, is faithful to the original's spirit, if a bit lacking in period sense. But the subject cries out for colour.

Ferrer is marvellous, with fencing ability to match. Producer Stanley Kramer is roadshowing *Cyrano* through his own set-up before United Artists handle the film worldwide, and that's a wise move. Word of mouth is already excellent, and people in the know are tipping Ferrer for the Oscar.

STAR QUOTES

Dalton Trumbo
HUAC victim in jail, in a letter to his wife.

"The sudden shucking off of all responsibility gives one a sense of almost exhilarating relief."

Roxanne (Mala Powers) learns that the dying Cyrano (Jose Ferrer) is the man she loves in Cyrano de Bergerac.

NO FAT BROAD

Garson Kanin's adaptation of the Pygmalion legend *Born Yesterday* is an immaculate transposition of its Broadway success. It wisely retains superb comedienne Judy Holliday.

Columbia's Harry Cohn originally intended the subject for contracted Queen of the Lot Rita Hayworth, but she ran off and married Aly Khan last May. Holliday had had a resounding success on stage as Billie Dawn, the not-so-dumb mistress of a racketeer, but Cohn wanted a more commercial name. He tested nearly half of Hollywood, closing in on Jean Hagen and Gloria Grahame. But director George Cukor wanted Holliday, and, mindful of Cohn's description of Judy as "a fat broad," had Holliday diet, screen-test, and peroxide her hair. Cohn capitulated, and the performance is something that Columbia's boss can truly be proud of.

Broderick Crawford's thinly-disguised portrait of Cohn as the racketeer seems to have been completely missed by the Columbia mogul. Perhaps Crawford's *All The King's Men* Oscar makes it all OK?

Judy Holliday, Broderick Crawford and William Holden in Born Yesterday.

BOX OFFICE

UK

1 The Blue Lamp
2 The Happiest Days of Your Life
3 Annie Get Your Gun
4 The Wooden Horse
5 Treasure Island
6 Odette
7 Jolson Sings Again
8 Little Women
9 The Forsyte Saga (*U.S. title*: That Forsyte Woman)
10 Father of the Bride

BOX OFFICE

US

1 Samson and Delilah
2 Battleground
3 King Solomon's Mines
4 Cheaper by the Dozen
5 Annie Get Your Gun
6 Cinderella
7 Father of the Bride
8 Sands of Iwo Jima
9 Broken Arrow
10 Twelve O'Clock High

Julie Andrews in The Sound of Music *(1965).*

Gene Kelly Singin' in the Rain *(1951).*

Judy Garland and pals search for The Wizard of Oz *(1939).*

The Jets dance up a storm in West Side Story *(1961).*

Mitzi Gaynor in a scene from South Pacific *(1958).*

Seven Brides for Seven Brothers *(1954).*

I GOT RHYTHM

The first integrated song-and-narrative musical was actually *The Wizard of Oz* (1939) – and all thanks to the singular vision of one man, uncredited associate producer Arthur Freed. He was to guide the Hollywood musical to a point where characters broke into song or dance as naturally as taking a breath. In the 1950s Freed was twice honoured as producer with Best Picture Oscar: for *An American in Paris* (1951), and for *Gigi* (1958).

Both were directed by Freed's protege, Vincente Minnelli, who had been brought to M-G-M from Broadway along with talents like dancer Gene Kelly and choreographer Stanley Donen. Freed also lured Fred Astaire; but the shining star at M-G-M was the mecurial Judy Garland, whose presence was to transform Freed's *Meet Me in St. Louis* (1944) from just an enchanting family drama into one of the most durable movies of all time.

Good News (1947), *Easter Parade* (1948), *Annie Get Your Gun* (1950), and *Show Boat* (1951) followed – marvellous entertainments all. Meanwhile, in *On the Town* (1949) Freed had encouraged a cinematic breakthrough, with directors Gene Kelly and Stanley Donen actually shooting on the streets of New York.

Singin' in the Rain (1952), which followed *An American in Paris*, has since been recognized as the finest-ever screen musical. Directors Kelly and Donen, and stars Kelly, Donald O'Connor and Debbie Reynolds managed the rare feat of perfectly meshing their talents as well as creating memorable solo spots – Kelly's title number alone is legendary.

Inevitably other studios lagged behind M-G-M. Warners patriotically offered James Cagney as *Yankee Doodle Dandy* (1942), while 20th Century-Fox permed Alice Faye and Betty Grable in garish items like *Down Argentine Way* and *Weekend in Havana* (both 1941), immensely popular but of little intrinsic merit. At Columbia, Kelly made an impact with Rita Hayworth in *Cover Girl* (1944), while at Paramount Bing Crosby starred in an array of vehicles, culminating in the massive *White Christmas* (1954).

At M-G-M no one could really compete with the taste and style of the elite Freed unit. But Jack Cummings struck lucky with virile baritone Howard Keel in both *Kiss Me Kate* (1953), shot in 3-D, and Stanley Donon's *Seven Brides for Seven Brothers* (1954).

Warners turned sparky band singer Doris Day into a major musical star, notably in *Calamity Jane* (1953) and *The Pajama Game* (1957). Also at Warners, Garland resurfaced in her finest role, *A Star Is Born* (1954), and the studio lovingly enshrined Broadway hits *Gypsy* and *The Music Man* (both 1962) for posterity.

The Broadway pedigree was significant. With ever-escalating costs, the collapse of the studio contract system, and the rise of rock 'n' roll, the Hollywood musical was in jeopardy. *Oklahoma!* (1955), *South Pacific* (1958), *West Side Story* (1961), and, especially, *The Sound of Music* (1965) were all enormously successful, their pre-sold scores boosted by the new and lucrative LP record market. But eventually the market yielded unacceptably modest profits.

There were exceptions: director-choreographer Bob Fosse attempted to redefine the musical with the acrid *Cabaret* (1972) and the autobiographical *All That Jazz* (1979). But apart from the success of the compilation film *That's Entertainment!* (1974), the traditional Hollywood musical had become moribund by the 1970s. The pop/rock disco musical, which grew out of low-budget "teenpics" of the 1960s, took its place – marketing exercises like *Saturday Night Fever* (1977) and *Flashdance* (1983) that were more like feature-length music videos.

Jennifer Beals in a striking scene from Flashdance *(1983).*

DID PARKS NAME NAMES?

The opening on 21 March of the second round of the House Un-American Activities Committee's investigations has proved the downfall of Columbia's top star Larry Parks. He had portrayed Al Jolson on screen, swashbuckled in *The Swordsman* (1948) and romanced Rita Hayworth in *Down to Earth* (1947).

But Parks had joined the American chapter of the Communist Party in 1941 when he was 25, because he said it was the "most liberal" of all parties. Disillusioned, he formally left the party in 1945, but with Reds now said to be under everyone's beds, Parks was pressed that March morning to name other alleged Communists. "I would prefer, if you would allow me, not to mention other people's names," he said. "This is not the American way."

Two days later, it was leaked that Parks had "named names." The details are still secret, but his career is clearly over. Parks has been branded a squealer, an informer, a disloyal friend. In a nutshell: Un-American.

PEERLESS PIER

A charming pair of soft Italian eyes are entrancing moviegoers in M-G-M's *Teresa*. They belong to Sardinian-born Pier Angeli, who seems just right as the war bride of GI John Ericson, as she suffers prejudice and pregnancy in Fred Zinnemann's documentary-style drama.

Born in 1932, she began her career as Anna Maria Pierangeli in two Italian movies about adolescent growing pains. But it's only now, since Zinnemann cast the fragile teenage beauty in the title role of *Teresa* that the world has sat up to the talents of the renamed Pier Angeli.

Metro is carefully grooming her, and her mother, over in Hollywood with her other daughter Marisa Pavan, is insisting the fetching twins are in bed at a reasonable hour, alone. It'll be interesting to see in Hollywood how long Pier Angeli can preserve that innocence that makes her so lovely on screen.

BIRTHS, DEATHS AND MARRIAGES

BIRTHS

Jane Seymour
15 Feb, Hillingdon, Middlesex

Kurt Russell
17 Mar, Springfield, Massachusetts

DEATHS

Jack Holt
19 Jan, Hollywood
Heart attack

MARRIAGES

Henry Fonda
Jan, *to* Susan Blanchard

Kirk Douglas as a sensation seeking reporter who delays the rescue of a man trapped in a cave (Richard Benedict) in Ace in the Hole.

ACE NO TRUMP

Ace in the Hole, Billy Wilder's acrid new movie, is a misanthropic retelling of the Floyd Collins story. It's told through the eyes of a reporter (Kirk Douglas) who, to prolong the newsworthiness of an "exclusive," tries to keep the Collins character entombed for ever. The tale is heavily fictionalized – Collins, played by Richard Benedict, is called Leo Minosa – and it's obvious that he could have been rescued from the cave-in in less than a day.

With Douglas playing reporter Charles "Chuck" Tatum, as tough as they come, Wilder and his co-writers have fashioned a gripping movie. The only tenderness is provided by Jan Sterling as the cold-hearted Lorraine, owner of a local diner; but her relationship with Douglas is hardly whipped cream. As Wilder says of screen females: "Unless she's a whore, she's a bore." So why doesn't he just dispense with women altogether and dress up fellas in drag for laughs? That would draw the crowds more than this one's doing.

ACADEMY AWARDS

PRESENTED ON 29 MARCH 1951

Best Picture
All About Eve

Best Director
Joseph L. Mankiewicz
All About Eve

Best Actor
Jose Ferrer
Cyrano de Bergerac

Best Actress
Judy Holliday
Born Yesterday

Best Sup Actor
George Sanders
All About Eve

Best Sup Actress
Josephine Hull
Harvey

ACROSS THE PACIFIC

When Thor Heyerdahl set out on a raft to try to prove that Polynesians originally migrated from South America and not from Asia, he had the shrewd idea of taking along some film stock as well. Expedition members took it in turns with the camera, and the footage, blown up to 35mm and trimmed to 68 mins, can now be seen in *Kon-Tiki*, distributed by RKO. Readers of Heyerdahl's best-selling book will know what to expect, as sharks, whales, and other sea creatures attack the raft on its perilous 4,300-mile Pacific voyage. The movie is a gripping record of a courageous achievement.

GOSSIP COLUMN

- **Ronald Reagan, who penned an article called "Reds Beaten in Hollywood", is currently starring with a chimpanzee in *Bedtime for Bonzo*.**
- **Elizabeth Taylor is refusing to speak to Nicky Hilton and, as their marriage crumbles, she's now squired round Hollywood by director Stanley Donen.**

Howark Hawk's sensational sci-fi chiller The Thing.

ANIMAL, VEGETABLE OR MINERAL?

Something's causing confusion at the North Pole. Scientists and weathermen find their compass readings are being disturbed and, after trekking through the snows in search of the solution, come across a creature that's neither vegetable nor mineral. "An intellectual carrot," says one of them. "The mind boggles."

That's just the start of Howard Hawks' raw chiller *The Thing*, from John W. Campbell's science fiction story *Who Goes There?* RKO, distributing the movie, have added the sub-title *From Another World* to the posters, just in case there's any confusion with the recent Hit Parade-topping ditty.

James Arness plays the walking carrot and is so strangely clad he's impossible to recognize as John Wayne's drinking buddy. His limp (from a bullet at Anzio) is positively helpful in the role.

Margaret Sheridan and Kenneth Tobey share top-billing, and if they seem a little lacklustre, blame producer Hawks, who decided not to cast name stars but to spend the budget on special effects. And this time he left the directorial chores to his former editor Christian Nyby, and contented himself with merely supervising the production.

ROYAL BELLS

Stanley Donen, former choreographer and directing partner of Gene Kelly, has made a breezy debut as solo director with *Royal Wedding*. It's about a pair of hoofers, the brother a perfectionist and the sister a man-chaser. Sounds like Fred and Adele Astaire? Could be. Fred Astaire plays Tom Bowen and his sister Ellen is pert Jane Powell. She proves she can dance as well as she can sing, which is just as well: at short notice she stepped in for June Allyson, who got pregnant, and Judy Garland, who got sick.

Astaire gets some super solos, notably a number in a ship's gym where his partner is a punching bag, and a knockout turn where he appears to dance on the ceiling. It'll take fans a long while to figure out how that was done!

The plot takes Astaire and Powell to a foggy studio London for the wedding of Princess Elizabeth and Prince Philip. But in order not to offend Buckingham Palace, the movie is going out as *Wedding Bells* in the UK.

Orson Welles

"I hate acting. I'd rather direct. I only act because I need myself in the parts in my pictures."

The great singing star Mario Lanza.

THE SINGING GROCER

The public are flocking to M-G-M's *The Great Caruso* and even film fans who have never heard of the mighty Enrico are lining the streets to see new lyric tenor Mario Lanza.

Lanza has just completed a sell-out concert tour following his two Technicolored outings for M-G-M, *That Midnight Kiss* (1949) and *The Toast of New Orleans* (1950), both opposite Kathryn Grayson.

He was born in Philadelphia in 1921, the son of a disabled war veteran and a poor seamstress. He had singing lessons while at school, but dropped out to work in the family grocery business run by his grandfather. Conductor Serge Koussevitsky heard him sing and invited to appear at Tanglewood summer school. An M-G-M contract followed after Second World War service.

Lanza is bringing opera to movie audiences, and that's no bad thing. But on set his success may have gone to his head: he's said to be truculent and rude, and refuses to bathe or use the lavatory in the proper manner. Warned about his weight problem, he keeps eating; told not to drink, he goes on benders; asked to sing, he regularly warbles sharp. How long M-G-M will put up with this kind of behaviour remains to be seen.

MAY
JUNE

JULY
AUGUST

BRANDO RAISES THE HEAT!

Vivien Leigh and Marlon Brando in A Streetcar Named Desire.

They said it couldn't be filmed, and certainly the screen censors have diluted the ending of Tennessee Williams' award-winning play *A Streetcar Named Desire*.

But what's left is still the steamiest concoction ever from Warners. Director Elia Kazan (he did *Streetcar* on Broadway) has kept most of the original cast, notably Marlon Brando as Stanley Kowalski, the brutish Polish-American husband of Stella (Kim Hunter).

In a torn T-shirt, alternately mumbling and shouting his dialogue, Brando performs as no one before. His virile presence makes you yearn for him when he's not on screen.

As faded Southern belle Blanche, Vivien Leigh is superb, though some have said it's cruel for the prone-to-disturbances Leigh to be cast as the mentally unstable Blanche, even though she played the role on the London stage. But with her first Southern accent since her Oscar-winning Scarlett O'Hara in *Gone with the Wind* (1939), Leigh looks set to pick up another Academy Award. If Hollywood's got any sense, it'll snap up all of Tennessee Williams' work: his plays make mighty fine cinema.

HOLLYWOOD'S NEW BAD BOY

After only two movies, it's already clear there's never been anyone quite like Marlon Brando. After taking Broadway by storm, he's now conquering the silver screen. But off-screen Brando hasn't exactly endeared himself to Hollywood. Tearing around on a motor-bike, clad in leather and T-shirt, he's drawing accusations of being rude.

Born in 1924 the young Brando was expelled from a series of military schools. But he attended the New York Dramatic Workshops for a year, and after a season of summer stock on Long Island, the young Nebraskan made his Broadway debut in 1944 in *I Remember Mama*, and went on to play with Paul Muni in Ben Hecht's infamous *A Flag Is Born*.

In 1947 Brando was director Elia Kazan's and author Tennessee Williams' choice for Stanley Kowalski in *A Streetcar Named Desire*, and Broadway history was made. He turned down several movie offers while in *Streetcar*, but accepted the role of the paraplegic in *The Men* (1950).

SCHARY REPLACES MAYER AT M-G-M

It was just a matter of time before Dore Schary, head of production at M-G-M, would be asked to take over the studio by East Coast Metro boss Nicholas Schenck. There was never any love lost between Schenck and flamboyant West Coast head Louis B. Mayer, who on 22 June officially bowed out of the studio he had helped to create back in 1924. Besides, *Battleground* (1949), Schary's personal picture, had proved a big hit, and M-G-M seems on a winning streak with movies like *Annie Get Your Gun* (1950), *King Solomon's Mines* (1950) and *Father of the Bride* (1950), all released since Schary arrived. Schary's love of "message" pictures may not equip him for a long-term tenure at glitz-and-gloss M-G-M, but at the moment he's the shareholders' blue-eyed-boy.

DANCING DUO

Despite a marvellous cast headed by Kathryn Grayson, Ava Gardner, and Howard Keel, it's husband-and-wife dance team of Marge and Gower Champion that's tiptoeing off with the reviews of M-G-M's new musical *Show Boat*.

But the duo isn't exactly new to the screen. Hollywood-born Marge is the daughter of Ernest Belcher, the respected ballet coach of many screen stars, and was billed as Marjorie Bell in the Astaire-Rogers movie *The Story of Vernon and Irene Castle* (1939). She was also the model for the heroine in Walt Disney's *Snow White and the Seven Dwarfs* (1937) and the Blue Fairy in *Pinocchio* (1940), posing for Walt's cartoonists.

In 1945 she met Gower Champion (born the same year as her, 1921) who had been dancing in Los Angeles nightclubs since he was 15. As Gower and Bell, they were a sensation; they married in 1947.

Gower had appeared in a few movies, including partnering Cyd Charisse in *Till The Clouds Roll By* (1946). But their two main duets in *Show Boat* have proved such Technicolor show-stoppers that M-G-M plans to star them in a remake of Jerome Kern's *Roberta* (1935) and to build them up as the Astaire-Rogers of the 1950s.

BIRTHS, DEATHS AND MARRIAGES

BIRTHS

Timothy Bottoms
30 Aug, Santa Barbara, California

DEATHS

Warner Baxter
7 May, Beverly Hills

Fanny Brice
29 May, Hollywood
Cerebral haemorrhage

Mayo Methot
9 Jun, Portland, Oregon
Alcohol

Louis Jouvet
16 Aug, Paris

Robert Walker
28 Aug, Brentwood, California
Respiratory failure

MARRIAGES

Tony Curtis
4 Jun, *to* **Janet Leigh**

Diana Dors
2 July, *to* Dennis Hamilton

CLIFT AND TAYLOR SCORE IN DREISER

Montgomery Clift and Elizabeth Taylor in A Place in the Sun.

George Stevens' new production *A Place in the Sun* updates Theodore Dreiser's novel *An American Tragedy*, previously filmed by Josef von Sternberg back in 1931, under its original title.

The plot is simple: a poor boy falls for a rich girl, but by the time she's interested in him he's got a new fiancee, and she's pregnant. A boating accident causes the fiancee's death, but he intended to drown her anyway. . . .

It's strong stuff, based on the now-forgotten notorious Chester Gillette murder trial. New star Montgomery Clift plays the troubled George Eastman, and his chemistry with Elizabeth Taylor (as Angela Vickers) is magnificent. In one sequence Stevens fills the screen with huge close-ups of Clift and the radiant 19-year-old Taylor, dissolving the two until the lovers seem to merge as one. It's a marvellously sensual use of cinema.

As the unfortunate Alice Tripp, Shelley Winters scores strongly, and there's also sterling work from Keefe Brasselle, Fred Clark (are there any major Paramount features without his burly presence these days?), and Raymond Burr. But it's Clift and Taylor you remember.

ROBERT WALKER DEAD

"From childhood I found myself up against mental walls," Robert Walker confessed to Hedda Hopper. "I was always trying to make an escape from life." But few were prepared for the sudden death of this popular young actor, on 28 August at the age of 32. Two doctors had tried to revive him with sodium amytol after a drinking binge.

Drink had long been Walker's escape valve. He never recovered from his first wife Jennifer Jones's leaving him for producer David Selznick, even though he was starring in hits like *See Here Private Hargrove* (1944) and *The Clock* (1945). He reprised Pete Hargrove in *What Next Corporal Hargrove?* (1945), was Jerome Kern in the all-star biopic *Till the Clouds Roll By* (1946), and scored heavily in *Song of Love* (1947) and *One Touch of Venus* (1948). In *Since You Went Away* (1944), he played a young soldier killed at Salerno, cast opposite estranged wife Jones in a Selznick production.

An impulse marriage to John Ford's daughter Barbara lasted a brief eight weeks in 1948, and Walker was sent to the Menninger Clinic, by M-G-M's Dore Schary.

His finest work was in Alfred Hitchcock's *Strangers on a Train* (1951), as the homosexual psychopath Bruno Anthony. At the time of his death Walker was playing a suspected Communist in Leo McCarey's *My Son John*. Out-takes and fragments of *Strangers on a Train* are to be spliced into the movie to complete his role, and the results should be on screens next spring.

EALING IN LAVENDER

Ealing Studios has done it again! After 1949's winning hat-trick of *Whisky Galore!*, *Passport to Pimlico* and *Kind Hearts and Coronets*, producer Michael Balcon and his talented team have come up with the delightful comedy *The Lavender Hill Mob*.

It's not exactly side-splitting, more gently mirthful. Alec Guinness plays Holland, a meek clerk who, abetted by Pendlebury (Stanley Holloway), plans the Perfect Crime: smuggling over one million pounds-worth of gold bullion out of the United Kingdom as souvenir models of the Eiffel Tower.

Charles Crichton directs this fable with restrained zest, and the London locations are as well photographed as in his excellent *Hue and Cry* (1947). A word of warning: there's no "mob" in *The Lavender Hill Mob*. Guinness and Holloway recruit lovable cockneys Sidney James and Alfie Bass, and that's it. The rest of the cast hardly gets a look-in, but John Gregson, Sidney Tafler, and a pretty brunette called Audrey Hepburn do wonders with cameos.

GOSSIP COLUMN

- **Howard Hughes has bought up J. Arthur Rank's share of Jean Simmons' contract. Hubby Stewart Granger has threatened to take action against Hughes, and a major court case is pending.**
- **Danny Kaye is No. 3040 in Paris' exclusive Casserole Club, an eating and drinking hole for celebrities. Danny himself is an excellent cook.**

SEPTEMBER
OCTOBER

NOVEMBER
DECEMBER

Peter Ustinov as Nero and Robert Taylor as Marcus Vicinius, a Roman commander, at the games in Quo Vadis.

BEAT THIS, TELEVISION!

"Colossal" shriek the ads, and for once they're not wrong. *Quo Vadis* is shaping up as M-G-M's mightiest hit ever, giving new boss Dore Schary another triumph after taking over in the summer from the ousted Louis B. Mayer.

As *Quo Vadis* settles into its blockbusting run, it's worth remembering the Roman epic started shooting well over a year ago, on 22 May 1950, directed by Mervyn LeRoy (replacing John Huston). It's a big break for Robert Taylor, who plays a part originally earmarked for Gregory Peck and then Stewart Granger. The word is that, to help Taylor play a Roman centurion, producer Sam Zimbalist showed him Granger's screen test, directed by Huston!

The Henryk Sienkiewicz novel has been filmed three times before (1902, 1912 and 1925, with Emil Jannings). But M-G-M's version, partly shot in Italy, tops them all. Peter Ustinov's flamboyant Nero and Leo Genn's noble Petronius take the acting honours, but the real star is the sheer scale of the spectacle, with a breathtaking Fire of Rome. So realistic are the circus scenes where hungry lions munch on Christians' bones, that in England the movie is forbidden to under-16s. This is *exactly* the kind of movie that can never be shown on television.

BIRTHS, DEATHS AND MARRIAGES

BIRTHS

Michael Keaton
5 Sep, Coraopolis, Pennsylvania

Sting
2 Oct, Newcastle

DEATHS

Maria Montez
7 Sep, Paris
Heart attack

MARRIAGES

Cornel Wilde
4 Sep, *to* Jean Wallace

Peter Sellers
15 Sep, *to* Anne Hayes

Leslie Caron
23 Sep, *to* George Hormel

Ava Gardner
7 Nov, *to* **Frank Sinatra**

BOX OFFICE

UK

1 The Great Caruso
2 Samson and Delilah
3 Laughter in Paradise
4 Worm's Eye View
5 Cinderella
6 Captain Horatio Hornblower
7 King Solomon's Mines
8 Toast of New Orleans
9 Kim
10 Soldiers Three

BOX OFFICE

US

1 David and Bathsheba
2 Showboat
3 An American in Paris
4 The Great Caruso
5 A Streetcar Named Desire
6 Born Yesterday
7 That's My Boy
8 A Place in the Sun
9 At War with the Army
10 Father's Little Dividend

MASON MAKES GOOD

One of the year's big surprises was the incongruous casting of Britain's James Mason as Field-Marshal Rommel in *The Desert Fox*, 20th Century-Fox's sombre account of the general's defeat at El-Alamein. Mason was superb in the role, his close-cropped hair and sophisticated demeanour entirely convincing as the leader of Hitler's Afrika Korps.

Born in the mill town of Huddersfield in 1909, Mason studied architecture at Cambridge and, after a spell in theatre, broke into films in the mid-1930s. He scored heavily in melodramas like *Fanny by Gaslight* (1944) and *The Seventh Veil* (1945), and by the time of *The Wicked Lady* (1946) was judged Britain's top box-office draw. But it was director Carol Reed's *Odd Man Out* (1947) that revealed his true depths as an actor, despite a wayward Irish accent. Hollywood called, but Mason intended to go on his own terms, staying as independent as possible in a system where a seven-year-contract is a way of life.

He teamed with émigré director Max Ophuls in a pair of movies that failed to set the box office alight, and co-starred in a couple of M-G-M mellers, including playing Flaubert for Vincente Minnelli in*Madame Bovary* (1949). But the Hollywood success of compatriots Stewart Granger, David Niven and Michael Wilding seemed to elude him. Deliberately uncooperative with Tinseltown's press, Mason looked like he was heading home, sharpish.

Now 20th Century-Fox is readying *Operation Cicero* for its new star, and there's a rumour that Rommel will be reprieved in a sequel. It looks like the 42-year-old Yorkshireman has found a niche in Hollywood after all.

MOVING MIRACLE

The Festival of Britain, held on London's South Bank exactly 100 years after the so-called Great Exhibition of Queen Victoria, is intended to herald a dynamic new future for Great Britain and the British Commonwealth. And in London's brand new Telekinema cinema next door under Waterloo Bridge, stereoscopic films are being shown to the public for the first time.

The British film industry is paying tribute to pioneer William Friese-Greene, whose story is told in the hit movie *The Magic Box*. The craftsman who virtually invented the motion-picture camera is played by Robert Donat.

Producer Ronald Neame cajoled the great names of London's stage and screen to appear in the film for a fixed rate of pay. There's Michael Redgrave, Eric Portman, Emlyn Williams, Richard Attenborough and Michael Denison, all in small parts. But most effective is Laurence Olivier as a London policeman called in to witness Friese-Greene's first exciting projection. On a sheet in a dingy attic, the London policeman watches the miracle that is moving pictures. Olivier and Donat together bring tears to the eyes with their combined artistry.

BOGIE & KATE'S AFRICAN SAFARI

Technicolor goes on safari again for the first time since last year's *King Solomon's Mines* in John Huston's *The African Queen*. Improbably cast as cockney Charlie Allnut is Humphrey Bogart, and if Marlon Brando's Stanley Kowalski weren't in the running, this is an Oscar-worthy performance if ever there was one. Seen in colour for the first time, Bogie is a delight, belching and cursing his way up river in the scow of the title, putting up with spinster Katharine Hepburn for much of the way, until his respect for her grows into affection and eventually love.

Bogart and Hepburn seem made for each other, and the film's a tribute to their stoicism as well, for the African locale was clearly no holiday. Hepburn kept a diary of her misfortunes which would make fascinating reading some day.

Movie critic James Agee is credited with the screenplay (from C.S. Forester's First World War tale) but the attitudes and dialogue seem to be very much Huston's: he's a tough buzzard who takes pleasure in tales of hardship like *The African Queen*, and is one of the few directors able to get a real performance from the casual Bogart. Remember them 10 years back in *The Maltese Falcon?*

Humphrey Bogart and Katharine Hepburn in The African Queen.

Gene Kelly and Leslie Caron dance by the Seine in An American in Paris.

KELLY'S DANCING LENS

M-G-M have their third mammoth hit musical in a row (after *The Great Caruso* and *Show Boat*) with *An American in Paris*. Could this be the movie that will break the Best Film Oscar taboo against musicals since *The Great Ziegfeld* (1936)?

The Arthur Freed production ransacks the works of George Gershwin, but the real joy of the movie is star Gene Kelly, who choreographed the climactic 18-minute ballet himself. It's an innovative ending for an American movie, encouraged by the box-office success of the British *Red Shoes* (1948) which also featured a sel-contained ballet. Kelly and director Vincente Minnelli take the audience on a spectacular trip through the world of artists Dufy, Manet, Utrillo, Rousseau, Van Gogh and Toulouse-Lautrec. Says the star: "If the camera is to make any contribution to dance, the focal point must be the pure background, giving the spectator an undistorted and all-encompassing view of dancer and background. To accomplish this, the camera must be made to move with the dancer, so that the lens becomes the eye of the spectator".

He's helped by a superb cast that includes newcomer Leslie Caron (in a role originally intended for Marge Champion). She was discovered by Kelly at the Roland Petit Ballet Company in Paris when she was only fifteen. Also starring are French matinee idol George Guetary (in a part turned down by Maurice Chevalier because he doesn't get the girl!); Nina Foch as a wealthy American collector of "talent" (a part intended for Celeste Holm!); and Oscar Levant, who (in a steal from Buster Keaton) performs Gershwin's Concerto in F playing every instrument in the orchestra.

METRO'S MUSICAL WIZARD

His current hit is *An American in Paris* and next spring he's hoping to repeat the magic with another Gene Kelly starrer, *Singin' in the Rain*, now getting its finishing touches at M-G-M. Born in 1894, in South Carolina, Arthur Freed started as a song plugger, occasionally writing ditties of his own without much success. He played piano in vaudeville, appeared on-stage with the Marx Brothers, and served in the First World War.

But in 1923 he wrote a hit song "I Cried For You", and in 1929, Irving Thalberg, the "Boy Wonder" producer at M-G-M, hired him as studio lyricist. The songs that Freed wrote with composer Nacio Herb Brown became part of the fabric of Hollywood itself: "Singin' in the Rain", "You Are My Lucky Star", "Pagan Love Song", "Would You?", and many more.

M-G-M tried out Freed as associate producer on *The Wizard of Oz* (1939), and he was responsible for the movie's fabulous use of music. Louis B. Mayer made him top musical producer at the studio, and Freed turned out classics like *Babes in Arms* (1939), *Best Foot Forward* (1943), and *Girl Crazy* (1943).

But it was *Meet Me in St. Louis* (1944) that made him. And he followed it with a string of hits such as *Easter Parade* (1948), *On The Town* (1949), *Annie Get Your Gun* (1950), and this year's *Show Boat* and *An American in Paris*. If Dore Schary will increase his budgets, there'll be no holding back Arthur Freed.

JANUARY
FEBRUARY

MARCH
APRIL

BIRTHS, DEATHS AND MARRIAGES

DEATHS

Polly Moran
24 Jan, Chicago

Gregory La Cava
1 Mar, Malibu, California

MARRIAGES

Elizabeth Taylor
21 Feb, *to* **Michael Wilding**

Ronald Reagan
4 Mar, *to* Nancy Davis

Vera Ralston
15 Mar, *to* Herbert J. Yates

Betty Hutton
18 Mar, *to* Charles O'Curran

ANSCO HUES

Those ever-so-rich M-G-M Technicolor movies may well soon be a thing of the past. Metro is experimenting with the Anscocolor process which uses single-negative shooting stock, instead of the three strips (magenta, yellow, cyan) of Technicolor.

It's cheaper, of course, and M-G-M executives are swearing by it. Audiences can judge for themselves in *The Wild North* (1952), an action-adventure shot in Canada, re-uniting the successful team from *King Solomon's Mines* (1950) star Stewart Granger, director Andrew Marton, and cameraman Robert Surtees.

Eastman-Kodak is also developing a single-strip base, as is DeLuxe laboratories. With the elimination, at last, of nitrate base for film, and the introduction of safety celluloid stock, it seems as though a genuine revolution is taking place in film itself.

Donald O'Connor, Debbie Reynolds and Gene Kelly in a scene from Singing in the Rain.

SINGIN' AND TALKIN'!

Those who have seen it are already raving about M-G-M's *Singin' in the Rain*. The Arthur Freed musical is being called the wittiest and inventive movie about movie-making to date.

Singin' in the Rain is about the coming of sound and deals with such incidents as silent idol John Gilbert's screen downfall (speaking the lines "I love you, I love you, I love you" in *His Glorious Night* (1929)) and the revelation of the Brooklyn twang of screen goddess Norma Talmadge as *Du Barry – Woman of Passion* (1930), her first and last talkie. The names, of course, are changed in the hilarious Betty Comden-Adolph Green screenplay.

Gene Kelly and Stanley Donen direct with verve and Kelly is glorious as the vain silent star of limited talent, relying on his stunting skills ("Dignity, always dignity") as a bridge to a career. Kelly's co-stars are Donald O'Connor, borrowed from Universal, and, in a starring role for the first time, vivacious 19-year-old Debbie Reynolds, who proved so popular in *Two Weeks - with Love* (1950).

The score largely consists of producer Freed's back catalogue, and there is a splendid "Broadway Ballet" in the centre of the movie. Is *Singin' in the Rain* the best musical ever made? Can you think of a better one?

KAZAN NAMES NAMES

Although best known as the director of *A Streetcar Named Desire* (1951), Elia Kazan boasts a distinguished New York career, notably for his work with the socially conscious Group Theater, as both actor and director. His movies include such "liberal" works as *Gentleman's Agreement* (1948) about anti-Semitism, *Pinky* (1949) about racial discrimination, and *Boomerang* (1947), about political obstruction of justice.

Kazan appeared before the House Un-American Activities Committee in January, when he answered all questions except the one about which people he knew to be members of the Communist Party. Kazan had been a communist between 1934 and 1936, and HUAC wanted the names of other party members in that period.

Then on 10 April in secret session, Kazan told HUAC what they wanted to know. He then placed an ad in the *New York Times* explaining his position.

A BOY NAMED KELLY

When *An American in Paris* premiered on 9 November last year, Gene Kelly's faith in himself was triumphantly justified. Once-and-for-all he'd proved that movie musicals were more than just lightweight fluff. They could flex their muscles in the boulevards of a Hollywood Paris, as they'd done in the New York streets of *On The Town* (1949) or the Caribbean alleyways in *The Pirate* (1948). And now, having given *American* an armful of Oscars, the Academy has finally given its stamp of respectability to the form.

Producer Arthur Freed has also been awarded the Irving G. Thalberg Memorial Award for Cinematic Achievement, and Kelly himself a statuette for "appreciation of his versatility as an actor, singer, director, and dancer, and specifically for his brilliant achievements in the art of choreography on film".

It's been a long haul for Kelly, a former dance instructor from Pittsburgh. He's had a lot of people to thank, many of them great choreographers themselves: Robert Alton, who first cast him in the chorus and gave him his stunning break on Broadway in 1940 in *Pal Joey*; Busby Berkeley, who starred him in *For Me and My Gal* (1942), as a vaudevillian who is shamed into heroics by his love for Judy Garland; and producer Arthur Freed, who recognized in Kelly and co-choreographer Stanley Donen the kind of invention and energy that movies need.

Kelly now wants to film a song-less musical of pure dance, and he's developing one along those lines. He's talking about starring in, and choreographing, a movie version of the 1947 Broadway hit musical *Brigadoon*, to be shot entirely in Scotland. And he wants to turn *An American in Paris* into a television series, to star his old *Pal Joey* mate Van Johnson. Can anything stop him now?

Charlton Heston and Betty Hutton in The Greatest Show on Earth.

THE CIRCUS COMES TO TOWN

The Greatest Show on Earth is very nearly that. At 151 Technicolored minutes, veteran Cecil B. DeMille pulls out every stop as he weaves a fictional tale of jealousy, romance, and murder under the big top of Ringling Bros.-Barnum & Bailey three-ring circus.

Stars on hand are Cornel Wilde (in a part first offered to Stewart Granger) as The Great Sebastian, daredevil aerialist whose spectacular missed double somersault is causing an audible gasp among audiences; Betty Hutton, rightly top-billed, proving once again that she's Paramount's gold-dust queen as Holly, who loves and loses Sebastian; newcomer Charlton Heston as circus manager Brad; and Dorothy Lamour, whose greatest fans, Bing Crosby and Bob Hope, make a surprising and delightful guest appearance.

There's also James Stewart, his all-American features permanently covered in whiteface, as a medic on the run disguised as a clown, and Gloria Grahame and Lyle Bettger as a couple with an elephant act. But the DeMille *pièce de résistance* is the most spectacular train wreck ever seen on the screen: the animals are unharmed, but the audience gets the thrill of a lifetime.

DON'T FENCE ME IN

Cornel Wilde's athleticism in *The Greatest Show on Earth* (1952) has surprised audiences who remember his Oscar-nominated performance as the sickly Chopin in *A Song to Remember* (1945), and his sterling work in all those Fox melodramas, like *Leave Her to Heaven* (1947), *Road House* (1948), and, of course, *Forever Amber* (1947). But Wilde trained as a champion fencer, and was chosen for the Olympic team in Berlin in 1936, fencing for America. That in itself was ironic, for he comes from Hungarian-Czech stock, although born in New York City in 1915.

Wilde quit the U.S. fencing team to become an actor, and received a break in 1940 when he was selected to be both fencing instructor to the cast and to play Tybalt in the Laurence Olivier production of *Romeo and Juliet* on Broadway, co-starring Olivier and Vivien Leigh. Rehearsals were held in Hollywood, and both Warners and Fox signed young Wilde, although it was on loan-out to Columbia that he scored his biggest success, opposite Paul Muni and Merle Oberon, as a Technicolored Chopin.

Wilde hopes to produce and direct feature films himself, and has already several ideas down on paper, including remakes of Robin Hood (he played his son in the 1946 *Bandits of Sherwood Forest*), Lancelot and Guinevere, and, of all people, Omar Khayyam.

DO NOT FORSAKE ME, DUKE . . .

Frank Miller arrives on the noonday train, to be met at Hadleyville station by three old cronies, and together the four of them seek revenge on Marshall Will Kane, who sent Frank Miller down. It's Kane's wedding day, and Tex Ritter's plaintive singing of the Dimitri Tiomkin-Ned Washington ballad ("Do Not Forsake Me, O My Darlin' . . .") forms a haunting background to Stanley Kramer's production *High Noon*.

As Kane, Gary Cooper makes a strong return after a slew of unworthy pot-boilers. As his lovely Quaker bride, newcomer Grace Kelly, shows a fetching combination of sexiness and innocence. And as Coop's former mistress Katy Jurado scores heavily.

The film is directed by Fred Zinnemann, who made the Marlon Brando starrer *The Men* two years ago. Some people, including John Wayne, reckon *High Noon* is actually about standing together against the McCarthy threat. The Duke has publicly castigated writer Carl Foreman and says he intends to make his version of the same story, where the Marshall takes all the help he can get.

Gary Cooper prepares for the showdown in High Noon.

ACADEMY AWARDS

PRESENTED ON 20 MARCH 1952

Best Picture
An American in Paris

Best Director
George Stevens
A Place in the Sun

Best Actor
Humphrey Bogart
The African Queen

Best Actress
Vivien Leigh
A Streetcar Named Desire

Best Sup Actor
Karl Malden
A Streetcar Named Desire

Best Sup Actress
Kim Hunter
A Streetcar Named Desire

MAY
JUNE

JULY
AUGUST

FOILED AGAIN!

This May's attraction at New York's Radio City Music Hall and London's Empire, Leicester Square, is a treat for all ages, M-G-M's swashbuckling remake of its 1923 Ramon Novarro hit *Scaramouche*.

The Rafael Sabatini novel begins with the words: "He was born with the gift of laughter, and a sense that the world was made". He might as well have been writing of Stewart Granger, who's superb as Scaramouche, a harlequin of the famed *commedia dell'arte* tradition, but who's really Andre Moreau, a Frenchman forced to avenge the death of a revolutionary buddy by disguising himself as the clown of the title.

The movie climaxes with an eight-minute duelling sequence in a packed theatre between Granger and villain Mel Ferrer. M-G-M and director George Sidney have spared nothing to make this one of the greatest fights in movie history. Granger did his own work; Jean Heremans doubled for Ferrer.

Both stars are complemented by the fiery Eleanor Parker, who reveals a nice line in ready wit; and lovely Janet Leigh is a treat as the lovelorn heroine.

PRETTY BOY GROWS A BEARD

The arrival of Stewart Granger at M-G-M has had a knock-on effect on the careers of the older generation of Metro stars. King of the lot Clark Gable is stepping into a remake of the 1932 *Red Dust* and matinee idol Robert Taylor has already taken over two roles once earmarked for Granger, last year's *Quo Vadis* and now *Ivanhoe*.

Ivanhoe was directed on the grand scale by Richard Thorpe at M-G-M's Borehamwood studios in Britain. There are fine performances from co-stars Elizabeth Taylor, Joan Fontaine, and George Sanders; but Taylor's playing of the courageous Saxon knight has restored his box-office value and won him new fans. They're too young to have remembered "The Man With the Perfect Profile" who partnered Garbo in *Camille* (1937) and caused a major sensation when he docked at Southampton to play *A Yank at Oxford* in 1938.

The brash, likeable Nebraskan became the screen's top romantic star in movies like *Magnificent Obsession* (1935) and *Waterloo Bridge* (1940). But Second World War service as a flight instructor hardened that "pretty boy" profile. He directed 17 navy training films while in service, and narrated the feature-length wartime documentary *The Fighting Lady* (1944).

Last year he divorced Barbara Stanwyck, whom he had married back in 1939. But they're still great friends and Taylor is busier now than he has ever been – and still under a long-term M-G-M contract. The studio has plans for a follow-up about King Arthur, with Taylor as Lancelot, and there's talk of a movie with Stewart Granger. Who will get top billing in that?

PIRATE PRANKSTERS

Shiver me timbers, if it isn't Burt Lancaster hanging from the yardarm, telling us a tale. And telling it spendidly too, as Vallo, in Warners' *The Crimson Pirate*. Vallo's privateers have captured a 30-gun galleon and plan to sell off the cargo of cannon to rebels trying to depose the King of Spain. But plot isn't what *The Crimson Pirate* is about: it's about action, romance and the fun of piracy. Douglas Fairbanks would have been proud.

Former circus athlete Lancaster cuts a fine figure, and reunites with old big-top and vaudeville chum Nick Cravat for some splendid stunt work.

The Harold Hecht production is directed by Robert Siodmak, better known for heavy-handed Teutonic melodramas like *The Spiral Staircase* (1945) and Lancaster's memorable movie debut, *The Killers* (1946). It's rumoured that Lancaster, writing friend Roland Kibbee, editor Jack Harris and second unit director Vernon Sewell took over the movie, and turned it into the roistering romp it's now become. Siodmak apparently thought he was making a serious study of piracy on the high seas!

Burt Lancaster is The Crimson Pirate.

MOVIE TALES

In England a run of movies based on W. Somerset Maugham's short stories has momentarily changed the shape of cinema. First, *Quartet*, with four episodes directed by different directors, appeared in 1949. When the mixture of actors like Dirk Bogarde, Mai Zetterling and Basil Radford and Naunton Wayne proved popular, it was followed by *Trio* (1950). Two directors shared the chores here and the casts included Jean Simmons, Nigel Patrick and Michael Rennie.

Now *Encore* has completed the Maugham series, with a further three tales, three directors, and players like Kay Walsh, Glynis Johns and Terence Morgan.

The "portmanteau" idea has spread to Hollywood. Ben Hecht has made *Actors and Sin* from two of his own short stories, starring Edward G. Robinson, Eddie Albert and Marsha Hunt. *Face to Face* is also a two-parter, with adaptations of Joseph Conrad's classic short story *The Secret Sharer*, with James Mason, and Stephen Crane's *The Bride Comes to Yellow Sky*, with Robert Preston bringing Marjorie Steele out West.

20th Century-Fox has an all-star affair in *O. Henry's Full House*, five tales from America's best-known short story writer, and directed by Henry Hathaway, Howard Hawks, Henry King, Henry Koster and Jean Negulesco. Distinguished author John Steinbeck links the tales, and the casts are superb: Charles Laughton, Marilyn Monroe, Richard Widmark, Anne Baxter, Fred Allen, Oscar Levant, Jeanne Crain, Farley Granger and Dale Robertson.

Finally, over at M-G-M, Vincente Minnelli and Gottfried Reinhardt are shooting *The Story of Three Loves*, with Pier Angeli, Kirk Douglas, James Mason, Leslie Caron, Moira Shearer, Ethel Barrymore and young Ricky Nelson. The first Technicolor portmanteau picture, it should be out next spring.

THE SCARECROW SCORES

To many Ray Bolger will forever be the lovable scarecrow in *The Wizard of Oz* (1939), singing "If I Only Had a Brain" and escorting Judy Garland down the Yellow Brick Road.

But this season the 48-year-old, Massachusetts-born hoofer has made a spectacular return in the leading role in *Where's Charley?*, the film version of his Broadway success.

Filmed in England at the ABPC studio, Elstree, the Warners movie caps quite a haul to big-screen stardom. Bolger made his professional debut back in 1922, touring New England towns in musical comedy summer stock. Vaudeville led to Broadway, including *George White's Scandals, Life Begins at 8.40*, and, famously, *On Your Toes*, in which he danced Richard Rodgers' "Slaughter on 10th Avenue".

That got him his movie debut in *The Great Ziegfeld* (1936), and *Rosalie* (1937) and *Sweethearts* (1938) followed. The success of *Where's Charley?* has led Warners to cast him opposite Doris Day in the song-fest *April in Paris*, due next year.

OIRLAND'S DARLIN'

Maureen O'Hara, Victor McLaglen, John Wayne and Barry Fitzgerald in The Quiet Man.

Director John Ford returns to his spiritual roots with *The Quiet Man*. The youngest child of Irish immigrants, Maine-born Ford has always shown a bit of the blarney in his movies' notably in the Oscar-winning *The Informer* (1935), but also in *The Plough and the Stars* (1936).

The Quiet Man is boxer Sean Thornton, played by Ford's favourite star John Wayne, returning to the homeland after killing an opponent in the ring. He falls for Mary Kate Danaher, and that's the end of his peace and quiet, for she refuses to, shall we say, honour the marriage bed, until her wild brother, "Red" Will Danaher, coughs up a dowry.

The feisty Danahers are Maureen O'Hara and Victor McLaglen, and with such Ford stalwarts as brothers Barry Fitzgerald and Arthur Shields, big Ward Bond, and Ford's own brother Francis in the cast, *The Quiet Man* shapes up as a romp for old pals to get together.

Ray Bolger in Where's Charley?

BIRTHS, DEATHS AND MARRIAGES

BIRTHS

Liam Neeson
7 Jun, Ballymena, Ireland

Carol Kane
18 Jun, Cleveland, Ohio

Isabella Rossellini
18 Jun, Rome

Dan Aykroyd
1 Jul, Ottawa, Canada

Robin Williams
21 Jul, Chicago

Patrick Swayze
18 Aug, Houston, Texas

DEATHS

John Garfield
21 May, New York
Heart attack

MARRIAGES

Judy Garland
Jun, *to* Sidney Luft

Zachary Scott
6 July, *to* Ruth Ford

Jack Carson
1 Aug, *to* **Lola Albright**

GARFIELD DEAD

On 21 May John Garfield was found dead in a friend's New York apartment, allegedly having had a heart attack while *in flagrante delicto*. He was only 39.

He's the fourth actor to die within the past three months who had been investigated by the House Un-American Activities Committee for alleged Communist affiliations. (The others were Mady Christians, Canada Lee, and J. Edward Bromberg.)

Garfield testified before HUAC last year as a "co-operative witness", and said he had never actually been a member of the Communist Party. Over the past two years the screen tough guy had seemed a shadow of his former self; he suffered his first heart attack in Hollywood in 1949, collapsing after a game of tennis.

A Jewish kid from the tough lower East Side of New York, the son of an immigrant tailor, he travelled the country on freight trains, later winning a *New York Times* debating contest and a scholarship to study drama with Maria Ouspenskaya.

He was really the first movie rebel, pre-dating Clift and Brando by a decade. In *Four Daughters* (1938), *Castle on the Hudson* (1940) and *Humoresque* (1946), he was Warners' resident tough cookie, a younger, brasher version of Bogart, Cagney and Robinson. He achieved stardom with a trio of hard-hitting movies: *The Postman Always Rings Twice* (1946), *Body and Soul* (1947) and *Force of Evil* (1948), in all of which he was excellent.

SEPTEMBER OCTOBER

NOVEMBER DECEMBER

Recreation of a Toulouse-Lautrec painting from John Huston's Moulin Rouge.

BIRTHS, DEATHS AND MARRIAGES

BIRTHS

Mark Hamill
25 Sep, Oakland, California

Christopher Reeve
25 Sep, New York

Melanie Mayron
20 Oct, Philadelphia

Jeff Goldblum
22 Oct, Pittsburgh

DEATHS

Gertrude Lawrence
6 Sep, New York
Yellow jaundice

Jack Conway
11 Oct, Pacific Palisades, California
Heart ailment

Basil Radford
20 Oct, London
Heart ailment

Susan Peters
23 Oct, Visalia, California

Hattie McDaniel
27 Oct, Hollywood
Cancer

Gladys George
8 Dec, Hollywood

MARRIAGES

Jane Wyman
1 Nov, *to* Freddie Karger

Pier Angeli
24 Nov, *to* **Vic Damone**

Brigitte Bardot
20 Dec, *to* **Roger Vadim**

SLEEPY-EYED JOE

With the Korean War drama *One Minute to Zero* and rodeo movie *The Lusty Men* sleepy-eyed Robert Mitchum has finally started to prove that he's more than just a serviceable RKO leading man. Earlier this year he also played an ersatz Howard Hughes squiring Jane Russell through a series of exotic locales in *Macao*.

Mitchum has been around for some time. Although he won a best supporting Oscar nomination for *The Story of G.I. Joe* (1945), it was actually his 25th film appearance!

Born in 1917, he joined the Long Beach Theater Guild in 1942, finally deciding to be an actor after a variety of odd jobs, including engine-wiper on a freighter, a promoter for a Californian astrologer, and a bouncer for a nightclub. He was also a poet and a published playwright. After a year on stage, he made his screen debut in a Hopalong Cassidy western, *Hoppy Serves a Writ*, one of 18 movies he made in 1943.

He showed a talent for singing in *Rachel and the Stranger* (1948), and had a double-sided hit record from the movie with "O-he-o-hi-o-ho" and "Just Like Me", featuring youngster Gary Gray. In films like *The Locket* (1946), *Crossfire* (1947), and *His Kind of Woman* (1951), he's proven someone to be reckoned with, especially in a trench-coat in the shadows. He's also been tender too, in *Holiday Affair* (1949) and the current *Lusty Men*, which *Variety* calls "his best performance yet". Next up is a part as an African hunter in *White Witch Doctor*, and he's also got a Fox contract in his pocket.

GOSSIP COLUMN

- **Frank Sinatra called in the police to remove his wife Ava Gardner from their home in Palm Springs. Ava and good friend Lana Turner were partying and, said Frank, "cutting him up."**
- **Shelley Winters seems to have dropped Farley Granger for Vittorio Gassman, Italy's latest heart-throb. "I wanna go where this guy is," says Shelley.**

ON YOUR KNEES, MEL

The first 20 minutes of *Moulin Rouge*, director John Huston's biopic of the painter Henri Toulouse-Lautrec, are among the most exciting and colourful in all cinema. As the cameras capture the swirl of the can-can in 1890s Montmartre, the smoky Technicolored night-club is magnificently re-created on the sound stages of Shepperton studios.

Jose Ferrer swaps his outsize conk in *Cyrano de Bergerac* (1950) for a part where he spends all his time on his knees. Lautrec was stunted by a hunting accident in his youth, and Ferrer's performance is a *tour-de-force*, even though a real dwarf clearly doubles him in the long shots.

Was it worth the effort? Handsome though it is to look at, *Moulin Rouge* is actually a trifle dull. The novel by Pierre La Mure was a best-seller but the sex has been diluted for the screen. However, the glamorous Colette Marchand and Suzanne Flon score heavily, and there's a marvellous depiction of Jane Avril by lovely newcomer Zsa Zsa Gabor.

A LOOK ALL HER OWN

It's turning into the year of Gloria Grahame. The cool, pouty-lipped beauty has been outstanding in four big hits – *The Greatest Show on Earth, Macao, Sudden Fear*, and as Dick Powell's Southern wife in *The Bad and the Beautiful*. She has been hotly tipped for an Academy Award for the last one.

Remember the moment in *The Greatest Show on Earth* where villainous Lyle Bettger nearly causes his elephant to trample on her face? Grahame hasn't had such a good role since *In a Lonely Place* (1950) opposite Humphrey Bogart (literally – she played the girl in the apartment opposite), directed by husband Nicholas Ray. The scenes between the two set a new high in adult relationships, particularly a romantic dialogue in the kitchen about straightening the grapefruit knife.

Grahame's English ancestry and show business background mark her out as something out of the usual Hollywood blonde rut. Born in 1925 in Los Angeles, she made her Broadway debut in 1943 and M-G-M signed her up. She's had choice moments in some good movies to date, and can play prostitutes or "other women" with ease: standouts have included *It's a Wonderful Life* (1946) and *Crossfire* (1947). She's clearly hard to cast, but has a look all her own.

Audiences experience the thrills of a new process in This Is Cinerama.

HOLD TIGHT, THIS IS CINERAMA!

The cinema's biggest challenge to television so far opened on 30 September at the converted Broadway Theater, New York. The venue has been turned into the world's first Cinerama showcase, and the first film in the new process is aptly titled *This Is Cinerama*.

So what *is* Cinerama? Basically it's three 35mm projectors showing a composite picture on a massive screen with an arc of 146°. Colour and grading has to be perfectly matched for the joins between the three projected images to be invisible. At the same time six stereophonic soundtracks are fed from two triple-track soundheads and the whole is projected at 26 frames a second (instead of the usual 24) to avoid flicker.

Inventor Fred Waller had been pushing his invention for some years, but it took producers Merian C. Cooper, of *King Kong* (1933) fame, and Robert L. Bendick to realize its potential.

The film itself begins with Lowell Thomas explaining the history of art and communication on a normal-size screen, then the image expands into a breathtaking sequence of a roller-coaster ride, shot from the front seat of the first car. That's the giddy sequence everyone's talking about. After that there's a selection of travelogues, including La Scala in Milan, Niagara Falls, a gondola ride on Venice's Grand Canal, a Madrid bullfight, and finally a tour across the good old U.S. of A., from the Great Plains to New York City. Is this the cinema of the future? And if so, can it ever be used to tell a real story?

HERE'S MUD IN YOUR EYE

"A lion in your lap" promise the ads for *Bwana Devil*. It's the first feature movie to use stereoscopic projection, christened by British pioneer Charles Smith "3-Dimension", or 3-D.

When *Bwana Devil* opened this November in downtown Los Angeles, the critics were hostile. Director-producer Arch Oboler's jungle epic is certainly inept, with poor African footage intercut with the cavortings of Robert Stack and Barbara Britton, but it's important for its gimmick.

The snag is that audiences have to wear Polaroid glasses, handed out on entry to the auditorium. With these, two colour images merge together and give a striking illusion of depth. It's so real you can almost reach out and touch the images.

It's only a matter of time before all cinemas are equipped with interlocked projectors and silver screens for true 3-D projection. That will be one more in the eye for television.

NO TALKING, PLEASE

It comes as a shock to realize – about 20 minutes in – that *The Thief* has no dialogue. It's certainly the first talkie to attempt this gimmick, and brings it off superbly.

Ray Milland is a nuclear scientist who tries to ship out secrets to foreign agents. Eventually the authorities discover the security leak, and the spies take flight. It's all very cleverly plotted by director and co-writer Russell Rouse (with Clarence Green): the key plot point is a ringing telephone, and other sounds play major parts, as well as Herschel Gilbert's musical score.

Co-starring are Martin Gabel, and New York newcomer Rita Gam as a temptress. She needs no dialogue. The Empire State Building in New York is the setting for the climax, as the FBI chases Milland to the top.

But how many more stories can be told like this? Even silent movies had dialogue in their intertitles.

Silent movie greats Buster Keaton and Charlie Chaplin team up in Chaplin's film Limelight.

CHAPLIN'S SAD CLOWN

Limelight is Charlie Chaplin's first new film since his black comedy about a Paris Bluebeard, *Monsieur Verdoux* (1947). It's the saga of a British music hall artiste (played, of course, by Chaplin) who finds that the great days are over, and that no one wants his brand of humour any more. He befriends a young would-be suicide, a beautiful ballerina played by exquisite 21-year-old Claire Bloom (from the London stage), and becomes her mentor and confidante as she becomes a top ballet star. There's no hanky-panky. As Chaplin says: "When you reach my age, a platonic friendship can be maintained on the highest platonic level". A comic highlight of the film is a musical double-act between Chaplin and another genius of the silent screen, Buster Keaton.

The wistful film gives an insight into a bygone age. But given that *Monsieur Verdoux* was boycotted and was a centre of attention from sub-HUAC right-wingers, it'll be interesting to see what happens to *Limelight*. Distributor United Artists isn't keen to open the movie in Los Angeles and it seems like it may well have more appeal outside the United States.

BOX OFFICE

UK

1. The Greatest Show on Earth
2. Where No Vultures Fly
3. Son of Paleface
4. Ivanhoe
5. Mandy
6. The Planter's Wife
7. The Quiet Man
8. The World in His Arms
9. Angels One Five
10. Reluctant Heroes

BOX OFFICE

US

1. The Greatest Show on Earth
2. Quo Vadis
3. Ivanhoe
4. The Snows of Kilimanjaro
5. Sailor Beware
6. The African Queen
7. Jumping Jacks
8. High Noon
9. Son of Paleface
10. Singin' in the Rain

Olivia Newton-John and John Travolta in the musical Grease *(1978).*

Jayne Mansfield and Tom Ewell in The Girl Can't Help It *(1956).*

Elvis swivels his pelvis in Jailhouse Rock *(1957).*

Dennis Quaid in the Jerry Lee Lewis biopic Great Balls of Fire! *(1989).*

John Travolta struts his stuff in Saturday Night Fever *(1977).*

A couple jive to Bill Haley and the Comets in Rock Around the Clock *(1956).*

ROCKIN 'N' ROLLIN

In 1955 M-G-M, contributing to the juvenile delinquency cycle started by Marlon Brando's *The Wild One* (1954), made *The Blackboard Jungle*, with Glenn Ford as an English teacher at New York's North Manual Trades High School. Instead of using an original score for the opening music, director Richard Brooks chose an existing record by the little-known Bill Haley and the Comets, "(We're Gonna) Rock Around the Clock".

Nobody could have foreseen the result: *The Blackboard Jungle*'s title music brought the newly-born rock 'n' roll to a mass audience, giving Bill Haley an instant million-selling gramophone record and leading immediately to a Columbia quickie called *Rock Around the Clock* (1956), starring the kiss-curled Mr Haley himself. This cheapo-cheapo production cost less than $200,000 and in North America grossed $1 million on first release.

Amazingly, considering its mildness, there were riots in cinemas all over the world as *Rock Around the Clock* went on release. It was swiftly followed by other low-budgeters that encouraged jiving in the aisles, like *Don't Knock the Rock* (1957), also with Haley, and such mini-epics as *Rock, Rock, Rock* and *Shake, Rattle and Roll* (both 1957), featuring "stars" like Fats Domino and Little Richard. 20th Century-Fox put 17 'pop' names, including Gene Vincent and Eddie Cochran, into the big-budget CinemaScoped *The Girl Can't Help It* (1956), although the tone was decidedly anti-rock.

But one performer snatched Bill Haley's self-styled crown of King of Rock 'n' Roll and wore it until his death in 1977: Elvis Presley, the teenage rage who fused black rhythm-and-blues with white country-and-gospel, to become the greatest pop performer ever. Hollywood rushed Elvis into a western, *Love Me Tender* (1956), then the semi-autobiographical *Loving You* (1957), swiftly followed by *Jailhouse Rock* (1957), in which Presley did his own choreography, and the excellent *King Creole* (1958). Then the army claimed him, and with Elvis Presley's call-up went the golden days of rock 'n' roll. Back in civvy street, Elvis fulfilled his contracts, and ground out 27 more movies, few of which had any merit.

While Elvis was in the army, a group of British teenagers who had grown up listening to Presley and the great rhythm-and-blues stars were making the world dance to their Mersey beat. The Beatles first hit the screen in *A Hard Day's Night* (1964), followed by the surreal *Help!* (1965). Their break-up was chronicled in *Let It Be* (1970), one of a batch of rock concert movies, that included *Monterey Pop* (1969) and *Woodstock* (1970). Even Elvis himself appeared in two notable examples, *Elvis – That's the Way It Is* (1970) and *Elvis on Tour* (1972).

While *Easy Rider* (1969) and *Zabriskie Point* (1970) used rock soundtracks instead of conventional film scores, several pop performers graduated to leading roles, with David Bowie, Kris Kristofferson, Art Garfunkel and Roger Daltrey all starring in major movies. Diana Ross and Bette Midler both won Oscar nominations. And *Saturday Night Fever* (1977) made a pop star of actor John Travolta.

Eventually a series of movies – *American Graffiti* (1973), *Grease* (1978), *Quadrophenia* (1979) – treated rock 'n' roll retrospectively, with great affection, and productions appeared about the great names of the era: notably *The Buddy Holly Story* (1979), and the Jerry Lee Lewis biopic *Great Balls of Fire!* (1989). Rock's archives were also plundered, with great skill, in films like *Let the Good Times Roll* (1973) and *This is Elvis* (1981).

Left: The Fab Four in their first film A Hard Day's Night *(1964).*

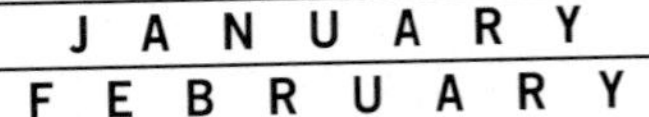

MARCH
APRIL

FALLING FOR MARILYN

"Marilyn Monroe and *Niagara* – a raging torrent of emotion that even nature can't control!" It's this season's most potent movie ad, with new star Monroe draped over the world's most famous falls. After years of stealing the notices in films like *The Asphalt Jungle* (1950), *Clash by Night* and Howard Hawks' *Monkey Business* (both 1952), she has finally got top billing. It was only a matter of time. Although miscast as the neurotic baby-sitter in last year's *Don't Bother to Knock*, Monroe still showed a strong presence. But as Rose Loomis, the nymphomaniac wife of war veteran Joseph Cotten, she reveals true potential in *Niagara*. Whether sultrily singing "Kiss" or tossing and turning, clearly unclad, in motel bedding, Monroe sets the screen alight.

Born in 1926, the daughter of Columbia negative cutter Gladys Pearl Baker (who had a history of mental disturbance), she married at 16 and was divorced in 1946.

Marilyn Monroe in seductive pose for Niagara, in which she has revealed her potential as an actress.

She became a pin-up model, and appeared on magazine covers, plus a notorious nude calendar ("I was hungry", she says).

A 20th Century-Fox contract led to several notable small parts, including one in *All about Eve* (1950). And a series of friendships with people like Elia Kazan and Darryl F. Zanuck gave her a high profile in the Hollywood community, spearheaded by a close relationship with an executive from the William-Morris Agency, Johnny Hyde.

Niagara puts her on the brink of stardom. She's currently co-starring with Jane Russell in Howard Hawks' Technicolor musical *Gentlemen Prefer Blondes*, and one number from that movie, "Diamonds Are a Girl's Best Friend", has been shown in Fox's new anamorphic process, CinemaScope, at trade previews. The word is that Marilyn and CinemaScope were made for each other.

ACADEMY AWARDS

PRESENTED ON 19 MARCH 1953

Best Picture
The Greatest Show on Earth

Best Director
John Ford
The Quiet Man

Best Actor
Gary Cooper
High Noon

Best Actress
Shirley Booth
Come Back, Little Sheba

Best Sup Actor
Anthony Quinn
Viva Zapata!

Best Sup Actress
Gloria Grahame
The Bad and the Beautiful

BIRTHS, DEATHS AND MARRIAGES

BIRTHS

Deborah Raffin
13 Mar, Los Angeles

DEATHS

Alan Curtis
1 Feb, New York
Complications following kidney operation

Herman Mankiewicz
5 Mar, Hollywood
Uremic poisoning

MARRIAGES

Ginger Rogers
7 Feb, *to* Jacques Bergerac

Joan Leslie
17 Mar, *to* William Caldwell

VIVAT REGINA!

In preparation for the Coronation of Queen Elizabeth II on 2 June, M-G-M's *Young Bess* is playing at London's Empire, Leicester Square, "The Showplace of the Nation." It's a Technicolor adaptation of Margaret Irwin's novel about a girl who would become the first Queen Elizabeth.

The Sidney Franklin production boasts a remarkable cast: Young Bess is played by Jean Simmons, while Stewart Granger, now married to her in real life and currently M-G-M's biggest box-office star, is the dashing Lord High Admiral, Thomas Seymour, in a startling array of blue velvet capes. Deborah Kerr is Catherine Parr, and Charles Laughton reprises Henry VIII, for the first time since his Oscar-winning role in *The Private Life of Henry VIII* (1933).

Director George Sidney, fresh from Granger's *Scaramouche* (1952), directs; and Miklos Rozsa's melodious score is truly fit for a Queen. Vivat Regina!

FRIENDS, ROMANS, MOVIEGOERS . . .

Despite its heavy subject-matter, M-G-M's *Julius Caesar* is a revelation. Director Joseph L. Mankiewicz has nabbed the finest talent around, aided and abetted by producer John Houseman. As Mark Antony, Marlon Brando silences those critics who accuse him of "mumbling", declaiming Shakespear's verse with all the clarity of a seasoned veteran. James Mason excels as Brutus, the "noblest Roman of them all", and John Gielgud makes a perfect "lean and hungry" Cassius. Americans Louis Calhern, as Caesar, and Edmund O'Brien, as Casca, are also superb, though their accents jar in the largely British cast. Greer Garson and Deborah Kerr add M-G-M female star power, and the former is especially good when she warns Caesar not to venture forth on the Ides of March.

But if you happen to catch the trailer for the movie, about all you'll hear is Miklos Rozsa's superb score. Metro seems curiously shy of telling moviegoers that the dialogue is by the Bard. Can Shakespeare really mean bad box office?

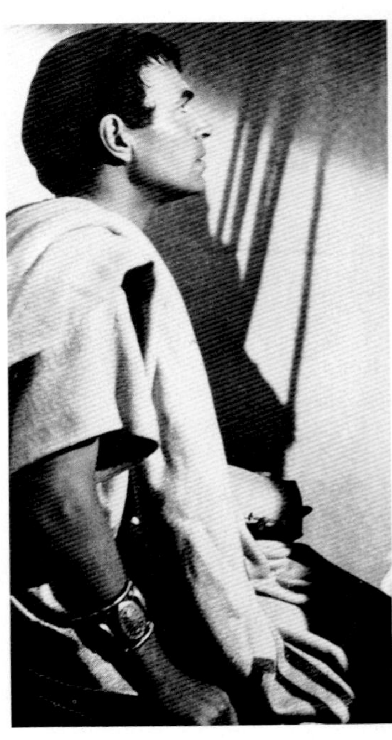

James Mason excels as Brutus in M-G-M's production of Julius Ceasar.

Above: Donald O'Connor, Ethel Merman, George Sanders and Vera-Ellen in Irving Berlin's Call Me Madam.

CALL ME MERMAN

Irving Berlin's 1950 smash hit musical *Call Me Madam* gets a faithful filming from 20th Century-Fox, happily retaining the powerhouse Ethel Merman in the lead. Like the lady says, "When you call me madam, smile".

It's smiles all round as the Technicolor movie tells the tale of ambassadress Mrs Sally Adams (based on President Truman's Minister to Luxembourg, Perle Mesta) to the fictional Grand Duchy of Lichtenburg, and how she follows that old *Merry Widow* plot of dispensing largesse.

Some critics feel a little of Merman goes an awful long way, and her performance at times does seem calculated, but Berlin's score couldn't be in safer hands. (It's also her real voice in the movie, after being replaced by Dinah Shore on the RCA original cast album.) Particularly charming is the contrapuntal duet "(You're not sick) You're just in love" that she shares with aide Donald O'Connor. Other highlights are O'Connor's wine cellar dance with Vera-Ellen, and his set-piece, here "What Chance Have I With Love?". But the revelation is George Sanders who, in a romantic role, reveals a lyric bass all his own. Musicals could benefit from more of the urbane Sanders.

DONALD'S LUCK

In last year's *Singin' in the Rain* and now *Call Me Madam* and *I Love Melvin*, versatile Donald O'Connor has shown he can hold the screen on his own, without help from Peggy Ryan, Gloria Jean, or Francis the Talking Mule.

He's been around a long time. Born in 1925, the son of vaudevillians who were former circus performers, he made his movie debut at the age of 11 in *Melody for Two* (1937). Other early roles included playing Gary Cooper as a child in *Beau Geste* (1939), and, from 1942 onwards, co-starring with Ryan in a string of low-budget Universal musicals, often alternating co-stars, including Jean, Ann Blyth, and Susanna Foster. In films like *It Comes Up Love* (1943) and *Are You With It?* (1948) O'Connor was building a strong following.

It was as the talking mule's co-star in *Francis* (1950) that he had his greatest success. But fortunately Gene Kelly needed a top dancer for *Singin' in the Rain* and M-G-M borrowed O'Connor from Universal.

Between movies, he's writing a symphony, *Reflections d'un Comique*, and plans to conduct the Los Angeles Philharmonic in its premiere. Meanwhile, there's *Francis Covers the Big Town* due out this summer. Seems there's just no escape from that talking mule.

Right: The diminutive Alan Ladd plays the part of the mysterious cowboy in George Steven's fine and beautifully crafted western Shane.

ONE MORE IN THE EYE

The first major studio 3-D movie is showing to packed houses at the 3,664-seater Broadway Paramount in New York. Despite the critics, it's clear the public wants 3-D, and Warners' *House of Wax* is a major crowd-pleaser, replete with WarnerPhonic (actually RCA) sound and the new single-strip WarnerColor.

The story has been filmed before, as *Mystery of the Wax Museum* (1933), but the plot's a hoary old stand-by. A wax museum owner (Vincent Price) tries to save his precious models in a fire, is himself burned, and has to wear a mask of wax over his own scarred features (shades of *Phantom of the Opera*).

All the 3-D stops are pulled out: chairs are flung into the audience, hunched villains leap out at you, can-can dancers pirouette towards camera, even a barker's ping-pong ball plays fast-and-loose with the cinema audience's nerves.

House of Wax was directed by Andre de Toth, who has only one eye. Maybe Warners was playing safe when they hired him, to make sure the movie works in 2-D as well. . . .

Versatile actor Donald O'Connor in I Love Melvin.

LONESOME LADD

With the Technicolored *Shane* director George Stevens has followed his series of urban dramas with the most beautifully-photographed western ever made.

Alan Ladd is Shane, a buckskin-clad gunman who rides into a Wyoming valley and offers to help a homesteading family in their battles against the cattle farmers and their hired killer, the sinister Jack Palance. He tries not to use his skill with six-shooters, until goaded. It's all beautifully observed through the eyes of the homesteader's son, played by young stage actor Brandon de Wilde.

Ladd finds dimensions in the character rare in a conventional westerner. No wonder Van Heflin's homesteading wife (Jean Arthur) secretly yearns for him.

Victor Young's main theme, "Call of the Faraway Hills", is already in the hit parades, and adds to the scale of the movie.

GOSSIP COLUMN

■ Lana Turner admits to being in love with Fernando Lamas, who has a wife in South America. "I am quite sure that around the corner there's something good," says recently-divorced Lana.

MAY
JUNE
1953
JULY
AUGUST

BEACH MANOEUVRES

Montgomery Clift entertains Frank Sinatra in From Here to Eternity.

From Here to Eternity is that rare item, an instant classic. It also keeps the tone and thrust of James Jones' tough novel about army brass well within Production Code requirements.

But it's much more than just a popularization of a steamy novel. It derives its great humanity and adult relationships from impeccable casting. Lancaster is Top Sergeant Milt Warden, and, in the key role of boxer/bugler Robert E. Lee Prewitt, Montgomery Clift is superb. Prewitt's credo, "If a man don't go his own way, he's nothin'", is similar to Clift's own.

But the revelations are the three other stars. In the role Joan Crawford rejected, British rose Deborah Kerr is the sultry nymphomaniac Karen Holmes who romps memorably on the beach with swim-suited Lancaster. As the prostitute from the New Congress Club, called "hostess" in the movie, little junior miss Donna Reed proves a cookie to reckon with. And best of all, as the beaten little Italian G.I. Maggio, Frank Sinatra – yes, *that* Frank Sinatra – is superb, revealing talent that could well bring him an Academy Award. An Oscar for the Crooner?

BIRTHS, DEATHS AND MARRIAGES

BIRTHS

Catherine Hicks
6 Jun, New York

DEATHS

William Farnum
5 Jun, Hollywood
Cancer

Roland Young
5 Jun, New York

MARRIAGES

Robert Donat
4 May, *to* Rene Asherson

Ann Blyth
27 Jun, *to* James McNulty

Rosemary Clooney
13 Jul, *to* **Jose Ferrer**

VIRGIN ON THE DANGEROUS

Producer-director Otto Preminger is daringly releasing his version of *The Moon Is Blue* without the requisite Production Code Seal.

Although many theatres won't play the movie, and the Catholic League of Decency have condemned the film from the pulpit, Preminger and author F. Hugh Herbert didn't want to compromise in adapting the Broadway comedy hit for the screen. Unlike recent movies like *A Streetcar Named Desire* (1951) and even *Annie Get Your Gun* (1950) – both bowdlerised for the screen – Preminger and Herbert stuck to their guns.

The three-hander (William Holden, David Niven and newcomer Maggie McNamara) revolves around the simple tale of a pick-up who lets her beau know that she's not opposed to kissing or even attempts at seduction, providing her virginity stays in place.

Words like "virgin" and "seduce" are strictly verboten in the Breen (formerly Hays) office. In retaining them Preminger knew he was severely testing the system.

THAT'S ENTERTAINMENT!

With *The Band Wagon* producer Arthur Freed and his M-G-M team have surpassed themselves. The Betty Comden-Adolph Green screenplay satirizes the "theatah" the way they did the movies in *Singin' in the Rain* last year. And director Vincente Minnelli improves on the ballet in *An American in Paris* (1951) with "Girl Hunt", a wicked take-off of the Mickey Spillane school of terpsichore ("She came at me in sections").

It also boasts a cast like no other. Impeccable Fred Astaire plays a former dance star famed for his top hat, white tie and tails trying out on Broadway with ravishing prima ballerina Cyd Charisse. Britain's Jack Buchanan is troupe boss Jeffrey Cordova, and there's also the laconic Oscar Levant and delectable Nanette Fabray in support. That's entertainment indeed. And "That's Entertainment" is the only new song in the great Arthur Schwartz-Howard Dietz 1931 score which includes showstoppers like "A Shine on Your Shoes" (Astaire in an amusement arcade), "Triplets" (Astaire, Fabray, and Buchanan – on their knees), "I Guess I'll Have to Change My Plan" (Astaire and Buchanan in trademark tuxedos) and, best of all, "Dancing in the Dark" (Astaire and Charisse in Central Park). Gene Kelly has already called that his all-time favourite moment of screen dance.

Fred Astaire as a veteran dancer joins forces with a temperamental producer to put on a show in The Band Wagon.

Above: Gregory Peck and Audrey Hepburn on a Roman Holiday.

COME RIDE WITH ME

Roman Holiday, the story of a princess falling in love with a commoner, is the most delightful comedy of the season. And if it bears more than a passing resemblance to the real-life romance between Princess Margaret and Group-Captain Peter Townsend, then it's the Eternal City to an ice-cream cornet that it's intentional.

Delightful newcomer Audrey Hepburn plays Princess Anne in a role originally intended for Jean Simmons. She embarks on a passionate, but sex-less, affair with American newspaperman Joe Bradley, played with charm by Gregory Peck, who was loaned by 20th Century-Fox to Paramount for the occasion. But the real star is Rome itself, as the lovers take off on a motor-scooter ride along the Tiber and director William Wyler, not generally renowned for comedy, works wonders with the lightest of touches.

GIGI GOES TO ROME

The wafer-thin gamine who enchanted Broadway in *Gigi* has made a remarkable American feature debut in *Roman Holiday*. She's proving that both the camera and movie audiences love Audrey Hepburn.

Left: Audrey Hepburn.

The daughter of a Dutch baroness and an English banker, she was born near Brussels, Belgium, in 1929. When the Second World War broke out, she was trapped in Nazi-occupied Arnhem, and took ballet training at Arnhem Conservatory. The long-legged beauty then went to London on a ballet scholarship, was spotted for fashion magazines and eventually became a chorus girl in the 1948 West End musical *High Button Shoes*. She followed that with another, the risque *Sauce Piquante*, and was spotted by producer-director Mario Zampi, who saw the show 14 times because of her.

Zampi cast her in *Laughter in Paradise*, and that led to walk-ons in *One Wild Oat* and *The Lavender Hill Mob* (all 1951). She tested for *Quo Vadis* that year but M-G-M over-ruled director Mervyn LeRoy's enthusiasm and turned her down.

However, the next year she appeared in the comedy *Young Wives' Tale*, the spy thriller *Secret People* and *Monte Carlo Baby*. While on location in the South of France she was spotted by authoress Colette for *Gigi*, in which she opened on Broadway to rapturous acclaim. Paramount screen-tested her, and when Jean Simmons turned down *Roman Holiday*, Hepburn stepped into the part of a lifetime.

AN UNLIKELY STAR

A genuine 'old crock' is providing British moviegoers with one of the season's big hits. *Genevieve* is a 1904 Darracq, entered in the London-to-Brighton veteran car run by John Gregson and Dinah Sheridan, and cared for as if it were their own child.

Gregson and Sheridan face competition from playboy Kenneth More and delightful trumpet-tooting girl friend Kay Kendall. Kenny Baker dubs the trumpet and the film's wistful harmonica theme is composed and played by maestro Larry Adler. (Ludicrously, he's not credited on American prints, as he's *persona non grata* with HUAC.)

Genevieve could herald a new wave in British comedy – parochial, but of universal appeal.

CAT AND MOUSE GAMES

Two versatile screen performers make their feature debut in the new M-G-M musical *Dangerous When Wet* (1953), swimming alongside Esther Williams. They're only on screen for about 10 minutes but for Tom and Jerry this may be their greatest moment.

The pair have been starring in their own cartoon shorts since Rudolph Ising produced a little gem for M-G-M called *Puss Gets the Boot* (1939). It was nominated for an Academy Award, which Tom and Jerry went on to win no less than seven times, from *Yankee Doodle Mouse* (1943) to *Johann Mouse* (1952).

Fred Quimby took over as their producer, and their efforts are now directed by William Hanna and Joseph Barbera. It was Barbera who named the couple, despite M-G-M's original monikers of Jasper and Jinx. He had helped to script a short back in 1932 with characters called Tom and Jerry, and he remembered the names.

STAR QUOTES

Paulette Goddard

"I have a rule – when in doubt about what you look your best in, wear tights."

Esther Williams with Tom and Jerry in Dangerous When Wet.

CALAMITY DORIS

One of the biggest, and most surprising, treats of the current season is a musical that begins with buckskin-clad Doris Day atop a stagecoach belting out "Oh, the Deadwood Stage is a headin' on over the hills. . . ." Yup, it's *Calamity Jane*. It's Warners' riposte to M-G-M's smash *Annie Get Your Gun* (1950) and Broadway's long-running *Oklahoma!* The studio borrowed *Annie*'s Frank Butler, handsome Howard Keel, to play Wild Bill Hickok and he and Day strike sparks off each other.

The Sammy Fain-Paul Francis Webster songs are likely to endure. But it's Day's movie. The former band singer, after years of light-weight Warners' vehicles like *Tea for Two* (1950), *On Moonlight Bay* (1951) and *April in Paris* (1952), finally gets her teeth into a movie, shakes it, and makes it hers. No wonder Warners is reprising her and choreographer Jack Donohue for the first original screen musical in CinemaScope, *Lucky Me*.

FEEL THE WIDTH

Jean Simmons and Richard Burton in The Robe, *the first film in CinemaScope.*

Almost a year to the day since the unveiling of *This Is Cinerama* (1952), 20th Century-Fox has opened another big-screen wonder at the 6,000-seat Roxy Theater in New York. *The Robe* is the first film in the new process, CinemaScope.

The robe in question is that worn by Christ on the Cross, the garment that a handful of Romans gambled for, and the symbol of the conversion to Christianity of centurion Marcellus Gallio, played by British import Richard Burton.

In a role originally intended for Gregory Peck, Burton shows he has the voice and physique for such historic pageantry. But it's Victor Mature, as his slave Demetrius, who steals the acting honours, and a sequel is already being planned for this character. Jean Simmons is a fetching love interest, and Michael Rennie adds stature as Simon called Peter. Jay Robinson hams it up as the loony Caligula.

Producer Frank Ross had wanted to film Lloyd C. Douglas' novel for a decade. In stereophonic sound, on the 65-foot by 25-foot screen, *The Robe* isn't short on spectacle. There's a striking storm scene, a fine trip through a slave market, and an impressive use of four white horses in the finale.

THROW AWAY THOSE GLASSES

"You see it without the aid of special glasses" says 20th Century-Fox. And that's the big plus of CinemaScope, the wide-screen anamorphic process that looks like killing off 3-D.

CinemaScope has actually been around since inventor Henri Chretien developed the process in the 1920s, but it was reckoned to have little commercial value. That was before the threat of TV.

CinemaScope squeezes an oblong image on conventional 35mm film, and then "unsqueezes" it during projection. It can give a screen ratio of 2.55:1 (with magnetic sound) or 2.33 or 2.35 (with optical sound). Compare this with the conventional 1.33, or the new "wide-screen" maskings of 1.75 or 1.85 as seen in films like *Young Bess* (1953) or *Thunder Bay* (1953).

So far, few theatres are equipped for it, but Fox plans to use its patented process exclusively. M-G-M and Universal are shooting twin versions of all their biggies at present, but Warners has just scrapped all footage on *A Star Is Born* and *Rebel without a Cause* and ordered them to be reshot in CinemaScope.

BRANDO'S BIKER BITES BACK

Based on an actual incident, when a mob of youths on motorcycles terrorized a small Californian town, Stanley Kramer's production *The Wild One* is already garnering a cult following despite its unsavoury, violent subject-matter.

Though he looks too old as gang boss Johnny, Marlon Brando is magnificent as the leather-clad, sideburned psycho, at one with his "sickle". He seems to distil the essence of disgruntled youth as he replies to Mary Murphy's question "What are you rebelling against?" with the line "Whatever you've got."

The movie has been banned by Britain's censors. But the enterprising young manager of Cambridge's Rex Cinema, Leslie Halliwell, has turned his theatre into a club to screen the film, and devoted moviegoers are flooding out of London to catch it.

The police question gang leader Marlon Brando in The Wild One.

Ava Gardner is an American showgirl on safari and Clark Gable is the Kenyan white hunter and guide in Mogambo.

THE AFRICAN KING

There can't be many stars who have played the same leading role 20-odd years apart. But that's what Clark Gable is doing for M-G-M this season with *Mogambo*. It's a remake of *Red Dust* (the title is Swahili for "speak").

This time out Gable plays Victor Marswell, a white hunter in Africa; his name last time was Dennis Carson, but that sounded like an amalgam of Warner's top team, Dennis Morgan and Jack Carson. Ava Gardner, in her best role to date is in the old Harlow role, though today's Production Code is stronger than it was in 1932, so her character has been changed from whore to showgirl. The Mary Astor "other woman" part is prettily filled by newcomer Grace Kelly; but on-set rumours suggested that for "King" Gable she was no "other woman". Gardner was busy with one Francis Albert Sinatra, who spent an awful lot of time visiting the African location.

Veteran John Ford had good reasons for directing the movie: "I'd never been to that part of Africa, and I liked the script and the story, so I just did it." He claims he never saw the original.

BIRTHS, DEATHS AND MARRIAGES

BIRTHS

Amy Irving
10 Sep, Palo Alto, California

Victoria Tennant
30 Sep, London

Peter Firth
27 Oct, Bradford, West Yorkshire

Roseanne Barr
3 Nov, Salt Lake City, Utah

Tatum O'Neal
5 Nov, Los Angeles

Tom Hulce
6 Dec, Wisconsin

Kim Basinger
8 Dec, Athens, Georgia

John Malkovich
9 Dec, Benton, New Jersey

DEATHS

Francis Ford
5 Sep, Hollywood

Lewis Stone
12 Sep, Beverly Hills
Heart attack

Nigel Bruce
8 Oct, Santa Monica, California
Heart attack

MARRIAGES

Lana Turner
7 Sep, *to* Lex Barker

Rita Hayworth
24 Sep, *to* Dick Haynes

Janet Blair
5 Oct, *to* Nick Mayo

Clint Eastwood
19 Dec, *to* Maggie Johnson

MISSED ME, MATE!

M-G-M's film version of Cole Porter's 1948 Broadway hit is *Kiss Me, Kate* the only true musical so far in 3-D. But 3-D is proving a problem with audiences. Folks who already wear glasses don't like wearing a second pair, and many people are complaining of headaches. The interval in 3-D movies, caused by the changeover in double projectors, is also beginning to infuriate moviegoers, plus the not-uncommon occurrence of the left or the right machine slipping out of synch.

Despite this, *Kiss Me, Kate* (based on Shakespeare's *Taming of the Shrew*) is still splendid. Ann Miller and Tommy Rall dance out over the audience on washing lines, Kathryn Grayson propels brass utensils into the stalls, and Howard Keel lobs fire-flashes into your lap.

In 3-D, that is. M-G-M is only playing *Kate* in 2-D at Radio City Music Hall, where it opened this November. But in its West Coast bow, at Loew's State Theater, Los Angeles, *Kate* is showing in 3-D. At London's prestigious Empire, Leicester Square, 3-D prints will also be used.

BOX OFFICE

UK

1. A Queen Is Crowned
2. Road to Bali
3. The Cruel Sea
4. Genevieve
5. The Red Beret (*U.S. title*: Paratrooper)
6. Because You're Mine
7. Shane
8. Quo Vadis
9. Moulin Rouge
10. Malta Story

BOX OFFICE

US

1. The Robe
2. From Here to Eternity
3. Shane
4. How to Marry a Millionaire
5. Peter Pan
6. Hans Christian Andersen
7. House of Wax
8. Mogambo
9. Gentlemen Prefer Blondes
10. Moulin Rouge

SENSITIVE BOY MAKES GOOD

Montgomery Clift is special. In films like *From Here to Eternity* (1953) and *A Place in the Sun* (1951) he's revealed a naturalistic acting talent alongside those Greek God looks that's unsurpassed. He's a far cry from the Pecks and Ladds and Grangers who dominate today's screens.

Born in 1920 in Nebraska, he was on stage with no formal training by the age of 14. The following year he made his Broadway debut, and eventually Hollywood beckoned. But Clift rejected a lucrative M-G-M contract to wait for the right role. Aware of his "sensitive" image, he chose to make his screen bow in a western opposite John Wayne, the majestic *Red River* (1948).

However, production problems delayed its release until after he had completed the postwar Berlin drama *The Search* (1948). He won an Oscar nomination for his role as an American soldier caring for a young concentration camp survivor.

Off-screen Clift has a reputation as a social climber with a penchant for alcohol. He loves fame, but seems to loath his own celebrity. Analysis, apparently, is helping him to cope.

JANUARY
FEBRUARY

MARCH
APRIL

ACADEMY AWARDS

PRESENTED ON 25 MARCH 1954

Best Picture
From Here to Eternity

Best Director
Fred Zinnemann
From Here to Eternity

Best Actor
William Holden
Stalag 17

Best Actress
Audrey Hepburn
Roman Holiday

Best Sup Actor
Frank Sinatra
From Here to Eternity

Best Sup Actress
Donna Reed
From Here to Eternity

LOOK, NO SETS!

First, there was the movie without dialogue – last year's *The Thief*. Now there's one without sets! Paramount's Technicolored *Red Garters* has characters walking through doorways without doors and dealing cards in saloons without walls. Amazingly, it all works brilliantly in the musical western comedy. Director is veteran George Marshall, of *Destry Rides Again* (1939) fame.

Rosemary Clooney and Guy Mitchell co-star with Jack Carson and Pat Crowley in the light-hearted movie, which *Variety* says "resembles a live-action UPA cartoon."

STEWART MIMES MILLER

Phil Garris, June Allyson and James Stewart in The Glenn Miller Story.

The director-star team of Anthony Mann and James Stewart have produced some fine movies for Universal, like *Winchester '73* (1950) and *Bend of the River* (1952). Their latest outing is far from being a western and is their best yet – *The Glenn Miller Story*. It's the fictionalized tale of the real-life bandleader and his quest for a new "sound", and the tragedy of his death when his aircraft vanished in heavy fog over the English Channel during the Second World War as he flew from London to Paris for a broadcast.

Stewart is charming as Miller, and June Allyson endearing as his wife Helen. The pair have been Mr. and Mrs. before, in *The Stratton Story* (1949). They seem made for each other.

The frighteningly accurate recreations of the Miller Sound are by young arrange Henry Mancini. All the music in the film was recorded stereophonically, but there are no plans to issue the movie that way at the moment.

FIRST WESTERN IN SCOPE

"All the might of the unconquerables and their seven days of daring." That's the Warners' tagline for the first western in CinemaScope, *The Command*. If you look closely at the advertising, you'll find the movie stars Guy Madison and Joan Weldon; but it's CinemaScope that gets top billing.

The Command is well-chosen to show off the new wide-screen process, with a magnificently staged 11-minute battle between Indians and a wagon train at the climax.

The process used for filming it was originally to be called Vistarama, and then WarnerScope. But 20th Century-Fox's *The Robe* created huge public interest in CinemaScope last year, so Warners decided to use the accepted trade name, billing it above the title in ads.

New star Guy Madison was also in the first major western in 3-D, *The Charge at Feather River* last year. But in both movies the technical aspects have made a greater impression on audiences than he has. Perhaps a small-scale drama in black-and-white might do more for his career.

A CHARMING TALE

The Kidnappers is a slight tale of two boys who "borrow" a year-old baby. But the film's charm, warmth, and marvellous performances by the two youngsters is making it a hit with audiences. In case American audiences expect a crime melo, the movie has been retitled *The Little Kidnappers* across the Atlantic.

The story is set in turn-of-the-century Nova Scotia, and deals with the clash of cultures between two sets of immigrants, the Scots and the Boers, with fine performances from Duncan MacRae and Theodore Bikel as the respective "tribal" elders. Into this mistrustful, unhappy atmosphere come the two young lads, whose real moments of happiness occur when they adopt, unofficially, the "bairn".

There's skilful direction by Philip Leacock, a former documentary-maker and member of John Grierson's Group 3 production unit, plus an un-mawkish screenplay by Neil Paterson. It's another example of the fine work at present in British commercial cinema – in this case, J. Arthur Rank and Pinewood Studios.

Duncan MacRae and Vincent Winter, grand father and grandson, in The Kidnappers.

Donald Sinden, Donald Huston, Kenneth More, Kay Kendall and Dirk Bogarde in Doctor in the House.

DOCTORS AND NURSES

Hot on the tracks of last year's *Genevieve* and the steps of this year's *The Kidnappers* comes director Ralph Thomas' hilarious adaptation of Dr. Richard Gordon's autobiographical best-seller *Doctor in the House*.

The doctor is one Simon Sparrow (Dirk Bogarde), who joins St. Swithin's Hospital medical school and is taken under the wing of three young veterans who have all failed their preliminary exams. They're played with relish by Kenneth More (from *Genevieve*), Donald Sinden and Donald Houston, the last so good in *The Blue Lagoon* (1949).

The jokes may be obvious ("Big breaths." "Yeth, and I'm only thixteen" – Bogarde and blonde stunner Shirley Eaton) but they're also very funny. Bogarde, freed at last from the psychopaths and loners that he's played in *The Blue Lamp* (1950) and *Desperate Moment* (1953), looks like heading for international stardom with his good looks and (at last) a sense of humour.

BIRTHS, DEATHS AND MARRIAGES

BIRTHS

John Travolta
18 Feb, Englewood, New Jersey

Ron Howard
1 Mar, Duncan, Oklahoma

Lesley-Ann Down
17 Mar, London

Dennis Quaid
9 Apr, Houston, Texas

James Belushi
14 Apr, Chicago

DEATHS

Sydney Greenstreet
18 Jan, Hollywood
Diabetes

MARRIAGES

Marilyn Monroe
14 Jan, *to* Joe Di Maggio

Linda Darnell
25 Feb, *to* Philip Leibmann

Peter Lawford
24 Apr, *to* Patricia Kennedy

Audrey Hepburn
29 Apr, *to* **Mel Ferrer**

TOP BANANA PHIL

The filming of the Broadway hit *Top Banana* may at long last give Phil Silvers, 41, the audience his talents deserve.

Top Banana has been filmed, literally from the stalls, at the Winter Gardens, New York, after the show ended its run. Some say Silvers' character Jerry Biffle is based on Milton Berle; but the style is all his own.

Young Brooklyn-born Phil appeared in some Warners' two-reelers before making his first appearance, aged 13, at Minsky's burlesque house, where he started as third banana. He made his big-screen debut in *Hit Parade of 1941* (1940), and his myopic and sharp-witted presence has enlivened many a movie since, notably *Tom, Dick and Harry* (1941), *Roxie Hart* (1942) and especially *Cover Girl* (1944), in which he performed "Make Way for Tomorrow" with Gene Kelly and Rita Hayworth.

The association with Kelly continued with *Summer Stock* (1950), and then in 1951 Silvers went into the lead in *Top Banana*, a series of musical numbers and vaudeville sketches directed by Jack Donohue.

Phil Silvers in Top Banana.

FROM COCHISE TO CENTURION

With his performance in Universal's *Sign of the Pagan*, as the Roman centurion who converts Attila the Hun (Jack Palance) to Christianity, Jeff Chandler takes a major stride forward in his movie career.

As one of Universal's three "beefcake boys", along with Rock Hudson and Tony Curtis, 6-foot 4-inch, rugged Chandler set female hearts a-flutter with tough roles in *Iron Man* (1951) and *Red Ball Express* (1952). But it was as Apache chief Cochise in *Broken Arrow* (1950) that he'd first scored a major success, and has since reprised the character in *Battle at Apache Pass* (1952) and in *Taza, Son of Cochise*, the Rock Hudson starrer.

Born in Brooklyn in 1918, he found he liked performing at his bar mitzvah. During the Second World War he took part in G.I. radio broadcasts, and eventually did much radio work. After peace came, he enrolled at the Feagin School of Dramatic Art, New York, and joined a Long Island repertory company. One of his school friends, Susan Hayward, was already gaining success in Hollywood, and his radio career was making his voice well-known, notably in the 1947 series *Michael Shayne, Detective*.

Universal was looking for a tall, good-looking Jewish leading man for their Israeli drama *Sword in the Desert* (1949) and the path was set for the prematurely grey-haired star.

STAR QUOTES

Audrey Hepburn

"I am 24 years old and I have lived a lifetime."

FOOT-STOMPIN' STUFF!

The surprise hit of the season is an M-G-M musical based on a yarn from Ancient Rome. Director Stanley Donen and choreographer Michael Kidd have taken the Rape of the Sabine Women story and turned it into a foot-stompin' backwoods American musical called *Seven Brides for Seven Brothers*.

Howard Keel, in a red rinse, plays Oregon backwoodsman Adam Pontipee, who rides into town one day and gets hitched to Milly (feisty Jane Powell). What she don't know is, he's got six brothers back at base, an' he expects her to do for 'em, an' all.

It's an infectious romp, despite the fact that M-G-M's Ansco Color still leaves something to be desired. But beware: the studio is also sending out non-CinemaScope versions, even though the movie really needs the new wide process – and nowhere less than in the stunning barn-building hoedown when the Pontipee brothers take on the town boys in dance.

Backwoods America in Seven Brides for Seven Brothers.

FOX'S LATEST BLONDE

She's billed as "The Queen of the Starlight Ballroom" on the ads, and she's sensational in the new Dean Martin-Jerry Lewis romp *Living It Up*. She's Hollywood-born blonde bombshell Sheree North, 21, who created that wild dance number in the original Broadway show, *Hazel Flagg*.

Although "introduced" in *Living It Up*, she's already made a couple of unbilled screen appearances, in the Red Skelton comedy *Excuse My Dust* (1951) and the Bob Hope romp *Here Come the Girls* (1953). But she had to go to Broadway to be "discovered".

In Hollywood she'd been a professional dancer at the age of 10, and married by 15. A mother at 16, she worked as a dancer and a model, and there are rumours (denied, of course, by 20th Century-Fox) that she even appeared in some stag movies before finding her way into *Excuse My Dust*.

Fox has now signed her up and cast her in two roles that its own Marilyn Monroe turned down – as Stormy Tornado with Betty Grable in *How to be Very, Very Popular* and opposite Tom Ewell in *The Lieutenant Wore Skirts*, both due out next year. Bubbly North is the studio's latest addition to a talent roster that includes Alice Faye, June Haver, Grable and Monroe. But it's always been Fox's policy to co-star their out-going blonde with their new in-coming one. Could this mean the end of Betty?

BIRTHS, DEATHS AND MARRIAGES

BIRTHS

Kathleen Turner
19 Jun, Springfield, Massachusetts

Sam Jones
12 Aug, Chicago

DEATHS

Gabriel Pascal
5 Jul, New York

MARRIAGES

Robert Taylor
24 May, *to* Ursula Thiess

Kirk Douglas
29 May, *to* Ann Buydens

Jack Lemmon
22 Jun, *to* Cynthia Stone

Fred MacMurray
29 Jun, *to* June Haver

GENTLE GIANT

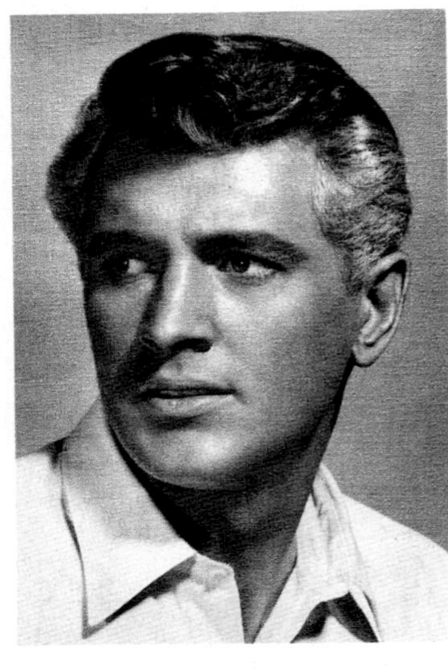

After years of toiling in the Universal vineyards, good-looking Rock Hudson, 29, has finally emerged as a fully-fledged star. It's taken one performance – as a drunken playboy who causes and then cures Jane Wyman's blindness in *Magnificent Obsession*, Douglas Sirk's remake of the 1935 Irene Dunne-Robert Taylor weepie.

Six-foot-four, fourteen-stone Rock hails from Winnetka, Illinois. As a teenager he idolized film star Jon Hall, but it wasn't until a truck-driver friend suggested he send his photograph to casting directors that he thought of putting his good looks to work in the movies. That got him nowhere. But when he heard there was a casting call at Selznick, he left his photograph with a secretary, who gave the picture to talent-spotter Henry Willson with the message: "You ought to see this kid – he's great."

Ironically, it was Willson who'd spotted Jon Hall. And Guy Madison. And Lana Turner. Willson liked what he saw. So the Gentle Giant's teeth were capped, and he was coached in acting, singing, dancing, fencing and riding. His one line in *Fighter Squadron* (1948) took 38 takes; but it led to a tiny part in the crime thriller *Undertow* the next year, seven movies in 1950, five in 1951, and then a Universal contract and leading roles in *Has Anybody Seen My Gal?* and *Horizons West* (both 1952).

As the fan letters poured in, he became a marquee name in movies like *The Lawless Breed* (1952) and the Canadian outdoors drama *Back to God's Country* (1953).

Future plans? Bachelor boy Rock is to marry Willson's secretary Phyllis Gates next year (they've already named the day) and another co-starring movie with Jane Wyman is planned.

Rossano Brazzi, Jean Peters, Maggie McNamara *in* Three Coins in the Fountain.

REAR VIEW

Imagine a movie with only one point of view. A news cameraman, laid up with a broken leg, looks out of his back window into the yard below and the tenement block across the way. Eventually he believes he's seen a murder. But he's laid up, he can't move. What should he do? A cop friend doesn't believe him, but his girl and the nurse who tend him trust his judgment.

In *Rear Window* master of suspense Alfred Hitchcock milks this situation for all it's worth. James Stewart is excellent as the voyeur, but radiant Grace Kelly as his fiancee is a revelation – in more senses than one when she dons a negligee for an overnight stay!

GOSSIP COLUMN

- **On 14 January Marilyn Monroe married baseball star Joltin' Joe di Maggio. Said studio publicity head at 20th Century-Fox: "We're not losing a star, we're gaining an outfielder."**
- **Marilyn Monroe and Joe Di Maggio divorced on 27 October. During the shooting of *The Seven Year Itch* Joe had been deeply disturbed by Marilyn flashing her undies in the sidewalk grating scene. On 5 October Marilyn told director Billy Wilder she was taking the day off because she was getting a divorce; "mental cruelty" was the official reason.**

WISH UPON A GUY

Three Coins in the Fountain is that old 20th Century-Fox standby – three girls and three guys. Director Jean Negulesco has been here before with *How to Marry a Millionaire* (1953); but this time he's taken his CinemaScope cameras to Europe. The fountain of the title is the Trevi in Rome, where it's said that a coin tossed in will grant a wish.

The girls with the loose change are Dorothy McGuire, Jean Peters and Maggie McNamara; the guys are Clifton Webb, Rossano Brazzi and suave Louis Jourdan. McGuire has a moving drunk scene at the end and Peters stretches the Production Code with some sensuous dialogue in her love-making scenes. But it's delightful 24-year-old McNamara, the revelation of last summer's saucy *The Moon Is Blue*, who has the main role, as an American secretary falling for Italian prince Jourdan – a neat switch on *Roman Holiday* (1953).

There's a bonus in the Sammy Cahn-Jule Styne title ballad, crooned uncredited by Frank Sinatra. Could this be the start of something new?

WATERFRONT SQUEALER

On the Waterfront doesn't pull its punches. Budd Schulberg's screenplay, based on a series of articles by Malcolm Johnson, is a hard-hitting expose of gangsterism amongst New York dock workers, with a great central role for Marlon Brando.

Prior to HUAC, playwright Arthur Miller had been preparing the subject at Columbia under the title *The Hook*. It deals with the dilemma of an illiterate former boxer, Terry Malloy, whether to turn against the thugs who have protected him and his family.

As Malloy, Brando's superb and his scenes with newcomers Rod Steiger as his brother and young Eva Marie Saint as the sister of a waterfront victim show his uncanny gift for memorable mumbling.

Most disturbing of all, however, is the name of the director of this movie which glorifies the role of the informer. It's none other than famed HUAC "squealer" Elia Kazan.

Marlon Brando is offered words of wisdom by Rod Steiger *in* On the Waterfront.

SEPTEMBER
OCTOBER

NOVEMBER
DECEMBER

OUR MAN FRIDAY

"Dum-da-dum-dum." It's the most famous musical call-sign in the land, as Sergeant Joe Friday (Jack Webb) cautions "Just the facts, ma'am" in yet another episode of the long-running TV series *Dragnet*. Now it's a movie in WarnerColor, with Webb starring and directing, and Ben Alexander as his trusty sidekick. Gone is the cheapskate look of the TV show; but the film is still a terse, gripping study of urban crime.

Webb, 34, is no stranger to movies. Before *Dragnet* broke on TV the former radio star had appeared in *The Men* (1949) and *Sunset Blvd.* (1950). The laconic Californian developed his delivery as an announcer on San Francisco local radio and by 1946 was starring in his own series, a forerunner of *Dragnet*.

His interest in jazz has led to Warners commissioning him to star in and direct his own story *Pete Kelly's Blues*, co-starring Janet Leigh and featuring Peggy Lee and Ella Fitzgerald. It's all a long way from local radio.

JUDY, REBORN!

It's a triumph. Forget those on-set rumours, and the tales of budget over-runs. Judy Garland's comeback movie is a three-hour tour-de-force of music and dramatics as she plays a rising star married to an ageing dipso. *A Star Is Born*, indeed.

The George Cukor movie is a remake of the 1937 Janet Gaynor-Fredric March starrer, but this time in WarnerColor. Garland's husband Sid Luft produced. It's the 32-year-old actress's first stint away from her home studio M-G-M, and her first movie since *Summer Stock* with Gene Kelly four years ago. Between times she's been treading the boards, in New York and London.

As her bottle-bashing, ex-swashbuckler husband, James Mason is both witty and desperate. Mason got the part only after Stewart Granger and Cary Grant begged off – but he gives the performance of his life. He and Garland will be Oscar front-runners next March. But word is, studio boss Jack Warner is a little worried about the film's length: he'd like to get in one more performance a day.

James Mason and Judy Garland in the remake of the 1937 romantic melodrama A Star Is Born.

MOVIE BUFFS

It's an exploitation movie with a "natural" gimmick – sunbathing in the nude. In *Garden of Eden* Jamie O'Hara's car manages to stall near – guess where? – a nudist camp, and she's helped out by sunbather Mickey Knox. Pretty soon her grizzled father-in-law R.G. Armstrong joins them in the buff, and they all romp away to the movie's theme tune "Let's Go Sunning".

Nudity on this scale has never been seen on the screen before, but the movie's not much more than simple-minded propaganda for naturism. (There's no full-frontal.) The biggest surprise is that it's this year's second movie from distinguished cameraman Boris Kaufman. The first? Why, *On the Waterfront*.

BIRTHS, DEATHS AND MARRIAGES

BIRTHS

Kathleen Quinlan
19 Nov, Pasadena, California

Denzel Washington
28 Dec, Mt. Vernon, New York

DEATHS

Eugene Pallette
3 Sep, Los Angeles
Cancer

Lionel Barrymore
15 Nov, Van Nuys, California
Heart attack

MARRIAGES

Shirley MacLaine
17 Sep, *to* Steve Parker

John Wayne
1 Nov, *to* Pilar Palette

Marilyn Maxwell
21 Nov, *to* Jerome Davis

CONTESSA FROM CAROLINA

She's "the world's most beautiful animal" in the ads for *The Barefoot Contessa*. The hair is tossed by some Mediterranean wind, the contours are unashamedly on display. Yes, folks, it's Ava Gardner.

There's more than one similarity between Gardner, 32, and contessa Maria Vargas. Both rose from humble beginnings to international stardom, both lustily enjoy public affaires with celebrities, and both have the hots for Italians.

Gardner was one of six children born to a poor tenant farmer in North Carolina. Her childhood was unhappy, but her life changed when her dimpled good looks drew the attention of an M-G-M talent scout in New York. In 1940 she found herself in Hollywood being groomed for stardom.

By the time she'd divorced Mickey Rooney in 1943 (a year after marrying him), she had already had walk-ons in six M-G-M movies. After a further 15 she was loaned out to play opposite Burt Lancaster in *The Killers* (1946), which shot her to stardom. Meanwhile, she married and divorced top bandleader Artie Shaw, and was soon the natural successor to Rita Hayworth.

In movies like *Show Boat* and *Pandora and the Flying Dutchman* (both 1951) she proved that she had talent as well as looks, and won an Oscar nomination simmering opposite Clark Gable in *Mogambo* (1953). Now, as Mrs. Frank Sinatra, she's spurring the former bobby-sox idol to new heights, as well as consolidating her own career.

HAVE A NICE DAY, SPENCE

It's only 81 minutes long, and it's set out west but not a western. *Bad Day at Black Rock* is as taut as buckwhip.

Personally produced by Dore Schary, the CinemaScope movie reunites John Sturges and Spencer Tracy, the director-star team of *The People against O'Hara* (1951) in a suspenseful tale of a crippled war veteran (Tracy) who arrives in the town of Black Rock to look for a Japanese farmer. He wants to give the farmer a medal won by his son in an action which cost the boy his life and Tracy his left arm. Hostility and resentment greets him everywhere, but eventually he finds out exactly what happened to the Japanese.

Tracy gets strong support from an arsenal of star-power – Robert Ryan, Anne Francis, Dean Jagger, Walter Brennan, John Ericson, Ernest Borgnine, and heavy Lee Marvin. The scene in which one-armed Tracy uses oriental martial arts to defeat plug-ugly Borgnine is tough as they come. Another feather in the Schary cap at M-G-M.

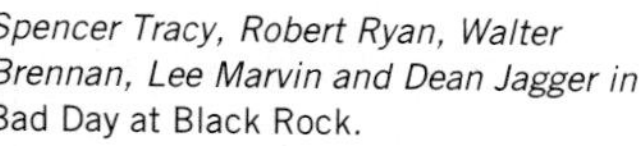

Spencer Tracy, Robert Ryan, Walter Brennan, Lee Marvin and Dean Jagger in Bad Day at Black Rock.

ALL-BLACK CARMEN

Otto Preminger's not short on courage. After flouting the Production Code with *The Moon Is Blue* last year, he's come up with an all-Negro version of the torrid *Carmen Jones*. This one won't play south of Dixie.

Pugnacious Preminger has used Oscar Hammerstein II's wartime update of the Bizet opera. As femme fatale Carmen, Dorothy Dandridge is hotter than hot, and there are even rumours that the married producer-director has installed her in an apartment and is paying the bills. Dandridge's singing voice is that of Metropolitan Opera newcomer Marilyn Horne, with the well-known "Habanera" number getting lyrics like "You Go for Me, I Go for You, But If I Do, and You're Taboo . . ."

Harry Belafonte – who was also with Dandridge last year in the Deep South drama *Bright Road* – is Joe/Jose. He's dubbed by La Verne Hutchinson, surprising given that Belafonte has a musical reputation of his own. In other roles, Olga James, Pearl Bailey, and former West Coast disc jockey Joe Adams (dubbed by Marvin Hayes) score mightily. Adams gives a showstopping performance with "Stand Up and Fight", a reworking of the Toreador Song.

STAR QUOTES

Zsa Zsa Gabor

"People say I don't belong in this century."

STAR QUOTES

John Wayne

"I'm no actor – I just react to situations and what's said to me."

Rosemary Clooney, Danny Kaye, Bing Crosby and Vera-Ellen in White Christmas.

SNOW BUSINESS

Paramount unveils its new VistaVision process with the Bing Crosby-Danny Kaye starrer, Irving Berlin's *White Christmas*. It's a tuneful cross between two old Berlin movies: *Holiday Inn* (1942), in which Crosby warbled the biggest-selling single of all time, "White Christmas", and *This Is the Army* (1943), Warners' all-star military revue.

VistaVision isn't "squeezed" like CinemaScope. Its 1.85:1 screen ratio comes from having 35mm film run sideways through both the camera and theatre projector. As Paramount's ads promise, it certainly gives "Motion Picture High Fidelity".

The plot? Crosby and Kaye rally round in peacetime to stir up business at the Vermont snow lodge of their old army commander, straight-as-a-dye Dean Jagger. Songbird sisters Rosemary Clooney and Vera-Ellen are on hand to supply the glitz – and from then on it's cosy log-fires all the way. Play it again, Irving!

BOX OFFICE

UK

1 The Robe
2 Doctor in the House
3 Trouble in Store

OTHER TOP BOX OFFICE FILMS

The Belles of St. Trinians
Calamity Jane
From Here to Eternity
The Glenn Miller Story
The Kidnappers (*U.S. title:* The Little Kidnappers)
Knock on Wood
Three Coins in the Fountain

BOX OFFICE

US

1 White Christmas
2 The Caine Mutiny
3 The Glenn Miller Story
4 The Egyptian
5 Rear Window
6 The High and the Mighty
7 Magnificent Obsession
8 Three Coins in the Fountain
9 Seven Brides for Seven Brothers
10 Desiree

The New Breed

The arrival of sound created the first revolution in screen acting. Gone forever were the effete Valentinos and John Gilberts. The Broadway stage was ransacked for Depression-era babies – actors who could speak as well as they could wear contemporary clothes, players like James Cagney, Paul Muni, Spencer Tracy and George Raft, and exciting newcomers like Joan Blondell, Robert Montgomery, Edward G. Robinson and Clark Gable.

And so they reigned, these gods and goddesses – Myrna Loy, Joan Crawford, Bette Davis, Barbara Stanwyck – throughout the 1930s and 1940s. Together with homegrown matinee idols like Robert Taylor and Tyrone Power the words "film star" became synonymous with unattainable good looks and glamour.

But in 1938, in *Four Daughters*, a young Jewish actor from New York made an indelible impression. John Garfield was no ordinary romantic lead: he was iconoclastic, bitter, laconic. In short, a rebel – a new naturalistic hero for the post-Depression era. Garfield starred memorably in a series of movies, notably *The Postman Always Rings Twice* (1946) and *Body and Soul* (1947). But later he fell victim of the McCarthy anti-communist witchhunt.

In 1950 Garfield had been offered the part of Stanley Kowalski in Tennessee Williams' Broadway play *A Streetcar Named Desire*. He turned it down, and the role went to Marlon Brando, a sensational young actor who had already made an impressive screen debut in *The Men* (1950) as a paraplegic war victim. Brando's reprised Kowalski in the bowdlerised 1951 movie of *Streetcar*, was a revelation, his animal magnetism and naturalistic acting creating a worldwide rush for his talents. The notoriously non-conformist Brando was both a graduate and promoter of New York's Actors' Studio, where Stanislavsky-inspired Lee Strasberg taught an acting "method" based on a semi-improvisational, internalised approach. It was to have a devastating effect on Hollywood.

Notable Strasberg graduates were Rod Steiger (*On the Waterfront*, 1954) Anthony Perkins (*Fear Strikes Out*, 1957), Eli Wallach (*Baby Doll*, 1956), Julie Harris (*East of Eden*, 1955), and Paul Newman (*Somebody Up There Likes Me*, 1956). Others included Karl Malden, Ben Gazzara, Joanne Woodward, Carroll Baker and Barbara Bel Geddes. Marilyn Monroe went to the Actors Studio to study, and appropriated Paula Strasberg as her acting coach. Other Hollywood stars whose styles changed post-method included Frank Sinatra, Glenn Ford, Anthony Quinn and Sidney Poitier.

Even before Brando had made his screen debut, an early alumnus of the Actors' Studio had already created a sensation – the sensitive, neurotic Montgomery Clift as John Wayne's prickly ward in *Red River* (1948). Clift went on to grace films like *A Place in the Sun* (1951), *From Here to Eternity* (1953) and *The Young Lions* (1958), the epitome of the rebel-star.

Brando, meanwhile, was showing astounding versatility in films like *Viva Zapata!* (1952), *Julius Caesar* (as Mark Antony, 1953), and his Oscar-winning *On the Waterfront* (1954), despite widespread criticism of his "mumbling".

But the most mythic graduate of the Actors' Studio was the mercurial James Dean, whose emotional intensity in his only three starring roles – *East of Eden*, *Rebel without a Cause* (both 1955) and *Giant* (1956) – lingers to this day. Dean also adopted a non-conformist image off-screen. His early death in 1955 boosted the careers of both Paul Newman and Steve McQueen, and it was those two actors who were to develop the naturalistic approach in the next decade.

Main picture: Montgomery Clift in From Here to Eternity *(1953).*

James Dean in East of Eden *(1955).*

Al Pacino and Marlon Brando in The Godfather *(1972).*

John Garfield in Body and Soul *(1947).*

Brando in On the Waterfront *(1954).*

JANUARY

FEBRUARY

MARCH

APRIL

RED-HOT ICEBERG

With four major movies last year, *The Bridges at Toko-Ri* (1955) on release, and *The Country Girl* (1954) tipped to win her an Oscar nomination, "ice-cool" Grace Kelly has really shot to stardom. The 26-year-old Philadelphian is the most beautiful and sophisticated blonde on the screen today. She can do more with a look or a raised eyebrow than certain blondes can do with their whole anatomy!

The daughter of former world champion oarsman Jack Kelly and niece of *Craig's Wife* playwright George Kelly, she was born with a silver spoon in her mouth. As a model in New York she appeared in many TV commercials, and played Raymond Massey's daughter on Broadway in *The Father* (1949). That led to her Hollywood debut in the suicide suspense drama *Fourteen Hours* (1951).

Despite her cool exterior, Kelly enjoyed a torrid off-screen romance with Gary Cooper during the making of *High Noon* (1952), and there were rumours that she and Clark Gable were close during *Mogambo* (1953). She then embarked on an affaire with Ray Milland that nearly shattered the actor's marriage. That was during Alfred Hitchcock's *Dial M for Murder* (1954), and so impressed was Hitch that he promptly cast her in the daring *Rear Window* (1954), opposite James Stewart. Said Hitch: "An actress like Grace gives a director certain advantages: he can afford to be more 'colourful' with a love scene played by a 'lady'."

She was de-glamourized for last year's *The Country Girl* but made up for her on-screen image by simultaneously involving herself romantically with both co-stars, Bing Crosby and William Holden. What next for the ravishing Kelly? She's off to the Cannes film festival, having fallen in love with the Riviera scenery while shooting her third Hitchcock movie, *To Catch a Thief* (1955), opposite Cary Grant.

GLENN'S SECOND WIND

Gone is the likable, chubby-cheeked juvenile from Columbia "B" movies. Gone is Rita Hayworth's amiable co-star in *Gilda* (1946) and the miscast Don Jose in *The Loves of Carmen* (1948). Instead, here's a star with a friendly grin and troubled brow who's making moviegoers feel comfortable in his presence. No wonder M-G-M is building Glenn Ford up big. So far this year he's been seen in *Blackboard Jungle* and the operatic biopic *Interrupted Melody*, with Eleanor Parker. Later this year he's got *Trial!* – all major roles in major movies.

Born in Quebec, Canada, in 1916, Ford moved to California at the age of eight and started acting at Santa Monica Junior High, eventually playing in various West Coast stock companies. In 1939 he was signed by Columbia and made his screen debut that year in *Heaven with a Barbed Wire Fence*, opposite Jean Rogers.

Columbia worked him hard. He quickly became a popular young star, and made 13 movies before joining the Marines at the outbreak of the Second World War. His comeback was in the fabulous *Gilda*, and he settled down to be a comfortable, though colourless, leading man, happily married in real life to M-G-M's premiere danseuse Eleanor Powell, whom he persuaded to hang up her dancing shoes.

But two dramas with director Fritz Lang – *The Big Heat* (1953) and *Human Desire* (1954) – showed there was steel under those smiling features. Now, as the teacher in the tough *Blackboard Jungle*, he's got his second wind as a movie star.

ROCK IT, TEACHER!

"One, two, three o'clock, four o'clock, rock. . . ." There's a new kind of music at the beginning of *Blackboard Jungle*, a tough drama about juvenile delinquency in a New York high school. It's called "Rock around the Clock", and it's by Bill Haley and His Comets. The record first came out in May last year, but its use here has created a minor revolution in the recording industry. Other rhythm-and-blues and country-and-western acts are being signed up as a result.

Blackboard Jungle, based on the best-seller by Evan Hunter, is a social drama about a young navy veteran's first teaching job at the North Manual Trades High School. Glenn Ford (in a crew cut) plays the teacher, Richard Dadier, who's immediately re-christened "Daddy-O" by his unruly class. Leading the student pack is Marlon Brando lookalike Vic Morrow, who comes at Dadier with a knife.

Glenn Ford and Sidney Poitier in Blackboard Jungle.

The movie has upset certain dignitaries, who reckon it gives an unfair image of America abroad. So M-G-M has added a prologue explaining that not all schools are like the one in the movie. Let's hope not.

WHADDYA WANNA DO, MARTY?

Now and again a movie comes along that touches the heart with its pure simplicity. *Marty* isn't in CinemaScope or Cinerama. It isn't even in colour. And it doesn't need to be.

The Ben Hecht-Burt Lancaster production tells of a Bronx butcher who meets a "dog", a girl who feels her average looks are working against her. He's no looker either, but they fall in love. That's it. The Italian background is beautifully etched, and the minor characters include the man's mother and a few friends.

Both Ernest Borgnine and Betsy Blair have been around for a while, but Borgnine is best known for playing heavies, as in *From Here to Eternity* (1953) and *Bad Day at Black Rock* (1954). Here he's a revelation.

The movie is said to have cost only $300,000. And Paddy Chayefsky's screenplay has been only slightly changed from NBC's Philco Television Playhouse version which had Rod Steiger as the butcher picking up a girl called Clara (Nancy Marchand) after she'd been ditched by her blind date. "Whaddya wanna do tonite, Marty?" has become the most-quoted line of the movie. And there's a simple answer: tonite, see *Marty*.

Tough guy Ernest Borgnine and Betsy Blair in Marty.

ACADEMY AWARDS

PRESENTED ON 30 MARCH 1955

Best Picture
On the Waterfront

Best Director
Elia Kazan
On the Waterfront

Best Actor
Marlon Brando
On the Waterfront

Best Actress
Grace Kelly
The Country Girl

Best Sup Actor
Edmond O'Brien
The Barefoot Contessa

Best Sup Actress
Eva Marie Saint
On the Waterfront

CANINE CANOODLING

After showing how CinemaScope can enhance animation with last year's musical featurette *Toot, Whistle, Plunk and Boom* (1954), Walt Disney has let the wide-screen process loose on a full feature, the delightful *Lady and the Tramp*.

Lady is a pedigree cocker spaniel who meets roguish mongrel Tramp and gets to visit the other side of the tracks. It's all done to a fine original score by Sonny Burke and Peggy Lee, who sings most of the songs herself, and in prime playdates audiences can enjoy sterophonic sound as well. Drawing in all that extra wide-screen detail added 30 per cent to the picture's cost. But it was worth it.

BIOPIC CRAZY

The Great Caruso started the revival back in 1951, and last year's *The Glenn Miller Story* helped it along. Now every studio seems to have a major biopic on, or ready for release. And they're not just about legendary people like Louis Pasteur, Thomas Edison or Babe Ruth.

20th Century-Fox has an Easter smash with *A Man Called Peter*, the life story of the late Peter Marshall, Protestant minister and chaplain to the U.S. Senate. Richard Todd delivers the sermons with skill and drama, and his scenes in the pulpit are the best in the movie.

At M-G-M Eleanor Parker plays crippled Australian opera star Marjorie Lawrence, with Glenn Ford as her beau, in *Interrupted Melody*; while Doris Day has left Warners to take on the role of "Ten Cents a Dance" torch singer Ruth Etting in *Love Me or Leave Me*, with James Cagney as her protector. Cameron Mitchell plays Etting's arranger Johnny Alderman – while over at UA he is to play drug-addicted boxer Barney Ross in *Monkey on My Back*, as soon as they get Production Code approval.

America's most-decorated war hero Audie Murphy is playing himself in Universal's *To Hell and Back* and Columbia has on release *The Long Gray Line*, with Tyrone Power as long-serving West Pointer Marty Maher.

Forthcoming from Fox is *The Girl in the Red Velvet Swing*, based on a notorious New York shooting incident; and from Warners Gary Cooper will be seen as pioneer airman Billy Mitchell in *The Court-Martial of Billy Mitchell*. It seems that Walt Disney is the only studio still feeding up fiction. Except, this summer there's *Davy Crockett*.

BIRTHS, DEATHS AND MARRIAGES

BIRTHS

Kirstie Alley
12 Jan, Wichita, Kansas

Kevin Costner
18 Jan, Los Angeles

Isabelle Huppert
16 Mar, Paris

Bruce Willis
19 Mar, Germany

DEATHS

S. K. Sakall
12 Feb, Hollywood
Heart ailment

Tom Moore
12 Feb, Santa Monica, California

Theda Bara
7 Apr, Los Angeles
Cancer

Constance Collier
25 Apr, New York

MARRIAGES

Sheree North
20 Feb, *to* John Freeman

Olivia de Havilland
2 Apr, *to* Pierre Galante

Carroll Baker
3 Apr, *to* Jack Garfein

A NEW STAR TO WATCH

Drawn from the last few pages of John Steinbeck's mammoth novel, *East of Eden* is a powerful, intense family drama, about rivalry between two sons for the love of their father. What makes director Elia Kazan's film so remarkable is the casting of virtual unknowns in the leading roles.

As Abra, the girl who comes between the brothers, top-billed Julie Harris creates a real, warm woman; and as the stern patriarch Adam Trask, Raymond Massey couldn't be bettered. Newcomer Richard Davalos, as the "sensitive" brother Aron, is also fine, if a little too contemporary looking. But it's the actor who plays Cal who really bears watching.

His name is James Dean, and he's from the New York stage and TV. He's done some movies – like *Has Anybody Seen My Gal?* (1952), in which he described an ice cream sundae to Rock Hudson – but nothing has prepared moviegoers for his work here. Dean, 24, is like a younger Brando, but more natural, open, and less mannered. Every movement, every expression, sweeps you into the troubled mind of Steinbeck's adolescent. It's a performance to reckon with – and a new star to watch.

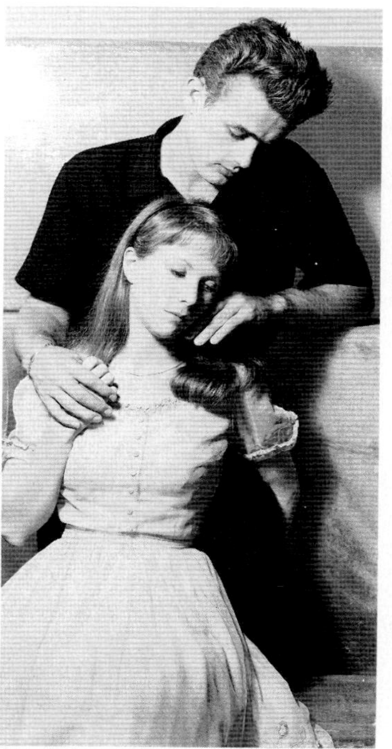

James Dean and Julie Harris in East of Eden, *from John Steinbeck's novel.*

MAY
JUNE
1955
JULY
AUGUST

SALTY TALES

Henry Fonda created the role of Lt. J. G. Roberts on the stage in 1948, and his success in the play effectively kept him off movie screens. Now he's back in his first film in seven years, and – surprise, surprise – it's *Mister Roberts*, a CinemaScope and WarnerColor version of the stage hit.

The salty dialogue of Thomas Heggen's novel hasn't all found its way on to the screen, but it is still a warm-hearted, irreverent saga of gobs at sea. Fonda is terrific, but those who saw Tyrone Power play the role on the London stage reckon he would have been equally fine. And the movie is stolen by a trio of supporting performances: James Cagney as the loathsome captain, William Powell as the bellicose doc, and, best of all, Jack Lemmon as the loud-mouthed, scheming Ensign Pulver.

John Ford and Mervyn LeRoy share the directing credit. The official reason is that Ford became ill and had to be replaced. But insiders say Ford and Fonda, who worked so well together in *The Grapes of Wrath* (1940), *The Fugitive* (1947) and *Fort Apache* (1948), fell out over the interpretation of the main character. Looks like Henry won.

William Powell, Henry Fonda and Jack Lemmon in Mister Roberts.

PLAIN JOE GETS THE GIRLS

Tom Ewell, Mr. Average American, gets all the luck. In *The Seven Year Itch* Marilyn Monroe keeps her panties in his refrigerator (it's an awfully hot summer) and he indulges in Noel Cowardish fantasies as they play *Chopsticks* together. There's a lot of chemistry going on here. And it certainly beats being a salesman at Macy's.

That was one of Ewell's jobs between working on Broadway, prior to being cast as the guy Judy Holliday shoots in *Adam's Rib* (1949), his screen debut. Born in Kentucky in 1909, he had got into acting while at Wisconsin University and made his professional debut in 1928.

After a few movies like *Up Front* (1951), he returned to Broadway in George Axelrod's comedy *The Seven Year Itch*. Billy Wilder saw the play, liked it, and next thing Tom Ewell was in the CinemaScope version with Monroe.

Mr Average American's next partners? He's currently making a Frank Tashlin comedy, with vivacious Sheree North, called *The Lieutenant Wore Skirts*. After that he's lined up for another Tashlin, as a press agent giving – wait for it – Jayne Mansfield a leg-up to stardom. Go, boy, go!

Marilyn Monroe and Tom Ewell in The Seven Year Itch.

LOVE & HATE

Charles Laughton makes his directing debut with *Night of the Hunter*, the terrifying story of a deranged backwoods preacher who kills in obedience to "messages from the Lord". Laughton has bedecked the tale (from David Grubb's novel) with all kinds of fantastic imagery, giving a curious spiritual overtone to a story of a sick killer.

Robert Mitchum is the preacher who has "LOVE" tattooed on one hand and "HATE" on the other. Shelley Winters plays the mother of two young children who is widowed at the start of the movie as her husband is hanged. The only character with any real warmth is Lillian Gish, as a fey guardian of children left alone in the world.

It's a rum movie for Laughton to choose for his first stint behind a camera. And with moviegoers giving it the cold shoulder, it could possibly be the portly thespian's last.

BIRTHS, DEATHS AND MARRIAGES

BIRTHS

Debra Winger
17 May, Cleveland, Ohio

Isabelle Adjani
27 Jun, Germany

Willem Dafoe
22 Jul, Appleton, Wisconsin

DEATHS

Carmen Miranda
5 Aug, Hollywood
Heart attack

MARRIAGES

Joan Crawford
10 May, *to* Al Steele

BABY-FACE MURPHY

Audie Murphy was America's most decorated soldier of the Second World War. Now married to lovely Wanda Hendrix, it's hard to imagine the laconic star of Universal westerns personally killing 240 Germans on his way through Europe. But at the end of the war he was one of only two left from his company, and called his book of experiences *To Hell – And Back!*

Now he's re-creating history in Universal's movie of the best-seller. *To Hell and Back* is a gripping action drama with Murphy himself in the lead, and it's setting box-offices alight.

The baby-faced Texan was born in 1924 into a poor share cropping family, and made his movie debut in *Beyond Glory* (1948), cashing in on his fame as America's war ace. But his clear kinship with guns led to a career in westerns, broken only by John Huston's Civil War drama *The Red Badge of Courage* (1951) in which he played The Youth. He's played both Jesse James and Billy the Kid, but his own life story is easily his best role to date.

Audie Murphy (right), the most decorated soldier of the Second World War, stars in the movie story of his own war experience, To Hell and Back.

Richard Todd as Wing-Commander Guy Gibson and Michael Redgrave as Barnes Wallis in The Dam Busters.

BOMBS AWAY!

The Dam Busters is the only film to get two complete circuit releases within the space of a few weeks on Britain's prestigious ABC circuit. It's a grimly realistic version of the heroic bombing raids on the Mohne and Eder dams in Germany's Ruhr valley.

The movie has two heroes. There's the inventor of the "flying bomb", Dr. Barnes Wallis, played by Michael Redgrave, and Wing-Commander Guy Gibson (Richard Todd), the pilot who led the mission. Todd was earmarked for the part when he first signed with Associated British five years back.

The film is based on Paul Brickhill's novelization and Gibson's own account, *Enemy Coast Ahead*. Young director Michael Anderson, 34, keeps sentimentality firmly at bay, and Eric Coates' stirring *Dam Busters March* is already high in the British hit parade.

FRANCIS KILLED IN PLANE CRASH

The death of Robert Francis on 31 July has shattered Hollywood. Blond-haired, blue-eyed Francis was one of Columbia's most popular rising stars, and was amassing a large female fan club. He was only 25 years old when he died, as the private plane carrying him and bit player Ann Russell crashed while trying to take off from an unused parking lot in Burbank, California.

Francis will be best remembered as Willie Keith in last year's *The Caine Mutiny*, based on Herman Wouk's novel, and, in *The Bamboo Prison*, as the prisoner-of-war brainwashed with communist ideas. Earlier this year he was seen in John Ford's West Point epic *The Long Gray Line*, as a young cadet under Tyrone Power's instruction.

KING OF THE WILD FRONTIER

Every kid on the block is wearing a Davy Crockett coonskin hat, and singing the song you can't get away from this season – "Born on a mountain-top in Tennessee . . ." And all because of a three-part television show that's now been released as a feature film, Walt Disney's *Davy Crockett – King of the Wild Frontier*.

In the United States, where the TV show was highly rated, the movie has been helped by the familiarity of the material – at least it's now in Technicolor and you can see how many extras are fighting at the Alamo. But *Davy* is also proving a sensation worldwide.

Bill Walsh's production is good, clean fun. But who'll remember tall Fess Parker, or "The Ballad of Davy Crockett", when the next craze rolls around?

GOSSIP COLUMN

■ Rita Hayworth's husband, crooner Dick Haymes, faces deportation because he claimed he was ineligible to fight in the war on account of his Argentinian citizenship. This has finished Haymes at the box office, and brought sadness to the Hayworth household, which includes nine-year-old Rebecca Welles and four-year-old Yasmin Khan, from Rita's former marriages.

SEPTEMBER
OCTOBER

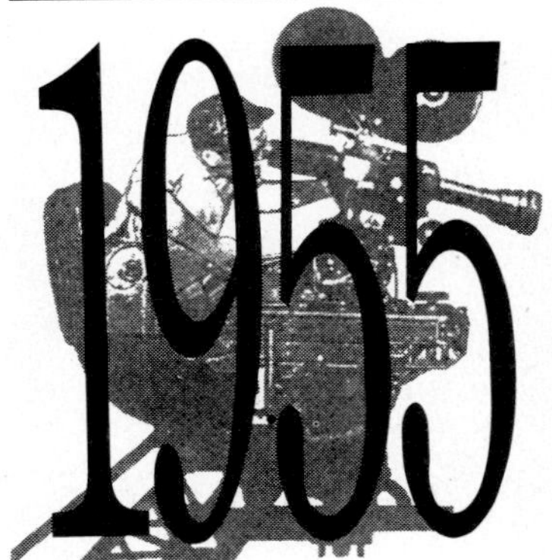

NOVEMBER
DECEMBER

BIRTHS, DEATHS AND MARRIAGES

BIRTHS

Glynis Barber
25 Oct, South Africa

DEATHS

James Dean
30 Sep, nr. Chalame, California
Road accident

Alice Joyce
9 Oct, Hollywood
Heart ailment

Lloyd Bacon
15 Nov, Burbank, California
Cerebral haemorrhage

John Hodiak
19 Nov, Hollywood
Heart attack

MARRIAGES

Rock Hudson
9 Nov, *to* Phyllis Gates

Gregory Peck
30 Dec, *to* Veronique Passani

A REBEL BEYOND DEATH

James Dean, Sal Mineo and Natalie Wood in Rebel without a Cause.

Just under a month before *Rebel without a Cause* premiered in New York its young star was already dead. At 5.45 p.m. on 30 September, at the intersection of routes 466 and 41, near Chalame, California, a Ford sedan collided with James Dean's Porsche Spyder 550. Dean was killed instantly.

It's impossible to watch *Rebel* without a deep sense of regret, of loss. His performance as Jim Stark – "the bad boy from a good family" as the ads have it – is a masterly achievement, fulfilling the promise shown in last year's *East of Eden*.

Dean plays the spoilt son of henpecked Jim Backus and shrewish Ann Doran. He forms a substitute "family" with girlfriend Natalie Wood and sulky Sal Mineo after a tragic incident – an automobile test-of-nerves known as the "chicken run" – has brought them together. It's a particularly scary sequence in the light of the young star's death, and the movie looks like becoming a beacon for today's troubled youngsters. *Rebel without a Cause* is more than a monument to its star: it's a movie for all time.

JEAN SIMMONS

The little girl from London's Golders Green has certainly "grown up" in Hollywood. Raven-haired beauty Jean Simmons, 26, has turned into one of Hollywood's hottest properties, something that couldn't have been foreseen when she was chosen from a group of dance students to play Margaret Lockwood's sister in *Give Us the Moon* (1944).

She spent her teenage years in movies: *Mr. Emmanuel* (1944), *Meet Sexton Black* (1944) and *Caesar and Cleopatra* (1945). On the set of the last she met Stewart Granger, soon to become M-G-M's top star, and after several movies – during which the pair tried to keep their burgeoning affaire hushed-up, she won some plum movie roles.

In David Lean's *Great Expectations* (1946) 17-year-old Simmons was suitably spoilt as the young Estella, and in Michael Powell's *Black Narcissus* (1947) she was a sultry Indian temptress. When Laurence Olivier chose her to play Ophelia in his film of *Hamlet* (1948), Granger opposed the casting but it won her an Oscar nomination.

After the Technicolor romance *The Blue Lagoon* she co-starred with Granger in *Adam and Evelyne* (both 1949). The pair were by now open lovers, and they married in 1950. She followed Granger to Hollywood and her success virtually equalled his. In *The Actress, Young Bess* and *The Robe* (all 1953) she showed a sharp acting talent that matched her beauty.

She also proved she could rise above historical rubbish like *The Egyptian* (1954) with her dignity intact. And she's now winning new plaudits for her uninhibited rendition of "If I Were a Bell' in the musical *Guys and Dolls*.

THE LEGEND LIVES ON

Though he never lived to see the premiere of even his second starring movie, James Dean has left quite a legacy behind. He was already acting in 1947, playing in Fairmount High School sophomore productions.

In 1951 he withdrew from Santa Monica City College to study acting under James Whitmore. He urged the 20-year-old youngster to go to New York, although Dean had already appeared in his first professional job – jiving in a Pepsi-Cola commercial. Before leaving for New York, Dean appeared in four Hollywood movies, and played St. John the Apostle in a TV Easter special, *Hill Number One*.

On Broadway he got a part in *See the Jaguar*, and was among the seven selected from over 200 for the Actors' Studio, foster-home of his idol, Marlon Brando. Then the jobs came quick and fast. In 1953 he appeared in 15 live TV dramas, including, memorably, Rod Serling's *A Long Time Till Dawn*.

When director Elia Kazan cast Dean (instead of Paul Newman) in last year's *East of Eden*, international stardom beckoned. He did four more TV dramas, and appeared on stage in Andre Gide's *The Immoralist* and Sophocles' *Women of Trachis* in one month.

Now he lives on in *Rebel without a Cause* and George Stevens' as-yet unfinished *Giant*, with Elizabeth Taylor and Rock Hudson, due next year. James Byron Dean, 8 February 1931-30 September 1955 – R.I.P.

OH, OH, TODD-AO!

Cinerama Holiday, with a projected $10 million gross, is shaping up to be the year's box-office hit. But yet another big-screen process is also drawing the crowds. Made in the remarkable new Todd-AO, the film version of Rodgers & Hammerstein's musical *Oklahoma!* is entrancing a new generation of fans.

Broadway's longest-running musical hardly needs any extra gimmicks. But Todd-AO makes it look – and sound – even more impressive on New York's giant Rivoli Theater screen.

Developed by producer Michael Todd and the American Optical Company, Todd-AO is a 70mm process with six-track magnetic stereophonic sound, projected faster than normal (30 rather than 24 frames a second) to avoid on-screen flickering. Todd plans to use it again for his forthcoming *Around the World in 80 Days* and *Don Quixote*, and Rodgers & Hammerstein want it for when *South Pacific* finally reaches the screen.

For theatres that can't show Todd-AO – and that means everywhere outside the Rivoli – director Fred Zinnemann shot a 35mm CinemaScope version in parallel. Close observers will spot tiny differences between the two. But there's no mistaking the strength of "Method"-actor Rod Steiger as the threatening "Pore" Jud Fry and, in her debut, Shirley Jones as the cornbred innocent Laurie. They're two brand new stars on the musical horizon.

Shirley Jones and Gordon MacRae in Rodgers & Hammerstein's Oklahoma!.

FROM TUBE TO SCREEN

In autumn 1947, NBC's Sunday 9 p.m. hour-long slot was given over to live drama for the first time. Certain sponsors offered some of the finest new plays ever seen on TV, and the best have already been made into movies.

The most famous was Philco Playhouse's *Marty* (1953), with Rod Steiger and Nancy Marchand. It catapulted Paddy Chayefsky into the front rank of screenwriters, and Delbert Mann went on to direct the movie version (with Ernest Borgnine and Betsy Blair) as well. Other writers who have emerged from that slot are Rod Serling, Calder Willingham, Horton Foote, Gore Vidal and Reginald Rose.

Among movies which started life on TV are *Cyrano de Bergerac* (1950) – Jose Ferrer, Christopher Plummer and Claire Bloom on television – and last year's *The Caine Mutiny* – Lloyd Nolan, Barry Sullivan and Frank Lovejoy in the TV original, *The Caine Mutiny Court Martial*. But it's also a two-way traffic.

CODE BUSTERS

Producer-director Otto Preminger has flouted the Production code for the second time by releasing a movie without a Seal of Approval. His earlier *The Moon Is Blue* (1953) now looks innocuous compared with *The Man with the Golden Arm*, a searing study of narcotic addiction, up to now a forbidden subject.

The junkie, played by Frank Sinatra, is a musician forced to work as a dealer in a small town professional poker game. He's shaken his heroin habit when we first meet him, but throughout the course of the film falls prey to Darren McGavin's insidious peddler. Eventually he goes cold turkey and these scenes are harrowing to watch.

Preminger is only one of many who reckon the Code has outlived its usefulness since the Hays Office pronounced those "dos and don'ts" back in July 1934. It looks like *the Moon Is Blue* and *The Man with the Golden Arm* are only the beginning.

BOX OFFICE

UK

1 The Dam Busters
2 White Christmas
3 Doctor at Sea

OTHER TOP BOX OFFICE FILMS

Above Us the Waves
The Colditz Story
A Kid for Two Farthings
Raising a Riot
Seven Brides for Seven Brothers
The Student Prince
20,000 Leagues Under the Sea

BOX OFFICE

US

1 Cinerama Holiday
2 Mister Roberts
3 Battle Cry
4 20,000 Leagues Under the Sea
5 Not as a Stranger
6 The Country Girl
7 Lady and the Tramp
8 Strategic Air Command
9 To Hell and Back
10 Sea Chase
A Star Is Born

Marlon Brando, Jean Simmons, Frank Sinatra and Vivian Blaine in the musical Guys and Dolls.

A MUSICAL FOR ADULTS

Never in the history of the movies has there been such a wave of mammoth musicals – virtually one a month, and all based on Broadway hits. Latest off the sound stages, following *Oklahoma!*, is *Guys and Dolls*, from Frank Loesser's 1950 smash-eroo. And it's packed with a cast of movie stars that Broadway could never buy.

Producer Sam Goldwyn wanted Gene Kelly to play gambler Sky Masterson but, ironically (as M-G-M has ended up distributing the film), Louis B. Mayer wouldn't let him go. So instead of the best dancer, Goldwyn went for the screen's best actor – Marlon Brando. He does a sensational job, even to using his own singing voice (pleasant, but not great) in songs like "Luck Be a Lady", and a ballad that Loesser wrote especially for the film, "A Woman in Love".

As Sister Sarah Brown of the Save-a-Soul Mission, British import Jean Simmons, 26, is fine. And it's not the first time she's either co-starred with Brando – she was a seamstress to his *Napoleon* in last year's *Desiree* – or sung on screen – she swung her way through "Let Him Go, Let Him Tarry" in the British airbase drama *The Way to the Stars* (1945).

Frank Sinatra's Nathan Detroit, shows he would have been a good Sky Masterson, but Broadway's Sam Levene is a hard act to follow. Retained from the original cast, however, is Vivian Blaine as "chantoose" Adelaide. She's a peach.

JANUARY FEBRUARY

MARCH APRIL

SIMPLY . . . SINATRA

Who'd have thought, when his vocal chords haemorrhaged in 1952, the agency MCA dropped him like a ton of bricks, and Columbia terminated his recording contract, that by 1956 Francis Albert Sinatra would be a bigger star than ever – "sitting on a rainbow, string around his finger". He's the Guv'nor alright.

The comeback trail started with his begging Columbia boss Harry Cohn to let him play Maggio in *From Here to Eternity* (1953), and that won him an Oscar. He'd already married Ava Gardner, and it was as if she inspired him. A contract with Capitol followed, and he became the first singer to use the new long-player as a "concept vehicle". Instant classics all: "Songs for Young Lovers", "Swing Easy", "In the Wee Small Hours of the Morning", and now the fabulous "Songs for Swingin' Lovers", the only album to climb up the singles chart.

But he's also had an unbroken run of good luck with his movie roles, showing a naturalistic ability in parts like the presidential assassin in *Suddenly* (1954); the old John Garfield role in the remake of *Four Daughters* (1938), this time called *Young at Heart* (1954); the medical student in Stanley Kramer's *Not as a Stranger* (1955); and M-G-M's snappy comedy *The Tender Trap* (1955), whose opening sequence was simply Sinatra walking towards the camera singing the title song.

In *The Man with the Golden Arm* (1955) he gives his most powerful performance to date as the heroin-addicted Frankie Machine, and is well in line for an Oscar nomination. The kid from New Jersey who was ripped from his mother's womb back in 1915, and still bears the scars on his face, has finally arrived. The Guv'nor.

MUSICAL MANTLE OF QUALITY

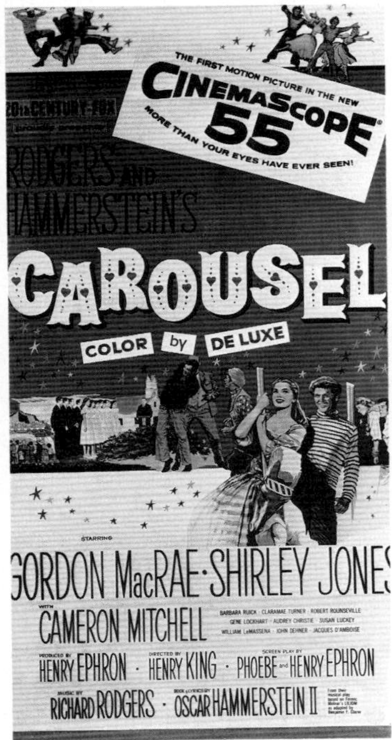

20th Century-Fox's version of *Carousel* has real clambake locations on the rocky Maine coast, and June "bustin' out all over" in CinemaScope 55 and six-channel stereophonic sound.

Shirley Jones is cast as Julie with her *Oklahoma!* partner Gordon MacRae. The story has actually been filmed twice before, as *Liliom* in both 1930 and 1934. But *Carousel* tells the tale of the fairground barker gone bad with vivid new motion-picture magic. With this Rodgers & Hammerstein gem, the 20th Century-Fox musical has finally lost its usual garishness and taken on the mantle of quality.

John Wayne in The Searchers.

RIDE AWAY, DUKE

John Ford's new western, *The Searchers*, is a bleak but impressive saga of a quest fulfilled. As the ads have it: "He had to find her. . . . He had to find her."

"He" is John Wayne, uncle of a girl kidnapped by a Comanche chief and brought up as an Indian. The moment when he recognises "her" (a grown-up Natalie Wood) is one of the most heart-stopping in all cinema.

The quest itself takes its time, and involves Wayne with Jeffrey Hunter as a young man taken in and brought up by Wayne; Vera Miles, as Hunter's romantic interest; Ward Bond as a colourful vigilante preacher; and most memorable of all, Hank Worden as a veteran Indian scout, "grateful for a rockin' chair".

It's handsomely photographed stuff, with an exciting raid on a Comanche camp, the action framed through bodies and guns. But Wayne's character may be too bitter for many, and there's an unpleasant hint of racialism running through the tale. But it continues the tradition of fine westerns like *Shane* (1953) and *High Noon* (1952) and has a closing shot that sums up a whole era gone by. The camera pulls back through a doorway leaving Wayne with no place to go, and Tex Ritter croons "Ride Away".

WHO WAS THAT MASKED MAN?

They've been a part of American popular culture over the past two decades – on the airwaves, in the pages of comic books, and since 1949 in ABC's long-running TV series. The Lone Ranger ("Hi-yo, Silver, Awaayy!") and his faithful Indian friend Tonto ("Keemo sabay") have a place next to Superman, Dick Tracy and Orphan Annie. Now they've made their big-screen debut in the WarnerColor western *The Lone Ranger*, a rattling good release timed to catch Yuletide family audiences before kids start the spring semester.

Clayton Moore is the blue-eyed hero, and indian actor Jay Silverheels is Tonto the Brave. The leading lady, intriguingly called Welcome, is played by former child star Bonita Granville, who just happens to be married to Jack Wrather, the producer. The villain is current Mr. Nasty, Lyle Bettger, from *The Greatest Show on Earth* (1952) and last year's *Destry* and *The Sea Chase*. Warners is already planning a follow-up, but the dynamic duo will have to shoot it between breaks in the TV series.

SLOE-EYED SAL

Talented Sal Mineo already has a Best Supporting Oscar nomination for his Plato in *Rebel without a Cause* (1955) and he's now in two of the toughest films around – *Crime in the Streets* with John Cassavetes, and *Somebody Up There Likes Me*, the biopic of Rocky Graziano. Not bad going for a kid who was once given the choice of going to a home for delinquents or attending a professional stage high school. Salvatore Mineo Jr, aged 11, chose the stage.

Born in 1939, sloe-eyed Sal grew up in the Bronx, on tough 217th Street. By eight he was in a street gang, and at 10 he planned a major caper. But the authorities nabbed him and gave him two choices.

At stage school he was spotted by producer Cheryl Crawford, who was looking for children to play in her production of Tennessee Williams' *The Rose Tattoo* with Maureen Stapleton and Eli Wallach. So at the age of 11 Mineo was on Broadway. Two years later he took over the role of Yul Brynner's son in *The King and I* and he finally made his movie debut, as a juvenile delinquent, in last year's *Six Bridges to Cross*, with Tony Curtis.

STAR QUOTES

Rock Hudson

"There was a time when Vera-Ellen and I were thinking about getting married. We even set the date. But later we both agreed that our marriage wouldn't work out."

BIRTHS, DEATHS AND MARRIAGES

BIRTHS

Mel Gibson
3 Jan, Peekskill, New York

Robby Benson
21 Jan, Dallas

Eric Roberts
18 Apr, Biloxi, Mississippi

DEATHS

Alexander Korda
23 Jan, London
Heart attack

Robert Newton
25 Mar, Beverly Hills

Edward Arnold
26 Apr, Encino, California

MARRIAGES

Grace Kelly
19 Apr, *to* Prince Rainier

BRIT APPEAL

Top M-G-M star Stewart Granger is becoming more trouble than he's worth. Having lambasted the studio to the world's press for not giving him the parts he thought he deserved (he hates costume roles, he says, and wants to do westerns), Granger is now refusing to sign a further seven-year contract, even though it's a deal most actors would die for.

But M-G-M has been grooming two new Brits to keep the errant Granger in line. Edmund Purdom replaced over-weight Mario Lanza in *The Student Prince*, and the good-looking actor also took over Marlon Brando's part at 20th Century-Fox in *The Egyptian* (both 1954). Although considered by many to be wooden and lacking in sex appeal, Purdom was rushed by M-G-M into two roles turned down by Granger, last year's *The King's Thief* and *The Prodigal*.

Also being groomed by the studio is tall Roger Moore, talent-spotted while on Broadway in *A Pin to See the Peepshow*. Elegant, well-spoken Moore was then rushed into three pictures: as the gigolo in *The Last Time I Saw Paris* (1954) with Elizabeth Taylor; opposite Eleanor Parker in the handsome *Interrupted Melody* (1955); and with fellow-Brits Purdom and David Niven in the CinemaScope swashbuckler *The King's Thief* (1955).

Stewart Granger? Who's he?

Danny Kaye and Angela Lansbury in the swashbuckling comedy-musical The Court Jester.

DANNY'S ONLY JESTING!

"The chalice from the palace. . . ." No, "the vessel with the pestle. . . ." The whole world's wondering, along with Danny Kaye as *The Court Jester*, where "the brew that is true" is hidden. The loony jingle that's caught the public's fancy is one of the many laughter highlights of the production for Paramount. It's written, directed and produced by masters of mirth Norman Panama and Melvin Frank.

The Court Jester is Kaye's best vehicle since the popular *Hans Christian Andersen* (1952). He plays Hawkins, a yokel mistaken for the Jester, and gets to guy swashbucklers alongside lovely Glynis Johns as Maid Jean, Basil Rathbone as villainous Sir Ravenshurst, Angela Lansbury as Princess Gwendolyn, and Cecil Parker as codger "King" Roderick, who has managed to oust the real Royal Family from the throne.

Kaye's wife Sylvia Fine contributes some fine numbers, like "They'll Never Outfox the Fox" and "Life Could Not Better Be". And even the name of the movie's production company – Dena - comes from his daughter. And, by the way, "the pellet with the poison's in the vessel with the pestle."

ACADEMY AWARDS

PRESENTED ON 31 MARCH 1956

Best Picture
Marty

Best Director
Delbert Mann
Marty

Best Actor
Ernest Borgnine
Marty

Best Actress
Anna Magnani
The Rose Tattoo

Best Sup Actor
Jack Lemmon
Mister Roberts

Best Sup Actress
Jo Van Fleet
East of Eden

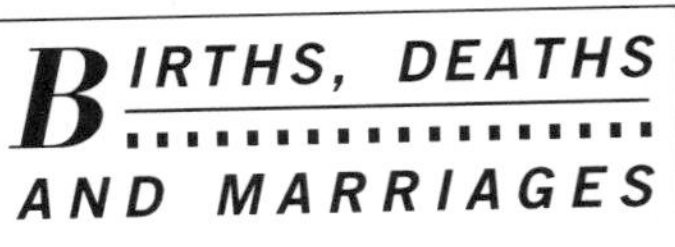

BIRTHS, DEATHS AND MARRIAGES

BIRTHS

Tom Hanks
9 Jul, Concord, California

DEATHS

Louis Calhern
12 May, Tokyo
Heart attack

Jean Hersholt
2 Jun, Beverly Hills
Cancer

Bela Lugosi
16 Aug, Los Angeles

MARRIAGES

Marilyn Monroe
29 Jun, *to* **Arthur Miller**

R & H SCORE AGAIN!

Yul Brynner and Deborah Kerr in Rodgers & Hammerstein's The King and I.

The King and I is the third Rogers & Hammerstein hit to reach the screen within a year. Of course, the story is not particularly new: Irene Dunne played the English schoolteacher and Rex Harrison was an unlikely King of Siam (in a part James Mason turned down) in the non-musical *Anna and the King of Siam* (1946). That had a plot that was simply a battle of wills between the two, set in the court of the despotic oriental monarch in the 1890s.

There's a subtle change in the film version of *The King and I*. Between Deborah Kerr's Anna and newcomer Yul Brynner's king (the role in created on Broadway in 1951) there's now more than a hint of a romance. That suggestion of a mutual, unfulfilled love makes the tale doubly moving.

The score itself is sumptuous, with famous numbers like "Hello, Young Lovers", "I Whistle a Happy Tune", "Getting to Know You", "Shall We Dance?", and the instrumental "March of the Siamese Children" in which the king's brats are wheeled out. Director Walter Lang may lack the flair of Vincente Minnelli but he knows when to stand back and let the piece speak for itself.

It's a pity the movie is let down by wobbly DeLuxe Color: if there's to be a single-strip replacement for Technicolor, it needs to be much better than this.

IS THIS THE LAST OF KELLY?

The Philadelphia Story (1940) was the scintillating film version of Philip Barry's Broadway success about love among the very rich. Katharine Hepburn recreated her stage role, Cary Grant was her ex-husband and James Stewart won a Best Actor Oscar as a budding Scott Fitzgerald. The whole thing was just "yar".

Now it's back – with Cole Porter songs – as *High Society*. And again the cast is a sparkler – Grace Kelly, Bing Crosby and Frank Sinatra. The story has been moved to Newport, Rhode Island, to incorporate its annual jazz festival. This gives the movie the chance to include Louis Armstrong and his All-Stars.

The all-new Porter score – except for "Well, Did You Evah?" from *Dubarry Was a Lady* (1943) – is fine, though Porter purists reckon it's below his best. Sadly it looks like being the last time Kelly will grace the screen. On 19 April she married Prince Rainier of Monaco and became Princess Grace. High Society, indeed!

FROM SWINDON TO TINSELTOWN

The mink bikini Diana Dors wore at the Venice film festival made more people aware of the blonde British sex-bomb than had ever seen her movies. It landed her a Hollywood contract, fulfilling her childhood dreams.

Britain's answer to MM was born in 1931. She studied at the Royal Academy of Dramatic Art, and made her movie debut at 15 in *The Shop at Sly Corner* (1947) as a plump, brunette teenager. She had good roles in David Lean's *Oliver Twist* (1948) and as a bar-room hostess in Rank's South African "western" *Diamond City* (1949), with David Farrar. But her image was beginning to change.

She dyed her hair blonde, lost weight, and started posing for pin-ups. Often wearing little more than a drape of fur and high heels, DD made the covers of every magazine from *Picturegoer* to *Picture Post*. There was even a booklet, issued with red-and-green glasses, called *Diana Dors in 3-D*. Every schoolboy wanted one.

But she can act. In Carol Reed's *A Kid for Two Farthings* (1955) and now, relatively deglamourized, in *Yield to the Night*, as a character based on Ruth Ellis, the last woman in England to be hanged, DD demands audiences take her seriously. With an RKO contract under her arm and a mission to report on Hollywood for *Picturegoer*, it seems the world's her oyster. But can the girl from Swindon conquer Tinseltown?

Diana Dors.

WHALE OF A TIME

John Huston's production of *Moby Dick* reaches the screen at last, after an agonizing shoot involving rotten Irish weather and at least one whale lost to the high seas. The movie has a striking, parchment-like look, achieved by British labs over-printing black-and-white on the Technicolor negative.

Most of the cast are well-chosen. Ishmael, the narrator and only survivor of the whaling ship *Pequod* out of New Bedford, is sensitively played by Richard Basehart, and first mate Starbuck is gently portrayed by Leo Genn. Among the supporting players aboard are Harry Andrews as Stubb, Noel Purcell as the Carpenter, and the bizarrely-cast Friedrich Ledebur as the multi-tattoed Queequeg. As Father Mapple, a fire-and-brimstone preacher, Orson Welles makes a splendid guest appearance.

But as the loony Captain Ahab, Gregory Peck lacks fire. Despite his height, his peg-leg and white-tinged Lincolnesque beard, he lacks stature. Huston's father, the late Walter, would have been fine; so would Spencer Tracy or even Charlton Heston. So, despite the movie's excellent dialogue, scripted by Ray Bradbury from the Herman Melville novel, *Moby Dick* is holed beneath the waterline.

Sterling Hayden in The Killing, *about a $2 million heist at a racetrack.*

Gregory Peck as Captain Ahab tries to kill the white whale in Moby Dick.

A KILLING AT THE RACES

On release in a double bill with the Robert Mitchum mystery drama *Foreign Intrigue* is a gripping little "B" movie that's well worth seeking out. *The Killing* is based on Lionel White's crime novel *Clean Break*, about an attempt to steal $2 million from a racetrack; it co-stars Sterling Hayden – reprising his hustler from *The Asphalt Jungle* (1950) – and Coleen Gray, who actually has very little screen time.

Noteworthy in an excellent cast are Elisha Cook, Jr and Marie Windsor as a timid little cashier and his frowzy wife; Vince Edwards as a small-timer trying to edge in on the deal; and the seemingly deranged Timothy Carey as Nikki Arane, a professional killer.

The film is the first for a new production team headed by producer James B. Harris and director Stanley Kubrick, whose previous screen credits include the barely-seen cheapies, *Killer's Kiss* (1955) and *Fear and Desire* (1953) and a couple of shorts, *Day of the Fight* (1950) and *The Flying Padre* (1951), none of which revealed any exceptional talent.

But *The Killing* is a beautifully directed movie, with fine black-and-white camerawork that's almost documentary-like at times. Unfortunately, the influence of TV's *Dragnet* makes itself felt with an over-used narration. But if Kubrick learns to tell stories in pictures alone, he could turn out to be a considerable talent.

THE BRYLCREEM KID

Born rich, 26-year-old Robert Wagner has the air of someone drifting through the real world, his dark-haired looks and amiable appeal ready-made for an executive position and a slew of women at his feet.

Known as "R.J." to his friends, he's the son of a wealthy steel executive and originally intended to go into business. But his handsome features were spotted by 20th Century-Fox, and he swiftly became a teenage idol. His early films included traditional action roles in *The Halls of Montezuma* (1950) and *The Frogmen* (1951). But it was *With a Song in My Heart*, when he was sung to by Susan Hayward, and *Stars and Stripes Forever* (both 1952), with Clifton Webb as John Philip Sousa, that drew audiences' attention. Both were in Technicolor, which benefited Wagner's tan and slicked-down hair.

Fox quickly realized what it had under contract, and starred him in the early CinemaScope *Beneath the 12 Mile Reef* (1953), in which the Brylcreemed hair went curly, and *Prince Valiant* (1954), in which the Brylcreem vanished under a pudding-basin wig. In *Broken Lance* (1954), a western version of *King Lear*, he was one of rancher Spencer Tracy's sons, and the two got along so well that Tracy asked for him to play his brother in the action drama *The Mountain* (1956). That's on screens this autumn, but meanwhile Wagner can be seen as the cool killer in *A Kiss before Dying*, from Ira Levin's chilling novel.

Long attached to Debbie Reynolds, Wagner later fell into the clutches of Barbara Stanwyck, his co-star in *Titanic* (1953). Still friendly with Stanwyck, Wagner has just announced his engagement to lovely Natalie Wood.

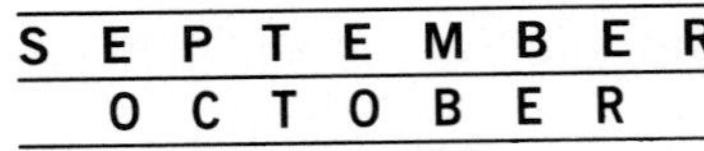

SEPTEMBER
OCTOBER

NOVEMBER
DECEMBER

BIRTHS, DEATHS AND MARRIAGES

BIRTHS

Fiona Fullerton
10 Oct, Kaduna, Nigeria

Carrie Fisher
21 Oct, Beverly Hills

Bo Derek
20 Nov, Torrance, California

DEATHS

Anne Crawford
18 Oct, London
Anaemia

Francis L. Sullivan
19 Nov, New York
Lung ailment

MARRIAGES

Diahann Carroll
Sep, *to* Monte Kay

Donald O'Connor
11 Oct, *to* Gloria Noble

Steve McQueen
1 Nov, *to* Neile Adams

Gig Young
Dec, *to* **Elizabeth Montgomery**

AROUND THE WORLD IN TODD-AO

David Niven and Cantinflas in Around the World in 80 Days.

Some reckoned Michael Todd would never actually finish his version of Jules Verne's *Around the World in 80 Days*, so complex was the filming and so errant were his pay cheques. But now unveiled on New York's giant Rivoli screen, the movie confounds all disbelievers. The producer-showman has come up with a real "show", a rollicking $5 million-plus adventure for all ages.

Using his own Todd-AO 70mm process, he's filled the big screen with wonder, as Phileas Fogg (David Niven) travels around the world on a bet, attended by his faithful manservant Passepartout (Mexican comedian Cantinflas). Todd peppers the movie with cameo appearances by star players, often appearing for a joke or a gift (say, a car or a painting). Making most impact are Noel Coward, Ronald Colman, Beatrice Lillie, Charles Boyer, Buster Keaton and, in a lusty San Francisco saloon, George Raft, Marlene Dietrich, and Frank Sinatra. Direction by Michael Anderson is seamless, and the use of magnetic stereophonic sound, particularly when Indians attack a railroad train, is breathtaking.

BLACK JACK

Once Jack Palance has crossed your celluloid horizon, you know that your time's up. He not only looks like a double-dyed villain, he invariably plays one. As the hired killer in *Shane* (1953), or menacing Joan Crawford in *Sudden Fear* (1952) – his two Oscar-nominated performances – or as Atilla the Hun in *Sign of the Pagan* (1954), Palance is the man you love to fear.

In fact, this kindly son of a Pennsylvania coal-miner is an intellectual, educated at both the University of North Carolina and Stanford University. He followed his father briefly into the mines before becoming a professional boxer but the Second World War cut short his sports career.

After replacing Marlon Brando in Elia Kazan's Broadway production of *A Streetcare Named Desire*, Kazan gave him his screen break in *Panic in the Streets* (1950). In 1955 he played the role that John Garfield created on stage in Clifford Odets' acerbic *The Big Knife*. His rapport with director Robert Aldrich led to this year's major acting triumph, *Attack!* where he's a psychotic lieutenant who takes advantage of a weak officer (Eddie Albert) and eventually causes his death.

BOX OFFICE

UK

1 Reach for the Sky
2 Private's Progress
3 A Town Like Alice
4 Trapeze

OTHER TOP BOX OFFICE FILMS

The Baby and the Battleship
Cockleshell Heroes
It's Great to Be Young
The King and I
Lady and the Tramp
The Searchers

BOX OFFICE

US

1 Guys and Dolls
2 The King and I
3 Trapeze
4 High Society
5 I'll Cry Tomorrow
6 Picnic
7 War and Peace
8 The Eddy Duchin Story
9 Moby Dick
10 The Searchers

ADULT MOVIES MAKE THE GRADE

If the Catholic League of Decency had simply given *Baby Doll* its infamous "C" rating (morally objectionable for all), the film might have sunk without trace, robbed of a large audience. But New York's Cardinal Spellman has blasted the movie from the pulpit, and so ensured its notoriety and commercial success.

Not that *Baby Doll* needed much help. Warners' giant billboard over Times Square has Carroll Baker sprawled across an iron bedstead, sucking her thumb, and wearing a short nightdress now christened the "Baby Doll Nightie".

Elia Kazan's movie of the Tennessee Williams shocker has Production Code approval, and shows the Breen (formerly Hays) Office is finally growing up. In fact, since Otto Preminger's double-barrelled blasting with *The Moon Is Blue* (1953) and *The Man with the Golden Arm* (1955), the Production Code has amended itself. "Adult" situations are now allowed, depending on the story. Drug-taking is now okay, as long as it is not made attractive. And adult dialogue can be spoken in unhushed tones. Watch out for a run of filmed "sensational" best-sellers.

STAR QUOTES

Karl Malden
referring to *Baby Doll* (1956)

"We've got to do something to get people away from TV."

DEBORAH'S NO LADY!

Despite being Oscar-nominated for her nymphomaniac in *From Here to Eternity* (1953), Deborah Kerr is still stuck with her image as a lady – or as she puts it, "high-minded, long-suffering, white-gloved, and decorative." But moviegoers have queued to watch those banked fires beneath that ladylike exterior, in hits like *King Solomon's Mines* (1950), *Quo Vadis* (1951), and *The Prisoner of Zenda* (1952).

But this year there's a new woman emerging. A spell on Broadway in Robert Anderson's daring *Tea and Sympathy* led to her being cast in Vincente Minnelli's movie version, as the headmaster's wife who awakens young John Kerr (no relation) into sexual awareness. This follows her Anna in *The King and I*, opposite Broadway's Yul Brynner, and eradicated memories of Gertrude Lawrence who created the part on Broadway in 1951.

"Her name will rhyme with star and not with cur" was Louis B. Meyer's memo when he signed her to an M-G-M contract in 1945. At that time she was a threat to the Queen of the Lot, another British redhead, Greer Garson. Born in 1921 in Scotland, Kerr trained as a dancer, and made her London debut at 17 in *Prometheus*. A film debut in *Major Barbara* (1941) followed at 20, and an affaire with director Michael Powell led to her playing three roles in *The Life and Death of Colonel Blimp* (1943) and the leading, sex-starved nun in *Black Narcissus* (1947).

Currently married to Tony Bartley, the tall star has now settled in California, and has a new two-picture deal at 20th Century-Fox, with both director and leading-man approval.

DeMILLE'S LAST COMMANDMENT?

In the biggest season of "big" movies ever, up comes veteran showman Cecil B. DeMille with a gargantuan remake of his own 1923 silent *The Ten Commandments*. At $13.5 million it's easily the most expensive movie ever made, beating recent items like M-G-M's $7 million *Quo Vadis* (1951) and Walt Disney's $9 million *20,000 Leagues under the Sea* (1954). DeMille also claims he used 25,000 extras.

All that's missing is taste. At 219 minutes DeMille's life of Moses is certainly all-embracing but it's often highly inventive as well – there's a 30-year gap in Moses' life in the Bible itself. But as the producer-director appears in the prologue and occasionally comments on the action, only a churl (or a biblical scholar) would dare challenge its veracity.

Apart from the awe-inspiring special effects like the parting of the Red Sea (actually miniature waterfalls in reverse), DeMille has a fine Moses in Charlton Heston, 33, who graduates from gusto to gravitas, from prince to patriarch. And as Rameses II, the pharoah who finally lets Moses' people go, Yul Brynner proves that his performance in this summer's *The King and I* was no fluke: here's an actor born to command, who can also convey human frailty.

Milling around as well are Edward G. Robinson, Debra Paget, Yvonne De Carlo and John Derek. Only Anne Baxter's Nefretiri strikes a ludicrous contemporary note. But could this be DeMille's swan song? Word is, the 75-year-old autocrat suffered a heart attack while filming the Exodus, and is not in the best of health.

Charlton Heston in Cecil B. DeMille's remake of The Ten Commandments.

Audrey Hepburn as Natasha in Paramount's War and Peace.

TOLSTOY'S BLOCKBUSTER COMES TO THE SCREEN

Dino De Laurentiis' sumptuous production for Paramount of Tolstoy's *War and Peace* is as fine a version of a Russian classic as ever attempted. With Audrey Hepburn a perfect Natasha, the three-and-a-half-hour sprawling epic by director King Vidor manages to encapsulate not just the mammoth plot but also its very soul.

The battle sequences involved 5,000-6,000 Italian troops playing French and Russian soldiers. They're the most impressive ever seen, but the spectacle doesn't dwarf the intimate scenes. Co-starring with Hepburn is real-life hubby Mel Ferrer as Prince Andrey, his saturnine looks well-suited to the moody portrayal, and Henry Fonda, as Pierre, is properly confused as his homeland is destroyed by the French. Others making a strong impression are Vittorio Gassman as Anatole, John Mills as Platon, Barry Jones as Count Rostov, Oscar Homolka as General Kutuzov and Herbert Lom as Napoleon.

Several new names also register strongly. Watch out for Anita Ekberg, Milly Vitale, Jeremy Brett, Sean Barrett and May Britt. Shot largely in Italy, at Cinecitta studios, the $6 million production restores to Italian cinema the spectacle that was part of its great tradition.

Watch The Skies!

Science fiction movies began almost as soon as the cinema was invented. The daddy of the genre was Frenchman Georges Melies whose *Trip to the Moon* (1903), *An Impossible Voyage* (1905), and *20,000 Leagues under the Sea* (1907) made clever and witty use of primitive special effects.

In *Metropolis* (1926) German director Fritz Lang revealed a vision of future society as chilling as it was inventive, but throughout the 1930s the elements of what came to be recognized as "science fiction" were relegated to serials, often using characters from comic strips, with the heroes of *Flash Gordon* (1936) and *Buck Rogers* (1939) battling mad scientists in a low-budget universe.

After the Second World War and the atomic devastation of Hiroshima and Nagasaki, the science fiction movie graduated from cheap serial status to that of co-feature. Space travel was now becoming a possibility and the Bomb had ushered in a new scientific age. Extra-terrestrial involvement in Earth affairs became a favourite theme – a cosmic variant on the 1950s fear of Communist infiltration into American suburbia.

The Day the Earth Stood Still (1951) with its visiting alien and robot sent to warn Earth to mend its ways, and the hysterical *Red Planet Mars* (1952) were typical of this period. Human mutations included *The Incredible Shrinking Man* (1957) and *The Fly* (1958), while *The Thing (from Another World)* (1951), *Them!* (1954) and the superior *Invasion of the Body Snatchers* (1956) dealt with the threat of the unknown on "civilized" society, be it giant ants or "pods" to replace the neighbours. *The Beast from 20,000 Fathoms* (1953) was the first of a string of giant-monsters-on-the-rampage movies, typified by the Japanese import *Godzilla* (1954).

The technical innovations of the 1950s lent themselves perfectly to sci-fi. 3-D was used in films like *It Came from Outer Space* (1953) and *Creature from the Black Lagoon* (1954), and their popularity made studios realize that more had to be spent on design and special effects. Many budgets were upped to A-feature level.

Paramount scored with a version of H.G. Wells' *War of the Worlds* (1954), and two movies which presaged the space travel cycle, *Destination Moon* (1950) and *When Worlds Collide* (1952). CinemaScope was used for two of the finest films of the decade, Disney's stylish *20,000 Leagues under the Sea* (1954), starring James Mason as Captain Nemo, and M-G-M's *Forbidden Planet* (1956), a handsome re-working of Shakespeare's "The Tempest" in outer space with Robby the Robot and the Monster from the Id.

But most sci-fi movies were still low-budget, often independently made, films with catchpenny titles like *The Monster That Challenged the World* (1957) or *Attack of the 50 Foot Woman* (1958) that tended to play double-bills at drive-ins.

Films like *On The Beach* (1959) proved that a bigger budget could help sell fantasy to larger audiences. Classier sci-fi product followed, like Alfred Hitchcock's *The Birds* (1963) and Stanley Kubrick's black joke *Dr. Strangelove (1964).*

Kubrick teamed with M-G-M, NASA, and Cinerama for 2001: A Space Odyssey (1968), and filmed sci-fi took one giant step forward. Other high-budget hits were *Fantastic Voyage* (1966) and *Planet of the Apes* (1968), the latter spawning four sequels. These movies paved the way for the next stage in screen sci-fi, when directors like Steven Spielberg and George Lucas – clearly influenced by past classics like *Metropolis* and *The Absent Minded Professor* (1961) – would put new life into the sagging genre. The age of *Star Wars* and *E.T.* was about to dawn.

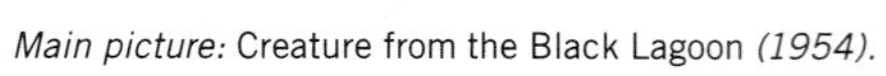

Main picture: Creature from the Black Lagoon *(1954).*

Giant ants attack in Them! *(1954).*

Walter Pidgeon and Robbie the Robot in Forbidden Planet *(1956).*

The Invasion of the Body Snatchers *(1955)*.

Comic book sci-fi hero Buck Rogers *(1939)*.

Attack of the 50 Foot Woman *(1958)*.

JANUARY
FEBRUARY

MARCH
APRIL

BIRTHS, DEATHS AND MARRIAGES

BIRTHS

Theresa Russell
Mar, San Diego, California

Amanda Plummer
23 Mar, New York

Christopher Lambert
29 Mar, New York

DEATHS

Humphrey Bogart
14 Jan, Hollywood
Cancer

Josephine Hull
12 Mar, New York

MARRIAGES

Elizabeth Taylor
2 Feb, *to* **Mike Todd**

Susan Hayward
8 Feb, *to* Floyd Eaton Chalkley

Henry Fonda
Mar, *to* Afdera Franchetti

Linda Darnell
3 Mar, *to* Merle Roy Robertson

BOGIE DEAD

"The trouble with Bogart," quipped John Huston, "is that he thinks he's Bogart." Not any more. The screen's greatest tough guy, who in real life was a man with a heart of gold, died in Hollywood on 14 January, from cancer of the oesophagus.

After years of playing minor parts on stage and screen, Bogart rose to prominence on Broadway as gun-toting Duke Mantee in Robert F. Sherwood's *The Petrified Forest*. When the play was filmed, Leslie Howard insisted Bogart recreate Mantee despite the studio's preference for Edward G. Robinson. Between 1936 and *High Sierra* (1941), the movie that George Raft turned down, Bogart appeared in 28 features, mainly as villains. But in *High Sierra* he played Roy Earle, a gangster with soul, and the public took him to its collective bosom.

A natural screen actor, he achieved great popularity in films like *The Maltese Falcon* (1941), *Casablanca* (1942), *To Have and Have Not* (1945) and *The Big Sleep* (1946). He was a better actor than he admitted, and his work in *The Treasure of the Sierra Madre* (1948), *In a Lonely Place* (1950), *The Caine Mutiny* (1954), and his Oscar-winning Charlie Allnutt in *The African Queen* (1951) attest to that. His fourth wife, Lauren Bacall, was also his perfect screen partner, and it was she who nursed him through his last, long final illness.

JIMMY STEWART FLIES SOLO

The biography of Charles A. Lindbergh, the first American to fly the Atlantic Ocean back in 1927, is the unlikely subject of the new Billy Wilder movie *The Spirit of St. Louis*, which takes its title from the name of Lindbergh's frail craft. The story of the "Lindy hop" is well-known, but Wilder's narrative is also remarkable: as the film is virtually a one-man show, flashbacks and voice-overs are used to open up the movie.

Ace aviator Lindbergh is played by James Stewart, perhaps a shade too elderly for the 25-year-old who flew 3,610 miles in a single-engined plane. But there's no doubting Stewart's expertise in conveying all the character's hopes, fears and joy. Most audiences will already know that Lindbergh arrived safely at Le Bourget airfield outside Paris, so all credit to Wilder for making it such a suspenseful yarn. But whether a one-man, one-plane movie will make money is anybody's guess. Warners clearly has doubts as well: after a disappointing preview in San Francisco, studio boss Jack Warner has already demanded changes to be made to the $6 million picture.

James Stewart as aviator Charles Lindbergh in The Spirit of St. Louis.

Lee J. Cobb and Henry Fonda face up to each other in a tense scene from the courtroom drama 12 Angry Men.

12 GOOD MEN AND TRUE

Reginald Rose's tense teleplay about a single juror (Robert Cummings) convincing the other 11 that they are too hasty in reaching a verdict proved to be fine TV. Henry Fonda recognized that the qualities of Juror No. 8 were very close to his own screen image – integrity and a sense of justice, seen in roles like his Young Mr. Lincoln, Kirby Yorke, Tom Joad, and Mister Roberts. So Fonda bought the rights to *12 Angry Men* and co-produced with Rose, ensuring the work was not subject to "Hollywoodization". There's none of the usual all-star cast, unnecessary inclusion of women, or symphonic underscoring.

12 Angry Men is a spare movie, brilliantly directed in a confined space (the jury room) by novice Sidney Lumet, who also made the TV drama. By casting little-known New York actors as jurors, producer Fonda has served actor Fonda well: Lee J. Cobb, Ed Begley, E.G. Marshall, Jack Warden and Martin Balsam are the names that will come to mind first when anyone is asked to name all *12 Angry Men* in some future film quiz. But the whole cast is flawless, and the movie gives valuable insights into what goes on when "12 good men and true" are locked up together with the power to decide the fate of an individual in the name of justice.

MYSTERY MAN YUL

Mystery surrounds the birth of bald heart-throb Yul Brynner. Is he Siamese, or is he Russian? When, exactly, was he born? And is he really bald? Brynner himself encourages all this; but seldom in the history of cinema has such a powerful presence arrived on the screen in three starring roles in one year. With *The King and I, The Ten Commandments* and *Anastasia* last year he made a huge impact.

Brynner claims he and his half-sister Vera were abducted by gypsies and brought to Paris, and it's certainly true that at 13 he was singing in Left Bank bistros. A recently discovered birth certificate is said to reveal he was born on 12 July 1915, on Sakhalin island, east of Siberia and north of Japan.

As a teenager in Paris, he worked in the theatre and studied at the Sorbonne. Michael Chekhov invited him to accompany him to the United States and join his Shakespearean troupe, and he accepted. He directed TV shows and made an early film appearance as a gangster (with hair) in *Port of New York* (1949). But a Broadway appearance in *Lute Song* with Mary Martin led to his being chosen in 1951 for the part of the king in *The King and I*, with Gertrude Lawrence. After 1,246 performances he repeated the role in the movie, for which he's now won a Best Actor Oscar.

He shaves his pate daily, but he'll sport a toupee for his next film part, as Jean Lafitte in Cecil B. DeMille's remake of his own 1938 *The Buccaneer*.

ACADEMY AWARDS

PRESENTED ON 27 MARCH 1957

Best Picture
Around the World in 80 Days

Best Director
George Stevens
Giant

Best Actor
Yul Brynner
The King and I

Best Actress
Ingrid Bergman
Anastasia

Best Sup Actor
Anthony Quinn
Lust for Life

Best Sup Actress
Dorothy Malone
Written on the Wind

WE FORGIVE YOU, INGRID

Ingrid Bergman's Best Actress Oscar for *Anastasia* (1956) is final proof of her redemption in the eyes of the American public. Before casting her, 20th Century-Fox polled theatre owners to find out if she would be acceptable, following the scandal when she left America to run off with and bear the children of Italian art-house director Roberto Rossellini.

The results were mixed; and Fox's sales force wanted Jennifer Jones in the role. But Fox boss Darryl F. Zanuck and director Anatole Litvak fought for her and she did the part for a mere $200,000. The movie's success has surprised everyone, and once again Bergman is the toast of Hollywood.

Photographer Fred Astaire with his protege Audrey Hepburn in Funny Face.

S'WONDERFUL!

Starring Fred Astaire, directed by Stanley Donen and produced by Roger Edens in Technicolor, with a marvellous Gershwin score, *Funny Face* sounds like an M-G-M musical. Except it isn't.

To get the services of radiant urchin Audrey Hepburn, the beatnik "Funny Face" of the title, Donen & Co. took their package to Paramount.

Astaire plays fashion photographer Dick Avery (based on Richard Avedon. He discovers Hepburn in a Greenwich Village bookshop, whisks her off to Paris as a top fashion model.

GOSSIP COLUMN

■ ***Confidential*, the scurrilous magazine first published out of New York in 1952, was finally sued – in February by actress Dorothy Dandridge. She asked for $2 million in damages for suggesting that she "partied" in a forest with some "naturalists". That was the moment other stars had waited for. But when it came down to it, only Maureen O'Hara joined the trial on 2 August, alleging that the magazine's story of her sexual encounter in Grauman's Chinese Theater was pure fiction. She said she'd been in Spain at the time.**

JAYNE IS BUSTIN' OUT ALL OVER!

Jayne Mansfield was well-known in showbiz circles long before she hit the screen in a pair of Warners movies in 1955. At the infamous premiere of one of them, the Jane Russell film *Underwater!*, it was Mansfield, not Russell, who grabbed the limelight. In a skin-tight, flesh-coloured swimming costume, her 40-21-36 curves were bustin' out all over.

Last year she got the star-making role of a lifetime, opposite Tom Ewell: *The Girl Can't Help It* was a veritable paean to her figure, surrounded by 22 rock 'n' roll performers.

Born in 1933 in Pennsylvania, she was married at 16, a mother at 17, and a pin-up and beauty queen as well. Those who knew her then say she had an all-consuming ambition to become a movie star, and to that end she went to drama classes at both the University of Texas and UCLA. She dyed her brunette hair platinum blonde, and there are even rumours she had a rib or two removed to stress that 40″ bust.

In 1955 on Broadway, clad in a Turkish towel for *Will Success Spoil Rock Hunter?* she gained some helpful notoriety, and Warners signed her up. After three movies it didn't pick up her option, but at 20th Century-Fox, studio of Hollywood's most famous blondes, she's gone from *The Girl Can't Help It* into three big movies. This year she'll be adorning John Steinbeck's *The Wayward Bus*, with Joan Collins, *Kiss Them for Me* opposite Cary Grant, and the movie version of *Will Success Spoil Rock Hunter?*.

LITTLE MISS INNOCENCE

MAY
JUNE

1957

JULY
AUGUST

"When Debbie Reynolds opens the refrigerator door and the light goes on," says Gene Kelly, "she does a 20-minute solo." Kelly should know: it was he who gave the sparkling young Texan her big break in *Singin' in the Rain* (1952).

Born in 1932, spunky Reynolds won a Miss Burbank contest, was signed up by Warners in 1948 and, after small parts in *June Bride* (1948) and *The Daughter of Rosie O'Grady* (1950), she fetched up at M-G-M. The studio was churning out just the product to which her talents were suited, although ironically she was dubbed (by Helen Kane, the original 1930s "Boop-boop-a-doop" girl) in her Metro debut, *Three Little Words* (1950), with Fred Astaire and Red Skelton. It was as Jane Powell's younger sister in the subsequent *Two Weeks – with Love* (1950) that she created her first real impact, as she and Carleton Carpenter took that "Abba-Dabba Honeymoon", resulting in screen stardom and a golden disc.

Reynolds seems to epitomize the perfect 1950s doll. But in *Susan Slept Here* (1954) and *The Tender Trap* (1955) she showed a maturing talent, and only last year she co-starred with her husband, singer Eddie Fisher, in *Bundle of Joy*, a remake of Ginger Rogers' comedy *Bachelor Mother* (1939).

Now with *Tammy and the Bachelor* she's found the ideal role, topping the hit parade with the title song and striking pay-dirt as the simple country girl in pigtails and gingham check. It'll be a tough image to shake off for the female half of America's Sweethearts.

FRANCIOSA GETS THE PLAUDITS

It's Don Murray who plays the morphine addict in *A Hatful of Rain*. But it's young New Yorker Anthony Franciosa, 28, who's stealing all the notices as his brother, the role he created in the play on Broadway two years ago.

Franciosa has so far appeared in three of this year's best movies, all with major directors – Robert Wise's *This Could Be the Night*, Elia Kazan's *A Face in the Crowd*, and now *A Hatful of Rain* for Fred Zinnemann. And coming later this year is George Cukor's *Wild Is the Wind*, in which he's a young Basque shepherd who has the hots for Anthony Quinn's bride, Italy's earthy Anna Magnani.

It took Franciosa five hard years of sweating in off-Broadway productions before he finally made his Great White Way debut in 1953. Then came *A Hatful of Rain*. This year he's also married screen sex tornado Shelley Winters. Now there's a volatile love-match if ever there was.

DORIS INTO PAJAMAS!

Labour relations in a pajamas factory sounds like an unusual subject for a musical. But Warners' *The Pajama Game* harnesses the theme to the naughtiest, most exuberant movie in ages. Based on the long-running 1954 Broadway show, it reprises most of the original cast, with John Raitt making his movie debut as the new boss who falls for the "chairman of the grievance committee" (Doris Day in Janis Paige's part). Also on hand from the original are Carol "Steam Heat" Haney, Eddie Foy, Jr and Reta Shaw.

Day proves she can be sexy as well as tender in numbers like "Hey, There", "Small Talk" and "I'm Not at All in Love". And the choreography that made young Bob Fosse a major name on Broadway is recreated for the movie, with the bonus of outdoor locations for the exciting "Once a Year Day" and a super-dark set for the flamboyant and funny "Hernando's Hideaway".

The Pajama Game is probably the best of the seemingly endless run of Broadway shows now being filmed. What's amazing is how co-director Stanley Donen managed to find the time to make it, *Funny Face* and the Cary Grant-Jayne Mansfield starrer, *Kiss Them for Me*, all within a space of 12 months.

Doris Day and John Raitt in The Pajama Game.

SAINT JEAN

Quite why Otto Preminger wanted to make a film version of Bernard Shaw's *Saint Joan* is a mystery. Even more amazing is his choice of lead actress. She's Jean Seberg, a 17-year-old shop-girl from Iowa.

She looks right, with her page-boy haircut, dressed in armour; but she never convinces that she's a creature of destiny, burning with a faith that can move mountains. Preminger has great faith in his new discovery, though, and has already cast her in his film of Francoise Sagan's scandalous French novel *Bonjour Tristesse*, due out early next year. Tinseltown's rumour-mill is already wondering whether she will follow in the paths of Dorothy Dandridge and Maggie McNamara, whose personal lives were reduced to shambles by the Austrian bully.

BIRTHS, DEATHS AND MARRIAGES

BIRTHS

Richard E. Grant
5 May, Mbabane, Swaziland

Melanie Griffith
9 Aug, New York

DEATHS

Erich von Stroheim
12 May, Paris
Cancer

James Whale
29 Jul, Hollywood
Drowned in swimming pool

Oliver Hardy
7 Aug, Sacramento, California
Stroke

MARRIAGES

Rex Harrison
23 Jun, *to* **Kay Kendall**

Merle Oberon
Jun, *to* Bruno Paglia

Laurence Olivier
26 Aug, *to* Joan Plowright

THE ACTOR AND THE SEX GODDESS

Sex goddess Marilyn Monroe and great actor Laurence Olivier co-star in *The Prince and the Showgirl*.

Laurence Olivier, Britain's greatest actor, and Marilyn Monroe, America's No. 1 sex goddess, in a movie together. Sounds like dynamite? Well, actually, no. It's not that the two of them don't work together on screen; it's that they sometimes seem to be in different movies. And the vehicle itself, adapted by Terence Rattigan himself from his Coronation play *The Sleeping Prince*, is not exactly a masterwork.

The Prince and the Showgirl is the first movie from Monroe's own production company, and she's cast and crewed it well. Sybil Thorndike, Richard Wattis and Jeremy Spenser (England's Sal Mineo) recreate their stage roles with wit and delicacy; and the technicians are among Britain's finest. The problem is with MM's choice of director.

Ever desperate for prestige, she hired Olivier for the job, and the Shakespearean was unnerved by his voluptuous co-star, especially as his wife, Vivien Leigh, created the role of the showgirl on stage. As the Balkan prince regent, Olivier offers an immaculate but one-note performance. Perhaps MM, clad throughout in a skintight, revealing dress, knew all along what was best, and made absolutely sure no one else got a look-in.

SHOOT-OUT IN TOMBSTONE

The most famous showdown in the history of the Old West is splendidly retold in Technicolor and VistaVision with *Gunfight at the O.K. Corral*. The gunfight itself takes up virtually the whole of the last reel, although the duel between Wyatt Earp and the Clantons actually lasted little over a minute. But western fans still have a real treat in store, as Burt Lancaster as Earp and Kirk Douglas as Doc Holliday face Lyle Bettger's Ike Clanton in the Tombstone, Arizona, shoot-out.

Kirk Douglas and Burt Lancaster in *Gunfight at the O.K. Corral*.

Leon Uris's screenplay fleshes out the strange friendship between Earp and Holliday, and involves famous westerners like Jimmy Ringo (John Ireland) and Big Nose Kate Fisher (Jo Van Fleet, from the 1955 *East of Eden*). Director John Sturges has already proved he's one of the finest outdoorsmen Hollywood has seen with *Escape from Fort Bravo* (1953) and *Bad Day at Black Rock* (1954). And with Frankie Laine singing the title song, what more could any western fan want?

BIOPIC BONANZA

Having successfully filmed biopics of Glenn Miller, Audie Murphy and Benny Goodman, Universal now takes a look at one of its former top names, Lon Chaney. He's best remembered for his extraordinary make-up in roles like *The Phantom of the Opera* (1925) and *The Hunchback of Notre Dame* (1923).

In *Man of a Thousand Faces* (1957) Chaney is played by James Cagney who, aided by make-up specialist Bud Westmore, recreates the silent star's triumphs. The movie traces the fascinating story of Chaney from his birth in Colorado to deaf-and-dumb parents to his tragic death in 1930 from throat cancer.

The Chaney story is one of a small spate of movie-star biopics this summer. Columbia has Kim Novak as *Jeanne Eagels*, the dope-addicted actress who was a sensation as Sadie Thompson in the stage and screen versions of Somerset Maugham's *Rain*, and Paramount let screenwriter Sidney Sheldon direct *The Buster Keaton Story*, with Donald O'Connor as The Great Stone Face.

But most interesting of all is Warners' *Too Much, Too Soon*, currently in production and due out next year. Dorothy Malone stars as alcoholic Diana Barrymore and Errol Flynn as her equally drunken father, John. Errol and John were old drinking buddies, so it'll be interesting to see whether fact or fiction reaches the screen.

GOSSIP COLUMN

- **The Oscar for the best original story this year went to Robert Rich for *The Brave One*. But no one came forward to pick up the award. Now it's been leaked that "Rich" was a pseudonym for blacklisted Dalton Trumbo.**
- **During the filming of *Raintree County* Montgomery Clift had a horrendous accident which permanently scarred both his face and his psyche. If you watch closely, you can see which sequences were shot before and after.**

SEPTEMBER OCTOBER 1957 NOVEMBER DECEMBER

James Donald and Alec Guinness in The Bridge on the River Kwai.

ZE BRIDGE ON ZE RIVAIR KWAI

British Second World War veterans will recognize the whistling theme in Sam Spiegel's gripping production *The Bridge on the River Kwai*. It had those unforgettable lyrics "Hitler, has only got one . . ."

The $3 million-plus movie tells the story of the prisoners of war who built the infamous Thai-Burmese "Death Railway" for the Japanese. The tough, all-male action adventure is a study of the futility of war. William Holden stars as an escapee from Sessue Hayakawa's prison camp, co-erced by British major Jack Hawkins into returning to the River Kwai camp, and blowing up the bridge built by Alec Guinness' Colonel Nicholson (a part originally intended for Charles Laughton). To re-create the infamous structure, the film-makers travelled to the steamy jungles of Ceylon.

Guinness, in his third picture with director David Lean, is magnificent as the colonel, obsessed with building the bridge to prove the mettle of British soldiers. The screenplay is also particularly fine and is credited to the author of the original novel, French writer Pierre Boulle. But he speaks no English at all. It all seems very strange, especially when there are so many unemployed American scriptwriters around since the HUAC witch-hunt a few years ago. . .

SAYONARA TO WAR MOVIES?

James Garner, Marlon Brando and Red Buttons in Sayonara.

"And then she said: 'I am not allowed to love, but I will love you, if that is your desire.'" Warners' ad slogan for *Sayonara* is torn straight from the pages of James A. Michener's best-seller about inter-racial romance, and director Joshua Logan spares audiences nothing in the bitter-sweet tale of a love that could never be.

Marlon Brando, replete with Southern drawl, is the race-conscious war ace who finally turns against the army he believes in. As the dedicated Japanese kabuki dancer, Miiko Taka is tender and touching as she begins by hating all things American and ends up in Brando's arms.

But the film is stolen by Red Buttons and Miyoshi Umeki, as an inter-racial couple who commit suicide rather than be split up. Former comedian Buttons shows unexpected warmth, and Umeki is a major discovery: watch out next year when the Best Supporting Oscar nominations are announced.

With Japanese locations sumptuously photographed in Technicolor and Technirama, and a haunting Irving Berlin theme song, *Sayonara* shapes up as one of the year's best. It's also the third major new movie this season with a military motif, and the second involving American/Japanese relationships. Time to give the war a rest?

FOLLIES OF WAR

Opening the same time as, and totally overshadowed by, *The Bridge on the River Kwai* is another remarkable war film. But where *Kwai* deals in heroics, *Paths of Glory* deals with cowardice; and where *Kwai* shows the follies of the Second World War, *Paths* exposes the follies of the First. Also, *Kwai* is in Technicolor and CinemaScope, whereas *Paths* is in austere black-and-white.

Made by the same team that produced last year's *The Killing*, *Paths of Glory* stars Kirk Douglas as former Paris lawyer Major Dax, now defending three men of his division charged with cowardice by arrogant General Mireau (George Macready) who ordered them "over the top" in a suicidal mission.

It's a grim tale, superbly told by young director Stanley Kubrick, aided by a fine screenplay by himself, Calder Willingham and Jim Thompson. Kubrick captures the hellish excitement of trench warfare with a realism unseen since *All Quiet on the Western Front* (1930). *Paths of Glory* is playing top half of a double bill with Don Siegel's *Baby Face Nelson*. Now there's a tough programme for those who can take it!

Kirk Douglas as Colonel Dax in Stanley Kubrick's Paths of Glory.

HOORAY FOR KAY

Graceful lady clowns don't grow on trees. So tall, beautiful, witty Kay Kendall is a cherishable talent. She's finally broken through to international stardom, plus an M-G-M contract and marriage to Rex Harrison earlier this year.

She's currently scintillating as one of *Les Girls*. But it's been a long trip to stardom, with several false starts. Born in 1926 near Hull, England, she is third-generation show business and, because of her height, managed to wangle her way into the London Palladium chorus line at the age of 13. After touring in a double act with her sister Kim, she landed some film parts in *Dreaming* (1944), *Waltz Time* (1945) and *London Town* (1946). But not much happened.

However, a nose-job resulted in a slew of parts, finally with Kenneth More in *Genevieve* (1953) in which, drunk, she memorably played the "plumpet" and won hearts everywhere. *Doctor in the House* (1954) followed, then *The Constant Husband* (1955) where she met Rex Harrison. And after playing the "perfect" TV couple with Peter Finch in the farce *Simon and Laura* (1955), Hollywood beckoned.

BOX OFFICE

UK

1 High Society
2 Doctor at Large
3 The Battle of the River Plate

OTHER TOP BOX OFFICE FILMS

Giant
Gunfight at the OK Corral
Ill Met by Moonlight
Island in the Sun
The Shiralee
The Story of Esther Costello
War and Peace

BOX OFFICE

US

1 The Ten Commandments
2 Around the World in 80 Days
3 Giant
4 Pal Joey
5 Seven Wonders of the World
6 The Teahouse of the August Moon
7 The Pride and the Passion
8 Anastasia
9 Island in the Sun
10 Love Me Tender

Gene Kelly and Kay Kendall in the comedy-musical Les Girls.

BIRTHS, DEATHS AND MARRIAGES

DEATHS

Jack Buchanan
20 Oct, London
Spinal arthritis

Louis B. Mayer
29 Oct, Los Angeles
Leukemia

Norma Talmadge
24 Dec, Las Vegas
Stroke

MARRIAGES

Marlon Brando
9 Oct, *to* Anna Kashfi

Bing Crosby
24 Oct, *to* Kathryn Grant

THE PELVIS ACTS, TOO

When veteran producer Hal B. Wallis signed rock 'n' roll phenomenon Elvis Presley to a seven-picture contract, he knew exactly what he was doing. Presley's ambition had always been to be a movie actor.

Presley swept across the country on the coat-tails of the rock 'n' roll craze. His records sold more than anyone else's, and his TV appearances last year kept America at home, glued to the small screen.

Wallis had him screen-test in a scene from *The Rainmaker* (the part Earl Holliman finally played in the 1956 movie) and Abe Lastfogel, head of the William Morris Agency, said "Elvis's screen test was one of the best I ever saw." But Wallis needed time to put together a film, so he loaned him out to 20th Century-Fox for *The Reno Brothers*, a western which was retitled *Love Me Tender* after one of Presley's four songs in the movie.

Wallis had writer-director Hal Kanter follow Elvis on tour, and the result was this summer's semi-biographical *Loving You*, about a young truck driver who becomes a singing sensation. Elvis proved he could act, even if he seemed a little influenced by the late James Dean.

Now, in the hit *Jailhouse Rock*, Elvis proves he's more than just a flash-in-the-pan. He gives a tough, relentless performance as young hoodlum Vince Everett.

KIM IS HOT!

Kim Novak, stunning blonde "discovered" by Columbia studio boss Harry Cohn.

When Rita Hayworth started doing things her own way at Columbia, studio boss Harry Cohn started looking around for a replacement, and found a stunning blonde who demonstrated refrigerators. She had no acting experience, nor any ambition in that direction, but she had already had bit parts in *The French Line* (1954) and *Son of Sinbad* (1955). Cohn liked what he saw and started to groom hazel-eyed Kim Novak for stardom.

Born in 1933, she's the daughter of Czech immigrants who settled in Chicago. Her father was a former history teacher who ended up working for the Chicago-Milwaukee railroad. She became a model at the age of 11, and the already voluptuous teenager with the 37-23-37½ figure met talent scout Maxwell Arnow who took her to Columbia.

In 1954 she was cast in the crime drama *Pushover*, with Fred MacMurray. Director Richard Quine defined her quality as that of the "proverbial lady in the parlour and the whore in the bedroom." She couldn't act, and seemed uneasy in front of the camera, but after *The Man with the Golden Arm*, *Picnic* (both 1955) and *The Eddy Duchin Story* (1956), she became America's No. 1 box-office attraction. This year, with *Jeanne Eagels* and *Pal Joey* already behind her, she's even more popular. Next up, between dating such notable Romeos as Prince Aly Khan, Frank Sinatra and General Rafael Trujillo, is an Alfred Hitchcock thriller, *Vertigo*, with James Stewart.

MITZI'S IN LOVE WITH A WONDERFUL GUY!

Francesca Mitzi Marlene de Charney von Gerber, descended from Balkan aristocracy, was born in Chicago. Her mother was a ballerina, and she started dancing at four. At 12 she joined the Los Angeles Civic Light Opera corps-de-ballet, and in 1950 made her screen debut in 20th Century-Fox's *My Blue Heaven*, with Betty Grable and Dan Dailey.

She is, of course, Mitzi Gaynor, and she's a bright, pert, singing-and-dancing gift to movie screens. Fox swiftly cast her in the title roles of *Golden Girl* (1951) and *The I Don't Care Girl* (1952), and in musicals like *Bloodhounds of Broadway* (1952) and Irving Berlin's all-star *There's No Business Like Show Business* (1954). She sparkled and revealed an exquisitely sexy figure; but her films didn't do well and Fox dropped her option in 1954.

But that year she married Jack Bean, who rejuvenated her career. First at Paramount, with Bing Crosby and Donald O'Connor in *Anything Goes* (1956), and then last year opposite Frank Sinatra in *The Joker Is Wild* and as one of M-G-M's *Les Girls*, with Kay Kendall, Taina Elg and Gene Kelly.

When Rodgers & Hammerstein set up the company Magna to bring their 1949 Broadway smash *South Pacific* to the screen, almost every star in Hollywood wanted to play Ensign Nellie Forbush who, "Some Enchanted Evening", fell for handsome plantation owner Emile de Becque. Gaynor auditioned with "I'm in Love with a Wonderful Guy" and "I'm Gonna Wash That Man Right Out-a My Hair", and *South Pacific* got its screen Nellie.

STAR QUOTES

Joanne Woodward
Best Actress for The Three Faces of Eve (1957)

"If I had an infinite amount of respect for the people who think I gave the greatest performance, then it would matter."

PELVIS MARK II

20th Century-Fox, which has already pioneered the way in rock 'n' roll movies with Elvis Presley in *Love Me Tender* (1956) and The Pelvis's biggest rival, Pat Boone, in *Bernardine* (1957), has now filmed the Kraft Sunday Night Theatre play *The Singin' Idol* as a movie, retitled *Sing, Boy, Sing*.

Star is Chicago-born rocker Tommy Sands, who was the ersatz Elvis in the TV original. The Capitol recording artiste has been performing since he was 11, and proves he can belt out numbers like "Soda Pop Pop" and the title tune nearly as well as Presley. Fox is next co-starring him with Boone and Gary Crosby in *Mardi Gras*, which sounds like a light, romantic trifle. Sands, 20, is worthy of better than that. But he's currently seeing a lot of Nancy Sinatra, whose dad is not without influence.

Marlon Brando as Christian, a young Nazi officer, in Edward Dmytryk's The Young Lions.

ANOTHER WAR CLASSIC

The Young Lions comes hot on the heels of last year's *Bridge on the River Kwai* and the stark *Paths of Glory*. But 20th Century-Fox's adaptation of Irwin Shaw's novel leaves both standing as a study of men in wartime.

Shaw's three interweaved stories have been softened for the screen, notably that of top Nazi Christian Diestl who in the book is unrepentant. In the movie, blond German-accented Marlon Brando has a change of heart before his inevitable death. But the story is merely made more interesting in contrast.

Montgomery Clift is young Jew Noah Ackerman, and the scene where he meets the father (Vaughn Taylor) of his girl friend (Hope Lange) is deeply touching. And as Broadway entertainer Michael Whiteacre, Dean Martin proves there is life without Jerry Lewis in a carefully casual performance. Under Edward Dmytryk's direction, in stark black-and-white CinemaScope, *The Young Lions* already looks like a classic of its kind.

ACADEMY AWARDS

PRESENTED ON 26 MARCH 1958

Best Picture
The Bridge on the River Kwai

Best Director
David Lean
The Bridge on the River Kwai

Best Actor
Alec Guinness
The Bridge on the River Kwai

Best Actress
Joanne Woodward
The Three Faces of Eve

Best Sup Actor
Red Buttons
Sayonara

Best Sup Actress
Miyoshi Umeki
Sayonara

Orson Welles as the local law enforcer with Joseph Calleia and Janet Leigh in Touch of Evil.

A TOUCH OF ORSON

Roped into a Universal double bill with the Patty McCormack frolic *Kathy O'* is a remarkable thriller. Shot as *Badge of Evil*, it's reached screens as *Touch of Evil* and is the latest quirky work from the unpredictable Orson Welles.

Welles himself plays a portly, mentally disturbed cop in a small Mexican border town. Government bigwig Charlton Heston (in moustache and swarthy make-up) is honeymooning down south with sexy Janet Leigh and gets involved in a narcotics racket that Welles is "investigating". His idea of that is to plant evidence all over town.

The movie has lots of odd touches to be expected from the director who stormed Tinseltown with *Citizen Kane* (1941) and *The Magnificent Ambersons* (1942). Standouts are the opening sequence, nearly 10 minutes without a cut, and some bizarre playing by veteran Marlene Dietrich. Spot unbilled cameos, too, by Joseph Cotten, Mercedes McCambridge and Ray Collins.

It's bizarre, arty stuff and, as usual with a Welles movie, the production had off-screen problems. The 93-minute version on release is apparently Universal's cut. Welles delivered a 108-minute film, and didn't expect to be double-billed with juve star Patty McCormack.

SEX & SALVATION, RUSSIAN STYLE

Dostoevsky's mighty Russian novel *The Brothers Karamazov* has finally arrived on screens in a sumptuous M-G-M production. But where's Marilyn?

Monroe made it clear at every one of her press calls last year that she wanted the female lead of Grushenka very badly. Her acting coach Paula Strasberg even recommended that she be given the part, despite one cynical pressman calling out to Monroe, "Can you spell it?" The movie has certainly benefited from all this free publicity: who in Middle America would have heard of *Karamazov* if MM hadn't kept mentioning it?

In the event the part is played by German import Maria Schell in her first American movie; she manages to suggest both innocence and depravity, something Monroe might have found difficult. Lusting after her are Yul Brynner, as the cruel elder Karamazov son, and Lee J. Cobb as his father. Richard Basehart and newcomer William Shatner are the other sons, and Claire Bloom the beauty who saves Brynner from debtors' prison. Richard Brooks directs.

Lana Turner (left) in Peyton Place, about the underlying emotions of a small New England town.

SMALL-TOWN LUSTS

Not so long ago scriptwriters would have had to take a chainsaw to Grace Metalious's sexy novel of small-town lust. But with changes in the Production Code, *Peyton Place* emerges as permissible entertainment for adults.

You still need a compass to follow the plot. But roughly it goes like this. New teacher in town Mike Rossi (newcomer Lee Philips) falls for widow Constance MacKenzie (top-billed Lana Turner), whose daughter Allison (terrific Diane Varsi) turns her birthday party – shock! – into a petting party. Allison's classmate Rodney Harrington (Barry Coe) marries Betty (Terry Moore), against the wishes of his father (Leon Ames), and Allison swims nude with Norman (Russ Tamblyn). Selena (striking newcomer Hope Lange) is raped by her father-in-law Lucas Cross (Arthur Kennedy), and stands trial when she accidentally kills him later on.

BIRTHS, DEATHS AND MARRIAGES

BIRTHS

Lorenzo Lamas
20 Jan, Los Angeles

James Wilby
20 Feb, Rangoon, Burma

Holly Hunter
20 Mar, Atlanta

DEATHS

Edna Purviance
13 Jan, Woodland Hills, California

MARRIAGES

Paul Newman
29 Jan, *to* **Joanne Woodward**

Paulette Goddard
25 Feb, *to* Erich Maria Remarque

CINEMIRACLE

The latest wide-screen wonder is Cinemiracle. The three-cameras-in-one process may not be the best, but it's certainly the biggest. At New York's Roxy theatre, the screen measures 100ft × 40ft, making *Windjammer* look enormous. The film is a semi-documentary, following the 18,000-mile journey of the square-rigger *Christian Radich* on a training cruise.

GOSSIP COLUMN

■ On Good Friday, 4 April, lawyer Jerry Giesler's phone rang. "This is Lana Turner. Something terrible has happened." What seems to have transpired is that Lana's 14-year-old daughter Cheryl had stabbed Lana's gangster lover, Johnny Stompanato, alias Johnny Valentine, with a nine-inch butcher's knife, and Stompanato's bloody corpse lay across the bed.

BB GOES MAINSTREAM

Stephen Boyd and French sex-kitten Brigitte Bardot in The Night Heaven Fell.

First there was America's MM, then England's DD. Now it's the turn of French sex-kitten BB! Ash-blonde stunner Brigitte Bardot was born in 1934 in Paris. She's 5ft 3in tall and 101 pounds with brown eyes. Those vital statistics are 36-20-36, and last December she finally divorced her mentor, French director Roger Vadim, after five years of marriage.

Bardot became an international sensation with Vadim's *And God Created Woman* (1957), which ran into censorship problems even in France. She was a revelation as she romped unclad across the CinemaScope screen, making mincemeat of Curd Jurgens and Jean-Louis Trintignant in a Riviera town.

She had posed for the cover of the magazine *Elle* at the age of 15 and married Vadim in 1952, making her movie debut the following year. Her nubile body appeared in several movies in quick succession, including the British comedy *Doctor at Sea* (1955), in which she took a sexy VistaVision shower, and halfway down the cast-list in Warners' *Helen of Troy* (also 1955), in which she was dubbed by an English actress. After gravitating to leading roles in French movies, there came the sensational *And Woman . . . Was Created*, the film that yanked French movies out of the art-houses and into mainstream cinemas.

This year BB and Vadim have followed it up with the Spanish adventure *The Night Heaven Fell* in which Stephen Boyd falls for her pert pout. Not bad for an industrialist's daughter who might have ended up as a prima ballerina had it not been for that *Elle* cover back in May 1949.

James Stewart in Hitchcock's Vertigo.

HIGH ON FEAR

Alfred Hitchcock's latest movie, *Vertigo*, is likely to divide audiences and critics. It's a slow-paced, haunting mystery, but its plot is genuinely original.

James Stewart is Scottie, a man obsessed with recreating the memory of a dead woman as he makes over Kim Novak in her likeness. If that isn't morbid enough, Stewart also suffers from vertigo, a neurotic fear of heights. The story is from a novel by two Gallic ghouls who also wrote the cult French spine-chiller, *The Fiends* (1955).

In the hands of master-craftsman Hitch, Stewart's vertigo is excitingly exploited with some special camera effects (tracking backwards and zooming in at the same time). And Novak displays plenty of animal-like carnality – even if few signs of acting ability – especially as Hitch keeps her bra-less throughout.

The other star of the movie is San Francisco. Scene after scene takes place at Nob Hill, Ernie's restaurant, Land's End, Muir Woods, the Mission Dolores and, most breathtakingly, the old mission of San Juan Bautista, where the dual climax is set.

NORSEMEN ON THE LOOSE

Kirk Douglas loses an eye, Tony Curtis loses an arm, and Ernest Borgnine ends up thrown to the wolves. Even bosomy Janet Leigh has her bodice ripped. It's all in *The Vikings*, a rousing 8th-century swashbuckler that's not short on comic-strip violence.

After a stirring introduction by Orson Welles, the film begins with a Viking invasion of Northumbrian England. Later, Leigh is kidnapped, setting up a romantic triangle with Douglas and Curtis. Director Richard Fleischer makes the most of some superb European locations, including the fjords of Norway; interiors were shot at West Germany's Bavaria Studios. Helping the proceedings along are a sterling supporting cast which includes James Donald, Alexander Knox and Australian actor Frank Thring, as "heavy" a heavy as ever was. Produced by Douglas himself, *The Vikings* is perfect bloodthirsty fare for schoolboys of all ages. It's certainly no history lesson.

Tony Curtis and Kirk Douglas as Viking half-brothers in The Vikings.

UNLIKELIEST STAR

The Matchmaker with (left to right) Wally Ford, Paul Ford, Shirley Booth, Perry Wilson, Shirley MacLaine, Robert Morse and Anthony Perkins (seated).

The most unlikely Hollywood star in ages is a dumpy lady who's been on amateur stages since the age of 12. New York-born Shirley Booth, 50, made her first professional appearance in a Hartford, Connecticut, production of *The Cat and the Canary* in 1923, and her Broadway debut in 1925 in *Hell's Bells*, in a supporting part with another stage newcomer, Humphrey Bogart.

This summer she's top-billed in two very different Paramount movies. In *Hot Spell* she's the dreamy mother of three grown-up children in the Deep South, a woman who has lost touch with reality. "Once we were all part of each other," she says, "but now we're all pulling in different directions." And in the screen version of Thornton Wilder's *The Matchmaker* she's the infamous Dolly Levi, out to entrap Horace Vandergelder (Paul Ford), the corn merchant of Yonkers.

Booth finally got to play important roles on Broadway in *Three Men on a Horse* (1935) and *My Sister Eileen* (1940). A successful career in radio followed, then came her biggest triumph, William Inge's play *Come Back, Little Sheba*. She repeated her role in the 1952 movie, opposite a miscast Burt Lancaster as "Doc", and she won a Best Actress Oscar.

Booth has a Hal Wallis contract in her pocket, but she's hard to cast and is also said to be a truculent talent. That could be Hollywood's loss.

MY FAIR COURTESAN

Just when every new musical seems to be a blockbusting recreation of a Broadway hit, along comes Arthur Freed's production of *Gigi*, an original musical by *My Fair Lady* authors Alan Jay Lerner and Frederick Loewe.

It's not quite original. *Gigi* started as a novel by French writer Colette and was a hit as a straight play on Broadway with Audrey Hepburn. Leslie Caron played the part in London and she makes a welcome return to M-G-M, for the first time since *Lili* (1953), as the young trainee courtesan who finally realizes a wedding ring is more important than being the perfect mistress.

The subject couldn't have been filmed without the recent changes in the Production Code. And there are some fine risque moments, like Gigi being taught how to prepare a symbolic cigar.

The elegant package was actually shot on Paris locations, and the Lerner-Loewe score bristles with memorable numbers like the nostalgic "I Remember It Well" and the up-beat "The Night They Invented Champagne" and "Thank Heaven for Little Girls". The last is performed by veteran Gallic charmer Maurice Chevalier, who also gets a personal anthem, "I'm Glad I'm Not Young Anymore".

Louis Jourdan is Gigi's lover Gaston (in the role Britain's Dirk Bogarde turned down) and other European performers like Hermione Gingold, Eve Gabor and Jacques Bergerac add to *Gigi*'s authentic "feel". But it's the costumes and sets of the great Cecil Beaton, making his first movie, that give *Gigi* its *fin-de-siècle* atmosphere.

Director Vincente Minnelli shows taste in handling the sensual tale. But apparently most of the best sequences, including Gaston's final soliloquy, were shot by Charles Walters, Caron's old director on *Lili*.

Louis Jourdan and Leslie Caron dine at Maxim's in Gigi.

GOODBYE, MR. CHIPS!

Robert Donat, best known for his Oscar-winning English schoolteacher in *Goodbye, Mr. Chips* (1939), died on 9 June in a London hospital. He was 53, and recently completed his role as a Chinese Mandarin opposite Ingrid Bergman in *The Inn of the Sixth Happiness*, due to be released later this year.

The son of Polish immigrants, Mancunian Donat started taking elocution lessons at the age of 11 to overcome a stutter. He grew to be a tall and handsome actor, but was plagued by self-doubt. He also suffered from asthma, which became the emphysema that finally killed him.

Donat turned down more roles than he accepted. Offered an M-G-M contract by Irving Thalberg, he rejected it for an Alexander Korda deal, appearing in British films like *The Private Life of Henry VIII* (1933) and *The Ghost Goes West* (1935). He turned down *Captain Blood* (1935), which made a star of Errol Flynn, and was *The Count of Monte Cristo* (1934), but he didn't care for Hollywood and went home to star in Hitchcock's *The 39 Steps* (1935) and King Vidor's *The Citadel* (1938).

A series of distinguished British films followed, including *Perfect Strangers* (1945) and *The Winslow Boy* (1948), and he directed and produced, as well as starring in, *The Cure for Love* (1949). He was a memorable William Friese-Greene in the Festival of Britain film *The Magic Box* (1951); but his asthma made the shoot a difficult one, and began to affect his choice of roles on both stage and screen.

BIRTHS, DEATHS AND MARRIAGES

BIRTHS

Frances Barber
13 May, Wolverhampton

Kelly McGillis
30 May, Newport Beach, California

Kevin Bacon
8 Jul, Philadelphia

Steve Guttenberg
24 Aug, Brooklyn, New York

DEATHS

Ronald Colman
19 May, Santa Barbara, California
Lung infection

Robert Donat
9 Jun, London
Emphysema

Bonar Colleano
17 Aug, Birkenhead, Merseyside
Car accident

STAR QUOTES

Oscar Hammerstein II

"If there were more movies like Witness for the Prosecution *(1957), I'd see more movies."*

SEPTEMBER OCTOBER

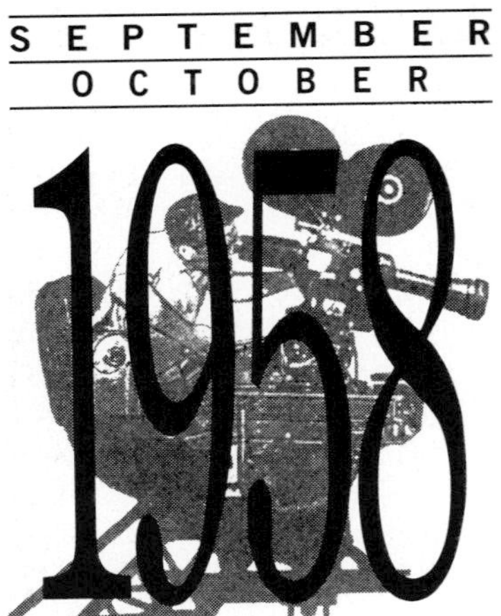

NOVEMBER DECEMBER

BIG CROWDS, BIG COUNTRY

The Big Country is as big as its title. Despite the popularity of westerns on TV at the moment, no amount of 21-inch black-and-white episodes of *Wagon Train, Cheyenne* or *Maverick* can compete with the size and grandeur of this William Wyler-Gregory Peck production, shot in Technicolor and Technirama.

The story is simple enough. Jean Simmons owns the only watering hole between two feuding ranchers, Charles Bickford and Burl Ives. Into this valley rides peaceful eastern dude Gregory Peck to marry Carroll Baker, Bickford's beautiful daughter, who's lusted after by chief ranch hand (Charlton Heston). Things get really complicated when Ives' son (Chuck Connors) tries to rape Simmons. . . .

The Big Country, *with Jean Simmons, Charlton Heston, Carroll Baker, Gregory Peck, Burl Ives and Chuck Connors.*

It's a starry cast, and director Wyler gives them all fine moments: a fist-fight between Peck and Heston amid the wide open spaces is especially watchable. The movie's sweeping orchestral theme by Jerome Moross is already among the most-requested radio music of the moment. The crowds lining up for the United Artists release seem to prove that the western is still one of the most popular forms of entertainment.

BIRTHS, DEATHS AND MARRIAGES

BIRTHS

Phil Daniels
25 Oct, London

Mary Elizabeth Mastrantonio
17 Nov, Oak Park, Illinois

Jamie Lee Curtis
22 Nov, Los Angeles

DEATHS

Carl Brisson
26 Sep, Copenhagen
Cancer

Marshall Neilan
27 Oct, Hollywood
Cancer

Tyrone Power
15 Nov, Madrid
Heart attack

H. B. Warner
21 Dec, Woodland Hills, California

MARRIAGES

Robert Redford
Sep, *to* Lola Von Wagenen

BOX OFFICE

UK

1 The Bridge on the River Kwai
2 Dunkirk
3 The Vikings

OTHER TOP BOX OFFICE FILMS

Carry on Sergeant
Carve Her Name with Pride
Ice Cold in Alex
Indiscreet
A Night to Remember
South Pacific
The Ten Commandments

BOX OFFICE

US

1 The Bridge on the River Kwai
2 Peyton Place
3 Sayonara
4 No Time for Sergeants
5 The Vikings
6 Search for Paradise
7 South Pacific
8 Cat on a Hot Tin Roof
9 Raintree County
10 Old Yeller

TYRONE POWER DEAD

Two months into shooting United Artists' *Solomon and Sheba*, with Gina Lollobrigida, Tyrone Power has died in Madrid following a heart attack on 15 November. The 44-year-old film star was stricken just after a strenuous duelling scene opposite George Sanders. Yul Brynner is to replace him in the $4 million epic.

Power was the last of the matinee idols. He had been very busy recently, on Broadway with Katherine Cornell in *The Dark Is Light Enough*, and touring in *Back to Methuselah* and *Mister Roberts*. He had also shown last year a new maturity on screen with *The Sun Also Rises*, as Hemingway's Jake Barnes, and in Billy Wilder's Agatha Christie adaptation *Witness for the Prosecution*.

Cincinnati-born Power followed his dad on stage, which led to a Fox contract and his movie debut in *Tom Brown of Culver* (1932). He swiftly became a popular romantic lead, and also showed his swashbuckling talents in *The Mark of Zorro* (1940), *Blood and Sand* (1941) and *The Black Swan* (1942). Despite revealing a deeper side in *Nightmare Alley* (1947), he found critical respect elusive and resorted to the stage as well.

Power's private life was stormy and, as well as affaires with Judy Garland and Lana Turner, he married three times, including Annabella (1939-48) and Linda Christian (1949-55).

UA LINES THEM UP

Decades in film history sometimes seem to belong to certain studios. The 1920s was the era of Paramount, the 1930s belonged to Warners, the 1940s was epitomised by 20th Century-Fox, while the current decade has seemed in the thrall of M-G-M.

But TV has made severe inroads into the studio system, and companies like Fox and M-G-M are letting their contract players leave when their usual seven-year options come up for renewal. The studios can't afford the overheads any more, and this year has seen the new emergence of United Artists, the "studio without a studio" set up in 1919 by Charlie Chaplin, D.W. Griffith, Mary Pickford and Douglas Fairbanks.

A syndicate headed by Arthur Krim and Robert Benjamin recently took over ailing UA and has encouraged independent producer-directors to seek work.

UA's deal with Stanley Kramer includes his current *The Defiant Ones* as well as his future film of Nevil Shute's novel *On The Beach* and his proposed movie about the Monkey Trial, *Inherit the Wind*. Billy Wilder and the Mirisch brothers plan a film based on the original premise of what happened to the apartment that Trevor Howard and Celia Johnson left in such a hurry in *Brief Encounter* (1945). And Mirisch also has the rights to the current Broadway musical *West Side Story*. Agreements with Gregory Peck, Lewis Milestone, Kirk Douglas, Robert Wise and William Wyler are also in hand.

NOT JUST A PRETTY FACE

Of Universal's three Beefcake Boys, Jeff Chandler and Rock Hudson have scored prestige and box-office success. But Tony Curtis, with his triple triumph in *The Vikings, Kings Go Forth* and now *The Defiant Ones*, looks like outstripping them both in the long-term talent stakes.

It was last year's *Sweet Smell of Success*, in which he played slimy small-time agent Sidney Falco, that really woke critics up to the fact that Curtis was more than just a pretty face. This was after years as a Universal contract player in movies like *The Black Shield of Falworth* (1954) and *The Purple Mask* (1955). It was British director Carol Reed who spotted his potential, casting him alongside Burt Lancaster and curvaceous Gina Lollobrigida in the circus drama *Trapeze* (1956).

Born in New York's Bronx in 1925, Curtis grew up in poverty, and at 11 was a member of a notorious street gang. It was in a neighbourhood settlement house that he got his first taste for acting and, after Second World War navy service, he began studying at New York's Dramatic Workshop. Disregarding "advice" from fellow-student Walter Matthau that his Bronx accent would handicap his chances, Curtis worked hard in the Catskill Mountains' "borscht circuit", and was eventually signed by Universal.

He first appeared dancing with Yvonne De Carlo in the Burt Lancaster thriller *Criss Cross* (1949), and the fan mail started flooding in. Since *The Prince Who Was a Thief* (1951), he's been in three movies a year, including *Houdini* (1953) and the Boston heist drama *Six Bridges to Cross* (1955).

THE BIGOT & THE NEGRO

Producer-director Stanley Kramer's *The Defiant Ones* (1958) is a chase movie that's also a study of racism. It shows the problems of two escaped convicts shackled together, one white, one black. Tony Curtis is a dyed-in-the-wool bigot from the Deep South, and Sidney Poitier is an intelligent but sullen jailbird who suddenly gets a chance to escape to the racially "safe" North. It's basically a two-hander. But Cara Williams, as a lonely woman who takes pity on the pair, is also very fine.

Cynic Billy Wilder has a story about the casting. "First, they offered the Tony Curtis part to Marlon Brando, but he turned it down because he wanted to play the Negro. Then it was offered to Kirk Douglas, who wanted to play both parts. Next, Robert Mitchum, who wouldn't act tied to a Negro. So they ended up with the Jew. . . ." Apocryphal? Certainly, but good Hollywood tittle-tattle to boost one of the year's most hard-hitting movies.

Sidney Poitier and Tony Curtis as escaped convicts in The Defiant Ones.

THE MAGNIFICENT AUNTIE ROZ

"Life is a banquet – and most poor suckers are starving to death!" That's the philosophy of Mame Dennis, immortalized on stage by Beatrice Lillie and now on screen by the magnificent Rosalind Russell. She played *Auntie Mame* on Broadway under the direction of Morton DaCosta, who here makes his directorial bow in film.

The Betty Comden-Adolph Green screenplay tries to compress the play's rambling structure, which deals with the impact of the Bohemian life-style of Mame on her nephew (Roger Smith). In fact, the screen version has been tamed, but Mame still emerges as all heart. And it's a handsome movie to look at.

Russell gets good support from Coral Browne as her dipso friend, Peggy Cass (reprising her helpless Agnes Gooch from the original), Fred Clark as a banker, and Forrest Tucker as Beauregard, Mame's beau. The movie's long (143 minutes) and episodic, but it's already shaping up to be one of the biggest money-makers of the year.

Rosalind Russell (centre) with Betty Comden and Adolph Green in Auntie Mame.

HANDSOME TAB

When "Young Love" topped this year's hit parade, it wasn't by Sonny James, who had the record out first on Capitol. It was movie star Tab Hunter on the Dot label who got the gold disc, and then followed it with "99 Ways". So it's no real surprise to find the blond good-looker playing baseball hero Joe Hardy in the film version of the 1955 smash musical *Damn Yankees*.

Hunter is just right as the confused young man who resists sexy witch Gwen Verdon, and Bob Fosse's choreography carefully disguises his lack of dance training. The 27-year-old New Yorker has already been seen this year as the young William Wellman in Warners' *Lafayette Escadrille* and with James Darren and Van Heflin in the western *Gunman's Walk*. Quite a year for someone with no acting training at all.

Hunter lied about his age when he was 15 to join the U.S. Coast Guard, and at 18 made his film debut in the Southern Californian fruit-picking drama *The Lawless* (1950). He was taken under the wing of Hollywood agent Henry Willson, who had also nurtured the young Rock Hudson, and went on to register strongly in the British-made *Saturday Island* (1952) with Linda Darnell. He won a Warners contract, appearing in *Track of the Cat* (1954), *Battle Cry* (1955), and two successful teamings with Natalie Wood in 1956, *The Burning Hills* and *The Girl He Left Behind*. Since then his recording debut has helped to turn him into a teenage idol, and his three 1958 movies look like making him as big a star as that other Willson discovery, Rock Hudson.

RIDIN' THE RANGE

"Sure-shot" Annie Oakley had actually appeared on film in 1894, but westerns really started with *The Great Train Robbery* (1903), which was also the first motion picture to tell a story. One of the actors was G. M. (Broncho Billy) Anderson who went on to appear in over 375 western shorts, his popularity equalled only by the laconic William S. Hart and the glamorous Tom Mix. These westerns were simplistic tales of goodies vs. baddies. Eventually bigger budgets were expended on more adult themes: *The Covered Wagon* (1923) and *The Iron Horse* (1924) were typical.

Sound brought an Oscar for Warner Baxter as The Cisco Kid in *In Old Arizona* (1929) and revealed the drawl of Gary Cooper in *The Virginian* (also 1929). *The Big Trail* (1931) marked the starring debut of John Wayne. *Cimarron* (1931) was the only western ever to win the Best Picture Oscar. Depression audiences seemed to prefer gangsters and chorines to cowboys.

Although Cooper played Wild Bill Hickok in *The Plainsman* (1936), it wasn't until John Ford directed John Wayne in *Stagecoach* (1939) that the western returned as mainstream adult entertainment. Ford and Wayne went on to make a remarkable series, including *She Wore a Yellow Ribbon* (1949) and *The Searchers* (1956). Ford also directed Henry Fonda as Wyatt Earp in *My Darling Clementine* (1946), and among the finest westerns of the 1940s was Howard Hawks' sprawling epic *Red River* (1949), starring John Wayne and introducing Montgomery Clift.

High Noon (1952) was intended as an anti-communist witchhunt allegory, and Gary Cooper won a popular Oscar as Marshal Will Kane, standing alone against a killer arriving on the midday train. The image of the loner was a constant theme of 1950s westerns, and featured in some of Hollywood's best work. Stars like James Stewart, Glenn Ford, and Randolph Scott appeared in several films for specific directors. Burt Lancaster and Kirk Douglas were Wyatt Earp and Doc Holliday in *Gunfight at the O.K. Corral* (1957), while Alan Ladd made his most popular film *Shane* (1963). Indians were at last treated sympathetically in films like *Broken Arrow* (1950) and Mexico was the setting for *Vera Cruz* (1954).

In the finely-wrought *Rio Bravo* (1959), Howard Hawks and John Wayne offered a riposte to *High Noon*, inverting both plot and characterizations, and followed up with the masterly *El Dorado* (1967) and *Rio Lobo* (1970).

The Magnificent Seven (1960), the westernized version of the Japanese film, *Seven Samurai* (1954), signalled the end of the classic western: killing became ritualized, and the already laconic dialogue became less necessary. Women, already marginalized, became redundant. *The Wild Bunch* (1969) was a raw, brilliant lament for the Old West, epitomized by John Wayne's Rooster Cogburn in *True Grit* (also 1969), for which Wayne finally won an Oscar.

The genre was moribund when the Italians guyed the conventions mercilessly in films like *Fistful of Dollars* (1964), which made an international star of Clint Eastwood.

Despite the occasional appearance of films like *The Outlaw Josey Wales* (1976), *Heaven's Gate* (1980) or *Silverado* (1985), there was no audience for a lone stranger on a horse operating by law of the gun. In Sam Peckinpah's epitaph for the western *Pat Garrett & Billy the Kid* (1973; re-issued full-length in 1989) Garrett tells the Kid that: "Times are changing, Bill". Despite the brat-packin' pair of *Young Guns* (1988, 1990) and rarities like Tom Selleck in *Quigley Down Under* (1990) and Kevin Costner's *Dances with Wolves* (1990), it's a mighty brave filmmaker who'll attempt a western nowadays.

Main picture: Burt Lancaster as Wyatt Earp in Gunfight at the OK Corral.

The seven stars of The Magnificent Seven *(1960).*

John Wayne (with Natalie Wood) in John Ford's The Searchers *(1956).*

The race for land by the homesteaders as depicted in Cimarron *(1931).*

Tom Selleck as a cowboy in Australia in Quigley Down Under *(1990).*

Clint Eastwood in the spagetti western A Fistful of Dollars *(1964).*

Gary Cooper won his second best actor Academy Award in High Noon *(1952).*

Alan Ladd in his best and most popular role as Shane *(1963).*

Ricky Nelson, John Wayne and Dean Martin in Rio Bravo *(1959).*

JANUARY
FEBRUARY
1959
MARCH
APRIL

ACADEMY AWARDS

PRESENTED ON 6 APRIL 1959

Best Picture
Gigi

Best Director
Vincente Minnelli
Gigi

Best Actor
David Niven
Separate Tables

Best Actress
Susan Hayward
I Want to Live!

Best Sup Actor
Burl Ives
The Big Country

Best Sup Actress
Wendy Hiller
Separate Tables

LIFE'S A DRAG!

Joe (Tony Curtis) and Jerry (Jack Lemmon) are jazz musicians. How they become Josephine and Daphne (yes, Daphne, not Geraldine) is the subject of Billy Wilder's sizzling new comedy *Some Like It Hot*.

The problem is that they witness the St. Valentine's Day Massacre and are seen by mobster Spats Colombo (George Raft). Desperate measures are needed. So they sign up with an all-girl band, Sweet Sue and Her Society Syncopaters, and head down towards the sheltering palms of Florida for the winter season, well out of the clutches of Chicago's gangsters.

Their female disguises work, but not without some problems. Joe is smitten by sexy Sugar Cane (Marilyn Monroe), the band's vocalist. She's got a drink problem and a millionaire complex. And how can Joe/Josephine make romantic overtures to another girl? By disguising himself/herself as Cary Grant and inviting her aboard his yacht, that's how.

Filmed in black and white ("Colour would have made it look phony," says Wilder), the sparkling comedy bristles with great dialogue and meaty playing. And the latter doesn't come any meatier than when MM croons "My Heart Belongs to Daddy". It's enough to make a guy bust a suspender!

Tony Curtis, Jack Lemmon and Marilyn Monroe in Some Like It Hot.

IF YOU KNEW SUSIE . . .

When Susan Hayward won this year's Best Actress Oscar, producer Walter Wanger said: "Thank heavens, now we can all relax. Susie got what she's been chasing for 20 years." Hayward won for her powerful performance in *I Want To Live*, the true story of Barbara Graham, the woman indicted for murder who went to the gas chamber.

Hayward was born in 1918 in Brooklyn, and after modelling made her screen debut in 1938. Sheer determination, akin to Joan Crawford's starrier version, got her through the 1940s – she'd arrived but still seemed to be getting nowhere in movies like *Reap the Wild Wind*, *I Married a Witch* (both 1942) and *The Hairy Ape* (1944). Then she married, had twins, was divorced and signed a contract with Walter Wanger, playing a lush in *Smash Up* (1947).

But real stardom still eluded her and she soldiered on opposite the likes of Tyrone Power, Robert Mitchum, Gregory Peck, Charlton Heston and Gary Cooper in *Rawhide* (1951), *The Lusty Men*, *The Snows of Kilamanjaro* (both 1952), *The President's Lady* (1953) and *Garden of Evil* (1954).

An overdose of sleeping pills put paid to her contract with 20th Century-Fox, and then she made something of a comeback as a singer and alcoholic in *I'll Cry Tomorrow* (1955). Now she's hot again, Wanger wants to cast her in his new production, *Cleopatra*.

ROMAN SCANDAL

Universal has announced that director Anthony Mann has been relieved of his duties on the studio's $12 million production of *Spartacus*. Less than two weeks after shooting began in Death Valley, California, the director of several classic westerns has been dismissed by Kirk Douglas, star and executive producer of *Spartacus*. His replacement will be 31-year-old Stanley Kubrick, who directed Douglas in *Paths of Glory* (1957) and recently quit as director on the Marlon Brando western *The Authentic Death of Hendry Jones*, which has yet to start shooting.

BIRTHS, DEATHS AND MARRIAGES

BIRTHS

Linda Blair
22 Jan, St. Louis

Aidan Quinn
8 Mar, Pasadena, California

Matthew Modine
22 Mar, Loma Linda, California

Emma Thompson
15 Apr, London

Michelle Pfeiffer
29 Apr, Santa Ana, California

DEATHS

Cecil B. DeMille
21 Jan, Hollywood
Heart attack

Lou Costello
4 Mar, Hollywood
Heart attack

MARRIAGES

Diana Dors
12 Apr, *to* Dickie Dawson

DEMILLE DEAD

Cecil B. DeMille has died of a heart attack, aged 77. One of the great pioneers of the American cinema, DeMille was the first major director to move from the East Coast to California – for *The Squaw Man* (1914) – and will always be remembered for his showmanship and his historical and religious epics, like *The King of Kings* (1927), *The Sign of the Cross* (1932), *Cleopatra* (1934) and *The Ten Commandments* which he made twice, in 1923 and 1956. Just weeks before his death on 21 January he had delivered his autobiography to his publishers.

Walter Brennan and John Wayne watch for raiders in Howard Hawks' Rio Bravo.

DUKE & DEAN'S HIGH NOON

"*Rio Bravo* is the story of a friendship between a sheriff and his drunken deputy and how the deputy is rehabilitated," says director Howard Hawks. "The crux of it is not Wayne – it is Dean Martin's story."

Martin plays Dude, the deputy, and drink has made him lose all self-respect. Wayne is John T. Chance, the sheriff, a tower of integrity and strength. When Wayne arrests one of the Burdett family for murder and throws him in jail, a siege begins. All Wayne has for help is Dude, the crippled old Stumpy (Walter Brennan) and, possibly, a flashy gunfighter called Colorado (Rick Nelson). There's a dame, of course, to add to Wayne's problems – that's Feathers (Angie Dickinson), a professional gambler.

Hawks' new western has none of the great outdoors of earlier movies like the classic *Red River* (1948). It's an indoor and unusually talkie western, spiked with lots of dry repartee. For Hawks, it all began with *High Noon* (1952): "Gary Cooper ran around trying to get help and no one would give him any. And that's a rather silly thing for a man to do. So I said, we'll do just the opposite and take a real professional viewpoint."

ANGIE GETS LUCKY

Angie Dickinson makes Big John Wayne real nervous in *Rio Bravo*. When he's out on the street waving his rifle around or sitting in the jailhouse with Dean Martin and Walter Brennan, the Duke is at peace with the world. It's when he enters Dickinson's hotel room, finding her dressed in slinky lingerie, that he gets all tongue-tied and awkward.

But then the sexy, sophisticated Dickinson is rather special, and it's amazing that Hollywood has taken so long to give her a really decent role. She was born in 1931 in North Dakota, and won a beauty competition. She went to college in California and broke into films as long ago as 1954, playing a bit part in the Doris Day musical *Lucky Me*. She next appeared way down the cast list of *Man with the Gun* (1955), a Robert Mitchum western, and then received second billing in a "B" western called *Gun the Man Down* (1957), for which she got decent notices as the woman who deserts James Arness and gets killed for doing it.

Next was Samuel Fuller's "B" thriller *China Gate* (1957), in which she played a Eurasian, Lucky Legs, followed by *Cry Terror* (1958). She could hardly look back to her first movie and say, "Lucky Me."

But then director Howard Hawks spotted her, liked her feistiness as much as her beauty, cast her in *Rio Bravo* as the gambler Feathers and got her to throw a huge vase out of a window. It could be the turning point in her career.

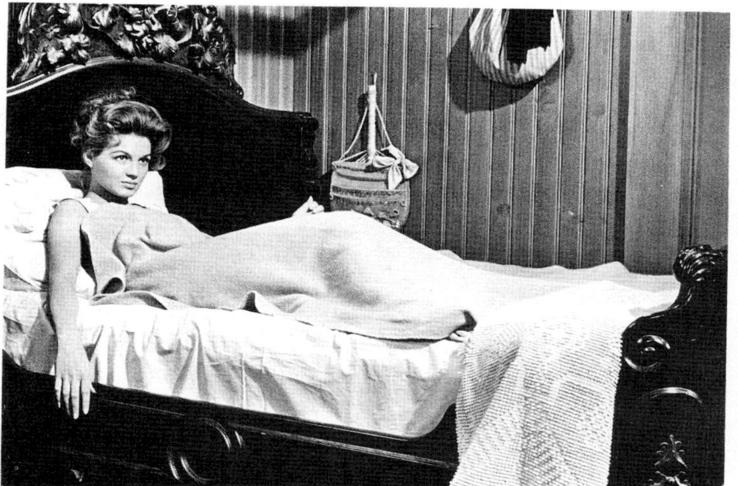

Angie Dickinson as the gambler Feathers in Rio Bravo.

A HERO FOR OUR TIMES?

Simone Signoret and Laurence Harvey in Room at the Top.

Meet Joe Lampton (Laurence Harvey), a new kind of British hero. He wants sex and success, at the same time, and he wants to escape his northern working-class origins by climbing to the top. But is there room for a man like Joe?

Based on John Braine's acclaimed, trail-blazing novel, *Room at the Top* charts Joe's all-consuming feelings of social inferiority and his inexorable rise. Arriving in dreary Warnley to take up a job in the Borough Treasurer's Department, his eyes quickly latch on to pretty Susan Brown (Heather Sears), the daughter of a local tycoon (Donald Wolfit). Against all advice, Joe starts courting Susan, until her father sends her abroad.

Then Joe takes up with an older and alcoholic married woman, Alice Aisgill (Simone Signoret). Susan returns, is quickly seduced by Joe and discovers she is pregnant. Brown then insists that Joe should marry his daughter and abandon Alice. That's when Joe has to choose between his driving ambition and the love of an older woman. It's a choice that ends in tragedy and triumph in this tough, cynical drama, directed by Jack Clayton.

STAR QUOTES

Tony Curtis
on working with Marilyn Monroe

"It was like kissing Hitler."

STAR QUOTES

Hedda Hopper

"Too bad Eddie Fisher isn't free to marry Liz. I give that union six months – you can't build a marriage on sex alone."

MAY
JUNE

JULY
AUGUST

BIRTHS, DEATHS AND MARRIAGES

BIRTHS

Rosanna Arquette
10 Aug, New York

DEATHS

Ethel Barrymore
18 Jun, Beverly Hills
Heart condition

Preston Sturges
6 Aug, New York
Heart attack

MARRIAGES

Julie Andrews
10 May, *to* Tony Walton

Elizabeth Taylor
12 May, *to* Eddie Fisher

Brigitte Bardot
19 Jun, *to* Jacques Charrier

Dorothy Malone
28 Jun, *to* Jacques Bergerac

Peter Finch
4 Jul, *to* Yolande Turner

STAR QUOTES

Alfred Hitchcock

"The length of a film should be directly related to the endurance of the human bladder."

STAR QUOTES

Charlton Heston

"I feel very strongly that the director is supposed to be the boss. Art was never created by democracy."

HOLD THAT MARTINI

Cary Grant gets lumbered with a corpse at the United Nations building in Alfred Hitchcock's North by Northwest.

In Alfred Hitchcock's new thriller *North by Northwest*, Cary Grant plays Roger Thornhill, a Madison Avenue man who's having his usual martini at New York's Plaza Hotel when, inexplicably, he's kidnapped by men who insist on calling him George Kaplan, a CIA agent.

At a house on Long Island, James Mason gets him drunk and sends him packing in his car. Tracking down the owner of the house to the United Nations, Grant is caught holding a knife over the murdered man. The chase is on – to Chicago, to the wheat belt, where Grant is almost murdered by a crop-dusting plane, and to Mount Rushmore, where the faces of the four presidents are the backdrop to the climax (Hitch wanted to call the film *The Man Who Sneezed in Lincoln's Nose*).

Just what are all these people up to? Eva Marie Saint, for instance, the cool mistress of Mason. Or Leo G. Carroll, the tight-lipped head of the CIA who's travelling in the same direction. And where is George Kaplan?

Ernest Lehman's screenplay has had several aliases. It was once called *Breathless* and, before that, the less-than-snappy *In a Northwesterly Direction*. But they all give an idea of the pace of Hitch's latest gripper.

CASTING CLEO

Producer Walter Wanger and 20th Century-Fox both agree that a film based on the life of the Egyptian Queen Cleopatra is a good idea. Wanger wants Elizabeth Taylor, Laurence Olivier (Caesar) and Richard Burton (Antony). But Fox chairman Spyros Skouras is said to prefer Joan Collins or Marilyn Monroe, supported by Cary Grant and Burt Lancaster. British novelist Nigel Balchin is currently writing the script for the picture, which is budgeted at $3 million.

THE NEW GRACE KELLY?

In Alfred Hitchcock's thriller *North by Northwest* Eva Marie Saint is the mystery woman – cool, resourceful, blonde – who shares a sleeping compartment with Cary Grant. It's a starry role for an actress who has made relatively few movies and has more talent than most. And critics are already comparing her with Grace Kelly.

Audiences will remember her as Marlon Brando's girlfriend in *On the Waterfront* (1954), for which she won a Best Supporting Oscar. It was her first film, and, accepting the award, heavily pregnant, she said: "I think I might have the baby right here."

She was born in 1924 in New Jersey and started acting on radio and in TV. Then she won the New York Drama Critics' Award for her performance in *The Trip to Bountiful*, which brought her to the attention of Elia Kazan, director of *On the Waterfront*. She struggled bravely in the Bob Hope comedy *That Certain Feeling* (1956), was more at home in Fred Zinnemann's drama *A Hatful of Rain*, and lost Montgomery Clift to Elizabeth Taylor in M-G-M's epic *Raintree County* (both 1957).

She's now under a three-picture contract with M-G-M, of which *North by Northwest* is the second. The third is to be *Exodus*, opposite Paul Newman, though Otto Preminger has bought the property from M-G-M and will produce and direct it for United Artists.

OTTO'S LATEST CODE-BUSTER

James Stewart, Lee Remick and Ben Gazzara in Anatomy of a Murder.

Anatomy of a Murder is based on the acclaimed novel by retired high court judge Robert Traver and was actually filmed in Ispeming and Marquette, Michigan, where Traver lives. When producer-director Otto Preminger wanted a real legal person to play the judge in the movie, he persuaded Boston lawyer Joseph N. Welch to play the part. Welch, says Preminger, represented the US army during the McCarthy hearings and became the hero of the American conscience.

But apart from Welch, it's Hollywood talent all the way in this powerful drama. James Stewart is the country-hick lawyer hired to defend army lieutenant Ben Gazzara, who has allegedly raped and beaten up wife Lee Remick. The medical examiner finds no physical evidence to support the charge and Stewart enters a plea of "temporary insanity". The prosecution is led by a big-city type Claude Dancer, played by chunky George C. Scott, in only his second screen role. As the trial develops, attention focuses on Remick's morals – and nothing is quite what it seems.

As with previous Preminger movies, like *The Moon Is Blue* (1953) and *The Man with the Golden Arm* (1955), *Anatomy of a Murder* breaks down Production Code taboos in its dialogue. Words like "panties", "contraception" and "spermatogenesis" are heard for the first time. And, at least for the first two, it looks like it won't be the last.

HAMMER HORRORMEISTER

Peter Cushing has the pallor of a funeral parlour. But his voice is powerful, testifying, like so many British actors, to formal dramatic training. Cushing has been making movies since 1939 (he was born in 1913) but has only recently become a star – as Baron Frankenstein in *The Curse of Frankenstein* (1957), as Dr. Van Helsing in *Dracula* (1958) and now as Sherlock Holmes in *The Hound of the Baskervilles*.

All these horrors come from British studio Hammer Films, and they're setting local box-offices alight. The films are exotic, violent and heavily sexual – a far cry from the drawing-room comedies and stiff-upper-lip war movies that have populated British screens this past decade. Cushing is Hammer's main star, but lofty Christopher Lee could well become his rival (he was the toothy Count in *Dracula*).

Cushing first made movies in Hollywood – he was in *The Man in the Iron Mask* (1939) and *A Chump at Oxford* (1940) – and returned home for war service and stage work. He made his British screen debut as Osric in Laurence Olivier's Oscar-winning *Hamlet* (1948) and then appeared in the Alan Ladd Arthurian romp *The Black Knight* (1954), the Grahame Greene romance *The End of the Affair* (1955) and the epic *Alexander the Great* (1956). But it's as the new Boris Karloff that he's finally found his niche.

HEPBURN GETS THE HABIT

Director Fred Zinnemann sums up his movies as stories about "conflicts of conscience". And having just returned from the Belgian Congo, where he shot part of *The Nun's Story*, he says: "The most exciting landscape is still the human face." When that face belongs to Audrey Hepburn you get Zinnemann's drift.

Hepburn plays Sister Luke, a novice nun who suffers from a lack of humility because her father is a celebrated physician and because she has no doubts about her own medical gifts. Accordingly, Mother Superior (Edith Evans) asks her deliberately to fail her exam in tropical medicine and sends her to tend the mentally ill in a nightmarish sanatorium.

Eventually, she gets to go to the Congo where she meets atheistic doctor Peter Finch and her troubles really begin. Handsome Finch has more on his mind than syringes . . .

It's a powerful drama, of epic scope, played with skill and sensitivity by Hepburn, and with a stirring score by veteran composer Franz Waxman. But relations between Waxman and Zinnemann didn't go completely smoothly – only late on did the director discover that Waxman secretly hated Catholicism and had deliberately written a triumphant ending for when Hepburn leaves the convent. Now, the movie ends in silence!

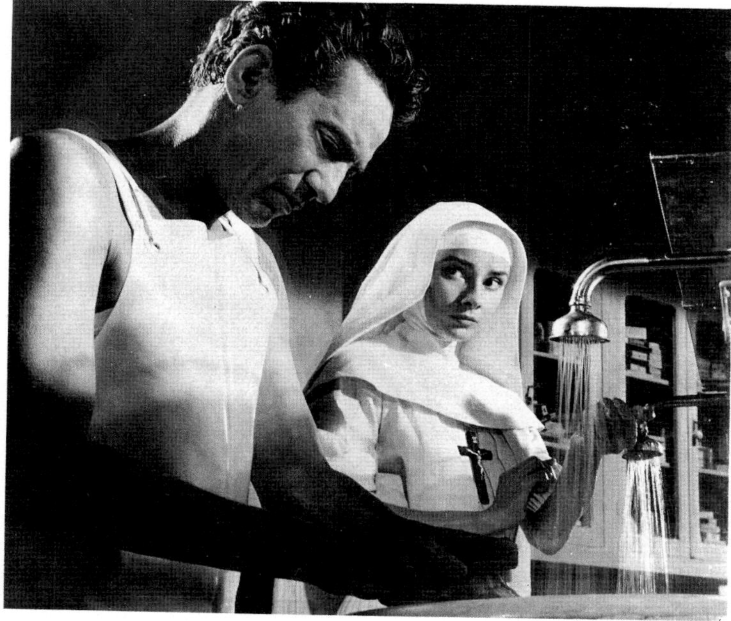

Peter Finch and Audrey Hepburn in The Nun's Story.

SEPTEMBER OCTOBER

1959

NOVEMBER DECEMBER

Above left: The recreation of the famous chariot race in Ben-Hur. *Above: Charlton Heston as Judah Ben-Hur.*

BREAD AND CIRCUSES

The future of M-G-M is riding on the mighty *Ben-Hur*. The ailing studio has invested an all-or-nothing $14.5 million in the production, which was filmed at Cinecitta studio in Rome. M-G-M last filmed Lew Wallace's story in 1925 and that, too, was the most expensive film of the time. Fortunately, none of the problems of that film have been repeated this time round, although insiders report that several uncredited writers were brought in to help fix the script, including British playwright Christopher Fry and American writer Gore Vidal.

Director William Wyler, who also took over as producer after the death of Sam Zimbalist, has brought it in safely. Charlton Heston stars as Jewish aristocrat Judah Ben-Hur who, at the time of Christ, falls victim to the ambitions of childhood friend Messala, played by iron-jawed Irish actor Stephen Boyd, 31. While his mother and sister languish in jail, Ben-Hur is condemned to the Roman galleys. But he saves the life of a Roman consul (Jack Hawkins), becomes a Roman citizen, and returns to Judaea to exact revenge on Messala and find his family.

Running 212 minutes – as long as *Gone with the Wind* – the Camera-65 production is filled with spectacular sequences, especially the ferocious chariot race, co-directed by Andrew Marton and veteran stuntman Yakima Canutt. This sequence alone involved weeks of arduous training for Heston and Boyd and was filmed on the largest outdoor set ever built. By a strange coincidence, Wyler was one of several assistants who worked on the chariot race in the 1925 version.

ROCK AND DORIS' HOTLINE!

Filmdom's No. 1 male and female stars, Doris Day and Rock Hudson, team up for the first time in the cheekily titled *Pillow Talk*. Both stars are cast slightly against type. Day abandons her wife-next-door look and is decked out in *haute-couture* and jewellery as bachelor lady Jan Morrow. Hudson plays philandering songwriter Brad Allen.

Pillow talk? Well, actually, they share a party phone line – and whenever Hudson wants to call one of his girlfriends he inevitably finds Day on the line. They meet at a dance and, rather than reveal his identity, Hudson passes himself off as a Texan called Rick Stetson. But Day still falls for him and Hudson has to decide whether or not to reveal his true identity. Produced by Ross Hunter, this bright CinemaScope comedy seems certain to set audiences talking.

FLEX THOSE PECS

In Italy, muscle-bound Steve Reeves has been a major star for almost two years. Now he's poised to become a star in America as well, thanks to a movie called *Hercules Unchained*.

Hollywood impresario Joseph E. Levine has bought this cheaply-made Italian spectacular and plans to spend more than its original budget on promotion. Its forerunner *Hercules* (1958), has already been a modest success in America this summer. Reeves plays the hunky hero in both and has also starred this year in *The Last Days of Pompeii*, *The Giant of Marathon* and *Goliath and the Barbarians*, all due Stateside in the next few months. Reeves performs extraordinary feats of strength – toppling columns of temples, playing tug-of-war with horses, and defeating armies of Italian extras. But he didn't learn to do this at the Actors' Studio in New York. A native of Montana, where he was born in 1926, he first flexed his muscles to become Mr. America, Mr. World and, finally, Mr. Universe. With no more body-building accolades to reach for, he went to Hollywood and made his debut in *Athena* (1954), a Jane Powell-Debbie Reynolds musical, in which he was billed as "Mr. Universe 1950."

Reeves is now firmly stuck in ancient history. The big question is, can he act in the 20th century?

CHINA STINKS

A documentary about Red China, *Behind the Great Wall*, has opened at the DeMille Theater, New York, in TotalScope and stereo sound. But visitors are lining up to experience Aroma-Rama, a new process that gives audiences the smells of China – which range from burning incense, jasmin and other spices to less alluring smells of the waterfront areas and farmyards. However, the theatre is having problems keeping the images and stinks in sync.

Fred Astaire, Gregory Peck and Ava Gardner in the domesday thriller *On the Beach*.

NO HAPPY ENDING

For weeks United Artists has been preparing moviegoers for *On the Beach*, with posters screaming "The Biggest Story Of Our Time!" The Stanley Kramer production is about nothing less than the end of the world – what happens when nuclear war breaks out in 1964.

Kramer, adapting a novel by Nevil Shute, doesn't immediately show the devastation of the United States or Soviet Union. Instead, the film is set in Australia, far from the battle zone. Surely everyone will be safe Down Under?

Not so. Clouds of radiation are drifting inexorably south and the movie shows how its characters and society in general cope with the knowledge that in five months time they will all be dead.

Gregory Peck stars as the captain of an American nuclear submarine who falls for Ava Gardner, a nervy and hard-drinking Melbourne girl. Leaving her behind, he sets sail for San Francisco in which everyone has already died. Returning to Melbourne, he's reunited with Gardner as the Australian government is issuing suicide pills to anyone wanting to avoid radiation sickness.

Co-starring Anthony Perkins, Donna Holmes and Fred Astaire as a guilt-ridden scientist who races cars with suicidal enthusiasm, *On the Beach* is a rarity in that no one lives happily ever after. That's its message.

BOX OFFICE

UK

1 Carry on Nurse
2 I'm All Right Jack
3 The Inn of the Sixth Happiness

OTHER TOP BOX OFFICE FILMS

The Big Country
Carry on Teacher
North West Frontier
Room at the Top
The Sheriff of Fractured Jaw
The 39 Steps
The Square Peg

BOX OFFICE

US

1 Auntie Mame
2 The Shaggy Dog
3 Some Like It Hot
4 Imitation of Life
5 The Nun's Story
6 Anatomy of a Murder
7 North by Northwest
8 Rio Bravo
9 Sleeping Beauty
10 Some Came Running

BIRTHS, DEATHS AND MARRIAGES

BIRTHS

Dolph Lundgren
3 Nov, Stockholm

Sean Young
20 Nov, Louisville, Kentucky

DEATHS

Kay Kendall
6 Sep, London
Leukemia

Edmund Gwenn
6 Sep, Woodland Hills, California

Paul Douglas
11 Sep, Hollywood
Heart attack

Mario Lanza
7 Oct, Rome
Heart attack

Errol Flynn
14 Oct, Vancouver
Heart attack

Victor McLaglen
7 Nov, Newport Beach, California
Heart failure

Gerard Philipe
25 Nov, Paris
Heart attack following surgery

Gilda Gray
22 Dec, Hollywood
Heart attack

MARRIAGES

Mickey Rooney
Dec, *to* Barbara Thomason

OUT LIKE FLYNN

Errol Flynn, star of such adventure movies as *The Adventures of Robin Hood* (1938), *The Dawn Patrol* (1938) and *The Sea Hawk* (1940), died of a heart attack on 14 October while waiting for a plane at Vancouver Airport.

As famous for his off-screen exploits – Flynn was a hard drinker and womanizer who was acquitted of a charge of statutory rape in 1942, which led to the catchphrase "In Like Flynn" – as much as for his ebullience on screen, Flynn was born in Tasmania in 1909 and made his screen debut as Fletcher Christian in the Australian movie *In the Wake of Bounty* (1933).

A major Warners contract player throughout the 1930s and 1940s, Flynn's career had recently declined because of marital problems and his troubles with alcohol and drug addiction. The Canadian coroner is quoted as saying that Flynn had the body of an 80-year-old.

LOLLO LUCK

Some say she's famous simply for being famous. The epitome of what the Italians call "busto provocante", sultry Gina Lollobrigida adorns fashion magazines and is constantly seen at parties and premieres. She also makes motion pictures.

There have been at least 40 of them since her first in 1946, when she was 19. She traded on her ravishing looks and a natural gift for comedy – in European movies she is the wife of mousy men or the equal of adventurers like France's dashing Gerard Philipe. Hollywood wanted her but she ran into bad luck, signing a contract with Howard Hughes which actually prevented her from making films there. But a way was found around that legal quagmire: Hollywood went to her.

She starred with Humphrey Bogart in *Beat the Devil* (1954), and then swung with Burt Lancaster and Tony Curtis in *Trapeze* (1956) and tempted plug-ugly Charles Laughton in the French-made *The Hunchback of Notre Dame* (1957). Now the Hughes problem is behind her and her charms can currently be seen on display in two major Hollywood productions: as the sensual Queen of Sheba in the epic *Solomon and Sheba* and opposite Frank Sinatra in the Second World War drama *Never So Few*.

Gina Lollobrigida, the busty Italian film star adored by many.

JANUARY
FEBRUARY

MARCH
APRIL

BRITS NIX PIX

Cinema admissions in Britain have slumped to below 600 million at an estimated 3,400 cinemas. The figures have caused despondency among industry leaders who blame the fall on increased audiences for the two television networks, which are showing an increasing number of films originally shown in cinemas. Production at British studios, however, remains fairly healthy, with 86 feature films made last year.

ACADEMY AWARDS

PRESENTED ON 4 APRIL 1960

Best Picture
Ben-Hur

Best Director
William Wyler
Ben-Hur

Best Actor
Charlton Heston
Ben-Hur

Best Actress
Simone Signoret
Room at the Top

Best Sup Actor
Hugh Griffith
Ben-Hur

Best Sup Actress
Shelley Winters
The Diary of Anne Frank

BEN-HUR WINS OSCAR RACE

M-G-M's $14.5 million blockbuster *Ben-Hur* has won a record 11 Oscars. The ceremony, held on 4 April at the RKO Pantages Theater in Hollywood and compered by Bob Hope, was televised live by ABC.

The picture, which has so far grossed over $20 million and has saved the famous studio from bankruptcy, carried away the coveted statuettes for Best Picture, Best Actor (Charlton Heston), Best Supporting Actor (Hugh Griffith), Best Director (William Wyler), Best Cinematography (Robert Surtees), Best Art Direction (William A. Horning, Edward Carfagno, Hugh Hunt), Best Sound (Franklin E. Milton), Best Music (Miklos Rozsa), Best Editing (Ralph E. Winters, John D. Dunning), Best Costume Design (Elizabeth Haffenden) and Best Special Effects (A. Arnold Gillespie, Robert MacDonald, Milo Lory).

The only major award to elude the picture was Best Screenplay. There was no nomination, owing to the large number of uncredited writers; but one of them, British playwright Christopher Fry, was publicly thanked by Heston during his acceptance speech. Quipped songwriters Sammy Cahn and Jimmy Van Heusen, who won Oscars for another film: "We're glad *Ben-Hur* didn't have a title song!"

PANHANDLE PREJUDICE

Based, like John Ford's *The Searchers* (1956), on a novel by Alan LeMay, *The Unforgiven* is a strong and starry western about the relationship between Whites and Indians. Produced by and starring Burt Lancaster, the story tells of a girl (Audrey Hepburn) who's been brought up by foster parents since she was a baby.

Her half-brother (Lancaster) is secretly in love with her and acts as the leader of the homesteaders who have settled in the Texas Panhandle after the Civil War. Their lives are made even harsher by the frequent attacks by Kiowa Indians, and then it's discovered that Hepburn is not, as supposed, a white survivor of an earlier massacre but an Indian.

Directed by John Huston and co-starring Audie Murphy as Hepburn's brother and veteran Lillian Gish as Hepburn's adopted mother, *The Unforgiven* is a notable addition to the ranks of "adult" westerns which deal with psychological issues as well as ridin' and shootin'.

Burt Lancaster in The Unforgiven, *the story of racial violence between Whites and Indians.*

THE GOSPEL ACCORDING TO BILLY

"I have 10 commandments," says director Billy Wilder. "The first nine are Thou Shalt Not Bore. The 10th is Thou Shalt Have Right Of Final Cut."

Wilder is one of America's best and most famous moviemakers, despite the fact that his definition of direction is something you don't notice. He's famous because of his wit – as William Holden, the star of three Wilder films, says, "He has a mind full of razor blades."

Wilder was born in Austria in 1906 and, like so many writers and artists, fled Nazi Germany and arrived in Hollywood in 1934. He teamed up with Charles Brackett and penned such sparkling comedies as *Bluebeard's Eighth Wife* (1938), *Midnight* and *Ninotchka* (both 1939) in which "Garbo laughs!" Wilder finally became a director in 1942 with the Ginger Rogers comedy *The Major and the Minor*.

There followed a string of classics, such as *Double Indemnity* (1944), *The Lost Weekend* (1945), *Sunset Blvd.* (1950), *Ace in the Hole* (1951) and *Stalag 17* (1953). In 1957 Wilder teamed up with another co-writer, I. A. L. Diamond, and produced last year's hit comedy *Some Like It Hot*.

There's no wittier nor sterner observer of American life than Wilder. He never bores and, thanks to his current contract with Mirisch and United Artists, he's one of Tinseltown's few directors with complete control.

A CUBAN COMEDY?

Celebrated novelist Graham Greene refused to sell the screen rights of *Our Man in Havana* to Hitchcock. Instead, they were sold to director Carol Reed who, with Greene, produced the classic thriller *The Third Man* (1949).

Their latest collaboration concerns a vacuum-cleaner salesman (Alec Guinness) who is financially induced to represent the British Secret Service in Cuba. Noel Coward is the Secret Service head who recruits him, Maureen O'Hara his new secretary sent from London, and Burl Ives his friend who is murdered by the Cuban police under the direction of Captain Segura (Ernie Kovacs).

Combining elements of thriller and comedy, *Our Man in Havana* was shot on location in Cuba, only two years after the revolution that swept Fidel Castro to power. A censor attached to the production demanded several changes to the script, and Reed and his camera team found it difficult to recreate the flavour of the earlier Cuban regime with its glitzy casinos and floorshows.

Says Reed: "They wanted to make sure that our story, which is set in the old regime, showed just what a police state it was then. We did that with odd little scenes and reference to torture of political prisoners. The authorities didn't want to make it appear that anything that happened under Batista could possibly happen again. But most of the plot is comedy and we couldn't make it too heavy."

BIRTHS, DEATHS AND MARRIAGES

BIRTHS

Nastassia Kinski
24 Jan, Berlin

James Spader
7 Feb, New York

Meg Tilly
14 Feb, Victoria, California

Greta Scacchi
18 Feb, Milan

Michael Praed
1 Apr, London

DEATHS

Margaret Sullavan
1 Jan, Connecticut
Overdose of barbiturates

Victor Seastrom
3 Jan, Stockholm

Hope Emerson
25 Apr, Hollywood
Liver ailment

MARRIAGES

Anne Baxter
18 Feb, *to* Randolph Galt

STAR QUOTES

Jayne Mansfield

"I can't sleep in anything but a pink bedroom."

STAR QUOTES

Jane Russell

"Let's say I've given up being moody magnificence, but my friends still say I'm mean."

CRITICS SLAM PEEPER SHOCKER

Anna Massey and Carl Boehm in Michael Powell's Peeping Tom.

In London *Peeping Tom* is creating a scandal. It's a sordid tale about a psychopathic film technician (Carl Boehm) who murders women with the sharpened leg of his camera tripod, and films their agonizing screams and deaths. It's directed by Michael Powell, who also plays Boehm's father, a professor studying the symptoms of terror. His cruelty towards his young son has clearly had disastrous results.

The violence and disturbing nature of the movie – when not killing, Boehm simply spies on and photographs young lovers (whence the title) – has shocked British film critics. Their attacks on Powell, director of such films as *The Life and Death of Colonel Blimp* (1943), *A Matter of Life and Death* (1946) and *The Red Shoes* (1948), is unprecedented.

Powell himself says it's "a tender film", but one critic has written: "The only really satisfactory way to dispose of *Peeping Tom* would be to shovel it up and flush it swiftly down the nearest sewer." Wrote another: "It's a long time since a film disgusted me as much. I don't propose to name the players in this beastly picture."

Yet another: "I was shocked to the core to find a director of this standing befouling the screen with such perverted nonsense. It is wholly evil." And yet another: "Sick minds will be highly stimulated."

But it seems there are plenty of sick minds in London at present – the Plaza cinema is doing good business. Due at the same cinema soon is Alfred Hitchcock's long-awaited shocker, *Psycho*.

MAY

JUNE

JULY

AUGUST

THE TROUBLE WITH MOTHER

"No one, not even the manager's brother, will be admitted after the film starts." So say the notices at theatres playing Alfred Hitchcock's *Psycho*, which the director calls "my first horror film". And at the end, after all the shocks, portly Hitch's familiar voice is heard in the foyer, ordering us not to reveal the ending.

That would spoil the fun – and *Psycho* is fun. It's a horror movie that Hitchcock also describes as a comedy. But it's comedy of the most macabre kind.

It all starts on a hot afternoon in Phoenix, Arizona, when Marion Crane (Janet Leigh) is spending her lunch-hour with boyfriend John Gavin. Back at work she's given $42,000 in cash to take to the bank. $42,000! Why not? So she takes off in her car and, driving into a storm, checks into a motel. The Bates Motel – 12 cabins, 12 vacancies, overlooked by a gingerbread house on the hill.

The owner is an old hag who can sometimes be heard yelling at her dedicated son Norman (Anthony Perkins), who runs the motel. He gives Marion cabin one, then a sandwich and a glass of milk. And they share a moment of mutual loneliness – Norman speaks of his fondness for stuffing birds and his love for his mother. Marion speaks of her desire for a private island.

But then it's time for her to take a shower and for him to spy on her through the wall. To say any more would be to spoil the thrills and surprises in this riveting shocker. And be warned: you'll never want to take a shower again with the curtain pulled.

MOTHER'S BOY

As Norman Bates, the bird-obsessed mother's boy in Alfred Hitchcock's shocker *Psycho*, Anthony Perkins has created a character that will remain in the minds of moviegoers for years to come. Born in 1932, Perkins is the son of actor Osgood Perkins and made his screen debut in William Wyler's *The Actress* (1953), as Jean Simmons's boyfriend.

His gangling looks and natural twitchiness seemed to work against him: he lost out to James Dean for *East of Eden* (1955) and next appeared in another Wyler film, *Friendly Persuasion* (1956), as Quaker preacher Gary Cooper's son who enlists in the army. He became the awkward adolescent – as a neurotic baseball player in *Fear Strikes Out*, an insecure marshal in *The Tin Star* (both 1957), and fumbling into an affair with Sophia Loren in *Desire under the Elms* (1958).

Now there's *Psycho*, in which Hitchcock cleverly builds on Perkins' screen personality. As for the famous shower sequence - Perkins was not even there for the shooting (he was rehearsing a part on Broadway). But then, Perkins wasn't needed. His mother was.

JESUS TALKS!

Filming has started in Spain on the first talkie screen biography of Christ, *King of Kings*. Producer Samuel Bronston denies it's a remake of the 1927 DeMille picture, claiming that he and director Nicholas Ray have decided on a more modern approach to the Gospels. The actor chosen to play Christ is 33-year-old Jeffrey Hunter, who's been forbidden to grant press interviews to preserve an air of reverence.

The spooky house behind the Bates Motel in Hitchcock's Psycho.

Anthony Perkins, who plays the lead in Psycho.

BIRTHS, DEATHS AND MARRIAGES

BIRTHS

Sean Penn
17 Aug, Burbank, California

DEATHS

Leo McCarey
5 Jul, Santa Monica, California
Emphysema

Hans Albers
24 Jul, Munich

MARRIAGES

Marlon Brando
4 Jun, *to* Movita Castenada

Gene Tierney
11 Jul, *to* Howard Lee

Deborah Kerr
23 Jul, *to* Peter Viertel

STAR QUOTES

Alfred Hitchcock

"If I made Cinderella, the audience would be looking for the body in the coach."

STAR QUOTES

Yul Brynner

"People don't know my real self and they're not about to find out."

Jack Lemmon and Shirley MacLaine in Billy Wilder's comedy The Apartment.

KEY TO SUCCESS

In Billy Wilder's new comedy *The Apartment* C. C. Baxter (Jack Lemmon) works in Premium Accounting and slaves away at his adding machine with the other 31,259 employees. So what makes him so special that managers start calling him "Buddy boy"? He has this little apartment in the West 60s, nothing fancy but cosy. "The only problem is," he says, "I can't always get in when I want to."

This is because Baxter loans out his apartment so that his bosses have somewhere to take their mistresses. While they make love and whoopee, Baxter snivels in Central Park. He always has a cold. But then personnel director J. D. Sheldrake (Fred MacMurray), latches on to Baxter's latch-key and promotion for buddy-boy is assured.

He gets his own office and . . . a heap of trouble. He rather likes elevator girl Fran Kubelik (Shirley MacLaine) but doesn't realize she's the girl Sheldrake takes to his apartment. That is, until they have a row and Fran takes a whole bottle of sleeping pills.

Can Baxter nurse her back to health and keep his self-respect – or should he become Sheldrake's personal assistant with a key to the executive washroom? All is revealed in this sparkling, if bitter-sweet, comedy from the team that produced last year's hit, *Some Like It Hot*.

LEMMON TWIST

Jack Lemmon was born in an elevator in Boston in 1925. It was clearly going up, for Lemmon has rapidly become one of Hollywood's greatest stars and finest screen actors.

He won an Oscar as Best Supporting Actor for his second film, *Mister Roberts* (1955) and has essayed the modern American male in a string of hit comedies: *Phffft!* (1954), *My Sister Eileen* (1955), *You Can't Run Away From It* (1956) – a remake of the 1934 Clark Gable-Claudette Colbert comedy *It Happened One Night* – and *Operation Mad Ball* (1957).

Only as a tenderfoot in *Cowboy* and as a warlock in *Bell, Book and Candle* (both 1958) has he seemed out of place. He looked great, though, in lipstick, wig and flapper outfit in Billy Wilder's *Some Like It Hot* (1959) and managed to transfer intact his image as a bag of nerves with reserves of charm and basic humanity.

Those qualities are much in evidence in his new film, *The Apartment*, in which he plays an insurance clerk with uncertain morals. Says Lemmon: "As I see it, he is ambitious, a nice guy but gullible, easily intimidated and fast to excuse his behaviour. In the end he faces up to having rationalized his morals. He realizes he's been a dumb kid, he's been had." Well, nobody's perfect – except, maybe, Lemmon's acting.

BIBLE BASHERS

At a time when religious epics are a dime a dozen (well, $12 million or so each), writer-director Richard Brooks has come up with a controversial film about religion that is not set at the time of Christ. And what's more, it is not even in CinemaScope.

Elmer Gantry is set in America in the 1920s and stars Burt Lancaster as an evangelist who works his way through the Bible Belt bringing the word of God to people hungering for salvation. But he's a crook, a con-man, and teams up with the equally dubious Sister Sharon (Jean Simmons).

Arthur Kennedy is a journalist who exposes Simmons's phony mission, Shirley Jones is a hooker redeemed by Lancaster, and singer Patti Page makes her screen debut as a singer in Simmons's choral group. Based on Sinclair Lewis's 1927 novel, which was inspired by the discrediting of evangelist Aimee Semple Macpherson, the film provides Lancaster with his most expansive role to date, and looks set to offend plenty of people in America's Bible Belt.

Both Burt Lancaster and Jean Simmons are not what they seem in Elmer Gantry.

Kirk Douglas in the title role of Spartacus as a gladiator who leads the slaves in revolt against Rome.

KIRK VS. ROME!

At $12 million, *Spartacus* has Universal executives hoping it will do *Ben-Hur*-type business. It's very much a personal project of executive producer Kirk Douglas, who also plays the Thracian slave who in 73 B.C. led an army of gladiators in revolt against the tyranny of Rome. Jean Simmons plays the beautiful slave-girl he loves and Tony Curtis his boyish best friend.

Matched against them is the might of Rome and British acting – Laurence Olivier as Roman general Crassus, Charles Laughton as Crassus' rival in the Senate, Peter Ustinov as a cowardly and scheming gladiator trainer, and John Gavin as a young Julius Caesar.

Written by former HUAC blacklistee Dalton Trumbo, directed by 31-year-old Stanley Kubrick (who replaced Anthony Mann when Douglas had him fired after a week's shooting) and photographed in Super Technirama-70, it has few equals as a screen spectacular, even though most of it was made on Universal's backlot. But critics are also praising the film as an intimate drama and a celebration of personal liberty. Says Douglas: "If *Spartacus* is a thrilling experience, $12 million was a drop in the bucket. If not, $12 was too much. There is no ratio between cost and artistic value. This helps explain why ulcers are as prevalent as California sunshine."

LIFE'S A BITCH

British novelist Alan Sillitoe went to Nottingham to watch the film being made of his sexually frank novel *Saturday Night and Sunday Morning*. "It gave me a wonderful emotional shock to see Albert Finney standing at exactly the same place at the bench in the Raleigh factory where I had worked," he says. Newcomer Finney plays Arthur Seaton, an angry young man. He makes bicycles and in his North Country brogue mutters: "No wonder I always have a bad back, though I'll soon be done. I'll have a fag in a bit. No sense working every minute God sends. I could get through it in half the time but they'd only slash me wages, so they can get stuffed. Don't let the bastards grind you down. That's one thing you learn. What I'm out for is a good time. All the rest is propaganda."

Shirley Anne Field, Albert Finney and Norman Rossington in Saturday Night and Sunday Morning.

Arthur lives for the weekend, when he can go fishing, go to the boozer, and have it off with his workmate's wife. His real love is pert Doreen – played by Shirley Anne Field, who was also with Finney in this summer's *The Entertainer*, with Laurence Olivier. But she's old fashioned and wants a ring on her finger first. It looks like he's stuck, ground down like he feared. Oh well, work tomorrah.

THE BIG SHAVE

As they used to say of Esther Williams: "Wet she's a star, dry she ain't." Nobody has yet said of Yul Brynner: "Bald he's a star, hairy he ain't" – but they might.

Audiences remember him as the bald King of Siam in the musical *The King and I* (1956) which won him a Best Actor Oscar. But Brynner's background is draped in mystery. "Just call me a nice, clean-cut Mongolian boy," he says.

He lived in the Soviet Union and Paris before arriving in America in 1941 as a guitar player. He played on Broadway and in London and made the "B" movie narcotics drama, *Port of New York*, in 1949. Then, in spring 1951, came his big break and his big shave: he starred opposite Mary Martin in the Broadway production of *The King and I*.

Movie offers flowed in – he starred as Pharaoh in Cecil B. DeMille's *The Ten Commandments* (1956), even though the film version of *The King and I* beat it into the cinemas. He played Russians in *Anastasia* (1956) and *The Brothers Karamazov* (1958), and wore a wig as Solomon in *Solomon and Sheba* (1959). The box-office failure of that last film was partially blamed on the fact that Brynner had hair.

Now he's shaved again for his new film, John Sturges' epic western *The Magnificent Seven*, in which he leads a gang of gunfighters who defend a poor Mexican farming village against a vicious bandit. Brynner is already a major star but the other six (Steve McQueen, James Coburn, Robert Vaughn, Horst Buchholz, Brad Dexter and Charles Bronson) look like becoming stars too.

CLEO SHUTS DOWN

20th Century-Fox announced on 18 November that owing to the illness of Elizabeth Taylor the $10 million production of *Cleopatra* has been closed down.

The Roman epic, produced by Walter Wanger, directed by Rouben Mamoulian and starring Taylor as the Egyptian Queen, Peter Finch as Julius Caesar and Stephen Boyd as Mark Antony, has been shooting at Pinewood Studios in England since 28 September.

The production has been dogged by delays and script problems – the latest version is by novelist Lawrence Durrell – and insiders suggest that Taylor's viral infection could not have come at a more convenient time.

BIRTHS, DEATHS AND MARRIAGES

BIRTHS

Colin Firth
10 Sep, Grayshott, Hampshire

Kenneth Branagh
10 Dec, Belfast

DEATHS

Ward Bond
5 Nov, Dallas, Texas
Heart attack

Mack Sennett
5 Nov, Hollywood
Heart attack following surgery

Clark Gable
17 Nov, Hollywood
Heart attack

Phyllis Haver
19 Nov, Falls Village, Connecticut
Suicide

MARRIAGES

Joan Caulfield
24 Nov, *to* Robert Peterson

Betty Hutton
24 Dec, *to* Peter Candoli

TEX-MEX FIGHTIN' FARE

John Wayne (who also directed) and Richard Widmark in The Alamo.

"*The Alamo* had to be made into a motion picture," says star, producer and first-time director John Wayne. "It has the raw and tender stuff of immortality, peopled by hard-living, hard-loving men whose women matched them in creating a pattern of freedom and liberty. Making this picture has given me great satisfaction because, paraphrasing Davy Crockett, it gave me the privilege of feeling useful in this old world. If there is anything better than that, I don't know what it is."

Making *The Alamo* – the legendary story of 185 men who were massacred by the Mexican army on 6 March 1836 – was a herculean task. To begin with, the Alamo itself had to be re-created, as the original now sits in the middle of downtown San Antonio. A site was found nearby, on James T. "Happy" Shahan's ranch, and the set will remain as a tourist attraction.

Then Richard Widmark was cast as knife-fighter Jim Bowie, Laurence Harvey (sporting an off-centre southern accent) as Colonel Travis, grizzled Richard Boone as General Sam Houston, and several thousand extras who went before the six Todd-AO camera units.

The siege of this Alamo lasted 91 days, seven times as long as the one in 1836. Now, $12 million later, it's finally reached the screen in a 3¼-hour homespun epic of American fortitude and patriotism.

MR. NASTY

In his film debut Richard Widmark liked to push old ladies in wheelchairs down the stairs. Just for kicks. That might have been the kiss of death for his career, but so compelling was Widmark's nastiness, so brutal was his face, and so appalling was his giggle, that stardom followed like night follows day.

He was 32, and had been a teacher and radio actor before he signed with 20th Century-Fox. The studio liked this sadistic little monster on their books and many more villains were to follow. He played heroes as well, but not so effectively as he played racist cops (*No Way Out*, 1950) or hoodlums (*Pickup on South Street*, 1953).

By now Widmark was wearying of the films that Fox cast him in. He wanted to extend his range and worked out his contract by appearing opposite Gary Cooper in the Mexican adventure *Garden of Evil* and as Spencer Tracy's psychotic son in *Broken Lance* (both 1954). Since then, as an independent, he's made some eccentric choices, including *Saint Joan*, as the Dauphin opposite Jean Seberg, the military thriller *Time Limit* (both 1957) and even a Doris Day comedy, *The Tunnel of Love* (1958).

Now audiences can see him as Jim Bowie, wielding a giant knife and killing hordes of Mexicans in John Wayne's epic *The Alamo*. And there isn't an old lady in a wheelchair in sight.

BLACKLIST BUSTERS

Hollywood screenwriter Dalton Trumbo has become the first blacklisted writer to receive a full film credit. Trumbo has scripted the Kirk Douglas production of *Spartacus* and Otto Preminger's *Exodus*, both expensive spectacles.

Trumbo served a 10-month jail sentence in 1948 for refusing to testify before the House Un-American Activities Committee about his alleged membership of the Communist Party. Until Douglas and Preminger decided to break the blacklist he had been working under a number of pseudonyms.

Trumbo's on-screen credits coincide with the announcement that another blacklisted writer, Michael Wilson, has been signed to write the forthcoming Sam Spiegel-David Lean epic, *Lawrence of Arabia*. Wilson is said to have been one of the writers who worked uncredited on Lean's *The Bridge on the River Kwai* (1957), so his script for *Lawrence* should make interesting reading.

BOX OFFICE

UK

1 Doctor in Love
2 Sink the Bismarck!
3 Carry on Constable

OTHER TOP BOX OFFICE FILMS

Conspiracy of Hearts
Dentist in the Chair
Hercules Unchained
The League of Gentlemen
Psycho
Two Way Stretch
Suddenly, Last Summer

BOX OFFICE

US

1 Ben-Hur
2 Psycho
3 Operation Petticoat
4 Suddenly, Last Summer
5 On the Beach
6 Solomon and Sheba
7 The Apartment
8 From the Terrace
9 Please Don't Eat the Daisies
10 Ocean's Eleven

Richard Burton (right) and Victor Mature in The Robe.

Magnificent set from The Fall of the Roman Empire.

Peter O'Toole (left) in Lawrence of Arabia *(1962).*

Scene from D. W. Griffith's silent epic The Birth of a Nation *(1915).*

The famous chariot race from the 1959 remake of Ben-Hur.

Epic Hollywood

During the 1950s and 1960s two words obsessed Hollywood – epic and blockbuster. The key to success was to spend enough to make the picture look lavish but not so much as to make a profit impossible. This was a lesson learned the hard way by 20th Century-Fox with *Cleopatra* (1963) and by independent mogul Samuel Bronston with *The Fall of the Roman Empire* (1964).

Epics were nothing new. The Italians were old hands at them and a version of *Quo Vadis* in 1912 impressed American director D. W. Griffith so much that he immediately embarked upon his immense *The Birth of a Nation* (1915) and the even bigger *Intolerance* (1916) which bankrupted him. In France, a lavish and lengthy film about *Napoleon* (1927) also bankrupted director Abel Gance. Cecil B. DeMille splurged on silent versions of *The Ten Commandments* (1923) and *The King of Kings* (1927) and the newly formed M-G-M mortgaged its future on *Ben-Hur* (1925). At $5 million it was one of the most expensive films ever made and it barely broke even.

During the 1930s and 1940s the epic was supplanted by other genres but in the 1950s it staged a dramatic comeback – M-G-M decided to remake *Quo Vadis* (1951) in Italy and 20th Century-Fox chose another religious subject, *The Robe*, to unveil their widescreen process CinemaScope in 1953. Both films were commercial successes and in their lavish sets, thousands of milling extras and packs of hungry lions they offered something television could not. DeMille and Paramount remade *The Ten Commandments* (1956), and its success encouraged M-G-M to risk solvency again by remaking *Ben-Hur* (1959). Like the original, it was at the time the most expensive movie ever made ($14.5 million); it turned a massive profit and won a still unbroken record of 11 Academy Awards.

By then every studio in Hollywood was ransacking the history books. And the Italians began making their own brand of epics – known as 'Pepla'. For a major producer like Dino De Laurentiis, epics were a way of joining forces with Hollywood and ultimately making a career there. He had made *Ulysses* in 1954, using Kirk Douglas and forging a distribution deal with Paramount. He went on to produce *War and Peace* (1956) for Paramount, *Barabbas* (1962) for Columbia and *The Bible in the beginning . . .* (1966) for Fox before setting up in the US.

A much sadder story unfolded in Spain, where producer Samuel Bronston set up his own studio, relied on frozen US money, the Franco regime and co-production deals with Hollywood studios. In five years (1960-4) he produced four historical epics – *King of Kings, El Cid, 55 Days at Peking* and *The Fall of the Roman Empire* – before his own empire collapsed soon afterwards.

Bronston's epics are among the best of their kind. But most film critics held epics in contempt, mainly because they could not take Hollywood actors in togas seriously and because the films were virtually critic proof. Only David Lean's *Lawrence of Arabia* (1962) got generally good notices.

By the late 1960s too many studios had had too many flops. The new, younger audience had little interest in historical yarns and the films themselves became too expensive to contemplate.

A real epic – in the classical sense of the word – deals with heroism, quest and the inevitable advance of history. Few of the blockbusters of the 1950s and 1960s aimed that high, apart from *Ben-Hur, El Cid* and *Lawrence of Arabia*. But the spirit of the epic survived in movies like *2001: A Space Odyssey* (1968), the *Star Wars* trilogy (1977-83) and *Heaven's Gate* (1980).

Main picture: Charlton Heston as 11th century warrior El Cid.

'it screen section from Abel Gance's restored Napoleon *(1927).*

Marilyn Monroe and Clark Gable in The Misfits, *which was Gable's last film and perhaps his finest performance.*

BIRTHS, DEATHS AND MARRIAGES

BIRTHS

Madonna
1 Jan, Pontiac, Illinois

Nicholas Lyndhurst
20 Apr, Emsworth, Hampshire

DEATHS

Anna May Wong
3 Feb, Santa Monica, California
Heart attack

Belinda Lee
13 Mar, San Bernadino, California
Road accident

Gail Russell
26 Apr, Los Angeles

ACADEMY AWARDS

PRESENTED ON 17 APRIL 1961

Best Picture
The Apartment

Best Director
Billy Wilder
The Apartment

Best Actor
Burt Lancaster
Elmer Gantry

Best Actress
Elizabeth Taylor
Butterfield 8

Best Sup Actor
Peter Ustinov
Spartacus

Best Sup Actress
Shirley Jones
Elmer Gantry

THE KING'S LAST HURRAH

Tragedy hangs over John Huston's production *The Misfits* as its star, Clark Gable, died of a heart attack on 17 November last year, aged 59. Although he saw a rough-cut of the film, he never saw the finished version of what many are hailing as his finest ever dramatic performance.

Nor will the star of *It Happened One Night* (1934), *Mutiny on the Bounty* (1935) and *Gone with the Wind* (1939) see his only child, John Clark Gable, born three months after his death. Let *The Misfits*, then, be a memorial to the undisputed King of Hollywood.

It's a prestige picture in every way, written by playwright Arthur Miller for his wife Marilyn Monroe. She plays a lonely divorcee who becomes the conscience of Gable and Montgomery Clift as rodeo-riders forced to round up wild horses and selling them for dog food.

Filmed in and around the gambling resort of Reno, Nevada, and containing a spectacular round-up sequence, *The Misfits* is by no means an ordinary western. "More of an anti-western," says Huston, who during shooting impulsively entered a camel race at Virginia City and won. "This movie is about a world in change. Now the cowboys drive pick-up trucks. Once they sold the wild horses for children's ponies. And now for dog food. This is a dog-eat-horse society."

AMIABLE FRED

Fred MacMurray as the man who invents flubber in The Absent Minded Professor.

There are two sides to Fred MacMurray. In Billy Wilder's *The Apartment* (1960) he played an insurance executive devoid of moral scruple. Now, in Walt Disney's *The Absent Minded Professor*, he plays Neddie the Nut, a science teacher devoid of memory. He's twice left his fiancee waiting at the church and his experiments tend to go dreadfully wrong. However, he does wind up commended on the White House Lawn.

In addition to this success, MacMurray has also just started a TV comedy series called *My Three Sons* which will bring him to a huge audience. Where did this amiable 52-year-old performer come from? A long way back.

MacMurray has more than 50 films to his credit, starting with his debut in 1934. They were mainly light comedies and musicals (he was a saxophonist and vocalist in a jazz band). But then, in 1944, Billy Wilder cast him as the bluff insurance salesman in *Double Indemnity* who commits murder after he gets a glimpse of Barbara Stanwyck.

This revealed MacMurray's considerable dramatic talents; but these lay fallow (apart from the occasional western and war movie) until *The Caine Mutiny* (1954). It's to be hoped it won't be years before MacMurray gets another dramatic opportunity. In the meantime, enjoy this actor's comic skills.

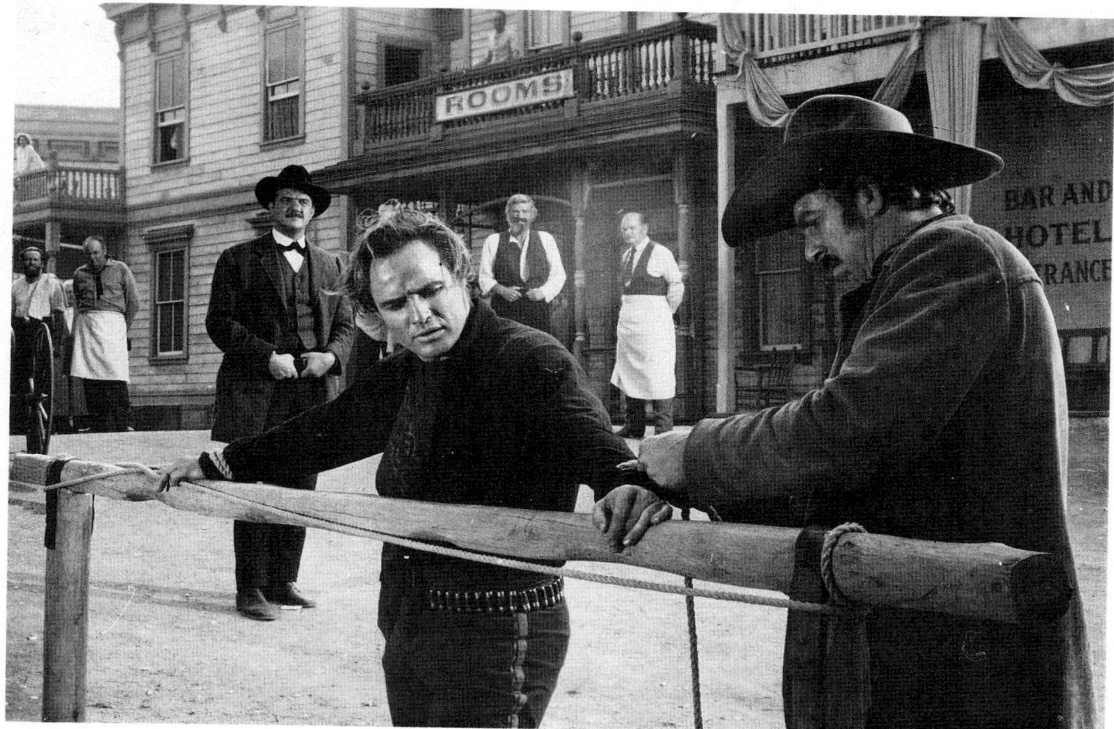

Karl Malden, Marlon Brando and Slim Pickens in One-Eyed Jacks.

BRANDO'S OUT FOR REVENGE!

Marlon Brando's western *One-Eyed Jacks* has had a long and difficult ride to the screen. Rumours abound that Paramount has hacked its running time from 240 to 141 minutes; but critics generally agree that it was well worth it.

It's Brando's first time behind the camera and the result has a different look from most westerns, being set beside the pounding Pacific surf at Big Sur and Monterey, with early sequences shot in Death Valley. Brando plays Rio, who gets out of jail following a robbery committed with his partner Dad (Karl Malden). He believes Dad still has the loot stashed away somewhere and that nothing has changed. But it has.

Dad has married and has a daughter, played by Mexican beauty Pina Pellicer. Dad is also marshal of the town and when Brando makes advances to his daughter he publicly whips and crushes his gun hand. The scene is set for revenge.

Brando started work on the movie three years ago when producer Frank P. Rosenberg brought him a screenplay by Sam Peckinpah based on Charles Neider's novel *The Authentic Death of Hendry Jones*. Stanley Kubrick was hired as director but after various disputes – amongst them, his choice of Spencer Tracy for the role of Dad – the tyro director quit. That was when Brando decided to direct it himself. The saturnine star is said to have foresworn directing for ever after his experiences on *One-Eyed Jacks*. That would be Tinseltown's loss.

JACK OF ALL PARTS

Karl Malden, 47, can claim to be America's finest character actor. An Oscar winner for his portrayal of Mitch in *A Streetcar Named Desire* (1951) and nominated for *On the Waterfront* (1954), he now makes his third screen appearance with Marlon Brando in the western *One-Eyed Jacks*. Asked what it was like being directed by an actor, he says: "Well, you know, I have done it myself, just the once, but I didn't cast myself in it."

That was the 1957 military thriller *Time Limit*, starring Richard Widmark. But he's been acting in movies since 1940 – among his credits are *The Gunfighter* (1950), Hitchcock's *I Confess* (1953), *Fear Strikes Out* (1957), as Anthony Perkin's forceful father, and the current *Parrish*, as a loony tobacco plantation boss.

Long associated with New York's Group Theater, he has had a fruitful collaboration with director Elia Kazan, in *Boomerang* (1947), *Streetcar, Waterfront* and *Baby Doll* (1956) as blonde nymphette Carroll Baker's tormented husband.

Potato-nosed Malden will probably never be a box-office draw by himself. But he can be relied upon to add dramatic weight to a movie, whether playing a character of moral conscience, as in *Waterfront*, or one of moral collapse, as in *Baby Doll*.

One of America's most versatile character actors Karl Malden.

FLATFOOT HOUNDS

One Hundred and One Dalmatians is destined to take its place alongside other Walt Disney immortals like *Snow White and the Seven Dwarfs* (1937), *Pinocchio, Fantasia* (both 1940) and *Bambi* (1942). The story takes place in London and the English countryside and concerns the heroic efforts of two dalmatian detectives to rescue 99 who are in the evil clutches of Cruella De Ville, a villainess likely to receive more boos from young audiences than the wicked witch in *Snow White*. The pups, though, will receive as many tears as cheers.

Costing $4 million, the picture is the result of three years' work at the Disney studio by some 300 artists – that's three artists a hound. And it seems certain to restore that old magic to the studio whose previous animated features, *Cinderella* (1949) and *Sleeping Beauty* (1959), were less than rapturously received by the public.

On a technical note, *Dalmatians* is the first feature to use the new Xerox camera, devised by Ub Iwerks, which saves time and money by enabling artwork to be transferred directly to film cels. When you have maybe 50 spotted dogs in a frame, all barking and wagging their tails, this new device is very welcome.

STAR QUOTES

Sophia Loren

"I'm glad I was born poor. Poverty gives one so much more than riches – the priceless gift of real ambition."

STAR QUOTES

Joan Collins

"Psychiatry has helped me tremendously as an actress.

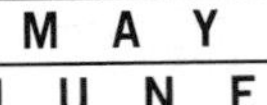

MAY
JUNE

JULY
AUGUST

BIRTHS, DEATHS AND MARRIAGES

BIRTHS

Michael J. Fox
9 Jun, Edmonton, Canada

Iain Glen
24 Jun, Edinburgh

DEATHS

Gary Cooper
13 May, Bel Air
Cancer

Joan Davis
23 May, Palm Springs, California
Heart attack

Jeff Chandler
18 Jun, Hollywood
Blood poisoning after surgery

Charles Coburn
30 Aug, New York
Heart attack

MARRIAGES

Lauren Bacall
4 Jul, *to* **Jason Robards**

"COOP" DEAD

Legendary screen star Gary Cooper died of cancer on 13 May, aged 60. Only last month he was honoured with a special Oscar by the Academy of Motion Picture Arts & Sciences, and rumours about his health began to spread after a tearful James Stewart collected the award on Cooper's behalf.

A major star since the early 1930s, tall and handsome Cooper, an expert at the slow delivery, embodied for many the American ideal. He won Oscars for his performances in *Sergeant York* (1941) and *High Noon* (1952) and recently finished work on a British-made thriller, *The Naked Edge*, with Deborah Kerr.

THE BIG GUN-DOWN

Stanley Baker, Anthony Quinn, David Niven and Gregory Peck in The Guns of Navarone.

The Guns of Navarone is the most spectacular war film since *The Bridge on the River Kwai* (1957). A star-studded cast, led by Gregory Peck, David Niven, Anthony Quinn, Stanley Baker, Anthony Quayle and James Darren, mounts a daring commando assault on the Greek island of Navarone in 1943 to destroy two giant radar-controlled guns which threaten the evacuation of 2,000 Allied troops from another nearby island. To add to the group's problems, it gradually becomes clear there's a traitor in their midst.

The film is produced and written by Carl Foreman, the writer of *High Noon* (1952), who was blacklisted during the McCarthy witch-hunts and, it is said, wrote the original screenplay for *Kwai*. Of his new CinemaScope and Technicolor picture he says, "It seems to me more than literary coincidence that Alastair MacLean's novel is set on the same stage as the legends of Jason and the Argonauts, and Theseus and the Minotaur, for this story tells of men who dare even the Gods."

The same could be said of the film-makers. Shot in Greece and at Pinewood Studios back in the UK, the $6 million production has tested everyone to the limit, with a last-minute scramble to make its royal première in late April. But it's set the box office alight, with two sequences in particular (a spectacular storm and the nail-biting climax in the gun cave) drawing great praise.

POOL GAMES

Meet Fast Eddie Felsen, a pool player who arrives in New York with one thought only – to beat the legendary Minnesota Fats. The first frames go badly for him and after he hustles another player he's beaten up and cared for by Sarah, a crippled, alcoholic.

Then Eddie is taken up by Bert Gordon, a professional gambler, who becomes his manager. They go down to Louisville where Eddie recovers his will to win, even if it destroys Sarah in the process. Now Eddie is ready to take on Minnesota Fats again.

Directed by Robert Rossen of *Body and Soul* (1947), *All the King's Men* (1949) and *Alexander the Great* (1956) fame, *The Hustler* looks set to provide another hit for star Paul Newman – no mean pool player himself – and gives Piper Laurie, as Sarah, and George C. Scott, as Gordon, superb supporting roles. And as Minnesota Fats there's hit TV comedian Jackie Gleason, who spent much of his own childhood in pool halls.

Paul Newman as pool shark Fast Eddie Felsen in The Hustler.

SHIRLEY TAKES A U-TURN

Shirley MacLaine has fizz and talent in spades and the critics adore her: the freckle-faced redhead can sing, act and dance.

Born in Virginia in 1934, she started dancing at the age of three and had her first major break in the theatre when she was understudying Carol Haney in the 1954 Broadway production of *The Pajama Game*. It was the Hollywood myth come true: a bigtime producer (Hal Wallis) was in the audience, and a screen test and starring role followed. That was in Hitchcock's *The Trouble with Harry* (1955), a box-office failure, but MacLaine had arrived (her wedding night was spent on the set).

She next made *Artists and Models* (1955), with Dean Martin and Jerry Lewis, and played a Hindu princess in Mike Todd's *Around the World in 80 Days* (1956). But it was as the sad-eyed floozie Ginny Moorhead, in *Some Came Running* (1958), and as the abused elevator operator Fran Kubelik, in *The Apartment* (1960), that she really came into her own, winning Oscar nominations for both.

Frank Sinatra, her co-star in *Some Came Running*, then insisted she play opposite him in the musical *Can-Can*. "MacLaine is bouncy, outgoing, scintillating, vivacious and appealing," said *Variety* last year. She's currently putting that reputation to the test with *Two Loves*, cast against type as a frigid American schoolteacher who gets amorous advances from handsome Laurence Harvey in rural New Zealand. So far Larry is having more luck than the box office.

Vincent Price and Barbara Steele in The Pit and the Pendulum.

SLICED HAM

Last year producer-director Roger Corman and American-International scored a box-office hit with Edgar Allen Poe's horror story *House of Usher*. They look like repeating the same business with *The Pit and the Pendulum*, another Poe story and again starring Vincent Price, who plays the evil Nicholas Medina as a nobleman who thinks he has accidentally buried his wife alive.

John Kerr, the juve lead in *South Pacific* (1958), arrives at Price's castle and eventually finds himself tied to a table above a deep pit. Above him a huge, razor-sharp pendulum swings. To his horror he realises that with every swing it gets closer.

Filmed in CinemaScope and colour, this is the 29th film Corman has directed in seven years. He specializes in speed (some of his movies took less than a week to shoot!) and in subjects likely appeal to the young, drive-in trade. He also seems to have noticed the success in Britain of Hammer Studios and its horror flicks like *Dracula* and *The Curse of Frankenstein*. Corman promises more until the appetite for gore runs out.

BOND ISSUE

British novelist Ian Fleming has sold the screen rights of his novels featuring secret agent James Bond. American producers Harry Saltzman and Albert R. Broccoli have optioned all of Fleming's novels with the exception of *Casino Royale*, which was made for American TV in 1955.

The deal guarantees Fleming $100,000 a film plus five per cent profit participation. First into production will be *Dr. No*, starring Scottish actor Sean Connery as Bond. He was chosen after David Niven, Richard Burton and Roger Moore were all considered for the part.

STAR QUOTES

Marilyn Monroe

"To put it bluntly, I seem to be a whole superstructure with no foundation . . . I'm working on the foundation."

STAR QUOTES

Billy Wilder

"I have never met anyone as utterly mean as Marilyn Monroe. Nor as utterly fabulous on screen."

TRUE BRIT

"He's a very, very bad actor, but he absolutely loves doing it," says David Niven of himself. That he enjoys it is evident in every performance Niven has given. That he is a very good actor is also evident.

Audiences love his easy charm and his utter Englishness. That's on display now in *The Guns of Navarone*, in which his Corporal Miller, an explosives expert, is always belly-aching, always feigning cowardice, but comes through at the end, a true hero.

Niven was born in 1909 and was set on an army career. But then he went to Canada and ended up in Hollywood because a friend told him he could make a living as an extra. That wasn't to be: he made a better living as a star, in swashbucklers like *The Prisoner of Zenda* (1937), dramas like *Wuthering Heights*, comedies like *Bachelor Mother* (both 1939) and, back in Britain, war movies like *The Way Ahead* (1944) and *A Matter of Life and Death* (1946).

The immediate post-war years seemed unkind to his career – unlike those of equally urbane contemporaries Cary Grant and Rex Harrison – but then he got the main role in *Around the World in 80 Days* (1956) and won a Best Actor Oscar for *Separate Tables* (1958), as a bogus army officer living in a drab seaside hotel.

It was the perfect role for him – a charade. As the veteran of more than 60 movies says: "Can you imagine being wonderfully paid for dressing up and playing games?"

SEPTEMBER
OCTOBER

NOVEMBER
DECEMBER

BOX OFFICE

UK

1 Swiss Family Robinson
2 The Magnificent Seven
3 Saturday Night and Sunday Morning

OTHER TOP BOX OFFICE FILMS

Carry on Regardless
G.I. Blues
One Hundred and One Dalmatians
The Parent Trap
Pollyanna
The Sundowners
Whistle Down the Wind

BOX OFFICE

US

1 The Guns of Navarone
2 The Absent Minded Professor
3 The Parent Trap
4 Swiss Family Robinson
5 Exodus
6 The World of Suzie Wong
7 The Alamo
8 Gone with the Wind (*reissue*)
9 One Hundred and One Dalmatians
10 Splendor in the Grass

AMERICA! AMERICA!

West Side Story is a new type of screen musical. Since the stage show opened at the Winter Garden, New York, on 26 September 1957, its blending of drama, music and dance has been hailed as a milestone in American musical theatre. Now movie critics will be saying the same thing about this $6 million, Panavision-70 motion-picture version.

The story, an updating of Shakespeare's *Romeo and Juliet*, is about the rivalry of two New York street gangs – the American "Jets" and Puerto Rican "Sharks" and how the former leader of the Jets, Tony, falls for Maria, sister of Sharks leader Bernardo. Co-directed by Robert Wise and Jerome Robbins, who choreographed and directed the stage production, the finger-snapping pulse of Leonard Bernstein's score and Stephen Sondheim's lyrics can now be heard in six-track Todd-AO sound.

A brilliant cast of young actors has been assembled – beautiful Natalie Wood as Maria, handsome Richard Beymer as Tony, pint-sized Russ Tamblyn as Jets leader Riff, sassy Rita Moreno as Bernardo's girlfriend, and flashing-eyed George Chakiris as Bernardo. Chakiris has actually changed sides for the Hollywood version – he played Riff in the London production.

Richard Beymer and Natalie Wood as the lovers in the film version of the hit musical West Side Story.

CLEO CRANKS UP AGAIN

20th Century-Fox's much-troubled *Cleopatra* re-started shooting on 25 September at Cinecitta studio in Rome under the direction of Joseph L. Mankiewicz, who is still re-writing the script and earning an estimated $1.5 million for his troubles. Elizabeth Taylor, whose illness shut down production in London last year, is getting more than $1 million for playing the Queen of the Nile.

Rex Harrison and Richard Burton have taken over from Peter Finch and Stephen Boyd as Caesar and Antony. The $14 million Todd-AO production is scheduled for a summer release next year.

BIRTHS, DEATHS AND MARRIAGES

BIRTHS

Scott Baio
22 Sep, New York

Meg Ryan
19 Nov, Bethel, Connecticut

Mariel Hemingway
22 Nov, Portland, Oregon

DEATHS

Marion Davies
22 Sep, Hollywood
Cancer

Chico Marx
11 Oct, Hollywood
Heart attack

SUMPTUOUS SOPHIA

Looking at Sophia Loren – which is something a lot of people like to do – it's hard to believe that she was a skinny kid living in the slum quarters of Naples. Her nickname was "*Stechetta*" – the stick. Skinny, but pretty, she entered a Miss Rome beauty contest at the age of 14 and came second. One of the judges was film producer Carlo Ponti, who set about filling her out, changing her name from Scicolone to Loren, and grooming her for international stardom.

Under Ponti's guidance, she was an Italian movie star by 1954 and started making American pictures in Europe a few years later – *Boy on a Dolphin*, *The Pride and the Passion*, with Cary Grant and Frank Sinatra, and *Legend of the Lost*, shot in Libya with John Wayne. All three appeared in 1957; and somehow, Loren and Ponti found time to marry the same year.

Now hailed as a sex goddess, she makes movies in Hollywood and Britain. This year has been a busy one for her: early on she starred in *Two Women* and received rave reviews from the critics as the woman bringing up her daughter in war-torn Italy. Then came *The Millionairess*, a comedy with Peter Sellers. And now she plays the sumptuous Chimene in *El Cid*, more than holding her own against Charlton Heston and hordes of extras.

Sophia Loren as Chimene, first the sweetheart then the wife of Rodrigo Diaz, otherwise known as El Cid.

Dirk Bogarde as a barrister with homosexual leanings in Victim.

DIRK'S QUIRK

Victim has opened in the middle of a London heatwave but that hasn't prevented people from queueing up from lunchtime to see this landmark film. Its controversial subject is homosexuality and its star is Dirk Bogarde, Britain's best-loved matinee idol, famous for light comedy roles such as the *Doctor* series.

Victim is a colossal departure for Bogarde: he plays a barrister, Meville Farr, whose homosexual leanings are known to his wife (Sylvia Sim) but become public when he is blackmailed over a youth who has committed suicide. Produced and directed by the team of Michael Relph and Basil Dearden, whose 1959 film *Sapphire* dealt with colour prejudice, *Victim* is crusading cinema.

The movie argues for a change in the British law on homosexuality because it leaves practitioners open to blackmail (the producers claim that 90 per cent of U.K. blackmail cases involve "queers"). Homosexuality is illegal and punishable by a jail sentence. Whether or not the film succeeds in changing the law remains to be seen; but Bogarde's career can never be the same again.

HELLO, YOUNG LOVER!

People are already labelling him the new James Dean for his moody young lover, opposite Natalie Wood, in *Splendor in the Grass*. But boyish Warren Beatty, 24, seems to be taking sudden stardom in his stride. He's got a contract to do several more pictures with director Elia Kazan, but that's all. Says Beatty: "I would prefer not to get committed for too many films. Somebody who goes under long-term contract now will still be under contract in 1968, by which time I think the movie industry will have undergone great changes."

He's the younger brother (by three years) of Shirley MacLaine, and owes much of his present success to playwright William Inge. When in stock in New Jersey he was spotted by Inge and director Joshua Logan and tested for *Parrish*, in the part later played by Troy Donahue under another director. After a further false start into movies, he was cast by Inge in his play *A Loss of Roses* (1959) on Broadway.

Now he's setting female hearts fluttering in the Inge-scripted *Splendor in the Grass*, a tale of thwarted sexual passion among young lovers in late 1920s Kansas. Later this year he'll be seen in a very different guise, as a handsome young gigolo in *The Roman Spring of Mrs Stone*, with Vivien Leigh. Virginia-born Beatty, who was a whizz on the football field in his schooldays, is also said to be quite a whizz off-screen with the girls. But ask him about his role in *Roman Spring* and all you get is: "I'm really playing the opposite of what I did in *Splendor*. It's like a field where you plant one thing one year and the next you have to plant something else."

Rising star Warren Beatty.

HISTORY INTO LEGEND

He was Rodrigo Diaz de Bivar, an 11th-century knight whose courage knew no bounds. While the Spanish royal family were in dispute with each other, Rodrigo gathered an army to help defend his beloved Spain against the Islamic hordes from the coast of Africa. The Moors, his greatest enemies, called him *El Cid* – the lord.

Independent producer Samuel Bronston has brought this stirring epic tale to the 70mm Super Technirama screen. Charlton Heston stars as El Cid and Sophia Loren plays his lady Chimene. Directed by Anthony Mann, the giant production is backed by years of historical research into a character whose life is difficult to disentangle from myth.

Filmed in Spain and in studios near Rome, *El Cid* involved 10,000 authentic costumes, $40,000 worth of jewellery, $150,000 worth of 11th-century artefacts, a full-scale reconstruction of the cathedral of Burgos and a monumental wooden gate that marks the entrance to the besieged city of Valencia. This is the setting for the memorable final sequence as the Cid rides out of the gates of history into legend.

Before that, Mann was in charge of 2,200 extras, 15 towering war machines and 35 Moorish ships for the ferocious final battle. Producer Bronston later donated the gates to the township of Peniscola, the film's location, where they remain today.

Charlton Heston in the lead role of El Cid.

Peter Lawford and Richard Todd as British paratroopers in The Longest Day.

ZANUCK'S D-DAY

D-Day is being fought all over again – and this time Darryl F. Zanuck's in charge. The cigar-chomping mogul, who in 1957 left 20th Century-Fox, the studio he helped to create in the 1930s, is currently re-creating the momentous day of 6 June 1944 when the Allies launched their massive armada and invaded the beaches of Normandy.

Turning this event into a motion picture is requiring 50 international stars, some 10,000 extras, 31 locations in France and innumerable studio sets, 48 technical advisors, enough planes, tanks and ships to start another war, and $10 million. All this makes *The Longest Day* the most expensive black-and-white film ever made.

Ken Annakin, Andrew Marton and Bernhard Wicki are responsible for directing the British, American and German sections respectively, but Zanuck uses a helicopter to visit the separate units, often more than 100 miles apart, and takes the opportunity to film scenes from the air. "This is my picture," he says. "When one wants to take the credit for something one must also take the responsibility. I don't mind the hard work. There is plenty of compensation in the pride one can feel when it's all over."

The result won't be on screens until the end of the year – after a world premiere in Paris – but you can bet Zanuck will sound the call to arms in good time.

THE FILM THAT STOPPED THE SUN

"Now, Barabbas was a robber." That's all the Bible says of the man who was freed instead of Christ that day in Jerusalem. But Swedish novelist Par Lagerkvist became intrigued by this mysterious man – saint or sinner and cast into historical limbo. Now *Barabbas* is a spectacular epic movie starring Anthony Quinn in the title role.

The Italian-made movie is drawing crowds in Rome, and will open in London this summer. Produced by Dino De Laurentiis, written by British playwright Christopher Fry, directed by Richard Fleischer and co-starring Silvana Mangano, Vittorio Gassman and Jack Palance as a blood-crazed gladiator, *Barabbas* will surprise audiences with its dark subject matter and its unusual levels of violence.

The arena scenes were shot over several weeks in the perfectly preserved amphitheatre in Verona; but for the equally stunning Crucifixion sequence, director Fleischer had only 20 minutes to get his shots. *Barabbas* started filming on 15 February 1961 when there was a total eclipse of the sun, against which Fleischer had decided to stage the key scene. No wonder wags nicknamed it "The Film That Stopped The Sun".

Silvana Mangano and Anthony Quinn in Barabbas.

SWAMPLAND SEX

American critics are calling it "amoral" and "brutal", and it's certain to be scissored if it's ever shown in more conservative countries like Britain. *Cape Fear* is a striking shocker which, like Alfred Hitchcock's *Psycho* (1960), is setting moviegoers' nerve ends on edge. And like Hitch's miniature masterpiece, it makes the most of being shot in black-and-white.

Taken from John D. MacDonald's novel *The Executioner* (serialized in magazines), it stars Robert Mitchum as a sadistic ex-convict who terrorizes a small-town Georgia lawyer (Gregory Peck), his wife (Polly Bergen) and teenage daughter (Lori Martin). Peck had testified against him eight years earlier, and now Mitchum is out for revenge.

First he poisons their dog, then rapes Peck's daughter (hints of forced sodomy); and there's nothing the law can do unless Peck puts the girl on the witness stand. But finally the worm turns: Peck sets a trap at their up-country swampland retreat, and the scene is set for the terrifying climax.

The director is actually a Briton, but one with much experience of nailbiters. He's J. Lee Thompson, 47, responsible for everything from last year's epic *The Guns of Navarone* to the Second World War drama *Ice Cold in Alex* (1958) and Hayley Mills' starring debut, *Tiger Bay* (1959). Says Thompson: "In *Cape Fear* I haven't tried to show any sympathy for the villain. He's a cut-and-dried black, no white, no shades at all. What interested me was the problem of parents whose daughter is raped. Do they or don't they accuse the rapist, because he will deny the crime. The film is told in thriller terms pure and simple, but it was that kernel, that idea, that enthralled me. The law is impersonal. The law doesn't have any feelings."

NO DUMB BLONDE

Says Shelley Winters: "It's not merely talent that brings good films your way in Hollywood. It's being noticed and talked about. So I discussed it with my press agent and quite cold-bloodedly we invented this personality – a dumb blonde with a body and a set of sayings."

Good films have always come Winters' way and so have awards and rave reviews. She's been acting in movies since 1943 but only when she played a waitress who was strangled by Ronald Colman, in *A Double Life* (1948), did she make a real impact. Her talent was firmly established in *A Place in the Sun* (1951), when she played a pregnant girl drowned by Montgomery Clift. She was drowned again by Robert Mitchum in Charles Laughton's eerie *Night of the Hunter* (1955) and won a Best Supporting Actress Oscar for *The Diary of Anne Frank* (1959).

Her latest role is in Stanley Kubrick's long-awaited film of *Lolita* (due out this summer) in which she plays the nymphet's mother, Charlotte Haze. Says Winters: "Kubrick wants me to look glamorous but I'm fighting it. The author, Vladimir Nabokov, said I was ideal for the role and I think I should play it looking a bit dowdy. This girl who plays Lolita – Sue Lyon – is gorgeous, a sort of young Bardot. I could murder her. Dammit, she makes me look like Marjorie Main."

FAIR PRICE FOR FAIR LADY?

Jack Warner, chairman of Warners, has bought the screen rights of the hit 1956 stage musical *My Fair Lady* for a record $5.5 million. Warner, who will personally produce the picture, hopes the Lerner & Loewe musical will do for his studio what *West Side Story* (1961) has done for United Artists' coffers. Insiders suggest that putting *My Fair Lady* on the screen will cost more than $15 million, making a profit far from certain.

Warner is said to favour Cary Grant as Professor Higgins over Rex Harrison, who has made the role his own on stage. A question mark also hangs over stage star Julie Andrews' suitability as the screen Eliza.

KANE TOPS CRITICS' POLL

Orson Welles' 1941 production of *Citizen Kane* has topped a poll of 100 international film critics conducted by the specialist British film magazine *Sight and Sound*. *Kane*, one of only two American films cited, narrowly beat Michelangelo Antonioni's *L'Avventura* (Italy, 1960) to claim the title of the greatest film ever made.

The other 10 top entries were *La regle du jeu* (France, 1939), *Greed* (U.S.A., 1924), *Ugetsu monogatari* (Japan, 1953), *The Battleship Potemkin* (U.S.S.R., 1925), *Bicycle Thieves* (Italy 1949), *Ivan the Terrible* (U.S.S.R., 1943-6), *La terra trema* (Italy, 1948) and *L'Atalante* (France, 1933).

Richard Beymer (left) is the hero of Hemingway's Adventures of a Young Man.

A NEW MONTY CLIFT?

"He is taller, but in many ways he is like young Montgomery Clift. He has a convincing naturalness," says director George Stevens of Richard Beymer. Stevens cast Beymer as Peter in *The Diary of Anne Frank* (1959) and the actor went on to star as Tony in the Oscar-winning *West Side Story* (1961).

Beymer seems to have it made: he left his hometown in Iowa at the age of 14 and arrived in Los Angeles for what he thought was a screen test for a commercial. Instead he was offered not only the role of Jennifer Jones' nephew in *Indiscretions of an American Wife* (1954), shot in Italy with Clift, but also a contract with Jones' husband, legendary producer David O. Selznick. In fact, Beymer was the last Selznick contract player: the producer wound down his studio, leaving Beymer to co-star as Jane Wyman's piano playing protege in *So Big* (1953), directed by *West Side Story*'s Robert Wise.

Since his demanding dance and dramatic work in the musical, the lanky, quietly intense actor has been seen in the comedy *Bachelor Flat* (1961), with Tuesday Weld and Terry-Thomas, and will be seen this summer in his most demanding dramatic role to date, as Nick Adams, the autobiographical hero of Ernest Hemingway's *Adventures of a Young Man*. Meanwhile, he's currently dodging the bullets in Darryl F. Zanuck's blockbuster *The Longest Day*, due out this winter.

STAR QUOTES

Paul Newman

"Acting is a question of absorbing other people's personalities and some of your own experience."

ACADEMY AWARDS

PRESENTED ON 9 APRIL 1962

Best Picture
West Side Story

Best Director
Robert Wise and Jerome Robbins
West Side Story

Best Actor
Maximilian Schell
Judgment at Nuremberg

Best Actress
Sophia Loren
Two Women

Best Sup Actor
George Chakiris
West Side Story

Best Sup Actress
Rita Moreno
West Side Story

BIRTHS, DEATHS AND MARRIAGES

DEATHS

Michael Curtiz
10 Apr, Hollywood
Cancer

Louise Fazenda
17 Apr, Beverly Hills
Cerebral haemorrhage

MARRIAGES

Rex Harrison
22 Mar, *to* **Rachel Roberts**

KISS AND TELL

James Mason and Sue Lyon in Stanley Kubrick's adaptation of Vladimir Nabokov's novel *Lolita*.

"How did they ever make a film of *Lolita?*" ask the posters of Stanley Kubrick's new film. Paedophilia is, of course, a controversial subject, and Vladimir Nabokov's 1960 novel caused headlines all around the world.

In the film James Mason plays Humbert Humbert, a university professor who moves to a new town and finds lodgings with the widowed Mrs Haze (Shelley Winters). Her 12-year-old daughter, Lolita, immediately catches Humbert's eye and he even marries Mrs Haze to keep Lolita near him. When Mrs Haze dies he takes Lolita away with him but tragedy looms: his relationship cannot be kept a secret and a famous writer, Clare Quilty, is also taking an interest in the beautiful young girl.

To make the film Kubrick went to England where censorship codes on sex are more relaxed than in America and where the Catholic Legion of Decency is unknown. He's also added humour to the story, notably by casting Peter Sellers as Quilty who, in the course of the story, adopts several hilarious disguises.

But the biggest problem for Kubrick was casting Lolita. After several actresses were considered, including Britain's leading juvenile Hayley Mills, he finally plumped for 15-year-old American Sue Lyon. Will this film do for her what *Baby Doll* (1956) did for Carroll Baker?

JOAN AND BETTE – FACE TO FACE!

Two of the cinema's greatest legends, Bette Davis and Joan Crawford, finally star together in *What Ever Happened to Baby Jane?* It promises to be the most sensational inside look at Hollywood since *Sunset Blvd.* way back in 1950.

Baby Jane was a child star in the old days of Hollywood until her sister, Blanche, forced her out of the limelight. Now, some 30 years later, the ageing hams live in a mutual hell in a shuttered mansion. Uptight Blanche (Crawford) is confined to a wheelchair while whisky-sodden Jane (Davis) serves her rats for dinner.

For producer-director Robert Aldrich, it's a second searing look at his own industry: he directed *The Big Knife* (1955), a fictional story about Columbia boss Harry Cohn, and previously worked with Crawford in *Autumn Leaves* (1956).

Bette Davis and Joan Crawford in *What Ever Happened to Baby Jane?*

Rumours are that Crawford and Davis upstaged each other just as much off-screen as on. Whatever the truth, it'll certainly draw the crowds when it's released later this year. And don't be late – Warners is planning not to let anyone in after the shocker has started.

Joan Crawford.

NATALIE GROWS UP

One of Hollywood's most beautiful stars, Natalie Wood made her screen debut at the age of five, in *Happy Land* (1943), shot in Santa Rosa where she lived. It was a tiny role but she impressed director Irving Pichel, who cast her three years later in *Tomorrow Is Forever*, with Orson Welles and Claudette Colbert.

While she never rose to the heights of Shirley Temple or Judy Garland, she disproves the adage that child stars never make it past their second set of teeth. In 1954 she won an Oscar nomination for her moving portrayal of adolescence in *Rebel without a Cause* (1955) opposite James Dean, and then played the girl kidnapped by Indians in John Ford's western *The Searchers* (1956).

A year later she married actor Robert Wagner, who co-starred with her in *All the Fine Young Cannibals* (1960). She starred as Maria in *West Side Story* (1961), adding dancing to her acting talents (but not singing – her voice there was dubbed by Marni Nixon) and the same year co-starred with newcomer Warren Beatty in *Splendor in the Grass*.

America has watched Natalie Wood grow up from a virtual toddler, and this autumn audiences will see her throwing off the vestiges of childhood forever. In fact, she throws everything off - she plays notorious stripper Gypsy Rose Lee the lavish screen version of the 1959 hit musical *Gypsy*, by Jule Styne and Stephen Sondheim, with Rosalind Russell in the role Ethel Merman created on Broadway.

John Kitzmiller, Ursula Andress and Sean Connery in Dr. No.

LICENCE TO THRILL

"My name is Bond . . . James Bond." Moviegoers hear these words for the first time in *Dr. No*. But probably not for the last. Ian Fleming's 1957 secret agent novel was his sixth, and the Eton-educated former Intelligence officer and journalist said he wrote his first, *Casino Royale*, to alleviate the shock of getting married at the age of 44.

His hero, James Bond, code-number 007 (licensed to kill), was named after an ornithologist whose book *Birds of the West Indies* is one of Fleming's favourites. British critics have summarized Fleming's novels as dealing with "sex, sadism and snobbery," a formula Fleming does not intend to change.

Bond is always sent out by his boss, "M", to do battle with the KGB or SMERSH and defeat megalomaniacal villains with names like Dr. No or Auric Goldfinger. The novels were not immediate best-sellers but Fleming received a boost in 1960 when President Kennedy named *From Russia, with Love* as one of his 10 favourite novels.

The wait for a movie James Bond has been a long one. But the producers found Scottish actor Sean Connery who, Fleming says, is "an absolute corker." Bond is sent from London to Jamaica to investigate a murder and ends up the prisoner of Dr. No (Joseph Wiseman), who is playing havoc with American space launches.

Directed by Terence Young, it's an ultra-modern thriller with deliberate echoes of the Cuban missile crisis. Fans of the novel may be disappointed that the giant squid has been dropped but they'll surely be delighted with curvaceous Swiss-German newcomer Ursula Andress, 26, who keeps Bond firmly on the job.

CINERAMA SPINS YARNS

M-G-M and Cinerama have unveiled *The Wonderful World of the Brothers Grimm*, the first story film in the Cinerama process. Until now the giant three-screen system has been used only for feature-length travelogues. The lavish fairy tale, directed by George Pal, bowed at the Cooper Theater in Denver, Colorado on 14 July. However, M-G-M seem to be placing more confidence in *How the West Was Won*, an all-star western also filmed in Cinerama, which will open before *Grimm* in major cities in the United States and abroad.

BIRTHS, DEATHS AND MARRIAGES

BIRTHS

Danny Huston
14 May, Rome

Ally Sheedy
13 Jun, New York

Tom Cruise
3 Jul, Syracuse, New York

Matthew Broderick
21 Aug, New York

DEATHS

Frank Borzage
19 Jun, Hollywood
Cancer

Marilyn Monroe
5 Aug, Hollywood
Overdose of barbiturates

Hoot Gibson
23 Aug, Woodland Hills, California
Cancer

MARRIAGES

Jack Lemmon
17 Aug, *to* Felicia Farr

MONROE DEAD

Screen goddess Marilyn Monroe was found dead from an overdose of barbiturates at her rented Brentwood, California, home in the early hours of 5 August. She was 36. Her naked body was found in bed by two doctors who had been alerted by a worried housekeeper. She had recently been fired by 20th Century-Fox from the production of *Something's Got to Give*.

Famous for her unpredictability and unpunctuality, the voluptuous actress-singer rose from a difficult childhood and an early marriage to be a model before her screen debut in 1948. She signed with Fox in 1952 and starred in several hits, including *Gentlemen Prefer Blondes*, *How to Marry a Millionaire* (both 1953), *The Seven Year Itch* (1955) and *Some Like It Hot* (1959).

She married baseball star Joe DiMaggio in 1952 amd then playwright Arthur Miller in 1956, following a year in which she abandoned Hollywood for the Actors' Studio in New York. Miller scripted her last completed film, *The Misfits* (1961), in which she co-starred with Clark Gable and Montgomery Clift. She'd been undergoing psychoanalysis since her divorce from Miller.

SEPTEMBER
OCTOBER

NOVEMBER
DECEMBER

HAWKINS IS YOUR MAN!

When *Lawrence of Arabia* was in pre-production it was announced that Cary Grant would play General Allenby and Jack Hawkins would play Colonel Newcombe. As it has turned out, Hawkins plays Allenby and no one plays Newcombe. But director David Lean reckons Hawkins gives his best-ever screen performance as the ruthless British general.

Hauling himself up through the ranks of British cinema since his debut in 1930, gravel-voiced Hawkins, 52, has had a lot of dress rehearsals for the role, notably in Lean's *The Bridge on the River Kwai* (1957), in which he played the neurotic commando, and in *The Cruel Sea* (1953), as a tormented corvette and destroyer captain. If you need a wonderfully expressive voice in an officer's uniform – even a Roman officer's tunic for *Ben-Hur* (1959) – Hawkins is your man, Sir!

LEGEND OF THE DESERT

Peter O'Toole as Lawrence and Anthony Quinn as Arab leader Auda Abu Tayi in Lawrence of Arabia.

"I deem him one of the greatest beings alive in our time. I fear whatever our need we shall never see his like again." So wrote Winston Churchill after the death in 1935 of T. E. Lawrence, known to the world as Lawrence of Arabia.

The legend and controversies surrounding Lawrence's life remain equally potent today; and they're likely to rage even more after the release of the Sam Spiegel-David Lean production of *Lawrence of Arabia*. The $15 million epic, three years in the making, is the most eagerly awaited event in a long time. It stars Alex Guinness as Prince Feisal, Jack Hawkins as General Allenby, and a roster of well-known names like Anthony Quinn, Arthur Kennedy and Anthony Quayle. In the title role, and his first starring part, is lanky, Irish-born Peter O'Toole, 30. And as his Arab friend Sherif Ali is Omar Sharif, well-known to moviegoers in his native Egypt and expected now to become a major star.

Lean's previous film, the Oscar-winning *Bridge on the River Kwai* (1957), took seven months to film in the jungles of Ceylon. For *Lawrence*, Lean took his Super Panavision-70 cameras to regions never before seen in a motion picture – the spectacular deserts of Jordan where Lawrence fought his campaigns during the First World War. Word is, there's never been a screen epic like *Lawrence of Arabia*. And we may, perhaps, never see its like again.

STAR QUOTES

Marlon Brando

"Acting is the expression of a neurotic impulse. It's a bum's life. Quitting acting, that's the sign of maturity."

LAUGHTON DEAD

Rotund British actor Charles Laughton died of cancer, in a Hollywood hospital on 15 December, aged 63. He was about to start work in Billy Wilder's *Irma La Douce* and had recently played King Lear on stage at Stratford-upon-Avon.

By no means the popular image of a movie star, Yorkshire-born Laughton's outsized talent made him one. Long remembered for his portrayals of Henry VIII, Captain Bligh and the Hunchback of Notre Dame, Laughton also directed the critically esteemed *Night of the Hunter* in 1955. His most recent screen appearances were as wily old senators in both *Spartacus* (1960) and *Advise and Consent* (1961). He had been married to British-born actress Elsa Lanchester since 1929; the couple had moved to the United States in 1934, becoming American citizens in 1950.

FROM WARNERS TO PEPSI

A major star since the 1930s, Joan Crawford shows no signs of letting up in *What Ever Happened to Baby Jane?*, the Gothic melodrama in which she finally co-stars with her old Warners rival Bette Davis. There was no arguing over top billing. "Bette gets it of course," Crawford told Hedda Hopper. "She plays the title role. No question about it."

Crawford, who joined Warners after leaving M-G-M in 1943, left the studio in 1951 and went independent. In 1956 she married her fourth husband, Pepsi-Cola chairman Alfred Steele; when he died in 1959, she was left to take an active role in the soft-drink company's affairs. Although she travels the world promoting Pepsi, she continues to star in movies, although few of them match her earlier achievements. *Baby Jane*, though, looks like it's attracting old fans as well as new ones. And for all of them she's just published her autobiography, *A Portrait of Joan*.

BIRTHS, DEATHS AND MARRIAGES

BIRTHS

Kristy McNichol
11 Sep, Los Angeles

Vincent Spano
18 Oct, New York

Cary Elwes
26 Oct, London

Ralph Macchio
4 Nov, Long Island, New York

Lori Singer
6 Nov, Corpus Christi, Texas

Demi Moore
11 Nov, Roswell, New Mexico

Jodie Foster
19 Nov, Los Angeles

Andrew McCarthy
29 Nov, Westfield, New Jersey

DEATHS

Tod Browning
6 Oct, Hollywood
Cancer

Charles Laughton
15 Dec, Hollywood
Cancer

Thomas Mitchell
17 Dec, Santa Monica, California
Cancer

MARRIAGES

Janet Leigh
15 Sep, *to* Robert Brant

Sean Connery
30 Nov, *to* **Diane Cilento**

BOUNTY SAILS AGAIN

Richard Harris, Marlon Brando and Trevor Howard in Mutiny on the Bounty.

In 1935 it was Clark Gable and Charles Laughton. Now, in M-G-M's lavish, much-fraught remake of *Mutiny on the Bounty*, it's Marlon Brando as mutineer Fletcher Christian and Trevor Howard as the sadistic Captain Bligh. British actor Richard Harris plays mutineer Mills and Tahitian beauty Tarita plays Princess Miamiti who captures Christian's love during the crew's sojourn in Tahiti.

Not a little of the vast $19.5 million budget was spent on HMS *Bounty* herself. The ship – at 118 feet long, 33 feet longer than the original vessel – was built at the Smith & Rhuland shipyard in Nova Scotia. It was launched in February 1960 and made a 7,327-mile voyage to the film's South Pacific locations in Tahiti and Bora Bora.

The original *Bounty* was burned by the mutineers after they had settled on Pitcairn Island, their remote and mis-charted refuge where their descendants still live. The new *Bounty* is to tour the world to promote the film and will then be moored permanently in St. Petersburg, Florida.

BOX OFFICE

UK

1 The Guns of Navarone
2 The Young Ones
3 Dr. No
4 Only Two Can Play

OTHER TOP BOX OFFICE FILMS

Carry on Cruising
Blue Hawaii
The Comancheros
A Kind of Loving
The Road to Hong Kong
That Touch of Mink

BOX OFFICE

US

1 Spartacus
2 West Side Story
3 Lover Come Back
4 That Touch of Mink
5 El Cid
6 The Music Man
7 King of Kings
8 Hatari!
9 Flower Drum Song
10 The Interns

LONG CLIMB TO THE TOP

People could be forgiven for thinking that Laurence Harvey's rise has been meteoric. He was the social-climbing Joe Lampton in *Room at the Top* (1959) and then went straight to Hollywood to play alongside John Wayne in the epic *The Alamo* (1960). He went back to England for *The Long and the Short and the Tall* (1961) and back to Hollywood for *Walk on the Wild Side, The Wonderful World of the Brothers Grimm* and *The Manchurian Candidate*, all released this year.

Meteoric? Possibly, except that Harvey has been making pictures since 1948. His tall, high-cheekboned looks give only a clue to his background: despite that chipped, British voice he was actually born in Lithuania to Jewish parents who moved to South Africa. At 14 he lied about his age and tried enlisting in the navy. He had better luck the following year when he made his stage debut with the Johannesburg Repertory Theatre. After military service in the Second World War he resumed acting in England, scoring a major success in *Henry V* at the Old Vic in 1958 and on tour in the United States.

He had already starred in several pictures; all he needed was a real breakthrough. That was *Room at the Top*. For Harvey, there clearly is, even if it's been a long climb.

Frank Sinatra and Laurence Harvey (standing) get the brainwashing treatment in The Manchurian Candidate.

HUMAN TIME-BOMB

Sergeant Raymond Shaw is a hero. He returns from the Korean War and is awarded a Congressional Medal of Honor. His mother and step-father, a U.S. senator, are inordinately proud. But Raymond has other things on his mind. In Korea, he and other members of his platoon have been brainwashed; programmed for an assassination, he is a bomb waiting to go off.

So too is *The Manchurian Candidate*, John Frankenheimer's latest film. It's based on Richard Condon's best-selling novel and is loaded with star-power. Laurence Harvey is Shaw, Angela Lansbury his mother, John Gregory is the senator, and Frank Sinatra is Major Marco, a member of Raymond's platoon whose brainwashing has been only partially successful.

Says Frankenheimer: "I wanted to do a picture that showed how ludicrous the whole McCarthy Far Right Syndrome was and how dangerous the Far Left syndrome is. I think our society is brainwashed by television commercials, by politicians, by censored press with its biased reporting. More and more I think our society is being manipulated and controlled."

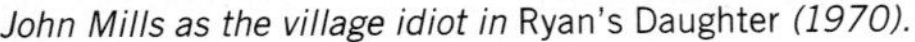

John Mills as the village idiot in Ryan's Daughter *(1970).*

David Niven as Phileas Fogg in Around the World in 80 Days *(1956).*

HIGH, WIDE & HANDSOME

Cinerama, Technirama, VistaVision, CinemaScope, Cinemiracle, Todd-AO, Dyaliscope, Camera-65, Panavision, Super-Panavision 70, Ultra-Panavision . . . these names were to be found on movie posters throughout the 1950s and 1960s. Inside the cinemas, the screens were growing ever wider, ever higher, ever more deeply curved and the sound came at you from all directions.

Hollywood's obsession with telling their stories on bigger screens was nothing new. As far back as 1900 pioneer photographer Louis Lumiere projected pictures on a 63 × 45-ft (19 × 14-metre) screen and in 1927 French director Abel Gance predated Cinerama for the triple-panel final sequences of his epic *Napoleon*. In the 1930s, Fox studio (later 20th Century-Fox) developed a process called Grandeur for a John Wayne western, *The Big Trail* (1930).

The problem in those days was to persuade cinema owners to instal large screens only a few years after they had wired their theatres for sound. Wide screens were really just a gimmick, better suited to the fun-fair. There was the same attitude in the early 1950s. Cinerama, first shown publicly in 1952, required special theatres, able to house the giant curved screen, the three 35mm projection booths and the six-track magnetic stereo sound system. In 1953 20th Century-Fox introduced CinemaScope with *The Robe* which required magnetic sound and a wide screen but only one projector. Paramount's rival system, VistaVision, originally needed equipment which ran the film horizontally.

The new medium television began making serious inroads on cinema attendances and wide screens seemed one way of luring them back. Of course, stories had to be found to fill the vast

on (1970), George C. Scott, lands in Sicily.

John Wayne in The Big Trail *(1930).*

Jean Simmons and Richard Burton in The Robe *(1953).*

The epic story and desert locations of Lawrence of Arabia's *(1962) suited the wide screen; it was filmed in Super-Panavision.*

expanses and the answer was historical epics, lavish war films, westerns and musicals.

The benefits to audiences came in 1956 when 65mm negative film was used to shoot *Around the World in 80 Days*. The 70mm projection prints (the extra 5mm was used for the soundtrack), produced a sharper and richer image that was almost three-dimensional (3-D itself was a three-year wonder of the early 1950s).

Throughout the late 1950s and the 1960s films such as *Ben-Hur* (1959), *El Cid* (1961), *Lawrence of Arabia, Mutiny on the Bounty* (both 1962), *The Sound of Music* (1965), *2001: A Space Odyssey* (1968) and *Patton* (1970) owed much of their impact to being shot in a variety of 65mm processes.

But there were disadvantages for filmmakers. The cameras were heavy and expensive, adding several hundred thousand dollars to production costs. At the same time, many 70mm blockbusters lost millions at the box-office and the general trend was moving towards smaller films. By this time, Hollywood had also conquered the television threat by buying it: every major studio now had its own TV affiliate.

The last major feature to be shot entirely on 65mm negative was David Lean's *Ryan's Daughter* (1970). Even 35mm widescreen – generally known as Panavision – is a rarity today because of the financial involvement of TV, video and cable stations. It is debatable whether movies are getting better or worse. But they have certainly got smaller, as the re-issues of *Lawrence of Arabia* and *Spartacus* (1960) in their original formats proved. And it may well be that *Lawrence* has brought about the second coming of 70mm. Big screens will always be a part of the magic of the movies, as shown by the international success of the Canadian IMAX system – a giant screen that towers in front of and *above* the audience.

BLOCKBUSTING CHUCK

Charlton Heston's latest role – his 25th – as Major Matt Lewis in *55 Days in Peking*, is quite unlike his previous Ben-Hur or El Cid. "After spending all of last winter in armour it's a great relief to wear a costume that bends," he quips about the stirring epic of the 1900 Boxer Rebellion in China.

But his portrayal of the marine who, with David Niven, holds out against impossible odds, proves once again that Heston is a star – possibly the only star – who fits the demands of the international blockbuster. It takes an actor of rare talent and physical stature not to be overwhelmed by thousands of extras and towering sets. Heston is exactly that.

He was born in Illinois in 1924 and began his career on Chicago radio and then on Broadway. After his screen debut in *Dark City* (1950) he became a star in his second picture, Cecil B. DeMille's circus spectacular *The Greatest Show on Earth* (1952). His second film for DeMille, *The Ten Commandments* (1956), in which he played Moses, was followed by Orson Welles' dark thriller *Touch of Evil* and the epic western *The Big Country* (both 1958). The director of the latter, William Wyler, then cast him in the title role of *Ben-Hur* (1959), for which he won a Best Actor Oscar.

Heston is currently on location for George Stevens' *The Greatest Story Ever Told* in which he plays another key historical role, that of John the Baptist. Rumour is, he's even directed one of his scenes himself. A presage of things to come?

ANCIENT ROME RISES TO FALL

Construction has finished on what is believed to be the largest single set ever built for a motion picture. It's the Roman Forum, designed by Veniero Colasanti and John Moore for producer Samuel Bronston's *The Fall of the Roman Empire*. The set stands on a 55-acre site outside Madrid and measures 1,312 x 754 feet, rises to a height of 260 feet and includes 27 full-sized buildings, 601 marble columns and 350 statues. Bronston plans to use the set as a tourist attraction after filming is completed.

ACADEMY AWARDS

PRESENTED ON 8 APRIL 1963

Best Picture
Lawrence of Arabia

Best Director
David Lean
Lawrence of Arabia

Best Actor
Gregory Peck
To Kill a Mockingbird

Best Actress
Anne Bancroft
The Miracle Worker

Best Sup Actor
Ed Begley
Sweet Bird of Youth

Best Sup Actress
Patty Duke
The Miracle Worker

Tippi Hedren is attacked in The Birds, *Alfred Hitchcock's adaptation of a Daphne du Maurier short story.*

PECKING ORDER

The Birds is unlike anything Alfred Hitchcock has done before: he set himself a technical challenge that many would have given up long before a foot of film was exposed.

The story is set in the picturesque community of Bodega Bay, north of San Francisco, where Rod Taylor, a lawyer, lives with his mother and young sister. New Hitchcock discovery, former TV model Tippi Hedren, meets Taylor in a bird shop and on impulse takes two small lovebirds to his home as a gift. For no apparent reason, a seagull swoops down on blonde Hedren and draws blood. That's just the beginning: eventually there are thousands of birds, attacking helpless school children, invading people's homes and causing many deaths.

The story caused innumerable technical problems which Hitchcock and his team solved in a variety of ways. Some scenes involve back projection, others animation, and still others remarkably lifelike mechanical birds. But for the scene in which Hedren is brutally attacked in a small room, real birds were tied to her body. Speaking of his characters, portly Hitch says: "They are the victims of Judgment Day. I felt that after *Psycho* people would expect something to top it."

BIRTHS, DEATHS AND MARRIAGES

BIRTHS

Jason Connery
11 Jan, London

DEATHS

Jack Carson
2 Jan, Encino, California

Dick Powell
3 Jan, Hollywood
Cancer

John Farrow
28 Jan, Beverly Hills
Heart attack

MARRIAGES

Tony Curtis
8 Feb, *to* Christine Kaufmann

ROBERTSON AS J.F.K.

Cliff Robertson is playing President Kennedy in Warners' dramatization of J.F.K.'s wartime exploits in the Pacific. Highlight of the drama is when Kennedy's boat, *PT 109*, is sliced in two by a Japanese destroyer. Robertson got the role after Kennedy's own choice – Warren Beatty – turned it down. Handsome Beatty drew accusations of arrogance and lack of patriotism.

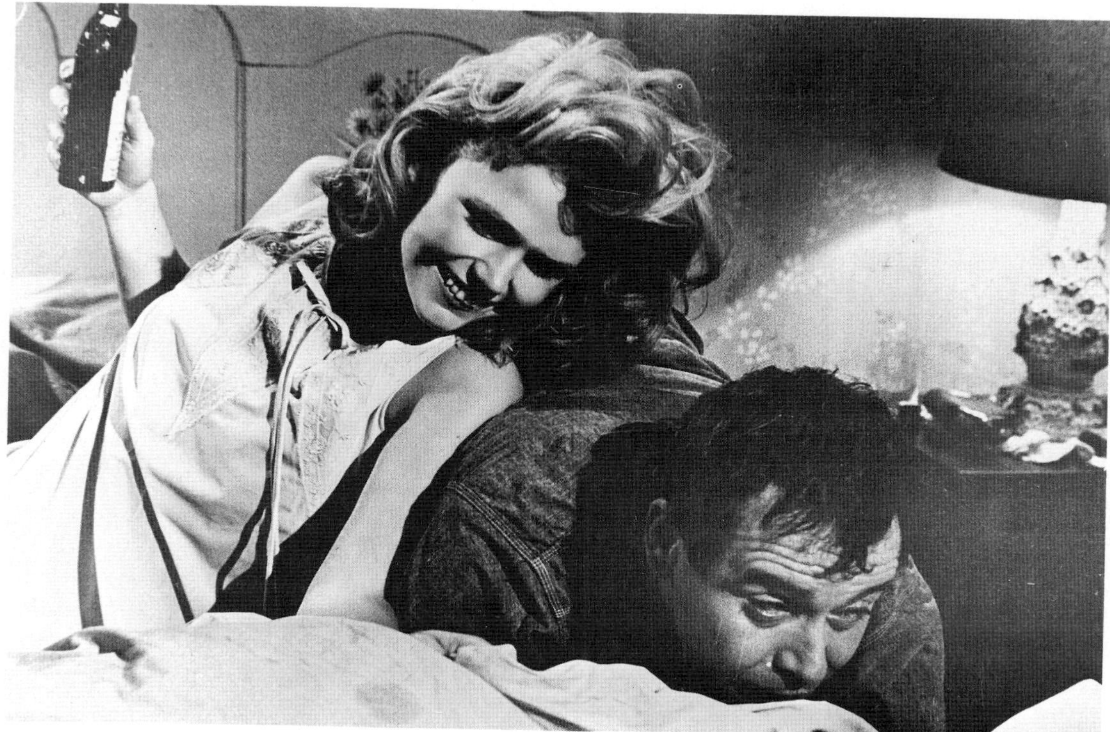

Lee Remick and Jack Lemmon on the bottle in Days of Wine and Roses.

LEMMON AND REMICK HIT THE BOTTLE

Not since *The Lost Weekend* in 1945 have the problems of alcoholism been so dramatically shown as in Blake Edwards' *Days of Wine and Roses*. Jack Lemmon and Lee Remick star as the married couple who, because of the pressures of modern life, graduate from being heavy drinkers into alcoholics. Their life in ruins, they attend AA meetings, enter Bellevue Hospital and, for a while, seem cured. Until one of them takes a drink, propelling them both on the downward spiral once more.

Edwards insisted the New York locations, including the hospital, should be authentic and that his stars had a full understanding of their roles. Says Remick: "I had the idea that AA meetings were just a lot of derelict drunks sitting around looking red-eyed and shaking. So the author of the novel, J.P. Miller, took us to a meeting on 64th and Park Avenue where all these people were drinking coffee, shaking a bit to be sure, but it was a marvellous experience.

"Then we went to see another sort on the Bowery in California and then I went to the jails in Los Angeles to the drunk tanks late at night, watching them bringing in people. It was very, very upsetting, very depressing."

MORE KITCHEN SINK

British critics are raving about *This Sporting Life*, the first feature of Lindsay Anderson, 40, a former critic who has directed many plays at the influential Royal Court theatre, including *Billy Liar!*, starring Albert Finney, and *The Long and the Short and the Tall*, starring Peter O'Toole.

The film is based on David Storey's novel and produced by Karel Reisz, director of *Saturday Night and Sunday Morning*. It stars Richard Harris as Frank Machin, a big, tough, inarticulate Rugby League player who rents a room from widowed Rachel Roberts. Their destructive relationship forms the core of the drama – Harris can't express himself in any way except violence and Roberts has cut herself off emotionally and sexually from the world around her.

Says Anderson: "It's an intimidating subject for a film." Whether or not audiences can stomach another dose of grim, kitchen-sink drama remains to be seen.

Richard Harris in This Sporting Life.

THE LAD FROM CROYDON

Says David Lean: "I hope the money-men don't find out that I'd pay *them* to let me do this." Lean, who's just won his second directing Oscar, for the epic *Lawrence of Arabia*, has been doing it for years. Alec Guinness, who also starred in the director's first Oscar winner, *The Bridge on the River Kwai* (1957), as well as his classic adaptations of *Great Expectations* (1946) and *Oliver Twist* (1948), has said: "David Lean is the most meticulous craftsman in the industry, the most painstaking in every department."

Born in Croydon, England, in 1908, Lean served a lengthy apprenticeship: he was a studio tea-boy, worked in the camera department and then the editing room. By 1940 he was regarded as the country's top cutter and was hired by Noel Coward to co-direct *In Which We Serve* (1942). Three further collaborations with Coward followed, culminating in the classic *Brief Encounter* (1945) for which Lean got his first Oscar nomination.

Summer Madness (1955), with Katharine Hepburn, launched Lean's international career and *Lawrence* has now put him among the world's foremost directors. Asked about the impact of his films, the tall and wiry Lean simply says: "All I hope for is that people take away with them something to think about and talk about." They're certainly doing that with *Lawrence*.

British director David Lean (right) discusses angles with his cameraman.

STAR QUOTES

Groucho Marx

"I've been around so long I can remember Doris Day before she was a virgin."

CLEO – AT LAST!

Cleopatra is so famous that 20th Century-Fox has not thought it necessary to put the title or the names on the stars of their first posters. "The film the whole world is waiting to see" is all it says. And they are unquestionably right. Another thing is certain: at $44 million, *Cleopatra* is the most expensive film ever made. Whether the studio can make a profit is another matter.

Running a record 243 minutes and filmed in the spectacular Todd-AO process, *Cleopatra* charts the life and times of the Queen of the Nile (Elizabeth Taylor) who captivated Julius Caesar (Rex Harrison) and, after his assassination, Mark Antony (Richard Burton), causing civil war in the Roman Republic and leading to the enthronement of the first Emperor, Augustus (Roddy McDowall). The subject of classic plays by Shakespeare and Bernard Shaw, it's basically a love story played out on the broadest possible stage, full of vast battles on land and on the sea.

Few productions have been so beset by so many problems or by so much gossip and speculation. Now the world needs wait no longer – even if other hands can't. There's already talk of experimentally cutting 21 minutes from the running-time by shortening some scenes.

Elizabeth Taylor, Rex Harrison and Richard Burton in Cleopatra.

QUEEN OF THE GALAXY

The words "movie star" and Elizabeth Taylor go together like turkey and cranberry sauce. No other actress has quite the same magic as Taylor: she's beautiful, dominating and vulnerable at the same time, and her private life and her frequent illnesses have become public property. She's also the first actress to get $1 million for a single movie.

That movie, of course, is *Cleopatra*. It's her 32nd screen appearance. She was born in London in 1932, evacuated to Hollywood during the Second World War, became a child actress at M-G-M and a child star in *National Velvet* (1944). She grew up quickly enough, playing the bride in the popular *Father of the Bride* (1950), the rich girl who snares Montgomery Clift in *A Place in the Sun* (1951), Rock Hudson's wife in *Giant* (1956), Paul Newman's nympho wife in *Cat on a Hot Tin Roof* (1958), a mental patient in *Suddenly, Last Summer* (1959) and a high-class hooker in *Butterfield 8* (1960). For the last she won an Oscar – less for her performance, it's said, than for her triumph over a near-fatal bout of pneumonia which helped to close down *Cleopatra* that year.

As well as those on-screen hitchings, in real life she's married four times: to hotelier Conrad Hilton (1950), actor Michael Wilding (1952), showman Mike Todd (1957), who died tragically in 1958, and singer Eddie Fisher (1958). As the world knows, she and Richard Burton fell in love during the filming of *Cleopatra* and M-G-M rushed into production their second film together, *The V.I.P.s*, due out later this summer.

Elizabeth Taylor.

BIRTHS, DEATHS AND MARRIAGES

BIRTHS

Natasha Richardson
11 May, London

DEATHS

Monty Woolley
6 May, New York
Heart ailment

ZaSu Pitts
7 Jun, Hollywood
Cancer

Richard Barthelmess
17 Aug, Southampton, New York
Cancer

SOMEBODY UP THERE LIKES PAUL

"Paul Newman *is* Hud," scream the posters. Hud Bannon spends his days driving his pink Cadillac convertible, drinking beer, getting into fights, womanizing in town and making passes at his housekeeper (Patricia Neal). He lets his old dad (Melvyn Douglas) and his young nephew (Brandon de Wilde) run the Texan cattle ranch. He is a hero for the times – as mean and as selfish as they come.

Hud is Ohio-born Newman's finest role to date and makes the handsome, clean-cut 38-year-old America's most sought-after actor. He's come a long way since an inauspicious debut in the biblical flop *The Silver Chalice* (1954). But Newman immediately got himself on the right track with his portrait of prizefighter Rocky Graziano in *Somebody Up There Likes Me* (1956).

His good looks, intense sexuality and instinctive rebelliousness (which has made people compare him with James Dean and Marlon Brando) were well to the fore in a trio of 1958 movies - *The Long Hot Summer, The Left-Handed Gun*, in which he played Billy the Kid, and *Cat on a Hot Tin Roof*, a steamy Tennessee Williams adaptation in which he co-starred with Elizabeth Taylor and won an Oscar nomination.

Exodus (1960) was his first foray into the international blockbuster, and he got a second Oscar nomination for his pool player in *The Hustler* (1961). Will *Hud* be third time lucky?

FLIGHT TO FREEDOM

Director John Sturges planned *The Great Escape* as the ultimate POW movie and admits that the formula set in his 1960 western *The Magnificent Seven* has been used again, as well as some of the same actors.

The Germans have an idea – to put "all our rotten eggs into one basket." That's Stalag Luft North, a huge prison-camp for those officers and men who persist in trying to break out. It's entirely escape-proof. Or is it? Among those working on a way out are Richard Attenborough, James Garner, Charles Bronson, James Coburn, Gordon Jackson, Donald Pleasence and David McCallum. Also, there is Steve McQueen, who plays "The Cooler King", so called because he spends most of his time in solitary confinement.

Each man has a speciality – Pleasence is a forger, Garner a scrounger, Bronson a tunneller – and all run rings around the German guards, causing diversions as work progresses on three tunnels, nicknamed Tom, Dick and Harry. Some 250 men succeed in breaking out. The extraordinary thing is, the film is based on fact and recounts in vivid detail the escape plan and subsequent flights – to freedom or death.

Susannah York, Hugh Griffith and Albert Finney in Tom Jones.

BAWDY TALES

"The whole world loves Tom Jones!" is United Artists' advertising slogan, referring to the numerous romatic conquests of the film's hero, gleefully played by Albert Finney. And it looks as if audiences love him too – a great relief to Woodfall Films as, at £350,000, it's a very costly British production.

The writer is John Osborne, whose play *Look Back in Anger* transformed British theatre overnight. Director is Tony Richardson, known for his dramas like *A Taste of Honey* (1961) and *The Loneliness of the Long Distance Runner* (1962). He calls *Tom Jones* "our holiday film." It's a boisterous comedy set in the 18th century and based on Henry Fielding's bawdy classic novel.

Tom is a foundling who lives on a farm and shocks everyone by his carefree attitudes to sex – attitudes which lead him into London society, the sudden realization of his true parentage, and the hangman's noose. Much attention has been paid to authenticity in the costumes and settings; but the filmic approach is entirely modern, using techniques developed by young French directors and utilizing a helicopter to film a spectacular hunting scene.

The cast also includes Hugh Griffith, who won an Oscar for *Ben-Hur* (1959), as well as Edith Evans, David Warner, and 24-year-old Susannah York as the English rose just waiting to be plucked by the hero.

Steve McQueen, Richard Attenborough and Gordon Jackson in The Great Escape.

DD REPLACES MM

20th Century-Fox has re-started production on the picture that closed down after the firing and subsequent death (in August last year) of Marilyn Monroe. Originally titled *Something's Got to Give*, it's now called *Move Over, Darling* and stars Doris Day and James Garner, currently on movie screens in the glossy farce *The Thrill of It All*.

Sources say the script has been substantially rewritten to accommodate Day, and Michael Gordon takes over as director from George Cukor, who's busy filming *My Fair Lady* for Warners.

SEPTEMBER
OCTOBER

NOVEMBER
DECEMBER

BIRTHS, DEATHS AND MARRIAGES

BIRTHS

Helen Slater
19 Dec, New York

Jennifer Beals
19 Dec, Chicago

DEATHS

Jean Cocteau
11 Oct, Milly-la-Floret, France
Heart attack

Adolphe Menjou
29 Oct, Beverly Hills
Hepatitis

Sabu
2 Dec, Hollywood
Heart attack

MARRIAGES

Harrison Ford
Sep, *to* Mary Ford

Barbra Streisand
13 Sep, *to* **Elliott Gould**

Joan Collins
11 Oct, *to* **Anthony Newley**

THE PERILS OF AUDREY

Cary Grant and Audrey Hepburn in Charade.

A comedy-thriller in the Hitchcock tradition, *Charade* places Audrey Hepburn in the direst danger and deepest confusion. She returns from holiday to find her Paris home stripped and her ex-husband murdered. Then she's called to the American embassy where local CIA head Walter Matthau says her husband vanished with $250,000 in gold that was intended for the French resistance during the war.

Three Americans – James Coburn, George Kennedy and Ned Glass - want the money and will kill to get it. A fourth man, Carson Dyle, has disappeared. Hepburn searches everywhere for the gold or the money but the only thing she has of her husband's possessions is an empty envelope. But she also has Cary Grant, whom she met on holiday, and he seems more than keen to help her in this time of crisis.

With its winning partnership of Hepburn and Grant, Stanley Donen's slick, romantic escapade has actually been ready for some months. But Universal has decided to make the most of its box-office potential by opening it at New York's prestigious Radio City Music Hall this Christmas.

LEOPARD ATTACKS FOX

Italian director Luchino Visconti has accused 20th Century-Fox of destroying his film *The Leopard*, which stars Burt Lancaster, France's Alain Delon and Italy's Claudia Cardinale. The film, which won the Golden Palm at the Cannes Festival in May, originally ran for 205 minutes and was photographed in Technirama and Technicolor. The release version, prepared by Fox, runs for 161 minutes and is in DeLuxe Color. Thunders Visconti in the London newspaper *Sunday Times*: "It is now a work for which I acknowledge no paternity at all."

BOX OFFICE

UK

SPECIAL PRESENTATION

1 Cleopatra
2 How the West Was Won
3 Lawrence of Arabia
4 The Longest Day

TOP GENERAL RELEASES

1 From Russia with Love
2 Summer Holiday
3 The Great Escape
4 Tom Jones

BOX OFFICE

US

1 Cleopatra
2 The Longest Day
3 Irma La Douce
4 Lawrence of Arabia
5 How the West Was Won
6 Mutiny on the Bounty
7 Son of Flubber
8 To Kill a Mockingbird
9 Bye Bye Birdie
10 Come Blow Your Horn

A.K.A. MOT SNEVETS

Terry-Thomas' real name is Thomas Terry Hoar-Stevens. That was a mouthful, so he thought of using Tom Stevens as a stage-name. But that lacked distinction. So he spelt it backwards, Mot Snevets. Then he tried Thomas Terry. Next, Terry Thomas. And then he added the hyphen.

Everyone knows him – the gap between the teeth (his 1959 autobiography was called *Filling the Gap*), the posh accent, the personification of the British upper-class twit, the raffish bounder and the schemer. He dabbled in greengrocery before acting on stage, on TV and in minor roles in movies. British moviegoers really took him to heart in the Boulting Brothers' satires on local institutions – the army in *Private's Progress* (1956), the legal profession in *Brothers in Law* (1957), the government in *Carlton-Browne of the F.O.*, industry and unions in *I'm All Right Jack* (both 1959), and education in *School for Scoundrels* (1960).

Inevitably Hollywood, which has always had a soft spot for this sort of "Englishness", wanted Terry-Thomas as well. Now critics are claiming he steals *It's a Mad Mad Mad Mad World* from the likes of Milton Berle, Phil Silvers and Sid Caesar. That's no mean achievement for a 52-year-old upper-class twit.

ENOUGH IS NOT ENOUGH

Stanley Kramer's It's a Mad Mad Mad Mad World.

Four "mads" may not be enough to describe Stanley Kramer's gargantuan, 190-minute comedy which, for the first time, offers Cinerama without the joins. *It's a Mad Mad Mad Mad World* has been filmed in Ultra Panavision 70, an extra-wide process for the giant curved screen.

The plot is simple: a crook (Jimmy Durante) dies in a car crash but not before he has told a group of four people that he has buried $350,000 "under a big W in Santa Rosita." The ract is on, gaining eager competitors by the minute. The case is the starriest ever assembled for a comedy: Milton Berle, Sid Caesar, Buddy Hackett, Ethel Merman, Mickey Rooney, Dick Shawn, Phil Silvers, Jonathan Winters, Dorothy Provine, Terry-Thomas, Edie Adams.

Those are the principals. Then add cameos from the likes of Buster Keaton, The Three Stooges and Joe E. Brown. And observing the madness, and playing the biggest joker in the pack, is police chief Spencer Tracy.

Filmed in 166 days, the production used almost all of Hollywood's stunt and special effects experts. Says stunt co-ordinator Carey Loftin: "You name a stunt – we did it. In airplanes, automobiles, tractors, trucks, fire engines, high dives, low dives, dives through plate glass windows, fisticuffs, fireworks, falls from fire escapes, ladders, palm trees and building tops."

Adds Kramer: "If this isn't the funniest motion picture ever made the fault will lie with the man I see in the mirror." But the biggest laugh of all is that the script was written by British-based William Rose, whose previous works include the classic *Genevieve* (1953). His original idea was for a chase around England and Scotland . . . .

MATINEE IDOL FIGHTS BACK

"I love the camera and it loves me. Well, not very much sometimes. But we're good friends." Dirk Bogarde and the camera have been friends since 1948, when he made his debut as a dashing young thing in *Esther Waters*, but his career has taken some unexpected turns.

Born in London of Dutch descent in 1920, he was signed to a contract at Rank Films where he beavered away in low-grade thrillers and adventure dramas until he shot to stardom as Dr. Simon Sparrow in the light comedy *Doctor in the House* (1954). Audiences – women especially – adored his good looks and charm and he became a matinee idol, starring in three more *Doctor* comedies, and as Sydney Carton in *A Tale of Two Cities* (1958). He then went to Hollywood to play composer Franz Liszt in *Song without End* (1960).

But Bogarde disliked Hollywood and returned to England for an abrupt change in his choice of roles. His blackmailed homosexual barrister in *Victim* (1961) created a stir and proved he was no longer just a light romantic comedian.

Earlier this year he was seen with Judy Garland in *I Could Go On Singing* and is now getting rave reviews for *The Servant*, another departure. Says Bogarde: "I'll only work with new people. If you stick with your contemporaries, you're dead."

British film idol and talented actor Dirk Bogarde.

Dirk Bogarde and James Fox in Joseph Losey's The Servant.

UPSTAIRS, DOWNSTAIRS

The Servant is Dirk Bogarde, in his most challenging role since *Victim* (1961). He is valet to an aristocratic young Englishman (James Fox) and gradually turns the tables on him, using his lover (Sarah Miles) as bait.

Directed by Joseph Losey, a previously blacklisted American now resident in Britain, *The Servant* has a pithy screenplay by famed playwright Harold Pinter, the first he's written for the screen. It's a searing, blackly humorous look at Britain's decadent ruling classes and resentful underclasses. Its release fortuitously coincides with scandals that have rocked the British government – the Vassall spy case and the Profumo affair.

GOSSIP COLUMN

■ **Tinseltown isn't dead. A recent survey shows that the major studios have 330 artists under long-term contract; M-G-M alone has 73. But for every six to eight months for a cinema feature, the studios can also grind out a TV episode of *Ben Casey* in five days.**

Murray Melvin and Rita Tushingham in *A Taste of Honey* (1961).

Saturday Night and Sunday Morning (1960).

Tom Courtenay and Julie Christie in Billy Liar! (1963).

Laurence Harvey and Simone Signoret in Room at the Top (1959).

Rachel Roberts and Richard Harris in This Sporting Life (1963).

Angry Young Brits

British cinema has always included the kitchen sink. It's a metaphor for real life: after breakfast, lunch and dinner, arguments break out and cups and saucers are there to be smashed during a squabble. The so-called "kitchen sink" movie reached its peak during 1958-63. Films like *Room at the Top* (1959), *Look Back in Anger* (1959), *Saturday Night and Sunday Morning* (1960), *A Taste of Honey* (1961), *Billy Liar!* (1963) and *This Sporting Life* (1963) focussed on the industrial North where the young men slaved away in factories, boozed in smoke-filled pubs, went to football matches, got into fights, had love affairs with the wives of older men and were generally pretty fed up with life. In short, they were angry.

The real angry young men, though, were artists and intellectuals, often from Northern backgrounds who began in the mid-1950s to revolutionize the London theatre and literary world. John Osborne's plays *Look Back in Anger* (1956) and *The Entertainer* (1957) changed the face of British theatre almost overnight, the latter starring establishment figure Laurence Olivier who gave the new movement its official stamp of approval. Similarly, John Braine's novel *Room at the Top* (1956) and Alan Sillitoe's *Saturday Night and Sunday Morning* (1958) gave new impetus to British fiction.

The films of these plays and novels were made on tiny budgets and became commercial hits, mainly because of their liberal approach to language and sex. A new breed of actor starred in them – Albert Finney, Richard Harris, Peter O'Toole, Tom Courtenay, Laurence Harvey, none of whom had Southern accents. And there were new directors as well – Lindsay Anderson, Karel Reisz, Tony Richardson, John Schlesinger, all of whom were influenced by the British documentary movement of the 1930s.

The movies spoke directly to the majority audience in Britain who lived "North of Watford," an imaginary line drawn on the northern fringe of Greater London which divided the world of complacency and plenty with the world of struggle and envy. Working-class characters were no longer just colourful additions.

They reflected the changes in Britain since the end of the Second World War. Unlike America, Britain had fallen into a deep recession – there was food rationing well into the 1950s – as well as years of stagnation as the country lost much of its industrial muscle. There were also a succession of sex and spying scandals which rocked the Conservative government, adding weight to the idea that the ruling class had lost its credibility.

Britain lost much of its international muscle too – the embarrassment of Suez and the inevitable collapse of its Empire in Africa and the Far East all led to a general apathy and disillusion. Against this background the "kitchen sinks" prospered.

But it didn't last long. In terms of cinema, much significance has been placed upon a scene in *Billy Liar!* when Julie Christie leaves dreary Nottingham for London and a brighter life. "Swinging London" was about to burst upon the world.

Coincidentally, Britain began to lead the world in fashion and music – Carnaby Street, the Beatles and James Bond. Realism transferred quietly to television, with plays like *Cathy Come Home* (1966) and soaps like *Coronation Street*, and the cinema entered into flights of fantasy with working-class heroes running trendy boutiques, performing to hordes of screaming fans or fighting enemy agents. The Bond movies in particular symbolized a Britain of fantasy and Imperial nostalgia. They had everything – sex, luxury, violence, exotic locations.

Claire Bloom, Richard Burton and kitchen sink in Look Back in Anger (1959).

JANUARY
FEBRUARY

MARCH
APRIL

ACADEMY AWARDS

PRESENTED ON 13 APRIL 1964

Best Picture
Tom Jones

Best Director
Tony Richardson
Tom Jones

Best Actor
Sidney Poitier
Lilies of the Field

Best Actress
Patricia Neal
Hud

Best Sup Actor
Melvyn Douglas
Hud

Best Sup Actress
Margaret Rutherford
The V.I.P.s

POITIER TRIUMPHS

Sidney Poitier has become the first black star to win the Best Actor Academy Award. Accepting his statuette from Anne Bancroft on 13 April, Poitier said, "It has been a long journey to this moment." The actor, who won for his performance as a handyman who builds a church in *Lilies of the Field* (1963), triumphed over fellow-nominees Albert Finney, Richard Harris, Rex Harrison and Paul Newman. Poitier's award is the first to a black performer since Hattie McDaniel won Best Supporting Actress for *Gone with the Wind* (1939).

WE'LL MEET AGAIN . . .

"I started with every intention of making a serious treatment of accidental nuclear war," says British-based producer-director Stanley Kubrick. "But as I kept trying to imagine the way things would happen ideas kept coming to me which I would discard because they were so ludicrous. I kept saying to myself, I can't do this. People will laugh." So was born *Dr. Strangelove*, subtitled *Or: How I Learned to Stop Worrying and Love the Bomb*, which Kubrick describes as a "nightmare comedy." Sterling Hayden plays General Jack D. Ripper who sends his bomb-wing to attack the Soviet Union. George C. Scott plays Pentagon General "Buck" Turgidson who welcomes the idea of a sneak-attack to nuke the "Commies". And Peter Sellers plays no less than three roles – a British Group Captain Lionel Mandrake, attached to Ripper's command, mild mannered US President Muffley, and weirdo Dr. Strangelove himself, a crippled, former Nazi scientist now employed by the Pentagon. The problem is that no way is found to decipher Ripper's cryptic recall codes, so the fate of the world hangs a single plane, piloted by Major T. J. "King" Kong (Slim Pickens), which evades Soviet radar. And just what is the Doomsday Machine that the Other Side has?

LADD DEAD

Alan Ladd was found dead at his home on 29 January from a fatal dose of sedatives and alcohol. He was aged 50. The diminutive star, whose leading ladies often had to stand in trenches built on the set, was one of the screen's leading tough-guys, starring in dozens of crime dramas, westerns and war films. Most famous for his thrillers, like *The Blue Dahlia* (1946), co-starring Veronica Lake and for playing the gunfighter *Shane* (1953), Ladd had already seen his career in decline at the time of his death.

STAR QUOTES

Sterling Hayden

"If I had the dough, I'd buy up the negative of every film I ever made and start one hell of a fire."

CLOUSEAU'S CLUEDO

The Pink Panther is a priceless jewel that belongs to Indian princess Claudia Cardinale. When she and the jewel take a holiday in the Swiss Alps they naturally become the target of the notorious jewel thief, the Phantom (David Niven) and his nephew (Robert Wagner). On the trail of the Phantom is French Detective-Inspector Jacques Clouseau (Peter Sellers), whose wife (Capucine) is also involved in the criminal side of the jewellery business. The scene is set for an eye-catching thriller by director Blake Edwards which turns into an uproarious comedy, thanks to Sellers' portrayal of the dedicated – but clumsy and incompetent – Clouseau. Sellers got the role only after Peter Ustinov turned it down. But so delighted is Edwards with Sellers' performance that a sequel, *A Shot in the Dark*, is already in production. His character could run and run.

Peter Sellers, with John Le Mesurier, as Inspector Clouseau in The Pink Panther.

BLONDE BOMBER

Sophia Loren and Stephen Boyd in Samuel Bronston's epic The Fall of the Roman Empire.

VELVET-VOICED HERO

As Livius in *The Fall of the Roman Empire*, Stephen Boyd finally becomes a hero. This latest excursion into ancient Rome, in which he makes a stand against the despotic Commodus while loving the Emperor's sister, is a far cry from his previous Roman role as the evil Messala who dies under horses' hooves and chariot wheels in the Oscar-encrusted *Ben-Hur* (1959).

The muscular, velvet-voiced Boyd was born in Belfast in 1928 and worked as a cinema doorman and a busker before a chance meeting with Michael Redgrave led him to Windsor Repertory Theatre. He acted on the stage, made his film debut in 1955 and then played the Irish agent in *The Man Who Never Was* (1956). Hollywood beckoned and Boyd appeared in the racial drama *Island in the Sun* (1957) and the western *The Bravados* (1958) before becoming a major star in *Ben-Hur*. But he's still surprised by his success. "I don't know what goes into being a star," he says. "Perhaps it's the ability to explain the character and story to any audience in any language in any country." He certainly shows it in *Roman Empire*.

ROME FALLS IN SPAIN

At $20 million, the Samuel Bronston production *The Fall of the Roman Empire* is one of the most expensive films ever made. To tell the fall of an Empire, Bronston first had to build one and the sets are on an unprecedented scale. The one for the Roman Forum alone took 1,100 men working daily for seven months to build 27 separate structures in what once were barley fields outside Madrid. Others include a massive wooden fort in the spectacular Sierra Guadarrama mountains near Segovia, which stand in for the empire's German frontier. In all, this spectacular epic took three years to bring to the screen.

Directed by Anthony Mann, who made Bronston's *El Cid* (1961), the story opens with the last days of the noble, philosophical Emperor Marcus Aurelius (Alec Guinness) on the Danube frontier, and then switches to Rome as Aurelius's heir, the Emperor Commodus (Christopher Plummer), destroys all his father's hopes for world peace and racial harmony. Stephen Boyd and Sophia Loren are the handsome lovers swept up in the larger story. Unlike most Roman epics, this one lacks any religious dimension, though there are the requisite number of battles and chariot races, thrillingly staged by veteran stunt director Joe Canutt.

BIRTHS, DEATHS AND MARRIAGES

BIRTHS

Nicolas Cage
7 Jan, Long Beach, California

Zack Galligan
14 Feb, New York

Matt Dillon
18 Feb, New Rochelle, New York

Rob Lowe
17 Mar, Charlottesville, Virginia

DEATHS

Joseph Schildkraut
21 Jan, New York
Heart attack

Alan Ladd
29 Jan, Palm Springs, California
Overdose of drugs and alcohol

Peter Lorre
23 Mar, Hollywood
Heart attack

Ben Hecht
18 Apr, New York
Heart attack

MARRIAGES

Peter Sellers
19 Feb, *to* **Britt Ekland**

Elizabeth Taylor
15 Mar, *to* **Richard Burton**

Carroll Baker shot to fame as the sultry, supine, thumb-sucking child-wife in *Baby Doll* (1956). And now Marilyn Monroe is no more, Baker is America's foremost sex symbol, rivalling Europe's Brigitte Bardot and Sophia Loren. In her latest film, *The Carpetbaggers*, based on Harold Robbins' steamy best-seller, Baker plays the seductive and destructive movie star Rina.

The blonde actress was born in 1931 in Johnstown, Pennsylvania, and studied as a dancer before making her screen debut in the Esther Williams musical *Easy to Love* (1953). She then joined the Actors' Studio, married director Jack Garfein and co-starred with Elizabeth Taylor, Rock Hudson and James Dean in *Giant* (1956). After *Baby Doll* came roles as a spoilt daughter in *The Big Country* (1958), as a rape victim in *Something Wild* (1961), directed by her husband, as a pioneer wife in *How the West Was Won* (1962) and, to be released later this year, *Station Six-Sahara* in which she raises the temperature as the only woman in a desert outpost. Since filming *The Carpetbaggers* she's also made a guest appearance as a harlot in *The Greatest Story Ever Told*, George Stevens' long-awaited film about Christ due sometime next year. She recently signed to play 1930s sexpot Jean Harlow.

MY FAIR AUDREY

Lerner and Loewe's *My Fair Lady*, based on Bernard Shaw's 1912 play *Pygmalion*, has become one of the most successful musicals ever, since it opened on Broadway in March 1956. Warners paid a record $5.5 million for the screen rights and now the $17 million production has finally reached the screen after two years of work. Rex Harrison, who starred in the Broadway and London productions as Professor Higgins, repeats his performance under the direction of veteran George Cukor, who started his career on Broadway before switching to Hollywood in the 1930s and becoming one of tinsel town's top comedy directors. The stage Eliza Dolittle, Julie Andrews, is replaced on film by Audrey Hepburn. That snub to Andrews has rebounded on Warners since her first film, *Mary Poppins*, has already proved a box-office smash. But Harrison and Hepburn are still a winning combination; the sets and costumes by Cecil Beaton are sumptuous; and the songs, of course, are evergreens. One name that doesn't appear on the screen is that of Marni Nixon, who does a perfect job dubbing Hepburn's singing voice. The best-known "ghost" in the business, she also dubbed Deborah Kerr in *The King and I* (1956) and Natalie Wood in *West Side Story* (1961).

Audrey Hepburn, Rex Harrison and Wilfred Hyde White in My Fair Lady.

BOYO BECKET

With the title role in this year's *Becket*, Richard Burton adds another great performance to an illustrious career. Peter O'Toole stars opposite him as Henry II, the impetuous king who mutters "Will no one rid me of this meddlesome priest?" and lives to regret it. Says director Peter Glenville: "Until now, Burton has never appeared in a screen role that has tested his remarkable talent. He is really a big, strong instrument for great heroic roles and in *Becket* those gifts are fully challenged." Those gifts, especially his voice, have been known to London audiences since the early 1950s. Hailed as the successor to Laurence Olivier, Burton gave performances in *Coriolanus, Hamlet, Othello* and *Henry V* at London's Old Vic theatre that are already legendary. He's since drawn a wider public with his performance as King Arthur in the stage musical *Camelot*. The 39-year-old Welshman, whose real name is Richard Jenkins, made his screen debut in *The Last Days of Dolwyn* (1949) and quickly became a sought-after actor in Britain and Hollywood. He went on to star in movies as diverse as *The Robe* (1953), *Alexander the Great* (1956) and *Look Back in Anger* (1959). But it was *Cleopatra* (1963), in which he played Mark Antony to Elizabeth Taylor's Queen of the Nile, which made him a world celebrity. Last year he and Taylor married and also starred in *The V.I.P.s*. He'll be seen next in John Huston's *The Night of the Iguana*, opposite Deborah Kerr, Ava Gardner and Sue Lyon, and in a Broadway production of *Hamlet* to be directed by John Gielgud.

DINO'S GENESIS

Italian producer Dino De Laurentiis has finally settled on John Huston as the sole director on *The Bible*. De Laurentiis first announced the project in 1962 as a 14-hour epic to be directed by such art-house favourites as Ingmar Bergman, Robert Bresson, Federico Fellini, Luchino Visconti and Orson Welles. Now the veteran Huston will be in sole charge and only the first few pages of Genesis are to be filmed, in a new wide-screen process called Dimension-150. Huston has approached Charlie Chaplin to play Noah and wants Laurence Olivier for the voice-over role of God. But nothing has been settled yet.

BEATLE POWER

The Fab Four – John, Paul, George and Ringo – make it to the screen in *A Hard Day's Night*, a fast-moving comedy-musical directed by American-born Richard Lester. He got the job because the Beatles admired his work with Peter Sellers and BBC Radio's *The Goon Show*. Queues have begun forming outside the London Pavilion cinema in Piccadilly Circus several days before the film's Royal Premiere and extra police have been called in to control the crowds. Beatlemaniacs will be rewarded with a close-up look at their heroes and, if the soundtrack can be heard above the screaming, with eight new songs.

BIRTHS, DEATHS AND MARRIAGES

DEATHS

Diana Wynyard
13 May, London
Kidney ailment

Cedric Hardwicke
6 Aug, New York
Emphysema

Gracie Allen
27 Aug, Hollywood
Heart attack

MARRIAGES

Robert Duvall
Aug, *to* Gail Youngs

Anne Bancroft
5 Aug, *to* **Mel Brooks**

Angie Dickinson
Sep, *to* **Burt Bacharach**

Tippi Hedren in Hitchcock's Marnie.

Henry Fonda and Larry Hagman in Fail Safe, *about the problems of nuclear war.*

HITCH'S ICEBERG

You last saw Tippi Hedren attacked by thousands of birds in Alfred Hitchcock's successful shocker *The Birds* (1963). Now she has the title role in this summer's *Marnie* (also directed by Hitchcock) which looks set to be the most demanding female part of the year. Marnie is a compulsive thief caught rifling businessman Sean Connery's safe. Rather than turn her over to the police, Connery is attracted to the ice-cool blonde, marries her and then discovers that she's frigid because of a childhood trauma.

Hedren is the latest in a long line of Hitchcock blondes and she's very much the director's discovery. Looking for an actress for *The Birds*, Hitch saw a TV commercial for the diet drink Sego and told his staff to find the tall, elegant actress. It was Tippi Hedren. A successful model who was born in 1935, Hedren's real Christian name is Nathalie (Tippi is her father's nickname for her). She has a daughter called Melanie Griffith, born in 1957. Hitch signed her up and has personally supervised her training and wardrobe. He's also embellished her further by putting quotes around her first name – "Tippi". Says Hedren: "It was never my ambition to be an actress, much less a movie star. I was a model and I had come to Los Angeles not only to try for better work than was available in New York but also because I wanted my daughter to grow up in a home with a yard and trees."

LAST BUT NOT LEAST

In January Columbia Pictures released *Dr. Strangelove*, Stanley Kubrick's black comedy about nuclear war, with Peter Sellers and George C. Scott. *Fail Safe*, also released by Columbia, has an identical subject and has been delayed until the autumn so that Kubrick's film can complete its run. But this powerful movie is no comedy. Henry Fonda plays the President of the United States faced with the ultimate nightmare – a technical failure that leads him and his Soviet counterpart into a terrible decision, whether or not to sacrifice New York for Moscow to avoid a world war. There are no jokes in director Sidney Lumet's film, only tension and anxious-looking co-stars like Walter Matthau, Dan O'Herlihy and (as Fonda's nervous Russian translator) Larry Hagman. It's faithfully based on the enormous best-seller by Eugene Burdick and Harvey Wheeler. Columbia was so worried by the similarity of its plot to *Strangelove*'s that it filed a Federal Court suit early last year against the authors and production company on the grounds of plagiarization. Columbia ended up taking over financing and distribution of the movie itself.

SUPERCALLY JULIE!

Walt Disney has come up with a glittering showcase for its animation skills with the groundbreaking family musical *Mary Poppins*, combining live action with cartoon backgrounds and characters. Julie Andrews, who created Eliza Dolittle on stage in *My Fair Lady*, makes her screen debut in the title role. She's governess to an Edwardian English family blessed with the ability to fly on broomsticks. But Mary Poppins is no witch; she's an angel who captivates the children in her charge and also a chimney-sweep played by Dick Van Dyke. Andrews gets plenty of chance to show her vocal talents in numbers like "Chim-Chim-Cheree", "Spoonful of Sugar", "Jolly Holiday" and the tongue-twisting "Supercalifragilisticexpialidocious". She's flying your way this autumn, and it looks like she will be cleaning up.

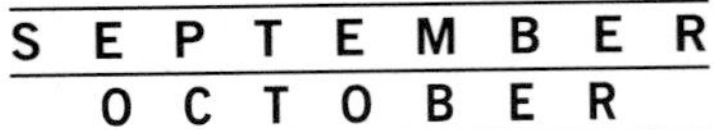

NOVEMBER
DECEMBER

KISS CONDEMNED

Billy Wilder's Christmas offering, *Kiss Me, Stupid*, starring Dean Martin and Kim Novak, has been denounced by America's powerful Catholic Legion of Decency as "indecent, immoral and an insult to Judaeo-Christian sensibilities". The legion has given the film, which is about a popular singer and a housewife who impersonates a prostitute, a "C" rating, last issued in 1956 to *Baby Doll*. Throughout the South and Middle West, theatre owners are cancelling screenings owing to pressure from religious groups. United Artists has decided to withdraw its name from the picture and distribute it nationally through a subsidiary, Lopert Pictures.

BIRTHS, DEATHS AND MARRIAGES

BIRTHS

Sophie Ward
30 Dec, London

DEATHS

Harpo Marx
28 Sep, Hollywood
Heart attack

Eddie Cantor
10 Oct, Hollywood
Heart problem

William Bendix
14 Dec, Hollywood
Pneumonia

MARRIAGES

Janet Gaynor
24 Dec, *to* Paul Gregory

Robert Duvall
30 Dec, *to* Barbara Brent

BOND APPEAL

Sean Connery in trouble as James Bond 007 in Goldfinger.

A frogman emerges from a lake, breaks into an oil refinery, sets the explosives, takes off his frogman suit to reveal an immaculate dinner suit (complete with red carnation), retires to a nearby bar and calmly waits for the big bang. Later, embracing a woman in his bedroom, he sees a killer reflected in her eyes. He throws the man into a bath and an electric heater as well. "Shocking, simply shocking," he says as the assassin goes up in smoke. James Bond is up to his old quips and tricks again in *Goldfinger*. And Bond is again played by Sean Connery, the rugged 34-year-old Scot who has become one of the world's most popular screen stars since donning the 007 mantle. The former bricklayer, milkman, lifeguard, coffin polisher and male model began his theatrical career in the chorus of a British stage production of the musical *South Pacific*. Minor beef roles followed in films like *Hell Drivers* (1957) and *Darby O'Gill and the Little People* (1959), but his career was not exactly taking off. Then he was cast as Ian Fleming's dapper spy in *Dr. No* (1962) and *From Russia with Love* (1963), and the rest is already history. Says Connery: "My only grumble about the Bond films is that they don't tax one as an actor. All one needs is the constitution of a rugby player to get through those 19 weeks of swimming, slugging and necking." Connery has already broken out of the Bond mould to star in *Woman of Straw* and Hitchcock's *Marnie*, both seen this summer. But it's back to 007 for *Thunderball* before he gets a crack at playing a tough, insubordinate soldier in the tense drama *The Hill*.

U OPENS ITS DOORS

Universal Studios in Burbank, California, has thrown open its doors to tourists. Visitors will be able to see movies in production, tour technical departments and visit the backlot, where many sets from old productions are still standing.

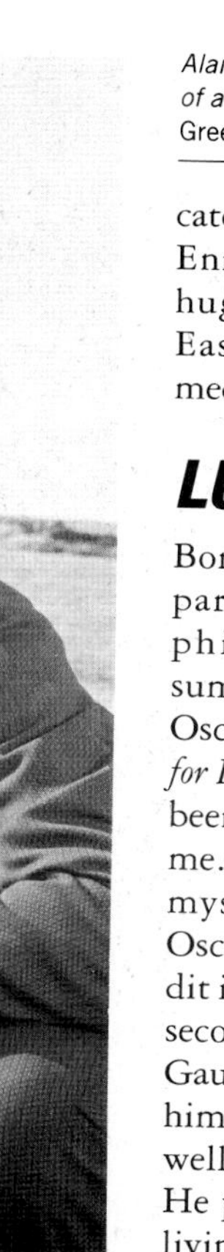

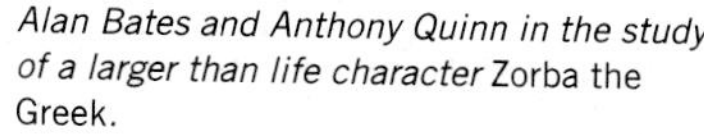

Alan Bates and Anthony Quinn in the study of a larger than life character Zorba the Greek.

BOUZOUKI BLUES

A glum English writer (Alan Bates) inherits some land and a mine in Greece. Unsure of what to do with them, he meets Zorba (Anthony Quinn), a fisherman whose lust for life provides Bates with a reason to go on living. Also on the island are Irene Papas, as a widow who attracts Bates's attention, and Lila Kedrova as an old hag still needing a man around the place in order to cheat death. A clear contender for acting and music Oscars (Mikis Theodorakis' dance music is on everyone's lips), *Zorba the Greek* is directed with zest by Cypriot Michael Caccoyannis from the best-selling novel by Nikos Kazantakis.

BOX OFFICE

UK

SPECIAL PRESENTATION

1 How the West was Won
2 Lawrence of Arabia
3 Cleopatra

TOP TEN GENERAL RELEASES

1 Goldfinger
2 A Hard Day's Night
3 Zulu
4 A Stitch in Time
5 Wonderful Life
6 The Pink Panther
7 The Long Ships
8 Marnie
9 The Sword in the Stone
10 633 Squadron

BOX OFFICE

US

1 The Carpetbaggers
2 It's a Mad Mad Mad Mad World
3 The Unsinkable Molly Brown
4 Charade
5 The Cardinal
6 Move Over Darling
7 My Fair Lady
8 What a Way to Go!
9 Good Neighbor Sam
10 The Pink Panther

NO NAME CLINT

With *Fistful of Dollars* the Italians are making a bid for that most American of movies, the western. Clint Eastwood, a tall, gaunt-looking, 34-year-old actor known to American TV audiences as Rowdy Yates in *Rawhide*, is The Man With No Name. The plot is a rehash of a Japanese film *Yojimbo* (1961).

This Italian-West German-Spanish co-production was actually filmed in Spain, where the desert scenery is a fair approximation to New Mexico, and directed by "Bob Robertson", a pseudonym for Sergio Leone, who did the action sequences in the sin-and-sword epic *Sodom and Gomorrah* (1962). The violent, heavily stylized film, with a catchy score by young composer Ennio Morricone, is drawing huge crowds in Rome where Eastwood has gained an immediate following.

LUST FOR LIFE

Born in 1915 of Irish-Mexican parentage, Anthony Quinn's philosophy of acting was summed up during his second Oscar acceptance speech for *Lust for Life* (1956). "Acting has never been a matter of competition to me. I am only competing with myself." Quinn won his first Oscar for playing a Mexican bandit in *Viva Zapata!* (1952) and his second for playing the artist Paul Gauguin. An accomplished artist himself, his autobiography could well be subtitled "Lust for Life". He plays men with a passion for living, as if to exorcise memories of a poor childhood and a speech impediment which had to be cured by an operation on his tongue. His first break came as a Red Indian in Cecil B. DeMille's *The Plainsman* (1937) and the following year he married the director's daughter, Katherine. Scores of films followed as well as celebrated stage appearances in *A Streetcar Named Desire* and *Becket*, opposite Laurence Olivier. Since his Oscars for Best Supporting Actor, he has played Quasimodo in *The Hunchback of Notre Dame* (1957), a Greek in *The Guns of Navarone* (1961), a Roman slave and gladiator in *Barabbas* and an Arab brigand in *Lawrence of Arabia* (both 1962). Quinn's looks make him ideal in ethnic parts. As Zorba, he's back to playing a Greek again – and a living life-force.

STAR QUOTES

Dean Martin

"I'd hate to be a teetotaller. Imagine getting up in the morning and knowing that's as good as you're going to feel all day."

THE SOUND OF MONEY?

Darryl F. Zanuck, boss of 20th Century-Fox, is gambling everything on the movie version of the 1959 stage hit *The Sound of Music*. He needs plenty of box-office dollars to wipe out some of the debts from *Cleopatra* (1963). The studio's back lot has already been sold off for offices.

Fox originally offered the project to Billy Wilder and William Wyler, but it was Robert Wise, co-director of *West Side Story* (1961), who finally took the Todd-AO cameras to Salzburg for exteriors. Filming wasn't exactly raindrops on roses. The local burgers were uneasy about having Nazi brownshirts and a swastika on display; the weather was terrible; and the young children in the cast refused to stop growing during the seven months they were on the picture.

Julie Andrews, fresh from her triumph as Mary Poppins, plays the children's governess Maria, and tall, handsome Canadian actor Christopher Plummer is the widowed Austrian naval officer, Captain Von Trapp, who takes Maria and his brood of seven across the border to escape the invading Nazis. Plummer and Peggy Wood (the Mother Superior) have had their songs dubbed.

Competition for the roles of the children was fierce: 1,000 kids turned up at the New York auditions, and a further 1,000 in Los Angeles. Most of the lucky ones are either child models or beauty pageant contestants. And just to make sure the movie's a success, Richard Rodgers has penned two new songs for the movie, "I Have Confidence in Me" and "Something Good." He also had to write the words: his partner died back in 1960.

OFF-THE-PEG BOND

Move over James Bond, the British secret service has a new recruit. He's called Harry Palmer and he is played by Michael Caine, the handsome young officer in last year's *Zulu*. Unlike 007, this spy does not wear Savile Row suits or drive an Aston Martin. Palmer dresses off-the-peg, wears glasses and even has a desk in a grubby office. Says Caine, who got the part after Christopher Plummer turned it down in favour of *The Sound of Music*: "Palmer would have regarded Bond as a bit of a toffee-nosed twit. But at the same time he'd have been a bit worried." The irony is that *The Ipcress File*, based on the 1962 novel by Len Deighton, is produced by Harry Saltzman and Albert R. Broccoli, who also make the Bond films. Obviously they have in mind a parallel series of spy dramas. Deighton has already written two more novels and the downbeat seediness of his stories makes a nice contrast to the glamorous fantasies of the late Ian Fleming.

WHAT'S NEW, PETER?

Since shooting to stardom as the enigmatic hero of *Lawrence of Arabia* (1962), lanky Peter O'Toole has been much in demand. Born in Connemara, Ireland, in 1932, the son of a bookie, O'Toole later moved with his family to Leeds in the north of England, where he worked for several years on a local newspaper as a reporter. After a spell in the navy, he won a scholarship to London's Royal Academy of Dramatic Arts, where his classmates included future stars Albert Finney, Alan Bates and Richard Harris. After considerable stage experience (including work for the Royal Shakespeare Company), he was chosen for the lead role in *Lawrence* – a part for which, ironically, Finney had also tested. Since then he hasn't looked back. In the epic *Lord Jim*, now on release, he plays a British seaman, court-martialled for cowardice, who finds a new chance in life by defending a village against a brutal warlord. Based on Joseph Conrad's novel, the film co-stars James Mason, Curt Jurgens, Eli Wallach, Jack Hawkins and beautiful Israeli newcomer Daliah Lavi and was filmed at the spectacular Angkor Wat temples in Cambodia. He'll also be seen this summer in the very different *What's New Pussycat*, a zany comedy in which he plays a libidinous playboy analysed by long-haired shrink Peter Sellers.

ACADEMY AWARDS

PRESENTED ON 5 APRIL 1965

Best Picture
My Fair Lady

Best Director
George Cukor
My Fair Lady

Best Actor
Rex Harrison
My Fair Lady

Best Actress
Julie Andrews
Mary Poppins

Best Sup Actor
Peter Ustinov
Topkapi

Best Sup Actress
Lila Kedrova
Zorba the Greek

Michael Caine is Len Deighton's Harry Palmer in The Ipcress File.

Peter O'Toole as Joseph Conrad's sailor Lord Jim.

Max Von Sydow is Jesus in the epic The Greatest Story Ever Told.

THE LONGEST STORY

George Stevens' *The Greatest Story Ever Told* is also the longest: four years in production, costing $20 million and running 225 minutes, this is the story of Christ writ larger than ever before. Because of Stevens' painstaking approach, several other directors are rumoured to have directed segments, including David Lean and Jean Negulesco.

Filmed in the single-lens Cinerama process entirely in the United States, the massive movie has a reverential approach but features, with one exception, dozens of major stars in the hope of recouping the huge budget. These include Charlton Heston as John the Baptist, Claude Rains as Herod, Sidney Poitier as Simon and John Wayne as a Roman centurion. The exception is Max Von Sydow, who plays Christ. Until now, the tall, saturnine 35-year-old has been known outside his native Sweden only as the favourite actor of director Ingmar Bergman in classics like *The Seventh Seal* (1957).

JULIE'S A TROUPER

As they say in the theatre, Julie Andrews is a trouper. Already a veteran at the age of 30, Andrews came from a British showbusiness family and made her stage debut aged 12. She was 19 when she made her Broadway debut in *The Boy Friend*. Two years later the fresh-faced, plum-voiced singer-actress starred opposite Rex Harrison in *My Fair Lady*. She played Eliza Dolittle in London and on Broadway for three years and in 1960 starred as Guinevere opposite Richard Burton's Arthur in Lerner and Loewe's *Camelot*. Another long run followed, during which she learned that Warners had passed her over in favour of Audrey Hepburn for the film version of *My Fair Lady* (1964). But Walt Disney turned her into a major movie star with *Mary Poppins*, one of last year's biggest grossers, for which she has won the Best Actress Oscar. A much less wholesome role opposite James Garner in the cynical Second World War drama *The Americanization of Emily* followed the same year and now Andrews can be seen in the lavish film version of Rodgers and Hammerstein's *The Sound of Music*.

KUBRICK REACHES FOR THE STARS

M-G-M and director Stanley Kubrick have announced a big-budget science fiction film called *Journey Beyond the Stars* to start shooting on 16 August on locations in Britain, Switzerland, Africa, West Germany and the United States. Interiors will be filmed at M-G-M's Elstree studios outside London. Kubrick, who is to write the script with famed science fiction author Arthur C. Clarke, says that *Journey* "will take place in the year 2001 and involves exploration of the solar system and the discovery of extraterrestrial intelligence". Says M-G-M president Robert H. O'Brien: "It won't be a Buck Rogers kind of space epic." The budget is set at $4.5 million.

BIRTHS, DEATHS AND MARRIAGES

BIRTHS

Robert Downey
4 Apr, New York

DEATHS

Jeanette MacDonald
14 Jan, Houston, Texas
Heart failure following surgery

Stan Laurel
23 Feb, Santa Monica, California
Heart attack

Margaret Dumont
23 Mar, Hollywood
Heart attack

Mae Murray
23 Mar, Hollywood
Stroke

Linda Darnell
10 Apr, Chicago
Fire accident

MARRIAGES

Kim Novak
15 Mar, *to* **Richard Johnson**

STAN LAUREL DEAD

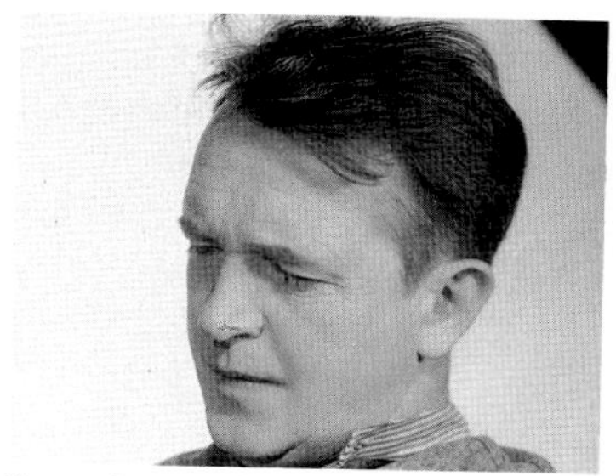

Stan Laurel, the thin half of Laurel and Hardy, died on 23 February, aged 74. Born in Ulverston, England, Laurel's real name was Arthur Stanley Jefferson. He worked the British music halls and after a stint as Charlie Chaplin's understudy on an American tour in 1912 he changed his name and made his screen debut in 1917. He teamed with Oliver Hardy in 1926 and they made more than 100 comedy pictures together, the last released in 1951. Long regarded as the more creative of the two, Laurel was said to be deeply distressed by Hardy's death in 1957 and had not worked since. He was presented with an honorary Academy Award in 1960 for "his creative pioneering in the field of cinema comedy".

MAY
JUNE

JULY
AUGUST

THE FALL OF THE BRONSTON EMPIRE

Samuel Bronston, the producer who made *King of Kings*, *El Cid* (both 1961), *55 Days at Peking* (1963) and *Circus World* (1964), has closed down his studio in Spain and filed for bankruptcy. Bronston's pictures were second to none in production values and generally well received by critics, but only *El Cid* was profitable. Most damaging to Bronston's organization has been the colossal commercial failure of *The Fall of the Roman Empire* (1964), which cost $19 million and earned less than $2 million in the United States.

STAR QUOTES

Steve McQueen

"In my own mind, I'm not sure that acting is something for a grown man to be doing."

STAR QUOTES

Jane Fonda

"You spend all your life trying to do something they put people into asylums for."

ACCENTS, NOT ANECDOTES

Peter Sellers and Capucine in the zany comedy What's New Pussycat?

Will the real Peter Sellers please stand up? A master of vocal mimicry and disguise, Sellers was born in 1925 and started clowning during his RAF service. In 1949 he joined forces with Spike Milligan, Harry Secombe and Michael Bentine, whose satirical and surreal BBC radio series *The Goons* ran for seven years and gained a cult following. Sellers was now getting small roles in comedy films and made his first major impression as a spiv in *The Ladykillers* (1956) and as an elderly drunken cinema projectionist in *The Smallest Show on Earth* (1957). His range is limitless – Cockneys, aristocrats, Indians, Italians – Sellers can play them all. But like many comedians, he's a deeply introspective man who says, "I feel safer with an accent than an anecdote." When director Stanley Kubrick cast him as Clare Quilty in *Lolita* (1962) – a role which required him to play an American writer, a detective and an Austrian psychiatrist – he reached a wider audience. In Kubrick's *Dr. Strangelove* (1963) he played three roles (stiff-upper-lip RAF officer, mad German scientist, and smooth American president) and would have played a fourth (American pilot) had not a broken ankle intervened. With his fumbling French detective Clouseau in last year's *The Pink Panther* and *A Shot in the Dark* he reached his widest audience so far. But tragedy befell his first Hollywood role – a heart attack put him out of Billy Wilder's *Kiss Me, Stupid* (1964) though he has made a swift recovery as the loony Dr. Fritz Fassbender in *What's New Pussycat?*

SELZNICK DEAD

David O. Selznick, the producer of *Gone with the Wind* (1939), died of a heart attack on 22 June at the Mount Sinai Hospital, California. Selznick was one of Hollywood's most powerful executives, famous for his creative gifts. The son of movie pioneer Lewis Selznick, he rose through the ranks of Paramount, M-G-M and RKO until he founded his own production company in 1937. He married Louis B. Mayer's daughter, Irene, and later the actress Jennifer Jones, who was with him when he died. His credits included *King Kong* (1933), *Intermezzo* (1939), *Rebecca* (1940), *Spellbound* (1945), *Duel in the Sun* (1946) and *A Star Is Born* (1954) – but he will always be remembered as the driving force behind *GWTW*, the most successful picture ever made. His last production was *A Farewell to Arms*, released in 1957.

BIRD APPEAL

Tolan (Ray Brooks) has the knack. Colin (Michael Crawford) doesn't, but he desperately wants it. The knack is the ability to have scores of women – every day, as Tolan does. Nancy (Rita Tushingham), just arrived in London, may offer Crawford a chance to get the knack, especially as she moves into the house which Tolan and Colin share with Tom (Donal Donelly) who isn't really interested in sex. He simply likes to paint everything virgin white. Following his success last summer with *A Hard Day's Night* (the next Beatles film, *Help!*, will be released in a few weeks' time), Richard Lester has already seen his zany comedy *The Knack . . . and how to get it* carry off the main prize at the Cannes Film Festival in the spring. Based on the play by Ann Jellicoe, it showcases four of Britain's brightest talents. Says Lester: "I don't think it's the kind of picture that needed bigger 'names'. We were allowed to have who we wanted. Rita was already committed before I arrived. The good thing about Ray is he can play a man who has sexual activity five hours a day but you know there is something absurd about it all the time."

BIRTHS, DEATHS AND MARRIAGES

BIRTHS

Brooke Shields
31 May, New York

Marlee Matlin
24 Aug, Morton Grove, Illinois

DEATHS

Judy Holliday
7 Jun, New York
Cancer

Steve Cochran
15 Jun, off Guatemala
Lung infection

David O. Selznick
22 Jun, Hollywood
Heart attack

Constance Bennett
24 Jul, New Jersey
Cerebral hemorrhage

Nancy Carroll
6 Aug, New York

MARRIAGES

Cary Grant
Jul, *to* **Dyan Cannon**

Jane Fonda
14 Aug, *to* **Roger Vadim**

JULIE CHRISTIE'S ROLES

Blonde British actress Julie Christie has landed two of the most demanding roles of the year – as the loose-living model/actress in *Darling*, for which she got rave reviews, and as Lara in David Lean's forthcoming epic *Doctor Zhivago*. Like many others, Lean saw Christie in *Billy Liar!* (1963), walking along the drab suburban street, swinging her handbag and embodying a free spirit, an independent spirit blowing away the cobwebs of British screen heroines.

Born in Assam, India, in 1940, Christie is the daughter of a tea planter. She came to England for her schooling, went to Paris to study art and then decided to become an actress, enrolling at the Central School of Music and Drama in London. Like so many British actors, she trod the boards at a provincial repertory theatre. Then she appeared in a BBC-TV science fiction series called *A for Andromeda*. At the same time she appeared in two run-of-the-mill comedies, *Crooks Anonymous* (1962) and *The Fast Lady* (1963). Director John Schlesinger had seen her at Drama School when he was casting *A Kind of Loving* (1962) and remembered her when he was casting *Billy Liar!* Schlesinger now wants her to play Bathsheba Everdene in *Far from the Madding Crowd*, and acclaimed French director Francois Truffaut has signed her for *Fahrenheit 451*. Her good looks and acting talent are much in demand and, along with Sarah Miles and the Redgrave sisters, Christie is spearheading the invasion of Hollywood by British actresses.

Julie Christie and Dirk Bogarde, one of her lovers, in Darling.

DOLCE, DARLING

Everyone calls Diana Scott (Julie Christie) "darling". She's gorgeous, vivacious and totally without moral scruples. She is determined to go places and leaps in and out of bed with Dirk Bogarde, a TV interviewer, and Laurence Harvey, an advertising man, becoming a famous model and finally settling down with an Italian prince. Written by Frederic Raphael and directed by John Schlesinger, *Darling* is an unflinching look at the *dolce vita* of today, with a juicy starring role for 24-year-old Christie, who first turned heads as the blonde "swinger" in Schlesinger's previous movie, *Billy Liar!*, two years ago. *Darling* caused a sensation at the Moscow Film Festival this summer, where it was shown with an entire sequence cut out. Even in Britain the "offending" section – where Diana is introduced to a sexual exhibition by the Paris smart set – has been modified after moans by the censor.

GOSSIP COLUMN

■ **Legendary mogul David O. Selznick, who died in June, had a secret ambition – to be a scriptwriter. In the mid-1950s he had a stab at scripting Dexter Masters' novel, *The Accident*, about the dangers of atomic lab work, but was warned off by nervous M-G-M executives.**

NIGHTMARE IN EARL'S COURT

Polish tyro Roman Polanski, 31, challenges Hitchcock for the title of Master of Suspense with his first English-language film *Repulsion*. It's the horrific story of a young manicurist, played by blonde French sensation Catherine Deneuve, who is left alone in a dingy Earl's Court flat when her sister goes on holiday. She slowly retreats deeper and deeper into sexual madness, leaving food to rot and then murdering first her boyfriend and then her landlord.

It's the first film in English by young Polanski, who was invited to England by producer Gene Gutowski, impressed by his art-house success, *Knife in the Water*, made in Poland in 1962. Says Polanski: "*Repulsion* will shock some people, jolt them. What interests me is the girl's disintegration, the withdrawal turning to violence. I'm concerned with exposing a bit of human behaviour that society likes to keep hidden, and by lifting the curtain on the forbidden subject I think one liberates it from secrecy and shame."

Yvonne Furneaux, Ian Hendry and Catherine Deneuve in Roman Polanski's Repulsion.

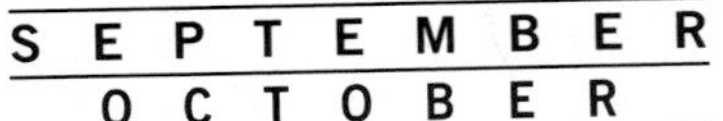

RED SNOW

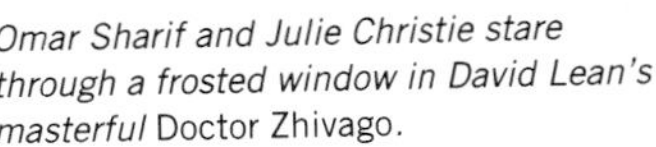

Omar Sharif and Julie Christie stare through a frosted window in David Lean's masterful Doctor Zhivago.

WILDEST WEST

Westerns don't come any wackier than *Cat Ballou*, in which Jane Fonda plays the title role, a prim schoolgirl who becomes the leader of a gang of outlaws in order to avenge the murder of her father by a notorious, silver-nosed gunslinger played by a snarling Lee Marvin. Marvin also plays Kid Shelleen, Fonda's sidekick, another gunslinger whose addiction to the bottle has seeped through his pants and saddle and into his horse – both are usually plastered. But they sober up when Jane, after robbing a train and avenging her father, is sentenced to be hanged. The title song, sung by the late Nat "King" Cole, who plays a wandering minstrel, is a surefire hit.

DISNEY IN FLORIDA

At a press conference on 15 November Walt and Roy Disney announced plans for a second theme park to be built in swampland between the cities of Orlando and Kissimmee in central Florida. The new facility, to be called Walt Disney World, will complement the 10-year-old Disneyland at Anaheim, California, and is scheduled to open in October 1971. It will cover 43 square miles, twice the area of Manhattan. Disney has paid $5 million for the land and will build its own hotels to lodge the visitors who will come mainly from the eastern United States. A key attraction of the new park will be an "Experimental Prototype Community of Tomorrow" (EPCOT), which Disney says "will take its cue from the new ideas and technologies emerging from American industry. It will be a place where people actually live a life they can't find anywhere else in the world."

With *Lawrence of Arabia*, director David Lean and screenwriter Robert Bolt gave us the sand. Now, with *Doctor Zhivago*, they have endured sub-zero temperatures to give us the snow. Boris Pasternak's Nobel Prize-winning novel is set at the time of the Russian Revolution which, Lean says, "provides the canvas against which is told a moving and highly personal love story". Omar Sharif plays Zhivago, the young, idealistic physician whose love for his wife (Geraldine Chaplin) and the beautiful Lara (Julie Christie) is engulfed by the tide of history. Co-starring Rod Steiger, Tom Courtenay, Alec Guinness and Ralph Richardson, the epic has taken nine months to film in the frozen wastes of Finland and in Spain, where a giant set depicting Moscow in 1917 was built.

OMAR SHARIF

Few actors could have wished for a finer entry into international stardom than Omar Sharif got in *Lawrence of Arabia* (1962). He emerged on a camel from a desert mirage, resplendent in his Harith robes and looking every inch the romantic hero of popular fiction. It should have been his screen debut. In fact, Sharif had already starred in more than 20 movies, all of them made in his native Egypt, where he was born in 1932. He was lucky to be cast as Sherif Ali in *Lawrence* – director David Lean had already cast Alain Delon in the role but things were not working out. So Lean plucked Sharif out of a book of Egyptian actors and made him a star. Since *Lawrence* he has starred as an Armenian in *The Fall of the Roman Empire* (1964), as a Spanish priest in *Behold a Pale Horse* (1964) and as *Genghis Khan* (1965). These roles were unworthy of the dusky-eyed star many critics have dubbed "the new Valentino", but his performance as the romantic poet-hero of Lean's *Doctor Zhivago* will undoubtedly put his career back on track. However, Sharif himself still sees acting as only a means to pursue his first love – championship bridge.

BIRTHS, DEATHS AND MARRIAGES

BIRTHS

Charlie Sheen
3 Sep, Los Angeles

DEATHS

Dorothy Dandridge
8 Sep, Hollywood
Barbiturate poisoning

Clara Bow
27 Sep, Los Angeles

Zachary Scott
3 Oct, Austin, Texas
Brain tumour

MARRIAGES

Judy Garland
15 Nov, *to* Mark Herron

Henry Fonda
3 Dec, *to* Shirlee Mae Adams

MARVY MARVIN

Ever since he threw scalding hot coffee in Gloria Grahame's face in *The Big Heat* (1953), Lee Marvin's been the bad guy you just love to hate. With a face that looks as if it was chiselled out of Mount Rushmore, and a voice that sounds as if it's coming from the bottom of an empty whisky bottle, he's gradually softened his image from the thugs of the 1950s but still isn't someone a girl would take home to meet mother. Only last year, as a hit man in *The Killers*, he tossed sultry Angie Dickinson out of her bedroom window.

Born in New York in 1924, he served as a marine in the South Pacific during the Second World War and started acting in off-Broadway productions thereafter. Following work in live TV, he made his debut (along with Charles Bronson) in the war comedy *You're in the Navy Now* (1951), and subsequently settled in Hollywood. Over the next decade he made almost 30 movies, ranging from westerns to thrillers – most memorably *The Big Heat*, *Bad Day at Black Rock* (1955) and *Attack!* (1956).

Three action movies with John Wayne – *The Comancheros* (1961), *The Man Who Shot Liberty Valance* (1962) and *Donovan's Reef* (1963) – showed him broadening his range and emerging as a star in his own right. This summer we've seen him in two more guises, as a drunken has-been baseball player in the all-star drama *Ship of Fools* and as a drunken has-been gunfighter in the comedy western *Cat Ballou*. But at the ripe old age of 41, this son of an ad executive and fashion writer looks as if he's only just beginning.

Jane Fonda and Lee Marvin in the way-out western Cat Ballou.

BOX OFFICE

UK

SPECIAL PRESENTATION

1 The Sound of Music
2 My Fair Lady
3 The Great Race

TOP TEN GENERAL RELEASES

1 Mary Poppins
2 Help!
3 Snow White and the Seven Dwarfs
4 What's New Pussycat
5 A Shot in the Dark
6 The Carpetbaggers
7 Von Ryan's Express
8 The Train
9 Operation Crossbow
10 Carry on Cleo

BOX OFFICE

US

1 Mary Poppins
2 The Sound of Music
3 Goldfinger
4 My Fair Lady
5 What's New Pussycat
6 Shenandoah
7 The Sandpiper
8 Father Goose
9 Von Ryan's Express
10 The Yellow Rolls-Royce

Richard Burton and Oskar Werner in The Spy Who Came in from the Cold.

COLD WAR TREACHERY

Richard Burton abandons the heroic, glamorous and historical roles of recent years to play seedy British secret agent Alec Leamas. The adaptation of John le Carre's best-selling novel *The Spy Who Came in from the Cold* marks a move away from the world of James Bond and Harry Palmer to create a realistic portrayal of the Cold War. Director Martin Ritt has eschewed all gadgets, fancy weaponry and even colour to enhance the downbeat mood. Burton's role requires him to sink into alcoholic despair and poverty, making him ripe for defection in order to expose a chain of treachery that leads to a bleak climax on the Berlin Wall. Claire Bloom plays a British communist who befriends him, and Rupert Davies, famous on British TV for playing Inspector Maigret, plays Burton's boss, George Smiley. Fans of the spy genre will enjoy the in-joke of casting Bernard Lee – "M" in the Bond films – as a shopkeeper whom Burton beats up.

JANUARY
FEBRUARY

MARCH
APRIL

SPEX APPEAL

With the likes of Sean Connery, Terence Stamp, Peter O'Toole, Albert Finney and, the least likely of all, Michael Caine, Britain has introduced a new breed of actor to movies. Caine is unmistakable: he's the one with the glasses.

You have to go back a long way – to Harold Lloyd in the silent era – to find a movie star wearing specs because he has to. Caine didn't wear any in *Zulu* (1964), in which he led a motley band of soldiers against hordes of Zulu warriors. But his portrayal of a toffee-nosed British officer got him noticed. Only later did audiences realize Caine was simply "playing posh".

Born in 1933 in a working-class district of South London, Caine is Cockney through and through. His parents worked in the local food markets, but he decided to become an actor, working his way through local repertory theatre. After serving in Korea, he made his first film in 1956, ironically enough in *A Hill in Korea*. Several minor roles followed until Stanley Baker saw him understudying O'Toole in the stage production of *The Long and the Short and the Tall*.

Baker offered him the co-starring role in *Zulu* and then came *The Ipcress File* (1965), in which he donned his glasses and natural accent as the antidote to James Bond. Now, with acclaim for his performance as the Cockney Casanova *Alfie*, Caine has no need to ask, "What's it all about?"

Julia Foster and Michael Caine (without glasses) as Cockney Casanova *Alfie*.

COCKNEY CASANOVA

"What's it all about, Alfie?" warbles Cilla Black in the title song. Well, it's about this Bermondsey bloke who's a regular Casanova, see. Birds fall for his cynical charm and end up in the back of a car and then a maternity ward or an abortion clinic.

Alfie is based on Bill Naughton's play, and it's a candid modern morality tale. Michael Caine is Alfie and Shelley Winters, Millicent Martin, Julia Foster, Jane Asher and Shirley Anne Field are his various sexual conquests. Says Caine, currently Britain's hottest young actor following *Zulu* (1964) and *The Ipcress File* (1965): "I wanted to show the sadness of a man who destroys others and destroys himself." But it's also very funny.

David Warner in *Morgan (A Suitable Case for Treatment)*.

MONKEY BUSINESS

"If I'd been planted in the womb of a chimpanzee, none of this would have happened," mutters Morgan (David Warner). The title character in *Morgan (A Suitable Case for Treatment)* is an artist and he's more than a little confused. He's haunted by visions of Tarzan movies and has a fondness for dressing up as King Kong.

This is due partly to his mother, a rabid Cockney Marxist, and partly to the fact that his marriage to posh Vanessa Redgrave is on the rocks. It's a riotous exercise in fantasy and social anarchy, based on a play by David Mercer. Director is Karel Reisz, who made the much glummer *Saturday Night and Sunday Morning* back in 1960.

ACADEMY AWARDS

PRESENTED ON 18 APRIL 1966

Best Picture
The Sound of Music

Best Director
Robert Wise
The Sound of Music

Best Actor
Lee Marvin
Cat Ballou

Best Actress
Julie Andrews
Darling

Best Sup Actor
Martin Balsam
A Thousand Clowns

Best Sup Actress
Shelley Winters
A Patch of Blue

BIRTHS, DEATHS AND MARRIAGES

BIRTHS

Laura Dern
10 Feb, Los Angeles

DEATHS

Hedda Hopper
1 Feb, Hollywood
Pneumonia

Buster Keaton
1 Feb, Hollywood
Cancer

MARRIAGES

Brian Donlevy
25 Feb, *to* Lillian Lugosi

Sophia Loren
9 Apr, *to* **Carlo Ponti**

BRANDO TAKES A BEATING!

Marlon Brando and Robert Redford in The Chase.

Sam Spiegel's first production since *Lawrence of Arabia* (1962), *The Chase* is a searing indictment of the violence in American society. Director Arthur Penn says it's a response to the Kennedy assassination and subsequent murder of Lee Harvey Oswald three years ago.

Marlon Brando plays the sheriff of a Texan town who has to defend an escaped convict from the local people, most of whom have a good reason to hate him. Alongside Brando, Spiegel has assembled a superb cast including up-and-coming Robert Redford (Natalie Wood's glamour boy in the current *Inside Daisy Clover*) as the convict, Jane Fonda as his wife and Angie Dickinson as Brando's wife. Lillian Hellman's script (from a novel and play by Horton Foote) takes in bigotry, adultery and racism before reaching its climax in which Brando receives the bloodiest beating of his career.

Jane Fonda in a scene from Arthur Penn's The Chase.

"STONE FACE" DEAD

Buster Keaton, one of the greatest comedy stars of the silent era, died of lung cancer at his home in California, on 1 February, aged 70. Known as "Stone Face" because he never smiled on screen, Keaton made scores of comedy shorts before turning to features in 1923. His credits include *Our Hospitality* (1923), *Sherlock, Jr., The Navigator* (1924) and *The General* (1926)

Unlike his rival Charlie Chaplin, he was a casualty of the sound era and his later years were largely unhappy, plagued with marital and alcohol problems brought on by his difficulty in finding work. But a screen biography starring Donald O'Connor in 1957 made him financially secure and aroused interest in his work, and in 1959 he received a special Oscar for his "unique talents".

He began to make cameo appearances in films such as *It's a Mad Mad Mad Mad World* (1963) and *A Funny Thing Happened on the Way to the Forum* (1966), and in September 1965 he was feted at the Venice film festival with a retrospective of his work. This will now travel the world, delighting new generations of filmgoers.

DEAN OF ALL TRADES?

Comedian, singer, serious actor – Dean Martin is all of these, drunk or sober. In his latest film *The Silencers*, with sexy Stella Stevens, he plays secret agent Matt Helm, a man who makes James Bond look like a monk – he's got a circular bed with a built-in bar, a TV screen and a special flap which tips him straight into his swimming pool, where his secretary waits to take a memo. A master of Okinawa Te, a form of martial arts, Helm saves the world from being irradiated by the Chinese. All this and songs too!

For Martin, it's an ideal role, and further adventures of the horny Helm seem inevitable. Martin's career in movies has gone hand-in-hand with his rise as a nightclub entertainer – his shows rival Frank Sinatra's at Las Vegas and since the late 1950s he's been a fully paid-up member of The Clan, co-starring with Sinatra, Sammy Davis, Jr. and Peter Lawford in such films as *Ocean's Eleven* (1960) and *Robin and the Seven Hoods* (1964). Before that he was Jerry Lewis's partner in 16 pictures, including their joint screen debut *My Friend Irma* (1949), *The Caddy* (1953) and *Hollywood or Bust* (1956).

But Martin showed what a fine actor he is in the classic western *Rio Bravo* (1959), in which he played a reformed drunk, and as a gambler in *Some Came Running* (1959). He also showed what a sport he was in Billy Wilder's controversial comedy *Kiss Me, Stupid* (1964), in which he played Dino Martini, a nightclub entertainer, movie star and lothario who sees life through a haze of bourbon and half-remembered women. Martin has the genius to maintain a facade without any cracks appearing.

THE SOUND OF MONEY

20th Century-Fox's *The Sound of Music* has become the highest-grossing motion picture of all time, finally displacing *Gone with the Wind* (1939) as all-time box-office champ. The Rogers & Hammerstein musical has racked up over $70 million in its first year of release and when foreign markets are taken into account it will have grossed $120 million.

The picture has ended Fox's financial problems caused mainly by *Cleopatra*. And on 18 April it got Hollywood's ultimate seal of approval by winning five Oscars, including Best Picture. This won't please most critics, though. One of them re-titled the picture *The Sound of Mucus*.

STAR QUOTES

Julie Andrews

"I don't want to be thought of as wholesome."

MAY
JUNE

JULY
AUGUST

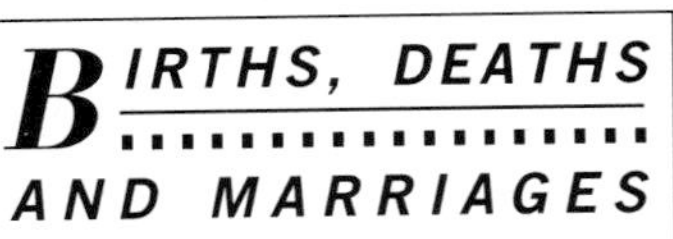

BIRTHS

Helena Bonham-Carter
26 May, London

DEATHS

Montgomery Clift
23 Jul, New York
Heart attack

Francis X. Bushman
23 Aug, Hollywood
Heart problem

MARRIAGES

Brigitte Bardot
13 July, *to* Gunther Sachs

CLIFT DEAD

Hollywood is in a state of shock at the announcement of the death of actor Montgomery Clift, on 23 July, at the age of 45. He had suffered a heart attack in his New York apartment.

Nominated for an Oscar for his screen debut in *The Search* (1948), Clift rapidly became one of Hollywood's most sought-after young actors. He was a forerunner of Marlon Brando and Paul Newman, specializing in emotionally demanding parts. His credits include *Red River* (1948), *A Place in the Sun* (1951), *From Here to Eternity* (1953), *Suddenly, Last Summer* (1959) and *The Misfits* (1961). In 1956 he was involved in a car accident, his injuries leading to recurrent bouts of ill-health and mental instability. Last month he completed work on the spy thriller *The Defector*, and he was due to start John Huston's *Reflections in a Golden Eye* this autumn.

ROCK OF AGES

We all know Rock Hudson. He's Hollywood's leading man – the romantic partner of Doris Day in *Pillow Talk* (1959), *Lover Come Back* (1961) and *Send Me No Flowers* (1964); the hero of westerns, adventure dramas and war films. And tear-jerkers like *Magnificent Obsession* (1954), *All That Heaven Allows* (1955) and *Written on the Wind* (1956). His director on those tear-jerkers, Douglas Sirk, realized that this "Baron of Beefcake," as a Universal publicity release once described him, had an emotional vulnerability that won the hearts of women everywhere.

Hudson's critics say he doesn't really have to act; but his performance in the epic *Giant* (1956), for which he was loaned to Warners by Universal for $250,000, stood up well beside Elizabeth Taylor and James Dean. Hudson's tall, square-jawed appeal placed him at or very near the top of Hollywood most popular stars from 1957 to 1964. Then his star began to wane ever so slightly – *Strange Bedfellows* (1964), with Gina Lolobrigida, and *A Very Special Favor* (1965), with Leslie Caron, were flops. Hudson's disdain for his image and for much of his career became known and he went looking for a change of role.

Now he's certainly found it in *Seconds*, John Frankenheimer's science-fiction drama about an ordinary, middle-aged man who undergoes plastic surgery and is reborn as a bohemian artist in Malibu. Hudson's performance is his bravest and most challenging work to date. You might say, a second Rock Hudson.

Dogfight scene from The Blue Max, *about a young German flying ace in the First World War.*

KNIGHTHOOD'S FINEST HOUR

One of the biggest pictures of the summer is a two-part, two-and-a-half-hour spectacular set among German air aces of the First World War. *The Blue Max* is the slang name for what every one of the Kaiser's flyers yearns – the highest award for bravery. And the most ambitious of all is Bruno Stachel (George Peppard), a lower-class heel who will stamp on anyone in his way to get it.

Based on a 1964 novel by Jack D. Hunter it's a dog-eat-dog drama of social snobbery among Germany's officer class. Jeremy Kemp is Peppard's chief rival and James Mason the count who uses Peppard for his own ends. Sexpot Ursula Andress (her husky Swiss-German tones put to authentic use for the first time in her career) is in for some torrid scenes with Peppard, and paralleling their bedroom action is a string of exciting air battles with Spads, Camels, Pfalzes and Fokkers.

Shot in Ireland and directed by Britain's John Guillermin, *The Blue Max* could be tough to sell – are moviegoers ready for a picture about German heroes? But it's another powerful role for 36-year-old Peppard who, after hitting the big time opposite Audrey Hepburn in the romantic *Breakfast at Tiffany's* (1961), is rapidly turning into a younger version of Richard Widmark with his steely-eyed playing in *The Carpetbaggers* (1964) and *Operation Crossbow* (1965).

Buck Taylor, Peter Fonda and Nancy Sinatra in The Wild Angels.

BEACH BIKERS

The Wild Angels is low-budget horror maestro Roger Corman's update on Marlon Brando's shocker *The Wild One* (1953). Peter Fonda, son of Henry and sister of Jane, is the leader of some Southern Californian Hell's Angels who terrorize a sleepy middle-class beach community.

Nancy Sinatra, daughter of Frank, plays his girl and Bruce Dern is a gang-member shot by the cops. The graphically violent film opens with a warning: "The picture you are about to see will shock and perhaps anger you. Although the events and characters are fictitious, the story is a reflection of our times." It's already been banned in Britain.

George Segal, Richard Burton, Sandy Dennis and Elizabeth Taylor in Who's Afraid of Virginia Woolf?

MATRIMONIAL FIREWORKS

The world's most famous married couple, Richard Burton and Elizabeth Taylor, are superbly cast in the powerful film version of Edward Albee's play, *Who's Afraid of Virginia Woolf?* Continually drunk and at each other's throats, history professor Burton and blousy wife Taylor entertain clean-cut student George Segal and twittering fiancee Sandy Dennis with an evening of verbal fireworks. Or at least, that's how it starts. As the younger couple fight back, it's no prisoners until dawn in this searing emotional drama.

This savage showcase for acting talent is the movie debut of Broadway director Mike Nichols, who says of the experience, "There was a very unpleasant aspect for all of us. We had to keep coming back to the same damn room, over and over, every day. And the poor Burtons had to spit at each other and hit each other for days."

Alfred Hitchcock takes a phone call with the help of his secretary while on location filming Torn Curtain.

HITCHCOCK'S CURTAIN

A new movie opens in town. What is it, a friend asks? A western, a comedy, a swashbuckler, a musical, you may say. But if the film is called *Torn Curtain*, you simply say "a Hitchcock".

Critics have been unkind to Hitch's 50th film, a Cold War thriller with Paul Newman and Julie Andrews. But what other director's name conjures up such a self-contained world? Of suspicion, vertigo, shadows of doubt, strangers on trains?

For more than 40 years and through 50 movies Hitchcock has held audiences spellbound. He's the one director who's as famous as the actors in his films. His portly, business-suited profile is known from scores of TV shows and his own laconic trailers; close our eyes and we hear his slow, Cockney voice. From humble origins in London, he worked in silent pictures, made the first British talkie (*Blackmail*, 1929) and a string of classic thrillers such as *The 39 Steps* (1935) and *The Lady Vanishes* (1938) before moving to Hollywood in 1940.

He's never won an Oscar but few have done so much to extend the range of cinema. Revered in France as a major artist and moralist, Hitchcock has recently been celebrated in a long interview book with by French director Francois Truffaut.

STAR QUOTES

Sean Connery

"I've always hated that James Bond. I'd like to kill him off."

STAR QUOTES

Elizabeth Taylor

"I don't pretend to be an ordinary housewife."

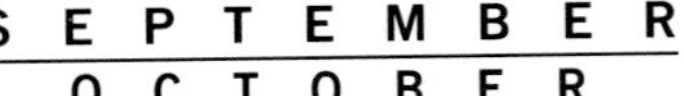

SEPTEMBER
OCTOBER

NOVEMBER
DECEMBER

RACING STAR

"Acting is like racing," says Steve McQueen. "You need the same absolute concentration." Audiences love watching McQueen concentrate: of all modern stars, his style proves the maxim that "less is more." His face is impassive, his movements economical, like a mountain lion. His range is limited, but his image of self-sufficiency has turned him into one of the most popular screen stars of his generation.

He's had touching love affairs on screen, most tellingly with Natalie Wood in *Love with the Proper Stranger* (1963) and Lee Remick in *Baby the Rain Must Fall* (1965). But moviegoers remember most his exhilaration and love of machines – the stolen Nazi motorcycle in *The Great Escape* (1963), which briefly unleashes him from solitary confinement in "The Cooler"; the plane in *The War Lover* (1962); and now the hot, grimy engine room of the USS *San Pablo* in *The Sand Pebbles*. They remember, too, his gunfighter in *The Magnificent Seven* (1960) and his card-player in *The Cincinnati Kid* (1965).

The 36-year-old star had a difficult childhood and after a spell in a reform school he became a merchant seaman, a marine, a lumberjack and a racing driver before stumbling into acting. He was an extra in *Somebody Up There Likes Me* (1956) and appeared (as Steven McQueen) in films like *Never Love a Stranger* and *The Blob* (both 1958).

But he became nationally famous in CBS-TV's western series *Wanted: Dead Or Alive* (1958). That led to his becoming one of *The Magnificent Seven* and a star to be reckoned with.

Richard Attenborough and Steve McQueen *in* The Sand Pebbles.

UP THE YANGTZE

For *The Sand Pebbles* director Robert Wise has meticulously reconstructed the Shanghai waterfront and the revolutionary chaos that was China in the late 1920s. Steve McQueen, Richard Attenborough and Richard Crenna are the crew of the USS *San Pablo*, an American gunship, which sails up the mighty Yangtze river to rescue a group of American missionaries threatened by feudal warlords. Not all of them survive the hazardous mission.

The 193-minute drama co-stars exciting 20-year-old newcomer Candice Bergen (who made her debut as the lesbian Lakey in *The Group* last spring) as a missionary teacher. A former fashion model, she was signed by director Wise after he saw her unsuccessful test for *The Chase*.

The production is a triumph of logistics. After examining the Sacramento river in California, the nearest river to Hollywood, Wise decided that only Far East locations would do. While waiting for negotiations to be completed, he directed *The Sound of Music* and then took his crew to Hong Kong and Taiwan, formerly the Chinese island of Formosa, where filming began on 22 November 1965 and lasted until 15 May this year.

Filming was frequently bogged down by weather and civil disturbances, and morale ran low. That explains an enigmatic credit in the titles – "Diversions by Irving Schwartz," said to be the name of an unknown letter-writer who kept the harassed crew's spirits up.

BIRTHS, DEATHS AND MARRIAGES

BIRTHS

C. Thomas Howell
7 Dec, Van Nuys, California

DEATHS

Wilfred Lawson
11 Oct, London
Heart attack

Clifton Webb
13 Oct, Beverly Hills
Heart attack

Walt Disney
15 Dec, Burbank, California
Heart attack

MARRIAGES

Mickey Rooney
Sep, *to* Margie Lane

REAGAN LANDSLIDE

Former Hollywood actor Ronald Reagan won a landslide victory on 9 November in the election for the governorship of California. His victory, by nearly 2 million votes, reflects a national trend towards the Republican party.

Reagan's last screen appearance was as a ruthless crook in *The Killers* (1964). Never a major screen actor, Reagan has for long involved himself with industry issues, becoming president of the Screen Actors' Guild in 1947-52 and again in 1959.

BOX OFFICE

UK

SPECIAL PRESENTATION

1 Doctor Zhivago
2 My Fair Lady
3 Khartoum

TOP TEN GENERAL RELEASES

1 The Sound of Music
2 Thunderball
3 Alfie
4 Born Free
5 Our Man Flint
6 Those Magnificent Men in Their Flying Machines
7 The Early Bird
8 One Spy Too Many
9 The Great St. Trinian's Train Robbery
10 Battle of the Bulge

BOX OFFICE

US

1 Thunderball
2 Doctor Zhivago
3 Who's Afraid of Virginia Woolf?
4 That Darn Cat
5 The Russians Are Coming! The Russians Are Coming!
6 Lt. Robin Crusoe, U.S.N.
7 The Silencers
8 Torn Curtain
9 Our Man Flint
10 A Patch of Blue

HANDSOME HENRY

Forget the corpulent, drumstick-chomping Merry Monarch as portrayed by Charles Laughton. In *A Man for All Seasons* Henry VIII, as played by Robert Shaw, is handsome and virile, a man in his prime. He wants to divorce Catherine of Aragon and marry Anne Boleyn (Vanessa Redgrave), which brings him into conflict with the Catholic Church and Sir Thomas More (Paul Scofield), the respected judge and Chancellor, who refuses to sanction the marriage and is threatened with execution for treason.

Such trials of conscience are a speciality of Fred Zinnemann, who directs this lavish historical drama. It co-stars Orson Welles and introduces to the cinema some new British faces, including John Hurt and Corin Redgrave, brother of Vanessa. The screenplay is by Robert Bolt (based on his own 1960 play) who previously scripted *Lawrence of Arabia* (1962) and *Doctor Zhivago* (1965).

Robert Shaw, Nigel Davenport, Susannah York, Paul Scofield in A Man for All Seasons.

John Huston as Noah plays his pipes as he leads animals of every kind toward the Ark in The Bible.

IN THE BEGINNING . . .

Costing $18 million and filmed in Dimension-150 in locations as far flung as Sicily, Iceland and the Galapagos Islands, *The Bible* tells the first 22 chapters of Genesis. Subtitled *in the beginning . . .*, it starts with the Creation and ends with God ordering Abraham to sacrifice his son Isaac. In between are the stories of Adam and Eve, Cain and Abel, Noah's Ark, The Tower of Babel, and Sodom and Gomorrah.

Director John Huston, who himself plays Noah because "the animals and I struck up a fine relationship", and producer Dino De Laurentiis have gathered an international cast of stars – Peter O'Toole, Ava Gardner, Richard Harris, George C. Scott – as well as two unknowns. Michael Parks and Ulla Bergryd are the young couple who are required to stroll decorously naked through the Garden of Eden.

SPREADING THE WORD OF GOD

The latest blockbuster to hit the screens is the adaptation of James Michener's door-stopping *Hawaii*. Originally to have been directed by Fred Zinnemann, the task finally fell to George Roy Hill and it stars Julie Andrews as the dedicated wife of a New England missionary played by Swedish actor Max Von Sydow. For the tall, blonde, gaunt-looking Sydow it's another major Hollywood role after his portrayal of Christ in *The Greatest Story Ever Told*, one of the most costly box-office failures in Hollywood history.

Long regarded as one of Europe's finest screen actors, 37-year-old Sydow is the son of a university professor and trained as an actor at Stockholm's Royal Dramatic Theatre School. He made his screen debut in 1949 and after several stage appearances came to the attention of famed Swedish director Ingmar Bergman.

Sydow's most celebrated role for Bergman is the mediaeval knight who challenges Death to a game of chess in the art-house classic *The Seventh Seal* (1957). But his other Bergman roles in films like *Wild Strawberries* (1957), *So Close to Life* (1958), *Through a Glass Darkly* (1961) and *Winter Light* (1963) are all searing examinations of urban man on the brink of moral and psychological breakdown.

Hollywood has not captured Sydow for good. Following the spy thriller *The Quiller Memorandum*, with George Segal, due out this winter, he's already back in Sweden working with Ingmar Bergman again.

UNCLE WALT DIES

Walt Disney, one of the most famous names in showbusiness, died in a Burbank, California, hospital on 15 December at the age of 65, following surgery for lung cancer. Disney's name is synonymous with family entertainment and the hugely successful cartoons produced by his studio, including the feature-length *Snow White and the Seven Dwarfs* (1937), *Pinocchio* (1940), *Fantasia* (1940), *Dumbo* (1940), *Bambi* (1942), *Lady and the Tramp* (1955), *One Hundred and One Dalmatians* (1961) and many others.

Disney's studio also specialized in nature documentaries, adventure dramas, and more recently musicals like *Mary Poppins*, which combined live action with animation. Known the world over as "Uncle Walt", he was also the mastermind behind Disneyland in Los Angeles and Walt Disney World, currently being built in Florida.

Play It Again, Man

Hollywood was recycling waste long before the Green movement. Even before today's studio executives were born, it was plagiarising and plundering its own vaults as well as those in Europe and Japan.

There are two main approaches to remakes. The writer and director's view is fairly subtle: they look at a tried and tested story, assess its contemporary relevance and change things if necessary. Examples here include the sci-fi *Star Wars* (1977) and *Outland* (1981), both of which transposed the plots of revered 1950s westerns (*The Searchers* and *High Noon*) because westerns were then unfashionable. Billy Wilder's 1974 remake of *The Front Page* kept its 1920s setting but was full of references to Watergate.

The studio's view is that a hit of 20 or 30 years ago may prove a hit again. Sometimes a remake can save money: the studio may own the original copyright, so they don't need to pay for an expensive original script which might cost $1 million.

In this way, *Grand Hotel* (1932) became *A Weekend at the Waldorf* (1945); *Love Affair* (1939) became *An Affair to Remember* (1957); *The Letter* (1940) became *The Unfaithful* (1947); *The Philadelphia Story* (1940) became *High Society* (1956) and of course, *What Price Hollywood?* (1932) became *A Star Is Born*, three times.

Fletcher Christian has mutinied on the *Bounty* once every other decade; The Hounds of Zaroff are always barking, King Kong is ever on the rampage, and the works of Dickens, Tolstoy and others are always being taken out of the studio library. Few remember that John Huston's *The Maltese Falcon* (1941) was the third (and not the last) version of Dashiell Hammett's detective story.

Another ploy is to remake a successful foreign picture: in 1939 Ingrid Bergman's Hollywood debut, *Intermezzo*, was a remake of her 1936 Swedish success; *Le Jour Se Lève* (1939) became *The Long Night* (1947); *Seven Samurai* (1954) became *The Magnificent Seven* (1960); *Rashomon* (1950) became *Valerie* (1957) and *The Outrage* (1965); and *Yojimbo* (1961) became *Fistful of Dollars* (1964). The list is endless, as is the ways of recycling old material: samurai films become westerns, comedies become musicals, war films become science fiction, but the story basically remains essentially the same.

In the 1970s there were some famous blunders. Director William Friedkin, on a roll after *The French Connection* (1971) and *The Exorcist* (1973), decided to remake the classic 1952 French thriller *The Wages of Fear* as *Sorcerer* (1977); the result was an all-round calamity. Producer Dino De Laurentiis, after having remade *King Kong* in 1976 and barely managing to recoup his costs, lavishly remade the 1937 South Seas melodrama *Hurricane* in 1979 but failed to create even a mild breeze at the box-office.

Remakes are especially popular today, as good original material becomes scarcer and costlier. Those of 1950s Hollywood pictures like *We're No Angels* (1955, 1989), *Desperate Hours* (1955, 1990) and *Narrow Margin* (1952, 1990) have all been box-office dodos. But those of European films like *Three Men and a Baby* (1988), *Cousins* (1989) and *Three Fugitives* (1989) have made money. There's no end in sight: remakes of *Lolita, Cape Fear, Born Yesterday, Father of the Bride,* and *Robin Hood* are due in 1991.

The general view is that remakes are seldom as good as the original; the same goes for sequels. But there are some exceptions. *Ben-Hur* (1925, 1959), *Mutiny on the Bounty* (1935, 1962) and *A Star Is Born* (1937, 1954) have improved on the originals. But few can claim, as Alfred Hitchcock did of his two versions of *The Man Who Knew Too Much* (1934, 1956) that "the first version is the work of a talented amateur and the second was made by a professional."

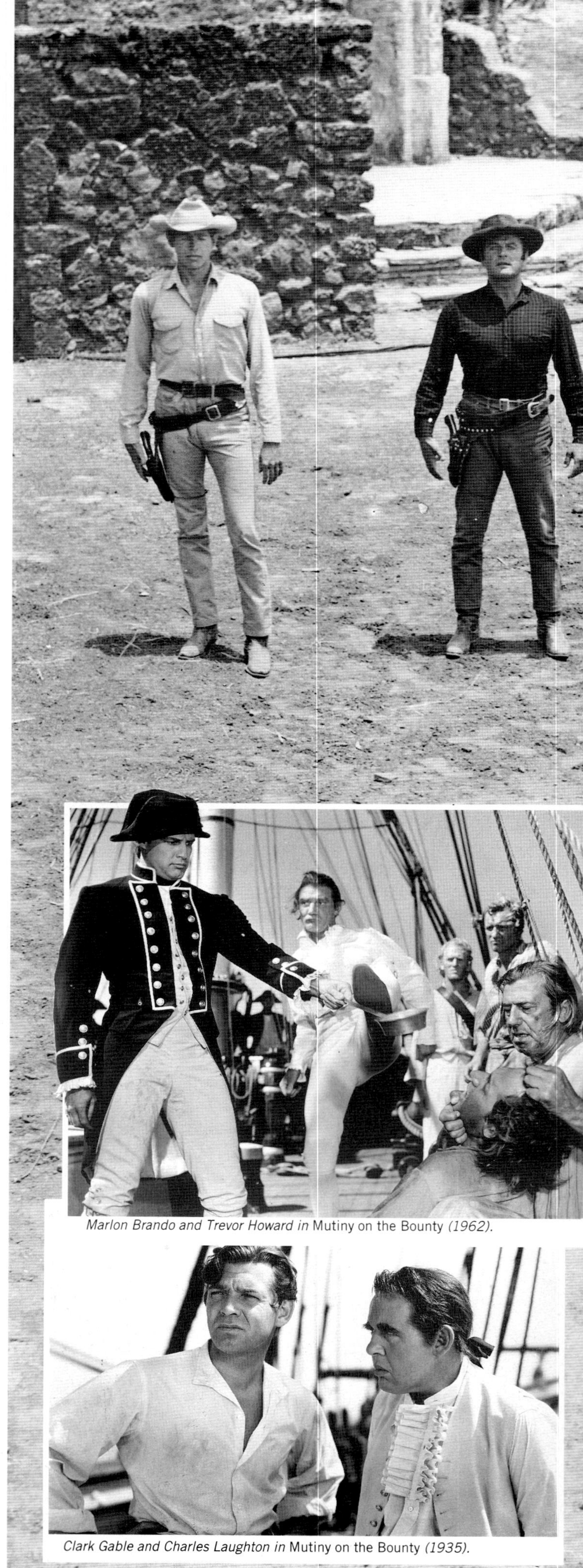

Main picture: James Coburn, Brad Dexter, Robert Vaughn, Charles Bronson, Horst Buchholz, Steve McQueen and Yul Brynner in The Magnificent Seven *(1960).*

Marlon Brando and Trevor Howard in Mutiny on the Bounty *(1962).*

Clark Gable and Charles Laughton in Mutiny on the Bounty *(1935).*

Academy-award winning A Star Is Born *(1937).*

What Price Hollywood? *(1932).*

Pat O'Brien in The Front Page *(1931).*

Jack Lemmon in Billy Wilder's remake of The Front Page *(1974).*

Akira Kurosawa's The Seven Samurai *(1954).*

JANUARY
FEBRUARY

MARCH
APRIL

IN LIKE COBURN

James Coburn's career has been rather tied to that of Steve McQueen – Coburn is taller, more athletic, but they both have close-cropped blonde hair and weather-beaten faces, and specialize in heroes who are experts in their field and have to be pushed to prove it.

They both became stars in *The Magnificent Seven* (1960) – Coburn was the gangly one whose trick was to outdraw a gunfighter by throwing a knife into him. And when he was forced to use a gun, he was critical of his performance: "I was aiming at the horse," he said after shooting down a bandit at a range of several hundred yards.

He played with McQueen in two war movies as well – *Hell Is for Heroes* (1962), in which he wore spectacles, and *The Great Escape* (1963), as the silent Australian who insists on taking a large suitcase with him.

Audiences love Coburn's minimalist efficiency and monosyllabic utterings. He was born in Nebraska in 1928 and studied acting at the University off Southern California and under Stella Adler in New York. But he found work hard to come by until he got small roles in westerns like *Ride Lonesome* (1959) and *Face of a Fugitive* (1959).

He's subsequently supported Cary Grant in *Charade* (1963) - with a knife again – James Garner and Julie Andrews in *The Americanization of Emily* (1964), and Charlton Heston in Sam Peckinpah's *Major Dundee* (1965), a film much cut by the studio. But it's only since his success as a laconic, ladykilling secret agent in *Our Man Flint* (1966) that he's become a real star in his own right. The second in the series, *In Like Flint* doesn't look like repeating the original's success, but there's no doubt that Coburn himself is "in" to stay.

ACADEMY AWARDS

PRESENTED ON 10 APRIL 1967

Best Picture
A Man for All Seasons

Best Director
Fred Zinnemann
A Man for All Seasons

Best Actor
Paul Scofield
A Man for All Seasons

Best Actress
Elizabeth Taylor
Who's Afraid of Virginia Woolf?

Best Sup Actor
Walter Matthau
The Fortune Cookie

Best Sup Actress
Sandy Dennis
Who's Afraid of Virginia Woolf?

ACCIDENT

Following their success in 1963 with *The Servant*, director Joseph Losey and writer Harold Pinter have now come up with *Accident*, an intense, darkly humorous drama that starts with a car crash and keeps flashing back to how it happened.

Newcomers Michael York, 24, and France's Jacqueline Sassard, 26, play students who become pawns in the sexual and professional rivalry between two Oxford University dons, played by Dirk Bogarde and Stanley Baker. The $1 million British production is a comparatively rarity in that no American company has invested in it.

Says Losey: "It's about a group of people who have a fairly profound knowledge of all sorts of aspects of life but still don't have many answers. They live in a kind of backwater, and then an accident occurs . . . . "

STAR QUOTES

Richard Burton

"Acting is a kind of showing off. And the best person to show off to is your wife."

BIRTHS, DEATHS AND MARRIAGES

DEATHS

Ann Sheridan
21 Jan, Woodland Hills, California
Cancer

Martine Carol
6 Feb, Monte Carlo
Heart attack

Anthony Mann
29 Apr, Berlin
Heart attack

MARRIAGES

Raquel Welch
14 Feb, *to* Patrick Curtis

Stanley Baker and Vivien Merchant in Accident.

AFI FOUNDED

Gregory Peck and George Stevens, Jr, son of the veteran film-maker, are to be chairman and director of the new American Film Institute. Based in Washington, DC, and funded to the tune of $5 million by the National Endowment for the Arts, Motion Picture Association of America and Ford Foundation, the AFI is charged to "preserve the heritage and advance the art of film in America." High on its agenda will be a film school to train new talent and a substantial, education-directed publishing list.

SWINGING STUFF

"Swinging London" comes under the microscope in *Blowup*, Italian art-house director Michelangelo Antonioni's first film in English. Boyish 25-year-old "newcomer" David Hemmings (he's actually been playing on screen since his early teens) stars as a fashion photographer who thinks he may have accidentally photographed a murder in a London park. And Vanessa Redgrave plays a strange girl who enters his life as he unravels the mystery.

In filming the sexually explicit drama, which features a sizzling romp between Hemmings and two naked models, Antonioni has had whole streets painted different colours. For the climax the intellectual Italian has even staged a tennis match played without balls or rackets. Whatever next?

David Hemmings and Vanessa Redgrave in Antonioni's mystery thriller Blowup, *about a photographer who discovers he has photographed a murder.*

LURE OF THE GREASEPAINT

The daughter of actors Michael Redgrave and Rachel Kempson, Vanessa Redgrave was born with thespian blood in her veins. So too were brother Corin and sister Lynn, and both sisters now find themselves nominated for Oscars – Lynn in the comedy *Georgy Girl* and Vanessa for *Morgan (A Suitable Case for Treatment)*.

Vanessa's birth in 1937 did not go unnoticed: her arrival was announced on stage at the Old Vic by Laurence Olivier who was playing Hamlet to Michael Redgrave's Laertes. She's grown into a tall, classically beautiful actress who was born for the big dramatic parts of Shakespeare, Chekhov and Ibsen. She made her screen debut aged 21 in *Behind the Mask* (1958), playing her real father's daughter, but the film was a flop and she devoted herself entirely to the theatre.

Last year's *Morgan* was her first major role and since then she's never left the camera's gaze – a cameo as Ann Boleyn in *A Man for All Seasons* (1966), the mystery girl in the current *Blowup*, and two forthcoming films for her husband, director Tony Richardson – *The Sailor from Gibraltar* and *Red and Blue*.

If these seem rather specialized films, she's currently fixing that too. Later this year she'll be seen with Richard Harris in Warners multi-million film version of the 1960 Lerner & Loewe musical *Camelot*.

Elizabeth Taylor and Richard Burton in The Taming of the Shrew.

BURTON TAMES LIZ!

Way back in 1929, the world's most famous married couple, Douglas Fairbanks and Mary Pickford, played Shakespeare's bickering Petruchio and Katherine. Now, following their portrait of a stormy modern marriage in last year's *Who's Afraid of Virginia Woolf?*, the world's currently most famous couple, Richard Burton and Elizabeth Taylor, give us their version of *The Taming of the Shrew*.

Filmed in colour and widescreen on authentic Italian locations, first-time director Franco Zeffirelli says of the characters (or perhaps the Burtons): "Their instincts are shrewd, decisive – black, white, yes, no, I love you, I hate you. Like cats. I would like adults to enjoy it as if it were a Christmas pantomine."

Faye Dunaway as Bonnie Parker in Bonnie and Clyde, *based on the true story of two young gangsters from Kansas.*

BIRTHS, DEATHS AND MARRIAGES

DEATHS

Claude Rains
30 May, New Hampshire
Intestinal haemorrhage

Spencer Tracy
10 Jun, Hollywood
Heart attack

Jayne Mansfield
29 Jun, New Orleans
Car crash

Vivien Leigh
8 Jul, London
Tuberculosis

Basil Rathbone
21 Jul, New York
Heart attack

Anton Walbrook
9 Aug, Germany
Heart attack

Jane Darwell
13 Aug, Hollywood
Heart attack

Paul Muni
25 Aug, Santa Barbara, California
Heart trouble

MARRIAGES

Elvis Presley
1 May, *to* Priscilla Beaulieu

"WE ROB BANKS"

Meet Clyde Barrow and Bonnie Parker. They rob banks. And they like having their pictures in the paper, together with the rest of their gang, their tommy-guns and their stolen loot. Robbing and shooting their way across Kansas during the Depression, they've become heroes to everyone except their blood-stained victims and Detective Frank Hamer, who is continuously on their trail.

Based on the real-life career of the youthful gangsters, who eventually died in a police ambush, *Bonnie and Clyde* stars Warren Beatty as Clyde and several relative unknowns as the rest of the gang – striking Faye Dunaway as Bonnie, Gene Hackman as Buck, Estelle Parsons as Blanche and Michael J. Pollard as C. W. Moss. Directed by Arthur Penn, the movie's blend of comedy and graphic violence will shock many audiences.

It also marks Beatty's debut as a producer. He admired Robert Benton and David Newman's script, offered it to France's Francois Truffaut to direct, even thought about directing it himself, and settled on Penn, who'd directed him in *Mickey One* (1965). Beatty brought in his friend, Robert Towne, to polish the script and then started to ponder the casting of Bonnie.

Natalie Wood maybe, his co-star in his first movie, *Splendor in the Grass* (1961)? But Wood disliked Texas. Tuesday Weld, then? She was pregnant. What about Carol Lynley? So many women . . . . The lucky winner was finally Faye Dunaway, a 26-year-old native of Florida who had some New York stage experience and was seen earlier this year as a lithe young kidnapper in *The Happening* and as John Phillip Law's wife in the racial drama *Hurry Sundown. Bonnie and Clyde* could rocket her to stardom.

VIVIEN LEIGH DEAD

Vivien Leigh, known the world over for her Oscar-winning portrayal of Scarlett O'Hara in *Gone with the Wind* (1939), died in London on 8 July of tuberculosis, aged 53. Her last screen appearance was in *Ship of Fools* (1965) and she had recently starred in a London stage production of *Camille*. London theatres darkened their lights the same night in tribute to her talent.

One of the screen's most radiant beauties, Leigh's career was dogged by bouts of mental and physical illness, though her much publicized marriage to Laurence Olivier (1940-60) and her roles in *Gone with the Wind* and as Blanche DuBois in *A Streetcar Named Desire* (1951) earned her a place in Hollywood's Hall of Fame.

TRACY DEAD

Spencer Tracy, star of over 70 pictures since his debut in 1930, died of a heart attack at his Beverly Hills home on 10 June, aged 67. Only a month ago he completed work on *Guess Who's Coming to Dinner*, in which he co-starred for the ninth time with long-time friend and companion Katharine Hepburn.

Winner of two Academy Awards and nominated on six other occasions, Milwaukee-born Tracy was one of Hollywood's most respected and loved figures. First signed by Fox in 1930, he became a star with *San Francisco* (1936), which he made for M-G-M, the studio he stayed with for 20 years. He first teamed with Hepburn in *Woman of the Year* (1942) and went on to star with her in classics like *State of the Union* (1948), *Adam's Rib* (1949) and *Pat and Mike* (1952). He'll also be remembered for his dramatic performances in films such as *Fury* (1936), as an innocent man corrupted by mob violence, *Captains Courageous* (1937), as an (Oscar-winning) Portuguese fisherman, *Bad Day at Black Rock* (1954), fighting small-town prejudice, and as a crusty judge in *Judgment at Nuremberg* (1961).

Hard-drinking, hard-living Tracy was a consummate professional, always line-perfect on set and not fond of going beyond one take on a scene. He once told Frank Sinatra: "All you have to know about acting school is know your lines and hit your mark."

Spencer Tracy.

GOSSIP COLUMN

- **As television demands all-colour material, film companies have come up with a novel way of selling their old black-and-white films – mechanical tinting. Universal is experimenting with a coloured version of the 1930 *All Quiet on the Western Front*.**
- **M-G-M has turned down $10 million for one airing of *Gone with the Wind* on US TV.**

Lee Marvin inspects *The Dirty Dozen*, which stars Donald Sutherland, Charles Bronson and Telly Savalas.

MISSION IMPOSSIBLE

Fans of *The Magnificent Seven* (1960) and *The Guns of Navarone* (1961) won't be disappointed by *The Dirty Dozen*. This tough Second World War drama sends a motley crew of experts and psychos on a mission impossible – to destroy a luxury weekend watering hole for high-ranking German officers.

Lee Marvin is the officer assigned this difficult task and his team are all condemned murderers, rapists and thieves. If they succeed, their sentences will be reduced; if they fail, well, the army executioner will be saved some work. Charles Bronson, Telly Savalas, John Cassavetes and Donald Sutherland are amongst the dirty; Robert Ryan and Ernest Borgnine the officers who dream up the exercise. Despite the all-American cast, the movie was actually shot in Britain.

SUPER STRUCTURE

Raquel Welch as prehistoric pin-up in *One Million Years B.C.*, a dramatic story with no dialogue except grunts.

Before becoming an actress, Raquel Welch modelled and served cocktails to pay for plastic surgery on her nose. But the Welch proboscis is one of her less prominent attributes. In the role that's made her the most famous pin-up of the age, the rest of the structure was clad only in a skimpy leather two-piece in *One Million Years B.C.*

Earlier last year, in *Fantastic Voyage*, she was miniaturised and injected into a man's body to perform internal brain surgery. While coursing through his lymphatic system in a tight rubber suit, she was groped by armies of leech-like anti-bodies.

The long period of special effects work on that movie meant audiences had to wait some time to see what all the Welch hype was about. The result was that she was incredibly famous before she ever starred in a movie. Born in 1940 of Bolivian-English parents, she won teenage beauty contests, married at 18, mothered two children, and was divorced by the time she was 21. She took acting classes, was seen fleetingly in *A House Is Not a Home* and Elvis Presley's *Roustabout* (both 1964) and then met Patrick Curtis, a press agent with whom she formed Curtwell Enterprises, a company devoted to promoting the Welch bod.

20th Century-Fox took the bait and promoted her without actually committing her to a film. She and Curtis married and toured Europe as celebrities without portfolio. Stranger things have happened in Tinseltown. But, to use the title of her new film – in which she's a voluptuous sky-diver – it's still hard to *Fathom*.

Sidney Poitier and Rod Steiger investigate a murder in *In the Heat of the Night*.

RAISING THE HEAT

When a local police chief can't solve a murder and a more experienced, senior officer is sent to help out, no one is surprised. But when that police chief is a racist and when the senior officer is black, there are obviously going to be some fireworks.

Set in Mississippi, *In the Heat of the Night* is a tough and provocative crime thriller that provides ample scope for its two stars – Rod Steiger, as the sweaty, bigoted Bill Gillespie, and Sidney Poitier as the cool, methodical cop Virgil Tibbs.

HEY, MRS ROBINSON!

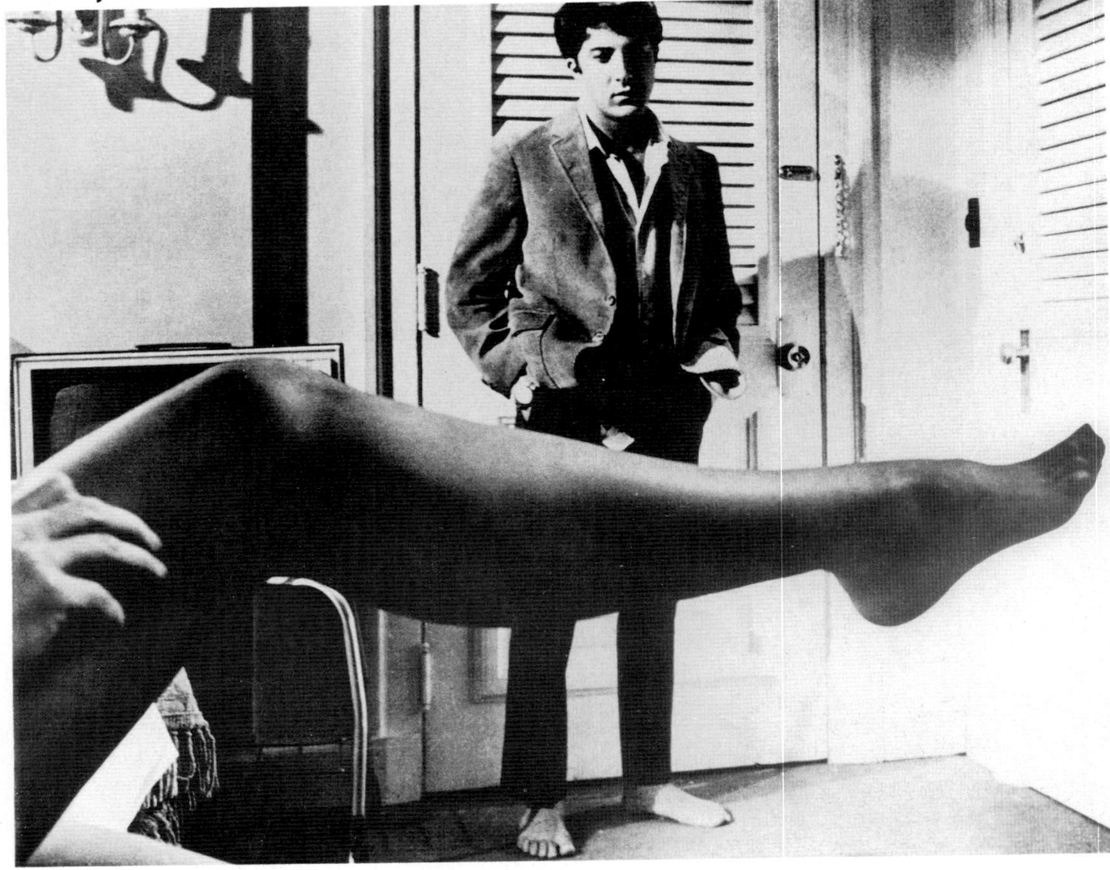

Dustin Hoffman discovers the pleasures of an older woman in The Graduate.

Benjamin Braddock (Dustin Hoffman) is a little worried about his future. He's left University with more degrees than a thermometer. His parents see a rosy future ahead, but all Benjamin sees is Mrs Robinson (Anne Bancroft), the mother of his high-school friend Elaine (Katharine Ross) and a close friend of his parents.

After initial nervousness on Benjamin's part, he and Mrs. Robinson have a clandestine affair. But Benjamin's troubles really begin when his parents insist that he start courting the lovely Elaine.

Directed by Mike Nichols (who last year made the very different *Who's Afraid of Virginia Woolf?*) and with songs by Simon & Garfunkel, *The Graduate* is a thoroughly modern comedy that's set box-offices alight. It speaks to an entire generation of Americans and looks like making a star out of diminutive Hoffman, a 30-year-old off-Broadway actor who's made only one previous film.

BANCROFT'S BACK

"Here's to you, Mrs Robinson," sing Simon & Garfunkel on the soundtrack of *The Graduate* – and actress Anne Bancroft will have a tough time living the role down. For years people will remember her swigging a dry martini, tossing her earrings down, and giving Dustin Hoffman a look up her dress.

It's a tragic role – a bored, alcoholic wife who envies her daughter's youth and beauty and has an affair with an inexperienced man who says she is the most attractive of his parents' friends. But Bancroft wasn't first choice for the role – the producers originally had French star Jeanne Moreau in mind, following Hollywood tradition that only European women can really play seductresses or prostitutes.

For Bancroft (and maybe for Hollywood too) it's a turning point in a career that so far has been rather understated. Married to comedian Mel Brooks since 1964, she originally trained as an actress and dancer. Under the name Anne Marno, she started her career on TV in 1950 and then had supporting parts in films like *Don't Bother to Knock* (1952), *Demetrius and the Gladiators* (1954) and *New York Confidential* (1955).

Unhappy with the roles she was getting, she returned to the New York stage, played opposite Henry Fonda in *Two for the Seesaw* and won a Tony award for *The Miracle Worker*, in which she was cast as the near-blind teacher of a deaf-mute blind girl. She won an Oscar for the 1962 film version, which led to starring roles in *The Pumpkin Eater* (1964) and John Ford's *7 Women* (1965).

BOX OFFICE

UK

SPECIAL PRESENTATION

1 Grand Prix
2 A Man for All Seasons
3 The Taming of the Shrew

TOP TEN GENERAL RELEASES

1 The Sound of Music
2 Doctor Zhivago
3 You Only Live Twice
4 The Dirty Dozen
5 My Fair Lady
6 The Family Way
7 Bonnie and Clyde
8 The Blue Max
9 El Dorado
10 The Professionals

BOX OFFICE

US

1 The Dirty Dozen
2 You Only Live Twice
3 Casino Royale
4 A Man for All Seasons
5 Thoroughly Modern Millie
6 Barefoot in the Park
7 Georgy Girl
8 To Sir With Love
9 Grand Prix
10 Hombre

IRISH GRIEF

There is an aptness in the fact that in *The Bible* (1966) Richard Harris played Cain. The actor is as famous for raising Cain as for his powerhouse acting talent. He crossed swords with Marlon Brando and Kirk Douglas on the sets of *Mutiny on the Bounty* (1962) and *The Heroes of Telemark* (1965) and has left many a bar in ruins.

His own nose shows the signs of bloody combat. But few deny Harris' talent. He was born in Ireland in 1933 and after acting school in London was hired by the influential Joan Littlewood Theatre Company. His physical presence impressed Associated British Pictures, which signed him to a seven-year contract. Harris was lucky: in *The Wreck of the Mary Deare* (1959) he held his own against Gary Cooper and Charlton Heston; he co-starred with Laurence Harvey in *The Long and the Short and the Tall* (1961); and he received special billing for the hit war adventure *The Guns of Navarone* (1961), in which he had a cameo as a foul-mouthed Australian.

M-G-M offered *Mutiny on the Bounty* and then came *This Sporting Life* (1963), Lindsay Anderson's powerful drama which won Harris the acting prize at the Cannes film festival. He then made *The Red Desert* (1964) in Italy for Antonioni, a decision he immediately regretted, and was recalled to Hollywood for the much cut-about western *Major Dundee* (1965), followed by *Hawaii* (1966).

Now comes his starriest role yet – as King Arthur in the musical *Camelot* (1967), a role he says he was destined to play. Says Harris: "I swim in a pool of my own neuroses. I carry love, grief and wrath deeply, like an Irishman."

GWTW BIGGER THAN EVER

M-G-M has re-issued the blockbuster *Gone with the Wind* in 70mm widescreen and stereo. The re-release of the 1939 classic comes two months after the death of Vivien Leigh, who played Scarlett O'Hara. Co-star Clark Gable and producer David O. Selznick are also no longer around, though Olivia de Havilland attended the film's glamorous unveiling.

M-G-M toiled for two years on the technical re-fit, but it's been given the thumbs down by critics. They say cropping the film's image to get the wide-screen ratio has clobbered the film's visual beauty.

Angie Dickenson

"I dress for women and I undress for men."

BIRTHS, DEATHS AND MARRIAGES

DEATHS

Charles Bickford
9 Nov, Los Angeles
Pneumonia

Sidney Poitier, Katharine Houghton, Spencer Tracy and Katharine Hepburn in Guess Who's Coming to Dinner.

TRACY'S LAST SUPPER

Sidney Poitier (having just survived his racial clash with Rod Steiger in *In the Heat of the Night*) is coming to dinner – and hosts Spencer Tracy and Katharine Hepburn are not entirely happy about it.

Their daughter, Katharine Houghton (Hepburn's real-life niece), has announced her engagement to Poitier, which is to prove a real test of her parent's liberal sensibilities. Also coming to dinner are Poitier's parents. The scene is set for a comedy-drama about inter-racial marriage, directed by Stanley Kramer whose 1958 drama *The Defiant Ones* addressed similar issues.

Opening in the wake of civil rights demonstrations in America, *Guess Who's Coming To Dinner* is a timely picture. It's a sad one, too, for it marks the last screen appearance of Spencer Tracy who died this summer, soon after completing his role.

Lee Marvin plays a gangster who takes an elaborate revenge on his cheating partner in Point Blank.

LEE ON THE LOOSE

Thrillers don't come any faster or more violent than *Point Blank*, the first Hollywood movie by British director John Boorman, who shot the picture on location in Los Angeles and San Francisco's Alcatraz prison.

Tough-guy Lee Marvin plays a crook who has been betrayed by his best pal and has ended up on the deserted island prison of Alcatraz. Swimming ashore, Marvin decides to bulldoze his way into the Mob's higher echelons and claim the money that is owed him.

Among the people who get in Lee Marvin's way in the M-G-M release are sexy Angie Dickinson, gruff Keenan Wynn and ultra-smooth Canadian actor John Vernon.

JANUARY
FEBRUARY

MARCH
APRIL

BEYOND THE INFINITE . . .

Three years and $10.5 million in the making, Stanley Kubrick's *2001: A Space Odyssey* sets new standards for cinematic special effects and will inspire debate for decades to come. Filmed in England in conditions of high security, because Kubrick and co-writer Arthur C. Clarke did not want information to leak out about the plot, the film is an epic speculation on intelligent life in the Universe, beginning in pre-historic times and ending with a mission to Jupiter and Beyond the Infinite.

Actors Keir Dullea and Gary Lockwood take second place to a talking computer called HAL9000 as well as mysterious black monoliths which appear whenever mankind is ready for a further step up the evolutionary ladder. Kubrick has thrown out an original score by Alex North, and has chosen classical tidbits like "The Blue Danube" waltz and pieces by modern composers.

Kubrick is refusing to give interviews to explain what his 70mm-Cinerama film actually means. Says the reclusive director: "I'd rather not discuss the film. The feel of the experience is the important thing, not the ability to verbalize or analyze it. Those who won't believe their eyes won't be able to appreciate this film."

Gary Lockwood and Keir Dullea discuss the problems of their mission computer HAL in 2001: A Space Odyssey.

ACADEMY AWARDS

PRESENTED ON 10 APRIL 1968

Best Picture
In the Heat of the Night

Best Director
Mike Nichols
The Graduate

Best Actor
Rod Steiger
In the Heat of the Night

Best Actress
Katharine Hepburn
Guess Who's Coming to Dinner

Best Sup Actor
George Kennedy
Cool Hand Luke

Best Sup Actress
Estelle Parsons
Bonnie and Clyde

BLACK & WHITE IN COLOUR

The Academy of Motion Picture Arts & Sciences has announced that distinctions will no longer be made between colour and black-and-white. Since 1939 the cinematography award has been divided into b&w and colour sections; art direction followed suit in 1940.

Now, in recognition of the total dominance of colour, the rules have changed again. Of this year's cinematography nominations only one – *In Cold Blood* – was filmed in black-and-white. The winner was *Bonnie and Clyde*.

THE BRAIN BEHIND 2001

"A director is a kind of idea and taste machine," says Stanley Kubrick. "A movie is a series of creative and technical decisions and it's the director's job to make the right decisions as frequently as possible."

Kubrick has made more right decisions than most directors, and his perfectionism and pursuit of complete control have become legendary. Significantly, his films tend to be stories about control and the loss of it, a theme taken to the ultimate in *Dr. Strangelove* (1964), which ends in nuclear war. Kubrick is always setting traps for his characters and watches their discomfiture sardonically and from a sardonic distance.

He's a self-taught director. Born in New York in 1928, he was a dud at school and became a photographer for *Look* magazine. He borrowed money from relatives to make two short films and then his first features, a war allegory called *Fear and Desire* (1953) and the thriller *Killer's Kiss* (1955). On all these films he was not only director but writer, cameraman and editor as well. Another thriller, *The Killing* (1956), was followed by the anti-war classic *Paths of Glory* (1957).

Its star, Kirk Douglas, hired Kubrick to direct the epic *Spartacus* (1960) after having original director Anthony Mann fired. Kubrick has subsequently disowned the movie, because he lacked total control. Since then he's been based in Britain, where he made *Lolita* (1962), *Dr. Strangelove* and now *2001*. After journeying to the stars Kubrick is to retreat into history for his next project – a screen biography of Napoleon.

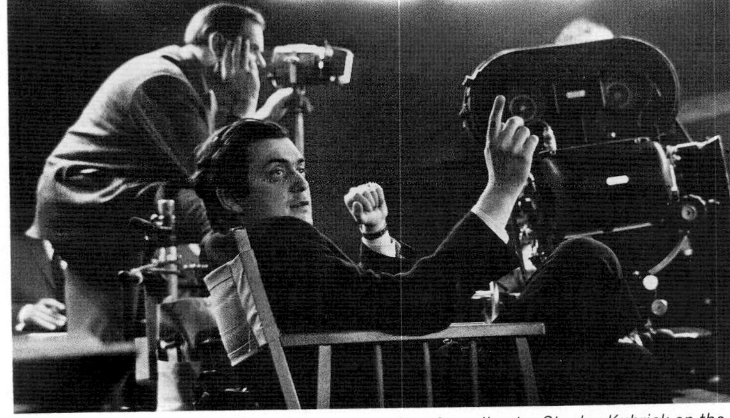

American director Stanley Kubrick on the set of his epic science fiction movie, 2001: A Space Odyssey.

DOING WHAT COMES EASILY

"I think I have a facility for acting," says Albert Finney. "My danger is that I do it too easily. In *Tom Jones* I just felt I was being used. I wasn't involved. I was bored most of the time. In *Two for the Road* I felt the same. I think it's a pity I haven't done more demanding work in the cinema."

His admirers would disagree – his factory worker in *Saturday Night and Sunday Morning* (1960), his sexual rogue in *Tom Jones* (1963), his psychopath in *Night Must Fall* (1964) and his architect with marital problems in the comedy *Two for the Road* (1967) testify to his versatility.

He's just completed his first film as a director, *Charlie Bubbles*, in which he plays a successful writer who returns to his roots in northern England. It's also a return for Finney himself, the Lancashire lad who was encouraged by a schoolmaster to take up acting and ended up at Stratford-upon-Avon playing opposite Olivier. Critics began calling him Olivier's natural heir and he was immediately cast as Olivier's son in his screen debut, *The Entertainer* (1960).

A lot would seem to rest on the success of *Charlie Bubbles*. Finney has used his own money (in addition to investing in race horses – his father was a bookmaker) to have complete control of his projects. If it fails, those self-doubts could turn Finney into a prestige star of films unworthy of his talent.

SECRET OF THE MONKEY PLANET

You are an astronaut and you have to crash-land on an unknown planet. And the first thing you see is an army of monkeys on horseback. This is the start of Charlton Heston's new picture, *Planet of the Apes*, which takes the actor as far from the historical epic as it is possible to go.

Dressed for most of the time in a loin-cloth, Heston is taken prisoner by the monkeys, is put on trial and finally has to escape to solve the terrible secret of the monkey planet. The sci-fi allegory from 20th Century-Fox, from a novel by *Kwai* author Pierre Boulle, features some of the most spectacular make-up effects ever designed: beneath those simian features are actors of the calibre of Kim Hunter and Roddy McDowall.

Charlton Heston as an American astronaut who is captured by simians in Planet of the Apes.

GOSSIP COLUMN

- **Director Tony Richardson announced that he would not show *The Charge of the Light Brigade* to British critics, branding them the worst in the world. Result? Headline news.**
- **Madness in his Method? Marlon Brando put on pounds for his role in last year's *Reflections in a Golden Eye.* Now he's sweated it all off for a part in *The Arrangement.***
- **Walt Disney is said to be preparing a series of educational films on contraception. The star? Donald Duck.**

BIRTHS, DEATHS AND MARRIAGES

BIRTHS

Molly Ringwald
14 Feb, Sacramento, California

Patsy Kensit
4 Mar, London

DEATHS

Mae Marsh
13 Feb, Hermosa Beach, California
Heart attack

Anthony Asquith
20 Feb, London

Fay Bainter
16 Apr, Los Angeles

MARRIAGES

Roman Polanski
20 Jan, *to* **Sharon Tate**

Tony Curtis
20 Jan, *to* Leslie Allen

Maureen O'Hara
11 Mar, *to* Charles Blair

Zero Mostel and Gene Wilder (seated) in Mel Brooks' satire on Broadway, The Producers.

HOW TO WRITE A FLOP

Mel Brooks, a former gag writer on some hit comedy TV series, could not have asked for a better advertisement for *The Producers*, his first outing as a movie writer-director. On the posters, Peter Sellers says, "Last night I saw the ultimate film . . . it is the essence of all great comedy, combined in a single motion picture!"

The essence is non-stop gags and dubious subject matter – how a Broadway producer (Zero Mostel) conspires with his accountant (Gene Wilder) to make money from a surefire flop. Their play, written by a former Nazi, claims Hitler was a regular, decent guy and includes a grand musical number "Springtime for Hitler" performed by a chorus in jackboots. Needless to say, the intended flop becomes a big hit. The movie could also be a hit for Brooks and make him as famous as his wife - none other than Anne "Mrs. Robinson" Bancroft.

McQUEEN & DUNAWAY ON THE JOB

Faye Dunaway and Steve McQueen in The Thomas Crown Affair.

The Thomas Crown Affair is as cool and hip as tomorrow's fashion. Steve McQueen is Crown – 36, divorced, worth $4 million and with a nice line in beach-buggies. Faye Dunaway is Vicky, an insurance investigator who dresses like a Paris fashion model and has only one thing on her mind – to nail Crown.

Her instinct, and her loins, tell her he's behind a daring $2.6 million Boston bank job. All she has to do is prove it. Crown knows the score and, again for the pure thrill of it, goes double or bust – making it with Vicky and pulling a second bank job at the same time.

It's super-sophisticated stuff, and looks set to clean up this summer. Directed by Norman Jewison, of *The Cincinnati Kid* (1965) and *In the Heat of the Night* (1967) fame, the movie crackles with sexuality, features a memorable title theme by Michel Legrand ("Windmills of Your Mind"), and makes clever use of multi-screen – first used, less imaginatively, in John Frankenheimer's *Grand Prix* (1966). And if you thought the famous eating scene in *Tom Jones* was suggestive, wait until you see McQueen and Dunaway's foreplay around a chess table.

BAD GUY MAKES GOOD

Until *The Fortune Cookie* (1966) Walter Matthau was often cast as the heavy, and sometimes as the hero's best friend. But never the hero. His face and posture were simply too slobbish and untrustworthy – or, as one critic put it, a cross between a bloodhound, Wallace Beery and Yogi Bear. It took director Billy Wilder to recognize Matthau's comic potential and, as the shyster lawyer who exploits his injured brother-in-law (Jack Lemmon) in *The Fortune Cookie*, Matthau won an Oscar as Best Supporting Actor.

Now he's back with Lemmon in *The Odd Couple* and, at the ripe old age of 48, is set on a glittering career. In fact, Wilder wanted to cast Matthau years ago, in *The Seven Year Itch* (1955) with Marilyn Monroe, but 20th Century-Fox wanted Tom Ewell, who'd played the part on stage. At that time Matthau was a New York stage actor yet to make his screen debut. He did so as the villain in Burt Lancaster's *The Kentuckian* (1955) "because I was desperately short of money."

He then kept solvent by essaying villains in films like *The Indian Fighter* (1955), *Slaughter on Tenth Avenue* (1957), *King Creole* (1958), *Gangster Story* (1960), which he somehow directed himself, *Lonely Are the Brave* (1962, as a sheriff) and *Charade* (1963). He was more or less on the level in *Bigger than Life* (1956), *A Face in the Crowd* (1957), *Fail Safe* (1964) and *Mirage* (1965). Matthau was dependable and solid; but he was bigger on Broadway, where he won a Tony award in 1962 for *A Shot in the Dark*. In 1965 he starred in the Broadway production of Neil Simon's *The Odd Couple* – and among the first-nighters was Billy Wilder . . . .

Walter Matthau as Oscar Madison and Jack Lemmon as Felix Unger are The Odd Couple.

LIVING APART TOGETHER

Remember the 1966 comedy *The Fortune Cookie*? Well, that brilliant teaming of Jack Lemmon and Walter Matthau (who won an Oscar) is back again in *The Odd Couple*, the screen version of Neil Simon's Broadway smash.

Lemmon plays Felix Unger, a decent, if neurotically house-proud man who becomes suicidal when his wife abruptly leaves him. Matthau plays his best friend Oscar Madison, a happily divorced sportswriter who lives in an apartment filled with month-old sandwiches and other garbage. Oscar takes pity on the finicky Felix and suggests they share the apartment together. The result is one of the stormiest and oddest marriages ever. This surely can't be the last time we'll see these two great comic actors working together on screen.

John Cassavetes, Mia Farrow and Ralph Bellamy in Roman Polanski's gothic melodrama Rosemary's Baby.

MIA – THE DEVIL'S DOLL!

Mia Farrow, the slender beauty best known for the long-running TV series *Peyton Place* and for marrying Frank Sinatra, has the year's most demanding female role so far in the supernatural shocker *Rosemary's Baby*. She plays the pregnant wife of John Cassavetes but believes that the father of her child might actually be the Devil. Ruth Gordon co-stars as a strange neighbour who offers to help the increasingly distraught Farrow.

Based on the best-selling novel by Ira Levin and produced by William Castle, who once wired cinema seats to provide audiences with electric shocks during *The Tingler* (1959), it's the first Hollywood movie of tyro Polish director Roman Polanski. Three years ago he shocked audiences with *Repulsion*, in which beautiful Catherine Deneuve slowly went bananas in a dingy London apartment. This time his heroine has better-appointed quarters: exteriors for *Rosemary's Baby* were filmed at the macabre-looking Dakota Apartment Building on Central Park West, New York.

BIRTHS, DEATHS AND MARRIAGES

DEATHS

Dorothy Gish
4 Jun, Italy
Pneumonia

Dan Duryea
7 Jun, Hollywood
Cancer

Kay Francis
22 Aug, New York
Cancer

TRANSAM BUYS UA

United Artists, the studio founded in 1919 by Charlie Chaplin, Douglas Fairbanks, Mary Pickford and D. W. Griffith, has been purchased by the giant San Francisco-based Transamerica Corporation. UA has been on a roll since senior executives Arthur Krim and Robert Benjamin bought the studio from Pickford in 1956.

Films such as *Some Like It Hot* (1959), *The Apartment, The Magnificent Seven* (both 1960), *West Side Story* (1961), the Clint Eastwood westerns, and the Beatles and James Bond films have made UA extremely profitable, leading to after-tax profits of $20 million in 1967. Transamerica's purchase of 98 per cent of UA stock follows Gulf & Western's purchase of Paramount and Seven Arts' merger with Warners in 1966.

NO CANNES DO

A chaotic press conference has effectively closed this May's Cannes film festival less than a week after it started. French director Jean-Luc Godard has led the campaign to halt the proceedings, which are usually noted for their glamour and starlets parading half-naked on the Côte d'Azure beachfront. In response to Godard's call, some jury members (including Roman Polanski, Monica Vitti and Louis Malle) have resigned and directors have withdrawn their films from the festival.

The chaos and occasional violence at Cannes reflect the student unrest and widespread strikes now sweeping across France. Godard insisted the festival should close to show solidarity with French workers and students. The cult director has proposed that all the films be shown free to these groups.

HENRY'S GIRL GROWS UP

Jane Fonda is no longer just the daughter of Henry. Maybe that's how audiences saw her in the early days; but not any longer. And certainly not after *Barbarella*, the comic-strip, sci-fi sextravaganza directed by her French husband Roger Vadim – the man who turned his former wife, Brigitte Bardot, into a world-famous sex symbol.

Fonda and Vadim married in Las Vegas in 1965, only months after Fonda had criticized the institution of marriage – "I don't want to possess anyone and I don't want to be possessed." *Barbarella* is actually her third film for hubby Vadim – after *Circle of Love* (1964) and *The Game Is Over* (1966). In it she plays a intergalactic innocent who saves the universe by engendering feelings of love. Looking very lovable in miniscule g-strings and metallic bras, she makes love to a crucified angel (John Phillip Law) and blows all the fuses in a pleasure machine played by mad Milo O'Shea.

The 31-year-old actress has come a long way since her screen debut in *Tall Story* (1960) and her appearances in comedies such as *Sunday in New York* (1963), *Cat Ballou* (1965) and *Barefoot in the Park* (1967). It remains to be seen whether her talents as a dramatic actress, revealed in *The Chase* (1966) and *Hurry Sundown* (1967), will ever match her striking physical assets. So far, the jury's out on that one.

SHOOTIN' STRAIGHT

Clint Eastwood as a hicksville sheriff in New York in Coogan's Bluff.

He is The Man with No Name – the lanky, laconic, cheroot-puffing, poncho-wearing hero of *Fistful of Dollars* (1964), *For a Few Dollars More* (1966) and *The Good, the Bad and the Ugly* (1967). The three violent "spaghetti" westerns, made in Spain by Italy's Sergio Leone, have made Clint Eastwood one of the world's most popular movie stars.

Hollywood had earlier been oblivious to his appeal and he took the job in Spain only because he had nothing better to do and the $15,000 was welcome. Born in San Francisco in 1933, Eastwood served in the army and was a lifeguard and luberjack before he got a Universal contract at $75 a week. His screen debut was inauspicious – as the creature in *Revenge of the Creature* – and bit parts in *Francis in the Navy* and *Tarantula* (all 1955) did little for his career. Universal dropped him and he went to RKO just as the studio was closing down. His acting career was at a standstill and he paid the rent by labouring.

Then, in 1958, he was suddenly signed by CBS-TV to star in a western series called *Rawhide*. As ramrod Rowdy Yates, Eastwood signed up for a cattledrive that was to last seven years, during which came the call from Leone. He currently has three films on release – *Hang 'Em High*, a Hollywood "spaghetti" western, the Second World War adventure *Where Eagles Dare* in which he's with Richard Burton, and *Coogan's Bluff*.

All three are already hits. His latest venture is another western, but with a twist – the film version of Lerner & Loewe's 1951 musical *Paint Your Wagon*. Can Clint sing as well as shoot?

Steve McQueen as a San Francisco homicide detective in Bullitt.

MAVERICK COPS

Two of Hollywood's best-loved tough guys, Steve McQueen and Clint Eastwood, play maverick cops in their latest releases. In *Bullitt* McQueen plays a San Francisco detective who has to play wet nurse to a gangster prior to testifying at a court hearing. When McQueen's charge is shot dead it unleashes a vicious spiral of violence that leads to corruption in high places. Directed by Britisher Peter Yates and co-starring Robert Vaughn as a ruthless politician and Jacqueline Bisset as McQueen's girlfriend, the film's highlight is a thrilling car chase which allows McQueen to drive his own custom-built Shelby Mustang at speeds of over 100mph.

In *Coogan's Bluff*, tall and laconic Eastwood plays a Texan marshall ordered to collect a prisoner from New York. The prisoner escapes and Eastwood has to use all his frontier expertise in the concrete canyons of Manhattan. Says director Don Siegel: "It's a western with cars, machine-guns and helicopters."

BRITS NIX PIX – AGAIN

Cinema admissions in Great Britain have slumped to 237 million at an estimated 1,600 cinemas. The figures have caused further despondency amongst industry leaders who continue to lay the blame on the rival attractions of television. Production in British studios continues to flourish despite worries that major Hollywood investment might be cut off.

INDOMITABLE KATE

Katharine Hepburn is entering her fifth decade as one of the screen's finest actresses and greatest stars. In the 1950s she went to the Congo to make *The African Queen* (1951) with Humphrey Bogart and director John Huston, then to Venice for *Summertime* (1955) with director David Lean, and in 1962 she starred in the powerful adaptation of Eugene O'Neill's *Long Day's Journey into Night*.

She was then absent from the screen owing to the illness of her close friend Spencer Tracy with whom she'd made eight memorable films. Tracy recovered enough to make one last film with her, *Guess Who's Coming to Dinner* (1967), but he died shortly after filming was completed. Now 59, Hepburn isn't letting up one bit, even making a return to Broadway in a musical based on the life of Coco Chanel.

In her new film, *The Lion in Winter*, she has one of the most demanding roles of her career and a record-breaking 12th Oscar nomination seems as predictable as tomorrow's sunrise. She plays Eleanor of Aquitaine to Peter O'Toole's Henry II, and their marital and regal squabbles over which of their sons (Anthony Hopkins or Timothy Dalton) should inherit the crown, make for some fine fireworks.

BIRTHS, DEATHS AND MARRIAGES

DEATHS

Franchot Tone
18 Sep, New York
Cancer

Lee Tracy
18 Oct, Santa Monica, California
Cancer

Ramon Navaro
30 Oct, Hollywood
Murdered

Talullah Bankhead
12 Dec, New York
Pneumonia

MARRIAGES

Charles Bronson
5 Oct, *to* **Jill Ireland**

Diana Dors
23 Nov, *to* Alan Lake

David Wood, Richard Warwick and Malcolm McDowell as rebellious public schoolboys in if. . . .

FUNNY BARBRA

Look out Julie Andrews, there's a new musical star in town! Her name is Barbra Streisand and she's as New York as a pretzel. After playing the famous singer and actress Fanny Brice on stage for two seasons, 26-year-old Streisand now stars in the movie version of *Funny Girl*. Directed by William Wyler and co-starring Omar Sharif as cardsharp Nicky Arnstein, the Columbia Pictures release is all set to challenge *The Sound of Music* as box-office champ.

Many of the Jule Styne-Bob Merrill numbers are already hits - "People", "I'm the Greatest Star", "Don't Rain on My Parade" amongst them – and now a new one, "Second-Hand Rose", seems destined for the charts. Speaking of her portrayal of the famous actress Fanny Brice, Streisand says: "I never studied her whole life. I felt that we were so instinctively alike that I didn't have to work to get her."

Barbra Streisand does the Roller Skate Rag in Funny Girl.

PUBLIC SCHOOL GUERRILLAS

Lindsay Anderson's previous movie was the powerful kitchen-sink drama *This Sporting Life* in 1963. In *if. . . .* the British director turns his attention to the public school (i.e. fee-paying) educational system and has produced a picture that catches the mood of student revolt surging through the West.

Newcomer Malcolm McDowell, 25, plays Mick Travis, a student at a traditional boarding school for boys. Travis and his friends form themselves into a revolutionary unit, inciting anger and punishment from the masters, until they launch a guerrilla war during the end-of-term ceremonies.

Mixing colour and black-and-white, the film is poetic, violent, erotic, anarchic and ambiguous. Says Anderson: "It is a metaphor, if you like, or life in Britain today – a reflection of a hierarchical society."

BOX OFFICE

UK

SPECIAL PRESENTATION

1 Thoroughly Modern Millie
2 Half a Sixpence
3 Doctor Dolittle

TOP TEN GENERAL RELEASES

1 Doctor Zhivago
2 The Sound of Music
3 The Jungle Book
4 Up the Junction
5 Barbarella
6 The Graduate
7 Poor Cow
8 Here We Go Round the Mulberry Bush
9 The Devil's Brigade
10 Guess Who's Coming to Dinner

BOX OFFICE

US

1 The Graduate
2 Guess Who's Coming to Dinner
3 Gone with the Wind (reissue)
4 Valley of the Dolls
5 The Odd Couple
6 Planet of the Apes
7 Rosemary's Baby
8 The Jungle Book
9 Yours, Mine and Ours
10 The Green Berets

Mogul Power

Louis B. Mayer, Sam Goldwyn, David O. Selznick, Darryl F. Zanuck, Carl Laemmle, Adolph Zukor, Jack Warner, Harry Cohn – these were the men who ruled Hollywood from the 1920s to the 1950s. They ran the dream factories, the Hollywood studios, and won great wealth, power and mystique. Mere directors and stars often had rude things to say about them; but nowadays these former scrap-metal dealers and glove salesmen are remembered with a deal of nostalgia and respect.

Richard Widmark called them "robber barons." Most of them came from East Europe – childhood refugees from anti-Semitism in Poland and Russia. They had no real code of practice to follow; Hollywood had to be invented. But by 1925 the corporate mould was established – the talent was in Hollywood and the money was in New York. The moguls churned out hundreds of pictures, year in year out, that made America out to be paradise; men like Mayer and Goldwyn themselves embodied the American Dream.

Hollywood lasted for perhaps three decades. The studios protected their people, fussed over the major stars, and served as both factory and social counselling service. Cracks began to appear in the system soon after the end of the Second World War. GIs started families and moved into new suburbs that lacked movie theatres. And by the 1950s they were also buying televisions.

But the most damaging event was in May 1948 when the Supreme Court found the studios guilty of restrictive practices with the chains of cinemas they either owned or had privileged access to. The Supreme Court ruled that the chains and the studios should be separated, forcing the latter to compete or bid for screen time.

Studio boardrooms quickly became battlegrounds – by the mid-1950s most of the major moguls were either ousted, had retired or died. An incident in 1950 pointed the way ahead when powerful talent agent Lew Wasserman clinched a deal with Universal that gave his client, James Stewart, a slice of the profits of *Winchester '73*. Similar deals followed and the agent slowly assumed more and more power. Wasserman himself eventually became head of mighty MCA, of which Universal is now a wholly-owned subsidiary.

Throughout the 1960s Hollywood was in even more turmoil – the battle against TV was fought with epics like *Ben-Hur* or lavish musicals like *The Sound of Music*. Production costs soared and several were huge flops. Studio heads rolled and the studios themselves became ripe for takeover. By the late 1980s Paramount was owned by an oil company, Columbia by Japan's Sony Corporation, Universal by MCA, and 20th Century-Fox by media tycoon Rupert Murdoch.

The directors and stars have the power now, and increasingly well-known writers as well. And they all have agents. Those like ICM's Jeff Berg and CAA's Michael Ovitz have built on the business acumen of 1950s and 1960s agents like Wasserman and David Begelman (who became head of Columbia and M-G-M) to become celebrities themselves. Ovitz was thanked by client Dustin Hoffman, in his 1989 Oscar acceptance speech, for being the driving force behind *Rain Man*.

That deal was a box-office triumph. But many others are not and, as they enter the 1990s, studios are questioning the value of agents' packages. They are more and more opting to develop projects in-house and doing deals with stars that reduces their basic fees. The golden age of Hollywood's dream factories is over, but some of the old ways of running them are making a comeback.

Louis B. Mayer in signing session.

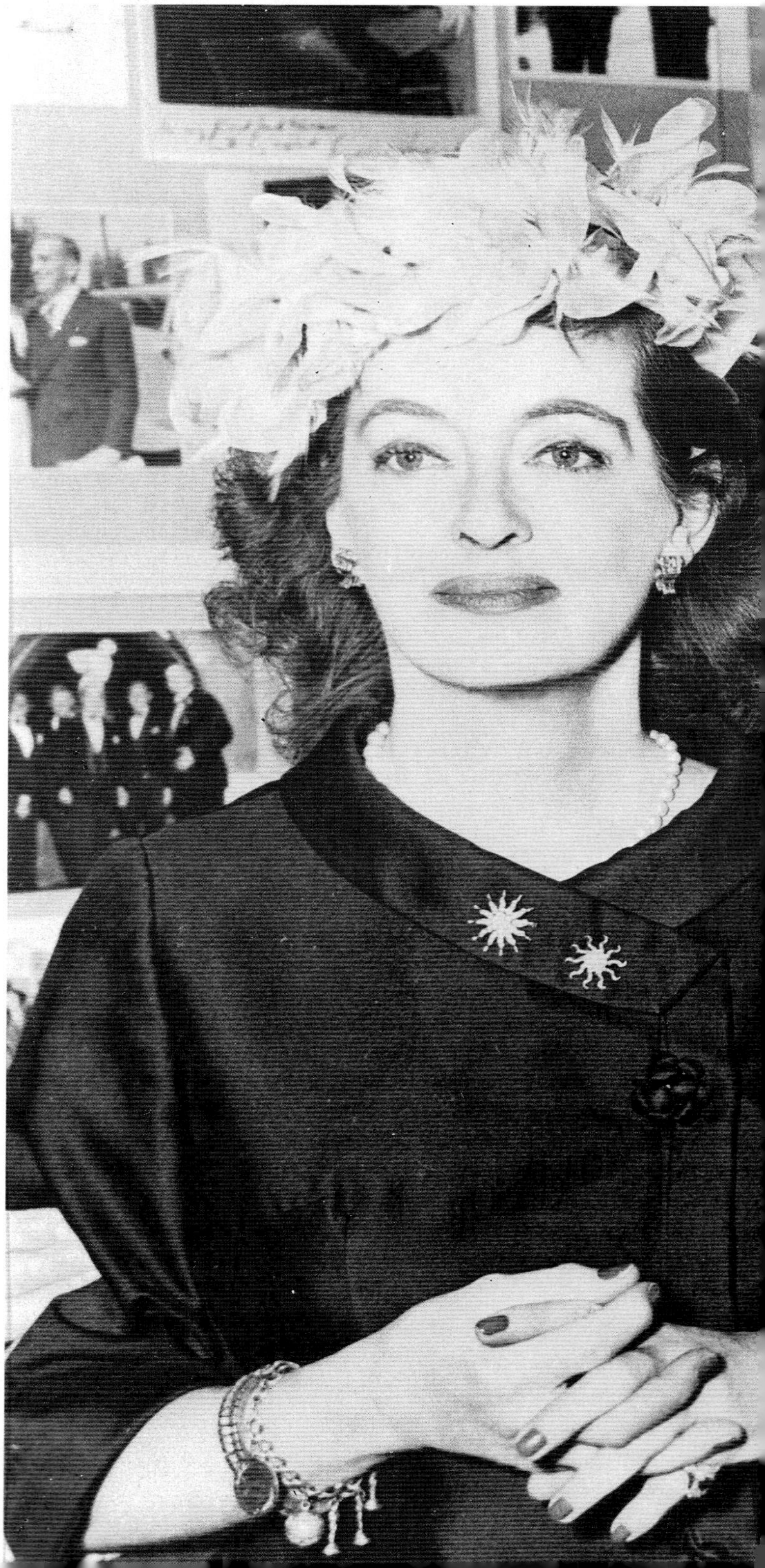

Jack Warner and two of his stars, Bette Davis and Joan Crawford.

Sam Goldwyn.

David O. Selznick.

Harry Cohn and starlet.

JANUARY
FEBRUARY

1969

MARCH
APRIL

SWEET SHIRLEY

Dance sequence on a Manhattan rooftop with Paula Kelly, Shirley MacLaine and Chita Rivera in Sweet Charity.

ACADEMY AWARDS

PRESENTED ON 14 APRIL 1969

Best Picture
Oliver!

Best Director
Carol Reed
Oliver!

Best Actor
Cliff Robertson
Charly

Best Actress
Katharine Hepburn
The Lion in Winter
Barbra Streisand
Funny Girl

Best Sup Actor
Jack Albertson
The Subject Was Roses

Best Sup Actress
Ruth Gordon
Rosemary's Baby

Originally it was a Federico Fellini movie, *The Nights of Cabiria* (1957), with his wife Giulietta Masina in the role of the prostitute who never loses hope despite all the adversities of life and love she has to endure. Then it became a 1966 Broadway musical, *Sweet Charity*, with songs by Cy Coleman and Dorothy Fields, and with Gwen Verdon as a dance hostess, Charity Hope Valentine. Now it's a movie again, a blockbusting musical with some prodigious talent both before and behind the camera.

Shirley MacLaine plays Charity. It's the first real chance she has been given to show off her dancing in movies since she was spotted by Hal Wallis in 1954 when understudying Carol Haney for a few performances in the Broadway production of *The Pajama Game*. It's also a first for Bob Fosse, who choreographed that production and went on to become one of the most successful choreographer-directors on the Broadway stage, with such hits as *How to Succeed in Business without Really Trying* (1961) and *Sweet Charity*. This is his first film as movie director, and he has taken pains to forget the work's stage origins and use every device of the new medium. "Big Spender" has been hailed as one of the film musical's best set pieces since *Singin' in the Rain*; and a rooftop routine, "There's Gotta Be Something Better" is as galvanizing as the "America" number in *West Side Story*.

Since *The Sound of Music*, the studios have been investing more and more in big musicals: in the last year alone, *Star!*, *Finian's Rainbow*, *Funny Girl* and *Hello, Dolly!* have either been completed or put into production. After the failure of *Star!* (1968), which was all the more surprising since it reunited the *Sound of Music* teaming of actress Julie Andrews and director Robert Wise, the studios are expected to become a little more wary about musicals. Universal has its fingers crossed over *Sweet Charity*.

GRADUATING WITH HONOURS

What was Dustin Hoffman doing before he became an instant star in *The Graduate* (1967)? Several things, including being a toy demonstrator at Macy's and an attendant in a hospital's mental ward. Fame rarely comes easily and it certainly did not to him.

Born in 1937 in Los Angeles, son of a furniture designer, Hoffman had taken an instant shine to acting and, by the age of 19, was performing at the Pasadena Playhouse. In 1958 he moved to New York, but work was harder to come by. Was he too short? Did he look too young? Bit parts alternated with odd jobs, until the turning point: a part in the offbeat comedy *Eh?* by British playwright Henry Livings off Broadway. Director Mike Nichols, who was casting *The Graduate*, saw it and knew he had found his Ben Braddock. The rest is movie history. The British connection continues in Hoffman's next two films – *Midnight Cowboy* (due this summer) and *John and Mary* (later in the year). Both are directed by Englishmen, John Schlesinger and Peter Yates. Hoffman is hoping they bring him as much luck as *Eh?*, and consolidate his new-found, hard-won stardom.

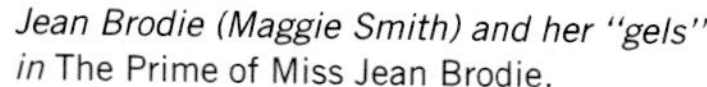

Jean Brodie (Maggie Smith) and her "gels" in The Prime of Miss Jean Brodie.

BIRTHS, DEATHS AND MARRIAGES

DEATHS

Boris Karloff
2 Feb, Sussex
Respiratory disease

Thelma Ritter
5 Feb, New York
Heart attack

Eric Portman
7 Feb, Cornwall
Heart ailment

John Boles
27 Feb, San Angelo, Texas
Heart attack

MARRIAGES

Audrey Hepburn
18 Jan, *to* Andrea Dotti

Mickey Rooney
17 Apr, *to* Caroline Hacket

IN HER PRIME

First a successful novel, then a hit play, now a movie. *The Prime of Miss Jean Brodie*, Muriel Spark's novel, about an opinionated but magnetic Edinburgh schoolmistress of the 1930s whose influence on her girls becomes of increasing concern to the school and to the headmistress, is a choice part for any actress and it has gone in the film to Maggie Smith, who is certainly a performer "in her prime."

The director is experienced British film-maker Ronald Neame, who produced a number of films for David Lean before branching into direction. As well as expressing delight with Smith's performance, Neame is pleased with his strong supporting cast: Robert Stephens as the school art teacher and Miss Brodie's former lover; Pamela Franklin as the girl Sandy, who betrays her teacher's Fascist sympathies; and Celia Johnson (never to be forgotten as the heroine of David Lean's *Brief Encounter*), playing the headmistress Miss Mackay, who will become Miss Brodie's greatest adversary.

The film is one more example of the cinema's current fascination with British education: *To Sir, with Love* (1967), *If. . . .* (1968) and the forthcoming musical, *Goodbye, Mr Chips* (1969) are others that spring to mind. Says Neame: "Everyone remembers their teachers and their schooldays. It's part of being a child and growing up. There's a Peter Sellers sketch that conveys this: he's a public school headmaster and he says to a parent: 'You may not realize this, sir, but some of our greatest men started out life as children'."

CARTOONS OR CHARACTERS?

The current smash-hit comedy success, *The Love Bug*, about a driver who finds that his Volkswagen has a mind of its own, has presented the people at Disney studios with a dilemma. Should they continue with feature-length animated cartoons, on which Disney's reputation has mainly rested, or should they commit themselves to more modestly budgeted family comedy, with a touch of fantasy and adventure?

In the past Alfred Hitchcock used to envy Walt Disney's freedom with his cartoon characters. "If he doesn't like someone," droned Hitch, "he just tears him up." But it was during the making of the live-action *Treasure Island* (1950) that Disney began to weigh up the commercial advantages of conventional features. "You guys take six months to draw a scene," he said playfully to his animators, "but with these actors in England, you give 'em the lines, they rehearse it a couple of times, and you've got it on film – finished."

But as veteran English film critic Dilys Powell wrote at the time of *Treasure Island*: "Disney can make us care far more about the fortunes of a painted duck, mouse, dog or elephant than the fate of all these honest chaps in search of pirate gold."

GOSSIP COLUMN

■ **A bio-pic of Fidel Castro's right-hand man, Che Guevara, is currently being filmed in a Caribbean rain forest. Title of the movie is *Che!* and it will tell the story of a man whose dreams of revolutionizing the world ended in execution in Bolivia. Playing the role is Omar Sharif, who might not identify with the politics but who is a dead ringer for Che.**

STAR QUOTES

Mel Brooks

"If you've got it, flaunt it."

THE NEW MARLOWE

As Raymond Chandler's chivalrous private eye in the updated *Marlowe*, James Garner is following in the footsteps of Humphrey Bogart, Dick Powell and Robert Montgomery, all of whom had a shot at the role. Garner's rugged good looks equip him well for a role that might give his career the boost it needs.

Born in Oklahoma in 1928, Garner was a high-school dropout, then Purple Heart hero (for service in the Korean War) before he finally turned his attention to acting. The breakthrough came when he starred in the satirical TV western series, *Maverick*, which suggested his forte was as much comedy as action. To date, however, his most memorable screen roles have been as action man, in films like *The Great Escape* (1963) and *Grand Prix* (1966) which have, as it were, garnered more attention than his sophisticated playing in movies like *The Children's Hour* (1961), *Move Over, Darling* (1963) and *The Americanization of Emily* (1964) opposite such lovely leading ladies as Audrey Hepburn, Doris Day and Julie Andrews. Is he the new Cary Grant, or the new Clark Gable? We shall see. Maybe he is the one and only James Garner.

M A Y
J U N E

J U L Y
A U G U S T

BIRTHS, DEATHS AND MARRIAGES

DEATHS

Jeffrey Hunter
26 May, Van Nuys, California
Unsuccessful surgery after accident

Robert Taylor
8 Jun, Hollywood
Cancer

Judy Garland
22 Jun, London
Cirrhosis of the liver

Sharon Tate
9 Aug, Bel Air, California
Murdered

MARRIAGES

Dustin Hoffman
4 May, *to* Anne Byrne

GARLAND, TATE DEAD

Judy Garland was found dead in her apartment in London on 22 June, at the age of 47. The cause of her death is believed to be an accidental overdose of sleeping pills. The body was discovered by her fifth husband, Mickey Deans, whom she married last year.

Garland's later years were clouded by drugs and divorces and stage disasters, but her legion of fans has remained loyal through thick and thin. For some she will always be the little girl with the big voice who sang "Over the Rainbow" in *The Wizard of Oz* (1939); for others, she will be remembered for that scintillating series of M-G-M musicals in the Forties that included *Meet Me in St. Louis* (1944) and *The Pirate* (1948); few would dispute that her finest hour on film was probably her performance in George Cukor's classic Hollywood backstage drama, *A Star is Born* (1954). Ray Bolger, her scarecrow friend in *Wizard of Oz*, comments sadly: "She just plain wore out."

Now, almost seven weeks later, Hollywood has reeled again from another body-blow. On 9 August young actress Sharon Tate, beautiful wife of controversial Polish director Roman Polanski, was found brutally murdered in her Los Angeles home. The body was found by her maid, Mrs Chapman. Adding to the horror is the fact that Tate was only one of a number of murdered bodies found. They appear to have been the victims of a crazed gang who broke into the actress's house. Dallas-born Tate, 26, who married Polanski last year, was eight-and-a-half months pregnant. Polanski has been in London preparing for his next film, following the success of his movie about Satan worshippers, *Rosemary's Baby* (1968). He is flying back to Los Angeles immediately.

LAUGHING GAS

Goldie Hawn, the dumb blonde of NBC-TV's *Laugh-In* who regularly steals the thunder from under the noses of hosts Dan Rowan and Dick Martin, makes her big screen debut in *Cactus Flower*. It's a light comedy, based on a play by Abe Burrows about a dentist who gets his secretary to pose as his wife in order to deceive his mistress. Things get complicated when the dentist begins to fall for his secretary.

When starting out in show-business, Jack Lemmon recalled a piece of advice his father had given him: "Try always to work with the best." Hawn might have been eavesdropping: her co-stars in *Cactus Flower* are Walter Matthau as the dentist and Ingrid Bergman, in an offbeat piece of casting as the gloomy secretary who slowly begins to bloom. Hopes are high that Hawn will follow in the tradition of such splendid screen comediennes as Monroe and Judy Holliday.

GOSSIP COLUMN

■ Director John Boorman is fed up with what the studio has done to the ending of his new film, *Hell in the Pacific*. It's about the uneasy friendship which slowly develops between an American pilot (Lee Marvin) and a Japanese naval officer (Toshiro Mifune) when they are stranded together on a Pacific island during the Second World War. Boorman wanted to end it with the two going their separate ways, but that seemed too anti-climatic for the production heads, and it now ends with them in the middle of an explosion. "The irony is," says Boorman, "that the film was partly inspired by T.S. Eliot's poem 'The Hollow Men,' which talks about the world ending 'not with a bang but with a whimper'. Now the whole thing ends with a bang."

Walter Matthau and secretary Ingrid Bergman in Cactus Flower.

Dennis Hopper and Karen Black in Easy Rider.

EASY HOPPER

"I'm just a dumb Kansas farmboy," says 32-year-old actor/director Dennis Hopper. Farmboy he may be; dumb he certainly is not. His debut as director, *Easy Rider*, has been the sensation of this year's Cannes festival and is one of the biggest commercial hits of the year.

But until recently Hopper was almost debarred from a movie studio. His acting career had begun with a small role in the James Dean classic, *Rebel without a Cause* (1955) and his admiration for Dean led him to study at Lee Strasberg's famous Actors' Studio, and then attempt to apply his theories in the more conservative arena of a Hollywood soundstage. It was after take 86 of a scene from the western *From Hell to Texas* (1958) that exasperated Hollywood veteran director Henry Hathaway told him: "Kid, there's one thing I can promise you – you'll never work in this town again." Sure enough, parts were very hard to come by in the next six years.

But it was Hathaway who gave his career its next fillip by casting him in the John Wayne western, *The Sons of Katie Elder* (1965). (He's also due to appear in another Wayne/Hathaway western next year, *True Grit*.) Nevertheless, Hopper always dreamed of making his own "different" movies, and *Easy Rider* is certainly that.

TICKET TO RIDE

"It isn't hard to make a successful movie," says Dennis Hopper, "just feed the elements into your computer and the answers will come out." His first film, *Easy Rider*, not only won him a directing prize at the Cannes Film Festival but looks set to become one of the most profitable low-budget cult movies of all time.

Previously an actor, Hopper both directs and stars in the film, sharing a leading role with his friend Peter Fonda, with whom he had previously worked on Roger Corman's psychedelic extravaganza *The Trip* (1966). The two play motor-cycling drop-outs who ride round the country, peddling drugs, picking up girls, and generally refusing to conform. On their travels they encounter an alcoholic Southern lawyer who comes to a violent end (Jack Nicholson in a striking performance) and also come up against the kind of bigots they dropped out of society to avoid.

Given that the film is star-less and plot-less, what reason can Hopper give for its enormous success? "The hippie generation dig it," he says. "They identify with Billy and Wyatt, their suspicion of the old values, their bid for freedom on the road." Its impact on Hollywood thinking could be immense.

THEATRE, FILM AND JOSH LOGAN

Now in his sixties, director Joshua Logan has the enthusiasm of a man half his age. "It's a preposterous story, lusty," he says happily about his new musical, *Paint Your Wagon*. "Two men and a woman get married, the three of them together. And what this implies is that civilization is no good; and so they do something uncivilized because they're really ahead of civilization. That's the comedy of it, and at the same time the ideal of it too." The three stars involved in this lusty show are Lee Marvin, Clint Eastwood and Jean Seberg.

Logan's association with the theatre goes back to the Thirties when he studied under Stanislavsky, but he has seriously begun to make films only since the mid-1950s. Most of his work consists of adaptations of stage hits of his like *Mister Roberts* (1954) – Logan was brought in when Henry Fonda fell out with director John Ford – or *South Pacific* (1958). He has nevertheless drawn magnificent and magical cinematic performances from Marilyn Monroe in *Bus Stop* (1956) and Marlon Brando in *Sayonara* (1957). Logan sees himself as essentially a man of the theatre, but he is no mean man with the movie camera either.

STAR QUOTES

Roman Polanski

"People call me a pessimist. I'm not pessimistic – I'm just serious."

Arlo Guthrie (with hat) goes before the draft board in the requiem for the Sixties Alice's Restaurant.

REQUIEM FOR THE 1960s?

It is not often that a song provides the inspiration for an entire movie. But, for his first film since *Bonnie and Clyde* (1967), director Arthur Penn has chosen to make a movie, *Alice's Restaurant*, based on Arlo Guthrie's talking blues, "The Alice's Restaurant Massacree." Penn himself co-wrote the screenplay with Venable Herndon and the film has mostly been shot where the original story took place.

Arlo Guthrie plays himself, wandering between New York, Montana and Massachusetts; visiting his dying father Woody in hospital; dodging the police, who are after him for dumping rubbish; being rejected for military service in Vietnam; and visiting his friends Ray (James Broderick) and Alice (Pat Quinn) who hold open house in a deconsecrated church. The movie is influenced by *Easy Rider*, but the theme is coherent enough, says Penn: the search of a drop-out generation for roots and values. Is the mood hopeful or pessimistic? "I would call it," says Penn, "a requiem for the Sixties."

SEPTEMBER OCTOBER

NOVEMBER DECEMBER

LAWRENCE WITH KNOBS ON

Glenda Jackson as Gudrun and Jennie Linden as Ursula in Ken Russell's Women in Love.

Since the trial in England over the alleged obscenity of the novel *Lady Chatterley's Lover* in 1960, film-makers have looked again at the works of D.H. Lawrence whose frankness about sex seems so much attuned to our permissive era. *Sons and Lovers* was made into a successful film in 1960, but *Women in Love* is likely to reach an even larger audience because of its sexual frankness and passionate performances.

The film is directed by Ken Russell, 42, who has built up a high reputation for his work on British television (a 1962 documentary on the composer Elgar for the BBC became an instant classic) but whose films to date have been rather routine – *French Dressing* in 1964, *Billion Dollar Brain* in 1967. *Women in Love* looks like changing all that. He has a strong cast. Alan Bates plays a school inspector, Birkin, a character who is generally believed to be a portrait of Lawrence himself; Jennie Linden plays Ursula, the woman Birkin will eventually marry. The most tempestuous relationship, however, is that between Ursula's sister, Gudrun, played by stage actress Glenda Jackson, and a coal-mine owner, Gerald, played by Oliver Reed.

Russell's daring flamboyance is at its most extreme in the film. There is a naked wrestling scene between the two men, and full-frontal nudity. The normally prudish British critics reckon it is the finest attempt to put on the screen Lawrence's passion and spirit. Says Russell: "Perhaps I should have turned the whole thing into a musical – it wasn't far off in some ways." He is hoping that his next film will be a biopic of Tchaikovsky.

BLUE ANGEL DIRECTOR DEAD

One of the most flamboyant visual stylists of Hollywood's Golden Age, director Josef von Sternberg, died in a Hollywood hospital on 22 December, aged 75. Vienna-born Sternberg (the "von" was added by a zealous press agent) moved to America at the age of seven with his parents and eventually settled in Hollywood. His first major success, however, came when he went to Germany to direct the great silent actor Emil Jannings in his first talkie, *The Blue Angel* (1930), and discovered a young actress from the Berlin stage, Marlene Dietrich. In the next five years, he was to make six films with Dietrich, including *Shanghai Express* (1932), *The Scarlet Empress* (1934) and *The Devil Is a Woman* (1935), richly photographed studies of obsession and desire.

STAR QUOTES

Lee Marvin

"Just give me my span of years and knock me down when it's all over."

BIRTHS, DEATHS AND MARRIAGES

DEATHS

Sonja Henie
13 Oct, Norway
Leukemia

Josef von Sternberg
22 Dec, Hollywood
Heart attack

MARRIAGES

Julie Andrews
12 Nov, *to* **Blake Edwards**

Esther Williams
31 Dec, *to* Fernando Lamas

OH-H-MMS!

Like Laurel without Hardy, or Jekyll without Hyde, it looks like James Bond is not the same without Sean Connery. The sixth Bond film in the series, and the first without Connery, *On Her Majesty's Secret Service* has opened to lukewarm business and reviews. The stunts are as spectacular as ever and, in a film that stretches well over two hours, there are more of them. Diana Rigg is a suitably sexy heroine, Telly Savalas a spicily hissable villain, but the consensus of opinion is that the new Bond confection has a hollow centre.

Fresh from TV commercials, Australian leading man George Lazenby is the new Bond, and the feeling is that he has looks but no personality. Rumours were flying during production of ill-feeling between him and his leading lady, with the latter supposedly eating a lot of garlic before her love scenes with the Aussie hero. There's probably enough action to satisfy Bond fans, but producer "Cubby" Broccoli is privately wondering if Connery can't be tempted back to the role. Connery has said he wants to avoid being typecast and go for more challenging dramatic roles, but Broccoli might make him an offer he can't refuse.

George Lazenby, as James Bond, faces up to arch criminal and rival Blofeld, played by Telly Savalas, in On Her Majesty's Secret Service.

Peter O'Toole as Mr Chips, with Petula Clark and pupils, in Goodbye Mr Chips.

A CHIPS WITH EVERYTHING

Thirty years ago Robert Donat won an Oscar for his performance as the diddery schoolmaster in *Goodbye, Mr Chips*, stealing the award from under the nose of Clark Gable whose immortal Rhett Butler in *Gone with the Wind* had been confidently tipped to win the prize. Now Peter O'Toole is hoping to emulate Donat in the remake of *Goodbye, Mr Chips*.

But this is a *Chips* with a difference. The story, which previously stretched from mid-Victorian times to the First World War, has now been updated to stretch from the 1920s to the present-day. Scriptwriter Terence Rattigan has drawn on incidents and memories of his own public-school days. But even more, the story has been turned into a musical.

Songs are by Leslie Bricusse, who composed those for *Doctor Dolittle* (1967), and first-time director is Herbert Ross, the choreographer of *Dolittle* and *Funny Girl* (1968). "I was very impressed by Mike Nichols' use of 'Mrs Robinson' in *The Graduate* to comment on the story," says Ross, and he is using a voice-over technique for the songs to reflect the main characters' interior personalities.

The plot simply concerns the schoolmaster's life and retirement and, in particular, his romance and marriage to a show-girl, played by Petula Clark. "A marvellous role," says O'Toole of Chips, "almost Chekhovian in its depth." He is delighted to be appearing with Petula Clark. "She's teaching me to act," he says sweetly, "and I'm teaching her to sing."

THE SUNDANCE STAR

"I can't help you, Sundance," says Butch to the Kid in *Butch Cassidy and the Sundance Kid*. Sundance, however, doesn't need any help and chances are that, from here on in, neither will Robert Redford. He's been knocking on the door of stardom for some time now, and the Sundance Kid might have opened it for him.

Born in 1936 in Santa Monica, California, son of an accountant, Redford's earliest ambition was to become a painter. However, he trained at the American Academy of Dramatic Arts, and small parts on Broadway began to come his way in the late Fifties. His blond, athletic good looks seem tailor-made for Hollywood, so it has been no surprise to see him make steady progress in films in such offbeat productions as *Inside Daisy Clover* (1965), *This Property Is Condemned* (1965) and *The Chase* (1966). Until Sundance, however, the star part seemed to elude him. Now, thanks to what is shaping up as the most successful western ever, the movie territory is his for the taking.

SHOOTING STARS

If asked politely, would you put a bullet through the head of someone to spare him or her any more suffering? After all, they shoot horses, don't they?

This is the sense behind the title of *They Shoot Horses, Don't They?*, whose action takes place during a six-day marathon dance contest during the American Depression. The film is based on a cult novel by Horace McCoy who is best known for this story, published in 1938, and *I Should Have Stayed Home* (1939), both of which offer tough evocations of life at that time in Los Angeles. The directing honours were originally to be granted to the experienced screenwriter James Poe, whose directing debut this would have been, but the assignment was eventually given to Sydney Pollack, whose work to date has ranged from Tennessee Williams (*This Property Is Condemned* in 1966) to comedy western (*The Scalphunters* in 1968).

The movie establishes Jane Fonda at last as one of the finest of current movie actresses, but most attention has been given to an eye-opening performance as the Machiavellian MC by Gig Young. Young has been in movies for nearly 30 years and has twice been nominated for supporting actor Oscars (for *Come Fill the Cup* in 1951 and *Teacher's Pet* in 1958) without ever making the transition to leading man. Some observers reckon his time might at last have come. It's Young who steals the show.

BOX OFFICE

UK

SPECIAL PRESENTATION

1. Oliver!
2. Gone With the Wind
3. Chitty Chitty Bang Bang

TOP TEN GENERAL RELEASES

1. Oliver!
2. Till Death Us Do Part
3. Carry on Camping
4. The Love Bug
5. Bullitt
6. Carry on Up the Khyber
7. The Virgin Soldiers
8. Shalako
9. Oh! What a Lovely War
10. Half a Sixpence

BOX OFFICE

US

1. The Love Bug
2. Funny Girl
3. Bullitt
4. Butch Cassidy and the Sundance Kid
5. Romeo and Juliet
6. True Grit
7. Midnight Cowboy
8. Oliver!
9. Goodbye Columbus
10. Chitty Chitty Bang Bang

PIONEERING PECKINPAH

Sam Peckinpah is a descendant of pioneering settlers of the old West, so it's not surprising he should have gravitated to westerns as a director. What has taken people aback has been the uncompromising vision he brought to last summer's *The Wild Bunch*. Some Hollywood veterans aren't impressed, though. "Oh, hell," says Howard Hawks, "I can kill five guys and have 'em buried in the time it takes him to kill one," alluding to Peckinpah's slow-motion, blood-spurting violence. But most audiences have seen the film as a breakthrough, a new vision of the West and its heroes and how things really were.

Born in 1925, Peckinpah began his career by writing screenplays for TV series such as the long-running *Gunsmoke* (1955) and serving as assistant to director Don Siegel. A chance to direct came along in the early Sixties, and he made a big impact with the elegiac *Ride the High Country* (1962). Producer trouble bedevilled his next project, *Major Dundee* (1965) – compromise does not come easily to him – but *The Wild Bunch* is much as Peckinpah would have it: raw, red-blooded, and revisionist. "He could be the new John Ford," comments one observer, adding, ". . . of the Vietnam age."

Director Sam Peckinpah during the filming of The Wild Bunch, *his stylish and exciting epitaph for the western.*

BANGERS AND M*A*S*H

"No one sees the war the way surgeons do." Thus producer Ingo Preminger on his new movie, *M*A*S*H*, a raucous comedy about surgeons at a mobile hospital in Korea during the Korean War. The initials stand for Mobile Army Surgical Hospital, and the film, moving between slaughterhouse and whorehouse, suggests that the proximity of death brings out the primitive and anarchic in all of us. (Movie chroniclers may also care to note that it features the first on-screen use of a four-letter word beginning with "f".)

Stars are the little-known Donald Sutherland, who is best known for a supporting role in *The Dirty Dozen* (1967), and Elliott Gould, who's best known for being the ex-husband of Barbra Streisand. The enthusiastic response to the film, however, suggests that the Seventies will be a good decade for them.

Has the film any modern relevance? "Sergeant Bilko in Vietnam" is one description of it, and director Robert Altman concurs. The screenplay is by Ring Lardner Jr, one of the famous "Hollywood Ten" sent to prison in the early Fifties for alleged Communist sympathies. Has America changed a lot since then? "Let me put it this way," says Lardner. "The man who prosecuted me then was Richard Nixon. He's now President of the United States."

ACADEMY AWARDS

PRESENTED ON 7 APRIL 1970

Best Picture
Midnight Cowboy

Best Director
John Schlesinger
Midnight Cowboy

Best Actor
John Wayne
True Grit

Best Actress
Maggie Smith
The Prime of Miss Jean Brodie

Best Sup Actor
Gig Young
They Shoot Horses, Don't They?

Best Sup Actress
Goldie Hawn
Cactus Flower

GRAND HOTEL OF THE SKY

Pilot Dean Martin and stewardess Jacqueline Bisset try to persuade a madman to let go of his bomb in Airport.

Veteran moviegoers who wonder whatever happened to the old-fashioned escapist entertainment movie may be reassured by the current hit, *Airport*. One American critic has already labelled it "the best film of 1944."

Based on Arthur Hailey's best-selling novel, *Airport* uses a formula that audiences have been entranced by since what one critic called the "super-rich pudding" of *Grand Hotel* (1932). Expensive actors and actresses are thrown together in a confined setting and, as they work out their romantic and financial problems, the audience can eavesdrop on a world of privilege and power, glamour and excitement.

Airport adds a touch of tension as well. Among those characters thrown together on a snowy night at an international airport are a pilot with marital problems, an eccentric grandmother, and a madman who plans to blow up passengers, plane and crew. The cast makes this one of the most prestigious airports ever: Burt Lancaster, Dean Martin, Jean Seberg, Van Heflin (as the madman) and Helen Hayes (as the lovable granny).

WARRIOR GENERAL

George C. Scott as Patton, *the story of the adventures of an aggressive and successful Second World War general.*

"Peace is hell." So said the most controversial American general of the Second World War, George S. Patton, whose wartime exploits are the subject of the new movie of director Franklin J. Schaffner, who had a big hit recently with *Planet of the Apes* (1968). *Patton* could not be more different; it's an epic character study more than a war adventure. Because of his strong dislike of Patton's views, Rod Steiger turned down the role, and the lead was taken by George C. Scott.

"Patton was a complicated, contradictory man," says Schaffner. "The classic warrior – religious, profane." Something of that complexity is reflected in the different views expressed of him by people involved in the movie. "The man was obviously nuts," says the writer, Francis Ford Coppola, adding that he saw Patton as "a man out of his times, a pathetic hero, a Don Quixote figure." The film is no whitewash job: the infamous incident when Patton accused a shell-shocked private of malingering and struck him is there in all its brutal force. The film pulls no punches: neither does Scott's performance.

WILD WEST

She was Snow White, she said – but she drifted. She was permissive before the "permissive" era had ever been dreamt of. She was called the Statue of Sexual Liberty. She was – still is – Mae West.

Now, wonder of wonders, she is returning to the screen after an absence of 26 years. The film is *Myra Breckinridge*, based on the novel by Gore Vidal and directed by a young Englishman, Mike Sarne. The novel was a Hollywood satire, and Mae West has always taken her screen image with a large pinch of salt – one of her most endearing characteristics. Her great period was the 1930s, when her co-stars included Cary Grant (whom she claimed to have discovered) and W.C. Fields. Now 78, she seems to have lost little of her sparkle and, as in her heyday, is writing her own dialogue. Whether the film will be any good remains to be seen, though, as Mae would say, goodness has nothing to do with it. Whatever happens, the return of Mae West is an event.

BOYO IN BREECHES

King Henry VIII has been a right royal role for actors. It won an Oscar for Charles Laughton back in 1932/33. More recently, Robert Shaw was nominated for an Academy Award in *A Man for All Seasons* (1966). Now Richard Burton is also in the running for an Oscar for his performance as Henry in *Anne of the Thousand Days*, co-starring beautiful French-Canadian actress Genevieve Bujold as Anne Boleyn.

Asked how his interpretation differs from his predecessors, Burton says: "In the past Henry has often been played as a lovable buffoon. But I have been reading a few books about him and I did not like the man at all: he seemed to me childish, arrogant and vain, full of peevish rages." What the King's descendants will make of the interpretation could soon become apparent: *Anne of the Thousand Days* has been chosen for this year's Royal Film Performance in London.

GOSSIP COLUMN

■ **After his Oscar-winning performance in *True Grit*, John Wayne is set to star in another western, *Rio Lobo*, directed by Hollywood veteran Howard Hawks. Hawks has directed Duke in some of his finest western roles – *Red River* (1948), *Rio Bravo* (1959) and *El Dorado* (1967).**

BIRTHS, DEATHS AND MARRIAGES

DEATHS

Cathy O'Donnell
11 Apr, Los Angeles

Anita Louise
25 Apr, Los Angeles
Stroke

Rock Hudson and Julie Andrews in the musical *Darling Lili*.

END OF THE RAINBOW?

Has the musical had its day? This is the question the industry's asking as the poor critical response and box-office returns trickle in for the new Julie Andrews movie, *Darling Lili*. After the runaway success of *The Sound of Music* and *Mary Poppins* in the mid-Sixties, it seemed as if the musical was what audiences most wanted. But now, with *Darling Lili* at the end of a string of musical box-office duds – *Star!*, *Finian's Rainbow* (both 1968), *Sweet Charity* (1969) among them – Hollywood is having another think. For one thing, musicals are expensive.

In *Darling Lili* Julie Andrews plays a musical Mata Hari, an entertainer of the Allied troops who is actually a German spy. Rock Hudson plays the American flier who falls for her. Maybe singing and spying don't go together? Yet the general view is that Henry Mancini's score, particularly the haunting theme, "Whistling in the Dark", is one of his most attractive. And one can hardly blame lack of rapport between actress and director: Andrews and director Blake Edwards fell in love during the making of the film and are due to marry this year. If music be the food of love. . . . But audiences are still not coming to see the movie.

FROM BERLIN TO BROADWAY

When Richard Burton and Elizabeth Taylor were looking for a director for the film version of Edward Albee's play *Who's Afraid of Virginia Woolf?* (1966) they were after someone who was new, fresh and brilliant, with a way with actors and a gift for comedy. Who better than Mike Nichols, clearly the brightest director on Broadway and surely just ripe for his debut as film director? How right they were. In his second film, *The Graduate* (1967), Nichols went on to win an Academy Award.

He was born in Berlin in 1931 and at the age of seven fled the Nazi terror with his family and emigrated to the United States. He discovered the delight of performing when a student at the University of Chicago, and this eventually led to a partnership with Elaine May, and a semi-improvised evening of revue sketches that bowled over Broadway. The *Virginia Woolf* offer came along after Nichols had directed a string of stage successes, and to date he has had the same magic touch with the movies. *Catch-22* should be right up his street: satire with a real cutting edge.

Mike Nichols, the director who won an Academy Award for his film debut *The Graduate*, at work on his latest film *Catch-22*.

Art Garfunkel and Alan Arkin in *Catch-22*.

WAR GAMES

Few novels of the past decade have had such acclaim as Joseph Heller's *Catch-22* since its publication in 1962. At one time mooted as a possible subject for Stanley Kubrick, whose black comedy *Dr Strangelove* (1964) was not far from Heller's style, the film version has finally materialized. It's directed by Mike Nichols, who made *Who's Afraid of Virginia Woolf?* (1966) and *The Graduate* (1967). The roll-call of actors is awesome: Alan Arkin as Yossarian, Jon Voight as Milo Minderbinder, Bob Newhart as Major Major, not to mention sizable roles for Anthony Perkins, Orson Welles, Art Garfunkel, Richard Benjamin and Martin Balsam.

The setting is a US Air Force base in the Mediterranean during the Second World War and, as the movie surveys the madness and brutality of war, its action shifts manically between hospital and headquarters, Roman nightlife and airborne horror. But will *Catch-22* catch on? There's a feeling in the trade that, as a military black comedy, *Catch-22* may have been upstaged by the enormous success earlier this year of *M*A*S*H*.

And what is Catch-22? A flyer asks to be grounded because he is crazy. But you can only be grounded if you make a formal request to be grounded; and if you make such a request – to avoid being killed – it proves you are *not* crazy. That's Catch-22. It's the best there is.

MR. VERSATILE

Alan Arkin hasn't been in films very long, but he's already been nominated for two Oscars. His roles have ranged from a bumbling detective in *Inspector Clouseau* to a poignant deaf-mute in *The Heart Is a Lonely Hunter* (both 1968). He has also played an endearingly friendly Russian in *The Russians Are Coming! The Russians Are Coming!* (1966), and a psychopathic killer who terrorizes blind Audrey Hepburn in *Wait Until Dark* (1967). To call him versatile is an understatement.

A New Yorker, born in 1934, Arkin first came to critical attention in 1963 when his debut on Broadway in *Enter Laughing* was a wild success. Since then he has alternated between stage and screen, between comedy and straight acting, between acting and directing. Is this man too gifted for his own good? It's a nice problem to have: better talent to burn – even if it burns out – than no talent at all. In the meantime, watch him as Yossarian in *Catch-22*, confidently holding his own in a high-powered cast that might have intimidated a lesser actor.

END OF AN ERA

Some have called it the end of an era – or at least the end of the studio system. In May M-G-M, the studio that had more stars than there were in heaven and epitomized the Hollywood dream factory, auctioned off some of its most famous props from over 45 years of filmmaking. Rhett Butler's top hat, Tarzan's loincloth and even the ruby slippers from *The Wizard of Oz* (1939) are being sold off. It looks likely that 20th Century-Fox will follow. The studios are claiming they need the money, but many film fans believe they are selling off the nation's heritage.

BIRTHS, DEATHS AND MARRIAGES

DEATHS

Billie Burke
14 May, Los Angeles

Frances Farmer
1 Aug, Indiana
Cancer

MARRIAGES

Peter Sellers
24 Aug, *to* Miranda Quarry

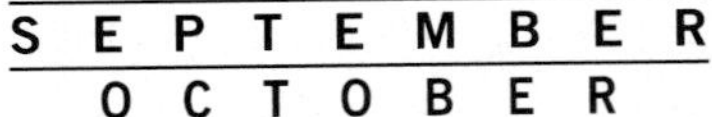

GET OUT YOUR HANKIES

NOVEMBER
DECEMBER

SEDUCTIVE SARAH

She tempted timid teacher Laurence Olivier in *Term of Trial* (1962) and seduced James Fox's aristocrat in *The Servant* (1963). Sarah Miles plays ladies who are bad, mad and dangerous to know. But in her new film, *Ryan's Daughter*, scripted by husband Robert Bolt, she shows a new romantic vulnerability and a growth as a dramatic actress.

Born on the last day of 1941, she enrolled at the Royal Academy of Dramatic Art in London at the age of 15. Her debut in *Term of Trial* launched her screen career. Although her trademark to date has been sultry sexuality – there have been few sirens in British cinema quite as explosive as her role in *The Servant* – her winsomeness in *Those Magnificent Men in their Flying Machines* (1965) and her sensitivity in *I Was Happy Here* (1966) suggest different sides and shades to her character. She needs someone to write her a new part: she has the husband to do it.

BIRTHS, DEATHS AND MARRIAGES

DEATHS

Edward Everett Horton
29 Sep, Encino, Calif
Cancer

Charles Ruggles
23 Dec, Hollywood
Cancer

MARRIAGES

Howard Keel
21 Dec, *to* Judy Magamoll

Ali MacGraw and Ryan O'Neal as young lovers in Paramount's three hankie weepy Love Story.

"Love means never having to say you're sorry." So says one of the star-crossed lovers in Paramount's new romantic weepy, *Love Story*, which seems to have tapped the tear-ducts of the nation. Ryan O'Neal and Ali MacGraw play the young lovers, who are first separated by class (he's the son of a wealthy banker, she the daughter of an Italian immigrant) and then by impending death as she is struck down by a fatal illness. Ray Milland and John Marley play the all-important parents.

The instant success of the film is a vindication of the faith in the project by studio executive Robert Evans. He spotted the potential of Erich Segal's story at an early stage, encouraged him to write it up as a novel, and then invested heavily in publicizing the book when it came out on St. Valentine's Day, helping it to become a number one best-seller. Why was he so confident, when six other studios had turned it down? "I think it has several potent ingredients," says Evans. "The death of a beautiful woman is always a poetic subject. I also see it as a modern *Romeo and Juliet*, where love is threatened by parental opposition and then by death."

BOX OFFICE

UK

SPECIAL PRESENTATION

1 Paint Your Wagon
2 Oliver!
3 Anne of the Thousand Days

TOP TEN GENERAL RELEASES

1 Battle of Britain
2 On Her Majesty's Secret Service
3 Butch Cassidy and the Sundance Kid
4 Where Eagles Dare
5 Women in Love
6 M*A*S*H
7 Carry On Up the Jungle
8 Midnight Cowboy
9 Funny Girl
10 Easy Rider

BOX OFFICE

US

1 Airport
2 M*A*S*H
3 Patton
4 Bob & Carol & Ted & Alice
5 Woodstock
6 Hello, Dolly!
7 Cactus Flower
8 Catch-22
9 On Her Majesty's Secret Service
10 The Reivers

DICKENS OF A MUSICAL

Two years ago the musical *Oliver!* captivated audiences and critics, and now there's a singing *Scrooge*. Albert Finney and Alec Guinness star in a new musical version of Charles Dickens' *A Christmas Carol*, and the film's rave reviews suggest it is likely to emulate the popularity of the earlier film.

Dickens has always been one of the most popular English novelists for screen adaptation, from the silent period onwards. In the Thirties, two performances were especially memorable: W.C. Fields' Mr Micawber in *David Copperfield* (1934) and Ronald Colman's Sidney Carton in *A Tale of Two Cities* (1935). Two adaptations stood out in the following decade, both by David Lean: *Great Expectations* (1946) and *Oliver Twist* (1948). Dickens is perfect screen fare: he creates memorable characters and his plots are full of incident. Music adds an extra dimension. We can expect other Dickensian characters to be breaking into song before long.

David Lean's *Ryan's Daughter* was shot in County Kerry, Ireland and stars Sarah Miles and Robert Mitchum.

EPIC FLOP?

After the enormous success of *Doctor Zhivago* (1965), which to audiences was the *Gone with the Wind* of the 1960s, M-G-M was looking to David Lean to repeat his triumph with *Ryan's Daughter*, particularly as the studio's fortunes have been so rocky of late. (There was the last minute cancellation of Fred Zinnemann's *Man's Fate*; the financial debacle of Michelangelo Antonioni's *Zabriskie Point*; the selling off of studio mementoes – to name but three crises.)

But auguries are not good. Critics in both London and America have savaged the film. "Gush made respectable by millions of dollars tastefully wasted," says *The New Yorker*. "Instead of looking like the money it cost to make," says London's *Evening Standard*, "the film feels like the time it took to shoot."

Ryan's Daughter was filmed in Ireland, around the Dingle peninsula, County Kerry, at a cost of $6 million. It took 10 months to write; five months for M-G-M to build the village of Kirrary; and 53 weeks to film. It tells a romantic story of an adulterous love affair between a village schoolmaster's wife (Sarah Miles) and a British officer (Christopher Jones), set against the background of the Irish troubles in 1916. Lean's writer is once again Robert Bolt, who wrote the screenplays for his *Lawrence of Arabia* (1962) and *Doctor Zhivago*; and a strong cast includes Robert Mitchum, John Mills (in a wordless part as the village idiot), Trevor Howard and Leo McKern.

Lean is confident that word-of-mouth will do the trick. "After all," he recalls, "none of the critics liked *Doctor Zhivago* when it first came out. But the studio had faith in it, and kept it running, and it's become the most popular film I've made." The cast, too, are fully supportive. "A great film," opines Howard emphatically. We'll see.

RED INDIAN REVIVAL

With the new film *Little Big Man* Hollywood continues its reappraisal of the role of the Red Indian. In the traditional western the Indian was invariably the painted savage threatening the white man's drive towards progress and civilization. Who can forget that moment in John Ford's classic *Stagecoach* (1939) when, just as the stage seems to be nearing safety, Ford pans to a tribe of Apaches preparing to mount an ambush?

Actually, this portrayal was not true of all westerns. *Broken Arrow* (1950), in which James Stewart falls in love with an Indian girl, showed the Indian in an unusually sympathetic light. During the Sixties, films like *The Unforgiven* (1960), with Audrey Hepburn as a half-breed, and *Flaming Star* (1960), in which Elvis Presley gave his best performance in a similar role, tried to show the destructiveness of prejudice, as did last year's *Tell Them Willie Boy Is Here* (1969), with Robert Redford. In *Cheyenne Autumn* (1964), John Ford himself showed the betrayal of Indians by the white community and their poignant longing for a homeland. Perhaps the western has got the Red Indian on its conscience. Maybe now's the time for owning up.

Dustin Hoffman in *Little Big Man*.

DUSTIN'S 121!

Based on Thomas Berger's best-selling novel, *Little Big Man* is another movie on a mission to revise our ideas of the American West and the western. The tale is narrated by a 121-year-old man (Dustin Hoffman under a remarkable make-up job) who claims to be the last living survivor of the Battle of the Little Big Horn, where General Custer and his men were wiped out by Indian braves. His name is Jack Crabb, a white man who, as a boy, was captured and brought up by the Indians and who has slipped back and forth between the two cultures ever since.

At the helm is *Bonnie and Clyde* director Arthur Penn. In his film it is the Indians who are referred to as "human beings" and are passive, and it is the whitemen who are "savages" and the aggressors. The film also strips the bogus glamour from the unsavory historical figures of Wild Bill Hickock and General Custer.

GOSSIP COLUMN

■ **Russ Meyer is due to direct his second major film for 20th Century-Fox, the first being the notorious *Beyond the Valley of the Dolls* (whose release in Britain is still delayed because of censorship problems). The new film is called *Seven Minutes*, and will it be different from *Dolls*? If Meyer's explanation of the title is anything to go by ("the time it takes for a woman to reach sexual climax"), it appears not.**

The Manchurian Candidate *(1962)*.

Jack Lemmon and Sissy Spacek in Missing *(1982)*.

Warren Beatty in The Parallax View *(1974)*.

High Anxiety

In the 1970s paranoia was contagious. The inconclusive Warren Commission Report on the assassination of President Kennedy, and the dark conspiracies of Watergate, seemed to show that simple truths and honesty had disappeared and that elected representatives were not to be trusted. The individual seemed vulnerable in the face of bureaucracy, political surveillance and corporate power.

Key conspiracy movies of this period included *Executive Action* (1973), *The Conversation* (1974), *The Parallax View* (1974), *Three Days of the Condor* (1975) from the US; while, from Europe, *Z* (1969), *Investigation of a Citizen above Suspicion* (1970) and *Illustrious Corpses* (1975) expressed their fears of a police state.

Very often a lone hero would try to uncover the facts behind a sinister death, only to find his own life threatened by an anonymous organization. By the end, if he wasn't dead, he was either crushed by the opposition or ready for the funny farm.

Paranoia may have been a disease of the 1970s but it had long been a subject of the movies. Earlier directors like Fritz Lang and Alfred Hitchcock had pitted characters against an implacable Fate or the Law in a way that seemed to call into question the whole notion of individual freedom. Don Siegel's *Invasion of the Body Snatchers* (1956) showed the takeover of a whole community in their sleep by an alien force (McCarthyism or Communism?). "You're next!" screamed the hero at the audience.

Director John Frankenheimer carried things a stage further in the 1960s. In *The Manchurian Candidate* (1962), an ostensible war hero is brainwashed into becoming a political assassin. In *Seconds* (1966), an organization fakes a client's death, for a fee, to give him the chance of a different life, but when it does not work out, his new identity has to be obliterated.

The forces arrayed against the individual seemed to grow ever vaster and more menacing in the 1970s. Cock-up and cover-up in the nuclear industry provided the suspense in *The China Syndrome* (1979): the tension seemed even more authentic when a similar nuclear accident took place for real at Three Mile Island. There was also a factual basis to *Silkwood* (1981), about the death in mysterious circumstances of a worker at a nuclear power plant who was preparing to reveal damaging evidence against the plant.

Perhaps the king of conspiracy thrillers is director Costa-Gavras: films like *Z* and *Stage of Siege* (1974) are withering exposes of the abuse of political power that goes unpunished. He reached his largest audience with *Missing* (1982), in which an American businessman searching for his son in Chile after the military coup, has to contend with a stonewalling American administration extremely economical with the truth.

Political double-talk hardly decreased in the 1980s; but the previous decade's anger and despair was replaced by resignation and cynicism. The British thriller *Defence of the Realm* (1985) tried to revive the form, and US director Peter Hyams has done conspiracy thrillers like *Capricorn One* (1978), about a faked space mission, and *The Star Chamber* (1983), about a secret society of judges taking the law into their own hands, in which the individual eventually comes out on top.

In the 1940s, the screen hero's enemy was Fate; in the 1970s it was the State. Is history conspiracy or cock-up? Are we just being paranoid, or are we *really* being persecuted?

Gabriel Byrne in Defence of the Realm *(1985).*

Sam Waterston, James Brolin and O.J. Simpson in Capricorn One *(1978).*

Main picture: Cliff Robertson and Robert Redford in Three Days of the Condor *(1975).*

MAY IN BLOOM

For a woman to be a director, screenwriter or actress in a male-dominated industry like Hollywood is hard. To be all three is virtually unprecedented. In *A New Leaf*, Elaine May does all of these things – and brilliantly.

She was born in 1932 in Philadelphia. Her showbusiness career took off when she partnered Mike Nichols, whom she had met at Chicago University. They conquered Broadway with a double-act of improvised wit of nonchalant brilliance. In 1961 they decided to go their own ways – though they have wound up going in the same direction. May made a hesitant cinematic start in the nondescript romantic comedy *Luv* (1967), but *A New Leaf* shows the range of her talents in full bloom. Will more women follow her example and will Hollywood turn over a new leaf? Time will tell.

GOSSIP COLUMN

■ **Dustin Hoffman has his strongest part yet, according to reports, in *Straw Dogs*, the new Sam Peckinpah movie being filmed in Cornwall in England. Hoffman plays an American mathematics professor who lives in a Cornish village with his English wife (Susan George) but whose idyll is shattered by an eruption of primitive savagery from the locals.**

GAMBLER SEEKS MADAME

Julie Christie and Warren Beatty in McCabe and Mrs Miller.

He brought laughing-gas to the war movie in *M*A*S*H* (1971), and now iconoclastic director Robert Altman is bringing an equally beady, fresh eye to the western in *McCabe and Mrs Miller*, due out in the summer. A small-time gambler drifts into a mining town and, with an opium-addicted madame, sets up a chain of frontier brothels. Warren Beatty is McCabe; Julie Christie is Mrs Miller.

Many westerns are about the birth of a nation but *McCabe* is about the birth of American capitalism. Says Altman: "It is less about the spirit of the pioneer than about the spirit of the entrepreneur." Leonard Cohen songs provide a moody backdrop to the action, and Altman has told cameraman Vilmos Zsigmond to use yellow filters for some scenes, perhaps to reflect the drug-addled vision of Mrs Miller. Most of the film's budget has gone on the sets and although it looks like being one of the most visually striking of westerns, will it provide the expected thrills? Is there, for example, a good shoot-out at the end? "Oh, yes," confirms Robert Altman, "a very long one, in the snow and very beautiful."

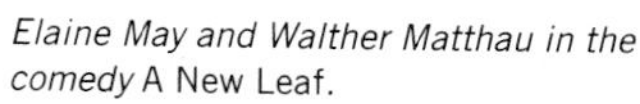

Elaine May and Walther Matthau in the comedy A New Leaf.

THE NEW WESTERN

A younger generation of American directors have got their hands on the western and are turning it inside out. It all started with Sam Peckinpah's ferocious *The Wild Bunch* (1969), which set a new level of violence for the genre; and it continued with Arthur Penn's *Little Big Man* (1970), with its sympathetic view of the Indian. Now comes Robert Altman's offbeat, downbeat *McCabe and Mrs Miller*, which analyzes how the entrepreneur, not the pioneer, brought capitalism, not civilisation, to the wilderness.

So are the old romantic western myths of good vs. evil finished? Perhaps not, but with recent American tragedies in mind modern directors are wary of simplifications. They question how America has got to the present from a pioneering past. They wonder about the place of violence in the development of American society. The western could develop into the most interesting film genre of the decade. Or it could be dead on its feet.

LEAFY LUV

There's a welcome whiff of Thirties screwball comedy in *A New Leaf*, a black farce about wealth and murder and the love between unhandsome people. Walter Matthau plays a bankrupt playboy who's searching for a wealthy mate to marry and then murder. He seems to have found an ideal candidate in a short-sighted botanist, but will fate have other plans?

Playing the part of the botanist and making her writer-director screen debut at the same time, is the brilliant Elaine May, one-time partner of Mike Nichols in an association that took the art of improvised comic duologue to new heights. Nichols turned to the cinema, and May has followed. An inauspicious co-starring role with Jack Lemmon in *Luv* (1967) is probably best forgotten, but *A New Leaf* is a much more personal project that might establish her in a rare niche in modern Hollywood: a woman director with a rare gift for comedy.

ACADEMY AWARDS

PRESENTED ON 15 APRIL 1971

Best Picture
Patton

Best Director
Franklin J. Schaffner
Patton

Best Actor
George C. Scott
Patton

Best Actress
Glenda Jackson
Women in Love

Best Sup Actor
John Mills
Ryan's Daughter

Best Sup Actress
Helen Hayes
Airport

BIRTHS, DEATHS AND MARRIAGES

DEATHS

Harold Lloyd
8 Mar, Hollywood
Cancer

Bebe Daniels
16 Mar, London
Cerebral haemorrhage

Edmund Lowe
22 Apr, Hollywood
Heart ailment

GREAT SCOTT

It was hardly surprising that George C. Scott refused his Oscar nomination for *Patton* (1970), denouncing the awards ceremony as a "meat parade" that degraded his profession. For one thing, he'd done it before, refusing his supporting actor nomination for *The Hustler* (1961). And it confirmed the seriousness with which Scott takes his craft. Unfortunately, in an industry that loves awards, he's bound to find himself being offered them: it's just that he's so very good.

Born in 1927, Scott served in the Marines before the acting bug bit him. A turning point came when his off-Broadway performance as Richard III created as much of a stir as the Olivier film version that had just opened. Otto Preminger quickly cast him as a needle-sharp prosecutor in his courtroom classic *Anatomy of a Murder* (1959), and many memorable parts followed, notably the Mephistophelian manager in *The Hustler* and the crazed General "Buck" Turgidson in *Dr Strangelove* (1964), gleefully anticipating nuclear combat with the Russkies. Even though he refused to accept it, Scott still won an Oscar for *Patton*.

MAY
JUNE

JULY
AUGUST

DICK STUCK IN BIG APPLE

Jane Fonda and Donald Sutherland in *Klute*, a thriller about a killer stalking a New York prostitute.

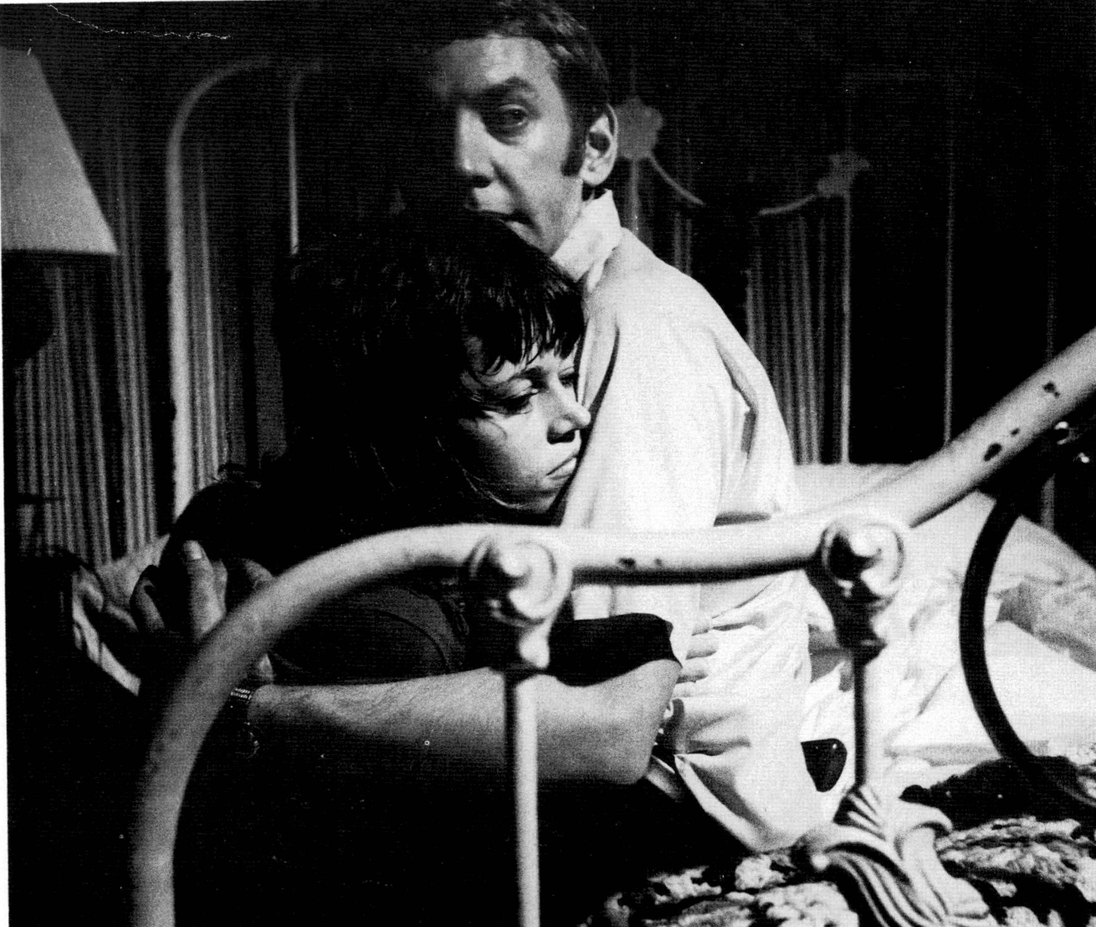

Is *film noir* making a comeback? The question seems relevant to one of the most stylish thrillers of the season, *Klute*, which is as visually dark and shadowy as its illustrious predecessors and has a suitably mysterious *femme fatale* at its centre. A man has disappeared; a sadistic killer is on the loose; and a small-town detective's search leads him to New York and to a callgirl who might hold the key to the mystery.

Donald Sutherland plays private eye Klute ("*very* private," says Sutherland) and Jane Fonda is prostitute Bree Daniels. It could be a highpoint of Fonda's career. Certainly director Alan Pakula is delighted. "We've been doing some improvisation, and Jane has been wonderful," he says. "There's a scene with her psychiatrist where Jane suddenly explodes and starts talking about how she is beginning to feel for this man Klute and how it frightens her because she's so used to being in control – and I could feel my skin beginning to crawl up my back, it was that moving and unexpected." It's certainly the most substantial female role for some time, and has found an actress in her prime.

CANADIAN ADVENTURER

You wouldn't think an imposing figure like Donald Sutherland, all 6ft 4in of him, would be so hard to discover, but he's come up through a long, hard path. He played a moron opposite Tallulah Bankhead in a horror opus, *Fanatic* (1964); was the brain's voice in Ken Russell's *Billion Dollar Brain* (1966); and ended up dubbed by British actor Patrick Allen when he played the leader of the chorus in *Oedipus the King* (1967). It was Sutherland's ears, says director Robert Aldrich, that prompted him to cast him in a minor breakthrough role in *The Dirty Dozen* (1967); but it was his comedy panache in *M*A*S*H* (1970) that finally catapulted him to stardom at the age of 35.

Canadian-born Sutherland had been waiting for this chance for nearly 15 years. He had studied acting at the London Academy of Music and Dramatic Art in 1956 – an experience he now looks back on with horror as one that also terminally shook his confidence. He acknowledges the encouragement of actor Christopher Plummer when the going was at its toughest at the time of *Oedipus*, and now *Klute* has come along, Sutherland is confident he can repay that encouragement with interest. So far his roles have ranged from anarchic antics to lanky laconic loner: he's an adventurer whose development should be fascinating to follow.

TWO'S COMPANY

Hollywood is always looking to cash in on a successful trend while it lasts, and one at the moment is the "buddy movie," a new name for an old theme in American movies. Deep friendship between two men goes back to Laurel & Hardy or Hope & Crosby; but recently there's been a whole spate of new films on the theme. Paul Newman and Robert Redford in *Butch Cassidy and the Sundance Kid* (1969), Dennis Hopper and Peter Fonda in *Easy Rider* (1969), Donald Sutherland and Elliott Gould in *M*A*S*H* (1970), Jon Voight and Dustin Hoffman in *Midnight Cowboy* (1969) are just a few recent examples in films of high quality, and there are more in the pipeline.

Several reasons have been advanced for the phenomenon. It's a reaction against the growing feminist movement in the States; it's an insurance against relying too heavily on *one* star to carry a film; it's a symptom of a less individualistic age; and so on. Whatever the reason, the films will continue until audiences tire of them, and the only people to lose out will probably be actresses, who are reduced in these movies to marginal interest. Unless, that is, they start a trend of their own. What's the feminine of "buddy"?

Ann-Margret and Jack Nicholson in Carnal Knowledge.

STAR QUOTES

Candice Bergen

"I may not be a great actress but I've become the greatest at screen orgasms – ten seconds' heavy breathing, roll you head from side to side, simulate a slight asthma attack and die a little."

BIRTHS, DEATHS AND MARRIAGES

BIRTHS

River Phoenix
23 Aug, Madras, Oregon

DEATHS

Glenda Farrell
1 May, New York

Audie Murphy
28 May, Virginia
Plane crash

Van Heflin
23 Jul, Hollywood
Heart attack

MARRIAGES

James Mason
Aug, *to* Clarissa Kaye

Rex Harrison
26 Aug, *to* Elizabeth Harris

MORALITY?

Permissiveness is dead: that's official. *Carnal Knowledge*, the new Mike Nichols movie scripted by Jules Feiffer, is a bitter morality play about sex that's more likely to leave audiences weak than aroused. Some industry insiders reckon there's a danger that exhibitors may be prosecuted for obscenity if they play this R-rated film. Says one: "It doesn't pull any punches."

Jack Nicholson plays Jonathan, a wheeler-dealing sexual athlete who is to wind up in middle-aged impotence. Art Garfunkel, who was in Nichols' *Catch-22* (1970), is his initially innocent friend to whom Nicholson gives the knack. The revelation amongst the performers, though, is Ann-Margret, previously just a Hollywood glamour queen, who reveals unsuspected depths as an actress. Critical consensus seems to be that it's a movie to be admired, but not one that goes out of its way to be liked. It could put people off sex for life. As one London critic advises: "Don't see it with anyone you love."

MORE THAN A SEX KITTEN

Carnal Knowledge, the controversial sex-drama directed by Mike Nichols, might be remembered less for what it has to say about morals than for what it reveals about Ann-Margret. Her sensitive performance will come as a revelation to all those who though she was just one of those decorative starlets born to play the girlfriend of Elvis Presley.

Swedish by birth (her full name is Ann Margaret Olsson), she's lived in America since the age of five. Her screen debut was as Bette Davis's daughter in *Pocketful of Miracles* (1961). She clocked up a number of smouldering parts in the Sixties, showing off her musical and dancing skills in *Bye Bye Birdie* (1963), wiggling opposite Elvis Presley in *Viva Las Vegas* (1964), and tempting Steve McQueen away from the poker table in *The Cincinnati Kid* (1965). But only the most diehard fans could have remembered the names of the characters she played: she decorated more than dominated her movies. But *Carnal Knowledge* has unearthed an authentic dramatic talent and that, coupled with her successful cabaret career, augurs well for the future. At 30, she's ready for more mature roles and clearly more than capable of doing them justice.

GOLDEN SUMMERS

Dominic Guard with Julie Christie in a scene from The Go-Between.

The Go-Between, based on the acclaimed 1953 novel by L.P. Hartley, won the top prize at this year's Cannes film festival. It's the third time writer Harold Pinter and director Joseph Losey have worked together and it could surpass the success of their previous *The Servant* (1963) and *Accident* (1967). Both brought a lot of prestige – if not a lot of money – to Britain's film industry.

Set in the golden summer of 1900, *The Go-Between* tells the story of a young boy who becomes a messenger for the love letters between aristocratic young Julie Christie and farmer Alan Bates. His role as go-between becomes increasingly compromised by his friendship with Christie's fiance Edward Fox and the suspicion of her mother Margaret Leighton, and the scene is set for tragedy. The movie was filmed on the story's actual locations in picturesque Norfolk.

On the surface, there seems to be little in common between a Londoner like Pinter and an American like Losey. But Pinter's Jewishness has made him aware of bigotry and class tensions; and Losey's expulsion from America during the McCarthy era for his political views put him in the firing-line of intolerance. They are both outsiders who can view a class-ridden conservative society with irony and scorn. How do they explain their success as collaborators? "He's superb at dialogue," says Losey of Pinter, "and does evoke the visual for me." Says Pinter of Losey: "His camera never becomes complacent, never says, 'I'm doing fine, I'm very happy where I am'. Even when it is still, you feel it really wants to move, but it can't; it's trapped. A kind of anxiety which I find is always stimulating."

SEPTEMBER OCTOBER

1971

NOVEMBER DECEMBER

LATE DEVELOPER

When *M*A*S*H* opened to almost instant acclaim last year, even well-informed observers were asking: who *is* Robert Altman? They were astonished to find that the driving force behind the film had been around for 15 years.

Born in Kansas City in 1925, son of an insurance salesman, Altman had begun working in showbusiness in the mid-Fifties. He had completed a ramshackle documentary on James Dean, and, for television, had directed episodes for popular series like *Alfred Hitchcock Presents* and *Bonanza*. He had had a mild success with two movies in the Sixties, the space thriller *Countdown* (1968) and the offbeat drama *That Cold Day in the Park* (1969). Even so, *M*A*S*H* producer Ingo Preminger (son of Otto) has admitted that Altman was about the thirteenth director he approached for the film. With *M*A*S*H* and now *McCabe and Mrs Miller* behind him, Altman's style is becoming clearer: comic and offbeat, independent and iconoclastic, and one that is likely to shake up a few sacred American institutions.

POPEYE GIVES CHASE

Detectives "Popeye" Doyle (Gene Hackman) and Russo (Roy Scheider) rough up a pusher in The French Connection.

People are calling it "the best cops-and-robbers film ever." *The French Connection* is a semi-documentary thriller based on the exploits of real-life cop Eddie Egan and his attempts to track down an international drugs trafficker. Gene Hackman plays the cop, here called "Popeye" Doyle, in a performance already tipped for Oscar honours. Spanish actor Fernando Rey is the trafficking boss.

The film was shot on location in New York and has the most spectacular chase scene since *Bullitt* (1968). Says producer Philip Antoni, whoe also produced *Bullitt*: "We wanted a chase scene that was different from the one between two cars, so we came up with the idea of a chase between a car and a subway train." Needless to say, it needed detailed negotiation with New York transport heads, and the shooting of this sequence alone took a total of six weeks, but it is integral to the film's excitement and success. Director William Friedkin, who began his career directing TV films for Alfred Hitchcock and whose films to date include adaptations of the plays, *The Birthday Party* (1969) and *The Boys in the Band* (1970), explains the intentions of the chase scene: "We had to come up with something different," he says, "something that not only fulfilled the needs of the story but that also defined the character of the man who was going to be doing the chasing – Popeye Doyle, an obsessive, self-righteous, driving, *driven* man."

BIRTHS, DEATHS AND MARRIAGES

BIRTHS

Emily Lloyd
29 Sep, London

DEATHS

Spring Byington
7 Sep, Hollywood
Heart attack

Pier Angeli
10 Sep, Beverly Hills
Barbiturate overdose

STAR QUOTES

Dirk Bogarde

"Someone from Warners saw Death in Venice *and was bowled over by the music. We told him it was Mahler. 'Terrific,' he said, 'we must sign him'."*

KUBRICK'S REAL HORROR-SHOW

In more senses than one, Stanley Kubrick is the director of the future. After the blackly comic prophecy of World War Three in *Dr Strangelove* (1964) and the futuristic visions of *2001: A Space Odyssey* (1968), Kubrick's new film is *A Clockwork Orange*, based on Anthony Burgess's novel about a young thug, Alex, in a society of the not-too-distant future. When Alex (Malcolm McDowell) is arrested and imprisoned for murder, he submits to the Lodovico treatment, where an aversion to sex and violence is instilled in him through a course of drugs.

"The central idea of the film," says Kubrick, "has to do with the question of free will." Do we become less human if deprived of the choice between good and evil? Do we become a "clockwork orange?" The film has been made with Kubrick's customary perfectionism and preserves the offbeat language invented by Burgess ("droogs," "devotchka," "viddy well," etc). And, as with *2001*, he's using music in a stylized way. A rape scene is choreographed to "Singin' in the Rain"; violent gang warfare takes place against a soundtrack of a sparkling Rossini overture; and even the thuggish hero professes a love of Beethoven. The violence is as extreme as in *Straw Dogs* (1970), but Kubrick hopes to avoid the controversy of Sam Peckinpah's film because of his stylized treatment. He may not be so lucky: there are those in Great Britain who are already sharpening their knives in readiness.

Ben Johnson, Timothy and Sam Bottoms at the local diner in Peter Bogdanovich's The Last Picture Show.

FLYING START

Many actors might be tempted to sell their soul for what Malcolm McDowell, 28, has achieved in the past three years: starring roles in major new films by three of the cinema's most exciting directors – for Lindsay Anderson in *If. . . .* (1968); Joseph Losey in *Figures in a Landscape* (1970); and now for Stanley Kubrick in *A Clockwork Orange*. No British actor has made a more significant impression since Albert Finney in the early Sixties.

Fame can hardly have been on young Malcolm's mind when he was serving drinks in his father's pub to earn a living or working as a salesman for a coffee factory. To escape, he joined a repertory company and then the Royal Shakespeare Company. A brief part in the Ken Loach working-class drama, *Poor Cow* (1967) got him spotted by Lindsay Anderson, who cast him as his chief public school rebel in the highly acclaimed *If. . . .* There's the same audacity in his inventive performance in *Clockwork Orange*, and the only question-mark about the future is whether the films can stay good enough to stretch his instinctive talent.

GOSSIP COLUMN

- **An extract from a press release about *Mary, Queen of Scots*, currently in production: "During a recent tour of Alnwick Castle, where the film is being shot, Vanessa Redgrave was particularly interested in a cap woven from the hair of the tragically beheaded Mary, executed by the orders of Queen Elizabeth in 1587, as was director Charles Jarrott."**
- **Lana Turner has revealed that she is a passionate believer in reincarnation. Possibly influenced by some of her roles in historic epics, she feels that she was a member of an Egyptian royal family in a former life. "Not any of the Cleopatra jazz," she insists, "but royal. Another time I was an American Indian."**

A FUTURE WELLES?

Newsweek has called *The Last Picture Show* "the most important work by a young director since Orson Welles's *Citizen Kane*." High praise, indeed. Based on a novel by Larry McMurtry, whose work also provided the basis of one of Paul Newman's finest movies, *Hud* (1963), *Picture Show* looks at the lives and loves of a small Texas community before one of them goes off to fight in Korea, and the picture house where they all used to meet will close. The cast has been uniformly acclaimed. Timothy Bottoms, Jeff Bridges and Cybill Shepherd (talented newcomers all) play the teenagers; the elders are played by experienced hands Ben Johnson, Ellen Burstyn, and Cloris Leachman.

The main raves, though, have gone to young director Peter Bogdanovich. Born in 1939, Bogdanovich has been a film fanatic since childhood. As a film journalist he's written monographs of some of his favourite directors like John Ford, Alfred Hitchcock and Howard Hawks. Encouraged to try his hand at direction by exploitation king, Roger Corman, he made a striking debut with *Targets* (1968), in which a star of horror films (Boris Karloff) comes face to face with a sniper at a drive-in cinema. Now, with his second film, Bogdanovich shows he can handle depth of emotion as well as melodrama. *Picture Show* has an authentic feel, partly because of the director's brave insistence that the film be shot in black-and-white. "Colour always has a tendency to prettify," he says, "and I didn't want that. I didn't want it to be a nostalgia piece."

BOX OFFICE

UK

SPECIAL PRESENTATION

1. Song of Norway
2. Love Story
3. Ryan's Daughter

TOP TEN GENERAL RELEASES

1. The Aristocats
2. On the Buses
3. Soldier Blue
4. There's a Girl in My Soup
5. Percy
6. The Railway Children
7. Too Late the Hero
8. Tales of Beatrix Potter
9. Up Pompeii
   The Last Valley

BOX OFFICE

US

1. Love Story
2. Little Big Man
3. Summer of '42
4. Ryan's Daughter
5. The Owl and the Pussycat
6. The Aristocats
7. Carnal Knowledge
8. Willard
9. The Andromeda Strain
   Big Jake

JANUARY
FEBRUARY

MARCH
APRIL

GOSSIP COLUMN

■ *Variety* reports that a substantial number of theatres showing Sam Peckinpah's bloody *Straw Dogs* are having to schedule five-minute breaks between showings. The reason is unclear, but presumably the audience needs time to recover from the movie's emotional impact – particularly the violent final minutes.

BIRTHS, DEATHS AND MARRIAGES

DEATHS

Maurice Chevalier
1 Jan, Paris
Heart attack

Marilyn Maxwell
20 Mar, Beverly Hills
Heart attack

Brian Donlevy
5 Apr, Woodland Hills, California
Cancer

George Sanders
25 Apr, Spain
Barbiturate overdose

STAR QUOTES

Marlon Brando

"Christ Almighty, look at what we did in the name of democracy to the American Indian. We just excised him from the human race."

MAGIC OF THE MAFIA

Brando is back. After 10 years in the doldrums and a string of unsuccessful films, he's made a triumphant return in *The Godfather*, Paramount's new epic gangster movie that is drawing unprecedented queues. Brando plays Don Corleone, the Mafia boss, who can simultaneously preside over his daughter's wedding and the brutal settling of scores on behalf of his friends and associates. James Caan, Robert Duvall and exciting young actor Al Pacino play younger members of his family.

What attracted Brando to a subject that might seem merely a Mafia melodrama? "I don't think the film is about the Mafia at all," he says (the word "Mafia" is conspicuously absent from the film's vocabulary). "I think it is about the corporate mind. Don Corleone is just any ordinary American business magnate who is trying to do the best he can for the group he represents and for his family."

The 31-year-old director Francis Ford Coppola agrees: "The Mafia is no different from any other big, greedy, profit-making corporation in America," he says. Coppola was considered a daring choice for such a massive project with such a volatile star, given that his previous films have tended to be big-budget flops like *Finian's Rainbow* (1968) or arty failures like *The Rain People* (1969). But critics agree that he has fashioned the most provocative and exciting American movie for some time.

When Corleone's men are planning to intimidate or terrorize a rival into delivering what they want, they say, with chilling understatement: "We'll make him an offer he can't refuse." Coppola's movie is making a similar offer to the American public – and they're lapping it up.

KANE SCRIPT FURORE

There has been a furore over the publication of the complete shooting script of the Orson Welles classic *Citizen Kane* (1941). Cause of the controversy has been a long introductory essay by fiery *New Yorker* film critic, Pauline Kael, who claims the screenplay was almost entirely the work of Herman J. Mankiewicz and not (as the credits say) co-written by Mankiewicz and Welles. Collaborators on the film, like composer Bernard Herrmann and actor George Coulouris, have rallied to Welles's defence. His secretary on the film has been quoted as saying: "If Welles didn't write it, I don't know what were those memos and scenes I was typing up from him every morning." Welles's friends are particularly incensed that Kael spoke to producer John Houseman about the film ("an old enemy of mine," is Welles's description of Houseman) but did not bother to interview Welles himself – who, as they say, is not the most inconspicuous of men.

LIZ AT 40

Elizabeth Taylor is 40 and philosophical about it. "Forty always sounded so important," she says. "It's halfway or more through life, but I find it so appealing. I've always wanted to be older." The years have seen her grow from a child star in *National Velvet* (1945) through being one of the cinema's most beautiful stars in films like *A Place in the Sun* (1951) and into a two-time Oscar-winning actress – *Butterfield 8* (1960), *Who's Afraid of Virginia Woolf?* (1966) – of considerable dramatic range. Through it all, she has always exuded the aura of a star and can be counted the Queen Mother of post-war Hollywood.

Her birthday party was a comparatively modest affair in Budapest, lasting a weekend, and with a guest list that included Ringo Starr and Princess Grace of Monaco. Her birthday present from husband Richard Burton? A heart-shaped diamond pendant at a cost of $50,000. "I think she likes it," he says. "She went over it with a magnifying glass." He's promised to match the sums spent on the gift and the party with a contribution to charity, and has said his wife intends gradually to withdraw from the screen to devote herself to the world of poverty.

Elizabeth Taylor, aged 40, goes from strength to strength.

DIRTY CLINT

The "rogue cop" cycle, which *The French Connection* began last year, has reached a new extreme with the controversial Clint Eastwood movie, *Dirty Harry*, a cop thriller shot through with savage violence and possibly dubious morals.

The title character is a San Francisco cop, Harry Callahan, who is constantly in trouble with his superiors for his rough idea of justice on the streets. He's "dirty" because he is given all the dirty jobs; but he's also "dirty" because of the methods he uses. He finally tracks down a mad sniper (Andy Robinson) who has been terrorizing the city, but his dubious methods allow the man to go free on a legal technicality, and Harry must go outside the law to stop him.

Says director Don Siegel: "I've never known an actor like Eastwood so keen to play an anti-hero." Eastwood's screen career was given a huge lift in the Sixties, of course, by his performance of "The Man With No Name" in Sergio Leone's violent spaghetti westerns. Siegel made fun of Eastwood's western image in his modern thriller *Coogan's Bluff* (1969). He reckons a film like *Dirty Harry* reflects a genuine worry that urban crime is out of control and may unleash the extreme actions of a Harry out of frustration and despair.

Michael York, Liza Minnelli and Helmut Griem in the story of 1930s Berlin, Cabaret.

Clint Eastwood, with Magnum revolver, as a maverick San Francisco police officer in Dirty Harry.

DIVINELY DECADENT

Bob Fosse's film *Cabaret* is being hailed as the most original screen musical since *West Side Story*. Based on episodes in two novels by Christopher Isherwood and with songs by John Kander and Fred Ebb from the 1966 Broadway show, the film follows singer Sally Bowles in the Germany of the early 1930s. Liza Minnelli plays Sally, Michael York is her English lover, and Helmut Griem plays a homosexual German baron who becomes involved with both of them.

Critics are in agreement that the musical numbers are stunning, and that the performances of Minnelli and Joel Grey as the MC of the Kit Kat Klub are outstanding. Fosse's previous film, *Sweet Charity* (his first as director after choreographing superb musicals like *Damn Yankees* and *The Pajama Game*), was highly praised but a commercial failure, though it has since been acquiring the status of a cult classic. Fosse takes his musicals seriously – life is *not* a cabaret in his world – and both his films look at the problems of innocence in a society of surrounding corruption. Yet no one can mount better musical set pieces (who can forget "Big Spender" from *Sweet Charity?*) and choreograph with such flair. He could turn out to be a successor to such musical masters as Vincente Minnelli (Liza's dad), Gene Kelly and Stanley Donen.

ACADEMY AWARDS

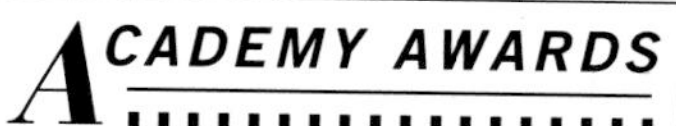

PRESENTED ON 10 APRIL 1972

Best Picture
The French Connection

Best Director
William Friedkin
The French Connection

Best Actor
Gene Hackman
The French Connection

Best Actress
Jane Fonda
Klute

Best Sup Actor
Ben Johnson
The Last Picture Show

Best Sup Actress
Cloris Leachman
The Last Picture Show

Barry Foster in Alfred Hitchcock's thriller Frenzy.

DAUGHTER OF JUDY

As daughter of Judy Garland and Vincente Minnelli, Liza Minnelli has a lot to live up to – and she seems to be living up to it.

Liza (and that's pronounced Lyza, not Leeza!) was born in a trunk that was destined for show-biz. Indeed her first screen appearance occurred when she was two-and-a-half, for her mother's movie, *In the Good Old Summertime* (1949). Her screen debut proper came in Albert Finney's unusual personal project, *Charlie Bubbles* (1967), and she won an Oscar nomination for her comic-neurotic performance in *The Sterile Cuckoo* (1969). What her screen career was really waiting for, however, was a big fat musical that could accommodate her powerhouse performing talents as singer and actress. *Cabaret* beckoned – right on cue. She's divinely decadent in a role tailor-made for her talents, which is some compliment to the role, and to her talents.

A HITCH IN TIME

Back in his native London again after a film break of 20 years (the last time was to film *Stage Fright* in 1950), Alfred Hitchcock looks set for a big success with his new thriller, *Frenzy*. A "necktie murderer" is stalking London and, as usual in Hitchcock, the police are busily hunting the wrong man, a brutal and disillusioned ex-RAF officer (Jon Finch), while the real culprit, a suave fruit merchant (Barry Foster), is wandering free.

Critics have been reminded of Hitch's 1930s British thrillers like *The 39 Steps* and *The Lady Vanishes* by the film's quaint atmosphere and dialogue. They have been delighted by the comic banter between the police inspector and his wife, played by Alec McCowen and Vivien Merchant, but there is some controversy over a ferocious rape and murder scene that is even more violent than the controversial killing in the Cold War thriller, *Torn Curtain* (1966). As always, Hitch is unrepentant. "I have brought murder back into the home," he drawls, "where it belongs."

One casualty has been the film's original score by Henry Mancini, composer of such classic movie scores as *Breakfast at Tiffany's* (1961) and *The Pink Panther* (1963). Hitch felt it was too heavy and replaced it with one by Ron Goodwin where he felt the score's pomp and sub-Elgarian main theme were more appropriate accompaniments to the film's setting and mood. It is his second major falling-out with a composer since his row with Bernard Herrmann in the mid-1960s. His rejection of Herrmann's score for *Torn Curtain* ended a relationship that lasted over 10 years and eight films.

BIRTHS, DEATHS AND MARRIAGES

DEATHS

Brandon de Wilde
6 Jul, Colorado
Road accident

STAR QUOTES

Barbra Streisand

"I arrived in Hollywood without having my nose fixed, my teeth capped or my name changed, and that is very gratifying to me."

GOSSIP COLUMN

■ Oscar-winning director Elia Kazan is delighted with his new film, *The Visitors*, written by his son Chris and shot on 16mm. Was it very cheap to make? "Let me put it this way," says Kazan. "Our shooting costs were less than what Faye Dunaway's agent got for my last picture, *The Arrangement*."

■ Roger Moore looks likely to be cast as the new James Bond. The new 007 adventure, due to start shooting shortly, is *Live and Let Die*, Ian Fleming's second novel, first published in 1954. The irony is that Moore was one of the actors originally considered for the role back in 1962.

Stacy Keach and Jeff Bridges in Fat City.

DOWN BUT NOT OUT

As Sam Goldwyn used to say: "I don't care if this film doesn't make a nickel, so long as every person in America goes to see it!" Producer Ray Stark feels almost the same about his new film, *Fat City*. He doesn't think it will make much money but it's the movie of which he's most proud.

Directed by John Huston, *Fat City* is basically the story of a boxer (Stacy Keach) on the way down, who strikes up a friendship with a promising newcomer (Jeff Bridges). Will the new boy do any better, or will he by the end be going the same way? Huston has said that the movie draws on his memory of his own early life when he had a spell as an amateur boxing champion (he also had a fight with Errol Flynn over a lady which has passed into Hollywood legend). He is delighted with his cast and once again proves himself to be the poet of the downbeat and the dispossessed. "I'm fascinated by the psychological processes of the defeated," he says, "people who have been battered to the floor by life but refuse to stay down."

Al Pacino as Michael Corleone in The Godfather.

NEW MASTER OF THE METHOD

It takes some actor to upstage Marlon Brando, especially Brando at pretty nearly his best. But in *The Godfather*, even Brando in many eyes has been eclipsed by the young man who, as his dutiful son, steps into his shoes after the Don has been shot – and proceeds to walk away with the movie. The young man's name? Al Pacino.

He was born in New York in 1940, his parents of Sicilian descent. He was a school drop-out and, while trying to pursue his great love, acting, he took in a variety of jobs from cinema usher to delivery boy. His luck changed when he was accepted by Lee Strasberg's legendary Actors' Studio in 1966: Pacino has since spoken of Strasberg as his spiritual and artistic godfather. After a minor role in the light comedy *Me, Natalie* (1969), he made an impact in the downbeat drugs drama, *Panic in Needle Park* (1971), and it was on the strength of this performance that he got *The Godfather* offer. Pacino is an actor, not a star, and there is Method in his mastery. He makes you think about the character.

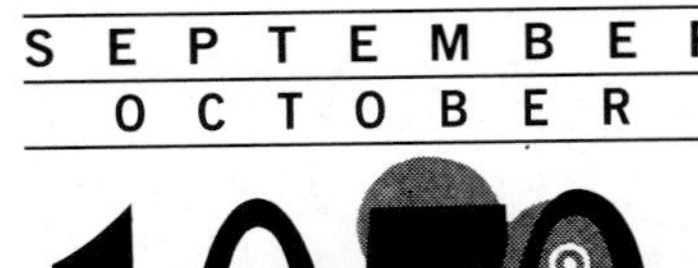

SEPTEMBER OCTOBER

NOVEMBER DECEMBER

FUNNY GIRL

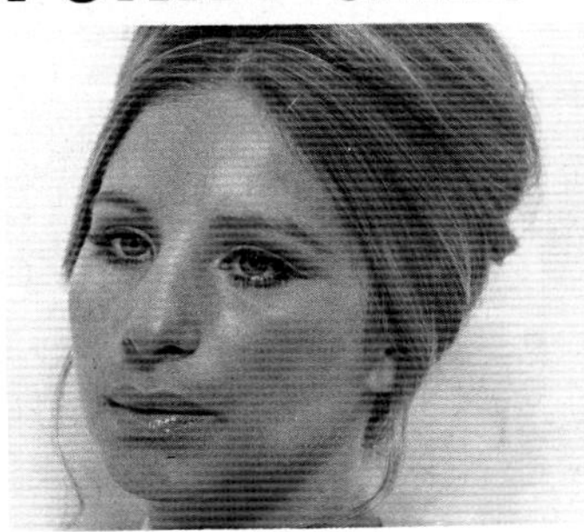

Says *The New Yorker* about her: "she is easily the best comedienne now working in American movies." Considering the fact that she has only been working in movies for four years, and that, of the five films she has so far made, only two are comedies, this is some considerable feat.

She was born plain "Barbara" Streisand in Brooklyn in 1942 and seems to have had showbusiness ambitions from the cradle. She appeared on the Broadway stage in 1962 in *I Can Get It for You Wholesale*, and although her part was not big, her success was: her zany clowning and vibrant singing stole the show. (Her co-star was Elliott Gould, whom she married but later divorced.) Two years later, she triumphed as Fanny Brice in the Broadway musical *Funny Girl* and, when a film was planned in 1968, she was the obvious choice. Her director was the exacting William Wyler, but they got on splendidly, both being perfectionists, and Streisand accomplished another feat: a best actress Academy Award for her first film. Since then she's made *Hello Dolly!* (1969), *On a Clear Day You Can See Forever* (1969), *The Owl and the Pussycat* (1970) and the recent big hit, *What's Up, Doc?* (1972).

GASPING AUDIENCE

14 October 1972 was a memorable night in movie history: *Last Tango in Paris* closed the New York Film Festival and left audiences gasping. It's the most sexually explicit yet made, about an obsessive relationship between a 45-year-old American and a 20-year-old girl whose only meeting point is their sexual need for each other. The girl is played by German newcomer Maria Schneider, but the American in Paris is played by Marlon Brando, in a performance critics are already calling as epoch-making as his Stanley Kowalski in *A Streetcar Named Desire* (1951). Brando's presence should ensure the film a large international audience, not just the art-house clique who follow the career of the director, Italy's Bernardo Bertolucci. But it's going to give the censors a few headaches.

BIRTHS, DEATHS AND MARRIAGES

DEATHS

Akim Tamiroff
17 Sep, Palm Springs. Florida

Miriam Hopkins
9 Oct, New York
Heart attack

Leo G. Carroll
16 Oct, Hollywood

Jack Lemmon and Juliet Mills in Billy Wilder's black comedy Avanti.

A TOUCH OF LEMMON

"My idea of Heaven," says directr Billy Wilder, "is working with Jack Lemmon." They had such immediate rapport on *Some Like It Hot* (1959) that Wilder wrote his next film, *The Apartment* (1960, with Lemmon in mind for the leading role, He did it so well that that character – decent urban man harrassed by ambition and self-disgust – has dominated Lemmon's career ever since. He went on to make *Irma la Douce* (1963) and *The Fortune Cookie* (1966) for Wilder, and now has the starring role in Wilder's new movie, *Avanti!*

In *Avanti!* Lemmon plays a bustling, brusque businessman who is called away from the golf course to Italy when he learns that his father has died in a car crash on holiday. While dealing with the local red tape, Lemmon finds his fathr was not alone in the car and that his companion was a lady with whom he had a holiday affair for years. Adding to the complications is the fact that the lady's daughter (Juliet Mills) has also come to claim her mother's body. Entranced by the romantic atmosphere on the island, Lemmon slowly begins to feel that history might repeat itself. . . .

Avanti! was shot on location in Ischia and also has a plum part for Clive Revill as the hotel manager who deftly deals with any crisis. So is Wilder, long renowned as Hollywood's resident cynic, mellowing? It would be an interesting development in the career of a director whom admirer William Holden once described as "a man who ate razor blades for breakfast."

BOX OFFICE

UK

1 Diamonds Are Forever
2 The Godfather
3 Fiddler on the Roof
4 Bedknobs and Broomsticks
5 The Devils
6 Steptoe and Son
7 The French Connection
8 Nicholas and Alexandra
9 Ryan's Daughter
10 Dirty Harry

BOX OFFICE

US

1 The Godfather
2 Fiddler on the Roof
3 Diamonds are Forever
4 What's Up, Doc?
5 Dirty Harry
6 The Last Picture Show
7 A Clockwork Orange
8 Cabaret
9 The Hospital
10 Everything You Always Wanted to Know About Sex, But Were Afraid to Ask

GOSSIP COLUMN

■ **After a gap of 20 years, Charles Chaplin's *Limelight* (1952) is due to open for the first time in Los Angeles in December. The film's initial release coincided with HUAC's pursuit of Chaplin for alleged Communist sympathies. While in London for the premiere of *Limelight* and hearing that he might be denied a re-entry visa to the United States, Chaplin decided to emigrate to Switzerland, and the film has never been shown to the general public in America.**

UPSIDE DOWN ADVENTURE

Imagine a combination of the drama of the *SS Titanic* with the glamour of *Grand Hotel*. That is what is offered in the new Irwin Allen extravaganza, *The Poseidon Adventure*, which has been adapted for the screen by Stirling Silliphant (Oscar-winner for *In the Heat of the Night*) and Wendell Mayes from the novel by Paul Gallico. A luxury ocean-liner is hit by a tidal wave and capsizes, leaving the surviving passengers to find their way out of a ship that has been turned upside down.

As befits a luxury liner, the cast is a glossily expensive one: Gene Hackman (as a practical preacher), Ernest Borgnine, Red Buttons, Carol Lynley and the indomitable Shelley Winters, whose underwater swim to save the others is one of the film's highlights. It is certainly a change of pace for soft-spoken British director Ronald Neame, whose most recent success has been *The Prime of Miss Jean Brodie* and who is probably best-known for his sterling studies of the British in films such as the Alec Guinness/John Mills drama, *Tunes of Glory* (1960). What does he think of this all-action melodrama? "Fun," he replies. "It's as much an adventure for me as it is for the characters."

STAR QUOTES

Robert Shaw

"Most of the films I've been in haven't taken any money at all. My record of commercial success is quite appalling, worse than any actor I can think of."

Carol Lynley and Red Buttons search the upside down ship in The Poseidon Adventure.

Laurence Olivier and Michael Caine in Sleuth, an adaptation of Anthony Shaffer's successful play.

CRY GOD FOR LARRY

The New York critics have given their best actor award this year to Laurence Olivier for his performance in *Sleuth*, in recognition no doubt not only for the excellent acting but for his return to a full-length film role after a run of cameos. But then, over the past decade, Olivier has been busy, to say the least. In 1963 he was appointed the first-ever director of England's National Theatre Company. One of his first productions was *Othello* (1965), which was subsequently put on film to preserve a memorable performance. A later production of Chekhov's *The Three Sisters* (1970) has also been filmed for posterity, directed by Olivier himself.

To add to his knighthood, Olivier was made a peer of the realm in 1970 and took his seat in the House of Lords in 1971, the only actor ever to have been granted this honour. (When asked how he should be addressed, he says: "How about Lord Larry?") Small wonder, then, that he has not had a lot of time for films lately, though recent ill-health has also taken its toll. Nevertheless, his role in *Sleuth* is one of his biggest in films, and a challenge even for so giant a talent. But then a challenge is always something he has relished. "He'll put himself out on a limb, totally out on a limb," said the young actor Anthony Hopkins about his idol Olivier recently. "In fact he'll put himself out on a twig of a tree; if it snaps off and falls, then the fall is very big. He'll risk being appalling, he'll risk being very bad. He *dares*."

AMAZING MAZE

"They got on famously," recalls Hollywood veteran Joseph L. Mankiewicz, talking of his teaming of Laurence Olivier and Michael Caine in his new film, *Sleuth*. "Michael did a little bow when he was introduced to Larry for the first time, which tickled Larry, and after that things went just fine."

Sleuth is an adaptation of the hugely successful stage play by Anthony Shaffer. Olivier plays a thriller writer who invites his wife's lover (Caine) to his home in order to make him the victim of a perfect murder, a plan that goes spectacularly awry.

Mankiewicz is pleased with the idea of having a maze in the writer's garden, which is a nice visual parallel to the intricacies and game-playing of the plot. There are also some other interesting names in the cast-list, such as Eve Channing, who is credited as the writer's wife. In the end titles her name mysteriously changes to Margot Channing – the Bette Davis character in Mankiewicz's bitchy 1950 classic *All About Eve*. Curiouser and curiouser. . . .

Glenn Close and Michael Douglas in Fatal Attraction *(1987).*

Maria Schneider and Brando in Last Tango in Paris *(1972).*

Fatal Attractions

Sex and the cinema have been uneasy bedfellows. Silent cinema rapidly discovered the erotic appeal of the film star. The close-up gave a unique intimacy to the relationship between performer and audience. Theda Bara as Vamp, Rudolph Valentino as Latin lover, Clara Bow as the "It" girl (named after her most successful film) were early stars celebrated for their sex appeal.

But sex on screen was to become less open-minded. This was partly due to public outrage at various scandals that rocked Hollywood in the early 1920s, notably the "Fatty" Arbuckle case in which the comedian was tried (and acquitted) of the rape and murder of a young actress. Then in 1934, partly as a reaction against the outrageous Mae West ("I was Snow White – but I drifted"), a new Motion Picture Code laid down stringent rules for sex on screen.

"Indecent or undue exposure is forbidden . . ."; "The sanctity of the institution of marriage and the home shall be upheld. . ." Husband and wife on screen could sleep in the same bedroom but not in the same bed. If they kissed, they had to have at least one foot on the floor.

The Code's influence lasted for decades: *From Here to Eternity* (1953) had a love scene on a beach – pounding waves equals pounding hearts – that was thought to be daring. It was films from Europe that threw down the gauntlet. There was no mistaking the allure of new screen goddesses like Brigitte Bardot, Sophia Loren or Gina Lollobrigida, especially when several of them graduated to American movies.

The permissiveness of the 1960s made coy nudity and sex more common, and a breakthrough of sorts came with *Last Tango in Paris* (1972): the presence of American star Marlon Brando in the film ensured a large, enthralled audience. *Don't Look Now* (1973) raised eyebrows with a passionate love scene between Donald Sutherland and Julie Christie that looked more lived than acted. And Jack Nicholson and Jessica Lange raised a few more as they wrestled on the kitchen table in the remake of *The Postman Always Rings Twice* (1981).

If the 1960s was the era of sexual liberation, the 1980s was the decade of sexual anxiety, perhaps because of pressure from feminism and AIDS. The decade's most successful sex film, *Fatal Attraction* (1987), came over as a lurid warning against promiscuity and adultery, with the "other woman" as dangerous as the AIDS virus. More recently *Henry & June* (1990) prompted a new category to be introduced in America (NC-17 – "No children under 17") to avoid the X rating that would have classed it as de facto pornography.

The arguments over sex on screen will never die. Some point to the hypocrisy of a situation where screen violence is treated much more liberally than sex. Others see sexual explicitness as a failure of imagination. Billy Wilder thought a sophisticated director like Ernst Lubitsch, who was risque without being rude, could do more with a closed door than most modern directors can manage with an entire bedroom.

For many, one of the cinema's most erotic scenes is still Rita Hayworth's "striptease" in *Gilda* (1946), where all she removes is a long black glove. Maybe in sex, as in other things, it is quality not quantity that counts.

ostman Always Rings Twice *(1981).*

Henry & June *(1990).*

Lancaster and Deborah Kerr in From Here to Eternity *(1953).*

Glenn Ford and Rita Hayworth in Gilda *(1946).*

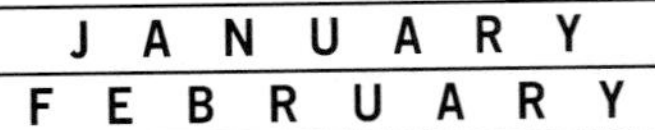

JANUARY
FEBRUARY

MARCH
APRIL

ACADEMY AWARDS

PRESENTED ON 27 MARCH 1973

Best Picture
The Godfather

Best Director
Bob Fosse
Cabaret

Best Actor
Marlon Brando
The Godfather

Best Actress
Liza Minnelli
Cabaret

Best Sup Actor
Joel Grey
Cabaret

Best Sup Actress
Eileen Heckart
Butterflies Are Free

BIRTHS, DEATHS AND MARRIAGES

DEATHS

Edward G. Robinson
26 Feb, Hollywood
Cancer

Robert Siodmak
10 Mar, Switzerland
Heart attack

Noel Coward
26 Mar, Jamaica
Heart attack

Lex Barker
11 Apr, New York
Heart attack

MARRIAGES

Michael Caine
Jan, *to* Shakira Bakish

Jane Fonda
21 Jan, *to* Tom Hayden

A HERO FOR OUR TIMES

Nina Van Pallandt and Elliott Gould in a 1970s update of a Raymond Chandler story The Long Goodbye.

One thing you can say about Elliott Gould: he's nobody's idea of a knight-errant private eye. That may be why oddball director Robert Altman cast him as Philip Marlowe in his updated version of *The Long Goodbye*. Gould is a hero for our times, with a confused look and a lived-in face. He's a shambling survivor.

Born in Brooklyn in 1938, he began drama lessons at eight, but had to sell vacuum cleaners and run a hotel elevator before making any impact on the American stage. His star role in *I Can Get It for You Wholesale* on Broadway was less of a break for him than for his supporting co-star Barbra Streisand. He married her in 1963 and watched in frustration as her career soared and his languished. When they separated, Gould's luck changed. A substantial role in *Bob & Carol & Ted & Alice* (1969) won him an Oscar nomination, and his role in *M*A*S*H* (1970) made him one of the year's most popular stars. Since then he's never stopped working.

Directors like Robert Altman and Alan Arkin, who directed him in *Little Murders* (1971), speak highly of his talent, intelligence and adaptability. To date, though, Gould's biggest compliment has been the decision of Swedish maestro Ingmar Bergman to cast him in *The Touch* (1971), the first time Bergman has ever cast an American actor in a leading role. "Very often you see American monsters created by the audiece," says Bergman. "Oh, they do have something, but it's only one dimension. What I want from the actors in my pictures is an ability to express the second and third dimensions, an ability to put the part together inside themselves and then materialize it. I want to get it from their faces, from their eyes, from their movements. I can see that Gould has it."

THE LAST GOODBYE?

Raymond Chandler purists are up in arms. The film of his novel, *The Long Goodbye*, with Elliott Gould as sleuth Philip Marlowe, is being called a spit in the eye to a great writer. Marlowe, they say, is shown not as a knight-errant but as an unshaven slob who, in the words of one film critic, "could not locate a missing skyscraper and would be refused service at a hot dog stand."

Director Robert Altman, after what he did to the war comedy in *M*A*S*H* (1970) and the western in *McCabe and Mrs Miller* (1971), is used to such controversy. "If you are updating the story to modern Los Angeles," he says, "you have to update the attitudes." He confesses to disliking Marlowe's moral certainties and his know-all attitude to detection. "We live in an era of political duplicity and corporate cover-up," he says. "Marlowe's purity and individualist solutions are a lie. It's about time he grew up." Sterling Hayden is also on hand to play a besotted writer not a million miles from Hemingway, and composer John Williams has written a score whose main theme turns up wherever Marlowe goes (even on a door chime), repetitive but crucially unfinished. "We were after something that reflected the film's own sense of search and fragmentation," he says.

TWO DOLLS

Back in 1960 there was a lot of fuss when two films about Oscar Wilde (one starring Robert Morley, the other Peter Finch) were premiered within a week of each other. Now there are two rival film versions of Ibsen's play *A Doll's House* in post-production. In one, directed by theatrical producer Patrick Garland, Claire Bloom repeats her stage triumph as Nora (a Women's Libber before her time), and she will be supported by Anthony Hopkins, Ralph Richardson and Denholm Elliott. The glossier of the two versions stars Jane Fonda as Nora, supported by David Warner, Trevor Howard and Edward Fox, and the director is the renowned Joseph Losey. Losey's sounds the livelier bet on paper, but everything hinges on the performance as Nora. It'll be interesting to see this summer if Fonda's youth can upstage the experience of Bloom.

STAR QUOTES

John Wayne

"I don't go for all this realism in movies, see. Pornography, violence, all that junk. Those goddam sons of bitches making that stuff are ruining the business."

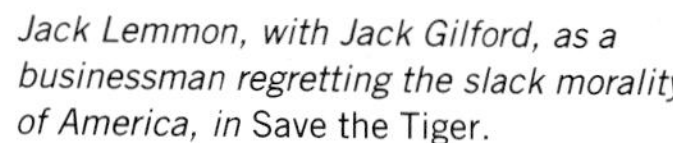

Jack Lemmon, with Jack Gilford, as a businessman regretting the slack morality of America, in Save the Tiger.

LEMMON'S ART MOVIE

"I had no idea what a remarkable straight actor Jack Lemmon was," said one critic after seeing his performance as an alcoholic in *Days of Wine and Roses* (1962). Although he is still best known for comedy, Lemmon's range is wide and in his new film, *Save the Tiger*, he has his strongest dramatic role in a decade. He plays a garment manufacturer who, during a day of wheeling and dealing and even considering arson as a solution to his financial problems, muses about the loss of idealism in himself and in his country.

The film is directed by relative newcomer John Avildsen, who had a modest success with *Joe* in 1970. It's scripted by Steve Shagan, who formerly was an assistant producer on a TV Tarzan series. The film was shot in chronological order on location in Los Angeles, and Lemmon's belief in the project was reflected in his agreement to work at a minimum scale plus a percentage of the gross, rather than for his usual salary. Paramount has been cagy about this somewhat downbeat project, setting a low $1 million budget, but strong critical support and word-of-mouth recommendation seem to be drawing appreciative audiences: an American art movie for the masses.

BRANDO SAYS NO

These days you can't give Oscars away. Two years ago George C. Scott refused his for *Patton*. Now Marlon Brando has refused his best actor Oscar for *The Godfather*. Instead he sent an Indian girl, Sasheen Littlefeather, to read out a statement accusing the motion picture industry of "degrading the Indian and making a mockery of his character" and saying that "I do not feel . . . I can accept an award here tonight."

Reactions seem to be that the gesture was sincere but misplaced. Some wonder why Brando didn't make the statement himself. Others, including Gregory Peck, suggested he could have helped the Indians more by donating some of his enormous salary for *The Godfather*. Still others feel the gesture focused less attention on the Indians than on Brando. Says Peter O'Toole: "I admire George C. Scott enormously, but for him to refuse awards, and for Marlon Brando to refuse awards, is another way of accepting them with more noise than is normal."

GOOD, BAD, OR PLAIN UGLY

Clint Eastwood is back in the saddle. He both directs and stars in *High Plains Drifter*, in which he plays a stranger who rides into a corrupt western community and proceeds to paint the town red. Is the town Hell? Is he the Devil?

The film has been scripted by Ernest Tidyman, who wrote the screenplay for *The French Connection*. Eastwood, whose directing debut *Play Misty for Me* (1971) won high praise from critics and fellow professionals alike, sees it as a traditional western in form but with a modern twist. "The drifter character is a little like Shane, in that no one knows where he comes from," says Eastwood. "The situation is also a bit like *High Noon*."

GOSSIP COLUMN

- **The trade mag *Variety* has revealed that *The Godfather* took three times as much money ($81.5 million) at the box-office last year as its nearest rival, *Fiddler on the Roof* ($25 million). Peter Bogdanovich had the biggest personal success with two films in the top six, *What's Up, Doc?* and *The Last Picture Show.***

Clint Eastwood as the mysterious stranger who rides into town and terrifies the locals in High Plains Drifter.

MAY
JUNE
1973
JULY
AUGUST

FORSYTH SAGA

Edward Fox as a professional assassin tries his new gun supplied by Cyril Cusack in The Day of the Jackal.

Frederick Forsyth's best-selling thriller *The Day of the Jackal* has been turned into one of the summer's most suspenseful films. It deals with a plot to assassinate President de Gaulle and the combined efforts of the British and French intelligence services to stop the hired killer, code-named "Jackal."

It's a welcome return to the screen for Hollywood veteran Fred Zinnemann, whose last film was the Oscar-winning *A Man for All Seasons* (1966). (His projected film version of Andre Malraux's novel, *Man's Fate*, was cancelled at the last moment by M-G-M in 1969, a move that precipitated an acrimonious legal dispute between director and studio which has been settled out of court.) His only other thriller has been the classic western, *High Noon* (1952). What attracted Zinnemann to *Jackal*? "I was intrigued by the dramatic challenge," he says. "Could you sustain the interest and attention of an audience in a story of which they already know the outcome?"

English gentleman-actor Edward Fox, best known for his role as Viscount Trimingham in *The Go-Between* (1971), is the unexpected choice to play the hitman. Is this another example of Zinnemann's fondness for casting against type, as he did so startingly in *From Here to Eternity* (1953), when he cast "English rose" Deborah Kerr in the role of an army major's nymphomaniac wife? "Partly," explains Zinnemann. "I wanted an actor who was not too well known, so that he could at certain stages in the film lose himself in a crowd, as the Jackal is required to do. I also had the idea of the Jackal as a particular anti-Establishment type: a kind of English public schoolboy gone wrong. Edward plays it perfectly."

BIRTHS, DEATHS AND MARRIAGES

DEATHS

Betty Grable
2 Jul, Santa Monica, California
Cancer

Veronica Lake
7 Jul, Vermont
Hepatitis

Robert Ryan
11 Jul, New York
Cancer

Jack Hawkins
18 Jul, London
Cancer

John Ford
31 Aug, Palm Springs, California
Cancer

MARRIAGES

Steve McQueen
Jul, *to* **Ali MacGraw**

GOSSIP COLUMN

■ **Not for the first time in his career, director Sam Peckinpah has asked for his name to be removed from the credits of his new film. He claims M-G-M has butchered *Pat Garrett and Billy the Kidd* in its re-edited version. By cutting a prologue and epilogue of Garrett's death at the hands of the people who hired him to kill the Kid, the film is robbed of its ironic dimension. The final film is now 20 minutes shorter than Peckinpah's version. M-G-M has also used more of Bob Dylan's music than Peckinpah wanted, no doubt to cash in on album sales: Dylan has a small role in the film. Peckinpah's *Major Dundee* (1965) was also heavily cut after he fell out with producer Jerry Bresler.**

THE NEW BOND

Now that Sean Connery's decision to stop playing Bond seems final, audiences can concentrate on his replacement. George Lazenby wasn't right but Roger Moore is proving a hit in his first outing in *Live and Let Die*.

Moore, 44, actually made his Hollywood debut in the 1954 Elizabeth Taylor melodrama *The Last Time I Saw Paris* when he was under contract to M-G-M. He describes himself in those early films as "window-dressing." "I was the last of the Englishmen, after Edmund Purdom and Stewart Granger," he says, "both of whom had been giving them trouble in Hollywood. I very quickly learned that I had to be highly humble and obsequious and grovel a lot." In fact, until Bond, television had been a happier hunting-ground for Moore than film, and it is likely that his leading role in TV's long-running *The Saint* (1962) influenced his selection for Bond more than anything in his film work. For the London-born actor, Bond is the biggest break of his career. An actor of limited range, as he himself admits, Moore nevertheless projects an enjoyment of what he is doing and the poise of the debonair Englishman. The search for Connery's replacement is surely over.

ALL-ROUND ENTERTAINER

George Segal has a touch of class. He can do dramatic roles, as his first starring part, in *King Rat* (1965), testified and his Oscar nomination for *Who's Afraid of Virginia Woolf?* (1966) amply confirmed. But his real forte is for sophisticated comedy, and his new film, *A Touch of Class*, opposite Glenda Jackson, looks like being his biggest hit yet.

Born in 1934, the New Yorker worked his way through the usual finishing schools of rep, off-Broadway productions, and TV bit-parts, while filling out his earnings with odd jobs from theatre dogsbody to jazz musician. The Sixties saw his career in the cinema take off in roles that varied from the lead in the unusual spy thriller *The Quiller Memorandum* (1966) to the Jewish cop trying to track down Rod Steiger's Method murderer in *No Way to Treat a Lady* (1968). His choice of comedy material tended to be the abrasive and bizarre, as in *The Owl and the Pussycat* (1970) opposite Barbra Streisand, and the cult black comedy, *Where's Poppa?* (1970). But he's always seemed to miss that popular hit that can change a familiar face to a household name. *A Touch of Class* may be it.

STAR QUOTES

Marlene Dietrich

"I liked Helmut Berger's impersonation of me in The Damned *– but then the boys were always better at it than the girls."*

Candy Clark, Charles Martin Smith and Ron Howard in American Graffiti.

RETURN TO THE SIXTIES

One of the surprise hits of the summer has been *American Graffiti*, only the second feature of young film-school graduate George Lucas (he made his directorial debut with the bleakly offbeat sci-fi fantasy, *THX-1138* in 1971). It's certainly surprised Warners, which was preparing to shelve it as unmarketable until Francis Ford Coppola rallied to his friend Lucas's defence. It cost less than $1 million to make and looks like taking many times that amount at the box-office.

"The time is 1962," says Lucas in a publicity note, "a period of transition for American youth. The kids are wearing ducktails and ponytails, and driving fast and flashy cars. We follow four buddies, age 17 to 20, who've grown up, played, joked together, and spent countless hours joining the traffic flowing up and down the neon-lit streets. The passing chrome-flashing cars become a dance. Cruising is a vehicle of fate which causes relationships to shift, form and separate by chance. Tonight marks the end of the group, a break from their old lives."

Lucas brings to the movie the authenticity of having lived through the era. A young cast of unknowns perform perfectly – big things are predicted for Richard Dreyfuss, Ronny Howard, Cindy Williams and Candy Clark – and the soundtrack songs create an irrestistible nostalgia. But most audiences feel the film has more to do with a world of innocence before political assassination, Vietnam and the Watergate scandal darkened America's mood.

NO KIDDING

"Never act with animals or children" is an old theatrical adage. "Never act with animals and *your own* children," became a popular variation after John Mills, in *Tiger Bay* (1959), found himself upstaged by little daughter Hayley. Now, in *Paper Moon*, Ryan O'Neal faces the same challenge from his daughter Tatum.

He plays a phony Bible salesman in the mid-1930s and she is a little girl who teams up with him to make the perfect con team. A variation on Charlie Chaplin and four-year-old Jackie Coogan in the silent classic *The Kid* (1921), perhaps. In any event, it's turning into one of the comedy hits of the summer and it's Tatum O'Neal's performance that is getting the praise. Pundits already predict she could become the youngest-ever winner of a performance Oscar.

Ryan O'Neal and his daughter Tatum as a couple of con artists in Paper Moon.

It is a complete change of pace and another triumph for young director Peter Bogdanovich, who made *The Last Picture Show* (1971). A former movie columnist and critic, he is proving as adept behind a camera as behind a typewriter.

SEPTEMBER OCTOBER

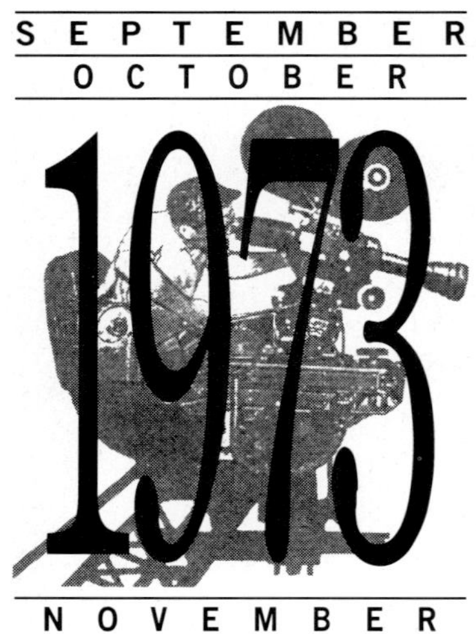

NOVEMBER DECEMBER

MAESTRO MARVIN

According to Andre Previn, the question all Hollywood composers used to ask was: "Do you want it good, or do you want it Thursday?" But what if you found a composer who could give it to you good *and* by Thursday? Tinseltown's latest wonderboy, Marvin Hamlisch, has two smash-hit scores adorning new movies – romantic stuff for *The Way We Were* (including a hit song for Barbra Streisand) and arrangements of Scott Joplin's piano rags for *The Sting*.

Hamlisch is a musical prodigy. How do you get to Carnegie Hall? Practice. But his career was underway almost before he had time to practise: he was the youngest-ever student accepted by Manhattan's famous Juilliard School of Music at the tender age of seven. Broadway beckoned, and a chance meeting with producer Sam Spiegel at a party led to him writing the music for *The Swimmer* (1968). Hamlisch has barely stopped since, seeming as slickly adept in Woody Allen comedies (*Take the Money and Run*, 1969; *Bananas*, 1971), as in Jack Lemmon dramas (*Kotch*, 1971; *Save the Tiger*, 1973). But it's still unusual for a composer to have two hit movies out at the same time – especially movies whose success is partly due to their music. And he is still only 28 years old!

DEMONS IN HOLLYWOOD

Few films have excited more controversy than *The Exorcist*. Critics are divided on its merits. The discussion has been taken up by anxious parents, child psychologists and eminent churchmen – and audiences are flocking to it in droves. As one patron told *Variety*: "I want to see what everybody is throwing up about."

As *Rosemary's Baby* proved in 1968, demonic possession is a subject with great box-office appeal. The Devil often has the best tunes, and in *The Exorcist* Satan is the star of the movie, entering the soul of a young girl, and causing beds to shake, heads to rotate, and bile to fly.

Director William Friedkin and author William Peter Blatty insist *The Exorcist* is basically religious. It argues that loss of faith can leave you susceptible to possession, but also shows the triumph of good over evil.

If Friedkin had any doubt about the difficulties of handling such disturbing subject matter, they were silenced by his sinister experiences while shooting the film. "An unexplained fire destroyed the set of the Georgetown house," he recalls. "A sprinkler broke down and flooded the set. The cast became accident prone. Ellen Burstyn wrenched her back; Jason Miller's son was in a serious car crash. And there were strange images and visions that showed up on film that were never planned. . . ." A movie about the making of *The Exorcist* is not at the moment planned: that would be tempting Providence.

STAR QUOTES

Walter Matthau

"I just found Barbra Streisand a terrible bore. I said something to her like 'I was acting before you were born, so please don't tell me how to act.' And she said, in her own inimitable way, 'Is this guy crazy or something?'"

BIRTHS, DEATHS AND MARRIAGES

DEATHS

Anna Magnani
26 Sep, Rome
Cancer

Laurence Harvey
25 Nov, London
Cancer

Bobby Darin
20 Dec, Los Angeles
Heart ailment

MARRIAGES

Peter Finch
Nov, *to* Eletha Barrett

WHAT A MOTHER!

The new Jack Nicholson movie, *The Last Detail*, in which he and Otis Young play seamen escorting a hapless young sailor (Randy Quaid) to the stockade, is causing a lot of raised eyebrows at its salty dialogue. Writer Robert Towne is unrepentant: he reckons it's a true reflection of how characters like that would talk. Columbia has asked him if he would consider reducing the number of "motherfuckers" to, say, 20, but Towne is adamant. "No," he says, "because you'd lose the point that these men can't do more than swear."

SEPTEMBER SONG

At the ripe old age of 71, producer John Houseman is embarking on a new career. He's just scored a resounding success as an actor, playing a crusty Harvard professor in *The Paper Chase*. He had a cameo role back in *Seven Days in May* (1964), but *The Paper Chase* is a full-blown part of award-winning potential.

It's strange it has taken Houseman so long to catch the acting bug. Bucharest-born, he founded the Mercury Theater in 1937 with Orson Welles, and has been around film and theatre actors for the best part of his working life. As a Hollywood producer, he has had a record of providing challenging and intelligent entertainment, working with first-rate directors like Max Ophuls, Nicholas Ray, Joseph L. Mankiewicz, Vincente Minnelli and Fritz Lang. Among his classics are *Letter from an Unknown Woman* (1948), *They Live By Night* (1948), *Julius Caesar* (1953) and *Lust for Life* (1956). Last year he published his autobiography, *Runthrough*, but *Paper Chase* may already have made it out-of-date. Perhaps he should add a new chapter: "John Houseman – Actor."

John Houseman as a Harvard law school professor in The Paper Chase.

Robert Redford and Barbra Streisand in The Way We Were.

THE UGLY DUCKLING & THE LONGHAIR

The ads proclaim "Streisand and Redford – Together!" No doubt about where the appeal of the new movie, *The Way We Were*, lies. Streisand is a left-wing ugly duckling and Redford is an apolitical literary intellectual who meet at college and fall in love. The movie then follows their romance, from ecstasy to divorce, through three decades of often turbulent political history: Second World War, and the "Red Menace" period in Hollywood when many artists were hounded for their alleged Communist affiliations.

"It's a romance," director Sydney Pollack insists, "but I hope audiences also ponder some of the movie's serious undertones." Writer Arthur Laurents had first-hand experience of the blacklist period in Hollywood: "The film doesn't exaggerate what it did to the Hollywood community," he says. However, with a hit title song by Marvin Hamlisch, Alan and Marilyn Bergman and the generally luxurious ambience of the film, Pollack's hope that the political themes will register might be a little optimistic. Signs are that the large audiences are flocking to the movie for one overriding reason: Streisand and Redford – together.

BOX OFFICE

UK

1 Live and Let Die
2 The Godfather
3 A Clockwork Orange
4 Snow White and the Seven Dwarfs
5 The Poseidon Adventure
6 Last Tango in Paris
7 Cabaret
8 The Day of the Jackal
9 Lady Caroline Lamb
10 That'll Be the Day

BOX OFFICE

US

1 The Poseidon Adventure
2 Deliverance
3 The Getaway
4 Live and Let Die
5 Paper Moon
6 Last Tango in Paris
7 The Sound of Music *(reissue)*
8 Jesus Christ Superstar
9 The World's Greatest Athlete
10 American Graffiti

Robert Shaw, Robert Redford and Paul Newman in The Sting.

THE WAY WE STUNG

It's courting disaster to predict success, but if any film looks like a surefire hit for the Christmas season, it's surely *The Sting*. The movie reunites Paul Newman, Robert Redford and director George Roy Hill for the first time since they made *Butch Cassidy and the Sundance Kid* four years ago. One might call it a racing certainty, except that part of the plot involves a scam involving the "fixing" of race results.

Newman and Redford play conmen who concoct an elaborate plan to fleece a New York gangster (Robert Shaw), who killed their friend. (How does Shaw feel about appearing opposite two such big stars? "I can hold my own", he says brusquely.) The plot is set in Al Capone's Chicago and the characters are clearly Damon Runyon types.

The film is tailored to cash in on two other trends. One is the "buddy movie", typified by *Easy Rider* (1969), *Midnight Cowboy* (1969) and *Papillon* (1973). The other is nostalgia. The film uses the piano rags of Scott Joplin, sparklingly rearranged by Hollywood's hottest composer, Marvin Hamlisch (he also scored *The Way We Were*). With the recent success of *Paper Moon* and *American Graffiti*, one can confidently say nostalgia *is* what it used to be.

THE OLD MASTER

"My name's John Ford," he would say. "I make westerns." It was a typically self-deprecating remark from the hard-nosed Hollywood director who died in California on 31 August at the age of 78 after a 50-odd year career and over 100 feature-length movies. Ford always disdained the high claims made for his work and simply called himself a professional doing a job.

But others thought differently. Orson Welles, for instance, reckoned Ford was the grand old master of American film – a poet, a genius and, without doubt (with his cap, eye-patch and Irish cussedness), a character. He was given directing Oscars more times than anyone: for *The Informer* (1935), *The Grapes of Wrath* (1940), *How Green Was My Valley* (1941) and *The Quiet Man* (1952), plus a couple of war documentaries. But it is for his westerns that he will be remembered. *Stagecoach* (1939) united him with a setting (Monument Valley) and a new star (John Wayne). Both were to play a large role in Ford's work, as he proceeded to make such classics as *Fort Apache* (1948), *She Wore a Yellow Ribbon* (1949) and *The Searchers* (1956). Nobody could match Ford for the measured pace, the visual grandeur, and the sense of history he brought to the western. He was the unsurpassed chronicler of the frontier days in America.

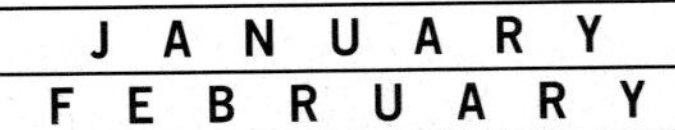

JANUARY
FEBRUARY

MARCH
APRIL

WIND ON THE PRAIRIE

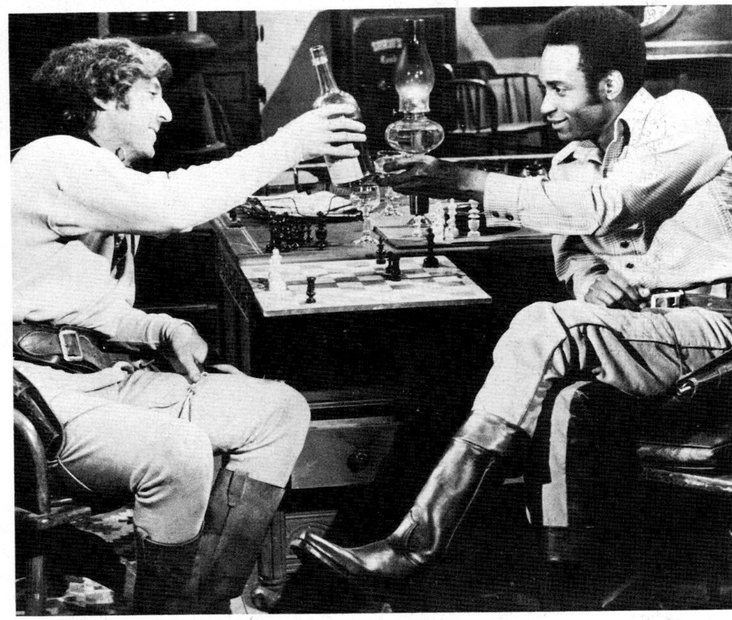

Gene Wilder and Cleavon Little in Mel Brooks's Blazing Saddles.

Mel Brooks has a perfect retort to those who say his movies are in bad taste. "Bad taste? Me?! Up yours!" His first, *The Producers* (1967), featured a memorable Busby Berkeley pastiche of Nazi paratroopers in "Springtime for Hitler". His latest, *Blazing Saddles*, is a raucous cowboy opus about a black railroad worker made sheriff to a corrupt, bigoted town. The West was wild, but not as wild as all this.

Cleavon Little plays the sheriff, replacing Brooks's original choice of Richard Pryor when Pryor had a nasty accident and had to go to hospital with burns. Gene Wilder is the alcoholic gunfighter who befriends the sheriff, and Madeline Kahn (who caught the eye with her sparkling comedy portrayal of Ryan O'Neal's girlfriend in last year's hit *Paper Moon*) is the Marlene Dietrich-type saloon singer who's assigned to seduce the sheriff.

"I just about got everything out of me in this picture," says Brooks, "all my furore, my frenzy, my insanity, my love of life and hatred of death." A lot is riding on *Blazing Saddles* after the resounding commercial failure of his previous movie, *The Twelve Chairs* (1970), but it looks like he has a big hit on his hands.

A wind-breaking campfire scene already rivals the "Springtime for Hitler" routine in controversy. Brooks is unfazed. "If cowboys had so many beans," he says, "it stands to reason there must have been *some* activity back there. I think audiences are a bit puzzled by the first fart, then start tittering on the fourth, and by the sixteenth. . . ." Is it raw comedy or cheap vulgarity? "It's a new phase in comedy," says Brooks, "a sign of the way the wind is blowing."

HOLLYWOOD CHILD

Mia Farrow is not everyone's idea of Scott Fitzgerald's Daisy in *The Great Gatsby* – who could be? – but Daisy's combination of frailty and allure is fundamentally Farrow. She is a Hollywood child (daughter of director John Farrow and actress Maureen O'Sullivan) who still looks like an undernourished war orphan. Shirley MacLaine has called her "a child, with a highly energetic brain, all tuned in and vulnerable. From the neck up, she's 80 years old."

She was among the thousands of kids who tried for a part in *The Sound of Music* (1965); but she was 19 when her acting career really started, playing Alison MacKenzie in ABC-TV's *Peyton Place* between 1964 and 1967. Her big-screen debut was in *Guns at Batasi* (1964), but she got much bigger headlines two years later when she married Frank Sinatra. They were divorced in 1968, and Farrow next united with conductor/composer Andre Previn in 1970, after having given birth to twin boys. Her private life seemed to be eclipsing her film career, except for an astonishing performance in Roman Polanski's satanic thriller, *Rosemary's Baby* (1968). That suggested that behind the child-like exterior lurked an actress of considerable power.

Nothing she has done since, even in prestigious movies like Joseph Losey's *Secret Ceremony* (1968) or opposite Dustin Hoffman in *John and Mary* (1969), has quite lived up to that promise. Yet her elfin presence may still hit on a role that strikes a chord. She could be the Audrey Hepburn for a more neurotic age.

BIRTHS, DEATHS AND MARRIAGES

DEATHS

Sam Goldwyn
31 Jan, Beverly Hills
Stroke

Bud Abbott
24 Apr, Woodland Hills, California
Cancer

Agnes Moorhead
30 Apr, Minnesota
Cancer

GOLDWYN DEAD

One of the legendary figures of Hollywood, producer Samuel Goldwyn, died on 31 January in Beverly Hills. He was 91 and had suffered a stroke five years ago. One of the European immigrants (he was born in Warsaw) who helped to establish Hollywood as the cinema capital in the early years of this century, Goldwyn became famous for his high-quality film production. He won a production Oscar for *The Best Years of Our Lives* (1946), directed by William Wyler, with whom Goldwyn had his most creative partnership, with such classics to their credit as *Dead End* (1937), *Wuthering Heights* (1939) and *The Little Foxes* (1941). Goldwyn was famous for his egotism ("*I* made *Wuthering Heights*," he snapped to an interviewer, "Wyler only directed it"), but even more for his legendary Goldwynisms ("Include me out", "A verbal agreement isn't worth the paper it's written on", etc). With his death an era ends in Hollywood.

ANOTHER CULT FLOP?

Few first films have made as big an impression on critics as *Badlands* about a James Dean lookalike and a sassy teenage girl who went on a killing spree across Montana in the Fifties. Some are claiming Terrence Malick's movie is the finest first work by an American since Orson Welles' *Citizen Kane*, and many are predicting stardom for the young leads, Martin Sheen and Sissy Spacek. But because of its grim subject, the industry is a little nervous about its commercial potential. Last year's *Mean Streets* was another young, vital movie that won critical bouquets but flopped at the box office.

STAR QUOTES

Sam Goldwyn

"Anyone who goes to see a psychiatrist needs his head examined."

Mia Farrow and Robert Redford in an adaption of the F. Scott Fitzgerald novel The Great Gatsby.

FITZGERALD'S REVENGE?

The great American novelist Scott Fitzgerald had a rough time in Hollywood in the Thirties, doing plenty work but getting only one screen credit. Perhaps his revenge has come in the form of his novels, which seem to defy successful filming.

The word is that the new version of *The Great Gatsby* has again missed the boat. Fitzgerald's great novel of the American Dream has been filmed before, most famously as a tentative *film noir* in 1949 with Alan Ladd as Gatsby. Here Robert Redford is Gatsby; Mia Farrow is the great love of his life (replacing Ali MacGraw who fell out of love with the film's producer, Robert Evans); and Bruce Dern plays Farrow's violently jealous husband. Redford and Farrow have strongly denied rumours that they did not get on during shooting. But the film does contain an odd mixture of talents. The writer is Francis Ford Coppola, whose adaptation is so slavishly faithful that the film lasts almost two-and-a-half hours; and the director is Englishman Jack Clayton, best known for *Room at the Top* (1959) and his stylish ghost story, *The Innocents* (1961).

The movie is lavishly upholstered, but maybe that's part of the problem. A $6.5 million budget doesn't guarantee artistic quality. *Gatsby* looks like having more influence on the future of fashion than on the future of film.

ONE-MAN RIOT

At one stage in Mel Brooks's cult comedy *The Producers* (1967), Zero Mostel moans that "I'm being sunk by a society demanding success when all I can offer is failure." After the flop of his second film, *The Twelve Chairs* (1970), Brooks confessed he felt rather like that himself. Happily *Blazing Saddles* is turning into a rip-roaring success.

"We were so poor, my mother couldn't afford to have me," says Mel. "The lady next door gave birth to me." Born in New York in 1926, he became friends as a young man with Sid Caesar and a writer on Caesar's epoch-making TV *Show of Shows*, joining a team that included Neil Simon and Woody Allen. When the show closed, Brooks found it hard to adjust. A film script for Jerry Lewis was shelved; a Broadway show failed. But he was rescued when "The 2,000-Year-Old Man", a brilliant comedy routine he had devised with Carl Reiner, was recorded to brilliant effect.

The upturn in his professional life was matched in his private life when he married actress Anne Bancroft in 1964. He has been directing since *The Producers* and it looks as if *Blazing Saddles* has fixed his career. To borrow the words of the movie's title song, he has conquered fear and he's conquered hate and he's turned dark night into day.

Oliver Reed, Michael York, Richard Chamberlain and Frank Finlay in Richard Lester's comic version of The Three Musketeers.

RETURN OF THE MUSKETEERS

A glittering cast that includes Michael York, Oliver Reed, Charlton Heston, Richard Chamberlain, Faye Dunaway and Raquel Welch brings lustre to a new version of the ageless Alexander Dumas classic, *The Three Musketeers*. The film is a return to pure escapism after the recent stomach-churners on exorcism.

It's also a return in strength for director Richard Lester, still best known for his Beatles films *A Hard Day's Night* (1964) and *Help!* (1965). His career seemed to languish after recent commercial failures like *Petulia* (1968) and *The Bed-Sitting Room* (1969).

Lester was unsure about whether he wanted to do the film. "I had seen the old Fairbanks version," he says, "and that seemed to me perfect of its kind." He was tempted when he saw the 1948 M-G-M remake, which he "loathed", but then he re-read Dumas' novel. "The Musketeers are really mercenaries, and Dumas doesn't like them all that much," Dick Lester says. "I thought I could work on that. All for one, and every man for himself."

One interesting footnote is that, although made as one film, *The Three Musketeers* is to be released in two parts. The first, *The Three Musketeers (The Queen's Diamonds)* is now on release, with a closing trailer for part two. *The Four Musketeers (The Revenge of Milady)* will be released later this year. The cast are happy: it means they get paid twice.

ACADEMY AWARDS

PRESENTED ON 2 APRIL 1974

Best Picture
The Sting

Best Director
George Roy Hill
The Sting

Best Actor
Jack Lemmon
Save the Tiger

Best Actress
Glenda Jackson
A Touch of Class

Best Sup Actor
John Houseman
The Paper Chase

Best Sup Actress
Tatum O'Neal
Paper Moon

GOSSIP COLUMN

■ After the head-spinning success of *The Exorcist*, the industry is brading itself for a batch of rip-offs. First off the mark is *Exorcism's Daughter*, now in production and already being heavily advertised. "Exorcism is only the beginning," scream the ads. "When there's no place left to go . . . you can always go mad."

MAY
JUNE

JULY
AUGUST

IN OLD CHINATOWN

It began in his mind, says writer Robert Towne, simply with the title and the image of a beautiful woman. He told producer Robert Evans of the idea, and the Paramount chief gave him money to develop it. The resulting film, *Chinatown*, is now one of the biggest hits of the summer.

Jack Nicholson heads the cast as a private investigator, J. J. Gittes, specializing in matrimonial affairs, who stumbles across a murder and then across a plot involving massive civic corruption. Faye Dunaway plays the beautiful mystery woman.

It's not only the plot that has unexpected twists. *Chinatown* is set in the 1930s, and its tribute to the detective movies of the past is underlined by its black-and-white credits in the style of the early talkies. There's also John Huston, veteran director of perhaps the greatest private eye movie, *The Maltese Falcon* (1941), as a sinister tycoon who holds the key to the mystery.

Production of the movie wasn't exactly smooth. Director Roman Polanski insisted on major changes to Towne's original script on which he's laboured for two years; and even after simplifying the complex plot, the pair still couldn't agree on the ending (Towne wanted a happy one, Polanski a darker one; Polanski won). And relations between Polanski and Dunaway during shooting are said to have been less than cordial.

A final twist is Polanski himself playing a weasel-like hood in a small role. He has his own solution to Nicholson's habit of poking his nose into other people's business. He slashes that nose with a knife. . . .

STAR QUOTES

Roman Polanski

"Faye Dunaway in Chinatown *was a gigantic pain in the ass. She demonstrated certifiable proof of insanity."*

GOSSIP COLUMN

■ **Shooting on the Universal thriller *Jaws*, about the hunt for a killer shark menacing the waters around a holiday resort, is said to have run into difficulties. It's being shot mainly on Martha's Vineyard off Cape Cod, and technical problems have doubled both the schedule and the budget. "It could turn out to be the flop of the year," actor Richard Dreyfuss has been heard to mutter, "because everything depends not on how well we act but on how well the shark acts." So far the mechanical model has sunk, exploded, developed cross eyes, and a jaw that won't shut. But young director Steven Spielberg, whose first feature film *The Sugarland Express*, a road movie with Goldie Hawn, has just opened to high praise from the critics, is keeping his head above water.**

Fred Astaire and Gene Kelly in That's Entertainment!

SEE IT, FEEL IT

A new disaster movie, *Earthquake*, about an earthquake that strikes Los Angeles, is to open in October. Say the ads: "You will *feel* it as well as see it in the startling new dimension of Sensurround. . . ."

BIRTHS, DEATHS AND MARRIAGES

MARRIAGES

Jennifer Jones
30 May, *to Norton Simon*

THAT WAS ENTERTAINMENT!

It was the studio that had "more stars than there are in heaven", and raised the art of the screen musical to new heights. M-G-M was synonymous with Hollywood glamour. But since its infamous auction of 1970, which sold off some of its most famous props (from the *Ben-Hur* chariot to a pair of Sophia Loren's bloomers from *Lady L*), the studio has lost a lot of its glitter. Now, to celebrate its 50th anniversary, M-G-M has produced *That's Entertainment!*, a dazzling compilation of some of its musical highlights.

And what highlights they are! There are classic moments from *The Wizard of Oz* (1939), *Meet Me in St. Louis* (1944), *Easter Parade* (1948), *On the Town* (1949), *An American in Paris* (1951), *Singin' in the Rain* (1952), *Seven Brides for Seven Brothers* (1954), *High Society* (1955), *Gigi* (1958), and many others. The items are linked by a glittering array of stars, including Fred Astaire, Gene Kelly and Frank Sinatra. And the concluding one is what many consider the highpoint of the M-G-M musical, the French Impressionist ballet sequence that concludes Vincente Minnelli's *An American in Paris*. It's a nostalgic feast for all lovers of film. As *Variety* has put it: "While many ponder the future of M-G-M, none can deny that it has one hell of a past."

Gene Hackman as a Watergate-style professional eavesdropper in Francis Ford Coppola's The Conversation.

WATERGATE REVISITED

"The best bugger in the business." That's how Gene Hackman is described in Francis Ford Coppola's new movie, *The Conversation*. He's a saxophone-playing professional eavesdropper who comes to suspect that the conversation he has been hired to record is actually a murder plot. It's Coppola's first movie since *The Godfather* (1972) and he's now reckoned as one of the hottest directors in the business. *The Conversation* won the top prize at the Cannes Film Festival in May, and part two of his *Godfather* saga is due later this year.

The theme of incriminating tapes is uncannily reminiscent of Watergate two years ago; but Coppola insists he had the idea for the film as far back as 1967. It was partly inspired by Michelangelo Antonioni's cult movie *Blowup* (1966) about a photographer who thinks he may have accidentally photographed a murder. "It's a modern horror story," says Coppola, "with a construction based on repetition rather than exposition, like a piece of music." He praises the work of sound editor Walter Murch who had a big hand in the film's structure and whose creative use of the soundtrack is so important. "In the second half of the film," says Murch, "there are only about five lines of actual dialogue: the rest is replay and analysis of the conversation itself. All the content of the film is being carried by the sound." It has all the hallmarks of a classic and has been already acclaimed as one of the most ingenious thrillers of recent years.

UNLIKELY STAR

Gene Hackman is an unlikely star. He's not handsome and not at all a romantic leading man. So what's his secret? "Well," says Warren Beatty, "he's the best screen actor in America."

Beatty should know. He appeared with Hackman in one scene in a little-seen but beautiful Jean Seberg movie, *Lilith* (1964), and was so impressed that he offered him the part of Clyde Barrow's brother when he came to produce and star in *Bonnie and Clyde* (1967). It won Hackman an Oscar nomination and lent considerable impetus to his career, culminating in a Best Actor Oscar for *The French Connection*.

Yet Hackman only decided on an acting career in his early 30s. Born in 1931, he had served in the Marines and then drifted around America, working in a variety of jobs that included truck driver and shoe salesman. Maybe this background is important: Hackman's acting has a rawness and authenticity that sets him apart from the "pretty boy" school of Hollywood heroes. His probing performance as the private hero of *The Conversation* is interior screen acting at its finest, but it's intriguing to learn too that he is auditioning for a comedy role in Mel Brooks' next film, *Young Frankenstein*. The best is yet to come.

THE CHARMING REBEL

These are golden days for Jack Nicholson as, with *Chinatown*, he chalks up another personal hit after his stand-out performance last year in *The Last Detail* won him a prize at the Cannes Festival. He's brought the rebel back to the American screen, but has given him a lazy charm and a cheeky smile.

Born in New Jersey in 1937, Nicholson had his first contact with the movies as an office boy in M-G-M's cartoon department. He was in countless Roger Corman B-movies before he was offered a part in *Easy Rider* (1969) after Rip Torn proved unavailable. His performance won him an Oscar nomination and moved his career to a completely different plane.

He has since excelled in some of America's most original recent movies, like *Five Easy Pieces* (1970) and *Carnal Knowledge* (1971), and had a creditable stab at direction with *Drive, He Said* (1971). "He's eccentric, but very interesting," says George C. Scott. "A unique kind of approach. He shines. A very fascinating actor." All ages need their anti-heroes. The Seventies have found theirs in Nicholson.

Jack Nicholson in Chinatown.

BETTER THAN THE ORIGINAL?

Robert Duvall and Al Pacino in The Godfather Part II.

The Godfather Part II is no ordinary sequel. It takes the original story back into the past (Don Corleone's arrival in America at the turn of the century and his gradual rise in the Mafia) and forward into the future (Michael Corleone's war with his rivals and his confrontation with American Senators' investigation into organized crime). Al Pacino continues his performance as Michael after his triumph in the original 1972 movie; and, as the young Corleone, there's exciting actor Robert De Niro, who made a big impression last year in *Mean Streets*.

Filming took place in Trieste, Sicily, Rome, Miami and Washington, DC. No expense was spared to enhance the film's visual impact, and director Francis Ford Coppola (riding high with the success this summer of *The Conversation*) reckons this is one sequel that's even finer than the original – less melodramatic and more probing. "I've had more freedom on this," he says. "I've not been threatened with the sack every three weeks, which is what happened on the first one." One intriguing piece of casting is that of Lee Strasberg as the head of Michael Corleone's rival organization. Strasberg is the head of the legendary Actors' Studio; apparently it was Al Pacino, a member of the Studio, who persuaded him to take the part. The battle of wits between the two bids fair to be the highlight of one of the year's most eagerly awaited films.

ALICE IN MOVIELAND

In *Alice Doesn't Live Here Anymore*, the identification between the character, Alice, and the actress playing her, Ellen Burstyn, is almost palpable.

So where was 42-year-old Burstyn before the Seventies? Working under a staggering array of aliases, that's where. In her bid for success, Detroit-born Edna Rae Gilhooly (of Irish parents) is said to have had 25 different names. She was simply Edna Rae as an 18-year-old model in Texas in 1950. She was Kerri Flynn as a dancer in a Montreal nightclub, and Erica Dean as a young actress and in commercials. In her first movie, the Tony Curtis-Debbie Reynolds comedy *Goodbye Charlie* (1964) she was billed as Ellen McRae, and only in *Tropic of Cancer* (1970), playing the tiny role of Henry Miller's wife, did she settle on her current moniker.

She was nominated for an Oscar for her role as Cybill Shepherd's mother in *The Last Picture Show* (1971), and again as mother of the demonic child in *The Exorcist* (1973).

CHRISTIE'S TRAIN

The Orient Express was always an exclusive form of transport, but it could never have dreamed of the passenger list for the film version of the Agatha Christie whodunit, *Murder on the Orient Express*. Passengers include Ingrid Bergman, Lauren Bacall, Wendy Hiller, Sean Connery, Vanessa Redgrave, John Gielgud, Michael York, Richard Widmark and Jacqueline Bisset. And let's not forget Albert Finney as Belgian sleuth Hercule Poirot whose skills are needed when a murder is committed. Sidney Lumet directs, and the period trappings of the Thirties and Richard Rodney Bennett's music all add up to good old-fashioned entertainment.

STAR QUOTES

Albert Finney

"Acting is a marriage between me and the person I'm asked to play. I just hope the wedding takes place without a hitch. Sometimes we don't even get to the altar."

BIRTHS, DEATHS AND MARRIAGES

DEATHS

Walter Brennan
21 Sep, Oxnard, Ventura County
Emphysema

Vittorio De Sica
13 Nov, Paris
Cancer

Clive Brook
17 Nov, London

Jack Benny
26 Dec, Beverly Hills
Cancer

MARRIAGES

Liza Minnelli
15 Sep, *to* Jack Haley Jr.

Steve McQueen tries to save a fellow fireman in The Towering Inferno.

THE CONTROVERSIAL COMIC

Saint or sinner? Lenny Bruce was either the most liberating stand-up comic of his time or a loudmouth who confused inanity with profanity. The legend has grown since his death from a drug overdose in 1966, and is likely to swell still further with *Lenny*, which has Dustin Hoffman in the title role.

Adapted by Julian Barry from his stage play, the film is directed by Bob Fosse, whose last movie, *Cabaret* (1972), won him an Oscar. Fosse once again examines the seedier side of showbiz, and he's filmed it in black-and-white to give the movie the feeling of a semi-documentary. Valerie Perrine plays the stripper Honey who will become his wife. Not for the straitlaced or faint-hearted, it's a film for lovers of gutsy comedy and provocative drama.

Dustin Hoffman in Lenny.

YOUNG BRIDGES

Jeff Bridges knows all about actors. His father, Lloyd, starred in the long-running TV series, *Sea Hunt* (1958) and has long been a reliable Hollywood character actor, most memorably as Gary Cooper's jealous deputy in *High Noon* (1952). Jeff's brother Beau was on screen at the age of eight in *The Red Pony* (1949) and has had good grown-up parts in *The Landlord* (1970) and *Child's Play* (1972). But will Jeff turn out the biggest star of them all?

He's certainly got off to a good start, with an Oscar nomination at 22 for his impetuous teenager of *The Last Picture Show* (1971). He followed it with a subtle portrait of an up-and-coming boxer who is soft inside in John Huston's *Fat City* (1972), and even stole some of Clint Eastwood's thunder as his joky sidekick in this summer's *Thunderbolt and Lightfoot*. "He's able to dissolve himself in a role and invest his characters with integrity and truth," says Robert Benton, who directed Bridges in the western *Bad Company* (1972). "Through imagination and instinct he can metamorphose into almost anybody." That's not necessarily a description of a star in the making, but it is one of an unusually fine actor.

HIGHER AND HOTTER

The latest disaster movie (or "group jeopardy" movie, as they're known in the trade), *The Towering Inferno*, looks likely to out-gross previous block-busters like *The Poseidon Adventure* (1972) and this season's *Earthquake*. Perhaps audiences more readily identify with a tower-block fire than typhoon or earthquake: they certainly relish the heroics of blue-eyed superstars, Paul Newman and Steve McQueen, the engineer and fireman trying to bring the blaze under control.

The movie represents a unique teaming of Warners and 20th Century-Fox, brought about when each found it was in the process of adapting similar novels. In addition to Newman and McQueen, the cast is exceptionally strong: William Holden, Faye Dunaway, Richard Chamberlain, Jennifer Jones and Robert Wagner all have leading roles. It even has Fred Astaire, who continues to ignore the advice of his friend, the late Spencer Tracy, who, on hearing that Astaire was to take a dramatic role in *On the Beach* (1959), cabled him: "Either you stop acting or I'll start dancing!"

BOX OFFICE

UK

1. The Sting
2. The Exorcist
3. Enter the Dragon
4. The Three Musketeers
5. Papillon
6. Herbie Rides Again
7. Robin Hood
8. The Great Gatsby
9. Mary Poppins
10. The Way We Were

BOX OFFICE

US

1. The Sting
2. The Exorcist
3. Papillon
4. Magnum Force
5. Herbie Rides Again
6. Blazing Saddles
7. The Trial of Billy Jack
8. The Great Gatsby
9. Serpico
10. Butch Cassidy and the Sundance Kid (*reissue*)

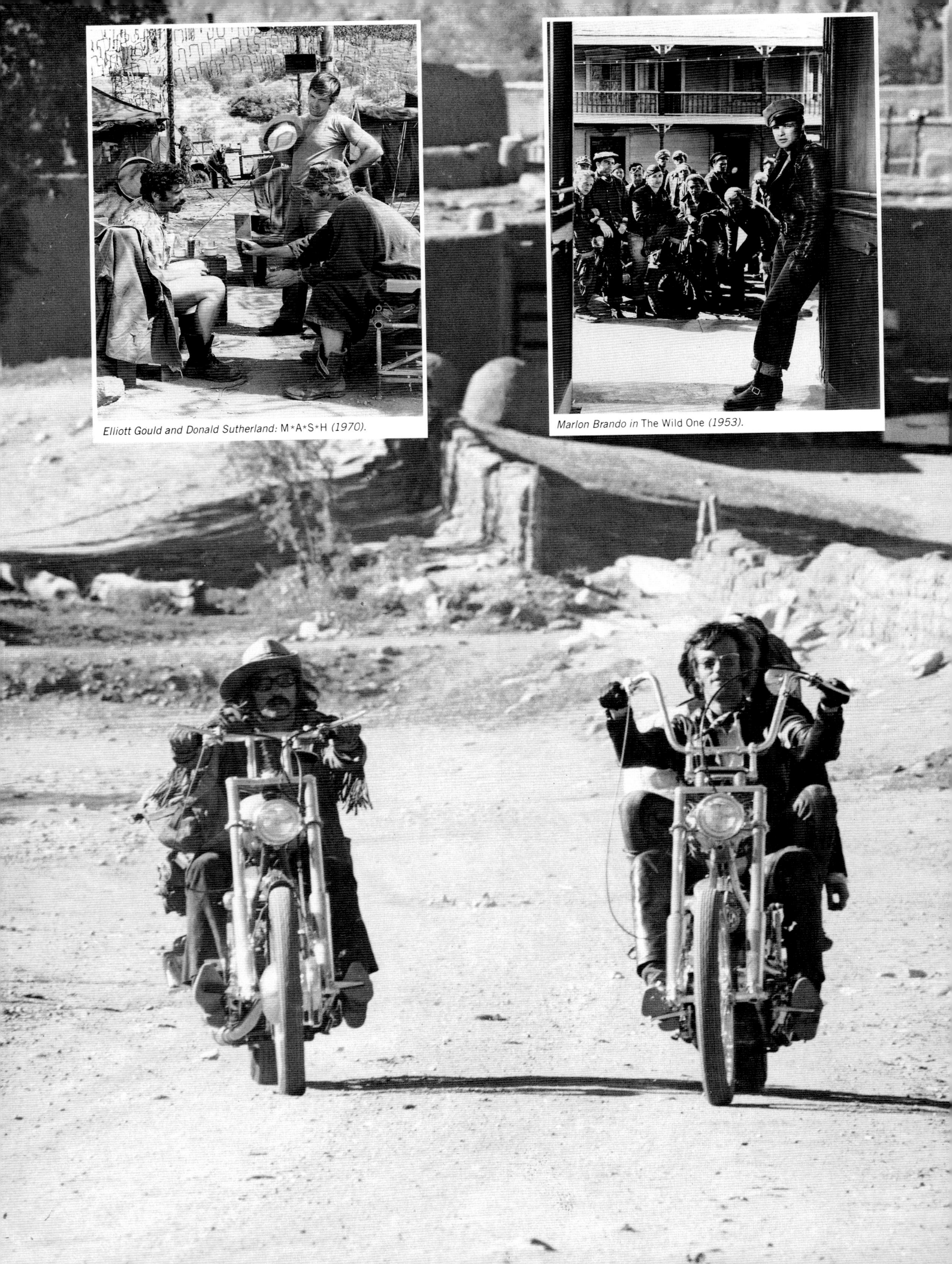

Elliott Gould and Donald Sutherland: M*A*S*H (1970).

Marlon Brando in The Wild One (1953).

Anne Bancroft and Dustin Hoffman: The Graduate (1967).

Woodstock (1970), the rock documentary.

James Woods and John Savage in Salvador (1986).

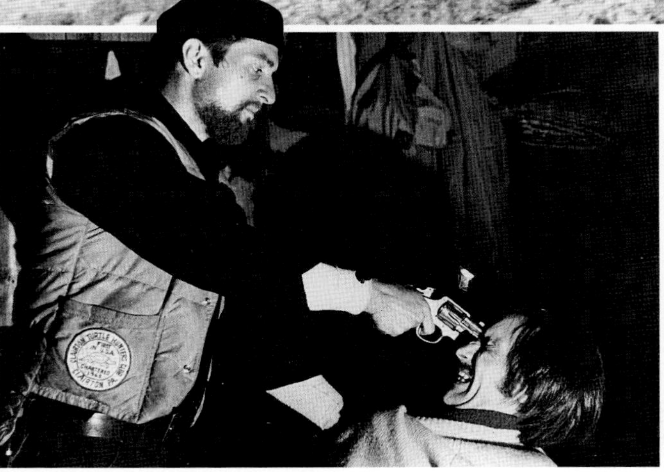
Robert De Niro and John Cazale in The Deer Hunter (1978).

Something To Shout About

"This used to be a helluva country. I can't tell you what's wrong. They're scared not of you but of what you represent: freedom." Jack Nicholson's middle-aged drop-out in *Easy Rider* (1969) was the voice of one of the most popular protest movies of the period. The heroes of the movie (Peter Fonda and Dennis Hopper) were rootless rebels on motorcycles, taking drugs and thumbing their noses at respectable society.

The 1960s was the decade of the protest movie. Times were a-changing. It was a time of political assassinations, campus riots, free love, flower power. And the increasingly unpopular war in Vietnam was a focus for all this rebellion and discontent against a bullying Establishment that was out of touch and out of date.

A number of movies caught the mood. Although set in the 1930s, *Bonnie and Clyde* (1967) was pugnaciously modern. Its leading characters were "hippies" of an earlier generation; but like the characters in *Easy Rider*, they suffered a violent backlash.

The Graduate (1967) also captured the spirit of disaffected youth, searching for alternative values. The rock documentary *Woodstock* (1970) was an epic hymn to youth and rock 'n' roll. And *Zabriskie Point* (1969) had an apocalyptic climax, imagining the explosion of old institutions and attitudes that had had their day.

At this stage Vietnam was an undercurrent of the Hollywood movie rather than a main theme. John Wayne's pro-Vietnam *The Green Berets* (1968) had run into a storm of criticism, partly through its crude, cowboys-and-Indians approach. More obliquely, the ferociously violent, anti-heroic western *The Wild Bunch* (1969) also seemed influenced by Vietnam: American adventurism without the usual uncomplicated vigour.

Although set during the Korean War, the military comedy *M*A*S*H* (1970) had a tone that reflected the anti-authoritarianism of the Vietnam era. But it was only later in the 1970s that Vietnam as a theme moved centre stage, in movies like *The Deer Hunter* (1978), *Coming Home* (1978) and *Apocalypse Now* (1979).

Protest was not new in American movies. The gangster film of the 1930s had some pungent things to say about the failures of the American Dream and the connections between poverty and crime. "What chance have they got in a place like this?" cries the social worker in *Dead End* (1937). In the 1950s a brooding anti-hero emerged, at war with society and family. "You're tearing me apart!" wails a tormented James Dean to his parents in *Rebel Without a Cause* (1955). And Marlon Brando's biker in *The Wild One* (1953) exudes insolence. "What are you rebelling against?" he's asked. "What have you got?" he snaps back.

The 1980s saw conservative values return to Hollywood cinema. But Vietnam is still a painful thorn in American culture. Former Vietnam vet Oliver Stone brought a bruising authenticity to the Vietnam conflict in *Platoon* (1986) and *Born on the Fourth of July* (1989). And he bluntly attacked American foreign policy in *Salvador* (1985). Dissent is not dead.

Main picture: Dennis Hopper and Peter Fonda in Easy Rider (1969).

LOOKING AFTER HIMSELF

Warren Beatty is a sharp operator. A gifted actor and said to be irresistible to women, he's also a canny businessman with an eye to his own career. He is not content with being a romantic heartthrob, he wants also to control his own films, which he did with enormous success on *Bonnie and Clyde* (1967), where he was actor and producer, and now has also done with *Shampoo*, in which he is actor, producer and co-writer. Direction is the logical next step.

Born in 1937, the younger brother of Shirley MacLaine, Beatty studied acting under Stella Adler before appearing on Broadway to great acclaim in William Inge's *A Loss of Roses*. Elia Kazan saw him and cast him opposite Natalie Wood in his film, *Splendor in the Grass* (1961); and, in the same year, he played an Italian gigolo in pursuit of Vivien Leigh in *The Roman Spring of Mrs. Stone* (1961). Since then he's alternated between esoteric drama like *All Fall Down* (1962) or *Mickey One* (1965) and frivolous comedy. Perhaps it was the danger of frittering away his talent that prompted him to take more charge of his career. He's more selective now with the movies he makes, either setting up his own projects or working with a director or co-star he admires. But, as *Shampoo* is showing, greater selectivity means no diminution of his popular appeal.

SEXY STYLING

Julie Christie and Warren Beatty, as a Beverly Hills hairdresser, in the sour comedy Shampoo.

Warren Beatty had his biggest success so far in 1967 when he not only starred in but produced *Bonnie and Clyde*. Now in *Shampoo*, he's gone one step further – starring in, producing and co-writing the film with Robert Towne, co-author of *Chinatown*. It's a comedy about sex, but with a sour and serious edge.

Beatty plays an LA Casanova who is hairstylist to the stars and is a master of juggling affairs, until he begins to sense the emptiness of his life. "There is an ambivalence in the character and his whole generation," says Beatty, "having been told in formative years that life should be led one way and that there were certain rules of sexuality and monogamy that had to be followed, then having been told later in life that the rules don't apply any more." The women in his life include Julie Christie, Goldie Hawn and Lee Grant.

The film is set on the eve of the 1968 Presidential election, which saw the victory of Richard Nixon. Why this period? "There's a kind of irony," says Towne. "We have Spiro Agnew, who had to resign, talking about the 'moral tone' of the country, and Nixon promising to bring the country together before becoming the first President to resign in office because of corruption. It's about not just a handful of characters but a whole country in a process of disintegration, through hypocrisy and a loss of leadership and values." Towne ran into trouble last year for his strong language for *The Last Detail*. Some of the lines he has put into the mouth of Julie Christie, in particular, in *Shampoo* will – well, make your hair curl.

ACADEMY AWARDS

PRESENTED ON 8 APRIL 1975

Best Picture
The Godfather Part II

Best Director
Francis Ford Coppola
The Godfather Part II

Best Actor
Art Carney
Harry and Tonto

Best Actress
Ellen Burstyn
Alice Doesn't Live Here Anymore

Best Sup Actor
Robert De Niro
The Godfather Part II

Best Sup Actress
Ingrid Bergman
Murder on the Orient Express

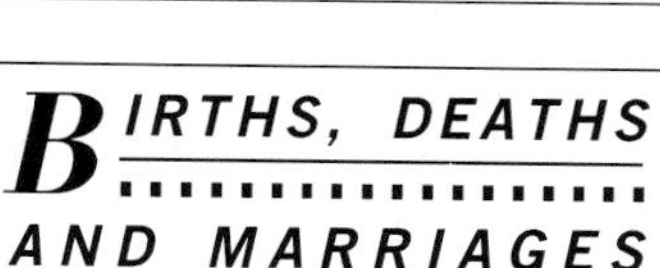

BIRTHS, DEATHS AND MARRIAGES

BIRTHS

Drew Barrymore
22 Feb, Los Angeles

DEATHS

George Stevens
8 Mar, Los Angeles
Heart attack

Susan Hayward
14 Mar, Beverly Hills
Brain tumour

Mary Ure
3 Apr, London
Accidental overdose

Fredric March
14 Apr, Los Angeles
Cancer

Richard Conte
15 Apr, Los Angeles
Heart attack

MARRIAGES

Malcolm McDowell
21 Apr, *to* Margot Dullea

STAR QUOTES

Bob Guccione

"Ken Russell is an arrogant, self-centred petulant individual, I don't say this in any demeaning way."

Oliver Reed, Roger Daltrey and Ann-Margret in Tommy.

ROCKING RUSSELL

Flamboyant British director Ken Russell – arguably the second oldest *enfant terrible* in the cinema – is back. His new musical extravaganza assails the ears, assaults the eyes and offends the sensibilities. The subject this time is *Tommy*, the rock opera of Pete Townshend and The Who about a deaf, dumb and blind child who becomes a rock celebrity. Roger Daltrey plays Tommy, and a strong supporting cast includes Ann-Margret and Oliver Reed and pop celebrities like Elton John and Eric Clapton.

The star, however, is likely to be Ken Russell, and the film is expected to cause the usual ruffling of feathers amongst Russell critics who sigh for the days of his BBC documentary on Elgar, when he seemed a more temperately creative young man.

MAD ABOUT TOWNE

Few screenwriters have made as big an impact in as short a time as Robert Towne. Relatively unknown until recently, though rumoured as one of the best uncredited script doctors in the business, who had even ministered to *Bonnie and Clyde*, he's shot to prominence with three major credits in the last two years: *The Last Detail* (1973), *Chinatown* (1974) and now *Shampoo*. Worth noting, too, is his writing credit for last year's Robert Mitchum Japanese gangster drama, *The Yakuza*.

In each of the three major films, his hero is a rebel ultimately defeated by the forces he either sought to overthrow or thought he controlled. The writer as chief author of the film? Not entirely. He and director Roman Polanski had a fierce argument over the last scene of *Chinatown*, which Polanski won: Towne had wanted a more upbeat ending. On the other hand, he does acknowledge Polanski's assistance on another scene which was giving him trouble. What could make his heroine confess the terrible secret that she has concealed all these years in *Chinatown* – that she has been raped by her father and her daughter is the incestuous product of that union? "Why not get the detective to beat it out of her?" Polanski suggested blithely. And that's what he does.

THE SPICE OF LIFE

Hollywood's inimitable trade paper *Variety* celebrated its 60th anniversary on 8 January. It has long been the bible of the film community and its language ("boffo b.o. prospects", "acceptable for lesser houses but not de luxe quality", "not strong enough for the upper bracket") has a flavour all its own. For its 60th anniversary edition it listed the top money-making films of all time, which are, in order: *The Godfather; The Sound of Music; Gone with the Wind; The Sting; The Exorcist; Love Story; The Graduate; Airport; Doctor Zhivago; Butch Cassidy and the Sundance Kid.* And out of all the directors, whose films have grossed most money overall? DeMille? Hitchcock? Ford? Perhaps surprisingly, the answer is the unassuming Disney director of *Mary Poppins* and many other films, Robert Stevenson.

MAY

JUNE

JULY

AUGUST

SHAW SUCCESS

How times change. Just over two years ago Robert Shaw said that "most of the films I've been in haven't taken any money at all. My record of commercial success is quite appalling: worse than any actor I can think of." Since then he's appeared in *The Sting*, one of the top box-office hits of 1973, *The Taking of Pelham One Two Three*, a smash hit last year, and he's currently appearing in *Jaws*, which is shaping up to be the biggest money-maker of all time. From being a bad omen, Shaw has turned into a lucky charm.

Shaw has always been a rugged, intimidating character. His haunted demeanour might be traceable to his memory of his father's suicide in 1939 when Robert was 12. He trained as an actor; appeared on stage at the Shakespeare Memorial Theatre at Stratford; and has written a number of highly acclaimed novels, such as *The Flag* (1965) and *The Man in the Glass Booth* (1975), a film of which is now being prepared with actor Maximilian Schell. Yet his film roles have fluctuated strangely, between the sensitive (*The Caretaker*, 1963) and the sensational (the blond killer in *From Russia with Love*, 1963). He has played everything from Henry VIII to General Custer, from a Nazi general in *Battle of the Bulge* (1965) to Churchill's father in *Young Winston* (1972). Now Hollywood seems at last to have figured out what to do with this English enigma. He can play the heavy – but with style.

Robert Shaw as Quint the shark-killer in Jaws.

BITE-SIZED BUSINESS

It looks as if *Jaws* is doing for sharks what Alfred Hitchcock's *Psycho* did for showers. It's certainly frightened summertime audiences off the beaches and into the movie theatres. In its first six weeks, one person in eight in America has already seen it.

Producers Richard Zanuck and David Brown have been taken aback by the success. The story is simple: a shark is menacing the beaches of a holiday resort and must be stopped. The cast is talented but not star-studded: Roy Scheider as the police chief, Robert Shaw as the ancient mariner, Richard Dreyfuss as the whizz-kid on sharks. Both book and film have been skilfully advertised and sold, and it is splendidly directed by Steven Spielberg. "Perhaps," says Zanuck, "as well as a chase, the film is about a restoration of communal confidence. We have a Watergate-type cover-up in the first part of the film, when the mayor doesn't tell the people about the danger for fear of losing money. The second part is not about analyzing problems: it's about annihilating them." He raises his eyebrows, quizzically, at his own explanation. "If it was that easy to define what makes a successful movie, everyone would be doing it."

THE STUFF OF LEGENDS

Can the epic make a comeback? It will if swashbuckling director John Milius has anything to do with it. His new film, *The Wind and the Lion*, is about a Berber brigand (Sean Connery) who kidnaps an American widow (Candice Bergen) and her children, thus provoking an international incident and America's first foray into international politics. It's loosely based on real events in 1904. Playing the Lion to Connery's Wind is Brian Keith as that grizzly bear of American politics, President Theodore Roosevelt, and some striking Spanish locations stand in for the tale's Moroccan setting.

Milius has also cast John Huston in a supporting role, as a way of thanking him for directing his script for *The Life and Times of Judge Roy Bean* (1972). "I had a terrible time on that film," says Milius. "When they cast Paul Newman as Roy Bean, I sort of sensed that their idea of the character was not mine. But I learnt a lot from Huston. I was really blooded on that movie."

Like a number of writer-directors of an earlier era, such as Preston Sturges and Billy Wilder, Milius took up direction as a means of protecting his own scripts. *Dillinger* (1973) was an impressive debut, and now his second movie suggests he is ready for the big time. His cinematic master, he says, is Akira Kurosawa. Whatever Milius comes up with in the future, it won't be ordinary and it won't be dull.

STAR QUOTES

The Who

"We would like to thank the film business for teaching us the gentle art of getting up at 6 o'clock in the morning in order to enjoy the dawn, drink coffee, and hang around until 10 o'clock when the work realy starts."

ALTMAN'S BEST?

His best film yet. That's the verdict of some critics on Robert Altman's new movie, *Nashville* which, against the background of a pop concert staged to support a political campaign, weaves a kaleidoscopic melodrama that lurches between adultery and assassination, desire and disillusionment. Many Altman regulars are in the cast – Geraldine Chaplin, Keith Carradine, Gwen Welles, with guest appearances from Julie Christie and Elliott Gould – and there's the usual smattering of improvisation and satire. What Nashville itself will make of it is another matter. But movie lovers will have to wait, as the film isn't ready for release yet.

Ronee Blakely, Henry Gibson and Barbara Baxley in Nashville.

GOSSIP COLUMN

■ **Bound to be one of the most controversial pieces of casting of the year: Robert Powell will play the leading role in Franco Zeffirelli's *The Life of Christ.* John the Baptist will be played by Peter O'Toole, and Zeffirelli hopes to find parts for Elizabeth Taylor and Laurence Olivier.**

BIRTHS, DEATHS AND MARRIAGES

DEATHS

Evelyn Brent
4 Jun, Los Angeles
Heart attack

Rod Serling
28 Jun, Rochester, New York
Complications following surgery

CREATOR OF CLOUSEAU

Inspector Clouseau might spell disaster for everyone within hailing-distance of him, but he has been a goldmine and a saviour for his creator, Blake Edwards. Yet, if Edwards is to be remembered mainly for Clouseau, this would be scant recognition of a highly versatile and original talent.

Born in 1922, Edwards first came to the attention of film buffs with his scripts for such Fifties delights as the musical *My Sister Eileen* (1955), with a singing Jack Lemmon, and the service comedy *Operation Mad Ball* (1957), also with Lemmon. His directing career hit its stride with the romantic *Breakfast at Tiffany's* (1961) and the alcoholic drama *Days of Wine and Roses* (1962). Then came *The Pink Panther* (1964). It's popularity was so phenomenal that it immediately spawned a successor, *A Shot in the Dark* (1964). Today, when the careers of Edwards and Peter Sellers seem to have sputtered a little, a dose of Clouseau may be all that is needed to restore them to former glory.

A former actor and son of a stage director, Edwards knows his business. He can turn his hand to thrillers – the gripping *Experiment in Terror* (1962) – to westerns (*Wild Rovers,* 1971), and to musicals (*Darling Lili*, 1970). But comedy is his forte, particularly slapstick where you can hear the bones break. Nobody directs party scenes better and few have got more out of such prodigious talents as Lemmon, Sellers and Julie Andrews. Truly, a survivor in a world of sharks.

Director Blake Edwards on the set of last year's The Tamarind Seed.

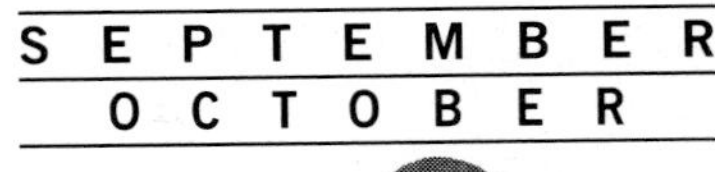

SEPTEMBER OCTOBER

1975

NOVEMBER DECEMBER

KING HUSTON

He first wanted to film it in the Fifties with Clark Gable and Humphrey Bogart. He finally got to do it in the Seventies with Sean Connery and Michael Caine. John Huston's *The Man Who Would Be King*, based on a story by Rudyard Kipling, is about two soldiers of fortune in India who set themselves up as kings of a remote tribe until a stroke of fate reveals them to be all too mortal – and vulnerable.

The story has long been a favourite of Huston's, and he is delighted with his two principals, and with Christopher Plummer who plays Kipling in the movie. Location filming was done in Morocco and Huston hopes audiences will respond to it with as much enthusiasm as they did for *The African Queen* (1951). It has similar ingredients: adventure, exotic locale, with characters who discover not the answers to their dreams but the secrets of their own personalities.

GOSSIP COLUMN

■ **Pornography or masterpiece? The film sensation of the moment is a Japanese movie, *Empire of the Senses*, made by "New Wave" tyro Nagisa Oshima. It features an orgy of love-making between an innkeeper and his ex-servant, who does amazing things with boiled eggs. Says one critic: "It makes *Last Tango in Paris* look like a vicarage tea-party."**

JACK'S MADHOUSE

It took some 14 years to get off the ground but now it's really flying. *One Flew over the Cuckoo's Nest*, about a battle of wills between an anarchic asylum inmate, McMurphy (Jack Nicholson), and an authoritarian matron, Nurse Ratched (Louise Fletcher), is based on an early Sixties cult novel by Ken Kesey. The lead role was played on Broadway by Kirk Douglas, who bought the film rights but could never get enough financial backing. The rights were eventually taken over by his son Michael, who has not only succeeded in bringing it to the screen but has made an altogether unexpected box-office bonanza with it.

"I think it's the film people have been waiting for from Jack Nicholson," says Douglas; "it fits classically into his non-conformist image." It is a performance already tipped to bring Nicholson his third consecutive Best Actor Oscar nomination (he was a loser in 1973 with *The Last Detail* and again last year with *Chinatown*). Director is Czech-born Milos Forman, who is equally delighted with Louise Fletcher's blood-chilling performance as the formidable Nurse Ratched. "She is dangerous," Forman says of the character, "because she really believes in what she is doing. I have seen this situation, and I know that authority in trouble will sacrifice anything and anyone to prove its point." Forman's anti-authoritarian instincts plus Nicholson's rebel hero are proving an intoxicating combination. You'd be cuckoo to miss this one.

Jack Nicholson as inmate McMurphy in One Flew over the Cuckoo's Nest.

BOX OFFICE

UK

1 The Towering Inferno
2 The Exorcist
3 The Man With the Golden Gun
4 Emmanuelle
5 Earthquake
6 Airport 1975
7 Murder on the Orient Express
8 Papillon
9 Stardust
10 The Island at the Top of the World

BOX OFFICE

US

1 Jaws
2 The Towering Inferno
3 Benji
4 Young Frankenstein
5 The Godfather Part II
6 Shampoo
7 Funny Lady
8 Murder on the Orient Express
9 The Return of the Pink Panther
10 Tommy

DEATH OF A GREAT COMPOSER

One of America's greatest film composers, Bernard Herrmann, died in Hollywood on Christmas Day at the age of 64. Composer of a symphony, a string quartet, an opera, and oratorios as well as numerous film scores, Herrmann was a great musician. He will be remembered most for his work with two great directors, Orson Welles and Alfred Hitchcock. Born in New York in 1911, Herrmann joined CBS in the 1930s where he met Welles. His first film score was for Welles' *Citizen Kane* (1941); and he wrote nine scores for Hitchcock, in particular helping to create atmospheres of throbbing romanticism in *Vertigo* (1958) and ice-cold terror in *Psycho* (1960).

PERRINE'S?

Beauty and talent are still a combination rare enough to make critics and audiences sit up and take notice. The voluptuous Valerie Perrine, who plays Lenny Bruce's stripper wife in *Lenny*, certainly has the looks for stardom but, as she charts the woman's descent into drug addiction, it is clear that what we're watching is also the blossoming of a fine dramatic actress.

Prior to *Lenny* Perrine had appeared in a small role as an other-wordly beauty in *Slaughterhouse Five* (1972), oozing sexuality from a fantastic planet; and as a racetrack groupie who seduces Jeff Bridges in *The Last American Hero* (1973). She's just finished shooting *W.C. Fields and Me*, playing the mistress of Rod Steiger's W.C. Fields, and has also been sounding off to the press about the inadequacy of the role. The 31-year-old actress has a mind of her own and is not afraid to express it, something which does not always go down well in Hollywood. But if a producer would be mad not to exploit her physical allure, he'd also be crazy not to let Perrine give full rein to her dramatic talents. Both are considerable.

Marisa Berenson and Ryan O'Neal *in* Barry Lyndon.

KUBRICK'S EPIC GAMBLE

After the sensational spectacle of *2001: A Space Odyssey* (1968) and the ferocious controversy over *A Clockwork Orange* (1971), a new movie by Stanley Kubrick is not simply news: it's an event. *Barry Lyndon* is a cautionary tale of a rake's progress and come-uppance in the high society of the 18th century. But this is no sex farce on the lines of *Tom Jones*: the pace is stately, the visuals awesome, the atmosphere ominous.

Warners backed Kubrick to the tune of $12 million to choose his own project and realize it on screen. As usual, Kubrick shot the movie in total secrecy, mainly in Ireland, and used special lenses to give a natural, candelit look to interior scenes. It is based on a novel by the Victorian author Thackeray which, Kubrick says, had an instant impact on him. In a surprising piece of casting, he chose Ryan O'Neal for the leading role, feeling that he could project the surface attraction but inner coldness of his hero. But really the star of *Barry Lyndon* is Stanley Kubrick. The film is his vision and it remains to be seen what audiences will make of the film's ravishing photography and deliberately *adagio* tempo.

PRETTY BOY

Ryan O'Neal is not just a pretty face, he's one of the most promising of the younger generation of Hollywood stars. No one who lands the title role, *Barry Lyndon*, in a new Stanley Kubrick movie can be an insignificant talent.

He was born in Los Angeles in 1941. A former life-guard, amateur boxer and even jailbird, he landed his first showbiz job as a TV stuntman and finally, like Mia Farrow, became a mainstay of the TV soap *Peyton Place*.

His big film break came with *Love Story* (1970), where his handsome features seemed to make him the ideal romantic hero for the weepie. The irony is, though, that he was sixth choice for the role after Jon Voight, Beau Bridges and the Michaels York, Sarrazin and Douglas. O'Neal has gone on to show a deft way with comedy opposite Barbra Streisand in *What's Up, Doc?* (1972) and with his daughter Tatum in *Paper Moon* (1973). Now with *Barry Lyndon*, another dramatic horizon is beckoning.

BIRTHS, DEATHS AND MARRIAGES

DEATHS

William Wellman
12 Dec, Los Angeles
Leukemia

William Lundigan
21 Dec, Duarte, California

Bernard Herrmann
25 Dec, Hollywood
Heart attack

PERSECUTION MANIA

Paranoia may be contagious, but these days it's becoming downright fashionable. Last summer Warren Beatty was pursued (by whom? by what?) in *The Parallax View*, and Gene Hackman wrecked his own apartment in *The Conversation* in vain search of a bug he was convinced had been planted there.

Now it's Robert Redford's turn. In *Three Days of the Condor* he plays a minor researcher for the CIA who returns to the office one day to find his colleagues murdered and himself the next target. Who did it, and why? And who can he trust? Faye Dunaway plays the lady who reluctantly harbours him; Cliff Robertson is a sinister CIA man who may know more than he shows; and Max Von Sydow and John Houseman are also in the cast. Director is Sydney Pollack, making his fourth film with Redford and hoping it repeats the success of their last collaboration, *The Way We Were* (1973).

So what are the reasons for the plethora of paranoid thrillers? Last summer the *New York Times* grumbled about the way the modern thriller was making audiences feel helpless and hysterical; surely they were shaken up enough by the cycle of assassination, corruption and cover-up in recent American history? But audiences seem to like them, and *Condor* provides reassurance of a sort. After all, if everyone is paranoid, you feel a little less alone.

Faye Dunaway, Cliff Robertson and Robert Redford *in* Three Days of the Condor.

THE ANTI-HERO IS BACK

The new movie everyone is talking about is *Taxi Driver*, in which the film's eponymous hero goes berserk in a shooting orgy in a New York he sees as a modern Inferno. Robert De Niro, recent Oscar-winner for *The Godfather Part II* (1974), plays the leading character with such power that he could have created the anti-hero of the decade. Director Martin Scorsese is amazed by audience response to the film. "We thought they would reject it as too unpleasant," he says, "but they seem to relate to the driver's state of loneliness."

The film is a personal triumph for producers Michael and Julia Phillips, who had difficulty getting Paul Schrader's script accepted by any studio. Originally they wanted Jeff Bridges as the taxi driver and, as director, Robert Mulligan, best known for sensitive dramas like *To Kill a Mockingbird* (1962) and *Summer of '42* (1971). Schrader didn't like that idea; and after seeing the raw and vibrant *Mean Streets* (1973), set in New York's Little Italy, the Phillipses felt sure they had found the right director (Scorsese) and actor (De Niro) for their material. But what they still lacked was studio finance, even on the strength of their recent success, *The Sting* (1973). Then Columbia stepped in, but at minimum risk – in other words, a low budget, which meant comparatively modest salaries. "Oh hell," the friends said, "let's not argue, let's just make the movie." It could be one of the best of the year.

BRANDO'S HEIR-APPARENT

They're calling him the new Brando. His name is actually Robert De Niro. He has already won a supporting actor Oscar for his performance as the young Vito Corleone in *The Godfather Part II*. Currently De Niro is roaming the New York streets in *Taxi Driver*, not so much as an accident waiting to happen as a bomb about to explode.

He was born in 1943 in New York City. As an actor, he studied under Lee Strasberg and Stella Adler and began making a steady reputation in off-Broadway productions and low-budget movies. It was not until his eighth movie that he really made an impression: as a small-time, volatile hood in *Mean Streets* (1973). It led to *Godfather II*, and also to *Taxi Driver*, where De Niro's volatility and barely suppressed violence seem a match for the nervous, neurotic energy of Martin Scorsese's direction.

BOWIE DEBUT

Although *The Man Who Fell to Earth* has got generally poor notices, critics have been impressed by the performance of pop star David Bowie as an outer space alien who is visiting earth on a secret mission. "He really does look and behave like someone from another planet," says one critic. It's what many have always said about his singing.

BIRTHS, DEATHS AND MARRIAGES

DEATHS

Paul Robeson
23 Jan, Philadelphia
Stroke

Sal Mineo
12 Feb, Hollywood
Stabbed on the way home from a rehearsal

Busby Berkeley
13 Mar, Palm Springs, California

Luchino Visconti
17 Mar, Rome
Influenza

Carol Reed
25 Apr, London
Heart attack

STAR QUOTES

Peter Bogdanovich

"Francis Ford Coppola is his own worst enemy. He equates success with sell-out and doesn't care to remember that nearly all the really good directors became successful."

Dustin Hoffman and Robert Redford in All the President's Men.

HOFFMAN & REDFORD GO WATERGATE

The political scandal of the century looks like making one of the films of the year. *All the President's Men* is based on the book by Bob Woodward and Carl Bernstein, the two *Washington Post* reporters whose investigations into the 1972 Watergate break-in led to the resignation of President Nixon. Robert Redford plays Woodward and Dustin Hoffman plays Bernstein, and Redford is also a producer on the film.

Recalls Redford: "I was first hearing about this story when I was making *The Candidate* in 1972" (another film about political manipulation). He bought the film rights to Woodward and Bernstein's book for $225,000; commissioned a screenplay from William Goldman (Oscar-winning writer of *Butch Cassidy and the Sundance Kid*); and persuaded Hoffman to play Bernstein on the strength of Goldman's script. Was it the political events that fascinated him about the book? "That," says Redford, "and the methodical routine of journalism." He went to great lengths to preserve authenticity in the film, spending time at the offices of the *Washington Post* and even arranging for the paper's rubbish to be shipped over to Burbank studios to add to the realism of the massive set for the paper's newsroom.

Both Redford and Hoffman agreed on Alan J. Pakula as director. He is a painstaking perfectionist, insisting on discussion and many takes, a method that appeals more to Hoffman than to Redford. But from Pakula's work on such films as *Klute* (1971) and *The Parallax View* (1974), Redford knew he could deliver the suspense and sense of paranoia the story requires. Watergate might have been a political scandal. It's also a helluva thriller.

ROBIN'S RETURN

Robin Hood is back in Sherwood Forest. But this time he is 20 years older, just back from the crusades, and can scarcely climb a tree, let alone ambush anybody from one. Moreover, Maid Marian has retired to a convent, and the Sheriff of Nottingham has become a grassroots liberal.

Such is *Robin and Marian*, in which Sean Connery plays Robin and Audrey Hepburn plays Marian. The strong supporting cast includes Robert Shaw as the Sheriff, Nicol Williamson as Little John and Richard Harris as King Richard. Directing is the bubbly Richard Lester, who has recently given a fresh gloss to historical comedy-adventure in films like *The Three Musketeers* (1973) and *Royal Flash* (1975). So is *Robin and Marian* a comedy? "Not at all," says Lester, "it's a sombre film of ideas." He's a bit concerned that the advertising slogan, "Love is the Greatest Adventure of all," misrepresents the film, and he doesn't care for the title. "I wanted to call it *The Death of Robin Hood*," he grumbles. The filming was done in Spain, and everyone seems delighted with Audrey Hepburn's return, which is one of her very best screen performances.

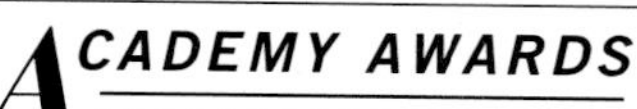

ACADEMY AWARDS

PRESENTED ON 29 MARCH 1976

Best Picture
One Flew over the Cuckoo's Nest

Best director
Milos Forman
One Flew over the Cuckoo's Nest

Best Actor
Jack Nicholson
One Flew over the Cuckoo's Nest

Best Actress
Louise Fletcher
One Flew over the Cuckoo's Nest

Best Sup Actor
George Burns
The Sunshine Boys

Best Sup Actress
Lee Grant
Shampoo

Sean Connery as an "older" Robin Hood and Audrey Hepburn as Maid Marian in Robin and Marian.

HOLLYWOOD ON HOLLYWOOD

After *Day of the Locust* and *Hearts of the West* last year, there is now another sudden spate of films dealing with Hollywood history. *Gable and Lombard* is a biopic about Clark Gable and Carole Lombard, whose marriage tragically ended when Lombard was killed in a plane crash in 1942. James Brolin plays Gable; Jill Clayburgh plays Lombard. Peter Bogdanovich has assembled some cronies like Ryan O'Neal and Burt Reynolds to investigate the early days of Hollywood in *Nickelodeon*, which takes us up to the 1915 premiere of D.W. Griffith's *The Birth of a Nation*. But most eagerly awaited of all is the Sam Spiegel-Elia Kazan production *The Last Tycoon*, adapted by Harold Pinter from Scott Fitzgerald's novel, with Robert De Niro as a studio head closely modelled on Irving Thalberg.

Will the films be hate-mail or valentines? When Billy Wilder's hard-hitting portrait of the Hollywood community *Sunset Blvd.* (1950) was shown, Louis B. Mayer shouted: "They should horse-whip this Wilder, he is biting the hand that feeds him!" The classic has survived intact, but so too has the unabashedly celebratory *Singin' in the Rain* (1952). Maybe it all comes down to quality. If any of the above can match those 1950s movies, a classic will have been born.

DIDN'T I SEE YOU WITH A SHARK?

You may not know the name but you'll probably recognize the face. Richard Dreyfuss was the whizz-kid ichthyologist in *Jaws*, and his boyish looks, charm and talent make him one of the rising stars of the younger generation of screen actors.

Dreyfuss was born in 1947 and grew up in Los Angeles. "I cannot remember a time," he says, "when I did not want to be an actor." After working on the stage, he had walk-on parts in *The Graduate* and *Valley of the Dolls* (both 1967), but made his first impression as Baby Face Nelson in *Dillinger* (1973). The main breakthrough came that same summer with *American Graffiti*: even with so many fresh and new faces in a film given over to youth, Dreyfuss' sprightly characterization stood out.

Will he be a star? If dedication and enthusiasm count, he will. He recently flew to London to see Albert Finney on the stage in *Hamlet*; and he says the best piece of advice he ever had was from Tony Randall, who, listening to the young Dreyfuss sounding off about acting, said to him: "May I ask you, have you ever seen real theatre? If not, then shut up." "Since then," says Dreyfuss, "I've tried to catch every major play within range."

Richard Dreyfuss

MAY
JUNE

JULY
AUGUST

MIND YOUR HEAD

First *The Exorcist*, now *The Omen*. No less a person than the U.S. Ambassador to Great Britain (Gregory Peck) comes to believe that his adopted son is diabolically possessed. Audiences are certainly swallowing it whole. The film was budgeted at $2.8 million and has taken $4 million in its first three days. Lee Remick also stars, as Peck's wife, and there's solid support from British actors like Billie Whitelaw, David Warner and Leo McKern.

For director Richard Donner it's an unexpected leap into the big time after a career in TV, and a decade as a film director that has been quite undistinguished. His Sammy Davis Jr comedy *Salt and Pepper* (1968) and sub-*Lolita* movie *Twinky* (1970) hardly prepared one for the shocks of this film, which include a startling death by decapitation from a flying sheet of plate glass. Interestingly Gregory Peck landed the leading role only after Charlton Heston turned it down. And writer David Selzer has said, disparagingly, "I did it strictly for the money." Such lack of belief in the project has not been shared by the producers, who have spent more on publicity than on the film. It is paying off handsomely, and Jerry Goldsmith's pounding, satanic music has already been hailed as a masterpiece of its kind.

Gregory Peck attempting to kill his son Damien (Harvey Stephens) in *The Omen*.

CZECH ON THE REBOUND

The extraordinary success of last year's *One Flew over the Cuckoo's Nest* has come as both a surprise and tremendous relief to its director, Czech-born Milos Forman. His previous American film, *Taking Off* (1971), was not a financial hit and, apart from directing the decathlon episode in the Olympic movie, *Visions of Eight* (1973), he's since been struggling to find the right material. Now he can take his pick.

Forman is no stranger to hardship, to say the least. His father was killed in Buchenwald and his mother died in Auschwitz when Forman was a child. As a young man, he became a graduate of the Prague Film School, and was at the forefront of the Czech New Wave in the 1960s, with such highly praised films as *Peter and Pavla* (1964), *A Blonde in Love* (1965) and *The Firemen's Ball* (1967). This flourish of freedom and talent was abruptly curtailed when the Russians invaded Czechoslovakia in 1968. Forman left Prague for New York in 1969, returning to visit his sons (he is separated from his wife). In 1971 he allowed his exit visa to expire without returning to Czechoslovakia, and he has since settled in the United States. "At first," he says, "I knew very little of the language but I learnt it from TV. My best teachers were Rona Barrett and Johnny Carson."

BIRTHS, DEATHS AND MARRIAGES

DEATHS

Adolph Zukor
10 Jun, Los Angeles

Stanley Baker
28 Jun, Malaga, Spain
Cancer

Fritz Lang
2 Aug, Beverly Hills, California

Alistair Sim
19 Aug, London
Cancer

MARRIAGES

Sting
1 May, *to* Frances Tomelty

Robert De Niro
Jun, *to* Diahne Abbott

Richard Burton
Aug, *to* Suzy Hunt

TAXI FAIR

Martin Scorsese's *Taxi Driver* has won the Grand Prix at this year's Cannes Film Festival. It stars Robert De Niro as a Vietnam vet who gets a job as a taxi driver because he cannot sleep at night, and becomes appalled by the squalor of what he sees. Action, he thinks, is called for – which leads to a tense and extremely violent climax. Jodie Foster, Harvey Keitel and Cybill Shepherd co-star, and it also boasts the last film score of the great Bernard Herrmann, who died last Christmas. Asked about the idea of the movie, writer Paul Schrader has said: "It came out of feelings I had at the time of loneliness and insomnia, and it translated itself into the image of this taxi driver. After that, scenes just seemed to pop up in my head as fast as I could write them down."

GOSSIP COLUMN

■ Can movie stars act? The question is now being asked in London, as a number have been appearing on the stage. Rock Hudson has been grumbling about the ungenerous reviews he got opposite Juliet Prowse in *I Do, I Do*; and, because of film commitments, Charlton Heston will not now be coming to do *Macbeth*. But there's one interesting production on the cards: Lee Remick and Keir Dullea in William Inge's *Bus Stop*. Marilyn Monroe and Don Murray starred in the 1956 film.

John Cassisi, Jodie Foster and Scott Baio in Alan Parker's Bugsy Malone.

DEATH BY CUSTARD PIE

"To make a musical with 200 kids, all but two of whom are first-timers, is just about the least safe kind of debut you could make," says young British director Alan Parker, who has done just that. His first feature, *Bugsy Malone*, is a gangster spoof set in 1929, in which Fat Sam fends with Dandy Dan over love and money. The twist is that the gangsters are played exclusively by children.

Parker had the basic idea, he says, back in Christmas 1973 and reckons he tested 10,000 children for the 200 roles. Most experienced of the young players is 13-year-old Jodie Foster, who hit the headlines earlier this year in a very different role – as a child prostitute in *Taxi Driver* – that won her an Oscar nomination. Her "My Name Is Tallulah" routine is one of the film's highlights. The songs are by Paul Williams, who scored and starred in the cult rock comedy *Phantom of the Paradise* (1974) and has recently written songs for the Barbra Streisand remake of *A Star Is Born*, due later this year. And the whole movie was actually shot in a British studio.

But is the gangster genre a little too violent for the involvement of children? Not in *Bugsy Malone*. The most destructive weapon is the splurge gun, and the most horrific death is by custard-pie in the face. Death means work for the confectioner, not the coroner: it's a kid's dream.

LUCKY 13

"That kid's no trouper," W.C. Fields used to say, when grumbling over and trying to sabotage the performance of a child co-star. But what would he have made of Jodie Foster, star of Alan Parker's kid-musical, *Bugsy Malone* and who, at the age of 13, has more experience than some actors twice her age? She starred in TV commercials before making a two-part Disney film, *Menace on the Mountain*. Her feature debut was in the Disney production *Napoleon and Samantha* (1972), with Kirk Douglas' son Michael, but the part that really got her noticed was as the androgynous friend of Alice's son in Martin Scorsese's *Alice Doesn't Live Here Anymore* (1974). Earlier this year she raised eyebrows with her remarkably assured performance as a child-prostitute in *Taxi Driver*, and she'll be seen next as a mysterious murderess in *The Little Girl Who Lives down the Lane*, shot in Canada with Martin Sheen, the young star of *Badlands* (1973).

Her comments reveal an old professional head on those slim young shoulders. She's disappointed her own singing voice was not used in *Bugsy Malone* – "I thought of sueing," she observes coolly, "but I decided against it in the long run." Her ambition? "To direct," she says. It's an unusual ambition for a woman in a male dominated industry, let alone a girl of 13; but, given what Foster has achieved so far, one wouldn't put it past her.

STAR QUOTES

Ryan O'Neal

"If things get really bad, I can always live off Tatum."

DISNEY FOR GROWN-UPS

The film of the moment to take your kids to see is *The Bad News Bears*, a comedy about a hopeless junior baseball team who are whipped into shape by a gruff coach (Walter Matthau) and by the introduction of a star player (Tatum O'Neal). But adults should stick around too: the film is witty and raw, and gives a real insight into the way kids talk and behave.

"It's not Disney," says director Michael Ritchie, "but I hope people will go away from it with the same kind of good feeling that you got from a good Disney movie." Like Ritchie's previous films, such as the Robert Redford political satire *The Candidate* (1972) and the beauty pageant send-up *Smile* (1975), it's based on a competition. But unlike his previous movies, it's drawing large audiences, which the director attributes, among other things, to the chemistry of his two stars and a sharp script from Bill (son of Burt) Lancaster. Given Ritchie's poor track record, how come Paramount approved him as director for *Bad News Bears*? "They'd seen the kids talking dirty in *Smile*," says Ritchie wryly, "and they figured, well, he can direct kids talking dirty. They don't look much beyond your last project."

Walter Matthau coaches Tatum O'Neal in The Bad News Bears.

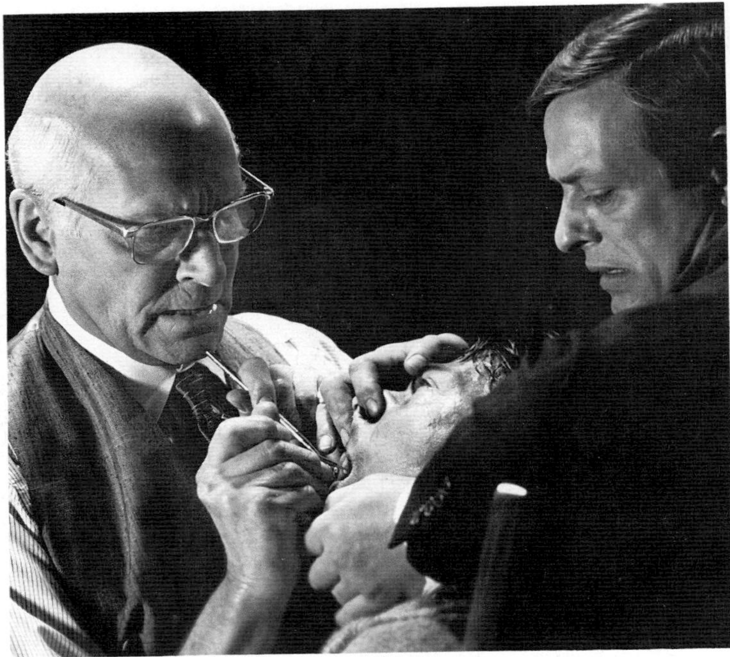

"Is it safe?" Laurence Olivier and Dustin Hoffman in Marathon Man.

MUSICAL CHAIRS

Two very different musicals are currently in production. Martin Scorsese is filming *New York, New York* at M-G-M's Culver City studio. It's an original music drama set in the post-Second World War era about the turbulent romance and marriage of a young band singer (Liza Minnelli) and a sax player (Robert De Niro). One spectacular scene of V-J Day celebrations at Radio City Music Hall (the scene with which the film will open) involves 550 costumed extras. Adding a certain piquancy to the occasion is the fact that Stage 29, where the film is being shot, was once the set of *The Pirate* (1948), directed by Liza's father, Vincente and starring her mother, Judy Garland. In a nostalgic gesture, M-G-M has given Liza her mother's dressing-room.

Over in Vienna is shooting the long-awaited film version of Stephen Sondheim's 1973 musical *A Little Night Music*, based on Ingmar Bergman's classic 1955 film, *Smiles of a Summer Night*. The film is budgeted at $7.5 million. The real surprise is in the casting, not so much in the supporting roles (Diana Rigg, Lesley-Anne Down and Len Cariou, who played the role of the middle-aged lawyer on Broadway) but in the choice of lead. Elizabeth Taylor stars and even sings, including the hit song "Send in the Clowns." Send in the voice coaches.

DRILLING FOR GOLD

The new Dustin Hoffman-Laurence Olivier thriller, *Marathon Man*, will have you on the edge of your seats – and you might not like it. Olivier is a former Nazi now at large in New York searching for hidden diamonds, and there's a key scene where innocent bystander Hoffman is tortured by Olivier, now a dentist, when he drills into Hoffman's good tooth. The scene has had to be trimmed somewhat: too many of the preview audiences were fainting.

William Goldman adapted his own novel for the screen, and John Schlesinger is the director. There is also an important role for Roy (*Jaws*) Scheider as Hoffman's brother, an American agent who is on Olivier's trail. But the main interest, say Goldman and Schlesinger, was watching the contrasting acting styles of Hoffman and Olivier in action. Hoffman's Method approach – though not quite as maddening to Olivier as his notorious encounter with Marilyn Monroe on *The Prince and the Showgirl* (1957) – was quite alien to Olivier. While waiting for his co-star to feel his way into the motivation of his scene, Olivier was said to mutter: "Dustin's very talented – but why doesn't he just get on and act?"

BOX OFFICE

UK

1. Jaws
2. One Flew over the Cuckoo's Nest
3. The Jungle Book
4. The Return of the Pink Panther
5. Emmanuelle
6. Rollerball
7. The Omen
8. It Shouldn't Happen to a Vet
9. The Outlaw Josey Wales
10. All the President's Men

BOX OFFICE

US

1. One Flew over the Cuckoo's Nest
2. All the President's Men
3. The Omen
4. The Bad News Bears
5. Silent Movie
6. Midway
7. Dog Day Afternoon
8. Murder by Death
9. Jaws (*reissue*)
10. Blazing Saddles (*reissue*)

METHOD IN HIS MADNESS

"Explosive" is the word to describe Harvey Keitel. Along with Al Pacino and Robert De Niro, he belongs to the new generation of actors who have given a tingling neurotic edge to recent American film. As the pimp in *Taxi Driver*, Keitel keeps you in a state of sweaty suspense. There is Method in his madness which makes the character seem uncomfortably true even when totally unpredictable.

Keitel was born in Brooklyn in 1945. He left school to join the Marines and, on his return to New York in 1967, he enrolled at the University, where he met Martin Scorsese. When Scorsese wanted an actor for the lead in his debut film, *Who's That Knocking at My Door* (1968), he cast Keitel.

Since then Keitel has appeared to great effect in three more Scorsese movies – *Mean Streets* (1973), *Alice Doesn't Live Here Anymore* (1974) and *Taxi Driver*. Coming shortly are two roles in which he should be in his element: as a demented concert pianist in *Fingers*, and as an officer pursuing a lifelong vendetta in *The Duellists*. You don't just watch Keitel: you watch out for him.

BIRTHS, DEATHS AND MARRIAGES

DEATHS

Jean Gabin
15 Nov, Neuilly, France
Heart attack

Rosalind Russell
28 Nov, Beverly Hills
Cancer

MARRIAGES

Elizabeth Taylor
4 Dec, *to* John Warner

STAR QUOTES

Arthur Hiller

"I don't mind Steven Spielberg being 28 years old. I don't mind him being brilliant. It's being both things at once that makes me hate him."

Blonde newcomer Jessica Lange is scooped up by King Kong in the remake of the 1933 classic.

WITH A KONG IN MY HEART

Movies are getting technologically more sophisticated, but does that mean they are getting better? The question arises with Dino De Laurentiis's *King Kong*, a remake of the 1933 classic that starred the most famous movie monster of them all. The new Kong is a more complex mechanism – 40 foot tall and weighing six tons – but is he more lovable?

The heroine this time whom Kong falls for is played by leggy blonde newcomer Jessica Lange, 27, who is a more liberated heroine than original star Fay Wray and enjoys being blown dry by Kong after her bath. This time the villains are the Petrox Oil Company, and the grand climax takes place at the World Trade Center, where director John Guillermin had to cope with 30,000 unpaid extras who had just turned up to watch. Even with its modern ecological theme and its topical references, from *Deep Throat* to male chauvinism, it may have problems recouping its massive $24 million cost. One critic has already dismissed it as "the story of a dumb blonde who falls for a huge plastic finger."

SCREAM WITH ME

New bumper-stickers which proclaim "I'm mad as hell and I'm not going to take it anymore!" are actually publicizing the new film *Network*, in which a television newcaster (Peter Finch) goes berserk one evening and invites viewers to lean out their windows and scream the slogan. "Originally we printed 25,000 of the stickers," said M-G-M's publicity vice-president, Richard Kahn. "We're now up to 80,000. There are a lot of mad people out there."

Michael Murphy and Woody Allen in The Front.

NO LAUGHING MATTER

Woody Allen and Zero Mostel in a film together sounds like a comic feast. But *The Front* is no laughing matter: it deals with the blacklisting of entertainment personalities during the Fifties for allegedly communist sympathies. Woody Allen plays a bookmaker who's asked to serve as a "front" by putting his name to scripts by blacklisted writers; Zero Mostel plays the host of a comedy series who is himself blacklisted and whose tragic suicide drives Allen from apathy to rebellion.

It is Woody Allen's first real dramatic role – and a break from his own writing and directing career – but he accepted it, he says, because he feels so strongly about the film's theme. Three of those involved in the film – Mostel, director Martin Ritt and writer Walter Bernstein – were actual victims of the blacklist, but it has taken until now to get the story on the screen. "It's the first time that the subject has been dealt with seriously and in detail in a major motion picture," claims Ritt. "We hope it will remind people of a dark period in American history."

ITALIAN STALLION

"He may be to acting what Mario Lanza was to singing," said the *New Yorker* of Sylvester Stallone, writer and star of the rags-to-riches boxing saga, *Rocky*. He may be, but Stallone is unlikely to mind very much. Born in 1946, and raised in Manhattan's Hell's Kitchen neighbourhood, he had a turbulent upbringing. "I wandered through 14 high schools and five colleges without getting a degree," he recalls, and his jobs ranged from zoo attendant to pizza demonstrator before he became an actor (reputedly in a 1968 porno movie). He had bit parts in *Bananas* (1971), in which he harassed Woody Allen on a subway train, in *The Prisoner of Second Avenue* (1975), where he was a jogger whom Jack Lemmon mistook for a mugger, and as a heavy in *Death Race 2000* (1975).

A more substantial part as a Brooklyn hood in *The Lords of Flatbush* (1974) failed to jumpstart his career, so one of the conditions Stallone made about his screenplay for *Rocky*, which he wrote in three days, was that he should play the part himself. It is about an unknown boxer who is given an unexpected chance and rises to the opportunity. Life is echoing fiction.

GOSSIP COLUMN

■ Robert Redford and Warren Beatty are at loggerheads. Beatty is preparing a film of the life of reclusive Hollywood millionaire Howard Hughes, who died recently. He'll produce as well as play Hughes. The trouble is that Redford was also planning a film on Hughes. Associates say he's angry with Beatty for stealing the project.

Brat Power

Kids with beards took over Hollywood in the early 1970s. These bright young directors had film diplomas in their pockets and celluloid in their veins. Hollywood was their finishing school, but on graduation they didn't just want to romp in the playground: they wanted to take over the classroom. They came to be known as the Movie Brats: Francis Coppola, Brian De Palma, George Lucas, John Milius, Steven Spielberg and Martin Scorsese.

The leader of the pack was Coppola and he had a flair for the epic and expansive. His two masterpieces of Mafia melodrama, *The Godfather* (1972) and *The Godfather Part II* (1974) revived the career of Marlon Brando, revitalized the gangster film and transformed Coppola's own career. His next film, *Apocalypse Now* (1979), was similarly stunning: an account of America's experience in Vietnam that turned into a haunting exploration of man's capacity for primitive evil.

Coppola was the brats' godfather, whose success and patronage eased the way for the others. Lucas was their toymaker. Like Coppola he was a film school graduate. Warners had signed him up on the strength of his short films and he gained an unexpected success with *American Graffiti* (1973), a semi-autobiographical study of youth in the early 1960s. But it paled into insignificance compared with his next film, *Star Wars* (1977), a triumph of new technology and old morality that touched a chord in the national psyche. It was the blockbuster of the decade.

The brats' wonderboy was Spielberg. He had the heart of a Peter Pan but the camera sense of an Alfred Hitchcock. *Jaws* (1975), about the hunt for a killer shark, brilliantly manipulated the audience's emotions. His sci-fi extravaganzas, *Close Encounters of the Third Kind* (1977) and *E.T. The Extra-Terrestrial* (1982), harnessed techno-wizardry with open-hearted wonder that touched the explorer in every child and the child in every adult. The age had found its new Disney.

De Palma represented the dark side. De Palma's speciality was horror rhapsodies like *Phantom of the Paradise* (1974) and his biggest hit *Carrie* (1975), which was a feverish adaptation of Stephen King's Gothic novel. The ending, with Carrie's bloodsoaked hand reaching out to grab us from beyond the grave, left audiences gasping.

Milius was the brat's warrior, a maverick celebrating fellow mavericks like *Dillinger* (1973) who robbed banks with style. He followed it with *The Wind and the Lion* (1975), an ironic, often brilliant epic about an Arab chieftain and an American president locked in a political struggle over hostages in 1912.

Scorsese was the Mafia priest. Films like *Mean Streets* (1973) and *Taxi Driver* (1976) were searing studies of Little Italy machismo and New York neurosis; but even in his most brutal films, like *Raging Bull* (1980), there was a strong religious undercurrent as manic and masochistic males sought salvation. Through his association with Scorsese, Robert De Niro became the major screen actor of the decade.

Their inventiveness flagged a little in the 1980s. Coppola lost his way; De Palma sold his soul to commerce; Lucas retired to his workshop; Milius went extreme; Spielberg grew up; and only Scorsese still surprised with his personal vision. But they had done their job. Orson Welles had described the Hollywood of that time as "a nervous old lady who needed young hands to guide her." The movie brats had yanked her into the 1980s.

Murray Hamilton, Roy Scheider and Richard Dreyfuss in Jaws *(1975).*

Candice Bergen and Sean Connery in The Wind and the Lion *(1975).*

Dennis Hopper, Martin Sheen and Frederic Forrest in Apocalypse Now *(1979).*

Main picture: Fifties nostalgia in George Lucas' American Graffiti *(1973).*

Robert De Niro and Martin Scorsese on set for *Taxi Driver* (1976).

Brian De Palma behind the camera.

Kris Kristofferson and Barbra Streisand in the latest update of A Star Is Born.

CATCH A FALLING STAR

That hardy perennial *A Star Is Born* has now been given a rock beat. At first a dramatic vehicle for Janet Gaynor and Fredric March in 1937, then a musical melodrama for Judy Garland and James Mason in 1954 (and even before either, a film, *What Price Hollywood?*, on the same theme had appeared in 1932), it is now a vehicle for the combined talents of Barbra Streisand and Kris Kristofferson. She plays a songstress on the way up; he's an alcoholic rock star on the way down.

The decibel drama on screen has been as nothing, apparently, compared with the drama on set. The film has been produced by Streisand in conjunction with her hairdresser and current consort Jon Peters, who, the rumour says, has been massaging her ego as well as her curls. Frank Pierson is the credited director, but the star has been in charge, much to the chagrin of her co-star Kristofferson, who has admitted he was in an alcoholic haze for much of the film (appropriate to the part, of course) and was developing deeply hostile feelings towards Streisand. *Village Voice* has called the movie "a bore is starred", but Streisand sings her big hit "Evergreen", and her fans are loving it.

A STAR IS PISSED OFF

Asked about working with Barbra Streisand on *A Star Is Born*, Kris Kristofferson is diplomatic but firm. "It has caused me to think about retiring from acting," he says. Which would be a shame, as this 40-year-old musician has been building a steady career for himself in movies. He already has two more in the pipeline: *Semi-Tough*, with Burt Reynolds, and *Convoy*, with Ali MacGraw, in which he is directed for the third time by Sam Peckinpah.

It was Peckinpah who really brought Kristofferson into movies. Previously he had been a top-selling and extremely popular songwriter-singer, whose biggest hit, "Help Me Make It through the Night" had been effectively used in the John Huston movie, *Fat City* (1972). Peckinpah, however, cast him as Billy the Kid in his *Pat Garrett and Billy the Kid* (1973), feeling that Kristofferson's image was right for the anti-authority, free-spirited, anarchic Billy. Since then he has had effective roles in *Alice Doesn't Live Here Anymore* (1974), *Blume in Love* (1974) with George Segal, and Peckinpah's modern western *Bring Me the Head of Alfredo Garcia* (1974) with Warren Oates. His steamy scenes with Sarah Miles in *The Sailor Who Fell from Grace with the Sea* (1976) also seem to have enhanced his popularity. A combination of drugs, drink and Streisand have taken their toll over the past few months. But it's nothing that a rest and a good new movie might not cure, and both seem in the offing. He has made it through the night.

THE OLDEST STAR

George Burns is God. No, this is not a fan speaking. It's a description of Burns' role in the new Carl Reiner comedy *Oh, God!*, in which the Divine Presence appears before John Denver's supermarket manager and proceeds to drive a cab, sweep up leaves and perform the odd miracle, like making it rain.

Eighty-year-old Burns is making one of the oldest comebacks in movie history. *The Sunshine Boys* (1975), in which he played with Walter Matthau, was his first film for 35 years, and dubbed "The Old Couple" by critics because it was scripted by Neil Simon. To the delight of everyone, it won Burns an Oscar. He has long been one of the most popular figures in entertainment, particularly through his shows on radio and TV with his wife Gracie Allen. *The Sunshine Boys* was congenial to him because he was playing an old vaudevillian that would remind Burns of his own vaudeville origins in showbiz as a singer in a children's quartet. He played it so well that a new movie career is opening up for him. As he says himself, "it couldn't happen to an older guy".

George Burns in Oh, God!

ACADEMY AWARDS

PRESENTED ON 29 MARCH 1977

Best Picture
Rocky

Best Director
John G. Avildsen
Rocky

Best Actor
Peter Finch
Network

Best Actress
Faye Dunaway
Network

Best Sup Actor
Jason Robards
All the President's Men

Best Sup Actress
Beatrice Straight
Network

BIRTHS, DEATHS AND MARRIAGES

DEATHS

Groucho Marx
1 Jan, Los Angeles
Pneumonia

Peter Finch
14 Jan, Los Angeles
Heart attack

Eddie "Rochester" Anderson
28 Feb, Woodland Hills, California
Heart attack

MARRIAGES

Peter Sellers
18 Feb, *to* Lynne Frederick

Michael Douglas
20 Mar, *to* Diandra Lucker

BEGINNING FROM ZERO

With his performance as Hecky Brown in *The Front*, a comic who is victimized by the blacklist, Zero Mostel closes a chapter on one episode of his life and may be starting another. He resurrects memories from the most difficult part of his own life, when he too was blacklisted, but in doing so, he reveals a dramatic range that adds poignancy to his usual wild New York Jewish comedy.

Born in 1915, Mostel started as a parlour comedian in New York and made his Hollywood debut in 1943. He had been developing a fine career as a character actor in movies like the crime thrillers *Panic in the Streets* (1950) and *The Enforcer* (1951) before the blacklist struck. He was out of work for several years, though his appearance before the House Un-American Activities Committee for alleged Communist affiliations did provide some rare humour during those proceedings (he referred to his employers as "18th Century-Fox"). His return to the Broadway stage in the early Sixties in productions of *Rhinoceros, Fiddler on the Roof* and *A Funny Thing Happened on the Way to the Forum* was a triumph, and he was to repeat his performance in *Forum* for the 1966 film version. Of his films since the blacklist, his performance in *The Producers* (1967) is the most memorable, his outsize personality seeming to match director Mel Brooks's grotesque humour. Sometimes his talents seem too big for the film frame, but *The Front* shows a new intimacy and subtlety. Welcome back, Zero.

SPORTING BEHAVIOUR

Paul Newman is hoping that his new movie with director George Roy Hill *Slap Shot*, will emulate the success of their previous films, *Butch Cassidy and the Sundance Kid* (1969) and *The Sting* (1973). But it's very different. Newman plays an ice-hockey coach who will stoop to any level, including dirty play, to get results. The film is violent and profane.

"It's a satire on sport, and what the pressures of commercialism have done to the sporting spirit," says director Hill. Female interest is provided by Jennifer Warren and Lindsay Crouse who play hockey wives. Perhaps the main feminine interest, though, lies in the fact that this raucous movie was scripted by a lady, Nancy Dowd. Her quality of profanity is not strained. It suggests she could hold her own in any male locker room.

Michael Ontkean and Paul Newman in the ice-hockey pic Slap Shot.

Diane Keaton and Woody Allen in Allen's latest comedy Annie Hall.

WOODY'S 2½

Everyone seems to agree: *Annie Hall*, the new film from Woody Allen, is his best yet. Billed as "a nervous romance," about a love affair that dies between a neurotic romantic and a nervous wreck, it's actually a semi-autobiography. Woody plays Alvy Singer, a stand-up comic like himself in his younger days. In the title role Diane Keaton plays someone, like herself, who starts her career as a singer; and Keaton's family name is Hall. As the relationship fades in the film, so Woody and Diane split up before the film's release.

Comparisons between his film and Italian master Federico Fellini leave Woody sceptical. "Hardly my *8½*," he says, "more like my *2½*." If a European master has influenced the film, he says, it is more probably Ingmar Bergman, and particularly Bergman's strategy in *Scenes from a Marriage* (1973): instead of fitting the actors to the parts, why not make a film in which you fit the parts to the actors? Characteristically, he deprecates his own film, feeling he got only 60 per cent of what he originally had in mind up there on screen. Critics and moviegoers disagree.

STAR QUOTES

Woody Allen

"I'm one of life's self-haters. I figure you've got to hate yourself if you've got any integbrity at all."

STAR DATE 25.5.1977

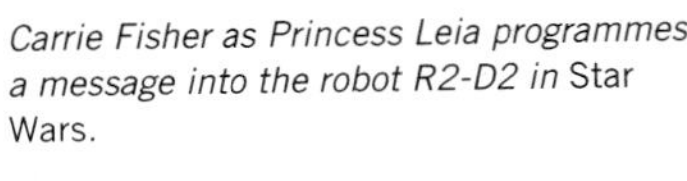
Carrie Fisher as Princess Leia programmes a message into the robot R2-D2 in Star Wars.

25 May 1977 is a date that looks like going down in Hollywood history. The reason? The opening of *Star Wars*, a sci-fi adventure that has clocked up $6 million in less than a fortnight and looks like being one of the phenomenal successes of all time. "It is a fairy-tale for modern youth," says director George Lucas. "It has a beautiful princess, and heroes and villains, and a struggle between Good and Evil, but it has been decked out with modern technology: special effects, robots, space-suits. . . ." There's also a swashbuckling score by *Jaws* composer John Williams that recalls classic movie music of the past.

Was it an easy film to get off the ground? Producer Gary Kurtz laughs. "There was even trouble over the title," he recalls. "The studio argued that no film with 'star' or 'wars' in the title had ever made any money." *Star Wars* was initially turned down by both Universal and United Artists and three years passed between inception and the beginning of shooting, by which time 20th Century-Fox had become interested. But shooting was so strung-out and troubled that the studio almost pulled the plug on the movie several times. Interiors were all shot at Britain's Elstree Studios, with location work in Tunisia, Guatemala and Death Valley.

"It is a homage to all the action adventure fantasies of the movies, particularly the Flash Gordon series," says Kurtz. Lucas calls it a "high-energy action movie uniting the hardware of contemporary space adventure with the romantic fantasies of sword and sorcery, plus a dash of wish fulfilment. . . ." The biggest name in the film is actually that of Alec Guinness, who plays a veteran knight, Ben Kenobi. Mark Hamill (from TV) plays Luke Skywalker, Harrison Ford (from *American Graffiti* and *The Conversation*) is Han Solo and Carrie Fisher (Debbie Reynolds' daughter) plays Princess Leia: their names may not mean much at the moment but the way things are going, they'll be on everyone's lips in no time. As will the robots, R2-D2 and C-3PO, whose comic interplay provides much of the film's humour: Laurel and Hardy for the space age.

GOSSIP COLUMN

■ **Veteran actor John Carradine has revealed that, at the age of 70, he has one outstanding ambition: to play in a movie with talented sons David and Keith. "A western perhaps," he says, though at the moment he is having a stage success in Florida in a very different role: Big Daddy in Tennessee Williams' *Cat on a Hot Tin Roof.***

CANDY STAR

Watch out for Candy Clark. She is one of those actresses who steals up on you unawares. Perhaps it is personality more than looks; but it might also be star quality.

She was born in 1949 and first appeared as the young lady who is about to domesticate and tame Jeff Bridges' young boxer in *Fat City* (1972). This was followed by what is to date her most famous role, as the sexy, gum-chewing teenager in *American Graffiti* (1973). It earned her an Oscar nomination. She has since co-starred opposite David Bowie's creature from another planet in *The Man Who Fell to Earth* (1976), so her career has been fascinatingly offbeat as well as versatile.

She is currently playing the younger daughter of General Sternwood in Michael Winner's London-based remake of *The Big Sleep*. The part isn't big but it's the kind that gets noticed, because the character is a loony and also holds the key to the mystery. Candy Clark has, it seems, a natural way of attracting attention. It could make for an exciting screen career.

BIRTHS, DEATHS AND MARRIAGES

DEATHS

Joan Crawford
11 May, New York
Heart attack

Elvis Presley
16 Aug, Memphis, Tennessee
Heart attack

Stephen Boyd
19 Aug, Los Angeles
Heart attack

One of the bridges is secured in A Bridge Too Far.

THE LONGEST WAR

After *Oh! What a Lovely War* (1969), Richard Attenborough's new film for producer Joseph E. Levine might be subtitled: "Oh, What a Lousy War." *A Bridge Too Far* is about Operation Market Garden, aimed at ending the Second World War by the winter of 1944, but which turned into almost total disaster at Arnhem.

The movie is based on a book by Cornelius Ryan, who wrote *The Longest Day* about the D-Day landings which was a successful movie back in 1962. As producer Darryl F. Zanuck did then, Attenborough has packed his film with stars: Dirk Bogarde, Michael Caine, Sean Connery, James Caan, Gene Hackman, Anthony Hopkins, Laurence Olivier, Robert Redford, Maximilian Schell and, as token feminine interest, Liv Ullmann. Attenborough feels that the film belongs to the tradition of a movie like *Patton* (1970) which was more analytical than action-packed. But will the fact that the operation was a disaster stop it recouping the massive $24 million budget? Attenborough hopes not. As George Orwell pointed out, the most popular war poem in the English language is Tennyson's "Charge of the Light Brigade" – and that's about soldiers who charged in the wrong direction and were annihilated.

LOOKING FOR DIANE

This could be the breakthrough year for kooky Diane Keaton. Born in 1946, she was first seen as just a good girl to have around: as Al Pacino's wife in *The Godfather* films, and as Woody Allen's romantic interest in *Play it Again, Sam* (1972), *Sleeper* (1973) and *Love and Death* (1975). But now her talents as actress, comedienne and even singer have burst forth most beautifully in *Annie Hall*, Woody Allen's semi-autobiographical confession that could turn out to be the unexpected romantic hit of the decade. Upcoming also is a strong dramatic role in writer-director Richard Brook's new movie.

Keaton was just completing *Annie Hall* when Brooks was casting around for a suitable lead for *Looking for Mr. Goodbar*, a dark and violent drama about a teacher who seems to have one personality by day but quite another by night, when she cruises singles bars for increasingly dangerous sexual encounters. "I wondered if Diane could handle the dark side of the character as well as the teacher side," says Brooks, "but she's sensational."

MAKE IT AGAIN, PHIL

This seems like the age of the remake. So far there's been *A Star Is Born*, just after a new version of *King Kong*, and currently British director Michael Winner is preparing a new version of Raymond Chandler's novel, *The Big Sleep*, last filmed in 1946 with Humphrey Bogart as world-weary private eye Philip Marlowe. In Winner's modern version, Robert Mitchum plays Marlowe, and he's supported by a glittering cast that includes James Stewart, Sarah Miles, Candy Clark, Oliver Reed and Joan Collins. One novelty is that the story will now take place in London – but a London, says Winner, that has "a timeless, illusory quality." The producer is Elliott Kastner, who also produced two other recent Chandler adaptations, *The Long Goodbye* (1973) and the remake of *Farewell, My Lovely* (1975).

But why do remakes at all? Director John Huston once said that he could never understand the point of re-making successful films: the ones that ought to be re-made are the ones that failed first time. Michael Winner has a different re-make philosophy. "Sir Henry Irving did a good *Hamlet* in 1874", he says, "but people still try again with different interpretations." Still, the Bogart/Lauren Bacall version is a tough act to follow.

SEPTEMBER OCTOBER

NOVEMBER DECEMBER

A "close encounter of the third kind" in Steven Spielberg's movie on UFOs.

WE ARE NOT ALONE!

A close encounter of the first kind is sighting a UFO; the second kind, physical evidence after the sighting; and the third kind, a confrontation with the species. The new movie from Steven (*Jaws*) Spielberg, due to open in mid-December, is *Close Encounters of the Third Kind*, a spectacular epic in the mode of *2001: A Space Odyssey* (1968). Douglas Trumbull, who helped on the special effects in *2001*, was responsible for those on the present movie, said by insiders to be breathtaking.

Excitement has been gathering over the film because it has been shot in the strictest secrecy. The sound stage, converted from an old Second World War aircraft hanger in Alabama, is the largest ever for a movie – 450 feet long, 250 feet wide, 90 feet high. Lighting it has been a problem: the film's electricity bills, apparently, have been the highest for a decade. The spectacular climax was shot at Devil's Tower, a mountain in Wyoming, and there's even a sequence in a remote part of India.

Richard Dreyfuss, the shark expert in *Jaws*, plays the suburban power-worker whose sighting of the UFOs changes his life. The aliens are the creation of Carlö Rambaldi and are played by 50 six-year-old girls. But the most unusual piece of casting is that of French film-maker Francois Truffaut in the role of a scientist who has come to monitor the UFO landings. "I wanted a man-child," explains Spielberg, "ingenuous and wise, a father-figure with this very wide-eyed outlook on life. I didn't want the stoic with the white hair and pipe." It was Truffaut's first experience of the slower way of making movies: during all the hanging around he managed to write the script for his next film.

BOX OFFICE

UK

1 The Spy Who Loved Me
2 A Star Is Born
3 When the North Wind Blows
4 The Pink Panther Strikes Again
5 A Bridge Too Far
6 Sinbad and the Eye of the Tiger
7 The Omen
8 King Kong
9 Airport '77
10 The Adventures of the Wilderness Family

BOX OFFICE

US

1 Star Wars
2 Rocky
3 Smokey and the Bandit
4 A Star Is Born
5 King Kong
6 The Deep
7 Silver Streak
8 The Enforcer
9 Close Encounters of the Third Kind
10 In Search of Noah's Ark

GOTTA JIVE!

Saturday Night Fever, the Bee Gees disco movie that's set box offices dancing, is a triumph of canny marketing. It's designed to get the 18- to 25-year-old age group that buys records out of the shops and into movie theatres. But it could not have worked without the charismatic central performance of 23-year-old John Travolta, who shows real screen magnetism.

"There's nothing glamourised about his personality," says Travolta about the part he plays. "He's neither macho nor withdrawn, neither heroic nor anti-heroic. He's universally identifiable." Travolta was actually seen on screen last year, as one of the school fraternity in *Carrie* (1976) who pushed Sissy Spacek just a little too far at the school prom. Indeed, he's quite a performing veteran, having made his stage debut in a rep production of *Bye Bye Birdie* at the age of nine. But it's *Saturday Night Fever* that has set youngsters' pulses racing. He'll next be seen in the film version of the musical *Grease*, opposite pop singer Olivia Newton-John, and he is then slated to star in an as-yet-untitled adult romance with comedienne Lily Tomlin.

Jane Fonda as Lillian Hellman and Vanessa Redgrave in the title role of *Julia*.

GREAT JANE

Her talent is a credit to her father, Henry, and one of the outstanding features of Seventies' American cinema. Jane Fonda's time has come and she's shaping up to be the Katharine Hepburn of the modern US screen – vibrant, intelligent, independent.

She'll be 40 on 21 December. Born in New York, she went to Vassar, to Europe (to study painting) and worked as a model to finance her spell at Lee Strasberg's classes. After decorative roles in Hollywood and France during the 1960s (including marriage to Roger Vadim), she became the cinema's bourgeois conscience in the early Seventies when she campaigned against the Vietnam war and made films about her views, like Jean-Luc Godard's *Tout va bien* (1972). It seemed for a while as if politics would claim her – though she managed an Oscar-winning performance in *Klute* (1971) – but she's slowly steered her career back with *Steelyard Blues* and *A Doll's House* (both 1973), and the acerbic comedy *Fun with Dick and Jane* earlier this year.

Her role as Lillian Hellman in *Julia* is congenial to her feminist and political beliefs, and offers a tremendous part to boot. "In the beginning you try too hard and end up showing too much," she has said. "It's only later that you learn that if you are truly experiencing and behaving, then it doesn't show." Look out for her early next year in *Coming Home*, as a nurse who campaigns with the crippled Jon Voight against the Vietnam war.

STRONGER THAN THE MALE?

Jane Fonda and Vanessa Redgrave in a movie together? That's the powerful teaming in *Julia*, which comes as a riposte to the flurry of buddy movies. Based on a chapter in Lillian Hellman's memoirs, *Pentimento*, it tells the story of her friendship in her youth with the beautiful and mysterious Julia, and particularly the latter's involvement of Lillian in a dangerous mission against the Nazis (smuggling money to help refugees to escape) in pre-war Berlin. Says Jane Fonda, who plays Hellman: "It demonstrates that, in her particular way, the female is every bit as capable of courage as the male."

Redgrave plays Julia and critics are saying it's her best movie performance yet. There are also important roles for Jason Robards, who plays Lillian's long-time lover, Dashiell Hammett, and Maximilian Schell, who has a key role as the messenger who will alert Lillian to Julia's danger. The director is one of Hollywood's most respected veterans, Fred Zinnemann, 70, never better than when dealing with lonely struggles of conscience and courage within the sensitive individual, as in his award-winning classics like *High Noon* (1952), *From Here to Eternity* (1953) and *A Man for All Seasons* (1966). Austria-born Zinnemann, however, modestly disclaims too much credit for the success of *Julia*, pointing instead to the performances of Jane Fonda and Vanessa Redgrave. "When you are working with people of that quality," he says, "directing is easy."

BIRTHS, DEATHS AND MARRIAGES

DEATHS

Zero Mostel
8 Sep, Philadelphia
Heart attack

Bing Crosby
14 Oct, Madrid
Heart attack

Charlie Chaplin
25 Dec, Vevey, Switzerland

Howard Hawks
26 Dec, Palm Springs, California
Complications following a fall

STAR QUOTES

Woody Allen

"This year I'm a star, but what will I be next year – a black hole?"

Shirley MacLaine and Anne Bancroft in a tense confrontation from The Turning Point.

FEMALE TROUBLES

Once we had "buddy movies": now it's "female bonding." The good news is that it means strong roles for strong actresses. Following *Julia* the latest is *The Turning Point*, with Shirley MacLaine and Anne Bancroft as two dancers who move from tender friendship to hair-pulling hatred. MacLaine plays the one who sacrificed her career and stayed at home; Bancroft is the one who stuck with it and became a star. The great Soviet ballet-dancer Mikhail Baryshnikov is also in the cast, and the film is made by Herbert Ross, who choreographed musicals like *Doctor Dolittle* (1967) and *Funny Girl* (1968) before turning director on *Goodbye, Mr Chips* (1969), *Play It Again, Sam* (1972) and *Funny Lady* (1975).

"This is not a feminist story," says MacLaine. "It's about two old friends who care about their lives and each other . . . . They're not holding up banks or wrestling each other in the mud; it's like an old-fashioned Hollywood film." It's MacLaine's first film for four years. What particularly attracted her to the project? "I think it's written with understanding and dimension," she explains, " and that's why I did it."

JANUARY
FEBRUARY

MARCH
APRIL

MY SON'S A CARPENTER

After eleven years in the movie business, Harrison Ford is an overnight success. His Han Solo in last year's *Star Wars* has brought recognition to an actor who several times has thought he might need to return to his first trade, carpentry.

Born in Chicago in 1942, he studied philosophy and English at Ripon College, Wisconsin, but chucked it in in 1963 to become an actor. "My first role," he recalls, "was in a 1966 movie, *Dead Heat on a Merry-Go-Round*. After it, a studio executive called me into his office and said: 'You ain't got it kid'." A seven-year contract with Columbia yielded only brief appearances in some of the least successful movies in the studio's history, such as the Jack Lemmon comedy *Luv* (1967) and the Civil War drama *A Time for Killing* (1968). A job as a student revolutionary extra in *Zabriskie Point* (1970) ended up on the cutting-room floor.

His luck has changed, however, through his association with two of the industry's brightest young talents, George Lucas and Francis Coppola. Modest but significant roles in Lucas's *American Graffiti* (1973) and Coppola's *The Conversation* (1974) and the long-awaited *Apocalypse Now* have consolidated his career. Now with *Star Wars*, it seems, the sky's the limit.

ACADEMY AWARDS

PRESENTED ON 3 APRIL 1978

Best Picture
Annie Hall

Best Director
Woody Allen
Annie Hall

Best Actor
Richard Dreyfuss
The Goodbye Girl

Best Actress
Diane Keaton
Annie Hall

Best Sup Actor
Jason Robards
Julia

Best Sup Actress
Vanessa Redgrave
Julia

STAR QUOTES

Mel Brooks

"Why should I indulge myself and do a David Lean-ish kind of film? I could do my little Jewish Brief Encounter *and disguise it – shorten the noses. But it wouldn't be as much fun as delivering my dish of insanity."*

GOSSIP COLUMN

■ ***Apocalypse Now***, **the epic movie with Marlon Brando about the Vietnam War, seems to be following in the footsteps of such troubled productions as *Mutiny on the Bounty* (1962) and *Cleopatra* (1963). Yet another announced opening date has been and gone and still no movie. *Godfather* director Francis Coppola (he officially got rid of his middle name "Ford" last year) is characteristically taking his time. The film, which began shooting in the Philippines in March 1976 and finished in May last year, is being referred to in the trade as *Apocalypse When?***

Mel Brooks attacked by birds in his spoof of Hitchcock movies High Anxiety.

DON'T HOLD THE MAYO

"Danger, Intrigue, Romance . . . and a Touch of Kinkiness!" proclaim the posters for *High Anxiety*. Yes, Mel Brooks is back. Having done dementedly hilarious spoofs of the Western (*Blazing Saddles*, 1974), the horror film (*Young Frankenstein*, 1974) and early film comedy (*Silent Movie*, 1976), he's now turned his attention to the suspense thriller. *High Anxiety* is affectionately dedicated to "the master of suspense, Alfred Hitchcock."

Brooks himself plays the leading role, the new head of the psycho-neurotic Institute for the Very, Very Nervous, who suffers from vertigo and whose predecessor died in suspicious circumstances. Brooks' usual leading lady, Madeline Kahn, plays the Hitchcockian cool blonde whose frigid facade conceals a fiery, passionate nature, and other Brooks' stalwarts such as Harvey Gorman and Cloris Leachman are on hand to play the more sinister staff at the institute.

"I get to sing the title song," says Brooks cheerfully. Asked if he will include parodies of such famous Hitchcock set-pieces as the shower murder in *Psycho* (1960), Brooks replies: "Oh certainly – only the camera will steam up." The hero will also find himself attacked by birds – or, more precisely, splattered by their deposits, which Brooks explains disarmingly are "made out of mayonnaise and chopped spinach." The man himself, Alfred Hitchcock, gave the production its blessing and even sent him a case of wine as good luck. Both men in fact share the same droll humour. When asked by a cringing reporter what he had used for the blood in the shower murder of *Psycho*, Hitch replied calmly: "Chocolate sauce".

BIRTHS, DEATHS AND MARRIAGES

DEATHS

Charlotte Greenwood
18 Jan,

Jack Oakie
23 Jan, Northridge, California
Heart attack

Oscar Homolka
27 Jan, Sussex
Pneumonia

Basil Dean
22 Apr, London
Heart attack

Alan Bates and Jill Clayburgh discuss art in An Unmarried Woman.

NEW WOMEN

After last year's *Julia* and *The Turning Point* comes *An Unmarried Woman*. It looks like women are back in fashion after a spate of "buddy movies." The film is directed by talented Paul Mazursky, who made *Bob & Carol & Ted & Alice* (1969) and *Harry and Tonto* (1974). Here he tells the story of a sophisticated New Yorker, devastated by the desertion of her husband, who finds a new life – and herself. In the leading role is a new star in the making, Jill Clayburgh.

Mazursky first remembers meeting Clayburgh when she unsuccessfully read for parts in his films. Marsha Mason was preferred to her in *Blume in Love* (1973) and Lois Smith was the choice for *Next Stop, Greenwich Village* (1976). "I knew she had genuine humour, intelligence, wit, beauty", recalls Mazursky, "but could she handle emotion, could she carry a whole picture?" She answers that with a resounding affirmative in *An Unmarried Woman*. The picture is an American entry in this year's Cannes Film Festival, and Clayburgh must surely be in contention for an acting prize.

MISS-COMFORT

Two sensations at the Oscars this year. The first is that Richard Burton did not win the best actor Oscar for *Equus*, as was strongly tipped: it went to Richard Dreyfuss for the Neil Simon comedy *The Goodbye Girl*. It was Burton's seventh nomination and he might have supposed his luck was in. What must his disappointment have been when he heard: "And the winner is: Richard. . . ."?

The other talking-point, less unexpected, has been Vanessa Redgrave's acceptance speech for her supporting actress Oscar in *Julia*. There had been some not too discreet lobbying against Redgrave's nomination, particularly because of her pro-Arab political sympathies in the Palestinian conflict. Much to the discomfort of Academy members, Redgrave thanked them for standing up to the "Zionist thugs" who had campaigned against her.

WE SHALL OVERCOME

A war cripple (Jon Voight) and a volunteer nurse (Jane Fonda) begin an affair. He's abrasive and embittered, and she's inhibited and respectable; but both start actively campaigning against the Vietnam war. They are put under surveillance and their liaison brought to the attention of the nurse's soldier husband (Bruce Dern).

This is the dramatic situation of the powerful new movie *Coming Home*, which also draws attention to the treatment of veterans who suffered as a result of the war. It is in the tradition of such classic Hollywood movies as *The Best Years of Our Lives* (1946) and *The Men* (1950), which looked at the physical and psychological effects of combat on men who had returned home. The project is a triumph for Fonda, who worked hard to get it off the ground and has drawn some brickbats in the process (her anti-Vietnam war campaigning of the early Seventies hasn't endeared her to all Vietnam vets, to say the least). It's also a great comeback for Voight, who has not had a hit since *Deliverance* (1972). "I felt down at the bottom of the totem pole in terms of viable commercial personalities," he said. "I couldn't get a film made." *Coming Home* has changed all that.

One ironic black mark, however. *Coming Home* has opened in San Francisco in a cinema with no access for wheelchairs. The film is being picketed by the disabled.

CHANGING TRACK

There are signs that the macho image of Burt Reynolds is being modified. The 42-year-old, part-Red Indian former football star, famed for his tough-guy roles in films like *Deliverance* (1972), *Hustle* (1975) and *Smokey and the Bandit* (1977), is turning director and also showing a growing hand at comedy. (Hands up who saw him in *At Long Last Love* and *Lucky Lady* back in 1975.) His latest three films, just released or due for release, show the multi-faceted hunk in different guises.

He has just completed *Semi-Tough* with Kris Kristofferson and Jill Clayburgh, and one critic has boldly suggested that Reynolds has the best light comedy touch in American film since Cary Grant. Coming soon is *The End*, which Reynolds stars in and directs and which is said to be inspired by his own recent illness, where bad chest pains made him at one stage fear for his life. He feels he might be upstaged, though, by a manic Dom DeLuise, who plays a failed suicide with a complex about his father's cultural ignorance ("he thought 'Moby Dick' was a venereal disease"). Finally there is *Hooper*, a film about Hollywood stuntmen, drawing on Reynold's own early career in that trade before superstardom. Comedy actor, director, or macho man? "Let the public decide," says Reynolds. "They always do."

Burt Reynolds as the Bandit.

MAY
JUNE

JULY
AUGUST

BIRTHS, DEATHS AND MARRIAGES

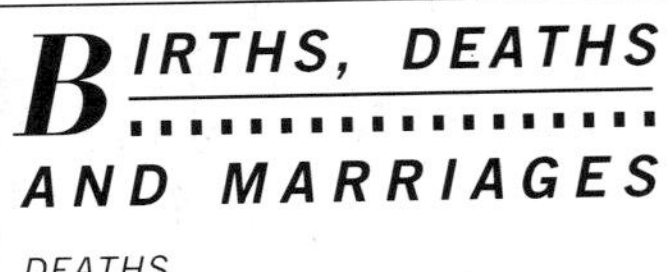

DEATHS

Charles Boyer
2 Jun, Phoenix, Arizona
Suicide

Nicholas Ray
16 Jun, New York
Cancer

Jack L. Warner
9 Aug, Los Angeles
Heart inflamation

Robert Shaw
28 Aug, Tourmakeady, Ireland
Heart attack

REEL LIVES

They call them "biopics", film biographies of real-life people but often sweetened and softened by Hollywood sentiment. Last year Jane Fonda played Lillian Hellman in *Julia*, a film which dramatized an incident in the young Hellman's life. This year Gary Busey is playing the tragic rock star Buddy Holly in *The Buddy Holly Story*, and Vanessa Redgrave is playing Agatha Christie in *Agatha*, a film which attempts to unravel a Christie-like mystery in the author's own life when she went missing for 10 days.

Ironically, a popular film like *Rocky* (1976) looks nearer the truth than Mohammed Ali's version of his own life story last year in *The Greatest*. But biopics will always do well. Audiences are interested in how the rich and famous *became* rich and famous. And truth is sometimes more interesting than fiction – though biopics have a habit of confusing the two.

HEAVENLY COMEDY

The hereafter is not ready yet for Warren Beatty. In *Heaven Can Wait* he plays a quarterback with the Los Angeles Rams who, due to celestial error, is called to Heaven prematurely. Discovering that in the meantime his body has been cremated, he now has to return to earth and occupy the body of a rich industrialist whose wife (Dyan Cannon) is trying to kill him. It's based on the 1941 hit comedy, *Here Comes Mr Jordan*, with Robert Montgomery, and is not to be confused with the Ernst Lubitsch period fantasy *Heaven Can Wait*, with Gene Tierney and Don Ameche which was released two years later.

Like *Bonnie and Clyde* (1967) and *Shampoo* (1975), it's another of those projects in which Beatty has taken an active interest. As well as starring in the film alongside Julie Christie and James Mason, he co-wrote the screenplay (with Elaine May) and co-directed the movie (with Buck Henry). At the ripe old age of 41, he even does his own quarterbacking, in a Superbowl sequence filmed in front of 60,000 fans at the LA Coliseum.

BEE MOVIE

The buzz about *The Swarm* is that it's one of those disaster movies that's truly disastrous. You can hardly fault the calibre of the cast: Michael Caine, Katherine Ross, Richard Widmark, Olivia de Havilland, Henry Fonda, Richard Chamberlain, Fred MacMurray. But the script? "Houston on fire," murmurs General Richard Widmark, "will history blame me or the bees?"

Warners spent $12 million on the project, partly out of pique at being the one major studio to have missed out on the disaster cycle. The movie has also antagonized America's beekeepers, with the result that Warners have had to insert a disclaimer on the end credits, saying in effect that any resemblance to a living American bee is purely coincidental. The villain, apparently, is the Africanized killer bee: does this make the film racist? Hitchcock never had this trouble with our feathered friends in *The Birds* (1963).

GOSSIP COLUMN

■ **Director Sydney Pollack and actor Robert Redford had to abandon their plans to make a film on the western character Tom Horn because Steve McQueen got there first. But now it appears Pollack and Redford will work together again after all. Martin Ritt has withdrawn from the directing job of *The Electric Horseman*, in which Redford stars, and Pollack has taken over the reins. Shooting begins in New Mexico in May.**

ALL-AMERICAN SURVIVOR

In the new Billy Wilder movie *Fedora*, the role of an embittered producer is played by William Holden. It seems a long way from Holden's gigolo in Wilder's *Sunset Blvd.* (1950); he is one of Hollywood's great survivors.

He was born in 1918, son of an industrial chemist and a schoolteacher. He never planned on an acting career: he always said that "my father is a success in the manure business and I can always go back with him if I don't make it." But after being spotted in a minor role at Pasadena Playhouse, he was cast to star in *Golden Boy* (1939) and his career was launched. For 10 years he was an undistinguished Paramount contract player until *Sunset Blvd.* dramatically raised his profile. His next film for Wilder, *Stalag 17* (1953), won him an Oscar, and a string of successful Fifties films, like *The Moon Is Blue* (1953), *Sabrina* (1954), *Love Is a Many-Splendored Thing* (1955), *Picnic* (1955) and *The Bridge on the River Kwai* (1957) made him one of the most popular stars of the decade. In the permissive Sixties, however, his clean-cut persona seemed to have had its day. Then he made a stunning comeback as the ruthless outlaw leader of *The Wild Bunch* (1969), and a superb Oscar-nominated performance in *Network* (1976).

The reunion with Wilder is especially apt, since both have such admiration of each other. "He is the ideal motion picture actor," says the director. "Like Jimmy Stewart or Gary Cooper, you never doubt or question what he is. He has presence."

Richard Widmark fends off an attack of killer bees in The Swarm.

THE FANTASTIC FIFTIES

There's nothing harder than trying to equal your first big success, but John Travolta has gone one better: he's topped it. His new musical, *Grease*, about the course of true love in a Fifties high school, is shaping up to be an even greater box-office smash than *Saturday Night Fever*. Travolta's co-star is British-born pop singer Olivia Newton-John, playing, as it were, Sandra Dee to Travolta's Elvis Presley. Audiences are finding it an irresistible combination.

Grease is based on the highly successful Broadway show by Jim Jacobs and Warren Casey with a few new numbers added. "The show's appeal," says Paramount head of production, Ned Tanen, "lay in its nostalgic look back to the Fifties – the early years of rock 'n' roll and an age of relative innocence before Vietnam and Watergate." He has packed the film with identification figures an older audience will remember from their youth in the Fifties – Joan Blondell, Sid Caesar, Edd Byrnes, Eve Arden and Frankie Avalon. It's all heady escapism. Maybe the Fifties weren't like this – but they ought to have been.

Olivia Newton-John and John Travolta in the musical Grease.

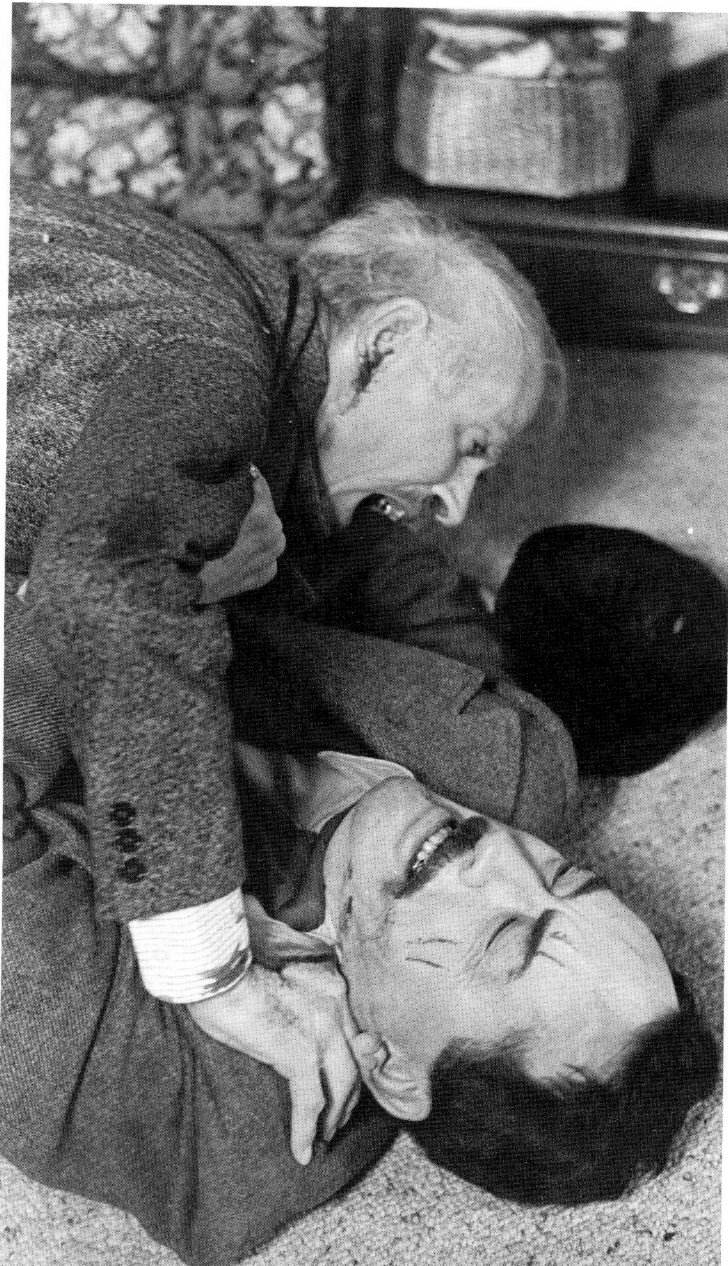

Laurence Olivier and Gregory Peck locked in combat in The Boys from Brazil.

PECK'S BADDIE

The Boys from Brazil has been called "Send in the Clones" within the industry. Based on a novel by *Rosemary's Baby* author Ira Levin, it tells a tale of the use of cloning as part of a sinister neo-Nazi plot to conquer the world. Laurence Olivier plays the Jewish Nazi-hunter who is alarmed when he gets wind of this scheme. It's a nice reversal for Olivier, who played a neo-Nazi with a mean dentist's drill two years ago in *The Marathon Man*. And in one of the year's most surprising pieces of casting, fanatical Nazi Josef Mengele (who's rumoured to be still alive somewhere in South America) is none other than Gregory Peck.

It is by no means Peck's first villain in films. He was a volatile, unpredictable outlaw in *Duel in the Sun* (1947), and he played the fearsome and obsessive Captain Ahab in *Moby Dick* (1956) – though one critic felt he would have been better cast as the whale. But he's still more associated with parts like the decent liberal lawyer in *To Kill a Mockingbird* (1962), for which he won an Academy Award. Casting against type can work two ways: it can succeed through surprise, or it can fail through an audience's incredulity.

THE AMERICAN WAY

Christopher Reeve as Superman and Margot Kidder as Lois Lane in Superman.

"You'll believe a man can fly" says the publicity for *Superman* – and if you have missed the publicity, you must have been on the planet Krypton. The $50 million blockbuster is delighting audiences and critics. The technical effects are predictably awesome, but the performances too have come in for a lot of praise, particularly Marlon Brando for his brief, million-dollar appearance at the beginning, and Christopher Reeve as Superman.

"I needed an actor who could play it as straight as you can within the fable," says director Richard Donner, who feels Christopher Reeve achieves that charmingly. Reeve says that he saw Superman as a "warm and humorous but solitary man with incredible powers, trying to fit into his adopted planet." He has to pit his power in this film against earthquakes, tidal waves and titanic villainy launched by Lex Luthor, played in sprightly comic-book fashion by Gene Hackman. He's also tempted by romance in the comely form of Lois Lane, whom Margot Kidder has made into a spunky, attractive heroine.

Asked to explain the popularity of the Superman character, producer Ilya Salkind says: "It's largely because of the spirit of the legend. Everybody wants to fly, everybody wants to feel free and totally on top of the world. In that sense, there's something of Superman in all of us." Audiences agree. It's a film to lift the spirits.

BOND IN BLUE TIGHTS?

Not only can the screen's Superman, Christopher Reeve, not get used to his new fame: he has yet, he says, to accustom himself to his new shape. Landing the role meant many hours in the gym building up his physique.

Reeve might seem an unlikely choice for this athletic all-American hero. His only previous film role has been a small part in the Charlton Heston submarine drama, *Gray Lady Down* (1976). But he had the fortitude to pit his ability against the redoubtable Katharine Hepburn on Broadway (in the Enid Bagnold play *A Matter of Gravity*), so he might not be as overawed as expected. When asked if he is intimidated by the prospect of working opposite the likes of Marlon Brando and Gene Hackman, he says: "Yes, but if the opportunity comes, what can you do? Either you decide to stay in the shallow end of the pool, playing with your toy sailboat, or you go out into the ocean." Wanting to stretch his wings as an actor, he feels the danger of typecasting is a greater problem. When reminded that Sean Connery made a good living out of 007, he replies: "Yes, but he didn't wear blue tights."

NO KIDDER

"I've had good parts in crummy movies up until now. Everyone keeps telling me this one is going to make me a star." So says 28-year-old Margot Kidder, who landed the key role of Superman's girlfriend, Lois Lane in this year's blockbuster *Superman*. She adds, however, "I still don't believe it."

Her caution is understandable for her career to date has developed in fits and starts. From her childhood days in Quebec she knew she wanted to be an actress, and she made her first impression in Norman Jewison's *Gaily, Gaily* (1969) about the early life of celebrated screenwriter Ben Hecht. She also gave a superb performance in Brian De Palma's disturbing thriller, *Blood Sisters* (1973), but marriage and maternity then intervened. Now she is committed to her career again, as feisty and ambitious as Lois Lane herself (perhaps why she landed the part). But stardom? "I'm not the star type," insists the brunette Canadian. "I think I'm a pretty good actress but sometimes I feel presentable and other times I feel like the biggest bag of potatoes on earth."

GOSSIP COLUMN

■ **After four years away from the screen sorting out his health, personal life and career, Steve McQueen is back, looking unrecognizable behind spectacles and beard. He plays the leading role in *An Enemy of the People*, an adaptation of a play by Norwegian dramatist Henrik ibsen about a doctor who runs into local opposition when he insists that the water supply of the local spa is contaminated. McQueen is also executive producer, so he obviously believes in it. Whether fans will believe *him* in it remains to be seen.**

WOODY'S SERIOUS STREAK

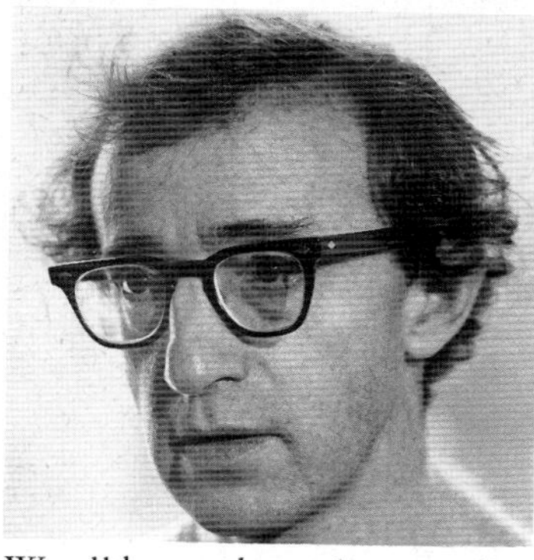

We all know about the comedian who wants to play Hamlet, but what about the comic who wants to direct Chekhov? Woody Allen's new film, *Interiors*, is like *Three Sisters*. There are no laughs and this time Allen isn't on screen: he confines himself to writing and directing.

There's a precedent for all this. One of Allen's great heroes, Charlie Chaplin, at the height of his comedy powers, suddenly made a serious film, *Woman of Paris* (1923). Like Chaplin, Allen is a natural performer so it is unlikely that he will be away from the screen for long. But it's an interesting development for the actor-writer-director, whose career, after the Oscar-winning success of *Annie Hall* earlier this year, seems to be entering a fascinating new phase.

Diane Keaton, Kristin Griffith and Mary Beth Hurt in Interiors.

NO PART LIKE HOLMES

The new Sherlock Holmes and Dr. Watson are Christopher Plummer and James Mason. The film is *Murder by Decree*, in which Holmes' deductive powers are tested to the full by the Jack the Ripper murders. Ten years ago, Billy Wilder tried to demystify the character by having Holmes (Robert Stephens) complain to Watson (Colin Blakely) about the "improbable costume" he has to wear, as well as grumble about Watson's exaggerated claims over Holmes's violin virtuosity and his drugs intake. The film was *The Private Life of Sherlock Holmes* (1969). We have since had a bizarre addition to Holmesiana in the form of *They Might Be Giants* (1971) with George C. Scott as an unhinged lawyer who thinks he may be Sherlock Holmes. But generally the myth resists debunking or updating, and *Murder by Decree* will be playing it straight.

STAR QUOTES

Meryl Streep

"I'm looking forward to bigger parts in the future, but I'm not doing soft-core scripts where the character emerges in half-light, half-dressed."

BIRTHS, DEATHS AND MARRIAGES

DEATHS

Dan Dailey
16 Oct, Los Angeles
Anemia

Gig Young
19 Oct, New York
Suicide

MARRIAGES

Meryl Streep
Sep, *to* Donald Gummer

WAR ROULETTE

The Deer Hunter, the latest feature film about Vietnam, has already been described as "amongst the most brilliant films ever made". It deals with the lives of steel-mill workers in Pennsylvania who go to fight in Vietnam and are shattered by the experience. Robert De Niro and Christopher Walker head the cast, and there's an important role too for up-and-coming actress Meryl Streep, who made a striking impression in her cameo in *Julia* (1977).

"It's not a political film," says writer-director Michael Cimino. "It's really about the resilience of the human spirit." But audiences are emerging shaken from the three-hour movie. Particularly disturbing are the scenes in Vietnam, where American soldiers are forced by their Vietnamese captors to play Russian roulette amongst each other. This takes America's gun obsession to its extreme. Cimino's only previous film as director was the Clint Eastwood starrer, *Thunderbolt and Lightfoot* (1974). With *The Deer Hunter*, he steps into the big league.

BOX OFFICE

UK

1. Star Wars
2. Grease
3. Close Encounters of the Third Kind
4. Saturday Night Fever
5. Revenge of the Pink Panther
6. The Rescuers
7. Abba the Movie
8. The Gauntlet
9. Herbie Goes to Monte Carlo
10. The Stud

BOX OFFICE

US

1. Grease
2. Close Encounters of the Third Kind
3. National Lampoon's Animal House
4. Jaws 2
5. Heaven Can Wait
6. The Goodbye Girl
7. Star Wars (*reissue*)
8. Hooper
9. Foul Play
10. Revenge of the Pink Panther

Henry Fonda and Katharine Hepburn *On Golden Pond* (1981).

Maurice Chevalier, Leslie Caron and Louis Jordan in *Gigi* (1958).

Jack Nicholson wins an award for *Terms of Endearment* (1983).

r O'Toole *in* The Last Emperor *(1987).*

UNCLE OSCAR

The Oscar is Hollywood's most glittering prize. It can put millions of dollars on a movie's box-office takings and on a star's earning power. It can also put years on a nominee's life as he or she waits for the envelope to be opened and the winner announced. "Oscar night," said Bob Hope, "is the night that war and politics are forgotten and we find out who we really hate."

The Oscar, or Academy Award, was a result of the formation of the Academy of Motion Picture Arts and Sciences in 1927. It was suggested that the Academy would gain increased prestige (and publicity) if every year awards were given for artistic and technical achievement. The first were handed out on 16 May 1929 in a modest ceremony. Over the years the award categories grew and so did interest in, and coverage of, the event.

The Oscar itself is a gold-plated statuette of a knight holding a crusader's sword and standing on a reel of film whose five spokes symbolise the original branches of the Academy (actors, directors, producers, technicians and writers). A secretary, Margaret Herrick, who later became an executive director of the Academy, said one day that the statuette "reminds me of my uncle Oscar."

The award ceremony has since become Hollywood's big night – sometimes of controversy. Marlon Brando sent a Red Indian to collect his Oscar for *The Godfather* (1972) in protest at Hollywood's treatment of the Indian on screen. George C. Scott publicly refused his nomination for *Patton* (1970) out of distaste for the ceremony itself (he still won, though). Other embarrassments have included Spencer Tracy collecting his Best Actor Oscar for *Captains Courageous* (1937), only to discover it was inscribed to "Dick Tracy"; or the moment when a delighted Frank Capra jumped up to collect a directing Oscar, to find that the presenter's cry, "Come and get it, Frank!" was meant not for him but for director Frank Lloyd for *Cavalcade* (1933).

Emotions can run high at such times. Disappointed at not winning the Best Director Oscar for *Double Indemnity* (1944), Billy Wilder stuck out a foot as Leo McCarey (for *Going My Way*) was heading for the stage and almost sent him flying.

Ben-Hur (1959) holds the record number of Oscars – 11. *West Side Story* (1961) won 10; *Gone with the Wind* (1939), *Gigi* (1958), and *The Last Emperor* (1987) each won nine. Katharine Hepburn has won more major acting Oscars than any other star, and was voted Best Actress for four films: *Morning Glory* (1934), *Guess Who's Coming to Dinner* (1967), *The Lion in Winter* (1968), and *On Golden Pond* (1981). Bette Davis, Louise Rainer, Olivia de Havilland, Ingrid Bergman and Sally Field have won Best Actress twice: Spencer Tracy, Fredric March, Gary Cooper and Dustin Hoffman have done the same as Best Actor.

Whether the Oscar reflects merit or commercial pressures is still a moot point. There have been some glaring omissions: Charles Chaplin and Greta Garbo never won an Oscar for their playing; Alfred Hitchcock and Orson Welles never won Best Director; and the "Best Ten" lists of critics and audiences rarely include many multi-Oscar winners.

In fact, the awards ceremony sometimes has more drama than the winning film. As Bob Hope drily remarked, when those famous words "And the winner is . . ." are heard, the best performances are always given by the losers.

Main picture: The Pantages Theater in Los Angeles hosts the 1959 Academy Awards presentations.

ey Maclaine wins Best Actress.

Gone with the Wind *(1939).*

MELTDOWN! MELTDOWN! MELTDOWN!

Reporter Jane Fonda and cameraman Michael Douglas investigate a nuclear plant in The China Syndrome.

They say it really could happen – and that's what makes Jane Fonda's new movie *The China Syndrome* so terrifying. It's a nuclear disaster story triggered off not by war but by an industrial accident. The "China syndrome" is what could happen if the core of a nuclear reactor melted down and the inferno could not be contained. Theoretically it could go on burning right through the Earth and come out the other side in China.

It's a perfect subject for this eager-beaver, trouble-stirring actress and to signal her faith in the project she has put it through her own production company, IPC Films. The tale is told not just as a thriller but as an ecological cover-up, unmasked through dogged investigative TV journalism. It's no surprise that Fonda takes the role of the crusading journo herself. A persistent and notorious anti-Vietnam War campaigner, she has a new cause to fight for now.

She is joined here by Jack Lemmon in one of his non-comic roles and by another famous offspring – Michael Douglas, son of Kirk. Lately he's been winning more kudos as a producer than as an actor. He co-produced *One Flew over the Cuckoo's Nest* in 1975, which won a slew of Oscars, including best film.

ACADEMY AWARDS

PRESENTED ON 9 APRIL 1979

Best Picture
The Deer Hunter

Best Director
Michael Cimino
The Deer Hunter

Best Actor
Jon Voight
Coming Home

Best Actress
Jane Fonda
Coming Home

Best Sup Actor
Christopher Walken
The Deer Hunter

Best Sup Actress
Maggie Smith
California Suite

GIDGET GOES POLITICAL

The daughter of former screen actress Margaret Field, Pasadena-born Sally Field broke into TV as a teenager in the title role of the series *Gidget* (1965), following it up with another popular role in *The Flying Nun* (1967). It wasn't until 1976 and *Stay Hungry* (she was 30) that her screen career began in earnest.

Not happy with her image she boned up on thesping at Lee Strasberg's Actors' Studio. Her combination of TV professionalism and solid technique equipped her to seize her chances when they finally came. A made-for-TV film *Sybil* in 1976 copped her an Emmy award as a schizophrenic with 16 personalities. Field's work caught the eye of director Martin Ritt, who rescued her from a foundering on-screen association with Burt Reynolds in movies like *Smokey and the Bandit* (1977) and *The End* (1978). He's now given her the role of a lifetime as the heroine of *Norma Rae*.

BLIND BIDDING WAR HOTS UP

Battle lines are being drawn between America's National Association of Theater Owners and the powerful Motion Picture Association of America (MPAA) on the subject of "blind bidding". This is the practice where exhibitors have to bid for an upcoming product sight unseen. Exhibitors hate it because sometimes they get burnt fingers when a would-be blockbuster bombs. Over the past few years the Theater Owners' Association has succeeded in pushing through anti-blind-bidding legislation in five southern states. Now Utah and West Virginia are set to follow suit, but MPAA boss Jack Valenti is unrepentant. He's going to the courts to try to upset the legislation.

FILLY ON THE PICKET LINE

Films about trade unions only set the box office alight if they also deal with corruption and crime, as in *On the Waterfront* (1954). *Norma Rae* isn't one of those. It's simply a very good drama about a Southern textile worker whose eyes open to the exploitation she daily undergoes. When she becomes active in union affairs she's fired, and she goes into battle to establish the workers' right to associate.

What gives the film a real lift is the spunky performance of Sally Field in the title role. It's the kind of showy, sympathetic part that often wins awards. And it's a natural subject for director Martin Ritt, whose films have always had a strong social conscience. His work goes back to the famous Group Theater of the 1930s and in the 1950s he was blacklisted during the McCarthy years – which he later made the subject of his film *The Front* (1978).

Ritt has once again worked with the husband-and-wife scriptwriting team Harriet Frank Jr and Irving Ravetch. They wrote his earlier *The Long Hot Summer* (1958), *The Sound and the Fury* (1959), *Hud* (1963), *Hombre* (1966) and *Conrack* (1974). In fact it's often been the writers who alerted Ritt to the potential in a subject. Says Ravetch: "We found all that material and brought it to Marty; we share those social concerns."

Sally Fields is Norma Rae.

Diane Keaton and Woody Allen in Allen's eulogy to his city – Manhattan.

HAVE A LITTLE FAITH IN PEOPLE

Woody Allen is right back on form with *Manhattan*, a bittersweet comedy that's his love letter to New York. Gleaming black-and-white 'scope photography (daring in these days of almost universal colour) and a soundtrack full of George Gershwin golden oldies make the Big Apple seem the ultimate romantic city – as big a "knockout" as it is to the director himself. It's a relief after the dead end of last year's *Interiors*, the maudlin non-comedy he made straight after his Oscar-winning *Annie Hall* (1977).

Allen has devised a touching little love story, played opposite Ernest Hemingway's granddaughter Mariel – a relationship whose future will hinge on whether he can, as she asks, "have a little faith in people." The last shot – a long, lingering, non-committal close-up of Allen's face pondering how to reply to that – winds the film up with the best open ending since Chaplin's *City Lights* (1931).

The tip-top cast includes Allen's ex-steady Diane Keaton, and striking newcomer Meryl Streep as his lesbian ex-wife. The comic one-liners are in the capable hands of Woody himself.

BIRTHS, DEATHS AND MARRIAGES

DEATHS

Jean Renoir
12 Feb, Beverly Hills
Heart ailment

Yvonne Mitchell
24 Mar, London
Cancer

THE NEBBISH TURNS

When 15-year-old Allen Stewart Konigsberg started sending jokes to newspaper columnists in 1950, he used the name Woody Allen. Earl Wilson liked his style and helped get him a job writing one-liners for comedians. This led to Allen becoming a stand-up comedian himself and ultimately, in 1965, actor and scriptwriter of the Peter O'Toole starrer *What's New Pussycat*.

By 1969 Woody was writing, directing and acting in his own movies, beginning with *Take the Money and Run*. His own part has always been the same – an undersized, whining, put-upon Jew. The fun of his films is the dreadful humiliations he goes through and his wry realisation that God somehow miscounted when numbering the Chosen People.

But there's an underlying seriousness to Woody too. He got the balance just right in *Annie Hall* (1977) and picked up a clutch of Oscars for it; then all wrong in last year's *Interiors*, a dark-night-of-the-soul movie that's like Ingmar Bergman having a bilious attack. But with *Manhattan* he's right back on form – a comedian who can be dead serious without losing his sense of humour.

STAR QUOTES

Sylvester Stallone

"People don't credit me with much of a brain, so why should I disillusion them?"

GOSSIP COLUMN

■ **Michael Cimino's *The Deer Hunter*, the runaway success in this year's Oscars, has run into a storm of controversy. Vietnam vets say the game of Russian roulette that provides the most dramatic scene was never played in 'Nam. What's more, Cimino claims poetic licence.**

THE HORROR, THE HORROR

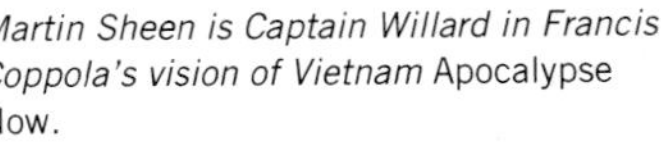
Martin Sheen is Captain Willard in Francis Coppola's vision of Vietnam Apocalypse Now.

SON OF SHANE GOES INDIE

Alan Ladd Jr, son of the actor Alan Ladd, best known for his performance as *Shane* (1953), is quitting 20th Century-Fox to strike out as an independent producer.

Under Ladd Jr Fox made some of its most successful recent films, including *Star Wars* and *The Turning Point* (both 1977). Part of his disgruntlement has to do with money – he feels he is entitled to more, much more. But it also reflects differences of management style between Ladd, who has been brought up in the informal approach of the West Coast, and Fox chairman Dennis Stanfill, a former investment banker for Lehman Brothers who hails from the East Coast. Versed in the more formal ways associated with New York investment banking, Stanfill has been getting in Ladd's hair by demanding written statements of his "management objectives."

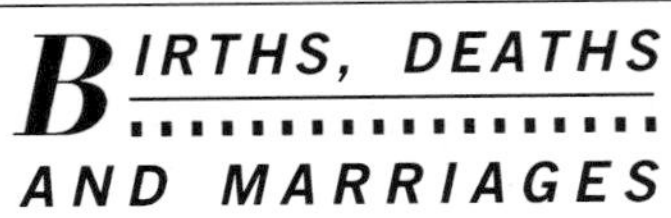

BIRTHS, DEATHS AND MARRIAGES

DEATHS

Mary Pickford
29 May, Santa Monica, California
Stroke

Jim Hutton
2 Jun, Los Angeles
Cancer

John Wayne
11 Jun, Los Angeles
Cancer

Michael Wilding
8 Jul, London
Complications following a fall

It came within an inch of bankrupting director Francis Coppola, but *Apocalypse Now*, the $31 million Vietnam war movie to end all Vietnam war movies, has turned out to be no white elephant. Wisely entering it at the Cannes festival as a "work in progress" (because there is still work to be done on it), Coppola shared the top prize with the German film *The Tin Drum*. It set the movie up as a work to be taken seriously by the art-house crowd and a dramatically engulfing entertainment to please wider audiences.

The bold venture was actually filmed in the Philippines from March 1976 to May 1977. The theme – a journey into the jungle in search of a soldier who has allegedly lost his mind – is from a story by Joseph Conrad, "Heart of Darkness" (which was also, incidentally, one of Orson Welles' early abortive projects). Coppola has also prepared a special 70mm version of the movie which is shorter and has no credit titles.

The star is Marlon Brando and his fee added one of the millions to the budget, even though he appears only in the last scenes. Now grossly bloated, he is seen only in shadow or in big close-up, but he still exudes true star quality. Martin Sheen, who has the biggest role as the soldier sent to execute him, is blown away as an actor, though not in the story, as soon as the two finally meet. Sheen suffered a heart attack during the latter stages of shooting but survived to fight another day, as do Brando and Coppola.

COSMIC HORRORS

"In space," goes the catchline, "no one can hear you scream." But at your neighbourhood movie theatre, when they're showing *Alien*, they can hear you a block away. Loosely based on the schlock quickie *It! The Terror from beyond Space* (1958), it's the scariest sci-fi picture ever. A bunch of astronauts, adrift in an unknown galaxy, become inadvertent hosts to an alien life form that hatches under the skin and bursts bloodily out of the abdomen. Rapidly evolving into a nightmare creature, it goes on the rampage and sets about devouring the crew one by one.

The creature, designed by H. R. Giger, master of the morbid and the sinister, is a vision out of hell. The direction, by Britain's Ridley Scott, who cut his teeth on advertisements (for Hovis bread, among other things) before his first feature *The Duellists* (1977), generates more thrills, tension and suspense than anything this side of Hitchcock. It was entirely shot at Pinewood Studios, near London. And the film marks the emergence of an impressive new actress, New York-born Sigourney Weaver. It's the first space movie in which the job of zapping the monster falls to a woman: she's the only one with gumption enough to know how to fight it. Feminists have mostly applauded, though they jibe at director Scott's "sexist" insistence on having her strip to her scanties before the final battle.

THE MOON IS DOWN

Actress Jill Clayburgh was born (in 1944) with a silver spoon in her mouth. Her parents were well-off socialites and sent her to Brearley School and Sarah Lawrence College for her top-drawer education. But she made it in movies by her own efforts.

While still at college she acted in summer stock and then signed on with a repertory company in Boston before graduating to off-Broadway productions in New York. In the early 1970s she appeared in Broadway musicals (*The Rothschilds* and *Pippin*) and then gravitated to the West coast, where her pixie charm graced a number of comedies, like *Portnoy's Complaint* (1972). The breakthrough came in 1976, when she had a critical success as Carole Lombard in *Gable and Lombard*.

It set up her career for her finest role to date: in last year's *An Unmarried Woman* she scooped the top acting prize at the Cannes film festival and got an Oscar nomination (she lost to Jane Fonda in *Coming Home*).

It certainly caught the eye of flamboyant Italian director Bernardo Bertolucci, who cast her spectacularly against type in his new film *La Luna* as an operatic diva engaged in a near-incestuous relationship with her son. For Clayburgh it looks like a watershed role – one that will make or break her.

A SLY ONE, THAT ROCKY

In the ring *Rocky* looks 10 feet tall; in real life actor Sylvester Stallone is only 5ft 7 in. Born in New York in 1946, he cooked pizzas and swept zoo cages on his way to a career in movies. His first, forgotten movie was *Party at Kitty and Studs* (1970) and in the early 1970s he did walk-ons in a variety of films, including Woody Allen's *Bananas* (1971) as a mugger.

His heavy-lidded, mouthful-of-tomatoes acting style made him perfect casting as a thug or hoodlum. Roger Corman used him several times in that way, as did Paul Bartel in *Death Race 2000* (1975) as Machine Gun Joe Vitebo.

Unexpectedly, however, Stallone could write. He hawked his boxing script *Rocky* all round Hollywood without much success until he at last persuaded United Artists to give it, and him, a whirl. The rest is history. *Rocky* (1976) took the Oscar, with audiences warming to the lunkhead with a kind of urban poetry all his own. But Stallone's ambitions did not stop there. He wanted to run the whole show, picking up the director's megaphone for the first time in the less than successful *Paradise Alley* (1978) and now going for the treble (writer, director and actor) in *Rocky II*.

TOMORROW DOWN UNDER

Australian cinema finally hits the big time with *Mad Max*, a post-nuclear sci-fi extravaganza that bids fair to define a new genre – punk trash. The Bomb's gone off, the world is destroyed and mad bikers rule the world, hotly pursued by the vestiges of law and order. It's a sci-fi movie that has no need of expensive hardware or special effects and that makes a virtue of its own minuscule budget. It kids the world that its lunar landscape cost a lot to deliver.

Mad Max himself is played by Mel Gibson, as handsome and promising an Oz actor as any since the young Errol Flynn. Like the rest of the cast, he's been dubbed into American for the movie's release outside Australia. The director is an antipodean doctor named George Miller who always hankered after a career in the movies and in fact began with a cod horror film, made at his own expense, called *Sex and Violence in the Cinema Part II*.

Just to confuse matters, there is another Australian director called George Miller. As Dr. Miller's *Mad Max* movie is starting its worldwide career, his namesake is putting together a Down Under western called *The Man from Snowy River*, to star the American veteran Kirk Douglas. This has all the makings of a smash in Australian terms, but on a world view it's Dr. Miller who looks the stronger bet.

Mel Gibson is the Road Warrior in Mad Max.

Lee Remick and Wesley Addy in the Merchant-Ivory film The Europeans.

FROM KEWPIE DOLL TO HENRY JAMES

Lee Remick's Eugenia in the current version of Henry James's *The Europeans* is making audiences look again at her as an actress. The flirtatiousness is familiar; it's her effortless projection of social superiority that's raising eyebrows. She really does make James's New Englanders look and feel like country bumpkins.

Remick's screen career was associated from the start with naked ambition and sexual rapacity. Her first bit part, in Elia Kazan's *A Face in the Crowd* (1975), was as a drum majorette, as a result of which she was typecast in such roles in many of her early films – *The Long Hot Summer* (1958), *Anatomy of a Murder* (1959) and *Sanctuary* (1961). She was the sex kitten who would not only claw your back but pluck your eyes out, given a chance.

But there was always a more mature actress waiting to pop out. There was a hint of it in *Days of Wine and Roses* (1962) in which she was Oscar-nominated for her performance as an alcoholic. But it's *The Europeans* that finally shows what she has in her. For this Boston-born actress, 44 years old this year, it's like a long-awaited homecoming.

THORN BIDS FOR EMI

Britain's giant electricals and TV rental group, Thorn International, has made a £169 million bid for EMI, the records-to-cinemas conglomerate that is one of the country's last surviving movie majors. It owns the former Associated British Pictures chain and effectively shares the U.K. exhibition market with Rank. It also makes movies, and last year scored a notable success with the Oscar-winning *The Deer Hunter*.

EMI's leisure interests were the only division last year to show increased profits, losses of £20 million having been sustained over the past two years in the body-scanner division. Thorn's original all-share offer was turned down as inadequate at £147 million, but the increased terms, which have now been agreed, include a cash sweetener.

BIRTHS, DEATHS AND MARRIAGES

DEATHS

Felix Aylmer
2 Sep, Sussex

Jean Seberg
8 Sep, Paris
Barbiturate overdose

Gracie Fields
27 Sep, Capri
Pneumonia

Merle Oberon
23 Nov, Malibu, California
Stroke

Joan Blondell
25 Nov, Santa Monica, California
Leukemia

TUG OF LOVE

Little movies, if they have strong enough casts, can sometimes knock big ones into a cocked hat – which is why Columbia is rushing out *Kramer vs Kramer* just before the year end to qualify for the Oscars and compete with the heavyweight candidate, *Apocalypse Now*. *Kramer* is a simple story of a marital crack-up and the battle between the parents for custody of their child.

Dustin Hoffman has been waiting for more than a decade for a role as good as his first in *The Graduate* (1967), and he gets it here. The movie also has a marvellous supporting part for the fast-rising Meryl Streep as Hoffman's ex-wife. Both are likely to be in line for Oscars next spring, along with young Justin Henry as the little boy who is the object of their embattled affections.

Director Robert Benton isn't too well known among moviegoers. He has a western (*Bad Company*, 1972) and a quirky thriller (*The Late Show*, 1977) to his credit, but his real talent is for writing. He had a hand in the scripts for *Bonnie and Clyde* (1967) and *Superman* (1978), and it's his way with words that gives his top-notch cast the bricks to build with.

Dustin Hoffman and Justin Henry in the tug-of-love weepie Kramer vs Kramer.

PIMPS AND SHARKS AND ALL THAT JAZZ

Roy Scheider is a contradiction in terms – a star without star quality. On screen he registers as a competent technician, a man born to play sidekicks. You believe in him as the earnest sheriff in *Jaws* (1975) and as Gene Hackman's partner in *The French Connection* (1971) because, with his craggy looks and air of solid dependability, he gives the impression of playing from life. He's a man, you feel, to whom things should be delegated, not a man to do the delegating. A broken nose, acquired in boxing bouts as a boy, reinforces the image.

He's equally at home playing seedy crooks, like Jane Fonda's pimp in *Klute* (1971), and slightly shifty individuals, like Dustin Hoffman's brother in *Marathon Man* (1976). But his background is wider than this. Born in 1935, he's played Mercutio on stage in *Romeo and Juliet* and many classic roles in repertory.

Now comes one unlike any other – effectively playing the director himself in Bob Fosse's autobiographical *All That Jazz*. The grey man in Hackman's shadow is now a prancing dynamo of a choreographer, erupting all over the screen and the Broadway stage. Is this the new Scheider bursting at last out of his shell, or a flash in the pan?

BOX OFFICE

UK

1. Moonraker
2. Superman
3. Jaws 2
4. Every Which Way But Loose
5. Alien
6. Watership Down
7. The Deer Hunter
8. Grease
9. Quadrophenia
10. Pete's Dragon

BOX OFFICE

US

1. Superman
2. Every Which Way But Loose
3. Rocky II
4. Alien
5. The Amityville Horror
6. Star Trek
7. Moonraker
8. The Muppet Movie
9. California Suite
10. The Deer Hunter

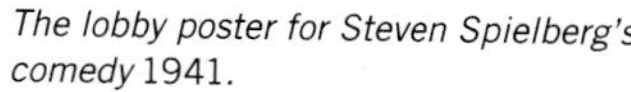
The lobby poster for Steven Spielberg's comedy 1941.

BOMBS AWAY

Wonderkid Steven Spielberg looks as if he's slipped on a banana skin in the wartime comedy *1941*. Like Stanley Kramer's *It's a Mad Mad Mad Mad World* (1963), it stars everybody who is anybody but leaves them mostly flailing for laughs. The story of the panic that hit Los Angeles in the wake of Pearl Harbor, when one stray Japanese submarine was thought to be the spearhead of a full-scale invasion, Spielberg's movie is an orgy of destruction. It's paid the penalty at the box office with nowhere near enough tickets sold so far to recover the $27 million that it cost to make.

Stars include Dan Aykroyd, Ned Beatty, Nancy Allen, Robert Stack, Christopher (Dracula) Lee and even Tokyo's Toshiro Mifune, hero of a million samurai sagas, as the Japanese captain. John Belushi's racist bomber pilot introduces a touch of vinegar to Robert Zemeckis's script. *1941* is the kind of folly that Spielberg, with two smash hits behind him (*Jaws* in 1975 and *Close Encounters of the Third Kind* in 1977), probably needed to make.

BEGELMAN BOUNCES BACK

You can't keep a good executive down. David Begelman is taking over as day-to-day boss of the film activities of M-G-M after a legal wrangle that would have sunk a lesser man. Formerly top gun at Columbia, Begelman was exposed by the actor Cliff Robertson in unorthodox financial transactions and eventually pleaded *nolo contendere* (that's to say, he wouldn't contest the charge) to the theft of $40,000 of company money, having forged cheques to that amount and cashed them to his own benefit. Begelman was fined $5,000, placed on three years' probation.

BEAM THEM UP, SCOTTY

It's taken Hollywood 13 years to get round to making a film of the most popular sci-fi TV series of all – *Star Trek*, which first went out on NBC in 1966. All the original cast, William Shatner, Leonard Nimoy, DeForest Kelley, Nichelle Nichols, George Takei et al, repeat their roles as the crew of the USS *Enterprise*.

Direction is in the capable hands of Robert Wise, who began as Orson Welles' editor on *Citizen Kane* (1941) and *The Magnificent Ambersons* (1942) and moved up through B pictures to become a Jack of many trades, including science fiction (*The Day the Earth Stood Still* in 1951 and *The Andromeda Strain* in 1970).

At the same time, Walt Disney has ventured into the sci-fi field with its most expensive picture to date – *The Black Hole*, costing $20 million, against *Star Trek's* $42 million. The actors, including Maximilian Schell, Anthony Perkins and Ernest Borgnine, come off a poor second to the robots. The cutest, in typical Disney fashion, is a saucer-eyed, anthropomorphized tin-can called Vincent (clearly modelled on R2-D2 from *Star Wars*), while the villain, a towering, visored humanoid called Maximilian, is based on designs for the Devil in Disney's 1940 movie *Fantasia*.

Where *The Black Hole* follows the all-action, comic-strip path of *Star Wars*, with laser guns blazing in stereo sound, *Star Trek – The Motion Picture* gets metaphysical towards the end, with an intergalactic union of human and alien (disguised in the shapely, shaven form of actress Persis Khambatta). Early box-office returns suggest there's room for both.

STAR QUOTES

Dustin Hoffman

"A good review from a critic is just another stay of execution."

THE NAME OF THE ROSE IS BETTE

Roll over Mae West, here comes the raunchiest, crudest comedienne since you hung up your corset. Her name is Bette Midler (named after Bette Davis, her mother's and in due course her own favourite actress). And don't you dare pronounce it Betty!

The Rose, in which she plays a spaced-out rock singer loosely based on Janis Joplin, launches her as a star. But she first had a bit part way back in *Hawaii* (1966). A native-born Hawaiian herself, she was "the only Jewish girl in an otherwise Samoan neighbourhood."

The money she earned on *Hawaii* took her to New York, where she performed around the coffee houses of Greenwich Village in the 1960s, singing loud songs, cracking lewd jokes and generally bringing the house down. She had guest spots on the "Johnny Carson Show", cut sought-after discs and did a $3 million cross-country tour before winding up with a one-woman show on Broadway that sold a record $160,000 worth of advance tickets in a single day. Her next show, *Clams on the Half Shell Review*, beat that with $200,000 and eventually ran for 10 weeks netting $1.8 million.

Her records have won Grammy awards and now she's taking Tinseltown by storm. What makes her tick? "I just try to have a good time", she says, "and let the audience in on the secret. It's like giving a party and I am the Grande Hostess."

JANUARY
FEBRUARY

1980

MARCH
APRIL

MOVING INTO TOP GERE

Richard Gere as a gigolo and Lauren Hutton in the stylish American Gigolo.

A TOUCH OF THE BRESSONS

If *American Gigolo* feels a tad different from most other Hollywood movies that's because the man who made it, Paul Schrader, is an intellectual who thinks more in art-house terms than of what will play in neighbourhood theatres. A Calvinist by upbringing, he was never allowed to see movies when young, so when he reached the age of reason, cinema burst over him like a tidal wave. In fact, he wrote a book about the movies he liked best – those of the Japanese Yasujiro Ozu, the Dane Carl Dreyer and the Frenchman Robert Bresson. He called it *Transcendental Style*.

All three are spiritual directors and when Schrader came to make his own movies, that was the line he followed. *American Gigolo*, starring Richard Gere as the nearest thing to a male prostitute and Lauren Hutton as the woman who redeems him, is like a remake of Bresson's *Pickpocket* (1959).

Schrader, who also wrote the script of *Taxi Driver*, describes Julian, the Richard Gere part in *American Gigolo*, as "an intellectual, the opposite of the taxi driver. Among other things, Julian doesn't explode, he implodes." Gere sees him in more practical terms than Schrader: "He's more of a companion, trading his company for objects. And he's always improving himself. Julian's one frustration is that he never had the blue blood of the people he runs with. But you root for Julian. At least I do."

In *American Gigolo* Richard Gere finds his best role to date, one that fully exploits the narcissistic quality that has sometime marred his work in the past. Born in 1949, he has had a distinguished theatrical career before making it in Hollywood. He made his stage debut in 1971 in the rock opera *Soon* and played the John Travolta part in both the Broadway and London productions of *Grease*. While in England he also played Christopher Sly in the Young Vic production of *The Taming of the Shrew*. A handsome, manly figure, he took the boldest step of his career by starring in the homosexual play *Bent*. His screen debut was in 1975 (*Report to the Commissioner*) and his early roles all drew on his physique and good looks – in films like *Looking for Mr Goodbar* (1977), *Days of Heaven* (1978) and *Yanks* (1979).

Says Gere, who keeps his off-screen life fiercely private: "Each character I've played came from me – and returns to me. Yes, they're all Richard Gere; they couldn't be anyone else. And the root character of Richard Gere also changes in the process. Of course, there are similarities, core-wise and drive-wise, between some of the characters I play. That's probably why I've ended up playing them."

ACADEMY AWARDS

PRESENTED ON 14 APRIL 1980

Best Picture
Kramer vs. Kramer

Best Director
Robert Benton
Kramer vs. Kramer

Best Actor
Dustin Hoffman
Kramer vs. Kramer

Best Actress
Sally Field
Norma Rae

Best Sup Actor
Melvyn Douglas
Being There

Best Sup Actress
Meryl Streep
Kramer vs. Kramer

HITCH DEAD

Alfred Hitchcock is dead. The Leytonstone lad who became the undisputed master of cinematic suspense called it a wrap on 29 April 1980, aged 79. Only a few months before he had received a knighthood.

Hitch, along with Charlie Chaplin, was one of Britain's greatest gifts to Hollywood. A distinguished pre-war career in London, which included classics like *The Lady Vanishes* (1938), was followed by an even more illustrious one in America, resulting in movies like *Strangers on a Train* (1951), *Psycho* (1960) and his last work, *Family Plot* (1976). His signature was a bit part, usually just a fleeting glimpse, in all his films. It helped to make him, with his portly frame, as instantly recognizable as the stars who played for him.

BIRTHS, DEATHS AND MARRIAGES

DEATHS

Alfred Hitchcock
29 Apr, Bel Air, California
Heart attack

MARRIAGES

Dustin Hoffman
Jan, *to* Lisa Gottsegen

STAR QUOTES

Alfred Hitchcock

"The length of the film should be directly related to the endurance of the human bladder."

Sissy Spacek as a Kentucky hillbilly who becomes a country and western star in Coal Miner's Daughter.

QUEEN OF COUNTRY MUSIC

Plain Sissy Spacek doesn't look much like country-and-western singer Loretta Lynn in *Coal Miner's Daughter*, but she comes uncannily close to copying the famous glottal catch that made Lynn's voice so memorable. Now 46, Lynn was born to a mountain miner in Butcher's Hollow, Kentucky and grew up in the Appalachians. Married at 13, she had her first child at 14 and by 18 she had three more – a tally that eventually grew to six.

The film cuts a straight path through her life and career, which really began when she started singing and travelling at the age of 26. A feature of her life is that she stayed married, through thick and thin, to the same Doolittle Lynn who made her his bride when she was barely into her teens.

Lynn's career took off when she started appearing on the Grand Ole Opry radio show, and British director Michael Apted skilfully captures the mood of those days. Was it difficult for a British filmmaker to enter into the spirit of rural America? Apparently not. "Appalachia," he says surprisingly, "is not so very different from the north of England. I spent seven years in Manchester working for Granada TV, and after that anything is possible." Perhaps so, though it is hard to imagine that for a Mancunian, too, there were only three things to do – "coal-mine, moonshine, or move on down the line."

THE LADY CARRIES A NOTE

After being around in movies for 10 years, beginning as an extra in *Trash* (1980), homely-looking Sissy Spacek hits a high note in *Coal Miner's Daughter*, the biopic of country-and-western singer Loretta Lynn. What's more, she sings all the songs herself – a legacy of her early years in New York in the 1960s as a budding rock singer, though she didn't get much beyond commercials.

A Texan, born in 1949, she laid a firm foundation for her career by enrolling at New York's Actors' Studio, where she studied under Lee Strasberg for eight months. In 1974 she married art director Jack Fisk, with whom she had worked on *Phantom of the Paradise*.

Spacek specializes in childlike roles, creatures with the body of a woman but the mind of a teenager. One of her best parts was in *Badlands* (1973) as the amoral child-bride Holly Sargis who, with her lover, drove across country killing at random. The horror was doubly disturbing because it looked as if butter wouldn't melt in her mouth. She has had a facility for working with gifted, sympathetic directors, like Robert Altman in *Three Women* (1977), Terrence Malick in *Badlands* and now Michael Apted in *Coal Miner's Daughter*. What's been missing till now is a personality of her own. Will the infant in Sissy Spacek grow up in the 1980s?

LANSING CALLS THE SHOTS

20th Century-Fox has broken with precedent and appointed a woman as head of production. Sherry Lansing is the first woman in Hollywood history to have the right of yea or nay over what films get made.

Lansing was a not-too-successful actress in her early days. She had a tiny role in Howard Hawks' last movie, *Rio Lobo* (1970). Though pretty enough, she left something to be desired in the acting stakes, so switched to management in mid-career. From M-G-M she moved to Columbia as production vice-president, which she was told was "almost Camelot", but made the leap to Fox at the invitation of her former boss, Alan Hirschfield, when he moved into the top slot left vacant by the departure of Alan Ladd, Jr as head of Fox's motion picture unit.

Theresa Russell and Art Garfunkel in Nicolas Roeg's Bad Timing.

ROEG ELEPHANT?

Cameraman-turned-director Nicolas Roeg pushes his fans' patience to the limits in his new film *Bad Timing*, an arty study of time and sexuality that includes, among other things, a rape scene involving a "dying" woman. It's not clear from the movie whether the rapist thinks she is already dead and that he is having relations with a corpse.

Roeg has been a distinguished cameraman, with a career stretching back to 1950, when he was clapper boy at the age of 22 on *The Miniver Story*. Among other films, he was responsible for the striking appearance of works like *The Masque of the Red Death* (1964), *Fahrenheit 451* (1966) and *Far from the Madding Crowd* (1967). He began as a director with *Performance* (1970), sharing the credit with Donald Cammell, and has since made *Walkabout* (1971) and the spooky *Don't Look Now* (1973). Some hail him as the white hope of British cinema.

So far he seems able to attract interesting casts. *Bad Timing* features Art Garfunkel in an unsympathetic dramatic role, Harvey Keitel and the voluptuous Theresa Russell, Roeg's wife.

MAY
JUNE

JULY
AUGUST

GONG WITH THE WIND

The Rank Organisation, one of Britain's last two surviving film conglomerates, has called a halt to film production. In future it's going to stick to distribution and exhibition. This means that "the man with the gong", the symbol of Rank films, can hang up his trunks.

Rank used to be known as the J. Arthur Rank group, after the flour miller who formed the company. He tried after the war to take on Hollywood and spent a fortune on what he hoped would be films of international appeal and on developing home-grown stars. These graduated through Rank's famous Charm School, but someone overlooked the fact that, for Americans, English-English was virtually a foreign language. Many of its films had to be dubbed for the U.S. market, giving them a phony art-house appeal.

Only once, with Laurence Olivier's *Hamlet* (1948), did Rank take the American market and the Oscars by storm. The rest was mid-Atlantic pap that pleased nobody. Calling quits is like a kindly vet putting an injured cur out of its misery.

BIRTHS, DEATHS AND MARRIAGES

DEATHS

Peter Sellers
24 Jul, London
Heart attack

FORCEFUL RETURN

The robots C3PO and R2D2 from the Star Wars *trilogy.*

Star Wars (1977) is the most profitable film ever made, with returns of $193 million on what's said to be less than $12 million investment. But its sequel, *The Empire Strikes Back*, has a tougher time ahead: the budget has ballooned to $32 million.

It was shot at Britain's Elstree Studios and on location in Finse, Norway, but the real work was done later at Industrial Light & Magic in California, producer George Lucas's state-of-the-art special effects factory. A special camera, called the Empireflex, was built to facilitate computer-assisted camera movements.

Star Wars director Lucas has again provided the script for the sequel but this time is only executive producer. The directorial reins are handled by Irvin Kershner whose most recent film was *Eyes of Laura Mars* (1978). He's had a long career stretching back to *Stakeout on Dope Street* (1958) but until now has never quite fulfilled his early promise.

The Empire Strikes Back resurrects all the old favourites from *Star Wars* except Peter Cushing and Alec Guinness, (though Guinness appears as a ghostly presence). It also introduces some new ones, like Han Solo's old sparring partner Lando Calrissian (played by black actor Billy Dee Williams) and a bat-eared Peter Lorre lookalike called Yoda, whose voice and "mechanical workings" are supplied by the talented Frank Oz.

HOLLYWOOD SHUTS DOWN AS ACTORS STRIKE

Hollywood has come to a standstill. The Screen Actors' Guild has called all its members out on strike in support of a 35 per cent pay claim (lowered from an initial 40 per cent), which the actors want paid in full in the first year of a new three-year contract. The producers are offering only 12 per cent in the first year, followed by 8 per cent in each of the next two. The actors also want to participate in residual money earned when the films reach the Pay-TV and video markets.

Barbra Streisand's new $14 million movie *All Night Long* has been hardest hit by the strike: it had only three days left to shoot. Thousands of studio employees have also been laid off, the stoppage is reckoned to be costing the industry $40 million a week.

SHIPPING WATER

Lord Grade's hope of turning his British film empire into a rival to the Hollywood majors is sinking fast. It's been holed below the water line by the disastrous overspending on *Raise the Titanic*, which eventually cost $36 million. Part of the trouble lay in building a giant model of the famous ship before enquiring whether there was a tank in existence large enough to float it. There wasn't, so one had to be built at vast expense.

Now that it's in release, few want to see the film. The sinking of the ship was a dramatic event that could have been spun out for some time; but raising it takes about 10 seconds and is about as exciting as playing in your bath.

STAR QUOTES

Lord Grade

"Raise the Titanic? It would have been cheaper to lower the Atlantic."

JACK THE CHOPPER

Five years after *Barry Lyndon* Stanley Kubrick has surfaced again with his most unusual film to date – an adaptation of the Stephen King horror novel *The Shining*. The story of a writer who takes a winter job as caretaker at a hotel in the mountains, it charts his gradual descent into madness under the influence of the spirits that still inhabit the premises.

Kubrick shot it at the Timberline Lodge, near Mount Hood in Oregon, and set the action in the non-existent Room 237, rather than the novel's Room 217. The hotel's management asked him to change it in case future guests refused to stay in it.

The film makes extensive use of the Steadicam camera, which allows smooth tracking shots with hand-held equipment. Says Kubrick: "The only trouble with the Steadicam is that it requires training, skill and a certain amount of fitness. You can't just pick it up and use it. I used Garrett Brown as the Steadicam operator. He has more experience than anyone with the Steadicam because he also happened to invent it."

Topping the cast are Jack Nicholson and Shelley Duvall. The role of the little boy, Jack Nicholson's son in the movie, is taken by a talented child of 5½, Danny Lloyd, son of a railway engineer from a small town in Illinois. The janitor who befriends him is played by Scatman Crothers, a celebrated black actor brought out of retirement for the occasion.

UNLUCKY FOR SOME

Horror movies don't come much gorier than *Friday the 13th*, an unabashed exploitation flick that is doing better business than the $18 million shocker *The Shining*, with which it is currently competing. Murder by axe, arrow, spear and butcher's knife are just a few of the bloodier means of execution by the maniac who is stalking the Camp Crystal Lake holiday resort. It seems that 20 years ago a child drowned there and every time anybody attempts to reopen the camp, a fresh epidemic of murders breaks out.

Friday the 13th was made on a shoe-string by director Sean Cunningham. Other than Betsy Palmer, a now largely forgotten actress from the 1950s, who appeared in movies like *The Tin Star* (1957), its cast is mostly young unknowns. This helps suspense because audiences cannot tell who are the stars and who, therefore, cannot wind up dead. In fact what looks like the heroine is one of the first victims (Cunningham has obviously taken a leaf out of *Psycho*).

The death of the killer at the end of the film would seem to rule out a sequel, but doubtless Hollywood can get round that little problem.

Scenes from Stanley Kubrick's The Shining. *Left: A menacing Jack Nicholson. Below: A terrorized Shelley Duvall.*

POPEYE'S GIRL

Tall, buck-toothed, gangling Shelley Duvall was born to play Olive Oyl, so mentor Robert Altman was typecasting when he picked her for the part in *Popeye* (1980). It's her seventh role for Altman, who discovered her in 1970 on location in Houston for *Brewster McCloud* and gave her a small part as an astrodome tour guide. A lawyer's daughter, she had no training as an actress, but it gave her a down-home naturalness in parts like Keechie in *Thieves Like Us* (1974).

For *Three Women* (1977) Altman encouraged her to write much of her own script and she researched it by reading dozens of popular magazines. It paid off with a Best Actress award at Cannes. Now she has her biggest part to date as Jack Nicholson's menaced and terrified wife in *The Shining*, one of the few films she has made for another director (Stanley Kubrick). In it she reveals new dramatic range. For TV she's also moving into production, with a series of Faerie Tale Theatre plays in which she'll also play occasional parts.

SEPTEMBER
OCTOBER

1980

NOVEMBER
DECEMBER

THE QUIET AMERICAN

Robert De Niro as Jake La Motta in Martin Scorsese's boxing study Raging Bull.

SCORSESE GOES THE DISTANCE

Picking up a tradition that died out in the late 1940s, director Martin Scorsese has turned the career of middleweight champion Jake La Motta into the most dynamic boxing film ever in *Raging Bull. Body and Soul* (1947), *Champion* and *The Set-Up* (both 1949) set standards of ringside realism that lasted for a generation, but none of them has the percussive impact of fist on flesh that makes Scorsese's film such a scorching experience. The sound effects were done by Frank Warner and are an art in themselves. He used the sound of rifle shots and melons breaking to give the effect of punches.

Robert De Niro is titanic in the main part. At the end he appears as La Motta was in later years, bloated and earning a living as a nightclub entertainer. In the interests of realism De Niro wolfed down pasta to add 55lb to his weight. Interestingly, the speech he's rehearsing in this sequence is the famous taxi scene in *On the Waterfront* (1954), in which Marlon Brando laments the end of his own boxing career.

Scorsese shot *Raging Bull* in black-and-white, except for some inserted home-movie shots in colour, because he's been campaigning against the rapid fading of modern colour stock. It's his way of ensuring that future audiences will be able to see his film as he shot it, and not through a puce haze.

Despite appearances in *Raging Bull*, Robert De Niro is a master of minimalisation. In *The Deer Hunter* (1978) he seemed to get rid of acting altogether and just gaze at the camera. Is there anything going on up top? His critics say there isn't: this is the real De Niro – as vacant and uncommunicative as he often seems in interviews.

But this is plainly an injustice. In the right context he can give quite different, dynamic performances. Most of them seem to be for Martin Scorsese, a director with whom he clearly has a fruitful relationship. They first worked together on *Mean Streets* (1973) and have since chalked up *Taxi Driver* (1976), *New York, New York* (1977) and *Raging Bull*, now doing the rounds.

GOSSIP COLUMN

■ What price realism? The cost is starting to emerge of actor Robert De Niro's quest for the ultimate in conviction. In *Raging Bull*, he ends the film as an obese caricature of the boxing champion Jake La Motta. De Niro's insistence on gaining 55lb instead of relying on prosthetics forced the production to shut down for four months while he ate his way round Northern Italy and France.

BOX OFFICE

UK

1 The Empire Strikes Back
2 Kramer vs. Kramer
3 Star Trek – The Motion Picture
4 Monty Python's Life of Brian
5 Airplane!
6 "10"
7 Escape from Alcatraz
8 The Black Hole
9 The Shining
10 Apocalypse Now

BOX OFFICE

US

1 The Empire Strikes Back
2 Kramer vs. Kramer
3 The Jerk
4 Airplane!
5 Smokey and the Bandit II
6 The Coal Miner's Daughter
7 Private Benjamin
8 The Blues Brothers
9 The Electric Horseman
10 The Shining

LAST OF THE BIG SPENDERS

Heaven's Gate is the first film by writer-director Michael Cimino since his Oscar-winning *The Deer Hunter* (1978). And it's turned into the biggest fiasco in Hollywood's history. Budgeted at $11.6 million, it wound up costing $36 million, thanks to Cimino's obsession with detail and accuracy ("If you don't get it right, what's the point?" he says). Based on the same cattlemen vs. homesteaders conflict that's in *Shane* (1953), the movie just wouldn't stop growing. At 219 minutes it's only a minute shorter than *Gone with the Wind*.

United Artists thought about stiffing the project several times along the way. But it was in so deep that it saw no alternative but to press on whatever the cost.

The critics hate it. When it opened this November the influential *New York Times* dismissed it as "something quite rare in movies these days – an unqualified disaster". Now, in a blue funk, United Artists and Cimino have withdrawn it after only a few days, promising to do more work on it – including reducing it to a manageable length. But that means throwing more money at it.

Mary Tyler Moore and Timothy Hutton attempt reconciliation in Ordinary People, Robert Redford's debut as a director.

REDFORD CALLS THE SHOTS

Ordinary People is just what you'd expect from Robert Redford in his first stint behind a camera. It's honest, unflashy and aimed at the same audience that responded to the commonplace qualities of last year's *Kramer vs Kramer*. Just like its title, in fact.

Redford found the story as an unpublished first novel by Minneapolis housewife Judith Guest, though the movie's success suggests it won't be long out of the bookshops. It's about mental disturbance within the home and touches on similar ground to Ken Loach's British art-house movie *Family Life* (1971). But where Loach's approach is Marxist and angry, Redford's is liberal and humane.

Redford's casting is unconventional but spot on. He has leaned on TV personalities rather than Hollywood types. Perhaps this makes them seem more homely – the kind of faces audiences are used to seeing regularly about the house. So Mary Tyler Moore plays the mother and Judd Hirsch, star of the long-running *Taxi* series, is a psychiatrist. Donald Sutherland is also well cast as the father, but the standout performance is by young Timothy Hutton as the disturbed son. He's the son of the late Jim Hutton, who played comedy and action roles in minor pictures in the 1960s and died last year at the age of only 45.

TEN-WEEK STRIKE COSTS HOLLYWOOD $400 MILLION

The actors' strike which left Hollywood like a ghost town for 10 weeks finally ended in September with a deal giving the actors an extra 15 per cent in each of the two 18-month halves of a new three-year contract. The actors had wanted 35 per cent, all to be paid from the start of the contract.

The overall cost to the industry in terms of work lost during the stoppage is being put at some $400 million. Barry Diller, Paramount's chairman, calls the strike: "A demarcation point. We all have to recognize that we cannot continue escalating our costs without a commensurate increase in revenues and survive as a healthy industry."

STAR QUOTES

Robert Redford

"All my life I've been dogged by guilt because I feel there is this difference between the way I look and the way I feel inside."

BIRTHS, DEATHS AND MARRIAGES

DEATHS

Steve McQueen
7 Nov, Juarez, Mexico
Cancer

Mae West
22 Nov, Los Angeles

George Raft
24 Nov, New York
Leukemia

Rachel Roberts
26 Nov, Bel Air, California
Barbiturate overdose

Raoul Walsh
31 Dec, Simi Valley, California
Heart attack

MARRIAGES

Malcolm MacDowell
Oct, *to* **Mary Steenburgen**

THE GIPPER IS THE GAFFER

America has overwhelmingly voted Ronald Reagan as its next president – the first actor ever to rise to the highest office. Born in 1911, Reagan was never more than an also-ran on the big screen in the 1940s, but he's been active in politics since being president of the Screen Actors' Guild from 1947 to 1952. Initially a liberal, he moved towards the right in the 1960s, backing the ill-starred Goldwater-for-president campaign and then becoming a conservative governor of California himself. As prospective presidential candidate, he lost out to Gerald Ford in the Republican primaries in 1976, but managed the winning combination in 1980. Let's hope he doesn't write his own scripts in the White House.

John Hurt as the hideously deformed John Merrick in David Lynch's The Elephant Man.

BORN TO PLAY THE AFFLICTED

Early attempts to turn John Hurt into a rollicking, swashbuckling hero in films like *Sinful Davey* (1968) were a disaster. The wan, 28-year-old British actor looked like he'd blow over in a mild breeze. But since then he's found his mark and stuck to it. He played a mental defective, Timothy Evans, in *10 Rillington Place* (1971), homosexual writer Quentin Crisp in *The Naked Civil Servant* (1975), also for television, the spaceman who gives birth to a monster in *Alien* (1979) and now the unfortunate John Merrick in this season's *The Elephant Man*.

CALL AGAIN ANOTHER DAY

The Postman Always Ring Twice, from the steamy Depression-era novel by James M. Cain, hasn't had much luck in the movies so far. First it was lifted, uncredited and unpaid for, by Italian director Luchino Visconti during the war. His version, called *Ossessione* (1942), was the most realistic, but reached only a small art-house audience after the war.

Hollywood then made it in 1946 as a vehicle for Lana Turner and John Garfield, but censorship left it watered down. That version was made by Tay Garnett. Now Bob Rafelson has had a third crack at it and there are no longer any taboos. So the story of a drifter (Jack Nicholson) sucked into a sordid domestic murder by his infatuation for a garage owner's wife (Jessica Lange) is sexually explicit as the Turner-Garfield version could never be. There are even rumours that Nicholson and Lange's acting was so realistic that Rafelson only used a portion of the more erotic scenes.

But despite all this hot air, audiences are seemingly curiously apathetic and the film is proving a box-office flop. Playwright David Mamet's script is closer to the novel than the earlier movie, but director Rafelson seems more in his element in modern yarns like *Five Easy Pieces* (1970) and *The King of Marvin Gardens* (1972), both of which also starred Nicholson.

IN THE RUNNING FOR AN OSCAR?

Ben Cross (as Harold Abrahams) and Nigel Havers (as Andrew Lindsay) race round the quadrangle of their Cambridge college in David Puttnam's Chariots of Fire.

Whizz-kid David Puttnam has produced one of those little pictures with a big heart that often win awards. *Chariots of Fire* is the unlikely story of two top athletes who ran in the 1924 Olympics – Jewish Cambridge student Harold Abrahams and devout Scottish missionary Eric Liddell. Religion, unexpectedly, is at the heart of the drama. Abrahams runs because he's racially snubbed and has something to prove; Liddell refuses to run because his event is set for a Sunday. He insists this is Biblically "the sabbath of the Lord thy God; in it thou shalt do no work."

Two little-known actors, Ben Cross and Ian Charleson, play Abrahams and Liddell and there are delightful cameos from John Gielgud and movie director Lindsay Anderson as the masters of rival Cambridge colleges. It's director Hugh Hudson's first film, one of a group (including Alan Parker and Ridley Scott) whom Puttnam has pulled from the world of advertising.

Producer Puttnam sees the two runners as twin sides of his own personality: "Eric Liddell is the kind of person I dream of being; Harold Abrahams is more similar to the kind of person I find myself, a pragmatist rather than an idealist." So it's a personal picture for him. He calls it "a reaction to having been the producer of *Midnight Express* [1978], a film in which I found no sense of identity other than the craftsmanship with which it was made."

Hollywood was snooty about the project at first. Puttnam hawked it round the studios and they all turned it down. Warners passed on it twice, but Alan Ladd Jr saw the potential and agreed to put up half the $1.2 million for the U.S. distribution rights. Warners (which handles all his movies) finally said yes at the third time of asking.

"HEART ATTACK" FOR COPPOLA

Not for the first time, disaster is starring Francis Coppola in the face. His relatively modest movie *One from the Heart* has ballooned to $23 million, thanks principally to some $4.5 million on sets to mimic Las Vegas's skyline. Unless he could line up a further $5 million in two weeks, Coppola was in danger of losing control not only of the film but also of his Zoetrope studios.

Enter Paramount, which had happily backed his hits *The Godfather* and *The Godfather Part II* in 1972 and 1974. It's now thrown him a $500,000 lifeline to get him off the hook and another $500,000 to buy an interest in a movie called *Interface*. The only trouble is that few people at Zoetrope seems to know what it is. A studio employee has described it as "a mind-boggling thing that has to do with the brain as well as the body." Quite.

But Paramount seems 100 per cent behind Coppola. "We would like to see him stay in business," says Paramount president Michael Eisner, "and *Interface* happens to be a project we have always loved."

BIRTHS, DEATHS AND MARRIAGES

DEATHS

Rene Clair
15 Mar, Neuilly, France

Norman Taurog
8 Apr, Rancho Mirage, CA

GOOD AND FILTHY

Former Baltimore hairdresser Harris Glen Milstead has carved out quite a career for himself as cinematic drag queen Divine. He was given the name by school chum John Waters, for whom he went on to make a series of underground movies in the 1960s and 1970s. He was once voted "the filthiest person alive" and once lived up to the title by eating dog pooh as a protest against American consumerism.

His best-known movies are *Pink Flamingos* (1972), *Female Trouble* (1974) and now *Polyester*, all made by Waters. Monstrously obese, and in cha-cha heels and spandex dresses, he looks far older than his 35 years. But the louche persona and gigantic "bosom" are simply part of the act. "I hate it when they call me a transvestite," he says. "These are my working clothes. That's how I make people laugh."

THUS SPAKE MERLIN

Sir Lancelot (Nicholas Clay) swears allegiance to King Arthur (Nigel Terry) in Excalibur.

John Boorman's Arthurian spectacle *Excalibur* is the first to take account of the fact that this is a Cornish legend. So Merlin the magician speaks as Cornishmen do – with a twang. Boorman was careful to avoid the pseudo-Shakespearean style into which many actors fall when making this kind of film. "I tried to avoid standard English as far as possible," he says, "and to distinguish each character with a regional accent, Scottish, Irish or Welsh. it gives them a special richness and density."

Excalibur is very Wagnerian. And with composer Trevor Jones, Boorman has even gone to pains to inject bleeding chunks of the maestro into the score. "Together, we selected extracts from Siegfried's death in *Götterdämmerung*, the prelude to *Tristan and Isolde* for the love story, and the prelude to *Parsifal*, which I've always adored," he says.

The film also had a Wagnerian pregnancy. The original script was written in 1975 but Warners turned up its nose because it would have run 4½ hours. Only when Boorman called in his old friend Rospo Pallenberg, who had already rewritten *Exorcist II: The Heretic* (1977) for him, was he able to make cuts, merge characters and make progress. It was Pallenberg's idea to have Uther Pendragon insert Excalibur into the stone, for example. Says Boorman: "It's in the nature of myths to be so powerful that you can change them and modify them and yet they remain essentially the same."

Divine as Francine Fishpaw in Polyester, *a film by John Waters.*

THE MARK OF CAIN

Hollywood didn't realise it at the time but it had a great actress nestling in a gorilla's paw. When producer Dino De Laurentiis picked Jessica Lange to play the Fay Wray part in his remake of *King Kong* (1976), critics wrote her off as just another leggy blonde floozy. Give her one or two more parts, they said, and she'll be gone, like a thousand others, with the wind.

It began to look like that. Her bit part in *All That Jazz* (1979) and supporting role in *How to Beat the High Cost of Living* (1980) has all the marks of celluloid flotsam. But with the current remake of *The Postman Always Rings Twice*, the 32-year-old, Minnesota-born actress is now being talked of as the real thing. Trained as a dancer, she lived in Paris from 1971 to 1973 and now has a daughter by Russian ballet defector Mikhail Baryshnikov.

ACADEMY AWARDS

PRESENTED ON 31 MARCH 1981

Best Picture
Ordinary People

Best Director
Robert Redford
Ordinary People

Best Actor
Robert De Niro
Raging Bull

Best Actress
Sissy Spacek
Coal Miner's Daughter

Best Sup Actor
Timothy Hutton
Ordinary People

Best Sup Actress
Mary Steenburgen
Melvin and Howard

MAN INTO FOX

Weighing in at 300lb, Denver oil tycoon Marvin Davis has made a $725 million takeover bid for 20th Century-Fox. He recently sold part of his Davis Oil Company stock to the Canadian group Hiram Walker Consumer Homes for $600 million, which will underpin most of the cost of buying out Fox.

The Fox studio itself sits on valuable real estate – some 63 acres, thought to be worth $280 million – but it also has property at Pebble Beach, on the Monterey peninsula south of San Francisco, standing in the books at a years-ago valuation of $40 million. Insiders reckon the true value of that land now could top $1 billion.

THE HEAVENS BURST

United Artists, the only major Hollywood distribution company without a studio, is no more. Transamerica,. the conglomerate that formerly owned it, has sold it to high-roller Kirk Kerkorian's M-G-M group for some $350 million.

United Artists was founded back in 1919 by Charlie Chaplin, D. W. Griffith, Mary Pickford and Douglas Fairbanks. It was one of the first attempts by bona fide artists to control what happened to their work. After a relatively fallow period in the Fifties, it had staged a comeback since the Sixties with the James Bond movies and Oscar-winners like *West Side Story* (1961) and *One Flew over the Cuckoo's Nest* (1975). What sank it was last year's *Heaven's Gate*, the sprawling Western that cost $36 million and made hardly a dime after the worst reviews in living memory. It left United Artists open to the first half-way reasonable offer on the table.

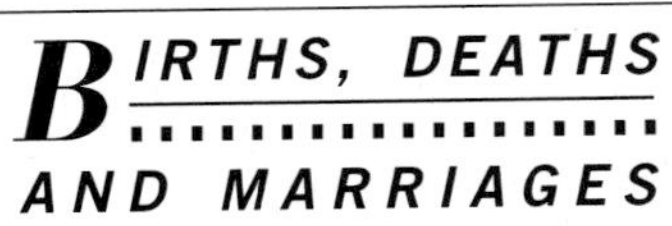

BIRTHS, DEATHS AND MARRIAGES

DEATHS

Melvyn Douglas
4 Aug, New York
Heart ailment

William Wyler
27 Jul, Beverly Hills
Heart attack

Vera-Ellen
30 Aug, Los Angeles
Cancer

Indiana Jones (Harrison Ford) lowers himself into an Egyptian tomb writhing with snakes in Raiders of the Lost Ark.

STAR JAWS TOPS $100M

Two of the most successful filmmakers of all time are behind the megabuck blockbuster *Raiders of the Lost Ark*. Director is Steven Spielberg, whose 1975 movie *Jaws* was the most profitable to date; producer is George Lucas, whose *Star Wars* overtook *Jaws* two years later.

Raiders is a throwback to the olden days of serials and B-picture adventures. The only difference is that it took $22 million to ensure that the thrills, spills and special effects are state-of-the-art. All that side was handled by Lucas's company Industrial Light and Magic in northern California. Shooting of the live action was spread over 73 days in France, Tunisia, Hawaii and Britain's Elstree Studios, where *Star Wars* was also filmed.

The elaborate yarn, set in prewar days, tells of the search for the famed Ark of the Covenant, source of unlimited power and (in the movie) laser beams and other sci-fi fireworks. The Nazis want it for world domination and archaeologist-cum-adventurer Indiana Jones for research.

Born and bred in the movie business, Spielberg has peppered his film with in-jokes. The film starts with a real-life equivalent of the Paramount mountain trademark and ends with the ark crated up in a warehouse like "Rosebud" in *Citizen Kane* (1941). Audiences are lapping it up and *Raiders* is set to join *Jaws* among the all-time box-office champs. Paramount is already rubbing its hands with glee as it carts $100 million or so off to the bank.

STEVEN HERO

At 34 Steven Spielberg is the most successful director the cinema has ever known. He made the most profitable film of its time – *Jaws* (1975), another blockbuster in *Close Encounters of the Third Kind* (1977) and now a hat-trick with *Raiders of the Lost Ark*. With a record like that, Hollywood ought to forgive him the flop of *1941* (1979). But Hollywood is a funny town. Though creatively dominated by Jews, it's controlled where it matters by gentiles. And for all his success, for some reason they don't like him. So his films are nominated for Oscars but he himself is not.

Critics say the Cincinnati-born wonder is the ultimate Peter Pan, the child who never grew up and who plays with the cinema like a giant train set – an image incidentally, that a much more respected director (Orson Welles) once invoked to describe his own work.

STAR QUOTES

Steven Spielberg

"I'd rather direct than produce. Any day. And twice on Sunday."

WYLER DIES

The death of William Wyler at his Beverly Hills home on 27 July marks the end of an era – an era of superb craftsmanship that brought Wyler three Oscars for best director. The first was in 1942 for *Mrs. Miniver*, followed by another in 1946 for *The Best Years of Our Lives* and, after 13 years, a final one for *Ben-Hur* (1959).

He should have won more. His 1939 adaptation of *Wuthering Heights*, his 1941 production of *The Little Foxes* (both with ace cameraman Gregg Toland), and the later, delightful comedy *Roman Holiday* (1953), which introduced Audrey Hepburn to America, reinforced his reputation as the finest craftsman in Hollywood.

Born in France in 1902, he arrived in New York in 1920 to work in Universal's publicity department, later moving to the West Coast to work on two-reelers. He became known as an actor's director. Thespians loved to work with him (even though he could be infuriatingly hard to satisfy) because they knew it might lead to an Oscar. He helped many to do so: Walter Brennan in *The Westerner* (1940), Greer Garson and Teresa Wright in *Mrs. Miniver*, Fredric March and Harold Russell in *The Best Years of Our Lives*, Olivia de Havilland in *The Heiress* (1949), Audrey Hepburn in *Roman Holiday*, Burl Ives in *The Big Country* (1958), Charlton Heston and Hugh Griffith in *Ben-Hur*, and Barbra Streisand in *Funny Girl* (1968). Hollywood will not see his like again.

PINTER LICKS A PROBLEM

How to film John Fowles' best-seller *The French Lieutenant's Woman* has been puzzling producers since it first came out in 1969. The snag is, it's two books in one – a Victorian love story and a 20th-century commentary on it. Lit.crit. isn't big news in the movies.

Playwright Harold Pinter has solved the problem by making the historical part a film being made by contemporary actors and actresses, whose own lives and romances reflect upon the story they are playing.

The production team is unusual. The director is Czech-born Karel Reisz, who brings a Central European perspective to the film, even though he has lived in Britain since arriving as a refugee from the Nazis in 1938. A former film critic and author of a classic book on film editing, he graduated from the British Free Cinema movement to commercial hits like *Saturday Night and Sunday Morning* (1960) and *Morgan (A Suitable Case for Treatment)* (1966). An infrequent film-maker, he's lately been working on the fringes of Hollywood, with films like *The Gambler* (1974) and *Who'll Stop the Rain* (1978), also known as *Dog Soldiers*.

Meryl Streep is Sarah, the French lieutenant's woman. The blonde 32-year-old New Jersey-ite has been building quite a following since the late 1970s, capped by a supporting actress Oscar last year for the very different *Kramer vs Kramer*. Her English accent is even more convincing than Marlon Brando's in *Julius Caesar* (1953) or Charlton Heston's in *Khartoum* (1966). After her Louisiana tones in *The Seduction of Joe Tynan* (1979) she seems an actress with an uncommonly keen ear for diction.

Meryl Streep and Jeremy Irons in The French Lieutenant's Woman.

EXPLETIVES EXQUISITELY UNDELETED

John Gielgud has had an on-and-off relationship with the cinema. Born in 1904, he early became one of the pillars of the London stage, a Shakespearean actor who alone could challenge Olivier as king of the boards. Yet movies neglected him. Footling parts in Hitchcock's *Secret Agent* (1936) and the film of J. B. Priestley's *The Good Companions* (1932) were almost all he had to show until he was chosen to immortalize his Cassius in *Julius Caesar* (1953).

It was a breakthrough, from which Gielgud never looked back. Orson Welles cast him as Henry IV in his film hewn out of the history plays, *Chimes at Midnight* (1966); in a 1969 remake of *Julius Caesar* he played the title role; and he made a marvellous novelist, puzzled at his failure to win the Nobel Prize for literature, in *Providence* (1977).

But it's in the Dudley Moore comedy *Arthur* that he's having his greatest triumph. Critics once said of Brando in *Julius Caesar* that the measure of his greatness as Mark Antony was the hash Gielgud might have made of a foul-mouthed slob. *Arthur* isn't quite that, but Gielgud's irrepressibly profrane valet, spewing expletives like Shakespearean *bons mots*, is a triumph of casting against type.

TRAVOLTA STRIKES BACK

In *Blow Out* John Travolta re-teams with Nancy Allen for the first time since *Carrie* (1976). It's also another threesome with director Brian De Palma, who's Allen's husband in real life. The movie is a pacy thriller with political overtones, plus (for those who can remember) conscious echoes of Italian director Michelangelo Antonioni's cult hit *Blow-up* (1966).

Travolta is a sound technician who overhears what he thinks is a gunshot just before a car crash involving a well-known politician and a young woman. Allen is a hooker who is drawn into the intrigue and pays the price. She ends up the most sympathetic character in the film, thanks largely to the actress's own contribution to the picture.

"When I read the script," she says, "Sally wasn't a likeable character and didn't have a sense of humour. What I brought to her was a good heart. I married the innocent Giulietta Masina played in *La Strada* [1954] with the Judy Holliday character in *Born Yesterday* [1950]."

She admits to only one reservation about her husband's movies: "What I felt was lacking until *Blow Out* was a strong relationship between two characters. John and I, by the nature of who we are, gave that element to the film." For Travolta it's a strong comeback after disappointments following *Saturday Night Fever* (1977) and *Grease* (1978). It proves that wiggling his bottom is not his only forte.

ARE YOU NOW? HAVE YOU EVER . . . ? WHO CARES?

Warren Beatty as American writer John Reed in Reds, which he also directed.

NOT JUST A PRETTY FACE

Warren Beatty, Shirley MacLaine's kid brother, has always hankered after respectability. Cast from the start in James Dean-type roles in *Splendor in the Grass* and *The Roman Spring of Mrs. Stone* (both 1961), he fought a long, hard battle to be taken seriously. It led the boyish Virginia-born actor, 44 this year, into more adventurous projects that would extend his range as an actor and an entrepreneur. The art-house movie *Mickey One* (1965) paved the way for a much more profitable association with director Arthur Penn in *Bonnie and Clyde* (1967) which Beatty also produced.

Beatty's input was extensive. "A lot of people worked uncredited on the screenplay of *Bonnie and Clyde*," he says. "When David Newman and Robert Benton brought their script to me, it didn't have quite the socio-economic underpinnings of the end product."

Beatty has made his fair share of commercial pap between more "personal" movies like *Shampoo* (1975); but his success as a producer persuaded him to direct himself, first with Buck Henry on *Heaven Can Wait* (1978), and now the mammoth biography of communist chronicler John Reed, *Reds*. That project was first announced way back in 1973.

Thirty years ago, actor-director Warren Beatty would have been hauled before the House Un-American Activities Committee and told to justify himself. *Reds* is the most unabashedly communist movie ever made by a major Hollywood studio (Paramount). It tells the story of John Reed (Beatty), one of the founders of the American Communist party, his long romance with activist Louise Bryant (Diane Keaton), and his chronicling of the Russian revolution in the classic book *Ten Days That Shook the World*.

Moodily shot by ace Italian cameraman Vittorio Storaro, *Reds* has wound up as an ultra-long movie (196 minutes) with a megabuck budget. It cost $35 million and looks like being lucky to see much of it back, despite the frisson of Beatty and Keaton being good companions off-screen as well as on.

Oddly enough, it's the supporting cast that registers most strongly. Maureen Stapleton is brilliant as the anarchist Emma Goldman, while Jack Nicholson pops up from time to time as Eugene O'Neill.

BOX OFFICE

UK

1 Superman II
2 For Your Eyes Only
3 Flash Gordon
4 Snow White and the Seven Dwarfs
5 Any Which Way You Can
6 Clash of the Titans
7 Private Benjamin
8 Raiders of the Lost Ark
9 The Elephant Man
10 Tess

BOX OFFICE

US

1 Raiders of the Lost Ark
2 Superman II
3 Stir Crazy
4 9 to 5
5 Stripes
6 Any Which Way You Can
7 Arthur
8 The Cannonball Run
9 Four Seasons
10 For Your Eyes Only

HOLLYWOOD'S DAISY DROWNED

Natalie Wood was found drowned off Santa Catalina Island, California, on 29 November. She was only 43 but had been a star for 38 years. Her first film, as a child star, was *Happy Land* in 1943. Her last, *Brainstorm*, is yet to be completed.

She was one of the few child actresses to enjoy a bigger career as an adult. She made her comeback as James Dean's girlfriend in *Rebel without a Cause* (1955) and went from strength to strength. Notable performances were in *Splendor in the Grass* and as Maria in *West Side Story* (both 1961), and the title roles in *Gypsy* (1962) and *Inside Daisy Clover* (1965).

LONG LIVE THE WRINKLIES!

A so-so play by Ernest Thompson, wearing its technique on its sleeve where its heart ought to be, is now a superior film entertainment thanks to inspired casting. A tetchy old man who cannot quite acknowledge the love that binds him to his fiercely independent daughter sounds like typecasting for Fondas, Henry and Jane. And the choice is leading to wet handkerchiefs all over the country.

But *On Golden Pond* isn't just a Fonda family showcase. Playing opposite 76-year-old Henry is another veteran – Katharine Hepburn, a mere junior at 74. She won her first Oscar (for *Morning Glory*) 48 years ago and went on to cop two more (for *Guess Who's Coming to Dinner* in 1967 and *The Lion in Winter* in 1968). Among actors, only Walter Brennan (in supporting roles) can match that. But the smart money is on Kate topping his record. Even if she doesn't win next spring, nobody doubts that Henry will finally get the statuette that's been due to him for nearly half a century.

On Golden Pond does have a director, but it's one of those not infrequent cases when a man of only modest gifts stumbles upon a surprise package. Mark Rydell's previous work includes the almost forgotten *Cinderella Liberty* (1973) and *The Rose* (1979). The latter is remembered only because it gave Bette Midler a star role.

THIS LITTLE PIGGY WAS A SLEEPER

Bob Clark, who made last year's sentimental, sanctimonious Jack Lemmon starrer *Tribute* has now come up with a low-budget, non-mainstream movie that looks like being the sensation of 1982. It's called *Porky's* and is about the rudest picture ever to get away with an R rating. In one scene, a horny adolescent who has been watching girls undress through a peephole pushes his member through the gap and has it unceremoniously grabbed and twisted by the gym mistress on the other side.

Porky's was shot where it is set, in southern Florida. The real Porky's was actually a raunchy bordello in director Clark's own youth. The film rewinds many moments from his younger days – like the scene in which a hooker walks up and down a line of kids comparing their vital equipment in fruity language.

Test-marketed in two towns in Colorado and South Carolina, the film has struck an immediate chord. Moviegoers have responded not only to the nostalgic elements (it's set in the Eisenhower years) but also to the promise of dirtier dialogue than usual. "Can you describe this movie in clean language?" ask the adverts. "No," comes the prompt reply. Get out those "House full" signs.

Dan Morahan as Pee Wee is about to be rudely ejected from Porky's, by Chuck Mitchell, the porky proprietor.

MORE JOAN THAN JOAN

Faye Dunaway's impersonation of Joan Crawford in *Mommie Dearest*, the sensational adaptation of the tell-all biography by the superstar's daughter, is more like Crawford than Crawford herself. Make-up has transformed her stunning features into a waxy replica of the real thing. And her barnstorming performance – chasing her daughter with an axe and beating her with wire coat-hangers – is in line with what we are now told was Crawford's regular behaviour. It's all way over the top.

Dunaway, now 40, got off to a flying start in the 1960s and gradually moved to more weighty parts, starting with *The Arrangement* (1969) for director Elia Kazan who had directed her on stage. But she's always had a tendency to go for broke. When a director can rein her back, as Arthur Penn did in *Bonnie and Clyde* (1967) and Roman Polanski (despite on-set squabbles) did in *Chinatown* (1974), she can be a compelling actress of the old school – a true heiress of Joan Crawford and Bette Davis. But when a director indulges her, as Sidney Lumet in her Oscar-winning *Network* (1976) and Frank Perry now in *Mommie Dearest*, the results seem less happy.

OZZIE MAKES THE GRADE

On 17 December media tycoon Robert Holmes a Court joined the board of Lord Grade's stricken entertainment company Associated Communications. Lurching from the losses of *Raise the Titanic*, its shares had nose-dived in the stock market, making them easy prey for the multi-millionaire Aussie, who now has 51 per cent of the non-voting stock and a strategic stake in the voting shares, too.

Holmes a Court is a well known takeover king, who tried to snap up Rolls-Royce and Times Newspapers in the late 1970s. He first met Grade in May 1980, when he told him: "What you're doing is all very exciting and I'm really pleased because I've just bought a million of your shares." But Grade says he doesn't feel threatened because most of Holmes a Court's shares carry no voting rights. "A coup?" laughs cigar-chomping Grade. "Who's going to lead a coup against me? I'm only 34, you know."

STAR QUOTES

Joan Collins

"Warren Beatty was insatiable. Three, four, five times a day was not unusual for him and he was able to accept telephone calls at the same time."

BIRTHS, DEATHS AND MARRIAGES

DEATHS

Ann Harding
1 Sep, Sherman Oaks, California

Robert Montgomery
27 Sep, New York
Cancer

Gloria Grahame
5 Oct, New York
Cancer

William Holden
16 Oct, Santa Monica, California
Accident

Natalie Wood
29 Nov, Santa Catalina Isl., California
Drowned

The Force Was With Them

Science fiction was considered a dead horse by the late 1970s. Costly disappointments like *Logan's Run* (1976) seemed only to confirm that audiences didn't want to know about the future. Then *Star Wars* (1977) changed all that. Nervously released at first by 20th Century-Fox, it became an instant sensation and to date has returned around $200 million to the distributors.

Funnily enough, *Star Wars* is not a futuristic film. The opening title makes it clear that it takes place 'A long time ago, in a galaxy far, far away'. Even so, audiences took it as set in the future.

Star Wars spawned two sequels – *The Empire Strikes Back* (1980) and *Return of the Jedi* (1983) – which were enormous hits, too, and made the leading characters, Luke Skywalker, Han Solo, Chewbacca, C-3PO, R2-D2 et al, household names among a whole generation of children.

On the back of these films' success, everybody jumped into the act. Within two years, Walt Disney was making its own *Star Wars*, called *The Black Hole*. State-of-the-art special effects, models and monsters became almost required ingredients. The old television series *Star Trek* was turned into a movie in 1979 and then into four sequels between 1982 and 1989. All boasted spectacular sets and effects undreamt of in its TV days. *Superman* was given the sci-fi works in 1978, with a dazzling prologue depicting the destruction of the planet Krypton, while in 1980 *Flash Gordon*, another comic-strip hero, was sent to do battle once again with Ming the Merciless. Soon after Superman had hung up his cape after three sequels, Batman took his out of the closet in a 1989 multi-million dollar razzler-dazzler.

Old genres that no longer appealed to modern moviegoers were skilfully dressed up in new clothes as sci-fi epics. When Sean Connery finds himself the only man prepared to make a stand against corruption on Jupiter in *Outland* (1981), he is playing Gary Cooper in *High Noon*. Another western, *The Magnificent Seven*, was revamped as *Battle beyond the Stars* (1980), while the Lee Marvin/Toshiro Mifune picture *Hell in the Pacific* (1969) became *Enemy Mine* (1985), with Dennis Quaid and Louis Gossett Jr.

In the wake of *Star Wars*, sci-fi in the 1980s went down two tracks. Picking up the child-like quality of that film, Disney's *Tron* (1982) was actually set inside an arcade game, with an elaborate use of computer graphics to tell the story. *The Last Starfighter* (1984) also treated inter-galactic dog-fights as a natural extension of computer games. (The hero is especially recruited to help the aliens because he is a wizard at zapping Pacmen.)

Slightly up-market from these, Steven Spielberg twice ventured into sci-fi for the family with *Close Encounters of the Third Kind* (1977) and *E.T. The Extra-Terrestrial* (1982). Both these films were Earth-bound stories about visitations from benevolent aliens. Audiences took them to their hearts and they became smash hits; the former returned over $80 million on an outlay of $21 million and the latter became the most profitable film of all time. *Starman* (1984) with Jeff Bridges, was another of this genre.

Parallel with these films, sci-fi developed the hardware and monsters element of *Star Wars* in movies like *Alien* (1979) and its sequel, *Aliens* (1986), in *Dune* (1984) and in the Arnold Schwarzenegger vehicle *Predator* (1987). Schwarzenegger has been a mainstay of 1980s sci-fi, whether as a robot in *The Terminator* (1984) or as a hologram in *Total Recall* (1990). In fact, replicants – the not quite human – were a staple of 1980s sci-fi, from *Blade Runner* (1982) to *RoboCop* (1987).

Classic image from Steven Spielberg's E.T. The Extra-Terrestrial.

Lance Guest and his navigator go into battle in The Last Starfighter *(1984).*

Chewbacca, Mark Hamill, Alec Guinness and Harrison Ford in Star Wars *(1977).*

Peter Weller as half-man/half-machine, the futuristic law enforcer Robocop *(1987).*

John Hurt discovers a cache of "eggs" in an alien spaceship in Alien *(1974).*

Harrison Ford on the track of a replicant in Blade Runner *(1982).*

Richard Dreyfuss in Steven Spielberg's Close Encounters of the Third Kind *(1977).*

JANUARY
FEBRUARY

MARCH
APRIL

GUN-FREAK MEETS MUSCLE-MAN

Arnold Schwarzenegger is the warrior in John Milius' Conan the Barbarian.

John Milius, the maverick film-maker who stacks his home with high-velocity weapons for the day the invasion comes, has found his ideal subject in *Conan the Barbarian*. It's adapted from the pulp-fiction novels of Robert E. Howard, and Conan is a hulking hero in the days of sword and sorcery with a physique that could fell dinosaurs.

Starring in the $19 million spectacular is Austrian-born Arnold Schwarzenegger, 34, the former multiple Mr Universe from *Stay Hungry* (1976) and *Pumping Iron* (1977). Both he and his leonine co-star Sandahl Bergman – the lead dancer in the steamy routine in *All That Jazz* (1979) – underwent gruelling training for their sword-wielding roles. Milius insisted that all the weapons in the movie should be real, not lightweight fakes, and injuries among the cast were common. Schwarzenegger was run over by horses, bitten by a camel, and had his knee ligaments torn; Bergman narrowly escaped permanent injury from a sword.

Milius has directed only three other films, though he was screenwriter on several more, including *Apocalypse Now* (1979). His first movie as director was *Dillinger* (1973), the story of how the FBI trapped and killed the famous bandit, followed by the Sean Connery desert drama *The Wind and the Lion* (1975).

Relations between him and producer Dino De Laurentiis were reported to be less than cordial during shooting in Spain (Segovia and Almeria). Milius even bought a statue of Mussolini and took it to meetings, saying: "Dino, while you talk to me, look at this."

ACADEMY AWARDS

PRESENTED ON 29 MARCH 1982

Best Picture
Chariots of Fire

Best Director
Warren Beatty
Reds

Best Actor
Henry Fonda
On Golden Pond

Best Actress
Katharine Hepburn
On Golden Pond

Best Sup Actor
John Gielgud
Arthur

Best Sup Actress
Maureen Stapleton
Reds

"THE BRITISH ARE COMING"

Chariots of Fire (1981), the modest British film about two runners at the 1924 Olympics, has put on a last-minute sprint and come from behind to win the Best Film award at the Oscars. Some think it slipped through because the vote was split between two thoroughbreds – *Reds* and *On Golden Pond*.

At the presentation scriptwriter Colin Welland, who also picked up an award, was adamant that this is no flash in the pan. "The British are coming!" he announced, as if throwing down the gauntlet to Hollywood. It remains to be seen what the Brits can make of this unexpected notoriety. Right now they are the talk of Tinseltown, but that won't last long.

MARIA GOES SLEAZY

After baring her breasts in last year's raunchy *S.O.B.*, Julie Andrews now plays a transvestite in the latest movie by her second husband, director Blake Edwards. *Victor/Victoria* actually began as a German film, *Viktor und Viktoria*, made by Reinhold Schunzel in 1933 and then became a vehicle for British Jessie Matthews as *First a Girl* (1935).

Both earlier versions don't shy away from the sexual misunderstandings, but the Blake Edwards film, set in the world of 1930s Paris cabarets, goes the whole hog. Julie Andrews' decision to don male attire is encouraged by gay entrepreneur Robert Preston and leads to acute embarrassment when macho James Garner falls in love with her – or does he think it's him? This is one of those movies that touch deeper chords than they know. Certainly for Blake Edwards, whose fame rests principally on the Pink Panther films, *Victor/Victoria* confirms the evidence of *"10"* (1979) that it's not too late for a 60-year-old to kick over the traces.

Julie Andrews is Victor/Victoria.

Nastassja Kinski, in One from the Heart.

ONE IN THE EYE

One from the Heart is a romantic little picture about a Las Vegas couple (Frederic Forrest and Teri Garr) who quarrel and spend the night with other partners (Nastassja Kinski, Raul Julia). No one thought it would end up costing $26 million. Part of the trouble was that it was used as a testing ground for new electronic equipment. Even before shooting began in February 1981, computers were brought into service. The screenplay was put onto floppy disks, a storyboard was committed to video, then Polaroid pictures of each scene were taken as rehearsals got under way. When shooting started, director Francis Coppola monitored the show from a portable home called The Silver Fish (with kitchenette and a tub, from which he actually directed one of the scenes). Video cameras recorded the shooting at the same time as movie cameras, with the hope that the film could be edited, much as live TV programmes are, by cutting from scene to scene.

Naturally, it didn't work out like that. Within four months, the budget had ballooned to $23 million and more money was required every day. For 32 days of additional shooting and more elaborate titles and special effects the cost was $4m alone.

When it was finally finished, the first screenings for exhibitors spelt disaster. One exhibitor, declining to bid for the picture at all, said: "I almost think the film is unreleasable. How can these very talented Big People be so wrong? Does Francis have people all around him mesmerized so that they can't even tell him the truth?"

Now it has hit the screens, the news is blacker still. In its first 20 days, it took only $804,000 at the box office and by 1 April, only one cinema was playing it in New York: there were 43 people in the audience!

BIRTHS, DEATHS AND MARRIAGES

DEATHS

Stanley Holloway
30 Jan, Littlehampton, Sussex

Eleanor Powell
11 Feb, Beverly Hills, California
Cancer

John Belushi
5 Mar, Los Angeles
Drugs and alcohol

Celia Johnson
26 Apr, Nettlebed
Stroke

DRUGS KILL JOHN BELUSHI

John Belushi, one of the most distinctive comedians to emerge in pictures in recent years, was found dead in a West Hollywood hotel room on 5 March of acute cocaine and heroin poisoning. He was only 33. Born in Illinois of Albanian parents, Belushi made his name with the Second City company in Chicago in the 1970s, then in stage and record productions by National Lampoon, and shot to fame in NBC-TV's *Saturday Night Live* (1975). He specialized in portraying slobs, often in association with fellow comedian Dan Aykroyd. Their only real teaming, however, was in *The Blues Brothers* (1980), an expensive flop but rapidly becoming a cult item.

Belushi's first film was a small part in Jack Nicholson's *Goin' South* (1978), for which Nicholson personally chose him. He is also remembered as the gross Bluto Blutarsky in *National Lampoon's Animal House* (1978) and as an alarmingly racist bomber pilot in *1941* (1979). His early death means we shall never know whether his range was limited to only one type of part. His brother, James Belushi, is also a rising young actor.

Z-MAN TAKES ON CHILE

Costa-Gavras, the French-based Greek-Russian filmmaker who's made a speciality of political thrillers, has directed his first Hollywood film. It turns out, not unexpectedly, to be another political thriller. *Missing* is the dramatic story of a father's quest to find out what has happened to his son, who has vanished in mysterious circumstances in Chile. As the film progresses, it begins to look as if, far from being innocently caught up in the unrest sweeping that country, he has actually been a dupe of the CIA.

The film stars Jack Lemmon and Sissy Spacek, but what gives it its special impact is the director's skill at making political cinema thrilling without blurring the issues involved. He first achieved it in *Z* (1969), set under the Greek military junta, which won an Oscar as best foreign film, and followed it with *The Confession* (1970), set in Czechoslovakia, *State of Siege* (1973), in Uruguay, and *Special Section (1975)*, in German-occupied Paris. His films hit the target because they are never simply highbrow art-house pieces but thrillers with genuinely popular stars – like Yves Montand in *Z* and Jack Lemmon here. Costa-Gavras' career will be worth watching.

EXIT THE CHARLESTON DANCER

Lord Grade's long and colourful career at the head of Associated Communications is at an end. The film and TV mogul, who began his career back in the 1920s as a Charleston dancer with his brother, Bernard Delfont, has agreed to sell out to Australian Robert Holmes a Court, who has been something of a Trojan horse since Grade first brought him into the business as a minority shareholder.

For his part, Holmes a Court has asked Grade to stay on, promising him a life presidency, a £203,000 a year contract until 1984 and the option to buy his £400,000 Knightsbridge flat for £105,000. 'Twixt cup and lip, however. . . . Somehow, when the chips are finally down, it turns out that Associated Communications has been acquired through a different Holmes a Court company. The offers to Grade were part of an earlier version of the bid involving Bell Group; now the ultimate owner is TVW Enterprises – and TVW has made no such promises.

STAR QUOTES

Arnold Schwarzenegger

"Maria Shriver is well-rounded and gorgeous. I tell her that, if we marry and have kids, with her body and my mind they'll have some real winners in the family."

TWO SIDES OF STEVEN

A doorway opens to the "other side" in the Steven Spielberg-produced Poltergeist.

Wonderkid Steven Spielberg has got two films out there earning for him this summer and the odd thing is that though they are quite different in tone, they both look rather the same. Spielberg himself directs *E.T. The Extra-Terrestrial* and acts as producer to *Poltergeist*, leaving the direction to Tobe Hooper, whose most notorious film is *The Texas Chain Saw Massacre* (1974). Both films seem to be set in an almost identical town and the way of photographing them is similar. Rumour has it – though nobody is saying anything – that Spielberg shot large chunks of *Poltergeist* while filming *E.T.*

E.T. is the perfect family film. The story of a benign creature from outer space who looks a bit like Snow White's Dopey with wrinkles and an indiarubber neck, it has caught the summer crowd and looks as if it will outlast its initial curiosity value. Spielberg calls it "a fairy tale for the 1980s, a love story between a young boy and a 600-800 year old extra-terrestrial." As well as the realistic creature (designed by Carlo Rambaldi), *E.T.* boasts some impressive special effects and an enchanting story that opens all tear ducts. The creature's catchphrase, "E.T. phone home," has already become a favourite.

Poltergeist has some even better special effects – a lights and ectoplasm show that recalls the climax of *Raiders of the Lost Ark* (1981), another Spielberg film. Especially interesting is that the film has more of a message than most horror movies. It suggests that the creatures waiting to get you live inside the TV set and will happily suck you in if you let them.

AN OSCAR BEFORE DYING

Henry Fonda, a Hollywood legend in his lifetime, died in Los Angeles, aged 77, on 12 August after a long illness. Months before, he had won his only Best Actor Oscar, for *On Golden Pond* (1981).

Born in Nebraska in 1905, Fonda did some of his finest work in the 1930s and 1940s for John Ford – performances for which he will always be remembered in films like *Young Mr. Lincoln* (1939), *The Grapes of Wrath* (1940) and (as Wyatt Earp) in *My Darling Clementine* (1946).

Between 1949 and 1955, Fonda quit the cinema and won fresh plaudits on Broadway, notably in the stage production of *Mister Roberts*, in which he played the title role. He returned for the film version in 1955, but it was an unhappy production begun by John Ford and finished by Mervyn LeRoy. Thereafter, he made a long and distinguished contribution to countless movies, including *Twelve Angry Men* (1957) and a rare excursion into villainy in the spaghetti western *Once Upon a Time in the West* (1969).

BLACKBOARD JUNGLE STAR DECAPITATED

Vic Morrow, the actor who shot to fame as a rebellious classroom kid in *The Blackboard Jungle* (1955), has died in an appalling accident during location filming north of Los Angeles for *Twilight Zone – The Movie*. On 23 July, explosions on the set knocked a helicopter out of the sky. Falling on Morrow and two child actors he was carrying to safety in a scene set in a river, it crushed one of the children and then the still whirling rotor blade decapitated 50-year-old Morrow and his other charge.

A portmanteau picture, with different sequences filmed by other directors, *Twilight Zone* is already attracting media attention as evidence of lax safety precautions on Hollywood movies. The episode in question was being directed by John Landis. Some want formal charges to be pressed.

BIRTHS, DEATHS AND MARRIAGES

DEATHS

Romy Schneider
29 May, Paris
Cardiac arrest

Rainer Werner Fassbinder
10 Jun, Munich
Accidental overdose

Henry King
29 Jun, Toluca Lake, California

Kenneth More
12 Jul, London
Parkinson's disease

Henry Fonda
12 Aug, Los Angeles
Heart ailment

STAR QUOTES

Jane Fonda

"Like a certain generation of men, my father had difficulty in expressing emotions."

GOSSIP COLUMN

■ **For the first time in Oscar history attempts are made to withdraw a nominee: Poland wants Andrzej Wajda's film *Man of Iron* pulled from the ballot for Best Foreign Film for being too soft on Solidarity. No dice, says the Academy, the nomination stands. But it gives the Oscar to the Hungarian film *Mephisto* anyway.**

Debra Winger and Richard Gere in An Officer and a Gentleman.

STEERS AND QUEERS

An Officer and a Gentleman has become a box-office bonanza, returning more than $55 million to distributors Lorimar and Paramount from the North American market alone. It's an extraordinary performance for a film that dares to force Richard Gere, one of Hollywood's most handsome younger actors, to prove on which side of the sexual fence he is sitting. Of course, at the end he proves to be the red-blooded male everyone thought him to be and sweeps Debra Winger off her feet; but along the way it has sometimes seemed touch and go whether Zack Mayo, the officer cadet he is playing, is, in the words of his tough, black drill sergeant, "a steer or a queer".

It's Gere's first movie since he took over from John Travolta the part of male prostitute in *American Gigolo* (1980). Winger was last widely seen straddling a mechanical bronco in *Urban Cowboy* (1980), though she took over from Raquel Welch in the adaptation of John Steinbeck's novel *Cannery Row* (1982), thinly released earlier this year. The real revelation is black actor Louis Gossett, Jr, as the drill sergeant who takes an evident delight in being able to humiliate, during training, men who are not only socially superior to himself but white as well. *An Officer and a Gentleman* is only the second film of Taylor Hackford, who's first was a study of power politics in the record industry called *The Idolmaker* (1980).

A flying car used by the police downtown is part of Ridley Scott's image of the future in Blade Runner.

SIMULATED FUTURES

Two new sci-fi films bring a whole new world of technology into the making of motion pictures. The most radical is *Tron*, a $17 million Disney picture that not only uses clever special effects but contains several sequences that are entirely computer-generated. Computer graphics techniques have hitherto been used only in animated logos and a few commercials.

The story of *Tron* takes place inside an arcade game. First, the live actors (Jeff Bridges, David Warner et al) were asked to perform against plain backcloths. Then these performances were integrated into the graphically simulated backgrounds and props by the use of masking and superimpositions. The result is visually unlike any other film. Each frame is given colour, shade and texture by assigning colour and intensity values to each point of light (pixel) on the screen. Says Larry Elin of MAGI, one of the firms that did the computer work: "It's no different from the way they light the big billboard on Times Square. The billboard has maybe 8,000 pixels, but one of our monitors can have over two million."

Blade Runner, starring Harrison Ford and dark, sexy newcomer Sean Young, is less innovative but equally effective in creating a future world through special effects (by Douglas Trumbull among others) and the production design of Lawrence G. Paull. This is Los Angeles *c.* 2019, a world drenched with rain and steam in which flying machines hover in the murky sky and "replicants" (androids) walk the streets. It's Ridley Scott's follow up to *Alien* (1979) and adapted from a novel by cult sci-fi writer Philip K. Dick called *Do Androids Dream of Electric Sheep?* Powerful visions of the future, both.

WHEN THE BOOT'S ON THE OTHER FOOT

Lou Gossett, who sometimes calls himself Louis Gossett, Jr, is the first black actor to be seen to play a dominant role over his white co-stars. In *An Officer and a Gentleman*, he plays an NCO with power for the duration over the officer cadets he is training. Thus racial stereotypes and class distinctions are turned on their heads. It's a notable breakthrough.

And it's significant that it has been the tough, no-nonsense Gossett rather than the more malleable Sidney Poitier and Harry Belafonte who has brought it about. Born in 1936, Gossett has specialized mainly in TV rather than the cinema. He first made his name playing Patrice Lumumba, the deposed and murdered prime minister of the Congo, in a Los Angeles production of Conor Cruise O'Brien's controversial play *Murderous Angels*. Then on TV he was Fiddler in *Roots* and is currently preparing a four-hour mini-series on the life of Anwar Sadat.

His screen roles have been few. He was in the comedy *The Landlord* (1970), with Beau Bridges, and in the black family drama *The River Niger* (1976). But it is *An Officer and a Gentleman* that has established him. The Hollywood grapevine is even talking of an Academy Award.

NOVEMBER
DECEMBER

WHO'S THAT GUY IN A GIRDLE?

Answer: Dustin Hoffman in *Tootsie*, a comedy that succeeds, by skilful direction and playing, in disarming any charges of bad taste. Hoffman plays an actor who dons women's clothing to prove a point about the paucity of good parts for an honest-to-goodness actor and then finds everyone taking a fancy to him – including his girlfriend!

Hoffman's performance in drag is a knockout and there's some sterling support from Jessica Lange as an actress who becomes "her" best friend and the film's director, Sydney Pollack, as Hoffman's long-suffering agent. The scene in which he meets Hoffman in the Russian Tea Room (famed New York feeding trough for the rich and famous) is a little masterpiece of comedy, in which Pollack proves himself a gifted comedian.

Pollack, in fact, began as an actor, with a leading role in the Korean War drama *War Hunt* (1962) – more famous now for being Robert Redford's first film – and progressed to direction three years later with *The Slender Thread*, with Sidney Poitier and Anne Bancroft. Since then his best films have included the Depression dance-marathon drama *They Shoot Horses, Don't They?* (1969) and the Redford-Streisand weepie *The Way We Were* (1973). His most recent film before *Tootsie* was *Absence of Malice* (1981), with Paul Newman and Sally Field.

TWO-MAN MULTI-RACIAL TEAM

The only thing that distinguishes *48HRS.* from a dozen other hard-bitten cop thrillers is that one of the two-man team "assigned" to bring the criminals to book is black. He's played by an actor new to the movies, 21-year-old Eddie Murphy, with a line in quick-talk repartee uniquely his own.

Murphy in the film is actually a jail-bird. He's sprung from the slammer to help policeman Nick Nolte track down his former associates. The movie is a highly efficient action piece directed by Walter Hill, a macho director who worked in construction and oil drilling before entering the cinema and whose most recent films are the violent western *The Long Riders* (1980) and Louisiana manhunt drama *Southern Comfort* (1981).

Nick Nolte is being hailed as the new Robert Redford for his performance in this film, but there's little similarity beyond craggy good looks. Where Redford is so righteous you can almost see the halo shining around his head, Nolte is tougher, more compromised and more like the way people are apt to be in real life. He was seen most recently in the grid-iron comedy-drama *North Dallas Forty* (1979), as singer Neal Cassady in *Heart Beat* (1980), and in this year's thinly-released *Cannery Row*, opposite rising young Debra Winger.

FAIRY-TALE PRINCESS DIES

Princess Grace of Monaco, the former filmstar Grace Kelly, has died of a cerebral haemorrhage the day after a car accident in the mountains above Monte Carlo on 14 September. She was 52. She had not made a film since *High Society* (1956), despite frequent talk of a comeback. She was, however, immensely popular in Monaco and had hosted a 1963 CBS-TV tour of the principality.

Born in Philadelphia in 1929, she was first seen in a small part in the suicide drama *Fourteen Hours* (1951). She made only 11 films in all, but was much admired for those she made with Alfred Hitchcock – *Rear Window* and *Dial M for Murder* (both 1954) and *To Catch a Thief* (1955). A cool blonde, she mussed up her coiffure for *The Country Girl* (1954) and won an Oscar for it. She met Monaco's Prince Rainier III while working on *To Catch a Thief*, which is set on the French Riviera, and after returning to Hollywood to make *High Society* (1956), her last film, she married him in April in a spectacular royal wedding. It was one of those fairy tales that just occasionally come true.

TALES OF HOFFMAN

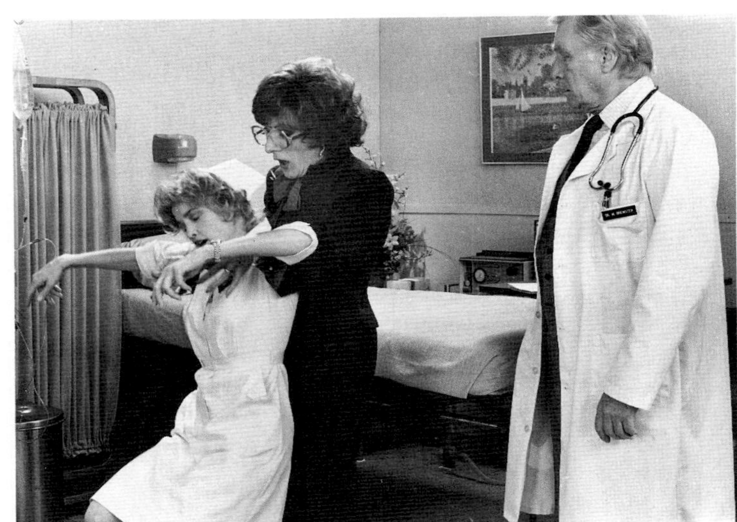

Jessica Lange and Dustin Hoffman in Tootsie.

Among actors, Dustin Hoffman, 45, is known as a perfectionist and as a man fanatically concerned with the minutiae of his own performances. Among directors, who want to get the film in the can, this has not always made him popular. But among ticketbuyers he's universally recognized as one of the finest American actors of today.

After hitting the headlines with his sensational performance as the gauche young hero of *The Graduate* (1967), educated in the ways of the world by the seductive Mrs Robinson, he went on to play crippled hobo Ratso Rizzo in *Midnight Cowboy* (1969). It was a startling transformation and many feel he might have taken the Oscar that year if the votes had not been split with his co-star John Voight. No less remarkable was his impersonation of comedian Lenny Bruce in *Lenny* (1974) – an extrovert performance that got full value from the comedian's notorious blue jokes and foul language.

He finally won an Oscar in 1979 for *Kramer vs Kramer*, a less showy performance but one so naturalistic that he hardly seemed to be acting at all. It's in complete contrast to his latest, which is one of his most flamboyant to date. *Tootsie* is not so much a female impersonator as an actor who dons drag to make a point about the kind of roles he is being given. It's a knockout and he will be lucky to find as good a part again.

BIRTHS, DEATHS AND MARRIAGES

DEATHS

Grace Kelly
14 Sep, Monaco
Car accident caused by cerebral haemorrhage

Jacques Tati
5 Nov, Paris
Pulmonary embolism

Marty Feldman
2 Dec, Mexico City
Heart attack

Rohini Hattangady, Ben Kingsley and Geraldine James in Gandhi.

A DREAM FULFILLED

Gandhi has long been a film that Richard Attenborough wanted to direct. The story of the father of modern India has an epic sweep ideally suited to the man who proved his mastery of logistics in *A Bridge Too Far* (1977) and his sympathy for the lives of great men in *Young Winston* (1972). It was the evident talent displayed in these films that encouraged the British company Goldcrest to give him his head after he'd been banging it against a brick wall for 20 years.

By UK standards it has proved expensive, eventually absorbing £9.5 million. It was still more of a risk for a company that entered into production without having world distribution deals fully sewn up. *Gandhi* turned out to be a film on which Goldcrest, until a late stage, bore all the risk.

The key to the film's success is inspired casting in the title role. Many actors tested for the part and John Hurt, in particular, is said to have given an outstanding reading. Yet it was not Gandhi – and Hurt had the good grace to accept it and stand down.

Ben Kingsley, who finally landed the part, is unknown in America, though slightly known in Britain as a leading player at the Royal Shakespeare. He has the double advantage of being Anglo-Indian himself.

The film's quality was not immediately apparent. 20th Century-Fox, which once had the option of picking it up for distribution, said, "It's wonderful, but it'll never sell." Technicians, however, are more perceptive. After a unit screening back in June, one of the construction boys came up to Attenborough and told him: "Tell you what, guv, I'd go back and do the whole bloody lot again if you asked me to. It's all right."

THE MAN WHO IS THE MAHATMA

Ben Kingsley, who plays *Gandhi* in Richard Attenborough's biopic of the great Indian statesman, is himself Anglo-Indian. He was born Krishna Banji, his father having emigrated to England and practised as a doctor in Manchester. (The English side of Ben Kingsley comes from Northampton.) Kingsley had never been to India before playing *Gandhi* and, as his career had been primarily in English parts, he had decided some years before to change his name by deed poll.

His career began in repertory at Chichester and Stoke-on-Trent, from which he joined the Royal Shakespeare Company and appeared in a number of well-known productions. These included Athol Fugard's play *Statements after an Arrest under the Immorality Act* and Peter Brook's production of *A Midsummer Night's Dream*.

"Athol was the most articulate man I'd ever met," says Kingsley. "He helped me articulate cries of pain." After this, he scored a big hit as Hamlet at Stratford-on-Avon in a production by Buzz Goodbody and began to appear from time to time in pictures. The idea that he was discovered for *Gandhi* is a myth. He had already appeared as John Vernon's henchman in the Alistair MacLean thriller *Fear Is the Key* (1972) and played the title role in the Anglo-Sri Lankan historical drama *The God King* (1975) before being replaced by British actor Leigh Lawson.

To prepare himself for *Gandhi*, Kingsley tried to live as near as he could to the way Gandhi did. So he sat cross-legged on a rush mat, ate the same kind of food, practised yoga, and so on. In the film it gives his performance a dimension over and above anything that make-up can provide.

A NEW NAME FOR THE EIGHTIES

First Blood is adapted from a novel by David Morrell, and perhaps it was felt that the name ought to be kept for the movie in order to attract those who might have read the book. But the name movie audiences are going to take away with them is John Rambo, the moniker of the leading character.

For Rambo is a killing machine, trained for Vietnam and unable to moderate his personality after the war. In post-Vietnam America he is a force for violence, who leads the police a merry dance after being falsely accused of petty crime. Rambo is played by Sylvester Stallone, more ox-like even than Arnold Schwarzenegger.

The movie's success is being deplored by do-gooders and sociologists. But it's giving audiences what they want in the form of almost non-stop violence. From their point of view, the only drawback is that he seems merely to want to maim people, not to kill them. A rare, wimpish trait that the inevitable sequel will no doubt suppress.

Sylvester Stallone in First Blood.

BOX OFFICE

UK

1 Arthur
2 Chariots of Fire
3 Gregory's Girl
4 Porky's
5 The Fox and the Hound
6 Condorman
7 Annie
8 Rocky III
9 Herbie Goes Bananas
10 Firefox

BOX OFFICE

US

1 E.T. The Extra-Terrestrial
2 Rocky III
3 On Golden Pond
4 Porky's
5 An Officer and a Gentleman
6 The Best Little Whorehouse in Texas
7 Star Trek II: The Wrath of Khan
8 Poltergeist
9 Annie
10 Chariots of Fire

s Doohan, Walter Koenig and William Shatner in Star Trek III *(1984).*

topher Reeve confronts Lex Luthor (Gene Hackman) in Superman IV *(1987).*

y the 13th Part V: – A New Beginning *(1985), the fifth in the series.*

ael J. Fox and Christopher Lloyd in Back to the Future Part II *(1989).*

Anything You Can Do

Sequels are as old as the cinema. What works once has always been reckoned likely to work again – and sometimes it does. From *Bulldog Drummond* in 1929, through *Frankenstein* in 1931 to *Tarzan the Ape Man* in 1932, every film hero or villain ever conceived has "returned", had his "revenge", or a "son", or a "daughter" or just plain "struck back".

In 1974, however, movies gave up the unequal struggle of trying to find variants for the simple number 2. With *The Godfather Part II*, Hollywood entered a new era of simply numbering each episode of the continuing saga by the next numeral in the series. *The Godfather Part II* is not just a sequel: it is a prequel-plus, to a large extent, a remake. It shows the early life of Vito Corleone and the career of his son Michael after his death. *The Godfather Part III:* (1990) is closer to a traditional sequel.

Rocky, which began life in 1976, never bothered to invent a new name for any of its five instalments – doubtless because the first three were simply straight remakes with a different ending. It's Sly Stallone v Carl Weathers three times in a row, with the decision going now to one guy, now to the other. *Superman* started that way, too. In 1980. he never "flew again", he just "twoed". Ditto with *Superman III* in 1983, but by 1987, the mantle of sobriety was clearly descending and the last episode to date in the series was called *Superman IV: The Quest for Peace. Star Trek* was never content with a mere numeral: at its fifth and increasingly arthritic outing it reached *The Final Frontier* (1989), which meant an audience with God. Next decision for Captain Kirk: to boldly pack it in perhaps.

Not all sequels are successful, and leaving it too long before picking up the threads can be a recipe for disaster. *Gremlins* was one of the unexpected delights of 1984 and a sequel in 1985 or 1986 might have been just as popular. But by 1990, a new generation had grown up that knew nothing of mogwais - so *Gremlins 2: The New Batch* proved one of the major disappointments of the year. *48HRS.* (1982) waited even longer for *Another 48 HRS.* (1990) and paid the penalty. The same fate awaited *Ghostbusters II*,the 1989 sequel to a film of five years before that had been among the top films of all time.

Sequels do best that capitalize on their goodwill while the going is good. How else to explain the ever-lengthening sequels to *A Nightmare on Elm Street* (1984) and *Friday the 13th* (1980)? Neither original was of great merit, but somebody had the good sense to follow them through while they were fresh in the audiences' mind – and they are still with us today. *Die Hard 2* (1990) is nowhere near as good a film as its 1988 model, but it followed as soon as practical on *Die Hard* itself and has reaped the reward.

The best sequels are those that carry the story forward rather than repeat the pattern of the original. The *Planet of the Apes* films are a case in point. Though each of the five films in the series, beginning in 1968, has a different writer and director, they add up to a surprisingly coherent narrative. The three *Star Wars* films beginning in 1977 and the three Indiana Jones films, beginning with *Raiders of the Lost Ark* (1981), are like that, too. Taken together, the latter add up to a biography of Indiana Jones.

Back to the Future, beginning in 1985 and concluding in 1990, is a trilogy that takes its hero, Marty McFly, into the past (1), the future (2) and the distant past (3). Though there's scope in *Back to the Future Part III* for yet another instalment, director Robert Zemeckis wisely called a halt. The closing credit is "The End". Knowing when to draw the line is the secret of all sequels.

Main picture: Harrison Ford faces a tight squeeze in Indiana Jones and the Last Crusade *(1990).*

JANUARY
FEBRUARY

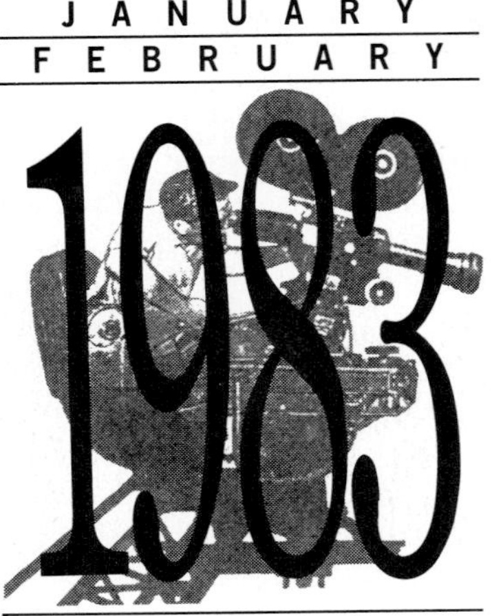

MARCH
APRIL

WHAT A FEELING!

Flashdance is the sensation of early 1983. It's one of those films that nobody held out any high hopes for yet has caught the imagination of young audiences everywhere and is raking in more money at the box office than many a long-haired movie. If it wins any Oscars, it can only be for Giorgio Moroder's pounding score, which includes the hit song, "What a Feeling".

Flashdance depicts a new kind of dancing – half way between ballet and break dancing – and it is this, probably, that has caught the kids' fancy. It looks as if anybody can do it if he or she has energy to spare.

The plot is some nonsense about a young woman who's a steel-welder by day, yearns to be a ballet star, and wins over the hoity-toity dance teachers at an audition by vitality and a thumping rock beat. The girl is played by newcomer Jennifer Beals, a knock-your-eye-out 19-year-old mulatto beauty who was discovered while still at college. Good though she is, however, that lithe body in the dance numbers actually belongs to France's Marine Jahan, not Beals – something the film-makers are keeping quiet about.

But the most unusual feature is that this ultra-American fairy tale is made by a Brit – and one, moreover, who cut his teeth on advertising. His name is Adrian Lyne, and he has said that he distrusts any film that panders to the intellect. For him, emotion is the key factor in his films – his first was the teen-drama *Foxes* (1980) – and, on the evidence, audiences seem to agree with him.

ACADEMY AWARDS

PRESENTED ON 11 APRIL 1983

Best Picture
Gandhi

Best Director
Richard Attenborough
Gandhi

Best Actor
Ben Kingsley
Gandhi

Best Actress
Meryl Streep
Sophie's Choice

Best Sup Actor
Louis Gossett, Jr.
An Officer and A Gentleman

Best Sup Actress
Jessica Lange
Tootsie

BIRTHS, DEATHS AND MARRIAGES

DEATHS

George Cukor
24 Jan, New York
Stroke

Gloria Swanson
4 Apr, New York
Heart ailment

Delores del Rio
11 Apr, Newport Beach, California

Buster Crabbe
23 Apr, Oakland, California
Heart failure

MARRIAGES

Harrison Ford
14 Mar, *to* Melissa Mathison

Rachel Ward
9 Apr, *to* Bryan Brown

IT'S THE PICTURES THAT GOT SMALL

Gloria Swanson, the silent star who made a spectacular one-off comeback in *Sunset Boulevard* (1950), died at New York Hospital on 4 April aged at least 84. In that film, in which she played a part rather similar to herself as an ageing star also trying to make a comeback, she insists that she never faded. "I'm still big," she says, "It's the pictures that got small."

Swanson started as a Mack Sennett bathing belle in 1915, but her career started to blossom when she appeared in Cecil B. DeMille sex comedies like *Don't Change Your Husband, For Better, For Worse* and *Male and Female* (all made in 1919). In 1928 she was star and producer of an Erich von Stroheim film *Queen Kelly*, which over-ran its budget so seriously that she pulled the plug on it. It wrecked Stroheim's career as a director and today only the first part and some scenes from the second survive. An excerpt from it is seen in *Sunset Blvd.* in which, ironically, Stroheim plays Swanson's chauffeur-cum-butler. It is thanks to this film that she is still remembered today, for her career had petered out in 1941 and even *Sunset Blvd.* led only to unworthy parts in costume and horror films like the TV movie *The Killer Bees* (1974). She last appeared, as herself, in *Airport 1975* (1974).

C. Thomas Howell, Tom Cruise and Emilio Estevez in The Outsiders.

COPPOLA STARTS A CRECHE

The Outsiders is not only Francis Coppola's attempt to make it back to the mainstream after the commercial and critical disaster of *One from the Heart* (1982). It's also an important training exercise for a number of young actors who show every sign of becoming big talents in their own right.

There isn't a dud among them. Emilio Estevez is the son of Martin Sheen (real name: Ramon Estevez) and first came to prominence in *Badlands* (1973) and was Coppola's choice for the lead role in *Apocalypse Now* (1979).

Estevez appears alongside a group of other young actors who play members of rival Oklahoma gangs: Matt Dillon, Patrick Swayze, Tom Cruise, Ralph Macchio, Rob Lowe and C. Thomas Howell. They are characters in a *West Side Story*-like novel that Susie Hinton wrote at the age of 15. When Coppola's company, Zoetrope, sought to acquire an option on it in 1967 it was too poor to pay the asking price of $5,000 and persuaded Hinton to accept $500 as a down payment. Shooting took place in Tulsa, beginning in March 1982, back to back with an adaptation of another Hinton novel, *Rumble Fish*, in which Matt Dillon also stars. That's due later this year.

GODFATHER TO HIS TRIBE

The son of the first flute in the NBC Symphony Orchestra under Toscanini, Francis Coppola has become a prime example in Hollywood of the director as superstar. Born in Detroit in 1939 to Italian-American parents, he studied in the film department of the University of California at Los Angeles (UCLA), during which time he made a soft-core nudie picture, *Tonight for Sure* (1961); then he moved into the film industry proper as one of Roger Corman's proteges, for whom he made a horror picture, *Dementia 13* (1963). Four years later, he presented his first mainstream picture, *You're a Big Boy Now*, as his MFA thesis at UCLA.

The breakthrough year was 1972, when he made *The Godfather* for Paramount. It became the most successful film ever made, overtaking the previous record-holder, *Jaws* (1975), and was named Best Film in the annual Oscar race. The following year *The Conversation* won the top prize at Cannes and the year after that *The Godfather Part II* became the first sequel ever to win an Oscar. It also netted him a Best Director award.

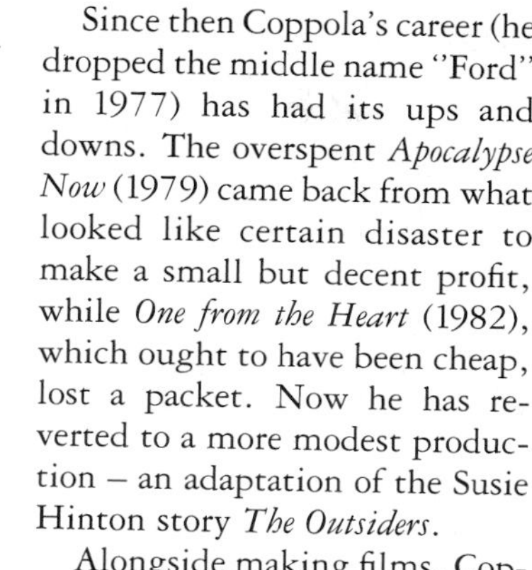

Since then Coppola's career (he dropped the middle name "Ford" in 1977) has had its ups and downs. The overspent *Apocalypse Now* (1979) came back from what looked like certain disaster to make a small but decent profit, while *One from the Heart* (1982), which ought to have been cheap, lost a packet. Now he has reverted to a more modest production – an adaptation of the Susie Hinton story *The Outsiders*.

Alongside making films, Coppola has operated a kind of creche for filmmakers (as Roger Corman had previously done at New World) at his Zoetrope studio. Carroll Ballard's *The Black Stallion* (1979) and Wim Wenders' *Hammett* (1982) were two films to benefit. Coppola has also provided work for his family – father Carmine as composer, younger sister Talia Shire and nephew Nicolas Cage as performers. Working for Coppola, says one of his technicians, is "a little bit of heaven for motion picture people".

Francis Coppola

E.T. IS CHAMP – STAR WARS BEATEN

The five-year reign of *Star Wars* (1977) is over. *E.T. The Extra-Terrestrial* (1982) is now officially the most successful film ever made. As measured by showbiz paper *Variety*, *E.T.'s* North American rentals topped $194 million at the end of last year, edging ahead of *Star Wars'* $193.5 million.

This is not the same as the box-office gross, which is much larger. Rentals are what accrues to the distributor after exhibitors have taken their cut. Also the figures are for North America only. The world-wide total will be much bigger, but is harder to collate.

Records are being broken more quickly than they used to be. *Gone with the Wind* (1939) was undisputed champ for 26 years until it was finally toppled by *The Sound of Music* in 1965. Since then, however, four films have worn the crown: *The Godfather* (1972), *Jaws* (1975), *Star Wars* and now *E.T.* Steven Spielberg, who directed *Jaws* and *E.T.* is the only filmmaker to win the title twice.

Jerry Lewis and Robert De Niro in The King of Comedy.

COMEDIAN STAGES COMEBACK

Jerry Lewis, once the more popular half of the Martin and Lewis double act, is trying to stage a comeback after his career went on the skids in the 1970s. In the prophetically entitled *Hardly Working* (1980) and now in a straight role opposite Robert De Niro in *The King of Comedy*, he is attempting to put the clock back. Ironically, though his role in *The King of Comedy* is as a stage comedian, the film sees him only off-stage as a rather grasping businessman.

Lewis was born in New Jersey in 1926. In the 1940s he began working in cabaret, met Dean Martin in 1946 and they worked together in night clubs from that time. Producer Hal Wallis saw them in 1948 and signed them up, putting them first into supporting roles in *My Friend Irma* (1949) and eventually star parts in *At War with the Army* (1951). A string of films followed but the act broke up in 1956, leaving Lewis to pursue a solo career as actor, producer and director, beginning with *The Delicate Delinquent* (1957).

Where Lewis in partnership with Dean Martin specialized in a form of lunatic comedy based on his ability to twist his indiarubber features into alarming shapes, on his own he became increasingly mawkish and aware of his duty to do good works. Though French critics started hailing him as *"le roi de Crazy"*, American audiences grew indifferent. Several films flopped, including *Which Way to the Front?* (1970) and *The Day the Clown Cried*, a project he aborted in 1972, in which he played a clown entertaining Jewish children on their way to the gas chambers.

SCORSESE SHOWS HIS FUNNY BONE

The King of Comedy, the new film by ex-movie brat Martin Scorsese, is his most unusual to date. It's a comedy about a stagestruck lummox who kidnaps a comedian and says he will release him only if he is allowed to appear and crack jokes on his show. It stars Jerry Lewis, who began his career as a nightclub performer, and Robert De Niro plays the fan.

The film took 20 weeks to shoot and was continually beset by production problems. "We didn't get one break from anybody in New York," Scorsese says, "or at least that's how it felt. If we wanted something, we had to pay for it and pay a lot." The script was written 14 years earlier with Dick Cavett in mind. Johnny Carson was later approached for the comedian part but turned it down. It was only when Lewis agreed that production went ahead.

STAR QUOTES

Dean Martin

"At some point Jerry Lewis said to himself, I'm extraordinary, like Chaplin. From then on nobody could tell him anything."

HOLLYWOOD ACQUIRES A NEW MAJOR

The face of Hollywood has been fixed, more or less, since the 1920s. Studios just don't rise any more (though some, like RKO and Republic, fall). Now, however, for the first time in more than 60 years, Hollywood has a new name to conjure with. Tri-Star is a brand-new major distribution company, differing from the other studios only in so far as it will not have sound stages and a back-lot of its own.

Tri-Star, as the name implies, is owned three ways. Columbia, itself a Hollywood major though now owned by Coca-Cola, is one of the partners, with CBS and Home Box Office. The idea behind the deal is that Tri-Star will be able to furnish its parents with assured product to meet their TV and video needs. Columbia executives will be heading the company (Victor Kaufman as chairman and David Matalon as president), but it will be operated independently of Columbia itself. Its logo will be Pegasus, the winged horse of Greek mythology.

STAR QUOTES

Roger Moore

"You're not a star till they can spell your name in Vladivostock."

STAR WARS – IT'S A WRAP

Return of the Jedi (allegedly episode six in a nine-part series) wraps up the story of Luke Skywalker, Han Solo, R2-D2 et al, and effectively brings *Star Wars* to a close, whatever the rolling title at the beginning may say. The most costly of the three films to date (at $32.5 million), it's as certain a box-office winner as any film can be.

The plot contains some surprises, notably that Darth Vader is Luke Skywalker's father and that the special relationship Luke feels for Princess Leia is based not on sexual attraction, but on the fact that they're twins. This, of course, leaves the way free for Han Solo to get chummy with the princess.

Special effects are variable – superb in the Sarlac pit in the first part of the film, less convincing in the scenes in the forest involving the Ewoks. The new characters are memorable: the Ewoks are the cutest creatures since Teddy bears, while Jabba the Hutt is an invention of genius. Jabba was mentioned in *Star Wars* in the scene when Han Solo zaps Greedo, who is working for Jabba. He is then forgotten until the final episode, but when he eventually appears, he lives up to expectations – a huge slug-like being with a giant mouth.

Each of the three films has had a different director (this one is made by Richard Marquand), but they are all of a piece thanks to the continuing control of producer George Lucas.

Carrie Fisher and Mark Hamill in The Return of the Jedi.

THIS IS THE WAY THE WORLD ENDS

Matthew Broderick and Ally Sheedy are the young stars of WarGames.

WarGames, M-G-M's new sci-fi thriller, is the kind of motion picture that one hopes is fantasy. It shows how a computer hacker might inadvertently break into America's nuclear defence system and trigger off a world war.

What's interesting is that it gives the impression of depicting a thermo-nuclear war in progress, yet shows nothing except arrows on a bank of TV monitors zeroing in on their targets. It's the cheapest world war ever fought.

The cast is made up of Brat Packers Matthew Broderick and Ally Sheedy to please the teen market and oldster Dabney Coleman to lend a touch of maturity for older audiences. It's directed by British-born, Alabama-raised John Badham, who made the Frank Langella version of *Dracula* (1979) but currently has another hi-tech movie in release, *Blue Thunder*, which suggests that he may be ready to take over this genre.

DEATH OF DAVID NIVEN

David Niven, one of the most popular British actors ever to make a home and a career for himself in Hollywood, died in Switzerland on 29 July, aged 73. He drifted into acting in the 1930s after being discharged from the British army. A physical resemblance to Ronald Colman persuaded Sam Goldwyn to put him under an M-G-M contract and he appeared in several Colman-like roles for him, notably *Raffles* (1939). During this time he was a close friend of both Errol Flynn and Douglas Fairbanks, Jr.

During the Second World War he re-enlisted in the British army and was later discharged with the rank of colonel. During this time, he made propaganda-cum-feature films like *The First of the Few* (1942) and *The Way Ahead* (1944). When he resumed his film career after the war he had a clause written into all his contracts specifying that the script should somewhere refer to a character named Trubshaw (a forces buddy). It became as identifiable a gimmick as Hitchcock's cameo performances.

He won an Oscar in 1958 for his performance as the bogus army officer in *Separate Tables* and proved remarkably durable throughout the 1960s and 1970s in films like *The Guns of Navarone* (1961), *55 Days at Peking* (1963) and *Death on the Nile* (1978). His autobiography, *The Moon's a Balloon*, published in 1971, was a best seller, and led to two other books.

BIRTHS, DEATHS AND MARRIAGES

DEATHS

Norma Shearer
12 Jun, Woodland Hills, California
Pneumonia

Luis Bunuel
29 Jun, Mexico City
Cirrhosis of the liver

David Niven
29 Jul, Geneva
Motor neurone disease

MARRIAGES

Richard Burton
Jul, *to* Sally Hay

Dan Aykroyd, Jamie Lee Curtis, Eddie Murphy and Denholm Elliott in Trading Places.

A FULLY FUNGIBLE FILM

Commodity and futures markets have a vocabulary of their own. *Trading Places*, the new Eddie Murphy-Dan Aykroyd comedy set in the Chicago futures markets, demonstrates the fact – though it manages not to make non-experts feel stupid.

The movie's title is a pun: it means both the place in which trading takes place and the act of swapping identity – becoming, in other words, something that, in the jargon of the futures business, is fully fungible (exchangeable) with something else. In the film, through a chapter of accidents, yuppie Aykroyd finds that he has changed places with tramp Murphy. The fun of the film lies in seeing how they respond to their dramatically changed roles, with Murphy the debonair know-it-all and Aykroyd a put-upon prole. The director is John Landis, currently fighting to clear his name in a legal case brought as a result of fatalities in his episode of the current *Twilight Zone – The Movie*.

Also starring are Don Ameche, a romantic star of the 1940s, now carving out a new career as a light comedian late in life, and Jamie Lee Curtis, daughter of Tony Curtis and Janet Leigh. For the newly-pneumatic Curtis her role as a hooker is quite a change from the *Halloween* screamers she's been making her name in.

CHIP OFF THE OLD BLOCKS

Jamie Lee Curtis comes with as good a pedigree as you can get in the movies. She's the daughter of not one but two stars. Her father is Tony Curtis and her mother Janet Leigh, who were married between 1951 and 1962.

Born in Los Angeles in 1958, she first drifted into show business in 1977 when she was signed up by Universal, her parents' old studio, during a break from college. After guest shots in *Columbo* and *The Nancy Drew Mysteries* she became a TV regular in the show *Operation Petticoat*, which, coincidentally, was a spinoff from the 1959 movie her father had originally starred in.

But Jamie Lee never seemed able to land a starring role herself. In part, perhaps, it was because she has unconventional features. "I have an odd face, which is good, actually, in the film business. It's uneven (offbeat, I'd say) and therefore it makes me interesting."

Her first big part was in *Halloween* (1978), a movie in which she is menaced by a maniac – just as her mother had been by Anthony Perkins in *Psycho* 18 years before. The trouble was that it led her to be typecast at the very beginning of her career. Four of her next five films were all of this type: *The Fog*, *Prom Night* and *Terror Train* (all 1980), and *Halloween II* (1981). Only *Road Games* (1981), a psychological thriller, broke the mould.

Now, however, it looks as if she will finally make the breakthrough with the Eddie Murphy comedy *Trading Places*, in which she plays a hooker and gets to strip for the camera. With luck, it can lend a whole new dimension to her career. "I don't want a little career," she says; "I plan to be around for a long time."

NICE GUY GOES ROBOTIC

"I have this kind of mild, nice-guy exterior but, inside, my heart is like a steel trap. I'm really quite robotic." So says Dan Aykroyd, the 33-year-old Canadian-born comedian who is currently the talk of the town as one half of a remarkable comic double act with black actor Eddie Murphy in *Trading Places*.

He first made his name in NBC-TV's *Saturday Night Live* and for several years developed a comedy routine with fellow actor John Belushi that was too rarely reflected in films. On screen they appeared together only twice. The first of these, Steven Spielberg's *1941* (1979), was essentially a series of individual acts, but the second, *The Blues Brothers* (1980), was a true marriage of minds. Unfortunately, it failed at the box office, and within two years Belushi was dead of drug abuse.

Aykroyd is made of sterner stuff. His skills as a comedian are a means to an end. He, of all comedians, is likely to end up in a different profession (politics perhaps?). For, as he says, "The entertainment business is not the be-all and end-all for me."

GOSSIP COLUMN

■ **Cannes this year has a spanking new edition, grandly known as the New Palais. But it's been an open invitation to gremlins. Projection equipment has gone on the blink, leaving films being shown on the curtains, while the entire market section has been banished to the (windowless) basement.**

SEPTEMBER
OCTOBER

NOVEMBER
DECEMBER

RIDE 'EM, COWBOY

Debra Winger has never been conventional. Born 1955 in Cleveland, she was told at the age of 14 that she had no class (by George Cukor, no less), enlisted in the Israeli army at 16, and two years later suffered severe paralysis and partial blindness when she feel off a truck. It was this that encouraged her to pursue her acting career on the grounds that she might not have much time remaining and had better get where she was going to get quickly.

After dropping out of college she made commercials and in 1976 played Wonder Girl to Lynda Carter's Wonder Woman in the TV series. But it was not until 1980 that she first caught audiences' eyes in the John Travolta film *Urban Cowboy*, in which she performed unmentionable things astride a mechanical bucking bronco. She took over Raquel Welch's part in the little-seen *Cannery Row* (1982) when the actress walked off the film, and was asked by her friend Steven Spielberg to supply the voice of the alien in *E.T.* (1982). A sympathetic performance in *An Officer and a Gentleman* followed the same year and now in *Terms of Endearment*, playing Shirley MacLaine's plucky but terminally ill daughter, gurus are talking at least of an Academy Award nomination.

Winger has been attracting almost as much attention for her outspokenness off-screen as for her husky tones on-screen. She has described Richard Gere, her co-star in *An Officer and a Gentleman* as "a brick wall. The producer was the only living person I had contact with, and he was a total pig."

SOAP, LOVE AND KISSES

Terms of Endearment is the kind of film that sweeps the board at Oscar time, and no one will be surprised if it does just that next spring. A laughter-and-tears saga of the up-and-down relationship between a kooky mother and her independent daughter, who ultimately dies of cancer, it's an unashamed crowd-pleaser.

What it does have is great parts for its hand-picked cast. Shirley MacLaine, who has been knocking on Oscar's door ever since she first appeared in Alfred Hitchcock's *The Trouble with Harry* (1955), may finally hit the winning combination this time. She is backed up by no less impressive performances from Debra Winger as her daughter and Jack Nicholson as a former astronaut neighbour with lust in his eyes and too many linguini round his waistline. Winger was last seen being swept off her feet by Richard Gere in *An Officer and a Gentleman* (1982). Nicholson, who won an Oscar in 1975 for *One Flew over the Cuckoo's Nest*, is now building a new reputation for himself as a scene-stealer in supporting roles – like his Eugene O'Neill in *Reds*.

The picture is directed by first-time film-maker James L. Brooks, who cut his teeth on TV shows like *The Mary Tyler Moore Show* and *Taxi* before graduating to the cinema as scriptwriter for *Starting Over* (1979), with Burt Reynolds. He gives the film the compulsive watchability of a TV soap; but don't get too carried away by all that lovey-dovey stuff between MacLaine and Winger – on-set relations between the duo were a little cooler than Alaska.

Jack Nicholson, an ex-astronaut, and neighbour Shirley MacLaine in Terms of Endearment.

GLAD TO SEE YOU AGAIN, SEAN

"Never again" is what Sean Connery is alleged to have said when he played what he thought would be his last James Bond – *Diamonds Are Forever* (1971). But, 12 years and a reputed fee of $5 million later, he's at it again. The aptly titled *Never Say Never Again* features Connery as 007 even though the present incumbent, Roger Moore, has not yet retired.

In fact, it's a remake. *Thunderball* (1965) was one of the few Ian Fleming novels in which movie tycoon "Cubby" Broccoli did not have rights. Producer Kevin McClory made it instead – and now he makes it again.

There are some good jokes. "Things have been awfully dull round here," says Q; "I hope we're going to have some gratuitous sex and violence." Twelve years, however, have thickened Connery's waistline a little and the film hasn't the terrific special effects that now enliven the Roger Moore films. But there's some compensation in Barbara Carrera's sexy assassin Fatima Blush, and Klaus Maria Brandauer's game-playing villain.

Connery himself, who had a hand in all stages of the new production, from writing to casting and editing, has never had much regard for the character that launched him to fame. "I don't really suppose I'd like Bond if I met him. He's not my kind of chap at all."

STAR QUOTES

Shirley MacLaine

"I've played so many hookers they don't pay me in the regular way any more. They leave it on the dresser."

BOX OFFICE

UK

1 E.T. The Extra-Terrestrial
2 Return of the Jedi
3 Octopussy
4 Gandhi
5 Tootsie
6 Superman III
7 An Officer and a Gentleman
8 Staying Alive
9 Airplane II the Sequel
10 Monty Python's Meaning of Life

BOX OFFICE

US

1 Return of the Jedi
2 Tootsie
3 Trading Places
4 WarGames
5 Superman III
6 Flashdance
7 Staying Alive
8 Octopussy
9 Mr. Mom
10 48HRS.

Meryl Streep, as Karen Silkwood, and Cher in the true story *Silkwood*.

COMEBACK FOR MIKE NICHOLS

When he won an Oscar for only his second film, *The Graduate* (1967), it looked as if Mike Nichols could demand an open cheque from Hollywood. It hasn't quite worked out like that. Of his succeeding films, only *Carnal Knowledge* (1971) performed well at the box office. The former night-club partner of Elaine May has somewhat squandered his chances and, apart from a straight record of the stage act of Gilda Radner in *Gilda Live* (1980), has not made a proper film for eight years.

Silkwood brings him right back into the limelight. It's a crusading picture about the life and mysterious death of Karen Silkwood, an employee at a plutonium processing plant. Made aware of the inadequate safety precautions at her workplace, she was about to blow the whistle on the plant when she died in November 1974 in what was described as a "one-car accident".

Nichols does not say it was anything other than that, but from the shots of another car attempting to overtake her in the moments before her death, he at least leaves other possibilities open. He has also lined up a terrific cast to put the story across. Meryl Streep's gum-chewing, mini-clad working girl adds yet another dimension to her range, while former singer Cher (once half of the Sonny and Cher pop duo) consolidates her growing reputation as an actress as Streep's lesbian workmate.

STREEP PUTS THE ACCENT ON QUALITY

Thirty-four-year-old Meryl Streep has come from nowhere to first lady of the American screen in six short years. Her first part, as Jane Fonda's society friend in *Julia* (1977), largely ended up on the cutting room floor. And for the first few years of her career, it looked as if she would be confined to supporting parts – Robert De Niro's girlfriend in *The Deer Hunter* (1978), Woody Allen's lesbian ex-wife in *Manhattan* (1979) and a Louisiana political activist in *The Seduction of Joe Tynan* (1979). One of these small parts, however, in *Kramer vs Kramer* (1979) was so telling that she won an Oscar for it.

Since then, Streep's career has never looked back. Recovering from the shock of losing her lover, John Cazale, to bone marrow cancer, she threw herself into her career and has tackled ever more challenging roles, most of which require the assumption of accents very different from her own New Jersey twang. In each of them she has won over critics who might have been expected to be sceptical. Her English accent for *The French Lieutenant's Woman* (1981) satisfied even the Brits, while her Polish one in *Sophie's Choice* (1982) was so convincing that the Academy gave her another Oscar, this time in the major league.

Her latest role breaks new ground yet again – she plays a factory worker in *Silkwood*. For this the Streep tones have changed yet again – to proletarian Texan.

CHARIOTEER BOWS OUT

Jake Eberts, the Canadian-born entrepreneur who has helped to build up Goldcrest from a one-horse outfit to a major Oscar-winner two years in a row, is quitting. He is standing down as chief executive in favour of his colleague James Lee and will join Embassy in America in the New Year.

Under Eberts' command, Goldcrest became the most conspicuous and extensive film production unit in Britain. Among the films with which it was associated were *Chariots of Fire* (1981) and *Gandhi* (1982), both Oscar winners.

It seems the company has grown too big for Eberts, who prefers striking small, individual deals to administering a huge production slate running to many millions of dollars. Says David Puttnam, one of Goldcrest's directors, "Jake didn't ever develop projects, and one thing that will now change stylistically is that at Goldcrest there will be less deal-making and more developing."

For his part, Eberts hints at burn-out. "In my heart I can't keep the level of energy and enthusiasm going night and day, every day. Suddenly I'm not so keen to be at my desk at 7.30 every morning. I want to get back to what I'm best at: doing film projects and individual deals."

LAST CURTAIN FOR FAMOUS STAGE KNIGHT

Ralph Richardson has died in London on 10 October, aged 80. He was one of that great trio of stage knights (Olivier and Gielgud were the others) who sometimes also made fine movies. Though his first film role was, unpromisingly, in *The Ghoul* (1933), he had three personal hits in a row in 1948 and 1949, shortly after he was knighted: as Baines the butler in *The Fallen Idol* (1948), as Tolstoy's icy Karenin in *Anna Karenina* (1948) and as Dr. Sloper in *The Heiress* (1949).

Classical parts found him at his best. He was a memorable James Tyrone in *Long Day's Journey into Night* (1962) and a fine Buckingham for Olivier in *Richard III* (1955). In later years he appeared in less worthy parts, such as Themistocles in *The 300 Spartans* (1961). But a sense of fun pervaded all of this later work. He was a known eccentric in life (and a great rider of motorbikes) and he went out in style in *Greystoke* (one of four films still to be released). Production stills show him, as Tarzan's noble grandfather, gleefully sliding downstairs on a tea-tray.

BIRTHS, DEATHS AND MARRIAGES

DEATHS

Ralph Richardson
10 Oct, London
Digestive ailment

Pat O'Brien
15 Oct, Santa Monica, California
Heart attack following surgery

Robert Aldrich
5 Dec, Los Angeles
Kidney failure

William Demarest
28 Dec, Palm Springs, California
Heart attack

GOSSIP COLUMN

■ Universal boss Lew Wasserman plans to turn Universal City in Los Angeles into a theme park a la Disneyland. Meanwhile, he is building a top-secret production unit for Steven Spielberg's Amblin outfit on the Universal lot. State-of-the-art facilities will include a computer hook-up to Lucas Films.

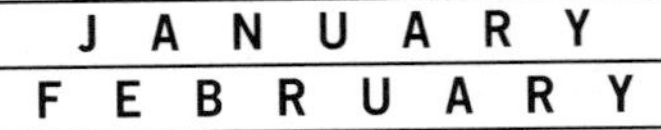

JANUARY
FEBRUARY

MARCH
APRIL

GETTING BACK TO THE "REAL" TARZAN?

Greystoke: The Legend of Tarzan Lord of the Apes, to give it its full title, is an attempt to strip away generations of movie accretions and get back to the Tarzan that originally figured in Edgar Rice Burroughs's 1915 novel *Tarzan of the Apes*. This means reviving the notion that he is the descendant of a noble English family who, through accident, was deprived of his parents at a young age and grew up in the jungle. The movie shows what might have happened if Tarzan had been reunited with his English family and been brought face to face with the contrast between primitive culture and the conventions of the English aristocracy.

Dedicated "in loving memory" to Ralph Richardson, one of the stars, it's Hugh Hudson's first film since *Chariots of Fire* (1981) and cost a packet ($33m) that Warners will be lucky to get back. It has been a troubled production, and Hudson's preferred version ran 20 minutes longer than the 130-odd at which it is finally being released. Another problem was that newcomer Andie MacDowell, who made her name modelling for L'Oreal, had a deep southern American drawl. Even though the character is American-born, her twang was replaced by the softer tones of actress Glenn Close.

Tarzan himself is played by another newcomer, French-American Christopher Lambert, also known as Christophe Lambert, who is most imposing – until he opens his mouth. The real stars of the film, shot in Cameroon and Scotland, are Tarzan's simian playmates in the huge forest set built at Elstree Studios. Real monkeys vie with mime artists in hairy suits – and you can't tell the difference.

Christopher Lambert as the "true" Tarzan in Greystoke.

TARZAN IS DEAD: LONG LIVE TARZAN

Johnny Weissmuller, best known of all the actors to play Tarzan of the Apes, died at his Acapulco home on 20 January. He was 79. Born in Pennsylvania in 1904, in his youth he was a champion swimmer and won five gold medals at the Olympic Games of 1924 and 1928. He first played Edgar Rice Burroughs's hero in *Tarzan, the Ape Man* (1932) and went on to play the role 11 more times, the last occasion being in *Tarzan and the Mermaids* (1948). After this he appeared as Jungle Jim and sometimes as himself, most recently in the 1920s Hollywood spoof, *Won Ton Ton, the Dog Who Saved Hollywood* (1975). Married five times, including once to fiery Mexican actress Lupe Velez, he always claimed: "I'm an athlete, not an actor." His death comes just as a new actor takes the role. Christopher Lambert plays Tarzan in *Greystoke*, which goes back to the character's origins as the son of a noble lord.

Daryl Hannah as beautiful mermaid Madison in Splash.

ACTRESS MAKES A SPLASH

Born and raised in Chicago, the tall and leggy 24-year-old Daryl Hannah has literally made waves in her first starring role. She plays a mermaid called Madison in the Disney comedy hit *Splash*, which is being released through the studio's new Touchstone arm – meant to signify films slightly more daring than those customarily associated with that studio.

Ballet-trained Hannah studied acting at the prestigious Goodman Theater and before she had finished high school had a small part in *The Fury* (1978), which was filmed in Chicago. She moved to Los Angeles to attend college and soon began to win parts in big pictures. She played a "replicant" (robot) in *Blade Runner* (1982) and showed off her dance skills opposite fast-rising Mickey Rourke in *The Pope of Greenwich Village* (1984). But it is her curvaceous, landlocked mermaid that shows for the first time what she is really made of.

BIRTHS, DEATHS AND MARRIAGES

DEATHS

Johnny Weissmuller
20 Jan, Acapulco, Mexico
Lung blockage

Ethel Merman
15 Feb, New York

William Powell
5 Mar, Palm Springs, California

WHAT'S IN A NAME?

When Steve Guttenberg (pronounce it Gootenberg, the German way) first came to Hollywood they wanted to call him Rock Venture. But figuring that one Rock was enough, he stuck by his name. "I hung in there," he says. "Ten years ago, would you have bet on Arnold Schwarzenegger becoming a movie star? And Arnold, for God's sake! It's a wimp's name."

Guttenberg, born in Brooklyn in 1958, arrived in Hollywood in 1977 and appeared in a number of now largely forgotten movies - like the high-school sex comedy *The Chicken Chronicles* (1977) and the Ali MacGraw tennis soap *Players* (1979). Never one to push himself, he seemed in danger of being overlooked, but he had the good sense to take part of his salary in one picture in the form of a share of the profits. That film was *Police Academy* and it's turning into the runaway success of the year. He's already being tipped as a big star, but he still keeps the common touch. He does not live it up in nightclubs and he doesn't punch photographers. "Nice doesn't make headlines," he says. "Nice is boring. But nice is low profile – and that's what I like."

Steve Guttenberg, Michael Winslow and G.W. Bailey in Police Academy.

COP OUT

Police Academy is the kind of comedy whose success nobody can quite explain but which has them queuing round the block. The story of a group of rookie cops and the personal and professional problems they encounter while undergoing training, the movie was shot in Canada by Hugh Wilson, who made his name on the show *WKRP in Cincinnati* and then went on to co-write a number of media satires, like *Tunnelvision*.

Steve Guttenberg is the star, but this splendidly vulgar, pratfall movie is essentially an ensemble piece. Trivia fans will spot porno star Georgina (*The Devil in Miss Jones*) Spelvin as a hooker, Bubba Smith (of Miller's Lite beer commercials) as a florist, and G.W. Bailey (transvestite Rizzo in TV's *M*A*S*H*) as a fanatical drill sergeant. It's also the first American movie to begin and end with a blow-job.

ACADEMY AWARDS

PRESENTED ON 9 APRIL 1984

Best Picture
Terms of Endearment

Best Director
James L. Brooks
Terms of Endearment

Best Actor
Robert Duvall
Tender Mercies

Best Actress
Shirley MacLaine
Terms of Endearment

Best Sup Actor
Jack Nicholson
Terms of Endearment

Best Sup Actress
Linda Hunt
The Year of Living Dangerously

STAR QUOTES

Ken Russell

"This is not the age of manners. This is the age of kicking people in the crotch and getting a reaction."

NOBODY WANTS A FIVE-FOOT-TALL CHARACTER ACTOR

"Nobody wants a five-foot-tall character actor," barked a Hollywood casting lady, throwing his picture back at him. That was the kind of reaction Danny DeVito had all too often when he was trying to break into the movies. A graduate of the American Academy of Dramatic Arts, he made his way to Hollywood in the 1960s only to be underwhelmed by its generosity.

He was so depressed that he made a Super-8 home movie of his experiences and called it *The Death of a Roach*, because insects were the only actors he could afford. He showed it to actress Rhea Perlman on a first date and she was so taken by it that she married him.

As an actor, DeVito first broke through off-Broadway with a production of *One Flew over the Cuckoo's Nest*. Then his old friend Michael Douglas asked him to repeat it for the screen version, which he was preparing to produce. Then came *Taxi*, a popular TV series that lasted for five seasons and brought him an Emmy for his performance as the tyrannical Louie de Palma. He even got to direct three episodes of the series and this has fired an ambition that he hopes one day to fulfil in the cinema. Besides last year's *Terms of Endearment*, he can be seen still clowning it up in the current hit *Romancing the Stone* with his old buddy Michael Douglas.

ROLL OVER, INDIANA

Romancing the Stone is an undisguised attempt to copy and go one better than Indiana Jones. It's a straight adventure movie, harking back to old-style serials and starring Michael Douglas in the Harrison Ford role. Douglas, the son of actor Kirk Douglas, has hitherto shown himself to have creative ambitions that are hardly touched here (he produced, among other things, the 1975 Oscar winner *One Flew over the Cuckoo's Nest*).

Here he plays opposite sexy Kathleen Turner, 29, who first set pulses racing in *Body Heat* (1981). The director is young Robert Zemeckis, a Steven Spielberg protege who cut his teeth on the pop musical *I Wanna Hold Your Hand* (1978) and the ultimate auto-smash comedy *Used Cars* (1980). Also in the cast is a pint-sized comedian named Danny DeVito, from the TV series *Taxi*, who is so funny in his own right that it cannot be long before he becomes a star.

Michael Douglas and Kathleen Turner.

MAY
JUNE

JULY
AUGUST

THE RETURN OF INDIANA JONES

The huge success of *Raiders of the Lost Ark* (1981), Steven Spielberg's tribute to the lost world of 1930s programmes and movie serials, made it inevitable that hero Indiana Jones would one day stage a comeback. He does so in *Indiana Jones and the Temple of Doom*, from a story by *Star Wars* creator George Lucas.

There are two big differences from *Raiders*. One is that the heroine (Kate Capshaw) is now a blonde bimbo, whereas Karen Allen in the earlier film was more than able to hold her own and trade blows with Indy. The second is that this prequel picks up the horror element rather than the simple thrills of the first picture. Among the grosser features are a dinner in which the delicacy is chilled monkey brains and a scene in which Indy's heart is apparently torn out of his chest.

Indy's second outing again stars Harrison Ford as the archaeologist-cum-adventurer. Although it starts in Shanghai, at a nightspot called the Club Obi Wan (geddit?), most of the story is set around an Indian maharajah's palace, beneath which is the terrible Temple of Doom. Apart from present-day Macau standing in for 1935 Shanghai, all exteriors were shot in Sri Lanka. It cost $27 million – $5 million more than *Raiders* – but early box-office indications are that it will again end comfortably in profit.

Dan Aykroyd, Bill Murray and Harold Ramis are Ghost Busters.

KARATE KID COMES OUT FIGHTING

For a whippersnapper, young Ralph Macchio has fought his way to the top in Hollywood in double-quick time. This summer he is one of Hollywood's hottest properties, thanks to *The Karate Kid*, in which he is taught the spiritual philosophy underlying martial arts by a venerable old Japanese American (Noriyuki "Pat" Morita).

Macchio, born in 1961, was raised in Suffolk County, New York, and found himself drawn at an early age to music and dance. In his teens he performed in local New York musical productions, at one of which, at Hofstra University, he was spotted by talent scout Marie Pastor. Soon after this he was doing commercials and appearing in small roles in television and films.

He made his debut in 1980 in a film called *Up the Academy*, a typical youth-orientated picture of the time, and then went on to become a regular member of the TV series *Eight Is Enough*. After appearing in a couple of TV movies of the week, *Journey to Survival* and *Dangerous Company*, he landed the role of Johnny Cade in Francis Coppola's Brat Pack movie *The Outsiders* (1983), which persuaded Columbia to give him the lead role in *The Karate Kid*.

HOLD THAT SPECTRE!

Ghost Busters boasts such amusing and impressive special effects that it is certain to finish up among the all-time Hollywood money-spinners. The idea is simple – a group of academic failures set up in business as ghostbusters and have a whale of a time winkling out ectoplasm and other spooky manifestations.

It cost a lost ($32 million), but always looked a dead cert to get its money back with interest. And that is how it's panning out as it becomes the box-office sensation of the summer.

Dan Aykroyd, Bill Murray and Harold Ramis play the ghostbusters, with Sigourney Weaver (monster-zapping heroine of the 1979 movie *Alien*) unable here to stop monsters having their way with her. The director is Canadian-born Ivan Reitman, who previously worked with Murray and Ramis in *Stripes* (1981), a parody of basic training in the army.

FUNNY GUY FROM CHICAGO

Bill Murray who, on the strength of *Ghost Busters*, can now virtually dictate terms to Hollywood, did not plan on a career in show business. In fact, while studying at the Jesuit-run Regis College in Colorado, the Illinois-born actor seriously considered a career either in medicine or on the baseball field.

Born in 1950, he was the black sheep of a family of five brothers, and a poor student. Life changed for him when he met John Belushi and Harold Ramis and joined Chicago's improvisational Second City Company. This led to work on *National Lampoon's Radio Hour* and NBC-TV's *Saturday Night Live*. That in turn brought him into the cinema when Ivan Reitman, who co-produced *National Lampoon's Animal House* (1978) for the movies, wanted to try his hand at direction with a broad-based spoof set in a boy's summer camp.

This was *Meatballs* (1979) and it was widely observed that Murray, as camp counsellor, held the show together. More success followed in *Stripes* (1981), a satire on military basic training, an unbilled role as Dustin Hoffman's room-mate in *Tootsie* (1982), and now in *Ghost Busters*. Murray made the latter as half of a package deal with Columbia that would also allow him to play his first dramatic role in a remake of *The Razor's Edge*, due out later this year.

Charlie Sheen and Patrick Swayze search for Russians in John Milius' Red Dawn.

THE RUSSIANS ARE COMING! THE RUSSIANS ARE COMING!

Red Dawn is the most controversial film of the summer. It's an unashamedly right-wing movie showing how the future of America and the free world might come to depend on teenagers if the Soviet Union started the Third World War. In the movie, the Russkies and their Cuban henchmen swoop into America by parachute and it's left to a small band of kids calling themselves the Wolverines to defend democracy.

This is the fantasy of the self-styled "zen-fascist" director, John Milius, whose life is a testimony to the importance of guns and other weapons of destruction. His films include *Dillinger* (1973) and *Conan the Barbarian* (1982).

What makes the film interesting is that it gives key roles to a number of young actors and actresses who, by virtue of their youth, are coming to be known as the Brat Pack (not to be confused with the Movie Brats, directors like Steven Spielberg, Brian De Palma and Francis Coppola). Starring in this film are Patrick Swayze and C. Thomas Howell – both of whom were in Coppola's *The Outsiders* (1983) – and a promising young actress called Jennifer Grey. But the most intriguing is Charlie Sheen, son of actor Martin Sheen and half-brother of Emilio Estevez, who appeared in *The Outsiders*: living proof that lightning does strike twice.

BYE BURTON

Richard Burton, who died on 5 August in a Geneva hospital, aged 58, ought to have been the greatest actor of his generation, the one British player to pick up and carry forward the torch borne by Laurence Olivier. Instead, he became the man who married Elizabeth Taylor twice (1964-74 and 1975-6) and attracted more publicity for the size of the diamonds he gave her than for the quality of his Hamlet.

Born Richard Jenkins in South Wales, 1925, Burton was the very image of a Shakespearean actor. His voice possessed an heroic Welsh timbre that seemed to point to a great theatrical career in the classical repertoire. Yet within a few years of going to Hollywood in 1952 he was driven to accept parts that were unworthy of him.

For every *Who's Afraid of Virginia Woolf?* (1966), in which he brought out the wonderful acrimony and wit of Edward Albee's play, there were a dozen *Anne of the Thousand Days* (1969) in which he played a stereotyped Henry VIII, and even more films like *The Klansman* (1974), in which he squandered his talent.

It would be good to think that his last film, *Nineteen Eighty-Four*, atoned for a lifetime of inadequacy, but it was not to be. Burton was an actor seemingly born to play Heathcliff but who did so only in the ephemeral medium of TV. He once claimed to be "pleased intellectually" with his performances in *The Spy Who Came in from the Cold* (1965), *Look Back in Anger* (1959), *Becket* (1964) and *Virginia Woolf*. He will, alas, be remembered more for his soppy Mark Antony in the overblown *Cleopatra* (1963) and action movies like *The Wild Geese* (1978). Truly, a great talent unfulfilled.

THE MONUMENTAL MASON

James Mason died in Lausanne, Switzerland, on 27 July, aged 75. He was one of the best-educated British actors of the 1940s, having taken a degree in architecture at Cambridge. Born in Yorkshire, he early lost all trace of a North Country accent.

He made his first film, *Late Extra*, in 1935. By 1946 he was Britain's highest-paid star and, with the release of *The Wicked Lady*, its top box-office draw. His greatest English role was as the wounded IRA man in *Odd Man Out* (1947); he then settled in Hollywood. He was a noble Brutus in *Julius Caesar* (1953), a surprisingly agile Rupert of Hentzau in the remake of *The Prisoner of Zenda* (1952), and a superb foil to Judy Garland in *A Star Is Born* (1954). His last, still to be released, is in *The Shooting Party*.

BIRTHS, DEATHS AND MARRIAGES

DEATHS

Diana Dors
4 May, Windsor, Berkshire
Cancer

Joseph Losey
22 Jun, London
Cancer

Carl Foreman
26 Jun, Los Angeles
Cancer

Flora Robson
7 Jul, East Sussex

James Mason
27 Jul, Lausanne, Switzerland
Heart attack

Richard Burton
5 Aug, Geneva, Switzerland
Brain haemorrhage

SEPTEMBER
OCTOBER

NOVEMBER
DECEMBER

EPIC TOUCH RETURNS TO BRITISH CINEMA

Sam Waterston and Haing S. Ngor in The Killing Fields.

David Puttnam's production of *The Killing Fields* marks a return to the epic tradition of British filmmaking that went into hibernation when David Lean virtually stopped making movies after *Ryan's Daughter* (1970). It's the true story of how *New York Times* journalist Sidney Schanberg was separated from and eventually re-united with his Cambodian friend, photographer Dith Pran, during the war in Cambodia.

It's an emotional movie (actually shot, for obvious reasons, in Thailand) and has a sweep that no British film has displayed in years. Astonishingly, it is the work of first-time movie director Roland Joffe, who had previously worked in theatre and television. But he has taken to movies as if his previous work was just a clearing of the throat. Here is a born filmmaker who has finally found his medium, though he is greatly helped by ace cameraman Chris Menges.

Sam Waterston, an American actor who appeared in *The Great Gatsby* (1974) but has not yet achieved star quality, plays Schanberg. But the film's biggest coup is to cast a Cambodian doctor (who was operating on a patient when the Khmer Rouge stormed into his hospital) as Dith Pran. He is Dr. Haing S. Ngor, who escaped with his niece to Thailand when Vietnam invaded Cambodia and worked as a doctor in refugee camps for 18 months before leaving for Los Angeles in 1980.

READY FOR FREDDY?

The most popular figure in American cinema today is a child molester with a hideously deformed face and finger-nails made of razors. He is Freddy Krueger, otherwise known as actor Robert Englund. Freddy is the central figure in a powerful new horror film called *A Nightmare on Elm Street*, in which he is incinerated by the matrons of a small American town in revenge for paedophilia. But Freddy won't lie down and is apt to be called back from the dead in nightmares.

For such a scary man, Robert Englund has a remarkably unsensational background. He was born in 1948, looks positively normal in real life and has done all the usual things that good actors do, including playing in Shakespeare. On television he won wide popularity in the maxi mini-series *V* (1983) as the most sympathetic of the lizard-like aliens who disguise themselves as humans.

Making up for the role of Freddy took Englund three hours every day. But it is him rather than the colourless heroine (Heather Langenkamp), that audiences are remembering, largely because he has a macabre sense of humour. Says Englund: "He doesn't say anything side-splitting, but his diabolical jokes relieve the tension. I let you laugh so I can scare you again."

BOX OFFICE

UK

1 Indiana Jones and the Temple of Doom
2 Never Say Never Again
3 The Jungle Book
4 Police Academy
5 Sudden Impact
6 Terms of Endearment
7 Educating Rita
8 Trading Places
9 Greystoke: The Legend of Tarzan Lord of the Apes
10 Jaws 3-D

BOX OFFICE

US

1 Ghostbusters
2 Indiana Jones and the Temple Of Doom
3 Gremlins
4 Beverly Hills Cop
5 Terms of Endearment
6 The Karate Kid
7 Star Trek III: The Search For Spock
8 Police Academy
9 Romancing The Stone
10 Sudden Impact

BIRTHS, DEATHS AND MARRIAGES

DEATHS

Janet Gaynor
14 Sep, Palm Springs, California
Pneumonia following a car crash

Richard Basehart
17 Sep, Los Angeles
Stroke

Walter Pidgeon
26 Sep, Santa Monica, California

Francois Truffaut
21 Oct, Neuilly, France
Cancer

Oskar Werner
23 Oct, Marbury, Germany
Heart attack

Sam Peckinpah
28 Dec, Inglewood, California
Heart attack

MARRIAGES

Gene Wilder
18 Sep, *to* **Gilda Radner**

Jamie Lee Curtis
Dec, *to* Christopher Guest

DOWN AMONG THE SHELTERING PALMS

One of the many odd things about Beverly Hills is that it is built on contradictions. A mosque lies cheek-by-jowl with one of the most famous hotels in the world (the Beverly Wilshire), and only a five-minute drive away is the futuristic office architecture of Century City. And all of it is within a stone's throw of tropical palm trees.

Beverly Hills Cop capitalizes on these contradictions and plunges a fast-talking black Detroit policeman into the laid-back life-style of southern California. Eddie Murphy is Axel Foley, whose every second word is an expletive and who operates a neat line in repartee that's like rap without the beat. Words cascade from his lips faster than anyone else in the movie can think, leaving fellow cop Judge Reinhold gasping with admiration.

STAR QUOTES

David Lean

"I wouldn't take the advice of a lot of so-called critics on how to shoot a close-up of a teapot."

COUNTRY MATTERS

When Hollywood gets a good idea it refuses to let it go – until, that is, it bombs at the box office and it is time to try a new fad. This year's flavour is, unexpectedly, rural America. Three current films are all based on country themes. One is actually called *Country* and stars the real-life team of actress Jessica Lange and playwright Sam Shepard. A second, *The River*, teams Sissy Spacek with rising young Australian star Mel Gibson. But the most ambitious – and the film that everybody is saying will be the one to beat come Oscar time – is *Places in the Heart*, based on director Robert Benton's recollections of life in Waxahachie, near Dallas, during the Depression. It stars Sally Field and young actor John Malkovich.

Peggy Ashcroft in David Lean's *A Passage to India*.

THE MAN WHO DID MOZART IN

Who would have thought it? A film about one of the world's greatest classical composers is shaping up as a big box-office hit. *Amadeus* is the film version of the Peter Shaffer play that focuses on the rivalry between Mozart and official court composer Salieri. The latter is a skilled musical technician and bitterly resents the kid prodigy, not just because he is a genius but because his gifts are far greater than his infantile behaviour implies. Mozart, in short, is a buffoon, whom God has chosen to favour, while Salieri is a hard-working, fundamentally decent man with talent but no spark of genius. The play and the film suggest that Salieri, consumed with envy, poisoned Mozart.

The movie is directed by Milos Forman, the Czech director who fled his country in the aftermath of the 1968 Soviet invasion and set about carving out a new career in America. His first American film, *Taking Off* (1971), demonstrated the quirky realism for which he was known at home. Then in 1975 he hit paydirt with *One Flew over the Cuckoo's Nest* which swept the board at the following spring's Oscars. After that he had difficulty finding a suitable subject: neither *Hair* (1979) nor *Ragtime* (1981) seemed quite right for him. But in *Amadeus* he has a subject that engages his full powers. The fact that much of the film was shot in his native Czechoslovakia must have had some bearing on the personal touch that shines through in every frame.

Tom Hulce is the composer Mozart in *Amadeus*.

INDIAN SUMMER FOR PEGGY ASHCROFT

Peggy Ashcroft, one of the great names of the British stage, an all too infrequent film actress, is receiving overdue recognition in the cinema in the autumn of her years. She plays a key role in David Lean's comeback picture, *A Passage to India*, as the highly-strung Mrs. Moore, who sails for England before she can give vital evidence in a court case. Curiously, this role comes hot on the heels of a no less impressive appearance in British TV's mammoth *Jewel in the Crown* series, also set in India.

She was born in 1907 and made her debut on the London stage at 20. She has been a great Shakespearean actress and is remembered to this day for her Juliet and her Cleopatra. On stage, unlike most actresses, she never wore heavier makeup than a woman would normally wear to walk down the street. It helped to lend her work a naturalism that stood out from the crowd.

Her film career has been patchy. She first appeared in *The Wandering Jew* in 1933 and was a murder victim in the Alfred Hitchcock version of *The 39 Steps* (1935). Since then her appearances have been rare, though they included supporting parts in *The Nun's Story* (1959), *3 into 2 Won't Go* (1969) and *Sunday Bloody Sunday* (1971). Now at last film-makers may offer her the kind of parts that are her due.

ROLE OF A LIFETIME

Some actors have to wait a lifetime for the one role that brings out all that they have in them. a prime example is Robert Preston, who capped a long career of second-lead parts with a personal triumph in the play (and subsequent film) *The Music Man* (1962).

F. Murray Abraham is the most recent case in point. Abraham, who was born in 1940, has been around for a long time without making a stir. His first film was *They Might Be Giants* (1971), and he also appeared in *Serpico* (1973) and *All the President's Men* (1976).

As a character actor he might have remained permanently in the background had he not been chosen to play Salieri in Milos Forman's film version of the Peter Shaffer play *Amadeus*. He is perfect in the part of the man who may, or may not, have poisoned Mozart (nobody is quite sure). But will he have anything more to offer?

Gore Blimey!

Violence has always been a vital ingredient of many movies, but under the old Hollywood Production Code, filmmakers had to imply rather than show it, often creating an atmosphere that felt more explosive than anything actually seen. When they got close to the knuckle, in films like *Brute Force* (1947), censorship bodies often stepped in and cut out the offending material. In that film, for example, few have seen the climax of the scene in which prison inmates turn their blow torches on the squealer who has betrayed them. In its day, *The Blackboard Jungle* (1955) was notorious for its frank depiction of classroom violence but on screen it amounts to little more than a feeling of simmering unrest.

Bonnie and Clyde (1967) was a watershed movie in the depiction of violence because, for the first time, it showed just what damage a hail of bullets can do to human flesh. Since then, physical destruction has never looked back. Director Sam Peckinpah made it look even bloodier by extending the death scenes with slow-motion photography, especially in *The Wild Bunch* (1969).

In the 1970s and 1980s, actors carved out careers based on beating people up and blowing them away with high-powered weapons. Charles Bronson became a one-man vigilante force in *Death Wish* (1974) and its sequels, visiting punishment on the criminals and the punks that the law seemed powerless to contain. Sylvester Stallone followed a similar path in *First Blood* (1982), the initial Rambo picture and later unleashed his destructive instincts on communists of all kinds. So did Chuck Norris in *Missing in Action* (1984) and its cousins. In all of these films the body count is high and the victims simply targets.

Arnold Schwarzenegger is presently the arch-exponent of the mindless mayhem picture. Whether as a mercenary in *Commando* (1985) or as a sci-fi hero in *Total Recall* (1990), all he does is to splatter his enemies over the wall. *Robocop* (1987) and *RoboCop 2* (1990) suffer from the same excess: when you've already seen a body dunked in toxic slime, you hardly react to the sound of a head being squelched in a giant metal fist.

There is little harm in these films because they are preposterous. More dangerous are those which have a grounding in reality and seem to encourage violence. Several of director Martin Scorsese's films fall into this category: *Taxi Driver* (1976), which climaxes with a bloodbath, and *GoodFellas* (1990), which starts with a still living body pulled out of a car boot, kicked and filled full of lead while the killers laugh at the crime, are much more insidious than the heroics of, say, *Die Hard* (1988) because nobody believes the latter could really happen.

Sexual and racial violence on screen are equally disturbing. Sam Peckinpah invited a sackload of controversy with *Straw Dogs* (1970), in which, in order to protect his wife, Dustin Hoffman is forced to become as vicious as the thugs who are menacing her. And in *A Clockwork Orange* (1971), director Stanley Kubrick came close to saying that without the ability to behave as beasts we would not be truly human.

The fine line between justified and gratuitous violence on screen is hard to draw. The "gang-bang" in *Casualties of War* (1989), for example, seems essential to the story, yet in *The Accused* (1988), where it is discussed at great length before finally being shown, it smacks of voyeurism. Our awareness of the effect on the victim would have been no less if it had not been shown. But *Do the Right Thing* (1989), Spike Lee's portrait of escalating racial violence, would have lost most of its impact without the horrific detail.

Charles Bronson and victim in Michael Winner's Deathwish *(1974).*

Robert De Niro as gun crazy Travis Bickle in Taxi Driver *(1976).*

Warren Oates' and Ben Johnson's death throes in The Wild Bunch *(1969).*

Dustin Hoffman at the centre of violence in Straw Dogs *(1970).*

Convicts on the rampage in brutal prison drama Brute Force *(1947).*

Faye Dunaway and Warren Beatty as Bonnie and Clyde *(1967).*

Malcolm McDowell in Stanley Kubrick's A Clockwork Orange *(1971).*

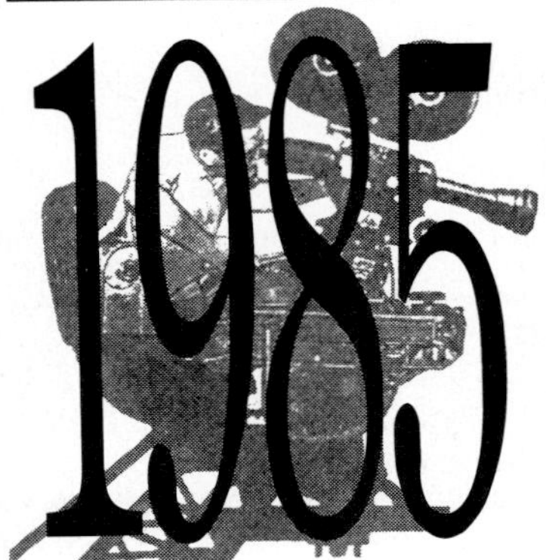

MINNOW GOES FOR THE BIG TIME

Goldcrest, the British company that won the Oscar two years running in 1981 and 1982 for *Chariots of Fire* and *Gandhi*, is venturing into territory far beyond its experience. After spending $15m on *The Killing Fields*, a film that has yet to recoup its costs, it is embarking on a massive production slate, including two films that will absorb $52.5m between them. These are *Revolution*, a story of the American War of Independence (also known as the American Revolution) and *The Mission*. They will cost $28m and $24.5m respectively, their budgets magnified by the fact that Goldcrest will be using big American stars for the first time – Al Pacino in the former and Robert De Niro in the latter. It's all part of the change of direction for Goldcrest since James Lee took over the helm from Jake Eberts in 1983. It's an open secret that some people within the company are concerned about its ability to shoulder such expense.

BIRTHS, DEATHS AND MARRIAGES

DEATHS

Louis Hayward
21 Feb, Palm Springs, California
Cancer

Michael Redgrave
2 Mar, Denham, Buckinghamshire
Parkinson's disease

COP MEETS BIBLE-BASHER

Kelly McGillis and Harrison Ford in Witness.

Witness is basically a thriller, but an unusual one. It focuses on the little-known fundamentalist community known as the Amish, who also featured in the 1955 Victor Mature thriller *Violent Saturday*. They dress and talk in the manner of the early pilgrim settlers and are strict pacifists in accordance with their interpretation of Christian teaching.

In the film one of their children is an inadvertent witness to a murder in a Philadelphia public convenience and a police cop (Harrison Ford) seeks to persuade him to testify, while he and the child are potentially the killer's next victims. Lending an extra dimension to the drama is the romantic attachment that springs up between the cop and the boy's widowed mother, played by striking 27-year-old Kelly McGillis, previously seen as Tom Conti's girlfriend in *Reuben, Reuben* (1983). Her steamy scenes with Ford mark the arrival of a major new talent.

KEPT IN AFTER SCHOOL

The Breakfast Club is the latest in a lengthening line of teenage movies made by John Hughes, often starring Molly Ringwald. The youth of the players and the frequency with which they act together has earned them a nickname: the Brat Pack. Though not all of them appear in this movie, quite a number do; so it can be considered the most typical of the Brat Pack genre.

The film action takes place one Saturday, when a group of five Chicago high-school students are brought in to write a 1,000-word essay on "who they are". From an initial atmosphere of resentment and frosty hostility towards authority and each other, they gradually unbend and come in the end to share a kind of friendship and respect.

Ringwald, who plays "Princess", a straight middle-class cheer leader, previously worked with Hughes on last year's *Sixteen Candles*. Others in the cast include sporty Emilio Estevez (son of actor Martin Sheen), from the 1984 cult success *Repo Man*, and as the weird loner "Basket-Case", Ally Sheedy, whose first film was *Bad Boys* opposite Sean Penn in 1983 and who starred in 1984 in *Oxford Blues*, a remake of *A Yank at Oxford* (1938).

ACADEMY AWARDS

PRESENTED ON 25 MARCH 1985

Best Picture
Amadeus

Best Director
Milos Forman
Amadeus

Best Actor
F. Murray Abraham
Amadeus

Best Actress
Sally Field
Places in the Heart

Best Sup Actor
Haing S. Ngor
The Killing Fields

Best Sup Actress
Peggy Ashcroft
A Passage to India

ON THE UN-SONNY SIDE OF THE STREET

Cherilyn La Pierre Sarkisian is the full name of the singer-turned-actress better known simply as Cher. Part-Armenian, part-Cherokee Indian, she was born in California in 1946. What has astonished everyone is that she's come back from a career that had ended, to an even bigger one in her late 30s.

Her mother married eight times and the young Cher spent time in a charitable institution because her father, a gambler and a junkie, was unable to care for her. She left school at 16, moved in with and subsequently married 27-year-old pop singer Sonny Bono. With him she made a number of hit records, including "I Got You, Babe", but the marriage ended in a messy divorce in 1973. After the break-up with Sonny, her career as a pop singer lost direction.

It was at this point that she took the bold step of angling for a straight acting career. A supporting part in the reunion drama *Come Back to the Five and Dime, Jimmy Dean, Jimmy Dean* (1982) took everyone by surprise.

As an actress Cher has a knack of letting vulnerability show through a hard-bitten surface. It made her ideal casting as Meryl Streep's lesbian friend in *Silkwood* (1983), for which she was nominated for an Oscar. Now she has her biggest part to date in the true-life drama *Mask*, as the barely responsible mother of a hideously disfigured son. It's going to Cannes and may well net her an acting prize.

STAR QUOTES

Cher

"If I'd been screwed by my husbands as I was by Warners, I'd still be married."

Rosanna Arquette and Madonna in the Susan Seidelman film Desperately Seeking Susan.

DESPERATELY SEEKING ROSANNA

Twenty-five-year-old Rosanna Arquette is one of the hottest stars of the moment following the unexpected success of her film *Desperately Seeking Susan*, in which she co-stars with pop star Madonna. Born in New York in 1960, she made her screen debut while still in her teens in the TV series *Shirley* in 1979 after acting in local theatre and being spotted in the play *Metamorphosis*.

She caught audiences' attention with a particularly erotic portrait of mass murderer Gary Gilmore's jailbait girlfriend Nicole Baker in *The Executioner's Song*, a more-than-three-hour adaptation of Norman Mailer's bestseller.

In the cinema, she began in bit parts in *American Graffiti* (1979) and *The World According to Garp* (1982) and had her first starring role in *Baby, It's You* (1983). Two years later, she has the best part of her career to date as one half of a team who meet only at the end in *Desperately Seeking Susan*. Her pixilated style of humour, however, may prove difficult to cast in future.

Cher plays tough "biker lady" Rusty Dennis, the mother of a boy with a badly disfigured face, in Mask.

A SAGA OF SUSANS

The sleeper of early 1985 is an out-to-lunch comedy called *Desperately Seeking Susan*, whose director is another Susan – Susan Seidelman; but that doesn't mean it's her own story. Far from it. The movie is two stories, which come close to meshing but finally meet up only in the last reel. Bored housewife Rosanna Arquette is intrigued by, an ad in the personal columns from someone who is "desperately seeking Susan" and decides to follow it up. Susan is a good-hearted doxy who lives by her wits, but circumstances prevent them from meeting until the end, when they join up to solve a crime.

Susan is played by rising young pop singer Madonna. It's officially her first film but rumours persist of another, less salubrious piece the blonde bomber made on the way up. In the film she does not sing, though her smash hit "Get into the Groove" is heard behind the end titles.

Susan Seidelman is a New York-based filmmaker who, in her teens, had every intention of becoming a fashion designer. But as she tells it, she and her sewing machine came to blows one day so she enrolled in film school instead. Realizing that film combined all her interests in design, storytelling and music, she switched careers there and then and never regretted it. Her first feature, *Smithereens* (1982), cost $60,000, but it was invited to Cannes, taken up for commercial distribution and paved the way for *Susan*.

MAY
JUNE

JULY
AUGUST

FIGHTING A LOST CAUSE

Something remarkable has happened to John Rambo since he appeared on screen in the film *First Blood* (1982). Then he was a Vietnam vet wrongly accused of a felony back home, who used his combat-training to lead the police a merry dance in the wilds of northwest America. It starred Sylvester Stallone, who already had three *Rockys* under his belt, was directed by Canadian-born Ted Kotcheff, and turned in a tidy profit.

In *Rambo: First Blood Part II*, however, he's transformed not just into a killing machine but also into a one-man army, still fighting the Vietnam War that America lost 10 years ago. Rambo is sent to Vietnam to release American MIAs that are still being held captive. This gives him the chance to kill or maim every communist in sight, making little distinction between foe and neutral so long as they have Asiatic features.

It's as if Rambo is being set up in the cinema to reassure those who lost loved ones in the war that they did not die in vain and that the might of America is still fighting their cause. Now barely under the control of director George Pan Cosmatos, who has previously made international mish-mashes like *The Cassandra Crossing* (1977), Stallone turns the film into a hymn to his own physique and physical prowess. But it'll clean up.

The $28 million production was filmed in and around Acapulco and in the Mexican jungle, whose mountainous terrain most resembles that of Vietnam. Stallone trained for five months to be in top physical shape for the demanding shoot in the sweltering location. Veteran Richard Crenna reprises his role as Rambo's ex-commanding officer, and beautiful Singapore-born model Julie Nickson, 26, of Chinese-English extraction, makes her big-screen debut as Co Bao, a Vietnamese agent who helps Rambo. British actor-director-writer Steven Berkoff plays the sadistic Russian lieutenant who battles Rambo in the explosive climax.

COPPOLA BACKS KUROSAWA

Francis Coppola, director of *The Godfather* (1972) and *Apocalypse Now* (1979), is coming, for the second time, to the aid of the great Japanese director Akira (*Seven Samurai*) Kurosawa, who's finding it difficult nowadays to raise money for his epics. Back in 1980, Coppola urged 20th Century-Fox to save Kurosawa's epic *Kagemusha* through buying distribution rights outside Japan in advance.

Kurosawa's new project, *Ran*, is a Japanese version of *King Lear*, and Coppola wants to put some money into that, too, even though the major financiers are French and Japanese. Coppola has a reputation for godfathering other talent. It was thanks to him that the silent French classic *Napoleon* (1927) was revived in America and that *Hitler: A Film from Germany* (1977) was taken up for U.S. distribution.

MATCH-MAKER TO MA AND PA

Back to the Future must be the only box-office smash that's aimed esseentially at children but hints at incest. Marty McFly (engagingly played by new teenage heart-throb Michael J. Fox, 24) travels back to his parents' day by boarding an invention devised by mad scientist Christopher Lloyd.

When he gets back to the 1950s, however, he finds his dad was a wimp and so bashful that he was unlikely to get to first base with his mum. If he can't arrange for the two to get married and procreate, where does that leave him? Meanwhile, his mother takes more than a casual interest in this new young boy in town. It seems she wouldn't in the least mind giving her all to Marty McFly.

Back to the Future is strong on special effects, especially those associated with time travel, and is a product of the Steven Spielberg factory. Though Spielberg didn't direct it himself, he gave full backing and encouragement to Robert Zemeckis, who was responsible for last year's hit *Romancing the Stone*. Zemeckis, still in his early 30s, is fast becoming the young director who, after Spielberg himself, has his finger most accurately on the box-office's youth pulse. Though it cost $22 million, *Back to the Future* is set to return almost five times as much to its lucky distributor, Universal. But how can they possibly make a sequel to such a story?

BIRTHS, DEATHS AND MARRIAGES

DEATHS

Louise Brooks
8 Aug, Rochester, New York
Heart attack

MARRIAGES

Madonna
16 Aug, *to* **Sean Penn**

Marty McFly (Michael J. Fox) and the Doc (Christopher Lloyd) witness the first test of the Doc's time machine in Back to the Future.

Lobby card for the Ron Howard science fantasy Cocoon.

OUT OF THE PAST

Don Ameche in Cocoon.

There's nothing new in well-known movie faces suddenly getting a second lease of life. Silent star Gloria Swanson made a memorable comeback in *Sunset Blvd.* (1950). Now it's Don Ameche's turn. *Cocoon* is about a group of wrinklies' close encounters of the third kind, and the 1940s matinee idol comes across just as debonair as he was in his youth. In fact, it's hardly a comeback at all: he was one of the scheming pair of brothers in the Dan Ayckroyd-Eddie Murphy hit comedy *Trading Places*, two summers back.

Born in Wisconsin in 1908, Ameche appeared briefly on Broadway before making his name in radio, where he developed an agreeable baritone voice that served him later in musicals, like *Alexander's Ragtime Band* (1938), *Swanee River* (1939) and *Moon over Miami* (1941). His most famous part was the title role in *The Story of Alexander Graham Bell* (1939), but his best film was the comedy *Heaven Can Wait* (1943), a wartime fantasy made by Ernst Lubitsch and co-starring Gene Tierney that has no connection other than the title with the 1978 Warren Beatty picture.

Ameche retired in 1970 after *The Boatniks* and *Suppose They Gave a War and Nobody Came?* His re-emergence has won him new friends in Hollywood and there's already talk of his performance in *Cocoon* being in line for a supporting Oscar. Whoever said old actors just fade away?

THE MAN WHO WAS A PLACE

For an American comedian to call himself Chevy Chase is like an Englishman calling himself Park Lane. Chase really is his name, but in life the handles are Cornelius Crane. Born in 1943, after entering showbusiness he developed a following on the satirical American TV show *Saturday Night Live*.

His first, now forgotten, film was *Tunnelvision* (1976), a parody of the future of television, but he began to attract a wide audience when he appeared in *National Lampoon's Vacation* (1983). He consolidates this now with *Fletch*, in which he plays an undercover reporter with aspirations to being a gumshoe. In America, Chase's reputation is assured but he's yet to win a big following overseas. "I guess I look so straight and normal," says Chase, "nobody expects me to pick my nose and fall."

HEY HO, SILVERADO!

Westerns could make a comeback if *Silverado* has its way. Once Hollywood's bread and butter, they reached their peak in 1943, when 143 were made – 30 per cent of all films made in Hollywood that year!

Their popularity had waned by the 1970s, but it was *Heaven's Gate* (1980) that dealt the knockout blow. The monumental $36 million flop made only $1.5 million in the North American market and forced United Artists into a shotgun wedding with M-G-M. After that hardly anyone was willing to take a chance on westerns again. The small budget *Barbarosa* (1982), directed by the Australian Fred Schepisi, was one of the few exceptions.

Silverado is the first big-budget western in years, clocking in at $26 million. It's strikingly shot, with plenty of widescreen vistas, and is certainly packed with star power: Kevin Kline, Kevin Costner, Scott Glenn, Danny Glover, lanky Jeff Goldblum and burly Brian Dennehy all have star parts, and Rosanna Arquette as the token love interest.

There are smaller parts, too, for tiny Linda Hunt, who won an Oscar in *The Year of Living Dangerously* (1983), and lofty British comedian John Cleese, who cuts a slightly incongruous figure as a western sheriff.

It's the same kind of pattern with which director Lawrence (*Body Heat*) Kasdan had such a success with *The Big Chill* (1983), also starring a selection of the rising young stars of the moment. Before becoming a director, he won fame as a screenwriter, notably for *Raiders of the Lost Ark* (1981) and *Return of the Jedi* (1983). Can he now kick-start the venerable western back to life?

Kevin Costner, Amanda Wyss, Linda Hunt, Jeff Fahey, Kevin Kline in Silverado.

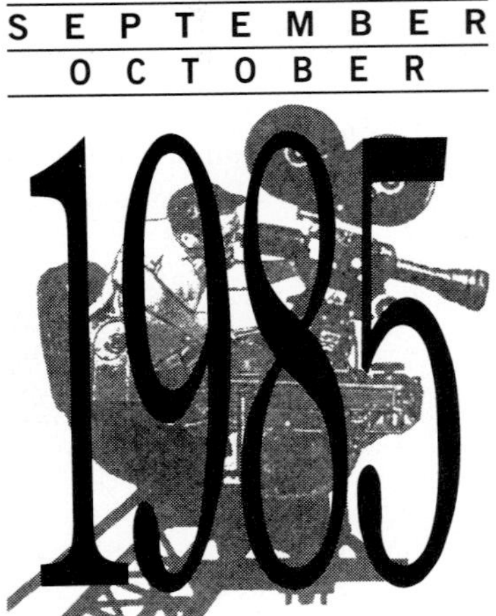

RETURN OF THE JEDI MASTER

Richard Marquand, the British filmmaker who was the surprise choice to put the final seal on the *Star Wars* trilogy as director of *Return of the Jedi* (1983), has turned his hand to courtroom drama and come up with a taut, thrilling piece of work called *Jagged Edge*. It stars Glenn Close as a lawyer who takes on the defence of Jeff Bridges, who may or may not have knifed to death his wife, a San Francisco newspaper heiress. Along the way she falls in love with her client, which makes it difficult to retain a clear perspective on the case.

Marquand skilfully plays on the easy charm of Bridges to confuse Close and the audience over whether he is guilty. Brother of Beau and son of Lloyd (*Sea Hunt*) Bridges, a hardy second-ranker of the 1950s, Jeff Bridges made his debut in 1970 and was nominated for an Oscar the following year in *The Last Picture Show*, when he was only 22. Close is of an earlier generation and the age gap between them adds piquancy to their relationship. She was nominated for supporting Oscars in each of her first three films, *The World according to Garp* (1982), *The Big Chill* (1983) and *The Natural* (1984), and is now rivalling Meryl Streep for the toughest women's parts on offer.

Scriptwriter Joe Eszterhas first came into prominence with the screenplay for the Sylvester Stallone union drama *F.I.S.T.* (1978), and has since written *Flashdance* (1983).

MERYL GOES DANISH

The latest accent for Meryl Streep is a Danish one – in a film called *Out of Africa*. In it she plays Karen Blixen, a Danish writer who went to live in Africa with her aristocrat husband and began writing short stories under the name Isak Dinesen. It's not a real Danish accent but an imitation of how a Dane might sound when speaking English. Some feel that Streep's constant pursuit of accents (Polish in *Sophie's Choice*, 1982, English in *The French Lieutenant's Woman*, 1981) has become a form of showing off.

Out of Africa shows Blixen's struggles as a farmer, her romance with a British adventurer (played by Robert Redford) and the treatment she was forced to undergo for syphilis, which she contracted from her husband (played by Klaus Maria Brandauer). It is a big, sweeping portrait of the continent, with fine photography, and a complete change of pace for director Sydney Pollack, whose last film was *Tootsie* (1982) starring Dustin Hoffman in drag.

Redford has been an increasingly reluctant actor since he directed his first movie, *Ordinary People* (1981). He has set up a training school (the Sundance Institute) and is still looking for a suitable follow-up movie to direct. Meanwhile, he's been rationing his appearances as an actor. He was last seen in the baseball drama *The Natural* (1984).

REVOLUTION OVERWHELMS THE KINSKI KID

Al Pacino and Nastassja Kinski in Hugh Hudson's *Revolution*.

Career-wise Nastassja Kinski's biggest mistake was to appear in *Revolution*, the story of the War of American Independence, also known as the American Revolution. It's been one of the all-time box-office flops, soaring way over budget at $36 million and recouping just $200,000 of that in the American market.

Until now, however, 24-year-old Kinski has been steadily establishing herself as a sultry actress owing little to the fact that her father is the well-known Klaus Kinski, star of the film *Aguirre, Wrath of God* (1973).

After a number of small roles in German films, and as a nymphet in the Hammer horror *To the Devil a Daughter* (1976), Kinski (who was known for a spell as Nastassia) met director Roman Polanski in 1976 and he groomed her to play *Tess* in his 1979 adaptation of the Thomas Hardy novel. Not the least of the movie's achievements (apart from making northern France look like Wessex) was Kinski's mastery of a West Country accent, remarkable for a girl who until then had spoken only German.

Her subsequent career has been less auspicious. She played a tightrope dancer in Francis Coppola's mega-flop *One from the Heart* (1981) and mostly pouted her way through Paul Schrader's 1982 remake of the old horror classic *Cat People*. Only last year's *Paris, Texas*, made in English by German director Wim Wenders (who gave her her first role back in 1975), and the delicate *Maria's Lovers*, with John Savage and Robert Mitchum, have recaptured the promise of *Tess*. If she can find the right parts, the actress whom Schrader once described as having "an Ingrid Bergman face, Brigitte Bardot lips and Katharine Hepburn's personality" still has a bright future ahead.

AIDS CLAIMS ROCK HUDSON

Rock Hudson, beefcake star of 1950s romantic melodramas like *Magnificent Obsession* (1954) and *All That Heaven Allows* (1955), has died of AIDS. He was the first major star to succumb to the disease and was only 59 when he passed away at his Beverly Hills home on 2 October. An actor of limited range, he achieved success in a series of glossy Universal comedies, such as *Pillow Talk* (1959) and *Send Me No Flowers* (1964) with Doris Day, and was nominated for an Oscar in *Giant* (1956). Despite these, the performance of which he was personally proudest was as the middle-aged businessman given a new lease of life in *Seconds* (1966), an artistic success but box-office flop.

The Illinois-born matinee idol was not what he seemed to his adoring female fans. Despite a three-year marriage to secretary Phyllis Gates, he was a confirmed homosexual. His willingness to reveal the cause of his illness some weeks before his death is seen as a courageous attempt to draw attention to the seriousness of the AIDS epidemic.

CITIZEN KANE IS DEAD

A giant of world cinema has died. Orson Welles, who revolutionized movie-making with his first Hollywood film, *Citizen Kane* (1941), was 70 when a heart attack felled him sitting at his typewriter on 10 October.

A 'young Turk' of the American stage and radio before he went to Hollywood at the age of only 25, he had achieved especial notoriety for a radio broadcast of *The War of the Worlds* on 30 October 1938. Its account of a Martian invasion – and especially its simulated "news flashes" – were taken as true by thousands of listeners, causing widespread panic. His career as a director after *Kane* was troubled. *The Magnificent Ambersons* (1942), was re-edited and shortened in his absence, with a new, more conventional ending added. His adaptations of Shakespeare – *Macbeth* (1948) and *Othello* (1952) – suffered from an inadequate budget and he left many films unfinished at the time of his death, including a *Don Quixote* that he had started filming in 1955.

After 1948, he worked in Hollywood only once as a director – on the typically quirky *Touch of Evil* (1958); but this too, underwent re-editing behind his back. Much of his later directorial career was in Europe, where he made a version of Kafka's *The Trial* (1963) and a brilliant film of the life of Falstaff, *Chimes at Midnight* (1966), taken from Shakespeare's history plays. Welles's last real film was an essay on illusion called *F for Fake* (1973).

Alongside his career as a director, Welles was a hugely talented actor, and he will always be remembered for his Harry Lime in *The Third Man* (1949). He had three marriages, including a turbulent one from 1943-7 to Rita Hayworth.

BIRTHS, DEATHS AND MARRIAGES

DEATHS

Simone Signoret
30 Sep, Normandy, France
Cancer

Rock Hudson
2 Oct, Beverly Hills
AIDS

Yul Brynner
10 Oct, New York
Cancer

Orson Welles
10 Oct, Hollywood
Heart attack

Phil Silvers
1 Nov, Century City, California

Anne Baxter
4 Dec, New York
Cerebral hemorrhage

MARRIAGES

Steven Spielberg
1 Nov, *to* Amy Irving

Sylvester Stallone
15 Dec, *to* **Brigitte Nielsen**

SPIELBERG FOR GROWN UPS

However much money Steven Spielberg's movies make, Hollywood (unlike the great moviegoing public) has never quite warmed to him. Carping critics say that all his films are for children and the product of a mind that has never outgrown the serials and action pictures he saw in his youth.

There's some truth in that. *Raiders of the Lost Ark* (1981) and *E.T.* (1982) had little to exercise the mind, but plenty of thrills, spills and tears. Now, however, Spielberg has attempted to answer his critics with his first film since *The Sugarland Express* (1974) to address grown up subjects. It's *The Color Purple*, an adaptation of Alice Walker's Pulitzer Prize-winning novel about growing up black in the Deep South.

It's a highly emotional picture with an all-black cast that introduces several new and exciting faces to the screen. These include 36-year-old Whoopi Goldberg, a homely-looking girl with a Panavision-sized smile, who's in fact been acting since the age of eight and on stage for the past decade. Another is Margaret Avery who plays a black singing star, though her songs were all dubbed in the film.

Whoopi Goldberg in Spielberg's The Color Purple.

BOX OFFICE

UK

1. Ghost Busters
2. A View to a Kill
3. Gremlins
4. Rambo/First Blood Part II
5. Beverly Hills Cop
6. Police Academy 2: Their First Assignment
7. Santa Claus The Movie
8. A Passage to India
9. Back to the Future
10. One Hundred and One Dalmatians

BOX OFFICE

US

1. Back to the Future
2. Rambo: First Blood, Part II
3. Rocky IV
4. Beverly Hills Cop
5. Cocoon
6. The Goonies
7. Witness
8. Police Academy 2: Their First Assignment
9. National Lampoon's European Vacation
10. A View to a Kill

MURDOCH ACQUIRES FOX

Rupert Murdoch, controversial Australian press and TV tycoon, has become an old-style Hollywood movie mogul. Six months ago, he paid $250 million for a half stake in ailing 20th Century-Fox, studio, formerly wholly owned by the legendary Denver oil magnate Marvin Davis. Now he has stumped up $325 million for the rest, leaving Marvin Davis only Fox's interests in holiday resorts at Pebble Beach, California, and Aspen, Colorado. Murdoch gets the studio (63 acres of prime real estate in Century City) and the valuable backlog of past Fox productions, which can fuel his TV channels worldwide. Murdoch's initial investment consisted of $162 million for the shares plus a cash injection of $88 million. It was clear from then on that he would not long be satisfied with only 50 per cent of the company.

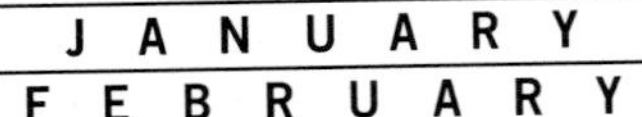

JANUARY
FEBRUARY

MARCH
APRIL

MERCHANT-IVORY'S CROSSOVER PICTURE

Julian Sands and Helena Bonham-Carter in A Room with a View.

The Merchant-Ivory production team (Ismail Merchant producing, James Ivory directing) has long been a stalwart of the art-house circuit. But with *A Room with a View* it's managed to turn an arty picture into a mainstream hit. On an outlay of less than $5 million, the movie has already pulled in $12 million for the distributor from the North American market alone. That's practically unknown for this kind of picture.

The film is adapted from the first novel of E.M. Forster, better known as the author of *A Passage to India*, which David Lean filmed in 1984. The adaptation is by another distinguished novelist, Ruth Prawer Jhabvala, whose Booker prize-winning *Heat and Dust* Merchant-Ivory filmed in 1983. She brings a literary quality to the script that provides marvellous lines for the hand-picked cast. Set largely in the late 19th century, with its early scenes in Florence, the film offers great scope for its art directors and costume designers and grateful settings for the likes of Maggie Smith, Denholm Elliott, Helena Bonham-Carter, Daniel Day-Lewis, Simon Callow and Judi Dench.

Merchant and Ivory joined forces in 1963 to make Jhabvala's *The Householder* and have been together ever since. Many of their earlier films, notably *Shakespeare Wallah* (1965), had an Indian setting, but latterly they've ventured into stylish adaptations of English and American literature. These have included two films from Henry James novels – *The Europeans* (1979) and *The Bostonians* (1984) – one from the recently "rediscovered" Jean Rhys – *Quartet* (1981) – and now one from E.M. Forster.

ACADEMY AWARDS

PRESENTED ON 24 MARCH 1986

Best Picture
Out of Africa

Best Director
Sydney Pollack
Out of Africa

Best Actor
William Hurt
Kiss of the Spider Woman

Best Actress
Geraldine Page
The Trip to Bountiful

Best Sup Actor
Don Ameche
Cocoon

Best Sup Actress
Anjelica Huston
Prizzi's Honor

BIRTHS, DEATHS AND MARRIAGES

DEATHS

Ray Milland
10 Mar, Torrance, California
Cancer

Robert Preston
21 Mar, Santa Barbara, California
Cancer

James Cagney
30 Mar, Duchess County, New York

Otto Preminger
23 Apr, New York
Cancer

Broderick Crawford
26 Apr, Palm Springs, California

Robert Stevenson
30 Apr, Santa Barbara, California

MARRIAGES

Arnold Schwarzenegger
26 Apr, *to* Maria Shriver

VIDEO IS KING

In January, for the first time, the volume of business generated in America through video rentals exceeded the money taken at the country's box offices. The significance of this is not that it points to a decline in cinemas but that it underlines a change in importance in the overall scheme of things. Where initially theatrical release was the only significant source of income, now the cinema is the showcase for the even more lucrative after-life in other forms – video, TV, cable, satellite, laser disc, and so on.

STAR QUOTES

Michael Caine

"I'll always be there because I'm a skilled professional actor. Whether or not I've any talent is beside the point."

FIFTH TIME LUCKY?

Michael Caine drove a wedge through the English acting tradition in the 1960s by refusing to modify his Cockney accent.

It served him well in *Alfie* (1966) and the Harry Palmer spy films and has since proved no impediment in Hollywood. He's been a deft comedian in films like *California Suite* (1978) and no less effective in Hitchcock-style melodrama like *Dressed to Kill* (1980). He also held his end up well opposite Laurence Olivier in the two-hander *Sleuth* (1972).

But despite being nominated four times for an Oscar, he's never won. His surprise casting in Woody Allen's *Hannah and Her Sisters* may get him nominated again. And this time he may even win.

FROM GAY PAREE TO RODEO DRIVE

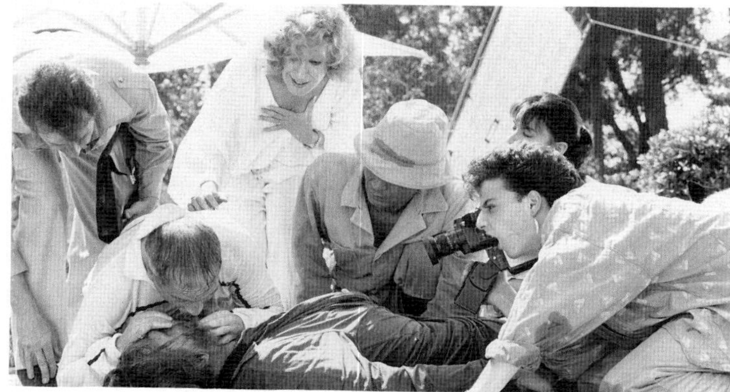

Richard Dreyfuss tries to resuscitate Nick Nolte in Down and Out in Beverly Hills.

Down and Out in Beverly Hills is one of a growing number of American movies adapted from French successes. Most of them are drawn from recent hits but this one is something else. Its model is the 1932 Jean Renoir film *Boudu Saved from Drowning* in which the great French actor Michel Simon gave a memorable performance as an old tramp whose arrival in the bosom of a staid and stuffy bourgeois family completely disrupts their lifestyle.

The Hollywood remake retains the basic situation, but it has undergone considerable change with the years – and with the change of location. The setting is no longer the Seine and the boulevards of Paris but Beverly Hills and Rodeo Drive – among the most fashionable bits of real estate in the world.

Nick Nolte plays the role of the bum who changes everybody's lives and Richard Dreyfuss and Bette Midler are the nouveau-riche couple who take him in. Dreyfuss' comeback after several years of illness shows his talents to be unimpaired; but Nolte cannot compare with Michel Simon. Director Paul Mazursky is a one-time actor who appeared in films like *The Blackboard Jungle* (1955) and made an immediate hit as a director with his first, and still most successful, film, *Bob & Carol & Ted & Alice* (1969).

TO HELL AND BACK

In *Down and Out in Beverly Hills* Richard Dreyfuss makes a determined comeback after several years' absence from the cinema as a result of a serious car accident and an arrest on drugs charges. Born in New York in 1947, he entered the movies in a small part as Dustin Hoffman's neighbour in *The Graduate* at the age of 20 and rose rapidly in the 1970s, playing the shark scientist in *Jaws* (1975), the star part in *Close Encounters of the Third Kind* (1977) and the male lead in the Neil Simon comedy *The Goodbye Girl* (1977), which won him an Oscar.

It seemed to go to his head. He became ultra-choosy about his roles, turning down *All That Jazz* (1979) and *Arthur* (1981), but giving a powerful performance in the film of *Whose Life Is It Anyway?* (1981), as a sculptor who's paralysed in an accident and becomes obsessed with euthanasia. At the same time, he was high on a cocktail of drink and drugs that led to the car crash in October 1982 that left him pinned for 15 minutes under the wreckage, unaware whether or not he had broken his spine. Says Dreyfuss: "I was doing two grammes of cocaine, 20 Percadon pills and about two quarts of alcohol a day. The only difference between John Belushi and me is that he's dead and I'm not."

With help, Dreyfuss was able to lick his drug dependency and resume his acting career, initially with a modest romantic comedy, *The Buddy System* (1984), opposite Susan Sarandon. *Down and Out in Beverly Hills* marks his first major stride on the road back.

CAGNEY DEAD

From the 1930s to the 1950s, James Cagney was one of the most famous of all screen tough guys. His death in upstate New York on 30 March, at the age of 86, brings an era to a close. He was the last of that trio of great screen actors that included Humphrey Bogart and Edward G. Robinson, all of whom made their names in hoodlum roles.

Cagney first played such a role in 1931 in *The Public Enemy* and later gave memorable performances in the same vein in *Angels with Dirty Faces* (1938) and *White Heat* (1949). Yet it was never more than an act. His cockiness and appalling behaviour (thrusting a grapefruit into a woman's face for venturing an opinion), bore no relation to the devoted husband he was in real life. He was also a talented dancer and finally got a chance to prove it in *Yankee Doodle Dandy* (1942), the story of showman George M. Cohan, for which he won his only Oscar. The movie remained his personal favourite. He was last seen on the big screen in *Ragtime* (1981), but subsequently made a moving farewell as a retired boxer in the TV movie *Terrible Joe Moran* (1984), opposite Ellen Barkin.

Hannah and her Sisters – *Mia Farrow, Barbara Hershey and Dianne Wiest.*

WOODY AND HIS REGULARS

When Woody Allen turns serious it's often had dire consequences at the box office. Few had a good word to say for his 1978 film *Interiors*, in which he came so close to imitating his favourite director, Ingmar Bergman, that it turned out like a parody.

Hannah and Her Sisters, however, is a serious film with a streak of humour that should please his fans as well as win him more critical respect. It's framed within three Thanksgiving celebrations and allows the lives of a variety of related and neurotic New Yorkers to intertwine, with new relationships being formed here, old ones dying there.

As always, Allen uses his "repertory company" of tried and trusted players, as well as introducing new faces. The newcomers are Britain's Michael Caine and Bergman's own favourite actor, the Swede Max von Sydow. Caine takes to Allen's world like a duck to water, perfectly complimenting more seasoned regulars like Mia Farrow and Dianne Wiest. Other familiar faces put in guest appearances, notably Julie Kavner, Tony Roberts and Sam Waterston, of whom the last doesn't even get a credit!

Among Hannah's sisters are Barbara Hershey (now turning into an accomplished actress, after her hippy days when she called herself Barbara Seagull) and Carrie Fisher, daughter of Debbie Reynolds and Eddie Fisher, who sprung to fame as Princess Leia in *Star Wars* (1977).

MAY
JUNE

JULY
AUGUST

IT'S THE REAL THING, DAVID

Coca-Cola has wooed and won British producer David Puttnam to run the show at Columbia, its film-making subsidiary. He'll have complete autonomy over any projects to which he gives the green light, up to a ceiling of $30 million on any one film.

Puttnam's rise has been meteoric. His early work, producing pictures like *Bugsy Malone* (1976), scarcely suggested that five years later he would be clutching an Oscar for *Chariots of Fire* and that by 1984 he would be handling blockbusters like *The Killing Fields*. His newest production, to be released later this summer, is *The Mission*, with Robert De Niro.

BIRTHS, DEATHS AND MARRIAGES

DEATHS

Anna Neagle
3 Jun, Surrey

Blanche Sweet
6 Jul, Los Angeles

Vincente Minnelli
21 Jul, Los Angeles

STAR QUOTES

Vanessa Redgrave

"I choose all my roles very carefully so that, when my career is finished, I will have covered all our recent history of oppression."

Ripley (Sigourney Weaver) shields Newt (Carrie Henn) from attack in Aliens.

MORE MONSTROUS THAN EVER

How do you make a sequel to *Alien* (1979), which ended with the terrifying creature being catapulted into outer space? Answer: by having Sigourney Weaver go back to the same planet with a bunch of commandos and find a whole colony of the critters. The appropriately titled *Aliens* is directed by James Cameron, who made the Arnold Schwarzenegger robot film *The Terminator* (1984). So this time the accent is on the fearsome hardware that is brought to bear against the monsters rather than the suspense that director Ridley Scott made the focal point of *Alien*. But there's still thrills a-plenty in the $21 million blockbuster, and it's already one of this summer's hottest items.

Another sci-fi film due out soon that also seems likely to rake in big money is *The Fly*, thinly based on the 1958 Vincent Price horror picture. Other than the central idea (a man gets crossed with a fly through an accident in a machine for transmitting matter), this remake is virtually a different movie. Canadian-born director David Cronenberg is the master of ick, the overlord of yuck. His movies, like *Videodrome* and *The Dead Zone* (both 1983), have specialized in unmentionable things that can happen to you in the most ordinary circumstances, so here the transformation of nice, healthy Jeff Goldblum into a fly is shown in appallingly graphic detail. Cronenberg takes special delight in depicting its eating habits – vomiting over the food before ingesting it. Sick? Maybe – but you can't keep it down!

Jeff Goldblum in David Cronenberg's update of The Fly.

THAT WAS WORLD WAR THREE THAT WAS

Top Gun is the most gung-ho, Reaganite movie since last year's *Rambo/First Blood Part Two*. Tom Cruise is a cocky young pilot being trained at Top Gun (where the Navy's elite fighter pilots are produced) who engages the enemy (Soviet MIG fighters) over the Indian Ocean and wards off the Communist threat to America virtually single handed.

It's a spectacularly shot movie and impressively directed by no less than a Brit – Tony Scott, who, like his brother Ridley, broke into movies via advertising. His early films, like *The Hunger* (1983), with David Bowie and Catherine Deneuve as kinky vampires, had an arty-crafty flavour that denied them a wide audience. But with *Top Gun* he's hit the jackpot. It's the smash-hit box-office movie of the summer, pulling in $79 million for Paramount on an investment of only $14 million.

The main plot virtually repeats that of *An Officer and a Gentleman* (1982), with Cruise playing the Richard Gere part. There's even some comparable love interest, with stunning Kelly McGillis (miles from her role in last year's *Witness*) taking the place of Debra Winger in the earlier film. But what moviegoers are taking away from the movie is more the visceral excitement of the flying scenes. Whatever happened to good old-fashioned sex?

FROM BRAT PACK TO BIG TIME

Top Gun catapults 24-year-old Tom Cruise right out of the Brat Pack mould and into the realm of the superstar able to demand more than $2 million a picture. Born in 1962, he once thought of becoming a priest and spent a year at a Franciscan seminary. But he was only 15 and soon realized "I loved women too much to give that up."

He discovered his vocation in a high school production of *Guys and Dolls* and, after a spell as a soda jerk in an ice cream parlour, came to New York to carve out a career in show business.

He made his first two films, *Endless Love* and *Taps*, back in 1981 but it was his good looks and grin in the yuppie teenage comedy *Risky Business* (1983) that set him on his way. He was visibly ill at ease as a mediaeval hero in *Legend* (1985), but *Top Gun* finds him back at his cocky best. For his part as a member of the elite fighter pilots of the U.S. Navy he spent weeks studying the gestures and body language of the crack Blue Angels flying team. Off screen he's also a speed fanatic. He rides a Ninja motorcycle called 'Crotchrocket' and for *Top Gun* had three outings in a F-14 fighter. As Cruise describes it, "It's very sexual. Your body contorts, you grab your legs and your ass and grunt as the sweat pours all over you." And the more he describes it, the more women like him.

NUMBER FIVE IS ALIVE

One of the stars of *Short Circuit* is Number Five, a military robot who gets struck by lightning during a demonstration to the Pentagon top brass and actually comes alive. He goes on the lam and is befriended by feisty Ally Sheedy, who seeks to protect him from the military who want to destroy him. Number Five is a kind of cross between R2-D2, metallic hero of *Star Wars* (1977), and *E.T.* (1982).

Says director John Badham: "Number Five is somebody that you'll fall in love with instantly. I did after I first read the script." Sheedy agrees: "Number Five just jumped off the page at me, he was so real."

Sheedy, 24, made her debut as Sean Penn's girl friend in *Bad Boys* (1983), is a leading actress in the so-called Brat Pack, appearing in last year's *The Breakfast Club*. She previously worked with director Badham on *WarGames* (1983) as a teenager trying to avert World War III.

Badham's other movies include the blockbuster *Saturday Night Fever* (1977), which made a star of John Travolta, and the Roy Scheider thriller *Blue Thunder* (1983). For the creation of Number Five, he went to a robotics convention in Japan and during filming the models were guarded as closely as any nuclear secret. "We wanted to be ahead of what is possible now," says Badham, "so we came up with a robot unlike anything ever seen on film before. No one will look at Number Five and say it's a guy in a costume."

ROAR OF THE CANNON

Are Menahem Golan and Yoram Globus off their trolley? That is the question bugging the British film industry this summer. The two cousins from Tiberias, Israel, recently paid £175 million for assets that the Australian tycoon Alan Bond had bought for £125 million only the week before. Essentially these assets comprise the film interests of Thorn EMI, including the 295-screen ABC chain (one of the two leading theatrical outlets in Britain).

Golan and Globus are the leading lights of a company called Cannon now registered in the United States. You can buy shares in it on Wall Street. It makes movies like *Invaders from Mars* (1986) and says it plans to step up production this year from 15 to 35 films at an estimated cost of $149 million. Does Cannon really have a bottomless purse?

RETURN OF THE VAMP

Low-down seductive dames, the kind Lana Turner and Barbara Stanwyck used to play, had been conspicuously absent in movies until Kathleen Turner sent the temperature rising in the 2film-noir-ish *Body Heat* (1981).

Born in Missouri in 1954, Kathleen Turner is the daughter of a foreign-service diplomat and had lived in five countries before she was 17. One of them was England, where she discovered a love of acting by theatregoing in the West End and at Stratford-on-Avon. Returning home after her father's death, she enrolled at Southwest Missouri State University, where she majored in dramatic arts.

She's had to fight for the parts she wanted. She was turned down at first for *Body Heat* on grounds of inexperience. And after that film she had to fight again not to be typecast. Actor-producer Michael Douglas initially had reservations about her for his adventure film *Romancing the Stone* (1984). But a screen test convinced him.

She has since been seen in more familiar roles as a prostitute-by-night in Ken Russell's *Crimes of Passion* and as a mobster's moll in *Prizzi's Honor* (both 1985). Her biggest challenge to date is her forthcoming film for Francis Coppola, *Peggy Sue Got Married*, in which she plays herself as she is now and as she was as a younger girl. Says Turner of her career: "I want it all. At the moment I can't seem to handle more than three films a year. I wish there were two of me."

GOSSIP COLUMN

- **Ex-critic turned director Paul Mayersberg has changed the name of his first film from *Heroine* to *Captive*. Seems that he wants to head off crummy jokes since the male lead is a Japanese named Hiro.**
- **Raquel Welch is richer by $11 million after proving in court that M-G-M "ruined her career" by firing her from the 1982 movie *Cannery Row*. It claimed that she had made up before coming to work instead of letting the studio handle it.**

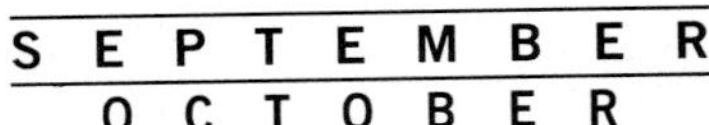

NOVEMBER
DECEMBER

IN THE PATHS OF THEIR PARENTS

In the build up to Christmas this year, movies seem dominated by young actors and actresses who are themselves the children of famous acting parents. *Platoon*, the hard-hitting Vietnam war movie, stars Charlie Sheen, the son of Martin Sheen, who in *Apocalypse Now* (1979) was the star of another Vietnam movie, directed by Francis Coppola.

Blue Velvet stars two such players. Laura Dern is the daughter of Bruce Dern and Diane Ladd, while Isabella Rossellini is the offspring of the controversial union between Ingrid Bergman and Italian film director Roberto Rossellini in the late 1940s and early 1950s. (Isabella and twin sister Ingrid were born in 1952.)

Rossellini's parents divorced when she was five and Bergman was granted custody of the children. Isabella's early career was not in acting. She was initially a sports journalist and then a TV producer in New York before landing a $2 million modelling contract for Lancome, spread over five years. That was in 1982 at the age of 30. But she drifted into acting and contracted two marriages (one to director Martin Scorsese) before meeting and settling in with David Lynch, her director on *Blue Velvet*.

Twenty-year-old Laura Dern never doubted she would be an actress, like her parents. She had a bit part as a child eating an ice cream cone in *Alice Doesn't Live Here Any More* (1975) and got herself an agent at the age of 11. Among her films before *Velvet* are *Smooth Talk* and *Mask* (both 1985), in the second of which she played a blind girl. She's picky about her roles. "I chose to act instead of having a college education," she says, "and I think that's why I like movies that educate me."

Charlie Sheen, now 21, was born in California and made his debut at the age of nine in the TV play *The Execution of Private Slovk*, which starred his father Martin. He has appeared in *Red Dawn* (1984) and, earlier this year, in *The Wraith*.

WILL NEWMAN POCKET THE OSCAR THIS TIME?

A quarter of a century after playing the role for the first time, Paul Newman again plays Fast Eddie Felson, the ultimate pool shark, in *The Color of Money*. It's the sequel to *The Hustler* (1961), for which many thought Newman should have won an Oscar. In the intervening 25 years, he has been nominated for an award several times but has never won.

In *The Color of Money* Fast Eddie is now an older, less energetic man (with a moustache and greying temples) who acts as coach to brash young Tom Cruise. Cruise aims to be as crafty a hustler now as Fast Eddie was then. Director is Martin Scorsese, best known for *Taxi Driver* (1976) and *Raging Bull* (1980); and there's a striking performance from rising young Mary Elizabeth Mastrantonio, 28, as Cruise's sexy girlfriend.

STAR QUOTES

Cary Grant

"Alfred Hitchcock couldn't have been a nicer fellow. I whistled coming to work on his films."

Dennis Hopper plays Isabella Rossellini's evil tormentor in David Lynch's sensual mystery thriller Blue Velvet.

WEIRD HAPPENINGS IN HICKSVILLE

Blue Velvet is like the kinky underside of *Peyton Place*. There's a severed ear lying in a cornfield, a young hero who acts as a voyeur through the slats of a dressing cupboard in a strange girl's bedroom, plenty of sado-masochism, and a villain so riddled with asthma that he has to gulp down oxygen from a respirator while performing unmentionable acts on a young woman.

It's all the work of arty-crafty director David Lynch, 40, who has something of an obsession with freaks. His first movie, the independently made *Eraserhead* (1977) was about a couple who sired a baby that looked like something out of *Alien* (1979). Then came *The Elephant Man* (1980) which told the true story of the grotesquely deformed John Merrick. *Dune* (1984), an unsuccessful adaptation of Frank Herbert's sci-fi classic, featured a monstrously fat man covered with sores.

GRUNT'S EYE VIEW

Unlike most of the other movies about the Vietnam war, *Platoon* is the work of a man who actually fought there – as a volunteer. Writer-director Oliver Stone signed on in 1967, was twice wounded and decorated. While there, however, he came to sympathize with the Vietnamese.

In 1975, as Saigon was falling, he wrote a script about the war that was too hot to handle. Eleven years later it has audiences queuing round the block.

Through a small incident in the war – a patrol and its consequences – Stone manages to debate the whole issue of America's presence there. A good cast helps, with Charlie Sheen (son of actor Martin Sheen) as a kind of Everyman figure torn between two NCOs (Tom Berenger and Willem Dafoe) who represent brutality and idealism.

Stone began as a writer, winning an Oscar for *Midnight Express* (1978). His previous film, the Central American political thriller *Salvador*, on view earlier this year, anticipated *Platoon* with its gutsy, sudden violence and radical outlook. His next? As the son of a stockbroker, Stone says he'll tackle corruption on Wall Street.

THE SHRIMP ON THE BARBIE

With *"Crocodile" Dundee*, Australian comedian Paul Hogan has made the most profitable foreign film ever released in the United States. That's sweet news to the man who, in his advertising days, promised to "slip another shrimp on the barbie" for his American guests. *"Crocodile" Dundee* was made for $5.6 million, which is high by Australian standards. Hogan and his partner John Cornell put up half the money, but since the film is expected to achieve a worldwide gross of more than $200 million, Hogan can count on a nest egg big enough to see him through the rest of his life.

Born in 1941, the second of three children of an army sergeant turned postman, Hogan grew up in a working-class suburb of Sydney and dropped out of school at 15. After accepting a dare to audition on the television programme *New Faces* in 1972, he was signed up for a regular series called *A Current Affair*.

From there he graduated to his own programme, *The Paul Hogan Show*, and advertisements for the tourist board and Foster's lager. Now he's a household name in America as well.

Paul Hogan proves he has got a bigger knife in "Crocodile" Dundee.

CARY GRANT DIES

Cary Grant, one of the Hollywood superstars, with a career that extended over four decades, died in Iowa on 29 November, from a stroke, at the age of 82. He had not acted in films since *Walk, Don't Run* (1966) so movie-goers still saw him as a seemingly ageless matinée idol – an image that he had been able to maintain for years. On a famous occasion, a columnist wired Grant's agent: "How old Cary Grant?" The star, who happened to be with his agent at that moment, wired back: "Old Cary Grant fine, how you?"

Grant was the epitome of the suave, romantic charmer in a whole series of sophisticated comedies, notably *The Philadelphia Story* (1940), with Katharine Hepburn and James Stewart. His other screen persona was best exemplified in his role as the unworldly professor in the hilarious *Bringing Up Baby* (1938), also with Hepburn, or the panic-stricken nephew in *Arsenic and Old Lace* (1944). Villainy was beyond his limited range, though there's a hint of it in Alfred Hitchcock's *Suspicion* (1941). He also starred in one of Hitch's finest, *North by Northwest* (1959). Grant was born in Bristol, England, but his voice (much imitated, notably by Tony Curtis in the 1959 comedy *Some Like It Hot*) was neither British nor truly American.

A master of comic timing, he made it all seem effortless. But it is untrue that he always played himself. The real Cary Grant was a more complex personality – as his five wives, including actresses Betsy Drake and Dyan Cannon, could testify.

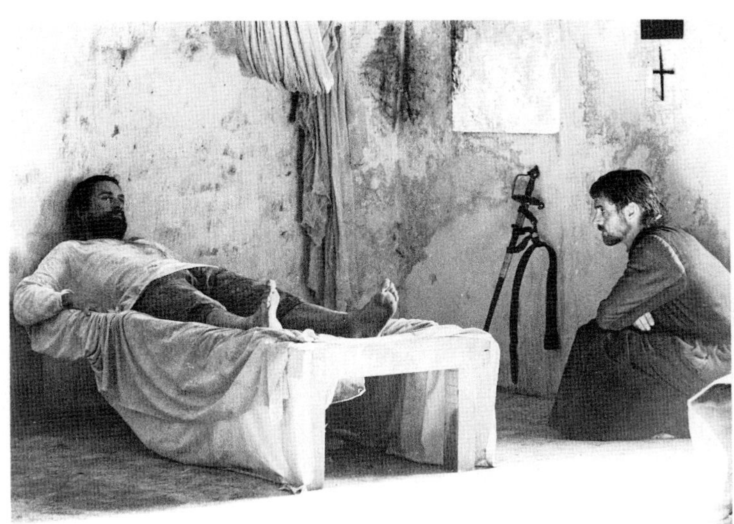

Robert De Niro and Jeremy Irons.

MISSION IMPOSSIBLE

After last year's mega-flop *Revolution*, the British company Goldcrest has a lot riding on *The Mission*. Set in the late 18th century, it's about the conflict between different branches of the Catholic church in South America. Some reckon it is too ambitious and costly to recoup its $24.5 million budget.

The production was beset with difficulties. It was filmed in Colombia and suffered from political unrest and from the illness, brought on by weather conditions, of the director, Roland Joffe, who previously made *The Killing Fields* (1984).

The film stars two contrasting actors – the classically trained Englishman Jeremy Irons and the more instinctive Robert De Niro. Irons puts their differences like this: "I think I'm quicker and have more technique, as I'm more of a theatre actor. Bob will tend to do few takes, but within them come up with extraordinary acting choices. He has an uncanny persistence in finding truthful moments."

The Mission was hastily unveiled at the Cannes Film Festival this summer in an unfinished version, and promptly won the top prize. But will audiences see it simply as an art-house epic?

BIRTHS, DEATHS AND MARRIAGES

DEATHS

Sterling Hayden
30 Sep, Sausalito, California
Cancer

Cary Grant
29 Nov, Davenport, Iowa
Stroke

MARRIAGES

Rosanna Arquette
Sep, *to* James Newton

Steve Martin
Nov, *to* **Victoria Tennant**

BOX OFFICE

UK

1. Back to the Future
2. Rocky IV
3. Out of Africa
4. Top Gun
5. Santa Claus The Movie
6. Aliens
7. Police Academy 3: Back in Training
8. Clockwise
9. Teen Wolf
10. The Jewel of the Nile

BOX OFFICE

US

1. Top Gun
2. The Karate Kid: Part II
3. "Crocodile" Dundee
4. Star Trek IV: The Voyage Home
5. Aliens
6. The Color Purple
7. Back To School
8. The Golden Child
9. Ruthless People
10. Out of Africa

Bruce Willis was highly paid for his work in sequel Die Hard 2 *(1990).*

Michael Keaton and Jack Nicholson in mega-blockbuster Batman *(1989).*

Chariot race from original silent version of Ben-Hur *(1925).*

Multi-million dollar loss-maker, The Adventures of Baron Munchausen *(1989).*

Beyond The Megasphere

Thanks to the cost of prints and advertising, films need to make 2½ times what they cost simply to break even. Box-office receipts cannot be measured directly against costs because the exhibitor is entitled to his cut and distributors regularly dock 30 per cent of the returns to cover their own fees. So big-budget pictures have to do very well indeed to show a profit.

Nowadays big pictures routinely cost close to $50 million, which can buy a *Batman* (1989), and some films cost even more. *Die Hard 2* (1990) and *Who Framed Roger Rabbit* (1988) presently hold the record at $70 million apiece, with *Total Recall* and *The Godfather Part III* (both 1990) weighing in at $65 million. Inflation, however, distorts comparison with earlier years and there is no doubt that in real terms, 20th Century-Fox's *Cleopatra*, made in 1963 for $44 million, leaves them all standing.

The million dollar barrier was broken very early. While D. W. Griffith's famous *Intolerance* cost only $386,000 in 1916, by 1924 *The Thief of Bagdad* cost $2 million and in 1925 the first *Ben-Hur* gobbled up $5 million, a record that was to stand for years (even *Gone with the Wind* in 1939 cost only $3.8 million).

The present phase of ultra-expensive movies began in the late 1970s, when films began to break through the $20 million ceiling that had been common in the 1960s. *Star Trek* cost $42 million in 1979 and *Superman* had already notched up $55 million the previous year. Even disasters proved unable to curb budgets. Both *Raise the Titanic* and *Heaven's Gate* swallowed up $36 million in 1980-81, of which they recovered only $6.8 million and $1.5 million respectively from their home markets. The former scuppered Lew Grade's international movie aspirations and the latter was a major factor in forcing United Artists into a shotgun wedding with M-G-M. Still budgets climbed and in 1988 alone *Rambo III* clocked in at $58 million and *The Adventures of Baron*

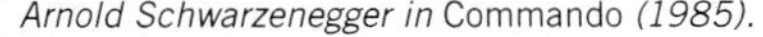

Arnold Schwarzenegger *in* Commando *(1985).*

James Stewart *in* The Far Country *(1955).*

Burton and Taylor *in* Cleopatra *(1953).*

Scene from Michael Cimino's controversial and costly Heaven's Gate *(1980).*

Munchausen at $52 million. *Rambo III* pulled in $28 million in North America, while *Munchausen* scored a mere $3.9 million.

Gone with the Wind remained the most successful film ever made for 26 years, when it was finally toppled by *The Sound of Music* (1965). But the $79.4 million *GWTW* had made by late 1990 would outstrip every other film if it were adjusted for more than 50 years of inflation. Since *The Sound of Music*, four other films have been all-time champs – *The Godfather* (1972, with $86.3 million), *Jaws* (1975, $129.5 million), *Star Wars* (1977, $193.5 million) and *E.T. The Extra-Terrestrial* (1982, $228.6 million).

Megabuck budgets are a product of megabuck stars. Their fees often account for a major slice of a film's total cost. Sylvester Stallone, for example, was paid $15 million to star in *Rocky IV* (1985), while Arnold Schwarzenegger has been paid $12 million for *Kindergarten Cop* (1990). Other big earners include Bruce Willis ($7.5 million for *Die Hard 2*) Richard Dreyfuss ($4 million per picture) and Kevin Costner ($7million for *Robin Hood*).

Since the break-up of the studio system, when actors were paid a weekly salary under contract, many performers have negotiated payments on a picture-by-picture basis, often involving a flat fee plus a percentage of the gross. If the film does well this can be worth much more than a single fee. James Stewart's revolutionary profit-sharing deal for *Winchester '73* (1950) made him a millionaire. Charlton Heston regularly accepted a comparatively modest $250,000 per picture plus 10 per cent. These percentages, known as "points", are extremely favourable because they are not dependent on the film making a profit.

Other actors who have negotiated tasty deals include Marlon Brando, who got $2.25 million for his cameo in *Superman* (1978), William Holden, whose 10 per cent of *The Bridge on the River Kwai* (1957) netted him $2 million, Richard Burton and Elizabeth Taylor, who could command $1 million a picture, and Paul Newman, who took $1 million plus 10 per cent of *The Towering Inferno* (1974), rising to 15 per cent when it broke even.

MAD MAX GOES HOLLYWOOD

Boyish-looking Mel Gibson is Australia's biggest gift to Hollywood since Errol Flynn. Or at least he would be if he weren't American already. Gibson, who shot to prominence in the Australian film *Mad Max* (1979) and its two sequels, *Mad Max 2* (1981) and *Mad Max beyond Thunderdome* (1985), was actually born in Peeskill, New York, in 1956, the sixth in a family of 11. His parents were of Irish-Catholic extraction and moved to Sydney when young Mel was 12.

He attended the National Institute of Dramatic Art, from which he graduated in 1977 and entered the Australian film industry, playing a beach bum in *Summer City* (1977). Joining the South Australian Theatre Company, he played in Shakespeare in Sydney.

Rapidly establishing himself in international productions and Australian pictures that achieved overseas distribution like *Gallipoli* (1981) and *The Year of Living Dangerously* (1983), he was snapped up by Hollywood, which did not at first know how to cast him. His initial American films, *The River* and *Mrs Soffel* (both 1984), ignored the macho qualities that had made him so popular in the *Mad Max* trilogy. His third American film, however, gets the formula just right. In *Lethal Weapon*, he plays a detective with such a kamikaze instinct that he himself is registered as a lethal weapon.

HEART OF THE MATTER

Mickey Rourke is Harry Angel, a down and out private eye in Angel Heart.

Alan Parker's *Angel Heart* is another 100 per cent American picture from a Cockney film maker, whose credits include *Bugsy Malone* (1976) and *Midnight Express* (1978). One of his earlier Hollywood pictures, *Shoot the Moon* (1982), with Albert Finney and Diane Keaton, was widely considered a failure.

Angel Heart is set in New Orleans and plugs into the strain of black magic that hovers just below the surface in that city. Indeed, one of the characters, Lou Cyphre (played by Robert De Niro in beard and talons) is a thinly veiled Devil figure. He's after the soul of Mickey Rourke.

Alan Parker first came across the subject in 1978, soon after the original book by William Hjortsberg was published. At the time, however, an option was acquired by one of the Hollywood studios and Parker forgot about it until he was re-introduced to it by Elliott Kastner, the Hollywood producer, who slipped a copy of it to him one lunchtime at Pinewood Studios in 1985.

It came at an opportune moment, when Parker was eager to get back to writing a script instead of re-writing somebody else's. Says Parker: "I have very eclectic tastes and have tended to react against the film I've just finished, avoiding the pigeon holes film journalists delight in stuffing you into. . . . I've always said that I'd like to tackle every genre and this novel embraced not one, but two. At any rate Kastner was very persuasive. Story has it that Marlon Brando finally said yes to *The Missouri Breaks* because he couldn't bear Elliott crying in front of him any more."

BODY AND MIND

"Are you an actress?" asks Ray Milland in Theresa Russell's first movie, *The Last Tycoon* (1976). No, she replies in that characteristically throaty voice, "I'm just Daddy's little girl." It's a fair self-description, in fact, for, after only one more Hollywood film (*Straight Time* in 1978), she flew in the face of her agent's advice and came to Britain to work for offbeat director Nicolas Roeg, whom she later married. He is twice her age.

Born in 1957 in San Diego, Russell spent most of her childhood in Burbank. Her parents divorced when she was six and she left home at 16 to pursue a modelling and acting career, enrolling at the Lee Strasberg Theatre Institute in Los Angeles.

Her first film for Roeg was the sexually explicit *Bad Timing*, in which she tempted and almost destroyed Art Garfunkel. Roeg set her early misgivings at rest and they went on together to make *Eureka* (1983), where she played the sexy younger wife of Gene Hackman, and *Insignificance* (1986), in which she vamped as Marilyn Monroe. This year she went back to America to appear in the thriller *Black Widow* as a scheming murderess being pursued by FBI agent Debra Winger, from whom she almost stole the film.

"I was always into older men," says the unconventional Russell, "but I don't believe in all this father figure stuff. Nic and I have a very physical relationship, but I was, and still remain, in awe of his mind."

Theresa Russell and Debra Winger in Black Widow.

A DEAD SET ON MILLIONAIRES

Black Widow, not to be confused with the 1954 Ginger Rogers thriller, is a fascinating study of an amoral murderess, who dispatches a stream of millionaire husbands, and of a Justice Department investigator who suspects that her prey's frequent bereavements are not as innocent as they appear.

The story becomes a kind of mirror image yarn in which the government agent (Debra Winger) eventually finds herself in conflict with her quarry (Theresa Russell) when they both fall in love with the same wealthy tycoon on vacation in the South Pacific. Gravel-voiced Winger and Russell strike sparks off each other throughout, and there's an interesting collection of moguls who make brief entrances before succumbing to the black widow's sting – America's Dennis Hopper, Britain's Nicol Williamson and France's Sami Frey.

The film is directed by Bob Rafelson, who made the Jack Nicholson starrers *Five Easy Pieces* (1970) and *The Postman Always Rings Twice* (1981). Though it is in some ways his least personal film, it is made with the panache that has distinguished Rafelson's career since his first film, *Head* (1968).

THE MAN WHO IS A WEAPON

In *Lethal Weapon*, the weapon in question is not some variant of a Magnum but a man. As played by Australian star Mel Gibson, he is a cop so affected by the death of his wife that he has developed a kamikaze instinct and is himself registered as a "lethal weapon" in the police arsenal.

In the film Gibson is teamed up with black Danny Glover (who featured in *The Color Purple*, 1985) and one of the most interesting features of the film is that nothing is made of their racial differences. Glover invites Gibson home and he assimilates instantly and completely. It's one of the first Hollywood films in which race is set up as a potential theme and then simply ignored as irrelevant.

Richard Donner, who directs, first attracted attention with *Superman* (1978) and spent nearly a decade looking for another project of comparable quality. The kiddies adventure *The Goonies* (1985), made for Steven Spielberg, didn't fit the bill. But with *Lethal Weapon*, he has a police thriller that works well in conventional action terms while contriving incidentally to make a point about racial equality.

BIRTHS, DEATHS AND MARRIAGES

DEATHS

Trevor Howard
7 Jan, Bushey, Hertfordshire
Bronchitis

Andy Warhol
22 Feb, New York
Cardiac arrest after surgery

Danny Kaye
3 Mar, Los Angeles
Heart attack

MARRIAGES

Burt Reynolds
29 Apr, *to* Loni Anderson

STAR QUOTES

Paul Newman
"A long time ago, winning an Oscar was important. But it's like chasing a beautiful woman. You hang in there for years, then finally she relents and you say: I'm too tired."

ACADEMY AWARDS

PRESENTED ON 30 MARCH 1987

Best Picture
Platoon

Best Director
Oliver Stone
Platoon

Best Actor
Paul Newman
The Color of Money

Best Actress
Marlee Matlin
Children of a Lesser God

Best Sup Actor
Michael Caine
Hannah and Her Sisters

Best Sup Actress
Dianne Wiest
Hannah and Her Sisters

Danny Glover and Mel Gibson are two L.A. cops in the action-thriller Lethal Weapon.

KEEP THE UNIVERSE, I'LL TAKE HOLLYWOOD

Nineteen years after he first arrived in America, Austrian-born muscle-man Arnold Schwarzenegger, 40, still speaks English as if he's got a mouthful of strudel. But it hasn't stopped him from rising to the heights in Hollywood. The winner of practically every body-building title in existence – Mr Universe, Mr Olympia – he has muscles where you wouldn't even think they existed. But he knows it, and his performances are like an act of comic collusion with the audience.

His first film, in 1969, was *Hercules in New York*, in which he appeared under the name Arnold Strong; but there was a long break until *Stay Hungry* (1976), where he played Sally Field's bodybuilder boyfriend, and the cult semi-documentary *Pumping Iron* (1977). Since then he has moved increasingly into mainstream action movies – sword and sorcery sagas like *Conan the Barbarian* (1982) and *Conan the Destroyer* (1984) and films that tread the same path as Sylvester Stallone, like *Commando* (1985). His newest, *Predator*, one of the summer's biggest hits, is an astute mixture of that type of picture and science fiction. And in April last year, he cemented his acceptance by the American establishment by marrying John F. Kennedy's niece, Maria Shriver.

KUBRICK'S VIETNAM

Matthew Modine (centre), a raw conscript, and Lee Ermey, a drill sergeant, in Full Metal Jacket.

Full Metal Jacket is Stanley Kubrick's first film since *The Shining* (1980) and there are those who say that the increasingly long intervals between his pictures (the one before that was *Barry Lyndon* in 1975) is making them more like museum pieces than true movies. He takes so long finding a subject, shooting it (generally on closed sets) and then editing and grading it afterwards that some of the spontaneity that marked his earlier work, like the racetrack robbery thriller *The Killing* (1956), is lost.

A "full metal jacket" is a type of bullet rather than a form of armour. It was used in the Vietnam war and Kubrick's film is about the training of draftees and their subsequent experiences in the field. Little of the film was shot in the Far East. The warscape was re-created in south London with imported palm trees; it's a Vietnam of the imagination only, though it is based on the novel *The Short-Timers* by real-life Vietnam veteran Gustav Hasford. Hue city was in fact constructed around an old gasworks at Beckton-on-Thames, and was blown up expressly for the movie.

The cast is relatively unknown, with only Matthew Modine striking any chord in the audience's memory. The standout performance is from Lee Ermey as the platoon's drill instructor – a role that he actually filled in real life. During the production he was injured in a car accident, which held up shooting for three months, pushing up the budget to $20 million.

THE NAME'S DALTON, TIMOTHY DALTON

There's a new man in James Bond's shoes. He's Timothy Dalton, who takes on the role of 007 for the first time in *The Living Daylights*. Born in 1944, Dalton has hitherto specialized in historical pictures like *The Lion in Winter* (1968), *Cromwell* (1970) and *Mary, Queen of Scots* (1971).

He is the fourth actor to portray Ian Fleming's hero. Sean Connery was the first, beginning with *Dr. No* (1962), and Roger Moore the latest, beginning with *Live and Let Die* (1973). In between, Australian George Lazenby filled the role in a single film, *On Her Majesty's Secret Service* (1969).

Does Connery have any advice for his newest successor? "Well, Timothy Dalton is an excellent actor," he says, "and I'm sure he doesn't need any advice from me. But I think primarily he should get a good lawyer."

RELEASED FROM BONDAGE

Until Sean Connery, no actor with such a pronounced Scottish accent had ever made it to the top in the international movie scene. Born in Edinburgh in 1930, he played James Bond seven times before crying "never again" after *Diamonds Are Forever* (1971). And he stuck by that decision for 12 years until a fat salary and extensive control over the production persuaded him to assume the role again in a remake of *Thunderball* (1965), appropriately called *Never Say Never Again* (1983).

Meanwhile, Connery had progressively established his right to be treated as an actor with a wider range than 007. He played in Alfred Hitchcock's *Marnie* (1964), in the sci-fi film *Zardoz* (1973) and distinguished himself playing Robin Hood in old age in *Robin and Marian* (1976), opposite the equally middle-aged Audrey Hepburn.

But during the 1980s he's steadily won the right to be regarded as one of the cinema's major screen presences. His newest film is a movie version of the old ABC-TV series *The Untouchables* (1959), in which he plays a shrewd Chicago policeman helping the FBI to nail Al Capone. His grizzled, confident performance puts most of today's beardless stars in their right place.

Sean Connery as Jimmy Malone.

BIRTHS, DEATHS AND MARRIAGES

DEATHS

Rita Hayworth
14 May, New York
Alzheimer's disease

Fred Astaire
22 Jun, Los Angeles
Pneumonia

Pola Negri
1 Aug, San Antonio, Texas

Rouben Mamoulian
4 Aug, Woodland Hills, California

John Huston
28 Aug, Middletown, Rhode Island
Emphysema

Lee Marvin
29 Aug, Tucson, Arizona
Heart attack

Joseph E. Levine
31 Aug, Greenwich, Connecticut

MARRIAGES

Tom Cruise
May, *to* **Mimi Rogers**

Tom Selleck
Aug, *to* Julie Makk

Cher, Jack Nicholson, Susan Sarandon and Michelle Pfeiffer in The Witches of Eastwick.

JOHN LANDIS CLEARED IN TWILIGHT CASE

On 29 May film director John Landis and four movie-making colleagues were acquitted of charges of involuntary manslaughter arising out of an incident during the filming, five years before, of *Twilight Zone The Movie*. On 23 July 1982 a helicopter had crashed during the shooting of a sequence purporting to be set in Vietnam. Vic Morrow, the actor, had been decapitated by the whirring rotor blades, along with a child he was carrying in the scene, and a second child had been crushed to death under the wreckage.

The trial had become a test case of whether safety precautions in Hollywood productions were being adequately adhered to. The evidence on this score has been variously interpreted. The Screen Actors' Guild has followed up the Landis verdict with statistics indicating that, between 1982 and 1986, annual injuries sustained by its members have declined from 214 to 65. But other figures published by the California Occupational Safety and Health Administration show that if all crew members are included in the survey, the numbers of injuries over this time has actually risen.

TALK OF THE DEVIL

The Witches of Eastwick lets Jack Nicholson finally play the role he often seems on the verge of – Old Nick, the Devil himself. In the film he is conjured up by three shapely New England women who find that they have a common gift – the power of witching – and decide to summon up the perfect man. Leeringly decadent and giving those circumflex eyebrows a full workout, Nicholson is in his element. He's matched by the comely Cher, Michelle Pfeiffer and Susan Sarandon as his initially sex-starved creators.

Adapted from the John Updike novel, the movie is a superior entertainment that should have audiences clamouring for more this summer. The special effects in the second half as Nicholson has to cope with the women's attempts to drive him away again are state-of-the-art.

The director is former Australian doctor George Miller, better known for *Mad Max* (1979) and its two sequels. He's not to be confused with another Australian director of the same name who made the Kirk Douglas Australian western, *The Man from Snowy River* (1982).

GOSSIP COLUMN

■ **Bob Dylan, guru of folk music, and Richard Marquand, director of the smash-hit *Return of the Jedi* have combined to make a movie – *Hearts of Fire*. But Fox has passed on it as distributor leaving it to Lorimar. Word has it that it's not only weird but pointless.**

ROAD TO RUIN

Ishtar is like some long-lost script from the Hope and Crosby *Road* series. It's about two untalented entertainers who are drawn into a world of intrigue in hot places. This time it is North Africa – and *Road to Morocco* (1942) comes instantly to mind.

The big difference is that Hope, Crosby and Dorothy Lamour were natural comedians, whereas their opposite numbers here are not. Warren Beatty, Dustin Hoffman and Isabelle Adjani have seldom been at their best in comedy and, for the most part, are upstaged here by a blind camel.

The film would not be worth mentioning if its budget had not also done a Topsy and ballooned to $55 million, thanks to the perfectionism of its two male stars and of its director, Elaine May. Unlike *Heaven's Gate* (1980), that other runaway production that became a byword for extravagance, audiences can't even see where the money went this time.

Neither of the two stars' careers seems likely to be affected, but it will make it difficult for Elaine May to work again in the cinema. Mike Nichols' erstwhile cabaret partner, she has had a sporadic movie career. Her early films, *A New Leaf* (1971), *The Heartbreak Kid* (1972) and *Mikey and Micky* (1976), have not led to the sustained body of work one might have expected. *Ishtar* will not make it easier for her to find suitable projects.

Warren Beatty and Dustin Hoffman in Ishtar.

SEPTEMBER OCTOBER

NOVEMBER DECEMBER

STAR QUOTES

Peter Weller

"You think you're indestructible when you're 28. When you're 10 years older you know there's a lot of other things you want to do with your life than be a big-shot on a 40-foot screen."

DIVORCE FOR PUTTNAM AND COLUMBIA

Little more than a year after Coca-Cola welcomed British producer David Puttnam as supremo of its Columbia film-making subsidiary, the two sides have filed for divorce. Puttnam's downfall was that he never fully understood where the power lay in Hollywood. In particular he rubbed powerful producer Ray Stark up the wrong way by refusing to sanction any longer the "special relationship" Stark had with Columbia. Puttnam also offended comedian Bill Murray.

Had he delivered some successful movies, Puttnam might have kept his job. But too many of those begun in his time were British (like *Hope and Glory*) or disappointing (like *Someone to Watch over Me*) or only of minority appeal (like *Housekeeping*). All these films opened this year to less than sensational business, and Puttnam's fate was sealed.

YUPPIE NIGHTMARE

Fatal Attraction is the kind of movie that will give yuppies nightmares. It shows the awful things that could befall a rising young executive who has what he imagines will be a mere fling. Unfortunately, his partner turns out to be a psychotic who, like the proverbial woman scorned, turns on her lover and threatens to wreak vengeance on him and his family.

The picture is clearly a calculated commercial affair, with some highly erotic copulation all over the kitchen range. But some see it as an allegory on the ability of AIDS, through a one-night stand, to destroy all those with whom the partners later have relations.

Its commercial side is reinforced by casting handsome Michael Douglas as the arbitrageur with the wandering libido. (This December he'll be seen as another yuppie type – the nasty kind – in *Wall Street*, with Charlie Sheen.) Playing opposite him is fast-rising Glenn Close, who has been thrice nominated for supporting Oscars and this time could be in for the major award. Anne Archer is the wife caught in the middle.

The director is Britain's Adrian Lyne, who cut his teeth on advertising but made a big impression with *Flashdance* (1983) and last year's *Nine ½ Weeks*. The eroticism of those was like a dry run for *Fatal Attraction*. Originally the movie had a more ironic ending than the bloody mayhem with which it now concludes, but it was altered after unfavourable reaction at a sneak preview.

SO CLOSE TO AN OSCAR

Glenn Close, tipped as the actress most likely to topple Meryl Streep as queen of Hollywood, got off to a flying start in the cinema. For each of her first three films, *The World according to Garp* (1982), *The Big Chill* (1983) and *The Natural* (1984), she was nominated for an Oscar in a supporting role. Now she's graduated to star parts and is still getting Oscar nominations. Her latest, in *Fatal Attraction*, is her most dramatic to date – a terrifying study of a vengeful woman destroyed by sexual obsession.

Born in Connecticut in 1945, she is a true Yankee, and in fact her forebears helped to found her home town of Greenwich in the 17th century. The daughter of a surgeon, she grew up on a 500-acre estate and was educated first at a Swiss boarding school and subsequently at a prep school in America.

Close sees clear similarities betwen herself and Streep: "We are both blondes. We both have long noses. We both play strong women. I feel confident of my ability and hope the day will come when Meryl will feel as much influenced by me as I am by her."

Glenn Close in Fatal Attraction.

THE SON ALSO RISES

Wheeler-dealer Ivan Boesky had not yet been disgraced when Michael Douglas agreed to play a part with close similarities to Boesky's career in *Wall Street*. It's one of the best roles of his career and confounds those who have accused him of being a mere lightweight riding on the coat-tails of his dad.

Michael Douglas is Kirk's eldest son, born in 1944. After studying drama at the University of California at Santa Barbara, he moved to New York and appeared in several off-Broadway plays before making his movie debut in *Hail, Hero* (1969).

For four years he appeared regularly in the TV series *The Streets of San Francisco*, two episodes of which he directed himself. Eager to produce as well as direct, he eventually got his chance with *One Flew over the Cuckoo's Nest* (1975), a project that took 4½ years to set up but was rewarded with a clean sweep at the Oscars. Since then, he has acted in and produced the nuclear drama *The China Syndrome* (1979), the escapist *Romancing the Stone* (1984) and its lame sequel, *Jewel of the Nile* (1985).

Charlie Sheen and Michael Douglas in Wall Street.

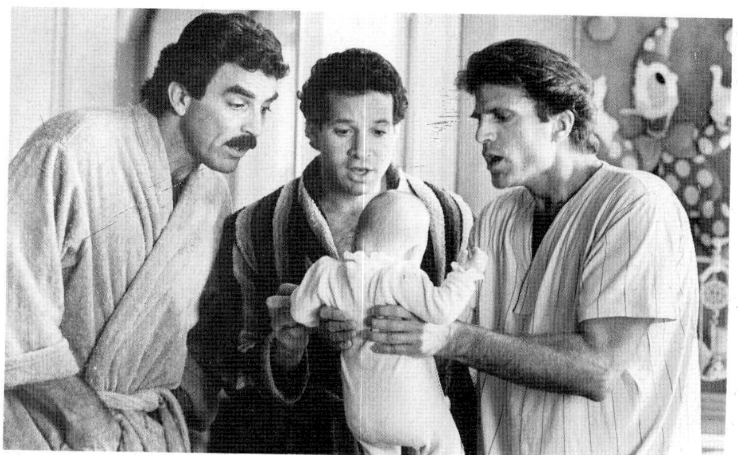

Tom Selleck, Steve Guttenberg and Ted Danson are left in the lurch in Three Men and a Baby.

TRANSATLANTIC CHANGELING

Three Men and a Baby, currently doing record business, is a remake of a French hit, *Three Men and a Cradle*, made by Coline Serreau in 1985. This is a growing trend in American movies – the Michael Caine comedy *Blame It on Rio* (1984) was a remake of the 1977 French film *One Wild Moment*, and Blake Edwards' *The Man Who Loved Women* (1983) a re-run of the Francois Truffaut comedy of 1977.

Three Men and a Baby plays up all the usual diaper-changing jokes and softens the original into a more slapstick mode. Coline Serreau was to have directed but, after spending time in America, she and Disney parted.

So the film was directed by Leonard Nimoy, better known as Mr Spock in the *Star Trek* movies. He shows a competent touch, though without the subtlety of the French original. Tom Selleck, Steve Guttenberg and Ted Danson play the three bachelors suddenly left in possession of a cooing infant.

BOX OFFICE

UK

1 "Crocodile" Dundee
2 The Living Daylights
3 Beverly Hills Cop II
4 Platoon
5 Police Academy 4: Citizens on Patrol
6 The Golden Child
7 Labyrinth
8 Superman IV: The Quest for Peace
9 Full Metal Jacket
10 Blind Date

BOX OFFICE

US

1 Beverly Hills Cop II
2 Platoon
3 Fatal Attraction
4 Three Men and a Baby
5 The Untouchables
6 The Witches of Eastwick
7 Predator
8 Dragnet
9 The Secret of My Success
10 Lethal Weapon

FUTURE LAW?

RoboCop is almost unprecedented in the American cinema - a full-blown action picture made by a European art-house director. Paul Verhoeven is a Dutchman whose first international picture, *Flesh + Blood*, made for Orion in 1987, suffered from his comparative unfamiliarity with English. But *RoboCop* is in a different league. For one thing, he was working with actors and actresses like Peter Weller and Nancy Allen, who already had considerable experience and were able to modify the script in ways that made it sound more realistic.

The basic idea of the film is arresting. In a Detroit of tomorrow, Police Officer Murphy is violently murdered. His innards are then cased in titanium, turning him into a metallic man who cannot be destroyed and is therefore the police department's ultimate law-enforcement weapon. There's only one thing wrong with him – he will not turn on his creators, even if they are crooks and have sewn up the police force as an enormous racket.

Despite the impressive special effects, including the robots stacked up against RoboCop that are entirely synthetic, the movie cost a relatively modest $14 million and is clunking towards a return of $23 million for Orion.

BIRTHS, DEATHS AND MARRIAGES

DEATHS

Mervyn LeRoy
13 Sep, Beverly Hills

Bob Fosse
23 Sep, Washington, DC
Heart attack

Richard Marquand
5 Dec, London
Stroke

Alice Terry
22 Dec, Burbank, California
Pneumonia

MARRIAGES

Bruce Willis
1 Nov, *to* **Demi Moore**

Bernardo Bertolucci's epic The Last Emperor tells the story of Pu Yi, the last Chinese royal ruler.

FIRST WESTERN MOVIE SHOT IN PEKING

Italian director Bernardo Bertolucci has all the right socialist credentials to be the first western director allowed to film in Peking. His *1900* (1977) was a Marxist interpretation of Italian history in the 20th century. Now, in *The Last Emperor*, he tells the story of Pu Yi, last of the old Chinese imperial line, who became a dupe of the Japanese during the Second World War and underwent a kind of conversion after the Communists took over, serving out the remainder of his life as a gardener.

The film is magnificently shot by ace Italian cameraman Vittorio Storaro and, especially in the early scenes, vividly brings to life the rituals of the Chinese imperial court.

The title role is played by John Lone, a Chinese actor who trained in Peking Opera, though he has been making a name for himself principally in the west. He's best remembered as the Chinese gangster in *Year of the Dragon* (1985). Among the supporting cast only Peter O'Toole is known, playing Lone's British teacher.

SPIELBERG'S VOICE BREAKS

Hollywood wonderkid Steven Spielberg is often taken to task for making movies that appeal primarily to teenies, tweenies and weenies. But in *Empire of the Sun* he stakes out his claim to be treated as a bona fide adult. It's adapted by Tom Stoppard from a semi-autobiographical novel by J.G. Ballard about his experiences in China during the Second World War.

The movie is told through the eyes of a child – marvellously well played by young British actor Christian Bale – who, after being separated from his parents in 1941 in Shanghai, falling in with some American soldiers and later being interned by the Japanese, evolves from a spoilt brat into a real member of the human race. It's an uplifting story that has more than a touch of David Lean about it, both in look and theme, especially in the prison camp sequences that contrast the behaviour of Brits and Americans. In fact, the original plan was for Lean to direct and Spielberg to produce; but in the event the two parted company at an early stage, despite Spielberg's long admiration for the veteran British director.

John Malkovich makes a vivid impression as the U.S. soldier young Bales comes to admire; and there are minor roles for Nigel Havers as a camp doctor and Miranda Richardson as an internee. The real quality, however, lies in Spielberg's direction and in particular his handling of the big set pieces – the fall of Shanghai to the Japanese, the bombing raid on the prisoner of war camp (filmed in one enormous tracking shot) and the detonation of the atomic bomb on Nagasaki, which seems to the boy so bright that it is "like God taking a photograph". You'd never guess that, apart from a few scenes in Shanghai, the whole of the movie was shot in Spain and south-east England.

Christian Bale thrills to the attack of US aircraft on the airbase next to his prison camp in Empire of the Sun.

A TOUCH OF THE POET

Daniel Day-Lewis comes with the very best credentials for a career in the movies. He is the son of actress Jill Balcon and the late poet laureate Cecil Day-Lewis, and the grandson of Michael Balcon, under whose wing Ealing Studios enjoyed its finest hour. With *The Unbearable Lightness of Being* we can see a promising character actor acquire star quality before our eyes.

Now 31, he was still a child when he made his screen debut in *Sunday Bloody Sunday* (1971) and more than 10 years later he was still playing bit parts in films like *Gandhi* (1982). The breakthrough has been sudden. One moment he was unknown, then he was a punk homosexual in *My Beautiful Laundrette* (1985) and prissy Cecil Vyse in *A Room with a View* (1986). His randy Czech surgeon in *Unbearable Lightness* further extends that range.

CZECH MATES

A three-hour movie about a rising young brain surgeon's experiences in Czechoslovakia at the time of the 1968 Prague Spring? Gulp, you say. But you'd be wrong. *The Unbearable Lightness of Being* is already being hailed as one of the sexiest, most dramatic movies of the year. And it has a peach of a part for young Irish actor Daniel Day-Lewis, whose handsome womanizer could hardly be more different from his punk homosexual in *My Beautiful Laundrette* (1985).

It's taken from a cult 1984 novel by exiled Czech writer Milan Kundera, and the story is essentially about enjoying life and sex to the full while they are still there. There's certainly plenty of the latter, in the shapely, bowler-hatted form of Swedish actress Lena Olin, plus fine playing from young French star Juliette Binoche as Day-Lewis' photographer wife.

Daniel Day-Lewis and Juliette Binoche in The Unbearable Lightness of Being.

Director of the film (from the producer who made *Amadeus*) is actually an American – Philip Kaufman. He's been responsible for a wide variety of movies over the years, from the Robert Duvall western, *The Great Northfield Minnesota Raid* (1972), through a remake of *Invasion of the Body Snatchers* (1978), with Donald Sutherland, to the epic of the birth of the American space programme, *The Right Stuff* (1983). Shot in the USA, France and Geneva, his latest film looks like breaking down the arbitrary division between mainstream and art-house movies.

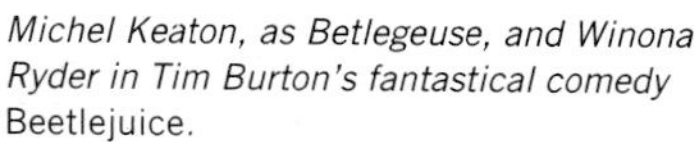

Michel Keaton, as Betlegeuse, and Winona Ryder in Tim Burton's fantastical comedy Beetlejuice.

CAN'T TAKE HIM ANYWHERE

Beetlejuice is a spook so decrepit and disreputable that he's not fit for polite society. The joke in this highly original comedy (the title's a corruption of the astronomical name Betelgeuse) is that because he's beyond the pale he is summoned up to scare away a family of nauseating yuppies who have bought a nice bourgeois house after the young owners have died in a car accident.

Beetlejuice is actually more like social satire. But it's also a special-effects picture in which the wraiths and ectoplasm are every bit as impressive as in *Ghost Busters* (1984).

Star of the show is Michael Keaton. He's truly disgusting – and should go far. The rest of the cast is impressive, too. Fast-rising Geena Davis and Alec Baldwin make the dead couple sympathetic, and striking Winona Ryder, one of the most talented child stars of recent years, makes an impact as the yuppie couple's feet-on-the-ground daughter. Veteran 1930s star Sylvia Sidney is also around as a harassed social worker from the hereafter.

Director Tim Burton began as an animator at Disney, working on *The Fox and the Hound* (1981) and *The Black Cauldron* (1985). His first movie was the wonderfully silly *Pee-wee's Big Adventure* (1985), with Paul Reubens, which was actually more like a live-action cartoon.

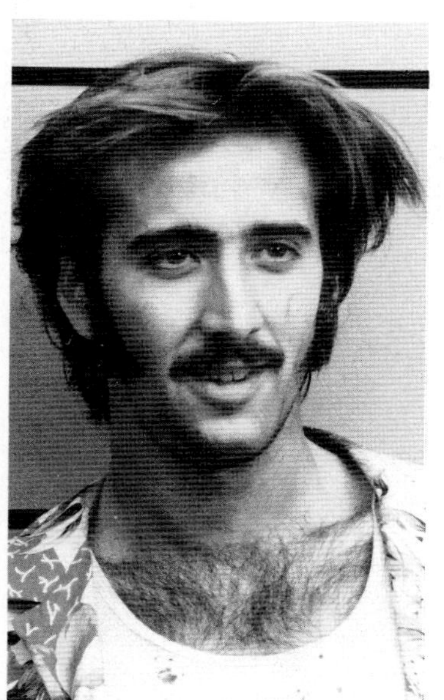

BREAKING FREE OF UNCLE FRANCIS

His real name is Nicolas Coppola and some will say that he has only got where he has thanks to strings pulled by his uncle, Francis Coppola. But that's why Nicolas Cage changed his name in the first place.

Born in 1964, the lantern-faced Cage began in high school plays and drifted into movies and television, though his first work, in *Fast Times at Ridgemont High* (1982), ended on the cutting room floor. He worked three times for his uncle, in *Rumble Fish* (1983), *The Cotton Club* (1984) and *Peggy Sue Got Married* (1986), but it was only in the last that his distinctive brand of comedy began to emerge. It was too much for co-star Kathleen Turner. Says Cage: "She was supposed to be with someone written as a suave and romantic young leading man. I turned the character into a cross between a nutty professor and Jerry Lewis. It freaked her out. She gave me the full ice treatment."

Since then he's been a manic ex-jailbird in *Raising Arizona* (1987), with Holly Hunter, and a one-armed, opera-loving Italian baker in *Moonstruck* (1987), jumping into the sack with Cher.

BIRTHS, DEATHS AND MARRIAGES

DEATHS

John Clements
6 Apr, Brighton, Sussex

Kenneth Williams
15 Apr, London
Heart attack

WHEN THE WORDS DRY UP

Eight years down the road from the punishing actors' strike that virtually brought Tinseltown to a halt in summer 1980, there comes a new threat with the decision of the Writers' Guild of America to strike from the beginning of March.

The strike is over three main issues: creative control, foreign residuals, and the actual amount paid for hour-long TV shows. Though the stoppage does not have the same immediate impact as the actors' strike, which paralysed films in progress, it means Hollywood is increasingly unable to develop new projects. Expect a hiatus in screenplays a year down the line.

ACADEMY AWARDS

PRESENTED ON 11 APRIL 1988

Best Picture
The Last Emperor

Best Director
Bernardo Bertolucci
The Last Emperor

Best Actor
Michael Douglas
Wall Street

Best Actress
Cher
Moonstruck

Best Sup Actor
Sean Connery
The Untouchables

Best Sup Actress
Olympia Dukakis
Moonstruck

BIRTHS, DEATHS AND MARRIAGES

MARRIAGES

Michael J. Fox
16 July, *to* Tracey Pollen

THE GOSPEL ACCORDING TO ST MARTIN

Even before his new film is shown, director Martin Scorsese has run into a barrage of flak from religious and moral pressure groups all over America, objecting to alleged elements in a film they haven't even seen. *The Last Temptation of Christ* is a film version of the novel by Greek writer Nicos Kazantzakis that Scorsese has been trying to set up for over 15 years.

Fundamentalists, on the basis of an early draft of the script that did not survive, say the picture depicts Christ as a crackpot who lusts after Mary Magdalene. Watch-dog committees have been besieging Universal, which made it, and even picketing the house of Lew Wasserman, chairman of MCA, the parent company. They want the film shelved; and one body, the Campus Crusade for Christ, has offered to buy the negative at cost ($10 million) and destroy it. Meanwhile, the Fundamentalist Baptist Tabernacle of Los Angeles has been picketing the studio protesting that the film stirs up race hatred by putting a Jewish gloss on the life of Jesus.

Bob Hoskins and Roger Rabbit in the integrated animation/live action feature Who Framed Roger Rabbit.

RUN RABBIT, RUN . . . .

Picking up a form of animation that goes back at least as far as *Anchors Aweigh* (1945), *Who Framed Roger Rabbit* integrates animated and real-life figures with such sophistication that the budget soared to $70 million. But all the signs are that Roger will run and run.

Director Robert Zemeckis, who made *Back to the Future* (1985), delights in the silliness of the idea. Roger yammers and stutters manically with the voice of Charles Fleischer, and is married to an animated seductress called Jessica, with an hour-glass figure and the throaty tones of (uncredited) Kathleen Turner. Her best line is "I'm not bad, I'm just drawn that way."

The co-production by Disney and Steven Spielberg unites famous cartoon figures from different studios. Daffy Duck, for example, co-stars with Donald Duck for the first time and the cast also includes Betty Boop and many other old favourites. Well-known British-based animator Richard Williams headed the team of cartoonists.

The logistics are mind-blowing. The credits list 739 people and to ensure that the live-action shots to be integrated with the animated material were crystal clear, an improved version of the old 1950s VistaVision camera was developed. The admen have even coined a new phrase with which to hype it: "multi-dimensional interactive character generation."

EALING GETS THE PYTHON SQUEEZE

A Fish Called Wanda is a caper movie not too different in subject matter from a thousand others. But it's been taken to the public's heart because it is a remarkable marriage between comedy styles of two different eras. The director is 78-year-old Charles Crichton, who was at his peak in the heyday of Ealing studios, for which he made the classic Alec Guinness comedy, *The Lavender Hill Mob* (1951). But the cast consists partly of actors who came to the fore with the *Monty Python* shows – John Cleese, Michael Palin and others. Trained in television, they subsequently transferred their anarchic brand of comedy to the screen in films like *Monty Python and the Holy Grail* (1974) and *Monty Python's The Meaning of Life* (1983).

A Fish Called Wanda is a story very like *The Lavender Hill Mob* but it has a savage streak as well – like the sequence in which the thieves try to induce a heart attack in an old lady by killing her pet corgis. It also has a transatlantic infusion: two of the stars are American and bring an extra dimension to this essentially British comedy. Jamie Lee Curtis adds a welcome touch of Hollywood glamour and Kevin Kline is a lunatic anarchist with several screws loose.

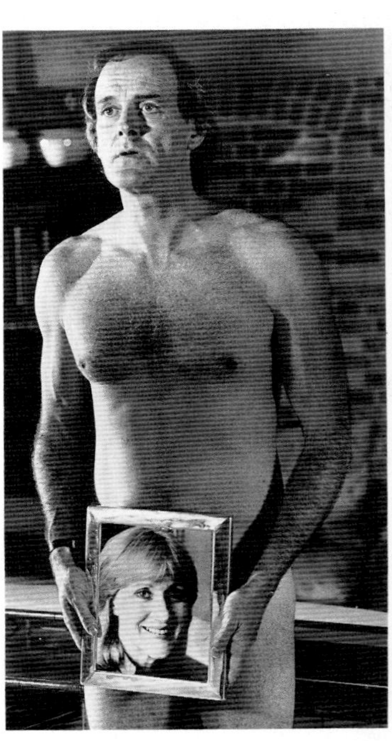
John Cleese in A Fish Called Wanda.

IS THIS A BLACK THING?

"Is this a black thing?" asks Eddie Murphy, with mockery hovering round his lips as he responds to a well-deserved put-down by a white cop in last year's *Beverly Hills Cop II*. Murphy is the undisputed black superstar of Hollywood and has been since he first exploded on the screen as Nick Nolte's wisecracking "partner" in *48HRS.* (1982), at the age of only 21.

Murphy's technique is formidable – a torrent of repartee, liberally punctuated with expletives. What makes him so refreshing among black actors is that he doesn't go for the "nice" parts as Sidney Poitier and Harry Belafonte did. He is randy, sly and nobody's Uncle Tom.

Hard to believe that *Beverly Hills Cop* (1984) was originally planned for Sylvester Stallone. But Murphy's sense of timing makes him a superb comic actor – seen to advantage in *Trading Places* (1983), a satire on social and racial distinction as well as on the shenanigans of the futures markets.

Now in *Coming to America* he is the black monarch of a banana kingdom who is used to having everything done for him by nubile young subjects. Few will see the early scene in which Murphy is washed by handmaidens, who proclaim the royal member clean, and fail to roll in the aisles.

STAR QUOTES

Eddie Murphy

"Wouldn't it be a helluva thing if this was burnt cork and you folk were being tolerant for nothing?"

THE THREE LIVES OF DEAN STOCKWELL

Few child stars are successful as actors when they grow up. Even fewer get two chances to make a comeback, but Dean Stockwell is the exception who proves the rule. Born in 1936, he was the curly-haired, bright-eyed child star of the 1940s who took over from Freddie Bartholomew when he grew too old to play such parts. He featured in films like *Anchors Aweigh* (1945), *The Green Years* (1946) and *Gentleman's Agreement* (1947), in which he asked his screen father Gregory Peck to explain anti-semitism to him. He made a virtual comeback in 1959 as a sensitive young man in *Compulsion*, the story of the Leopold/Loeb killers, which he had already played in 140 performances on Broadway.

After films like *Sons and Lovers* (1960) and *Long Day's Journey into Night* (1962), he slipped from view again and barely surfaced until the mid-1980s. He played an effete homosexual in *Blue Velvet* (1986), was Harry Dean Stanton's brother in *Paris, Texas* (1984), and now he is a ruthless but comic gangster in *Married to the Mob*, opposite Michelle Pfeiffer.

A lifelong pal of Dennis Hopper, Stockwell went through his drop-out phase at the same time. "We caroused together in the Sixties," Stockwell says, "and we were both virtually written off. No one expected us to survive because of the way we were living."

Bruce Willis as New York detective John McClane in Die Hard.

THE MAKING OF BRUCE WILLIS

Die Hard looks like the movie that will make Bruce Willis a big-screen star. His previous films, like *Blind Date* (1987) and this summer's *Sunset*, seemed unsure how to use the wise-cracking gumshoe of TV's *Moonlighting* (1985). Now we know: he comes over best as a breezy Clark Gable-type figure, with a sideline in sub-Stallone heroics.

Die Hard is a cross between *Lethal Weapon* (1987) and *The Towering Inferno* (1974). It's a tense thriller set within a California tower block in which a group of hostages are held prisoner on one of the upper storeys by a gang of loony terrorists. Only Bruce Willis, as a New York cop accidentally trapped within the building over Christmas, can frustrate the terrorists' plans, while outside the L.A. police with the FBI make a botch of things.

Director is John McTiernan, who cut his teeth on commercials and was responsible for the violent Arnold Schwarzenegger sci-fi thriller *Predator* (1987). The supporting cast includes Russian ballet dancer Alexander Godunov (last seen in *Witness*, 1985) as a strong-arm terrorist and Alan Rickman as the ultra-smooth heavy. He played the nasty Valmont in the London stage production of *Dangerous Liaisons*, the part that has gone to John Malkovich in the film.

SEPTEMBER
OCTOBER

NOVEMBER
DECEMBER

ELSTREE FINDS ITS WHITE KNIGHT

The saddest story of the summer has a happy ending. Elstree, the British film-making factory responsible for all the special effects work on *Star Wars* (1977), and the preferred studio of Hollywood whiz-kid Steven Spielberg, is not to be bulldozed after all. George Walker, the former fish-market porter who turned prize-fighter and rose to become chairman of the Brent Walker entertainment group, has come to its rescue with $32.5 million.

Elstree studios was acquired by Cannon as part of the film division of Thorn-EMI. Cannon's leading lights, the Israeli mini-moguls Menahem Golan and Yoram Globus, promised to fill the studio with new product but circumstances forced them to change their plans.

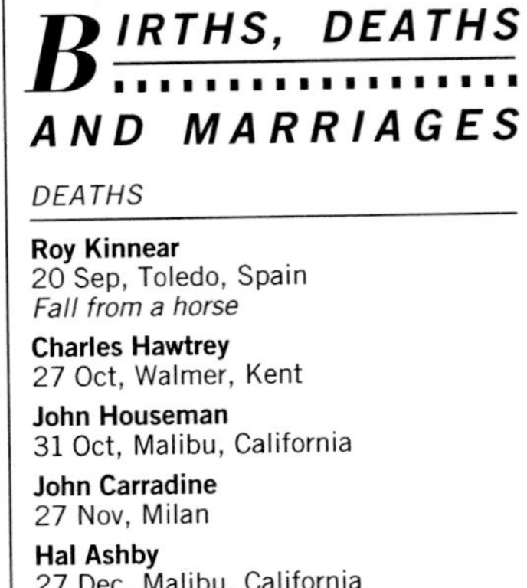

BIRTHS, DEATHS AND MARRIAGES

DEATHS

Roy Kinnear
20 Sep, Toledo, Spain
Fall from a horse

Charles Hawtrey
27 Oct, Walmer, Kent

John Houseman
31 Oct, Malibu, California

John Carradine
27 Nov, Milan

Hal Ashby
27 Dec, Malibu, California

BOX OFFICE

UK

1 Fatal Attraction
2 "Crocodile" Dundee
3 Three Men and a Baby
4 A Fish Called Wanda
5 Coming to America
6 Good Morning, Vietnam
7 The Last Emperor
8 The Jungle Book
9 Buster
10 Beetlejuice

BOX OFFICE

US

1 Who Framed Roger Rabbit
2 Coming to America
3 Good Morning, Vietnam
4 Crocodile Dundee II
5 Big
6 Three Men and a Baby
7 Die Hard
8 Cocktail
9 Moonstruck
10 Beetlejuice

COCKNEY DOWN SOUTH

The most unusual thing about *Mississippi Burning*, a powerful tale of the workings of the Ku Klux Klan in the Deep South, is that it is made by a Cockney lad called Alan Parker. Parker, who began his career in Britain with films like *Bugsy Malone* (1976), made an international breakthrough with *Midnight Express* (1978) and then went to Hollywood, where his first films were less impressive. *Shoot the Moon* (1982), a domestic drama with Albert Finney and Diane Keaton, never felt convincingly American; and even last year's thriller *Angel Heart*, with Mickey Rourke and Robert De Niro in New Orleans, seemed to catch the Cajun atmosphere less well than Jim McBride's sassy *The Big Easy*, which appeared at the same time.

But *Mississippi Burning* does not feel like the work of an outsider looking in. It's strongly written and cast, with two big roles for Gene Hackman and Willem Dafoe, as law enforcers with different ideas of how to discover and trap a killer in the Deep South. Dafoe's Yankee liberalism is contrasted with Hackman's more pragmatic Southern kind.

Dafoe comes straight from playing Jesus in the controversial *The Last Temptation of Christ*. Unkind critics are saying that all his roles are variations on Jesus: in *Platoon* (1986) he was the soldier representing peace and casting doubt on America's warlike role in Vietnam.

Gene Hackman and Willem Dafoe in Alan Parker's Mississippi Burning.

MELANIE COMES BACK FIGHTING

Melanie Griffith has her best role to date in *Working Girl*, in which she plays a secretary with "a head made for business and a body made for sin". She uses her native intelligence to rise to the boardroom over the head of office rival Sigourney Weaver. She seems to have triumphantly overcome the drinking problem that often caused her to take time off.

Born in New York, she moved to Los Angeles when she was four, attended various private Catholic schools, then the Hollywood Professional School and finally made her screen debut in *Night Moves* (1975) at the age of 17. She is the step-daughter of Tippi Hedren, blonde star of Alfred Hitchcock's *The Birds* (1963) and *Marnie* (1964).

Griffith took time off in 1981 to study acting with Stella Adler. Her black-wigged kook in *Something Wild* (1986) won her many new fans, while *Body Double* (1984), in which she played a porno star with a mind of her own, was in some respects a dry run for *Working Girl*.

STAR QUOTES

Gene Hackman

"I did nothing but work because I could never believe that an ugly schmuck like me could stay so lucky."

FROM ALIENS TO ANIMALS

Thirty-nine-year-old Sigourney Weaver has had to wait almost a decade for a part as good as her role in *Alien* (1979), where she was alone in the galaxy with a creature of pure evil. This year she's had two. She stars in *Gorillas in the Mist*, the story of primatologist Dian Fossey who fought for the future of the African gorilla, and she has one of the two key female roles in *Working Girl*, as a ruthless young boardroom executive who's not above stealing her secretary's best ideas and passing them off as her own.

Born in New York in 1949, she is the daughter of the actress Elizabeth Inglia (a contemporary of Vivien Leigh) and of Sylvester "Pat" Weaver, president of NBC and responsible for the *Today* and *Tonight* shows.

She trod the boards for the first time in a production of *King Lear* staged as a Japanese Noh drama. After studying at the Yale School of Drama, she was discouraged from seeking an acting career on account of her height. "I was crushed when they said I had no future," she says, "because I assumed they knew what they were talking about."

She made her debut (blink and you'll miss her) as Woody Allen's date in *Annie Hall* (1977). But until recently it has only been the role of Ripley in *Alien* and its 1986 sequel *Aliens* that has shown her potential. Now, at last, she has parts that are worthy of her – though she has Jessica Lange's pregnancy to thank for the part in *Gorillas in the Mist*.

ONLY THEIR MOTHER CAN TELL THEM APART

Twins is the ultimate "high-concept" movie. This means its story is so simple that a busy mogul can get the gist of it in a few seconds. The concept here can be told in two sentences. Danny DeVito and Arnold Schwarzenegger are twins. Only their mother can tell them apart.

It's a rib-tickling idea. Squat, fat DeVito must be all of five foot two. Towering, muscular Schwarzenegger tops him by more than a foot. They are as alike as bagels and sauerkraut.

Schwarzenegger has always had a sense of humour about the neanderthal parts he has played. DeVito is a natural comedian who last year ventured into direction for the first time with *Throw Momma from the Train*, a Hitchcock parody in which he also starred. In *Twins* the two actors are genetically designed siblings, unaware of each other's existence until they reach the age of 35.

Directing *Twins* is Ivan Reitman, a Canadian who has had his biggest successes in the United States, notably *Ghost Busters* (1984), which became the sixth most profitable film of all time.

Kelly McGillis (centre) shields Jodie Foster, a rape victim, in the powerful drama The Accused.

WHEN IS A RAPE NOT A RAPE?

The most controversial film of the moment is a modest little piece about a gang-bang called *The Accused*.

What makes it hot is that the incident itself is saved till near the end and then staged in unblinking detail. Some say this is pandering to voyeurs. Others feel that, as the point of the film is to indict those who only stand and watch as well as those who actually perform the act, the movie makes the audience into participants.

Jodie Foster is the teaser who expects men to comply with her wishes when she says thus far but no farther. Whether she asked for what she got is the subject of the first part of the film. Foster was originally a child star who appeared in the spoof gangster film *Bugsy Malone* and as a teenage streetwalker in *Taxi Driver* (both 1976) at the age of only 13.

It's one of those showy parts that often garner Oscars. The only other figure of note in the film is her lawyer, played by Kelly McGillis – a feisty part very different from the Amish heroine of *Witness* (1985). McGillis had an extra interest in taking her part in *The Accused*: she, too, has been a victim of rape.

Dustin Hoffman plays the autistic brother of sharp-dealing Tom Cruise in Rain Man.

KEEP RAINING ON MY PARADE

Rain Man is meant to represent the child-like attempt of an autistic to pronounce his name, Raymond. A troubled production that went through multiple re-writes, it's one of those inspirational movies that always seem to win Oscars.

Raymond is played by Dustin Hoffman, who did months of research among the autistic people to reproduce their behaviour. It's the kind of meaty role he hasn't had for years. Some of the ballyhoo leading up to the Oscars, however, is seen by some as distasteful. "Does he or does he not deserve an Academy Award?" asked chat-show host Oprah Winfrey, leaving her audience in no doubt how she expected them to respond.

Hoffman's co-star is Tom Cruise, making a strong bid to be taken more seriously than in his macho roles in films like *Top Gun* (1986). The director is Barry Levinson, marking a major step forward from the quirky little pictures, like *Diner* (1982) and *Tin Men* (1987), with which he first attracted attention.

Matthew Broderick and Ally Sheedy in *WarGames* (1982).

Tom Cruise in *Top Gun*, (1986).

Molly Ringwald and Judd Nelson in *The Breakfast Club*.

The Young Ones

They called them The Brat Pack, but that was never more than a convenient label to bracket together a bunch of new faces that began to appear in movies in the early 1980s. They formed no club or clan and each went a different way after the early films in which they starred together. All they had in common was their youth.

Three films formed a channel through which a great number of them passed on their way to (mostly) finer things. Francis Coppola's 1983 movie *The Outsiders* brought together an extraordinary number of young unknowns, all of whom later carved out substantial careers, with at least one major hit apiece. They included Tom Cruise, who went on to hit the jackpot in *Top Gun* (1986), *Rain Man* (1988) and *Born on the Fourth of July* (1989); Patrick Swayze, the star of *Dirty Dancing* (1987) and *Ghost* (1990); Ralph Macchio (*The Karate Kid*, 1984); and Matt Dillon.

Two other stars of *The Outsiders* (Rob Lowe and Emilio Estevez) appeared two years later in another film that acted as a focus for a new generation of exciting actors and actresses. This was *St Elmo's Fire*, a story of newly graduated college kids, with meaty parts for Demi Moore, Ally Sheedy and Andrew McCarthy. Both Moore and Sheedy have moved on to bigger roles, like *We're No Angels* (1989) and *Ghost* (1990).

Sheedy has developed into the great caring figure of the Brat Pack fraternity. She's the one in *WarGames* (1983) who cares whether fellow Brat Packer Matthew Broderick inadvertently starts the Third World War; she's the one in *Short Circuit* (1986) who cares what becomes of the smart robot Number 5; and in *Betsy's Wedding* (1990) she's a cop whose heart can be melted by the old-world courtesy of Anthony LaPaglia's gentleman mobster.

Young Guns (1988) *enhanced the careers of several young stars.*

St Elmo's Fire (1985) *starred Ally Sheedy, Emilio Estevez, Demi Moore and Rob Lowe.*

Emilio Estevez, Rob Lowe, C. Thomas Howell, Matt Dillon, Ralph Macchio, Patrick Swayze and Tom Cruise in Coppola's The Outsiders *(1983).*

Sheedy also stars in *The Breakfast Club* (1985) along with the young Molly Ringwald from *Betsy's Wedding* and Emilio Estevez from *The Outsiders*. Though she plays a bride in *Betsy's Wedding*, Ringwald has yet to grow up on screen. She remains a juvenile lead, while Moore and Sheedy are starting to fill adult roles. Emilio Estevez, however, has made greater strides than most.

He is the son of the actor Martin Sheen and some of his father's talent has evidently rubbed off. He made a stunning impression in *Repo Man* (1984) and tried his hand at direction in *Wisdom* (1984) with Demi Moore, though with mixed results. More recently he has played in *Young Guns* (1988) as Billy the Kid.

Charlie Sheen, another son of Martin Sheen, has also been pursuing an acting career. He, too, played in *Young Guns* though his finest work has been in the two Oliver Stone films, *Platoon* (1986) and *Wall Street* (1987). Another second-generation movie star in *Young Guns* is Kiefer Sutherland, son of Donald, and rapidly rising in the cinema of the 1990s if *Flatliners* (1990) is anything to go by. And yet another is Phoebe Cates, star of *Gremlins* (1984) and *Shag* (1989). She is the daughter of Gilbert Cates, director of *Summer Wishes, Winter Dreams* (1973), but registers strongly in her own right. Her account of how Daddy got stuck up the chimney and putrefied on Christmas Eve in *Gremlins* is a masterpiece of dead-pan humour.

Other members of the Brat Pack have yet to consolidate their early successes make the same impression. John Cusack's way with lightweight comedy in films like *One Crazy Summer* (1986) and *Sixteen Candles* (1984) did not adapt well to the heavyweight drama of the atom bomb movie *Fat Man and Little Boy* (1989); and Lou Diamond Phillips, one of the stars of *Young Guns*, has yet to recapture the dynamic quality he achieved in *La Bamba* (1987).

JANUARY

FEBRUARY

MARCH

APRIL

MR. E.T.'S RECORD DIVORCE

After 34 months of marriage, Steven Spielberg and actress wife Amy Irving have called it quits. Under Californian law Irving is entitled not only to half his assets but to a proportion of his earnings during the time they lived together before marriage. This means that she will trawl close to $100 million in all – the biggest settlement in Hollywood history. Previous record settlements, involving the entertainers Wayne Newton and John Carson amounted to less than a quarter of this.

Amy Irving, who is divorcing Steven Spielberg for a record settlement.

OLD GREG

Old Gringo, in which Gregory Peck plays 19th-century American writer Ambrose Bierce, is the crowning point of his long career. The performance is hardly effortless (it's an old man's part) but it comes with a lifetime's experience in acting technique and is as mellow as vintage port. He's 73 years young this year.

Born in California in 1916, Peck made his first film, *Days of Glory*, in 1944 and became a popular leading man through two decades in the 1940s and 1950s. His good looks and patent sincerity more than compensated for what some took to be a wooden acting style. Highlights of his early career included *Gentleman's Agreement* (1947), *Twelve O'Clock High* (1949) and *The Gunfighter* (1950).

He was miscast as the obsessive Captain Ahab in *Moby Dick* (1956), but in 1962 he found the perfect part as the lawyer defending a black boy on a murder charge in the Deep South in *To Kill a Mocking Bird*. It earned him the Oscar that had long eluded him.

In mid-career Peck also branched out into production – initially on the William Wyler western *The Big Country* (1958), whose peace-loving, humanitarian message meshed with his own thinking. Later films he produced included *The Trial of the Catonsville Nine* (1972), from a play about Vietnam draft-dodgers, and the eco-odyssey *The Dove* (1974).

THREE SLICES OF THE APPLE

New York Stories is one of those ideas that sounded a lot of fun before anybody got down to giving it shape. The theme is that the Big Apple is such a stimulating place that it ought to offer a challenge to any film-maker.

Three of them are involved here: Martin Scorsese, Francis Coppola and Woody Allen. Allen's episode, which closes the picture, is a brilliant short story built on the notion of the impossibility of escaping a Jewish mother. Even after she is dead she won't let her son lead his own life.

Allen has a mastery of the short-story form that eludes Coppola and Scorsese. The latter's section, about an artist (Nick Nolte) who falls out with his girlfriend (Rosanna Arquette), is inconsequential; while Coppola's, about a rich kid who helps to reunite her parents, suffocates under Vittorio Storaro's opulent photography. So-called "portmanteau" movies, which reached a peak of popularity in Europe in the 1960s, don't look like catching on again: so far moviegoers have resisted this three-course meal.

Woody Allen and Mia Farrow in his segment of New York Stories.

ACADEMY AWARDS

PRESENTED ON 26 MARCH 1989

Best Picture
Rain Man

Best Director
Barry Levinson
Rain Man

Best Actor
Dustin Hoffman
Rain Man

Best Actress
Jodie Foster
The Accused

Best Sup Actor
Kevin Kline
A Fish Called Wanda

Best Sup Actress
Geena Davis
The Accidental Tourist

STAR QUOTES

Kevin Costner

"I go with good writing and good writing has always served me well. I haven't picked the movies that go over the $100 million mark, but my movies have done okay."

BIRTHS, DEATHS AND MARRIAGES

DEATHS

John Cassavetes
3 Feb, Los Angeles
Cirrhosis of the liver

Lucille Ball
26 Apr, Los Angeles
Heart attack

Sergio Leone
30 Apr, Rome
Heart attack

WARNERS IN TWO-WAY TAKEOVER TUSSLE

Warners, the studio that gave you *Casablanca* (1942) and *My Fair Lady* (1964), is at the centre of a furious two-way bidding war involving rival studio Paramount and the magazine publishing empire Time Inc.

Both sides have since raised their terms and currently Time's offer of $14 billion outranks Paramount's $12.2 billion. Though Paramount threatens legal action in the Delaware courts, challenging Warners' action in rejecting an initially higher offer, it looks as if Time will carry the day.

SOUNDS GOOD

At this year's Academy Awards ceremony, a special Oscar was awarded to the British-based team of Dr. Ray Dolby and Joan Allen "for their continued contribution to motion picture sound through the research programmes of Dolby Laboratories." It's a remarkable tribute to an organization that Dolby (an American) set up in London in 1965, initially with no thought of motion pictures. It was a noise-reduction system intended to clean up the sound of LP records on the turntable.

Five years later the first steps were taken to see if the principles could be applied to cinema sound. The TV movie of *Jane Eyre* (1970), starring George C. Scott and Susannah York, was the first to incorporate what we now take for granted as Dolby sound. The improvement in range and frequency, coupled with the reduction in distortion, immediately confirmed the system's pre-eminence (although magnetic soundtracks from the early days of CinemaScope in the mid-1950s had a much more "immediate" feel and greater separation than modern optical tracks).

The first mainstream movie to show off Dolby to the full was Ken Russell's *Lisztomania* (1975), which had a Dolby Stereo optical soundtrack. Three years later, Dolby carried off the Oscar for the best sound recording, for *Star Wars*. Since then, the process has gone from strength to strength.

The annus mirabilis was 1979, when Dolby was first used to dub into a second language (*Hair*), first used to record an opera on film (*Don Giovanni*) and first used for 70mm Surround sound (*Apocalypse Now*). Japan took it up in 1981 and China in 1987. Today 100 studios in 25 countries and 27 languages can offer Dolby facilities and more than 2,500 films have been made worldwide in the system.

Amy Madigan and Kevin Costner in Field of Dreams, *about a farmer who builds a baseball pitch in a field.*

ANGELS IN THE OUTFIELD

Field of Dreams is a picture that *just* manages to stay the right side of yuck. It's about a simple, baseball-loving, pioneering type who hears the voice of God in an Iowa field which tells him to build a baseball diamond and, if he does, "he will come". "He" is legendary Shoeless Joe Jackson, the greatest of a clutch of Chicago White Sox players banned for life in 1919 after being found guilty of accepting bribes.

Adapted from a book by W.P. Kinsella, the movie is heavy with nostalgia for baseball in its golden years, and the supporting cast is studded with old timers and character actors. Burt Lancaster puts in a brief appearance as Dr. "Moonlight" Graham and the black actor James Earl Jones (whose coal-black tones were the voice of Darth Vader in *Star Wars*, 1977) is cast as a writer, loosely based on J.D. Salinger.

In the lead role fresh-faced Kevin Costner is perfectly matched to the part of Ray Kinsella, who builds the diamond. A star since *The Untouchables* and *No Way Out* (both 1987), Costner is one of the major discoveries of the late 1980s. Here he's well supported by husky Amy Jones as his understanding wife.

John Neville is Munchausen in Terry Gilliam's multi-million dollar The Adventures of Baron Munchausen.

TALL TALES IN CHRISTENDOM

The Adventures of Baron Munchausen is among the most popular fantasy stories in the cinema. The 18th-century teller of tall tales has been the hero of at least two films before – one made in Nazi Germany in 1943 and a part-animated one filmed in Czechoslovakia in 1962. Neither had the budget of Terry Gilliam for this version. At $25 million, it was to be one of the most expensive independent pictures ever made. Once production got under way delays and almost superhuman logistical problems caused the cost to soar to $52 million.

Production was halted in November 1987 for two weeks in hope of getting everything back under control. Gilliam – whose previous work includes the cult fantasy *Brazil* (1985) – was forced to throw out whole sequences and rein back hard on the planned special effects. Communications on set were also fraught with difficulty. Much of the film was shot in Rome at Cinecitta studios with Italian technicians who could no more understand the director's English than he could understand their Italian. Sean Connery left the movie in exasperation.

When asked whether he had anything to look forward to after this film, Gilliam replied: "Death. This may cure me of filmmaking for all I know."

MAY
JUNE

JULY
AUGUST

OLIVIER DEAD

Laurence Olivier died on 11 July, aged 82. The greatest Shakespearean actor of his age, he did more than anybody to popularize the Bard in the cinema. In *Henry V* (1944), *Hamlet* (1948) and *Richard III* (1955) he directed as well as playing the lead and showed a sharp eye for cinematic detail. *Hamlet* won two Academy Awards.

He was an actor of extraordinary range. His Heathcliff in *Wuthering Heights* (1939) was powerfully romantic; in *The Beggar's Opera* (1953) he displayed an attractive light baritone; and in *The Entertainer* (1960) he was transformed into a seedy cockney music-hall comedian.

As an actor he had two manners – the barn-storming one best seen in his *Othello* (1965) and in movies like *Marathon Man* (1976) as a sadistic Nazi dentist, and the almost self-effacing naturalist one of *Carrie* (1952) and *Bunny Lake Is Missing* (1965). He was married three times – to Jill Esmond, to Vivien Leigh in a turbulent 20-year marriage from 1940 to 1960, and finally to the actress Joan Plowright, who survives him.

BIRTHS, DEATHS AND MARRIAGES

DEATHS

Anton Diffring
20 May, Chateauneuf de Grasse, France

Gilda Radner
20 May, Los Angeles
Cancer

Laurence Olivier
11 Jul, Steyning, Sussex

MARRIAGES

Don Johnson
26 Jun, *to* **Melanie Griffith**

Kenneth Branagh
20 Aug, *to* **Emma Thompson**

YEAR OF THE CAPED CRUSADER

More than 10 years after DC Comics was approached for the rights to make a film about the Caped Crusader, the $50 million film of *Batman* has finally reached the screen. But neither the star nor the director had any experience in filming comic strips. Michael Keaton has specialized in comedy, and director Tim Burton, who made last year's *Beetlejuice* with him and before that *Pee-wee's Big Adventure* (1985), began as an animator at Disney. In fact it's Jack Nicholson, as Batman's arch-enemy The Joker who steals the show, and sexy Kim Basinger is the blonde in Batman's spokes.

Gotham City was built on most of the 18 sound stages at Pinewood studios – a sprawling 95-acre backlot in England. The set was designed by Anton Furst, who also provided the sets for *Full Metal Jacket* (1987). The idea, says Furst, was to evoke a city that looked "like hell had erupted through the pavements and kept on growing." In this respect the movie is closer to the strip's original concept than later versions.

The first Batman comic was published in May 1939 and two serial films of his adventures were made in 1943 and 1949, followed by a campy TV series in the 1960s that culminated in a *Batman* movie (1966) with Adam West. Missing from the latest version, however, is the character of Robin, Batman's boy assistant. Perhaps it was felt that Bruce Wayne had hang-ups enough without this.

Michael Keaton and Kim Basinger in Batman.

Robin Williams as an unconventional English teacher in Dead Poets Society.

LIVE COMICS' SOCIETY

Robin Williams has come a long way since he worked the beer and wine houses of San Francisco as a standup comedian. And in *Dead Poets Society*, where he's an unconventional English teacher whose methods lead to tragedy, he has one of his best roles to date.

The son of a Ford Motor Company executive, he was born in 1952 in Chicago but educated in California. After graduating, he worked at the Los Angeles Comedy Store, a showcase for young talent, and then won a guest spot on the TV show *Happy Days* as an extra-terrestrial called Mork. The character was so popular that it was revived for a series called *Mork and Mindy*.

Director Robert Altman signed him for the part of *Popeye* (1980) but his next few films, including *Moscow on the Hudson* (1984) and *The Best of Times* (1985), were only moderately successful.

It was *Good Morning, Vietnam* (1987) that brought him success. Real-life radio DJ Adrian Cronauer, on whose Vietnam experiences the film is based, is quite different from the manic character Williams creates for the film. Says Williams: "When Cronauer first saw the film he said, 'Jeez, you made me look so funny. That wasn't me at all'." Williams takes that as a compliment.

STAR QUOTES

Robin Williams

"Cocaine is God's way of saying you're making too much money."

Steve Martin and Mary Steenburgen in Ron Howard's story of family life *Parenthood*.

THE WILD AND CRAZY GUY

Texas-born Steve Martin, 44, is better known in the United States than in Britain. But his new film *Parenthood*, a family comedy that seems to be repeating its American success in Britain, may change that.

He grew up within a stone's throw of Disneyland and at the age of 10 sold official guidebooks to the then-new theme park. He was so good at it that he once shifted a record 625 in a day and was promoted to Merlin's Magic Shop, where he performed tricks.

His first major film was *The Jerk* (1979), which he made for Carl Reiner, once straight man to Mel Brooks. A hilarious story about a white boy who thinks he is black (but with a pale complexion), it featured a fair bit of pretty pointed racial humour and was not universally popular.

His other early films were also of minority appeal, none more so than *The Man with Two Brains* (1983), in which he played the brilliant surgeon Dr Hfuhruhurr who falls in love with a disembodied brain in a jam jar. *Dead Men Don't Wear Plaid* (1982), in which he intervened in famous old movies of the past, and *Pennies from Heaven* (1981), an adaptation of a British TV series, were also small-audience pictures, but the tide began to turn with *Roxanne* (1987), a modern American version of *Cyrano de Bergerac*.

SEPARATE BEDS

When Harry Met Sally . . . is a late-1980s variant on the war-between-the-sexes comedies that were once a Hollywood staple. Two nice young people (Meg Ryan and Billy Crystal) spend the whole film in a more or less platonic relationship and find every excuse over a period of some 10 years for not consummating it. Blame AIDS, perhaps, for that.

The two leads are very likeable. Ryan is evidently on the up-and-up since her performance in last year's remake of *D.O.A.*, where she played opposite her real-life companion Dennis Quaid. In *When Harry Met Sally . . .* she has the film's funniest sequence: in a crowded restaurant she conclusively demonstrates that it's possible to fake an orgasm.

Her partner, Crystal, is a hangdog Jewish comedian whose best role was as the luckless hero of Danny DeVito's comedy *Throw Momma from the Train* (1987), in which he tries to fight off the murderous suggestions of a man who has seen *Strangers on a Train* (1951) once too often. Also in the cast is Carrie Fisher, daughter of Debbie Reynolds and Eddie Fisher, and still best known as Princess Leia in *Star Wars* (1977).

Meg Ryan and Billy Crystal in *When Harry Met Sally*.

. . . AND DADDY CAME, TOO

Harrison Ford and Sean Connery in *Indiana Jones and the Last Crusade*.

Indiana Jones' dad is none other than Sean Connery. He and Harrison Ford strike sparks off each other and help to make *Indiana Jones and the Last Crusade* the most enjoyable of the three chapters.

The film was shot in Spain, Italy, Jordan, the United States and at Elstree studios in Britain, where all the elaborate sets were built. Special effects were filmed at Industrial Light & Magic, George Lucas' facility in Marin County, north of San Francisco. The sets and props were formidable, involving tanks, zeppelins, horses, camels, facilities for explosions and 7,000 custom-bred rodents. One tank, the International Mark 7 tank of 1917, was built in replica at a cost of £110,000.

Indy is now seeking the Holy Grail and is once more in conflict with the Nazis. In the early scenes we also see him as a boy, played by young actor River Phoenix, who starred in *Running on Empty* (1988). It seems likely this will be the last in the series as Ford no longer cuts quite the youthful figure he did back in 1981.

LITTLE BIG FILM

A small, independent American film costing only $1.2 million has snatched top prize at the Cannes Film Festival. It is called *sex, lies, and videotape*, a first feature by owlish Steven Soderbergh, 26. A deceptively casual affair about everyday people's sexual hangups, it has no big stars (Andie MacDowell and James Spader) and not much plot. Solderbergh's reaction to the award? "It's all downhill from here."

SEPTEMBER OCTOBER

NOVEMBER DECEMBER

BIRTHS, DEATHS AND MARRIAGES

DEATHS

Bette Davis
7 Oct, Neuilly, France
Cancer

Cornel Wilde
16 Oct, Los Angeles
Leukemia

Anthony Quayle
20 Oct, London
Cancer

John Payne
6 Dec, Malibu, California
Heart attack

Silvano Mangano
16 Dec, Madrid
Cancer

THE FABULOUS PFEIFFER

At 31 Michelle Pfeiffer is the toast of Hollywood, the fifth-ranked female star in America and able to command a multi-million dollar fee for every picture. In *The Fabulous Baker Boys* she's a cabaret singer who puts the sex appeal into a tired act being put across one too many times by the brothers Bridges, Jeff and Beau. In it she gets to sprawl seductively across a grand piano and croon "Makin' Whoopee" in husky tones reminiscent of Marilyn Monroe. To prepare for her role she installed a karaoke machine in her living room and practised singing to it night after night.

She first ventured into show business after winning a Miss Orange County beauty contest and taking a few acting lessons. After memorably strutting her stuff (and singing) in *Grease 2* (1982) her career soon moved into overdrive. She co-starred with Al Pacino in *Scarface* (1983) and was one of the three hexes who conjure up Jack Nicholson in *The Witches of Eastwick* (1987). Roles since then include the gangster's widow in *Married to the Mob* (1988) and a costume part in *Dangerous Liaisons* (1989), for which she was nominated for an Academy Award.

This was perhaps her most challenging part for, as she freely admits, "I don't have a Shakespeare background. I had to learn a whole new language of rhythms and stylized delivery. With this kind of period dialogue, if the ball is dropped, you really hear it. Clunk."

REVENGE FOR HIROSHIMA

The *Black Rain* of the title is fall-out – the inky substance that fell on Hiroshima and Nagasaki in the aftermath of the atomic bomb. Scott's film is the story of how a group of Japanese gangsters in the 1980s try to avenge Hiroshima by flooding the world with counterfeit dollars and undermining the American currency. Michael Douglas is the cop out to stop them.

The film brings out the most American aspects of modern Japanese society – the neon, the designer clothes and durables. Osaka, where the film is set, looks like New York.

On the Japanese side is Takakura Ken, star of a million Japanese gangster movies and already seen in the West in *The Yakuza* (1975), with Robert Mitchum. On the American side, Douglas' partner is rising young Andy Garcia who leaped to prominence in a small part in the Los Angeles barrio student drama *Stand and Deliver* (1987). He'll next be seen as an honest cop in *Internal Affairs*, opposite Richard Gere.

COLUMBIA GOES JAPANESE

Columbia Pictures has become the first Hollywood studio to pass under Japanese control under the terms of an agreed $3.4 billion takeover bid from the video and electronics giant Sony. Coca-Cola, owner of 49 per cent of the stock, will recommend the deal and Allen & Co, key holders of another 3 per cent, have indicated that they will accept.

A marriage between product and outlet is at the heart of the Sony/Columbia deal. Columbia has a library of 2,700 films and 23,000 television shows. Sony, which pioneered the Walkman and bought CBS Records for $2 billion two years ago, is now no longer just a hardware company.

Michael Douglas and Andy Garcia are menaced by a Japanese motorcycle gang in Black Rain.

BARKIN UP THE RIGHT TREE

Ellen Barkin in Sea of Love.

Look out, Kathleen Turner. Your title as the sexiest woman on screen is under attack on two flanks. On my left is the slinky Michelle Pfeiffer; on my right is the spunky but equally sizzling Ellen Barkin, 35. In *Sea of Love*, blonde Barkin (who may or may not be a murderess) reduces tough, no-nonsense cop Al Pacino to a quivering jelly, and in *Johnny Handsome* she goes round-for-round against Mickey Rourke with guns, guts and four-letter words.

In these latest movies and in *The Big Easy* (1987), in which she starred opposite corrupt New Orleans cop Dennis Quaid, Barkin raises the love scenes to almost spontaneous combustion. Married to Irish actor Gabriel Byrne (whom she met while appearing in *Siesta*, 1987) and mother of their young child, she picks her roles with care.

After a stint in a TV soap and a small role in *Diner* (1982), the actress with the lop-sized grin has steadily built up a portfolio of compelling performances on screen – a small part as Robert Duvall's daughter in *Tender Mercies* (1983), as Timothy Hutton's wife in *Daniel* (also 1983) and as the toenail-painting divorcee in the 1950s nuclear drama *Desert Bloom* (1986), with Jon Voight.

STAR QUOTES

Al Pacino

"I'm coming back, out of hibernation. It's going to be interesting to see how the audiences accept me back."

STONE RETURNS TO VIETNAM

Three years after the Oscar-winning *Platoon*, director Oliver Stone has returned to the scene of his greatest triumph. *Born on the Fourth of July* is the harrowing story of Ron Kovic, who went proudly from high school straight into the marines and suffered spinal injury in the Vietnam war that left him crippled from the chest down.

The subject mirrors Stone's own sentiments. He was himself a Vietnam volunteer, wounded and decorated, who came to reject the gung-ho philosophy curent when he enlisted.

Lending great impact is an unexpectedly dramatic performance from ex-Brat Packer Tom Cruise. The charm and the toothsome grin that he used in the hawkish *Top Gun* (1986) are here submerged beneath lank, straggly hair, a moustache and beard.

Tom Cruise as disabled Viet vet Ron Kovic in Born on the Fourth of July.

Dan Aykroyd, Jessica Tandy and Morgan Freeman in Driving Miss Daisy.

YES'M

Driving Miss Daisy is a picture that doesn't look like a blockbuster but has turned out to be one. Adapted from a long-running off-Broadway play by Alfred Uhry, it's the story of a 72-year-old Jewish widow from Atlanta, Georgia, who learns the meaning of friendship and racial understanding through being driven everywhere over the years by a 60-year-old, deferential black chauffeur.

The film, directed by Australian Bruce Beresford, provides the role of a lifetime for 80-year-old Jessica Tandy, who has had a distinguished stage career since the 1930s and was the original Blanche du Bois in Tennessee Williams's play *A Streetcar Named Desire*. Formerly married to Jack Hawkins, she's been the wife of Hume Cronyn since 1942 and they have often appeared together on Broadway. Her film roles have been few, though she and her husband co-starred in 1987 in **batteries not included*.

Her driver is played by black actor Morgan Freeman, also on view this season in the civil war drama *Glory*. In *Daisy* he's subservient to a fault, forever touching his cap and murmuring 'Yes'm' to his boss's every whim. How black audiences down South will react to his performance remains to be seen.

BOX OFFICE

UK

1. Indiana Jones and the Last Crusade
2. Who Framed Roger Rabbit
3. Batman
4. Rain Man
5. The Naked Gun
6. Licence to Kill
7. Lethal Weapon 2
8. Twins
9. Dead Poets Society
10. Cocktail

BOX OFFICE

US

1. Batman
2. Indiana Jones and the Last Crusade
3. Lethal Weapon 2
4. Honey, I Shrunk the Kids
5. Rain Man
6. Back to the Future Part II
7. Ghostbusters II
8. Look Who's Talking
9. Parenthood
10. Dead Poets Society

BETTE'S LAST BOW

Bette Davis, queen of Hollywood in the 1930s and 1940s and a star for more than half a century, has died aged 82. She won two Oscars, for *Dangerous* (1935) and *Jezebel* (1938), but her best work was as the murderous Regina in *The Little Foxes* (1941) and as the fading Broadway star in *All about Eve* (1950). In both these parts her natural inclination to strut and ham was harnessed to parts that demanded these qualities. In the 1940s, she suffered nobly in weepies like *Now, Voyager* (1942) and fought an epic battle with Warners for better parts. She continued acting, from time to time, till the last and was seen most recently opposite veteran Lillian Gish in *The Whales of August* (1987). Relations with Gish were far smoother than with her long-time rival, Joan Crawford, in the 1940s – a battle later mirrored in their only pairing, *What Ever Happened to Baby Jane?* (1962), in which their on-screen antics were paralleled by equally acid upstaging off-screen.

JANUARY
FEBRUARY

MARCH
APRIL

COWABUNGA!

If nobody expected *Pretty Woman* to be a smash hit, still fewer would have put money on *Teenage Mutant Ninja Turtles*, produced by Hong Kong's Golden Harvest, shot at Dino De Laurentiis' studio in North Carolina, and distributed in America by New Line. (20th Century-Fox must be kicking itself for passing on this one.) Though it cost close to $15 million, more than twice its original budget of $6 million, it pulled in $25 million at the box office in its first weekend.

The film is absolutely barking: four baby turtles fall into a New York sewer filled with radioactive sludge and are miraculously changed into human-sized turtle superheroes with the power of speech. They have a vocabulary, including 'bodacious', 'mondo to the max', 'tubular' and 'cowabunga', and an insatiable appetite for pizza preferably with banana-sausage topping. Raphael, Michelangelo, Donatello and Leonardo have learnt martial arts from a ninja-master called Splinter, an outsized rat.

The original ninja turtles were a comic strip of the early 1980s, invented by Peter Laird and Kevin Eastman. It was Tom Gray, Golden Harvest's LA managing director, who had the idea of making a movie. Says tycoon Raymond Chow, who runs Golden Harvest: "You can really stretch your imagination with this kind of film."

SIDEWALK CINDERELLA

Few would have predicted that this spring's hottest property would be a Disney-made romantic comedy about a millionaire and a hooker. The plot of *Pretty Woman* is rather like *My Fair Lady*. Richard Gere plays a millionaire tycoon who hires a prostitute to escort him for a week, wining, dining and clothing her in the manner to which he is accustomed.

Now greying with distinction, Gere has restored himself in one leap to the number one heart-throb position, following a contrasting performance earlier this year in *Internal Affairs* as a corrupt policeman ready to kill to protect his privileges.

But the sensation of *Pretty Woman* is Julia Roberts as the hooker-with-a-heart. She's been hovering on the edge of stardom for some time and made a strong impression last year in *Steel Magnolias*. But *Pretty Woman* puts her in the major league. As spring edges into summer, it's already clocked up nearly $72 million in revenue and is still the hottest ticket of 1990.

Julia Roberts has shot to stardom in the hugely successful Pretty Woman.

ERIC'S LITTLE SISTER

In one year Julia Roberts has bounded from being actor Eric Robert's kid sister to a fully-fledged star asking more than $1 million a picture. Last year's *Steel Magnolias*, for which she was nominated for a supporting Oscar, set her on the right track, but it is *Pretty Woman* that has put her in the fast lane. She's already deep in production of a new film, *Flatliners*, with her steady, Kiefer Sutherland. All this and she's still only 22.

She was born in Georgia. Her parents divorced when she was young and brother Eric went to live with their father in Atlanta. Julia was just an average scholar and at 17 joined her sister Lisa in New York. She took a few acting classes and hung around for about 18 months, auditioning for commercials and TV without great success.

Eric got her her first part in *Blood Red*, which led to some television work (an episode of *Crime Story*) and a couple of turkeys in 1988 – *Satisfaction* and *Baja Oklahoma*. In her third film that year, however, she starred as the sexy waitress Daisy in *Mystic Pizza* and the Roberts personality – wide-mouthed, leggy, long-haired and effervescent – was established. *Flatliners* director Joel Schumacher says she is a master of the dirty-joke – "but she never seems to come off vulgar in any way, shape or form."

STAR QUOTES

Mickey Rourke

"I'll never go back to Cannes – that whole thing is as phony as the Academy Awards."

ACADEMY AWARDS

PRESENTED ON 29 MARCH 1990

Best Picture
Driving Miss Daisy

Best Director
Oliver Stone
Born on the Fourth of July

Best Actor
Daniel Day-Lewis
My Left Foot

Best Actress
Jessica Tandy
Driving Miss Daisy

Best Sup Actor
Denzel Washington
Glory

Best Sup Actress
Brenda Fricker
My Left Foot

Sean Connery, Alec Baldwin and Scott Glenn in *The Hunt for Red October*, about a Russian submarine.

GODFATHER SEEKS GODFATHER

Once again Francis Coppola has bankruptcy staring him in the face. Unless he can stump up $12 million in short order, the courts will seize his assets, including his much-loved vineyards in California's Napa Valley. The debts stem from 1982, when Coppola was filming *One From the Heart*.

All of which casts new light on Coppola's decision to return to the theme of his most successful film. This year he will film *The Godfather Part III*. His fee, as writer and director, will be $6 million, but that will go only half way to meet his debts.

ECHOES FROM THE PAST

The Hunt for Red October is the luckiest film of the year. Its Cold War story about a Communist submarine commander who defects with his vessel to the West seems almost to belong to another era. While communism is loosening its hold on the world and President Gorbachev is America's favourite socialist, an old-fashioned better-dead-than-red story is almost an antique.

But audiences seem not to mind. It has become the first blockbuster of the new decade. Sean Connery gives a commanding performance as the Soviet officer but the rest of the cast is unimpressive.

Director John McTiernan hasn't been able to get the sheer thrills he brought to *Predator* (1987) and *Die Hard* (1988). Why word-of-mouth has built in the movie's favour is one of the early mysteries of the year.

GARBO IS DEAD

Greta Garbo, one of the greatest legends of the cinema, is dead. She passed away in New York on 15 April, aged 84, as famous today as when she made her last film, *Two-Faced Woman*, in 1941. She was then only 36 and, despite repeated attempts to lure her out of retirement she stuck by her decision and never filmed again.

Born in Stockholm in 1905, she acted in a few films in Europe before going to America in 1925 with her mentor, Mauritz Stiller. M-G-M, which originally took her as part of the cost of acquiring Stiller, then a hot director in Sweden, soon realized that his protegee was the real jewel.

When sound arrived, she proved to have a deep, attractive voice that recorded well, and the studio plugged her first sound movie, *Anna Christie* (1930), with the slogan "Garbo talks!" Her first line was "Gimme a visky, ginger ale on the side and don' be stingy, baby."

Throughout the 1930s she starred in a stream of classical weepies, of which *Queen Christina* (1933), *Anna Karenina* (1935) and *Camille* (1937) were the finest.

She also had a wry sense of comedy and both her last two films were in this mould – the successful *Ninotchka* (1939), billed as "Garbo laughs!" and the flop *Two-Faced Woman*, which persuaded her to retire. She never married and jealously guarded her privacy and seclusion. Though she never in fact said it, "I want to be alone" became the catch-phrase by which she was remembered.

Jack Nicholson and Harvey Keitel in *The Two Jakes*, the sequel to *Chinatown*.

JAKE HITS THE REEF

The Two Jakes, planned as a sequel to Roman Polanski's *Chinatown* (1974), was to have been made five years ago with scriptwriter Robert Towne directing. It foundered when Towne fell out with producer Robert Evans, who was also to have played one of the Jakes.

It was Jack Nicholson who resurrected the project, this time with himself directing. Towne agreed to do six more months' work on the project, but in the end Nicholson found himself rewriting more and more of the script himself. Towne walked off the set and left Nicholson to pull the project together as best he could. Many times, says co-star Meg Tilly, "he'd be up all night, go to bed at five and be up by six. We would have stuff being written at the last minute and have no idea what we were going to be doing."

Nicholson finally replaced Evans with Harvey Keitel, but wanted Evans to coach him in his very personal way of humming.

Matters went from bad to worse and the official opening was put back from Christmas 1989 to this March. Now word has it that because of extensive reshooting it won't be ready until August. Oh dear.

DEAD CERT AT THE BOX OFFICE

What a difference six months can make. Last Christmas, movie wonder-kid Steven Spielberg sought to open the tear ducts and the purse strings with *Always*, a remake of the 1944 Spencer Tracy movie *A Guy Named Joe*, about a pilot who comes back from the grave to play guardian angel to his girl friend. But audiences turned their backs on the notion of Richard Dreyfuss steering Holly Hunter into a new romance under the watchful eye of Audrey Hepburn, in her first part since *They All Laughed* (1981).

Now, however, director Jerry Zucker has told a remarkably similar story in *Ghost* and it's proving the smash hit of the summer. In the long run it could beat *Pretty Woman*, so far the most successful film of the year. *Ghost* is about a lover who dies and comes back to Earth to protect his girl friend from those who would harm her. The cast is attractive: Demi Moore, Patrick Swayze, and Whoopi Goldberg as a comic black fortune teller. But other than the youthfulness of the cast, nobody can explain why this film is succeeding where *Always* failed.

Perhaps audiences are in a more sombre mood; another film about death has since started to do good business. This is *Flatliners*, directed by Joel Schumacher, who made *St Elmo's Fire* and *The Lost Boys* (1987). In *Flatliners* a group of medical students (including *Lost Boy* Kiefer Sutherland) subject themselves to experiments in which they suspend each other's heartbeats to experience what may lie beyond the threshold of death. It sounds morbid, but not a little of the film's appeal can be attributed to Hollywood's latest sex symbol Julia Roberts, in her first film since *Pretty Woman*.

THE OTHER HALF

Demi Moore, whose name is stressed like the French word for "half", has made the headlines this summer for two things. First, she's one of the stars of surprise hit *Ghost*; second, she issued an ultimatum to hubby Bruce Willis on the set of his new movie *Hudson Hawk*. Basically she wanted the leading actress, torrid Belgian Maruschka Detmers, replaced with a less threatening thespian. Married mother Andie MacDowell got the job.

Husky Moore, 26, has always insisted that any hint of nudity must be justified by the context. It is an attitude she has maintained since her early show business days, when she modelled in Los Angeles for European magazines, although undraped photos of her are rumoured to exist.

She was born in 1963 in Roswell, New Mexico, as Demi Guynes (the Moore comes from her first husband, musician Rick Moore) and at the age of 15 acquired an agent. But it was a while before she made her first real movie – the limp sex comedy *Blame It on Rio* (1984), as Michael Caine's daughter.

After this she spent some years acting in Brat Pack movies like *St Elmo's Fire* (1985), *Wisdom* (1987) and *About Last Night . . .* (1986). In the first two of these she played opposite Emilio Estevez, to whom she was for a time engaged. The success of *Ghost* now makes her the hottest property in Hollywood – for the moment.

Demi Moore and Patrick Swayze in *Ghost*.

MOONLIGHTING NO LONGER

While wife Demi Moore stars in the summer blockbuster *Ghost*, Bruce Willis is in one of the few big-budget hits, *Die Hard 2*, again playing a cop trying to rescue his wife from terrorists.

Willis, 32, has made relatively few films. His first major movie was *Blind Date* in 1987, following bit parts in *The Verdict* (1982) and *Prince of the City* (1981). In 1988, he was in the modestly successful comedy *Sunset*, as legendary western hero Tom Mix; but it was *Die Hard* which changed the course of his big-screen career. His role as the carefree private eye David Addison in the TV series *Moonlighting* (1985), opposite Cybill Shepherd, was the break he had been looking for.

After studying at Montclair State College, New Jersey, Willis left school in 1977 and moved to New York, where he made his off-Broadway debut in *Heaven and Earth*. He also worked as a bartender, made TV commercials for Seagrams and was beginning to make a name for himself as a pop singer before breaking into films.

Currently he's starring in a new film called *Hudson Hawk*. It's intended to be a major attraction for summer 1991, but it's already run into cost and production over-runs.

THE LONG COLD SUMMER

Hollywood will look back at the summer of 1990 as the year when all its fondest predictions went awry. The two unqualified hits, *Pretty Woman* and *Ghost*, are average-budgeted movies. As summer shades into fall, the second has clocked up $103 million, while the first already has $168 million on the tally board.

It's those with megabuck budgets that have been either disappointments or disasters. The latter category includes *The Two Jakes* (less than $9 million) and *The Exorcist III* ($18 million); *Air America*, the Mel Gibson action picture, is already flagging at $23 million.

Sequels, like *RoboCop 2* ($44 million), *Gremlins 2* ($40 million), and *Back to the Future Part III* ($83 million), leaped out of the gate but soon ran out of puff. The biggest disappointment was the Tom Cruise vehicle *Days of Thunder*, which cost $55 million to make. Paramount had expected this *Top Gun* on wheels to clean up at the box office. Instead, it fell well short of expectations (with $80 million to date).

Of all the would-be blockbusters, only *Dick Tracy*, *Die Hard 2* ($108 million) and *Total Recall* ($116 million) have performed strongly. But they cost so much that in some cases they may have trouble ending in profit.

MATERIAL GIRL BACK IN VOGUE?

Madonna as the seductive chantoose Breathless Mahoney in Warren Beatty's Dick Tracy.

Will *Dick Tracy* finally give pop superstar Madonna the career she's so far been unable to find in the cinema? Ignoring a few minutes in the 1985 film *Vision Quest*, and an earlier skinflick, *A Certain Sacrifice* (1980), her first real part was in the highly successful *Desperately Seeking Susan* (1985), in which she played a bimbo living on her wits. A big movie future was predicted for her, but it never really happened.

Shanghai Surprise (1986), an ill-fated venture made during her brief and stormy marriage to co-star Sean Penn, was followed by the even more incompetent *Who's That Girl?* (1987) and the Damon Runyonesque comedy *Bloodhounds of Broadway* (1989).

Madonna Louise Ciccone was born in 1959 near Detroit, where her father was an engineer in the Chrysler factory. Sent to a Catholic school and brought up in the faith, she soon earned a name for herself as a rebel.

In 1978 she won a bursary to study dance in New York with the Alvin Ailey company. She spent two years with the Pearl Lang Dance Company but then turned to writing and performing songs. Now the raunchy warbler of "Like a Virgin," "Material Girl", "Borderline" and "Like a Prayer" gets to sing four new Stephen Sondheim numbers as *Dick Tracy* chantoose Breathless Mahoney. It's the kind of dramatic switch that may kick-start a new career for her on the big screen.

COMING OUT SHOOTING

The big hurdles *Dick Tracy* will have to vault at the box office are the fact that Chester Gould's comic strip on which it is based is some 60 years old, while star and director Warren Beatty is now an ageing matinee idol whom younger audiences can barely recall. *Ishtar*, his 1987 mega-flop with Dustin Hoffman, isn't even a memory, and his Oscar-winning *Reds* is now nine years old.

The $27 million Disney movie certainly looks expensive, and many of Gould's figures have been faithfully reproduced with elaborate masks and prosthetics. Most striking of all is Al Pacino as Big Boy Caprice, a gangster whose features completely transform the actor's appearance.

The snag is that Dick Tracy himself is almost characterless, and his resistance to Madonna's seductress Breathless Mahoney is positively monastic. It remains to be seen whether the T-shirts and other merchandising will stop this Dick going limp at the box office.

GOSSIP COLUMN

■ When is a mumble as good as a copyright? Answer (maybe) when it's Marlon Brando who is doing the mumbling. His mafia don in the new Tri-Star film *The Freshman* sounds and looks so like his Don Corleone in Paramount's *The Godfather* (1972) that characters in the film remark upon the resemblance. Which doesn't please Paramount at all. Legal eagles are already totting up the pickings should the case come to court.

Arnold Schwarzenegger in the sci-fi adventure Total Recall, *based on a story by cult writer Philip K. Dick.*

TOTAL RECOUP?

At $65 million, the new Arnold Schwarzenegger sci-fi picture *Total Recall* is the second most expensive film made this year. (*Die Hard 2* cost $5 million more, and *The Godfather Part III* looks like equalling it.)

Set in 2084, it's about a sinister company that enables you to travel to distant planets in your mind's eye and feel as if you have actually been there. The original story was by cult sci-fi author Philip K. Dick (who also provided the story for *Blade Runner*, 1982) and there are also overtones of the earlier *Westworld* (1973).

The project has been around for a long time. Disney had first option on it but walked away. A total of $7 million was wasted on false starts and abortive scripts. Among the actors at one time slated for the Schwarzenegger part were Richard Dreyfuss and Patrick Swayze. Schwarzenegger finally stepped in and persuaded Carolco to buy the rights for $3 million, with a view to making a $50 million picture, directed by Paul Verhoeven, who made *RoboCop* (1987).

But costs soared. There were more than 50 different drafts of the script and the movie was shot at the Churubusco studios in Mexico City, prone to power cuts. Says one wag: "*Total Recall* probably employed more Mexican labour than went into building the Mayan pyramids."

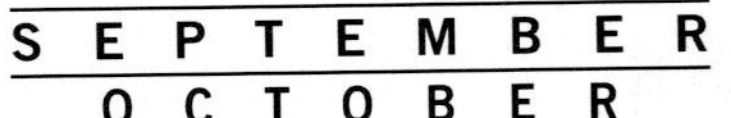

SEPTEMBER OCTOBER

NOVEMBER DECEMBER

A WILLOWY AIR OF DEBAUCHERY

Some found American actor John Malkovich miscast as Valmont in the film of *Dangerous Liaisons* (1988); yet his demeanour, conveying the impression of a willowy air of debauchery, made him eminently suitable for the part. He gives a rather similar performance, but this time in modern dress, in the new Bernardo Bertolucci movie *The Sheltering Sky*, adapted from the Paul Bowles novel.

Malkovich was born in 1953 in Illinois. One of his girl friends persuaded him to seek a theatrical career and he became a member of the Steppenwold Theater Company, which in turn led to off-Broadway productions and eventually the role of Biff in the Dustin Hoffman production of *Death of a Salesman*. This was eventually filmed for television in 1985.

Meanwhile, Malkovich was starting to attract attention for his work in feature films, beginning with *Places in the Heart* and *The Killing Fields* in 1984 and continuing with a notable contribution as Tom Wingfield to the Paul Newman film of Tennessee Williams' *The Glass Menagerie* (1987). His prisoner of war in the Steven Spielberg movie *Empire of the Sun* was also memorable. A side of his personality that the cinema has so far little tapped is his sense of humour, though Susan Seidelman recognized it in *Making Mr Right* (1987), casting him as a randy robot.

WISE GUYS CLEAN UP

Al Pacino as Michael Corleone with Andy Garcia as Vincent Mancini in Francis Coppola's The Godfather Part III.

It's been the year of the mobsters in the cinemas. Earlier in the year Britain came up with a movie about the notorious gangster twins *The Krays*, while this winter America has had an epidemic of such movies. *The King of New York*, with Christopher Walken, did least well, but at least two major gangster movies look like being among the year's big winners come Oscar time.

Martin Scorsese's *GoodFellas*, the true story of ex-mobster Henry Hill, reunites the director with his favourite actor, Robert De Niro, for the first time since *The King of Comedy* (1983). It also stars Joe Pesci, who previously worked with Scorsese and De Niro in *Raging Bull* (1980), and the rising Ray Liotta, who gave a terrifying performance as a psychotic in *Something Wild* (1986) and a gentler one as an old baseball player in *Field of Dreams* (1989). A long movie, *GoodFellas* (which is one of the names Mafia members use to describe each other) takes Scorsese back to the florid, operatic style of his earliest films, like *Mean Streets* (1973). It has already won a clutch of awards from the New York and Los Angeles critics' circles.

The other big Mafia movie is *The Godfather Part III*, Francis Coppola's return to the story he last tackled in 1974. It has managed to qualify for the Oscars by the skin of its teeth, with a Christmas Day launch and a magnificent $14 million take in just its first three days. At one Long Island cinema a real-life shoot-out in the stalls left a 15-year-old dead and another shot in the eye.

Originally budgeted at $44 million, the film rocketed to $65 million in production and suffered many delays and hiccups. One early one was the departure of young Winona Ryder, pleading exhaustion, as shooting was about to begin; Coppola replaced her with his own daughter, Sofia (critics say he should have looked elsewhere). But all agree that Al Pacino, playing Michael Corleone for the third time, has never been better.

NEARLY A STAR IN HIS OWN RIGHT

Director Alan Parker at first wanted Jack Nicholson to play the lead in his new film *Come See the Paradise*. He should be grateful Jack wasn't available and he had to settle for Dennis Quaid instead. For Quaid brings an emotional quality to this moving inter-racial love story, set during the Second World War, that the more cynical Nicholson could hardly have matched. For all his curled lip and air of opportunism, Quaid cares.

Born in 1954, he's the younger brother of Randy Quaid, with whom he has acted on screen only in *The Long Riders* (1980). Born in Houston, Dennis Quaid left university for Los Angeles and enjoyed his first big movie part in *Breaking Away* (1976), a little picture about racing cyclists that became an unexpected sleeper.

The film that he thought would be his breakthrough was *The Right Stuff* (1983), from Tom Wolfe's epic account of the birth and growth of the American space programme, but it bombed at the box office.

Climbing back from there has been hard and not all the steps along the way were well taken. For every success like *The Big Easy* (1987), Quaid has made his share of mistakes. Among these could be mentioned the sci-fi remake of *Hell in the Pacific* (1968) called *Enemy Mine* (1985), another remake (*DOA*, 1988) and the bio-pic of Jerry Lee Lewis, *Great Balls of Fire!* (1989).

AN X BY ANY OTHER NAME

This year a number of highly sexually explicit films have called the whole U.S. rating system into question. They include the British film *The Cook, The Thief, His Wife and Her Lover* and the Spanish *Tie Me Up! Tie Me Down!* (both 1989). Both gained an X certificate, making them hard to advertise and gain an audience.

The turning point was *Henry & June*, the film about writer Henry Miller's relationship with Anaïs Nin that includes several steamy lesbian scenes. This, too, received an X but, in the face of growing opposition, the Motion Picture Association of America, which imposes the ratings, suddenly announced that it was introducing a new category – NC-17 ("no children under the age of 17"). *Henry & June* became the first film to carry the new rating, and both the British and Spanish films were reclassified.

BOX OFFICE

UK

1. Ghost
2. Pretty Woman
3. Look Who's Talking
4. Honey, I Shrunk the Kids
5. Total Recall
6. Ghostbusters II
7. Back to the Future: Part III
8. Gremlins 2: The New Batch
9. Back to the Future Part II
10. When Harry Met Sally . . .

BOX OFFICE

US

1. Ghost
2. Pretty Woman
3. Home Alone
4. Die Hard 2
5. Total Recall
6. Teenage Mutant Ninja Turtles
7. Dick Tracy
8. The Hunt for Red October
9. Driving Miss Daisy
10. Back to the Future Part III

Kevin Costner in Dances with Wolves, *the epic three-hour western.*

COSTNER IN SENSATIONAL DIRECTING DEBUT

Dances with Wolves is the 1990 movie that has taken the biggest risks (it's a three-hour western); but there is every indication that the $16 million film will make money and win awards.

"Dances with Wolves" is the name taken by a white Union officer (played by Kevin Costner) who opts to live with the Sioux. The picture was shot in South Dakota over a careful 17-week span and has the epic sweep and grandeur too long missing from Hollywood movies.

For star and first-time director Costner it is a triumph. His career as an actor was slow to start. One of his first parts, in *The Big Chill* (1983), ended up on the cutting-room floor (he played the dead friend) and neither *Silverado* (1984) nor *American Flyers* (1985), a western and a film about bicycle racing, set the box office alight. His two back-to-back baseball films, *Bull Durham* (1988) and *Field of Dreams* (1989), were better received; but it was *The Untouchables*, in which he played FBI agent Eliot Ness, and *No Way Out* (both 1987) that established him as a romantic hero. In the latter, he hires a cab for a torrid back-seat tryst with Sean Young. Limo rentals reputedly soared in the States after the movie came out.

Kim Cattrall and Tom Hanks in The Bonfire of the Vanities.

THE BONFIRE AND THE BRAT

Latest in a long line of "can't miss" movies that have headed straight for Palookaville is *The Bonfire of the Vanities*, director Brian De Palma's star-studded adaptation of the Tom Wolfe best-seller regarded by some as the ultimate novel of the greedy Eighties.

Criticism has been unrelieved. "No one cast in this movie ever stood a chance," says *Newsweek*, "they all go down with the ship." R.I.P. Tom Hanks, Bruce Willis and Melanie Griffith.

But even as *Bonfire* fizzles out, Hollywood has bounced back with a Christmas stocking-filler that's rocketed in less than a month to become the third biggest hit of 1990. When the final accounts are drawn *Home Alone* might even prove the top movie of 1990. Where the John Hughes/Chris Columbus movie, about a little boy inadvertently left behind while his family fly to Paris for Christmas, ends up will depend on how far audiences see the subject to be good only for the holiday season.

MUSICAL CHAIRS IN TINSELTOWN

Universal is the second movie major to fall into Japanese hands under a $6.1 billion deal that will give the Osaka-based electronics concern Matsushita control of MCA, Universal's parent company. Last year, Columbia was acquired by Sony in a $3.4 billion deal.

The Matsushita takeover comes just as Universal has suffered a catastrophic fire that gutted large stretches of the 420-acre studio. Initial estimates indicate that a fifth of the sets on the lot have been destroyed, including the famous street scene where *Dick Tracy* was shot and sets from *The Sting* (1973) and *Conan the Barbarian* (1982).

Another famous Hollywood studio has also changed hands. M-G-M/UA, until recently controlled by Kirk Kerkorian, has been bought by Italian financier Giancarlo Parretti, for $1.3 billion through his company Pathe Communications. Hollywood is still wondering how he managed to raise the money.

STAR QUOTES

Clint Eastwood

"I'm not unduly obsessed with stardom or the industry. The secret to success is not to fill your mind with your own self-importance."

JANUARY
FEBRUARY

MARCH
APRIL

BAGS I PLAY STORMIN' NORMAN

They were on red alert in Hollywood on 16 January, the day the Gulf War broke out. Fearful of terrorist reprisals, all production in and around Los Angeles airport was shut down. The film *Serious Money*, which was to have been shot there, was put on indefinite hold, while in Israel production was halted on *The Prodigal Father*, a US/Hungarian/Israeli feature starring Michael York and Liv Ullmann. Intensive security was put into operation for the Golden Globe awards on 19 January and extra precautions were lined up for the Oscar ceremony, scheduled for 25 March.

Cinema attendances, despite an initial fall-off, held up remarkably well, notwithstanding the irritation of increased security checks in theatres. But the studios were taking no chances with their high-powered executives or stars. For many studios, visits to film festivals were out, causing problems at the first-ever contest in an undivided Berlin (17-26 February).

Now the successful outcome of the war has prompted Hollywood studios to rush to be the first to put the conflict on screen. At least half a dozen low-budget quickies are underway.

Spare a tear, though, for mogul Menahem Golan: he bought exclusive rights to the title Desert Shield, only to find it changed to Desert Storm.

Scott Glenn, Anthony Hopkins and Jodie Foster in The Silence of the Lambs.

SKINNING THE BOX OFFICE

The biggest box office hit of 1991 to date is *The Silence of the Lambs*, for which Jonathan Demme shared the best director prize at the Berlin film festival. From a best-seller by Thomas Harris, the original author of *Manhunter* (1986), it's about the search for a serial killer who skins and eats his female victims.

In both films the police co-opt as an assistant the man best equipped to think himself into the killer's mind. In *Manhunter* it's a retired FBI agent, in *Lambs* it's another sex fiend who, until then, had been safely locked up. When he escapes, the police have two killers on the loose.

Exceptionally grisly, the movie features Anthony Hopkins as convicted sex murderer Hannibal Lecter, who is evil personified. Hopkins, who made his film debut in *The Lion in Winter* (1968) and has been seen most recently in *Desperate Hours* (1990) opposite Mickey Rourke, gives the kind of malevolent performance that makes the film compulsively watchable. A flamboyant actor in the British theatrical tradition, he is to dub Laurence Olivier in some restored scenes for the re-issue of *Spartacus* (1960) for which the original soundtrack no longer exists.

Jodie Foster is a police officer who finds herself more closely involved with Hopkins than duty or safety requires. It's another dramatic role for the 28-year-old actress who picked up an Oscar for her blistering performance as a rape victim in *The Accused* (1988).

STAR QUOTES

David Warner

"Now, at last, I can look my daughter's friends in the face. When they ask me what I do, I can say I was in Teenage Mutant Ninja Turtles 2."

DYNASTIC DAUGHTER

Three generations of the Huston family have won Oscars. Director John won his for *The Treasure of the Sierra Madre* (1948), in which he also coaxed an award-winning supporting performance from his father Walter. Thirty-seven years later he did the same thing for his daughter Anjelica in *Prizzi's Honor*.

Anjelica Huston was not always so admired. When she made her debut in 1969 in her father's *A Walk with Love and Death*, opposite General Dayan's son Assaf, she received the same crucifying reviews that are now handed out to Francis Coppola's daughter Sofia in *her* dad's film *The Godfather Part III* (1990).

That undoubtedly shook Anjelica's confidence and for many years she languished on the sidelines, better known as Jack Nicholson's off-screen girlfriend than for anything she did on-screen. As a star she's crept up on Hollywood, but this past year has been a vintage one. She has been in Woody Allen's *Crimes and Misdemeanors*, a superbly over-the-top hex in *The Witches* and a hardened gangster's moll in *The Grifters*, for which she picked up another Oscar nomination.

She'll next be seen as another kind of monster in *The Addams Family*. This year she is 40, but age does not bother her. "I never want to be one of those women with old-looking hands and pulled-in faces," she says. "It's like silicone for breast enlargement. They look sexier with silicone, but it lessens sensitivity."

Patrick Bergin and Julia Roberts as estranged husband and wife in *Sleeping with the Enemy*.

NEW SMASH FOR JULIA ROBERTS

Julia Roberts, sister of actor Eric Roberts but better known now in her own right after last year's hits *Pretty Woman* and *Flatliners*, has started 1991 with another smash hit. *Sleeping with the Enemy*, from the novel by Nancy Price, opened to torrid business in February and within three weeks overhauled the box-office tally of *Look Who's Talking Too*, the John Travolta/ Kirstie Alley co-starrer of which much had been expected.

It's a chilling story about a young wife whose obsessive, chauvinist husband makes her life a misery by constant carping and physical abuse. So much so that one stormy night she fakes her own death in a sailing accident and runs away to start a new life. But tell-tale signs lead her husband to conclude that she is still alive and he sets off to inflict a terrible punishment on her.

Cast opposite Julia Roberts is Irish actor Patrick Bergin, who first came to prominence with *Mountains of the Moon* (1990), playing famed explorer Richard Burton, and has now gone on to play Robin Hood in one of two movies about the Sherwood Forest bandit due out this year. Here he plays a very different role – Roberts' psychotic husband.

The film was shot in North and South Carolina, with the seaside resort of Wilmington for the early scenes in the couple's beach house. As no suitable property could be found, a custom-built five-room house was erected in nine weeks. To mimic the appearance of Cedar Falls, Iowa, further scenes were shot in Abbeville, South Carolina, which looked more like the Midwest than the Midwest itself.

The dramatic finale was shot in a disused hospital in Spartanburg, South Carolina. For director Joseph Ruben, the film consolidates the reputation he won on a previous thriller, *The Stepfather*, in 1987.

OUT OF AFRIKA

They meet in the Afrika Cafe and it's wedding bells at first sight. She's up-tight horticulturist Andie MacDowell (from *sex, lies, and videotape*, 1989), he's laid-back French musician Gerard Depardieu (from *Cyrano de Bergerac*, 1990). And, they hope, it's a lifetime of never getting to know one another thereafter.

This is a marriage of convenience. He gets the green card he needs to live and work in the US and she gets the money to buy her coveted rooftop greenhouse. But then Cupid takes a hand.

This is the formula for *Green Card*, which is being called the most heart-warming love story since *Pretty Woman* (1990). Not surprising, really, as there haven't been many others. It's directed by Peter Weir, the Australian filmmaker who put his country's cinema on the map in 1975 with *Picnic at Hanging Rock* and has since made a big splash in Hollywood with films like *Witness* (1985) and *Dead Poets Society* (1989).

The big surprise of the film is Depardieu. Huge and overweight, he looks about as sexy as John Candy; but women can't resist his Gallic charm. *Green Card* and *Cyrano de Bergerac* make him currently the biggest, if most unlikely, heart-throb in American movies. If only they could pronounce his name right – "Deppardoo" doesn't get within hailing distance.

LEAN DIES

Sir David Lean, veteran British filmmaker, died on 16 April aged 83. He had been working to the last on what would have been a film of Joseph Conrad's *Nostromo*. He made many kinds of movies – from love stories like *Brief Encounter* (1945) to classic Dickens adaptations like *Great Expectations* (1946). But his fame rests on his epics: *Bridge on the River Kwai* (1957), *Lawrence of Arabia* (1965), *Doctor Zhivago* (1965) and *A Passage to India* (1984).

ACADEMY AWARDS

PRESENTED ON 25 MARCH 1991

Best Picture
Dances with Wolves

Best Director
Kevin Costner
Dances with Wolves

Best Actor
Jeremy Irons
Reversal of Fortune

Best Actress
Kathy Bates
Misery

Best Sup Actor
Joe Pesci
GoodFellas

Best Sup Actress
Whoopi Goldberg
Ghost

Gerard Depardieu and Andie MacDowell in Peter Weir's *Green Card*.

INDEX

Page numbers in *italic* refer to picture captions

Abba the Movie 353
Abbott and Costello in the Navy 96
About Last Night . . . 434
Above Suspicion 104
Above Us the Waves 193
Abraham Lincoln 24
Absence of Malice 380
Absent Minded Professor, The 200, *230*, 234
Accident *272*, 303
Accidental Tourist, The 426
Accused, The 396, *423*, 426, 438
Ace in the Hole *160*, 222
Action in the North Atlantic 121
Actress, The 192, 224
Adam and Evelyne 192
Adam's Rib 151, 156, 190, 274
Addams Family, The 438
Adventure 118, 131
Adventures of a Young Man 232, *237*
Adventures of Baron Munchausen, The *410*, 411, *427*
Adventures of Robin Hood, The *56*, 57, 73, 76, 77, 83, 221
Adventures of Tartu, The 108
Adventures of the Wilderness Family, The 346
Advise and Consent 240
Affairs of Cellini, The 56
Affair to Remember, An 270
Affectionately Yours 92
African Queen, The *165*, 167, 171, 202, 282, 332
After Office Hours 50
Agatha 350
Aguirre, Wrath of God 402
Air America 434
Air Force 121
Airplane! 366
Airplane II: The Sequel 388
Airport *293*, 296, 301, 329
Airport 1975 332, 384
Airport '77 346
Alamo, The *227*, 234, 241
Alexander the Great 219, 232, 254
Alexander's Ragtime Band *28*, 29, 74, 77, 401
Alfie *264*, 268, 404
Algiers *75*
Ali Baba and the 40 Thieves 56
Alice Adams *55*
Alice Doesn't Live Here Anymore 324, 329, 337, 338, 342, 408
Alice's Restaurant *289*
Alien 358, 360, 367, 374, *375*, 379, 392, 406, 408, 423
Aliens 374, *406*, 409, 423
All About Eve 156, 160, 174, 311, 431
All Fall Down 328
All Night Long 364
All Quiet on the Western Front 18, 19, 20, 206
All That Heaven Allows 266, 403
All That Jazz 159, 360, 369, 376, 405
All the Fine Young Cannibals 239
All the King's Men 146, 152, 157, 332
All the President's Men *334*, 338, 342, 395
All This, and Heaven Too 96
All Woman 59
Always 434
Amadeus *395*, 398, 418
American Citizen, An 23
American Flyers 437
American Gigolo *362*, 379
American Graffiti 173, *317*, 319, 335, *340*, 344, 348, 399
American in Paris, An 159, 164, *165*, 166, 167, 176, 322
Americanization of Emily, The 259, 272, 287
American Tragedy, An *25*
Amityville Horror, The 360
Anastasia 203, 207, 226
Anatomy of a Murder *219*, 221, 301
Anchors Aweigh 120, 122, 131, 146, 420, 421
And God Created Woman 210
And Woman . . . Was Created 210
Andromeda Strain, The 305, 361
Andy Hardy (series) 81
Andy Hardy's Double Life 115
Angel Heart *412*, 422
Angels One Five 171
Angels over Broadway 92
Angels with Dirty Faces 70, 77, 405
Animal Crackers 41
Anna and the King of Siam 196
Anna Christie 16, 20, 46, 433
Anna Karenina 53, 54, 63, 389, 433
Anne of the Thousand Days 293, 296, 393
Annie 381
Annie Get Your Gun 147, 154, 157, 159, 162, 165, 176, 178
Annie Hall *343*, 345, 348, 353, 357, 423
Another 48 HRS 383
Another Thin Man 62
A nous la liberte 59
Anthony Adverse *61*, 65
Anything Goes 208
Any Which Way You Can 372
Apartment, The *225*, 227, 230, 233, 281, 310
Apocalypse Now *340*, 348, *358*, 360, 366, 376, 384, 385, 400, 408, 427
April in Paris 178
Arabian Nights 56
Arch of Triumph 153
Are You With It? 175
Aristocats, The 305
Arizona 88
Around the World in 80 Days 193, *198*, 203, 207, 233, *242*, *243*
Arrangement, The 279, 308, 373
Arrowsmith 61
Arsenic and Old Lace 409
Arthur *371*, 372, 381, 405
Artists and Models 233
Asphalt Jungle, The *70*, *154*, 174, 197
As the Earth Turns 45
At Long Last Love 349
At War with the Army 164, 385
Athena 220
Atonement of Gosta Berling, The 53
Attack! 111, 263
Attack of the 50 Foot Woman 200, *201*
Auntie Mame *213*, 221
Authentic Death of Hendry Jones: *see* One-Eyed Jacks
Autumn Leaves 238
Avanti! *310*
Awful Truth, The *69*, 73

Babes in Arms 83, 109, 165
Babes on Broadway 103
Baby and the Battleship, The 198
Baby Doll 186, 198, 231, 238, 253
Baby Face 38
Baby Face Nelson 206
Baby, It's You 399
Baby the Rain Must Fall 268
Bachelor Flat 237
Bachelor Mother 204, 233
Back Street *33*
Back to God's Country 182
Back to School 409
Back to the Future 383, *400*, 403, 409, 420
Back to the Future Part II *383*, 431, 437
Back to the Future Part III 383, 434, 437
Bad and the Beautiful, The 170, 174
Bad Boys 398, 407
Bad Company 360
Bad Day at Black Rock *185*, 189, 205, 263, 274
Bad Girl 25, 34
Badlands 320, 337, 363, 384
Bad News Bears, The *337*, 338
Bad Sister 72
Bad Timing *363*, 412
Baja Oklahoma 432
Ball of Fire 94
Bambi 103, 231, 269
Bamboo Prison, The 191
Bananas 318, 339, 359
Band Concert, The 50
Bandits of Sherwood Forest 167
Band Wagon, The 159, *176*
Barabbas 229, 236, *236*, 257
Barbarella 281, 283
Barbarosa 401
Barbed Wire 31
Barefoot Contessa, The 184, 189
Barefoot in the Park 276, 281
Barkleys of Broadway, The 147
Barretts of Wimpole Street, The 48, *49*, 72
Barry Lyndon *333*, 365
Bat Whispers, The 20
Bataan 111
Bathing Beauty 115
Batman (1966) 428; (1989) *410*, *428*, 431
Batteries not included 431
Battle at Apache Pass 181
Battle Beyond the Stars 374
Battle Cry 193, 213
Battleground 147, 157, 162
Battle of Britain 296
Battle of the Bulge 268, 330
Battle of the River Plate, The 207
Beast from 20,000 Fathoms, The 200
Beast of the City, The 32
Beat the Devil 221
Beau Brummell 23
Beau Geste 94, 175
Beaver Valley 155
Because You're Mine 179
Becket 254, 393
Becky Sharp 52, 86
Bedknobs and Broomsticks 310
Bed of Roses *38*
Bed-Sitting Room, The 321
Bedtime for Bonzo 160
Beetlejuice *419*, 422, 428
Behind the Great Wall 220
Behind the Mask 273
Behold a Pale Horse 262
Being There 362
Bell, Book and Candle 225
Belles of St. Trinians, The 185
Bells of St. Mary's, The 131
Bend of the River 180
Beneath the 12 Mile Reef 197
Ben-Hur (1925) 62, 229, *410*; (1959) 156, *220*, 222, 226, 227, *229*, 243, 244, 247, 253, 322, 355, 370
Benji 332
Bergkatze, Die 73
Bernardine 208
Best Foot Forward 165
Best Little Whorehouse in Texas, The 381
Best of Times, The 428
Best Years of Our Lives, The *130*, 132, 137, 144, 320, 349, 370
Betsy's Wedding 0
Beverly Hills Cop 394, 403, 421
Beverly Hills Cop II 417, 421
Beyond Glory 191
Bible, The 229, 254, *269*, 277
Big 422
Big Broadcast, The 34
Big Chill, The 401, 402, 416, 437
Big Country, The *212*, 216, 221, 244, 253, 370, 426
Big Easy, The 422, 430, 436
Bigger Than Life 280
Big Heat, The 70, 188, 263
Big House, The *19*, 20, 70
Big Jake 305
Big Knife, The 198, 238
Big Parade, The 18, 58
Big Pond, The *17*
Big Sleep, The (1946) *128*, 202; (1977) 344, 345
Big Trail, The 20, 38, 79, 242, *243*
Billion Dollar Brain 289, 302
Bill of Divorcement, A 39
Billy Liar 245, *251*, 261
Billy the Kid 20
Birds, The 200, *244*, 255, 422
Birthday Party, The 304
Birth of a Nation, The 24, *228*, 229
Bitter Tea of General Yen, The 36, *37*
Blackboard Jungle 173, *188*, 378, 396, 405
Black Cauldron, The 419
Black Hole, The 361, 366, 374
Blackmail 12, 267
Black Narcissus 144, 192, 199
Black Night, The 219
Black Pirate, The 56
Black Rain *430*
Black Shield of Falworth, The 213
Black Stallion, The 385
Black Swan, The 56, 212
Black Waters 12
Black Widow 412, *413*
Blade Runner 374, *375*, 379, 390, 435
Blame It on Rio 417, 434
Blazing Saddles *320*, 321, 325, 338, 348
Blessed Event 46
Blind Date 417, 421, 434
Blob, The 268
Blonde in Love, A 336
Blonde Venus 34
Blood and Sand *95*, 212
Bloodhounds of Broadway 208, 435
Blood Red 432
Blood Sisters 352
Blow Out 371
Blowup *273*, 323, 371
Blue Angel, The *16*, 22, 290
Bluebeard's Eighth Wife *73*, 222
Blue Dahlia, The 252
Blue Hawaii 241
Blue Lagoon, The 151, 181, 192
Blue Lamp, The 157, 181
Blue Max, The *266*, 276
Blue Skies 131, 137
Blue Thunder 386, 407
Blue Velvet *408*, 421
Blues Brothers, The 366, 377, 387
Blume in Love 342, 349
Boatniks, The 401
Bob & Carol & Ted & Alice 296 314, 349, 405
Body and Soul *135*, 169, 186, *187*, 232, 366
Body Heat 391, 401, 407
Bombshell 41, 42
Bonfire of the Vanities, The 437, *437*
Bonjour Tristesse 204
Bonnie and Clyde *70*, *274*, 276, 278, 289, 297, 323, 328, 329, 350, 360, 372, 373, 396, *397*
Boomerang 133, 166, 231
Boom Town 114
Bordertown 72
Born Free 268
Born on the Fourth of July 424, *431*, 432
Born Yesterday 156, *157*, 160, 164, 371
Bostonians, The 404
Boudu Saved from Drowning 405
Bought 25
Bowery, The 41
Boy on a Dolphin 234
Boys from Brazil 351, *351*
Boys in the Band 304
Boys Town 77, 78, 83, 114
Brainstorm 372
Bravados, The 253
Brave One, The 205
Brazil 427
Breakfast at Tiffany's 266, 308, 331
Breakfast Club, The 398, 407, *424*, 425
Breaking Away 436
Brewster McCloud 365
Bridge on the River Kwai, The *110*, 111, *206*, 208, 212, 227, 232, 240, 245, 350, 411
Bridge Too Far, A *345*, 346, 381
Bridges at Toko-Ri, The 111, 188
Brief Encounter *123*, 131, 212, 245, 287, 348
Brigadoon 166
Bright Road 185
Bright Shawl, The 27
Bringing Up Baby 42, *43*, 72, *74*, 409
Bring Me the Head of Alfredo Garcia 342
Broadway *12*
Broadway Melody, The 11, 12, 13, 15
Broadway Melody of 1936 63
Broadway Melody of 1938 66, *66*
Broadway Nights 31
Broken Arrow 154, 157, 181, 297
Broken Blossoms 24, 37
Broken Lance 197, 227
Brothers in Law 248
Brothers Karamazov, The 209, 226
Brute Force 396, *397*
Buccaneer, The (1938) 56, 57, 203; (1956) 203
Buck Privates *92*, 111
Buck Rogers *201*
Buddy Holly Story, The 173, 350
Buddy System, The 405
Bugsy Malone *337*, 406, 412, 420, 423
Bulldog Drummond 13, 383
Bull Durham 437
Bullets or Ballots 70
Bullitt *282*, 291
Bundle of Joy 204
Burning Hills, The 213
Bus Stop 289
Buster 422
Buster Keaton Story, The 205
Butch Cassidy and the Sundance Kid 291, 296, 302, 319, 325, 329, 334, 343
Butterfield 8 230, 246, 306
Butterflies Are Free 314
Bwana Devil 171
Bye Bye Birdie 248, 303

Cabaret 159, *307*, 308, 310, 314, 319, 325
Cabin in the Sky *105*
Cabinet of Dr Caligari, The 16, 104
Cactus Flower *288*, 292, 296
Caddy, The 265
Caesar and Cleopatra 131, 192
Caine Mutiny, The 111, 185, 191, 193, 202, 230
Calamity Jane 159, 178, 185
California Suite 356, 360, 404
Call Me Madam *175*
Camelot 273, 277
Cameo Kirby 66
Camille *65*, 68, 168, 433
Can-Can 233
Candidate, The 334, 337
Cannery Row 379, 380, 388, 407
Cannonball Run, The 372
Cape Fear 236
Capricorn One *299*
Captain Blood 56, 76, 211
Captain from Castile 144
Captain Hates the Sea, The 58
Captain Horatio Hornblower 164
Captains Courageous 73, 77, 114,

146, 274, 355
Captains of the Clouds 103
Captive 407
Caravan 75
Caretaker, The 330
Carlton-Browne of the F.O. 248
Carmen Jones 185
Carnal Knowledge *303*, 305, 323, 389
Carousel 194
Carpetbaggers, The 253, 263, 266
Carrie 340, 346, 371
Carry On Camping 291
Carry On Cleo 263
Carry On Constable 227
Carry On Cruising 241
Carry On Nurse 221
Carry On Regardless 234
Carry On Sergeant 212
Carry On Teacher 221
Carry On Up the Jungle 296
Carry On Up the Khyber 291
Carve Her Name with Pride 212
Casablanca *102*, 104, 108, 112, 116, 202, 427
Case of the Curious Bride, The 76
Casino Royale 239, 276
Cassandra Crossing, The 400
Cass Timberlane 144
Castle Keep 111
Castle on the Hudson 169
Casualties of War 396
Cat and the Fiddle, The 64
Cat Ballou 262, *263*, 264, 281
Catch-22 *294*, *295*, 303
Cat on a Hot Tin Roof 212, 246
Cat People 402
Caught in the Draft 111
Cavalcade 36, 41, 44, 355
Certain Sacrifice, A 435
Chained 48
Champ, The *26*, 34
Champion *147*, 148, 155, 366
Chang 13, 36
Change of Heart 44
Chant of Jimmy Blacksmith, The 439
Charade *248*, 272, 280
Charge at Feather River, The 180
Charge of the Light Brigade, The (1936) 56, *62*; (1968) 279
Chariots of Fire *368*, 376, 381, 389, 390, 398, 406
Charlie Bubbles 279, 308
Charly 286
Chase, The *265*, 268, 281, 291
Che! 287
Cheaper by the Dozen 157
Cheat, The 53
Cheyenne Autumn 297
Chicago 99
Chicken Chronicles, The 391
Children of a Lesser God 413
Children's Hour, The 287
Child's Play 325
Chimes at Midnight 371, 403
China Gate 217
China Seas 53, 54
China Syndrome, The 299, *356*, 416
Chinatown 322, 323, 328, 332, 373, *433*
Chitty Chitty Bang Bang 291
Christmas in July 93
Christopher Strong 39
Chump at Oxford, A 219
Cimarron 22, 26, 63
Cincinnati Kid, The 268, 280, 303
Cinderella 155, 157, 164, 231
Cinderella Liberty 373
Cinerama Holiday 193
Circle of Love 281
Circus, The 12
Circus World 260
Citadel, The 77, 81, 83, 211
Citizen Kane *92*, 98, 99, 102, 209, 236, 305, 306, 320, 332, 361, 370, 403
City Lights 26, 35, 59, 357
Clash by Night 174
Clash of the Titans 372
Claudia 107
Cleopatra (1934) 49, 53, 216; (1963) 216, 227, 229, 234, *246*, 248, 258, 265, 348, 393, 410, *411*
Clive of India 51
Clock, The 163
Clockwise 409
Clockwork Orange, A 304, 305, 310, 319, 333, 396, *397*
Close Encounters of the Third Kind 340, *346*, 353, 361, 370, 374, *375*, 405
Cluny Brown 137
Coal Miner's Daughter, The *363*, 366, 369
Cockeyed World, The 15
Cockleshell Heroes, The 198
Cocktail 422, 431
Cocoanuts, The 41
Cocoon *401*, 403, 404
Cohens and Kellys in Hollywood, The 32
Colditz Story, The 193
Color of Money, The 408, 413
Color Purple, The *403*, 409, 413
Comancheros, The 241, 263
Come and Get It 65
Come Back to the Five and Dime, Jimmy Dean, Jimmy Dean 399
Come Back, Little Sheba 174, 211
Come Blow Your Horn 248
Come Fill the Cup 291
Come See the Paradise 436
Coming Home 349, 356, 359
Coming to America 421, 422
Command, The 180
Commando 396, *411*, 414
Commandos Strike at Dawn, The 108
Common Clay 20
Compulsion 421
Conan the Barbarian 229, *376*, 393, 414, 437
Conan the Destroyer 229, 414
Condorman 381
Coney Island 108
Confession, The 377
Confessions of a Nazi Spy 81, 97, 106
Conquest 75
Conrack 357
Conspiracy of Hearts 227
Constant Husband 207
Contraband 88
Conversation, The 299, *323*, 324, 333, 344, 348, 385
Convoy (1940) 88
Convoy (1977) 342
Coogan's Bluff *282*, 307
Cook, The Thief, His Wife and Her Lover, The 436
Cool Hand Luke 278
Coquette 10, 11, 13 15
Cotton Club, The 419
Counsellor-at-Large 66
Countdown 330
Count of Monte Cristo, The 56, 211
Country 395
Country Girl, The 188, 189, 193, 380
Court Jester, The *195*
Court-Martial of Billy Mitchell 189
Courtneys of Curzon Street, The 137, 153
Cousins 270
Cover Girl 117, 159, 181
Covered Wagon, The 15, 101
Cowboy 225
Crash Dive 112
Creation 36
Creature from the Black Lagoon, The *200*
Crime in the Streets 195
Crimes and Misdemeanours 438
Crimes of Passion 407
Criminal Code, The 32
Crimson Pirate, The 56, 168, *168*
Criss Cross 213
"Crocodile" Dundee *409*, 417, 422
"Crocodile" Dundee II 422
Cromwell 414
Crooks Anonymous 261
Crooner, The 46
Crossfire *135*, 147, 151, 170
Crowd, The 10, 13
Cruel Sea, The 179, 240
Crusade, The 53, 54
Cry Terror 217
Cure for Love, The 211
Curse of Frankenstein, The 219, 233
Cyrano de Bergerac 148, *157*, 160, 170, 193; (1991) 439
Cytherea 38

D.O.A. 429
Daddy Long Legs 26
Dam Busters, The *191*, 193
Dames 46
Damned, The 3, 17
Damn Yankees 213, 307
Dance, Fools, Dance 24
Dance of Life, The 18
Dances with Wolves 437, *437*, 439
Dancing Co-Ed 126
Dancing Lady, 29, 41, 60
Dangerous 58, 72, 431
Dangerous Liaisons 421, 430, 436
Dangerous When Wet *177*
Darby O'Gill and the Little People 256
Dark City 244
Dark Mirror, The 151
Dark Passage *137*
Darling *261*, 264
Darling Lili *294*, 331
Date with Judy, A 144
Daughter of Rosie O'Grady, The 204
David and Bathsheba 156, 164
David Copperfield *51*, 54, 61, 296
Davy Crockett – King of the Wild Frontier 189, 191
Dawn Patrol, The (1930) 19, 24; (1938) 76, 83, 221
Day of the Fight 197
Day of the Jackal, The *316*, 319
Day of the Locust, The 335
Day the Clown Cried, The 385
Day the Earth Stood Still, The 200, 361
Days of Glory 111, *115*, 136, 426
Days of Heaven 362
Days of Thunder 434
Days of Wine and Roses *245*, 315, 331
Dead End 67, *67*, 68, 81, 320
Deadline at Dawn 132
Dead Heat on a Merry-Go-Round 348
Dead Men Don't Wear Plaid 429
Dead of Night 122
Dead Poets Society *428*, 431, 439
Dead Reckoning *133*
Dead Zone, The 406
Death in Venice 304
Death of a Roach, The 391
Death of a Salesman 148
Death on the Nile 387
Death Race 2000 339, 359
Deathwish *396*
Deception 73
Deep, The 346
Deep Throat 339
Deer Hunter, The 353, 357, 360, 366, 389
Defector, The 266
Defence of the Realm *299*
Defiant Ones, The 212, *213*, 277
Delicate Delinquent, The 385
Deliverance 319, 349
Dementia 13 385
Demetrios and the Gladiators 276
Dentist in the Chair 227
Desert Fox, The *110*, 111, 164
Desire *58*
Desiree 193
Desire under the Elms 224
Desperate Hours, The 270, 438
Desperately Seeking Susan *399*, 435
Desperate Moment 181
Destination Moon 200
Destination Tokyo 121
Destry 195
Destry Rides Again 83, 180
Devil in Miss Jones, The 391
Devil Is a Woman, The 127, 290
Devils, The 310
Devil's Brigade, The 283
Devil's Doorway 154
Devil's Holiday 18
Dial M for Murder 188, 380
Diamond City 196
Diamonds Are Forever 388, 414
Diary of a Lost Girl 17
Diary of Anne Frank, The 222, 237
Dick Tracy 434, *435*, 437
Dick Tracy's G-Men (serial) 108
Die Hard 383, 396, *421*, 422, 433
Die Hard 2 383, *410*, 411, 434, 435
Dillinger 330, 335, 340, 376, 393
Diner 423, 430
Dinner at Eight *38*, 74
Dirty Dancing 424
Dirty Dozen, The 111, *275*, 276, 292, 302
Dirty Harry *307*, 310
Dishonored 25
Disraeli 16, 20
Divine Lady, The 13
Divorcee, The 17, 20
Docks of New York, The 25
Doctor at Large 207
Doctor at Sea 193, 210
Doctor Bull 53
Doctor Dolittle 283, 291, 347
Dr. Ehrlich's Magic Bullet 107
Doctor in Love 227
Doctor in the House *181*, 185, 207, 249
Dr. Jekyll and Mr. Hyde (1920) 23; (1932) 34; (1941) *95*, 146
Dr. Kildare (series) 81
Dr. No *239*, 241, 256, 414
Dr. Socrates 66
Dr. Strangelove, or: How I Learned to Stop Worrying and Love the Bomb *110*, 111, 200, 252, 255, 260, 278, 295, 301, 304
Doctor Zhivago 261, *262*, 268, 269, 276, 283, 297, 329
Dodsworth *61*, 63, 89
Dog Day Afternoon 338
Dog Soldiers 371
Doll's House, A 314, 347
Dolly Sisters, The 122
Don Giovanni 427
Don Juan *8*, 9
Donovan Affair, The 11
Donovan's Reef 263
Don Q., Son of Zorro 1925
Don Quixote 193, 403
Don't Bother to Knock 174, 276
Don't Change Your Husband 27, 53, 384
Don't Knock the Rock 173
Doomsday 94
Doorway to Hell 70
Do the Right Thing 396
Double Indemnity 113, 222, 230, 355
Double Life, A 140, 237
Dove, The 426
Down and Out in Beverly Hills *405*
Down Argentine Way 88, 96, 159
Downstairs 35, 58
Down to Earth 160
Dracula (1931) 27, 32; (1958) 219, 233; (1979) 386
Dragnet 184, 417
Dreaming 207
Dressed to Kill 404
Drive, He Said 323
Driving Miss Daisy *431*, 432, 439
Drums Along the Mohawk 83
Drunkard's Reformation, A 24
Du Barry Was a Lady 196
Du Barry – Woman of Passion 21, 166
Duck Soup 41
Duel in the Sun *132*, 137, 260, 351
Duellists, The 338, 358
Dumbo 269
Dune 374, 408
Dunkirk 212

Early Bird, The 268
Earthquake 322, 325, 332
Easiest Way, The 24
Easter Parade 144, 147, 151, 159, 165, 322
East of Eden *186*, 186, *189*, 192, 195, 205, 224
Easy Living 42, 66
Easy Rider 173, *289*, 296, 302, 319, 323
Easy to Love 253
Easy to Wed 131
Eddy Duchin Story, The 198, 207
Edison the Man 84, 107
Educating Rita 394
Egg and I, The 149
Egyptian, The 185, 192, 195
El Cid 229, *234*, *235*, 241, 253, 260
El Dorado 276, 293
Electric Horseman, The 350, 366
Elephant Man, The *367*, 372, 408
Elmer Gantry *225*, 230
Elvis – That's the Way It Is 173
Elvis on Tour 173
Emma 34
Emmanuelle 332, 338
Emperor Waltz, The 144
Empire of the Senses 332
Empire of the Sun *418*, 436
Empire Strikes Back, The 364, 366, 374
Employees' Entrance 36
Enchanted Hill, The 94
End, The 349, 356
Endless Love 407
End of the Affair, The 219
Enemy Mine 374, 436
Enemy of the People, An 352
Enforcer, The 343, 346
Entertainer, The 226, 279
Enter the Dragon 325
Equus 349
Eraserhead 408
Escape 97
Escape from Alcatraz 366
Escape from Fort Bravo 205
Esther Waters 249
E.T. The Extra-Terrestrial 200, 340, *374*, 378, 381, 385, 388, 403, 410
Eureka 412
Europeans, The *359*, 404
Evensong 149
Evergreen 50
Every Sunday 66, 68
Everything You Always Wanted to Know About Sex But Were Afraid to Ask 310
Every Which Way But Loose 360
Excalibur *369*
Excuse My Dust 182
Executioner's Song, The 399
Executive Action 299
Exodus 218, 227, 234, 246
Exorcism's Daughter 321
Exorcist, The 318, 321, 324, 325, 329, 332, 336
Exorcist II: The Heretic 369
Exorcist III, The 434
Experiment in Terror 331
Eyes of Laura Mars 364

Fabulous Baker Boys, The 430
Face in the Crowd 204, 280
Face of a Fugitive 272
Fahrenheit 451 261, 363
Fail-Safe 111, *255*, 280
Falcon Takes Over, The 118
Falcon's Brother, The 101

Fallen Idol, The 144, 389
Fall of the Roman Empire *228*, 229, 244, *253*, 262
Family Affair, A 75
Family Life 367
Family Plot 362
Family Way, The 276
Fanatic 302
Fanny by Gaslight 164
Fantasia 88, 96, 145, 231, 269, 361
Fantastic Voyage 275
Fantastic Voyage 200
Far Country, The 411
Farewell to Arms, A (1932) 34; (1957) 260
Farewell, My Lovely 118, 345
Far from the Madding Crowd 261, 363
Farmer's Daughter, The 140
Farmer Takes a Wife, The 59
Fast Lady, The 261
Fast Times at Ridgemont High 419
Fast Workers 58
Fatal Attraction *416*, 417, 422
Fat City *309*, 325, 342, 344
Father Goose 263
Father of the Bride 157, 162, 246
Father's Little Dividend 164
Fathom 275
Fat Man and Little Boy 425
Fear and Desire 197, 278
Fear Is the Key 381
Fear Strikes Out 186, 224, 231
Feel My Pulse 14
Feet First *20*
F for Fake 403
Female Trouble 369
Fiddler on the Roof 310, 315
Field of Dreams *427*, 436, 437
Fiends, The 210
55 Days in Peking 229, 244, 260, 387
Fighter Squadron 182
Fighting Lady 168
Fighting 69th, The 88
Figures in a Landscape 305
Finger Points, The 24
Fingers 338
Finian's Rainbow 286, 294, 306
Firefly 77
Firefox 381
Firemen's Ball, The 336
First a Girl 376
First Blood *381*, 396, 400
First Love 143
First of the Few, The 103, 106, 387
First Yank into Tokyo, The 120
Fish Called Wanda, A *420*, 422, 426
F.I.S.T. 402
Fistful of Dollars 257, 270, 282
Five Easy Pieces 323, 368, 413
Five Graves to Cairo *107*
Five Star Final *27*
Fixed Bayonets 111
Flame and the Arrow, The 56
Flaming Star 297
Flashdance 159, 384, 402, 416
Flash Gordon 200, 372, 374
Flatliners 425, 432, 434, 439
Fleet's In, The 103
Flesh 123
Flesh & Blood 417
Flesh and the Devil 58
Fletch 401
Flower Drum Song 241
Flowers and Trees 39
Fly, The (1958) 200; (1986) *406*
Flying Down to Rio 29, 60
Flying Leathernecks 111
Flying Padre, The 197
Fog, The 387
Follow the Fleet 29, 60
Follow Thru 18
Footlight Parade *29*, 40, 41
For a Few Dollars More 282
For Better, For Worse 384
Forbidden 31
Forbidden Planet *200*
Force of Evil 169
Foreign Correspondent 88
Foreign Intrigue 197
Forever Amber *136*, 144, 167
Forever and a Day *105*
For Me and My Gal 103, 166
Forsythe Saga, The 157
Fort Apache *141*, 190, 319
For the Love of Mike 54
For Them That Trespass 153
Fortune Cookie, The 272, 280, 310
48HRS 380, 383, 388
49th Parallel 96, 106
42nd Street *29*, 40, 41, 46
For Whom the Bell Tolls 108, 112, 117, 136
For Your Eyes Only 372
Foul Play 353
Four Daughters 169, 186, 194
Four Feathers, The (1930) 13; (1939) *81*, 83
Four Frightened People 53
Four Jills in a Jeep 142
Four Musketeers, The 321
Four's a Crowd 76
Four Seasons 372
Fourteen Hours 188, 380
Fox and the Hound, The 381, 419
Fox Movietone Follies 19
Fox Movietone Follies of 1930 19
Foxes 384
Francis 149, 175
Francis Covers the Big Town 175
Francis in the Navy 282
Frankenstein 26, 27, 32, 34, 35, 383
Freaks 32
Free Soul, A *24*, 25, 26
French Connection, The *304*, 307, 310, 315, 360
French Dressing 290
French Lieutenant's Woman, The *371*, 389, 402
French Line, The 207
Frenzy *308*
Freshman, The 20, 133
Friday the 13th 365, *383*
Frieda 137
Friendly Persuasion 224
Frogmen, The 197
From Hell to Texas 289
From Here to Eternity *176*, 179, 180, 185, *186*, 189, 194, 199, 266, 316, 347
From Russia with Love 248, 256, 330
From the Terrace 227
Front, The 339, 343, 357
Front Page, The (1931) 23, *271*; (1974) 270, *271*
Fugitive, The 141, 190
Full Metal Jacket *414*, 417, 428
Funny Face *203*, 204
Funny Girl *283*, 286, 291, 296, 310, 347, 370
Funny Lady 332, 347
Funny Thing Happened on the Way to the Forum, A 265, 343
Fun with Dick and Jane 347
Fury 65, 114, 274
Fury, The 390

Gable and Lombard 335, 359
Gabriel Over the White House *36*
Gaily, Gaily 352
Gallipoli 412
Gambler, The 371
Game Is Over, The 281
Ghandi *381*, 384, 388, 389, 398, 418
Gangster Story 280
Garden of Allah, The 75
Garden of Eden 184
Garden of Evil 227
Gaslight 118
Gaucho, The 56, 116
Gauntlet, The 353
Gay Divorcee, The 29, 60
General, The *11*, 265
Genevieve 177, 179, 181, 207, 249
Genghis Khan 262
Gentlemen of the Press 32, 45
Gentlemen Prefer Blondes 174, 179, 239
Gentleman's Agreement *136*, 140, 144, 166, 421, 426
Gentle Sex, The 106, 108
George White's Scandals, 45, 64
Georgy Girl 273, 276
Getaway, The 319
Ghost 424, 434, *434*, 437, 439
Ghost Busters *392*, 394, 403, 419, 423
Ghostbusters II 383, 431, 437
Ghost Goes West, The 63, 211
Ghoul, The 389
Giant 186, 192, 203, 207, 246, 253, 266
Giant of Marathon, The 220
G.I. Blues 234
Gigi 159, 177, *211*, 216, 322, *354*, 355
Gilda *127*, 131, 188
Gilda Live 389
Girl Can't Help It, The *172*, 173, 203
Girl Crazy 165
Girl He Left Behind, The 213
Girl in the Red Velvet Swing, The 189
Girl Shy 20
Girls on Probation 132
Give Us the Moon 192
Glass Menagerie, The 436
Glenn Miller Story, The *180*, 185, 189
Glorifying the American Girl 21
Glory 431, 432
Go-Between, The *303*, 316
Godfather, The 70, *186*, 306, *309*, 310, 314, 315, 319, 323, 329, 340, 345, 355, 368, 385, 396, 400, 411
Godfather Part II, The *324*, 329, 332, 334, 340, 368, 383, 385
Godfather Part III, The 383, 410, 433, 435, 436, *436*, 438
God King, The 381
Godzilla 200
Going My Way *112*, 117, 355
Goin' South 377
Gold Diggers of 1933 *29*, 40, 41
Gold Diggers of 1935 29
Golden Boy 350
Golden Child, The 409, 417
Golden Girl 208
Goldfinger *256*, 263
Goldwyn's Follies 77
Goliath and the Barbarian 220
Gone With the Wind 68, 76, 78, 80, *82*, 83, 84, 85, 86, 96, 107, 116, 132, 146, 151, 162, 220, 230, 234, 252, 260, 265, 274, 277, 283, 291, 297, 329, *355*, 366, 385, 410
Goodbye Charlie 324
Goodbye Columbus 291
Goodbye Girl, The 348, 349, 353, 405
Goodbye, Mr. Chips (1939) *81*, 83, 85, 211; (1969) 287, *291*, 347
Good Companions, The 371
Good Earth, The 65, 66, 68, 73, 77
Good Fairy, The 49
Good Morning, Vietnam 422, 428
Good News 159
GoodFellas 396, 436
Good, the Bad and the Ugly, The 282
Goonies, The 403, 413
Gorillas in the Mist 423
Graduate, The *6*, 7, *276*, 278, 283, *294*, 295, 329, 335, 360, 380, 389, 405
Grand Hotel 30, 31, 34, 44, 270, 293
Grandma's Boy 20
Grand Prix 276, 280, 287
Grapes of Wrath, The 84, 93, 190, 319, 378
Grass 36
Gray Lady Down 352
Grease *172*, 173, 346, 351, *351*, 353, 360, 371, 430
Great Balls of Fire! 172, 173, 436
Great Caruso, The 161, 164, 165, 189
Great Dictator *89*, 96, 133
Great Escape, The *247*, 248, 268, 272, 287
Greatest Show on Earth, The 167, *167*, 170, 171, 174, 195, 244, 269
Greatest Story Every Told, The 244, 253, *259*
Great Expectations 134, 137, 149, 192, 245, 296
Great Gabbo, The *15*
Great Gatsby, The (1926) 59; (1974) 320, *321*, 325, 394
Great Lie, The 98
Great McGinty, The *87*, 93
Great Northfield Minnesota Raid, The 418
Great Profile, The 86
Great Race, The 263
Great St. Trinian's Train Robbery, The 268
Great Ziegfeld, The 60, 65, 68, 165, 169
Greed 15
Green Berets, The 283
Green Card 439, *439*
Green Dolphin Street 137
Green Goddess, The 16
Green Hat, The 45
Green Pastures 105
Green Years, The 131, 421
Greenwich Village 156
Gregory's Girl 381
Gremlins 394, 403, 425
Gremlins 2: The New Batch 383, 425, 434, 437
Greystoke: The Legend of Tarzan, Lord of the Apes 389, *390*, 394
Grifters, The 438, *438*
Group, The 268
Guadalcanal Diary 111
Guardsman, The 27, 34
Guess Who's Coming to Dinner 274, *277*, 278, 282, 283, 355, 373
Gunfight at the O.K. Corral *205*, 207
Gunfighter, The 231, 426
Gunga Din 78, 83
Gunman's Walk 213
Guns at Batasi 320
Guns of Navarone, The *232*, 233, 234, 236, 241, 257, 275, 277, 387
Gun the Man Down 217
Guy Named Joe, A 107, *109*, 115, 117, 146, 434
Guys and Dolls 192, *193*, 198
Gypsy 159, 239, 372

Hail, Hero 416
Hair 395, 427
Hairy Ape, The 216
Half a Sixpence 283, 291
Hallelujah! *13*
Hallelujah, I'm a Bum 41
Halloween 387
Halloween II 387
Halls of Montezuma, The 111, 197
Hamlet 146, 192, 219, 364
Hammett 385
Hands Across the Table 60
Handy Andy 55
Hang 'Em High 282
Hannah and Her Sisters 404, *405*, 413
Hans Christian Andersen 179, 195
Happening, The 274
Happiest Days of Your Life, The 157
Happy Days 19
Happy Land 239, 372
Happy Landing 77
Hard Day's Night, A *173*, 254, 260, 321
Hardly Working 385
Hard to Handle *37*
Harry and Tonto 329, 349
Harvey 156, 160
Has Anybody Seen My Gal? 182, 189
Hasty Heart, The 153
Hatari! 241
Hatful of Rain, A 204, 218
Hawaii 269, 277, 361
Head 413
Heart Beat 380
Heartbreak Kid, The 415
Heart Is a Lonely Hunter, The 295
Hearts of Fire 415
Hearts of the West 335
Heat and Dust 404
Heaven Can Wait (1943) 350, 401, (1978) 350, 353, 372
Heaven's Gate 366, 370, 401, 410, *411*, 415
Heaven with a Barbed Wire Fence 188
Heidi *68*
Heiress, The *151*, 153, 370, 389
Helen of Troy 210
Hell in the Pacific 288, 374, 436
Hell Is for Heroes 272
Hello, Dolly! 286, 296, 310
Hello, Frisco, Hello 108
Hell's Angels *18*, 19, 20, 67
Hellzapoppin' 96
Help! 260, 263, 321
Henry & June 436
Henry V *117*, 134, 155
Herbie Goes Bananas 381
Herbie Goes to Monte Carlo 353
Herbie Rides Again 325
Hercules 220
Hercules in New York 414
Hercules Unchained 220, 227
Here Comes Mr. Jordan 350
Here Come the Girls 182
Here We Go Round the Mulberry Bush 283
Heroes for Sale 41
Heroes of Telemark, The 277
High and Dizzy 20
High and the Mighty, The 185
High Anxiety 348, *348*
Higher and Higher 120
High Noon 167, *167*, 171, 174, 188, 195, 217, 232, 270, 315, 316, 325, 347, 374
High Plains Drifter *315*
High Sierra *93*, 202
High Society 196, 198, 207, 270, 322, 380
Hill, The 256
Hill in Korea, A 264
Hi, Nellie 66
His Girl Friday *42*, 43, *85*
His Glorious Night 15, 166
His Kind of Woman 170
History Is Made at Night 66, 75
Hitler: A Film from Germany 400
Hitler's Children 103, 108
Hit Parade of 1941 181
Hole in the Wall, The 27
Holiday Affair 170
Holiday Camp 137
Holiday Inn *101*, 103, 185
Hollywood Canteen 117, 123
Hollywood or Bust 265
Hollywood Revue of 1929, The 19
Hombre 276, 357
Home Alone 437
Homecoming 144
Home of the Brave 148, 154
Homme du large, L' 75
Honey, I Shrunk the Kids 431, 437
Honky Tonk 126
Hooper 349, 353
Hope and Glory 416
Hoppy Serves a Writ 170
Horizons West 182
Horse Feathers 41
Hospital, The 310
Hot Spell 211
Hotel Imperial 31, 107
Houdini 213
Hound of the Baskervilles, The

(1939) 80; (1959) 219
House Divided, A 32
Householder, The 404
House Is Not a Home, A 275
Housekeeper's Daughter, The 150
Housekeeping 416
House of Rothschild, The *45*
House of Usher, The 233
House of Wax 175, 179
House on 92nd Street, The 141
How Green Was My Valley 96, 97, 98, 103, 319
How the West Was Won *6*, 7, 239, 248, 253
How to Beat the High Cost of Living 369
How to be Very, Very Popular 182
How to Marry a Millionaire 179, 183, 239
Hud 246, 252, 305, 357
Hudson Hawk 434
Hue and Cry 163
Human Desire 188
Humoresque 169
Hunchback of Notre Dame, The (1923) 19; (1939) 83, 205; (1957) 221, 257
Hunger, The 407
Hunt for Red October, The *433*
Hurricane, The (1937) 68, *69*, 74; (1979) 270
Hurry Sundown 274, 281
Hustler, The *232*, 246, 301, 408

I Am a Fugitive from a Chain Gang *35*, 41, 66
I Am Suzanne 45
I Can Get It for You Wholesale 314
Ice Cold in Alex 212, 236
I, Claudius 290
I Confess 231
I Could Go On Singing 249
Idolmaker, The 379
I Don't Care Girl, The 208
If . . . *283*, 287, 305
If I Had a Million 34
If Only You Could Cook 65
If You Feel Like Singing: *see* Summer Stock
I Live in Grosvenor Square 122
I'll Be Seeing You 146
I'll Be Your Sweetheart 122
I'll Cry Tomorrow 198, 216
I Love Melvin *175*
Ill Met by Moonlight 207
Illustrious Corpses 299
I'm All Right Jack 221, 248
I Married a Communist 151
I Married a Witch 216
Imitation of Life *49*, 221
Immortal Sergeant, The 111
I'm No Angel 40, 41
Impossible Voyage, An 200
Incredible Shrinking Man, The 200
Indian Fighter, The 280
Indiana Jones and the Last Crusade *383*, *429*, 431
Indiana Jones and the Temple of Doom 392, 394
Indiscreet 27, 212
Indiscretions of an American Wife 237
Informer, The 58, 63, 169, 319
Inherit the Wind 212
In Like Flint 272
Inn of the Sixth Happiness, The 211, 221
Innocents of Paris 17
In Old Arizona *11*, 13, 59
In Old Chicago 73, 74, 77
In Old Kentucky 54
In Search of Noah's Ark 346
Inside Daisy Clover 265, 291, 372
Insignificance 412
Inspector Clouseau 295
Interface 368
Interiors *353*, 357, 405
Intermezzo 83, 106, 260, 270
Internal Affairs 430
International Squadron 97
Interns, The 241
Interrupted Journey 153
Interrupted Melody 188, 189, 195
In the Good Old Summertime 308
In the Heat of the Night *275*, 277, 278, 280, 311
In the Wake of the Bounty 76, 221
Into the Blue 153
Intolerance 10, 23, 229, 410
Invaders from Mars 407
Invasion of the Body Snatchers 200, *201*, 299, 418
Investigation of a Citizen above Suspicion 299
In Which We Serve *102*, 108, 245
Ipcress File, The *258*, 264
Irma La Douce 240, 248, 310
I Remember Mama 147
Iron Curtain, The *143*
Iron Man 181
Iron Mask, The 56
I Should Have Stayed Home 291
Ishtar *415*, 435
Island at the Top of the World, The 332
Island in the Sun 207, 253
I Take This Woman 93
It Always Rains on Sunday 144
It Came from Outer Space 200
It Comes Up Love 175
It Happened One Night 42, *43*, 46, 47, 48, 50, 54, 225, 230
It's a Gift *48*
It's a Mad Mad Mad Mad World 248, *249*, 265, 361
It's a Wonderful Life 130, 170
It's a Wonderful World 42
It's Great to be Young 198
It Shouldn't Happen to a Vet 338
It! The Terror from beyond Space 358
Ivanhoe 168, 171
I Wanna Hold Your Hand 391
I Want to Live! 216
I Was a Male War Bride 151
I Was Happy Here 296

Jagged Edge 402
Jailhouse Rock *172*, 173, 207
Jane Eyre (1944) 117, 118; (1970) 427
Janice Meredith 48
Jassy 137
Jaws 322, *330*, 332, 335, 338, *340*, 344, 346, 360, 361, 370, 385
Jaws 2 353, 360
Jaws 3-D 394
Jazz Singer, The (1927) 9, 131, 157
Jeanne Eagels 205, 207
Jenny 12
Jerk, The 366, 429
Jesse James 79, 83, 87
Jesus Christ Superstar 319
Jewel of the Nile, The 409, 416
Jezebel 72, 78, 89, 108, 431
Joan of Arc 146, 151
Joan of Paris 99
Joan the Woman 53
Joe 315
Johann Mouse 177
John and Mary 320
Johnny Belinda *144*, 146, 151
Johnny Eager 105
Johnny Handsome 430
Joker Is Wild, The 208
Jolson Sings Again *149*, 151, 157
Jolson Story, The *131*, 137, 149
Journey Beyond the Stars: *see* 2001: A Space Odyssey
Joy Girls, The 46
Judge Hardy's Children 75
Judge Priest 48, 53
Judgment at Nuremberg 237, 274
Julia *347*, 348, 349, 350, 353, 389
Julius Caesar *174*, 186, 318, 371, 393
Jumping Jacks 171
June Bride 204
Jungle Book, The 283, 338, 394, 429

Kagemusha 400
Karate Kid, The 392, 394, 424
Karate Kid: Part II, The 409
Kathy O' 209
Kentuckian, The 280
Kentucky 77, 78
Key Largo *143*, 146
Keys of the Kingdom, The 115, 136
Khartoum 371
Kid, The 317
Kid Boots 21
Kid Brother, The 20
Kid for Two Farthings, A 193, 196
Kid from Spain, The 34
Kidnappers, The *180*, 181, 185
Killer Bees, The 384
Killer's Kiss 197, 378
Killers, The *129*, 168, 184, 263, 268
Killing, The 70, *197*, 206, 278, 414
Killing Fields, The *394*, 398, 406, 409, 436
Kim 164
Kindergarten Cop 411
Kind Hearts and Coronets 149, 150, 163
Kind of Loving, A 241, 261
King and I, The *196*, 198, 199, 203, 226, 254
King Creole 173, 280
King Kong (1933) 36, 52, 171, 260; (1976) *339*, 345, 346, 369
King of Burlesque *59*
King of Comedy, The *385*, 436
King of Jazz, The *17*, 120
King of Kings, The (1927) 53, 216, 229; (1960) 224, 229, 241, 260
King of Marvin Gardens, The 368
King of New York, The 436
King Rat 317
Kings Go Forth 213
King Solomon's Mines 56, *156*, 157, 162, 164, 165, 166, 199
Kings Row 97, 103
King's Thief, The 195
Kiss Before Dying, A 197
Kiss Before the Mirror, The 39
Kiss Me Kate 159, 179
Kiss Me, Stupid 256, 260, 265
Kiss of Death 134
Kiss of the Spider Woman 404
Kiss Them For Me 203, 204
Kitty Foyle 88, 93
Klansman, The 393
Klute *302*, 307, 334, 347, 360
Knack . . . and How to Get It, The 260
Knife in the Water 261
Knight Without Armour 81, 411
Knock on Any Door 146
Knock on Wood 185
Kon-Tiki 160
Korea Patrol 111
Kotch 318
Kramer vs Kramer *360*, 362, 366, 367, 371, 380, 389
Krays, The 436

La Bamba 425
La Boheme 58
Labyrinth 417
Ladies Must Dress 18
Ladies of Leisure 31
Lady and the Tramp 189, 193, 198, 269
Lady Caroline Lamb 319
Lady Eve, The 42, *93*
Lady from Shanghai, The *141*
Lady Hamilton: *see* That Hamilton Woman
Lady in Question 92
Lady in the Dark 117, 122
Lady in the Lake, The 137
Lady Is Willing, The 51
Ladykillers, The 260
Lady L 322
Lady's Morals, A 47
Lady Vanishes, The 76, 83, 267, 308, 362
Lady With a Past 38
Lafayette Escadrille 213
La Luna 359
Lamp Still Burns, The 106
Landlord, The 325, 379
Lassie Come Home 118
Last American Hero, The 332
Last Command, The 25
Last Days of Dolwyn, The 254
Last Days of Pompeii 220
Last Detail, The 318, 323, 328, 329, 332
Last Emperor, The *355*, *417*, 419, 422
Last Flight, The *24*
Last Laugh, The 16
Last Mile, The 50
Last of Mrs. Cheyney, The 153
Last Picture Show, The *305*, 307, 310, 315, 317, 324, 325, 402
La Strada 371
Last Starfighter, The 374, *374*
Last Tango in Paris 310, 319, 332
Last Temptation of Christ, The 420, 422
Last Time I Saw Paris, The 195, 316
Last Tycoon, The 335, 412
Last Valley, The 305
Late Extra 393
Late Show, The 360
Laugh, Clown, Laugh 36
Laughter 18
Laughter in Paradise 164, 177
Laura *117*, 140
Lavender Hill Mob, The 163, 177, 420
Lawless, The 213
Lawless Breed, The 182
Lawrence of Arabia *6*, 227, *228*, 229, *240*, *243*, 245, 248, 257, 258, 262, 265, 269, 297
League of Gentlemen, The 227
Leathernecking 63
Leave Her to Heaven 122, 131, 167
Left-Handed Gun, The 246
Legend 407
Legend of the Lost 234
Le Jour Se Leve 270
Lenny *325*, 332, 380
Leopard, The 248
Les Girls *207*, 208
Les Miserables *50*, 54
Let George Do It! 88
Let It Be 173
Let the Good Times Roll 173
Lethal Weapon 412, *413*, 417, 421
Lethal Weapon 2 431
Letter, The 34, 95, 270
Letter from an Unknown Woman 318
Letter to Three Wives, A *145*, 153
Libeled Lady 62, 68
Licence to Kill 431
Lieutenant Wore Skirts, The 182, 190
Life and Death of Colonel Blimp, The 144, 199, 223
Life and Times of Judge Roy Bean, The 330
Life of Christ, The 331
Life of Emile Zola, The 66, 68, 73
Life with Father 137
Lili 211
Lilies of the Field 252
Liliom (1930) 195; (1934) 195
Lilith 323
Limelight *171*, 310
Lion Has Wings, The 83
Lion in Winter, The 282, 286, 355, 373, 414, 438
Lisztomania 427
Little Annie Rooney 11
Little Big Man *297*, 301, 305
Little Caesar *21*, 26, 27, 32, 70, 93
Little Foxes, The *95*, 96, 320, 370, 431
Little Girl Who Lives Down The Lane, The 337
Little Kidnappers, The: *see* Kidnappers, The
Little Lord Fauntleroy 11, 54
Little Man, What Now? 47
Little Miss Marker 68
Little Murder 314
Little Night Music, A 338
Littlest Rebel, The 54, 63
Little Women (1933) 39, 41, 61; (1949) 151, 157
Live and Let Die 308, 316, 319, 414
Lives of a Bengal Lancer *51*, 54, 94
Living Daylights 414, 417
Living It Up 182
Lloyds of London 101
Locked Door, The 31
Locket, The 170
Lodger, The (1927) 12; (1944) *113*
Logan's Run 374
Lolita 237, *238*, 260, 278
London Town 207
Lone Ranger, The 195
Loneliness of the Long Distance Runner 247
Lonely Are the Brave 280
Lonesome 12
Long and the Short and the Tall, The 241, 245, 264, 277
Long Day's Journey into Night 282, 389, 421
Longest Day, The *110*, 111, 236, *236*, 248, 345
Long Goodbye, The *314*, 345
Long Gray Line, The 189, 191
Long Hot Summer, The 246, 357
Long Night, The 270
Long Riders, The 380, 436
Look Back in Anger 247, 251, 254, 393
Look Who's Talking 431, 437
Look Who's Talking Too 439
Looking for Mr. Goodbar 345, 362
Lord Jim *258*
Lords of Flatbush, The 339
Lost Boys, The 434
Lost Horizon 68, *69*
Lost Patrol, The 63
Lost Weekend, The *120*, 127, 132, 222, 245
Lost World, The 36
Love 53
Love Affair 270
Love and Death 345
Love Bug, The 287, 291
Love Finds Andy Hardy 75
Love Is a Many-Splendored Thing 356
Love Laughs at Andy Hardy 144
Love Me or Leave Me 189
Love Me Tender 173, 208
Love Me Tonight 29
Love on the Dole 96
Love Parade, The 14, *28*, 29
Lover Come Back 266
Loves of Carmen, The 188
Love Story *296*, 305, 329, 333
Love with the Proper Stranger 268
Loving You 173, 207
Lt. Robin Crusoe, U.S.N. 268
Lucky Lady 349
Lucky Me 178, 217
Lust for Life 203, 257, 318
Lusty Men, The 170, 216
Luv 300, 301, 348

Macao 170
Macbeth 403
Mad Max *359*, 412, 415
Mad Max 2 412
Mad Max Beyond the Thunderdome 412
Mad Miss Manton, The 42
Madame Bovary 164
Madame Curie 107, 117
Madonna of the Seven Moons 122

Magic Box, The 165, 211
Magnificent Ambersons, The 98, 209, 361, 403
Magnificent Obsession 168, 182, 185, 266, 403
Magnificent Seven, The 226, 234, 247, 268, *270*, 272, 275, 281, 374
Magnum Force 325
Major and the Minor, The 120, 222
Major Barbara 96
Major Dundee 272, 277, 292, 316
Make Way for Tomorrow 67
Making Mr. Right 436
Male and Female 53, 384
Malta Story 179
Maltese Falcon, The 96, 165, 202, 270, 322
Man Called Peter, A 189
Manchurian Candidate, The *241*, *298*, 299
Mandalay 45
Mandy 171
Man for All Seasons, A *269*, 272, 273, 276, 293, 316, 347
Man from Montana, The 83
Man from Snowy River, The 359, 415
Manhandled 27
Manhattan *357*, 389
Manhattan Melodrama 46
Manhunter 438
Man I Killed, The 73
Man in Grey, The 108
Man in the Glass Booth, The 330
Man in the Iron Mask, The 219
Man of a Thousand Faces 205
Man of Iron 378
Manpower *94*
Man's Castle 41
Man's Castle, A 114
Man's Fate *(abandoned project)* 297, 316
Man's Genesis 87
Man Who Came Back, The 23
Man Who Fell to Earth, The 334, 344
Man Who Knew Too Much, The 52, 270
Man Who Loved Women, The (1977) 417; (1987) 417
Man Who Never Was, The 253
Man Who Played God, The 34, 72
Man Who Shot Liberty Valance, The 263
Man Who Would Be King, The 332
Man With the Golden Arm, The 193, 195, 198, 207, 219
Man with the Golden Gun, The 332
Man With the Gun 217
Man With Two Brains, The 429
Marathon Man *338*, 351, 360
March of Time (series) 61, 133
Mardi Gras 208
Maria's Lovers 402
Marie Antoinette *74*
Mark of Zorro, The (1920) 56, *57*; (1940) 56, 95, 212
Marlowe 287
Marnie *255*, 256, 414, 422
Married to the Mob 421, 430
Marty *189*, 193, 195
Mary of Scotland 63
Mary Poppins 254, 255, 258, 259, 263, 269, 294, 325, 329
Mary, Queen of Scots 305, 414
M*A*S*H 292, 295, 296, 300, 302, 304, 314
Mask *399*, 408
Mask of Fu Manchu 32
Masque of the Red Death 363
Matchmaker, The *211*
Matter of Life and Death, A 137, 223, 233
Maytime *64*, 68
Maytime in Mayfair 151, 153
McCabe and Mrs Miller *300*, 301, 304, 314
Mean Streets 320, 334, 338, 340, 366, 436
Meatballs 392
Meet John Doe 94
Meet Me in St. Louis *117*, 122, 159, 165, 288, 322
Meet Sexton Blake 192
Melody for Two 175
Melvin and Howard 369
Memphis Belle 130
Men, The 111, *155*, 162, 167, 184, 186, 349
Menace on the Moutain 337
Me, Natalie 309
Mephisto 378
Merrily We Live 42, *72*
Merry Widow, The 14, 15, 29, 48, 58
Merry-Go-Round 15
Metropolis 200
Mexican Spitfire (series) 116
Mickey One 274, 328, 372
Midnight 42, 78, *79*, 222
Midnight Angel: *see* Pacific Blackout
Midnight Cowboy 291, 292, 296, 302, 319, 380
Midnight Express 368, 408, 412, 422
Midsummer Night's Dream, A *54*, 61, 63, 151
Midway 338
Mikey and Micky 415
Mildred Pierce 123, 127, 131
Millionairess, The 234
Min and Bill 20, *21*, 26, 38, 42
Ministry of Fear, The 120
Miniver Story, The 363
Miracle Man, The 19
Miracle of Morgan's Creek, The 111, 117
Miracle on 34th Street *134*, 140
Miracle Rider, The 89
Miracle Worker, The 276
Mirage 280
Misery 439
Misfits, The *230*, 239, 266
Miss Bluebeard 14
Missing *298*, 299, 377
Missing in Action 396
Mission, The 398, *409*
Mission to Moscow 111
Mississippi Burning *422*
Missouri Breaks, The 412
Mr. and Mrs. Smith 93
Mr. Belvedere Goes to College 151
Mr. Deeds Goes to Town *42*, 59, 63, 65, 66, 94
Mr. Emmanuel 192
Mister Johnson 439
Mr. Mom 388
Mister Roberts 190, 193, 195, 289, 378
Mr. Smith Goes to Washington *83*
Mrs. Miniver 100, 103, 105, 115, 370
Mrs. Soffel 412
Moby Dick *197*, 198, 351, 426
Modern Hero, A 47
Modern Times 89
Mogambo *179*, 184, 188
Mommie Dearest 373
Monkey Business (1931) 41
Monkey Business (1952) 171
Monkey on My Back 189
Monsieur Beaucaire 14
Monsieur Verdoux *133*, 171
Monster That Challenged the World, The 200
Monte Carlo Baby 177
Monterey Pop 173
Monty Python and the Holy Grail 420
Monty Python's Life of Brian 366
Monty Python's The Meaning of Life 420
Moon and Sixpence, The 148
Moon Is Blue, The 176, 183, 185, 193, 198, 219, 350
Moon Is Down, The 111
Moon over Miami 401
Moon's Our Home, The 59
Moonraker 360
Moonstruck 419, 422
More the Merrier, The 111, 112
Morgan (A Suitable Case for Treatment) *264*, 273, 371
Morning Glory *39*, 44, 355, 373
Morocco 22
Mortal Storm, The 97
Moscow on the Hudson 428
Mother Machree 79
Moulin Rouge *170*, 179
Mountain, The 197
Mountains of the Moon 439
Mourning Becomes Electra 141
Move Over, Darling 247, 287
Muppet Movie, The 360
Murder at Monte Carlo 76
Murder by Death 338
Murder by Decree 353
Murder, My Sweet *118*
Murder on the Orient Express 324, 329, 332
Music Box, The 35
Music Man, The 159, 241, 395
Musketeers of Pig Alley, The 70
Mutiny on the Bounty (1935) 55, 58, 63, 69, 152, 230, *270*; (1962) *241*, 243, 248, *270*, 277, 348
My Beautiful Laundrette 418
My Best Girl 11, 15
My Blue Heaven 208
My Brother Jonathan 144
My Darling Clementine 131
My Fair Lady 211, 236, 247, *254*, 255, 258, 259, 263, 268, 276, 427, 432
My Favorite Blonde 103
My Friend Irma 149, 265, 385
My Friend Irma Goes West 149
My Gal Sal 103
My Left Foot 432
My Little Chickadee *85*
My Man Godfrey 42, *43*, 60, 68, 72, 98
Myra Breckinridge 293
My Sister Eileen 225, 331
My Son John 163
Mystery of the Wax Museum 175
Mystic Pizza 432
My Weakness 45

Naked City, The 140, *141*
Naked Civil Servant, The 367
Naked Edge, The 232
Naked Gun, The 431
Napoleon *229*, 242, 400
Napoleon and Samantha 337
Narrow Margin 270
Nashville *331*
National Lampoon's Animal House 353, 377, 392
National Lampoon's Vacation 401
National Velvet 118, 127, 246, 306
Natural, The 402, 416
Naughty Marietta 29, 64
Navigator, The 265
Neptune's Daughter 151
Network 339, 342, 350, 373
Never Give a Sucker an Even Break 130
Never Love a Stranger 268
Never Say Never Again 388, 394, 414
Never So Few 221
New Frontier 108
New Leaf, A 300, *301*, 415
New Moon 47
New York Confidential 276
New York, New York 338
New York Stories *426*
Next Stop, Greenwich Village 349
Niagara *174*
Nicholas and Alexandra 310
Nickelodeon 335
Night After Night 34, 40
Night and Day *129*
Night at the Opera, A 54, *55*
Night Heaven Fell, The *210*
Nightmare Alley 212
Nightmare on Elm Street, A 383, 394
Night Moves 422
Night Must Fall 279
Night Nurse 24
Night of the Hunter 190, 237, 240
Night of the Iguana, The 254
Nights of Cabiria, The 286
Night to Remember, A 212
9 ½ Weeks 416
Nine Lives Are Not Enough 97
Nineteen Eighty-Four 393
1900 417
1941 *361*, 370, 387
9 to 5 372
Ninotchka 42, *82*, 88, 97, 222, 433
Noah's Ark *10*
None But the Lonely Heart 118
No, No, Nanette 150
Norma Rae *357*, 362
North by Northwest *218*, 221, 409
North Dallas Forty 380
North Star, The 111
Northwest Mounted Police 88
North West Passage 88, 221
Not as a Stranger 193, 194
Nothing Sacred *42*, 69, 98
No Time for Sergeants 212
Notorious 131, 132
No Way Out (1950) 154, 227; (1987) 427, 437
No Way to Treat a Lady 317
Now, Voyager 103, 108, 431
Nun's Story, The *219*, 221, 395
Nuts in May 35

Objective Burma *119*
Ocean's Eleven 227, 265
Octopussy 388
Odd Couple, The *280*, 283
Odd Man Out 137, 155, 164, 393
Odette 157
Oedipus the King 302
Officer and a Gentleman, An *379*, 381, 384, 388, 407
Of Human Bondage 45, 51, 72
Of Mice and Men *84*
Oh, God! *342*
Oh, Mr Porter! 77
Oh! What a Lovely War 291, 345
Oklahoma! 159, *193*, 194
Old Acquaintance 108
Old Dark House, The *32*, 39
Old Gringo 426
Old Homestead, The 119
Old Maid, The 83
Old Yeller 212
Oliver Twist 144, 149, 155, 196, 245, 296
Oliver! 286, 291, 296
Omen, The *336*, 338, 346
On a Clear Day You Can See Forever 310
Once Upon a Time in the West 378
One Crazy Summer 425
One-Eyed Jacks *231*
One Flew over the Cuckoo's Nest *332*, 336, 338, 356, 370, 388, 391, 395, 416
One from the Heart 368, *377*, 384, 385, 402, 433
One Hour With You 29, *31*, 34
One Hundred and One Dalmatians 231, 234, 269, 403
One Hundred Men and a Girl *68*, 77
One in a Million 77
One Million Years B.C. 87, 142, 150, *275*
One Minute to Zero 170
One Night in the Tropics 92
One Night of Love *47*, 48
One of Our Aircraft Is Missing 103
One Spy Too Many 268
One Sunday Afternoon 92
One Touch of Venus 163
One Way Passage 33
One Wild Moment 417
One Wild Oat 177
On Golden Pond *354*, 355, 373, 376, 381
On Her Majesty's Secret Service *290*, 296, 414
Only Angels Have Wings 92
Only Two Can Play 241
Only Yesterday 74
On Moonlight Bay 178
On the Avenue 29, *64*
On the Beach 200, 212, *221*, 227, 325
On the Buses 305
On the Town 146, *150*, 159, 165, 166, 322
On the Waterfront *183*, 184, 186, *187*, 189, 218, 231, 357, 366
Operation Cicero 164
Operation Crossbow 263, 266
Operation Mad Ball 225, 331
Operation Petticoat 227, 387
Ordinary People *367*, 369, 402
Orphans of the Storm 24
Othello 311, 403
Our Daily Bread 47
Our Dancing Daughter 35
Our Hospitality 265
Our Man Flint 268, 272
Our Man in Havana *223*
Our Modern Maidens 35
Outland 270, 374
Outlaw Josey Wales, The 338
Outlaw, The *104*, 132, 145
Out of Africa 402, 404, 409
Outrage, The 270
Outsiders, The *384*, 385, 392, 393, *425*
Outward Bound 20, 21
Out West with the Hardys 75, 77
Owl and the Pussycat, The 305, 310, 317
Ox-Bow Incident, The *106*
Oxford Blues 398

Pacific Blackout 97
Pack Up Your Troubles 35
Paint Your Wagon 282, 289, 296
Painted Desert, The 24
Painted Veil, The 49
Pajama Game, The 159, *204*, 286, 307
Paleface, The *145*, 151
Pal Joey 166, 207
Palm Beach Story, The 42, *43*
Palmy Days 26
Pandora and the Flying Dutchman 184
Pandora's Box 17
Panic in Needle Park 309
Panic in the Streets 198, 343
Paper Chase, The 318, 321
Paper Moon *317*, 319, 320, 321, 333
Papillon 319, 325, 332
Paradise Alley 359
Parallax View, The *298*, 299, 333, 334
Paramount on Parade 17, 19
Paratrooper: *see* Red Beret, The
Parent Trap, The 234
Parenthood *429*
Paris Bound 31
Paris, Texas 402, 421
Parrish 231, 235
Party at Kitty and Studs 359
Passage to India, A *395*, 398, 403, 404
Passion 73
Passport to Pimlico 150, 163
Pat and Mike 274
Patch of Blue, A 264, 268
Pat Garrett and Billy the Kid 316, 342
Paths of Glory *111*, *206*, 208, 216, 278
Patton *243*, *293*, 296, 301, 315, 345, 355
Peeping Tom *223*
Pee-wee's Big Adventure 419, 428
Peggy Sue Got Married *407*, 419
Penalty, The 19
Pennies from Heaven 429
Penny Arcade 37

People against O'Hara, The 185
Pepe Le Moko 75
Percy 305
Perfect Crime, The 60
Perfect Strangers 122, 211
Performance 363
Pete Kelly's Blues 184
Peter and Pavla 336
Peter Pan 179
Pete's Dragon 360
Petrified Forest, The 58, *70*, 202
Petulia 321
Peyton Place *209*, 212
Phantom of the Opera 19, 175, 205
Phantom of the Paradise 337, 340, 363
Phantom President, The 34
Phfft! 225
Philadelphia Story, The 93, 96, 98, 196, 270, 409
Piccadilly Incident 131
Pickpocket 362
Pickup on South Street 227
Picnic 198, 207, 350
Picnic at Hanging Rock 439
Pigskin Parade 66
Pilgrimage 63
Pillow Talk 220, 266, 403
Pimpernel Smith 96, 106
Pink Flamingoes 369
Pink Panther, The *252*, 260, 308, 331
Pink Panther Strikes Again, The 346
Pinky 151, 154, 166
Pinocchio 88, 162, 231, 269
Pin to See the Peepshow, A 195
Pin Up Girl 114
Pirate, The 56, 166, 338
Pirates 56, *57*
Pit and the Pendulum, The *233*
Place in the Sun, A *163*, 164, 167, 179, 186, 237, 246, 266, 306
Places in the Heart 395, 398, 436
Plainsman, The *63*, 94, 257
Planet of the Apes 200, *279*, 283, 293, 383
Planter's Wife, The 171
Platinum Blonde 26
Platoon 408, 413, 417, 422, 425, 431
Players 391
Play it Again, Sam 345, 347
Playmates 100
Play Misty for Me 315
Please Don't Eat the Daisies 227
Pleasure Mad 44
Plough and the Stars, The 63, 169
Pockerful of Miracles 303
Point Blank *277*
Police Academy *391*, 394
Police Academy 2: Their First Assignment 403
Police Academy 3: Back in Training 409
Police Academy 4: Citizens on Patrol 417
Pollyanna 11, 234
Poltergeist *378*, 381
Polyester *369*
Pool Shark 48
Poor Cow 283
Poor Jake's Demise 19
Pope of Greenwich Village, The 390
Popeye 365
Porky's *373*, 381
Portnoy's Complaint 359
Port of New York 203, 226
Poseidon Adventure, The *311*, 319, 325
Possessed 24, 35
Postman Always Rings Twice, The (1946) *126*, 169, 186; (1981) 368, 369, 413
Predator 374, 414, 417, 421, 433
President's Lady 216
Prestige 31
Pretty Ladies 35
Pretty Woman *432*, 434, 437, 439
Pride and the Passion, The 207, 234
Pride of the Marines *121*
Pride of the Yankees *101*
Prime of Miss Jean Brodie, The *287*, 292, 311
Prince and the Showgirl, The *205*, 338
Prince of the City 434
Princess O'Rourke 107
Prince Valiant 197
Prince Who Was a Thief, The 213
Prisoner of Second Avenue, The 339
Prisoner of Shark Island, The 59
Prisoner of Zenda, The (1913) 56; (1922) 56 (1937) 69, 77, 233; (1952) 156, 199, 393
Private Benjamin 366, 372
Private Life of Don Juan, The 63
Private Life of Henry VIII, The 40, 44, 63, 174, 211
Private Life of Sherlock Holmes, The 353
Private's Progress 198, 248
Private Worlds 54
Prix de Beaute 17
Prizzi's Honor 404, 407, 438
Prodigal, The 195
Prodigal Father, The 438
Producers, The *279*, 320, 321, 343
Professionals, The 276
Professional Sweetheart 60
Professor Beware 133
Prom Night 387
Providence 371
Psycho 223, *224*, 227, 244, 330, 332, 348, 362, 365, 387
PT 109 244
Public Enemy, The 23, 26, 32, 37, 70, *71*, 149, 405
Pumping Iron 376, 414
Pumpkin Eater, The 276
Purple Mask, The 213
Pushover 207
Puss Gets the Boot 177
Putting Pants on Philip 35
Pygmalion 76, 83

Quadrophenia 173, 360
Quartet (1949) 168; (1981) 404
Quasimodo 27
Queen Christina *41*, 48, 433
Queen Is Crowned, A 179
Queen Kelly 14, 384
Quick Millions *23*, 70
Quiet Man, The 169, *169*, 171, 174, 319
Quiller Memorandum, The 269, 317
Quo Vadis (1912) 229; (1951) 156, *164*, 168, 171, 177, 179, 199, 229

Rachel and the Stranger 170
Radio Revue of 1930, The 19
Raffles 387
Raging Bull 340, *366*, 369, 408, 436
Ragtime 395, 405
Raiders of the Lost Ark *370*, 372, 378, 383, 392, 401, 403
Railway Children, The 305
Rain 35, 205
Rainmaker, The 207
Rain Man 284, *423*, 424, 426, 431
Rain People, The 306
Rains Came, The 83
Raintree County 205, 212, 218
Raise the Titanic 364, 373, 410
Raising a Riot 193
Raising Arizona 419
Rambo: First Blood Part II 400, 403, 407
Rambo III 410
Ran 400
Random Harvest *103*, 108
Rashomon 270
Rawhide 216
Razor's Edge, The (1947) *130*, 132, 137; (1984) 392
Reach for the Sky 198
Reaching for the Moon 29
Reap the Wild Wind *99*, 103, 216
Rear Window 183, 185, 188, 380
Rebecca *84*, 88, 93, 260
Rebel Without a Cause 178, 186, *192*, 195, 239, 289, 372
Reckless 53
Red and Blue 273
Red Badge of Courage, The 191
Red Ball Express 181
Red Beret, The 179
Red Danube, The 151
Red Dawn *393*, 408
Red Desert, The 277
Red Dust 35, 168, 179
Red Garters 180
Red-Headed Woman *33*, 75
Red Menace, The 151
Red Planet Mars 200
Red Pony, The 325
Red River *142*, 144, 148, 151, 179, 186, 217, 266, 293
Reds *372*, 376, 388, 435
Red Shoes, The 144, *145*, 165, 223
Redskin 22
Reflections in a Golden Eye 266, 279
Reivers, The 296
Reluctant Heroes 171
Rembrandt 63
Reno Brothers, The: *see* Love Me Tender
Repo Man 398, 425
Report to the Commissioner 362
Repulsion *261*, 281
Rescuers, The 353
Return of Frank James *87*, 117
Return of the Jedi 374, *386*, 388, 401, 402, 415
Return of the Pink Panther, The 332, 338
Reuben, Reuben 398
Revenge of the Creature 282
Revenge of the Pink Panther 353
Reversal of Fortune 439
Revolution 398, *402*, 409
Rhapsody in Blue 120, 129
Richard III 389
Ride Lonesome 272
Riders of Destiny 79
Ride the High Country 292
Right Stuff, The 418, 436
Rio Bravo *217*, 221, 265, 293
Rio Lobo 293, 363
Rio Rita 14, 26
Riptide *44*, 48
Risky Business 407
River Niger, The 379
River, The 395, 412
Road Games 387
Road House 167
Road to Bali 179
Road to Hong Kong 241
Road to Rio 144, 145
Road to Singapore *85*, 88
Road to Utopia 122, 131
Road to Zanzibar 96
Roaring Twenties, The 70
Robe, The *178*, 179, 180, 185, 192, *228*, 229, 242, *243*, 254
Roberta 60, 63, 162
Robin and Marian *335*, 414
Robin and the Seven Hoods 265
Robin Hood (1922) 56; (1974) 325
Robin Hood of Eldorado 59
RoboCop *374*, 396, 417
RoboCop 2 396, 434
Rock Around the Clock *173*
Rock, Rock, Rock 173
Rocky 339, 342, 346, 350, 359, 383
Rocky II 360
Rocky III 381
Rocky IV 403, 409, 411
Rollerball 338
Roman Holiday *177*, 180, 183, 279, 370
Roman Scandals 41
Romancing the Stone 391, 394, 400, 407, 416
Roman Spring of Mrs. Stone, The 235, 328, 372
Romeo and Juliet (1936) 61, 74; (1969) 291
Room at the Top *217*, 221, 222, 241, *251*, 321
Room with a View, A *404*, 418
Rosalie 169
Rose, The 361, 373
Rose Marie 63, 64
Rosemary's Baby *281*, 283, 286, 288, 318, 320
Rose Tattoo, The 195
Rosita 73
Rough Riders (series) 103
Roustabout 275
Roxanne 429
Roxie Hart 99, 181
Royal Flash 335
Royal Scandal, A 137
Royal Wedding 161
Ruggles of Red Gap 51
Rumble Fish 384, 419
Running on Empty 429
Russians Are Coming! The Russians Are Coming!, The 268, 295
Russia House, The 439
Ruthless People 409
Ryan's Daughter *242*, 243, *297*, 301, 305, 310, 394

Safrina 350
Sadie Thompson 27
Safety Last 20
Sailor Beware 171
Sailor from Gibraltar, The 273
Sailor Who Fell from Grace with the Sea, The 342
St Elmo's Fire 424, *425*, 434
Saint Joan 204, 227
Saint Strikes Back, The 101
Salt and Pepper 336
Salvador 408
Salvation Hunters, The 25
Samson and Delilah 150, 164
Sand Pebbles, The *268*
Sandpiper, The 263
Sands of Iwo Jima 111, 148, 157
San Francisco *60*, 63, 68, 74, 274
Santa Claus The Movie 403, 409
Santa Fe Trail 88
Sapphire 235
Saratoga 67, 68
Satan Met a Lady 96
Satisfaction 432
Saturday Island 213
Saturday Night and Sunday Morning *226*, 234, 245, *250*, 251, 279, 371
Saturday Night Fever 159, *172*, 173, 346, 351, 353, 371, 407
Save the Tiger *315*, 318, 321
Sayonara *206*, 208, 212, 289
Scalphunters, The 291
Scaramouche (1923) 56, 156; (1952) *57*, 168, 174
Scarface (1932) 32, 66, 70, 71; (1983) 430
Scarlet Empress, The 49, 290
Scarlet Pimpernel, The 51
Scenes from a Marriage 343
School for Scoundrels 248
Scott of the Antarctic 151
Sea Chase, The 193, 194
Sea Hawk, The 56, *57*, 221
Sea Hunt 402
Seal Island 155
Sea of Love *430*
Search, The 142, 179, 266
Searchers, The *194*, 196, 198, 239, 270, 319
Search for Paradise 212
Seconds 266, 299, 403
Secret Agent 63, 373
Secret Ceremony 320
Secret Life of Walter Mitty, The *135*, 151
Secret of My Success, The 417
Secret People 177
Secrets 37
Seduction of Joe Tynan, The 371, 389
See Here, Private Hargrove 163
Semi-Tough 342, 349
Send Me No Flowers 266, 403
Separate Tables 216, 233, 387
Sergeant York *94*, 95, 96, 97, 98, 103, *110*, 111, 232
Serious Money 438
Serpico 325, 395
Servant, The *249*, 272, 296, 303
Service for Ladies 51
Set-Up, The 366
Seven Brides for Seven Brothers *159*, *182*, 193, 322
Seven Days in May 318
Seven Faces 66
Seven Samurai, The 270, *271*, 400
Seventh Cross, The 111, *114*
Seventh Heaven *8*,*9*, 15, 23, 25, 44
Seventh Seal, The 259, 269
Seventh Veil, The 122, 134, 164
Seven Wonders of the World, The 207
Seven Year Itch, The 183, *190*, 239, 280
7 Women 276
Sex and Violence in the Cinema Part II 359
Sex, Lies and Videotape 429, 439
Shadow of a Doubt 105
Shag 425
Shaggy Dog, The 221
Shake, Rattle and Roll 173
Shakespeare Wallah 404
Shalako 291
Shall We Dance 68
Shampoo 328, *329*, 332, 350, 372
Shane *175*, 179, 195, 198, 252, 358, 366
Shanghai Express *30*, 34, 290
Shanghai Surprise 435
She 52
She Done Him Wrong *40*, 41
Sheltering Sky, The 436
She Married Her Boss 54
Shenandoah 263
Sheriff of Fractured Jaw, The 221
Sherlock Holmes 62
Sherlock, Jr 11, 265
She's a Sheik 14
She Wore a Yellow Ribbon *148*, 319
Shining, The *365*, 366, 414
Ship of Fools 263
Shiralee, The 207
Shooting Party, The 393
Shoot the Moon 412, 422
Shop at Sly Corner, The 196
Shopworn 34
Shopworn Angel, The 18, 74
Short Circuit 407, 424
Shot in the Dark, A 252, 260, 263, 331
Show Boat (1936) 63; (1951) 162, 164, 165, 184
Show of Shows, The 19
Siesta 430
Sign of the Cross,The 34, 53, 216
Sign of the Pagan 181
Silence of the Lambs, The 438, *438*
Silencers, The 265, 268
Silent Movie 338, 348
Silkwood 299, *389*
Silverado *401*,437
Silver Chalice, The 246
Silver Streak 346
Simon and Laura 207
Sinbad and the Eye of the Tiger 346
Since You Went Away *115*, 146, 163
Sinful Davey 367
Sing As We Go 48
Sing, Baby, Sing 64
Sing, Boy, Sing 208
Singin' in the Rain *158*, 159, 165, 166, *166*, 171, 175, 176, 204, 286, 322, 335

Singing Fool, The 9, 12
Sink the Bismarck! 227
Sinner's Holiday 37
Sin of Harold Diddlebock, The 133
Sin of Madelon Claudet, The 34
Sisters, The 76
Sitting Pretty *140*
Six Bridges to Cross 213
Six of a Kind *44*
Sixteen Candles 398, 425
Sixty Glorious Years 76, 77
Skippy 26
Slap Shot *343*
Slaughter on Tenth Avenue 280
Slaughterhouse Five 332
Sleeper 345
Sleeping Beauty 221, 231
Sleeping with the Enemy 439, *439*
Slender Thread, The 380
Sleuth *311*, 404
Slight Case of Murder, A *72*
Smallest Show on Earth, The 260
Smart Money 27
Smash-Up, The Story of a Woman *132*
Smile 337
Smiles of a Summer Night 338
Smiling Lieutenant, The 26
Smithereens 399
Smokey and the Bandit 346, 349, *349*, 356
Smokey and the Bandit II 366
Smooth Talk 408
Snake Pit, The *147*, 151
Snows of Kilimanjaro, The 171, 216
Snow White and the Seven Dwarfs 68, 77, 94, 162, 231, 263, 269, 319, 372
S.O.B. 376
So Big 237
So Close to Life 269
Sodom and Gomorrah 257
So Ends Our Night 148
Soldier Blue 305
Soldiers Three 164
Solomon and Sheba 212, 221, 226, 227
Somebody Up There Likes Me 186, 195, 246, 268
Some Came Running 221, 233, 265
Some Like It Hot *216*, 221, 222, 224, 239, 281, 310, 409
Someone to Watch over Me 416
Something Wild 436
Something's Got to Give: *see* Move Over Darling
Somewhere I'll Find You 100, 126
Song of Bernadette, The *108*, 112, 117
Song of Love 163
Song of Norway 305
Song of the South 129
Song to Remember, A *119*, 167
Song Without End 249
Son of Flubber 248
Son of Paleface 171
Son of Sinbad 207
Sons and Lovers 290, 421
Sons of Katie Elder, The 289
Sons of the Desert 48
Sophie's Choice 384, 389, 402
So Proudly We Hail 105
Sorcerer 270
So This Is New York 148
Sound and the Fury, The 357
Sound of Music, The *158*, 159, 243, 258, 259, 263, 264, 265, 268, 276, 283, 286, 294, 319, 320, 358, 385, 411
South American George 96
Southern Comfort 380
South Pacific *159*, 193, 208, 212, 233, 289
Sparrows 11
Spartacus 216, *226*, 227, 230, 240, 241, 243, 278, 438
Special Delivery 21
Special Section 377
Spellbound *122*, 131, 260
Spiral Staircase, The *127*, 168
Spirit of St. Louis, The *202*
Spite Marriage 11
Spitfire 47
Splash *390*
Splendor in the Grass 234, 235, 239, 274, 328, 372
Sporting Blood 24
Spring in Park Lane 144, 153
Spy in Black, The 104, 144
Spy Who Came in from the Cold, The *263*, 393
Spy Who Loved Me, The 346
Square Peg, The 221
Squaw Man, The 53, 216
Stagecoach 79, 83, 85, 131, 297, 319
Stage Door 69
Stagedoor Canteen 108
Stage Fright *153*, 308
Stage Struck 27
Stakeout on Dope Street 364
Stalag 17 111, 180, 222, 350
Stand and Deliver 430
Stand-In 69
Stand Up and Cheer 68
Star Chamber, The 299
Star! 286, 294
Stardust 332
Star Is Born, A (1937) *65*, 77, 270, *271*, 342; (1954) 159, 178, *184*, 193, 260, 277, 342, 345, 346; (1976) 337, *342*
Starman 374
Stars and Stripes Forever 197
Star Spangled Rhythm 108
Star Trek – The Motion Picture 360, 361, 366, 374, 410, 417
Star Trek II: The Wrath of Khan 381
Star Trek III: The Search For Spock *383*, 394
Star Trek IV: The Voyage Home 409
Star Trek V: The Final Frontier 383
Star Wars 200, 229, 271, 340, *344*, 346, 348, 353, 358, *364*, 370, *374*, 375, 383, 385, 386, 392, 407, 411, 422, 427, 429
Star Witness, The 32
State Fair 41, 53 (1933); 122 (1945)
State of Siege 299, 377
State of the Union 274
Station Six-Sahara 253
Stay Hungry 356, 376, 414
Staying Alive 388
Stealers, The 44
Steamboat 'Round the Bend 53
Steel Helmet, The 111
Steel Magnolias 432
Steelyard Blues 347
Stella Dallas 67, *67*, 68
Stepfather, The 439
Steptoe and Son 310
Sterile Cuckoo, The 308
Sting, The 318, *319*, 321, 325, 329, 330,334, 343, 437
Stir Crazy 372
Story of Alexander Graham Bell, The 107, 401
Story of Dr. Wassell, The 117
Story of Esther Costello, The 207
Story of GI Joe, The *121*
Story of Louis Pasteur, The 65, 66, 107
Story of Three Loves, The 168
Story of Vernon and Irene Castle, The 147, 162
Stowaway 64
Straight Time 412
Stranded in Paris 14
Strange Bedfellows 266
Strange Cargo 88
Strange Love of Martha Ivers, The 126
Strangers on a Train 163, 362, 429
Strategic Air Command 193
Stratton Story, The 151, 180
Straw Dogs, 300, 304, 306, 396, *397*
Strawberry Blonde, The 92
Streetcar Named Desire, A *162*, 164, 166, 167, 176, 186, 231, 274, 310
Strike Me Pink 63
Strike Up the Band 88
Stripes 372, 392
Strong Man, The 116
Struggle, The 24
Stud, The 353
Student of Prague, The 104
Student Prince, The 193, 195
Subject Was Roses, The 286
Submarine 11
Sudden Fear 170
Sudden Impact 394
Suddenly 195
Suddenly, Last Summer 227, 246, 266
Sugarland Express, The 322, 403
Summer City 412
Summer Holiday 248
Summer Madness 245
Summer of '42 305, 334
Summer Stock 181, 184
Summertime 282
Summer Wishes, Winter Dreams 425
Sun Also Rises, The 212
Sunday Bloody Sunday 395, 418
Sunday in New York 281
Sundowners, The 234
Sunny Side Up *15*, 20
Sunrise 10
Sunset 421
Sunset Blvd 6, 7, *152*, 184, 222, 238, 335, 350, 384, 401
Sunshine Boys, The 342
Superman *352*, 360, 374, 383, 410, 411, 413
Superman II 372
Superman III 383, 388
Superman IV: The Quest for Peace *383*, 417
Suppose They Gave a War and Nobody Came? 401
Susan and God 92
Susan Lennox: Her Fall and Rise 24
Susan Slept Here 204
Suspicion 98, 409
Svengali 23
Swanee River 401
Swarm, The 350, *350*
Swashbuckler 56
Sweet Adeline 63
Sweet Charity *286*, 294, 307
Sweethearts 169
Sweet Rosie O'Grady 117
Swimmer, The 318
Swingin' on a Rainbow 116
Swing Shift Maisie 111
Swing Time 29, 60, 63
Swiss Family Robinson 234
Sword in the Desert 181
Swordsman, The 160
Sybil 356
Symphony of Six Million 49

Take Me Out to the Ball Game *146*, 150
Take the Money and Run 318, 357
Taking of Pelham One Two Three, The 330
Taking Off 336, 395
Tale of Two Cities, A (1935) 55, 63, 296; (1958) 249
Tales of Beatrix Potter 305
Tall Story 281
Tamarind Seed, The *331*
Taming of the Shrew, The (1929) 15; (1967) *273*, 276
Tammy and the Bachelor 204
Taps 407
Tarantula 282
Targets 305
Tarzan and the Mermaids 390
Tarzan, the Ape Man *30*, 34, 383, 390
Taste of Honey, A 247, *250*, 251
Taxi Driver 334, 336, 337, 338, 340, *341*, 362, 366, 396, *397*, 408, 423
Taza, Son of Cochise 181
Tea for Two 178
Teacher's Pet 291
Teahouse of the August Moon, The 207
Teen Wolf 409
Teenage Mutant Ninja Turtles 432
Tell Them Willie Boy Is Here 297, 366
Ten Commandments, The (1923) 10, 22, 53, 216, 229; (1956) *199*, 203, 207, 212, 216, 226, 229, 244
Tender Comrade *109*, 111
Tender Mercies 391
Tender Trap, The 194, 204
10 Rillington Place 367
Teresa 160
Term of Trial 296
Terminator, The 374, 406
Terms of Endearment *354*, *388*, 391, 394
Terrible Joe Moran 405
Terror Train 387
Tess 372, 402
Test Pilot *73*, 77
Texas Chainsaw Massacre, The 378
That Certain Feeling 218
That Certain Thing 11
That Cold Day in the Park 304
That Darn Cat 268
That Hamilton Woman 92, 96, 111
That'll Be the Day 319
That Midnight Kiss 161
That's Entertainment! 159, *322*
That's My Boy 164
That Touch of Mink 241
Them! *200*
Theodora Goes Wild 63
There's a Girl in My Soup 305
There's Always Tomorrow 55
There's No Business Like Show Business 208
There's One Born Every Minute 118
These Three 61
They All Laughed 434
They Had to See Paris 53
They Live By Night 318
They Might Be Giants 353, 395
They Shoot Horses, Don't They? 291, 292, 380
They Were Expendable *110*, 123
They Were Sisters 122
They Won't Forget 67, 126
Thief, The 171, 180
Thief of Bagdad, The (1924) *56*, 410; (1940) 56, *88*, 104
Thieves Like Us 365
Things [from Another World], The *161*, 200
Things To Come 63
Thin Ice 77
Thin Man, The 42, *46*, 48, 62
Third Man, The 151, *152*, 223, 403
39 Steps, The *52*, 81, 211, 221, 267, 308, 395
Thirty Seconds over Tokyo 117
This Could Be the Night 204
This Day and Age 53
This Gun for Hire *99*
This Happy Breed 117, 155
This Is Cinerama *171*, 178
This Is Elvis 173
This Is the Army 117, 121, 185
This Is the Navy 108
This Lane Is Mine 111
This Property Is Condemned 291
This Sporting Life *245*, *251*, 277, 283
Thomas Crown Affair, The *280*
Thoroughly Modern Millie 276, 283
Those Magnificent Men in Their Flying Machines 268, 296
Thousand Clowns, A 264
Thousands Cheer 109, 117
Three Coins in the Fountain *183*, 185
Three Comrades *74*
Three Days of the Condor *299*, *333*
Three Faces of Eve, The 208
Three Fugitives 270
300 Spartans, The 389
3 into 2 Won't Go 395
Three Little Pigs, The 39
Three Little Words 204
Three Men and a Baby 270, *417*, 422
Three Men and a Cradle 417
Three Mesquiteers 79
Three Musketeers, The (1921) 56; (1948) 144; (1974) *321*, 325, 335
Three Sisters, The 311
Three Smart Girls 29, 65, 68
Three Smart Girls Grow Up 83
Three Women 363, 365
Thrill of a Romance 122
Thrill of It All, The 247
Through a Glass Darkly 269
Throw Momma from the Train 423, 429
Thunder Bay 178
Thunderball 256, 268, 388, 414
Thunderbolt 25
Thunderbolt and Lightfoot 325, 353
THX-1138 317
Tie Me Up! Tie Me Down! 436
Tiger Bay 236, 317
Tiger Shark 94
Till Death Us Do Part 291
Till The Clouds Roll By 162, 163
Tillie's Punctured Romance 46
Time for Killing, A 348
Time Limit 227, 231
Tin Drum, The 358
Tingler, The 281
Tin Men 423
Tin Star, The 224, 365
Titanic 197
T-Men 141
Toast of New Orleans, The 161, 164
To Be or Not to Be 98
To Catch a Thief 188, 380
To Each His Own 132, 151
To Have and Have Not *116*, 128, 202
To Hell and Back 189, *191*, 193
To Kill a Mockingbird 248, 334, 351, 426
Tom Brown of Culver 212
Tom Jones *247*, 248, 252, 279, 280, 333
Tom, Dick and Harry 181
Tommy *329*, 332
Tomorrow Is Forever 239
Tonight for Sure 385
Tonight or Never 27
Too Late the Hero 305
Too Much, Too Soon 205
Toot, Whistle, Plunk and Boom 189
Tootsie *380*, 384, 388, 392, 402
Top Banana *181*
Top Gun 407, 409, 423, 431, *424*, 434
Top Hat *28*, 29, 54, 60
Top of the Town 65
Topkapi 258
Topper 42, 69
Torn Curtain *267*, 268, 308
Tortilla Flat 146
To Sir, with Love 276, 287
Total Recall 374, 396, 410, 434, *435*, 437
To the Devil a Daughter 402
To the Shores of Tripoli 103
Touch of Class, A 317, 321
Touch of Evil *209*, 244, 403
Touch, The 313
Tout va bien 347
Tovarich 75
Towering Inferno, The *325*, 332, 411, 421
Town Like Alice, A 198
Track of the Cat 213

Trade Winds 116
Trader Horn 10, 20, *22*, 30, 56
Trading Places *387*, 388, 394, 400, 421
Trail of the Lonesome Pine, The 59, 63
Tramp, Tramp, Tramp 116
Trapeze 198, 213, 221
Trash 363
Treasure Island 155, 157, 287
Treasure of the Sierra Madre, The *140*, 146, 202, 438
Tree Grows in Brooklyn, A *119*, 127
Trial! 188
Trial, The 403
Trial of Billy Jack, The 325
Trial of the Catonsville Nine, The 426
Tribute 373
Trio 168
Trip, The 289
Trip to Bountiful, The 404
Trip to the Moon 200
Tron 374, 379
Tropic of Cancer 324
Trouble in Paradise *34*
Trouble in Store 185
Trouble with Harry, The 233, 388
True Confession 42, 69
True Grit 289, 291, 292, 293
Tugboat Annie 38, 42
Tunes of Glory 311
Tunnel of Love, The 227
Tunnelvision 401
Turning Point, The *347*, 349, 358
12 Angry Men *202*, 378
Twelve Chairs, The 320, 321
Twelve O'Clock High 153, 157, 426
Twentieth Century 42, *47*, 51, 60, 98
20,000 Leagues Under the Sea (1907) 200; (1954) 193, 199, 200
20,000 Years in Sing Sing 114
Twilight Zone – The Movie 378, 387, 415
Twinky 336
Twins 423, 431
Two for the Road 279
Two Jakes, The *433*, 434
Two Loves 233
Two Way Stretch 227
Two Weeks – with Love 166, 204
Two Women 234
Two Years Before the Mast 131
Two-Faced Woman 97, 433
2001: A Space Odyssey 6, 7, 200, 229, 243, *278*, 304, 333, 346

Ulysses 229
Unbearable Lightness of Being, The *418*
Unconquered 137
Undertow 182
Underwater! 203
Under Western Stars 119
Undertow 182
Underworld 70
Unfaithful, The 270
Unforgiven, The *222*, 297
Unholy Three, The 19
Unmarried Woman, An 349, *349*, 359
Untouchables, The *70*, 414, 417, 419, 427, 437
Up Front 190
Up in Arms 113
Up Pompeii 305
Up the Academy 392
Up the Junction 283
Up the River 114
Urban Cowboy 379, 388
Used Cars 391

Valerie 270
Valiant, The 66
Valley of Decision 122
Valley of the Dolls 283, 335
Vanishing American, The 22
Variete 16
Vera Cruz 411
Verdict, The 434
Vertigo 207, *210*, 332
Very Special Favor, A 266
Victim *235*, 249
Victoria the Great 68, 76
Victor/Victoria *376*
Videodrome 406
View to a Kill, A 403
Vikings, The *210*, 212, 213
Viktor und Viktoria 376
Violent Saturday 398
V.I.P.s, The 246, 252
Virgin Soldiers, The 291
Virginian, The *14*, 22, 94
Vision Quest 435
Visions of Eight 336
Visitors, The 308
Viva Las Vegas 303
Viva Villa! 41, 45
Viva Zapata! 186, 257
Von Ryan's Express 263

W.C. Fields and Me 332
Wages of Fear, The 270
Wait Until Dark 295
Wake Island 101
Walk in the Sun, A 142
Walk on the Wild Side 241
Walk, Don't Run 409
Walk with Love and Death, A 438
Wall Street *416*, 419, 425
Waltz Time 122, 207
Wandering Jew, The 395
War and Peace 198, *199*, 207, 229
War Brides 19
War Games *386*, 388, 407, *424*
War Hunt 380
War Lover, The 268
War of the Worlds, The 200
Warrior Husband, The 39
Watch on the Rhine 112, 121
Waterloo Bridge (1931) 86; (1940) *86*, 88, 168
Waterloo Road 122
Watership Down 360
Way Ahead, The 233, 387
Way Down East 24
Way to the Stars, The 122, 134, 193
Wayward Bus, The 203
Way We Were, The 318, *319*, 325, 333, 380
Wedding Bells: *see* Royal Wedding
Wedding March, The 15
Wee Willie Winkie 68, 141
Weekend at the Waldorf 122, 270
Weekend in Havana 159
Welcome Danger 11, 20
Welcome Stranger 137
Wells Fargo 68
We're Going to Be Rich 73
We're No Angels 270, 424
Westerner, The *89*, 93, 94, 370
West of Broadway 58
West Side Story 6, 7, *159*, 234, 236, 239, 258, 281, 286, 307, 355, 370, 372
Westward Passage 31
Westworld 435
Wet Parade, The 32
Whales of August, The 431
What Ever Happened to Baby Jane? *238*, 240, 431
What Next, Corporal Hargrove? 163
What Price Glory? *9*, 18, 148
What Price Hollywood? *65*, *271*, 342
What's New Pussycat 258, *260*, 263, 357
What's Up, Doc? 310, 315, 333
When Harry Met Sally . . . *429*, 437
When the North Wind Blows 346
When Worlds Collide 200
Where Eagles Dare 282, 296
Where No Vultures Fly 171
Where's Charley? 169, *169*
Where's Poppa? 317
Where the River Bends: *see* Bend in the River
Which Way to the Front? 385
Whisky Galore! 150, 163
Whistle Down the Wind 234
White Christmas 159, *185*, 193
White Cliffs of Dover, The 117, 118
White Heat *70*, 149, 405
White Shadow of the South Seas 22
White Witch Doctor 170
Who Framed Roger Rabbit 410, *420*, 422, 431
Whole Town's Talking, The 66
Who'll Stop the Rain?: *see* Dog Soldiers
Whoopee 20, 21
Who's Afraid of Virginia Woolf? *267*, 268, 272, 273, 276, 294, 295, 306, 317, 393
Whose Life Is It Anyway? 405
Who's That Girl? 435
Who's That Knocking at My Door? 338
Who's Who 68
Wicked Lady, The 131, 134, 164, 393
Wicked Woman, A 55
Wild Angels, The *267*
Wild Boys of the Road 41
Wild Bunch, The *292*, 301, 350, 396, *397*
Wild Geese, The 393
Wild Is the Wind 204
Wild North 166
Wild One, The 173, *178*, 267
Wild Party, The 12
Wild Rovers 331
Wild Strawberries 269
Willard 305
Will Success Spoil Rock Hunter? 203
Wilson 115
Winchester '73 180, 284, 411
Wind and the Lion, The 330, *340*, 376
Wings 64, 68
Wings of the Morning 64
Winslow Boy, The 144, 211
Winter Light 269
Winterset 63
Wisdom 425, 434
Witches, The 438
Witches of Eastwick, The *415*, 417, 430, 439
With a Song in My Heart 197
Witness *398*, 403, 407, 421, 423
Witness for the Prosecution 212
Wizard of Oz, The 29, *80*, 86, 146, *159*, 165, 169, 288, 295, 322
Wolf Man, The 96
Woman Commands, A 31
Woman in the Window, The *116*, 117
Woman of Paris 353
Woman of Straw 256
Woman of the Sea, A 25
Woman of the Year *98*, 103, 114, 274
Woman on Pier 13, The: *see* I Married a Communist
Woman's Face, A 104
Woman to Woman 67
Women, The 88
Women in Love *290*, 296, 301
Won Ton Ton, the Dog Who Saved Hollywood 390
Wonder Bar 44, 48
Wonderful World of the Brothers Grimm, The 239, 241
Wonder Man 122, 131, 135
Wooden Horse, The 157
Woodstock 173, 296
Words and Music 151
Working Girl 422, 423
World According to Garp, The 399, 402, 416
World in His Arms, The 171
World of Suzie Wong, The 234
World's Greatest Athlete, The 319
Worm's Eye View 164
Wraith, The 408
Wreck of the Mary Deare, The 277
Written on the Wind 203, 266
Wuthering Heights 76, *78*, 89, 233, 320, 372

Yakuza, The 329, 430
Yank at Oxford, A 67, *76*, 77, 86, 153, 168, 398
Yankee Doodle Dandy *100*, 103, 105, 159, 405
Yankee Doodle Mouse 177
Yank in the RAF, A 96, 111
Yank on the Burma Road, A 97
Yanks 362
Yearling, The *131*, 137
Year of Living Dangerously, The 391, 401, 412
Year of the Dragon 417
Yellow Rolls-Royce, The 263
Yield to the Night 196
Yojimbo 257, 270
Yolanda and the Thief 122
You Can't Run Away From It 225
You Can't Sleep Here: *see* I Was a Male War Bride
You Can't Take It with You *75*, 77, 78
Young at Heart 194
Young Bess 174, 178, 192
Young Frankenstein 323, 332, 348
Young Guns *425*
Young in Heart, The 76
Young Lions, The 186, *208*
Young Man of Manhattan 60
Young Mr. Lincoln 378
Young Ones, The 241
Young Tom Edison 84
Young Winston 330, 381
Young Wives' Tale 177
You Only Live Twice 276
You're a Big Boy Now 385
You're in the Navy Now 263
You're Only Young Once 75
You're Telling Me 44
Yours, Mine and Ours 283

Z 299, 377
Zabriskie Point 173, 297, 348
Zardoz 414
Ziegfeld Girl 126
Zoo in Budapest 36
Zorba the Greek *257*, 258
Zulu 258, 264

ACKNOWLEDGMENTS

Picture acknowledgments

All the photographs in this book have been supplied by The Kobal Collection with the exception of the photographs appearing on the following pages:

Octopus Publishing Group Ltd 17 top, 21 bottom, 39 top, 46 left, 48, 77 top right, 82 top left, 83 left, 89 bottom, 94 top, 97 top, 100, 102 top, 116 bottom, 117 top left, 124 centre top inset, 133 left, 169 left, 174 bottom, 176 bottom, 183 bottom right, 192 top left, 197 top left, 204 right, 206 bottom left, 211 bottom, 213 top centre, 217 bottom left, 219 top left, 225 top left, 230 top, 232 top, 235 left, 246 left, 249 top, 249 bottom left, 252 right, 254, 260, 261 bottom, 263 bottom, 273 top, 275 right, 275 bottom right, 277 right, 278 top, 289 right, 290 top left, 290 bottom, 293 top left, 308 right, 311 left, 317 bottom, 320 left, 321 right, 333 bottom, 334 bottom, 357 top, 415 bottom.

Photographs

The Publishers would like to thank all the film production and distribution companies both past and present, whose publicity-photographs appear in this book. Although every effort has been made to name all the film companies, we apologise in advance for any unintentional omissions and would be pleased to insert the appropriate acknowledgement in any subsequent editions of this publication.

A.A./P.E.A./U.A. 312 right inset; ABC, ABC/Allied Artists 307 top, 308 left; ABP 196 bottom; ABP/Woodfall 250-251; ABPC 191 bottom; A.I.P. 233 centre, 267 top left; Allied Artists 201 top left inset, 201 bottom inset; Anglo-Amalgamated 223 bottom; Art Cinema 35 bottom right; Associated General/Lew Grade 299 bottom right; Avco 317 top left; Avco-Embassy 282 top right, 303 top; Avco/Springtime/MGM 279 bottom; British Lion 264 bottom; British Lion/Bryanston/Woodfall 250 top inset; Samuel Bronston 228 top centre inset, 228-229, 234 bottom, 235 bottom right, 244 top, 253 left; Bryanston/Woodfall 226 bottom, 250 bottom inset; Cannon 57 bottom left inset, 383 top centre inset; Carolco 381 right; Castle Rock/Nelson Ent. 429 right; Charles Chaplin 89 left, 133 left, 171 right; Cinema Center 297 bottom; Cineguild 123; Circle Films 419 bottom; Columbia 30 bottom, 31 left, 37 top, 41 bottom, 42 top inset, 42-43, 43 right inset; 47 top, 47 bottom, 69 left, 69 top right, 75 top, 83 top, 85 top right, 110 left bottom centre inset, 119 bottom, 125 left inset, 127 right, 131 top, 133 bottom right, 141 top right, 149 top, 157 left, 173 inset, 176 top, 187, 187 bottom inset, 219 top, 255 right, 258 right, 263 top, 269 top left, 273 bottom right, 278, 288 top, 288 bottom, 312-313, 313 bottom inset, 326 right inset, 341 left inset, 355 top inset, 356 right, 360, 375 bottom inset, 392, 397 top left inset, 401 bottom right, 410 bottom right inset, 415, 417 right, 425 right inset, 426 top; Columbia/De Laurentiis 236 bottom; Columbia/EMI 346; Columbia/Carl Foreman 232 top, Columbia/Goldcrest 381 left; Columbia/Horizon 228 top right inset, 240 left, 240 right, 242-243; Columbia/Kingsmead 223 top; Columbia/Kramer 274 bottom, 277 bottom left; Columbia/LPS/BBS 305; Columbia/MGM 340 centre inset; Columbia/Mirage/Punch 380; Columbia/Pando/Raybert 289 left, 326-327; Columbia/Persky-Bright 328, 339 right; Columbia/Rastar 283 bottom, 309 top, 319 left, 335 top; Columbia/Sam Spiegel 110 top right inset, 183 bottom, 206 top, 265 top, 265 bottom; Columbia/Tri-Star 427 right; Columbia/Universal/A-Team 361 left; Compton Tekli 261 bottom; Cruze 15; Dino de Laurentiis 339 left, 376 top, 408; Cecil B. De Mille 150 left; Cecil B. De Mille/Paramount 167 left; Du Art 374 bottom inset; Ealing 149 bottom; Edenflow 393 right; Elstree/Springbok 249 bottom left; Embassy 261 top; EMI 293 bottom right, 303 bottom, 367 bottom, 395 top; Enigma/NFFC 299 top inset; Enterprise 187 top inset; Eon/Danjaq 290 bottom; Eon/United Artists 239 right, 256, 316 bottom; Epoch 228 bottom inset; Falcon International 139 bottom inset; Film Trust 321 right; Fox 8 top inset, 9 top inset, 11 top, 15 top, 23, 243 centre inset; Gaumont British 52; Geffen Film Co./Warner Bros. 419 top; Goetz-Pennebaker 206 bottom left; Goldcrest/Enigma 394 right; Samuel Goldwyn 61 bottom, 67 top, 67 bottom, 69 bottom right, 78 top, 89 right, 95 bottom right, 101 top, 130 top, 135 top right, 193 right; Guild Films 427 left; Hammer 219 bottom left, 275 left; Hemdale 327 bottom centre inset; Hemdale/Robert Stigwood 329 top; Howard Hughes 18 right, 71 right inset, 271 top left inset; Howard Hughes/RKO 161 top; ITC/IPC 354 top left inset, 378 left; ITC/Producers Circle 351 right; Stanley Kramer 155 top, 157 right, 167 right, 215 top right inset; Stanley Kramer/Columbia 178 bottom; Stanley Kramer/United Artists 147 top; Lam Ping 439 bottom; Levy Prods./Columbia 210 top right; London Films 81 top, 88 right; London Independent Producers 272 bottom; Lucas Film/Paramount 429 bottom left; Lux Galatea 220 bottom; Merchant/Ivory 359 top right, 404; MGM 11 bottom, 13, 19 left, 21 top, 22 top, 24 top, 26, 30 bottom, 33 right, 36, 38 bottom, 41 top, 44 top, 46, 49 left, 51 left, 55 left, 57 top right inset, 60, 64 top, 65 left, 66 right, 70 bottom inset, 73 top, 74 top, 74 bottom right, 76 bottom 77 left, 77 top right, 80 top, 81 bottom, 82 bottom, 86 right, 90 top inset, 90-91, 91 bottom inset, 95 top right, 98, 103 bottom left, 105 right, 109 top, 110 bottom right inset, 114 right, 115 top right, 116 bottom, 118 right, 122 left, 125 right inset, 126 top, 126 bottom left, 131 bottom left, 139 top inset, 146 right, 150 right, 154, 156 left, 158 right inset, 159 top inset, 159 bottom inset, 161 bottom, 164, 165 top, 166 top, 168 top, 170 bottom, 172 top centre inset, 174 bottom, 175 bottom, 176 bottom, 177 bottom right, 179 top, 182 centre, 185 top, 188 bottom, 199 top left, 200 bottom inset, 207 top, 211 bottom, 218 left, 220 top left, 220 top right, 229 top inset, 238 top, 242 left inset, 262, 270 top inset, 270 bottom inset, 275 top right, 277 right, 297 top, 322 bottom, 354 right inset, 376 bottom, 410 bottom left inset, 420 bottom; MGM/APJAC 291; MGM/Arcola 241 top left; MGM/Cinerama 6 top; MGM/Enterprise 135 bottom right; MGM/Stanley Kubrick 6 bottom, 278 top; MGM/Carlo Ponti 273 top, 273 bottom left; MGM/Hal Roach 72 bottom; MGM/David O. Selznick 82 top left, 82 top right, 355 bottom right inset; MGM/SLM 378 right; MGM/United Artists 393 left, 424 left inset; MGM-United Artists/Sherwood 386 bottom; Miramax/Palace 438 right; Mirisch/Seven Arts/United Artists 6 centre, 234 top; Morgan Creek/Vestron 425 left inset; New Line 139, 369 bottom; Northstar/Lorimar 313 top left inset; Omni Zoetrope 340 bottom inset, 358; Orion 172 bottom centre inset, 399 top, 405 right, 421 top right, 422 bottom, 437 right, 438 left; Orion-Nova 202 right; Orion/Warner Bros. 369 top, 371 top; Palomar 311 top; Paramount 6 left centre, 14 right, 17 bottom, 18 left, 25, 28 right inset, 30 top, 31 top, 34, 40, 43 centre right inset, 44 bottom, 48, 51 right, 58, 59 bottom, 70 centre top inset, 73 bottom, 79, 85 bottom left, 91 top inset, 93 right, 99 top, 99 bottom, 101 bottom, 107, 112, 120, 124 top inset, 124 top centre inset, 138 top inset, 145 top left, 151, 152 top, 158-159, 160, 163, 175 top right, 177 top, 185 bottom, 186 bottom inset, 203 centre, 210 left, 211 top, 215 bottom left inset, 231 top, 252 left, 253 right, 263 bottom, 264 top left, 264 top right, 280 left, 280 right, 294 top, 296, 298 right inset, 312 left inset, 315 top, 317 bottom, 322 top, 323, 334 top right, 337 bottom, 338, 362, 367 top, 372 top, 373 top, 383 top inset, 387, 388 right, 414 bottom, 416 top, 421 top left, 423 bottom left, 424 centre inset, 433 top, 433 bottom, 434, 436 top; Paramount/ABC 331 top; Paramount/Alfran 309 bottom; Paramount/Aries/Elkins 301 left; Paramount/William Castle 281 left; Paramount/Coppola Co. 324 right; Paramount/De Laurentiis 298-299, 333 bottom right, 396-397; Paramount/Cecil B. De Mille 57 left centre inset, 63, 199 bottom left; Paramount/Dena 195 right; Paramount/Feldman 398; Paramount/Filmways 295; Paramount/Jaffe-Lansing 430 bottom; Paramount/Lorimar 379 left; Paramount/Lucas Film 370 top, 382-383; Paramount/Memorial 283 top; Paramount/Newdon 320 right, 321 left; Paramount/Salem/Dover 246 top right; Paramount/Stigwood 172 top left inset, 172 bottom inset; Paramount/Stigwood-Carr 351 left; Paramount/Hal B. Wallis 205 bottom, 215, 281 right; Pathe 214 bottom inset; Ponti/De Laurentiis 199 right; Rank 180 bottom, 181 top, 245 right, 251 bottom inset, 258 top, 337 top; Rank/Allied Film Makers/Parkway 235 top left; Rank/Recorder Picture Company 363 bottom; Rank/Two Cities 102 bottom, 117 top left; Remus 217 bottom left; Remus/British Lion 251 centre inset; Republic/Argosy 167 left; Rimfire/Paramount 409 left; RKO 14 left, 22 bottom, 28-29, 38 top, 39 top, 43 centre left inset, 55, 74 bottom left, 92 top right, 104 right, 105 left, 109, 115 bottom, 116 bottom, 118 left, 127 left, 135 left, 141 top left, 148, 214, bottom inset, 271 centre right inset; Hal Roach 35 right, 87 top; Rodgers & Hammerstein 193 left; Romulus 170 top right; Romulus-Horizon/IFD 165 bottom; David O. Selznick 42 bottom inset, 65 right, 84 left, 115 left, 122 top, 132 right, 271 top right inset; Selznick/London Films/British Lion 152 bottom; Shamley/Universal 224 top; Simon Films 373 bottom; Talent Assocs. 397 centre left inset; Terror/Paramount 383 bottom centre inset; The Archers/G.F.D. 145 bottom; Toho 271 bottom right inset; Touchstone Pictures 390 bottom, 405 left, 417 top, 426 right, 428 top, 432, 435 left; Touchstone Pictures/Amblin Ent. 420 top; Tri-Star 407, 412; Tri-Star/Carolco 435 right; Twentieth Century Fox 28 left inset, 45 top, 50, 59 top, 64 bottom, 68 top, 80 bottom left, 86 left, 87 bottom left, 88 left, 90 centre inset, 95 left, 97 top, 106 right, 108 top, 110 left top centre inset, 110 bottom left inset, 113, 114 left, 130 bottom, 132 top right, 134 left, 134 right, 136 right, 137 top, 140 bottom, 143 top right, 145 top right, 147 bottom, 158 left inset, 159 centre bottom inset, 172 top right inset, 174 top, 175 top left, 178 top right, 183 top, 190 bottom, 194 left, 196 top, 203 right, 208 top, 208 left, 208 right, 209 right, 222, 228 top left inset, 232 bottom, 236 top, 237 right, 243 left inset, 243 right inset, 246 top left, 257 top, 266 bottom, 268 left, 268 top, 272 top, 279 top left, 287, 293 right, 304 left, 311 bottom, 318, 326 left inset, 336, 346 left, 349 top, 350 top, 356 left, 357 bottom, 361 right, 375 top inset, 391 bottom right, 406 top, 406 bottom, 410 top left inset, 411 left inset, 411 right inset, 413 top, 416 bottom, 421 bottom, 422 top, 436 bottom, 439 left; Twentieth Century Fox/Apjac 279 top right; Twentieth Century Fox/Crossbow 348; Twentieth Century Fox/Dino de Laurentiis 269 right; Twentieth Century Fox/Embassy 385 top right; Twentieth Century Fox/Enigma 368; Twentieth Century Fox/Hera 347 right; Twentieth Century Fox/Lucas Film 344 top, 364, 374 centre inset, 386 top; Twentieth Century Fox/Warner Bros. 325 left; Twentieth Century Fox/Zanuck-Brown 401 top left, 401 bottom left; UFA 16; United Artists 27 bottom, 84 right, 110-111, 121 top, 159 centre top inset, 184 top right, 189 top, 197 right, 197 bottom, 198 left, 198 right, 210 bottom right, 212, 215 top right inset, 222 bottom, 225 bottom right, 227 left, 241 bottom left, 241 right, 242 right inset, 257 bottom, 260, 280 top, 298 top left inset, 301 right, 314, 325 right, 327 top inset, 353 left, 357 top, 359 left, 366, 371 bottom, 410-411, 423 right; United Artists/Brandywine 290 top; United Artists/Bryna 206 bottom right; United Artists/Embassy 6 centre right, 276 left, 276 right; United Artists/Douglas Fairbanks 56 inset, 57 bottom right inset; United Artists/Fantasy Films 332; United Artists/Florin 289 right; United Artists/Stanley Kramer 213 top left, 213 top centre, 221 top, 249 top; United Artists/Joseph Levine 345; United Artists/Mirisch 214 top inset, 225 top, 226 top right, 230, 252 right, 269 bottom, 270-271, 275 bottom right, 310 right; United Artists/Mirisch/Alpha 247 bottom; United Artists/Monterey 142; United Artists/Proscenium 172-173; United Artists/Rollins-Joffe 343 top, 353 left, 353 right, United Artists/Seven Arts 230 top; United Artists/George Stevens 259; United Artists/Walter Wanger 79 top; United Artists/Woodfall 247 top; Universal 12 left, 17 top, 32 right, 33 left, 43 left inset, 49 right, 68 bottom, 85 bottom right, 92 centre, 96, 124 bottom centre inset, 129 bottom, 138 top centre inset, 138 bottom inset, 141 bottom, 180 top, 191 top, 200-201, 201 right inset, 204 top, 207 left, 220 centre left, 226 top left, 244 bottom, 248 left, 255 left, 267 top right, 271 bottom left inset, 282 top left, 286 top, 298 bottom left inset, 308 right, 313 top right inset, 316 top, 340-341, 343 bottom, 362 top, 374 top inset, 374-375, 377 right, 397 centre right inset, 399 bottom, 411 centre inset, 424 right inset, 429 top left, 430 top, 431 left; Universal/Lorimar 374 top inset; Universal/Lucas Film/Coppola Co. 317 top right; Universal/Malpaso 315 bottom; Universal/Rampart 143 top left; Universal/Rastar 349 bottom; Universal/Steven Spielberg 383 bottom inset, 400; Universal/Walter Wanger 132 bottom; Universal/Warner Bros. 423 top; Universal/Zanuck-Brown 319 right, 330 top, 330 bottom, 335 bottom, 340 top inset; Vic Films 251 top inset; Michael Wadleigh 327 top centre inset; Walter Wanger 66 left; Walter Wanger/United Artists 2-3, 75 bottom; Warner Bros. 8 bottom inset, 8-9, 9 bottom inset, 10, 19 right, 21 bottom, 24 bottom, 27 top, 29 top inset, 29 centre inset, 29 bottom inset, 35 left, 37 bottom, 45 left, 54, 56-57, 57 top left inset, 61 top, 62, 70 top inset, 70-71, 71 left inset, 72 top, 72 centre, 76 top, 77 bottom, 90 bottom inset, 92 left, 93 left, 94 top, 94 bottom, 97 bottom, 100, 102 top, 110 top left inset, 116 top, 119 right, 121 bottom, 124 bottom inset, 128 top, 129 top right, 137 bottom, 138 bottom centre inset, 140 top, 143 bottom, 144 bottom, 162 left, 168 bottom, 169 right, 178 left, 184 left, 184 centre, 186 top inset, 189 bottom, 190 top, 192 top left, 192 top right, 194 right, 195 left, 197 top left, 200 top inset, 202 left, 204 right, 205 top, 213 bottom, 214 top centre inset, 215 bottom right inset, 219 bottom right, 239 left, 245 top, 254, 267 bottom left, 277 top left, 293 left, 300, 302, 310 left, 342 bottom, 350 bottom, 359 bottom right, 365 top, 365 bottom, 391 top, 402, 409 right, 410 top right inset, 413 bottom, 414 top, 415 top, 418 top right, 426 bottom left, 437 left; Warner Bros./ABPC 153; Warner Bros./Amblin Entertainment 403; Warner Bros./Armada 217 top left, 217 right; Warner Bros./Arwin 194 top; Warner Bros./Barwood/First Artists 342 top; Warner Bros./Crossbow 320 left; Warner Bros./Gruber-Peters 428 bottom; Warner Bros./Hawk/Peregrine 333 top; Warner Bros./Ladd Co. 124-125, 375 centre inset, 379 right; Warner Bros./Malpaso 307 bottom; Warner Bros./Polaris 397 bottom right inset; Warner Bros./Alexander Salkind 352; Warner Bros./Saticoy 310; Warner Bros./Seven Arts 70 centre bottom inset, 274 top, 397 top left inset, 397 bottom left inset; Warner Bros./Seven Arts/Aldrich Association 238 bottom left; Warner Bros./Solar 282 bottom; Warner Bros./WEA 390 top; Warner Bros./Wildwood 334 centre; Warner Bros./Zanuck Co. 431 right; WESTI/SGF 229 bottom inset; Saul Zaentz Company 395 bottom, 418 left, 418 bottom right; Zoetrope 377 left; Zoetrope/Warner Bros. 384, 424-425.